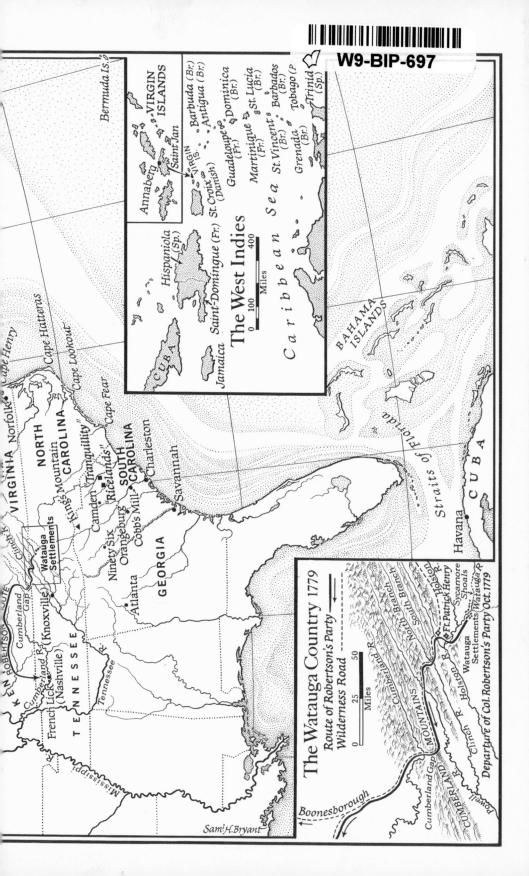

The West Indies

VIRGIN ISLANDS

Annaberg
Saint Jan
VIRGIN IS.
St. Croix (Danish)
Barbuda (Br.)
Antigua (Br.)
Guadeloupe (Fr.)
Dominica (Br.)
Martinique (Fr.)
St. Lucia (Br.)
St. Vincent (Br.)
Barbados (Br.)
Grenada (Br.)
Tobago (Br.)
Trinid. (Sp.)

Bermuda Is.

Hispaniola (Sp.)
Saint-Domingue (Fr.)

Caribbean Sea

Miles
0   100   400

CUBA

Jamaica

BAHAMA ISLANDS

Straits of Florida

CUBA

Havana

Cape Henry
Cape Hatteras
Cape Lookout
Cape Fear

VIRGINIA
NORTH CAROLINA
Norfolk

Clinch R.
Watauga Settlements
Kings Mountain
Camden
"Tranquillity"
"Ricelands"
SOUTH CAROLINA
Charleston
Ninety Six
Orangeburg
Cobb's Mill
Savannah

GEORGIA
Atlanta

Cumberland Gap
KENTUCKY
ROBERTSON'S ROUTE
French Lick (Nashville)
Knoxville
Cumberland R.
TENNESSEE
Tennessee R.

Mississippi R.

The Watauga Country 1779

Route of Robertson's Party ⟶
Wilderness Road ---

Miles
0   25   50

Holston R.
North Branch
South Branch
Cumberland R.
CUMBERLAND MOUNTAINS
Cumberland Gap
Powell R.
Clinch R.
Holston R.
Watauga Settlements
Sycamore Shoals
Ft. Patrick Henry
Departure of Col. Robertson's Party Oct. 1779

Boonesborough

Sam'l H. Bryant

Roads to Liberty

Roads to Liberty

F. van Wyck Mason

Illustrated with sketches by John Alan Maxwell

LITTLE, BROWN AND COMPANY · BOSTON · TORONTO

FIRST EDITION
T10/72

This book is dedicated to my wife
JEANNE-LOUISE HAND MASON
with much enduring love

Library of Congress Cataloging in Publication Data

Mason, Francis van Wyck, 1901-
    Roads to liberty.

    CONTENTS: Three harbors.—Stars on the sea.—
Wild horizon.—Eagle in the sky.
    I. Title.
PZ3.M3855Ro [PS3525.A7943]   813'.5'2   72-5353
ISBN 0-316-54930-4

Published simultaneously in Canada
by Little, Brown & Company (Canada) Limited

PRINTED IN THE UNITED STATES OF AMERICA

Contents

Introduction

Over the years I have written some eleven volumes describing historically significant and exciting events taking place in British North America colonies previous to and during the War for American Independence — a term which I believe more accurately describes the nature of the conflict than simply "the Revolution" or "the American Revolutionary War." Some of the above-mentioned works are not included in *Roads to Liberty* — an anthology which confines itself to that period extending from 1774 to 1782 — since they deal with pre-Revolutionary development of the colonies. Nevertheless, these efforts offer invaluable material towards understanding why rebellion against the Crown came about.

Incidentally, I prefer to classify these above books of mine as "dramatic history" rather than as "historical fiction," since I hold those two terms to be contradictory in their exact meaning. A novel largely is the product of an author's imagination, and he cannot ethically distort history to suit his plot. History is history; therefore, the historian is forced to include all manner of dull facts if his account is to be complete and accurate. When writing "dramatic history" I have, using modern phraseology, attempted to re-create an era relating significant and dramatically appealing but historically authentic events. I feel that humans living long ago experienced the same emotions, fears and aspirations as do we in modern times. Never for the sake of plot have I distorted descriptions of historical figures or of events and have stuck to facts derived from extensive researches based on the best accredited sources. While writing *Three Harbors* — my first attempt at creating dramatic history — I evolved the practice of giving patronyms to my fictional characters representative of families living in a given locality at the time described.

In the four books included in *Roads to Liberty* major historical figures appear comparatively rarely and then only long enough to explain how their decisions affected the course of recorded events. Many more minor historical figures have been included than a reader might surmise. Such are intended to express in a convincing, readable fashion trends of thought and ways of life peculiar to that period and region. To my mind it seems a great pity that in all too many schools, colleges and universities history is taught so unimaginatively — that intensely exciting and colorful events are reduced to the memorization of dates identifying various administrations, reigns, wars and battles. As a rule students are only to learn *when* an event took place, rather than what forces were brought into being or what were its lasting effects.

In order to obtain a better understanding of that period covered by *Roads to Liberty* — 1774 to 1782 — I feel it essential briefly to describe in this preface conditions in British North America which drove the original thirteen colonies — developing along separate but roughly parallel lines — to unite more or less uncertainly on that perilous road which led towards liberty and eventual independence. And in order to understand why hundreds of thousands of freeborn British subjects hopefully abandoned the only surroundings they were familiar with to venture across the Atlantic and start life anew amid a vast and terrifying wilderness, one must consider the pressures and conditions then prevailing in the mother country.

By the late seventeenth century Britain already was well on the way towards establishing a vast and generally beneficient colonial empire. Factors which greatly assisted in creating Britain's hegemony were the rapid decline of Spain's military might and the fact that Portugal's imperialistic ambitions were directed towards Brazil and the East Indies rather than to the Caribbean area. Aside from stubborn but generally spasmodic and ineffective resistance offered by the French and Dutch, little remained to hinder the blundering and often quite unplanned expansion of Britain's overseas empire. A series of great dynastic wars waged upon the Continent invariably were won by England and her allies of the moment — the powers often switched sides. These conflicts left Britain's countryside unravaged and her economic capabilities enhanced, while countries on the Continent had been so devastated they were slow to recover. By the time Louis XIV was nearing the end of his long and glittering reign, Britain had all but achieved undisputed supremacy on the high seas and so had entered upon an age of unprecedented prosperity which hastened intellectual and artistic if not political enlightenment.

Thanks to such economic advantages, Britain's population expanded by leaps and bounds, but alas, these new riches soon became concentrated in the hands of a relatively small minority — the royal family, powerful nobles, great merchants, landed gentry and politicians as influential as they were unscrupulous. Prosperous rural landowners set about ruthlessly expanding their holdings through the often forced purchase of countless small farms and businesses, thus creating swarms of landless and usually almost destitute commonfolk. These flocked into towns and cities; embittered, hampered by lack of education and social tradition, they were desperate concerning their future. Some also were barred from public office or private employment because of religious prejudices. In short, the plight of such Englishmen had become all but intolerable. What could they do? Various answers were offered, none of them easy. Long since, explorers and adventurers sent out by the Crown, powerful nobles, and various mercantile guilds had reported the natural riches of limitless and almost uninhabited North America, and always there existed the possibility of becoming rich overnight through discovery of silver, gold and precious stones so abundant farther south. Companies were formed and shares sold after charters had been obtained from the Crown authorizing the establishment of colonies in North America.

Such charters only vaguely defined those rights, privileges and powers prospective settlers might expect to enjoy; even less exactly did these grants describe the boundaries of such a colony. In New England, especially, immigrants soon became accustomed to regulating local affairs through the election of "select men" at town meetings. Such select men customarily chose from among their number a representative or representatives to vote for them at sessions of a popularly elected colonial assembly — or General Court, as such a body was termed in Massachusetts. Thus New Englanders gradually achieved a greater degree of self-government than ever had been intended under the royal charter — especially while the English civil war was raging. The northern colonies had made the most of what Robert Walpole later described as "salutory neglect." Massachusettsers soon came to consider these rights, often illegal, as inherent, and proved extremely unwilling to have them curtailed in any degree.

With intention of presenting a dispassionate and well-rounded picture of that period covered in *Roads to Liberty*, I adopted the practice of describing events taking place concurrently in a Northern, a Southern and an English colony which remained loyal to the Crown. For example, in *Three Harbors* I used Virginia, Massachusetts and Bermuda; in *Stars on the Sea* I employed Rhode Island, South Carolina and the Bahamas for backgrounds. In *Wild Horizon* I departed from this pattern for only good and sufficient reasons. A fallacy which persists even to this day is that Virginia, Maryland and South Carolina largely were colonized by aristocrats. True, there was a handful of gentry among the early settlers who quickly became dominant in the above-mentioned colonies. A vast majority of immigrants, however, were ordinary folk, illiterate or poorly educated at best.

Because Britain's North American colonies had flourished beyond all expectation, critical shortages of labor, both skilled and unskilled, soon developed. One reason for this scarcity of manpower and consumers was that only English-speaking colonists were encouraged or forced to emigrate to North America. There were exceptions, such as the sturdy inhabitants of Dutch settlements established in New Jersey, on Long Island and up the Hudson River Valley. Less numerous were the Swedes, who for a time maintained a solid foothold in what is now the state of Delaware. Such non-English outposts, however, soon became overwhelmed and absorbed by their Anglo-Saxon neighbors.

As time passed, the number of non-English immigrants gradually increased. French Huguenots and Acadians settled in South Carolina and Louisiana. Religious refugees such as the Mennonites, Amish and Moravians came from Germany to help populate and strengthen the colonies of Georgia, Maryland and especially Pennsylvania.

Also numerous and eventually much more influential were contingents of fierce Scottish Highlanders captured during the Jacobite wars and other rebellions. To begin with, these hardy and bellicose mountaineers settled principally along the frontiers of Georgia and among the mountains of Virginia and the Carolinas and proved to be the most adaptable and durable of pioneers. It is not surprising to note how many American Civil War generals bore Scottish names. Later arrived a flood of Scotch-Irish-Lowland Scots who had dwelt for a time in Ulster. Also came groups of shrewd and scholarly Sephardic Jews — mostly of Portuguese origin. Although relatively few in number, these Semitic immigrants quickly made the most of their special abilities, especially throughout the Southern colonies. To give a more detailed description of the distribution and influence of such non-English arrivals lies beyond the scope of this anthology.

It may now be appropriate to list some of those forces which impelled so many uneducated but self-reliant members of the English lower classes to seek a better life amid the dangers of a vast and unknown land. In various ways all were seeking the right to possess unlimited amounts of land, free from limitations imposed in the mother country through social traditions and religious restraints. Also, they craved freedom to pursue trades or professions to the limits of their ability and then to be allowed to enjoy the fruits of their skill or labor unhampered. Members of all classes demanded opportunity to receive an education at low cost. Many sought to escape the awful fate of incarceration in debtors' prison. Others fled risk of enforced military service such as that imposed by press gangs for the Royal Navy. Prisoners of civil wars — virtual slaves of the government — and persons of both sexes who had been convicted of petty crimes also yearned to make a fresh start.

A majority of the categories mentioned above lacked anything like the price of transportation across the Atlantic and so were forced to indenture themselves as bondsmen or bondswomen. This meant that they must labor as virtual slaves for whoever purchased their bond. During this time, for from four to seven years, they enjoyed no civil rights whatsoever, but at the expiration of their indenture, they became enfranchised and by law were furnished with arms, clothing, food, seeds and, in some regions, even oxen to help them get started on their own. Some unsuspecting would-be emigrants fell victim to rascally "scawbankers" — rogues who cheated the unwary about the terms of indenture and heartless kidnappers encouraged by planters to supply badly needed labor by whatever means they chose.

Many members of the middle class, younger sons of the minor nobility and educated professional men were prompted to emigrate for quite different reasons. Among these were the law of primogeniture, which settled on the oldest son of a noble family the title and properties, if any, pertaining to it. This practice forced younger sons of the nobility and landed gentry to seek their fortune overseas unless they elected to serve in the armed forces, make the church their career, or to follow some other profession. The possibility of lucrative adventure in unknown lands proved well-nigh irresistible attraction for many full-blooded younger sons.

Then there were professional officers and soldiers who had fallen onto hard times due to slow advancement in times of peace, and the sale, through corruption and influence, of high military command to often incompetent court favorites. Capable but impecunious lawyers as well sought greener fields and richer rewards on learning that in America existed a dearth of well-trained legal practitioners. Another class of emigrants consisted of bankrupt investors in fraudulent schemes for getting rich quick abroad.

While thus reviewing the development of the original colonies along generally parallel but all-too-often separate lines, it may prove rewarding to consider in general terms those goals they held in common.

All the settlers craved civil order under a government controlled by popularly elected representatives which would ensure them the right to pursue occupations without legal, religious or social restriction. All the colonists resisted the imposition of taxes, especially when they had no say in the matter, such as direct imposts levied by the king's government in faraway England.

All along the Atlantic seaboard, ordinary men resented the privileges of great property holders and political leaders, many of whom rewarded obedient adherents and underlings with liberal grants of land within the colony's dubious boundaries situated in undeveloped and vaguely-defined territories to the westward claimed under its particular royal charter. Everywhere, descendants of the original settlers came instinctively to mistrust Crown-appointed governors, most of whom were military men who understood little or nothing about practical civil administration. Of such that great humanitarian, Sir James Oglethorpe, governor of Georgia, was a notable exception.

The British North American colonies suffered in common from an acute shortage of scrupulous lawyers, able politicians on a high level, and military leaders adaptable to the style of warfare peculiar to North America. Almost without exception, when a colonist deemed himself unduly taxed or discriminated against, he packed up his family, called the dog and set out on the perilous westward journey toward what he believed to be free and unclaimed territory. This ever-increasing movement over the Alleghenies aggravated the already critical shortage of manpower in the scantily populated seacoast colonies.

It having long been the Crown's policy to discourage development of large industries in their North American possessions, all colonies were kept dependent upon the mother country for manufactured goods of every description.

As the westward trend of migration gathered momentum, the dehumanizing effects of the wilderness began to manifest themselves. Early pioneers of course had been subjected to multiple dangers and discomforts undreamed of in the mother country, but the farther pioneers, disgruntled by conditions prevailing along the East Coast, penetrated into the endless silent forests of the Ohio country, the more poignant became the brutalizing effect of constant contact with a primitive and barbaric society. Lack of education, civilized social contacts and the waning effectiveness of religious restraint added to isolation, primitive living conditions and the ever-present dangers of hideously painful death caused harsh transformations in the character of these frontiersmen. Instead of seeking orderly adjudication in a dispute through legal processes, inhabitants of newly-settled territories resorted to physical violence at the least provocation. What legal forces existed to restrain them from taking the law into their own hands?

This way of thinking reached a climax in incredible atrocities committed by Tories and patriots alike during the War for Independence — as described in *Wild Horizon*. The outward appearance of these migrants to the West became filthy and unkempt to a deplorable degree — to be halfway decently dressed became a matter for contempt and ridicule. These frontiersmen became harsh, their speech and vocabularies pitifully limited and adulterated with Indian words — in fact, they soon evolved a lingo peculiar to the region occupied by themselves. In short, these rugged people carried a conception of what constituted personal independence much too far. It is amazing that inhabitants of the original thirteen colonies, often separated from each other by hundreds if not thousands of miles of rugged territory, finally "touched hands," partially resolved individual differences, and, agreeing on principles held in common, at length formed a workable union of sorts.

Many differences arose from the nature of that charter under which a given province, colony or "plantation" had been settled and governed. Climatic conditions also played a decisive part in shaping differences in views developed by successive waves of immigrants to British North America. In principle, a typical royal charter reaffirmed most of those rights which a freeborn British subject had enjoyed back in England. If a colony was a "royal" one, then its inhabitants owed loyalty and the payment of taxes directly to the Crown and its representatives.

Under such a charter the king requested his privy ministers to nominate for appointment royal governors, judges, custom officers, military commanders and highly placed civil servants to enforce laws passed by Parliament.

The royal governor usually selected a governor's council drawn from Colonials desirous of, or dependent upon, royal favor. With few exceptions these councillors came from among great landowners, influential merchants and members of the local gentry. Essentially, the governor's council was intended to mediate differences between the Crown and the colonial assembly. The members of this latter body, on the other hand, had been *locally elected* once they had met a varying number of requirements regarding religion and certain property qualifications.

The one great power vested in a colonial assembly was that it and it alone had the power to *vote local taxes* which supported the colony's government and for a long time paid the salaries of the king's appointed representatives. Through this control of a colony's pursestrings, popularly elected assemblies pretty much had their way. Should a governor and his council attempt to force an unpopular measure into law, the assembly simply refused to vote taxes till their views were respected.

The original Massachusetts charter was extremely liberal, so much so that when Charles II came to the throne at the end of the English civil war he discovered the unpleasant fact that, to all intents and purposes, his Massachusetts Bay colony was all but self-governing internally, so by the time the period covered in this anthology arrived, a demand for self-determination expressed through popular elections had become deeply ingrained, especially in the New England character.

It is almost impossible for the present-day reader, as a citizen of a great nation now numbering well over two hundred million inhabitants, to visualize how very scant was the population of British North America. In fact when the War for Independence commenced, the entire white population of the thirteen colonies numbered only around eight million white persons, plus about half as many blacks. The Indian population of North America at the time when Jamestown, Plymouth and St. Mary's City were settled has been estimated at some three hundred thousand, but by 1770 their numbers had declined by half through interminable tribal wars and the introduction of European diseases such as scarlet fever, chicken pox, typhoid and smallpox; even chicken pox and mumps usually were fatal to the redman. One might travel even in comparatively well-populated regions for days without sighting the smoke of a white settler's cabin. A coasting vessel might cruise for a week without sighting a craft of any description be it a shallop, a skiff or even a canoe.

The Northern and Middle colonies permitted Negro slavery, but only in a mild form probably because of Puritan tenets and the fact that blacks among them were relatively few. Indeed, in many parts of New England Negro slaves often were treated as members of the family and usually manumitted upon the death of their owners. Slaves also were afforded at least a modicum of education, welcomed into church membership, and accorded far more social protection than that accorded to European serfs of that era.

However, south of the Mason-Dixon line the condition of slaves underwent a sharp and degrading transformation; the cultivation of rice, cotton, tobacco and indigo required huge labor forces. Much as the Southerners cherished and demanded self-government and personal freedom for themselves, they just as intently denied their black chattels even the most basic of human rights. So for generations Southern colonists existed in constant dread of servile insurrection in addition to the hazards of Indian attacks and invasion by French and Spanish neighbors.

When the probability of armed rebellion against royal authority became more apparent, colonists of all classes gradually came to appreciate that their only hope for the future lay in united action.

As if to aggravate the situation, powerful and socially prominent British-Americans in England were looked down upon, even though many of them had been educated in the mother country! No small part of the bitter and eventually decisive resentment towards royal governors and other officials appointed by the Crown was due to the home-grown English-man's haughty and arrogant manners not only in civilian but in military matters. A particular irritation to the colonists was the presence of regular army units, which in ever-increasing numbers arrived during the later 1700's to garrison military installations and to enforce the edicts of Parliament. Many of these behaved in ever so overbearing a fashion that Bostonians complained to the king that his troops behaved as if they were occupying a conquered country rather than protecting fellow British subjects.

At this point it may be advisable to list those acts which the American colonists resented most.

Once France had ceded all of Canada, the age-old threat to British-America's security had been forever removed. No longer would New Englanders shudder over the possibility of French-led Indian incursions, no longer would their all-important maritime trade and fisheries be harried by French cruisers, privateers and corsairs. Some one hundred forty million pounds had been expended to wage and win the third French and Indian War — in Europe termed the Seven Years War — which huge expense had to be defrayed by one means or another. When native Englishmen protested that British-Americans had not been taxed at all, Parliament reduced war taxes in Britain and then set about enacting a series of measures designed to produce revenue from North America. All fair enough, but the methods employed were politically unwise and so offensive they sowed the seeds of armed rebellion. Why should not the colonists who had benefited so greatly from the war help pay for their new-found security? It is only fair to state that the rate of taxes arbitrarily imposed on the colonies was reasonable — much lower than that levied on subjects in the British Isles.

As a result of the Peace of Paris signed in 1763, commerce and industry boomed along the Atlantic seaboard and fresh waves of immigrants arrived to participate in this new prosperity. As a result a general westward movement sent little bands of settlers haphazardly fighting their way over the Appalachians to claim land in unoccupied territories supposedly owned and controlled by the so-called Ohio Company, which corporation immediately opposed intrusion by ordering such persons "forwith to remove themselves" and at the same time firmly forbade pioneers from purchasing land from resident Indians. The first of those measures which eventually were to lead to an armed conflict was too-sudden enforcement of regulations known as the Acts of Trade — which laws had long been on the books but never had been seriously enforced — undoubtedly royal customs collectors had been bribed to look the other way. Suddenly these officials were severely reprimanded, increased in number and ordered from now on to collect *all* tariffs due the British government.

Serious trouble next was caused by Parliament's passage of the Sugar Act in 1764, which in effect ordered North American colonists to purchase sugar and molasses *only* from the British West Indies, at the same time denying them the right to buy from French, Spanish and Dutch colonies at lower prices. Further, very high import duties were placed on non-British textiles, coffee and indigo.

While outrage mounted over these arbitrary regulations — all imposed without colonial knowledge or consent — it was as nothing compared to the howls raised over Parliament's passage of the so-called Townshend Acts of 1767. These, among other provisions, imposed import duties on such essentials such as glass, lead, paper, tea and similar necessities. What really stirred up a tempest of protest and goaded British-Americans to desperation was that law which decreed that colonial exporters wishing to do business with a foreign country must cause their vessels to stop first at a British port and pay export duties on colonial-made merchandise and produce.

All thirteen colonies emitted roars of indignation, and through their various assemblies appointed Committees of Correspondence charged with the responsibility of deciding how best to cope with Parliament's so-called Intolerable Acts. These committees soon agreed that by far the most effective reply would be for all Colonials to refuse to import or to buy any merchandise of English origin until the obnoxious laws were repealed. Thus the first practical step was taken towards achieving unity of action among British-Americans.

As if determined to alienate the Crown's American subjects once and for all, Parliament next passed the Currency Act, which in effect forbade the colonies — always critically short of any standard or ready medium of exchange — to strike coinage or to print paper money on their own.

As if to cap this folly came enactment of the Quartering Act — another money-saving device — which required the king's regular troops in North America to be fed, housed and otherwise supplied at the inhabitants' expense.

Finally, a point of no return was achieved through the enactment of the Quebec Act, which law in effect placed the enormous, loosely defined and very rich Ohio country under the administration of the British government in Quebec and once more forbade colonists from along the East Coast to occupy lands lying west of the Appalachians, thus frustrating settlers and speculators eager to share in the enormously lucrative fur trade.

Further, this measure threatened to create a *second* group of North American colonies which might prove less intractable than the older ones along the Atlantic seaboard. Also under the Quebec Act, the Roman Catholic religion became recognized by law and subjects of French descent were permitted to continue native customs, legally to teach and employ their own language and to preserve traditional forms of local government. The worst aspect of this law lay in the fact that from the start it was utterly unenforceable.

Another wildly unpopular law enacted by Parliament in hopes of extracting revenue was the Stamp Act, which, passed in 1765, required the use of tax stamps on newspapers, almanacs, pamphlets, legal documents, insurance policies, ships' papers and, oddly enough, on such unessential items as cards and dice. So once again Parliament, lacking colonial knowledge or approval had levied a direct tax. Worse still, violators of this law now could be tried before courts of vice-admiralty, which operated without a jury, thus violating one of the Englishman's most cherished rights — that of public trial by a jury of his peers. Reaction to this measure was instantaneous and violent. Nowhere would the colonists buy stamps; in some places stamp agents were threatened, tarred and feathered and otherwise molested with the result the Stamp Act hurriedly was repealed.

British-Americans, now thoroughly alarmed, set about re-forming and adding to the powers of their previous Committees of Safety and otherwise consulted how best to oppose suppression of what they now felt to be inalienable rights and liberties. Such ad hoc committees renewed non-importation agreements and even went further by adopting the policy of "nonintercourse," which halted all trade — import or export — with or to the mother country.

So great were the reactions that Parliament was driven to annulling all the Townshend Acts saving for an insignificant import duty on tea; but by this time the damage had been done. Groups of colonists naming themselves "Patriots," "Defenders of Freedom" and "Sons of Liberty" started to collect arms and to drill in such rough-and-ready fashion that European professional soldiers held their musters to be ineffective, if not ludicrous.

In October 1768 two British line regiments plus artillery troops arrived in Boston to reinforce the already strong garrison there. Steadily tension mounted until in March 1771 the so-called Boston Massacre occurred when British troops on duty were so threatened by a riotous mob they opened fire with the result that three rioters were killed outright and two died later. The farther news of this occurrence traveled the more lurid and distorted grew accounts of what actually had taken place. Armed rebellion undoubtedly would have broken had not the acting royal governor promptly withdrawn his redcoated troops to islands scattered about Boston Harbor.

With the repeal of the Townshend Acts and the Nonimportation Agreements lapsed, comparative peace had been restored, but in 1773 the "Tea Act" was passed because certain corrupt ministers had large interests in the East India Company. During the period of nonimportation a surplus — some seventeen million pounds of tea — had accumulated in English warehouses and that had to be sold to save the "John Company" from bankruptcy. Therefore, it was decided to force half a million pounds of tea upon the colonies, to be taxed at the rate of three pence per pound. Outraged, British-Americans refused not only to buy but in some instances even to allow this tea to be landed, and further burned the tea ship *Peggy Stewart* in Annapolis, Maryland. The famous Boston Tea Party was another example of such extreme measures.

Perhaps the worst of Parliament's mistakes was the enactment of the law which made it possible to transport a colonist accused of certain crimes to England for trial. This, added to increased irritations caused by more stringent provisions of the Quartering Act and reaffirmation of the obnoxious Quebec Act, was too much, especially when more British regulars arrived in Boston.

In September 1774, the First Continental Congress, including representatives from twelve of the thirteen original colonies, convened in Philadelphia.

Parliament then enacted the Coercive Acts, which closed the port of Boston and ordered still more troops dispatched to the rebellious colonies. Tensions mounted and matters went from bad to worse until at Lexington, Massachusetts, on the nineteenth of April, 1775, the flames of war became ignited by the "shot heard around the world." After this, the uncertain and hazardous roads to liberty became stained by rivers of blood.

Three Harbors

Preface

It is perhaps inevitable that some readers will wonder how closely I have adhered to the rigid pattern of history. To these I would say that the main facts, dates, and historical figures are as nearly correct as a painstaking and selective research can make them. The same applies to such details as uniforms, military movements, legal proceedings, customs, currency and documents.

The writer of a novel which employs an historical setting is, I believe, to the careful historian somewhat as a landscape painter is to an architect. While a painter is at liberty to present and to emphasize those details of a scene which attract and interest him, an architect must present the most minute details of his plan. Therefore, in the selection of incidents used in this tale I have necessarily omitted or glossed over some historical events of great importance which unfortunately did not bear on the story.

My underlying purpose has been to tell how the early merchants of America's eastern coast lived, to show what they did and, on occasion, what they suffered. I have exaggerated their activities not at all. Every event reproduced has had its historical counterpart. Prices, rates of exchange, the nature of cargoes carried and the names of ships and their captains were selected from contemporary newspapers, journals and broadsides.

In no place have I consciously played the partisan. It has been my earnest endeavor to show the Virginians, Scots, English, New Englanders and Bermudians of that day as they were. All were selfish in a greater or a lesser degree, all were suspicious or contemptuous of anything unfamiliar and very outspoken about it.

The Ashton family is in its entirety imaginary and so are Katie Tryon and Colonel Fortescue. It goes without saying that the bulk of the minor characters are imaginary.

Should a moralist insist on seeking a raison d'être for this tale, he may find it in the thesis that events on occasion can drive peaceful Americans to taking up arms in defense of their rights.

It means much to be reasonably free in the conduct of a business or of a profession. So thought the colonial merchants during 1774–1775. They met a crisis and defeated it without aid of a paternalistic regime. Should American merchants of the present generation be called to do likewise, let us hope they will meet the problem as courageously as did their forebears.

[3]

Plume's Creek

It had just occurred to Rob Ashton that for a young fellow of twenty-seven he had recently bitten off a big mouthful. To get himself married and to start building his first ship within a few months of each other — even with the best of luck — was a large order. It seemed like tempting providence. Still, his wife was mighty level-headed, healthy, cheerful and he guessed Peggy loved him plenty. When it came to the new brig, his plans for her — her? Quietly he chuckled. Sounded kind of polygamous having two female things on his hands at the same time. Maybe that explained why women and ships were so often antagonistic. The blood mounted in his normally high-colored cheeks. He surely hoped Peggy and the brig would get on. They should; both were designed from first-rate materials.

The shipwrights had gone home, but smoke from a forge still climbed, mingling with low, steel-colored clouds. They suggested snow or sleet. He hoped the storm would not break soon; he hadn't seen his wife since six that morning and was in a hurry to get home. It was something to feel her smooth, warm arms go sliding up about his neck.

Momentarily he diverted his attention from the ship's hull, towering, nearly completed, above a forest of raw yellow shores, and considered the man he had an hour earlier signed on as master of his brigantine. The Yankee, huddled against the mast foot, was watching Norfolk's bluish-black outline recede. Rob Ashton was thinking the sea captain looked mighty like a shivery blue chipmunk with a blunt red nose. He would probably amuse Peggy no end. She hadn't met many Yankees, so his way of talking should tickle her ready sense of humor. Rob nodded, smiled and drew his short-skirted coat tighter.

The skiff was rounding a reed-grown reach of the creek and the wind blew in stronger, more penetrating puffs. Ahead gleamed the warm yellow-red lights of Noatan, Robert Gilmorin's ambitious estate. Everyone along Water Street knew that molasses smuggled from the foreign West Indies had laid its foundations. They admired Gilmorin's cleverness.

Rob reckoned Peggy was going to have a home just as fine as Noatan some day. Then he grinned at his own cocksureness.

"Quite a sight," remarked the Yankee chafing big hands. Upstream was rising a great snarl of ducks scared from feeding in the lee of the shore. To a sibilant whistle of wings they raced by the skiff, breasts gleaming white and rust-colored necks stretched far out. Canvasbacks, by their long wedge-shaped heads. In a few weeks now Chesapeake Bay would crawl with waterfowl migrating northwards.

[5]

Game never had been more plentiful. Over at Williamsburg, the provincial capital, the burgesses had enacted a law forbidding owners to feed their slaves either canvasback or terrapin more than twice a week. Good thing Peggy was serving ham for dinner. Wouldn't do to put such poor man's fodder as wild duck before the new captain.

Why was Captain Farish still watching the ducks? What could he find so absorbing about a flight of canvasbacks? A queer customer; but then, most New Englanders were.

He hadn't wanted to sign on a Yankee master. It was running a big risk. But old Willoughby's rheumatics this time had tied him up into true lover's knots. He hadn't been able to run down a native master who would sign on at the rate he could afford to pay.

Farish he had first encountered on Boutetourt Street. He was swinging along brisk and trim as a gamecock. Though a scant five feet five, the little New Englander stood so straight he gave no impression of under size; middle-aged, he was bald as any capstan. What Rob chiefly liked in his prospective master was the shrewd gleam in his wintry blue eyes; it suggested that he not only saw but observed what was going on. Stephen Farish had declared himself willing to sign on as master and supercargo at sixty Spanish milled dollars a month — and found. Times were so good Norfolk captains were laughing at less than eighty. He didn't know much about Stephen Farish yet, but he did know how much twenty dollars meant right now. The Yankee's credentials were first rate and he had once owned his own ship and had papers to prove it. He was short all right, but on occasion an amazing big voice would come rolling out of his small frame.

Pity he was a Yankee — a damned shame. Everyone knew a Bostonian would charge his mother for a drink even if he owned a lake. Rob knew first hand they weren't above dealing in goods stolen by slaves, indentured servants and other riffraff. Another thing: Farish had been reluctant to tell how he had lost his own ship, but in the end he admitted a court of revenue commissioners had condemned him for landing a cargo of Cuban molasses at Ipswich one dark night. Farish was bitter, but philosophical.

Rob, guiding his skiff around a weed-draped snag, again wondered what Peggy would make of the Yankee. Barely seventeen, she was proving a shrewd judge of character. Well, descended as she was from generations of tight-fisted Scots, she ought to be.

Flinging occasional flecks of spray over her bow, the skiff skimmed up the creek, weathering a series of miniature headlands formed by acres of reeds and wild rice. These, gone a sere yellow-brown, were sagging low over the water, as if cowed by an incessant lashing of winter winds.

Rob sat straighter. Any moment now they should sight the house — really an improved settler's cabin — he had bought. Tideover, Peggy had christened it in a flash of unexpected humor. He always got a thrill at spying Peggy's kitchen smoke in the lee of a giant oak rising behind their

[6]

home. Tideover was, sure enough, nothing to be ashamed about; every young couple had to make a beginning. Most of the ten acres which went with the house fronted the creek; they ought to be worth something soon if Norfolk kept on growing at its present rate. His spirits warmed.

At first Peggy had been reluctant about moving so far out of Norfolk, but when she saw how rich the earth was and how well placed was Boush's Pasture grant, she said he had better buy. She was glad, too, he suspected, to be out of the range of her family. Only a few days back, in mimicking an acid old aunt to the life, she gave the show away.

"If you marry him, you'll regret it all your life, Margaret Fleming. The idyeh your burying yourself 'way out on Plume's Creek. And in such a miserable little cabin. Plenty of Negroes would turn up their noses at it. Besides, those Ashtons are a wild, unreliable lot. Take old St. John, Robert's own father. What did he do? Why, he ran off and married a bound maid! And an Irish wench at that!

" — Look at David. *There* is a mighty fine brother-in-law for you! A proud record he's made, gaming away the fortune his father left him to the last thin farthing! Too bad Rob wasn't left a tenth as much. Mark my words, Margaret, there is no trusting those Ashtons — even the best of them."

There were other pointers. For instance that night Mrs. Fleming's contemptuous tones came drifting out to the Fleming's veranda. Rob was sitting there thinking how lovely, how very lovely Peggy was.

"Andrew, as I have said before, and will always say, such a marriage is not to be considered! I won't have it! Peg shall not lower herself so. It would do all of us harm! You must admit his family — well, it has gone to pieces! Who are the Ashtons now? Nobodies!"

Suddenly too somber eyed for her sixteen years, Peggy burst out, "That's not so! Oh, Rob, I'm *so* sorry! Mamma doesn't mean it. She doesn't know you."

"Perhaps, ma'am, it will prove a salutory experience," was the somewhat surprising suggestion of Major Fleming, Peggy's father. "All her life Mistress Peggy has been cosseted. I fancy she will miss the old comforts. Just wait, ma'am, just wait. He will find it no easy time," the major continued comfortably. "Today political winds back and shift so fast the cleverest of us along the waterfront can't tell for sure how to trim sail. Young Ashton will overreach himself. That is my guess. Remember one thing, ma'am. All the business he does is with Boston!"

"Boston? I don't understand you, Andrew. The trade always profited St. John Ashton."

"So it did," agreed her husband, lifting a decorous pinch from a small silver snuff locker on the mantelpiece. "But in the army I learned that 'always' is a treacherous word, ma'am. In the *Intelligence* today is more news from Boston. Two weeks ago a mob burnt more tea." His large, rather severe features tightened and his slash of a mouth grew thinner,

[7]

more colorless. "That, mark you, comes to cap outrages on the *Dartmouth* and *Beaver*. John Brown tells me the Bostonians have defied Gage to suppress their own meetings. Fancy that!"

"It sounds like downright sedition to me," Mrs. Fleming agreed dutifully. But her mind was on Peggy.

"Aye. Sedition it is. Parliament will not take it lying down. It's — why, damn, ma'am, it's more — it's defiance!"

Farish said, squirting to leeward a deft parabola of tobacco juice, "Saw you studying that shipyard a piece back. Craft on the stocks ain't — ?"

"No. She's building for John Brown. My brig's only just been stemmed in Tom Newton's yard."

"Um." Farish's brown features fell into deep lines; it was rather like watching an apple age before one's eyes. "Well, Mr. Ashton, I figger you'd do well to careen the *Assistance*. You don't mind my saying so? She's got some mighty spry leaks." He blinked utterly hairless lids. "Don't fancy navigating by sail and by pump handle. Not in wintertime."

Despite a tight feeling about his heart, Rob shrugged. "She'll do as she is for a while yet. Because she'll have to. Besides, she's hardly worth patching up. Her papers say she was laid down in Bristol — back in 1737. Most likely half her bottom needs replanking."

"Well, I must say there's no call to dwell on her rottenness. If I fetch her to Boston, I can get her repaired cheap up there. I have friends. Your rice and tobacco will bring a tidy sum, shouldn't wonder. What with the troubles lately, vessels are beginning to steer clear o' Boston and land cargoes at Salem, Ipswich and Falmouth. Wish you would tell me why the governor keeps acrowding more customs cutters into Massachusetts Bay. It stumps me. The way the *Gaspée* got burnt ought to have showed those dumblocks in Parliament how the wind blows over New England. But did it? No siree, it didn't! Every time a sea captain turns 'round he's got a new ordinance to fear, a new paper to make out, and a new tax to pay. You heard of their latest notion?"

Rob said he hadn't.

"Suppose a skipper ships a cargo for Spain or Germany or Sweden, on the way he has to touch at a British port, enter his cargo and pay duty! Means he has to sail 'way out of his course and lose a mort of money in wages and food. Now, what do you make of that?"

Rob considered, spoke equably. "In the end, Parliament generally does the fair thing. They repealed the Townshend Acts."

The New Englander made no immediate reply. Later he asked, "Suppose I get you above middling price on your cargo? You'll let me patch the *Assistance*?"

Rob hesitated. To finance the building of his new brig would require strenuous efforts; at the same time, the ancient brigantine was his sole source of income.

[8]

"We'll see. In any case, you'll only do what's got to be done." He reckoned he had better throw out his bait right now. He looked Farish square in his slightly bulbous blue eyes. "I'll tell you something, Captain. If we get on and make money, you'll have the new brig."

To his surprise, the Yankee's expression did not change. "I'll put in my best licks, Mr. Ashton, and pare expenses all I can. Always have done my durndest for my owners — got my vessel that way."

A puff heeled the skiff over and Rob eased her into the wind a little.

"Well, here we are," said he cheerfully.

Farish, turning on his seat, could make out a small, white-painted dwelling on a wooded point. The owner's home lay dead ahead and looked tiny under the great oak back of it.

Tideover

The house was part frame, part log cabin, but the cabin part was clapboarded and framed in. Its walls and half its roof were overgrown with English ivy which still shone a dull green; but the surrounding shrubbery was brown and lifeless. As the skiff neared a rickety pier, white with a littering of oyster shells, Captain Farish decided that the best thing about Mr. Ashton's property was its location. From the cottage a body could make out three distinct reaches of the creek and, beyond them, the far-off steeples of Norfolk. You could even make out a dim tangle of spars, wharves and warehouses.

When young Mr. Ashton had first shown him the *Assistance* lying to Ashton & Co.'s wharf, he'd felt he was in luck. The brigantine's paint and bright work had been kept up, but what a turn he'd got when he saw her running gear! Land o' Goshen! It was frayed and gray as a wharf rat's whiskers. Some of her spars looked as if they'd come out of the Ark. Worse still, her bottom was foul; a regular marine hayfield. But it was good to sign on as master once more.

"Evening, sah!" hailed a thin voice. A Negro was shuffling, loose-kneed, down to the landing. He was very old. So old his eyes seemed veiled by a bluish film. A small gold ring hung from his right ear. The old man stood at the end of the pier, waiting for Rob to round the skiff up.

"Captain Farish, this is Absalom," Rob explained, stepping ashore. "I shouldn't wonder but he's voyaged almost as far as you."

"Now do tell!"

"Lom was my father's cabin steward, then his body servant when he went ashore." Rob's voice held an undertone of affection. "He taught Dave and me to sail."

[9]

"Howdy, Mr. Absalom." Farish extended a stubby, big-veined hand; Lom only stared at it in stupid surprise. He made no motion to take it.

"All right. Lom, just you rake a mess of oysters before you come."

Rob's progress, hampered by Toby's welcoming leaps, commenced as a bone-weary walk, but the further he followed the path of crushed oyster shells, the more he felt his fatigue ebb.

"Supper ready?"

"Mercy! Rob, how you startled me!"

Heated by the fire, the alert oval of Peggy's face was glowing. His eyes lingered on her white linen blouse, blue bodice and full yellow skirt. She looked dainty, doll-like and she had tucked a pair of blue-dyed straw flowers into the dark hair above her ear. More color rushed into her face when she saw his solid figure nearly filling the door frame.

He saw that the rims of her large, dark-blue eyes were red from the smoke driven out of the fireplace. He must take a look at its flue the first chance he got.

"Where is your Yankee captain?" she queried. "Don't you dare tell me you left him in Norfolk! I am dying to see what he is like."

His face broke into a boyish, infectious grin. "Down at the landing. Coast's clear." He snatched her off her feet, dripping ladle and all, and, despite perfunctory kicks of protest, kissed her so thoroughly that when he put her down she dropped the ladle and, blushing, began retrieving a windfall of hairpins.

"Really, Rob, if you fail as a merchant you needn't worry. You would make a grand buccaneer! What *will* your captain be thinking?"

"The truth most likely," he chuckled. "Farish ain't much to look at, but he's smarter than an old he-'coon. Come in, Captain, come in! We don't put on much style just yet, but I hope you won't mind. Ma'am, may I present Captain Farish?" He felt right proud of Peggy and the friendly way she smiled even if Farish was just a Yankee sea captain.

The newcomer whipped off his leather hat and jerked a solemn bow. "Servant, ma'am. A pleasure and a privilege."

He paused in the doorway, a small erect figure in canvas trousers, worn blue serge and pewter buttons. As soon as she got a good look at the bandy-legged little figure, Peggy knew what he reminded her of. David Ashton's champion gamecock, Hannibal, had the same self-confident stance, the same quick, bright eye and alert air. But the gamecock had no traces of tobacco at the corners of his beak. Peggy felt her cordiality wilt when she noticed a brown splash marking the captain's turkey-red waistcoat.

Captain Farish sighed, settled comfortably into a chair and tilted. He wished it was a rocker. Missus Ashton was a girl of sense, it appeared. Another tot of the Medford would go well, but he didn't dare hint again. Watching the play of firelight on a frosty windowpane, he fell to wondering whether maybe he could smuggle aboard a half cask of powder without being seen. Gunpowder was fetching breathtaking prices around Boston.

She's a smart piece, no cornstarch airs, Farish appraised. But maybe a mite too smart for her husband. He asked casually enough, "You are not king's people here, ma'am?"

"No," Rob replied quickly. "And we're not Whigs, either."

"That's a sensible way to look at things — as long as you can." Stooping, the New Englander patted the spaniel which had come to sniff at the heavy white metal buckles on his shoes. Farish was watching his words, Rob sensed. "I'll try to explain, ma'am, and I can give you two answers. First off, this here tea tax gives the big mouths like Sam Adams, Dr. Joe Warren, Ruggles and Jimmy Otis — he's half cracked anyhow — something to caterwaul over. 'Taxation without representation,' says they. But that ain't the trouble." Farish pursed his lips to spit but remembered in time. "Three-quarters of the people in England ain't represented in Parliament no more than us."

"Then their talk is of no great moment?"

"Not yet, ma'am. But the Stamp Act of 'Sixty-seven put the lawyers, printers and writers on the side of the big mouths, mostly. The real reason has to do with trade — it most always does. It's the East India Act." Farish paused to tuck his feet on the rungs of his chair; there was a strong draught beneath the door. It was blowing harder. He could hear the wind roaring among dead leaves on the giant oak. "That there act gives the East India Company the *sole* right to import tea and some other goods direct and *in their own ships!* That is, they can import tea without going to pay duty in England first. Anybody else has to pay duty here and in England. By law, we ain't allowed to import Dutch or Russian tea — only English. Right now the East India people are selling tea dirt cheap — cheaper even than Hancock and the rest of the bigwigs can smuggle it. It slips in slick as a string without knots. Won't take you long to figger how long an independent tea trader, paying a double tax and freightage, will stay in the business."

"Just a minute," Rob objected. "The East India people have to pay freight, too."

Farish snorted. "Not by a jugful. Didn't you hear what I said just now? The company owns its own vessels and mans them with brown Sepoys. Don't pay them poor fellers 'nough to keep a roach going, either."

"It won't last, Captain," Rob said slowly.

"It has in India," Farish maintained emphatically. "Just you wait. In a few years a handful of big companies will own America lock, stock and barrel. The Hutchingses, Tom and Elisha, they're the old governor's sons; Richard Clarke & Sons, and a few others."

At length Farish sighed, belching delicately behind his hand, and

[11]

made an effort at polite conversation. "Norfolk's a likely spot for a port — in peace times."

"Why only in peace times?" Rob asked, holding his Madeira to the light.

"British navy. If there's trouble, I'll give Norfolk a wide berth."

"Now I mind me of a voyage to Dominica," Farish began and Rob sighed. God help them! The Yankee looked like one of those long-winded sea captains who could only be shut up with an ax handle. Drowsily, he again considered his wife. The bodice of her dress had lifted her breasts a little under the frills, making them seem riper than they really were. Suddenly he took to wondering how many petticoats she might be wearing. Anywhere from three to five. It was right good fun to make a guess — even more to check up.

"Never did see a hearth set high like that. Throws the heat fine," remarked Farish.

"They build them that way in the Bermuda Islands," Rob explained not without pride. "My father came from an island called Somerset. Some of my family is still living there."

"I wish you would build one like this in the kitchen," Peggy smiled. "A high fireplace saves a woman's back more than you lazy men ever think."

There was a pause and then Farish innocently inquired, "Do we — er, refit before I clear?"

Rob stared into the flames a little before he said, "No, Captain. Any work that is done will have to be done in Boston. It — well, you said yourself — it will be done cheaper there."

"For a fact, sir, I wish you'd heed what I've said." The captain's lowered voice was almost pleading. "Your vessel's pumps ain't fit to dry a canoe." He would have said more, only Rob's wooden expression warned him to press the point no longer. His arguments were getting him nowhere fast. Hanged if young Ashton wasn't proving as careless and easygoing as the rest of the Chesapeakers. Up till now he hadn't given the impression.

A lull in the booming of the wind let the three of them catch a distant clatter of hoofs. On the frozen ground the horseshoes sounded staccato.

"Who will that be?" Farish asked, toasting legs incased in coarse gray stockings.

"Some Sons of Liberty," Peggy told him with a little laugh. "They'll be coming back from their muster at Thoroughgood's."

"How can you tell that, ma'am?"

"Nobody else would be so drunk. Can't you hear them yelling?"

Farish could, by cupping his hand to his ear, catch a few wild whoops. The spaniel kept on growling. When Rob peered out of the kitchen door, he dashed through it and set up an excited barking.

"Oh, hush your fuss, you old fool. They've gone on."

When the dog refused to be silenced, Rob gave his wife a level look and crossed to an earthenware jar with a lid. It said GINGER in blue letters, but what Rob took out of it was a big old-fashioned horse pistol. After snapping open the frizzen to look at its priming, he said, "Reckon I'll find out what's worrying him. Pour the captain a bit more Madeira, my dear."

"You've something on your mind, ma'am?"

She nodded, stepped closer. "Yes. The *Assistance* really is as bad as you make out? Please tell me the truth."

"I hate to say it, ma'am, but she's a sight worse. She's so leaky I'll warrant some of her cargo will suffer."

"Well," Peggy spoke hurriedly, "you go ahead and get the pumps fixed. Replace the worst cordage and buy the sail you spoke of. Of course those rotten planks will have to come out."

Farish looked sharply at her. "Yes, ma'am. But where will I find the money?"

To his surprise the girl's fingers closed on his wrist. Right now she was a determined-looking piece. She was looking years older.

"I — I will bring it to you tomorrow morning. Have the carpentry done in the late afternoon and don't you dare use any new sails till you've passed the Rip-Raps. I want to surprise Mr. Ashton. You'll say nothing to anybody. Understand?"

"Nary a word, ma'am." He grinned.

From the next room came Ashton's voice "I can't take you in, Jemmy." He was talking low and quick. "You know I would if I could, but I can't. You know how things are these days. Everyone has got to be careful. Look, here's a duck and a slab of cornbread. Go down past the spring in Shawl's hollow and you'll find a leanto. I use it hunting. You ought to be able to make out there till you decide what to do."

"Thankee, sir, and Gawd bless yer. Thankee."

"Who is that?" demanded Peggy's clear, efficient voice.

"It's Jemmy Potter, the ostler at the Crossed Keys."

"Well, mister, you look a mite ruffled. What's happened?" Farish inquired, as he and Peggy came over to the door.

Jemmy Potter's uneven yellow teeth sank eagerly into the wedge of cornbread and when he spoke, little crumbs tumbled through lips swollen as from a blow.

"The Sons of Liberty, blarst 'em all to 'ell, was 'olding muster over at Thoroughgood's place. This a'ternoon, it bein' me day orf, I goes over to Flora's meadow for to watch 'em." He sought Rob's eye. "I didn't do nothink but larf, sir. I swear to God I didn't! I couldn't 'elp it. Them militia was that comical wot with their defaulter's parade uniforms and their firelocks canting every which way." The way Jemmy straightened as he spoke showed Rob he had all of an ex-regular's contempt for militia. "So 'elp me, at a simple 'right wheel,' they fell orl over themselves like a calf on a picket rope."

[13]

Rob couldn't hide a grin. He, too, had watched the Independent Company of Princess Anne at their exercises. But Farish wasn't smiling.

Jemmy shot Peggy a glance from anxious, bloodshot eyes. "I just larfed a little. Surely there weren't nothink so orful in that, were there, mum? A big, loud-mouthed sergeant named Leeming leaped orf 'is 'orse and grabbed me by the scruff of me neck. 'Larf at the Sons of Liberty, will yer, ye bloody Tory? We'll teach you respeck.'" Jemmy fumbled the crumbs from his mouth and blinked in the light from the kitchen. "You knows 'im?"

"Yes, I know Leeming. Get on with it," Rob said impatiently.

"They locks me in a room 'til their manoovers is done, then they fetches Mr. Jarvis. 'See to it,' says Mr. Phipp — 'e's a leftenant in the Winston troop — 'you don't employ no more traitors at the Crossed Keys or some fine day you'll wake up and find your inn ain't 'ere anymore.'"

"Where are you heading now, Jemmy?" Rob asked.

"For the Great Dismal Swamp, I guess."

Peggy lingered in the doorway, one hand clenched tight against her breast as Jemmy walked away. "Oh, the cowards! How dare they persecute an old soldier just for laughing! Sons of Liberty indeed!"

"Margaret! Be quiet!" Rob ordered sharply. "Come inside."

The Sons of Liberty

Captain Farish returned quickly to the sitting room and, idly at first, then in deepening interest, fingered what must be a set of plans for the new brig. The fact that Mr. Ashton had drawn plans for so small a vessel was in itself unusual. At Salem, Ipswich and Marblehead, where the best ships in America were built, a shipwright planned his vessel as he went along. He would mount stem and stern posts first, then lay the keel and commence framing out from amidships. Any inspirations would be more or less spontaneous and only then put into execution. What Farish beheld neatly rendered in India ink caused him to bend his hairless head in admiring concentration.

What with his specifications for pickled and boiled timbers, Mr. Ashton was aiming mighty high. Imagine calling for copper treenails below a merchantman's waterline! Crimanently! What did Mr. Ashton think he was building? A yacht? A ship of the line? Tapping hands softly behind back, Farish considered the way the brig's bow was to be sheered. Why in Tunket was he planning to step his mainmast so far forward? Involuntarily, he moved his head in disapproving jerks. Suddenly he recognized her. She was the *Grand Turk* drawn to a working scale!

[14]

Farish straightened hurriedly when the young couple appeared, she with color high and he with jaw set at a stubborn angle.

"Hope you don't mind, but I've been taking a look — " Farish broke off. Mrs. Ashton's eyes were growing very tense and round.

Horses, several of them, were advancing down the lane beside the meadow. When Peggy started up, her husband warned in a low voice:

"Stay where you are!" His eyes sought Farish's, asked a number of silent questions. Then because the riders seemed to have halted, he went to look out of a window. Turning, he said over his shoulder, "Nobody's been here, understand?"

He made out four riders whose horses were blowing and snuffling in the darkness. One of them swung off, looped the bridle over his arm and led his mount right up to the door. The beast shied back and the man cursed under his breath as Toby suddenly appeared and began a shrill series of yelps.

Rob watched a second horseman dismount, a big fellow with a sagging stomach. He wore a uniform of some sort. He began to stamp his feet and the others swung their arms as they sat in the saddle. The leader, wearing a triple-caped riding coat, rapped loudly on the door with his riding whip handle; the gesture irritated Rob no end. What right did he have coming to pound on a man's door at nine of the night?

Rob felt a little better on recognizing the leader as Matthew Phipp. A dark, sardonic fellow, he would much rather preach Rousseau's philosophies at the Spread Eagle, the worst rebels' hangout in Norfolk, than tend to his law practice.

"Hi, Rob! Will you open up, please?"

"Who is it?"

"Lieutenant Phipp, Sergeant Leeming, an' two more Sons of Liberty, by God!" rasped the second dismounted man. "Open up or you'll get to hear from some more of us."

Lieutenant Phipp cleared his throat. "Sorry to disturb you. Seen anybody about just now?"

"Why, no," Rob replied easily. "Why?"

The two men on horseback put their heads together, muttering something Rob could not catch. The fellow called Leeming started to speak but Phipp cut him short with a peremptory gesture.

"We're hunting for a fellow, an Englishman, named Potter — Jemmy Potter. He is — was — ostler over to the Crossed Keys." Ill at ease, the lawyer pulled off his hat, studied its interior a moment. He brushed a hand over his forehead. His breath, rising in small white puffs, became gilded by firelight beating through the open door. It revealed handsome intense eyes, a tangle of dark red hair and a wide red scar along his cheekbone.

Rob grinned. "I don't use the Crossed Keys much. What's he done?"

Swelling his chest until the tarnished brass buttons of an old blue milita uniform threatened to burst, the sergeant swaggered forward. Rob could see that the coat's scarlet facing and his waistcoat of the same color were peppered with food stains.

"He was spying on our muster! That's what he was! By Jesus!"

"Spying?" Rob laughed, incredulous. "Why, he's only a groom. Where do you get such crazy ideas?"

A pasty-faced, thin fellow in a dingy gray hunting shirt leaned forward in the saddle. Said he in a hoarse, passionate voice, "After we drove him out of Thoroughgood's, we searched his room. There was British army papers in his ditty bag! He was corporal in the 5th Dragoons."

"But he's been discharged, hasn't he?" Rob pointed out. "He isn't in the army anymore."

"Maybe. But that don't keep Potter from being a spy," the hunting-shirt man insisted.

Sergeant Leeming's small pale eyes narrowed to either side of a colorful nose. "Once a bloody-back, always a bloody-back, says us. We aim to find Potter, eh bub?"

"You'll be fools then," Rob said. "Anyway, I haven't laid eyes on him."

"You're sure about that?" Phipp sounded very suspicious.

"Of course. Why shouldn't I be?"

Capture

From their white tunic facings and lace, the Redcoats were marines, not regular infantry. Phipp now was able to distinguish curious low caps of scarlet. He had never seen any like them before. To the front of each brimless cap was fixed a visor-shaped pewter plate bearing a monogram. Big pewter buckles stamped with an anchor secured the intersection of white crossbelts. The marines were marching with bayonets fixed, forming a rough square about a prisoner who, despite the biting wind, wore only breeches and shirt.

Bub, staring ill-at-ease, kept hoping Mr. Matt would ride off, but he sure pitied that prisoner. He was a big, thick-limbed fellow and the wind was blowing his unbound hair all over his face. He clumped along with head hanging on breast. No wonder. About the captive's neck a length of fuzzy old rope had been knotted and his powerful-looking arms were lashed behind him. Every now and then one of the marines would lower his musket and give the bound man a little jab with his bayonet, not for any particular reason, but merely to see him wince. Through hair on the prisoner's left leg, bared where his white woolen stocking had fallen, two dark lines were meandering down into his shoe.

Suddenly aware of the two horsemen waiting in the lee of a bank, the sergeant ordered his detachment to halt. Silvered buttons on his cuff glittered as he saluted.

"Begging yer pardon, sir. Is it much further into Norfolk? The leftenant marched us out by a different road."

"No," Phipp told him. "Only about two miles. You are in command?"

"Yes, sir. The leftenant got cold and rode on into town."

By spurring his mare further out onto the road, Phipp was able to see what the handbarrow contained. A keg of French powder — CHARLEVILLE L^{ier} QUALITÉ was stenciled in white on its end — three or four pistols, and maybe half a dozen rusty old muskets and Spanish fuzees.

"See you've been busy," was Phipp's dry comment.

"Aye, sir. An informer warned the provost marshal there was illegal arms concealed in Pitson's boat house. We dropped in after dark." He glanced at the barrow, then at the shivering prisoner. "Fancy. We found this here Aaron Weaver hiding in the sail loft, and him carrying three-pound reward on his head."

"A deserter?"

"Yes. Jumped the *Liverpool* frigate five days back, he did, which he'll live to regret."

"Three pound for us," one of the marines amplified, "and, since it's second offense, three hundred with the cat for him."

Quick as a released spring, the prisoner spun half about, got free and ran over to raise a desperate, quivering face beside the mare's shoulder. "Save me, sir! For God's sake, save me! The cat — they — they'll cut me to ribbons with it this time. Oh God! God! I — I can't stand it again. They'll kill me!"

In Weaver's terror Matt Phipp recognized a frantic, animal-like quality. The back of his neck began to tingle. The man's panic was all the more dreadful because his was essentially a strong, kindly face suggestive of habitual self-control.

"Why did you desert?"

"I never enlisted," the prisoner gurgled. "They'd never the right to take me! I'm not a Britisher, sir; I'm a free, law-abiding citizen of Massachusetts." A tear began to course uglily down the prisoner's swollen cheeks and his chin quivered pitifully. Snarling annoyance, his guards closed in. Weaver flinched closer to Matt Phipp's horse. "You're Provincial, too. For the love of God, do something! Save me! They'll flog me to death aboard the ship. Sackville's a devil! My family's starv — "

Phipp said, "On occasion all of us meet with bad luck. A smart man makes the best of it."

Like light from a blown-out lamp hope vanished from the prisoner's eyes and his body resumed its slack, beaten attitude.

The sergeant coughed, husked and then spat. "Nah then, you mothers' mistakes. Form *threes!*"

The marine detachment, Phipp noticed, was moving at a faster pace.

They seemed uneasy, too; kept looking off into the gloom and marched closed in together. Rhythmically their muddied black gaiters swung back and forth behind the sergeant's lantern. They seemed eager to reach the security of Norfolk.

"They act scared," Phipp told Bub. "Maybe they'll have reason to be."

Game Cocks at the Spread Eagle

New and solidly built of brick, the Spread Eagle Ordinary loomed flush to a narrow brick sidewalk separating it from the mire and often pig-infested bog holes of Cumberland Street.

Tom MacSherry was inordinately proud of his tavern's leaded windows, of the blue and white eagle screaming on its signboard, of its pine-paneled taproom; and of a huge roasting spit in his kitchen. A fat old mongrel, running on a treadmill, turned it. The Spread Eagle's six comfortable beds could, and often did, accommodate as many as eighteen travelers. But MacSherry's greatest pride was what he called the "four-barreled" privy out back. It was brick, too, and had a flagstone walk leading to it clear across the backyard.

"No standing in line of a morning for my guests," he boasted, looking Ma Coverly, who ran the Harp and Crown at the corner of First and Mariner Streets, bang in the eye.

Lulled by dancing flames and the spicy odor of Madeira mulling on a little brass trivet, David Ashton mused on his favorite seat by the taproom's chimney corner. Only vaguely Rob Ashton's brother heard an occasional horse go clip-clopping over the frozen mud of Cumberland Street, the distant rattle of some watchman's staff as he dragged it along a picket fence, and the soft *slap-slap* of cards falling on the other side of the room.

But David Ashton didn't look. Instead, he abstractedly watched the barmaid dab at her stringy yellow hair, smooth her apron, and rearrange a set of dingy ruffles edging her bosom. He smiled faintly at the familiar routine. Katie wouldn't be a bad-looking piece, ran the undercurrent of his thoughts, if she'd half take care of her appearance. The wench had been blessed with a luscious, almost Junoesque figure and her regular features bore an inexplicable suggestion of breeding. She had, moreover, a complexion most women would give their best earbobs to possess. But what attracted him most to Katie was the genuine warmth of her smile and certain changeable lights in her very wide-set gray-green eyes. Lucky their lashes were long and several shades darker than the girl's tawny mane.

Katie fixed a look, unconsciously wistful, on David Ashton's six feet of stature as, garbed in an elegant bottle-green satin coat and white silk breeches, he lounged not ungracefully across the chimney-corner bench.

For a thousandth time she noticed how his right brow, set a bit higher than its companion, lent young Mr. Ashton a quizzical expression. It set girls asighing. And the way the dark brown hair grew into a point on his forehead. It wasn't powdered tonight, but was neatly clubbed at the nape of his neck with a broad, swallow-tailed grosgrain ribbon of Lincoln green. She pondered again what kind of weapon could have given his rather thick nose that slight swerve to the left. Once more she decided that it was attractive rather than disfiguring.

"Out of curiosity, Katie; just when did you last take a bath?" David asked.

"Oh la, sir, that was in October. River water's been colder'n Blixen ever since."

"Did you ever consider heating any?" David queried, tapping strong white teeth against the mouthpiece of a German porcelain pipe he favored.

"La, Mr. Ashton," protested the girl in frank surprise, "wouldn't that be getting above myself?"

"You are, I believe, aware of how often I bathe?" David came back.

Katie ducked her yellow head and, giggling, returned to her tumblers. She knew, none better. Every other day she toted a tin bath and seven pails of scalding water to the young gentleman's semipermanent quarters upstairs.

A deep sort, Mr. Ashton, she reflected. A girl couldn't ever tell what he was really thinking, or how much he meant of what he said; and he said the funniest things. The funniest thing of all about him was the way he kept his hands to himself. On occasion she had experienced a secret sense of grievance. Maybe she wasn't good enough for a young gentleman who had once been a rake-hell about London? Maybe that was it, but every other buck in town, young or old, would get his hand under her petticoats given half the chance. Not that she minded it a great deal. That was as much a part of her job as the squeal and half slap she gave in return.

Into the taproom stepped a broad-shouldered gentleman nearing forty. He was beginning to put on fat, but his build yet suggested activity and alertness. Above the collar of his mulberry-hued surtout Mr. George Leavitt's features, still lean of outline, shone a peculiar copper red. High and prominent cheekbones, straight jet hair, and eyes of the same hue prompted the assumption that a few generations ago some Leavitt had taken a squaw to share his cabin.

"Well, Davey. How's the bully boy tonight?" he called, limping the length of the taproom. Doc Gordon had never been able to extract the Frenchman's bullet from his knee joint. "Hell's fire! It's fit to freeze a man's heart out on the river — damned tide was running dead against us towards the last. Katie! A brace of rumbullions! Fast as you can brew 'em!"

"Welcome. La, Mr. Leavitt, you are looking real elegant tonight." Katie came bouncing out from the bar and bobbed an awkward curtsy. Easygoing Mr. Leavitt was a favorite of hers and was, without question, the most generous of the James River planters who from time to time liked a drink "brought up late."

"How's my darling chick tonight?" Laughing, Leavitt flung an arm about Katie's waist and, without effort, heaved her up to a seat on the bar. Her breathless giggles grew louder when, after fumbling in his pocket, Leavitt pulled out some money and began to grope beneath the grimy hems of her voluminous petticoats. "Dammit, wench, where *is* that garter?"

"Oh, Mr. Leavitt, ain't you awful?" Katie wriggled down and, laughing, ran for the shelter of the bar.

"And now, my dear, don't forget those rumbullions. Ask the other gentlemen present what they fancy."

Two more slaves dressed like Plato came shuffling in, their skins gone slate gray with cold. One carried a portmanteau and the other lugged a bundle, shapeless because it was so swathed in blankets.

David's crooked brow arose. "What have you got in there? The last remaining virgin along the Jeems?"

A low, wicked, delightful chuckle arose from Leavitt. "What Virgil carries, my boy, is the one and only gamecock along the Chesapeake who can whip the lights and livers out of Hannibal!"

"So?" David's dark face was losing its lonesome look. "I presume you have more of that pretty new currency?"

Briskly the plump planter rubbed his hands. "Aye, but I'm warning you, Davey, Ginger's a regular hellion. He killed Billy Rountree's Caesar last week and never got scratched himself. How's your bird?"

"Hannibal and I stand eager to oblige."

Half an hour later the low-ceilinged taproom reeked of tobacco smoke, wet wool, liquor fumes and pungent body odors. Already two pairs of stags — green birds never before pitted — had been matched and fought.

"Number two was a real fast fight," Captain Ben Rudder opined. He looked very spruce and well set up in a suit of new seagoing serge. "Kind of like a couple of privateer sloops in action."

Katie, hard put to fill so many mugs and tankards, was sweating like a June bride, as Tom Newton put it.

Towards the end of the second bout Katie's marine corporal, blue-lipped and running at the nose, pushed his way into the ordinary and, stripping off his scarlet tunic, tied a green baize apron about his middle. Whistling cheerily, he set to work at Katie's side, very matter-of-fact.

"You're late tonight, Mr. Pepperill," she chided, slapping aside the hand with which he pinched her rear.

"We was ordered out without notice." He wiped his sharp little nose on his sleeve and gave her a sly, foxy look. "Took a bleedin' deserter, we did; means three quid split among eight."

"Then I can have the blue petticoat?"

He nodded halfheartedly. "Ye'd do better with a ribbon for yer hair.

Looks like a bloomin' last year's rat nest." Though perspiration had beaded Katie's features and was staining dark half moons under her bodice's armholes, Pepperill cast her a lecherous look. "Gawd, ducky, yer a sight for sore eyes. When will MacSherry leave you go?"

"With this main on 'twon't be until late. You're tired, Mike. Why don't you go up to the loft? I'll wake you when I come in."

The corporal went on washing tumblers. "All right. For Gawd's sake, wash yer neck. You smell like a mink."

"Dirty Shirts was riding tonight," he volunteered. "Sergeant heard they mustered down to Thoroughgood's."

David Ashton, lace cuffs stripped back from forearms dark with hair, was entirely serious for once. He used a piece of broken glass to scrape Hannibal's spurs to a carefully calculated point. The horny growths were thin now and keen; nearly as deadly as the steel gaffs favored in the West Indies.

MacSherry beamed, roared welcome; rum and Holland gin were going faster than ale now.

David, satisfied, tucked his bird under one arm and, after relighting his queer porcelain pipe, called, "Heyo, George! Reckon we're ready." The red bird pecked savagely at his wrist, then flicked his head, glaring defiance at the crowd from clear, sherry-colored eyes.

The fanciers crowded in. "Ain't the red quill an ornery little cuss?" "Look at them spurs." "And them eyes! Crooler nor old Satan's." "Some bird, Mr. Ashton; good luck to ye." "Who'll take two to one on the red quill?"

"Weights, gi'e us weights," called some renegade Scot. "I'll no' bet till we hear the weight."

Leavitt's bird, a wiry Dominique, weighed four pounds six ounces, giving him an advantage of three ounces. This caused some shifting of odds, but confidence never deserted David's dark, intense face.

"Rush it to him, General," he whispered while lifting Hannibal, restless and belligerent, off the scales. "Our war chest is getting mighty low."

"Will you judge, Tom?" David asked MacSherry, then hastily added, "You agreeable, George?"

Leavitt, busy biting gently at Ginger's close-clipped comb, nodded his narrow blue-black head. The white cock struggled, glaring at the glossy red-brown bird between David's hands.

"Gentlemen, bill your cocks!" MacSherry called, and in an instant silence fell. Briefly the two birds were held at arm's length, just close enough to permit them to peck at each other. Between his hands David could feel Hannibal's muscles tightening, the bird's whole wiry body aquiver. It was just as well; his shot at the Spread Eagle hadn't been paid in two weeks.

"On the line!" MacSherry ordered. Sinking onto their heels in their respective corners, the owners set their birds on the floor, but still restrained them.

[21]

"One — two — three. Go!"

Leavitt and Ashton stood up, hands flung wide apart, watching. At their feet a feathered tornado was sweeping the floor. Mouths open, the onlookers surged forward and began to yell.

Twice, thrice the fighting cocks leaped into the air, fanning shortened wings in a furious effort to maintain equilibrium. Meanwhile, their legs worked in a series of lightning jabs driving the spurs forward. Only the trained eyes of veteran fanciers could follow such a rain of blows. Almost at once, however, the knowing began to offer odds as one gamecock or the other got in a telling blow.

"Three to five on the red! Three to five on Ashton!"

"Take you!"

"Ten shillings even money on the Dom!"

"Done!"

The first flurry did no real damage, left both warriors circling, necks outstretched, clipped ruffs flaring. Lazily, white feathers and red went drifting off among the damp and muddy feet of the onlookers.

Another two flurries slowed the cocks enough to make them pause and glare at each other. They held their wings half extended for better balance. A sudden shout made pewter mugs along the walls rattle. The Dominique had charged and, fighting a savage flurry, tumbled Hannibal onto his back. In a flash the white gamecock sprang up on his enemy, pecking and slashing like a demon in feathers.

In a murderous hurry to press his advantage, the Dominique charged in, and rising into the air, made a buzz saw of his spurs. Instead of rising to meet him, Hannibal this time ducked, passed cleanly under his adversary.

No sooner had the white, disconcerted, landed off balance, than the red bird pounced on his back and drove a spur into the upriver gamecock's neck. A resounding roar billowed about the taproom. Bright scarlet blood spurting from among his feathers, the Dominique floundered and made a valiant effort to stand. He ended by toppling crazily onto his side. Panting, punished by Hannibal's relentless spurs and beak, he tried to scrabble away, but the keel of his breast only sketched a pathetic groove through the scattered sand and feathers.

Tautly, Hannibal was strutting, one fiery eye fixed on the ungainly snarl of pinkish red feathers. At last the red bird threw back his head, beat his wings and emitted a strident crow. The crowd bellowed, pounded one another on the back, called each other to witness.

Still smiling, David lifted his bird. Gleefully he suffered a series of vicious pecks delivered when he began sponging off Hannibal's cuts with a mixture of rum and water. Just before he picked up the bird, he took a small mouthful of rum and squirted a bit into the gamecock's bloodied beak.

After a hard fight Hannibal enjoyed his tot of grog as much as any prizefighter.

[22]

H. M. S. Liverpool

In the frigate's lockup far forward, the song reached Aaron Weaver as little more than an elusive undertone. He blinked and shivered. Plague take them! Their caterwauling had roused him from that not unpleasant lethargy into which he had sunk at sundown. Now his brain again was stirring the bitter broth of Fact. It seemed ages since two marines had marched him forward from the wardroom; the court-martial had sat there. He blinked. He still could see the court ever so clear, sitting beyond a wide mess table. White wigs, gold epaulets, navy-blue tunics and marine scarlet. All the faces glaring, staring at him like a row of images. No mercy in any of those eyes.

Three times a hundred lashes with the cat! The heavy irons on his wrists conveyed their bitter cold into his arteries.

Three hundred lashes! Weaver's manacled hands joined themselves. They were big-knuckled and purpled by old gurry sores and fashioned to handle nine-foot oars. Well, he guessed he'd never again go salmon spearing along the Kennebec in the spring, nor feel his back tendons crackle under the drag of a well-filled net. There would be no more net mending at night and on stormy days.

What had he done? God Almighty knew he had not hurt nary a one of His creatures. Of course fish weren't creatures, just reptiles. All he had wanted was to get back to Falmouth in the province of Maine.

He was not afraid to die. He really wasn't. All his simple, hard-working life Aaron Weaver had feared a jealous God, just as the parson and the Bible said he should. He had paid his taxes and, back in '60, he'd served the Crown with the militia against Montcalm. A year ago he had been elected a deacon of the church because he kept the Commandments and only cursed when a seal got into the nets.

A flogging was bad enough, but the degradation of being dragged across the deck like a common criminal, that was what he really minded. Very well he knew what to expect. Hardly a week went by but some unfortunate wretch had his sentence read to him at the foot of the mainmast. Aaron knew very well what happened after that. The bosun's mate would strip off the culprit's shirt and lash him, spread-eagled, to a hatch grating. The bosun would pipe all hands on deck. If any other men-o'-war were in harbor, details from their crew arrived to witness the punishment.

He prayed. Our Father, which art in Heaven, I know I ain't much 'count, but I've tried to live right. I know You mean it all for the best, but it does seem a mite hard on Serena and the children. For myself, I don't ask anything, but please, Heavenly Father, keep an eye on Serena. She ain't so strong and her folks are all dead. And if You can, try to look the other way for a while, because I don't want You to see. It's just that I guess I ain't nigh so strong as I thought. And — and — it was an effort to get the next out — please forgive the British captain and his officers and all those who have trespassed against me, as I do forgive now. Amen.

Heavy boot soles clumped in the dark corridor, a keyring jingled and the singing in the wardroom swelled very loud as a bulkhead door creaked back. A light partially dispelled the gloom of Weaver's cubicle. A square window had been let into the cell door. It was set with two thick iron bars. Between them appeared the sergeant's not unfriendly face. A lantern held below lit his chin, the tip of his nose and the pewter plate on his cap.

"They were over-'ard on yer, Weaver," said he. "Captain Sackville's orlways 'ard." Putting his mouth to the bars, he whispered, "If ye've any money, I'll try to find yer some opium pills. Yer don't feel the knots so bad."

"It's mighty friendly of you, Sergeant," Aaron said in his faintly nasal voice, "but I ain't got a penny. I'll make out, though. I'll make out somehow."

Soothing music began to sound in Aaron Weaver's ears. He commenced to undo his belt. Fortunately it was long. During the afternoon he had noticed an eye bolt let into the deck beams. What it was for, he couldn't guess, but he knew it was there. His fetters hampered him so it took some time to locate the iron eye by sense of touch. When he found it he threaded the loose end of his belt through the buckle and made it fast. Good job the lockup was situated in the bow. The upsweep of the deck gave more head room here than in other parts of the ship.

Aaron Weaver climbed up on the biscuit box and slipped the leather noose over his head. That sweet, ineffably peaceful humming noise grew louder, like a swarm of bees drawing near. He drew a deep breath, then expelled it before he kicked the box backwards and out of reach.

The humming noises swelled to a deafening crescendo.

Rob and his wife stood alone at the end of the empty wharf, shivering in the raw February wind. They were watching the brigantine's slave crew warp her out into the *Elizabeth*'s greenish-yellow current.

Farish and the pilot were standing by the wheel, the former bellowing, brazen-lunged, through a leather trumpet at hands casting off topsail clews. The pilot was busily whirling the wheel. The ebb, running now at top speed, rounded the *Assistance* up to a sheet anchor which had been rowed far out into the stream.

Buff, Peggy noticed with inward satisfaction, was pushing hard against his capstan bar, helping hoist the green old cable inboard.

Rob said nothing. He was too dog-tired. He was thinking that the brigantine wasn't much to look at. She looked terribly shabby and old. Farish had been dead right about the main topmast. It *was* sprung — no doubt of it. He hoped it would last to Boston.

Well, for better or for worse, there she went. The words struck a chord of memory; he groped until he found Peggy's hand. They stood closer together.

As happened uncannily often, she expressed the words in his mind. "Well, honey, for better or worse, there she goes."

"And she will come back," Rob muttered. "She must!"

Talk in a Bedroom

David Ashton opened a tentative blue eye but shut it promptly, stifling a small groan. God's teeth! His head throbbed like the clapper of Big Ben. Why in blazes had he thought it so clever to toss off a pot of alicante on top of a double basin of Johnny Gilmorin's kill-devil? The belated wisdom only made him feel worse.

David was becoming disappointed at the turn of political events. During the past month not one event promising excitement had taken place. The damned Bostonians hadn't rioted in weeks, and what few letters reached the committee were sterile, tiresome reports, recommending this and deploring that. God's teeth, it looked as if Parliament actually didn't dare to monkey with those blue-nosed psalm-shouters up in Massachusetts.

He yawned and stretched until the tendons in his arms crackled. Plague take the Yankees anyhow!

In the street below, he heard jingling bells and the clopping hoofs of a pack train setting out for a trading journey among the new villages beyond the Blue Ridge Mountains. Maybe he would go out to the far west, too. Out to Ohio — to Illinois, even. Plenty of fighting there, all right.

Suddenly Katie appeared, broadly smiling over a tray set with copper chocolate pot and crumpets.

"O fairest Hebe in all this southern realm, I give thee greetings." Waving a derisive brown hand, David hoisted himself up on his elbows. Then, groaning a little, he slipped long and wiry arms into a bedjacket of cerise silk. He pulled off the nightcap and began vigorously to rumple his dark hair. Perceptibly his bloodshot eyes grew lusty with life.

"La, sir, you gentlemen made a big night of it. Cat ain't come down off the cupboard even yet, and Mr. MacSherry's that sick to his belly he says he's tasting hair!"

He drew a breath in exaggerated amazement. The wench looked uncommon pretty in her crisp white mobcap; beneath it curls, formerly dusty yellow, shone golden. She was wearing a frilled yellow apron and a shortgown of clean blue calico.

"God's teeth, Katie! Does my nose — er, do my eyes — deceive me? You — you bathed?"

"Ye-yes, sir. Last night."

[25]

"Well, damn my blood! We live in an age of miracles! And you've even washed your hair!"

A tide of scarlet flooded the barmaid's face and breast. "You was right, Mr. David. It felt kind of good. I — I'm fixing to wash every other week — all of me," she announced with a sort of desperate determination. "And — and I aim to better my education."

She took her birch twig broom over to the fireplace and commenced to sweep a powdering of blown ashes into the hearth. "I never had no home — a home, I mean. Ma, she said my papa was Squire Tryon."

"A squire?" David exclaimed, then cursed because he had spilled chocolate onto his bedjacket. "Which one?"

"Squire Hugh Tryon," Katie said without turning her head. "He, well, he wasn't exactly married to my ma."

"Oh! Who was she?"

"I — I couldn't say for sure. Ma Shannahan 'lowed the squire's wife sent her packing right after I was born. She put me out to live with her — Ma Shannahan, I mean. Squire got himself scalped in the Indian wars of Sixty-five. Anyways, the family moved away, but I stayed on with Ma Shannahan. She was drunk most of the time."

"And how old are you, my dear?"

Her gray-green eyes widened, wavered to the floor. Never before had Mr. David called her "my dear." Not like just now, anyways. A warm flush of pleasure swept over skin which felt strangely fresh and smooth.

"About nineteen, Mr. David, but I ain't exactly sure."

"Do I gather you have small affection for this Mrs. Skillings?"

Katie's eyes narrowed and a sullen twist deadened her wide mouth. "I hate her. She treated me something terrible. She beat me for nothing. No matter how early I kindled fires, it wasn't early enough. The water wasn't hot enough, not even when it was boiling, and she'd fetch me a box on the ear if I used a leaf of tea more than she reckoned was enough. I hate her — one of the children was always getting lost, but I couldn't help it; there was five of 'em."

"But what about the other servants? Did she treat them the same way?"

"Oh la, sir," she laughed. "There wasn't no other servants — not after old black Julia died. Just me."

The barmaid's voice dropped and she made a deliberate ceremony of measuring out a cup of cracked corn for the gamecock. "One day I was picking huckleberries in the back pasture. Mr. Skillings he comes up and says, 'Come with me, Katie. I got somethin' pretty to show you.' He took me over in the bushes awhile — when we came out I — wasn't the same. Mrs. Skillings was awful mad when she found out about it."

"But how did she find out?"

"Why, why, I reckon I was acting kind of scared — and — and my clothes — That was the first time she tied me when she beat me."

"God's teeth!" David's eyes flashed. "You mean to say she beat you on top of — of the other?"

"Sure she did, Mr. David; she called me bad names — a — a trollop, a lustful whore; that was only some of them. She promised I would end my days in prison."

"Did she whip you often?"

"Pretty near every week, even when I — I was sick. She's a powerful woman, is Mrs. Skillings. I reckon she must find pleasure in giving a whipping; she used to flog the children something awful, too. I stood it as long as I could, Mr. David. Honest I did. I wanted to serve out my time — honestlike. Maybe I could have stood the whippings, but what with Mr. Skillings always fixing to get me out in the bushes, I had to get away. The black people helped me to get here."

David inquired, "What's become of that weasel-faced corporal who used to hang around you?"

Katie tossed her head. "Oh, *him!* He was too dirty and ignorant. He couldn't even sign his name. I got rid of him."

Considering how often Katie and the corporal had shared the stable loft, David found the objections amusingly significant.

"Don't go too fast, my dear. Pepperill wasn't so bad as many. Gets drunk only twice a month, and he doesn't toss his money about — except on you. I'd venture the fellow's really in love with you."

"Maybe you'd be right kind and advise me about something?"

Laughing, David threw back his head. Strong and regular teeth gleamed. "Gads my life! Can there be someone in this world who values my advice?"

"My sergeant's ship is for Boston next week. He lets on he will be lonely without me. Should I go?"

David, one brow raised, studied her face. "Does he want you to go — married?"

"Why — why no."

"Good! Then by all means go," came the surprising advice.

Very quietly Katie slipped from the room.

Feeling the wisest of beings, David sighed. Unmarried, Katie might better herself, but then on the other hand she would probably get herself knocked up someday soon and then she'd be really bad off. It was a wonder she hadn't had a baby long since. Whatever she did, he would miss her soft slurring voice and her bursts of breathtaking frankness. A courageous creature, Katie, come to think of it. In Boston there would be more soldiers, and the larger town would give more scope.

Suddenly a series of wild whoops and Indian yells were making nearby houses resound. Heads were thrust out of windows and people opened their doors.

It was some damned sailor on a spree, David decided, going once to the window:

[27]

"Yow! Yow! Wow!" A figure raced into sight, hatless, running as if all the seven devils were at his heels. Twice, three times in midstride he bounded into the air like a boy on the last day of school. Horses standing at hitching posts turned mildly curious heads, then cocked their ears. Panting, round-eyed, Robert Ashton bore down on the Spread Eagle, oblivious to the frantic yipping of a playful mongrel running alongside.

David went hurrying down. "Easy on, old fellow. What's wrong?"

"Wrong? Nothing! Nothing is wrong in all the world! The *Assistance* is back!"

Tolling Bells

"Yes, siree! We made a plagued slow passage up — with that fished top-mast. I dared not crack on much canvas." Farish, fingering a chin dark before its weekly shave, glanced out of the stern ports. "It took considerable hunting 'round to land the right buyer. Them furs for instance — but I made a forty instead of twenty-five per cent profit on them. Same with the turpentine and salt. Then I had to wait a week to find room at Will Gibson's yard. He gave me far and away the lowest estimate for repairs, so 'twouldn't have been good business to go elsewhere."

Three days later Rob went aboard, found Farish on his quarterdeck running through a sheaf of papers.

"What would you say about a trip to Charles Town?"

"Massachusetts?"

"No. Charles Town, South Carolina. What do you think?"

"I'd say no, Mr. Ashton. Boston is the spot. Prices everywhere down east are higher nor a seventy-four's skysails. If you could contrive to dig up some gunpowder — even a few barrels." The sea captain dropped his voice. "Man alive, it's selling for two dollars the pound!"

"Why mention it?" Rob demanded, a trifle irritated. "I've told you there's not a smitch around Norfolk. Powder can't be bought for love nor money."

"You don't reckon on any delays this trip?"

"Shouldn't meet a one," Farish promised. "This ship's as trim now as Solace on Sunday. And the crew I've shipped this trip has gumption enough to discharge the cargo themselves."

By Godfreys, the new vessel sure promised to be a slick sailer. All morning he'd poked and nosed around Newton's shipyard, though he knew durned well he ought to be down to Aldrich's buying stockfish and sea-biscuit. Yes. There was something mighty tidy about that there brig's lines. The graceful forward rush of her bow got him all het up inside, like a third glass of rum.

[28]

Only one thing went against him. As he had guessed, Mr. Ashton was set on calling his new vessel *Grand Turk II*. While he was watching that morning some carpenters had stepped her figurehead. Though it was a tidy bit of craftsmanship, he still held, and always would hold, that *Grand Turk* was no fit name for a Christian vessel.

Farish straightened first, rubbed his bare scalp and stifled a yawn. "Wal, we ought to clear a pretty this voyage. But mind you, I mustn't lose a day — not with all them lemons and limes aboard. They're pretty near ripe already — some of 'em, and — "

He broke off. Somewhere ashore a deep-voiced bell had begun to toll. *Blong — blong — blong!* The tone of it was definitely funereal; long instants passed between each stroke of its muffled clapper.

When a second bell joined in the tolling, Rob looked up. A third joined in the lugubrious lament. "Hear that? Must be a bigwig who's dead."

"Yes. I guess likely."

"Maybe," Rob said suddenly, "we had better find out what's happened?"

The two went aloft and along the wharf through the warehouse and out towards Lawson Street.

The shipping clerk came running out to meet them. "Look — Mr. Ashton! Look over there! They're putting up the shutters on Neil Jameison's warehouse."

"Then it's him who must have died," Farish said.

Sharply Rob shook his head. "It couldn't be. I talked with him not two hours ago. Besides, see there?"

He pointed. At intervals down the street various freight sheds, warehouses, and stores were closing their shutters. People were congregating on street corners under the whale oil lamps rigged there.

"Hi! Johnny, what's happened?" Rob hailed young Gilmorin, David's friend. Oddly enough, he was wearing a sword in midafternoon.

"This! This!" Excitedly he ran up, brandishing a single sheet of paper marked with a broad black mourning band. "The Marblehead schooner brought it this morning, but the news has just got out. It means fighting for sure! Everybody says so!" He started off, but Farish's hand shot out, gripping him by the elbow.

"You ain't said what's happened, son."

Johnny flushed angrily, then grinned. "Why, that's so. Here, read it!"

With the force of a blow, black headlines sprang to meet Rob's eye.

BLOCKADE OF BOSTON!

Port Ordered Closed to Trade From June 1st, 1774.
Gen'l Gage Proclaims Rigid Blockade.

A shiver started under Rob's collar, coursed down his back and branched into many little icicles.

[29]

"Godfreys! It can't be so!" Farish exclaimed. "The Britishers wouldn't dast!"

"But it is so!" Johnny exulted. His lively brown eyes were snapping. "Read what it says! Read it! The ministers say Boston ain't to be the capital of Massachusetts any longer — it's Salem now."

He snatched back the paper and read aloud, " 'His Majesty's Customs House and Courts of Vice-Admiralty will be transferred to Marblehead.' Do you know, Rob, not even a skiff will be allowed across Boston Harbor? Not till the Yankees pay damages to the East India Company and sue for the king's pardon!"

Farish's plain little figure seemed to gain stature. Said he gravely, "Wal, mister, you can write this down on the tail of your shirt. Boston stands on her bounden rights. She won't sue. She'll rot first!"

Runaway

One day it was said the province of Massachusetts had defied England. The next day the statement was denied. A report stated that a thousand British troops had been ordered from Halifax to Boston. Tom MacSherry, to make the item more arresting, quietly raised the estimate to twenty-five hundred. Later it was proved that only a few hundred infantry had arrived, but earlier arguments had dried many a throat.

A few items admitted no doubt. It was undoubtedly true that independent companies were raising all over Virginia, Maryland and Pennsylvania. They were called "independent" because, being privately raised, paid and equipped, they needed brook no orders from the royal governor. Their recruits swore allegiance to the Crown, and only to the Crown. Parliament, the governor and everybody else could go hang. They paid no attention to orders issued by commanders of the Provincial militia.

David Ashton, promised the lieutenancy of a company in the process of raising, had purchased and was, with unaccustomed earnestness, undertaking the study of a handbook by one Roger Stevenson. Frowning, he scanned its title: *Military Instructions for Officers Detached in Full. Scheme for Forming Corps of Partisans, Illustrated with Twelve Plates of Maneuver Necessary in Carrying on the Petit Guerre.*

For Katie Tryon news items appearing on the Spread Eagle's notice board served a double purpose. They were also her primer. There was no one in the taproom, so slowly and painfully she began spelling the words out loud.

"RUNAWAY
£10 reward. Mulatto boy. Sam, 16 to 17 years.
A great Villain but a very good Barber.

John Bland."

Katie nodded to herself. She was beginning to read pretty good now — even long words like "re-ward" and "mu-lat-to." The sergeant said breaking up a word that way made it easier.

Mr. David had been right, of course. She had done as he advised when her sergeant of marines said something about getting spliced. The minute she said no to the idea, the big Englishman bought her a lovely picture of a place called Naples — a real steel engraving. She hung it over her bed where she could lie still and admire it. Even better; the sergeant now was spending near twice as much time with her over a greasy primer he'd bought her. She knew he was vastly tickled to feel that she thought enough of him to go along.

What a smart man Mr. David was! He'd been right about washing all over, too; nowadays the planters who wanted a drink late at night — with company — tucked five and even ten shillings into her stockings. Before, she had felt lucky to get two or three. Hidden in the lining of a little clothes chest she'd bought against the voyage to Boston was amassed a growing sum. Nine pounds so far, and most of it in silver! Paper didn't feel like real money, somehow, no matter what people said. Money of her own! She thrilled at the very thought of owning property. That very afternoon she intended buying a cloak. She wanted red, but it would have to be gray because Mr. David said gray went well with her eyes. She was pleasantly aghast at the thought of spending a whole pound all at once.

It was only ten of the morning and business hadn't begun to pick up yet, so, laboriously, she commenced to decipher the fact that a Mr. Thomas Shore was offering to an eager public "Keyser's famous Pills for Removing and Eradicating the most Confirm'd Veneral Disorders." She was pondering the exact nature of "Veneral Disorder" when she heard the door open. She turned and her welcoming smile became a grimace of terror. Her legs froze into stark rigidity.

There, framed in the door, towered Mrs. Skillings's forbidding figure! Her mealy-mouthed husband was there, too. Worse yet, Mr. Goodwilling, the assistant sheriff, stood behind them, his official halbert in one hand and an important looking piece of paper in the other.

Mrs. Skillings flung out a wiry arm, pointed. "*There* she is! The dishonest, ungrateful slut!"

Katie wanted to run, but fear held her motionless.

"The i-dee your running off from such a nice comfortable home! Come here, you outrageous cozening doxy!"

"Oh, Mr. Tom! Help me!"

"Here, here! What's all this?" Katie's gurgling cry of despair was an efficient spur. "What do you think you're doing to my girl?"

"*Your* girl, you outrageous, immoral publican!" shrilled the gaunt woman at the doorway. "I'll have the law on ye!" Mrs. Skillings's hard black eyes glittered with menace.

MacSherry was fond of Katie and fonder still of the trade she undeni-

[31]

ably attracted. As yet he hadn't noticed the sheriff standing out on the sidewalk, red and uncomfortable looking.

"Law for what? What ails you to stand in front of a respectable ordinary, screeching like a scalded cat?"

"Scalded cat!" Mrs. Skillings snarled. Her nostrils were opening and shutting like the gills of a fish. Her sallow complexion actually assumed some color as she glared down a long reddish nose at the angry landlord. "Don't you misname me, you wrinkle-belly rumblegut of a innkeeper! I'm a lady, I am! I warrant it was you encouraged this poor misguided creature to desert her home and her obligations. Don't you dare deny it!"

MacSherry took off his glasses and prepared to shed also his self-restraint. "Desert what? You cockeyed bag of bones!"

"Her's a runaway!" Mr. Skillings piped up. "Her's bound to us for two years, three months and five days more!"

"Katie!" Honest Tom MacSherry's outrage became deflated. He looked badly worried as in a paternal gesture he put a big red hand to the girl's shoulder. "Is this so? Tell me true. If it ain't, me and Mr. David will fight for you till the cows come home."

Katie choked, gave him a bewildered, tear-drowned look, then nodding, commenced to blubber.

"Leave be awhile, ma'am." The innkeeper pushed aside Mrs. Skillings's grabbing hand. "There's a mistake somewheres. Katie's a good true girl."

Not until now did the sheriff rest his halbert against the door frame and step inside the inn. He unfolded the paper as he came.

"No, this here is a boney fide indenture contract, doo and properly executed. Mrs. Skillings has the right. And this here's a warrant of arrest issued by the sheriff of Roanoke County. I got to respect it. I reckon you will have to turn this Katie Tryon over to her folks. It's the law."

"She's just like one of our children to us," Mrs. Skillings announced.

"I — damn, I'll buy her contract! Give you twenty pound' Virginia currency," MacSherry offered; he couldn't stand the sight of great round tears sliding over Katie's fresh cheeks, one by one.

"No!" Mrs. Skillings's narrow jaw clicked shut. It sounded kind of like a sprung trap, MacSherry thought. "We might maybe do business at fifty pounds, but I won't take one farthing less."

"M-Mr. MacSherry," Katie gasped, clung convulsively to his arm. "P-please b-buy me! I — I got nine pound I c-can give you. I sa-sa — "

Mrs. Skillings whirled, beady eyes lighting. "Oh, you have? Nine pound! Well, now ain't that nice?"

"You'll take it?" Katie choked.

"You can be sure I will. I'd have you know, you greedy doxy, them nine pound is mine! Anything you earn while you're indentured to me is mine. You can't own property. You've no more rights than a nigger. Where is that money?"

"God damn it, Harry, this ain't right," MacSherry snarled, catching the sheriff by his arm. "I took her in starving, and look at her now. That girl's been happy here and she's been doing right well by herself. Them folks is poor white louses."

"Reckon they be, Tom, but it ain't for me to interfere," the sheriff stated, wiping his forehead. "Law's law and I'm hired to make it respected and obeyed."

Once they all three stood in the Skillingses' sour-smelling bedroom, Mrs. Skillings turned with a dreadful smile and spoke in honeyed accents.

"Katie, I reckon yer needing to be learned to appreciate a good home when you got one. Come here, dearie, I'm agoing to put some color back in them purty cheeks of yourn."

Five, six cracking slaps snapped Katie's head back and forth. Dazed, she reeled to one corner of the room, cowering there behind a fending elbow.

"How's that?"

"Well, well, praise the Lord! To think our prodigal daughter's been found." Skillings's thin voice quavered with anticipation. Having peeled off his threadbare coat, he was unbuttoning a shirt the bedraggled frill of which was stained with splotches of egg. Jesus God, but it was fine to see the wench again! She sure had grown into an eyeful! He had forgot how pretty she was; having filled out helped her looks. Yes sir, she'd make a hot armful when they got back to the hayloft. He bet she'd been learned any number of cute whore's tricks in Norfolk. Norfolk was a bang-up sailors' town; the best south of Phillydelphy. Everybody said so.

"There," panted Mrs. Skillings, "that maybe will bring you back now, my high-flown fancy-Nancy. Now just you march your big backside over to that creek and cut me half a dozen switches — so big." She held up a big-knuckled, water-withered forefinger. "For every one that's too small you'll fetch me a extry, understand?"

Hampered by blurring tears, Katie commenced selecting switches. This must just be the end of everything. She reckoned now she'd never get to learn to read and write good now; she'd never get to show Mr. David — Pepperill had been right, she'd never amount to more than a camp girl.

She wondered what the sergeant would do when he found her gone. Probably nothing. Most English were sticklers for the law — till they'd lived in the colonies awhile. But Mr. David? He was smart and well educated, and he knew 'most everybody. Slowly a vague idea began to take shape. She had better make no trouble now. Her tousled head nodded several times.

Finally she found enough switches, terribly pliant and smooth, and slunk back to the house, tendons in the backs of her legs taut and her arms twitching.

The lumpy old bed had been pushed to one side and Skillings was taking some coats from a stout hook let into the room's greasy-looking wall. Lips compressed beneath a faint mustache, Mrs. Skillings tested the switches, accepted them.

Said she, stripping off her jacket and rolling up her sleeves, "Just you peel off them petticoats."

Somehow Katie's bungling, trembling fingers undid the strings securing three of them and they fell with soft impacts onto the gritty floor. Her skin went hot, then got pebbly it felt so cold. The scrape of the falling cloth sent shivers up the insides of her legs. One white petticoat, clean save for a rust stain in its hem, remained.

The sight of it seemed to enrage Mrs. Skillings. "Will you look at our fancy lady? White underpinnings — and lawn! She must ha' rolled with half the town to earn such."

Clumsily Skillings tied Katie's hands together, tight, then lifted them over the hook, forcing the victim to teeter on the tips of solid, square-toed pumps. She squirmed when she felt Mrs. Skillings's rough fingers breaking the strings of her blouse. The cold air came rushing in over her breasts. She felt the ripped garment hauled up over her head, blinding her and ready to muffle outcries. Naked, she shivered; felt goose pimples prickling her shoulders.

"Oh — don't hurt me — " Panic seized her. "Don't — ! I know you'll kill me!"

"Hush, you ungrateful piece. You're going to learn obedience and appreciation for the care me and Mr. Skillings gives you." Her switch hissed like an angry snake across the helpless girl's thigh. "Cheat me — ?" *Swish-crack!* "Run off — will you?" *Swish-crack!*

Mrs. Skillings did a cruelly efficient job. Diabolical was the cunning with which she made the limber willows lick about the runaway's body. Katie began to moan, then screamed outright. The withes felt like red-hot wires licking around the tenderest, most intimate regions of her body. In vain she danced, writhed and twisted first one way then the other.

"Mercy! For God's sake, mercy!" she babbled, sure that the woman meant to kill her.

"Easy does it, Ma," Skillings warned. "You'll have her unfit for travel." He didn't want her permanently marked — as it was, her backside would be livid for weeks. He was remembering the pale sheen of her buttocks.

"Fasting, Humiliation and Prayer"

On May twenty-fourth the House of Burgesses considered the plight of Boston. The Massachusetts capital was facing a fate as tragic and final as that of any ruined city along the Mediterranean. Reports had it that not even a waterman would be allowed to row his boat of vegetables from one wharf to the next. British harbor guards, so the rumors went, would impound every small boat they could lay their hands on. Dusty post riders reported that starvation faced the Bostonians; food which could have reached them after a half mile's sail would have to be carted thirty miles by land.

Promptly the Burgesses designated June first, 1774, as a day of fasting, humiliation and prayer. As promptly the royal governor ordered the House of Burgesses dissolved.

Defiant, Peyton Randolph, Lee, and some seventy others reconvened in the Long Room of the Raleigh Tavern. It was comfortable, familiar, and just around the corner from the ivy-draped capitol. There a defiant legislature listened to the eloquence of Patrick Henry and George Mason. Ignoring the disapproval of merchants, factors and sundry Crown employees, they there considered a circular letter penned by the despairing but undaunted Boston Committee of Correspondence. It was entitled, "A Resolution Taken on May 13th." Patrick Henry made a lot of one of its paragraphs:

— "If other Colonies come to a joint Resolution to stop all Importation from Great Britain, and Exportations to Great Britain and every Port of the West Indies, till the Act for blocking up this Harbour be repealed, the same will prove the Salvation of North America and her Liberties. Otherwise there is high Reason to fear Fraud, Power and most odious Oppression will rise triumphant over Right, Justice, Social Happiness and Freedom!"

To commercial men only one thing was certain; trading was becoming a very hazardous occupation. As a result, the town's tobacco sheds, warehouses and lofts bulged with an influx of prohibited goods which could only be sold at auction, and on the orders of the Committee of Correspondence. English ships were ordered back to sea with cargoes unbroken. Virginian vessels laden with British produce were given the same treatment. Vessels hardly docked than their owners sent them ploughing back over the Atlantic, deep with colonial produce. Exportation was not yet forbidden. The price of Negroes soared on a well-founded rumor that the new Virginia Assembly would pass laws against continuing African slave trade. Consequently, slave stevedores, carpenters and sailors earned their masters handsome wages, even two Virginia dollars a day.

Tom MacSherry was first to nail a copy of "The Continental Association" to his bulletin board. Almost at once he regretted this haste. Both of the Spread Eagle's leaded front windows got smashed by a jostling, cursing crowd trying to get near enough to read the news.

Rob Ashton, one of the early comers, lost his hat and had his pocket picked of a sixpence. On the point of suffocation, he could only brace himself against the doorjamb and try to shove his way clear.

"My spectacles!" wailed an old man. "Pray don't break them; they cost three pound!" But nobody heeded him.

[35]

A swarm of ship's carpenters on the fringes of the crowd began yelling. "Read it, somebody! Hey there! Read it out!"

"Sure, read it!" panted a gangling farmer carrying a manure fork.

"Better read it, mister," gasped a one-eyed seaman struggling at Rob's left. "Quick — we'll get mashed, else."

"No!" roared another voice. "Don't let no bloody Tory read it!"

"Tory? Who's a Tory? Where is he?" Luckily the jam was so great no one could move forward or back, but Rob felt a savage grip on his shoulder loosen the seam of his coat sleeve.

Just then a shout went up. "Hurrah! Here's Cap'n Brush. Come on, committeeman, you read it!" "Sure, let old Slow-and-Steady read it!"

"It's as you wish, boys, but I can't fly over there."

A way was made for Brush. He drew near the door and the notice board alongside of it, outwardly jovial, though his wig was askew and half his coat buttons were torn off.

"All right, boys, if you'll leave me a rag to my back and keep still, I'll read it." In a hurried undertone he added to Rob, "Get into the inn — out back door — "

The independent company's captain braced powerful shoulders against the crowd and made room for Rob to push by him.

Somebody yelled, "Don't let that damned Tory go! Keep him till later!" But the big committeeman had put a hand to either side of the notice board and was shouting for silence.

The Congress, it appeared, insisted that Parliament repeal their duties on tea, wine, molasses, etc.; their act extending the Admiralty Court's powers beyond their ancient limits; the act under which a person charged with an offense in America might be transported to England for trial; the oppressive Acts of 1774 respecting Boston town and Massachusetts Bay; and last, but not least, the obnoxious Quebec Act.

Bending, Brush squinted, then ran his fingers along a paragraph. "It says here we can go on exporting till next September tenth, 1775."

"Does this mean our West India trade, too?" Captain Rudder, unshaven and more than a little drunk, bellowed his question from the front of a shoemaker's shop. He had not been the same since the revenuers had seized his vessel.

Brush hesitated, then said, "I'm afraid it does."

Abruptly the crowd's jubilation evaporated. Why, eight-tenths of the livestock and nearly all the lumber and grain exported from Virginia went to feed slaves and otherwise to maintain the great plantations in Jamaica, Dominica and Barbados.

John Brush, fumbling for the buttons missing from his coat, was looking mighty grave. If he saw Major Fleming duck back out of sight into the entrance of North & Sandys's shipping office, he gave no sign of it.

Matthew Phipp was climbing the steps of Barstow's stationery store.

"Now you know what we aim to do." Phipp's voice rang out inspiring as the shrilling of a fife. "In the name of liberty will you enforce this decree?"

"Aye!" "To the last Tory dollar in town!" "Aye, I'm set to burn my tea right away."

"Where? I'll join you."

"In front of Gilmorin's store. Let's singe the old bugger's wig!"

Leeming pushed forward his lumpy face, all a-sweat. "That's the ticket! Come on, boys, now's the time to smoke out every Tory's rat nest in the town!"

Cargo Northward

In the late afternoon David appeared at the gangway of the *Assistance*. Dark eyes intense, he drew Rob aside.

"Committee has ordered me to Boston. They want me to see what's really going on," he went on with a quick flash of strong white teeth. "Mind my going up on the *Assistance?*"

So there it was! Rob felt relieved. Davey hadn't had the price of a passage and had been too damned proud to admit it.

"Why should I?" He grinned, unbuttoning the top buttons of his breeches and resetting shirttails dislocated by exertion. "You've done me a fair turn, Davey, a fine fair turn." With regard to himself, it wouldn't be a bad thing for people to know he was doing the committee's chief of couriers a favor.

David clapped his brother between the shoulders. "Obliged, Rob. So long as we Ashtons stick together, we'll do; no matter how the Congress and Parliament get along." In the same breath he continued, "I would like to take Johnny Gilmorin along with me. If you have room?"

"Johnny?" Rob hesitated, but could find no valid objection. "Well, I suppose it can be arranged. Oh, one thing; if a man-o'-war stops my ship, there won't be any talking out of turn?"

David stiffened. "You really don't think I would?"

Rob shook his head. "It wasn't you I was thinking of. Johnny gets heated up mighty quick."

It was a beautiful evening. Rob thought it one of the finest he could ever recall. Though this October weather grew crisp with the falling of the sun, the atmosphere was yet not cold and damp. The sweet scent of marsh grass and the acrid smell of fallen leaves burnt in the town made an elusive, delicate perfume. Again from the end of the wharf he and Peggy, she all but worn out, watched the *Assistance* drop downstream, her patched and weathered canvas yellow-gold in the sunset.

[37]

"Ain't much breeze," Rob commented, "but the tide's making out good and strong."

So it was. It swept the brigantine past three great men-o'-war which just that morning had dropped anchor off the gray old fortifications on Four Farthing Point. For better ventilation the nearest frigate had triced up her ports; as she swung to her anchors, the sunset successively glanced from the iron muzzles of her cannons.

The effect was so startling Peggy gasped, "Look! Rob! Don't those flashes look as if she were firing on Norfolk?"

Rob, groping for one of his omens, nodded, but said nothing. Prophetic? On the *Assistance*'s stern poop they could make out David in his gay yellow coat. He looked soberer than usual. Johnny Gilmorin in a dashing light blue cloak with a scarlet lining, however, acted excited enough for two. He might have been off to China instead of only to Boston.

"He's so young and gay," Peggy sighed, seating herself on a nearby bollard. "He's an incurable romantic. I fear Boston won't meet his expectations."

Rob squared his shoulders in a characteristic, familiar gesture, and turned. He flung an arm about his wife's waist and kissed her gravely. "What say, honey, shall we go by Tom Newton's and take a look? They are supposed to step the *Grand Turk*'s foremast today."

'Oh, Rob, I'm so awfully tired — " Peggy began, but there was such eager expectancy in his look she managed a damp smile. "All right, let's. We can sleep late and go over accounts tomorrow."

She faltered then sat down quite heavily, though in a boat she was generally easy enough.

"What's the matter, honey? You're looking a bit peaked."

"It was awfully close in the office." She smiled ruefully at her ink-marked fingers. "I will feel better as soon's we get out on the river. Oh, Rob! I am so anxious to see the brig. It's been a week since I've been over."

Rob sailed his skiff right up into the shadows of the brig's stern, so close Peggy could touch her rudder. His brig's stern, he judged, was the most graceful ever seen in Norfolk — a symphony of imagination, workmanship and design. Inordinate pride filled him when he pointed to a pair of carved sea horses and long tridents supporting the scroll on which her name was painted.

Above, there were more sea horses and an anchor, just as they appeared on the Frenchman's ivory model. If you compared it to the elaborate poop of a man-of-war, or an East Indiaman, the adornment wasn't so much, but it beat all hollow the looks of any other ship out of Norfolk.

Her name, *Grand Turk II of Norfolk*, was done in sturdy block letters black against the hull's white paint. Holt's paper had described her as "an elegant vessel, lovely as a modern Argo."

It was the first time Peggy had looked at the brig from the water. From there she could appreciate how well Rob had done; she could admire the wonderfully graceful sweep from under her bilges, the subtle blending of lines towards the bow.

"You have done it!" She spoke in a strange, unfamiliar voice. "You have the model — magnified a thousand times. She'll bring us all the good things in life, won't she, Rob? When will she be finished?"

"Soon as I get money from the Salem shipment. Call it another two months, honey."

"I'll be so very proud when she's launched; so proud of her — and of you," Peggy sighed. "None of the other merchants will have a — have a — a vessel to touch — " She was going to say more, but didn't. As she looked at the *Grand Turk*, the brig grew bigger and bigger, huge as a ship of the line! Her sides heaved as if she were breathing. Why, her single bare mast was reaching high into the heavens, higher than the steeple on St. James's Church. All at once her stern rose up — up.

"Come on," Rob's far off voice was saying, "hop ashore. I want to see if Newton's built the mast step like I told him. Oh — !"

Peggy's small body quietly slumped off the seat into a puddle of muddy water on the skiff's bottom. Lazily her limbs relaxed and her head fell over sidewise against a box of fishing gear; her skirts began to blot up the bilge water. Panic-stricken, he jammed the skiff onto the sloping, chip-littered beach, then lifted her onto the stern locker.

"Peggy, darling! What's wrong?"

She managed the ghost of a smile, spoke in the faintest imaginable voice. "Reckon we'll be havin' — baby sometime next spring. Must be twins — I feel so bad."

Major Bouquet

Her yards whining comfortably against their parrels, the *Assistance*, brigantine, bowled under full canvas. She ploughed a white ruler mark down the Chesapeake, stretching yellow-brown between low-lying streaks of shore. Great clouds of migrating ducks, geese and brant passing before the setting sun cast a shadow over the bay. By tens of thousands they roared into flight, filling the air with the sound of wings, then broke up into disordered squadrons, whirling black as death against a salmon-tinted sky.

By Gad, this was more like it, David thought. He had been getting uncommon fed up with Norfolk. Especially since poor Katie had dropped out of sight. He had missed her — her crude tact on mornings after, her cheerfulness, her flattering respect for his judgment. Her going had left quite a gap. When he got back he would really try to learn where she was.

Captain Farish had counted without the moon when he ordered the helm put over and set a course to nor'-nor'east. The brigantine was logging seven knots when, like a ghost of doom, a small frigate stood out from behind a headland. Her lanterns signaled, "Heave to, or take the consequences!" Farish astounded his passengers with the lividness of his language, but hauled his wind and waited for a boat put over by the man-of-war.

A lantern in her bow, the warship's boat came swinging and bumping alongside. Ashton and Gilmorin kept so mighty calm they weren't convincing. They went over to sit on the molasses barrels, capes gathered in their laps. If Farish hadn't been so busy backing his topsails, he would have seen the muzzle of a pistol peeping out from beneath young Gilmorin's blue cloak.

Farish, leaning over the rail, could make out a black-browed young lieutenant sitting in the stern, vastly self-assured and truculent. His single epaulet sparkled bright in the light of a second lantern on the boat's floor gratings.

"I cal'late you want a peek at my papers, sir?"

"Where are you bound?"

"For Salem, sir."

"Thought so from your course."

"Here's my log and other papers."

"The devil take your papers! Save them for some ratted customs officer's backside. Lower a ladder. You're to take Major Bouquet aboard."

Without affection, the provincial sailors viewed the jersied, barefooted seamen below, noted their blue shell jackets, their varnished, black-painted straw hats and the brass hilts of cutlasses lying on the floor beside them. A tough lot, David thought, but not half so husky as the *Assistance*'s mariners.

Farish, torn between anxiety and relief, called down, "Well, sir, I don't know as I have room aboard."

"Room!" snapped the naval officer. "Damn my eyes, you're bloody well going to make room! Rig a ladder in a hurry, you confounded farmers. How is Major Bouquet to climb up the side?" While the frigate's jolly boat swung and splashed under the brigantine's counter, the dark-browed lieutenant cursed everything mercantile and colonial.

A few minutes later an officer, portly and purple-faced in his starched ruffles and regimentals, came wheezing up a rope ladder rigged for his benefit. David watched him teeter on the rail an instant like an outrageous Humpty Dumpty in scarlet, then he lurched inboard. He would have hit the deck had not Mr. Turner, the mate, and two of the crew eased his fall.

Angrily, Major Bouquet set straight a silver-laced cocked hat. "What is your charge for a passage on this dung barge?"

"Three pounds." Farish spoke softly, but he was boiling to dot the Britisher. Big as he was, he cal'lated he could take him all right.

Breathing through his nose, the major directed bulbous, boiled-looking blue eyes upon the lieutenant who had scrambled aboard with catlike agility.

"I say, is three pounds proper fare to Salem?"

By the lantern light David could see the lieutenant scratch his long blue-black jaw. "Cursed if I know, Major. This rascal talks like a Yankee so I'd give him half what he asks — be on the safe side. Look at the hangdog phiz on him. Yes, I'd pay the rogue one pound ten and dock him five shillings any time he shows cheek."

"Now that ain't fair," Farish began. "My owner said — "

" — Plague take your owner, fellow," the lieutenant said coldly. "He should feel uncommon honored to accommodate one of His Majesty's officers."

The lieutenant in blue and white put down the manifest, stood glaring suspiciously. He seemed about to speak when Farish said:

"If you wish, sir, you can stow this gentleman's luggage in my cabin. It's larger than Mr. Ashton's. Me and Turner will bunk elsewhere."

The Assistance, Brigantine

Stephen Farish, stolidly pacing the poopdeck, was of two minds. By and large, this fog wasn't such a bad thing; it exempted his brigantine from molestation by roving patrol ships. Still, no skipper in his right mind enjoyed cruising blind near the treacherous shoals off Cape Cod. He cal'lated pretty soon he'd take in the courses, slow down and keep the lead going; it'd be a sin and a shame to have weathered the voyage so far and then come to grief.

Nodding to himself, he mechanically checked the quartermaster's course with the compass. Yes, sir, he guessed he could, when the time got ripe, argue Mr. Ashton into piercing the *Grand Turk* and applying for a letter of marque's commission. Jericho! What a dandy handy privateer she'd make. The *Turk* should have the heels of any cruiser, French or British, he'd ever seen; provided of course the brig didn't turn out to be crank. Yes, sir. Him and Ashton could make a fortune gobbling up slow-sailing, big-bellied English merchantmen. Imagine Serena in a fine big house like Gardiner Green's on Pemberton Hill. There was a lot of cash in privateering. But he still didn't favor the new brig's name — too heathen sounding.

Below, David Ashton was repacking his sea chest. When he had done, he used a worm to draw the charges from his pistols. Next he wiped their flints and frizzens with a dry wool rag. Then he reloaded and reprimed the pans with fine Charleroi powder.

He could hear Major Bouquet's snores resounding in the next cabin. So Homeric was their volume, they fairly made the bulkheads rattle.

[41]

David didn't wonder. All last night that bloated swine had sat alone in his cabin guzzling port. Around midnight he fell off his chair and his black servant went in to heave the worthy major onto his bunk. He still lay on it with his wig lying on the deck and his black, close-cropped hair looking somehow obscene against the vivid pink of his scalp. An hour ago he'd been sick. The stench made David's nostrils wrinkle. Grateful to be free of this cramped, bug-ruled cabin, David softly whistled "Petticoatee" and threw his last odds and ends into a pair of fine English saddlebags.

"*Cuck! Cuck!*" observed Hannibal, executing a belligerent shuffle in his wicker coop. He was spoiling for a fight and pecked viciously at David's hand when he offered some cracked corn.

At the head of the companion, David hesitated, peering aft, then to either side. Farish himself had taken the wheel, replacing the quartermaster. He stood, a dim, alert silhouette amid the drifting mist, craning his neck to starboard. His profile was outthrust and tense. A second booming report came rolling and skipping over the ocean like a flat stone flung by a boy. It sounded much nearer.

"It's two ships, sir," grunted the mate, cupping a hand to his ear. "That other couldn't have come up so quick."

Farish snatched a leather speaking trumpet. "Masthead! Ahoy!" he bawled. "Can you see anything?"

"No, suh! It's thick like wool up heah."

Farish made no comment, but shifted his course two points to port. Presently he said, "Charge the signal cannon, Mr. Turner. If she fires again, we had better answer."

Farish seemed to be thinking aloud. "They may take us for another man-of-war and leave us be. If we ring a bell she'll know certain sure we are merchantmen. Wish to God the bulldog would fire again."

"Why?" David asked, studying the fog.

"Because I hear breakers again. Means we can't be but two spits and a jump off Province Town. I don't dast carry a port helm much longer."

David stepped closer. "Captain, I reckon we'd better take a chance of getting run down."

"Eh?" The New Englander's head swung sharp to face him and hard lines went slanting down from the corners of his nose to his chin. "What's that you're saying?"

"Tell Turner not to fire."

"I am master of this ship! Hold your peace."

Farish's blue eyes became more wintry; he looked dangerous for all his small stature. "Stand aside. Touch her off, Turner. Quick!"

Everyone could hear the rhythmic rushing swash of a ship ploughing over the water — fast. From dreadfully near, the screech of a block and tackle came knifing through the wall of fog.

"Drop that match!"

Turner spun about and gave a little startled yelp. He was looking down the muzzle of one of David's pistols.

"Drop it! Step back!" Like reports made by a drover's lash the words snapped from David's lips.

"Now by the eternal — !" Farish exploded, but checked his rush when the pistol and the deadly eyes behind it swung in line with him.

No fool, he halted, then went back to the wheel.

The soft hiss of the mate's linstock glowing on the damp deck sounded very loud. The little signal gun gleamed dully, looked out of its port at the shifting murk.

"If everyone keeps still, we'll get out of this," David said.

All three men on the quarterdeck of the brigantine heard the creak and groan of cordage grow louder. They could catch the tramp of feet, voices. It would be a near thing.

"Deck ahoy!" the lookout hailed, a frantic urgency in his tone. "Port your helm! Port! Port! *For God's sake!*"

David only glanced aloft, but Farish was on him. He slapped the pistol clattering into the scuppers. In one quick bound the master then caught up the gunner's match and jammed it into the touch-hole of the signal gun. An orange flame spurted vertically and the little cannon surged back against its recoil ropes just as a member of the crew screamed, "Jesus! There's her bowsprit!"

Quick as a swooping hawk a tall ship materialized out of the smoky atmosphere, rushed straight at the brigantine. Spouting frantic curses, Farish spun his wheel away from that thrusting wooden finger. Wise members of the crew flung themselves flat.

David could only gape through the signal cannon's bitter-smelling smoke in helpless dismay. That onrushing bowsprit, dolphin striker and diamond-shaped netting were almost overhead.

He heard the stranger's Officer of the Deck yell, "Starboard helm! Starboard!" But the great brown hull kept on, the sea boiling past her stem. A yellow streak punctuated by gun ports swept into sight; the muzzles of two bow chasers peered out of their ports like sinister eyes. The crews of both vessels were yelling and shouting. Turner helped Farish grind the wheel over as far as it would go. His hat had fallen off and his bald head glimmered in the ghostly light.

A grinding, rending crash as of a tall pine falling in a forest filled David's ears. The whole vessel lurched like a fish struck by a spear. Aloft ensued a furious snapping and crackling as overstrained cordage broke and writhed. Canvas ripped, snarling like a mad dog. Over, and still further over, heeled the brigantine's deck. Everything loose went tumbling. A yard crashed down amidships; smashed the longboat.

In a daze David glimpsed gilded scroll work, freshly scarred and gashed, rush by; also the name *Falcon*. A great wave spewed up between the colliding vessels. Spray flew yards high, drenching the lesser craft's deck. The grinding diminished as the merchantman staggered off to port. Farish, it turned out, had been able to change his course enough to avoid worse than a hard, glancing blow.

David told himself that if Farish hadn't taken time to fire the gun, he could have avoided a collision altogether.

An enraged voice began bellowing, "They fired on us, sir!"

"Then fire back! Sink the lousy dogs!"

That high, brown-painted side and its line of gaping gun ports were falling away fast now.

"Down for your lives! Down, everyone!" Farish flung himself flat to the deck. Turner followed his example.

David was too stunned by the swiftness of the catastrophe to grasp the little Yankee's meaning. Into his face sprang fountains of flame. A cannon-ball screamed by him, sucked the air from his lungs. Then followed a deafening roar. As he reeled back through a choking blast of smoke, he heard a devastating *crack!* near the foremast.

"Don't fire!" Farish's voice was hoarse and frantically he waved his hands. "For God's sake, don't fire again! We are unarmed!"

But again and yet again the *Falcon*'s guns slammed projectiles at the brigantine, smashed her gig and tore a great ragged hole through the fore-course. From their shattered coop several hens flew right over the rail and landed in the water. Others raced crazily about the deck. One missile struck the bulwarks and showered the merchantman's deck with a mur-derous shower of splinters. The *thud-thud* of debris falling onto the deck kept the terrified crew cowering. Someone had set up a series of shrill screams — one strident, agonized cry on the tail of the last. The acute agony of them set David's teeth on edge.

"Heave to!" Astern lay the man-of-war, a big sloop. Seen in the fog and smoke she presented an infinitely menacing silhouette.

Farish scrambled to his feet once the foremast began to give out a strange grinding sound. Crackling, the spar swung in an eccentric semi-circle, rocked until the overstrained stays gave way, then toppled over the port bow and raised a smother of spray. Snapped lines, blocks and hal-yards rained onto the deck; then, as suddenly as if she had run aground, the stricken merchantman lost way. To David's nose came the pungent odor of burning pine. Gasping, he noticed that the cook's fire had been spilled over the deck. Here and there the fallen forecourse was beginning to smolder.

No more firing took place; the *Assistance* was too obviously helpless. In the trough of the sea she rolled sullenly as a rain-filled canoe.

Farish never gave David a glance. He picked up his hat, all dripping, from the water and stood shaking it. "Git up, Mr. Turner, they'll not shoot anymore." His face was like granite as he helped the ashen-faced mate to his feet. "What ails you? Scairt?"

"Hell no! Swallered my chaw when the fo'mast went."

[44]

A grim, tough-looking lieutenant of marines was first to clamber over the shattered bulwark. He leveled an espantoon, a sort of short-hafted pike, and two of his sergeants presented blunderbusses.

"Who is master?"

"Me."

"Say 'sir' when you address me!"

"Very well, sir," Farish replied in a grating voice. "Maybe you'll explain why you fired into me? I'm a peaceful merchantman."

The marine lieutenant did not reply at once. Coolly he was estimating the brigantine's situation, the damage done her.

"What can you expect if you fire into one of His Majesty's ships?"

Farish wet his lips. "We only fired a signal gun, then you ran us down."

A violent scuffling and a roar of rage preceded the appearance of Major Bouquet. In stocking feet, breeches and rumpled shirt, he burst out of the companionway, brandishing a dress sword.

"What's this? What's this? Mutiny? Piracy?" Blinking shortsightedly, he gaped at the wreckage all about.

On recognizing the marine officer's uniform, he started waddling over to the poop ladder. "Well, sir, who locked me in my cabin? Had to break damn' door — I'll see someone hanged for this! I'll — "

The lieutenant asked, "Who is he?"

"Major Ponsonby Bouquet of the 52nd Line Regiment," David told him. "Every inch of him."

"Gad, that barrel's sharp slatted!" Rubbing his stern, Bouquet turned to stare at the ruined casks. Suddenly the gross figure stooped and everyone could see a smear of blood dyeing his soiled white breeches. "Damn my eyes, what's this?" With his free hand Major Bouquet drew from among the broken staves a molasses-covered bayonet, then a pike head and a pair of pistols. Bouquet squinted at the bayonet, rubbed a section of it clean. " 'Fabrique de L. Aguiel, St. Malo,' " he read. "French weapons!"

The lieutenant's jaw clicked. "Smuggling foreign arms? Well, well! French arms. That alters matters. You are, I perceive, an extrapeaceful merchantman, Captain." The marine's sarcasm was deadly. "Sergeant, fetch a rope and secure these honest mariners."

Into Salem

H. M. S. *Falcon*, sloop of war, took her prize in tow. By consequence, the brigantine set up a sullen heave and toss which endured over to Chatham. The trip was a nightmare to the sixteen men who found themselves jammed indiscriminately into a forecastle designed for eight.

The prisoners had to wait all day for their single ration of food and water, but Johnny Gilmorin's irrepressible cheerfulness went a long way towards helping people through the ordeal. He sang bawdy tavern ballads and quoted Sir John Suckling until Farish, inexpressibly shocked, begged him for God's sake to be still. Good-humoredly, Johnny switched to riddles and guessing games. Then, declaring they all should deem it a privilege to suffer like this in the name of liberty, he goaded Farish into an argument which lasted for hours.

The boatswain momentarily floored them both by drawling, "What's all this to-do about liberty, Mr. Gilmorin? Once you've seen a Boston town meeting, ye'd know we wouldn't know what to do with liberty if we got it. The British make some mistakes; we all do. But they been figgerin' out this liberty business nigh on five hundred years, so they tell me, and so far they done it purty well. I wish you'd cast an eye over some of the plugs calling 'emselves Sons o' Liberty."

Snow, light and feathery as winged seeds, was falling in the prison courtyard when, after securing the middle of their ankle chains to their belts with strips of rag, the prisoners started for the courthouse. A month's beard darkened their cheeks and they still stood in the clothes they had worn when they were captured. The stench of them was by now appalling. Only the *Assistance*'s officers and passengers had been permitted to shave once a week.

Lining the narrow, snow-muffled street stood a band of youngsters; schoolbooks under arms, they sniffled in the cold. Briefly they surveyed this line of blue-lipped men tramping along between red-coated guards. The sight was becoming too common to hold their interest long. They started off, casting wistful glances at fortunate little illiterates coasting on the hills back of Salem. Their shrill and joyous whoops echoed and re-echoed among the severe and generally unpainted clapboard dwellings.

It was pleasantly warm in the courtroom. David, looking about, realized this with a sense of surprise. After nearly a month in Salem jail, one forgot there were such things as soap, hot water, clean linen and beds. In grim amusement he stared at his hands. Could these grimy paws with black crescents of dirt under each broken nail be his? He looked sidewise at Johnny, then suddenly squirmed. God's teeth! Thanks to the heat, lice in his clothes were becoming active. As it warmed, Johnny's body began to exude the indescribably foul odors of flesh long unwashed. Johnny noticed it himself and looked so apologetic David grinned.

"Reckon I'm no rose myself."

On the bench sat three judges appointed to adjudicate the libel's validity. The grim, hawk-featured presiding justice looked mighty impressive in scarlet robes and a full-bottomed wig.

The Court Cryer called for order, began reading an order to hold court:

[46]

" 'By his Excellency Lieutenant-General Thomas Gage, Governor, Commander-in-Chief and Vice-Admiral of this Colony, to the Honorable Peter Oliver, Jonathan Sewall and Charles Paxton, judges of His Majesty's Court of Vice-Admiralty:

" 'Whereas Captain John Linzee, Commander of His Majesty's sloop of war called the *Falcon* by his humble petition to me exhibited setting forth that the said John Linzee in pursuance of his duty against His Majesty's enemies did on, or about, the 11th day of November last past, attack, seize and take a certain vessel called the *Assistance* belonging to one Robert Ashton, a subject of His Majesty residing in Norfolk in the Colony of Virginia, laden with divers goods and merchandizes and contraband arms and hath brought said same ship and lading into this port of Salem in order of adjudication and condemnation. And by said petition hath prayed for a Court of Admiralty to be holden for trial of the same at His Majesty's Court of Vice-Admiralty held at the courthouse upon a libel exhibited by John Linzee, Commander of His Majesty's sloop of war the *Falcon*. The officers, mariners and marines belonging to the Same

Against

A certain vessel called the *Assistance*, the property of a British subject one Robert Ashton, and also against all and singular the cargo and lading on board. Her tackle, apparel and furniture kindsoever.

Officers attending: Wm. Woolen, Marshall
Ed. Winston, Register
John S. Petit, Cryer

Given under my hand and the Public seal of this colony this 18th day of December, 1774/5 in the fourteenth year of His Majesty's reign.' "

Captain Linzee of the *Falcon* stated his version of the affair in blunt nautical terms. The brigantine, he swore, had made desperate attempts to evade capture.

The lieutenant of marines, next being sworn, described his boarding of the brigantine. Firmly he maintained that the signal cannon, so-called, had been charged with ball.

"Was this ball ever found?" demanded Mr. Gray for the defendants.

The missile had not penetrated the *Falcon*'s side, Captain Linzee asserted, but had nonetheless smashed several planks before rebounding into the sea.

"Were there other balls in evidence — on the deck?"

"No, but balls fitting said cannon were discovered in a nearby chest."

Farish and Turner, Mr. Alexander implied, had been too lazy or too disloyal to investigate the cargo's true nature.

Turner got angry and his chains rattled loudly when he sprang up. "By God, suh, do you expect us to drain every molasses barrel?"

"Silence! The prisoner will not interrupt." Judge Oliver's gavel thumped heavily.

Mr. Alexander made an obsequious bow. "Your honors, the facts are as I have represented them. These men were transporting a cargo of foreign arms destined to strike at the authority of our most gracious king." His voice rang in every corner of the bare and musty smelling courtroom. "On behalf of my clients I implore you to find their libel a true bill. I hold that the owner, Robert Ashton, the prisoners Stephen Farish, David Ashton, John Gilmorin and Andrew Turner have, beyond a doubt, been proved guilty of a treasonable conspiracy to smuggle arms into this colony!"

"Your honors!" David struggled to his feet. "May I speak?"

Judge Oliver's slash of a mouth thinned ominously, but he ended by nodding.

"While it is entirely true," David began in a low-pitched voice, "that Mr. Gilmorin and I planned to import illicit arms into this colony, it is also true that I misrepresented the nature of this cargo, not only to the officers of the *Assistance*, but to her owner. The owner, gentlemen, is my brother."

Soldiers surrounding the prisoners glanced sidewise, looking at him from dully interested eyes.

"The prisoner may proceed," snapped the presiding judge.

"I beg of you, your honors, to dismiss the other prisoners. They are indeed innocent of any illegal intent. The fault is John Gilmorin's and mine; but principally mine, because I collected the arms and arranged for their transportation."

David stood erect, a grimy unkempt figure outlined against the whitewashed wall. Everyone was looking at him now, especially a pretty girl in the second row. She reminded him a bit of Katie, but she wasn't as large and her gray eyes lacked the greenish tinge. The scratching of the court clerk's pen continued.

"Your honors, I beg mercy for these men, if you may find none for me. Most of my fellow defendants have families. The owner of the slave members of this crew will suffer through no fault of his." Gripped by the swing of his peroration, David prolonged it. It was a glittering moment. Even the *Falcon*'s officers were looking at him in astonishment. "As a last inducement, may I state that my brother, Robert, is a most loyal subject of His Majesty?" David drove home his main point with triumphant emphasis. "That, gentlemen, is why I did not inform him about the arms. He never would have allowed them aboard his vessel."

In Stephen Farish's opinion the deliberation of the judges appeared ominously brief. Within ten minutes the jurists entered, resumed their places. Judge Oliver peered the length of the now stuffily hot courtroom, then cast a glance out at the windows. A furious snowstorm was raging. He cleared his throat and passed a sheet of paper down to the bailiff.

A stillness descended, impressive in its completeness. The bailiff had a bad cold but all could hear him read:

"Verdict of this court. We do unanimously find the libel against the *Assistance* brigantine of Norfolk to be a true bill. She is hereby condemned, together with all her cargo, tackle, furniture and appurtenances kindsoever. Proceeds of the sale shall be divided as prize money among the officers, marines and mariners of the *Falcon*, man-of-war, according to the rules and regulations therefor prescribed. Because of extenuating circumstances, we hold Robert Ashton acquitted of treasonable intent and exempt from further prosecution. We do find Stephen Farish, captain of said vessel, Andrew Turner, mate, guilty of firing shot at a ship of the Royal Navy. David Mountford Ashton and John Pingree Gilmorin, owners of the contraband materials of war, we find guilty of a conspiracy to violate the laws of this province. We do hold the remainder of the crew of said vessel guiltless of wilfully transporting illicit arms; but, as a warning, their personal property aboard the vessel condemned is hereby forfeited. They are hereby discharged! David Ashton, John Gilmorin, Stephen Farish and Andrew Turner, rise and hear the sentence of this court!"

Hands tightly gripped before him, David obeyed; somehow the drama of the moment had completely evaporated. The irons on his legs felt extra heavy and he became overwhelmingly aware that he was very hungry and dirty.

" — As a warning to other disaffected, dishonest subjects of the Crown, and as an example of the fate awaiting such, this court herewith sentences David Mountford Ashton to ten years' penal servitude and to transportation from this province to a destination later to be decided. John Gilmorin, to five years' penal servitude and transportation. Stephen Farish — in view of the prisoner David Ashton's statement, we do hold you, Stephen Farish, not guilty of wilful conspiracy. But — " blood rushed through Farish's arteries — "we do find you guilty of a criminal negligence at a time when all loyal subjects of the Crown should be alert against treason and rebellion. We do, therefore, sentence you, Stephen Farish, to serve one year at hard labor in His Majesty's prison at Boston."

Spring Scene

It had been one of the coldest winters even the oldsters of Norfolk could recall. The ice became so jammed up people could walk across the Chesapeake clear to the Maryland shore. There had never been finer skating on Plume's Creek; everybody agreed on that. But otherwise it was such a winter as none of the city's six thousand inhabitants wished to experience again.

The population, cooped indoors by bitter winds, fairly stewed in politics. Party lines became more sharply drawn. On December first a ship bringing imported goods had been turned back with her bulk unbroken, for once the embargo got under way, the Norfolk Committee kept fast sailing boats cruising off the mouth of the Elizabeth River. Every vessel which would stop was boarded and searched for embargoed goods.

Everybody, even his worst enemies, admired Robert Ashton for one thing. Not once did he ever reproach his brother. He made no attempt to explain David's astounding duplicity, even to himself. When people offered sympathy or expressed indignation he only turned aside in silence. His wife and possibly Matt Phipp alone guessed the depth of his bitterness. It was unfortunate that his undemonstrative temperament made it impossible to break loose with a stream of relieving curses. Instead he strove to forget the fact of David's existence. No matter how he looked at the matter, the facts remained.

Mr. Abel Hovey of Hovey & Sons, who had attended the prize court sitting, took pains to forward a transcript of David Ashton's testimony. Rob read it, then used it to kindle a fire. What had happened to Farish troubled Rob deeply. He'd grown mighty fond of his dry, dependable little master, even if he was a Yankee.

A good while would have to elapse before he could forget that night he'd gone stumping over frozen roads out to Tideover. Peggy, showing her pregnancy in more ways than one, staged a tearful scene and uttered bitter, unreasonable reproaches when he told her he must sell Tideover. Only in that way would he be able to finish the brig. She knew it as well as he did.

"Oh, the devil take that wretched ship!" she wailed.

"Peggy!" Rob groaned. "Don't say that! For God's sake, don't!"

"I mean it! *I hate her!*"

It in nowise helped matters that when Peggy on her own initiative asked help of her father, the old man curtly quoted the cruel old saw about making a bed and lying on it. Major Fleming considered her husband an out-and-out rebel.

"A smart merchant like Robert would certainly know whether his vessel carried contraband, and you can't tell me otherwise!" he stormed, beating the back of a chair. "French arms, mark you, for use against the Crown! I can't forgive that! No, Margaret, you will have to choose between the loyalty every self-respecting English subject owes his king, and Robert Ashton. He may be, as you say, a sound apple from a rotten tree, but he is a rebel through and through! I daresay you are proud to have a condemned felon for your brother-in-law? Bad blood always shows —"

Peggy thought of her baby and fainted.

[50]

Mrs. Fleming bent above the limp figure and, for one of the few times in her life, flared up at her husband.

"You are a brute, Andrew Fleming, a heartless brute to treat her so! And with her in the family way! If she had married the devil himself, she is still our daughter. Mine, anyway."

But Andrew Fleming only snorted. "I'd liefer have her married to the devil, ma'am, than to an enemy of my sovereign!"

The night he learned the prize court's verdict Rob looked up Tom Newton. They worked till dawn revising plans and estimates for the *Grand Turk*. By a ruthless elimination of nonessentials, by reducing spare gear and by refiguring the sailmaker's bill on the basis of lighter weight canvas, they cut the original estimate by a third.

The following day Rob roamed Norfolk and the adjacent countryside. It took him three days to locate the right buyer for Tideover. He was one Llewellyn Jones, a wizened Welsh corn broker.

"Aye, I know what is brewing in the trade world," he cackled. "I am selling out. The politicians don't bother with a small farmer much."

Though the sale brought enough to complete the *Grand Turk*, there wasn't any money left. At least, not enough to rent them a room in even the meanest ordinary. When the blow fell in December it was Peggy who recalled a small storeroom to the rear of Ashton & Co.'s office.

"There is a fireplace in it. I'm sure there is. It backs up against the flue in the office. There are some old sails in the loft. Why couldn't we hang them 'round the walls and nail a tarpaulin over the floor? We would be very snug in there. Besides, it would be something new to live out over the water." Desperately, she had tried to make light of their impoverishment. "We would be by ourselves, then, dear — much better off than in some messy, noisy inn."

Rob seemed to live with but one thought — to rush the completion of his brig.

"As soon after she's launched as it's possible, we'll live aboard her," Rob said. "I am building her stern cabin extra big. You should be more comfortable there; for a few months more I reckon we'll not be taking chances about the baby. After that — " he forced a confident smile — "well, I will be back on my feet again."

Launching Day

Right after breakfast Rob began looking about for an omen. He believed it was at hand when someone began to rap loudly at the office door. The caller proved to be a lanky, big-faced seafaring man wearing a shipmaster's coat and a ring in his left ear.

"Captain Trott, at your service, sir," he announced.

"Come in, Captain. What can I do for you?" Rob was conscious of being subjected to the intent inspection of two bloodshot gray eyes. There was an indefinable foreign air about this red-haired fellow. It might be his old-fashioned cut clothes and his footgear, square toed pumps sporting huge brass buckles. Captain Trott came closer, narrowing his eyes.

"You Mr. Ashton?"

"Yes."

"Robert Ashton, son of St. John Ashton?"

"To the best of my belief," smiled Rob. "Take a seat, won't you?"

"I made 'e port yesterday in 'e *Active*," the caller volunteered, running an eye over the little office. "Notice her?"

"The Bermuda-built sloop that anchored in the afternoon?"

"Aye." Employing his cuff, Captain Trott wiped a drop from the end of his blunt nose. He began fumbling in his coat. "Should have knowed ye straight off; you're 'e spit and image o' Mr. Hereward." Captain Trott nodded a big battered-looking head several times. "But you're bigger."

After handing Rob a letter, the Bermudian captain swung over to the fireplace. He lingered there toasting badly bowed legs and gazing at the ivory model on the shelf.

Here sure enough was his omen! Tingling with suspense, Rob went over to the window and slipped his thumbnail under a seal of blue wax. Fingers quivering a little, he unfolded a letter.

February 6th, 1775
Gaunt New House, Summers Isles

Most Respkt'd Cousin Robert:

It has ocured to Me that there is Small proffitt in prolonging a Family quarrell wich is none of our jeneration's making. Your Papa I hear, is dead & so is mine. Hereward, my oldest Bro. is becom somewhat Soften'd with advancing yeres. Therfor, I ofer you the Olive Branch in high hopes that you are as Reddy to take it as I am to ofer it.

A Virginia ship tuched hear not long past and having had ocassion to dyne with her Mast'r, lerned he knue you well & that your Affairs do Prossper. I do asshure you, Cousin, I am vastly pleased to lern of your Suckcess & am mov'd to wonder why it would not be to our mutewel Adv'tage to Conduct a Commerce between these Ilands and the fare Colonie you enhabit.

Most ridicklous rumours circulate amongst us. To witt: ere long Comerce between England & the W. Indees will ceese with America. You can beleive we in Bermuda are grately exerciz'd, since we can not for six Months survive without vittels & those other necesitties of Life wich come from America. We are so feeble and few we Dare not speak out 'gainst the inikwities of Parlament, but thar are many sleber (Do you understand?) amongst us.

That gave Rob pause. Sleber? The twerp can't spell. What in the world? Then he saw how the word should be read and, conscious of Captain Trott's intent regard, returned his attention to the letter.

Here, dear Cousin, is what I purpose. Ship as heavy a cargoe of Vittels as you may, salt meat, pottatos, and flower in partikular. I will undertake to bring you such Prices as will make your Mouth water. Gainst this I have to ofer Salt & a comoddity I hear you are most desirus of prokuring — gunpowder.

Gunpowder? Rob whistled softly. Not entirely a fool, this cousin.

I scarce need warn you to be most seekret about this. The crying Need of vittels in these Ilands will soon become known in America. Then prices must fall, but I believe, most respeck'd Cousin, that this epissel is the first inteligence America has of the dire straights of these Ilands respeckting true feeling. Should you decide to make this Ventur pleas send word by Captain Trott.

A final warning. You had Best ship no Sgnik sdneirf. Our Governor has an Eager ear for trechery.

Pray present my compli'ts to the Virtuous Female who is your Wife. Am sorely vex'd Mountford wrote such a breef acc't of your Wedding. I would it had been my Good Fortune to atend it.

Yr. respt. aff. Cousin,
Peter Ashton

Captain Trott promised to return for an answer and went swaggering off up Main Street towards the Pied Bull. Rob in his delight relented and told Peggy all about it.

She was wholly delighted and chuckled so hard over Peter Ashton's spelling that tears gathered in her eyes.

"Heavens! Haven't they any schools in Bermuda?"

"He's probably a good fisherman," Rob grinned, "and there's plenty of sense to his suggestion."

By God! This was like finding money in the bank. He began to figure on how early the brig might be put in commission.

Rob wondered, as he stood there fingering the letter, what the Bermudas were really like. Waterfront gossip wasn't any too flattering to the inhabitants. Most sailors called them a parcel of pirates, wreckers and sharp dealers. Old Mr. Gilmorin always maintained that a 'Mudian's word wasn't worth a thin damn unless you got him tied down and backed into a corner. Exaggerations of course. But where smoke arises? He reckoned he would move cautiously, find out more as soon as he could about this group of little-known islands lying some six hundred miles out to sea.

"It's a sign!" Peggy's voice recalled him. "Oh Rob, I'm sure it's a sign! Wasn't it fine of your cousin to write like this?"

"It was mighty handsome," Rob observed dryly. "You'll notice there's a little profit involved?"

[53]

"Oh, you Ashtons are all alike — merchants! Merchants! All of you except — " She had started to say "David" but turned away, instead, to smooth the coverlet.

Petition

Not since the return of the *Assistance* almost a year ago had Peggy seen Rob so entirely happy. It was almost as if their dark hours following the brigantine's loss had never been. Every morning he was up at dawn and over at the shipyard where the *Grand Turk* rose and fell with the tide.

Peggy took his food over to him until the day Mrs. Fleming paid the "Construction Camp," as Rob called their one-room quarters, her one and only visit.

"Mrs. Rudder came to call."

"Call? The wife of a common sea captain — and a drunken one at that?"

"Oh, she meant all right. I really felt sorry for her. She was trying to get the new brig for Ben. So many ships are tied up, she is near desperate."

"But surely, my dear, one hears of some ships sailing?"

"Only coastwise vessels trade, and vessels in the Bermuda and West Indies trade. The embargo don't affect them yet, not till next November."

"Why do you say Bermuda *and* the West Indies? Surely Bermuda is one of the islands, isn't it?"

Peggy unpinned her apron and stepped into a plain yellow skirt. She'd been washing in a shawl and petticoats.

"Rob says Bermuda ain't a West Indie, and it's really not an island, but a whole lot of little ones. The old charts call them the Summer Islands."

"You seem to know a lot about it, my dear."

"Rob's father came from there."

"What else, pray?"

"Years ago Bermuda belonged to the old Virginia Company, but now they are self-governing, like a little Rhode Island 'way out in the Atlantic."

Mrs. Fleming put out a feeler. "Has — have — well, Rob has heard from his relations in Bermuda?"

Peggy told her yes but refused to be drawn out. It had not been pleasant to watch Rob repent that revelation of what Peter Ashton had written. Very well she knew he hadn't yet got over her going to her father about the brigantine's supplies. He didn't wholly trust her. She wondered whether he ever would again.

"Margaret, I can't abide you to live in this rude place. You are alone too much of the time."

"La, Mamma, it's not so bad as it seems, though sometimes I'd give my silver shoe buckles to eat breakfast in bed, to have clean clothes just appear like — that." She snapped her fingers.

Betsy Fleming spoke quickly. "You know you can, my dear."

Peggy slowly shook her small head. "We are going to live aboard the brig soon. It will be nicer there."

"What! Live on a ship — a girl in your condition?"

"Yes, Mamma, a girl in my condition. The *Grand Turk* won't be ready for sea for another month anyhow and then — " the half smile faded from her lips. "Well, I'll give you my answer. I love Rob, but I'll not have my baby suffer."

"My dear," said Mrs. Fleming softly, "I have with me a great chance to help your husband."

"Why, Mamma, what do you mean?"

"He will thank you some day; you see if he doesn't."

Parchment rustled softly as Mrs. Fleming held out a scroll.

"You must read this carefully, Margaret. It is a petition to the Throne. All the leading loyal merchants in town have signed it. You can see their names — even Dr. Gordon's."

Peggy read slowly, carefully, the list of signatures. It was imposing.

"But what does this have to do with Rob? You know he favors neither one side nor the other."

"When the day of retribution comes," Mrs. Fleming began in a confident voice, "as surely it must come, the traitors and rebels who now are making our lives so miserable will be brought to book. They will see their estates confiscated; they will see their ringleaders hanged; they will feel the just and awful wrath of our king."

Peggy was impressed. "Well, I still don't see — "

"If Rob's name was to appear on this petition it would act as a — a sort of assurance."

Peggy's eyes traveled rapidly over the roll of parchment. It seemed entirely harmless — merely a reaffirmation of loyalty to His Majesty King George III and a respectful plea that something be done to ameliorate "the distressful condition of his Most Loyal Subjeckts in His Colonie of Virginia."

"I had better talk this over with Rob."

Mrs. Fleming shook her head, but smiled at the same time. "Oh, cat's foot! You know Robert can never make up his mind on politics. Besides, this petition doesn't commit him to anything. You can see that."

"It doesn't seem to."

"It doesn't commit him to *do* a thing, does it?"

"No, but I really daren't sign his name, Mamma. I daren't."

Mrs. Fleming's thin features beamed on her daughter. "There is no call to, my dear. That is where you can be helpful to him. Sign it as Mrs. Robert Butler Ashton. You have the right to, you know. Here is the beauty of it. If things go wrong for the King's Friends, you can vow you signed

[55]

it without Rob's knowledge — which is perfectly true. But when his Majesty sends troops, you can say Robert was busy, or away on his ship and told you to sign it for him."

Still Peggy hesitated, pondering a decision from every possible angle. In the end the persistent urgings of a woman even more determined than herself made her waver — and in wavering, she surrendered. This wasn't a bit like what she'd done before, Peggy assured herself. She wasn't signing Rob's own name. It was for his good, too. She took the parchment into the office and, after repointing a quill, wrote in a firm hand *Mrs. Robert B. Ashton.* There was no smile on her face as she sanded the document.

Articles of Association

Two days later as Rob was going home Matthew Phipp came up to him on the street. From the look of him, Rob knew this was no chance encounter.

Phipp indulged in no sociable preliminaries. Said he, "Rob, we must have a talk."

"About what?"

"Tell you later. Come with me."

"What the devil is this about? You talk like the second act of a theater piece." Rob wasn't finding the situation pleasant. He was dog-tired and hungry. Peggy had said they were going to have baked ham from Smithfield for supper.

"Why did Peggy sign that petition?"

"Don't talk riddles, man." Rob began to get irritated. "What petition?"

"A loyalist petition to the king."

"Are you crazy, or am I?" Rob forgot his fatigue. In the back of his mind was a terrible premonition. "She has signed no petition."

There was incredulity in the lawyer's tone. "Do you mean to sit there and tell me that your wife signed old Fleming's petition to the Throne without your knowing about it?"

"Peggy signed — !" Rob's naturally high color deepened. "Just a minute. Let me see it!"

"Here is a copy." Grimly the committeeman handed over a sheet of paper with the printer's ink still wet upon it.

Rob looked Phipp bang in the eye. "I had no idea my wife signed such a thing."

"You will have to act fast. Leeming and his crew of radicals are burning for action. They will interpret the major's petition as an invitation for ships and ministerial troops to come here."

"But that's insane! Nobody wants troops sent here."

Phipp nodded. "Of course they don't. Just the same, you are now in serious danger. Resentment against Tories gets stronger every day. Some of the news from Boston isn't pretty. They say the British soldiers up there are raising merry hell with the Whig inhabitants. Some women have been raped — whores probably — but the effect's the same. Then again, the patriots in Boston are going broke by the hundred."

Rob rose from his chair, then sat down again heavily. "What do you think is going to happen about this?"

"We don't know for sure. Almost anything. With so many people hungry and out of work, it won't take a lot to get them excited. I expect the radicals will try to force the committee to jail everybody who signed that petition. The signers will be blacklisted — that much is sure."

"What do you reckon I'd better do?"

"Stop being a damned political eunuch and do what I advised nearly a year ago," Phipp said sharply. "You can't dodge picking sides any longer."

"But how can I when near as I can make out neither one side nor the other is right? Why in hell can't people leave me alone? I don't give two damns who runs the colony. All I want is to trade. I've got a right to trade, haven't I?"

"What you want isn't important any longer. No one can live a wholly private life these days. Whether we want it or not, we are becoming small parts of a new theory of government. You know what people are saying?"

"No. What?"

"They say your brig has been built for a ship-of-war. The radicals claim you intend to sell her to the British."

"Phipp, what do you reckon I'd better do? I couldn't stand to lose my brig. I'd sooner lose my right hand!"

"If you aim to keep your ship and to do business in Norfolk, you will have to sign a copy of the Articles of Association as quick as you can. A pile of them is over there."

Rob's fingertips felt curiously numb. Odd, a man signed his name so many times without its meaning much. But now whether he did or did not make a few loops and lines with a quill might change the course of his whole life.

Phipp's manner was more friendly. "You are showing good sense, Rob, and I'm glad. The only reason the committee has left you alone so far is because we felt sure you were playing fair with both sides. I am truly delighted that you see the justice of our cause. Our liberties — "

Rob's laugh was rasping, devoid of mirth. "Let the liberties go. You know damned well such high-sounding talk is just a side issue. Fact is, a lot of Virginians want to get rid of the factors because they owe the factors money. Again, most of our homegrown merchants ain't clever or dishonest enough to compete with the Scotch. The people here are sore because Parliament and the East India people are trying to squeeze more revenues out of them without making a profitable return for them. Reckon they are 'most as greedy as the so-called patriots."

Phipp made an impatient gesture. "Talk all you please, but you will still have to make up your mind. Let me tell you something; if you don't sign the association, your brig won't be allowed to sail! But if you come in with us I undertake to convince the rest of the committee that you didn't know about Peggy's signing. I can, and will, play up that you lost your ship through carrying arms for the patriots in Boston." A bleak smile twisted the lawyer's lips. " — Even though I know damned well you knew nothing about the munitions."

At last he'd been driven into a corner. There was nothing to do but to sign. Rob crossed to a nearby desk, dipped the pen on it, then hesitated, looking over his shoulder.

"If I sign this, you will guarantee everything will be all right?"

"Yes, everything will be all right. You have my word on it."

"You are sure you can handle Leeming?"

"I'll find him as soon as I can. He will have to listen to me; I'm his superior."

The pen's slow scratching filled the musty smelling office with sound.

Rob blew on the wet ink. "Now can I go on trading?"

Matthew Phipp cast him a glance of sympathy. "Why, certainly — if the British will let you."

The Cruise of the Grand Turk

"Ashton! Wake up! Hey, in there! Mr. Ashton!" Dimly voices penetrated Rob's profound slumber.

"Someone's out there," Peggy murmured sleepily. "Better see what they want."

Whoever was banging on the office door must be in a tearing hurry. The hammering of his blows shook the whole building.

"Mr. Ashton! Come quick!" More voices, hoarse with excitement joined in.

When he reached the front of the office, he was startled to see gables and roofs across Lawson Street in silhouette. They showed up sharp against a dull pink glow. Even as he fumbled at the lock the pink brightened to a throbbing orange-red. As he opened the door, he saw a lot of people running towards the harbor.

"What's wrong? House afire? Lumber yard?"

"Jesus, no!" panted Bub Jensen's deep voice. "You better come quick. It's your new ship!"

She made such a terrifying spectacle that Norfolk people in later days declared the *Grand Turk*'s burning was the greatest sight they had ever witnessed — barring none! As if propelled by a great bellows, sheets of flame beat out of the brig's ports, roared up from her hatches and licked prettily out of her hawse holes.

Her yards crashing down, one by one, the *Grand Turk* cruised over a surface dyed scarlet as a sea of molten lava. Warehouses, dwellings and ships reflected the infernal glare. White-painted steeples far back from the water looked as if they had been done in rose tints. People staring in open-mouthed awe could read each other's expressions by the flames.

"Ain't it awful?" they asked one another in hushed voices. But they were thrilled and enjoying the spectacle.

Soon the doomed vessel's freshly tarred rigging caught, sketched fiery patterns amid clouds of rosy smoke. Over a thunderous crackle of the brig's burning timbers, the explosion of turpentine barrels made the harbor resound.

"Sounds like a bleedin' skirmish," Sergeant Jemmy Potter grunted to his men as he turned them out. "This will rooin poor Mr. Ashton. Seems like he leaned too much on the Tory side."

Vessels anchored in the *Grand Turk*'s probable path slipped their cables and, hastily setting jibs and staysails, strove to get out of the way.

Until dawn the *Grand Turk* lay burning to the water's edge, sending up a dense, leisurely pillar of smoke and steam.

Salvage

Major John Brush took the initiative and at his own expense dispatched laborers who salvaged a not inconsiderable supply of metal from among the *Grand Turk*'s gaunt charred timbers. Without coming near to the office, Brush ordered the several tons of iron unloaded on Rob's wharf. Left there it made an ugly, rusty mound.

The very day the salvage was delivered, Norfolk was thrown into a turmoil by rumors of a pitched battle having been fought between British regulars and a kind of troops called minute men. The struggle had taken place, so the mud-spattered courier declared, near some villages called Lexington and Concord, in Massachusetts. The villages were not far outside of Boston, he thought. More reports arrived, fantastic, contradictory and hopelessly biased; but one accepted fact emerged. Armed rebellion had begun!

A mustering of the Dirty Shirts, as the Tories dubbed them, was a colorful affair what with the fox tails, buck tails and coon tails in the hats of these lantern jawed, tobacco spitting gentry. Some wore the words "Liberty or Death" painted on their chests in white.

Some few men from back in the swamps turned up in war paint and wearing scalps to their belts. A scalping knife or a war hatchet was the usual supplement to the long-barreled rifle most of them had brought along. They looked, and were, a hard lot, and independent as all get out when it came to obeying orders.

Everywhere appeared lists of those who had signed the Articles of Association — and of those who had not. The price of arms, powder and ordinary iron skyrocketed.

When final reports about the Concord fight came through, the war fever mounted. Crowds gathered every day before the Spread Eagle's notice board and the governor began threatening to arrest John Holt for printing seditious news. No matter who said what, the fact remained that British regulars had been made to run by a parcel of Yankee militia, and if Yankees could do that, my God! what wouldn't Virginians do to the Lobsterbacks?

A few days after news of the Lexington fight, Neil Jameison strode in, the gold seals of his watch fob all ajingle. Rob mechanically greeted him, shook hands and indicated a chair. Beaming, the older man removed his hat and took out a snuff box.

"Try a pinch?"

"Thanks. Don't use it, sir."

"Well, my boy," began Jameison closing the box lid with a small snap. "As we all know, you have had a spell of bad luck; too long a spell. Possibly the tide has turned. The iron out of the wreck should bring top prices. Know that?"

"Prices?" Rob's meaningless smile dissolved and he stood straighter. "Do you mean that iron prices are going up?"

"Just that, Mr. Ashton. Just that. A blind idiot can foretell it. You've got a lot of good iron here on your wharf." Neil Jameison gave him a sharp look. "Suppose I offer you a hundred pounds for it? What do you say?"

One hundred pounds? he reflected. Must be worth twenty or thirty pounds more, at the least. Let's see now, who'd most likely be wanting iron? Of course, that Lexington fight has brought this about. Gunmakers must be crying for iron.

"Thank you, Mr. Jameison. Come to think of it, I could do with a mug of ale." He put on his cap.

To start over with he had a hundred pounds, about five hundred Spanish dollars that was, left from the *Grand Turk*'s building costs. Walking down Cove Street in the gay spring sunshine he towered above Neil Jameison's sparrowlike stature.

He let Jameison stand him to three tankards of ale and at the same time worked his host's offer up to one hundred and twenty pounds cash, or one hundred and thirty credit. He began feeling better. It was something to get around Jameison. Few men did.

"I'm much obliged for the ale," he told the dapper little man in black. "And I will consider your offer with care. Suppose I let you know tonight?"

"I'll give you one hundred forty pounds for the iron. What do you say?"

But Rob shook his head, smiled and went out.

Down at the wharf, Joel Faree threw up pudgy hands with a fervent, *"Behüt mich Gott!"* when Phillip Wolfheimer without warning offered Rob one hundred and sixty pounds in hard money. He offered to pay in Portuguese escudos. *Gold!* Rob felt like throwing both arms around the gunsmith's fat little body. Gold would buy a lot more per unit than Virginia paper — no matter how sound the bankers claimed their Provincial currency to be.

Phillip Wolfheimer took no chances. All within an hour he not only sent a cart and a gang of Negroes, but produced a small stack of broad yellow pieces.

Retreat

Rob heard of a little schooner belonging to one Christian Southeby, a patriot trader ruined by the embargo; he had been in the cloth trade with Glasgow. Rob sailed over to Portsmouth to look at her. The schooner, as Rob had fully expected, was small and damp and her sails were very, very old, but she did have a wide stern cabin and there was plenty of room in her holds.

He didn't cotton to the *Desdemona* at all, at all; with such an awful stink in her bilges, she must be leaky. That her bottom was foul he could see from where he stood on Southeby's tumbledown dock. Discouraged, he went below and jabbed his clasp knife into her ribs, knees and sheathing. He struck sound wood every time. That made him feel better, because he had to have a ship; even a bull-nosed old bitch like this. The schooner's rigging was a sight to frighten the Dutch, but she could be chartered for six months dirt cheap. Seventy-five dollars a month. A pitiable rate, but Southeby was a sick man; so sick that the toothless old mulatto with whom he lived 'lowed she reckoned he'd never live to see the snow fly again.

When the *Desdemona*'s registry papers were produced, Rob found further cause for hesitation. Holy sailor! He hadn't guessed she could be so old! She had been built in Glasgow back in 1739!

Yes, it was fine to be back! Katie felt it was almost like coming home. The idea of seeing Mr. David Ashton right soon made her almost forget the ache of her feet. Craftily, Katie walked bent over. She had always held herself straight in Norfolk, and was taller than most girls. Crimanently! but she was thirsty.

Heart pounding, she peered up at Mr. David's windows. A warming flood of joyousness banished her fatigue. They were lighted! Straw on the stable floor felt fine on her swollen feet so, after setting down her bundle, she went over to see if Maggie still stood in the second stall. Sight of the beast's furry white rump did her heart good.

"You old darling! I'm *that* pleased to see you!" She felt so happy she slipped an arm about the mare's shaggy neck and hugged it hard. There was a strange horse in George's stall.

She had dried her feet and was finishing the last of her bread, ham and cheese when a door opened and heels rang in the cobbled yard. Suppose this wasn't MacSherry? Heart thumping, she darted into the harness room; she remembered it had a second door. But she had no sooner reached it than she recognized the landlord's shuffling step and the little sucking noises he made through his teeth after supper.

He carried a cruize lamp in his hand and he nearly dropped it onto a pile of hay when Katie called, "Mr. MacSherry. Please, sir, I — I've come back."

"What? Who? Why, Katie girl!" He put the lamp down and, taking her in his big fat arms, kissed her hard on her cheek. "Well, God bless my soul! I'm some tickled to see you." He pinched her bottom. "Um. Seems a bit thin." He backed her off to arms' length, running his eyes over the gold-yellow hair braided and coiled about her head, at her wide features and honest gray-green eyes. "You look fine, my dear. Ah, it's often I've wondered, but I've never worried over you."

"Never worried, Mr. Tom?"

"No, my girl. You've something to you that will carry you on so long as the breath stays in your body."

"I can have my job back, can't I?"

"Surest thing you — " MacSherry began, then broke off frowning. "That is — Katie, you know I'd give anything to tell you yes. But yesterday and the day before bailiffs from the sheriff's office have been over. They were looking for you and there's a twenty-five-dollar reward up."

"But can't you take me on — later? I — I'll hide a week somewhere."

"I — I wouldn't dare. They'd fine me cruel if I was caught harboring a runaway, deliberate-like. There, there, girl, don't cry. I'll have to think on what can be done."

"Oh, thank you!" She gave his hand a grateful little squeeze then brightened. "Why don't you ask Mr. David what to do? He's clever. He knows a way to manage 'most everything."

MacSherry put down the hay fork. "Mr. Ashton ain't here nowadays. He — he's in Boston. The British threw him in jail for helping the patriots up there, so they say."

"In jail!" Katie was horror-stricken. Mr. David in jail! Why, it was just as if Mr. Tom said they had put the king in jail. "Why — why — that's impossible!"

"But it's true just the same."

A horse stabled down the line turned, whinnying softly, its eyes dully afire in the lamp light.

"Then I hate the British!" Katie burst out. "I'd like to kill them all."

MacSherry laughed and wiped his hands on his leather apron. "Ain't that a pretty large order?"

"I don't care. I would. Every one of them! The idear their putting Mr. David in prison!"

"Maybe you'd better leave Virginia and start again somewhere else? Tomorrow I guess maybe I can scare you up some identification papers." For over a year now the clerk of the court had owed Tom MacSherry five pounds. He might as well collect it this way. He never would otherwise. "You can stay on the top floor tonight — nobody'll look there." He lived there by himself.

"Listen." MacSherry wiped his face and seated himself on a corner of the bran bin. His fat bottom ran over the edge, drooping comfortably. "Listen; you remember Mr. David had a brother?"

"Oh yes, sir. Mr. Bob, wasn't it?"

"That's near enough. Well, anyhow, tomorrow afternoon he's sailing for the Bermudas. He's a good man, right kind to people in trouble. Maybe, if I talked with him, he might take you along. In the Bermudas, where ever it is, you could make something of yourself."

"The Bermudas? Are they British?"

"They say so. They're some islands away out to sea."

To his surprise she burst into tears and clung to him. "Oh, Mr. Tom, I — I'm afeared to leave Norfolk. Norfolk's so fine. I love Norfolk."

MacSherry said he would talk to Robert Ashton that very night, then by the back stairs he sent Katie to the top floor.

Because folks said Mrs. Ashton was going on the chartered schooner, Tom MacSherry calculated she would be right glad of another female's company — especially with her as big as a beer keg. At the same time, he decided he wouldn't tell Ashton about Katie's having been his barmaid, not unless he was asked a direct question. Chances were Mr. Rob would never in the world recognize the girl. During Mr. David's stay he had never been anything more than a casual patron.

Mr. Rob Ashton fairly jumped at MacSherry's suggestion that another woman aboard would help matters all around.

"Who is this Katherine Tryon? What's her background?"

"She has been a bound maid, but she is good plain stuff. My word on that, Mr. Ashton! Her mistress abused her, beat hell out of her all the time so she is running away and I'm helping her. Wouldn't do it if I didn't think it was the right thing."

"I see. Well, I'll take your word on the rights of the matter, MacSherry. Has she any money? I'm right hard up."

"Here is two pounds against her passage. And it would be handsome of you to let her come for that."

" — She is to wash Mrs. Ashton's clothes, serve meals and make up the bunks in our cabin," Rob quickly reminded.

"You'll find her willing enough to do anything to help."

"All right," Rob spoke succinctly. "Bring her down to the *Desdemona* tonight."

"What time?"

"Around three o'clock."

A strong westerly wind blew down Chesapeake Bay and, filling the *Desdemona*'s sails, drove her past the pine-crowned dunes of Cape Charles. Rob stood beside Captain Ben Rudder in somber silence watching the outline of Norfolk blur, then sink slowly into the bay. Aloft, reef points tapped smartly against straining canvas. The yellow-green water murmured increasingly loud along the schooner's sides as swells, beating in from the sea, charged under the bow.

The tide, Rob noticed, was just turning. Slowly it swung about a red-painted channel buoy until, like an index finger, the spar pointed out to sea.

The Wars of Hannibal

To Buff, anxiously trimming Hannibal, it seemed on this mid-June evening as if the whole world had taken on a scarlet tinge. None of the other matches in Boston had attracted half such a multitude of officers. Though he couldn't read insignia, Buff reckoned about every rank in the British army was represented.

He wondered how Hannibal liked this ruckus. Not much, he reckoned. The red quill was actin' mighty nervous. All this red about most likely caused it. For luck, Buff spat on the stumps of the bird's natural spur. Using a little scroll saw, he had just sawed them off. He sure didn't like the idea of fighting Hannibal with steel gaffs on and he was only doing it because Mr. David told him he must. Mr. David must know best, but wrinkles cut across the chevron-shaped cicatrices on Buff's cheeks as he inspected the terrible little swords he must lash to Hannibal's legs. Slender, two inches long and double-edged, the gaffs were in addition needlepointed and sharp as razors.

If anything happened no one could blame it on Buff. No suh. He had begged Mr. David, "Please, suh, ah take mah chances, but doan' fight Hannibal wid none ob dem cutleries. Dey t'row him off balance, sho' nuff. He ain' used to dem."

David Ashton had hesitated, biting his lip, but when he looked across his noisome cell and saw Johnny sitting limply by the window and looking out, so mighty sad, at some green islands dotting the empty harbor, he held to his decision. The black shadow of a bar falling on Johnny's face emphasized his waxen pallor. A few hours earlier Corporal Shaun Mahoney had settled all doubts.

"Mr. Ashton," he whispered when he brought the food at evening. "It's ordered to Halifax I am; the transport sails in two days. If I'm to help yez, I've got to finger me money tomorrey night."

All in all, the wars of Hannibal had gone well and a bag of bills and silver hidden in the chimney of David's cell was growing.

There were times when Buff felt tempted. Often he found in his great, blunt fingered paws enough to buy freedom, but he didn't know what steps to take and he didn't dast try to find out. Yankee niggers were a treacherous, back-biting lot. Right smart, too — most likely they'd get his money somehow, then turn him over to a sheriff.

So always he gave Mr. David all of Hannibal's winnings excepting enough to pay for food and lodging. He hung onto a few shillings in case he got took with a misery and needed a mess of snake oil or something. He'd his eye on a monstrous big knife, too. You could take the parts off a flea with it, it was so sharp.

Buff worked hard to align the steel spurs. He reckoned they ought to set pretty near like natural ones. But Hannibal didn't like it and kept pecking Buff's fingers when, using the linen threads, he tied the leather wraps around his legs. Were they too tight? He reckoned so. He overheard one of the resplendent officers saying if the ties were too tight a chicken's leg got numb. He loosened them, hoping it wasn't too much. Golly, how he'd like to carve up that purple-faced Major Bouquet. He was doin' Hannibal dirty — that was what. Cutleries!

Buff felt powerful shaky when those damp red faces above the scarlet coats came crowding closer. Laws! The snapping of snuffboxes sounded like dry kindling thrown on a hot fire.

"Li'l bird," Buff muttered, "dey's just de two of us 'gin all dese heah Redcoats. But doan' you git skeered an' doan' you try no tricks till you gits used to dem cutleries dat damn' major man say you got weah. Jest you look sharp, li'l bird, till you cotches on dat gray chicken how he fight."

A referee was appointed and promptly called the handlers into the ring. Bets flew like hailstones among officers crowding four deep. The size of the wagers terrified Buff. Why, these men were betting his own purchase price on a couple of chickens most of them had never seen before.

"Beak your birds!" called the umpire.

Hannibal, battle lights glowing red in his eyes, was quick enough to nail the gray chicken by its comb. He gave it such a yank the enemy bird emitted an outraged squawk.

"Dey's ten pounds ob Misto David's money on you, li'l bird," Buff breathed as he stepped back into his corner. "Win dis heah fight an' ah reckon you won't have to fight no mo'."

It was an epic battle. Long afterwards among forests of the Mohawk Valley, on the banks of the Hudson and in the dreary, muddy entrenchments at Yorktown, British officers recalled that cockfight in Waller's hayloft.

Rumor had not lied concerning the gray cock's ability. Moon, as his handler called him, was fast; fast as greased lightning. Buff uttered a little moan when, during the third flurry, his trained eye caught sight of the Jamaican bird's gaff disappearing into Hannibal's side. It was so quick he couldn't tell how much Hannibal was hurt. Not much, he reckoned, because the Virginia gamecock never faltered and rallied furiously.

Once again the cocks squared away, necks outstretched, bloodied hackles flaring. The silver bird started his charge and Hannibal ducked. In the last split second Moon saw what his enemy was up to, swerved aside and raked Hannibal as the astounded red bird flashed by.

Beaks parted with fatigue, panting wildly, the chickens battled on, inspiring the officers to such an uproar that horses stabled below took fright and began whinneying and kicking at their stalls. Wigs slipped awry, perspiration coursed in streams down the faces of onlookers.

A deep groan went up when finally Hannibal tottered helplessly over onto his side, his yellow beak blood-streaked and his sides working like those of a bellows. Though the gray bird punished him cruelly, Hannibal lay still, glaring defiance.

"Count!" snapped the officer in the blue waistcoat, and the umpire counted slowly up to ten.

"One count for the gray! Handle your birds," he directed.

Hannibal must be hurt bad, Buff reckoned. When he set him down the chicken toppled over on his side as if his legs wouldn't work. Again the gray bird hammered him with a punishing beak.

"Count!" Buff begged.

The umpire nodded.

"Seven — eight — nine — ten! Two counts for the gray."

"Please, Misto Major, cain't ah have time loosen dem lashin's jes' a little?"

"No!" Bouquet snapped. "Count, umpire."

"Swine!" someone said in a clear voice.

"The rules are in Major Bouquet's favor," rasped the lieutenant colonel.

Bouquet, his eyes popping more than ever, turned to Buff. "Nigger, this time your chicken had better show fight or you will have lost."

"Yassuh, yassuh." In his excitement Buff began talking in a strange guttural language. He implored Ogune, Mambani and Kleh to lead strength to the blood-bathed bird between his hands.

Hannibal this time remained on his feet and when the gray, also badly winded, came lumbering in, the red gamecock unexpectedly sprang into the air. Moon ducked and tried to dash out from under but first one then the other needlepointed gaff struck home.

"I believe, Major Bouquet, you owe me fifty pounds?" drawled a wolfish lieutenant colonel. "Your bird has been hit in the brain."

This was so. The gray cock had rolled over on his back and though his legs still worked feebly, the marine made no effort to pick him up.

Buff's pockets bumped his legs as he walked; now and then gave off a faint clinking noise. Golly! He was fit to sink what with all them gold and silver coins! Carrying Hannibal under his coat and next to his skin, the blue Negro stepped out of the stable and went shambling off to his quarters in Fish Alley. His face was wreathed in an immense grin, but in his free hand he carried a short iron bar.

Buff emptied his pockets and counted the coins as high as he could count. He was not sure how much Hannibal had won, but it was fifty pounds easy. Mr. David had only asked for forty.

The River

A small canvas bag of coins dropped into Corporal Shaun Mahoney's hands wrought the miracle.

"Heah's half," Buff told him. "Misto David give you de res' when he ready. An' doan' you try no tricks, soljer!" Buff scowled. "Er ah'll cut yo' ha'ht out." In the dim light, he looked really ferocious.

"Faith, then, 'tis meself will be careful."

At two o'clock the corporal came walking down the cell block. His heavy tread echoed hollowly amid the damp silence.

"A fine evening it is," said he, peering through a little barred window let into the wooden door of cell number twelve. Quickly entering, he set down his lantern. "Hold out yer feet, sorr."

Heart pounding, David obeyed.

Corporal Mahoney made a deft selection of keys. The gyves fell away.

"Now you, sor-r." Mahoney crossed to Johnny Gilmorin and the orange facings of his uniform were briefly bright in the candlelight. Two keys clicked and another set of gyves lay, useless metal serpents, on the bug-infested straw. Mahoney might be doing nothing more dramatic than un-locking a woodshed door. It was lucky he was calm, David thought. Johnny was shaking like a colt the first time it smells a bear.

[67]

"Plaze to come wid me. Niver a noise now," pleaded the Irishman.

At length the red-coated figure stepped into a storeroom. Down from pegs he lifted two officers' cocked hats, one edged with tarnished silver and the other with gold. Next he pulled a pair of gray military cloaks out of a refuse barrel. Admirably they served to conceal the tatters and rags in which both prisoners now stood.

For the first time since he could remember David felt an urge to weep. The letdown was too great. The nightmare was over — or promised to be. The unbearable monotony, the dirt, the hunger, the lice, the gnawing fear of that moment when he and Johnny would be dragged away for transportation to God knew where.

"Follow me," Mahoney directed softly, then caught up a small bundle. "Ye will plaze walk straight like officers. If any guards stop us, say yer out o' the 47th. It's thim pants-rabbits o' the 6th have guard tonight. Talk Englishlike and curse to beat the divil. They'll lave yez be."

They made their way through an open gate and out into a street which was very black except for distant whale-oil lamps. Before David realized it, the Irishman was following a path leading towards the water's edge.

"Now if the blessed saints are kind, we will find our boat and be off."

"*Our* boat?" That Corporal Mahoney intended to go along was a complete surprise.

"Faith, yes — there'll be the divil to pay around that jail tomorrow."

Hidden among some high weeds and half under a deserted dock lay a rowboat. Once it was launched Mahoney prepared to take up the oars.

Farish stripped off his cloak and spoke for the first time. "I'll take them oars. I can row quiet and I know the harbor currents."

"Fine. 'Tis the divil's own pull over to Lechmere's Point." Mahoney shrugged, settling comfortably onto the bow seat. "Now, we'll be waiting till the three o'clock patrol rows by."

It was wise that they had waited. The night was so dangerously fine one could see trees on the other side of the Charles. Millions of stars cast a perceptible sheen over the river. Frogs along the Boston shore grumped and grunted.

Never, David thought, had he smelt a sweeter wind. His legs felt unfamiliar without the customary twenty-pound weight to them. Absently he reached down and felt his ankle. He had no difficulty whatever in locating calloused ridges raised by his gyves. Small wonder. From December until June they had been there.

Johnny was all excitement. He kept saying to David in eager undertones, "Isn't it amazing? We are actually free! Think of it! We can go where we like, eat what we like, drink what we like! By God, I'm going to eat for a week!"

"On what?" David inquired, watching the jet water slip by more rapidly now that the skiff's triangular sail was filling.

Johnny threw back his head in the old careless gesture. "The fat of the land, my lad. America is rich; there will be plenty of food. Soldiers get fed."

The Irishman reflected, scratching his close-cropped head. "First off, I'm for chucking these rigimentals and bad 'cess to their orange facings!" He sighed gustily. "Next, I'm going to buy me the two prettiest doxies I kin find and the three av us will go to bed for wan whole week."

"And then?" Johnny was fascinated.

"Next I'll buy me a wee bit av farming land wid some big trees to it."

" — And then?"

"Then, savin' the captain's presence, I'll be going back to that bed again. Afther which I will join Gineral Ward's army. If there's any fighting going on this year, 'tis the fond hope o' Shaun Mahoney he will be mixed into it."

They were halfway up a crumbling bank when the sea captain flinched back. Above him a dark figure in a three-cornered hat blotted out a segment of the Milky Way. Another head and shoulders popped into sight. It was bisected by a long barrel held at the diagonal. Still another.

A voice called, "Halt! Halt where you are, or we shoot!"

Mahoney dropped his bayonet and held up empty hands. "Go easy on thim trigger fingers, bhoys," he begged, "or ye'll be losing Gineral Ward four av the smartest recroots he'll enlist in a dog's age."

"He talks Irish," snapped a deep voice from the depths of an alder thicket. "Careful, it's likely a patrol from the 18th. They are rank with bog-trotters! I'm going down and see. Blow them to bits if they make a move."

"Shall we rush them?" Johnny breathed. "He talks like a Britisher."

All at once Farish heaved a little sigh. He could tell that the man coming down the bank wasn't in uniform.

"Praise Mary!" Mahoney murmured. " 'Tis ten years I'm aged."

Farish called in flat nasal tones, "Any of you know Captain MacKintosh of Butcher's Hall? He was captain general of the Liberty Tree."

"Yes. Who are you?"

"Stephen Farish. One of the Committee of Fifty One till the British jailed me."

"That's as may be," the unknown grunted and, having reached the water's edge, drew near.

Johnny drew himself up. "My name is Gilmorin, sir. My friend Mr. Ashton and I have come to dedicate our swords to the sacred cause of Liberty."

"My arse!" grunted the man with the bayonet. "Durned if I like the look of 'em, Cap. Do you? They don't talk New England."

"Of course not. We are Virginians, both of us," David explained. "Since Captain Farish is a New Englander, you had really better listen to him."

"All right. Go ahead, you."

[69]

"Don't know's I blame you for suspicionin' us, but I cal'late I can explain," Farish began. "We have just come across the Charles. This Irishman is deserting. Helped us escape from the Stone Jail."

"My land! You ain't really excaped prisoners?" When the boy shuffled closer, starlight glinted on a clumsy old fowling piece. The barrel of it was nearly as tall as he.

"Sure enough," Johnny replied in a friendly sort of way. "Ever felt fetter scars?"

"I have," the old man's reedy voice broke in. "Durned French held me and Billy Forrester in Quee-bec Castle two hull years. Lemme feel." Stooping, he closed his fingers over Johnny's ankle and slid them up and down two or three times.

"He ent lying, Cap. The ridges and smooth skin is there all right. Prison stink's on him, too."

Cambridge

By sunup David, Johnny Gilmorin and Shaun Mahoney, too, set foot on their way to Cambridge. But they followed the upper road inland from the Charles. They were feeling like new men, thanks to the hospitality of some Massachusetts troops detailed to the defense of a crude earthwork unimaginatively christened Fort Number Three. To Johnny's disappointment, the commander had packed them off before it was light enough to see much of what was going on. David, however, laughed when he heard picks and shovels going by lantern light.

"There's the Yankees for you! Even work at night, like a dose of castor oil."

Soon they began to meet parties of sunburned men under arms. The majority seemed to be farmers marching in any sort of order and wearing the oddest imaginable miscellany of homespun. They were traveling in both directions; some to Cambridge and others out to Fort Number Three which, David learned, had been constructed to thwart a British attempt on Cambridge. Colonel Gridley had said it could command a small bottleneck barely joining Charles Town Point with the shore.

All along the line they kept meeting men who urged them to join this regiment or that. No recognizable officers directed this great swarming of humans. Uniforms, tents or flags were nowhere in evidence. Only rarely did some unit on the march preserve even a semblance of organization. Twice they came across companies engaged at drill. The travelers sat on a stone wall for a while watching one of them maneuver to the wheezed commands of a big pompous-acting fellow. He was wearing a sort of scarf knotted over the shoulder of a snuff-colored coat. The scarf was made of red cheesecloth.

Johnny groaned softly. "Ever see anything like it? My God, and to think old Fleming called our company exercises the vague wanderings of a pack of clumsy cowherds! Compared to those lads, I reckon we drill like guardsmen."

David nodded absently. "Maybe, but look at their faces. Ain't one squad laughing or fooling."

Not far from the outermost houses of the village of Cambridge the road was barred by a long, high, yellow-brown earthwork. Through a grove of maples it stretched far off to left and right. Men with picks and shovels were swarming all over the entrenchment. They were like ants. Another fortification was being thrown up on a hill a few hundred feet to the right. The first defense, a couple of freckled boys said, was called the Cambridge Lines and the second Butler's Hill Redoubt.

A sudden doubt gave David pause. "Suppose the Yankees won't let us into Cambridge? What the hell of a joke if we came all this way for nothing."

They came upon a group of militiamen nearby. One of the men approached them and introduced himself as the corporal.

"Now you appear to be likely fellers, but you're strangers 'round here," he said. "So are we Connecticuters. Stands to reason you'd be at home with us. Don't it?"

"Maybe."

"So just you keep on into the village. There's a college there, but I forgit its name. We've got us a headquarters detailed in one of the buildings. Hollis Hall. Ask for Knowlton, Cap'n Tom Knowlton. You'll ketch him there if he ain't already left for Inman's. Rest of our boys are there. Can you remember?"

The corporal was eager to enlist two such able-looking recruits, even if they were southerners and probably Church of England.

"Captain Knowlton at Hollis Hall. Right. I reckon we can remember. Thank you." David held out his hand. "There's a lot of sense in what you just said."

Captain Knowlton

On the outskirts of the village — Cambridge only sheltered some sixteen hundred souls — the prospective recruits became involved in throngs of villagers, farmers, soldiers, commissioners, sutlers, children, carts and dogs.

It was a pretty, tidy village built about a square. David liked the way the churches thrust their slender white steeples through the vivid green branches into the June sky.

Johnny, with something like awe in his voice, remarked, "My God,

[71]

Davey, I never guessed there were half so many people in America. Where do you reckon they came from?"

"Mostly Massachusetts," David hazarded. He paused, watching a squad of men awkwardly setting up a marquee. "Notice something queer?"

"Quite a few things. Which especially?"

"No horses around. Haven't seen a single cavalry troop yet."

Something must be in the wind, David deduced. Every little while levies in from the back country marched by on their way to camp along the Concord road. They weren't prepossessing; just a lot of sunburned men walking along under gun barrels of every length and pattern. Powder flasks slatted on their hips; blankets and quilts were rolled about their shoulders. They tramped by behind fifes shrilling "The White Cockade." One company got a big laugh because they followed the martial strains of a fiddle and a flute.

"How'd you like riding to hounds on that?" Johnny demanded, flattening to let pass an aide bumping along on a heavy-footed farmer's horse.

He commenced making a mental map of the village. In four directions long, maple-shaded streets diverged from a central square; where they led there seemed no way of telling. All of them were lined with brick or clapboard houses of sturdy and often handsome proportions. Usually a picket fence guarded the residences from the street. Diamond-paned and leaded windows were the rule. Framing the manure-speckled square were the village's few shops and a single tavern, the Blue Anchor.

All the streets, David saw, were much broader than Norfolk's and, though unsurfaced, were edged by curbs of rough-hewn gray granite. Tethered to hitching posts commonplace riding horses stamped and switched at flies. There wasn't a blooded nag in the lot. Flower beds decorated nearly all the front yards and a few houses boasted little lilac plants, recent importations from China.

"Ain't that the college?" Johnny asked over a rattle of drums.

"Yes, I reckon so."

"You know what it's called? The Connecticut man didn't say."

"My God, Johnny, you ought to know. It's Harvard College. Harvard is the biggest college in America. It has been standing over a hundred and thirty years."

"How do you know?"

"Fellow in jail told me so. Used to go here."

"William and Mary is older," Johnny maintained. "And eleganter, too."

"Maybe." David shrugged. He felt very tired after the long inactivity. His feet hurt like blazes and he was wishing he could find a brook to cool them in. He looked up the road. "Good God above! That building must be big as the Capitol at Williamsburg."

A carpenter emerged from a doorway and came shuffling over a lawn of dusty, discouraged looking grass.

[72]

"Are either of these Hollis Hall?"

"No. One with the belfry is called Harvard Hall; t'other is Massachusetts. Hollis is the third building to yer left. Better hurry. Rate these goddamn chicken thieves they call militia are wrecking them, won't be but a few bricks left standing come another week. There now. Just look!" A bearded soldier went tramping by, lugging an armload of fence pickets. "Them is from in front of President Langdon's house."

On passing between Massachusetts and Harvard halls, they found themselves facing a rough quadrangle.

"Hey!" David hailed a workman leisurely repairing one of many broken windows. "Which is Hollis Hall?"

The glazier set down his putty knife. "Hi, Mr. Coffin!" He beckoned a hearty, red-haired young fellow trudging by. He carried a pickax over his shoulder. "Show these gents where you used to chamber, will you?"

The red-haired youth nodded, though he sharply eyed David's greasy coat.

"Come along. Have you just come in?"

"Yes. From quite a distance."

"Didn't bring along any powder, did you? We are getting plagued short."

"I tried to," came the dry reply. "But the British got it first."

"Is that a fact?" the youth demanded in precise English. Johnny could see he was too polite to exhibit undue curiosity. "Well, if you want to fight, you are just about in time. They tell us a big battle must be fought soon. I resigned from college two weeks ago to enlist. Prescott's regiment."

"Resigned from Harvard?"

Young Coffin's healthy brown features relaxed. "Yes. I am — or was, rather — a junior sophister here, class of seventy-six. But for me no bachelor's degree. I prefer swords to Sully and drums to Demosthenes. *Tam Marte, quam Minerva.*" He passed a grimy wrist over his forehead, pushed back a battered cocked hat. "Perhaps *tibi seris, tibi metis* is more apt? Like most of our fellow islanders my father is, most unfortunately for me, a damned, uncompromising loyalist."

Johnny grinned. "Mine is, too. Did he disinherit you?"

"Down to the uttermost root and branch, Mr. — ?"

"John Gilmorin of Norfolk, Virginia, sir. And at your service."

"The pleasure is mine, sir. I am Nathaniel Tristram Coffin of Nantucket Island and a confounded bad bargain if you care to believe the proctors of Harvard College. I fear they were deuced glad to read my resignation." He made a wide gesture. "Verily, 'man proposes, God disposes.' I resigned to escape these cloistered walls and lo! the Fates lead me back into the yard."

The minute David Ashton saw the entrance to Hollis Hall he felt his judgment had not been far off. The usual litter of rags, papers and broken equipment was not lying about and the entry stoop was so clean a man could sit on it in white breeches. Many of this big brick building's windows were mended with paper and from them a colorful array of quilts and blankets was airing. A good sign. No other unit was doing this.

A serious-appearing young fellow in gray homespun was on guard and when David started up the steps he smartly lowered his musket, holding it crosswise to bar the entrance. Deliberately he scanned the two men from untrimmed hair to their shoes.

"Your business?"

"We want to enlist," David explained. "Where do we go?"

"You aren't asking commissions?"

"Whatever made you imagine that?"

"I believe I know educated men when I see them."

"You sound like an educated man yourself."

"I will be sometime, I hope," returned the bespectacled young man with the gun. "At present I am only a college tutor."

David Ashton walked into a bare little office equipped with three tables and a bed. Two men were sleeping on it. A pair of secretaries drove their quills over sheaves of paper.

"Captain Knowlton?"

"Here. What can I do for you?" The speaker was a tall, brown-featured man with a face like that of a Seneca Indian. Though he had on a soft leather shirt instead of ruffles and had clubbed his own hair without powder, he was strongly reminiscent of George Leavitt.

"Speak up," Knowlton invited. "What do you want to sell? We need cartridge boxes if you've got any."

"We haven't any, Captain. Last I saw were down in Norfolk."

The Connecticut captain sat straighter and his two secretaries looked up, blinking behind their spectacles.

"Eh? Where are you from?"

David told him.

"So you want to enlist, eh? Well, I suppose you can." Then, suspicious all in an instant, he asked. "What rank would you want?"

Johnny started to say "sergeant" but David checked him. In the Stone Jail he had had plenty of time to revise his scale of values.

"Suppose, Captain, we talk about that after our first battle? Maybe you can decide better. We neither of us know much about soldiering — "

A flush sprang to Johnny's sensitive features. "Why, how can you say that? You drilled with the company over a year — and I for six months. Don't you call that soldiering?"

"Opinions differ," Knowlton smiled. "Some folks around here would say so; old Put wouldn't." He seemed pleased, though, and looked at David narrowly. "Can you shoot?"

A slow grin slid over David's dark features. It was a blessing to speak with confidence. "Mr. Gilmorin here has won the Norfolk County turkey shoot three years running."

"That's good — capital! What about yourself, Mr. — "

[74]

"Ashton. David Ashton, sir. Well, I can 'most always hit a Spanish dollar at fifty yards."

"Eh?" Knowlton's satisfaction vanished.

"— With a rifle, of course," David hastened to amplify.

"Couldn't be done with a smooth bore."

"It couldn't — except by accident, sir."

"Down in Virginia," Johnny put in, "we mostly use rifles."

"I hear they are very precise. We have none around here, worse luck. Bellinger." Briskly he faced a round-shouldered man laboring behind a knife-scarred desk. "Enroll these men in my company. You have brought no weapons of your own, I take it?"

"No, sir," Johnny said. "We only got out of Boston jail last night."

Thomas Knowlton's thin lips formed no smile and he spoke sharply, "You were in prison? Why?"

When the Connecticut captain learned, he offered his hand with gravity. "We are honored, gentlemen, to number you in this company. It has not yet been the privilege of any of us to suffer so much in the sacred cause of liberty."

A gleam danced in Johnny's eye and he nudged David. There wasn't a grain of nonsense about Captain Knowlton, yet he spoke of the "sacred cause of liberty!" By God, this was the kind of a man to fight under!

Fate of a Gladiator

When, after a meal of succotash, salt pork, and apple pie, the Virginians still found themselves in solitary possession of a squad room on the floor of Hollis Hall, David sat up. Johnny, however, remained sprawled in comfort upon bright yellow wheat straw which, scattered knee deep, served as bedding. He yawned when David came over and spoke.

"Here is five dollars, Massachusetts. You'd better buy us some kerchiefs and shirts — extra pair of stockings for me, and a comb."

"Where are you going?"

"Take a look around for Buff. Ought to be out here by this time."

To find Hannibal's handler was surprisingly easy. The Negro was too tall and his blue-black complexion too unusual. A woman marketing said she had seen him loitering beside the bridge that led across the Charles River towards Boston. This bridge, David found, was heavily defended. To command it three cannons had been emplaced and, on a bend downstream, a mound of raw brown earth marked the existence of Fort Number Two. Further downstream another redoubt was being thrown up.

In a little field not far from the guard tent — one of the few in Cambridge — he found the Negro snoozing at the foot of a big oak. Hat over eyes and mouth open, Buff snored though flies explored and drank at his eye corners. A chip basket, carefully covered, lay in the tall grass beside him.

"Wake up, you no-'count rascal," David called. "Wake up, Buff!" He felt mighty uncomfortable at owing so much to the big, simple creature now scrambling to his feet.

"Yassuh, Misto David. Yeh! Yeh! Yeh! Bin lookin' all over dis measly li'l town fo' you, suh."

"Thank you. Was it difficult getting out of Boston?"

"Oh, no suh. Ah jes' let on ah was goin' out buying hens fo' Gen'ral Burgoyme. He powerful pernickity 'bout his vittels, 'at gentleman. My! My! Lots Yankees 'round, ain't hit? Heerd tell de British is fixin' to cross de ribber an' burn Charles Town!"

David whistled softly. "The devil you say! Where did you pick that up?"

"At de chicken fight las' night."

Under the stab of conscience David forgot all about Charles Town. He was astounded to realize he had hardly given Hannibal a thought since the night before. "Hannibal is all right?"

Sable doubt clouded Buff's features. "Well now, Misto David, ah cain't rightly say. 'At gray bird he give Hammibal couple right mean licks."

"He — he's alive?"

"Oh, yassuh. He plenty cussed dis mawnin'."

Taking the basket, David moved further away from the dusty road, to the shade of a big chestnut. When he lifted the cover his heart swelled. The red gamecock was lying on his side, beak resting on the bottom of the basket. A single ruby drop glistened on its point. The bird's feathers of burnished bronze were barely stirring.

"How — how did this happen?" David demanded through a sudden blur of tears.

"'Twas dem newfangled cutleries dat major man 'sisted on, suh," Buff muttered, awed to see tears slipping down a white man's cheeks. "Ah done told you ah was 'feared ob dem. Wahn't mah fault, suh, 'deed hit wahn't."

"No. Of course not. It was my fault — all my fault. You just did as you were told. You find out who insisted on steel spurs?"

Buff, in the acme of distress, raised on crumpled shred of a felt hat and scratched the fuzz on his skull. "Mebbe you-all doan' remember, suh, but dey wuz a English officer on de ol' 'Sistance? Hit wuz him."

"Bouquet, by God!" David's eyes lost their whites. They looked black as smutty fingerprints in his thin face. His whole body set up a gentle trembling.

"Yassuh. He 'low he fit our way an' los', so he say 'Fight mah way, black boy, er ah turns you ovah to de sheriff man.'"

David said nothing, only slid the cover farther off the basket. When the warm sunlight struck the gamecock, a breeze beating down the glassy river lightly ruffled his feathers. He stirred a little. Half a hundred fights were mirroring themselves in David's memory. Battles at Belle Meade, Bizarre, Powhatan, Truxton, and big mains in Baltimore and Wilmington, North Carolina. Never once had Hannibal so much as flinched. Game clean through! Big, small, tough and tender, he'd licked them all. And now he was dying. There could be no doubt about it. The rose of his lacerated comb was fading to a dim pinkish gray.

"*Cuck! Cuck!*" David called softly. "Remember me, little warrior?"

One sherry-red eye raised a translucent film shielding it from the light. Hannibal lifted his head the merest fraction of an inch then, wearily, it sank again. The ruby drop dripped from his beak and smeared the wickerwork.

Madelaine

Eli Haskins, corporal of the 4th squad in Captain Knowlton's company, had the bluest nose and the reddest cheeks David had ever seen. He was jolly and plump and surprisingly efficient. Quite the reverse was Johnny Gilmorin's corporal, Hiram Edgell, a lean and bitter Methodist circuit rider. Johnny figured his corporal was fighting the Church of England just as hard as he was fighting the Ministerial troops; maybe more so.

"I'm sorry," Captain Knowlton had said, "but we can't enlist your black friend."

"Friend?" David had stiffened. "What do you mean, sir? He's just a nigger — a *damned* good one!"

"We don't allow swearing in the orderly room." Knowlton's black brows met over his beak of a nose. Like a majority of company commanders in a more than generally religious army, he discouraged profanity at all times. "About enlisting Negroes — the Congress has not yet adopted a policy. Of course, if he wants to hang around and make himself useful, he is welcome to his food and keep." Just the trace of a smile tugged at the corner of the Connecticut captain's mouth.

Two o'clock of the afternoon of Thursday, June 15th, found David stripped to the waist and perspiring heavily over a bullet mold. He reckoned Johnny was lucky. Johnny had been detailed to visit the armorer of a Massachusetts company with an armful of disabled muskets. He was also to get a worn-out pan-cover spring replaced on the Spanish fuzee left behind by the Connecticut man whose mother needed him.

On such a warm day it was hot work melting down pewter mugs and ladles, leaden saltcellars, ink wells, and porringers. One and all they were chucked into an iron melting pot. David worked the bellows hard and the metal bubbled like silver soup. When it was hot enough, the alloy was run into a series of hand molds. Belying sectionalism, patriotic residents of Weston had that day presented the Connecticut men with a pillowcase full of precious odds and ends. One tiny porringer drew a wry smile to David's lips. It was engraved "G. D. B. TO H. B. B. — 1732."

When the lead had solidified, Haskins pried open the molds and dropped the hot castings, hissing, into a pail of water.

"Why do we run all this buckshot?" David queried, blowing a drop of sweat from the tip of his nose. "I should think musket balls would be what's needed."

Haskins shifted his quid and spat into the fire. "Wal, when we was fighting the French and Injuns outside of Quee-bec, we most gen'rally used to drop six buckshot in under a musket ball. They fans out effective-like."

The Blue Anchor was so jammed one had literally to fight one's way into that same taproom in which Lord Percy had, not so long ago, rested on his way to Lexington.

"He's a member of the Committee of Safety." Someone identified the speaker to the newcomers.

" — And I say again, each one of you is doubly armed. The minions of Parliament have their weapons, but you not only have firelocks, but the Lord God fighting on your side. Lord North's hirelings march only for base silver and gold, but you go forward for our freedom and for our very lives!" The committeeman waved his arms. "Shall we become paupers? Shall we fall slaves to the East India Company, like the miserable Sepoys of India? Never! Shall we permit the king's godless and débauched ministers to fatten forever on the fruits of our toil?"

"Never!" A shout went up, momentarily stilling all other noises in the tavern.

"We have petitioned humbly, decently, to the Throne," the orator resumed in a lower voice. "To what effect? I ask you — to what effect? Jeers! Abuse! The ruin of our shipping, the theft of all New England's trade."

He fell briefly silent.

"Fellow Americans, I declare before God Almighty, we must fight for our very existence — all of us!" Haloed by smoke, the committeeman glared down from his vantage point. "I tell you the British *must* be kept in Boston! If they march out and beat us, the bloodybacks will ravage and burn all the country, just like Injuns. They will shoot down our people in cold blood. You remember Concord? Lexington?"

A deafening clamor was his answer.

"Well, we licked them there and, with God's help, we can lick them again!"

David realized he was feeling pretty high. Under normal conditions he could have handled twice as much brandy as he already had aboard. Why, he would never even have felt it; but his long abstinence had fooled him.

Johnny, too, must have been feeling his cups, for he strayed away immediately they quitted the Blue Anchor.

Everywhere flew rumors. The British were sending three great armies to America. One was to be composed exclusively of Russians. If John Hancock, Sam Adams and the other leading makers of the association were caught they would be sorry. General Gage had sworn to hang them on the spot. A great battle had been fought in New York, someone declared.

"That's a bloody lie," retorted another man. "I was there that day. There wasn't any battle."

David took a swig from a bottle of brandy he'd bought and, standing still, laughed right out until passersby gaped at him. Gad! He was feeling more like his old self than he had in months! Who-e-ee! He took another pull of brandy, shivering as the liquid grated on his throat. Yah — yah — e-e-e-o! He gave the view halloo, then checked himself with an effort.

He bore down on a group of New Hampshire men beckoning from the glow of a hut cleverly constructed of sods and canvas.

"I'm going to challenge Gage — call him out," he announced. "He's no gen'leman. I'll lick him, that's what!"

"Hurray!" cried the New Hampshire men. "Come in, pardner. That talks like good likker."

"Sure is. Brandy. Have some?" He plunked himself on a food locker and, with alcoholic frankness, spoke of his trouble.

"Comin' in from drill I noticed a gal lookin' at us," volunteered a gap-toothed youth with a squint.

"You did? Where?"

"Out on the west edge of town — on the road to Concord. She was peeking out the blinds this afternoon lookin' kind of longing like at the boys. Maybe I'm wrong; she didn't say anything. Lives in a little brown stone house."

"Pretty?"

"Yep — kind of. Big brown eyes."

"Brown eyes are beau'ful," David announced. "I love brown eyes."

As if following a line of thought, David then said, "Gen'leman, le's drink to Virginia, God bless her!"

"Sure. Who's Virginia?" asked the gap-toothed boy. Everybody laughed and laughed. Then they began laughing all over again; when the brandy bottle had completed its circuit of the squad it was much lighter.

All at once David remembered Katie. By God, he sure wished he had Katie handy tonight. Katie Tryon. What a bloody fool he'd been never to take her, and she honing to slide in bed with him. Would have, anytime, if he had even so much as crooked a finger. What the devil had become of her after her owners took her away? Funny, he could remember how once the sun had struck her yellow hair when she was opening his window.

After another pull David decided on his course. It was very simple. If he saw a light at the brown house, he woud go up and knock. If there wasn't any, he was going back to Chamber 34, Hollis Hall. He reckoned he wasn't really drunk or he could not have remembered that number.

When at last he saw the house, a small square affair hiding under two tall walnut trees, he was aware of his body as no body at all — just one terrible, burning hunger. He used his fingers to comb his dark hair. Must look nice. Mechanically he fumbled for nonexistent lace at his wrists, then reset the plain black stock about his throat. In rapid succession he gulped deep breaths of the night air. He would say very politely, "Excuse me, madam, I wonder if I might have — " Have what? What would a man be asking for at ten of the night? Milk? Tea? Food?

Damn! No light. Standing at the end of a short walk leading up from the road, he vacilated. No light. Wouldn't that beat the Dutch? After six months, no light! No girl.

He was about to take another drink when he noticed a faint gleam penetrating a shutter to the left of the front door. Allowing himself no time to reconsider, he crammed the bottle into his pocket, marched right up to the door and knocked. No answer. He knocked again, harder.

His heart hammered louder than echoes resounding faintly inside. No one appeared. He waited, counting twenty slowly. Rapped again. "Always rap three times," the wags of Norfolk used to say.

"Who — who is there?"

"David Trelawney, of Williamsburg, Virginia," he announced with portentous gravity. David Trelawney for years had been his *nom d'amour*.

A chain rattled before the door opened just a crack and the light of a single candle revealed a not unattractive young woman in a neat brown dress with a white kerchief pinned crosswise over her breast. The New Hampshire boy was right; she had brown eyes. Big ones. This girl was so very small she reminded him of Rob's wife, Peggy.

"What — what do you require, sir?

"Why — why, I was wondering — " He stood there, almost filling the door frame. Slightly parted lips gave his mouth an eager boyish expression. His eyes, still sunken, were masterful, yet at the same time appealing and avid of kindness. She was so demure and genteel looking David was sure he'd made a bad mistake until he noticed just a trace of paint on her lips. "What do you think I want?"

The girl in brown looked at him slowly, and candlelight beating upward revealed a pulsing throat, the outline of strong high breasts, and a short and passionate upper lip. She caught her breath and her shoulders sagged.

"Pray come in, Mr. Trelawney," she invited with a forlorn attempt at jauntiness. "After all, I have been trying to get up my courage to say this all day. Somehow, to you it seems not so — so strange."

He remembered amenities. "I — I have with me some cognac," he told her in a voice unfamiliar to himself. "Would you care to try a little?"

"I would rather have some food," the girl murmured. "But let that pass."

For the first time he noticed faint blue shadows beneath her eyes, but just now they only made her the more intriguing; they were like faint reflections of her smooth, wing-like brows.

"Where shall we find some glasses, my dear?"

"My name is Madelaine," the young woman told him nervously. She began to pump water from a pump built over the sink. The candlelight was poor but it revealed neat ankles and small feet. Madelaine turned, resting both hands on the edge of the sink behind her. So perfect was the circle of white around her pupils they reminded David of owl's eyes when she said in a barely audible tone. "You — have money? A little money?"

"Is that enough?" Hurriedly he placed three gold sovereigns on a checkered cloth on the kitchen table. The drip of the pump tinkled into a basin set below it.

She nodded, then drew a deep breath like a swimmer wading into cold water. "You are very generous — darling. Tell me, do you really like me?"

For a moment he did not move — did not dare. Still he could not believe after so many tortured, barren hours that an end had come to them. And in such a delightful way. Miracle of miracles! This girl, all warm and soft, was going to be his in a very few moments. All his. He could do with her as he pleased. He could feel the blood surging up into his head as he tilted brandy into two glasses. Hers he diluted with water. His hand was shaking so the bottle neck jingled against the rim of the tumbler. He sat down.

Madelaine came and sat on his lap. Great warm currents eddied about his brain. Again and again he crushed her mouth in voracious kisses. "Darling!" The softness of her arms and scented firmness at the base of her throat. Lower. In his eagerness to undo a pin securing the kerchief concealing her bare breasts, he tore it.

They lay on the bed, lax, exhausted. A great greenish white star looking in an open window sketched a dim high light on the girl's forehead, ever so faintly outlined the contours of a small breast. It was a warm night.

"Look," said he presently, "do you see that greenish star?"

Drowsily her head moved against his shoulder. "Yes. It is very lovely."

"I'd like to take it out of the sky, darling," he murmured, "and tuck it into your hair."

"I'd always wear your green star, David."

He drew her closer. "I know, but suppose we leave it up in the sky where we both can look at it? It will still be our own private star."

"Always," she breathed.

"Why did you speak of food a while back?"

"Because, dear, I haven't had much to eat — not for nearly two days," came the simple reply. "I am a Tory and a Tory's widow. None of my God-fearing neighbors will sell me anything."

"A widow?"

"Yes. My world ended two months ago. At Lexington. My husband was killed in the retreat." She raised slim naked arms and, locking fingers under her head, talked to the great greenish star. "That is why — I must find money to get away — to England."

David murmured, "I have more gold — a lot more of it. Enough, I think. I need you, Madelaine — dear God — I do — kiss me."

Benediction

The 4th squad of Captain Knowlton's company was busy making as many cartridges as it could from a miserably insufficient issue of powder. When each man drew only a gill of the coarse black stuff, David cocked his eyebrow.

"Is that all? God's teeth! Down in Virginia a man takes more than this to a turkey shoot!"

"Wish to God we was going turkey shooting," Haskins grunted.

Around five of the afternoon an orderly, running streams of sweat from under his wig, came clumping up into the north entry of Hollis Hall and inquired for the commanding officer. Alert in an instant, Knowlton came out, thin-lipped mouth still full of bread and honey.

"What is it?"

"General Ward says you should fall in your men on the parade ground right away," the orderly puffed. "No fifes or drums. Bring along any axes or spades you've got." With that the messenger spun on his heel and went clumping off. He walked on the side of his boots as if his feet hurt.

"That's a newfangled way of delivering marching orders," Captain Knowlton complained. "Bellinger!" He licked his fingers free of honey and went behind his desk. "The company will fall in within fifteen minutes. Every man will carry at least five flints and as much powder and ball as he can lay hold of. Lieutenant Bisley will take command of this detachment. I'm riding over to Inman's farm."

"Hey! What about food, Cap'n?" called Billy Colgate from the stairs.

"Let the men bring whatever is handy," Knowlton advised. "They may get fed — but more likely they won't."

Drums rattled in all directions. Voices shouted. The Harvard yard began to fume with activity. Out on the edge of town conch shells, carried as bugles by the Salem company, began to moan. They made an eerie sound.

A great majority of the Provincial troops were in homespun: gray, brown and neutral. Many favored three-cornered hats. The evening being sultry, they wore their coats knotted about their waists. Hardly any type of firearm manufactured within the past hundred years was not represented in the ranks, but as far as David could see there was not a single rifle in sight!

An hour passed and still the Provincials waited about in the dusk. Finally the last stragglers showed up.

"Must be at least three thousand of us," Billy Colgate cried, white-eyed.

Mahoney ran a practiced eye over the muster. "Sonny, if there is here wan man over a thousan' I'll kiss yer butt before the whole brigade." Turning solemn, the Irishman tilted his flat, rather comical face in Corporal Haskins's direction. "Faith, 'tis wings ye'd best be fitting to yer feet. God help these poor bhoys whin they faces up wid regulars. *Wurrah!* If he wasn't down to his last sixpence, Shaun Mahoney would niver be finding himself here!"

The commander-in-chief turned heavily to a straight, handsome old man in a black surplice.

"Dr. Langdon, will you lead us in prayer?"

The snowy-haired president of Harvard stepped forward. Removing his scholar's cap, he knelt and clasped his hands before him. Slowly he raised tight-shut eyes to the evening sky. Hats whispered off by the hundred as militiamen followed suit, saving only those adhering to some denomination which forbade kneeling.

Mahoney fumbled until he found a rosary. That was no proper priest out there, he reflected, but he might as well draw a ration of salvation with the rest. As Dr. Samuel Langdon commenced to pray, beads began to slip through the deserter's calloused fingers.

"O Heavenly Father," the old man's deep and reverent voice rang far out over the crowded field, "grant to these, Thy unworthy servants, Thy blessing. Grant to them strength each man to do his part. Comfort those which are in fear, O Lord, and support them in their hour of trial.

"Make the light of Thy countenance to shine upon their arms, O Lord, and grant wisdom to their leaders. I do humbly beseech Thee to grant eternal salvation to any of Thy servants who may be called in judgment before Thy awful throne. Forgive them their many trespasses against Thy law, O Lord, and sustain Thy servants as they enter into the valley of the shadow of death. For the sake of our Lord Jesus Christ, Amen."

Night March

Before the troops were well clear of the village, continual halts and delays began. At such times the men would light pipes and sit by the roadside, speculating on what was likely to happen. The veterans lay down full length. Mahoney, too. Little Billy Colgate was yawning, but tried to hide it. Several men kept wanting to move their bowels.

Now and then a horseman went clumping back towards the village.

[83]

" 'Tis lucky we are 'tis a dark night," remarked Mahoney, puffing on a short clay pipe. "A blindman could see the dust we're raising clear across Amurica."

From various fields along the route waiting units fell in, steadily augmenting the column's length. By the time the van of the army had passed a bridge over Willet's Creek, the river of men flowed as far back as one could see.

David decided it was typical of Knowlton and Israel Putnam that when Mr. Inman's farm buildings hove in sight the remainder of the Connecticut men were waiting just where they should be and ready to march. Unlike some units, they did not indulge in loud talk.

The nearer the Provincials drew to Charles Town Neck, the fewer grew the trees. Above and below the road the terrain was now composed of well-grazed pastures which soon resolved into a series of long smooth ridges.

From the crest of a low hill more men began to make out the lights of Boston blinking far away, across the Charles.

"No lights. No pipes," Knowlton kept warning.

The starlight was just strong enough on Charles Town Neck to let the Provincials glimpse wet boulders and seaweed littering beaches to either side. After all, the neck was less than forty feet wide, so the army had to slow up and jam together to cross it dry shod. As the van passed on over and found room again in a wide field lying behind the loom of Bunker's Hill, some killdeers whistled. Charles Town, David learned, was built on the point of a spoon-shaped peninsula, dominated by two grassy, treeless hills.*

At the foot of Bunker's Hill General Israel Putnam and Colonels Prescott and Gridley were engaged in heated argument. Now and then one of them would refer to a map by the light of a carefully hooded dark lantern. They were in deadly earnest. When he wasn't beating the palm of his left hand with his fist, Putnam, the Connecticut general, kept pointing towards Charles Town and Boston.

"Plague take a fort on Bunker's Hill!" he was rasping. "From Breed's Hill we can fire straight into Boston and singe Gage's wig. From Bunker's the range is too great, eh, Gridley?"

The engineer nodded reluctantly. "But there are no flanks to be covered and — "

Putnam's roundish face glowed a deep red. "To hell with the flanks! Gage will be too worried getting out of our range. Look!" He sank onto his heels and began jabbing at a map with the ferrule of his scabbard. "A

---

* Due to an error on the part of certain British Army cartographers, notably Montresor, Page, and de Bernière, Breed's Hill, lower and much nearer to Boston, was mismarked "Bunker's Hill." The real Bunker's Hill stood to the rear of Breed's Hill and was the scene of no fighting at all. Thus, the Battle of Bunker's Hill should properly be known as the Battle of Breed's Hill. — Author.

battery on Breed's will drive the British ships out of the Mystic, out of the Charles, out of Boston Harbor — clear down to the castle!"

Vehemently, Colonel Frye shook his head. "Nonsense! All you will accomplish is to sting Gage into action. A redoubt on Bunker's Hill would keep him where we want him — in Boston, and it wouldn't alarm him!"

"Where I want Gage," Putnam rasped, "is charging up to our muskets! There's been too confounded much shilly-shallying. Eh?"

Colonel Bridge had shoved forward a paper. "Those are the Committee of Safety's orders. Read them again, General." He was tired, and the skin was gray around his mouth. "It says, 'A strong redoubt is to be raised on Bunker's Hill.' See? There it is. *Bunker's* Hill! 'With cannon planted to annoy the enemy coming out of Charles Town — ' "

All at once Prescott, run out of the same mold as Israel Putnam, stooped over. His black eyes were hard and bright as he whispered into the Connecticut general's ear. Gridley fidgeted, stared anxiously out over the Mystic. The killdeers had fallen silent and only the grunting of bullfrogs in a mill pond off to the right broke the stillness. Uneasily, the troops on the beach and on the neck waited.

Putnam got up, a hard grin on his mouth. "Gentlemen, we will obey the committee's orders. We *will* fortify Bunker's Hill — after we have taken possession of Breed's Hill! Colonel Prescott will attend to it."

"You're a pigheaded old fool!" snarled Frye. "You'll get us all massacred."

"Silence! You'll answer for that later!"

"So will you" Bridge cut in. "Look! A child can see how easy it is to get outflanked on Breed's. I know! I have been there!"

The Redoubt

Marching in loose order, Knowlton's company toiled over the side of Bunker's Hill and followed Prescott and Gridley down a long slope across a series of pastures separated by low fences built of glacial stones. In them cow droppings lay thick and the stones and the grass were so soaking with dew that the men were glad to get back onto a road even if it was only a cart track used at haying time. Passing under an occasional willow tree, the track led straight towards the lights of Boston.

"Say, can anybody see a man-o'-war?" It was Bellinger, the company clerk. Though his blunderbuss was much heavier than most of the firearms, he had kept up very well considering his thin, badly bowed legs.

"There's one," Billy Colgate replied in a quivering whisper. "A great big sucker!"

[85]

"Where?" demanded a dozen voices, several of them sounded nervous.

"If you'll sight right down this little valley, you can just make her out layin' off a point."

"Ye've good eyes, Bub," Haskins croaked. "I can't see a blessed thing."

Presently a man with a dark lantern came slipping and sliding down from the summit of Breed's Hill. It was Colonel Prescott; the men immediately recognized him by his stature and straight carriage.

"Captain Knowlton?" he hailed in a cautious undertone.

"Here, sir!"

"Take your men and their tools to the top of Breed's Hill. Report to Colonel Gridley." And he hurried along the column.

The men began to sit up and look about.

"I don't feel so good," one of the Connecticut men announced suddenly. "I got a complaint in my bowels. Maybe I'd better go back?"

"I allow what you've got, Lem Barker, is the running complaint." Corporal Haskins spoke in a fierce undertone. "Just you bide where you are!"

On the top of Breed's Hill Captain Knowlton pulled off his coat, spat on broad hands and drove his spade deep into the ground, saying, "Some of you fellows are dod-gasted clumsy with a firelock, but you ought to be jim-dandies with a shovel. Remember one thing — if sunrise catches us aboveground, we'll be nothing but a lot of dead heroes."

Dirt flew in a dark spray. Knowlton had been entirely right. With these tools the Connecticut farmers felt right at home.

Every half hour Captain Knowlton would lift a hand and call softly, "Catch your wind awhile, boys." He never seemed to get excited or tired. And he never swore.

For a while the men would lie flat, chewing grass stems and listening to the long-drawn calls of sentries posted only twelve hundred yards away over in Boston. On men-of-war nearer but still swinging unalarmed to their anchors, the watch called, "All's well."

After a while somebody remarked, "It's going to get light any minute." As if to bear him out robins commenced to chirp among some apple trees at the foot of a slope to the left.

"Why don't somebody come up and spell us?" Bellinger demanded wearily.

"Yes. Why don't they?" Haskins said. "Why the hell should we do all the work for the army?"

Billy Colgate sank trembling onto a pile of dirt. "What chances for some food?"

"The hell wid food — 'tis watter I want," Mahoney panted. "Ain't there no watter near?"

Captain Knowlton said to Johnny, "Gilmorin, suppose you scout around, see if you can locate a spring." The young Virginian was patently exhausted but he was so very game the captain felt sorry for him.

[86]

"Yes, sir," Johnny smiled and, after saluting, went trotting off down the slope.

A dim milky quality was invading the darkness. The sky lightened perceptibly. Then up from the river floated a noise so thin and shrill as to sound ludicrous.

"*Peep! Peep! Peep!*"

"Bosun's pipe," Mahoney commented. "The lobsterbacks will have seen us at last. Now watch what happens."

Bom-m-m! A cannon shattered the predawn stillness to atoms. Its report reverberated about Boston Harbor like a stroke on a titanic kettledrum. The startled Provincials were still catching their breaths when the man-of-war's whole starboard side seemed to explode into a blinding sheet of yellow flame. In minutest detail her spars, shrouds and masts revealed themselves. Lower on the hill sounded a terrific crackle of branches. It was followed by a succession of heavy thuds.

The Provincials for the most part flung themselves flat or, in frantic haste, sought the half-finished redoubt. A few, kneeling, began to pray wildly. One man clutched his head, sobbing that he was killed.

"Dig, boys." Knowlton came stalking along, his face harsh and rigid as the ceremonial mask of an Iroquois sachem. "A cannon's bark is a hundred times worse than its bite. See what Colonel Prescott thinks of them? He's an old soldier, too."

The militiamen looked up. There, walking quietly on the yielding earth of the parapet, was the Massachusetts colonel! He was pointing down the slope at something and when a third broadside boomed he calmly stooped, picked up a pebble and chucked it in the direction of the enemy.

The milky gray quality of the sky was turning pink, so the militiamen made their shovels fly. The men-o'-war Mahoney identified as the *Lively*, twenty guns; the *Symmetry*, twenty guns; and a huge ship of the line, the *Somerset*, sixty-eight guns. They maintained a noisy but almost ineffectual bombardment.

Knowlton nodded several times and before the aide had climbed up a half-completed gun platform to rejoin Colonel Prescott, he called: "Get your guns and clothes, boys. We're going to be moved."

This order the 4th squad promptly obeyed. A breathing spell would come very welcome indeed. They were aching in every muscle and trembling with fatigue. When the captain led them straggling out of the redoubt and down the back of Breed's Hill, they had an opportunity to look about. David could see all three, no, there were four men-of-war! The fourth ship, a sloop, had been hidden by the buildings of Charles Town. She was lying off a little point. The ship looked so familiar he wanted to ask Johnny about it. Johnny, however, hadn't returned from hunting a spring.

The Connecticut regiment having reached a little meadow halfway between Breed's and Bunker's, Captain Knowlton indicated a stone wall and called out, "We are to wait here for orders. Don't stray off. Rest as much as you can. If any man has food, let him share it."

He came over to David, who was trying, without much success, to bandage his blistered hands. "You've done fine, Ashton; especially when those fool cannons began. Where has your friend got to? I sent him to hunt water over an hour ago."

David sprang up, looking very tall. "Sir, I do not know where he is." His jaw took an aggressive angle. "I trust you are not implying that a friend of mine would run away?"

The captain smiled, shook his head in a tired gesture. "I imply nothing, Ashton. I merely asked."

Around eight of the morning the warships ceased firing. Their bombardment had not caused any real damage. In Prescott's little redoubt — it was hardly fifty yards on a side — the ringing thump of hammers and a hurried rasping of saws told of cannon emplacements nearing completion.

"Hurray!" someone cried excitedly. "By Crikey! Look, boys! We got cannons, too!"

Skirting the base of Bunker's Hill progressed a short column of cannon dragged by oxen and horses. Men trotted over from adjoining fields and clustered about, staring at the harnesses of the gun teams. They were wonderful contrivances devised from odd straps, traces, and many lengths of faded and often frayed rope. No two sets were even remotely similar. The sunburned militiamen looked with some awe upon the dully shining iron tubes, but laughed at the homemade carriages upon which they were mounted. They had been built of new, unpainted oak and hand-forged iron, and the clumsy wheels of farm carts had been attached to them.

A man with an ax cut in his leg limped by. "The British are coming over," he yelled.

All in a moment the digging noises had stopped. Carpenters working on the gun platforms scrambled up onto the parapet. The buzz of voices swelled and swelled and swelled until men behind Breed's Hill came running to see what was the matter.

"Look there, by the North Battery! The British are going to cross! My God, will you look at all them boats?"

Johnny felt his last doubts disappear. Definitely there would be a battle. On a long wharf bodies of troops were moving like red checkers in an intricate play. Big barges propelled by leglike oars began to crawl away from various piers and jetties, out over the Charles.

"How d'you know?"

"On the hill you can hear drums going to beat the band over in Boston."

Breathless, the men on Breed's Hill watched hundreds of red figures climbing down into more and still more boats. Bells in Boston were striking a single note each. The sun beat down hotter than ever.

The Rail Fence

When he became certain that those long lines of barges ferrying the British army were going to put in at Morton's Point, Colonel William Prescott was at once relieved and alarmed. So General Gage wasn't going to try to seize the neck? Good! He was throwing away his one chance for a cheap victory. But so many regulars! Prescott hadn't figured Gage would deign to send more than a regiment or two to dislodge a pack of rebels.

To General Joseph Warren, who had just come up carrying not a sword but a musket, he called, "You are senior, sir. Will you assume command?"

But the Boston ex-doctor shook his head. Hard running had left him gasping. "Thank you, no, Colonel. I'm here as a volunteer — no more. Wouldn't think of supplanting an officer who has accomplished so much." But he was worried all the same. Pretty soon he asked, "What do you propose doing about that interval to our left?"

"Don't know what I can do about that interval," said Prescott as if to himself. "I haven't any reserve, except some Connecticut men under Captain Knowlton."

"How many of them are there?" Warren wanted to know.

"Only about two hundred."

"They can't hope to hold a fence two hundred yards long. Not against British regulars."

Around two o'clock of the afternoon, a runner came panting up to Captain Knowlton, comfortably smoking his pipe in the shade of a small pear tree.

"Urgent orders! The colonel says take your men over behind the rail fence yonder. Build it higher."

Ten minutes later Knowlton's tired command set to work. It lent them energy to know that the British were actually landing in force farther down the peninsula. Soon they would be coming this way. The fence, as they found it, was no higher than a man's knees. It consisted of stones and two wooden rails which raised it waist high.

David's hands began bleeding and soon his nails split from dislodging and replacing the smooth glacial stones of which the fence was built. Billy Colgate and Bellinger were in no better way. All three of them were on the extreme left of line. From where they stood they could see the beach and the slimy green stones on it.

Advancing along the shore of the Mystic some Provincial troops came slogging along. It turned out to be Jonathan Stark's New Hampshire regiment. Some more Connecticut men were with him. They arrived surprisingly fresh.

A rhythmic beating of drums drew David's attention. Then many fifes began to shrill "Britons Strike Home!" They were real drummers off there. Their flams fell precisely together — *a rattle-tat-tat-tat! a rattle-tat-*

tat-tat! The Provincials raised heads in broad-brimmed straws and felts and tricornes, but they couldn't see anything because of the slope of ground down to the beach.

No ammunition arrived for the two fieldpieces.

Colonel Stark climbed up on one of the cannons, clapped his hands for attention. "You boys better form teams of three. When the first man shoots, the one next behind him will step forward and fire." He raised his voice over an insistent dull thunder raised by the fleet's broadsides. "Remember, we have very few rounds a man, so every shot has got to tell! Now look alive all of you and pick out their officers. You can tell 'em by their pretty uniforms and they don't wear crossbelts. They'll have silver half moons hung over their throats and will carry swords or spears. Got that? Shoot at their officers and *aim low!*"

Everyone was listening, squinting up at Colonel Stark's chunky figure up there on the gun carriage.

"Best place to hit the rest is where their white belts cross. If any man fires afore I give the word, I'll kick his pants up to his shoulders." He said it as if he meant it. "Now take your positions and remember why we're here. If the British get past us, we may as well go home and fit handcuffs on ourselves."

On Morton's Point the martial shrilling of fifes grew more strident. Up on Breed's Hill breathless silence reigned. The defenders evidently were watching something.

"My God," croaked Haskins. "Look at that!"

In stately array two scarlet streams began trickling away from the great red pool collected on the grayish sand of Morton's Point. One division started climbing very slowly towards the redoubt on Breed's Hill. The other moved off trampling the beach grass and gray-white sand along the bank of the Mystic. They came straight towards the breastwork of boulders the New Hampshire men had just raised, and at the rail fence.

It was an awesome, breathtaking spectacle, a terrifying exhibition of power. In the distance British weapons gave off brief, thin, pale sparkles of light. The scarlet of their tunics as yet obscured the white of their breeches and gaiters. Formed in column, company after company swung into sight, officers marching stiff and proud alongside. The drummer boys looked like midgets. Nobody who saw it ever forgot the spectacle of old England's troops on parade.

A veteran of the Louisburg expedition said to the Colgate boy, "If you hold spare musketballs between the knuckles of your left hand, you can save time reloading. They won't fall out, either."

For a space the 4th squad was given time to watch the British left wing deploying at the base of Breed's Hill. They were having trouble in their advance. Time and again the ruler-straight ranks were forced to break up in order to scale a pasture fence. The British pulled down the rails whenever they could, but often they had to scramble over and re-form on the far side.

"By God, they're slow as kids on the way to school," grunted a bald old man two places down from David.

"Ye'd move slow, too," Mahoney grunted. "What wid thim packs and heavy coats, ivry mother's son is carryin' a hundred pounds or better, or I'm a nigger."

The other enemy column which advanced along the beach found the going much easier. The British came steadily on behind their drums, the hollow beat of which was reverberating between the two hills. Larks flew up out of the grass before them, sped low towards the rail fence, then, seeing more men there, circled terror-stricken into the blazing sky.

A gorgeous officer moved over to a big patch of greenish white grass that rose to his knees. He shouted a command. The light-infantry column halted. Like some movement of a precise machine, steel rippled and a metallic rattle marked the fixing of bayonets.

"To hell with them!" Colonel Stark bellowed down the line. "If you hold your fire, boys, the bloodybacks will never get close enough to use those cheese knives!"

Like spilled water widening on a floor, tension spread behind the rail fence. The earth-marked militiamen pulled off their hats and, swallowing hard, sank low behind the tumbled stones of their fence. Many men knelt or crouched over like a valet peeking in a keyhole.

At a trot grenadier companies in tall bearskin shakoes began to deploy over the hay stubble some eighty yards away from the rail fence. Everyone could see the buttoned-back tails of their coats aswing, and brass-tipped bayonet scabbards wagging like the tails of so many dogs. In that big meadow there didn't seem to be quite so many of them. But there were still plenty.

The big grenadiers formed a long triple line, shoulder brushing shoulder, their white-gaitered legs swinging in time to the thumping drums. They halted and the brass plates on the fronts of their hats flashed in the eyes of the Provincials, bright as the mirror of a mischievous child. Out in front of them marched white-wigged officers gleaming with gold and silver. These also halted and, turning, supervised last-minute preparations.

Down on the beach the British light companies had not halted. Their advance continued. It was breathtaking, unforgettable, seemingly inexorable. Still in column they resembled a long scarlet tide sweeping up along the beach. White wigs, glittering epaulets, flashing musket barrels. Stiff as posts, the officers marched many feet in advance of their men. Faces set, scarlet with heat and exertion. Closer. The swishing of their feet over the sand was clearly to be heard now.

In David's squad, farthest to the left along the rail fence, there was a hurried shifting of musket barrels back to the front. Let Stark's men on the beach look out for themselves! The carpet of cut hay separating the grenadiers from the rail fence was growing narrower.

From behind came Captain Knowlton's sharp, "Take *sight!*"

David rested the Tower musket on the top rail and through his improvised rear sight watched square red faces all bright with sweat take shape. The officer nearest him was a big hairy fellow. He was loudly cursing the heat.

The wood of David's musket felt very hot to his cheek when he settled its butt more firmly into his shoulder, but the skin on his shoulders felt cold as if they had been rubbed with ice. Swallowing hard, he swung his front sight until he saw, as if balanced upon it, the gorget of a very tall major. As in a dream he watched the Englishman's face draw near. He had a big livid scar across his chin. A curl of his wig had fetched loose from its pins and was bobbing to his every stride. All the rest of the world became obliterated by that figure in scarlet with light blue cuffs, light blue lapels and a white waistcoat. The gorget grew simply enormous.

Why in hell didn't Stark give the command? The damned British were right on top of them! *Why didn't he?* A Virginia rifle company would have fired minutes ago. Closer! Closer! The dancing half moon of gilt silver and a lace jabot under it looked to be hovering right above him.

Jonathan Stark's husky voice suddenly roared out. "Pick the officers! Aim crossbelts. Ready — fire!"

Banging reports slapped at David's cheeks like invisible hands, but he held steady on the gorget, and by tightening his whole hand squeezed the trigger. The clumsy Tower musket kicked him like a curried horse with a ticklish belly and a swirl of rank, rotten-smelling powder smoke beat back in his face. He couldn't help a series of hard, racking coughs. A swirling hurricane of flame and smoke spurted from between the fence rails. All in an instant a gray-white miasma eclipsed nearly the whole of that glittering parade in the meadow.

"Fer the love av Mary! Get out av me way!" Mahoney was grabbing at his arm, hauling him back. At once the Irishman poked his firelock through the hay-covered rails.

David remembered his ramrod and had bent forward to grab it when a rift appeared in the wall of smoke. The hatless head and hunched shoulders of an officer showed up. He was clutching his cheeks and dazedly swaying back and forth, his sword adangle from a knot fastening it to his wrist. Out there the lines of muskets were wavering and bayonets were swaying like steel reeds under a gale of death. More heads materialized in the murk, some streaming blood, some yelling.

Terrible, animal-like noises arose beyond the curtain of smoke. Then a puff of wind from off the Mystic brushed aside the fumes. David felt his heart heave and he gasped as if a foot had been driven into the pit of his stomach. Not over sixty feet off lay a long squirming windrow of bodies dressed in scarlet and white.

The *click! clock!* of Provincial firearms being hurriedly cocked sounded on all sides. There was need of haste. Eyes ablaze, cheering, the second line of grenadiers was charging, hurdling their fallen comrades. David saw dark blue lapels out there this time — some white — a very few light blue. Here and there a survivor of the first wave staggered up, gray-faced, to join them. God! Too clearly he was remembering the way those deadly black holes had appeared in the tall major's gorget.

Bayonets, murderously atwinkle, shone amid the dust and smoke. Again the rail fence spouted fire. Before the smoke shut down, David, trying to tilt a powder charge into his gun, beheld the further effects of the Provincial fire.

No less effectively than before, the second volley had knocked the heavy companies backwards off their feet, had torn murderous gaps in their array. Howls, screams and curses became mixed in a fearful cacophony. As with trembling hands he poised a handful of buckshot over his musket muzzle, David watched a tough-looking grenadier's bearskin fly off. A small package fell out of it. He wondered what it contained.

"Come on! Oh damn you for bloody cowards! *Come on!*" A red-coated major, wig canted over one ear, became visible in the meadow. With the side of his sword he was hammering at some privates who, hatless, were reeling back, coughing, and black with burnt powder grains.

It was somehow appalling for David to watch the British third line come up, carrying with it broken remnants of the first and second ranks. Again a murderous volley smashed full into hot faces atwitch with desperation.

Then there were no more redcoats and crossbelts to shoot at. The few British left on their feet were running or staggering back over the meadow. Of all the officers who had participated in this attack, David could see only two and these were still pleading with their men to come back.

The cloying, musty-sweet smell of blood and the nauseous stench of torn entrails hung heavy in the lifeless air. Some forty feet away a drummer boy lay crumpled, his small face a pulp. In a scarlet cataract his blood was draining across the smudged head of his drum. Agonized shrieks from the pile of men on the meadow made an inferno of sound.

The young lieutenant whom David had noticed suddenly came crawling out from behind a tangled pile of bodies. On his gray and shining face was a look of awful astonishment at what had happened to him.

A wounded sergeant flopped up on one elbow, cried, "Mr. Bruère, go back! They will kill you! Go back!"

"Water! Water!" New gorget swinging, the young lieutenant came crawling on hands and knees over the grass, and the daisies were not whiter than his teeth, bared in agony.

"Stop, Mr. Bruère! That's the wrong way!" yelled the sergeant and tried to wave his arm in warning, but the pinkish and jagged end of a bone was sticking out just above his elbow, and his forearm dangled dreadfully limp.

"Don't shoot," gurgled the wounded boy. "Water! Kind friends, Oh, for the love of God! Water!"

Twenty feet short of the fence the young officer slowed, stopped his crawling. Then, like a frightened cat, he humped his back. He began to vomit such incredible torrents of blood it seemed as if he must be pumping from an inexhaustible reservoir. The flying gore splashed back from the ground, spattered his face, his white waistcoat. All at once he crumpled onto his side and lay still.

Charles Town

Immediately after the repulse of the British the wind died away entirely. Wounded men felt the sun grow scorching hot, howled and screamed for water. Only the sullen, futile bombardment of the redoubt by their ships and by a battery somewhere over in Boston marked any British activity.

Buff, shuffling loose-jointed and watchful over the neck, kept a sharp lookout across a tidal millpond to his right. Yonder, some men — he didn't know which side they were fighting on — were poling two big barges into shallow water among some reeds. Each had a cannon mounted behind by a sort of wooden shield. Who-e-e! If them things started shooting, this neck would be no place for a certain nigger. He looked up and watched a great lot of men swarming around the top of Bunker's Hill. Laws! They didn't seem to know where they was heading, no-how. Bluish heat haze, he realized, was obscuring the far end of this point of land.

A bony-faced farmer came shuffling to the rear. He was biting his lip and his face was a queer yellow-bronze color. Buff's eyes grew white. Blood dripped slowly from the farmer's shattered forearm. Eagerly, the dust closed over each drop, as if to hide it.

"Please suh, whe'h at is Cap'n Kno'len's people?" He repeated the query he had been asking all the way out from Cambridge.

"He Connecticut?"

"Yas, *suh!* He Connecticut!"

"Wal, you might come acrost him over there on our right — towards Charles Town. They say 'tis Massachusetts in the fort."

His information could not have been more erroneous, but Buff had no way of knowing it. The sight of that wounded arm was evoking unfamiliar, long-dormant impulses. Buff's clumsy-looking fingers crept up to rub the chevrons of scars on his cheeks. He had no idea he came from a fighting tribe in Senegal, but he did know he was different from his lazy, good-natured, brown-black companions in slavery in lots of ways. "Stupid bushmen" he called them. It was queer, but he really enjoyed a fight — a taste which had earned him shackles and many a session at Candless's whipping post. That, and the stigma of being a "bad nigger."

His conical-shaped head settled lower between his shoulders, but his step lightened. "Keep yo' eyes skinned, boy," he muttered. "'At's a pow'ful lot o' shootin' up yander."

Along the cart track he was following came another wounded militiaman. He was profanely protesting to not less than eight chalk-faced Provincials.

"Git back to the fight, you consarned yellow-bellies! Git away from me. I don't need help half so much as the boys up to the fort." He halted and, leaning on his weapon — an old duck gun with an enormously long barrel — glared appealingly about. "Won't any of you dad-burned heroes go back?"

"Shucks," boomed a gloomy-visaged fellow in undirtied nankeens, "we ain't going to allow a suffering comrade die on the road to safety."

"Won't one of you go back?" The wounded man's face was bitter, twitching.

"Whut for? Anyhow the British have run. They're whipped."

"They'll come back — damn yer ugly eyes! They're British regulars!"

Despite greasy duroy breeches and a very dirty red-and-white-striped jersey, Buff made an impressive figure when he came padding up on bare feet. His smooth blue-black skin was glossy with sweat and the great muscles of his chest and arms stood out like sculptured bronze. Though his features revealed nothing, he was thinking, developing a crafty scheme.

"Please, suh, ah heered whut you jes' said. Ah sho' would admire to go an' fight, but ah ain't got me no gun."

The wounded militiaman jerked his head at the old fowling piece. "If you'll fight, nigger, she's yours. Here are some bullets and you'd better take along my powder horn."

"Thank you, suh! Thank you, kindly." Buff ducked his head several times.

Once he had unstrung his cowhorn of powder, the wounded man glared at the skulkers in bitter contempt. "Go on home and tell your mas to put your diapers back on." He spat in their direction then said, "Good luck, boy, and give 'em hell!" He nodded to Buff and resumed his slow retreat.

Buff hadn't the vaguest notion about how to load a gun, but he climbed over the hot stones of a fence and took up a trot. He was heading for the gray-white roofs of Charles Town and the treetops poking up between them.

Presently he overtook a man tramping in the same direction. This one was wearing the blue shell jacket and white canvas breeches of a mariner. When Buff asked him about loading, the seaman stared, then squirted tobacco all over a clump of fireweed before he said,

"Sure, I'll teach anybody who'll go ahead."

In the shade of a little grove behind Charles Town they paused. Buff tried to remember the instructions, but it was hard work. To make matters more awkward, the duck gun's barrel was long, and five or six times the little man — whose name, it appeared, was Metcalfe — had to prompt him.

"*Je-sus!*" he exploded. "Can't you remember *nothing?* I never did see such a dumb nigger! Look here, we better set down by that fence while I show you how to prime."

Metcalfe reached up, pulled a green apple off a limb, inspected it, threw it away and got to his feet.

"What's your name?"

"Buff, suh."

"Well, come along, Buff. I guess the redcoats will have pulled themselves together by now. Maybe we can find us a bagnet or two down in Charles Town. They come in handy sometimes."

The big Negro attracted no end of curious stares with his scarred cheeks and pointed teeth. In a red-and-white-striped jersey and carrying a six-foot ducking gun, he made quite a picture. When he saw how cannonballs had knocked in the roof of a big schoolhouse, his broad nostrils began opening faster. From a gaping hole threads of blue smoke were spiraling slowly into the cloudless sky.

Pretty soon they reached an orchard and found many Provincials gathered among the trees. They were all staring anxiously across at Boston and at a line of boats rowing over. They were filled with red uniforms. Reserves.

Men skirmishing slowly out from Charles Town were just in time to see a second assault on the redoubt take shape. Once its reserve had been landed, the British command lumped together the decimated units which had already attacked.

The British drums were *slam-slamming* again, but not so evenly, and the squeaking of their fifes held hysterical overtones.

"Where would we be the most use?" Metcalfe asked of the crowd.

"Right here," said a man in a decent gray coat. "Since during the first attack we stung the British flank a lot, it stands to reason Gage will order Charles Town bombarded. We figure he will likely send troops to drive us out of here — or try to. It's my guess we will see plenty of action before long."

Buff was surprised to find how calm he felt. Who-e-e! In a little while he'd maybe be killing someone. All though the pear orchard sounded the thin slithering of steel slipping over steel; many ramrods were being driven home.

Buff felt his stomach tighten and his nostrils stiffen. He looked about and pretty soon he found what looked like a fine vantagepoint behind a stone well. The coping faced a rather wet cow pasture over which a British force coming to clear Charles Town must advance. Metcalfe came up to him.

"This is a dandy spot. Why, it ain't forty yards to the nearest of them dead Britishers," he grunted. "Remember to hold low."

Heart-stilling crashes sounded among the houses. Buff, shaking like a frightened colt, watched bricks fly from a chimney and fall into the street. Some of the bricks smashed windows clear across the road, scaring hell out of some militiamen. Under a steady rain of cannonballs, boards, shingles, shutters scaled up into the sky. A whole series of terrific smashing crackles reached the orchard.

Why, Buff wondered, had he ever been such a no-sense fool as to come looking for this sort of a death? Peeking around the well top, through the rough trunks of the fruit trees, he could see Provincials sprinting out of the village at a dead run. Every time a shot landed near they'd give such a funny little jump that Metcalfe and the rest of the fifty or sixty men lying hidden and safe in the orchard began to laugh.

Within ten minutes Charles Town was blazing in a dozen places, then the breeze sprang up and began to blow a great blue-black pall of smoke over the Charles River and into the faces of the naval gunners. Immediately their aim got bad and some cannonballs began smashing through the young pear trees. But they hurt no one. Soon the bombardment ceased and only the fierce crackle and roar of the flames consuming Charles Town beat against Buff's eardrums.

Metcalfe emitted a startled grunt. "Look alive, boys. Here they come!"

Battalion on battalion, regiment on regiment, the British, thirty-four hundred of them, were on the move, swinging over a succession of fields, and climbing fences. Metcalfe's party on the flank could see how very slow the advance was. With livelier interest they also watched the maneuvers of a body of marines. Because of their black leggings and white lapels they were easily recognizable. In column they came tramping along the beach; obviously detailed to drive the last Provincials out of the village.

"Boys, you had better close in a mite," Metcalfe called. "There are a lot of redcoats headed this way."

And there were, nearly two hundred in number. Buff, too terrified now even to run, beheld coming towards them two whole companies of marines in low caps with silvered ornaments and white facings to their scarlet tunics. That they had taken part in the first attack could be told at a glance. Some of the men wore bloodied rags tied about head or limbs. Not a few were limping. When they came closer, the Provincials in the orchard could read a sort of stunned expression on many of the sweat-bright faces.

A few impatient Provincials popped heads from behind the woodpile, stared mesmerized at the brilliant array moving forward across the cow pasture. The Royal Marines were now so close Metcalfe could make out an anchor and some oak leaves on their cap badges.

The officer saw the lurking skirmishers and yelled something. With a precise one-two-three the red and white ranks came to a halt. Like corn under a reaper, brown-mounted musket barrels swept down until the marines, holding their weapons waist high, were pointing in the general direction of the woodpile. Buff held his breath, cowered flatter than flat and felt his pants grow damp.

"Fire!"

The British volley struck only one of the Provincials. But he, a dark, unshaven fellow, was struck in the belly and began to scream shrilly, horribly, like a hurt horse. Whirling, rotten-smelling smoke shut out all sight of the enemy.

"Get ready, boys!" Metcalfe called out. "Aim for their belt buckles."

About sixty militiamen rose up out of the tall hay grass, some standing right up, others sighting from one knee. They took steady aim, waited for the smoke to thin out. Buff put up his duck gun and squared his shoulder against its butt. Dim figures coughed and wavered around in the gloom. The marines' second rank was slipping through the first, in a hurry to fire.

"Come on, marines, for God's sake! Don't run!" The only surviving officer ran back waving his little halbert. "Come back!" But the retrograde movement was gaining momentum. "Thompson! Harker! Stop those men!" he yelled. "Oh God! Why am I condemned to lead such wretched cowards!"

In a passion the hatless lieutenant reached up and tore off his remaining epaulet.

"There, damn you! I'm no officer of yours! Don't call yourselves marines! You act like damned frog-eating pimps!"

Buff was trying to tamp home a charge when someone who swore he came from Colonel Prescott himself ran up and told the men in the orchard to fall back. More troops had been seen embarking in Boston. This time it was certain they meant to strike Charles Town in force.

He advised, "You had better retreat along the road that runs across the back of Breed's Hill. There is a barn over there. You might make a stand in it."

Buff caught at his arm. "Misto, whea's de Connecticuters? Ah's jes' *got* to find Misto David."

"Clear around on the other side of this point," the messenger called over his shoulder.

With the other men from Charles Town, Buff retreated. He had started to skirt the rear of Breed's Hill when a terrible old man with two big horse pistols in his belt pointed to the redoubt.

"Go up there! No back talk!"

"Strike Britons Home!"

To David, Lord Howe's second attack on the rail fence seemed but the stupid repetition of an initial error. Somehow, the unflinching discipline

[98]

of those regulars in the face of certain destruction was more appalling than admirable. Good thing he felt numbed to ghastly sights and piteous sounds. In some places the grenadiers had fallen in easily discernible lines. They lay huddled like game arranged after a drive.

From everywhere arose anxious, urgent cries for powder. Captain Knowlton went striding across a gap between the end of the breastwork above and the rail fence. Some stragglers had built three crude *flèches* of rails there. He asked the sunburnt militiamen if they had any to spare.

"Jesus, no, mister. We got less'n two rounds apiece."

Knowlton hurried back and said, "Ashton! Get up to the redoubt — find whether they have any powder to spare. Even a horn or two would help. If there's none there, wait. Somebody might think to send some forward."

As he climbed Breed's Hill, David was surprised to note that the afternoon was well advanced. Shadows were lengthening, deepening.

He found Buff hovering outside the sallyport.

"Misto David!" If Buff had had a tail he would be wagging it, thought the Virginian.

"What the devil you doing here, boy? Haven't you got good sense?"

"Oh, Misto David, is you all right? You doan' look so brash."

"I reckon I don't." David's eyes were hollow and red-rimmed. His throat felt as if someone had gone over it with sandpaper. The one drink of water he'd swallowed came from a brackish pool and tasted as if it had lain overnight in an old boot.

David was debating whether he should go back and report to Knowlton that there was slim chance of any powder being sent when Johnny Gilmorin saw him.

"Davey!" He rushed forward, barely recognizable. David couldn't help laughing. Johnny's shirt was torn half off; his long, light brown hair was unclubbed and flying wild. One naked shoulder was black and blue from the recoil of his musket. A far cry, this, from the Johnny who doted on gay cockades and wigs of the latest *ton*. His face was so coated with burnt powder grains that the whites of his eyes showed up even brighter than Buff's.

"Hi, Johnny! Did I say something about the Yankees being scared to fight?"

Cried Johnny, a fine clear flame in his eyes, "They can fight! Damned if they flinched, even when some Britishers got right up to the parapet." He lowered his voice, licked his lips in puzzled fashion. "But, hang it all, Davey, they don't seem to take any pleasure in fighting. They're so — so damn' *serious* about it!"

Suddenly Johnny felt a thousand years old, very tired and, now that those distant drums were tapping for the third time, just a little scared. That was wrong, too. Long since, the British should have admitted that they were beaten.

David, having read a measure of his disillusion, put a hand to Johnny's damp shoulder. "One more repulse, Johnny, and even those damned brave bastards down there will have had enough."

Other voices, croaking with thirst, called, "Powder! Where in hell is some powder?" "Damned committee's sent no powder all day!" "We've been betrayed — I told you so!"

"This time they mean business," an officer in muddied breeches said. The British array was not so colorful. At last they had shed their heavy packs and a lot of them had removed smotheringly hot uniform coats. Not a few infantrymen had stripped to the waist, slinging over naked shoulders the crossbelts which supported their cartouche boxes and bayonets. With their tall bearskins and powdered hair the effect was grotesque.

The officers, however, had disdained to remove either coat or shirt, but their finery was sadly stained and their white leggings had taken on a pink-ish hue from the bloodied grass stems which had brushed them. David, resting his musket across the berm of the earthwork, noted how motion-less patches of white and scarlet dotted the slope from the crest of Breed's Hill all the way to Morton's Point.

"Any men having bayonets had better fix them," Warren called.

"I got a war hatchet," proclaimed a man in a buckskin shirt. "That's better'n a baynit any time!"

When the British in their long lines again started climbing that series of stone walls which had gone so far to exhaust them in their previous efforts, no drums were beating. Grenadiers and light infantry were all mixed up with the regular line companies. David saw tall shakoes stand out like dark stumps in a red and white field. The short-skirted light-infantry coats looked frivolous among the longer ones of regular length.

"Will you look at 'em come?" somebody muttered.

The British raised a cheer and kept on without waiting to re-form every time they crossed a fence; previously they had always realigned their ranks. The officers, though they must have realized their especial peril, were again well out in front.

Down by the rail fence, Shaun Mahoney, having used the last of his powder, dropped his musket and ran like hell. He intended to get over the neck in time.

Unhampered by packs, the English scaled the slope dotted with daisies and mustard flowers almost rapidly and, at sixty yards' range, commenced firing very coolly. After each volley they would advance ten yards and fire again. The bloodied corpses among the flowering hay grass might not have been there.

David, peering over the tumbled earth, picked out an officer, a gross, fat-shouldered fellow with a big belly wabbling beneath a buff waistcoat. By God! That was Bouquet! The major's heavy features were shining as if lacquered and since he wore a soggy red bandage about his left arm, he must have been this way at least once before.

"Fire!"

The weird assortment of firearms in the redoubt roared, and like dominoes the first rank of the British began spinning and tumbling about. But the other lines came on. A few scattered shots roared in an effort to check them. David thought of Hannibal, and took a careful bead on Major Bouquet's chest. This was the last of his powder.

In a hot rage he squeezed the trigger and must have pulled too hard. His ball merely tore some gold bullion from Bouquet's shoulder. The major roared and shook his sword at the redoubt. David had to hand it to that Englishman the way he kept on coming!

Johnny, not recognizing him, instead picked off a captain 'way down on the right. He winked at Coffin, said, "Pay me!"

"Forward, lads — got them!" Bouquet was struggling across a ditch below the parapet. He was dreadfully out of breath, but still could make himself heard. "Forward! Forward!"

Meanwhile the Provincial fire had gone out like an old candle. The attackers, too, stopped shooting for fear of hurting their own men. To climb up onto the parapet the English were forced to use both hands. To do it some of them, unwisely, laid their muskets on the berm of the redoubt. David and some others snatched these up and began smashing at the powdered heads which came clambering up.

"Oh God, isn't there *any* more powder?" Johnny began yelling crazily. "Powder! Give me powder!"

Right above David a figure scrambled into sight! Major Bouquet!

He seemed tall as the Colossus of Rhodes when he brandished his sword and roared, "Surrender, you rebels!"

"We are not rebels!" Colonel Prescott shouted.

Raising his rapier, he started forward, but Buff, crouched by a cannon's trail, heard Bouquet's voice and glimpsed him against the sky. In a flash he whipped up the duck gun and fired.

A full load of ball and buckshot struck Major Ponsonby Bouquet under his raised right arm. It ripped his scarlet coat into tatters, front and back.

"Dere's cutleries fer you!" snarled the Negro, then dropped his gun and joined a mob of fugitives fighting to get out of the sallyport.

A dying British officer falling into the redoubt dropped his sword almost at Johnny's feet. A sword! He snatched eagerly at it. This was more like it. Ha! The grip, though slippery with its late owner's sweat, felt fine in his hand — reassuring. Shouting, he turned with some others to dispute the British advance.

By tens and twenties attackers swept over the parapet and jumped down behind leveled bayonets. Dust rose in blinding eddies, figures disappeared, reappeared — red, homespun, white. Thumping sounds. Curses.

Johnny parried a bayonet's point and drove his blade in hard. It pierced through the fellow's throat. Why, this was easy!

"Forward! Forward!" he screamed. The captured blade shivered, but he beat aside another bayonet and slashed back. Missed this time.

An eddy of Royal Marines swept up from the right, driving a few Provincials before them. Leaping backward, the Yankees were swinging desperately with their clubbed muskets.

"Nah then, ye bleedin' rebel!" Johnny saw a towering sergeant gather himself behind his musket, and fell back a step to win elbow room. His heel struck an abandoned pickax and he lurched backward off balance. All the world resolved into a long brown face set with blazing blue eyes, snaggle teeth and writhing lips. A shooting star of steel materialized between him and it.

"Don't!" Johnny screamed and, using his left hand, tried to deflect the down-rushing bayonet, but the point caught on his palm, punched clean through it. Drove onwards. Johnny felt his arm slammed tight against his chest.. He suffered an excruciating, unbelievable pang, then distinctly felt the grating of steel against one of his ribs. The big sergeant had all his weight behind his bayonet, so quite easily he pinned Johnny Gilmorin to the dusty trampled ground.

Magically the tumult faded. Johnny caught a fleeting glimpse of a white-pillared mansion and of a paddock nearer at hand. Some mares and their foals stood in it, switching flies beneath a summer sun. He heard a tender, beloved voice murmur, "You must go to sleep now, Johnny. You are tired and it is very late."

Nothing more.

David, fighting alongside Colonel Prescott, was much too busy to see what had happened elsewhere. Supported by a handful of men, Prescott was trying to delay the enemy until Provincials without bayonets could escape through the sallyport. Surprisingly enough, the more he whirled his Brown Bess by its barrel, the more strength David felt welling back into his body. There was, he discovered, a fierce and unsuspected satisfaction in this business of killing people.

He made such an iron windmill of his musket that the British began to give way before him. At once some Provincials rallied and were starting forward, but a British light infantryman slipped in behind David and shot him straight through the back. As he fell, a snarl of panting grenadiers closed in and a whole constellation of steel stars hovered above him. One of the grenadiers ran up and, cursing, drove his bayonet into David's heart. The stars suddenly spun around faster, then all at once went out.

Ben

Presently Captain Rudder went below to write up his log book.

Yes, the *Desdemona* was proving a better sailer than Rob had been expecting. Seven knots. Not bad speed for such an old relic. The wind was fair, blowing fresh and not cold. If it held, he reckoned they ought to raise the Bermudas inside of ten days — nine maybe. The last of North America had been seen at twilight. He had been feeling better ever since.

He wondered what was keeping Rudder below. In the matter of officers the *Desdemona* would, for the outward voyage at least, be deplorably shorthanded. The after guard consisted of Rudder and himself. He had signed on Rudder because he had to. The master had been so long out of a ship he was damned glad to sign on at a minimum wage. He had fallen all over himself to get his name on the papers. It was further understood he was to complete and to correct Rob's faulty knowledge of navigation.

Rudder appeared, his nose ludicrously bright in the sunlight. Cheerily he touched the brim of his cap.

"Well, Mr. Ashton, I'm damned if we ain't got a stowaway!"

Holy Sailor! Rob was hanged if he hadn't forgotten Katherine Tryon's existence. "Really?" He smiled. "Fetch her up on deck and let's see what's what."

"Yes, sir." Rudder's figure, long and lanky in blue and white, started off, then paused. "What was that you said about fetching a 'her,' Mr. Ashton?"

"I said fetch her on deck. Don't worry. I know the wench is aboard."

"You *knew?*"

"Yes, I'm helping — " He stiffened.

Rudder's loose grin faded and he spoke seriously. "You've misread your signals, then, sir. The stowaway ain't a her — it's a him."

"What!"

"Yes, sir. A no-'count shrimp of a nigger. He was hiding in the forehold 'mongst the sacked onions."

"The devil you say! Where is he?"

"Forrad, sir. Hey, Qumana! Fetch that 'coon aft."

Emitting a gurgle of terror, the stowaway flung himself onto the deck. "Please — please, massa, doan' hu't me! Las' week ol' compoun' boss done whupped me turrible bad!" In a frenzy of haste the runaway slave tugged up his jersey and when he turned around Rob felt his stomach go queasy. The stowaway's back was a crisscrossed pattern of half-healed scars. Some of the scabs had cracked across and tiny drops of blood were seeping through them. In the strong sunlight they looked like little rubies.

"Stop that damn' whimpering," Rob ordered. "Who are you?"

"Doan' you 'member me, Misto Ashton? Yo' mistis done sign me on de ol' *'Sistance* las' yea'h. Mah name is Ben."

Ever since the schooner had begun to rock and the sea to gurgle beyond the sheathing, Katie Tryon's sense of joyful relief had augmented steadily. It was grand to be so surely beyond reach of the Skillingses! Mr. Tom had been right. In Norfolk she would have been forever anxious, always peering fearfully over her shoulder. Everything would be simply perfect if only Mr. David had been the owner of this boat instead of his brother; not that Mr. Rob wasn't being almighty kind, she hurriedly reproached herself. She felt so grateful she intended working for him and Mrs. Ashton when they got to Bermuda as long as he wanted — for nothing. She hoped Mrs. Ashton had got over the grouch she'd had that day at the Spread Eagle. If she hadn't, she allowed she could bear it; the worst Mrs. Ashton could say or do wouldn't be a patch on Ma Skillings's efforts.

People like Mr. MacSherry and the Ashton brothers made a girl realize men weren't always the selfish brutes she used to think.

The second day out of Norfolk proved fair and, better still, a strong westerly breeze drove the schooner along at a comfortable pace.

"At this rate we ought to be raising the Bermudas in eight days," Rudder confidently predicted. "See if we don't."

"Ever put into the Bermudas before?" Rob queried. "St. George's, Port Royal, or Eli's Harbor?"

"Can't say as I have touched there, sir. They're out o' the way, them islands, kind of. But I've heard tell a master has to look lively once he's made his landfall. There's plenty of reefs offshore and Job Waller 'lows the navy charts ain't worth the paper they're drawed on. If this here wind holds forty-eight hours more, we'll come near making a record passage. Even if that *Speedwell* was freighting victuals, prices will still be kite high, and we will be next in. Yessiree, you ought to clear a tidy sum, Mr. Ashton. On the voyage back you oughter do better still. All over the Tidewater they's an almighty holler for salt rising. If 'taint for salt, they're beggin' for gunpowder. You heard? Committee of Safety has sent to France to bring over any powder can be bought." Rudder chuckled, blew a blue spiral at the cabin lamp. "Independent companies ain't got but ten rounds a man. That's the hell of a fix for men who whack off salutes like they do."

Next day the wind was blowing not quite so fresh, but the weather was fair and seas kept boiling out from under the *Desdemona's* clumsy stern. Captain Rudder assured Rob the schooner was well out in the Gulf Stream. In proof he pointed to the water. It had turned a bright, vital blue and, continually, the schooner sheared through vast meadows of gulf weed meandering over the ocean in bright yellow streamers.

Katie, on her way to draw water from the scuttlebutt, saw a flying fish leap out of a swell. She uttered a delighted squeal and set down her bucket.

[104]

"Oh my God, now ain't *that* something to see? Why, it's so pretty and little and light." It filled her heart with the same inexplicable delight as the sight of hummingbirds sipping from a honeysuckle vine behind Ma Skillings's corn crib.

Pity Mrs. Ashton kept on acting so mean. She was just cutting off her nose to spite her face. The poor tiny little thing sure was swollen all out of shape with her baby. There were a lot of things Katie itched to do for her. Why, she could comb out Mrs. Ashton's hair and dress it prettylike; she could help her in and out of her clothes and wash her things. Best of all, she could bring her breakfast down to her bunk. Mrs. Ashton, she was certain, couldn't cotton much to smelly little Ben and his juicy nose. That nigger sure had a bad cold. He kept sniffling and rubbing at his eyes all the time. When he had come to fetch the food at breakfast time, he had talked kind of silly, but not fresh.

A shadow darkened her shoulder, and turning, she found George Wincapaw standing behind her, smiling. The mulatto had come up so quietly she was startled and annoyed.

"Well, pussyfoot," she demanded, "what do you want?"

"Splitting kindling is hot work, miss. I might do it for you."

Katie was ashamed of her irritation. The nigger was only trying to be friendly and today sure was going to be a scorcher. "Why, that would be mighty kind of you."

"Mis' Katie?"

In the shade of the port bulwarks Ben was lying on an old sail.

"What is it?"

"Please come heah, jes' a minute?" The steward's voice sounded thin, reedy.

Bare feet softly slapping, Katie crossed the deck to him and inquired kindly, "What's the matter, boy? Is your cold worse?"

"Ah — ah reckons so." Ben sighed, rubbed red-rimmed eyes. "Ask Misto Ashton can he git someone — wait on table tonight?"

Katie, squatting down, looked hard at him. "Where do you feel bad?"

The little Negro smothered a moan. "Ah dunno, Mis' Katie, but ah jus' now got sick over de side."

"Shucks, boy, that's the seasickness!"

"No, Mis' Katie, ain' dat. Ah been to sea. Feel lak de ol' debbil drivin' red-hot nails thoo mah haid."

"You got a headache?"

The Negro's lips, gone a faint lavender, moved slowly. "Hit's wusser dat, missy. Hit's a turrible misery."

Captain Rudder appeared at the head of the poop ladder. "What ails that nigger? Why ain't he working?"

Ben nodded his melon-shaped head. "No. Gib pasture twenty blue — will next — ah runs lightnin' not was."

[105]

Rudder looked sharply at Katie. "Why didn't you tell me he was out of his head?"

The girl looked at him, round-eyed. "Why, Captain, he was talking all right just now."

Rudder, coming closer, noticed a heavy dewing of perspiration on the gray-black features. Bending, he looked narrowly at the Negro's eyes. They were running big tears.

"My God!"

Katie saw Captain Rudder's face grow old and faded-looking like a print left too long in strong sunlight. He fell back half a dozen steps, fumbling for a bandanna. He clapped it over his nose — tight.

"Fetch Mr. Ashton!"

By the time Rob appeared on deck, damp with sleep and rubbing his eyes in the bright light, the watch stood grouped in a brown-black cluster at the foot of the mainmast. All of them were staring at the steward who sprawled, twisting slowly, on the gray canvas topsail. Ben kept moaning and muttering. Now and then his toes would buckle over in slow flections and successively their broad pinkish purple nails would catch the sunlight.

Rob locked his teeth, tried to forget the steward's fetid breath in concentrating on his pulse count. It was away over normal. Um. When he examined the little Negro's neck, scalp and arms, he found several small swellings.

Suddenly Ben screamed and doubled, working his thin legs in a series of futile jerks.

When Rob straightened, his face was as wet as if he had dipped it into a basin of water.

"He's sick all right. A hard case of measles most likely," Rob said extra loud. At the same time he winked at Rudder. "Maybe we had better keep him away from the crew."

Rudder kept on backing away, his heels loud on the sunlit deck. "You can't fool me! Listen to me, you niggers. He ain't got measles! *It's the pox!* Your only chance is to pitch him over!"

"T'row him over! Please, Misto' Ashton, T'row dat hoodoo feller over! Dey's a chanct fo' us. Ben ent bruk out yet."

Rob jerked a pair of belaying pins from the mainmast pinrail. "Get back, you fools!" Then he muttered to Katie, "Fetch the pistol under my pillow."

He commenced talking against time. Rob could always recall what followed. Creating a pattern of checkered and striped jerseys and ragged pants, the crew started aft. When the schooner rolled, their bodies all canted in the same direction, like so many parallel pendulums. Against the white deck the slaves looked mighty big and black.

Where in the blue blazes was Katie?

Rob began talking faster, louder. "Don't be fools! If you boys mutiny, you'll get hanged. Hear? Every damned one of you. If you're going to catch it, you're going to catch it. You've all been plenty exposed. Murdering Ben won't help you any."

Never in his life had he been so glad to hear anything as a quick patter of footsteps behind him.

Katie shoved the big pistol into his hand, but he noticed it had lost its flint. He hoped the Negroes were too excited to notice. Straight off they stopped where they were and fell back; without raising the weapon he started forward.

"There's an old tarpaulin on top the cargo in the forehold. You, Mohgreb! Jason! Fetch it!" A further inspiration came. "Squeegee, and you, Bullhead! Rig a tent over the main hatch. Hump yourselves!"

When Rob thought of how Ben had handled the cabin's dishes and food cups, little icebergs started floating about in his stomach.

We got the nigger isolated in time, he assured himself for the dozenth time, but as an extra precaution he ordered Katie to wash all the tableware in vinegar.

Next morning a breathless calm was ironing out the sea. The Atlantic was like a limitless mesa of hot and oily water. It stirred only vaguely under the impulse of rollers lifted somewhere below the horizon. As the sun climbed, it gave off rays of fierce, penetrating heat. Scorching sunbeams beat through the schooner's sides, through her decks, raised more blisters on her faded paint work.

Despite the breathless heat and the persistent calm, the crew seemed quiet. Maybe it was because Rudder kept them busy reeving new gear and found other odd jobs. The captain seemed, indeed, to have pulled himself together.

Only Peggy lingered in the grip of that terror which had swept the ship like a noxious squall. She insisted that the cabin door be kept tight locked and a blanket hung to either side of it.

At night when an uncanny stillness ruled the sea and the heat was less blasting, the patient, because his eyelids were swollen tight shut, often struggled up, shrieking of blindness. At such times his wails echoed and re-echoed through the schooner, rousing the crew from uneasy slumber on the foredeck. Even after sundown, the forecastle was too smothering to be tolerated and in this torrid atmosphere the few insects surviving fumigation multiplied by the hundreds of thousands.

"Oh, make him stop!" Peggy pressed moist palms tight over her ears. "Can't you make that damned nigger stop it?"

"He can't help it, honey. I know it's awful — but I can't do anything. We've no laudanum aboard."

Peggy would lie panting, feeling perspiration course down her neck and between her swollen breasts. In the morning Rob saw purplish crescents her fingernails had dug into her palms

Amid blistering afternoon heat Peggy pulled up the sweaty folds of her nightgown and listlessly waved a palmetto leaf over her naked body. Her gaze wandered through the stern ports, but she was finding the sea hideous. She hated its glaring, metallic copper blue and the horizon, all crazed and wavering with heat. Sniffling, she arose and sought her mirror. A dark red rash was breaking out on her forehead! Horror chilled the skin on her forearms into goose pimples. Though the cabin swam about her, she rallied, clutching the back of her armchair. Eyes wide and staring, she examined her neck. Oh God! It too was speckled! She put out her tongue. It was gray and mottled with furry patches. Lightnings played in her brain. By a supreme effort she unlocked the door before her knees gave way entirely.

"Rob!" she shrieked. "Rob! Help! Help!"

When first she saw her, he felt hairs rise on the back of his neck. But then he looked more carefully, and tenderly picked up his wife's small damp figure.

"Darling, darling! Don't take on so. Please don't. All you've got is a heat rash — a common heat rash. It's nothing to fear."

She clung to him, torn by spasmodic sobs. "Oh, it's not! I know b-better. You're trying to f-fool me. Oh, I don't want to d-die." Her arms were almost strangling in their pressure.

"You're not going to, darling. It's a heat rash, only a heat rash. Nothing more."

She pressed her head, oily with neglect, against his cheek. "Oh, Rob, take me home! I was so safe, so happy there! Why did you ever take me away?"

Having no answer to that, he kept quiet, but went on trying to soothe her.

June 9, 1775

POSITION: 71° 6m Long. 31° 12m Lat.
DISTANCE LOGGED THIS DAY: None
WEATHER: Clear and hot.
WIND: None.

REMARKS: Flat calm for fourth Day. Have never beheld Sea so unnatural still. Sick Man much worser. Today great white pustules broke out on Face and Shulders. Crew very uneasy, but through God's Mercy Pox has not Spread. Mohgreb, Bullhead extra sullen. Will bear watching.

A drop of sweat fell from Rudder's chin and exploded into smaller drops, blurring the fresh ink. Cursing, he used a penknife laboriously to scrape away the spots. In the old days he'd always been proud of the neat way he kept his log. After burnishing the rough places with his thumbnail, he resumed his slow and painful writing.

Vegetables in cargoe spoiling Fast. If God does not send us a Breeze soon, we shall lose the Half of them.

[108]

After tucking the goosequill behind his ear, Rudder blew on the page till it was dry. Then methodically he closed the logbook, locked it in his sea chest.

In spitting through the porthole, he noticed the sunset sky. It suggested nothing so much as an inverted brass bowl. Licking lips cracked by sunburn, he bent over a chart unrolled across his bunk and plotted his course for the next twenty-four hours.

Oh goddamn it! That bloody nigger was raising his holler again. Captain Rudder suddenly dropped his parallel rulers and lunged over to his sea chest. After spitting out his chew, he fished out a wicker-covered demijohn and poured out half a cupful of red-brown Jamaica rum. It tasted good, by God! Mighty good. Fine as silk. It was just what a man needed under a strain like this. No more today, though. This would have to be all. He tilted up the cup, straining for the last drop. That burning sensation in his belly made him feel right good, better than he had in a hell of a while. But he must take care not to look too cheery; Mr. Ashton had been keeping a weather eye on him.

Katie sat on the hard little bunk built across one end of the galley. She was deeply worried. Tomorrow, Wincapaw predicted, the ship's company would know for sure if anybody had taken the pox. Cramps in the belly or a splitting headache were ominous signs. Nausea, the mulatto had warned, was even more to be feared. He had insisted she wear a charm, a string of thirty-nine blue beads, to ward off the disease. Gladly she added it to her own necklace of Job's tears — those smooth brown seeds which had kept her well for so long.

Another cramp! Oh damn! Had she caught it? Just when she was learning to spell pretty good. If only a wind, a howling gale, would rise up and blow the pestilence away. But there were no signs of the calm's ending.

Too bad the poor lady below had to take on so about her being along, especially when there wasn't any call. Having a baby any time was no fun — but on a pest ship! Katie rested her elbows on the scarred bulwarks and wondered why no man had ever got her in the family way.

Reckon it must be the Lord's way of looking out for me, she concluded.

On the morning of June 11, the eighth day out of Norfolk, two deckhands came down with smallpox. They were Jason and a nondescript black known as Squeegee. A riot broke out when their plight was discovered and Rob was forced to use an oaken pump handle in quelling it.

In a dangerous state of despair, the balance of the crew took possession of the foredeck and defied authority. Pistols in hand, Rob then seated himself on the fore hatch patiently waiting for thirst to reinforce him. Around noon the mutineers, parched for a drink, gave up. Before he let them at the scuttlebutt he kicked each one on the shins until he screamed. Then he invented tasks to occupy their minds.

In the stern cabin Rob found Peggy lounging, more slatternly than ever, in a food-spotted nightrail and rumpled mobcap. To his surprise, she showed a measure of animation.

"I've just remembered something," said she.

"What?"

"Inoculation!"

"What's that?"

"Why, every time the pox broke loose in Norfolk, Dr. Gordon went 'round inoculating folks. He gave people light cases. He inoculated Papa when the pox broke out three years ago."

"Yes." Rob yawned, but asked patiently enough, "But how is it done?"

"I know," Peggy said in her old, self-sufficient manner. "You thread a needle, run it through a lister on somebody who has the pox but who is getting better — like Ben."

Rob was aghast. "Have you gone crazy?"

"No! Inoculation is my only chance. It's safe. They used to have regular boarders come to Dr. Aspinwall's for it."

Through a mist of fatigue Rob said, "But, honey, you may not catch it at all."

"I will!" Her voice grew clear, hard. "I know I will!"

"I won't stand for such nonsense."

"You will! You'll do as I say!"

"No. You had better take your chance."

"I know! You want to kill me!" Peggy's shiny, heated features began twitching. "You want me to die! That's what you want! You want to get rid of me. Then you can lie in bed with that yellow-haired trollop any time you please." She worked herself to such a pitch her words tore at Rob's eardrums like steel claws.

She knew what should be done, she sobbed, and he didn't. In the old days — two years back — Dr. Alexander Gordon had been one of Major Fleming's closest friends. He had told her how inoculating was done.

It required all Rob's resolution to pass the threaded needle Peggy gave him through a bleb on Ben's forearm. He hoped he was doing it right; his hurricane lantern wasn't any too bright.

On reentering the ovenlike heat in the stern cabin, a revulsion seized Rob. Hoarsely he begged, "Peggy, for God's sake, listen to me. You mustn't risk this. You can't know for sure if — "

Her head went back to the old stubborn angle he had learned to dread. "I do! I *will* have an inoculation!" Suddenly she smashed a tumbler on the floor. It shattered like an exploding shell and, stooping, she grabbed up a long and dusty splinter of glass.

"Don't!"

Before he could stop her, she dragged the jagged shard across her left arm. Against the pallor of her skin a thin scarlet arc appeared, widened.

"There!" She slashed again, and a third time. Deeper still. Bloody tears gathered, started to slide over the contour of her arm.

Katie, round-eyed among the shadows, winced when Peggy Ashton snatched the needle and its dangling, polluted thread from Rob's fingers.

"For God's sake — "

"Be quiet. I know what I'm doing!" Peggy clamped her teeth on her lips, pressed the matter-clotted thread into the deepest scratch and drew it back and forth. Rob watched her, shaking. Was she right? Probably. Most inoculated people got light doses, they said. It was sure that if Peggy got the disease full strength, neither she nor the baby could hope to survive.

In the Horse Latitudes

Though a hand was tugging at his naked shoulder, Rob awoke reluctantly.

"Come on deck! Quick! Quick!" Katie, flushed and breathless, was bending above him and dawn was beating through the stern ports.

He got on his feet in an instant. "What's happened?"

"They — they've gone!"

"Who's gone? Damn it, girl, don't stand there sniveling! Who's gone? Speak up!"

But Katie only hid her face in her hands and burst into terrified wails.

Rob cursed briefly, then clattered up the companion and looked about. Save for Ben in his little tent, the deck was completely deserted.

"Rudder! Captain Rudder!"

It was only five-thirty but already he could feel the sun's heat on the nape of his neck. Ben's voice was weak and thin as the mew of a new kitten, but in the breathless silence of ship and sea Rob heard him say, "He gone, Misto Rob. He gone."

Aghast, Rob wheeled. The longboat was gone! Its davits were empty and the falls trailed slack over the side. Shoes clumping loud, he searched the deck and was cheered to discover the quartermaster sound asleep on the galley bunk. All through the epidemic the mulatto had worked hard without complaining much, so he let him go on sleeping. Most likely Rudder had figured it was a risk to trust a hand so loyal to his owner.

Around noon a gentle creaking drew Rob's attention. Looking up, he felt astounded, almost awed, at the simple sight of the fore boom swinging slowly over to port. By God! Though the sails sagged, the air was losing its breathless quality. The sea was still flat as any dinner table, but it had lost its burnished look.

By two o'clock more clouds lifted over the southeastern horizon and brought with them a very gentle southerly breeze. Once more the *Des-*

demona began to creep towards Bermuda along the 33° latitude. Towards sundown the wind freshened, then held steady, but against the risk of a sudden squall, Rob deemed it wise to reef in. In a stiff breeze two men and a girl wouldn't be able to do much.

Rob's main concern was whether his newly acquired knowledge of navigation would prove adequate. It was a pity the Bermudas made such a tiny fleck on the chart. Even a minor error would send the *Desdemona* cruising far out into the Atlantic. If he didn't raise the Bermudas within a week, Rob decided, he would come about.

He reckoned even a poor navigator could hit the coast of North America somewhere.

"Rob! Rob! Wake up — oh, Rob! I need you."

He roused on the transom, turned up a lantern swinging in gimbals from the cabin beam, came stumbling over. "What is it?"

"I — I'm burning up! my arm, it — it hurts so I can't stand it."

He bent over then recoiled despite himself. Her face was flushed and a bright scarlet stain was dying her neck on the left side. It was not a rash. About the scratches she had made, the flesh was ballooning up, feverish, poisoned looking.

"Oh, Rob, Rob! My arm is killing me — Help! I'm burning up. I'm on fire — I'm so — so afraid — "

In an effort to reduce the fearful swelling of her arm he wrung out cloths in cold water but when he touched her ever so gently, she screamed outright.

"Cut it off!" she moaned. "Please cut it off. I can't stand this any longer!"

If only a doctor were aboard! Distracted, Rob shook his head. A fool could tell that the arm ought to come off, but for him to attempt such an operation would be tantamount to murder.

He gave her a drink and, heart in mouth, said, "I'm going aloft just a second to tell Wincapaw he must stand my trick. I'll be right back, honey, and I won't leave you till you feel better."

When he returned he found Peggy tossing in a wild delirium. Heavily her ungainly figure writhed and twisted on the sheet. By the whale-oil lantern the infected arm looked black and had become swollen to gigantic proportions all the way to the shoulder. Her skin had gone dry and shiny and was like hot iron to his touch. The delirium gripped her with greater violence and she sat up, babbled incoherently of skating, of a party dress of blue lutestring, of her mother.

Presently a stupor claimed the patient and she sank into a lethargy so deep Rob had no difficulty in stripping back the sleeve on her good arm. When Katie appeared, anxious but blessedly silent, he told her to fetch a basin.

"Reckon the only thing is to try bleeding," he spoke as if to himself. "Mind you hold that basin steady."

When he had drawn off a pint and a half of blood, Peggy seemed to grow quieter, so he tied up the awkward incision. For hours he sat motionless, watching the purplish features of his wife.

Pearly streaks of light had commenced to erase stars of the lesser magnitude when Margaret Fleming Ashton abruptly abandoned her labored struggles to draw breath.

Harbor Lights

Several nights after the death of Peggy Ashton, George Wincapaw stood at the wheel, watching stars break out by the hundreds of thousands. The moon, he knew, would be rising very late. He yawned. Christ, but he was tired! So was everybody aboard. For a green officer, Captain Ashton seemed to be doing fine with his navigation. His calculations showed the *Desdemona* to be sailing just about where she should. If the new navigator hadn't been making errors all along the line, Wincapaw figured they should raise Wreck Hill around daylight.

The quartermaster bent to pick up a stop lying at the foot of the binnacle, but checked himself in midmotion. Had a very faint sparkle of light shone ahead? He glanced at the compass. Northeast-by-east, by Jesus. It was right on the course! He looked again and this time saw the light for sure before the *Desdemona* lost it by nosing down the back of a long swell.

Wincapaw craned his sinewy neck. Was that a ship under way, or a light on shore? At the end of five minutes he saw another light wink into existence.

As loud as he could, he yelled, "Land-ho!" down the companionway.

Almost immediately Rob came on deck carrying a couple of charts under his arm.

He flattened a chart under the binnacle light and checked the course. "That must be the Bermudas. Couldn't be anything else."

Katie awoke and, all excited, followed Mr. Rob right out onto the jib boom. Her promised land! She felt feverishly impatient to see what these islands might be like.

When he returned, Wincapaw called out, "We're all right, sir. What we see is vessels laying in the harbor. If you skin your eyes, you can just make out Wreck Hill 'way off to port." With one hand he shaded the binnacle light and they all stared into the darkness.

"How could you tell so soon those were anchored ships?" Rob queried, interestedly.

"Why, sir, they're live."

"Live?" Katie asked.

"See them two lights off to port? They lie low to the water and they don't stay still. If you'll watch the space between 'em, you'll notice."

"Why is that?"

"It's because vessels swing to their anchors." Wincapaw's spirits were rising with the thought that this hoodooed voyage was near an end. "Well, sir, you hit Eli's Harbor square on the nose. Prettiest navigatin' ever I see."

"Good luck more than good management." Rob nodded and watched the harbor lights grow brighter. Around fifteen lanterns were ricocheting their rays over the water. He turned his head and called, "Katie, take the wheel and hold her as she is. Come along, Wincapaw, we'll strike the foresail. Reckon we had better not go in much farther."

"We're all right, sir. We can go — "

The quartermaster's further words were jolted out of his mouth, for without warning the *Desdemona* suddenly bucked like a spurred stallion and her bow shot high into the air. Her whole hull shuddered and her masts tottered. Then, as she settled back on an even keel, from below arose a dull grinding and rasping. In Rob's ears sounded the successive, terrifying crashes of objects falling about below. As quickly as it had begun, the tumult subsided except for a sibilant hissing sound. The schooner resumed her smooth and silent progress.

"Christ!" Wincapaw picked himself up from the deck as Rob let go the brace he had grabbed. "There just *can't* be a reef 'way out here! We're on the course and there's the lights of Eli's Harbor."

"You're the hell of a fine quartermaster!" Rob snarled at Wincapaw. "I'll skin you alive for this! You've punched a hole in her bottom."

Desperately Wincapaw shook his head as he grabbed the wheel. "Can't make it out, sir. 'Fore God, we're on the right course! I can't figure — "

"Shut up! Where's the nearest shallow water?"

"To port — should be," Wincapaw gasped, sawing hard on the wheel. "Can't — "

Searching his soul for curses, Rob dashed aft, stood ready to drop the mainsail in the same brutally effective manner as quickly as another reef revealed itself. There seemed to be none near.

"Look! My God, *look!*" As he stared ahead the quartermaster's eyes became concentric rings of white. "See that?"

"See what?"

"The harbor lights! They're going out!"

"Wreckers — " Wincapaw choked. "The real harbor must lie somewheres to starboard — " He felt better. It really wasn't his fault the schooner had broke her back on the coral.

Katie came feeling her way aft, showing a bruise on her chin. A trickle of blood dripped from a corner of her mouth. Though she looked frightened, she only asked quietly:

"Are — are we fixing to drown, Mister Ashton?"

"I don't reckon so; it's not rough, and there must be more reefs around."

When the schooner struck for a second time, her bottom made the same dull grinding noise. Long rollers lifted her, jacked her high onto a pan of coral. The impact was not too hard, Rob hoped. A second big sea roared up, heaved the wreck higher, then piled over her bulwarks like a line of enemy boarders. With an angry swirl the Atlantic began cascading down the forecastle companionway. Incredibly soon the whole foredeck was underwater. The sea became littered with flotsam. Twice more the *Desdemona* was lifted farther onto the reef then, with stern fairly high, she came to rest.

Salvage

Ben, sleeping on the poop deck, awoke in the early morning with the distinctive thud of oars against thole pins in his ears. He managed to rouse Katie, sleeping a few yards away.

Pulling over the flattening sea were three big whale boats. They carried no lights. Katie looked just long enough to make sure there were three, then fled below.

"Wreckers!" she gasped. "They're rowing out!"

Rob reached for Rudder's blunderbuss, but ended by leaving it where it was. Said he with a weary grin, "To the devil with it. All we need is daylight."

Wincapaw was up and looking very uneasy. Katie guessed he was scared stiff the wreckers were coming out to make a clean job of it. Survivors had an awkward way of disputing salvage charges.

The moon, combined with the first rays of dawn, gave enough illumination to let Rob make out three white-painted whale boats expertly skirting a line of reefs. The foremost had six men at her oars and at least as many passengers. These sat crouched on the bottom.

Two boats hung back in the gloom, but the other came pulling along in the lee of the reefs. The man at the steering oar had a not pleasing aspect. The leader, a burly fellow in a bright green shirt, got to his feet and, swaying, shouted:

"Vha-ant help?"

Rob waited awhile before calling back, "What the hell would you think?"

Rocking in the whale boat's stern, the Bermudian yelled, "Take you ashore! Five pound' a head!"

From his vantage point on the stern Rob shouted, "You *are* a slimy swine!"

"You got my price!" the leader shouted. "And you got no small boat!"

"Go to hell!"

"Vell, call it three pound' apiece. That's werry reasonable," the spokesman offered, as the steerer, a brutal fellow lacking his front teeth, sheered the boat away a little.

Rob took pleasure in the moment. "Your ma must be mighty proud of you, mister. Your pa, too, if you know who he is."

From another of the predatory whale boats arose a hail. "Say, Bill, she's from Virginia!"

"Ve are sorry for you," said he. "Too bad you should lose your ship dis vhey."

Seesawing over the waves, the other boats pulled closer. Their crews for the most part wore checkered shirts and wide, very dirty canvas breeches. Quite a few of them carried little gold rings in their earlobes and at least a dozen wore brass-hilted naval cutlasses strapped over their hips. Contrary to the mode prevailing in America and England, several of the Bermudians wore beards. Although no pistols were in evidence, Rob was very certain that enough lay under the thwarts to blow the *Desdemona*'s company into eternity.

The man in the green silk shirt grunted something which sent his boat nosing through a bright patch of gulf weed in the direction of the wreck. When she lay but ten feet off the beam, he looked up at Rob. There was no trifling in his manner and his gap teeth showed in a taut grin.

"You going to do business vith us?"

Rob affected sulkiness. "Sure. How else are we going to get ashore?"

"Vhut can you pay?" demanded the Bermudian. "Ve dun't vant to be hard on anyvon."

"Come aboard, Captain. We'll talk it over."

The islanders brought their big whale boat up under the lee of the wreck as deftly as a jolly boat. But she was indeed a whale boat, Rob noted. Rusted harpoons rested in racks, hatchets, a lug sail, water beakers and bailing scoops all were to be seen. There were in addition four tubs for line, but these at the moment were empty.

"Say fifteen shillings?" offered Rob.

"Maybe. How many aboard, Captain?"

"Four. A deckhand, the young woman over there, the quartermaster and myself."

"Only four?" A measure of the Bermudian's alert jauntiness departed. "Vhere's 'e rest?"

"Why?"

"For Jesus Christ's sake, you couldn't come all 'e wheh from America vith a crew this size!"

"The others jumped ship," Rob explained curtly. "Suppose you come aft, Captain. I'll need help in moving one of my deckhands."

[116]

The islander's stubby jaw closed with a little click. "Help? Vhut's 'e matter vith him?"

"Don't rightly know," Rob drawled. "Maybe you can tell."

It wasn't reassuring to see the other whale boats, each manned by twelve men, come bobbing alongside. The occupants looked just as whiskery and weather-beaten as the first lot. Resting on their oars, they craned necks to see over the bulwarks or grabbed at bits of flotsam. A few watched the blue-green water surge over and then retreat across the *Desdemona's* submerged bow. As Wincapaw had predicted, the visitors were for the most part small and lean; nearly all had bad teeth. The second boat's helmsman lacked an eye and three fingers of his left hand.

"Here he is," Rob said, throwing back the rough canopy they had rigged over the convalescent. "Can't imagine what ails him."

When he saw Ben goggling fearfully up at him, the Bermudian's expression became such a comic blend of horror and disappointed greed that Katie and Wincapaw, grinning expectantly from behind the wheel, laughed themselves wet-eyed.

The patient was certainly no vision of beauty. All his face, shoulders and the upper part of his body were encrusted with flaking scabs. He resembled some ungainly and loathsome reptile.

"Oh, my God, it's 'e pox!" screamed the Bermudian, and wheeling, ran back down the deck so fast he lost his cocked hat but never stopped to pick it up.

"She's a pest ship!" Green shirt billowing with haste, he vaulted over the rail and landed in the whaler on all fours, shouting, "Shove off, you club-footed baboons! Pull, for God's sake, pull!"

Quarantine

Around three of the afternoon a breeze sprang up. It blew from the island and brought an elusive fragrance the like of which Katie had never smelled. She lifted her short nose and sniffed eagerly.

Wincapaw roused her. "Boat's heading this way."

He took up Rob's spyglass and, after studying the distant craft, invited, "Here, take a look."

What Katie saw was a boat differing sharply from those which had appeared at dawn. Long and low in the water, she was painted white and boasted gunwales of bright blue. At her oars were six blacks wearing bright yellow shirts. A seventh Negro stood behind and above a canopy rigged over the stern. He was steering with a brass-bound tiller. She could distinguish two men under the yellow canopy. One of them was dressed all in white, but the other wore a red coat and blue breeches. In the bow of the barge crouched three white men with muskets lying across their laps. What chiefly attracted Katie's attention was the Union Jack fluttering from a short jack staff.

"She does look like a government barge," Rob agreed when they wakened him. After watching the leisurely, well-measured rhythm of her oars awhile, he went below and scraped the light brown fuzz from his cheeks. Also he dug out a decent suit and put on fresh linen.

When he got back on deck, the barge was drifting perhaps fifty yards abeam of the wreck. Upon command the grinning black rowers flipped their dripping sweeps to the vertical in ragged imitation of a man-of-war's crew.

Katie noticed that the white-clad man was decidedly plump and wore a bright blue bandanna knotted about his head beneath a broad-brimmed straw hat. He was young, thirty perhaps. In one pudgy hand he carried a palm leaf fan.

"Ahoy! What ship is that?" He spoke without bothering to bend forward. Ashton told him.

"Heard you have plague aboard. That right?"

"Yes, we've had smallpox."

"Any new cases?"

"No. Not in a week."

"That's good." The young man in the straw hat seemed relieved. "Put us alongside," he yelled at the black coxswain.

"Yassuh!" He bent forward. "Pull sta-bohd, back po't! Easy — now — easy all!"

The minute Rob laid eyes on the foremost caller, he felt an instinctive attraction. He was so very jolly looking with his bright blue eyes, the humorous expression of his wide mouth and the healthy pink complexion of a baby.

Arriving on the poop, he jerked a bow. "Servant, sir."

Rob returned the bow and declared himself delighted.

"You seem to have received an ill welcome from Bermuda. My sympathy, sir." There was dignity in the way the plump young man offered his hand.

Rob warned, "We've smallpox aboard, remember."

"Had it. So has Dr. Chamberlain. By the bye, I am deputy customs collector for this parish," he announced. "My name is Ashton — Peter Ashton."

In no single particular did he resemble the man Rob's imagination had pictured.

"You'll excuse my not wearing a wig?" he apologized. "It's just too blasted hot."

Rob shook his cousin's plump but surprisingly firm hand. "This is a pleasure, Cousin Peter."

"Cousin? Gad's my life! You can't be Robert Ashton?"

[118]

"I'm what's left of him."

"Why, my dear fellow, I'm charmed, delighted. Welcome! Welcome! Chamberlain! This is my cousin — the one I was speaking of." An instant later Peter Ashton's manner changed. He looked acutely unhappy. "How did this happen?"

"A runaway slave brought the disease aboard in Norfolk."

When Peter Ashton shook his head, his shadow mimicked him on the deck. "I don't mean that. How did you come to get piled up like this?"

Rob explained the manner in which his quartermaster had been deceived into taking false lights for those of Eli's Harbor, into mistaking the loom of Daniel's Head for Wreck Hill.

"False lights!" Peter Ashton's fingers snapped loud as a pistol's report. The doctor, looking uneasy, watched his companion face the shore. "Just where did you see those lights?"

"Where that long beach is — the one with all the white sand on it."

"You could swear the lights were there?"

"No. But if you'll show some lanterns there after dark, I could be sure. There's a hamper of Fayal wine below. Suppose we sample it?"

Peter beamed. "Why not? May as well feel comfortable while figuring out what's to be done."

Soon Katie was filling three glasses.

Rubbing his pink chin, Peter considered. "Suppose, Cousin Rob, we reckon the girl's exposure from the date of the original outbreak? Say, Charlie, what is the usual quarantine for the pox?"

"Eighteen days, I think, but it may be twenty."

"Eighteen, eh?" The Bermudian's eye wandered up to the main top. "First case was on the sixth. Um. That would call for only three more days in quarantine. Right?" His blue eyes flickered over to Chamberlain.

The physician smacked his lips. "That's right," said he. It had been a long time since he had tasted wine as good as this.

Peter accepted a second glass. "We can do one of two things, Cousin Robert. I can either send a boat to carry you to our regular quarantine station on Marshall's Island, or you can stay aboard. At this time of year you ought to be safe enough. If the glass starts to fall, I will come out and take you off in plenty of time." He grinned. "You've your choice, but I might tell you our quarantine station is no palace. What do you want to do?"

Rob's gaze wandered from Katie over to Wincapaw. He reckoned he could handle that situation all right.

"I reckon we will stay aboard, then."

Tomorrow morning the quarantine would be lifted. George Wincapaw was considering this prospect with no enthusiasm. He knew what to expect ashore. At best, he'd be sent to some hutch in the slave quarters, even though he had been born free.

[119]

Life aboard the *Desdemona* hadn't been bad at all. Both Captain Ashton and Miss Katie had trusted him, had treated him almost like a white man. They never had adopted a snotty manner when he came around — most white people did, though. They treated him the same way they would a dog that was too valuable just to be kicked about. All his life it had made him sore. Couldn't he read and write? Didn't he know more about ships and navigation than many a so-called master mariner?

Sitting on the wreck's canting deck and comfortably propped against her mainmast, Wincapaw took another slug from a brandy bottle he had swiped when Captain Ashton had left the liquor locker unfastened. The spirits made him feel at once better — and worse.

What would happen when they got ashore? The skipper must be pretty near broke. The cargo salvage wouldn't amount to much. His own future wasn't bright at all, at all. What with trade dead or dying all along the American Coast, he'd find trouble landing a decent berth. White Bermudians who didn't follow the sea were precious few. They bred slaves to get as many sound seamen as they could. Normally there was a shortage of deckhands on the islands. This was so because nowadays the islanders were building and manning so many sloops and snows each year.

Over the sibilant rush and retreat of seas across the sunken bow he heard Captain Ashton say "Good night." When he had gone, Katie stood up, stretched lazily, then lingered with face lifted to the sky. In that moment the quartermaster decided to take her even if it cost him his neck. He slipped off his shoes and, silent as a shadow, sought the poopdeck.

"Katie!"

"La! How you startled me." Katie whirled, made out the quartermaster's bony face and the two gold rings in his ear. He was standing right at her shoulder and his nostrils were opening and shutting like the gills of a stranded hornpout.

"Katie, honey, I'm just crazy 'bout you. I'm burning up." He held out his arms.

"Why, you damn' fresh nigger!" Her hand caught him a smack across his mouth; a hard resounding slap which sent fiery pinpoints shooting across his eyeballs.

It was a mistake. In a flash he pinned her in such a grip she couldn't move. Then he jerked out his knife and shoved it against her. With that point digging into the underside of her left breast, she didn't dare move a muscle. One shove on that knife handle and she'd be dead.

"You squawk, I'll kill you."

Wincapaw began thinking fast. Katie had been using Captain Rudder's old cabin. There was no key to its door because Rudder had lost it or taken it away with him in the longboat. If she didn't show up soon, the skipper might come up looking for her.

The soft pressure of Katie's stomach against his thickened his voice. "In a minute I'm going to your cabin. Hear? You follow right after." His teeth glistened and she could feel the furious hammering of his heart. "Try to get by or raise a holler, and I'll slip in and kill the skipper. He can't move near so quick as me."

Katie stood stockstill. She was more scared than she had ever been in her life. Wincapaw wasn't fooling and you never could tell what a nigger might do when he got this way.

She nodded mechanically. "All right. I'll follow you, but don't you dast hurt Mr. Rob!"

Hard as the jaws of a pair of pincers Wincapaw's fingers closed over Katie's wrists. "You make one little noise — I — I'll cut your heart out!" Slipping his knife back in its sheath, the mulatto turned and disappeared down the cabin companionway.

First testing her bruised forearm, then the little bloody spot his knife-point had caused on her breast, Katie remained rigid. If she just waited there, Wincapaw sure enough would come back and kill her. What to do? She didn't want any truck with a nigger. As a rule, she could think pretty fast. But not now. She never had looked a potential murderer in the face before. The nigger was liquored up, too, she realized dully. That made things extra bad.

This was what she got for having been so decent with Wincapaw. She had been a bloody fool. In sickened helplessness her gaze swept the deck and she saw light from Mr. Rob's cabin reflected in the water astern.

Then her eye lit on one of the empty kegs most skippers kept ready to heave to anyone who fell overboard. She was relieved to find the keg not so heavy as she had been expecting. Lugging it in both arms, she moved forward along the slanting deck.

She didn't even wait to take off her dress; she just waded out along the sunken foredeck until the water rose to her knees, to her thighs. Twisting one hand in a loop of rope secured to the keg, she commenced awkwardly to paddle. Good thing the tide was making, not falling.

It was a very long way to shore.

Colonel Fortescue

Katie Tryon felt pretty thoroughly exhausted by the time sand rose under her feet, but she didn't dare leave the water just yet, for away off to the left glowed the quarantine guard's watch fire. Looking backwards she could see lights were moving about on the wreck. Mr. Rob and Wincapaw must be hunting her.

Tired but decidedly pleased with her solution of the problem, Katie tottered up a beach of soft fine sand and sank onto a patch of grass. She stayed quiet, listening to the slow rushing of the sea up the shore and to the nearer *pat-pat-pat* of water dripping from her clothes. Maybe she wasn't such a complete numbskull as Mrs. Skillings always said she was. Here she'd freed Mr. Rob of any further responsibility for her and at the same time had left Wincapaw to whistle for his fun. She felt a little sick, though, when she remembered the sting of his knifepoint.

She lay panting awhile, gathering fresh strength and wondering what she had better do. First thing was to get warm. Though her fingers trembled with exhaustion, she stripped off her dress and petticoats. She wrung them out hard as she could, then draped them on a limb to dry. They'd still be damp by morning, but this warm onshore breeze should start the drying process.

With hair slatting soggily between her shoulderblades, Katie ran mother naked up and down the beach five or six times, fast as she could. That got her circulation started and her skin dried rapidly. At last, gasping and almost hot, she dropped down in the lee of an overhanging rock. It was a surprise to find how much heat the stone had retained. Why, in this little hollow the air felt right warm and the grass very soft. Since there seemed small use in lying awake worrying over what might happen, she went to sleep.

Aboard the *Desdemona* she had, among her reading lessons, seen Mr. Rob's chart of the island. Therefore, she knew that the Bermudas were an archipelago arranged roughly in the shape of a fishhook and consisting of some two hundred islands of varying size. Somerset Island, she knew, lay at the west, or barb, end of the group and St. George's at the east, or eye, end. Since Mr. Rob's family was settled on Somerset, it seemed only logical to seek work in the direction of St. George's. After all, the colonial capital lay only eighteen miles away; hardly more than a good day's walk.

Accordingly, Katie pulled on her dry clothes and struck off to her right down the road. The soil was so red and rich-looking it interested her. What did the islanders grow? Cotton? Tobacco? Rice? The surface of the road right here was sandy, but often soft limestone shone through. It had been ground and scarred by wagon wheels.

Not yet lost to curiosities, she gaped at a remarkable tree growing beside the road. It grew straight as any beanpole and, beyond an absurd topknot of leaves sprouting at its very tip, it boasted no foliage at all. The bark was rough patterned, like the belly of an alligator. Clustering like bats under an eaves, hung perhaps a dozen yellowish fruits. They looked like golden pears, kind of. Were they good to eat? Katie wished Wincapaw had told her. She was still craning her neck at the pawpaws when she blundered upon a solid figure halted at the entrance to a driveway. Twin pillars displayed the name "Eli's."

The stranger held the reins of a saddle horse looped over his elbow. He had been digging to dislodge a stone from his mount's near front hoof when Katie materialized suddenly around a clump of bushes. Startled, the animal snorted and reared.

Perforce, the man released the hoof, crying, "Steady! Confound you, steady!"

"Oh, I'm sorry!" Katie gasped when the animal's curvetings knocked off the stranger's hat. "I'll get it."

"Eh?" He turned so angrily to face the road that she flinched back from the hat. "Damn, why don't you look where you are going?"

He was not young, Katie saw; he must be tapping sixty, anyhow. Beneath a carefully curled white wig, strong, almost severe features glowed scarlet as any love apple.

"I'm so sorry!" she gasped, gray-green eyes flying wide open.

She started to hurry away, but he bellowed, "Stop there!" in such a terrifyingly loud voice she obeyed. She halted, not daring to turn around.

"Come back here, Buttercup. I won't eat you." When still she hesitated, the stranger rasped, "Damn it, girl, do as I say!"

His boots, Katie noticed, were expensive, English sewn; and so was his saddle. Tom MacSherry always said you could judge a man very well by the state of his leather goods and by the way he considered his horse.

"One of the Harvey girls?"

"Oh, no, sir."

"Jennings?"

"No, sir."

"Damn! Then you *must* be a Tucker. In Somerset, can't toss a pebble any direction and not raise lumps on a Tucker."

"No, sir, I'm not a Tucker, either."

"Not a Tucker?" He seemed inclined to take the denial as a personal affront. "Not really?"

"Yes, sir, really."

"Well, then I'm damned! Who are you?"

Katie floundered, then characteristically took refuge in the truth.

"Katherine Tryon? Not a bad name, Tryon, not a bad name. Still I'm hanged if Jerry has mentioned any Tryons in Somerset."

"Your friend Mr. Jerry has never seen me, Mr. — "

"Name is Fortescue, Colonel Hugh Fortescue." From his pocket he produced an apple, fed it to his sturdy-looking mare. "Newcomer?"

"Yes, sir," she said hurriedly.

He regarded her more critically. "You ain't English. Don't talk Bermudian, either. What are you?"

"I — I come from Maryland."

"Maryland? Eh, where in the world is Maryland?"

"Maryland is one of the American Colonies — one of the best."

Colonel Fortescue used his handkerchief to flick a minute speck of dust from his boot top. It was a very elegant gesture. "And how may I be of service to so lovely a lady?"

[123]

"Why, why — sir, I am right hungry and thirsty."

"Hungry? Thirsty? Shouldn't wonder. Dry work trudging along in the hot sun. Learned that in India. Well, swing up on Molly behind me. Have you to your destination in no time."

"Thank you, sir, but that's hardly possible."

"Eh? What's that? Hardly possible? And why not?" He looked at her down a rather large nose netted with tiny blue veins. "Why?"

"Because I haven't any place to go."

"No place to go? God's blood! Do you talk riddles?"

"Oh, no, sir," Katie replied as cheerfully as she could. "I — I'm on my way to St. George's. I hope to find employment there."

Colonel Fortescue stared, snorted, then quite deliberately unbuckled a rein and with it tethered his mare to a limb. Round-eyed, she watched him producue from his saddlebags a small paper package and a green bottle with a very long neck.

"Now then, Buttercup. Look like one, you know. Cheery, yellow hair; that sort of thing. Don't mind my calling you Buttercup?"

"Not when you tack a 'ma'am' onto it," Katie managed to get out, utterly astounded at her temerity.

Colonel Fortescue caught his breath, reddened and started to say something. Instead, he grinned.

"Very well, Buttercup ma'am. Fancy we might converse on your problems? Bad thing not to know where one is going. Like marching a regiment out of barracks without learning who you're going to fight, or where. When planning a campaign, Buttercup ma'am, I find it wise to do so on a full stomach, provided there is food about. There is now. While you refresh yourself, I will tell you something of myself. When I have done, you may return the compliment — as far as you deem discreet."

Though the sun, soaring higher, beat down on the island with pitiless intensity, the temperature did not perceptibly increase in the shade of the giant cedar. Colonel Fortescue, clay pipe between fingers, eased his belt and sat with yellow shoulders resting against the tree. Thrust out before him, well-varnished boots reflected patches of white clouds and green foliage.

Katie sat sidewise, trying to hide dust-whitened feet under the hem of her dress. She tried not to make a pig of herself. But it was hard work.

" — And so," Colonel Fortescue remarked between puffs on his pipe, "I said 'to hell with India!' No place for a white man. Stayed out there, though, till the mounseers were licked. Smashed 'em at Wandewash, by Gad, but it took Plassey to do the trick for good and all." His ruddy features relaxed in a grin. "Got my share of the loot, too, for a wonder. It's all banked in London with two stick-sucking macaroni nephews of mine watching it like perfumed cats at a rat hole." The colonel wiggled his toe and considered it with interest. "Like to boot them both. Do 'em good. I say, Buttercup ma'am, don't eat so damned fast—give you the bellyache."

Katie hurriedly put down the chicken leg and wiped her mouth on the hem of her skirt.

"Skirt to mouth existence, what?" Colonel Fortescue laughed till he turned purple and Katie wished she were ten feet underground. Aware of her embarrassment, the colonel calmed, relit his pipe and demanded, "Said you were an American, didn't you?"

"Yes, sir." Katie began to plait some of the coarse native grass. "But I've never met any Bermudians."

"Eh? Met no Bermudians? Gad's life! Nothing else here, is there, but blacks and land crabs?"

"But it's true," Katie insisted. "I have only been in Bermuda since last night." Spurred by the wine and by Colonel Fortescue's frank interest, she found herself telling him everything — almost. He listened in silence, his mulberry-tinted features now tightening, now relaxing.

"So you ran away — a second time?" He was looking at her intently.

"Yes, I did."

"Why? Don't you know you can be branded for it?"

"Yes. But I couldn't go on, not like that. Me, I'm going to live — I'm going to get someplace," Katie informed him serenely. She peered up through the branches at a ragged shred of blue. Not without pride she added, "Mr. David said so. I've learned myself to read and write."

At last he said, "Need a roof over you, food in your stomach. I need companionship. Rented a great barn of a house near St. George's. Got more money than I know what to do with." He glared at her from slightly yellowish gray eyes and went, "Harrumph!" in his throat. "How'd you fancy — er — keeping house for me?"

She heard him saying, "Suppose, Buttercup ma'am, suppose we say you are my niece? Barring old Jerry, nobody on Bermuda knows anything about me or my family. Jerry won't talk."

When she remained silent, he began talking faster to cover his own uneasiness. "You can be my niece, though no Fortescue ever had your looks. All our women look like horses — nice horses," he added loyally.

Henry of Somerset

From inland came a noise of hoofs rapidly approaching and the peculiar ringing sound made by iron wheel tires.

Said Peter Ashton to his boy, "Run to the gate entrance and find out if it's anybody but Mr. Henry Tucker." The little darky vanished like a shot. "I expect we will have quite a few callers tonight. I tried to keep them off till you were rested," he explained, smothering another belch, "but they're all anxious for news. Own ships and all that."

"Suh, hit's Mr. Henry Tucker ob 'e Bridge House," panted the tiger. "An' ah heerd mo' horses on 'e rhud."

Groaning softly, Peter got to his feet. "You are about to meet the leading Whig of the West End. Also, the most loyal of His Majesty's subjects. Cousin of ours by marriage."

"Your humble obedient servant, gentlemen." Walking across the coarse lawn appeared a long-nosed individual. He was leaning heavily on a stick and his jet eyes, Rob thought, were bold and dark as any Indian's. A Negro holding a hurricane lantern slouched along before him. Another followed, bearing a coat and a small handbag.

Peter actually walked fast to greet the caller. Once Rob had been introduced, Henry Tucker lowered himself into a chair with such an air of fatigue it seemed doubtful he could muster energy to rise again. He was really younger than he appeared, for his wig was old, carelessly powdered and tied with a rather dingy yellow swallowtail.

"And what might we be drinking, Peter?" he inquired, settling back to let his tiger fan him.

"Some of Aunt Lyd's Noyo punch."

"Good. My stomach has been none too steady these days." After the caller had lifted off his wig and had given it to a Negro waiting at his elbow, he wearily mopped his head. Dark hair on it had been clipped so close as to make him appear bald. Already he had scanned the Virginian from head to foot. "Is June in Norfolk as hot as this, Mr. Ashton?"

On occasion it was, Rob admitted. For all Peter's deference, he was damned if this narrow-headed, sharp-eyed fellow impressed him. His manner was just a shade too affable.

"I met your father once when he touched at Kingston, years ago. A smart trader — very. Always delivered his horses where they would bring a good price."

"Indeed?"

"Yes." The thin mouth narrowed, then relaxed. "Seems to me you favor him, Mr. Ashton."

"I would be flattered to think so, Mr. Tucker."

Two men wearing loose linen coats and trousers came tramping up behind their link boys. Small boats bumped and several sets of oars rattled down at the landing steps. Slaves came running out of Gaunt New House bringing rattan chairs. Under Zeke's direction many pitchers and bottles were brought out. Beneath a glowing fanlight Aunt Lydia's severe figure was supervising. A bright crack in an upstairs shutter suggested that Mistress Susan was eavesdropping.

A series of hearty greetings, gibes, and queries about the position of ships rang over the terrace. Perspiring mildly, Peter presented callers — George Lusher, Frank Morgan, John Harvey and a couple each of Gilberts and Bascombes. In all their small talk there was a definite undercurrent of

[126]

seriousness. Significant, too, was the way most of them, even the older men, deferred to Henry Tucker.

It was to him Rob addressed a question, "Is it true the Bermudas are hard pressed for food?"

Henry Tucker's sloping shoulders shrugged. "Some people are always hungry. Every one of us has felt the pinch in one way or another. All our food comes from America and two-thirds of our trade. Except for a few mossbacks creeping about the Colonial Secretary's office, England don't know Bermuda exists, and cares less. Me, I've two ships in the rice trade to Carolina and Trinidad. Where am I to send them if Congress claps this embargo on us?"

"Why not the West Indies?" Rob asked.

"No market. No prices there for limestone and salt. They've already more slaves there than they can feed." He gave a little barking laugh. "Don't you think the West Indies will feel the pinch worse than us, Mr. Ashton?"

Rob agreed. He said the Antilles couldn't get along without hard lumber, corn and livestock. There was no place they could get them but in the American Colonies.

Henry Tucker tapped his teeth with the head of his stick, looked up sharply. "Mr. Ashton, do you mind if I ask your opinion about a private matter? It concerns a neighbor, a young Bermudian. Here is what has happened. He is poor and weak and small for his age. His two bigger cousins each have property." Tucker paused and slapped a mosquito from his cheek. "Because he was willed a little cottage, he is forced to live on the property of his Cousin John, but John won't give him anything to eat. The boy's Cousin Silas isn't so big and important as John, but he's more friendly. He buys what this boy carves out of wood and gives him food for it. But here is what has happened just recently. His cousins have got to be on very bad terms; in fact, they quarrel whenever they meet. Each wants the boy to side with him. Now if you were going to advise this young fellow, what would you say?"

Rob considered. "The boy hasn't other friends?"

"No. He'll go hungry if he sides against Silas, but if he rows with John, he will be driven from his cottage."

The Virginian considered. "I reckon he had better avoid picking sides — no matter what."

Henry Tucker broke into a cackling laugh and looked at the men about him. "There's your answer, boys."

Rob blinked, then grasped the gist of Henry Tucker's little story.

"You see, Mr. Ashton," Bascombe said, crossing the *t*'s and dotting the *i*'s, "we figure we'd make out better by cutting adrift from England. But how can we? The Bermudas measure only eighteen square miles with only five thousand white men and about as many blacks. The American colonies lie six hundred miles away, so we can't expect help from them. Though we don't like the idea of it, the tea tax doesn't bother us much because we buy our tea direct at the Canary Islands rendezvous. And to us the coercive acts of Parliament weren't harmful until they stopped our trade with Boston." Bascombe shrugged perplexedly. "We're losing a lot of money here because nobody knows what laws have been made by whom. Only reason we have any vessels left is because most of our ships can show their heels to a committee boat or a man-o'-war."

"Why don't you tell Mr. Ashton about our petition to the Congress?" suggested a dumpy little man whose shirt lay open down to his navel. He spoke sharply to the Negro fanning him and the black quickened the beat of his fan.

The invalid hesitated. Obviously, he didn't like having his hand forced. "Well, it's this way. Last month, some of us decided we knew which way the cat is going to jump. If the American Congress includes us in their embargo on the West Indies trade, we'll be sunk, permanently ruined." Henry Tucker spoke impressively. "So we called a meeting down in Paget's Tribe — one of our middle parishes," he explained. "We composed a petition to the Congress avowing friendliness and sympathy." As Tucker talked, Rob felt his black eyes boring into him. "We informed the Congress that, while unable to take active part in a rebellion, we will abstain from buying the British articles banned in America."

" — Such as tea?" Rob could not resist suggesting. Everyone laughed, but not heartily. Peter regarded his cousin in astonishment.

"We wrote that we would give American vessels every assistance. We offered to sell the Congress Bermuda-built sloops — they, ahem — would make excellent privateers."

Henry Tucker leaned forward, looking at Rob through narrowed eyes. "We have even offered to pass on to the Congress information we pick up. We are eager to make life as hard for the bloody English as we dare. We have already begun, eh, boys?"

Several men nodded. "Yes, indeed, Mr. Tucker, we sure have."

"Well, sir, a delegation was appointed, headed by my estimable father-in-law, Colonel Tucker. It sailed for Philadelphia Tuesday last." Henry Tucker sighed, loosened his neck cloth. "We thought we had better send George Bascombe along. He's a smart enough lawyer to worry even the Yankees. Take a Jew to skin a Bermudian, but a Yankee to skin a Jew — or so they say." Everybody laughed and had another drink.

—"Always provided a bulldog don't catch our delegates — they'll get hanged as traitors if that happens!" spoke one of the men.

"I assume your sentiments represent those of all Bermuda. Is that correct?" Rob questioned.

"Well, not quite," James Fowle admitted. "But I'm damned if we don't represent the most important end of the islands. Those Tories hanging to old Bruere's petticuts don't own enough vessels to take notice of. Most of the smart folks live in the West End." He grinned, then continued. "Yes,

Mr. Ashton, we have old Bruere's hands tied. Last month we — er, some West Enders — pulled down the fort on Wreck Hill. The governor hasn't dared send anybody to repair it."

"Then the East End is Tory and the West End is pro-Congress?"

"You've got the size of it about!" Bascombe admitted, lighting a tabaco almost a foot long and as thick as his thumb. "Any more fights since Lexington?"

"Not that I've heard of," Rob told him. "They say a Yankee army is blockading the British in Boston — from the land, of course. Reckon there will be some sort of a fight when Gage comes out."

As if by tacit understanding, all but two of the guests began to say good night, strode off down the terrace, calling for link boys and grooms, or coxswains. Soon only Henry Tucker, Peter and two others remained talking and drinking on the terrace.

The Mercury Makes Port

"A war has begun, all right," the Mercury's captain told them, stepping ashore. Everyone noticed he was wearing a cutlass in a sheath of brass and scuffed black leather. "Don't make no mistake about that! First I got chased halfway down the Delaware by a Pennsylvania committee boat, then, by God, a damned British sloop of war tried to heave me to. Would of, too, if we hadn't had the heels of him."

Around the outskirts of the crowd hovered a fringe of slaves, ring-eyed in curiosity. They looked mighty pleased when John Gilbert shouted, "Hi there, tell us what happened at Charles Town! Tell us again."

"Why," the captain said, striking an attitude and resting one hand on the wide brass guard of his cutlass, "one night last month — the seventeenth, I think — the Yankees fortified a hill outside of Boston and Gen'l Gage attacked."

"Send his regulars — or was it militia?"

"Regulars, but they whipped him twice." Captain Lightbourn grinned. Right now he was the most important man in Bermuda and he enjoyed the sensation. "I reckon the Yankees would have gone on whipping him till all the British was dead, only they run out of powder."

"Who run out of powder?"

"The Provincials, you numbskull," the captain replied irritably. "It was too bad."

Captain Lightbourn's greasy gray cuffs showed when he raised his hand. "Listen! That ain't all. Listen! I got more news. A paper in Philadelphia said Parliament — "

"To hell with Parliament!" "Hang North!" "Horray for the Yankees!"

Peter Ashton climbed up onto an empty whale-oil barrel. "Quiet, please! Quiet! What was it happened?" he yelled over the heads of the crowd. Right now he looked a different man. He didn't seem so fat. He looked big, anxious and determined. "What about Parliament?"

"You remember them fool laws the Parliament passed last April? About the American fisheries?"

"No!" someone shouted. "I was to sea then."

"Well, the king's ministers says ain't none of the Massachusetts people allowed to fish in the sea. Guess they claim the ocean belongs to the king."

A great clamor went up. Someone at Rob's side began to curse. "No fish to cure means no salt."

Another man growled, "The prices will go to hell!"

The speaker glared desperately about. "What can we do if the salt market goes to the devil? Somebody tell me!"

Nobody answered. They were all listening to Captain Lightbourn.

"This same month the Royal Navy has been ordered to enforce the Fisheries law. They say the American Congress is so mad they ain't going to sell the English *and us* nothing more."

"I vow, I would never have dreamt a rabble of farmers and mechanics could beat troops the French, the Spanish, and the Germans couldn't whip. What can it be?"

"What can what be?"

"In what can those plain people believe so hard that they would face our army?"

Rob, recalling Braddock's fate, the failure of Abercrombie at Ticonderoga and the skirmishes at Concord and Lexington, looked unimpressed.

"Gage won the battlefield," John Gilbert reminded, coming from the throng.

"Reckon he did," Rob was astonished to hear his own voice say. "He bought a hill for a thousand men. Mr. Gilbert, I wonder if you know how many hills there are in America?"

Colonel Fortescue's Niece

Katherine Tryon had never suspected life could contain so many delightful surprises. Every day new and fascinating vistas became unclosed to her wondering gray-green eyes. To be mistress of such a magnificent — in her eyes — residence as Glen Duror was in itself dazzling. That she was in fact mistress in it, as well as of it, she was too practical ever to forget. Her every deed, her every thought, her every speech was dedicated to pleasing Hugh Fortescue.

What sheer rapture it was to climb into a bed boasting snowy white sheets! Imagine lying on a real mattress instead of on a bag of corn shucks. The business of lolling in bed until seven was in itself an undreamed of luxury. Imagine having all the pins she wanted — and soap! And a mirror with no flaws.

A sempstress was engaged and it was from Miss Harrington of the busy hands and busier tongue that Katie picked up many a useful item of information. She learned a great deal, too, about the people of the East End: for instance, who was making money, and who wasn't; which of the shopkeepers could be trusted; who owned a mulatto mistress and who didn't.

Selection of her slippers afforded Katie particular delight. For her, shoes had always held a strange, almost sensual fascination. Never in her life had she owned more than a single pair at a time — clumsy, cowhide affairs stitched by country cobblers.

"You will need that pair of slippers," Colonel Fortescue said, indicating a pair of black satin ones mighty pert because of scarlet heels and black rosettes.

He even bought for her a pair of high-heeled French pumps. They were sinfully expensive, Katie thought, but she was charmed with their fragility, even though they were just a little small and her ankles wobbled about to start with. Over her protests, Colonel Fortescue went on buying until she was genuinely dismayed, but the shopkeepers undulated in all directions.

"La! Uncle Hugh" — she had so practiced the term it slipped out with convincing naturalness —"you have bought enough for a harem."

"A bare beginning, my dear Kitty — " He had become fond of calling her so. "That scarlet cloak with the puffed and ruffled sleeves will favor you."

No fool, Hugh Fortescue moved with discretion in launching his "niece." He began inviting male friends to dinner. Mostly stodgy old fellows, they did not ask many leading questions. He took high delight in their praise of his Kitty's Junoesque beauty. One and all made much the same remark.

"Gad, Hugh, how could a line of plain mugs like yours breed such a beauty?"

Chuckling, he would invariably explain Kitty's looks as coming from his brother-in-law, a famous beau of Maryland. "One of the Merrymans." He had adopted the name from Katie who remembered having served — in more ways than one — a horse fancier by that name at the Spread Eagle. Once the colonel was given a bad moment by the master of a ship.

"Merryman? Merryman? Hmm. Know the name well. A Baltimore County family. Great sportsmen, ride their foxes and wenches clean into the ground."

From her window Katie noticed a ship dropping anchor in the harbor. She was a black, fast-appearing brig and flew the blue ensign at her main gaff.

She and the colonel were only half through breakfast when someone began pounding on the front door.

"Rat the scoundrel! Can't a chap bolt his eggs in peace? Tell whoever it is to wait."

But the insistence of the caller's rapping set Katie's heart pounding queerly. Had she, somehow, been traced? She cast a questioning glance at Fortescue. "Suppose I go see what he wants?"

Colonel Fortescue irritably prodded into a nest of sausages. "Better. Bloody fool will break down the door, else."

The butler was admitting a seafaring man who, when he saw Katie, swept off his round leather hat and jerked a clumsy bow.

"Servant, ma'am. Colonel Fortescue live here?"

"Yes." Katie sighed in overwhelming relief.

"I brought letters for him." Reaching into a breast pocket, the mariner produced a pair of envelopes. One of them was large and formidable with great blobs of scarlet sealing wax.

"Har-rumph! Dash it, Kitty, where have I left my spectacles?"

Immediately she said, "They're on the sideboard," and ran to fetch the steel-rimmed, square-lensed affairs Colonel Fortescue fancied he needed.

When she returned, he was fingering the larger envelope. "Hmm! News from the War Office; about the regiment I expect. High time."

" — And the other?"

"From a friend in Boston, I judge. Now, by God, I will get at the truth of Charles Town. Won't believe militia stood against the regulars. Never have. No age of miracles nowadays."

Katie could see he was torn with indecision over which envelope to inspect first. The one from the War Office was his choice. Slipping a broad thumbnail beneath its flap, he sent the wax seals flying. Anxious, well aware of what this meant to Hugh Fortescue, Katie studied his expression. His eyes narrowed, then widened and in a series of little jerks followed the written sentences.

All of a sudden he gave a great shout. "It's mine! They accepted my offer! By Gad, Kitty, the 63rd is mine!"

"Oh, darling, I am so very glad." Katie flung arms about his neck, kissed him a resounding smack. "You wanted it so much! Where is your regiment?" she faltered. Of course these orders in his hand were for duty in some faraway place like India, Africa, or the West Indies! As fearfully as she'd used to watch Ma Skillings's switch, she watched him search the War Office letter.

"Hum. Let's see. Let's see. Lord Barrington says the 63rd sailed from Ireland last May to — Gad's my life, why it's in Boston!" He pulled the napkin from his neck. "Means active duty. Good. Want to smell powder again before I get put on the shelf. Kitty, my purse please.

"Now, my dear, we shall hear what Frothingham has to say. Frothingham is leftenant colonel in temporary command of my regiment. Gad, it's good to say 'my regiment'! Looked forward to it for years. Stout fellow, Frothingham. A bit too partial to Malaga, though. Drinking is all right in barracks, but not in field. 'Tend to him when I get there."

The colonel's smile vanished. Settled deeper into his wide winged chair, he was reading intently over the tops of the precious spectacles. Katie's depression deepened. Anxious lines were creeping over Hugh Fortescue's claret-tinted features. He sat up, wrinkles creasing his forehead. All at once he exploded.

"Incredible! Can't be so! Howe deserves to be cashiered! Bloody idiot ordered three frontal attacks on entrenchments!" He put down the letter, stared blankly into the fireplace. "Where to find replacements? There's the problem."

For many minutes he sat lost in thought, but in the end looked up and said, "Must face it, Kitty. Seems impossible, but the rebels whipped us. Actually, though not technically. Charley says Provincials lost only four hundred and forty men; thirty of them prisoners." He passed a hand over his eyes, drew a deep breath. "Know our casualties? One thousand and fifty-four men killed and wounded! Damned fine showing, what? Didn't flinch, though. Mark that. Men came back a third time after the rebels shot them to hell twice."

He read aloud:

"These people show a spirit and conduct against us they never showed against the French, and everybody had judged of them from their former appearance and behavior when joined with the King's forces in the last war which has led many into great mistakes. They are now spirited by a rage and enthusiasm as great as ever people were possessed of. We must proceed in earnest or give the business up. The loss we have sustained is greater than we can bear. Small armies can't afford such losses. The troops are sent out too late. The rebels were at least two months before hand with us. I wish this cursed place was burnt."

Two weeks later they set sail for Boston.

Colonel Tucker Returns

A voice called out, "Where's Mr. Ashton? Well, never mind — tell him he's to come straight away to the Grove. Colonel Henry is back!"

[133]

"It's Jim Fowle," Peter said. Reluctantly he pushed away his plate, pulled the napkin from his neck and arose. Already the rider's hoofbeats were diminishing in the direction of the Gilberts' place. "Jim don't fancy moving fast any more than me. Come along, Rob."

In the distance someone had begun to blow on a conch shell. Three blasts, then two short ones. Making a doleful wailing, another conch answered the first.

Peter heaved himself up into the saddle and the beast grunted under his weight. Gathering the reins, he said, "What Colonel Henry Tucker has to tell us means make or break for us West Enders."

His cousin must be terribly anxious, Rob realized; few things could have induced him to ride at a gallop. But he was galloping now, his fat bottom slap-slapping hard against the saddle.

They met other riders traveling the road to Somerset Bridge: Joseph Gilbert, Richard Jennings, Thomas Dickinson and Sam Harvey. All of them, Rob knew, had signed that petition to the Congress in Philadelphia. They looked plenty worried — just as worried as Peter. Without looking much to the right or left, they plugged along towards the Grove, Colonel Henry Tucker's property in Southampton Parish.

"Guess the delegation came back on her," someone said, pointing.

Rob saw a small rakish sloop, lying in the lee of a row of reefs. Beyond her the stripped skeletons of two whales lay like wrecked ships on a sandy beach. They gave off a powerful stench but sea birds were quarreling loudly over shreds of meat adhering to the massive yellow-white bones. Further away still, and shadowed by heavy yellow-brown smoke from a try works, stood the Flemish Wreck House. It had, Jennings remarked, been built almost entirely from the timbers of a vessel lost among the boilers opposite.

The scene began to remind Rob of that day the Lexington fight news had reached Norfolk. Looking around, he recognized grimly expectant expressions. By the time the cavalcade from Mangrove Bay had reached a private road leading into Colonel Tucker's property it numbered about thirty people. More West Enders were waiting, hot and impatient, before Grove House. The property, Peter pointed out, lay in a rich, fertile little valley well sheltered from hurricanes.

Immediately the cousins dismounted and led their animals to a walless shed already crowded with horses. Slaves were busy trying to keep the fly-tortured creatures from biting and kicking each other. Subdued greetings arose.

"The boys brought back an answer?"

"I ain't heard. What about it, Harry?"

"Ain't heard neither."

"I have! The Congress is going to help us."

"If they do, it will cost us a pretty penny. Thum Yankees are closer than the bark on a cedar."

Weary lines momentarily aged Colonel Tucker's countenance. He nodded, and after draining a half mug of beer, stepped out onto a long, low veranda.

"Hi, Colonel!" "Nice trip, Harry?" "How did you make out?" Respect combined with affection was in the greetings.

Colonel Tucker told his listeners that the delegation's westward passage had been swift, had required only eleven days. On July 11th the delegation had presented its petition to the Congress. He had had several interviews with a Mr. Robert Morris and a Mr. Benjamin Franklin, men high in the affairs of the colonies. Speaking in low, carrying tones, Colonel Tucker went on to say that he had pictured to the Congressional committee Bermuda's difficult situation; her willingness to coöperate in a general embargo on trade with England and the West Indies.

"I told 'em," Colonel Tucker said, "we would agree to ship nothing that the Congress didn't approve. I also told 'em we would furnish the colonies with salt, ships, and would help American vessels touching here."

A breathless voice put the query everyone was dreading. "Well, what did they say to that?"

Colonel Tucker hesitated, spread his hands. "They said they sure enough didn't want us to side with the Crown. At the same time, Mr. Franklin made it clear it was all right for us to stay, outwardly, loyal subjects." Politicianlike, he glanced about quickly, trying to gauge the general reaction.

"That's good." "That's smart." "True." The cries sounded devoid of sarcasm.

"Mr. Franklin promised the Congress will exempt us from the embargo. When they asked for proof of our friendship, I promised we would go on shipping salt. They've got to have it. They know it, too. Then Mr. Franklin pointed out a loophole in the embargo."

"What loophole?" Richard Jennings wanted to know.

"The colonies will pass the cargo of any ship bringing in arms and ammunition! Mr. Morris admitted the Provincial armies are devilish short."

A thoughtful silence settled on the crowd.

"There's the whole story," the colonel concluded. "Exemption and food against salt, arms and statistics. Now, I guess we'd better all go home and think this over." He turned to Henry Tucker. "When can we have another meeting?"

"Today is Tuesday, July twenty-fifth," stated the parchment-complexioned master of Bridge House. "Is Thursday all right?"

" — At your place?"

Henry Tucker shook his head. He was a careful man. "No, it wouldn't do."

"Where then?"

"You can meet aboard the *Daphne*," suggested a man on the edge of the crowd. "She won't be sailing until Friday." He wore expensive blue serge and spoke with a Pennsylvanian accent. He was a sharp-nosed, wide-eyed chap with burnt powder grains speckling one side of his face. His expression was aggressive, but thoughtful, too, and his eyes were suggestive of infinite patience. His name, somebody said, was Mr. Peacock. He was a delegate from Philadelphia to the Continental Congress.

Henry of Bridge House looked his gratitude. "Thank you, Mr. Peacock. We will meet aboard the *Daphne* in Eli's Harbor."

Mr. Peacock

Because the sky clouded over and the atmosphere was like a sweaty hand on his brow, Rob opened the living room windows. He lingered there, watching distant flares of lightning and listening to thunder sullenly rumbling out to sea. Caught up on his sleep by now, he was increasingly restless, more like his old self.

Something went *tink!* against a windowpane above him. He turned more quickly than he would have a year ago. Because the Betty lamp's glare was in his eyes, it took him a few seconds to discern a figure standing just outside a fan-shaped area of lighted lawn.

"Who is that?" he demanded sharply.

"Peacock," replied a cautious voice. "Been waiting for a talk. Can you come out?"

Rob's breathing quickened. "Reckon so. What's up?"

Mr. Peacock, however, was already retreating across the lawn. Rob, feeling a bit foolish, climbed out through the window. What ailed the Philadelphian to come mousing about at this hour, and so secretly? Thunder was muttering louder than ever and brighter flashes of light cast motionless cedars and palms into silhouette.

On the sea steps Mr. Peacock stood waiting. Said he without a by-your-leave or anything, "We will go down to the beach."

Rob demurred, asked, "What do you want?"

"Just come along."

The congressional delegate led along the shore to a log half buried on the beach and lying in the lee of some nets drying on a rack.

"Since I don't dare trust a Bermudian," Peacock began, "I — "

"You can trust my cousin," Rob interrupted sharply.

"No doubt, Mr. Ashton, no doubt. Please don't get angry. You see, my ships once traded with these islands. I know the local people better than you — or ought to," Peacock added grimly.

"What do you want with me?"

"You are an American," the Pennsylvania owner replied simply, "so I

[136]

hope you can be trusted. God knows, we have plenty of sneaks and spys in America."

"Well?" Rob was irritated by the other's delay in coming to the point.

"You stand in with the Bermudians, don't you? I hear you do."

"I suppose I do. Why?"

Through the cloud muffled moonlight Rob could see Mr. Peacock's eyes white in the dark of his lean, powder-stained features. "I am asking you to lend me a hand."

"Why should I? What is the Congress to me?"

In the dim light he could see Mr. Peacock sit straighter. "The Continental Congress is the mouthpiece of a people fighting for their rights, fighting to maintain their self-respect."

" — And trade," Rob supplemented.

" — And trade," the Philadelphian agreed with a bitter little laugh. He was considering Rob more carefully now. The Virginian's last observation had both surprised and pleased him, it seemed. "Well, Mr. Ashton, the United Provinces need help, every bit of help they can get. Probably you have not heard that Parliament is bent on hiring Russian troops, barbarous savages, to beat us into submission? If they fail in that, they are sure to buy troops from old George's German cousins. Mercenaries shipped to America! How would you like to see them let loose in Norfolk?"

In the gloom Rob's jaw tightened. "Why, that — that can't be so! The king wouldn't send foreigners to kill his own subjects."

"Wouldn't he? Wait and see. They say in London it is not worth wasting good English lives on a pack of mangy Provincial rebels." Mr. Peacock smiled a sardonic smile. "Not after what happened at Bunker's Hill." Shoulders hunched forward, Mr. Peacock considered the play of lightning on the silver gray and empty harbor. "Yes, Mr. Ashton, our point of view in America is radically different from that of a year ago. Lord North's stupid threats and the king's indifference to all our petitions have made the change. Do you know that a good many people are talking independence?"

Rob shook his head, said slowly, "They will never win it. Out here it's easy to see why."

"On the contrary, Mr. Ashton, we have a chance, a good chance," Mr. Peacock declared so earnestly he carried a measure of conviction. "For one thing, we feel we have the right on our side. In Pennsylvania many thousands of us would sooner die than become slaves to the India Company."

"That goes for Virginia, too, I reckon."

"You see how it is? We must fight because we can't do anything else."

Rob shifted on the log, caught up a handful of sand and absently poured it from one hand into the other.

Mr. Peacock went on talking. "I don't know if it has occurred to you that we have a strong ally in the ministry. North and Germain and the rest are hopelessly ignorant of America and they won't listen. They won't learn.

Best of all, they won't work! The only real interest of most of them is the feathering of their nests. The king is stubborn about dismissing them, so their dishonesty and stupidity will be worth many regiments to us. Such men should not be too hard to defeat."

Mr. Peacock peered along the shore, then at the barren reef of Ireland Island briefly revealed by lightning. "But to even begin to fight, we must have powder."

"Do you know there is powder on this island?" Rob queried suddenly.

"How much?" Mr. Peacock's voice was eager, sharply anxious.

"A lot of it."

"Are you sure? How do you know?"

"An officer of the governor's family said so the other night. He was hopping mad, so I guess he didn't invent it."

"How much?"

"He didn't say. But from the way he spoke, it was a lot."

"Can you find out?"

"I reckon so. I might even find out where it's stored."

The Pennsylvanian's cleanly chiseled head inclined twice. "I know where it should be. What I must learn is whether it is still there."

"Why are you so curious about this?"

"The Pennsylvania Committee wants that powder, has *got* to get it. And to seize it, I must have dependable help. I can't rely on Bermudians to do the job; they will argue and waste time until somebody catches on. Again, I am not sure how many of them would risk their hides in a raid. They know St. George's Town swarms with Tories. That is why I have come to you."

Rob deliberated and ended by saying, "What do you want me to do?"

"Find out for sure which of these West Enders really want to help America. Most of them are only figuring to save their own skins — not that I blame them for it."

"I will do that," Rob said, but without enthusiasm.

"Very well." Mr. Peacock acted as if he had been expecting an acceptance all along. "Now listen, and *keep this to yourself!* Somewhere on her way here is a sloop out of Philadelphia; Robert Morris's *Lady Catherine*. George Ord may be a hard-a-weather captain, but he is also a fine navigator." Mr. Peacock's forefinger tapped Rob's knee. "Aboard the *Lady* are forty men — hand picked by the Pennsylvania Committee. We didn't dare send a larger craft for fear of her being noticed off Bermuda." Rob listened in growing curiosity. "Ord is coming to carry off the powder you mentioned. Colonel Tucker's son, St. George, told Peyton Randolph about it in Virginia. Randolph told Robert Morris."

The Pennsylvanian fell silent as if revolving something in his mind.

"When will this sloop appear?" Rob still poured sand from one hand to the other.

"Within a few days — three at the most. No sooner I hope, because I haven't made the progress I had expected," Mr. Peacock confessed. "You, of course, understand that the *Lady Catherine* must do her work and clear out promptly. You and I must get everything ready for Ord. We must make certain the powder is still there and how heavily it is guarded. I entertain serious suspicions of several of the biggest-talking Whigs around here. If you can discover who can be trusted all the way, Mr. Ashton, you will have performed a great and inestimable service to America. It's your country, you know."

"I will do what I can. Tell me, how do you feel about Colonel Tucker?"

In the darkness Mr. Peacock hesitated, rubbing his powder-blued cheek. "Hanged if I understand just where he fits. I am sure of only one thing about him. He will hesitate a good while before he will do anything downright treasonable — such as stealing powder for use against the king. Colonel Tucker has fine ideals and a keen mind; therefore I don't envy him these days." He pulled out a snuffbox and spilled a little on his thumbnail. "What's your opinion on this other Henry Tucker — the one living near Somerset Bridge?"

Rob grinned. "What is powder bringing in Philadelphia?"

"Around one and one half Spanish dollars a pound," came the instant reply. "Why?"

"At a dollar fifty a pound, you can rely on Henry Tucker. I was wondering why he's been scratching about so."

"I don't understand you."

"He has bought eight half barrels within the last ten days. He must have learned the Philadelphia price."

"Yes. I told him."

"There is your answer. With a profit like that to be cleared, he will never back down."

The Carolinians

On the morning of August twelfth a strange vessel appeared off Somerset. Since she was schooner rigged and big enough for a British cruiser, alarm in the West End was lively until the stranger backed her topsails and sent a boat ashore. To the vast relief of Peter, the Gilberts and the Harveys, the stranger proved to be the *Charles Town and Savannah Packet* out of South Carolina. John Turner was her master and said he would like to meet the Whig leaders of the vicinity.

Accordingly, at sundown there gathered on the beach a deputation headed by Henry Tucker of Bridge House. Mr. Peacock sat in the background saying not a word. It was plain he was trying to figure how to take this unexpected intrusion.

[139]

Henry Tucker directed a shrewd glance at him. "Well, sir, and where is this precious vessel you have been telling us about? If she were here, the business could be done in a hurry."

"Hanged if I know," grunted the Philadelphian. "She is two days overdue."

Rob, present at Mr. Peacock's insistence, only listened, and, watching the faces, noted uneasiness in the manner of one Joseph Jennings. He acted as committeeman from the Flatts, a village situated on the north shore near the center of the archipelago. His curiosity concerning the number of men and cannons carried by the *Packet* Rob thought were a trifle persistent.

"Could you keep your ship lying off and on for a few days?" Henry Tucker wanted to know.

Turner, burned almost black by the sun, squirted tobacco juice onto the sand, hooked big thumbs into a belt supporting a brace of boarding pistols. "Why, seh, I reckon I could tarry maybe three days mo'. Then I must git for Cha'les Town or mah owners will keel-haul me. This hyer venture is putting them gentlemen out of pocket. Yes, seh, it sho'ly is." He hitched his belt higher. "Still, I hanker to singe that damn' governor's nose. When we was layin' in St. Geo'ge's last week, he sho'ly made life a nuisance. From the way he kep' watch on the *Packet*, I reckon he maybe smelled a nigger in our woodpile."

"You don't say so!" Peter cried, looking very disturbed.

"Yes, seh, I do say so! That revenoo boat of his was always triflin' 'round."

Henry Tucker's expression grew graver. Rob could tell he, too, didn't like this news.

Peter said, "You're sure you didn't hint around about the powder?"

Captain Turner grinned. "No, seh. Warn't no need. Every nigger in town knows it's stowed in a garden back o' the governor's mansion."

Joseph Jennings coughed, ran a finger around the inside of his stock. "Boys, I don't like the sound of Bruere's being so suspicious. If you stop and think it over, this is pretty risky business. If we was to get caught stealing the king's powder, it will mean the gallows. That's treason."

Next day the whole situation changed. Late in the afternoon a large sloop lifted topsails above the aching blue of the horizon and as soon as she showed a green flag at her foretop and a red one at her main, Rob guessed her to be the *Lady Catherine*. At twilight the sloop's anchor had gone plunging onto the sand at the entrance to Mangrove Bay and Mr. Peacock had nearly ruined a horse in getting over from Eli's Harbor. He discovered Rob fishing at the end of the dock, apparently indolent.

"Thank God, she's got here!" the Philadelphian sighed, studying the sloop lying with rigging etched against the violet sky. "Soon as George Ord gets ashore, we'll have a talk, Mr. Ashton. Meantime, please ask your cousin to hoist the lantern signals; I want the *Packet* to stand in."

[140]

When the Whigs gathered in Peter's warehouse, the others from force of habit granted Henry of the Bridge a conversational right of way. Quite a number of men were present; more than Rob deemed wise considering the seriousness of the topic under discussion.

"Our only chance is to strike before Bruere hears of ships arriving at this end," declared Henry Tucker, more pasty-faced than ever. "We must make our try tomorrow night."

Heartily Mr. Peacock concurred, saying he thought the West End was crawling with informers.

Captain Ord tilted back in his chair, scratched a broad red nose. "How many men are we going to need?"

"Between sixty and seventy," was the prompt reply. "How many hands can you spare for the shore party?"

"Not over thirty," Ord replied, staring at Henry Tucker as if he were something he had never seen before. "Need the rest to navigate."

"And you?"

If it was a fair night, Captain Turner reckoned he could make out with five men.

A pair of rats began scuffling behind a pile of hides while Henry Tucker considered. "Well, I judge we can count on about six good men from here — and as many slaves as you want. Incidentally, I intend going along."

"Eh?" Peter looked amazed at the idea of Henry Tucker's risking his neck.

"Yes. I am familiar with Government House and its grounds. Also Tobacco Bay."

"Tobacco Bay?" Bascombe queried sharply. "I was thinking of Catherine's Point."

"Fewer houses face Tobacco Bay."

"What about boats?" Mr. Peacock wanted to know. "We have got to have quite a few."

"I don't mind risking my skin," someone grunted, "but whale boats costs money. I only got two. If I lose dem, my family vould go hungry."

Someone else said, "Mine is too old and slow."

Richard Jennings said, "Never mind. Joe has plenty of boats. We won't need any others. Besides, his place lies halfway to St. George's; he will save us a damned long row."

"Now here's what I figure," the chairman said, and leaning further forward, was dwarfed by his shadow. In the lantern light the white of his eyes looked lemon yellow. "We will cruise along the north shore as far as Burnt Point. You judge that would be safe, Colonel?"

Colonel Tucker, who had come in late, said, "It should be."

"We can row Joe Jennings's boats from there to Tobacco Bay and make our try for the powder."

In the *Lady Catherine*'s stuffy stern cabin Captain Ord held forth over mugs of lukewarm ale. Though the night was suffocating despite occasional spatters of rain, he still wore his coat. Captain John Turner, however, had undone his shirt clean down to his belt, exposing a weird design tattooed across his chest. It had been done in the South Seas, he said with pride. Mr. Peacock had shed his coat, but endured a waistcoat above his blue-and-white-checked shirt.

Outside the door the sloop's quartermaster stood guard, but Captains Turner and Ord had taken further precautions. Both their vessels had springs rigged to their cables and could be off within a few moments. What guns they mounted had been double shotted and in the cook's galley a nest of coals glowed, ready to light a gunner's match. Aloft, lookouts remained constantly on the alert.

Mr. Peacock had learned of no men-of-war at St. George's, but reported the three armed merchantmen Rob had noticed still there.

Captain Ord, rubbing his palm, snapped, "Mr. Peacock, I'm double damned if I like the look of things. Ever try to get a straight answer to a plain question 'round here?"

Captain Turner, though apparently absorbed in trimming his fingers with a sheath knife, looked up slowly. "Hell of a tune if we-uns was heave-to off St. George's and find a couple of batteries opening up on us."

Mr. Peacock turned to Captain Ord. "Everything depends, George, on how much the 'Mudians can expect to clear on the powder. I wish I could be sure the profits are high enough to keep them straight. As it is, I have quoted Henry Tucker a shilling a pound above the market." He chuckled. "I guess they will be disappointed when they learn what their infernal powder will really bring in America."

"*If* it gets to America," Captain Turner growled. "I don't mind tellin' you, Mr. Peacock, I ain't trustin' these heah 'Mudians too far. I dassent. Not with the skimpy little crew I got aboa'd. Tudor Tucker, he oughtn't have let me sail so God-damned shorthanded. It warn't right!"

Ord picked up a pipe, turned it sidewise to light it at a candle flame. "Wish to hell we could manage this by ourselves."

He was badly worried, was Captain George Ord. Mr. Franklin and Mr. Robert Morris had taken him and Mr. Peacock into their confidence. They had disclosed figures, appalling, eloquent of impending doom.

"Upon the success of this expedition," Mr. Franklin had reminded them in his low, impressive voice, "depends the existence of our troops. Not until many weeks have passed can we secure gunpowder from any other source. The army besieging Boston has not enough ammunition to fight a hard skirmish. Should the British learn this, as they well may, even our valorous enemy General Gage will make a sortie and crush our people."

Aloud Ord suggested, "Suppose we keep most the slaves aboard? They are handy sailors. Won't let them keep even a jackknife. They would be more useful here than ashore; niggers scare easy if things get tight."

Turner's grin bared big tobacco-yellowed teeth. "An' we'd take the white 'Mudians along with us?"

"That's my notion. It would leave most of our crews free for shore operations."

"Suppose we try pulling off the raid all by ourselves?"

Mr. Peacock shook his head. "If we try to freeze them out, the people ashore will turn ugly. Can't blame them, either. They want the powder's price — "

One by one, lights on the *Lady Catherine* and the *Packet* blinked out. They rode in solitary possession of the harbor; owners, chary of such dangerous company, had shifted all other vessels to safer anchorages. The perfume of cedar sawed in the shipyards hung strong in the air.

August 14th, 1775

"Now what the blazes has gone wrong?" Peter exclaimed in a low voice.

Sallow features flushed, neck cloth awry, Henry of Somerset stamped in, dust-powdered and trembling in his fury.

"We're in the devil's own mess!"

"What's wrong?" the cousins demanded in unison.

"It's Joe Jennings! The bloody bastard!"

Rob's breath stuck in his throat. Mr. Peacock, it seemed, had been right about the gangling committeeman from the Flatts.

"What's he done?"

Tucker glared about as if he would attack any movement. "What has he done? The crotch-blistered coward has ruined all my plans!"

"You mean he can't let us have the whalers tonight?"

"He can, but he won't! Blast his crooked soul to hell!" Henry Tucker was outraged as only a shifty man can be when for once he is the victim of trickery. Panting, he sank onto a meat cask. "My cousin Jim sailed down to Flatts this morning to give him last instructions." Narrow chest aheave, Henry Tucker cursed dreadfully. "But Jennings tells Jim he's sorry, he has changed his mind and doesn't want any part of the business. He even had the confounded gall to tell Jim he might get a reward from the governor if he'd peach on me!"

Peter joined in a flow of really artistic profanity.

Rob looked at his watch and saw it was four o'clock. Aware that the expedition was scheduled to set out at eight, he asked, "Well, Tucker, what is to be done about it?" Recalling Peacock's distrust of the islanders, he was seriously disturbed.

"Try to scratch up enough whalers 'round Somerset," Henry Tucker growled. "Doubt if it will be possible, though. People around here are too poor to go risking their boats."

Rob said, "If it will help matters, I'll agree to underwrite such losses."

"You will? You mean that?" Henry Tucker looked incredulous. "Why should you? Your loss might run into hundreds of pounds."

"Call it a gamble, Mr. Tucker."

"Then you really mean your offer?"

"Especially in business matters I mean what I say. It has been a failing with me."

"In that case we'd better be getting out and hump ourselves," Peter commented. "What about boat crews?"

"You and Bascombe will have to attend to that," Henry Tucker said, "and Colonel Henry and I will collect boats and see they get here on time."

Brushing away a fly which was skating over his close-clipped scalp, Peter inquired, "How do you think the American captains are going to take this change?"

"I'll attend to that," Rob promised. It was invigorating, it boosted his self-respect to feel the sense of responsibility. "Let me get this straight. I presume the ships will take the whale boats in tow and stand down along the north shore?"

"Yes, as far as Crawl Point," Henry Tucker replied. "The *Packet* first and the *Lady* following. If the night wind blows strong enough, we can follow the inner passage. Ships would not be so noticeable from shore then. As soon as it gets dark, the whale boats will pull for Tobacco Bay."

"I hope you'll let me take charge of one," Rob said.

"That can be managed." Henry Tucker closed his eyes, spoke as if he were consulting a mental map. "Around eleven, both vessels will move further east, but they had better not go any nearer St. George's than Burnt Point." He mopped his face briefly and asked Rob, "Well, sir, and why do you look at me like that?"

"I was just wondering," Rob confessed, "whether Joe Jennings might take it into his head to ride on into St. George's?"

"He is a cowardly dog, and after what he's done today I guess he would sell his sister to a Jew," the Bermudian stated, then added, "but he must live on these islands with the colonel and me. It all depends on how much he figures the governor might pay him for peaching. In any case, it is one chance we must run. In another day's time the venture will be too risky. Someone is bound to inform Bruere of American ships having been here."

It was, Rob realized, surprisingly pleasant to be aboard ship again. The *Lady Catherine*'s gentle rolling and the creaking of blocks and tackles played a familiar tune. Mangrove Bay and Gaunt New House now lay astern; they had passed Spanish Point. A dim veneer of clouds obscured the sky but later there should be quite a bit of moonlight. The only thing troubling Rob was Captain Ord's stiffness with him all along. The master's aloofness abated somewhat when he had asked to engage passage. Perhaps that was Ord's natural manner.

He was setting foot to the quarterdeck ladder when Captain Ord checked him with a peremptory, "Ain't no one allowed on my quarterdeck but the after guard of this ship."

Rob nodded. "It is as you wish, of course. I only want to know in which boat I'm to go?"

"In good time you will be given orders."

Puzzled and troubled, Rob went to the rail and looked astern. Towing easily, and with a steersman in the stern of each, four big dirty white whale boats trailed after the *Lady Catherine*. Because she was smaller and less likely to attract attention, the *Packet* had set sail earlier. They could see the gleam of her mainsail nearly a mile ahead. She was towing three whale boats of smaller size.

Rob looked at Negro seamen squatting on the deck amidships. Peter's slaves were fine big fellows. To his relief the four or five white Bermudians aboard acted very calm. Once the *Lady* got close inshore Ord called one of them up to act as pilot. It was just as well for just ahead lay the Stags, a wicked scattering of reefs. Surprisingly soon Crawl Point loomed through the afterglow. They could see the *Packet* heaving to off it. Already the Carolinian schooner's crew was pulling the whale boats up alongside.

Rob could visualize Henry Tucker of the Bridge, his thin face tight, directing the movements over there. Opportunist he might be, but there was no denying he was a capable man in a pinch; capable and by no stretch of the imagination timorous.

Very soon the *Lady Catherine* drew up to her consort and with canvas slatting came up into the wind.

Dressed in dark clothes, Peter Ashton came over to his cousin. His expression was somber and he looked angry. "What's eating Captain Ord? Fellow keeps looking at me as if he expects me to shove one of these," he tapped the butt of one of the pistols Rob had given him, "into his ribs."

"He is just nervous, I reckon," Rob ventured. "After all, we've a ticklish job ahead." His eyes probed the indistinct shoreline. Right here the coast was bold with an inlet slashing deep into its dark mass.

"Flatts is over yonder," Peter said. "That bugger Joe Jennings lives in the little house to the left. Hope to hell he hasn't got to Bruere — "

"Avast there!" came a sibilant order from the quarterdeck.

Swiftly the whale boats were brought alongside and then Rob got a jolt. More than half the blacks destined to act as rowers were ordered to stay on board and a corresponding number of white sailors took up their place. Captain Ord would remain aboard, but Mr. Peacock was for the shore party. Rob immediately sensed the reason for this sudden increase in the number of Provincials going ashore. He hoped Peter did not; Ord's maneuver was scarcely flattering to the Bermudians. It was rather dangerous, too, he thought, considering how utterly at the mercy of Henry Tucker they all were. Without Bermudian whale boats, without native pilots, without the help of slave labor and without volunteers, the Americans could have accomplished nothing.

The whalers shoved off without putting out oars. The breeze being favorable, a leg-of-mutton sail was raised in each boat. Under the propulsion of brown, often patched canvas the whalers slid quickly out from under the *Lady Catherine*'s towering yards.

The sea was silver-gray, like French paper, and the flotilla steering inshore formed little black blots on its surface. Along the shore only some pale sand beaches and a very few lights were visible. Rob, seated on a thwart, wondered what was going to happen. The next hour would tell a lot. Recently he had given up trying to find omens.

For about half an hour the whale boats cruised in silence. Everyone kept staring at the cedar-shrouded slopes above the water. Now and then a man would shift his position and a weapon would clink. Rob could see the coxswain in the boat alongside throwing his weight on the long steering oar; a blue-and-white-striped jersey he wore showed up surprisingly clear. He was a fool to have worn such a thing. Astern, the schooner and the sloop cruised slowly back and forth, remained barely discernible.

Rob strained his eyes at the shore ahead but could see no lights. For clearer vision he shoved aside the handle of a pickax destined for use later. Peter's heavy figure sat slouched in the stern of a whaler to port. He certainly must believe in the necessity of this expedition. He was risking a fortune, everything, to take part. Damned lucky the interests of Bermuda and America, for the present at least, ran in parallel grooves.

One of the black men whispered over the *hush-hush* of waves alongside, "'At's Burnt Point ovah yander, suh, 'n, 'at's Vale Bone Beh off sta'boa'd."

The steersman, second mate of the *Lady Catherine*, uttered a small sigh. "Abner," said he to the man beside him, "I do believe we are in luck. If this wind holds we ought to fetch the beach 'thout touching an oar. It would save us making any racket at all."

The other agreed, but kept sticking out his head, as if he were expecting to see some threatening object.

The flotilla was sailing along, bunched like a flock of wild ducks startled by a hostile sound. Henry of Somerset sat in the stern of the foremost talking to Captain Turner. Everyone could see his thin arm pointing ahead at a glimmer of white. This, Rob deduced, must be Tobacco Bay beach, for on some heights beyond it battlements showed as a series of gray and black planes. From his study of charts Rob knew this for Fort St. Catherine. The guns in it commanded the beach. The Bermudians, too, were painfully aware of the fact and kept looking in that direction.

Soon the land commenced to cut off the wind and the boats slowed. A sailor started to pick up his oar but was ordered to desist. On a low-pitched command from Captain Turner all the boats formed in line abreast and steered for the beach. Every one of the raiders knew that if an ambush had been arranged, its fire must any instant now crash into their faces. If that happened, not many men could hope to get away. The stillness became incredible — only the lazy wash of wavelets on the beach, a stirring of cedar branches and a merry gurgle rising in the wakes of the seven whalers.

Rob got a curious impression that his boat lay motionless while the shore moved out to meet her. A few seconds before land inserted itself under the keel, the steersman in a hoarse undertone ordered the sail lowered. Jumping overboard, the crew laid hold of the gunwales and they all heaved the big whaler further up on shore. It was a good thing the tide was making, Peter muttered.

The crews gathered at once, blotting out the white sand with their numbers. Acid and quite calm, Henry Tucker strode along the line of stranded boats. He leaned rather heavily on a cane.

Rob said to his boat captain, "Aren't we taking along those pickaxes?"

The other gave him a grateful look. "Jerusha! Clean forgot about 'em." He trotted over to the next boat. "Don't forget them shovels."

Rob was greatly surprised when Henry Tucker came to him and said, "Come with me."

The advance party consisted of seven men; Henry Tucker, Richard Jennings, Dan and James Tucker, Captain Turner, the first mate of the *Lady Catherine* and Rob.

Soon a wall loomed ahead, but as Henry Tucker had predicted, it was neither high nor defended by the usual collection of broken glass set in its top. The whole party scaled it without delay.

"We must be very still now. Government House lies right over there," Henry Tucker warned.

The men were panting, glad momentarily to ease the drag of weapons at their belts. They stood peering anxiously in all directions.

"Where is the magazine?"

"To our left. Now, Captain, suppose you post a lookout among those bushes. Two more men had better cross to the other side of the magazine."

The King's Powder

That the Provincials intended to run no unnecessary risk was patent from the careful way they arranged a ring of their own men as lookouts. Henry Tucker insisted, however, that one post be watched by his cousin. It was on a walk leading directly to Government House. The hot and anxious party could glimpse the faint loom of its roof through the trees. Rob deemed it a rather insignificant edifice.

Men thirty strong came up from the beach, handling their tools and weapons. They followed Henry Tucker towards what seemed to be a gate let into a rise in the ground. It was an eternal instant. Everybody braced himself for a hoarse, "Halt! Who goes there?" A twig snapping under Peter's heel set half the party swinging about. Rob saw in the stone façade a massive double grille of iron bars secured by a chain and padlock. Behind it was a door of sheet iron. The raiders came crowding up. Some of the slaves standing white-eyed in the background were so scared their teeth chattered.

"God in Heaven," Richard Jennings groaned. "How the blazes are we going to get into the damned thing?"

Henry Tucker beckoned one of his own slaves, a little runt of a Negro. "Stilicho, you see that ventilator up on top?" He pointed to the summit of a grassy mound behind the entrance.

"Yassuh."

"You and Justin take crowbars and scramble up there — pry the roof off the ventilator. You can slide down a rope. I hear the inner door can be unlocked from the inside."

"You sure about that?" the mate of the *Lady Catherine* asked. He was so nervous his voice shook.

"Haven't time to answer fool questions." Henry Tucker sank on a stone curb lining the little road up to the entrance. "You men use your crowbars to snap off that chain. Hurry — it's after eleven."

Everyone's heart faltered at the resounding *crack!* one of the ventilator's roof boards made when Henry Tucker's slave levered hard. Rob could see the two Negroes heaving and straining up there against the stars. Meanwhile, a crowbar twisted windlass-fashion through the chain was being turned. The pressure only resulted in a gradual bending of two of the grille bars. All at once the chain gave a sharp *tang!* and broke, raising a shower of sparks. In front of the magazine sounded muffled stampings, the clank of iron on iron and the whispering of the Negroes above. Stilicho had rigged a rope and now only his head and shoulders remained visible. It was a tight squeeze, but he was able to get through.

From within the vault sounded a metallic scraping, then the noise of kicking. Gradually the inner door swung open and freed a rush of damp, dank air. Two huge toads hopped frantically about, scuttling at last to safety.

"Hell!" grunted the mate. "Why don't the bloodybacks store their powder in a dry place! Must be plenty of it spoiled!"

"Quit talking and get your men going," snapped Henry Tucker.

To deaden sounds of barrels being rolled over stone flooring, the raiders arranged a path of canvas strips, brought for the purpose, out to the entrance. Rob marshaled slaves and seamen impartially into a line. Fortune again smiled. His Majesty's powder was for the most part packed in half barrels. One such keg was just small enough for a single man to manage. Rob's duty was to keep the line moving, to arrange for transportation of the larger barrels.

One after another the whites and Negroes vanished into the gaping blackness of the magazine, reappeared bent under a burden. It was like watching ants at work on a hill. A thin line flowed steadily down Retreat Hill, disappeared in the direction of Tobacco Bay.

As they tired, the raiders made more noise, a lot of it. They would blunder into a low branch or stumble. Sometimes they fell and their keg would crash off into the dark, making a terrific racket. At such times everybody froze in his tracks, stayed deathly still, listened for all he was worth. They could hear dogs barking in St. George's on the far side of the hill. Behind Government House an amorous cat made the welkin ring.

It was such hard work rolling out the heavier, iron-bound barrels and manhandling them over the rocky ground that nobody realized when two hours had passed. No matter what the raiders did, the big barrels gave off an alarmingly loud rumbling.

Peter, dusty and puffing like a grampus, looked about, noted that the lookouts were over their first tension. Diffused moonlight shone faintly on pistol barrels and on the cutlasses that some of them had drawn.

Henry Tucker put aside a bottle of medicine from which he had been dosing himself. He beckoned Rob. "Mr. Ashton, suppose you go take a look and see how much more the whalers can manage? We will have to clear out very soon."

Lugging a small keg, Rob started down the beach. He could see fine now. Deer shooting at home, it often was like this. He felt relieved on Peter's account; so far the Bermudians had made a fine showing.

He had passed through the pungent body aura of a big barefooted Negro and was starting down the beach when some branches moved, *against* the wind, in a thicket beside the path. Without seeming to take alarm, he swung out of line as far as he might. Yes, by God, somebody was in there! All in one motion Rob dropped his keg, leaped at the thicket.

The fellow gave a frightened cry, jumped up and began to run along a path. He was foolish. Had he dodged into the underbrush, he must have escaped in the thick gloom of branches, but apparently the fellow reckoned he could pull away. It was no wonder. Inside the first ten yards they covered Rob knew he was a damned fast runner. But he must be silenced! If he got away, he would raise the town.

Rob put on a burst of speed, concentrated on driving his legs. He began to close in. The fellow flashed a look back over his shoulder. He was either a white man or a very light mulatto. When he saw Rob coming up, he put on a spurt himself, began to draw away down a path which now traversed a small clearing. In it corn grew waist high to either side. Damn! If it came to matching sprints, Rob could tell right off the other would get away.

Since the fellow was wearing a striped waistcoat he was probably a house servant. From Government House? Rob began to tire. The fellow was a scant thirty feet ahead, but he might as well have led by a mile. And he was running faster. Rob made his decision, halted, grabbed up one of the many loose stones which had been hampering them both. Bracing himself, he heaved with all his might. He was good at throwing.

The rock took the man in the striped waistcoat at the back of the head. He went bowling over and over through the young corn like a shot rabbit. Rob jumped on him with both feet, hoping to drive enough breath out of his lungs so he couldn't raise a yell. He dropped flat beside his motionless adversary's warm, sour-smelling form. He listened because ahead voices had sounded.

Someone said, "Where in hell did Sam get to?"

"Down to the shack," a voice replied. "Sam's been laying that yellow-haired kid of Coolson's."

Rob deliberated only an instant before jerking out a handkerchief. He crammed it into the servant's slack jaws hoping it wouldn't choke him. Next he took the fellow's belt for wrist lashings and sacrificed a bandanna as hobbles. Only with difficulty was he able to pull the unconscious man off among the dew-covered cornstalks.

When Rob reached the shore he saw that both Provincial vessels were standing in almost dangerously close to the beach. In fact, they lay under backed topsails not two hundred yards out, their canvas lustrous in the moonlight. Whale boats were continually pulling out to and from them. The thump made by barrels hoisted up the *Lady*'s side sounded so loud it seemed a miracle no alarm had been raised. There was room, one of the Gilbert boys said, for about fifteen more small barrels — six big ones.

By three o'clock His Majesty's magazine stood all but empty; only eight or ten large barrels remained. Captain Turner wanted to take them too, but Henry Tucker was peremptory.

"No. By sunup you must both be out of sight of land. It is half past three now. Besides, the wind acts like it might fail."

By four o'clock all the stolen powder was safely aboard ship; two-thirds of it in the *Lady Catherine*, one-third in the *Packet*. All beaming smiles, his stiffness vanished as dew under the sun, Captain Ord swung down a Jacob's ladder and got into the stern sheets of the whaler containing Henry Tucker. He gave him a heavy bag of coins. Clapped him on the back and said loud enough for plenty of witnesses to hear, "Well, sir, here's your advance. One thousand Spanish dollars. The Congress will be delighted."

Henry Tucker called Peter over from another boat. He said, "Suppose you and Dan help me count this? Ord ain't trusted us so there's no use trusting him."

[150]

Mr. Peacock frowned. "You will find the amount correct, sir," said he sharply. "You will receive your balance within a month."

But Captain Ord wasn't upset; he offered his hand. "That was fine work, Mr. Tucker, smart, every bit of it. Wish you were an American."

The other looked up from the stack of coins dully agleam in the seat. "I'm damned glad I'm not." Presently when he and Peter had cast up the total, he said, "I will call it correct — even if some of the coins are thin. Now, get out of here as fast as you can. We'll go back up the shore in the whale boats."

The sloop's yards were braced in a hurry, but long before the *Lady Catherine* stood out for the northeast channel her crew could see the Bermudian flotilla scurrying up along the coast to the westward. It was a long way to Mangrove Bay and they knew they must put the whalers away before daylight.

To the deep concern of all aboard the *Lady Catherine*, dawn broke with Bermuda still uncomfortably high on the horizon. Rob could even distinguish the white roof of Government House. At intervals a sullen booming of alarm guns reached the sloop, and it did not help matters to feel the wind fading.

Captain Ord looked thoughtful, then very uneasy. Said he, "If a breeze rises from over the Bermudas, they can overtake us."

The House on Garden Court Street

From the first, Katie Tryon had fallen in love with the neat little house Colonel Fortescue's adjutant had found for them on Garden Court Street. Its brick and slate construction charmed Katie. Their new residence was set back quite a way from the street and had a towering walnut to shade the front porch. In the rear yard was a chicken run, but its former tenants had long since vanished down the gullets of marauding soldiers. She liked, too, the chestnut trees shading the street and the severe cleanliness of her new home, and the way great morning glories smothered the back porch and the tool shed. There was even an enormous gray cat, Peter, which condescended to let them live with it. When fish was on the menu Peter became markedly affectionate.

The passage from Bermuda hadn't been an easy one. Though it should have been completed in around ten days, the voyage had consumed over three weeks.

To Katie Boston proved a disappointment. From the way she had heard people talk, she had pictured Boston as a great, crowded city. Instead she landed in a modest town that failed to cover all of the narrow peninsula on which it was built. When she saw those wide fields and the woods fringing the great expanse of Boston Harbor the town seemed more insignificant than ever. Of course some of the streets were cobbled, the mark of a real metropolis, and there were lots of inns and rich-looking houses. After living in St. George's and Roanoke County, Boston seemed lively; especially in the morning when guard details were tramping to and from their posts. On the Common troops freshly arrived from England were forever drilling and cursing beneath the summer sun. Boston might once have been a rich, important port, but she didn't think it was a patch on Norfolk.

She was looking a different girl now that she had a maid to curl and set her hair and to keep her ruffles ironed. Her voice was softer and her slips in grammar came only when she got excited or very tired. On shipboard 'most everybody took her for what the colonel said she was — his niece. He had taught her to walk and to curtsy and to say, "It is the *ton*," "I do protest" and "Oh, you naughty fellow!" She worked hard at her writing and had read all of A *History of Greece from the Earliest Period*.

Almost every day new earthworks were thrown up by the Provincials, inexorably tightening the ring about the doubly blockaded port. That it was a dreadfully weak ring Lord Howe either failed to learn or ignored. Nor did he seem to guess that the besiegers, now under Washington, a Virginia general, were reorganizing their whole military establishment.

Around the middle of August the weather took an unseasonably ill turn. In from the Grand Banks an east wind drove a series of fogs, cold, damp, and bone-chilling. It shrouded Boston in a dismal, irritating pall. The garrison grew still more apprehensive. Rumors were flying that the Americans, stimulated by the arrival of some rifle companies from the South, were preparing to make a boat attack under cover of the mist. The nerves of officers and men wore thin.

It wasn't until seven of the morning that Colonel Fortescue came home, irritable and furious at the incapacity of his company commanders. When he came stumping in, water dripping from the skirts of his dressing gown trailed down the hall and into the library.

"Hate to do it, but there will have to be changes! Horton ain't fit to handle a squad, let alone a company. Silly ass lost his head, ordered the men to fire on one of our own patrol boats. Dash it all, Kitty, can't have that sort of thing!"

"Come to bed, darling, and rest." Katie slipped an arm through his, began shepherding him towards the staircase. "You are soaked to the skin and you look dead tired."

"Damn, let go my arm, girl." He gave her a weary smile, then shook his head. "Can't stop. Harrington, my last major, is down with a flux. Hitchcock hinted that the smallpox is loose in my grenadier company."

Katie shuddered. "Smallpox" was a word that would always give her the blue creevils. There was, she knew, a lot of it about. The epidemic was getting steadily worse. Hardly any hour of the day but you could see a funeral on its way to Copp's Hill burying ground.

"Was a fool ever to leave warm countries," reflected Hugh Fortescue. "Blood's thin. Hang such a climate!" He was shivering now. To forget about it, he began planning. "Ain't sensible sending all the best men to the flank companies. Recruits need stiffening of the old hands. Yes, damn, I'll put some grenadiers back into the line companies."

Katie was mending a rip in the lace on the colonel's second-best uniform. At the sound of a carriage stopping at the curb, she glanced up. That in itself was noteworthy; what with fodder so scarce, carriages were very few. Her heart missed a beat. Two red-coated officers got out, helping a third; Fortescue. Then came a man in black who carried a leather case under one arm. She flew out to open the front door. Eyes very round, she called,

"Oh, Hugh, are you wounded?"

The colonel was walking all bent over to the right. From halfway down the front walk she could hear his painful gasps for breath. "No. Just a damned bad pain in my side. Nothing — worry about. Silly business. Be all right tomorrow."

The doctor sighed, shook his head. "Lung fever and a very heavy case, I fear, Miss Tryon. I daren't bleed your uncle again."

Wiping a bloodied scalpel on his handkerchief, he turned from the big four-poster on which Hugh Fortescue lay shifting, talking in gasping, disjointed sentences of Madagascar, of Madras and of a place called Cuddapah. Occasionally he would struggle up, roaring furious, unintelligible commands in a strange language. He was fighting on the left wing at Fontenoy once more. When the delirium took firmer hold, he called for Jerry — his old friend.

In the early morning Colonel Fortescue opened his eyes and saw Katie sitting beside him. She was looking at her folded hands. The nearness of her was restful, but he felt very, very tired. Just before he waked, he had been reliving some marches he had made. For the first time in years he had recalled Dettingen and the bullet that had torn through his hat, and the time his horse shied on a dike in Belgium. The damned brute had reared into a swamp; another horse came plunging down on top. Then there was that near thing at Mindeh. He had seen again a French grenadier in white and blue holding a musket right at his chest; had it not misfired, the trail would have ended then. Dozens of times death had passed him by, but now he knew the dark angel was at hand. Why, or how, he was so sure he could not tell, but he knew it.

It wasn't uncomfortable just lying still. Even yet, Katie had not noticed that his eyes were open. Katie. And before her Rachel, and before her

Chloë, and before her Mameena of the mirrored thumbs and before her Zuleika, warm, brown and so very adept in bed. He smiled when he thought of blonde little Gretel waiting for him under the big windmill's arms.

"Oh, Hugh, honey! You are feeling better?"

"Capital, capital! Pray send for Hallam — regimental clark, billeted Mrs. Cartney — next street." To speak, it seemed he must relay what he wanted to say to a second person, who in turn passed the idea on to another man who spoke the words.

Katie gave him one long look, then crossed to the door and told Zuleem to wake the doctor.

"Come back in half an hour. No later." The doctor pointed his last words.

Katie went out.

There were quite a few people in her house when she came back up the bricked walk, including many officers, one of them very splendid in gold and white and scarlet. The doctor came hurrying out on the porch. He took her by the arm.

"My dear, he has been asking for you."

The way the doctor spoke put stitches in Katie's heart, and as she set foot to the stairs and fairly flew up them, she saw people waiting in the hall below stare at her. There were more men in uniform talking in undertones in the upper hall. When she passed, they too stepped back and looked curious, but she took no notice of them.

"My own sweet Kitty." He smiled from the depths of a huge feather pillow. "Kiss me, and listen."

When she had done so, she sank onto the side of the bed looking down into the face she had always admired, and had recently come to cherish.

"Kitty, plagued sawbones here says I must report to a new C.-in-C."

"Oh, no, no!"

"Sorry," Fortescue gasped, but looked quite cheerful. "Orders."

One of the captains began to blow his nose, made a honking noise.

The minister stepped forward. "My dear," said he, "let me spare the patient strength. It is Colonel Fortescue's earnest wish that I join you to him in holy matrimony."

Had the roof came crashing down, Katie could not have been more supremely astounded. Married? *Married* to Colonel Fortescue? To a real fine gentlemen like him? Katie Tryon a colonel's lady?

"Oh no!" she choked. "Not me. I couldn't. It wouldn't be right. I — I ain't fit."

"Bother!" the colonel wheezed. "Rubbish! Damned miserable return — for happiness you've given — old crock. Don't like stick-sucking nephews. You — courage, breeding. Make something of your life. Dammit girl — give me your hand!"

The minister drew a deep breath. "Dearly beloved," he began very softly, "we are gathered here in the sight of God and this company to join together in holy matrimony this man and this woman — "

In the Delaware

A frigate chased the *Lady Catherine*. Cracking on sail after sail, the man-of-war pursued her right into the entrance of Delaware Bay. She even harried the sloop past Point Norris. But when a big earthwork mounting cannons loomed below the village of Selem, she slowed. Then, as a trio of row-galleys began pulling out from shore, she sullenly came about. Just for spite, her commander fired a broadside, and because his trajectory was very flat, everyone could see the cannonballs come skipping over the river, like stones scaled by a small boy. They sank, however, before they reached the *Lady Catherine*.

"I'm a hundred years older, by God!" Captain Ord sighed, surrendering the wheel to his quartermaster. He shook as if seized by an ague. Rob, too, was mighty relieved to see the brown-and-blue-painted man-of-war standing out to sea. From the *Lady Catherine*'s people he had had accounts of the way prisoners were treated aboard His Majesty's ships and he had no desire for first-hand experience. Looking white about the mouth, Mr. Peacock came up from below and quietly ground out a gunner's match under his heel.

"What in tarnation you thinking of?" Ord roared. "You know it's against orders to go below with an open spark. Want to blow us all to hell?"

Mr. Peacock smiled. "No. But that powder wasn't going to get back into British hands."

Rob stared, felt his mouth go dry. Good God! Why, the idiot had been ready to blow them all to hell!

Ever since they had parted from the *Packet* off the Bermudas, the voyage had been speedy, and everyone felt fine over having lifted so much powder. The officers and the crew never got tired of telling one another what they had done. Every time, the teller's part grew more heroic. One night Rob lost patience.

Said he, "You couldn't have done a blamed thing without whale boats and Henry Tucker's running things like he did. Just remember that when you get ashore."

Mr. Peacock nodded. "You're right, Ashton. I'll admit I didn't trust them any farther than I can heave a bull by the tail, but they did their share."

Without waiting for orders, Captain Ord brought his sloop into the wind and let go an anchor. Evidently satisfied that they were not needed, two gundelos put back towards a little cove in the low-rising riverbank. Upstream sprawled Salem, a neat-appearing village of red-painted houses. The whole riverbank and a forest of soft-looking trees behind it was veiled in a blue-bronze haze.

It was ten — no, eleven days ago that they had dropped the Bermudas below the horizon. Today, therefore, must be the twenty-fifth.

Raggedly shipping her starboard oars, the leading gundelo came alongside. A well-dressed fellow caught a rope ladder and swarmed up the side with remarkable agility. He wore a definite air of authority and his deeply pitted face was tense. Without acknowledging Captain Ord's salute, he ran over to Mr. Peacock, and looking him square in the eye, asked, "Did you?"

"Yes, Mr. Duane," the other replied, offering his hand.

The newcomer beamed, flung ecstatic arms about Mr. Peacock's shoulders, then pumped his hands so hard it looked as if he wanted to wring the arms off.

"Splendid work, sir! You have no idea how relieved everyone will be." Then Mr. Duane rushed over and shook Ord's hand just as enthusiastically. "Capital work. Capital, Captain! How in the world did you manage?"

Mr. Peacock interrupted quickly, "That is a long story, sir, and the report must be made to Mr. Franklin and Mr. Morris."

The other smiled his apology. "Of course. Stupid of me to forget. Got carried away."

Of the conversation Rob heard only the beginning. He had become absorbed in the approach of a second gundelo. There seemed something familiar about a figure on the row-galley's steering transom. A suspicion formed, grew quickly.

He turned to Mr. Duane. "Sir, can you tell me who that fellow is? The short man?"

The Pennsylvanian answered carelessly. "He? Oh, he's a Yankee delegate to Congress. Massachusetts Committee sent him down to advise us on naval matters."

He was right. It was Stephen Farish yonder. He was mighty pleased, tickled no end at finding him again. What ages had passed since last he had seen Farish sailing off in the *Assistance* with David and Johnny Gilmorin.

"Well, Captain," he yelled, "you're a long way off your course!"

The New Englander goggled. "Well, I'm a son of a seacook!"

He turned to the gundelo's captain and immediately the oars quickened their beat. Quick as a squirrel, Captain Farish scaled the *Lady Catherine*'s salt-streaked side, paused on the rail until he spied Rob.

"Jumping Jehosophat!" he exclaimed. "This is mighty fine. How are you, sir?"

"Right well," Rob gripped Farish's fist very hard. "And you?"

[156]

"Tolerable, sir, tolerable. I wrote down to Mr. Jameison and was plumb took aback when he said you had pulled out of Norfolk lock, stock, and barrel. Said you'd sailed for furrin parts. That correct?"

"It was," Rob admitted slowly. "Things got pretty bad for me. But I'm back."

Mr. Duane of the Pennsylvania Committee of Safety began to look restless.

"Mr. Peacock," said he. "I guess you had better move your cargo to Philadelphia as quickly as possible. Committee's orders."

Rob noticed how careful he was not to use the word "powder."

A lantern burned late in Rob's cabin. Long since, he and Farish had laid aside coats and waistcoats. The remnants of a meal and a third bottle of port stood between them. Sachem had yawned and yawned until Rob bade him clear up and be off. But instead of going to bed, the half-breed went on deck and lingered there, staring eagerly at this new land. Laws! It seemed to go on forever. And there *were* forests and rivers.

Rob lounged on his new trunk and the sea captain sat on a locker sucking at a peculiarly rank clay pipe. They could, when they chose to look, see the riverbank slipping steadily by.

"Well," Farish was concluding, "like I said, your brother got us jailed but he got us out. I'll say that for him and, now that I look back on it, I don't abominate him the way I did. I guess maybe I, well, I see what he was driving at."

Rob sighed, passed a hand over his eyes, then rubbed their lids. Now that he had money again he wasn't feeling so bitter. He wanted to see David again.

Once Rob had finished talking, Farish relit his pipe and described how he had tackled the Massachusetts Committee about fitting out some cruisers. Once he had pointed out how British transports were, all unarmed, bringing supplies to the enemy, they got to work and fitted out the *Margaretta*. In quick succession she captured the *Diligent* and *Tattamagouche*, supply vessels. The stores they took pleased General Washington as much as the loss of them depressed the English cooped up in Boston.

"Seeing how things worked out on the bay, the Pennsylvanians wanted to do the same, and I got sent down here to tell 'em how. Says I to Mr. Benjamin Franklin, "If us fellers make the water unhealthy for the king's ships, his troops will just naturally starve. Why don't we build ships of our own, real men-of-war?"

Rob sat up and, shaking his head, poured a glass of port. "We couldn't hope to fight the Royal Navy! They'd blow us out of the water."

Philadelphia

On arising, Rob went straight up on deck. He found it fine to smell the land again, to see familiar types of houses and barns. Even the muddy current stirred warming memories. Above a bend in the river showed the steeples and roofs of a great city. Philadelphia with a population of almost twenty thousand was the largest and richest city in British America. Mr. Peacock said it boasted several theaters and nobody knew how many taverns. British naval officers liked Philadelphia best of all American ports; the girls there were jolly and some of them not above an unpremeditated cruise between the sheets.

Captain Ord, Mr. Peacock and Mr. Duane hurriedly disembarked and joined a knot of serious-looking men in dark blue uniforms. To the opposite side of the wharf a small sloop was tied up with hatches open, crew ready and whips rigged. Even while the *Lady*'s hawsers were being made fast, laborers began dropping onto her deck and took off the new arrival's hatches. Without delay they commenced to hoist out the powder and a low murmur went up when the sun shone on broad white arrows done on the keg ends — it was the government mark. In rapid succession barrels were heaved on deck, weighed and checked by an officer in a dingy blue and white tunic. A good half of the king's powder was sent rumbling and bumping over to the smaller vessel.

Rob was superintending Sachem's efforts to pack the last of his gear when Farish hunted him out. The New Englander was grinning, showing all the gaps in his teeth.

"You should hear what that Peacock feller has been telling the committeemen about you. I cal'late he's a sprier storyteller than Dan'l Dee-foe."

"Reckon he must be. Why all this hurry over trans-shipping?"

Farish looked grave, closed the door. "You'll not let on?"

"Never a word."

"Well then, the ordinance officer at Cambridge made return of thirty-six rounds a man but when the general checked up he found there weren't but eight! If the British take a mind to come out and fight, they can whip our troops all to hollow. May have done so already. There's rumors about that the siege is going to be lifted right away. Now you understand?"

"Yes. But in that case why don't they take all our load? Washington must need every speck of it."

"You ain't dealt with the Congress yet. A bunch of delegates are dead set to send an expedition against Canada. Maybe two. It's a pet idea of old Ben Franklin's. I ain't none too sure this much powder will do any good. Still, like we say to home, 'half a bed is better than none.'"

Mr. Peacock and Captain Ord had already departed when Rob followed Farish on deck, but they were in time to see the powder sloop cast off. Could it slip past that frigate lurking between Cape Henlopen and Cape May? Suddenly it came to him that this might be Mr. Franklin's real reason for holding back so much of the cargo.

On the wharf he paused, looked about. It was at once familiar and depressing to see so many dismantled ships. There were even more in sight than in Norfolk. Paradoxically, a shipyard across the river was going full blast. When Rob remarked on it and on the size of two vessels being laid down, the mariner winked and looked wise.

That same morning word was brought that Mr. Franklin wished a few words with Mr. Ashton. Would he be good enough to call? Captain Farish might stop by also. It was with some trepidation that Rob accepted, and around three of the afternoon set off.

Outside Mechanics' Hall, Farish halted, squinting up at its ivy-hung walls of red brick.

"Better take a good look," the New Englander advised, head cocked to one side. "History is being made in there; some good, some bad." His big voice thickened. "But this Congress will not disband until Parliament guarantees our rights."

Dr. Benjamin Franklin was working in a dark banyan and a Turkey-red turban, the day being too hot for a wig. Beside him stood an austere, severely aristocratic gentleman in black and white. Mr. Peacock came forward from the background, presented Rob. Farish they had met before.

Rob, taking Mr. Franklin's hand, felt his fears vanish. Whatever he tried to say he reckoned would be taken in the right way. What a depth of humanity and humor lurked in the septuagenarian's gray eyes. His head was big and its forehead was so lofty it swept up like the dome of a building. Gold-rimmed spectacles with square lenses had been pushed above the old man's brows. A trace of sensuousness marked the set of Mr. Franklin's mouth, but it served rather to mellow than to weaken his serene, surprisingly alert expression.

Smiling, he waved Rob to a chair, set down the quill with which he had been writing and said, "Mr. Peacock has been telling Mr. Morris and me about the assistance you afforded him in the matter of the Bermuda powder." Mr. Franklin pulled down his spectacles, shot Mr. Morris a fleeting glance. "Our friends in Bermuda will not regret their part. I am sure the Congress will prove — in a practical sense — how sensible it is of their genuine goodwill." The old man's manner was entirely grave, but a faint twinkle danced at the backs of his eyes. It conveyed knowledge that Franklin very well understood the true motives of the West Enders.

Morris smiled pallidly. "Indeed, Mr. Ashton, this powder could not have arrived at a more propitious moment. Perhaps someday you will do me the honor of dining with me?"

Rob shook hands all around and prepared to leave, but Mr. Franklin looked over the tops of his spectacles. "A moment more of your time, my dear Mr. Ashton. I have come to believe that abstract praise is stimulating, but not nourishing. Is there perhaps some concrete matter in which I might, to your advantage, use my inconsiderable influence?"

Rob's heart lifted. "Why, yes sir. I would like mighty well to come across eight twelve-pound cannon, six swivels, and powder and shot enough for them."

Mr. Morris wheeled, definitely startled. "God bless my soul! Well, sir, and what can you be wanting with cannon?"

"I fear that is not the point," Franklin interposed. "The point is that Mr. Ashton wants them. From the exactitude of his request one might infer that he knows what he is about." A fold of the turban flapped when he inclined his head. "Rest assured, Mr. Ashton, that I shall do my best. Pray, where can one communicate with you?"

Rob told him; then, perspiring heavily into his stock, went out. Mr. Morris's voice, sharp and petulant, followed him.

"But hang it, Ben, it's illegal, downright illegal to sell cannons to private individuals, and you know it!"

"Tut, tut," came the memorable voice. "If we wait for lawyers to pass on our decisions, we shall find about our necks something less pleasing than linen."

During the next week Rob devoted his time to combing shipyards and little estuaries along the pleasant banks of the Delaware. He wanted only one type of vessel and about her he had definite ideas. She must be fairly new, very fast, roomy in her hold, and big enough to mount eight guns. She must have a good-sized forecastle to accommodate the big crew a privateer called for. Copper sheathing, too.

Time and again a sloop or a brig came reasonably near filling his requirements, but always there was something wrong and Rob wouldn't have her. Even when the owners cut their asking price to shreds, the solid young Virginian would not listen and went rowing off in his chartered barge. He offered so good a price, three hundred Spanish dollars per ton, that men came from 'way downriver, from over in Jersey, from the upper Chesapeake inviting him to their yards.

Whenever Farish could get away from manifold sessions with the committee Congress had appointed to study the question of a navy, he would join Rob in rowing about the harbor. Every few days there would be new vessels to look at. By the dozen, ships were being confiscated by Provincial Committees of Safety for violations of the association.

The Speedwell

Next morning at breakfast Rob picked up his host's copy of the *Pennsylvania Gazette* and idly ran through it. He perused the usual advertisements for runaway slaves and bound boys, the rewards offered for deserters from this or that regiment. A woman with "a young breast of milk" begged possible clients to inquire of the printer.

Brig *Speedwell* to be sold at publick Vendue by order of Penna. Comm. Safety. 300 T. burthen, now lying in the River at Gloucester. Very fast. Bermuda-built of cedar.

Speedwell? Rob fumbled an instant then as soon as he remembered, grabbed his hat and rushed out. Like a bull of Bashan he charged into Farish's quarters at the Bunch of Grapes and routed him out.

"Come along!" he cried. "I must have your opinion."

Being of cedar and therefore wormproof, the *Speedwell* required no sheathing, either of lead or of more expensive copper. The weight thus saved should help her footing, Farish argued. There were so many ships idle only two other bidders put in an appearance, and the auctioneer was all for postponing his vendue until Farish stalked over and said a few words in his ear. Strangely enough, he changed his mind then.

From truck to keelson, from stem to stern Rob examined the prize. Then he went over every bit of the planking he could get at; studied the masts and yards for cracks; had the sails set down and the cables brought on deck. He sniffed at the bilges and found them sweet. The pumps were adequate and worked well when he tested them. He couldn't believe his offer of eighteen thousand dollars would be snapped up by the vendue agent.

"Mr. Ashton, you were overhasty," Farish reproved. "With a little haggling you might have got her for seventeen thousand or maybe sixteen thousand five hundred."

Rob said, "What's the difference? The cash goes to the committee and they will buy supplies for the army with it."

Farish chuckled. "You ain't such a dumblock, Mr. Ashton, even if you are a Virginian."

Rob grinned and cocked an eye at the rigging, freshly tarred and bright in the sunlight. "What do you mean?"

"Next month you'll be importing supplies that Congress needs, and get it all back."

"Do you think those bulwarks are solid enough to stand shot?" was Rob's innocent query.

Farish laughed and slapped his thigh. "You're pretty smart, by God-

[161]

freys. Eh? Oh yes, they're solid enough, but I'd support the deck beams below. In a heavy sea, gun carriages can throw a lot of weight about."

A weight lifted from Rob's heart. It was easy to visualize the *Speedwell* mounting eight guns and carrying half a dozen swivels on her rails. Provided he could find a good-sized crew of the right sort, it would take a big man-of-war to make him heave to. But the problem of manning his brig gave him little concern. Privateering had not yet begun and hundreds of able-bodied merchant seamen were hungrily tramping the streets.

Though Rob hadn't said a word of what he was planning, Farish marked his enthusiasm.

"Don't run on too fast," he advised. "Like I told you, the Congress ain't ready to issue letters of marque."

Rob looked into Farish's bright blue eyes. "When did I say anything about taking prizes?"

"Nary a word, but I guessed you were figuring on it."

"Not for a while. Right now I only want guns so's I can drive off anybody who tries meddling with my trading. Seems a man has to fight these days for the right to carry a cargo of goods."

"I'd say it took a smart feller like you a good while to figger that out," was Farish's dry comment.

"I reckon it did, Stephen, but from now on — God help anyone who gets in my way!"

Stars on the Sea

Preface

The further one delves into the history of the War for Independence, the more ample, and therefore the more contradictory, the evidence becomes. At the outset of this struggle few people bothered to make observations or to record their impressions. Officers were then too inexperienced to realize the vital necessity of preserving the orders they issued and received. In crossing the boundary from 1775 to 1776, an author's early difficulty in securing any accounts whatsoever changes to a perplexity over the proper evaluation of too much information. A writer in this position, therefore, is forced to analyze and interpret as accurately as possible all available material.

In the matter of the siege of Charleston, for example, it was necessary to study, item by item, eight authentic accounts, all of which varied sharply as to detail. When an eyewitness to a battle or an event is proved to have occupied a given position, and then calmly tells of happenings which logically he could not possibly have seen, one is inclined to question his accuracy — even though the balance of his account may be flawless.

Other than patently historical characters, the men and women appearing in *Stars on the Sea* are wholly fictional — the Bennetts, the Percivals, the Proveaux, the Dulacs are imaginary families. They do, however, represent families typical of the time and region. Incredible as some of the episodes described in Saint-Domingue may seem, they are nevertheless based on well-substantiated accounts.

To the author it has long been a disappointment that the attack on the Bahamas — the first expedition ever attempted by an American naval force — has been so seldom and so inadequately recounted. In attempting to correct this situation, it has been the author's purpose to picture America as she was when she lacked a strong navy and to show how deeply an enemy blockade can affect every walk of American life.

Sergeant Bennett

The clouds darkening Boston Harbor looked so low and ghostlike Sergeant Timothy Bennett guessed snow would soon begin falling. In fact, the jumbled dark roofs and church spires of distant Cambridge were already graying out of sight. He would welcome the snow. The cantonments around Roxbury were becoming mighty foul and unsightly, so the fall of a few inches of snow would be like spreading a clean cloth over a table marked by wet glasses. A snowstorm would please Lucy, too. Somehow the sight of falling flakes exhilarated, animated her.

The sergeant's red, useful-looking hands tightened about his musket. He would have welcomed a pair of mittens, knitted loose, the way Desire Harmony worked them. Good thing his sister had been a handy knitter ever since she'd been big enough to hold a set of needles. At the sting of his chapped fingers, Bennett grimaced. Should have dosed them with bear's grease before reporting for guard duty. Lucy surely couldn't find much to admire in such rough hunks of redness.

Shouldering Abner Hull's musket, he set off down the fire platform towards an eighteen-pound cannon marking the further limit of post number six. Halting, he once again painstakingly studied the vast gray and white panorama below the Heights of Roxbury. In a field beyond a system of bastions protecting the British position on Boston Neck, some crows briskly explored the snow between rows of tattered cornstalks.

In succession, the crows arose and, cawing, flapped heavily off in the direction of Charlestown. The sergeant's wide-set gray eyes narrowed. An enemy detail was relieving sentries shivering in a pair of *flèches* the British engineers had erected in advance of their main defenses on the neck. For all their high bearskin hats and gray greatcoats, the enemy grenadiers looked small and insignificant from the summit of Roxbury Hill.

Timothy Bennett rested the firelock against a timber bracing the parapet, began to flail his arms. Damn! His homemade sergeant's epaulet of red worsted was fetching loose again.

Crimanently! Tonight the wind had teeth like a ferret. It must be a real blizzard blowing up, his wounded leg was aching so. Still, he mustn't show it. Not many fellows of twenty-two were sergeants.

The crows, he noticed, still beat into the wind over a pair of floating batteries which had been caught by a cold snap and frozen into the ice of Back Bay. Now vicious flurries were powdering that redoubt on Breed's Hill which last summer had cost General Gage a thousand and more good men in winning.

Sergeant Bennett swung sharply at a sound of a muffled cadence. He

[167]

made out a line of figures advancing from the direction of camp. Heads held low, the relief bucked the gale until they found a measure of shelter in the lee of the firing platform. They had begun stamping their feet when from somewhere upwind came a flat, quick report. Bennett sighed in his relief. That had been a rifle, and the British had no rifle companies. He wondered why a rifle didn't give off a fine big-bellied *boom!* like a smooth-bore musket.

"Hear that?" asked one of the relief.

"Yes," grunted the corporal of the guard. "'Pears like them goddamn riflers must be drunk again." The corporal had knotted a muffler over his hat and under his chin. It gave him a mumpy appearance.

"Them Pennsylvany Dirty Shirts ain't ever satisfied les'n they are bragging or carving somebody up. Sure act crazy as loons. Fall out, number six!"

Most of the Second Rhode Island's cantonments were miserable; just three·tiers of logs laid cabin fashion and capped by one of the canvas tents which had sheltered the regiment ever since June. Colonel Daniel Hitchcock had ordered the company streets to be laid out in orderly fashion, even if most of his fellow colonels didn't take the bother.

Striding down Prospect Hill towards Roxbury village, Bennett noted that many sentries had of necessity built watch fires. He figured the blizzard would surely last all night; as fast as it fell, the snow kept blowing off the roofs — an ominous sign.

On the outskirts of the village, Tim Bennett became aware of yells and shouts emanating from beyond a snow-haloed cluster of lights.

A drunken voice began bawling, "Guard! Help! Help! Wheresh them damn' guards?"

Unfortunately, the road led directly toward a blur of men milling about in front of the Red Bull. It was a miserable place, and Joe Child claimed that the liquor served there wasn't fit to rub on a dog's backside. When he saw the frightened way the crowd kept backing away, he began to walk warily. This looked like no ordinary brawl.

A bottle came crashing through a windowpane, disappeared into the snowdrift.

Inside the inn a woman was screeching, "He's gone crazy! Stop him. Oh, my Gawd, he'll slay someone! Don't, Sam, don't ye dare! Don't, fer Gawd's sake!"

A weird cry, unearthly and more fear-inspiring than Bennett had ever heard, beat out into the street. There was an animal savagery in its quality that set the hair to twisting and ingling on his neck. Only thing comparable was the cry of a catamount he'd heard screech years ago when visiting Grandpa up in Deerfield, Massachusetts.

Men were calling through the driving snow, "What's up?"

"Ranger's drunk."

Furniture crashed over and the woman screamed shriller than ever when into the bright yellow rectangle of the inn's door swayed a loose-jointed figure. Sleeve and cape fringes aswing, the rifleman glared about until a Connecticut corporal in a calfskin coat made a grab at him. Tim had never seen anyone move with such amazing speed. All in one motion the rifleman freed a long knife; his arm licked out with the speed of a snake's tongue. Forearm squirting streams of blood over the dirty snow, the corporal staggered back.

Though a few men seemed too astonished to move, most of the crowd broke and ran. So for the first time Tim Bennett got a clear impression of that gaunt figure in buckskins. Dark features convulsed, wild mane of black hair flying, the rifleman hesitated. Something like a horse's tail was in his left hand. He was fighting drunk all right. Suddenly he sprang out into the street and, brandishing his broad-bladed knife, he backed a recruit against the inn wall.

"You got it?"

"G-got w-what, mister?"

"You stole my skelp, you no-'count piss-ant!"

The boy wriggled, his eyes enormous. "No! No! Don't hurt me. I ain't got it. I ain't seen it." In his eagerness to get away, the recruit fell sprawling in the snow.

"I'm a r'arin', tearin' wolverine!" roared the man in greasy buckskins, "and I c'n lick any ten o' you psalm-shoutin' sons o' smoothbores." He lurched violently sidewise and long rawhide thrums decorating the front of his hunting shirt fell apart, revealing the word LIBERTY printed in white across his chest.

From an upstairs window the innkeeper began yelling, "Guard! Fetch the guard! Oh, my God, why don't somebody shoot that Pennsylvany son of a bitch?"

"Shut up," snarled the ranger. "Some Yankee whoreson has stole one o' my skelps. Had six, all good Tuscarora and Cherokee hair — one's gone."

At the Congress Inn

Through a layer of steam and frost dimming the diapered and leaded window panes of the Congress Inn, Sergeant Bennett saw that the taproom was jampacked. After brushing flakes from his bottle-green riding cape, he stepped into an atmosphere rank with beer and tobacco fumes. He felt as if someone in a hot and smoky cloak had flung both arms about him. Voices pitched to a fourth or fifth drink rang in his ears.

"Yassah? Tek yo' cape, suh?" Lately the Widow Haskins had given up

[169]

serving wenches, had bought some little black boys. Her wenches, she declared, became pregnant so often she couldn't ever keep her staff full.

Heated faces swung to consider him when he clumped into the candle-light and began kicking the snow from his shoes. "Hey! Shut that damn' door!"

Behind the bar glowed the Widow Haskins' winter apple of a face. Right now it might have been freshly varnished, it was so shiny. Her white linen blouse was stained with sweat and splashings.

"Hi, Rhode Island," a nasal voice greeted. "Been over to Breed's Hill yet? Didn't see you there the seventh of June. Where was you?"

The taproom bellowed. All the army knew that on the day of the great battle both Rhode Island regiments had been kept cursing and sweating in idleness on Jamaica Plain.

Bennett's chilled lips formed a stiff grin. He made the stock reply, "We were too busy sleeping with your sister."

Ensign Joe Child came from the corner table at which he had been solemnly rolling dice, left hand against right. "Hi, Tim. You're so prettied I hardly knew you."

"Lucy here?"

"Yep. Her ma, too."

"Where is she? How does she look?"

Joe Child removed the churchwarden pipe and looked solemn. "Why, I should say Mrs. Percival looks positively elegant. Wearing a beaver tippet, green bombazine, and that same old be-damned-to-you look. You're the lucky boy, my lad."

"You go to hell, Joe," Bennett snapped. This was no time for jesting. He sought the widow.

"They are sharing my three-shilling room, front." Thrusting out her lower lip, the proprietress blew a drop of sweat from the end of her nose. "Lord's mercy, young man, but that old lady's a tartar. Went on a rare rampage, she did, when I told her she and her daughter would have to share a big bed with the colonel's lady, Mrs. Hitchcock. As if beds 'round Roxbury weren't skurce as honest niggers."

Tim Bennett perplexedly nursed bruised knuckles. Mrs. Percival in a temper was a fine person to steer clear of. He drew a deep breath, smiled, "Pray inform Miss Percival that Sergeant Bennett is — er — here."

"Inform? Fiddlesticks. Pray tell her yourself." She heaved up a tray of brass-bound leathern mugs. "I'm busier than a cat with its fur afire." By the cider barrel she paused and filled a brace of pewter tankards.

Intuition told Tim Bennett it wouldn't do to knock at Lucy's door like a confounded chambermaid. Behind the bar a small Negro was sleepily burnishing pewter with sand and a handful of rushes. He had a bad cold, was snuffling drearily, but, glimpsing a half penny in Bennett's palm, he brightened right up. "Yassuh?"

"Convey Sergeant Bennett's compliments to Mistress Percival —"

Smiling shyly, the slave cocked a bullet head to one side. "Mi'tess who, suh?"

"Mistress Percival. Inform her that I await her — er, below."

"Yassuh!"

At the foot of the stair Bennett cocked a hopeful ear.

"For pity's sake, child," came Mrs. Percival's staccato inflection. "Blow your nose, then tell Mr. Bennett I will be down directly."

Tim Bennett wanted to cuss. Why in blazes did Lucy's ma forever have to keep butting in? She must have been young and in love once — or had she? Maybe not. Folks claimed old Ike had only married to save himself the salary of a good bookkeeper. If ever two people were adept in coaxing a sixpence into doing a shilling's work, it was Lizzie and Ike Percival.

So Mrs. Percival would be down directly? Choked with disappointment he plunked himself down at Joe Child's table. "Be patient," he advised himself. "Lucy will come down soon." She must know how desperately he awaited the sight of her. Damnation! This evening wasn't going at all as he had anticipated. First that rifleman, then the crowded inn, now Mrs. Percival's interference. The gilt was fast rubbing off of this shining hour.

"You hear what is going on in Sullivan's brigade?"

"No."

"Well, they say the New Hampshire officers ain't rejoining. Damned hay-shakers figure they stand to get slighted in the New Army. One of their majors heard he would only rate a captaincy in the Continental Service so he hiked himself off home. Fact."

"Good riddance," grunted Bennett.

"Maybe," Child agreed, "but he took a whole battalion with him. They were all from the same county. It's bad. We shouldn't have so many men from the same district in one regiment."

"But it's only natural, Joe. The gentleman from Virginia will find it hard to alter that."

The ensign wagged his fair head. "It will have to be changed — along with short enlistments, different pay rates, and the men's electing company officers.

"Now take these lunar month enlistments —" Joe Child went on.

"What's wrong with them? My company enlisted lunar month. Works all right with us."

"Of course. Why should you men cavil at getting paid for twenty-eight days? New Hampshire, Massachusetts, and the rest of us Rhode Islanders must serve thirty or thirty-one days for the same pay. 'Tisn't fair, or sensible."

Suddenly Joe Child's foot nudged Tim Bennett's. "Make ready your sword, St. George," he chuckled. "Here comes your dragon."

Her high-bridged nose wrinkled in distaste, Mrs. Percival was advancing into the taproom with the air of a martyr exploring a den of lions.

[171]

Bennett jumped up and made the erect, gaunt figure a formal bow — like that of the officers off the royal ships — but it was an awkward attempt. The Society of Friends did not approve of salutes, bows and curtseys. Expressions of respect, they maintained, must be reserved for the Creator alone.

A mirthless smile briefly disarranged the habitual "prunes, prisms and persimmons" set to Mrs. Percival's mouth. "I trust I find you in good health, Timothy?"

"Yes, ma'am. I hope —"

"Oh, dear, such a dreadful, common place. Pah! How can a body breathe such air? Just you answer me that, Joe Child, and don't go sneaking off." Her expression relaxed. "I don't bite — often. Believe it or not."

Joe abandoned his furtive retreat, looked more like a schoolboy than a commissioned officer as he said, "The entire Rhode Island Army regrets, ma'am, that Roxbury is so small a village. Its comforts are — er — deucedly limited."

Mrs. Percival looked levelly about. "I have seen worse inns. Well, Timothy?"

"I am most sensible of your tarrying here on your journey home, ma'am." The words came out not at all as Tim Bennett had rehearsed them. Hang it! Lizzie Percival's small dark eyes were appraising him to the last detail. She must be seeing how really dirty he was, for all his pitiful attempts to slick up.

"You look older by two years," she announced. "Thinned out, kind of. You have not been acquiring loose habits, I trust?"

"Er — Lucy? Is she well, ma'am?"

"Thriving." Mrs. Percival's ruler mark of a mouth relaxed. "At present, my vain child is prettying herself in your honor." Without change of expression, she suddenly demanded, "Are your father's ships safe? Two of them are so long overdue, people in Newport are — well, wondering."

"They must be secure, ma'am, else I would have heard." Though Tim Bennett spoke easily, he was no little disturbed at Mrs. Percival's manner.

Wouldn't it be politer to tell Mrs. Percival his great news about the commission rather than save it for Lucy? The question bothered him. Women admired uniforms, even the older women.

"The reason I ventured into this bedlam, Timothy, was for a brief word with you," Mrs. Percival briskly informed him over the hum of conversation. "It's my opinion that the sooner you quit this playing at soldier the better. Between the Congress and the king's ministers, anything can happen these days. If a body is to keep his trade, he is wise to be Johnny-on-the-spot."

To Tim Bennett, the atmosphere grew suddenly smothering.

"Your enlistment expires December first, don't it?" Mrs. Percival was fixing him with a penetrating look. For all she must be near sixty, her hair was still black as an Indian's.

Falling all over himself mentally, he blurted, "Why, why, no, ma'am. We all enrolled for eight months; means we must serve till the tenth. But I had something I wanted to tell — "

" — Never mind about that," she cut in. "You get back home by the *first week* in December or you'll regret it!" Lizzie Percival's jaw muscles softened a trifle. "Now don't go telling everyone I advised you so. If you and Lucy weren't promised, wild horses wouldn't get me to talk like this. Lucy and I are heading home day after tomorrow."

"But — please. I — had something to tell you —"

The Commander-in-Chief

It was only a quarter past ten when Tim Bennett reached a low, white-painted dwelling doing duty as headquarters for the "Rhode Island Army of Observation." He stepped by two privates on guard at the entrance. They made a smart appearance, thanks to new blue and white uniforms. For a miracle they had bayonets fixed to their King's Arm muskets.

"Sergeant Bennett, sir, reporting to General Greene."

The adjutant, a yellow-complexioned, solemn young fellow with a bad squint, inclined his head slightly. "General Greene is occupied; take a seat."

"Will I have to wait long, sir? You see — I — "

"How in blazes would I know?" snapped the adjutant. "Am I a mind-reader?"

A single colorless drop clung to the end of this officer's nose, Tim observed. Every time he signed a document the drop trembled and threatened to fall. But it never did.

Here it was almost half after eleven. Damn all generals! Why couldn't Greene see a man straight off? Even now he still could make it to the Congress Inn, but he'd have no time to wash.

He was waiting for Greene's orderly when, outside, the sentries' hands went *slap! slap!* on their firelocks. That extra loud click of their heels argued someone of rank.

From the head of the stairs an orderly called, "The general will see Sergeant Bennett."

Tim felt better. His report shouldn't require five minutes to deliver. Now he was sure of seeing Lucy and if he described what had happened in the Connecticut camp, she ought to understand why he couldn't possibly come home now.

He had started upstairs when the adjutant got up so quickly he overset his chair. "Atten-shun, there!"

Something in his voice immobilized Tim and he stood to rigid attention beside the newel-post. A blinding glare off the snow flooded the hall. Feet stamped and spurs jingled, then a square-shouldered figure in a wide cloak entered. Tim noted he was so tall he had to incline his head to avoid knocking a blue and buff cockade against the lintel.

He was the Commander-in-Chief of all the Provincial Armies. To the last detail General Washington's uniform appeared faultless. Every last button glittered and the smother of French lace at his throat and wrists fairly sparkled.

There was no doubt that General Washington was chilled through. His lips, tight drawn over ill-fitting false teeth, were of a purplish blue and his clear gray-blue eyes were watering so hard that a succession of tears traced bright channels over the vivid pink of his cheeks.

He smiled stiffly and said to the adjutant, "Pray present my compliments to General Greene. Will he devote to me a moment of his time?"

The adjutant fairly bounded upstairs.

"Beastly cold," the general remarked to his staff officers, then sought the fireplace. As he stood warming himself, his heavy riding cape fell open, revealing a light blue ribbon of watered silk slanting across his waistcoat.

Tim remained at attention though the general's aides began pulling off gloves and blowing on their fingers.

After a bit Washington called, "Pray stand at ease. One forgets on occasion that you Rhode Islanders are so well disciplined."

Tim Bennett covertly surveyed the Southerner. Crimanently! There was something mighty impressive about the C.-in-C. — even if he was a Virginian.

Frantic activity was ensuing upstairs; chairs scraped back and forth, feet raced about. General Washington's eyes flickered upwards and a smile tugged briefly at the corners of his mouth.

"It would appear that General Greene is not expecting company," he remarked, drawing his thick cloak further back. Tim now saw broad lapels of pale buff secured by golden buttons and the guard of the French dress sword. It was of gold and handsomely jeweled. Flecks of mud, however, dappled the general's boots clear up to his knees.

"You will reenlist, I presume?" The general's voice was grave and even and without a trace of the pompousness or ill-temper you generally got from a general officer.

"Why — why, yes, sir. I expect to."

"Capital! The New Army stands in great need of experienced men. Young ones endure a hard campaign better than oldsters."

The general's aides crossed to the window and stood looking down a row of gray beeches edging the drive. The general turned back to the fire, wiped his cheeks on the back of his hand. "You have served since when, Sergeant?"

"Since last May, sir."

"Then you must have fought at Breed's Hill?"

"No, sir. We were ordered — to Jamaica Plain."

"Well, then, you men still have an opportunity to demonstrate your mettle. Perhaps it is just as well." He sighed. "Quite a few of the gentry who fought there seem inclined to rest forever on their laurels. But you were at Lechmere's Point?"

"Yes, sir." Under the general's reserved friendliness, Tim felt less ill at ease.

"Your regiment was little hurt?"

"Yes, sir. We had only one wounded."

"Who was he?"

"I, sir."

The general's smile widened and Tim noted that, sure enough, his teeth were not his own. "My compliments, Sergeant. Most men would long since have been describing their wound."

Greene's adjutant reappeared, hurried downstairs. At his heels was the sturdy, squarish figure of the Rhode Island brigadier. Tim guessed that Greene and the commander-in-chief understood one another, despite the fact that one was a Virginia aristocrat and the other had begun life as a Quaker blacksmith.

"Good morning, sir. Rhode Island is unduly honored," Greene declared. Both were of above-average height; the Northerner broader across the shoulders and shorter in the leg. Greene had a slight limp. Even though it didn't hamper the brigadier it had kept him out of the militia a long while. "I was contemplating a ride to Cambridge even as you rode up."

General Washington's smile faded. "I have heard of this trouble among Colonel Spencer's men. I am most eager to gain your impressions." As a delicate hint, the general's level gaze wandered over to the staircase. "Shall we repair to my office?"

"With pleasure, sir," General Washington replied, making a courteous suggestion of a bow.

Before they reappeared the clock stood at a quarter past two.

Suppose he decided to go home? Tim thought. He couldn't. His enlistment wasn't up until December fifteenth. Pure bad luck it carried eight days over that date, which in Newport appeared to be of such considerable significance.

He seated himself on the musket chest, drummed fingers on its greasy lid. The Connecticut men must be well on their way home. For all that Lee had said about them, they had been perfectly within their rights. It had required the courage of their convictions to march off. Pa certainly did need him; there was no getting around that.

There isn't a doubt but my enlistment is up, he thought. Just to make sure — "Thirty days hath September, April, June and November." Thirty-one days in May gives a three days' credit. In June I get two more, July and August six more days. Why, right now I've exceeded my enlistment, served thirteen extra days with no pay. Um. All I'm asking is the use of eight of these days — and I'm coming back, too. No one can reasonably find fault. Nobody can say I ain't patriotic.

He sanded, sealed the letter he had written with candle grease, then stuffed it into Captain Allen's pigeonhole.

When he closed the kitchen door on the supply sergeant's snufflings, the stars were very bright; it was so cold the snow creaked under his feet. For a staff he selected a tall stick from the fuel supply.

Light-heartedly Tim Bennett struck off along the icy road to Dedham.

The Blue Hills

Sam Higsby, late private in Thompson's Pennsylvania Rangers, felt elegant at being shut of civilization. Being cooped up, living on fat rations tied a man's bowels up, his spirit too. In the woods like this, a feller felt more like a man, less like some damned herded sheep.

By force of habit his jet, faintly oblique eyes explored a line of dark green firs crowning the next ridge. He laughed silently. As if there was an Injun worth worrying over within a hundred miles.

What a crowded gawd-forsaken land! Why, since sunup he hadn't noticed more than fifteen or twenty deer and a bear or two. 'Round these parts the wild things had grown almighty 'cute. Must have been hunted hard for a long time. Wouldn't be any elk or buffalo in these woods, he reckoned. Plenty of foxes, though, and bobcats. There were tracks all over the place.

For reasons sufficient unto himself, Higsby was traveling a series of rocky ridges running parallel to and above the stage road winding down from Boston to Providence, in Rhode Island. For one thing, the snow didn't drift on ridgetops. Of course, there weren't any Indians about; in western Pennsylvania or Kentucky no ranger in his right mind would have walked a ridgetop — not if he wanted to wear his hair for a while. Yesterday's blizzard had left the tree trunks white on the west side.

Higsby's eyes, black and narrow and bright in his long, flat countenance, traveled in restless semicircles. They noted even minor details without effort. It was growing so cold he reckoned pretty soon tree branches would start cracking. Yonder a buck had stropped his horns against a gray beech. Further away lay the remains of some rabbit an owl had got to. The approach of sundown put an edge to the wind. Higsby's brown complexion was turning coppery under it. Rhythmically, his hastily contrived snowshoes *whiss-whissed* along the powdery slopes.

Sam Higsby was thinking — and, as he often did on a long trip, he began to talk to himself.

"Ain't nobody goin' make me salute any snot-nosed lawyer who happens to wear a gorget. I didn't promise, either, I'd freeze my butt in a hole in the ground 'thout naught to shoot at. Never swore to do that. Not on the Bible, leastways. "Come along, boys,' says the recruiting feller. 'Ye'll get yer bellies full o' fighting. We'll set up a row of live, red-coated targets fer ye to fire at every day, an' twice on Sundays.' 'Twas lies, all damned, dirty lies. Ain't had me one shot at a live target in near on three months."

Even though the shortest line home was by the Springfield road, Higsby reckoned it would be smart to cut a trail closer to the sea. Were fewer provost patrols posted in this direction.

"Shore is colder 'n a old maid's bed," he grunted as hairs on the inside of his nostrils began to congeal. He shifted his Leman — one of the two long rifles he was lugging — to the crook of his left arm. At the same time he eased the thong to which he slung the extra weapon. It was a fine piece built by Adam Foulke of Allentown. Most folks would have claimed it was better than his Leman. But he knew his old rifle's balance, and Bella had a fine steady trigger pull.

"Oughter be a road somewheres down yonder," he reasoned. "Country falls that way."

Sure enough, in about twenty minutes the trail debouched on a traveled but unplowed road. He didn't know where it might lead but he knew which direction to take.

Despite frozen ruts hidden under the snow, Higsby made such good time that a haversack containing his bullet mold, powder gauge and pig lead began to pound his hip. A track branched off to the left, and since the smoke appeared to be rising in that direction, he left the main road. Um. His caution grew. Quite a few people had passed this way; ox and horse droppings darkly marred the snow.

In the center of a sizable clearing stood a large dwelling house. Because its second floor projected over the entrance, Higsby reckoned it must have been built when there were still Indians in the country.

The smoke which had attracted his attention was curling up from one of the largest brick chimneys he had ever seen. This place sure did look mighty homely with a bar of lamplight beating towards him across the snow. A down puff of smoke brought him odors of onions and frying meat. Goddamn! Springs of saliva rushed in his mouth.

Higsby shook a dusting of snow from his leggings, eased the blue wool muffler Effie Shindler had knit him, and hiked his belt straight. If them there folks expected money, he'd have to think fast, but maybe they would stand him to a free meal and lodging. Flipping open the pan of his rifle, he made sure the priming hadn't sifted out.

Mechanically he lifted his war hatchet free of its sling, then knocked on the door and jerked its latchstring almost simultaneously. No use letting people get set if they aimed to make trouble. Rifle held carelesslike yet ready, he stepped inside. A flurry of wind-driven snow swept by his feet onto the flooring of the rough boards ahead of him.

All the people sitting at a trestle table jumped up; an old sharp-nosed woman working before the big open fireplace screamed, "My Jesus, it's a Injun!"

"Howdy, folks." Slipping a hand from its rabbit-skin mitten Higsby raised it palm outwards. "Cold, ain't it?" Listening for noises upstairs, he stood quietly in the light of a bullseye lantern and two or three tallow dips. So there were only three able-bodied men in the place? He could handle them all right.

A barrel-chested fellow in patched leather breeches and a heavy gray flannel shirt started forward.

"For pity's sake shut that door," called the old woman's nasal voice. "Don't stand like a ninnyhammer letting in all outdoors."

Higsby closed the door then swept off his fur cap, gave its buck's tail a special flourish as he bowed a trifle.

"Servant, ma'am." He tried to say it like the Tidewater planters. "I was wonderin' whether you folks could obleege me with a meal of vittles? 'Pears like that ordinary up on the highroad has kind of gone out o' business."

Goddamn! A couple of wenches were coming out of a shadow. One of them was pretty as a young fawn and her color was high from the heat of the roaring fireplace. The other was well built but plain as a sod house.

The men at the table still said nothing. Beside the farmer who had come forward there was a fellow wearing a homespun suit and a leather jerkin. The third man was dressed almost dandy in his black suit and lace jabot. Right off Higsby set him down as a foreigner.

Without invitation the rifleman stood his two rifles near the door and everyone watched him unsling first his haversack, then powder horn and camp kettle. He kept his war hatchet and skinning knife to his belt, though. Grinning amiably, he swung over towards the fireplace and stood there toasting his hands.

"Well, folks, reckon I could lean into a platter o' that there ham an' chitterlings mighty easy. An' some of them elegant-looking turnips."

Then came the question Higsby had been dreading. The farmer still glowered, was slowly opening and closing big red hands as he asked, "Kin you pay?"

"Sho'," the ranger lied easily. "Just been discharged. Got most o' my pay."

"Ye'd better not be lying," the farmer rumbled. "Else I'll beat the tarnal tripes out of ye." He was big enough to do it, too.

The rifleman took no offense, declared affably, "I only lie to Injuns."

The two girls, giggling, bright-eyed and patently unfamiliar with rangers and their ways, watched him eat and brought him more as soon as his wooden trencher was empty.

Soon Higsby sighed, let out his belt, and slowed down his eating. Now he felt more inclined to look about.

The daughter called Betty, a bold, pretty piece nearing eighteen, was sly for her age. Whenever she passed, she always brushed his shoulder with her thigh. Once when she backed against him, he slipped a hand up among her petticoats. Goddamn! The girl only wriggled. Had on three petticoats near as he could tell — all of common cotton.

Aggie, the elder sister, had a really fine figure, but the smallpox hadn't helped her looks any. At first he reckoned she was shy but soon it seemed to him that for all Betty's tricks, Aggie looked more like a going concern. When she bent over to pop a popper of corn, he thought he saw a strip of lawn beneath her striped show petticoat. Um! Lawn? Now that was right interesting.

Anderson belched, turned a fire-red face and stared hard at Higsby. "Say, stranger, you ever fit any Injuns? Or you only dress like that?"

"Only last spring, me an' the Shain boys an' a couple of Tomkinses raided old Oconostota's village at Keowee all by ourselves."

"Kill any?" demanded the man in gray from the depths of his cider noggin.

"I got me half a dozen skelps."

Anderson started, narrowed his bloodshot eyes beneath dense brows.

"Six? You sure are a plain and fancy liar."

Higsby started to rouse his dander, but Betty was smiling at him from the shadows so he only stalked over to his haversack.

"Am I?"

He flung six snakelike lengths of braided black hair among the dishes. At the thick end of each was a ragged circle of what looked like a piece of dry calfskin.

"Oh my!" Betty's blue eyes flew wide open and Agatha gasped over the spiced cider she was mulling.

"*Mon dieu!*" for the first time the man in black seemed aware of Higsby's presence. "Those are scalps from human heads?"

Higsby's teeth flashed in his dark face. "They ain't horse tails." Highly enjoying the moment, he shoved aside the tableware and arranged his trophies in a row. He held a scalp to the light, loosened the lock near the big end.

"Lookey here, mounseer. Kin you see how these hairs sort of swing around in a circle — like a little whirlpool?"

The Frenchman's intense eyes narrowed. "But yes."

"That's the poll piece. Nuthin' else don't really count, 'cause there's only one poll to each head. Hair don't grow like that nowheres else."

The man in gray remarked, "I was wonderin' where you got that mouse over your eye. Who done it?"

The rifleman laughed shortly and his jaw muscles tightened. "Wisht I knew. I was in likker. If ever I come acrost him, I'll shorely cut his lights out. I claim 'tain't sportin' to hit a man when he's in likker."

Higsby, looking very tall in the center of the low-ceilinged room, bowed to the farmer's wife. "Ma'am, I kin say with all modesty that Higsby in likker is a r'arin', tearin' whirlwind of destruction."

"*Je crois bien*," murmured the foreigner, fingering a wineglass from which he took an occasional sip. "Tell me, *mon ami*, the siege of Boston, how does he progress?"

Higsby pursed thin lips, became cautious. "We-e-ell, suh, things is dead. Deader 'n ditch water. Most o' the home boys are right disgusted." The Pennsylvanian's voice deepened, filled the whole firelit room. "Ain't no sense to this war, anyway. What'd we march north fer? To fight the Britainers, o' course. What do we do most of the time? We just set around wearin' out the seats of our britches waitin' for orders, havin' to turn out an' salute a lot of snots who don't know a deer trace from a hog track."

Ostentatiously, the old woman blew out the bulls-eye lantern and snuffed one of the candles.

Conscious of the Frenchman's bright-eyed interest, Higsby went on. "Yessuh, them Yankee sons of bitches tried to make us, the fightin'est men in America, stand out in the wet when even a bug-tit would know there wouldn't be a hostile for miles around. Will them Britainers come out and give a feller a target? Hell an' destruction, no!" The Pennsylvanian squirted a long parabola of brown juice into the fireplace, watched it sizzle on the end of a log. "Will these psalm-shouting Massachusetters attack an' make 'em fight? Hell no! Me, I'm headin' somewheres where a feller kin keep his fightin' eye in."

Betty came over and stood so close alongside Higsby he made sure that, though her thigh was smooth and soft, her petticoats were undoubtedly of cotton.

The merchant's semibald head wagged. "Don't tell me New England privateers can't whip the British," he belched. "Back in Fifty-six I took six prizes off you frog-eaters my own self."

M. Pliarne inquired quite unruffled, "And among them, how many were ships of war?"

The merchant blinked suspiciously.

"The mounseers didn't have none cruising this coast; we'd have tooken them along o' the rest, I expect."

The man in gray hiccoughed, scowled in an attempt to recover dignity. "Suppose we don't always hold with what the Congress does? We don't want a lot of gold-laced whoresons of navy officers threatening us plain folks. Nossir!"

"Hear! Hear!" Anderson rumbled. "Folk 'round here is dead set agin a navy. Too dear."

Ma Anderson grabbed the dog by the ear, hauled him yelping to the door and shoved him out into the starlit cold. Whew! The draught that came beating in was like the blade of a sword laid across one's face.

"A navy is most assuredly costly," the Frenchman admitted. "Yet consider the costly destruction of your seaport towns."

Higsby reluctantly took his eyes off Betty. Screeching catamounts! She was scouring a pot, and a fine pair of rising beauties were jiggling tantalizingly to the circular movements of her scraper.

"Reckon yer mistaken, mounseer," said he. "The Britishers won't burn helpless towns. That's the Injun way o' fightin'."

A twinkle shone in M. Pliarne's pale gray eyes. "Ah? It appears that monsieur has not yet learned what has occurred at Bristol in the colony of Rhode Island? Nor of what has more recently been done at Falmouth in the Maine District? The one port was bombarded; the other burned to the ground — quite destructed. My point, if you will permit, is that a single American man-of-war might well have driven off the English and so have preserved both towns."

Then the merchant got up mumbling, "Privateers is good enough for us. When a war's done, a privateersman can go back to peaceful tradin'. Don't have to be fed by us taxpayers till some more trouble starts. Well — good night, all — "

Shortly Higsby and the two girls were left in the kitchen. The sisters suddenly acted shy but kept stealing glances at that virile figure standing so rangy, so easy-like, before the chimney place.

Betty rolled her eyes at the sleek blackness of the hair tumbling about the fringed cape of his sumac-colored shirt. Mercy, it shone like a crow's wing. There was a sort of freshness about this gaunt stranger and he smelt of wood smoke rather than of food fumes. That word LIBERTY across the chest of his outer shirt was impressive, even if the white paint was faded and the lettering all caterwampus. Betty wondered what had caused those gaps in the long fringes down his legs. The buckskin had had hard use; thorn scratches, snags and patches showed and the skin was glazed and greasy at elbow and knee.

Mrs. Anderson came thumping downstairs, a pellucid drop trembling on the end of her sharp red nose.

"Waal, young man and where you figger to sleep?"

"Why, ma'am, since you ain't said nothin', I don't rightly know."

The old woman blinked suspiciously in the candle's smoky red light. "You sure you've plenty of money?"

"Yes, ma'am."

"Hard money?"

Higsby laughed easily, slapped his pocket as if it contained more than a couple of walnuts and a curb chain.

"Sho'. Plenty an' to spare."

"You got — " Mrs. Anderson hesitated, licked her lips — "six shillings?"

[181]

Higsby got cooney. "Sho', ma'am, but not fer a single night's lodgin'."
She looked relieved. "Three, then?"

"Sho' 'nuff."

"I don't know wheres I could bed you unless I let you bundle with one of the girls."

The sharp way she looked at him set Higsby to thinking. "That would be mighty handsome of you, ma'am."

"Well, which one you want to bundle with? Aggie or Betty?"

Immediately Higsby drawled, "Why it don't greatly matter, ma'am, does it? But since you ask, I reckon Miss Aggie an' I might get along."

He could catch the amazed click of Betty's jaw. She turned scarlet. The idee! Passing her up for poor plain Aggie. Why, everyone held Betty Anderson one of the prettiest girls in Suffolk County. Pity's sake, this ranger fellow must be clean out of his senses.

Mrs. Anderson was so surprised she came dangerously near smiling as she beckoned Higsby towards the staircase.

"Guess you mean all right, young feller. Betty, you go get the trundle out from under our bed. You can bed with Pa and keep my side o' the bed warm."

Still red with anger, Betty tossed her head, lit a Phoebe lamp with a splinter from the fire, then with a disdainful flounce of her cotton petticoats, disappeared up the hollowly resounding stairs.

When Higsby reached a small room built right under the eaves, Aggie was already between the covers. According to custom, she had, with the exception of her shoes, kept on all her clothes. Mrs. Anderson was just finishing stitching the out edges of the blankets.

"What's that thing, ma'am? A deadfall?"

Higsby grinned at a narrow hickory plank fixed edgewise the length of the bed. One end fitted into a groove nailed like an inverted U onto the headboard of the bed. A staple and a hasp at the other end made it possible for Mrs. Anderson to secure the barrier to the footboard, thus dividing the bed into uncompromisingly separate units.

"For all you chose Aggie, I don't trust any man further'n I can throw a bull by the tail," Mrs. Anderson snuffled. "You get under the covers now, young man."

When he had done so, she stooped over the fire and began heating a stick of red sealing wax.

"Some women would be fools enough just to stitch a center seam," she remarked. "I ain't."

Slowly, because her fingers were cold, Mrs. Anderson passed a red and white thread through the hasp and secured its end to the footboard with sealing wax. From her petticoat pocket she fished a coin, spat on it, then used it as a seal. She held it up.

"That's a pine tree shilling and there ain't three more this side o' Boston.

If I find yonder seal so much as cracked in the morning, Mr. Anderson will surely beat the lights out o' you afore we turn you over to the law. Whoring," she glanced first at Aggie, then at Higsby, "ain't laughed at in these parts."

Without a word of good night, she stamped off down the stairs taking the candle with her.

Who would ever have guessed the girl would go to bed with all her clothes on? That was one thing he hadn't figured on. She might at least have shed a couple of petticoats. That fine lawn one for instance. Hell's bells an' panther tracks! This wasn't the way he'd reckoned things would go at all, at all.

By turning his head a little, he could glimpse Aggie's profile. Why, she'd a pert, well-shaped nose, a prettily curved chin, and her teeth weren't bad. Her eyes opened suddenly and she whispered, "You makin' out all right, Mister Higsby?"

"Can't say 'yep' or 'nope' to that, ma'am. Mighty cold, ain't it?"

"Yes, terrible. Been cold all week. Gets so I hate getting up and I hate going to bed. The bed's so awful cold and Ma won't grant me a warming pan. I'm — " she heaved a slow sigh, and a gray plume of breath vapor went swirling up. "I — I'm still kind of cold."

Imagine this handsome stranger having preferred her over Betty! Why was he so quiet? Right now he was staring hard at the ceiling as if he was doing some tall thinking. Why was he so slow? A local boy would have been at her bodice laces by now.

All at once he gave a little sigh and took her hand. She wished it wasn't so hard and chapped.

Maybe a good way to get him interested would be to ask what Indian women were like.

"Most of 'em ain't much," he explained in his deep, leisurely accents. "Their skin's tough an' leatherlike — what with the b'ar's grease an' other stuff they put on their hair, they stink somethin' fierce. Once in the Creek nation I bought me a winter wife, an' she wasn't bad. Toyota was plump, an' paler than most."

"Why, Mister Higsby! You *bought* her."

"Sho'. Cost me a cross fox an' ten prime beaver. I built us a cabin an' she kept house for me a hull winter. We had so much fun I spent too little time trappin'. Lost money that season. Yep, Toyota was — "

"Never mind about her." By now Aggie knew she'd made a mistake. "You — do you like me?"

Higsby sighed again. Hell's bells, was there no other way? "Sho' do, Miss Aggie. Wish this board wasn't here."

"So do I," Aggie whispered. "Guess we'd both be more comfortable if only that old board wasn't there."

"I wisht there was some way to outsmart that there sealing wax. Too bad. Reckon you don't get much fun."

They had to settle back. The air was too insufferably icy.

All at once Aggie began to snicker softly. "La, Mr. Higsby, ain't you the biggest stupid?"

"Reckon so — " he smiled in the dark. All right to let her think so; just like in Injun trading.

"I know a way; the clerk of the court up to Dedham showed me — "

"I'll bet — "

"No, it's about the sealing wax. You got your knife along?"

"Yep. Why?"

"Then you kin get the seal off easy. Go get it."

Out of bed he felt like he'd fallen through the ice on the Allegheny again, but he got his knife.

"Go on, heat the blade in the embers," Aggie's voice directed.

"Spoil its temper," he objected.

"You only have to warm it." Her voice was muffled because she'd ducked under the blankets. "Just push the hot edge of the knife gently under that seal. It should come off easy — but for God's sake be careful. Ma will skin me alive if it's disturbed."

Guiding his knife's point with his left thumb, Higsby urged it under the seal. Sure enough, the wax came away with ridiculous ease, hung dangling at the thread's end.

His feet were growing numb by the time he had slipped the seal through the hasp and had gingerly leaned the board against the wall. To keep the tiny fire going, he threw a couple of sticks on. Later, he reckoned, he would need the flames again.

Aggie snuggled up to him like a kitten. "More comfortable with that old board gone, ain't it?"

"A heap sight." He drew a deep breath, prepared to make the big gamble. "But it'd be a sight pleasanter if you'd shed just a couple o' them petticuts. It's like bein' in bed with a draper's store."

Without a word Aggie wriggled out of bed and untied her blue-and-white-striped outer petticoat and the lawn one, which left her one and her shift.

God, but she was a fine armful, and her breath was sweet. On the march up from Pennsylvania, he'd had fun and to spare, but nothing like this.

Aggie kept calling him "darling," not "honey" like the gals further south. It wasn't long before he learned that Aggie Anderson could teach those other gals quite a few tricks.

When Sam Higsby waked himself, it was colder than ever. Off in the woods he could hear branches snapping like pistol shots. Far away a fox was barking. By stopping his breath and lying right still, Higsby could hear variously pitched snores from other parts of the house. Out in the barn a restless horse was stirring in its stall.

Aggie lay fast asleep, her face pressed against his shoulder. Instinctively he knew it must be going on five. Damn. Time to get moving. It was so fine and warm here in bed. He loathed the thought of going. Very gingerly he removed his hand from her breast; but when he edged away she did not even stir. Only wrinkled her nose and made a little noise deep in her throat.

The fire had nearly died, so, shivering, he fed pine splinters to the few remaining embers. The resultant flame was like a single hot spike driven into the iciness of the room, but it served to reheat his knife blade. When he reaffixed the seal, he inspected his work by the light of a pine splinter. It was a pretty job.

While he warmed his moccasins and knee-length hunting shirt, Aggie snored softly — like the spindle of a hard-driven spinning wheel. It was half past four, he reckoned, when he went over to the far side of the bed and fumbled until he came across the petticoats. He had it. It hadn't been an easy prize, but he had it.

It was a real treat to feel such fine lawn between his fingers. That petticoat should make the jim-dandiest rifle patches. A lawn patch burned off clean, didn't leave behind smoldering shreds that would ignite a charge poured too hurriedly down one's rifle barrel.

Quiet as an owl ranging a forest, Higsby descended to the kitchen. There he paused long enough to tuck some bread and the heel of a ham into his shirt front. As an afterthought he stuffed a couple of cold sweet potatoes into his mouth.

The Road to Tiverton

Even if the Fall River was gray and all clabbered with ice, ex-Sergeant Timothy Bennett found it gratifying to be back in Rhode Island. The four days he'd spent in traveling down from Roxbury had been tiring, but tonight, if nothing happened, he would sleep in his own room.

He experienced a sudden craving for the deep peace of Pa's white clapboard farm house on Conanicut Island.

Peaceful Haven was well named. Of course Asa Bennett could have afforded a handsome brick or stone house in the English style just as well as Mr. John Bannister on Pelham Street, or Captain Maudsley on Spring Street. The Society of Friends, however, were dead set against ostentation or show of any sort, so he had built a plain, square house. Its only distinction were pairs of well-proportioned Doric pillars rising to either side of the entrance.

Presently the road crawled down into a small valley lying between two bare and rolling hills. A Y-shaped intersection lay ahead. Following the other arm was another lone traveler. Eager for companionship, Tim lengthened his stride and reached the fork a moment before the other.

Not wishing to seem overforward in striking up an acquaintance, he stared hard at some irregularly lettered finger signs. One of them, streaked with droppings of long-departed summer birds, read: TO NEW PORT, 8½ MILES. Another, to FALL RIVER, 10 MILES. The largest and newest sign stated that Tiverton lay but two miles ahead.

"Howdy, friend," the other traveler hailed cheerfully enough. "Cold enough fer you?"

Crimanently! It was the very rifleman who'd been in a drunken rage back in Roxbury.

"Hello," Tim greeted in that flat voice a schoolboy uses when he decides to stand up to the class bully.

The man in buckskins looked at him hard, suddenly diverted his gaze towards the distant river, then looked at him again.

Drawled he, "Back a piece folks said there's a town called Nooport somewheres along this road. That correct?" The buck's tail on his cap stirred to a damp wind beating in from the ocean.

Wondering why the ranger should be carrying two rifles and so little traveling gear, Tim relaxed. Also why was he traveling *away* from the siege?

"Yes, that's true."

"Is it likely a feller kin take ship there an' get back to God's country?"

"You're in God's country right here," Tim smiled. "We've the best land in America in Rhode Island."

Suddenly the rifleman extended his hand. "My name's Higsby, Sam Higsby. How's fer keepin' together a piece?"

"Glad to." Tim gave Higsby his name.

"You been up to Boston?"

Tim nodded. "My 'listment ran out." And it had. There was no doubt of it.

"So did mine." Higsby grinned like a winter wolf, wiped a drop from his nose on his cuff. "By my ratin', that was the hell of a poor war. Where's the profit just settin' 'round freezin' in ditches, killin' nobody? Why, you ain't allowed to take a skelp. By God, up there a feller has to get leave to visit the backhouse!"

Just before getting into Tiverton, Higsby looked Tim bang in the eye. "Friend, I figger I kin trust you with my spare rifle. Take care of her 'cause she was built by Adam Foulke of Allentown. Next to Bella, my Leman-made, I reckon she's the shootin'est weepon you will find this side of Pennsylvany."

Tiverton's rutted and muddy main street was busy, filled with a noonday crowd. From the Bower Anchor's chimney poured greasy billows of smoke; the delectable odor of a stewing fowl perfumed the air. Outside the inn waited half a dozen ox spans; standing close by, a postrider's nag gnawed at a hitching post while his master tried to collect fees from the innkeeper.

"Well," Higsby grunted, "here goes for a mess of vittles." Drawing out his war hatchet he tilted back his head and sent winging down the street the same eerie, terrifying screech Tim had heard in Roxbury. People froze in their tracks. Some horses shied, others tried to run away.

"E-e-e-e! Yah-yah! O-o-nah! Oo-nah!" Twice more Higsby raised his scalp yell, then commenced a furious whirling dance which gradually brought him to the main crossroads in the village. The ranger threatened the sky with his war hatchet, whirled, and bent over; then, fringes fluttering, brandished his long rifle at arm's length. All the while he screeched an unintelligible chant. Tim saw muscles along the ranger's throat standing out rigid.

Children squalled, scattered in terror when, as a grand finale, the rifleman raised a terrific yell and flung his war hatchet across the street. Spinning, it passed between a couple of townsmen and lodged quivering in the door frame of the Bower Anchor.

When a pair of serving wenches who had run out to see what was amiss uttered squeals and ducked back inside, Higsby burst into panting shouts of laughter.

"Heyo, friends! Come one, come all, an' I'll l'arn ye how us timberbeasts shoots along the Clinch River. Yonder, it's a mighty pore day a man don't get to cure a half dozen fresh skelps." He beat himself on the chest, dropped into the Indian mode of brag. "Brothers attend! Brothers attend! I kin shoot the eye out'n a gnat, the leg off'n a louse, the head off'n a pin! Brothers attend! In my lodge hang twenty-six skelps — all warrior hair."

Homecoming

A fisherman, mighty glad of a sixpence, rowed them over to Conanicut Island from Coddington Point. He had to work, though, because an ebb tide kept pushing pieces of floe ice across their course.

"Yonder is Conanicut — straight ahead." Tim, seated beside Higsby in the stern, indicated a long narrow island.

The Pennsylvanian saw that it was subdivided into pastures by rough stone fences, and dominated by three softly rounded hills. Beyond low places between these rises, they glimpsed the further, or western, passage of Narragansett Bay. Though a few clumps of fine tall trees remained, a greater part of the virgin stand had long ago been timbered away.

Over his left shoulder Tim could see Newport downstream, sprawling down its hillside to the harbor. The town looked very familiar. The windmills on the bluff back of town still swung their arms: one above the burying ground; one behind Jew Street; finally, Mr. Young's fine new mill. To think of Lucy being barely a mile distant. Lucy, sweet, sweet Lucy!

Mechanically, Tim's gaze sought Redwood's wharf. When the Bennett vessels didn't go straight to Pa's big warehouse over on Conanicut, they usually tied up there. None of the vessels moored at Redwood's looked familiar.

There was some sort of flag flying from the lookout of the courthouse, but what its design might mean he couldn't guess.

Today so many strange flags were flying over the United Provinces. One heard of pine trees, of anchors, of rattlesnakes and gridirons. They inspired wit and plenty of confusion, too.

Higsby's gaze took in row on row of neat and shining shingle roofs. Here and there clumps of leafless trees spurted up between the housetops like jets of water from between the boards of a landing stage built too low to the water. A bluish pall of kitchen smoke hung over Newport.

In the harbor, more ships swung to their moorings: pinks, snows, stumpy bluff-bowed whalers, tiny fishermen, broad-beamed coasters, and any quantity of riverboats. Tim pointed them all out.

"What's them long thin sheds up under the hill — look like Iroquois longhouses?"

"Ropewalks. When we get home you'll see one close to." He forgot his Quaker precepts. "Pa has one of the biggest in Rhode Island."

The fisherman, momentarily relieved by a favorable current, flicked the sweat from his face. "Should have been hereabouts last month. That goddamn Captain Wallace turned ugly, brought the *Rose* frigate, a bomb brig and a couple of armed schooners upstream and bombarded the b'Jesus out o' Bristol."

"Dunno, lest 'twas to scare the folks up there into feeding his crews."

"Didn't they fight back?"

"Couldn't. Was only a little battery there. Both our cruisers was up the bay to Providence."

"Cruisers?"

"Yep. Didn't ye know? We got a couple of them. They're the Rhode Island navy: the *Washington* an' the *Katy*. Old Abe Whipple commands the *Katy*. He sailed her clean down to Bermuda last summer."

"What for?"

Expertly the fisherman fended off a jagged ice cake and kept his eyes on the stream as he said, " 'Pears someone warned Governor Cooke the British had a powder magazine there."

"Whipple got the powder?" Tim demanded.

The fisherman resumed the oars and took up his characteristically choppy stroke. "Naw, a vessel out of Philadelphy, and 'nother from one of them there southern colonies beat him to it. A marine commissioner from the Congress last week spread the news."

Newport having always been a favored port for His Majesty's men-of-war, it seemed quite natural to Tim that a British squadron should be anchored in the harbor. But it was a shock to note gun ports triced up, cannon trained on the town. His misgivings increased. Under such conditions it wouldn't take much of a spark, Tim figured, to touch off a fight.

By God! Here was the siege of Boston all over again. The enemy within reach and nothing being done. Still, he *could* see the sense in Newport's understanding with Captain Wallace. Even a brief bombardment could erase the results of a hundred years' arduous trading, slaving and privateering.

As for Higsby, he was remembering what that yellow-faced mounseer had said about keeping an enemy offshore. Looked like he was right about that, too.

Desire Harmony

Sam Higsby remarked suddenly, "Right old-lookin' 'round these parts. Folks must have dwelled here since the year one."

"Well, it's near on a hundred and fifty years, anyway." Tim smiled. "Folks claim this end of Rhode Island was settled 'round 1639."

As they swung along over the muddy road, the Foulke slanted ever so comfortably over his shoulder. For one thing, the long rifle was lighter than the ten-and-a-half-pound Brown Bess he'd left in Roxbury — maybe by three pounds.

"Rich country," Higsby opined as they tramped past a plain, unpainted house and the well-filled barn behind it. A yard was crowded with fat brown and white cows. "Enough to make a Tuscarora's or a Cherokee's mouth water."

From the crest of a hillock they could see into Fox Hill Cove. A grateful warmth flooded Tim's being at the sight of the familiar farmhouses, orchards and pastures. Why he could even recognize Billy, Mark Remington's hunchbacked brother, working at his ferry landing.

"That's our place." Tim tried hard to suppress his pride.

Higsby saw a big, white square house set under fine tall trees. Beyond it a barn, also white and with a big cupola, proudly dominating a cluster of lesser structures — henhouses, pigstys, corncribs, carriage sheds and privies.

"Say! Ain't *that* sumpin'?" The ranger was definitely impressed.

"Further over are Pa's wharf and warehouse, and that's the ropewalk." He indicated a long shed which for a hundred yards paralleled the gray sand beach of a small cove.

"Thank God!" Tim sighed and a big load dropped from his shoulders when he saw lying to the wharf a three-masted schooner of about ninety tons' burden.

In keeping with Quaker tenets, the exterior of Peaceful Haven boasted no graceful pilasters, no elaborate cornices. Yet the house possessed distinction, the dignity of handsome proportions and good taste divorced from ostentation.

By the back door a very thin old Negress, Mamba, made a hatchet twinkle in the pale winter sunshine as she split kindling. About her graying head was knotted a yellow kerchief of the sort imported from Santiago in the captaincy general of Cuba. Preoccupied, she failed to notice the two figures descending the lane, vanished indoors leaving a flock of absurdly fat white ducks to inspect the chips she had made.

"Suppose I raise a warwhoop to let the folks know you're home?" Higsby suggested amiably.

"Heavens, no! Pa's a Friend. You mustn't ever forget it, either."

Behind the white barn — the only painted one for miles — Tim made hurried explanations concerning his prospective purchase of the Foulke. "Killing and war are dead contrary to Pa's principles. I'll have to play carefully to get that money."

"That's yore funeral," the rifleman conceded slowly, "but goddamn me if I kin understand folks who claim it's sinful to fight. Fightin' is a natural state. Didn't God give a b'ar claws, a wolf teeth and us guns to fight with?"

Mamba thrust a grizzled head out of the kitchen door. "Heabben's glory! Mister Tim! Mister Tim! Thank Gawd my sweet l'il boy is safe back. Praise Jesus, praise de good Jesus!"

The old Negress flung both arms about Tim and kissed him.

Right queer people, these Quakers, thought Higsby. Imagine letting a nigger act so familiar!

Where was Pa? In the setting room. Miss Desire was upstairs.

"Well, Mamba, you fix us a snack, we'll lean into it pretty soon. Come along, Sam."

As they circled around to the front door, he turned an anxious face. "Try and remember, won't you? No cussing, no talk about war, scalps, or killing 'less Pa asks."

A handsomely carved fanlight lent the main entrance distinction. Tim was reaching for a knob of silvered glass when the door swung open revealing Asa Bennett.

"Pa!" Tim's throat closed spasmodically.

"My son, my son!" For all it was contrary to Quaker teaching to betray undue emotion, the old man flung open his arms and his big, blue-veined hands quivered as they patted Tim's shoulder blades.

Asa Bennett then kissed his son on the forehead in the biblical fashion, raised faded blue eyes to the sky. "I praise the Lord, I praise the Lord my God that He hath brought safe home my son." His square, strangely unlined face quivered. "Oh, Timothy, Timothy, how worried we have been, thy sister and I." He broke off, controlled himself with an effort. "Pray, who is this? A friend of thine?"

No sharper contrast could have been presented than the old Quaker in a long-skirted, buttonless brown coat, long vest, gray thread stockings, and the ranger in fur cap, butternut-tinted hunting shirt, fringed leggings and warlike gear.

Higsby leaned his rifle against one of the porch pillars, whipped off his cap, said shyly in his soft voice, "My name's Sam Higsby, an' I'm proud, all-fired proud, to shake hands with Tim's pa. Him an' me are friends."

If Asa Bennett felt any misgivings over the long rifle leaning against his front porch, he concealed them. "Friend Higsby, thee is welcome to our poor home. Are thee ahungered?"

"Thanky, suh. Reckon me an' Tim *could* pack away a meal."

Tim stood aside to let the Pennsylvanian pass by. Higsby entered, took two steps, then halted suddenly. Tim bumped into him.

A young girl was descending a flight of stairs so lightly that she seemed to float. She was dressed, Quaker fashion, in dove gray. The strings of a fresh white apron deftly emphasized the slenderness of her waist, much as starched cuffs did for her wrists. Though the dress had been cut on severely simple lines, the maker had endowed this semiuniform with a subtle individuality. Primly it hinted the existence of high and full young breasts, long legs and arms.

Yet all that Higsby noticed was this girl's eyes. It seemed he had never before beheld such merry, sensitive, lovely brown eyes, nor such very long lashes. There were small splinters of golden light in them — Tim had such splinters, too, but the brother's eyes were gray and smaller.

So this was Desire Harmony. Goddamn, she was pretty as a speckled pup! In a second glance he realized that her face was broad across the brows, but narrowed down towards the chin. Her nose was short and straight, and her nostrils took a little upward lift which pleased him strangely.

From beneath a small gray cap edged in white, some curls escaped. Sunlight beating in the front door made her hair shine like good but unpolished copper.

The rifleman all at once became aware of the intensity of the look Tim's sister was fixing on him. Goddamn, she was lovely! All fresh and clean and bright. Like an October hillside at sunup.

Suddenly her lids fluttered, and running down the last few steps, she sped by him.

"Oh, Tim, Tim, praise the Lord thee has been spared!" Her surprisingly deep voice trembled. "If only I had laurels with which to deck thy brow. Oh, Tim, thee looks — looks like Achilles home from battle!"

The old Quaker coughed, interrupted mildly, "My dear, pray restrain the language. Friend Higsby, this is my daughter, Desire Harmony."

Desire Harmony smiled, dropped a demure curtsey and turned those disturbing golden-brown eyes on the dazzled Pennsylvanian.

After a welcome supper prepared by Mamba, Higsby decided that Tim most likely would want to talk to his sister, so he presently swung off upstairs, carefully shielding his candle flame.

Desire began to talk rapidly. "Tim, I have decided there's no sense in our 'theeing' and 'thying' each other in private. The simple language may suit Pa and his friends, but — well, it makes me feel silly." Her eyes narrowed, faintly defiant. "How can anyone be sure that 'you' is an improper word? It appears to me that by this talk we set ourselves above people, and a true Friend doesn't encourage that."

"I have pondered just that question, too, Dee. Pa would say it is not for us to question. But be careful. It would hurt Pa terribly if you became one of the world's people. Zeke and I — well, we *had* to." Tim gazed into the flames. "Why was Pa so dead set to get me home by the seventh?"

Desire was genuinely astonished. "What did he say?"

"Only that," Tim replied. "I was wondering. As usual the old man will tell me when he gets god-damned — er — er, thy pardon, Dee — when he gets good and ready."

His sister giggled, suggested hopefully, "You must have had plenty of fun at the siege."

He frowned, then grinned. "Not so much as you'd think, still there were moments — "

"What is our army like? Are the officers very brutal with their men? When they're displeased do they have their soldiers tied to cannons and flogged?"

"Why, no. Wherever — ?"

In the firelight, Desire's naturally high color glowed brighter still. She spoke eagerly, as if avid for information. "Do the American officers game? I hope not. Last week a leftenant in the *Swan* lost a whole year's pay at pharo — "

"— And just how did you learn all this?" Tim inquired sharply.

Desire slipped a walnut between teeth no less white and sparkling than Sam Higsby's.

"With trade gone and done for, what else is there left to do in Newport but to gossip?" she queried easily. "Tell me, did you actually kill anybody?"

"Guess I tried plenty hard, but I ain't sure," Tim admitted. "Most all our firing was by volleys."

"Tim," Desire inquired slowly, "why can't this trouble be mended? It would be so nice if there were no more fighting and we could still have our king."

"The king's refusal to accept our petition has made this impossible, Dee.

I mean the one Mr. Dickson sent," Tim explained soberly. "His Majesty's attitude has made the Congress feel entirely hopeless; it has made them feel that we must stand on our own feet."

"You mean the army is for — " she hesitated as if awed to utter the words — "for independence?"

Tim replied, "Independence is the only way out. Now what could have been softer than that last petition? Good Lord, Dee, old Dickson fairly groveled, just about licked the king's boots for the mere privilege of addressing His Majesty. What happened? His Majesty flatly refused to even hear the petition, though every Englishman is supposed to have the right of petition to the Throne."

"But what else can we do? We haven't a single frigate or a sloop of war, let alone a ship of the line."

Her brother's voice deepened. "If we drive the British from our shores, then their ships will *have* to starve."

The House on Bannister Street

Throat ready to burst, Tim followed Isaac Percival's walk of slate slabs. Clorinda, the Percivals' mulatto serving wench, opened the door about as soon as he had knocked. She was fairly wriggling with excitement. "Come right in, Mist' Bennett. Come right in! Us has been expecting you some time."

"Tim! Tim, darling! I *knew* you'd return!"

Small features eloquent of an inexpressible happiness, Lucy dissolved into his hungry grasp. "You came back! Oh, how I prayed and — "

Pressing her tight to him, he swam in the heady delight of Lucy's nearness. Couldn't find a thing to say — could only dwell in the radiant aura of overwhelming love.

The wench giggled and fled, leaving an orange-colored angora cat to watch the proceedings with aloof interest.

"Darling — I — I can't believe you're back. I didn't dare to believe you would give up your commission. I — I — almost wish you hadn't. It must have meant so much to you."

"Sweetheart — "

"Oh, you *are* unselfish and kind — too kind, I fear." Passionately, Lucy pressed her face against his. "I will try so hard never to make you sorry of your choice. Please believe that." Her long-lashed eyes swung upwards. "And you gave it up for *my* sake — "

"Yes — " he whispered and, for the moment, he honestly thought he had. "Let's look at you, dearest. I need another portrait in my private gallery."

"La, sir, what nonsense is this?"

"During the siege I used to look at memory pictures of you — ever so often. I have one of you in the pearch orchard. Remember? And another when you wore a green and a yellow chip hat." The intensity of her gaze betrayed her rapturous interest. "Then, at Captain Whipple's ball you wore gray silk and a red — "

" — Claret, dear."

" — Claret shawl, and God knows how many petticoats. And you had an ivory and silk fan."

"Oh, Timothy. To think of you remembering all that! You shall have your new picture — "

Lucy retreated, slowly spreading wide a skirt of pale blue challis. A fichu of Valenciennes rushed, like a sea foaming over a reef, from her shoulders to cross over her breast. As an added bit of jauntiness she had fixed a pair of blue-dyed everlastings in her hair. The blue enamel and silver brooch he had given her secured her collar.

Superbly bored, the cat yawned, cocked an ear backwards.

"Lucy!" He wanted to kiss her, but she whirled aside on tiny heelless slippers and the scarlet circle of her lips blew him a kiss.

Riot

"Come on! You cursed bloodybacks," roared a printer's devil, "or do you always wait for night before you steal our pigs and burn our barns?"

By the time Timothy Bennett crossed Spring Street, he realized that the British were not plundering Newport — not yet, at any rate. The trouble, he gathered, was taking place at the waterfront.

By climbing a stoop Tim glimpsed, over the shifting heads of the mob, some twenty-five or thirty Royal Marines lined up under a weather-beaten sign reading MOSES LOPEZ & BROTHER. HIDES, WINES, & SALT FISH. In the door of the warehouse at their backs lay huge heaps of sacked potatoes, turnips, hams, sides of beef and great brown bunches of smoked salmon.

The lieutenant in command was young, with a sensitive, classically handsome profile and a wiry, erect figure. Breeding showed in the last detail of his bearing. Right now, he was with no great success attempting to appear unconcerned by the savage temper of the crowd. He gripped an ivory-hilted sword just a little too tight to be quite convincing. It was a silly sort of sword to carry on duty, Tim thought; all that fine carving on the guard would be useless in stopping a cudgel.

Everywhere the townsfolk called questions, milled about with apparent aimlessness. A majority carried weapons; a poker, a cudgel, an ax, or even a hanger left over from privateering days. Very few firearms were visible.

"Go home, you damned pirates!" shrieked an old woman.

"Figger to burn us out, like Falmouth, don't you? Well, just you try!"

"Leftenant St. Clair, sir!" Red-faced, a sergeant strode over to the slim young officer and fiercely urged some step, but the lieutenant shook his head so sharply that his scarlet and black cockade fluttered.

Inside Lopez's warehouse more marines in scarlet, black, and white guarded a party of ill-dressed and barefooted seamen who were sullenly lowering supplies into the Rose's longboats. These marines had to keep a sharp lookout lest the seamen run into the crowd and so desert.

A marine lieutenant took a turn across the landing stage. His manner was so calm, so infuriatingly contemptuous, Tim felt a sneaking admiration. Why, he was acting as if this swarm of angry Provincials were no more than so many yapping puppies.

He was ill-advised, though, Tim knew. Too many of these people held a real grievance: a son impressed into the Royal Navy; a handsome wood lot hacked down; a drove of sheep or a herd of beef oxen driven off without a by-your-leave, let alone a penny in payment.

The crowd began to back up as if gathering for a rush. Someone grabbed at Tim's arm. It was Lucy, great-eyed, vigilant and anxious.

Exasperation flooded him. "You should have stayed at home. You're apt to get hurt."

"So are you," she retorted. "If anyone's going to hurt you, I — well, I want to get at him."

Away down Thames Street bayonets appeared swinging, flashing in the sun. Apparently another detachment of the troops, sent to draw rations under Captain Wallace's treaty with the town, had visited the inner harbor and were having a hard time. Tim could see missiles raining on the redcoats.

Better get out of this. God! If anybody got crazy enough to fire a shot. In Boston they still talked of the Massacre, which as he saw it had been no massacre at all, but troops shooting in self-defense.

Lucy's grip tightened on his wrist as a window opened just above and a well-dressed man called out, "Let us have no violence — not until our treaty with Wallace is honorably expired!"

A cobblestone smashed a pane above the speaker's head and he ducked hurriedly out of sight. Some people laughed, but others shouted, "No renewal! No more treaties with the bloodybacks!"

Commands, curses, and the furious trampling of feet reverberated among the tall warehouses lining Thames Street. A second shower of stones was hurled at Lieutenant St. Clair's men.

"Want vittles do they? All right, let's feed 'em — cold iron and hot lead!"

A shriveled little man to Tim's left suddenly jerked a boarding pistol out of his coattail pocket.

Tim's arteries froze. He was soldier enough to foresee the deadly effect of a volley in this packed street. Worse still, the instant that damned idiot

[195]

snapped his shot, the squadron out yonder would commence a bombardment. Swinging his fists, ignoring angry shouts, he lurched after the little man.

"Poise firelocks!" The marine lieutenant's voice was taut and penetrating. He had lost his languid look, was using the ivory-hilted sword to dress his handful of men into a thin double rank barring the warehouse entrance.

"Take aim!" called Lieutenant St. Clair. A line of twinkling muzzles swung in line with the rioters' eyes. The officer's sharply etched features were tense as those of a boxer waiting to deliver a killing blow.

As the young lieutenant caught his next breath, Tim prepared to throw himself flat. Still the marine lieutenant gave no command to fire, only called out, "Stand fast, Provincials. There will be no firing unless you shoot!"

Isaac Percival

On Friday afternoon Lucy and her father came over to pay a visit. To sort of settle things, Tim figured happily.

In the Quaker's living room the two merchants took each other's measure with respect tinged by suspicion. Ike Percival clapped the old Quaker on his shoulder, went into roars of laughter.

"When I heard how quiet and smart you'd got the *Hope* to sea, I like to split my waistcoat laughing. My *Jolly Beggar* didn't get off till noonday. Guess we kind of showed up the rest of the boys, didn't we?"

Percival was full of good spirits, even discussed the marriage date. The twenty-eighth was a Thursday. A good day. Trade would be slack then. He would see that everyone had cause to remember the wedding supper. The missis had even ordered Lucy's nuptial dress.

"I've got our table linen all hemmed," Lucy murmured to Tim in the study after dinner, her pale head bright on his shoulder, "and Mama is going to make us a compliment of that silver service our *Juno* captured in the old French war. Wine glasses, too. And Papa is being very generous. He says he will furnish a little setting room. Grandma Warren — it was she we went up to see at Concord —is going to send bed linen and a pair of elegant patchwork quilts she made all herself!"

Tim said, "Let me know if anybody gives us kitchen coppers. I'm counting on making you a Christmas gift of some."

Lucy hugged his arm, wrinkled her nose at him. "Aren't we the big stupids to go marrying right after Christmas? I guess plenty of people will combine their Christmas and wedding gifts. Ain't I the greedy little pig?"

"*Oink!*" he grunted, and kissed her soundly.

"Tell you a secret," Lucy said, looking a little scared. "This time I know what Papa intends telling you. I overheard him talking to a commissioner from Philadelphia. The sooner you know about it the greater chance you — I mean *we* — stand of profiting."

He looked at her with suspicion. "Are you serious?"

"As ever in my life, dear." She put her mouth so close to his ear that it tickled. He forgot about that when he heard her next words:

"Does your father know that the Congress intends to *build a navy?*"

"A what?"

Her blue eyes very round, Lucy nodded. "Yes, I heard Stephen Hopkins telling Papa. And two of the warships are to be built and outfitted in Rhode Island!"

Outfitted! Bennett & Son were ship chandlers, among other things. She began to talk in a rapid undertone.

"Next week Pa is going to meet the commissioners. Mr. Hopkins said some merchantmen will be armed as a stopgap until we can build real men-o'-war."

"That's right. We couldn't start work for a good while. Not until spring."

"Mr. Hopkins told Papa some ships have already been bought in Baltimore, in Maryland. One has been purchased here, and two in New York."

"Naval building means good profits for the shipyards," Tim said, thinking aloud.

"We had better take our profit while we can." Lucy was very like her mother now. "Papa fears the merchants of America will be taxed blue in the face to keep this navy afloat. Personally, he stands for fortifying our harbors. Forts would keep the enemy off, wouldn't they?"

"I guess so," Tim agreed absently. "It would be fine to see the *Rose*, the *Glasgow*, and the rest driven away."

The Leanto

When it was a quarter past four, Desire Harmony settled her shawl, then tied on a cloak equipped with a hood. In the twilight quiet of the woods she would feel that John was nearer. Weeks ago they had agreed to think very hard of each other at precisely half past four of each afternoon. Surely the intensity of their love must create vibrations that could span the space between them. Walking lightly, heels twinkling as usual, she hurried off through a grove of young birches growing beyond the barn.

Oh, dear Lord, why have you ordained that I must live in such troublous times? Young people *ought* to have a good time. We are young for so short a time. It isn't fair that Tim and Lucy are free to kiss and fondle whenever they want, while John and I are forbidden just because he's British.

[197]

From the edge of the birch grove she glimpsed a figure so long and supple that it must be Mr. Higsby, working at something out near the tip of Fox Hill Point. Her boredom vanished. With cloak whipping about her legs, Desire guessed she must look quite dramatic — perhaps like poor Mary, luckless Queen of Scots, reviewing her troops?

Once among the fir trees she was quick to discern an unfamiliar outline. Beside a huge spruce just above the floor of the ravine a triangular structure sloped back to a long point. This must be Mr. Higsby's leanto Tim had mentioned.

Naturally observant, Desire wondered why there were no cut branches or ax marks on any of the nearby trees. When the local boys went camping, you couldn't miss the place for blazes and hacked limbs. Plenty of times when she was a little girl she had been able to crawl up close without any of the boys suspecting her presence. It was once when the Gardner boys made ready to go swimming that she learned that boys were constructed differently.

How would a timber beast, as he called himself, arrange his quarters? She half fancied that he might be given to worshiping strange graven idols — like an Indian.

A small pile of firewood stood beside the leanto. A breathless temptation to inspect his quarters presented itself. Why not? Mr. Higsby was way down on Fox Hill Point and this all came under the head of learning about people. An actress must understand a wide variety of characters if she was to become famous.

Timidly, Desire descended into the hollow and paused briefly to inspect a fireplace cleverly contrived of smooth glacial boulders. A slightly charred lugpole of green elm canted over the ashes and blackened stick ends. A small, scrupulously clean brass kettle lay to one side; the frozen carcasses of three rabbits dangled pathetically from a branch. Stretched on hoops, the pelts of a big raccoon and three red foxes were drying.

Heart hammering, Desire thrust her head past an old cowhide doing duty as a door. Um-m. It was dark in the leanto and the air was fragrant with spruce. She also recognized the smell of tobacco and an odor pungent yet not unpleasant. It resembled that of a clean dog.

Hanging from a peg was the shirt that had been dyed with sumac. Its rich red-brown hue delighted her. Why in the world had the Friends long since decided that anything colorful was necessarily evil? What with Mr. Higsby's soft voice, black hair, and such a red shirt she stood ready to wager he could catch the eye of almost any girl. She stepped inside.

A dull sheen attracted her attention.

"Well, I never!" she burst out when she realized that it was a petticoat — a fine lawn one. Now why in the world would a good third of it have been so carefully trimmed away? This must mean that Mr. Higsby *was* what John called a lady killer! Funny part of it was, she'd guessed this was so all along. She giggled.

[198]

Curiosity mounting, Desire inspected his bed, even sat on it and jounced once or twice. Most surprisingly, it was almost as soft as her own. On a rough shelf lay a razor, a little bag of salt and a twist of tobacco bearing toothmarks.

If only it were possible to meet John in so cozy a hideaway. They both felt it monstrous humiliating to slink about, to meet in the barn or in that dusty recess behind Mr. Southwick's book cases. Love shouldn't be furtive. Love should be brave and straightforward! It afforded her considerable consolation to know that in another fortnight she and John could face the world unafraid, unashamed.

When Desire put down her hand to straighten herself from the bed her fingers encountered a hard object among the sprucetips. Why, it was a rifle's lock! What in heaven's name could Mr. Higsby want with two guns? Or was it just a pistol? Cautiously, she began to burrow.

"Oh-h!" Someone fetched her a resounding cut across the bottom. Another, impartially to the other buttock. In a mixture of terror and outrage, she whirled about.

Lean of jaw and very forbidding of expression, Higsby was squatting in the doorway, a long willow switch in his hand.

"Well, Miss curiosity, if you've done rummagin' my affairs, you kin come out."

He aims to whip me! was Desire's panic-stricken thought. He'd a perfect right too. Why, oh why, had she ever forgot herself enough to go prying about a stranger's private effects?

"Oh, please, Mr. Higsby — don't — I — I — I — di-didn't mean any h-harm — "

The ranger reached in at her, but hesitated, settled back on one knee. Obviously suspicious, he watched a long minute, then said anxiously, "Don't carry on that way, Miss Desire. I didn't aim to strike so hard, only you hadn't no business in my affairs."

More wails and sobs. "Oh, dear, I know you — you're g-going to — to — whip me — "

" — Not if you hush that fuss."

"Y-you won't tell P-Papa?" Great dark eyes swimming, she peeped over the crook of her elbow.

"Come out here an' — an' we'll talk about it." Pity she was Tim's sister. Them light brown shadows under her eyes shore warmed a man.

It was only when Desire had emerged that he noticed her cheeks were not even damp.

"Well, I'm damned!" he growled. Fancy getting took in like this. "You're smarter'n a she-fox with pups! You shore took me in."

"Did I, Mr. Higsby?" Desire began to smile, a bit breathlessly. "Did I sound as if I was really crying?"

"Sounded like you was bein' skinned alive." He kept sober with an effort. "You'd ought to be ashamed messin' 'round a man's kit."

"Tim told me what a wonderful Indian fighter you are. I — oh — dear, I did *so* want to see a scalp, to really touch one."

He stared. For the first time a girl was proving one too many for him. Great guns! What a way she had with her. When she got older, he bet she'd set the boys a pretty pace. "You wouldn't really want to see a skelp?"

"Oh, please, Mr. Higsby — " Her face was right at his shoulder, trustful, eager. " — If I'm not overbold."

A quarter of an hour later she was still hearing just how he'd killed the Tuscarora subchief. Higsby, squatting comfortably on his heels, was drawing designs on the ground with a stick. Here was where he had first cut the Tuscarora's trail. Now this was the way he had circled to head him off.

"How prodigiously clever of you." She smiled. "Were you ever in love, Mr. Higsby?"

He was so taken aback he almost cussed. "Shucks! You ain't even been listenin'. An' it's lots harder to lift a Injun's skelp than it is to roll — er — court a gal."

" —Some girls," Desire corrected primly.

She let him talk another ten minutes then, sedately, departed for home.

December 10, 1775

Oh, bother! thought Desire. The grandmother clock on the landing was chiming half after eight. Better pretend to go to bed else Mamba would notice. The old Negro woman had monstrous sharp ears and a curiosity to match.

The treads beneath her feet felt as if made of wool. La! In a very little time now John's dear arms would be close about her and banish all things save love. Would he wear his new wig? The one with the tight little curls over his ears? John had lovely small ears which lay crisp and flat against his skull.

Without undressing, she got into bed, and lay there listening to the wind rattling the privy door. There would be a moon later if the clouds didn't hide it. Nine o'clock. Only an hour more!

She would coax him to recite poetry. John really had a prodigious fine speaking voice, like warm honey spread on a hot biscuit.

"Had to walk over — worth it, though." John St. Clair's slim outline materialized among a grove of apple trees standing in silhouette back of the barn.

"Darling!" Desire rushed to him, felt a gloved hand at the back of her head. It pressed her face tight, almost cruelly tight, against his.

"Ah, sweeting — so many eternities." His boat cloak whipping about them, they clung to each other a timeless interval. At last she took his hand.

"Come, out here we will soon freeze."

"Quite right — it *is* a bit airy!"

The Right Honourable John St. Clair, sub-lieutenant in His Britannic Majesty's Regiment of Marine Light Infantry, followed her into the comparative warmth of the barn. He sighed. How deliciously sweet and homely it was here; forcefully reminiscent of those mews behind the great Norman castle which had sheltered the St. Clairs since Rufus the Red had ruled.

Desire, all breathless, cried, "John. Pray stand against that wall. Stand quite still, it's for only a moment."

Obediently, Lieutenant the Right Honourable John St. Clair remained with chin up, feet together. Abruptly his hand flickered to his sword. A slim blade hissed free, flashed up and he held an ivory guard carved in the shape of a mermaid in line with his lips. "Salute! Tender commander of my destiny."

Then she guided him past the three cows solemnly chewing their cuds in their stalls, past a pair of broad-sterned farm horses.

"This way one ascends again to heaven," he murmured. "Pray lead the way."

Although he couldn't see a thing, the Honourable John nimbly scaled a ladder leading to the loft and found it easier than climbing a ship's side in a seaway. After the biting wind beating up the East Passage and along the Ferry Road, it felt deliciously warm in the loft.

He had never thought it possible to tumble head-over-heels in love like this. But, pox take it, he had. He was simply mad for this adorable little Quaker. Come what might, he would have her to wife. By Gad! She would make a lovelier bride than had either of his brothers'.

The Honourable John hurried to unhook his cloak. He spread it on the hay then eased Desire to a seat beside him. Just enough light seeped through the dusty panes of a small window to create outlines.

"At last, my Thetis, at last!" John swept her into his arms, kissed her again and again.

His lips were so close she could feel their vibrations when he talked. Suddenly, a violent internal trembling seized her legs. The arteries in her throat began pounding so hard she couldn't hear John's voice. Fierce, warm currents invaded her cheeks, her breasts, her thighs. An inexorable force began to bend her over backwards, backwards onto the cloak.

Her hands, groping for support, met only his face and slipped hungrily about his neck. Darkness, fragrant of a thousand dried blossoms. Hundreds of tiny comets, flashing and spinning.

"John — dearest John," she gasped, "you — I — "

"Dee, this can't — this won't — "

His lips brushed the lids of her tight-closed eyes. She shivered. When his hands entered her bodice they were cold and rough, yet so welcome.

[201]

"Dee — ?"

"What difference?" she heard her own voice ask of the dark. "There is no reason — John — in two days more. Can't bear waiting — for fulfilment — ah, gently, adored lover."

He sounded breathless as a spent runner. "Dee, — my sweet wife." His hands fumbled further, deliciously eager and awkward. "And you *are* my wife — have been in soul — these three months! Soul is what really counts. Rest — stupid formality."

A torrid whirlwind began to blow through the loft. It beat through the folds of the cloak, penetrated the cloth covering their bodies, bared them, fused them.

The whole world began to spin — faster — faster.

Raid

When, shortly after midnight, he heard a voice below his window, Tim guessed Higsby had routed himself out early, really too early, and was waiting to go wild fowling. Snapper was growling, though, and raising his hackles. Self-deception ended at once. It could not be just the rifleman. Below sounded not one but many voices.

"Open! Open!" a muffled voice was calling.

From his window Tim was startled to see the lane, the barnyard and the front lawn swarming with dark figures. They showed up remarkably clearly against the snow.

There was a shattering thud as of an ax being driven hard into the front door. Voices were bellowing, "Open up! Open up! Get out, or fry in your own juice!"

In the rear of the house Mamba began to raise peal on peal of terror-stricken screams. Snapper set up a frenzied barking.

British raiders! The sickening realization hit Tim. Looked like a mixed landing party. Seamen, marines, and a handful of soldiers. Most numerous were the sailors in their distinctive petticoat breeches and a ragged miscellany of coats and jerkins. They wore big, brass-hilted navy hangers, and had boarding pistols jammed into wide leather belts.

He made out quite a few Negroes milling about in striped jerseys. These carried axes and candle lanterns. Drawn up in the front yard waited a file of Royal Marines.

"Turn out! In the king's name!" The voice was incisive, particularly ominous because of its lack of excitement. "Turn out, you confounded rebels!"

Tim encountered his father at the head of the stairs. Pa was blinking short-sightedly, making small, aimless motions. His long night cap dangled over thin shoulders.

"Timothy," he quavered, "what can this mean? What offense have we committed? The committee cannot call us to account."

"Pa, it's not the Sons of Liberty. It's the British."

At the foot of the stairs a red-coated figure was flashing a whale-oil lantern. He saw the two Bennetts standing there in their nightshirts.

"In just three minutes," he called, "my men will fire this house. You had better make haste."

Coughing in the smoke of the pine-knot torches, Tim calculated that that distant glare must be the Widow Hull's house afire — or was it Ben Elley's place?

"Come down, both of you, or I shall not be responsible." The officer saw Tim's scarlet, twitching face and immediately leveled a big brass-mounted pistol. Said he evenly, "One bit of resistance, my lad, and I will shoot you dead."

In the dining room sounded the clink of silver, the heavy crash of a cabinet overturned.

Asa Bennett shuffled forward. He looked as if someone had just hit him on the head.

"Rebels forfeit protection," roared the officer, a bony-faced lieutenant with a great brown wen on the point of his jaw. "Get outside!"

Hatless, a ragged seaman burst out of the dining room lugging a window curtain draped over one shoulder and waving Mrs. Bennett's most prized wedding gift, a real silver teapot.

When he saw that, Tim uttered a strangled grunt and, vaulting over the stair rail, smashed the fellow flat. Berserk, he flailed at the looters, who hampered by their plunder gave way. He felt the nosebones of a gap-toothed black crush under his blow. The swine was lugging a whole armful of Desire's dresses!

"Restrain that madman," the officer directed hurriedly.

A trio of marines leaped forward and one of them brought a blunderbuss barrel smacking down on Tim's head. His knees buckled, and desperately he clung to the stair rail, a torrent of hot blood pouring from his lacerated scalp.

That blow did a strange thing to Tim. He was able to tell what was going on, but for the life of him he could not command his limbs. Any ability to move of his own volition had left him. He could do nothing to the pair of marines who frog-marched him out into the front yard.

The Orchard Fight

Sam Higsby awoke at the very first impact of a musket butt against Asa Bennett's door. Despite the wind, he could hear hammering continue in the distance. From the summit of the ravine, he saw lights weaving crazy patterns about the Bennett place. Faint shouts.

By Jesus, if this wasn't New England, he'd say this disturbance had all the signs of a Injun attack. But what the hell? In these parts there weren't no savages worth mentioning.

He hesitated until, back of the road, a dull glow began to show. Sifting through the trees, he saw the glare of several other fires. Their light began to tint the tops of the spruces all about. Running back to his camp, he got busy. By the time he had slung his equipment and had regained the ridge, its whole crest was penciled in a bright pink which steadily deepened to a throbbing orange red. He could see terrified stock galloping about in the fields nearest the houses. He recognized such firelight.

No doubt now that the Britainers were pulling off a raid. Great screeching catamounts! Farms were blazing all along the Ferry Road. This promised to develop into a real interesting skirmish. His heart lifted and softly he began to hum a Cherokee chant old Standing Turkey had taught him. After tightening his laces, the Pennsylvanian started off towards the northeast. He halted almost at once. Somewhere to the left six, eight, ten shots were fired.

They formed no part of a volley, just a scattered, irregular popping. Survivors putting up a fight would fire like that. He began to grin.

He lingered just an instant studying over that little valley which, bisecting Conanicut Island, sheltered the Ferry Road. From the East Ferry on the Newport side of Conanicut to the West Ferry on the Narragansett side was less than a mile, but it was still a good long way to retreat if folks were shooting at you.

As the ranger broke into a run, he bit off a chew of tobacco, then fed rifle balls into his cheeks until they bulged like a squirrel's in acorn time.

Higsby's grin faded the minute he saw fire spurting from old Mr. Bennett's fine house. One of the plow horses dashed out of the barn and, in blind terror, charged straight across the meadow, tail up, mane flying. When it reached some boulders edging a little creek, the great, clumsy beast fell heavily and floundered about but could not regain its feet. Higsby reckoned the critter must have broken a leg.

Hitching his big powder horn around where it would be easier to get at, the rifleman advanced, ghosting forward among rows of twisted trunks in the apple orchard. Quite unnoticed, he reached a stone wall just below the barn. Though he waited quite a spell for a crack at an officer, he couldn't see one. In the firelit barnyard was only a tangle of red coats, white crossbelts and a swarm of blacks and sailors. The bastards! They were fixin to touch off the barn, too.

At last he glimpsed a sergeant — a big fellow carrying a sort of light spear, the kind the Indians had made copies of near Fort Ninety-Six. The Britainer was only forty yards off but with this blizzard blowing he offered no easy mark. Stomach tightening with pleasure, he leveled the Leman over a row of snowy stones. He took aim for the sergeant's heart, but since he was raiding Tim's pa's place, he sent the ball through the Britainer's belly instead.

As Higsby had calculated, the fellow's shrieks of agony diverted attention from the stone wall and the puff of gray smoke drifting above it. Before anybody spotted him, he had more than half reloaded.

"There he is! Down behind the wall. Come on. Kill the bleeding swine!"

Checking their priming as they ran, a trio of marines started down towards him, their bayonets agleam in flames that were lighting the whole countryside.

Deliberately Higsby permitted them to come within thirty yards, then threw his sights on the second man in line. Between the eyes. When he fired, the marine's arms flew violently apart, and dropping his musket, he collapsed in a regular bellywhopper that sent the snow flying far out from under him.

The leader was only ten yards off and yelling his head off in triumph. He knew his enemy couldn't possibly have time to reload. Higsby began to run back among the apple trees.

"Nah, then, yer bleedin' skulker!" The marine halted and deliberately leveled his musket, but before he could pull the trigger a bright object skimmed at him and his head snapped back so hard it might have been kicked by a mule.

Heavily, he fell.

The third private slowed, halted his advance, seemed disconcerted because Higsby, instead of continuing his retreat, was running forward. Setting one foot to his latest victim's shoulders, the rifleman began jerking to free his war hatchet from the marine's skull.

When it wouldn't come loose, Higsby raised a scalp yell so terrifyingly fierce that the third man never even fired his musket but began to run away. He was foolish. Higsby snatched up the musket of the Englishman he had just killed and took a snap shot.

The clumsy Brown Bess's recoil made the rifleman's teeth rattle, and he cursed in disappointment because the last of his enemies only screamed, dropped his musket and ran on, clutching a shattered arm.

Higsby's flat features lit as he reloaded his rifle. Knocking over three hostiles in five minutes wasn't bad; it made him feel finer than silk.

Aware that the enemy were in hurried retreat from the Bennett place and in no mood further to molest him, he went over to his second victim. Gripping the corpse by its hair, he lifted the dead man's face out of the snow. By the light of the burning buildings, he could see snow adhering to the fellow's eyelashes.

A small black hole showed, a shade to the right of a center shot, 'twixt the eyes. Drops of blood fell slowly from between the dead man's teeth.

Mechanically, the ranger freed his knife and posed its blade to make the initial incision above the Britainer's left ear, but he checked himself. God-damn it, people in these parts didn't hold with skelping.

Oh, hell's roaring bells! Without his having proof, the fellers back in Keowee would never credit his having done for three redcoats inside as many minutes. He had to have proof of some kind, so he cut away the pewter plate from the front of the marine's cap and slipped it into his war-bag. As evidence the plate wasn't up to hair, yet it was something.

The Barn

Reluctantly, Lieutenant the Right Honourable John St. Clair roused from blissful semiconsciousness. Somewhere something was causing a rhythmic clinking noise. Couldn't be anything important.

He turned, tried to see Desire's face amid the fragrant gloom. Exhausted, apparently asleep, she was nestled so close beside him that he could feel her breath fanning the rumpled lace of his shirt front. This was his wife, the Lady Desire. Between them they certainly should get a goodly number of strong and handsome children.

Suddenly he heard a voice just outside the barn, and not an unfamiliar one either, snap, "Henderson, tell off six men and go on down to the ware-house. You have your instructions."

"Yes, sir!"

Blood in the Right Honourable John's ears commenced to surge and pound like the surf on the shore. Great God in heaven! That was George Sneyd out there, commander of H.M.S. *Bolton*. What the deuce had brought him over on Conanicut?

Rallying his perceptions, he sat bolt upright, but Desire, childlike, slept on. To his ears came a host of subtle, significant sounds: the clink of a musket butt against a belt buckle, the soft *zwe-e-ep* of a cutlass sliding out of its sheath.

Desire awoke, sat up and turned eyes that were concentric rings of white. In a tense whisper, she asked, "What — what is happening?"

His hand slipped none too gently over her mouth. It was shaking.

"Quiet, for God's sake. Landing party — our ships," he barely enun-ciated. Didn't want to call it a raid. Even now he wasn't sure about what was afoot. The Right Honourable John kept telling himself he wasn't frightened. He and Dee would get out of this somehow. Of course they would.

Desperately, the Honourable John sat staring into the dark, trying to find some encouragement in the situation. He must present a ridiculous figure with his wig full of hay, his uniform dusty, and his stock twisted around under one ear. The heat of their love was still upon him and his cambric shirt was damp beneath his tunic.

"What's that?" A rising glare beat through cracks in the wall.

"Bad business," he breathed. "Must keep our heads, dear. Any other way out of this loft?"

"Only down the ladder." Her hand closed confidently on his. "I — I'm not afraid, John."

John sat rigid, listening, trying to guess what was going on at the house.

Suddenly everyone in the yard began yelling. Smoke drifted in the open door of the barn, stung Desire's eyes. A bright glare began to beat in the dusty window beside them.

"Oh, John, they're burning my home. Stop them! They mustn't. Papa has never harmed the British — or anyone. He wouldn't even pay war taxes. Quakers don't fight!"

"I can't — daren't show myself — " he whispered savagely. "This is a blunder. A stupid blunder. I can promise you there will be the devil to pay when news of this reaches home. We have influence in Parliament, strong influence." His unsheathed sword lay like a silver ruler mark across the hay.

"What must we do?"

"Wait. That's all. If Sneyd doesn't burn the barn we will be safe."

The Right Honourable John heaved a great sigh, wiped a heavy beading of sweat from his forehead.

"We're safe. Sneyd's falling in his men. They will be gone soon."

Someone ran in bringing bright patches of light. It was a Negro carrying a blazing brand.

"Hya! Hya!" he chuckled and disappeared. Almost at once swift spirals of fire began to lick up at the far end of the loft where the grain chutes were. Billows of smoke filled the barn. Outside sounded a single staccato shot, and just beyond the door a Yorkshireman clutched his belly and collapsed. He began to scream, to writhe and jerk. Men ran to bend him over. Others ran about.

Burning hay flung sheets of flame towards clusters of feed corn tied to the rafters and infernally hot waves of smoke beat at the two in the loft. Coughing, they figured to hold out awhile longer.

"They've gone. Come." His fingers closed over her wrist, but she thought that someone might still be out there in the firelight and flinched back.

"You sure?" she choked. "What would people say?"

"Jolly well say we're dead if — don't leave. Come." As he ran over to the ladder Desire saw that John had done up his waistcoat buttons all wrong.

Just inside the door John picked her up, slid an arm under her armpits. Because the wind was being drawn in to feed the flames, they had got fresh air—a second's respite. Dashing water from his eyes, the Right Honourable John saw the yard empty save for a weird miscellany of abandoned plunder.

"All clear, my chick," said he. "We will round the barn and run parallel to the road. Come. There is nobody about."

Lieutenant St. Clair was wrong. On the far side of the ring of firelight six men were coming up, and out of sight, on the opposite side of the barn, Asa Bennett, Tim and the two servants remained in stunned reaction.

"Faster, darling," pleaded the Right Honourable John as they ran along the Ferry Road. "You must run faster if we are to come up with Sneyd."

"Can't — hurt my knee," gasped Desire. Her legs felt all weak and uncertain, like a newborn foal's, and her lungs appeared to be drawing in no air at all.

"You run — ahead." She halted, began rubbing at her injured leg. "I — wait — here. You bring back some men."

John St. Clair saw that she really was winded and incapable of further flight. "Capital idea; wait here beside road. I'll fetch squad back — five minutes."

When Sam Higsby spotted the Right Honourable John, he halted in the lee of a haycock. The rifleman had been moving parallel to the Ferry Road waiting for a skirmish to develop and still hoping to pick off an officer. Certainly he should get a shot at some straggler. This was good frontier tactics.

The range he estimated as close on fifty yards and since the fellow was running fast, Higsby whipped out his ramrod and gave his charge a couple of extra hard *whams* just to seat his ball tighter.

By God, that Britainer, for all his silly hampering uniform, was coming on most as fast as an Injun. He'd pass, he now judged, near sixty yards off. Say, wouldn't it be grand if only Miss Desire was here? For a gal she had exhibited a real interest in rifles and marksmanship.

Yessir, just for the sake of them shadowed eyes of hers, he would make this one a real sporting shot. He would let the Britainer go by and take him going away — if he was able. The moon was at this moment near to breaking through the snow clouds. It illuminated the whole scene with a silvery radiance.

Distinctly, he heard the impact of the runner's feet grow louder. When he passed the haycock, Higsby drew a shallow breath. The long rifle's barrel went out and steadied itself. Sighting at the center of the Britainer's back, he knew he was a fool to have let the fellow go by. In jumping to avoid frozen puddles, the runner made a crazy mark to try to shoot at. Nor did the falling snow make sighting any easier.

Now! He squeezed steadily with his whole hand until a pencil of flame spurted up from the pan. The Leman's cold stock rapped smartly against Higsby's cheek as, seventy yards away, Lieutenant the Right Honourable

John St. Clair faltered. The speed of his running made him roll over and over — just like a shot rabbit. He lay sprawled on the road, arms twitching spasmodically.

Reloading as he ran, Higsby pelted over to the road. His face lit. Jesus Christ! What a sweet honey of a shot, and — yes — *he had got him a officer!* When he reached him the Britainer was stone dead and lay on his belly with his thin, handsome face twisted 'way over to one side.

Say, wouldn't Miss Desire be tickled particular pink when she heard of his picking off an officer at near seventy paces?

If he figgered on improving his tally, he knew he had better shake a leg. What could he take for proof? Hell, this officer hadn't no hat. But there was a sword lying a few feet back. The Pennsylvanian picked it up. Shucks, 'twas much too light to be of any use in a free-for-all. Its ivory grip was pretty, though, carved in a queer shape, half fish and half girl. Placing the blade against the earth, he set a heel on the steel and pulled. The blade broke off just below the guard.

Yessir, this hilt would make a damned fine trophy to give Miss Desire.

Though the snow was lessening, Desire realized it was growing colder. Now that she was losing the warmth gained by running, she began to shiver. Had there ever been another night so dreadful?

Her knees, as well as other parts of her, ached and burned. Why hadn't she had the wit to bring along her shawl? It must have got lost in the hay. The only redeeming element to this dreadful business was the way John had acted. How very splendid he had been during the crisis. She would love him more intensely than ever now.

Good thing they had a refuge aboard the *Swan*. After tonight she could never stay on Conanicut. The Gardners had seen her, of course. The rest, too. By morning the scandal would be all over Newport. What she and John had done hadn't been wrong; she was convinced of that. True love was sacred. When people felt as they did, nothing else mattered. If she wished it, they would be married tomorrow. John had promised so and was just as eager as she.

Homes destroyed earlier had resolved to mounds of embers furiously smoking and glowing in the center of rings of black and trampled earth. In a field opposite, some loose horses had gathered and stood with tails turned to the rising wind. Up the road someone fired a shot.

What could be delaying John? She got very worried because now a straggling string of reports marked the beginning of a skirmish of some sort.

May as well walk to meet him, Desire told herself, and began to limp towards the East Ferry. Though she wanted to turn, the fear suddenly came that she, too, might be transformed into a pillar of salt, like the wife of Lot, the Sodomite. She didn't dare look back to see what was left of her home.

Onwards. Where *was* John? Surely he must have started back for her?

A clock, a pair of woman's stays, a brass candlestick and the droppings of stolen cattle marked the new snow.

At a sound of hurrying feet, her heart quickened. John and the squad! But then she was aware that these men were coming up from behind. From where she stood on the summit she could see eight or nine of them coming along at a slow trot — British stragglers.

A snow squall cut off all distant objects.

Something big and dark lay in the road some distance ahead. At first she thought that somebody must have lost his coat but a few more strides told her that it was a man who lay across the frozen ruts. This was strange. The British were conscientious about bringing off their dead and wounded.

Heavens! That shooting she'd heard! John's party must have been attacked and driven back. The dead man *was a marine* — his black-gaitered legs and the white lining of his tunic left no room for doubt.

All at once Desire became appallingly convinced that she would never become Lady St. Clair. A few more faltering steps told her that never again in this life would John's arms go about her. The intoxicating pressure of his lips would be forever lost. Never! Never! Incredulously, she regarded the slender, clean-limbed body at her feet.

Somewhere, millions of miles away, an owl began hooting.

Like an icicle of steel, the broken blade of John's sword lay beside him. What could have happened to its hilt? Somewhere she had read that a dead officer must be buried with hands clasped on his sword. The blade would have to do.

Trying not to see that soggy little hole between John's shoulders, Desire Harmony tugged his body onto its back and straightened the disordered buttons. She couldn't help noticing how John's blood went creeping off down a wagon rut, sketching an erratic course.

Dimly she became aware of men calling in the distance. She only knew that John was looking up at her, with lips slightly parted. There was only a drop or two of blood on them, which she hurriedly wiped away.

"Well, I'm damned! It's Dee Bennett," exclaimed Jed Franklin, as he came up to her. Then angrily, "Say, what you doin' with this goddamned lobsterback?"

Looking up she saw a dark ring of faces gathered above her. The neighbors were carrying muskets and were breathing hard.

"He is dead," she told them dully. "John has been killed."

"Good riddance," young John Gardner snarled. "Come along, fellers, we must be gettin' close to 'em, now."

Old John Gardner hesitated. "Walt, maybe you had better take Miss Bennett down to Ma at our boat shed. She will freeze to death out here."

"Let her freeze!" Walt snapped. "I'll have no lobsterback's fancy girl mingling with my sisters." He had always hated the Bennetts, had envied their superior way of life. "I'm going. Coming along?"

Fancy girl! Desire winced and her fingers sought John's hand. It was so chilly it failed to lend her the strength she had hoped for.

"You oughter get whipped through town," Mark Remington growled. He didn't really think so, but he was still mad about losing those fine oxen.

Jed Franklin shouldered his musket. "Aw, let her be. She can peddle her arse through the hull British navy for all I care."

"Judge not lest ye, too, be judged," warned old John. "I am sorry for the child! Go to our boat shed, Miss Bennett; we have a fire there."

Ashes

Mr. Isaac Percival chipped away the top of his egg, sniffed it suspiciously as he always did. Mrs. Percival, ramrod straight at her end of the table, watched him narrowly. So far she hadn't tasted a morsel. Since that glare of fires had begun to glow across the East Passage, she had been up and about.

"Well, Mr. Percival, what do you hear about Captain Wallace's doings on Conanicut?"

Isaac Percival employed a horn egg spoon with deliberation, swallowed a mouthful. "A wretched business, my dear — wretched, for *some*." He regarded his wife expectantly. "You follow my meaning?"

" — Of course, I'm no numskull." Across a white expanse of tablecloth their eyes met. Though they had never loved, they enjoyed a community of understanding. "You mean such a — a brutal deed will benefit us?"

Ike Percival made a clunking noise in the back of his throat. "How can it fail to? The Provincial legislature will — must, in retaliation — authorize an outfitting of letters of marque and privateers. The Continental Congress — ahem — may follow suit."

"Shouldn't wonder."

"In that case, my dear, I shall sell our chandler's stores at a neat profit. Yes, a *very* neat profit."

Lizzie Percival cocked her head to one side and her jet earrings flashed. "It would help me to understand the precise definition of a letter of marque."

Mr. Percival's thin arm prolonged itself in the direction of the honey pot. He was careful, however, to keep his wrist lace free of the butter.

"A letter of marque, Mrs. P., is an armed merchantman. Her chief function is — ahem — to transport merchandise. She is armed essentially to preserve her from attack. Of course, should she chance to fall in with a weak vessel belonging to the enemy — ahem — a letter of marque's commission entitles her to attack and capture such a craft."

" — And a privateer?" Lizzie Percival knew perfectly well, but equally well she was aware that it flattered Isaac to appear wise at the breakfast table. Desperately, she wanted him in a good humor on this of all mornings.

"A privateer; my dear, is either built as a vessel of war or is converted to the purpose from a fast merchantman. Ahem. She signs a crew twice to three times as large as an ordinary merchantman and a double complement of officers." His sparse gray brows knit themselves. "Expensive, my dear, very expensive — especially those extra officers."

"And her purpose?"

" — Is to cruise, not trade. She sails to seize as many enemy vessels as she may — ahem — with the least possible risk to herself."

"Mr. Percival?" When Lizzie used that tone of voice, Isaac knew she'd something on her mind. "What will happen to the Bennetts?"

There it was! He had hoped Lizzie would say nothing until he had gleaned further. Sighing, he wiped his mouth, leaving a yellow crescent on the napkin.

"I have been pondering that question, my dear, with due attention."

"They are ruined?" Shrewd black eyes met sly gray ones.

"Inevitably, Elizabeth, inevitably. Asa Bennett is — er — beggared. Must be. And there is all this talk about Tim's having deserted."

"Under the circumstances, ahem, well — wouldn't it seem advisable to — er-r — ?"

" — To postpone the nuptials?" The merchant spread honey thickly over a crumpet. "You are entirely right. For some time to come, I fear, Timothy will be in no state to assume — ahem — additional responsibilities."

Mrs. Percival looked her spouse squarely in the eye. "But what of Lucy? She dotes on Timothy."

"As always," came the bland reply, "Lucy will do as we tell her. I am entirely confident on the point."

Mrs. Percival sat quite still.

He glanced up, surprised. "Do you imply that our child will not obey?"

Mrs. Percival pursed lips of the palest pink. "I have brought her up so well I presume she likely will. But — "

" — But?"

"Young people in love — well — sometimes they don't see the common sense of things."

"Love? Rubbish! Silly twaddle."

Mrs. Percival's wax-hued features softened and, as her color rose, she became almost handsome.

"Love? What do you know of love, Isaac? What do I, for that matter? We know nothing about it. Guess we — well, we hadn't time for love. That has been our loss."

"Whatever has got you so addled?

"Can't rightly say. It's that — well, maybe I'd like for Lucy to enjoy some of the things I missed — and you missed, Mr. Percival."

When Lucy appeared she had stopped crying but her eyes were bloodshot and her nose pink and swollen.

"Well, child, and how is my favorite daughter this morning?"

Eyes brimming suddenly, she wailed, "Oh, Papa, it's so awful not knowing. Tim may be hurt, even dead!"

Mr. Percival cleared his throat and his pale eyes sought the window. He hated a display of emotion.

"We trust not. Shortly, we will become informed as to just what has taken place. Ahem, Benson has been up since dawn. I gave him instructions to question anyone arriving from the island."

The girl slipped her napkin from its ring, dropped heavily onto her chair. "But what is known to have chanced?"

Her father shook his head dolefully. "Only that Captain Wallace's men ravaged the island — ahem — with fire and sword." He liked the sound of that. "Fire and sword" was a fine, round phrase.

"But, why, *why?*"

"As an object lesson, my dear, as an object lesson. Captain Wallace intends, ahem, to force us into supplying the king's ships. First Conanicut, then Newport, if the food treaty is not renewed. If we continue to supply his ships, he will spare this port."

As footsteps shuffled nearer along the back hall Mrs. Percival's hand came to rest on her daughter's. Big brown freckles dotted its back. It was a plain, strong hand, unornamented save for a narrow wedding band.

"Whatever chances," she whispered, "you *must* believe that I act in the interests of your eventual happiness."

Lizzie Percival was surprised at herself. Till this moment she hadn't realized that she cared tuppence about what went on inside Lucy's blonde head.

A furtive, round-shouldered little man in a dingy scratch wig shuffled in. His blunt nose was purple and moist from the cold.

Benson bowed hurriedly to his employers. "Sarvice, sir; sarvice, ma'am, miss."

Ike Percival sat straight and glared, as he always did at his employees. The rascals never understood kindness.

"Well? Speak up! Speak up, man!"

"Yes, Mr. Percival, sir." Nervously, Benson began revolving a battered fur cap. "It were an awful thing, that raid. 'Pears that near midnight Cap'n Wallace's people drove the Conanicut folks right out of their houses into the snow. 'Twas a monstrous thing — "

A gesture from Isaac Percival cut him short: "Dispense with dramatics, Benson. Tell me what was done with Mr. Bennett's property."

Lucy's hands gripped the sides of her chair fit to snap its arms off. She guessed she knew now how an accused person felt when he stood up to hear the verdict. Wasn't Benson ever going to speak? Oh, curse him! Why did he have to stand there, stupidly crumpling his cap?

"For pity's sake, speak!" she blurted out. "Answer Mr. Percival."

As from a long distance she heard Benson reply, "Pardon, miss, I — I hates to say it, but they — well, they burned down Mr. Bennett's house and barn. They cut out a schooner he had laying to the wharf; then they fired the warehouse — "

"Did they burn his ropewalk, too?" Mrs. Percival demanded.

"Yes, ma'am. Mr. Bennett ain't got nothink left, not a stiver! It's cruel hard on one so old."

Nothing left? It seemed as if hard, blunt fingers were being jammed into Lucy's ears.

"But the family?" she managed to ask. "Mr. Bennett and his family are safe?"

Benson misunderstood. "The old gent' took a chill, but they've brought him, and the wounded, safe to Mr. Warner's."

"Then there *was* fighting?" Percival interjected.

"Yessir, five or six of the bloodybacks was slain. One was a officer. And quite a parcel of them wounded."

"Don't be stupid," Mrs. Percival interrupted. "Is Mr. Timothy — old Mr. Bennett's son — safe?"

Benson forgot himself, scratched under a wig on which inky goose quills had created a smudge. "Why, ma'am, somebody said he got himself hurted bad."

"Badly! How badly?" Lucy felt the table, the whole room, sway before her.

Benson jumped, curled his cap brim into a desperately tight roll. "Why, mistress, some says one thing, some says another."

"Damn it, man, why don't you know?" Ike Percival shouted. "Why did I send you down to the harbor?"

So young Bennett was wounded, maybe incapacitated for weeks. Um. Should be easy as rolling off a log to snap up Bennett's old customers.

"They say he got hit in the head, was kind of stunned."

Lucy got up, chin quivering. "I must go to Tim — "

"You will not! Lucy, sit down!" said Ike Percival.

Trying to smooth things over, Mrs. Percival said, "I trust Mistress Bennett suffered no harm?"

"Why, ma'am, I guess she is all right." Benson shuffled. Embarrassed, his eyes sought the floor.

"What does that mean?"

"Please, ma'am, if I may make so bold — I — well, I ain't given to tale bearing."

"Go on, man, speak up," Isaac Percival roared. "What in blazes holds you gawping there?"

The clerk looked helplessly at Lucy but, aware of Mr. Percival's baleful

[214]

stare, stuttered, "When the Englishmen set fire to Mr. Bennett's b-barn, Mistress B-Bennett came running out."

"Well, what of that, you idiot?"

"A B-Br-British officer was with her!"

A faint, acid smile flitted over Isaac Percival's narrow mouth and he spoke softly, to himself it seemed.

"So Mistress Desire hides a scarlet letter beneath her Quaker's gray? What a pity. The Bennetts used to be a fine, respectable family. I pity Asa, one of his children a deserter, the other a trollop!"

Plunder

When she awoke around eight of the morning, Desire couldn't for the life of her think where she was. This wasn't her room with light yellow walls. Though she listened, she couldn't hear Mamba grumbling, rattling pots and pans downstairs. Where in the world?

Last thing she recalled was closing John's stiffening fingers over his sword blade. This undoubtedly was a woodshed, and she was terribly cold. Whose? Oh, yes — she half remembered creeping up to warm herself at the ashes of John Martin's house.

Mr. Martin's house had not burned entirely because a tabby stone wall had separated his kitchen from a sort of walled back porch. In this she discovered a sheaf of smoked salmon hanging from a roof beam. Also some frozen potatoes and onions in a little bin. This encouraged her to forget the snow in her shoes, her wet stockings and numb fingers.

A further search yielded a wooden noggin and a pewter plate containing a nondescript sticky mess. This she scrubbed as clean as possible.

Desire lowered the well sweep and drew a half bucket of icy water. After taking a long drink, she bathed her face. The water did clear her mind a bit and she perked up enough to tie a torn horse blanket about her.

When the sun slanted low over the Narragansett shore, Desire decided it was safe to reconnoiter. Nothing moved on the road now, save crows picking at some refuse. John St. Clair's body had been removed, but at the spot where he had lain a claret-colored stain marked the trampled snow. A cold, empty feeling invaded her with the realization that their married life had begun and ended within the span of one hundred and twenty minutes.

The half blanket about her shoulders, she hurried past the ruins of the Remingtons' and the Widow Hull's houses. Down by the river, Gardner's tanyard was still giving off smoke. Very likely the piles of bark there would smoulder for days.

Of Peaceful Haven nothing remained save the big chimney and four elms which would never leaf again. For yards about, the snow was black with burned-out brands. Down in the pasture beyond the apple orchard one of the plow team lay dead. The poor beast's legs poked queerly up out of the snow.

She found that the snow had been helpful in burying no end of useful objects: two blankets, a bundle of her own clothes containing a blouse, three petticoats, a shawl, three pairs of stockings — one pair silk — and a pair of shoes with heavy sterling silver buckles. Luckily they were solidly sewn and Boston cobbled. Her search also yielded the big silver spoon with which Papa had always ladled gravy and, best of all, a comb.

Utterly fantastic, incredible, all this. Yesterday at this time she had had a comfortable home, servants, plenty of food and a bed to sleep in.

And John.

Ruins

Two days went by before Tim Bennett could even raise his head without feeling all the world go spinning about. His split scalp itched and burned so he fell into a feverish doze which endured for interminable hours.

Somehow Sam Higsby had found him, had taken him away. To accommodate his guest the ranger must have widened and lengthened his leanto, besides raising a log front to it. Now it resembled a rough, triangular cabin. Sometimes Higsby went out and would be gone hours at a time. Where he went was of no interest to the patient.

Often Tim failed to hear the Pennsylvanian leave or arrive. It seemed incredible that anyone could move so softly.

From practically every absence he returned carrying a shirt, a blanket, or a soft cloth with which to dress his friend's raw and angry scalp.

"You sho' have a powerful thick skull," Higsby drawled. "That Britainer fetched you a mighty mean lick."

A jay began screeching up the hollow. Further off, a second jay taunted in reply.

Did Lucy know of the calamity? Dear Lucy, if only she could be here now. His bandage wanted changing, and despite the best of intentions, Sam was anything but gentle about the task.

Feeling mighty thirsty, Tim edged himself to a sitting position and drank from a birch-bark cup set beside the wooden water bucket. He was still drinking when the jay squawked again just outside and Sam Higsby's flat brown face darkened the door. He pitched a limp turkey gobbler onto the floor and slipped in. He had a parcel tucked under one arm.

He grinned. "Heyo. So you figger to sit up an' take notice?"

"Feel some better. Head don't whirl so bad anymore. Where did you find that turkey?" Tim knew a wild one hadn't been seen on the island in years.

Higsby looked very innocent. "Well, I was driftin' through that patch o' woods above the main road when I see this bird feedin' in a field. Sez I to myself, 'Sam, that pore critter looks god-awful cold an' lonesome out there. Wouldn't he look better all browned on a sassafras stick?' "

Admiringly, he extended a bronze-tinted wing. "Purty, ain't he? An' fatter'n a squaw in the family way."

Higsby was trying to act casual and cheerful-like because Tim was in for some very bad news and the poor feller didn't look fit to endure it.

Sinking onto his heels the ranger commenced vigorously to pluck the turkey onto an old blanket. "Now I wouldn't mind a lickin' an' I'd head back fer Boston right now, if I only was certain to see some fightin'." He grinned over his shoulder. "That there little brush with the redcoats t'other night pleasured me more than a kag of Mr. Booze's best whiskey. Wish't folks in this neck o' the woods wasn't so pernickety. I picked me off a officer an' under his wig he'd the softest skelp lock I ever laid a hand to."

At last Tim asked, "There's not much left of Pa's place?"

"Nope."

"Warehouse burnt?"

"Yep."

"Ropewalk, too?"

"Uh-huh." On the bed of spruce tips, Tim's face looked ghostly.

Sam frowned. He had done picking the turkey's back and was starting in on a leg. "Fine fowls, ain't they? These tame critters is different colored from the wild ones. They're redder an' smaller. Injuns, Conestogas 'specially, favor turkey-cock feathers in their headdress."

Tim wasn't to be diverted. "Sam, did you learn where my sister has gone? She came through safe, of course?"

"Heard tell so." Higsby studied to keep his voice steady. "Folks saw her after the fire was over." She was a cute piece, all right. Her wide, little-girl eyes sure had fooled him. Imagine Miss Desire gettin' flushed out of a loft, an' with a goddamn Britainer!

Yep. He was a fool not to have tumbled her when she came pesterin' about his camp the way she had. Of course those shadows under her eyes should have told him, but who would have figgered what she really wanted? He guessed he'd still plenty to learn about gals an' their 'cute little ways.

"Did you find out where Pa is?"

Higsby stopped plucking and his gaze wandered out of the doorway. Damn! He reckoned he'd have to spit it out after all.

"Yer pa was stayin' with a feller name of Redwood, a elder in yer church."

"*Was?* Where is he now?"

Higsby's hand, all fluffy with small feathers, came to rest on Tim's shoulder. "Tim, I —I'd ruther be skun alive than tell you — but, well — I guess I got to. Yer pa is dead. He died day after the raid."

Since he couldn't think of anything further to say, Higsby went on plucking the turkey. Little feathers drifted about, settled on Tim's bandage and unshaven cheeks.

At last he asked in a strained voice, "They — they wounded him?"

"Nope. Yer pa got took off with the lung fever. Doctor claimed 'twas caused by standin' 'round in the weather so long. A woman named Hull died o' the same ailment." He plucked faster. "They planted yer pa this mornin'. I'm — I'm right sorry, Tim. Yer pa was a fine old feller, mighty fine — even if he didn't hold with fightin'."

Next day Tim was set on going over to Newport. Though Higsby wouldn't let out a word, he sensed that something was wrong about Desire Harmony.

It was a bitter surprise to have had no word from Lucy. Wasn't it strange she had made no effort to find him? Then came the reassuring suspicion that the British had forbidden all traffic in the harbor.

Tim broke the news to Higsby by saying, "I'm going over to town and collect some debts that were owed Pa."

"You'd better," the rifleman agreed. "Some folks hev a short memory. Here, see if you can get into these."

From a canvas sack he dragged out a blue woolen jersey, some linsey-woolsey stockings, shoes and a pair of brown duroy breeches. All the clothes were in pretty good condition save the jersey. It had a small hole under its left arm; not a worn hole, either.

"Where did you get these things?"

Higsby spat tobacco juice at the fire. "Off'n a sailor."

"What did they cost? I want to pay you back."

"Nawthin'."

"Nothing?"

"Nope. He'd no use for 'em."

Tim gazed at the clothes. "You killed him?"

Higsby held up the jersey and, running his finger through the hole, wiggled it gently. "Naw, a bee stung him."

At the Pitt's Head

Tim decided that his bandaged head, sunken eyes and unshaven features were to thank for the absence of comment which attended his slow progress up Mill Street. Every few rods he had to stop, panting, to rest.

He knew he should stop in at a friseur's and have his week-old beard removed. But he was in too great a hurry to find Lucy. Of course, she could not have been told about what really had been done at Peaceful Haven.

The Percivals, through mistaken kindness, probably had given her false hopes and reassurances. Both of them imagined their daughter to be much more fragile and high-strung than she actually was. Lizzie Percival was forever insisting, "Lucy is so sensitive! The slightest excitement sends her into the vapors."

The snow was melting from nearby roofs, especially near the chimneys. Times must be hard when some shopkeepers dared offer such cheap and miserable Christmas gifts. Their stock was nothing but battered, unsalable, leftover merchandise. To whip up trade, Messrs. Hinchley & Bell had posted inviting broadsides offering. "A fine piece of Barley sugar with every Purchase amounting to ⅙ or more."

Each stride was taking him closer to Lucy of the smoky-blue eyes and the white-blonde hair. Never had he realized she lived so far out on the edge of town. Damn this weakness!

When he saw the big brick and clapboard Percival house beyond the Congregational Meeting House he wanted to run but his legs felt heavy as lead. Little bright points of fire began wavering before his eyes.

To Tim's vast surprise, Mrs. Percival herself, brown taffeta skirts rustling primly, answered the door.

She made no gesture to kiss him, only gave him a look of deep compassion. "Pray enter, Timothy, and accept my heartfelt sympathy."

Once they had seated themselves in the study, Mrs. Percival spoke at length, reviewed in surprising detail Asa Bennett's fine character and many kindly deeds.

When she discovered that Tim was in complete ignorance of how his father's last hours had been passed, she related everything of importance.

There was little to tell. The old Quaker's chill had progressed swiftly into lung fever and very quickly he had become delirious and had died without uttering a coherent phrase.

Since tokens of mourning and pomp of any sort were abhorred by the Society of Friends there had been no black, no wailing music, not even a choir. Nevertheless, the burial service had been impressive. Great quantities of people, Quakers and the World's People alike, had attended. Folks had come all the way from Tiverton, Narragansett and Little Compton.

Nearly every merchant and shipmaster in Newport had been among the multitude which gathered on the bleak hillside burying ground to hear "solid" Friends testify before the Lord that seldom had a more godly and generous man "traveled in the service of truth."

Now Asa Bennett was resting in an unmarked grave. The Friends did not hold with elaborate monuments. Of late, though, it had been conceded to those who yearned to mark a last resting place that they might, in propriety, raise an "unmarked stone no greater than eight by fourteen inches."

Tim listened heavily. It still seemed impossible that Pa would never again read from the Book in his deep, memorable voice. Presently he blurted out, "Where is Lucy? I — I need to see her."

Mrs. Percival's mouth tightened. She had been steeling herself for this. "Timothy. she is away — on a visit."

"*Away!*" The misery in the young fellow's bloodshot eyes gave Lizzie Percival a twinge. "She went away — now?"

"Don't you dare to misjudge her," Mrs. Percival warned sharply. "My daughter has only adopted a course which we all deem wise under the circumstances."

Had a mortar shell exploded at his feet, Tim could not have been more stunned. The only thing that had held together his courage, his reason, had been the prospect of curing his hurts with Lucy. How easily her gentle nature could have smoothed his anguish.

And now Lucy wasn't there with the expected encouragement and confidence. She had run away! "What we *all* deem wise —" that was what Mrs. Percival had said. "*All.*"

Mrs. Percival put forth a hand. "You, a man of the world, surely understand how unwise, how impossible, it is for you two to be wedded under the circumstances? Especially — "

" — Especially what?"

"There is the matter of your — I hesitate to mention the matter, Timothy, but it seems that I must — the matter of your having — er — come home early. People are saying hard things of you — quite unjustly, of course. Yet it will now be extra hard for you to undertake a fresh beginning."

"But Lucy, what does she say?"

"Your answer is that Lucy has gone away."

"Where is she?"

Mrs. Percival merely looked aside.

Angry color began to creep up along his bearded cheeks. "You better tell me where she is!"

The ruler-backed figure stiffened and the black eyes flickered back to him. "Timothy, pray don't make the situation more difficult than necessary. Anger will mend nothing."

She half held out a hand. "Believe me, I reasoned with Mr. Percival as long and hard as I dared; the most I was able to persuade him to grant was this: he will not oppose your wedding, if, *within a year,* he feels assured you can properly provide for Lucy. After all, Timothy, a year will pass — "

"A year?" A truculent twist hardened his wide mouth. "Aye, what's a year to people like you and old Ike? What's a year to a pair of dead, dried-up trees?"

"Timothy! How dare you!"

"I won't believe she has gone. She wouldn't leave me like this!"

"Lucy!" his voice grew hoarse as he called, "Lucy? Are you here? For God's sake answer — tell me you haven't gone away — I need you, Lucy!"

All the reply he got was a startled clatter of dishes in the pantry.

Ignoring Mrs. Percival's outraged protests, he climbed the stairs, wrenched open a door, "Lucy, where are you?" Another door. "Lucy! Come out. I can't stand this."

When he came at last to her room and he felt how cold it was, the truth sank in. The fireplace could not have been lit in some days.

It made matters no better that, stuck into a red, heart-shaped cushion, he recognized a silver and coral pin he had bought in Cambridge for her. He had posted it that September day when first he had been able to limp along without a stick.

"Ah, this can't be so — can't be — " His voice trailed miserably away. But it was.

He didn't even see Lizzie Percival when she put a hand on his shoulder and guided him back downstairs. She was silent. It was so bitterly true, what he'd said about dead, dried-up trees. That had hurt. She felt desperately sorry for this big, bewildered young fellow.

"Don't take on so, Timothy. Life is really not so brief as it must appear to a soldier."

To hell with her false sympathy! It wasn't as if she and old Ike hadn't enough idle money to help half a dozen daughters through the first difficult years of marriage. Ike could help if he would, and he knew that Tim Bennett was no idler, that he came of sound merchant stock.

In desperation he pleaded for a loan, for a modest measure of cooperation in getting Bennett & Son back on its feet. That now he was sailing a wrong tack he guessed by the way Mrs. Percival's face froze.

"There is only one sound way for a young couple to get ahead." She switched her petticoats. "They must make their own way, asking favors of no one. We did. Can't say I admire this carrying on, Timothy. Mightn't it be more profitable if you made some provision for your precious, innocent little sister?"

He looked at her sharply. "Why do you talk like that?"

Lizzie Percival scanned him. "You want me to believe you don't know?"

"Know what? Take care. She's my sister."

"You needn't speak so tart," Mrs. Percival snapped, "and I shall say what I choose in my own home. I will only repeat what was reported by several of your neighbors who chanced by your Pa's place when it was burning."

Tim caught his breath. Had this to do with Sam Higsby's reluctance to talk about Desire? "Well, what did they say?"

"When fire was set to your father's barn near midnight," her acid tones emphasized the hour, "your sister got smoked out of it — in company with a British officer!"

The accusation was too enormous to have been unfounded. Tim could only gape.

"The Englishman got shot during the retreat, they say. God's swift judgment against lust, no doubt!"

Desire. How could she — his own sister — have been in the hay — like that? Bringing disgrace on a name which had been honored since Rhode Island was settled. What had happened to the world? First Lucy, then Desire. He would never trust another woman — never!

Mrs. Percival's voice impinged on his misery. "And now, young man, you can march yourself right out of here. Though I have tried to be kind and civil, it has got me nowhere."

Gone all cold in his insides, Tim halted, gray-faced, at the door and said slowly and distinctly, "You are wrong. Thank you for reminding me that there never was a Percival worth a Bennett's little finger. Not Ike, your ex-slaver of a husband, nor your precious, faithless daughter! And by the great Jehovah *I'll prove it!*"

The front door slammed.

Man from Congress

Such a big crowd had gathered before the old Town Hall in Newport Tim figured at first that another ration drawing party from the fleet must be preparing to land. But a seaman said, "Naw. It's some fellers from Congress speechifying."

Four men were standing on a rude platform made of planks laid across some barrel heads. At first glance Tim recognized General Charles Lee as one of them. The adventurer's stock was as carelessly tied as ever, his tunic as wrinkled and the purple sash across his chest discolored with food spots.

Narrow jaw thrust far out, Lee was glaring at the crowd, evidently concluding a burst of oratory which had attracted people from all directions. His voice was shrill with passion and his untidy wig curls fluttered. "What species of patriotism is it to spare yourselves at the expense of your suffering brethren in Connecticut, Massachusetts, and New Hampshire? Shame! Purge yourselves of all faint-hearts, Tories and traitors! Turn out the rascals in your high places! Make them swear the awful oath I forced on the doubtful in Providence. See to it that this disgraceful private covenant with the enemy is expunged by the fierce, hot flame of patriotism!"

When Lee descended grandly from the platform, the crowd cheered like mad. Behind him he left a civilian and a pair of officers in uniform. Tim had no trouble in recognizing these last as two of the most famous privateer captains in New England: Esek Hopkins and Captain Tom Hazard.

In short, badly-mumbled sentences, Captain Hazard proudly reviewed the efforts of the tiny Rhode Island navy. It had captured the *Rose* frigate's tender; better still, the two Provincial men-o'-war recaptured a dozen or more prizes from the British. Why, on the night of June thirteenth alone, it had rescued three Rhode Island merchantmen.

"Bully f'r you, Tom!" roared a drunken voice. "Hurray for the Rhode Island navy! More ships, lads! Le's drive ol' Wallace out to sea!"

Tom Hazard shook his head, waved his cutlass. "Reckon we might, friends, if we weren't too poor to build big enough vessels."

"The hell with big ships!" It was Polypus Hammond yelling from a stoop across the street. "Give me enough men and I'll guarantee to carry the *Rose* by boarding."

Captain Tom Hazard shook a shrewd, somewhat brutal-appearing head. "Like hell you could, Polypus. No, friends, the only thing will help these colonies are stout, fast ships that were built to fight: sloops, frigates and, maybe sometime, ships of the line!"

Everybody stared at Tom Hazard. It was absurd even to dream of the weak little province building a three-decker. Why, to construct a single such vessel would cost more than to equip three regiments of troops.

Polypus Hammond sang out angrily, "Aw, quit raving, Tom. Tell the Congress to grant us privateer commissions and we'll wind up the king's clock in a hurry!"

"Granting what you say is gospel, Cap'n, but war vessels cost money. Shucks! We hear this colony is hard put to supply even the *Katy* and the *Washington*. Where will we find money?"

"Now, I wanted someone to ask just that." Captain Hazard placed a broad tattooed hand on the shoulder of the civilian at his left. "Friends, this here is Cap'n Steve Farish of Boston, delegated by the Marine Committee of the Congress to bring us some important news. I can promise you he won't talk tootle."

"Hurray for the Congress!" "Bully for Steve Hopkins and the Marine Committee!"

A small individual wearing a sea captain's worn blue serge coat stepped forward. A tougher-looking little man Tim had never seen. Like an old-style mariner, he wore a tiny gold ring in his left ear. While he waited for the crowd to quiet he fished out a red bandanna and began to mop an utterly hairless head. He had a strong face burnt brown by the sun of many an ocean, and fierce gray-blue eyes set beneath hairless lids.

For a man of his inches, Captain Farish owned the biggest voice Tim had ever heard. The effect was ludicrous — like a canary bird singing bass. But when the delegate from the Congress spoke, they forgot all about that.

"Now, we fellers hold conviction we're good fighters, don't we?"

"We'll stand up to them lousy lobsterbacks any time."

Captain Farish cocked his hairless head and studied a weathervane above the market. "Suppose I tell you the British ain't so convinced? Queer, but they ain't."

"Proved it at Bunker Hill, didn't we?"

The little delegate in threadbare serge had his answer pat. " 'Pears we were lucky in the British generals. We lost the hill, too, if you'll rec'lect. Now here's something you may not know — the English never have cottoned to their army like they do to their navy. No, fellers, we'll never convince the English us Americans amount to a pinch of ashes till we've fought 'em ship to ship, gun for gun, on deep salt water *and trounced 'em!* Your true-blue Britisher fancies that on the sea he's God's own gift to creation!" Farish's voice boomed on, "Just an' right, right an' just, say you. But where do us Americans come across the ships and guns to fight with?"

The throng was really impatient to hear; it fell quiet.

"Listen, all of you! Listen hard. *The Congress has voted to build a navy.*" Such deafening uproar followed that Esek Hopkins stopped scratching a bulbous red nose and looked solemn.

Echoes came flying from the hill back of the town. The speaker talked faster, thumped his hairy hand against its mate. "I seen the plans the Congress has voted." The small delegate's eyes glistened like the blade of the cutlass Hazard had forgotten to sheathe. "First off, we're going to lay down a fleet of thirteen men-o'-war. One for each of the United Colonies."

"What rig?" Polypus Hammond bellowed through cupped hands.

"Five thirty-two-gun frigates, five twenty-eight-gun frigates and three corvettes all of twenty-four guns, and ship rigged!" Captain Farish bellowed back. " 'Tain't much, but it's a beginning. Now here's some news will please you better still. Two of them vessels are to be built right here in Rhode Island! While them thirteen vessels I spoke of is abuilding, a temporary fleet will be equipped and put to sea. It may look queer, but jumping Jehoshaphat, 'twill be a genu-ine navy!

"Now fellers, I'll belay and make way for a gentleman who now ranks equal with the great and respected General Washington — only he's a Yankee and therefore better! Come on now, three cheers for Esek Hopkins, Commander-in-Chief of the Navy of the United Colonies!"

The new commander-in-chief stood up, resplendent in a high-collared blue uniform coat that was nattily turned back in turkey red. His red waistcoat was brave with yellow lace and his breeches were blue. Esek's older brother Stephen had been governor and now sat in the Congress. But it was Esek everybody looked up to. In the old French war he had made such a daring privateer captain.

"Fellow inhabitants of Rhode Island, under orders from the Marine Committee I sail in three days' time to take command of the new fleet which is to rendezvous at Phillydelphy."

"Hey, Commodore," yelled a one-eyed sailor. "What's a seaman's wage?"

"A handsome sum, my lad," Hopkins replied easily. "Sixteen shillings a month — and found."

"— And prize money?" a dozen voices demanded. Everyone listened for the new commander's reply. It was important — it meant everything.

Esek Hopkins hesitated, reached up and scratched a red spot on his chin. "Why, men, you can count on the Congress always being generous with patriotical-minded men."

"Yes, but what's the share rate to be? Stop being cooney and spit it out!"

Hopkins shot an unhappy glance at Hazard, then said, "Why, one-half the worth of a captured man-o'-war goes to the crew, other half to the Congress."

So? The crowd sobered. Everyone knew there was small profit and a big risk in tackling a man-o'-war.

"What share on merchantmen?" Polypus Hammond called. "That's where the fat lays!"

"Why, it's a third to the crew — "

Whistles and groans drowned out the rest of Hopkins's words. "Only a third! Plague take such a measly share!" rasped the young sailor's voice.

"Balls!" jeered the one-eyed man turning away. "We ain't that gullible. Aboard a privateer, the ship's company goes shares on the whole value!"

"Do you always have to think of shares?" Esek Hopkins demanded, his neck thick over his stock. He was mad clean through. "To join the navy is a patriotic duty!"

"Sure, it's easy for you and some others to tell us so — you got plenty of privateering money salted away!"

A young sailor whose broken nose had been slewed around to one side of his face came up to the speaker. "There will be fighting — real fighting? We will really go against the English?"

The new commander-in-chief laughed raspingly. "You'll get a bellyfull of broadsides, honor bright. Any man don't join up right away will be sorry, because there will be quick promotions soon as the new ships are commissioned. There will be fun and to spare in port and you will have money to spend. You will see the world at no expense — the Indies, Europe, Africa, maybe India."

"Catting?"

"There'll be no flogging worth mention," Hopkins beamed; he was away from the most dangerous subject. "Limit is to be twelve strokes! No real mariner would even notice that.

"Yes, boys; join the navy and you'll see strange sights, better yourselves and have a fine time. And, best of all, you will be a credit to Rhode Island. Your folks will be proud."

Hopkins looked about, began briskly rubbing his hands. "Every man jack who signs today will be given a glass of rum with my compliments. My quartermaster and an officer are at the Sabin Inn."

A whooping began at the far end of Anne Street. That, and a clatter of hoofs. Heads jerked about when the yelling continued.

"News! Hey! I got great news!" Jim Trumbull, the post rider, astride a blown and lathered nag, came riding up the outer edges of the crowd. He was bursting with a rare self-importance. "Hey, fellers, listen! I just heard the news up to Tiverton."

"Well, don't stand there bellerin' like a bull calf," Farish snapped. "Speak up and get out. You're interfering with the commodore's speech."

"All right then. Listen, fellers, listen!"

People crowded in around the panting horse.

"Know what? *The Congress is going to allow privateering!*"

"Oh God!" Captain Hazard looked ready to kill the post rider. "Some bloody fool in Phillydelphy has blabbed!"

" — And old Adams promised us a fortnight's start," Hopkins began cursing under his breath.

Farish scowled. "Wager 'twas that slippery-tongued Si Deane — I never did trust a Connecticuter."

Shouts which had risen heretofore were by comparison like the chirping of crickets in a wood pile.

"When?"

"Don't know yet," Jim Trumbull beamed. "But 'twill be soon, they say."

Ten minutes later, John Clarke tacked a sign to his warehouse door. It was so wet he smeared quite a few letters.

WANTED!
Able-bodied recruits for
the Private arm'd brig-of-war,
D E F I A N C E
Guranteed to be ready for sea when
Commissions arrive.
FULL PRIZE MONEY! LIBERAL SHARES!
HIGH WAGES

Men had begun fighting to get near Clarke's warehouse when down the street Abner Coffin began calling through a leather speaking trumpet.

"Hi, fellers! Come this way! This way! The *Defiance* is only a brig. Sign on for my *Retaliation.* She's a full-rigged ship and will mount eighteen carriage guns. This way, lads! Abner Coffin starts paying wages the minute you sign articles!"

A swarm of ragged seamen deserted Clarke's, but most of them kept on past Coffin because Ira Thaxter was swinging a big dinner bell and yelling in his thin voice: "To every man signing up on my vessels *Gamecock* and *Diamond,* I grant a four-shilling cash bonus. Hurry on, lads! Offer expires in an hour. Hurry, for the glory of old Newport!"

They hurried.

The Oystering Skiff

It was lucky for her, Desire Harmony realized, that the weather had remained windless. Even so, it was dreadfully cold in the woodshed at night. Suppose a hard blizzard came? She guessed she would freeze to death without ever waking up.

One fact had to be faced: she simply couldn't endure living like a hunted wild creature any longer. It was the being alone that bothered her most. For hours and hours she would just sit thinking of Pa and Tim and most of all about John lying dead across the frozen ruts. She lay awake long hours in her nest of straw. Was it possible to recall every last moment they had spent together? That was what always started her crying as she huddled shivering.

During a foraging expedition above the West Ferry Desire discovered an oystering skiff. Half full of water and ice, it lay in Great Creek Gut. It had belonged to Paul Clarke, who had sailed in the *Patience*. She figured he must have been captured and imprisoned the night of the raid.

By ranging patiently along the shore, she pretty soon discovered Clarke's oars and a sprit-sail in the depths of a juniper thicket. Her breath began to come faster. Tomorrow she would leave Conanicut, would dare a plunge into those blinding fogs concealing the future. Moping over John and her lost family certainly wasn't getting her anywhere.

When she got back to the woodshed she cried a little. The great world she had talked of so bravely now seemed monstrous formidable. Wiping her eyes, she calmed down and took stock of her resources. They were slim enough: a silver ladle, a pair of silver shoe buckles and a silver thimble and three shillings she had found on a dead marine. If used sparingly, the silver should preserve her from starvation until she found employment.

A gentle southeast breeze blew so steadily that in midafternoon, Desire saw Providence dead ahead. Many rows of buildings were crawling up a hillside beyond Fox Point. Some of her fright evaporated. Though the port looked strange, there was an unexpected and reassuring familiarity about the distant waterfront. Certainly that shipping at anchor in the river looked peaceful and unmenacing.

Just as at Newport, wharves, docks and warehouses edged the waterfront. Behind them rose a barricade of treetops, roofs and chimneys. From what Tim had said, that handsome brick building up on the hill must be New University Hall of Rhode Island College.

On tiptoes Desire Bennett threaded her way ashore, skirted a big warehouse and started along Water Street, outwardly as prim and confident as if she had lived in Providence all her life. But she was so scared her teeth clicked together. How did one go about finding cheap food and lodging? Probably the poorer districts, as in Newport, would be along the edges of town.

She knew she must look a fright. Her hands were black with charcoal and dirt that wouldn't come off, no matter how hard she rubbed with plain water. Her hair she guessed looked like a rat's nest, and her clothes — well, under her spare petticoat they were scorched, stained and greasy. Of course, her face must show smudges — she had no mirror to tell her where. Carrying her bundle, she must look like a storybook orphan. No help for it, though.

At last she found a baker's shop which didn't look formidable in any way. A single loaf and a few stale-looking buns were exposed in its window. Most encouraging was the fact that a woman and not a man was inside. Perhaps she might know of a situation suitable for a respectable young widow.

When the door closed the baker's wife stopped trimming the wick of a mutton-fat lamp and squinted over her shoulder.

"Well," she demanded sharply, "what do you want?"

Desire had to force herself to speak.

"I — I — please, how much are those b-buns in the window?"

"A penny apiece. Flour is very dear nowadays."

"Well, please let me have — t-two." Desire hated herself for stammering, but she hadn't the least notion how to get onto the real purpose of her visit.

Snuffling dismally, the baker's wife plunked the two discouraged-looking buns onto the counter and stared suspiciously at the firm oval of Desire's face. In the large brown eyes, the soft shadows beneath them, and the naturally bright lips, she found grounds for inaudible disapproval. Muttering, she carried Desire's shilling over to the candlelight.

Desire felt a flash of anger.

"My money is all right!"

"A body can't take no chances," she sniffed. "There's too many raggle-taggle girls coming to town nowadays."

"A raggle-taggle girl!" Desire gasped. "You'll not say such things to me! I'm a respectable married woman."

"Indeed? Then where's your ring?"

"When my husband died I had to sell it. We were very poor."

Though she wasn't in fact married, she would always think of herself as John St. Clair's widow.

The baker's wife hesitated, but when she saw real tears trickling through Desire's grubby fingers, she sucked in her breath and said softly, "There, there, child. Maybe things ain't quite so hard as I let on. Just you sit by the fire, my pretty, and eat your buns while I fetch you a mug of milk."

When Desire had swallowed the last crumb, she felt a little braver and even mustered an uncertain smile. "Perhaps, ma'am, you could tell me of a lodging house where a bed wouldn't — wouldn't cost very much?" Then she added brightly, "I shall find work tomorrow, I know."

The baker's wife showed gapped teeth in what was supposed to be a look of encouragement. "Now, I mind me of a woman, name of Norton. She keeps a lodging house up towards north end of town. Number nine, James Street."

Her plump hand patted Desire's shoulder, and she nodded to herself as if enjoying some private satisfaction. "I don't know this Mrs. Norton real well, but I heard tell she lets the rooms real cheap. I figure she might take pity on you."

Mrs. Norton

Even though Mrs. Norton's dwelling stood on James Street in a neighborhood where grog shops outnumbered private homes by two to one, number nine proved to be a neatly shingled structure with white trim and a certain air of respectability about it.

Plucking up courage, Desire knocked timidly at the clean, green-painted door. Sedately, the geese waddled off down the street to resting places in yards and under doorsteps.

Two sailors came reeling up James Street and, spying the girl, tilted hats at a rakish angle and swaggered up.

The taller of the pair nudged his companion. "Ahoy, mate — curse me if yonder ain't a pair o' the trimmest spars I see in a year."

"By Jeesus, ain't she something?"

Fear held Desire rigid when they teetered closer, tarred pigtails waggling over greasy coat collars.

"Hi, sweetheart, how's for a cruise in the goosedown?"

Desire grabbed desperately at the doorknob and said, "Please go away. Please! I — I'm respectable."

"Say," demanded the shorter one scratching his head. "Is this here Jim Str — "

The door burst open. "Clear out of here, you slimy scum of bilge brothels!"

On the threshold appeared one of the fattest women Desire had ever beheld. The apparition had heavy black brows and a perceptible mustache. Between amber and gold earbobs her face, above a starched white collar, glowed red as any love apple.

"Of course she's respectable! Now clear out of here, you bowlegged mother's mistakes!" The seamen fell back before the big woman's advance.

She shook her fist with such force that a ring of keys hitched to her belt began jingling. "Scat! Away with you or I'll call the watch. It would appear, my dear, that you told those — those specimens the truth. One would hazard that you are a good girl, good as of habit, at least. What age have you?"

For the first time, Desire noticed an unfamiliar accent to her benefactress's speech. "Sixteen, ma'am. Close on seventeen."

"Seventeen? That is well," the woman in green nodded emphatically. "And may one inquire what brings you here — to my home?"

Looking small and very scared, Desire launched into an explanation she had evolved during the voyage up from Conanicut. She was a widow, she explained; her husband had been killed in the British raid on Falmouth.

"So young and a widow already! Ah, my poor child, that is very sad. I know very well how it is." She dropped her eyes. "Mr. Norton died many years ago. The life of a widow is not one of the easiest." Mrs. Norton sighed, then cocked her head a little to one side. "You have parents — family, that is to say — living nearby?"

"No one, ma'am."

"And now, is it not time to tell me why you knocked at my house?"

Having risen at dawn, Desire was dead tired. It had been no easy matter to sail the skiff, either. To make matters worse, she was still terribly hungry.

"I was seeking lodgings but I — I fear, ma'am, this is too nice a place for my purse." Her dark red lips drew back from her teeth in a slow, rippling motion.

"Why?"

"I am looking for a situation, you see."

"Ah? One perceives your difficulty. Let us consider — "

Mrs. Norton bent her head in thought.

"My child, you have come to Providence before an ill wind," Mrs. Norton sighed. "The good God alone knows how the cursed English have stopped our trade. Ah! If only they could be driven away. What is your occupation?"

Desire put up a bold front. She would work at anything, she declared, anything that was respectable.

"That," Mrs. Norton declared comfortably, "is fortunate. Nice, fresh, clean-minded girls are scarce in a seaport. You sew?"

Desire sat very straight on the chair, her bundle on the floor beside her. "Oh yes, ma'am, I can sew very elegant on silk, on flowered muslin, on catgut. I can do satin stitch, quince stitch, tent stitch, cross stitch, tambour, and embroidery on curtains or chairs. I — I think I could make flowers and profiles out of wax if anybody would instruct me."

"Let me see your ankles — "

Desire flushed, but obediently thrust out a foot. In its damp, clumsy shoe and torn woolen stocking, it didn't make much of a showing.

"Ah, as I thought, small like your hands. You could not do heavy work."

Lord, she mustn't let Mrs. Norton suspect her bundle contained only a comb, old clothes, shoe buckles, two shillings, and a silver spoon. She wasn't counting the thimble of her mother's among her assets.

"You can cook? Bake?"

[230]

"Not very well, Mrs. Norton," Desire admitted honestly. Then added, "But I learn quickly, and I can spin a yarn better than most."

Mrs. Norton, stooping to pluck a thread from her knee, momentarily exposed a small gold crucifix caught between breasts resembling batter puddings as to size and texture.

Pursing up her lips, she studied the ceiling so hard, Desire guessed she must be reaching a decision. Would there be work? She bit her lips to hide their frightened trembling.

"Genevieve Norton is a fool of the worst sort — a soft-hearted old fool. I should not trust a strange girl for a week's rooming. Definitely not!"

There it was. Desire felt she would burst right out crying. "Oh, Mrs. Norton — please — "

"Do not interrupt me, little one, because I shall be a great, soft-hearted fool and trust you for your lodging. I shall even tell Chloë to give you a fine hot meal! *Mon dieu*, you look as if you had been pulled through a keyhole."

The room to which Mrs. Norton led Desire was narrow and sparingly furnished, but its bed was surprisingly wide and comfortable-looking; it boasted maple posts. A couple of chairs, a washstand and a tiny chiffonier lurking beneath a huge horizontal mirror completed the furnishings.

Desire guessed she ought to inquire into the rent but it seemed ungracious; besides she felt just too tired and weary to bargain. Hadn't the baker's wife said Mrs. Norton let rooms very cheap? Tomorrow would be time enough.

"This chamber is not large, little one," Mrs. Norton's tiny jet eyes twinkled, "but neither are you. Ha ha!"

In the doorway the landlady turned, hesitated, one huge breast swaying to either side of the doorframe. "And did you say what your name is?"

"Mrs. St. Clair — John St. Clair."

"But no, my little one, your saint's — your own name."

"Desire Harmony."

"How pretty!" She tilted her smooth black head to one side. "I am sure your husband, if he was even part French, called you Désirée. I shall call you so. The name is pretty, even intriguing." Mrs. Norton sniffed like a cat at a mouse hole. "My faith! Where can you have been to smell so of fish, sweat and wood smoke? Chloë will bring you some buckets of water. Name of God, use it well."

The Privateersmen

A fire of damp logs smoldered in a small meeting room on the second floor of the old Town Hall, but it didn't do more than take an edge off the chill. The body heat of the thirty-odd men present really did more to dispel it.

Tim, seated in a far corner beside Captain Lawson, recalled Pa's oft-repeated advice to do plenty of listening and precious little talking. It had been a relief to find the town's animosity diminished from active and often abusive contempt to a passive tolerance. Tim figured that the results of the raid and Pa's sudden death were mostly responsible.

Esek Hopkins wasn't present, but he had sent his stolid, persevering son, John B. Hopkins. Rumor ran that John B. would captain a vessel in the new Continental Navy. The Hopkinses were famous for looking out for their kinfolk.

George Irish, the town councilman, had the floor and was saying, "I believe we should back up this navy idea. We've damned well got to!"

"Got to?" Ike Percival cut in. "May I inquire why?"

"Because the army needs such support! How in hell are they going to whip Lord Howe while he remains free to import all the supplies and men he wants? If we don't put a stop to it, General Washington will get snowed under."

Up jumped Major John Handy, spic and span in his new Continental uniform. He had just that day arrived from Cambridge.

"Gentlemen, I want to say that Mr. Irish is right, dead right! We must cut off Howe from his base in Europe. It can be done. Look at what Manley, Martindale and the others have accomplished in Massachusetts Bay! Not one of their vessels measures seventy foot over all, yet they have captured above fifteen British transports!"

Abed Thaxter shrugged. "You go ahead; talk all you please, Handy, but I'll still be dead against building a fleet."

"Why?"

"Because a navy tends to create an officer class which will soon begin to lord it over us merchants."

Nicholas Brown of Providence rubbed his bald head. "Wal, there's something to such a notion, but you'll never run such a danger from privateer officers." He looked challengingly about. "When a war is over, what do the privateersmen do? Why, they go back into sailing merchantmen. Most private-armed vessels can return to trading without much trouble — not like frigates and sloops of war. *I* vote to put every penny into arming and equipping privateers."

Tim couldn't see why, if there were enough of them, privateers couldn't so hamstring Great Britain's trade that the Parliament would have to give up.

He got up and, obtaining recognition from Irish, made his point.

"Aye! Bennett is right," Abed Thaxter cried. "Let our privateers bleed Britain's commerce awhile. Once the Jamaica, Liverpool and London nabobs find their profits shrinking and their assurance rates rising, they'll force the ministry to listen to reason."

Isaac Percival looked the other way. It was clear he was astonished to find Tim Bennett here and well received.

By now the rank smoke from a dozen churchwarden pipes was clouding the air. The fire blazed higher, revealing half models of many designs of vessels, yellowed tariff schedules secured to the walls. Men began to shed their hats, to unbutton their coats.

"You fellers seem to forget a very important argument against this navy scheme," Ira Thaxter's bleating voice penetrated the hum of discussion. "Us New Englanders would be called on to furnish the bulk of ships, men, and pretty near all the money. The Southern and Middle colonies will derive benefit of our risk free for nothing."

Captain Farish glared across the meeting room. "That's a comical notion, young feller. And why do you presume that might be so?"

"Southerners ain't seafaring."

"That's right!" someone agreed. "Virginians ship in British bottoms."

"All the more reason for them to favor a Continental Navy," Farish countered. "With no foreign vessels to lug their merchandise, they'll be forced to build their own ships or go under. Stands to reason the Virginians will be anxious to see those new ships protected, don't it?"

Farish walked over to the Thaxters, looked at them steadily. "Meantime, 'pears to me like you Newporters might pick up a pretty penny carrying freight for them!"

Solomon Southwick spoke up and everybody listened with the attention due an educated man.

"Fellow patriots, history has a queer way of repeating itself. Consider another young country which once sought to maintain its freedom against a tyrannical sea power. Friends, I refer to the Roman republic. Now, the Romans at that time were a united people. It made no difference whether the men hailed from Rome, Naples, Tarentum, Salerno, or Marsala. They were all Roman citizens. By their union they founded a great central power."

Everybody was so quiet feet could be heard climbing the stairs.

"In the second and greatest of the three Punic wars, matters went from bad to worse for the Roman republic until those Romans built a united fleet which went out and whipped the pants off the Carthaginians — if they had pants, which I doubt. Anyhow, they cut Hannibal off from his base and he had to git for home. In the end, Rome won!

"We may reckon ourselves smart and handy at sea, but considered separately, these colonies are poor and weak." Looking over his spectacles, he reminded Tim of the old Quaker who had taught him the three R's. "A navy of the United Colonies can, and should be, strong!

"Gentlemen, I don't see that our situation is one whit different from that of the Roman republic."

Captain Farish ran over and wrung the printer's hand. "Jumping Jehoshaphat! That's prettily put. I call for a vote. Who's for a Continental Navy?"

He was smart enough to guess that Southwick's talk had made a deep impression. His motion of support was carried but most of the big priva-teer owners were still in opposition.

Tim didn't vote. Figured he didn't yet understand the rights of the case. After what he'd seen in the army, it was mighty doubtful if thirteen colonies scattered along two thousand miles of seacoast could ever be brought together.

Nadir

On the evening of Desire Harmony's fourth day in Providence, disaster met her face to face. The soles of her shoes had worn through and there were big raw blisters all over her feet. They hurt her so she limped and had to lock her teeth to keep from crying. Though her last ha'penny had been spent, she was so hungry she was ready to faint.

The long horizontal mirror above her bed warned her of lost weight. Those shadows beneath her eyes which had so intrigued Mr. Higsby — all the men for that matter — had deepened from a soft buff to a dark brown.

As if enough had not already gone wrong, she was now pretty sure of another cause for worry. Somehow her rhapsody with John had upset an otherwise regular routine.

By careful calculation she should have gone under the weather the day she sailed for Providence. Of course the delay might be entirely normal — due to hunger and fatigue. On the other hand could what she and John did have any connection with these circumstances? Strange how details of that heaven-sent experience escaped her.

It was odd Mrs. Norton made no mention of her room rent, even though every evening she would happen by and plunk her massive body onto the bed. About the only cheering element these days was the sympa-thetic way the widow would, with ready sympathy, listen to her account of disappointments.

Mrs. Norton must be truly kind or she would have long since demanded her board money. It must be, as she said, her great, foolish heart at work. Probably lots of tenants had taken advantage of her. Here was one who wouldn't. The Bennetts always honored their debts — just ones. She would pay Mrs. Norton every farthing — indeed she would.

What should she do for money? All at once she sat right up on the bed. For pity's sake! How could she have forgotten about the sterling silver ladle and the other things? Warmth flooded her. So much silver must be worth a fair amount, because silver was scarce these days. Papa had said so many times.

First thing she'd buy would be a big bowl of stew. A good meal would grant her strength to hunt work in the morning. Maybe the ladle would bring enough to let her run a notice in the *Providence Gazette & Country Journal*. That would give her standing. Something like: "A young Widow in Straitn'd Circumstances desires genteel Employment as Preceptress to Young Females, or as Sempstress."

Her heart sang as she ran over to the chiffonier and opened the top drawer. When her fingers encountered no hard objects, her heart sailed up in her breast like a deer jumping a pasture fence.

In frantic haste, she emptied the drawer onto the bed. Then sobbing, she searched her room from floor to ceiling. She had been robbed! Like a cold downpour, the fact chilled her.

A thief had taken her silver! *Her* silver. The things couldn't have been misplaced. Very distinctly she recalled putting the ladle and buckles at the back of the top drawer. Panic-stricken, she wrenched open the inner door. "Help! Help! I've been robbed!"

Almost instantly Chloë appeared. "Hush yo' mouth!" The mulatto glared, her previous deferential air quite vanished. "Mrs. Norton sayin' prayers."

Desire gripped the door frame, panted, "I don't care what she's doing. I must see her at once! I have been robbed! I'll call the law!"

"Hush!" Chloë ran forward, tried to clap a hand over Desire's mouth. "Mis' Margaret's got comp'ny!"

"I don't care," Desire's voice rose in anguish. "My silver spoon and buckles are gone. I want them! Do you understand? I've *got* to have my things back!"

Like a ship of the line sailing into action, Mrs. Norton loomed down the corridor. In one hand she had a crucifix on the end of a string of beads. A stick of kindling wood was in the other. Considering her bulk, the landlady moved with astonishing rapidity.

"*Fiche moi le camp!*" she hissed at Chloë. The yellow girl cringed, vanished like a wraith, closing the door behind her.

"What is the meaning of this?" The landlady's bright black eyes were menacing. "How dare you stand screaming robbery in my house?"

"But I *have* been robbed! My — my silver! I'll tell the watch — I'll — "

Lights exploded as the piece of kindling flashed down, caught Desire a smack across the cheek. "*Tais-toi, misérable!* How dare you make such accusations?"

The blow stung and burned like fire, confused everything. Desire wanted to hit back but she was too weak. She could only stagger back until she tripped onto the bed. Pressed against the farther wall she tried to shield her head as, puffing heavily, Mrs. Norton dealt her three or four more stinging blows across thighs and legs.

"Pay me my money and leave this instant! No person shall stay in my house and accuse me of such things. My money, where is my rent money? I want it this minute. Give it to me!"

To steady herself, Desire gripped the headboard. It seemed as if her stomach were bloated by a black acid which, welling up, up, was poisoning her heart and brain.

"But — I — I can't!"

"*Comment?* No money? What nonsense!"

"Oh, Mrs. Norton, I haven't been able to find work. I — I've tried, but there isn't any!"

"Of course, there is work to be had. Bah! You are just lazy! If you fancy one can cheat Genevieve Norton, you are in error. Come, I want my money!"

"I — I haven't got it."

"*Nom de dieu!*" Mrs. Norton raised the stick, bent over the bed and grabbed Desire's ankle. She hit her only twice, then paused fluttering in her struggles for breath. "So, miserable one, you plotted to cheat an honest woman? Well, we shall see. Now attend! If I am not paid every penny of your debt by tomorrow, you will find yourself in the debtors' prison."

Panting, Desire stared up fearfully. "Prison? Oh no! No, I couldn't stand it." Asa Bennett's daughter in jail! She could never endure such a disgrace, never would.

"Then pay me my money."

"Oh dear, I *can't!*" Desire couldn't see things clearly. Her head was ringing like an anvil under a blacksmith's hammer.

Mrs. Norton relaxed a trifle, slipped the rosary into her belt beside the big brass hoop of keys. "Either you are the most unprincipled little liar I have ever seen or you are an utter fool. No girl your age could be so incredibly naïve." Her beady little eyes stabbed like stilettos! "You were never married, of course — just in love and a little indiscreet. This is the right tune, no?" She must have read a confession by the misery in those large brown eyes. "I am sorry for you, Désirée, but I am not rich. I must have one pound ten shillings tomorrow — or you go to the debtors' prison. It is a question of setting an example lest others attempt to copy your method."

The widow straightened, smoothed her hair and glanced at herself in the mirror. She seemed her old kindly self as she said, "Now then, it is but half after seven of the evening. No more nonsense. If you care to entertain a friend in your room I shall not disapprove."

If once Mrs. Norton got her committed to the debtors' prison, she might never be freed. People said women in such a position had to do awful things to get out. Well, it was clear she had to find the money.

Suddenly came a heaven-sent inspiration. Through her recent study of poetry, she could recite verse on verse of it, could declaim long speeches from half a hundred plays. Her voice, she felt, was good even if it had not been trained.

Suppose she prettied herself up and then made a round of the Stirrup & Spur and the other better-class ordinaries? She should be able to earn some money singing or giving recitations. She was practical enough, however, to see that she could never earn so much as one pound ten shillings in a single night — not unless she was amazingly lucky.

Surprisingly enough her silk stockings had not been stolen and she found among her things some unfamiliar lengths of silk ribbon. The sensation of the silk stockings sliding up her legs plucked up her courage. Why, this was an adventure. She was like the poor orphan girl in Mr. Hallam's play.

By the light of a candle Chloë brought, Desire dressed her hair with great care. No Quaker cap now. Had all the disasters which had befallen the Bennetts been due to her backsliding? Poor Papa. Lucky he was in Newport and couldn't know that she was going to playact, sing even, in a public house.

Her position became luminously clear. Desire Harmony was about to play her first role — that of Mademoiselle Désirée. Whatever Mlle. Désirée was called upon to say or do must be considered just a part of the role in no way affecting the real girl — Desire Harmony St. Clair. Queer that the fates thus, willy-nilly, had summoned her onto the broad stage of the world.

A conviction came that, ere she was retired, she must play many parts.

Imitating with dreadful skill the gait of the girls she had seen in One Gun Lane, Désirée began sauntering along Wickenden Street.

In a soft soprano, she commenced to sing:

> "Foolish Swallow, what dost thou
> So early, at my window do?
> Cruel bird, thou'st ta'en away
> A dream out from my arms today;
> A dream that ne'er must equal'd be,
> By all but waking eyes — "

Around the first corner loomed a broad-shouldered young fellow in uniform. He was a lieutenant, Désirée judged by his single epaulet. The facings to his blue tunic were a gay turkey red. A nearby fanlight drew brief flashes from the guard of a sword.

Touching his tricorne, he halted in front of her, blocking the footpath but applauding gently at the same time. "May I, a poor soldier, venture the opinion that you enjoy a rare fine voice?"

Mlle. Désirée, aware that her heart was galloping up her throat, twisted her lips into what she hoped resembled a shy little smile. "La, sir, I am charmed that my p-poor accomplishment should p-please you."

"There are more verses?"

"Oh yes, sir." She kept her eyes modestly dropped so didn't see his quizzical, sardonic smile. She knew though that this officer, while not exactly handsome, was yet far from ugly.

"And how many more verses are there, mistress?"

"F-four or five, sir." Hot impulses bathed her neck and breast but she forced herself to say, "It — it would be pleasant to sing them."

His laugh was soft. "*Est modus in rebus!* You see, mistress, until now I never knew that Mr. Cowley's 'Swallow' had more than one stanza and I would like to hear them."

"Pray don't be mean," Désirée shrugged, turned aside her head. Then rallied. "It is scarcely gallant to force a lady to confess that she would even invent some verses to please so appreciative an audience."

In almost no time they had turned into the little lane off James Street and Désirée was fumbling in her stocking for the side door key. Though she exhibited a stimulating length of limb — she felt her role called for such tactics — the officer remained standing among the shadows, admirably restraining any eagerness he might have felt.

With one hand on the latch she hesitated and had to remind herself this night was dedicated to avoiding the debtors' prison. To get out her next words was a struggle, but she managed it.

"Pray, sir, do not misunderstand, but I — I am not wealthy. If you wish wine, I shall — I shall have to send out for it."

"Of course, we must have wine, my dear. And of the best. What poet worthy of the name ever declaimed, what siren ever sang, unblest by Bacchus's gracious gift?" He spoke it lightly; she liked him for that.

"For once, the lack of filthy lucre troubles me not." He brought out a bulging purse. "Of pounds, shillings and pence I have sufficient to finance a few excursions into Elysium. Tonight, an the tender goddess consents, we may find surcease from those 'alarums and excursions' of which Messer Shakespere is so prodigal."

In manners and bearing, this tall auburn-haired fellow was so like John that Désirée felt all shaken. Yet at the same time, this lieutenant was entirely different. At the back of his speech lay a hint of mockery; he seemed to laugh at himself, at her, at the whole wide world.

When she lit the candle, she blushed clear down to her bodice when he smiled at the wet stockings and muddied petticoats she had left lying beside the bed. In hurrying to the door to summon Chloë, she managed to kick them out of sight.

When the mulatto knocked she said, "I find that a fire would be pleasant," just as if she were in the habit of having a fire every night.

"Yes, ma'am." Chloë's quick eyes appraised the lieutenant. "Right away. It is one cold night."

Five minutes later the serving wench brought in a pair of fine wax tapers and kindled a generous blaze. Meantime the officer shed his cloak and hung his hat on a hook let into the wall. Next he carelessly straightened his hair before the looking glass.

"And what kind of a wine would you fancy, Mr. — ?"

"Co — er — Colebourne. Lieutenant Nathaniel Colebourne, at your service, ma'am." He made her quite an elegant bow, but it was not as graceful as John's. "Perhaps a bottle of Burgundy, and possibly a speck of cognac?" But for all his careless way, Colebourne seemed not entirely at his ease.

"Yes, sir." A striking figure in her yellow skirt and scarlet waist, Chloë actually curtsied. "Will you an' Mistress St. Clair require supper?"

"Oh, yes. Yes." Désirée nearly choked in trying to conceal her terrible eagerness. "What have we?"

Teeth and golden hoop earrings flashed. "Dey's ham and roas' fowl, and dey's maybe roas' beef left."

"Beef for me."

"I would prefer chicken. May I?"

Colebourne smiled, "Of course, chicken. *Sua cuique voluptas.*"

Chloë looked doubtful. "Reckon Amélie don' know dat way cookin' a fowl."

"Ah, my dusky Hebe, I fear you mistake me. What I said was, in effect, 'everyone has his own pleasure.'"

Désirée smiled, said, "Mind you hurry, Chloë."

Once the latch had fallen Nat Colebourne came over, took both her hands, studied her from his grave yet lively brown eyes. "While we wait suppose you sing me that second and third verse of 'The Swallow'?"

Désirée laughed. How strange to be really laughing once more, not just manufacturing a noise.

"After dinner, perhaps, Mr. Colebourne. You are from the army before Boston?"

He went over and seated himself beside the fireplace. "Was. You observe an ex-lieutenant — in Colonel Prescott's regiment," he added with a touch of pride.

"Prescott's? Then you fought at Bunker Hill?"

He nodded! "Aye, but it was not a pretty affair for anyone that day. I venture I shortened my age by ten years. War is an exacting profession, my dear. For its pomp and glory we pay a heavy fee in bitterness, discomfort and lost illusions."

Steam began rising from his half boots and, perceptibly, the familiar and homely odor of horses commenced to invade the room.

She sat beside him. The warmth from the fire increased, prompting her to ask, "Would you care to remove your tunic?"

"My humble gratitude." He smiled and, after standing a sturdy leather-scabbarded sword in a corner, stripped off his coat.

Gravely, Lieutenant Colebourne informed her that he hailed from Tuckernuck, a windswept island in Buzzard's Bay. His father, a fierce uncompromising man, was well to do, a Loyalist, and had cast him out "root and branch."

Smiling, he let his finger impale a curl that had fallen over her forehead. "So, gentle lady, you perceive poor Nat cast utterly adrift on the sea of an uncaring world. *Mobilis in mobile,* as it were."

[239]

In addition she learned that Nathaniel Colebourne had been a student at Harvard College when the Lexington fight took place.

"For the heinous crime of keeping a fowling piece in my chambers," he explained, "the Honorable President and Fellows of Harvard College doomed me to rustication. I had scarce survived this disgrace than the passing of the Boston Port Act prompted the Overseers to move the college to Concord, lest a brutal and licentious soldiery corrupt the students' tender morals."

In a medium-deep voice, rather like Tim's, he described the stagnant deadlock the siege had become; the wretched quarters, and the quarrels between various Provincial armies before Boston. That he could not say enough against the rifle companies amazed her.

Her guest declared, quite without heat, that most Provincial troops would liefer be brigaded with wild Indians than with Cresap's and Morgan's rangers. Thompson, their colonel, had less control over his rifle companies than a boy had over a herd of unbroken colts in an open field.

Désirée, her head at rest against his shoulder, remembering Sam Higsby's slow speech and quiet ways, protested. "But really, Mr. Colebourne, they can't be just showoffs. They are prodigious fine shots and tireless fighters."

She suddenly realized that, all unnoticed, he had contrived to undo her garter — a discovery at once pleasurable and frightening.

"And why should you rise in their defense, most Desired Lady?"

"Why, I — I have heard that no one could outmarch or outshoot these rangers. Some of them are handsome and gentle towards ladies."

"I have never met with such, *mirabile dictu*. A spot more wine, an you please, Desired Lady? Actually, they've not yet fought even a skirmish. Unless one is an utter ass, he won't credit a word a ranger says. They are the champion liars in creation. Quite a few of them have deserted to the enemy."

He found the other garter knot; slipped it.

"Deserted?" Somehow, after having known Mr. Higsby, she couldn't believe that any rifleman would do a thing so cowardly. "La, sir, such a report is hard to credit." His hand on her bare knee felt rough; the skin there tingled.

"I do not exaggerate. At sharpshooting I'll grant you they have no equals, but they quarrel, mutiny, kill each other and anybody else. When in liquor they become beasts! Like wolves and savages of the frontier, they are doomed once civilization catches up with them. What a devilish futile existence mine has been this past year. Soon must it recommence. So pray sing to me again, Desired Lady — something soft and gentle."

Timidly fingers crept up, brushed his cheek. " — You return to the siege?"

"No. War is not pleasant, but one can derive from it experience, ideas of lasting worth. I fear that beneath yonder regimentals there remains a scholar, a philosopher in embryo. Having studied the ways of men engaged in slaughtering each other on land, I have sent in my commission."

"Why?"

"I would learn what men think and do when they plan to slay each other on the ocean."

"But you can't like fighting?"

To her surprise he deliberated a considerable time over that. "I must confess that, at times, I derive a certain awful pleasure in the primordial lust of inflicting suffering and death." Hurriedly he added, "As a rule, I would not harm a mouse."

"You see, I know nothing concerning the management of a vessel of war, yet it would be foolish not to profit by my previous service. Marines, my dear, are in effect but soldiers afloat. At Tun's Tavern in Philadelphia, we shall learn whether their recruiting officer will accept an ex-sophister of Harvard College and an ex-lieutenant of Colonel Prescott's Massachusetts Regiment. And now, pray, a song for me."

With his head in her lap, his hand on her breast, Désirée sang:

> " 'If rightly tuneful bards decide,
> If it be fix'd in Love's decrees,
> That Beauty ought not to be tried
> But by its native power to please,
> Then tell me, youths and lovers, tell —
> What fair can Amoret excel?' "

The fire faded to a ruby glow. It was not impossible or unpleasant to pretend that she was only meeting John again.

Her lips of dark red felt like smooth, fragrant fruit warmed in the sun. He kissed her, long, hungrily, sighed. "It would be uncommon fine to think of you waiting for me to return from sea."

Next morning she cried impulsively, "Oh, Nat, you are so good, so — so understanding. Why must we part? Why can't I go to Philadelphia with you? There is nothing to keep me here — nothing!"

Ships Southward

FOR THE CAROLINAS
Peace & Plenty, Brigantine
Jno. Wentworth, Master
Hath good passenger accommodations.
Ready to sail December the Twenty-seventh.
J. Russell & Co., Agents

Without even inquiring the price, the red-haired lieutenant engaged a passage for his "married sister." He looked so concerned when he bade Mr. Russell to "look after her with the vastest consideration" that Désirée wondered why.

She wasn't in love with him, at least not yet. But she did very earnestly enjoy his company, his wit, and profound intelligence.

Yes, she had become monstrous fond of him. If only Nat Colebourne would shake off that bitterness, would give up his attempts to rationalize this crazy business of war. What he needed to do was to stop laughing at life in such a detached way, to unbend and to enjoy it.

On Christmas day they held a small celebration all their own. Nat made her the compliment of some handsome coral and gold earbobs and she presented him with a gorgeous red silk sash which he knew he would never be allowed to wear in uniform.

In the afternoon, they attended church — his church — like a truly married pair; no one had so much as raised an eyebrow at this muscular young lieutenant and the soberly clad young woman at his side.

Above her mantelpiece, Désirée had hung a spray of holly, bright with berries. They ate a little plum pudding, sipped cognac and grew merry over it. Désirée sang all the songs she knew and Nathaniel praised her voice until she blushed.

It was then that he confessed his true family name. All he had told her about himself was so, except that Nantucket was where his people lived and his name was Coffin, not Colebourne. Désirée felt a little hurt but soon got over it.

She wondered what sort of a Christmas Tim and Papa were having.

To watch Nathaniel climb onto the Newport stage next day was frightening. Désirée knew it meant a return to loneliness. Handing up his bundles, she figured she had not let slip anything which might have betrayed her true name — not unless she had talked in her sleep.

Though her affair with John was nothing to be ashamed of, Newport must never learn that Desire Harmony Bennett had ever lain with a man for the sake of money.

When the coachman blew his bugle, Nat Coffin leaned out of the window and kissed the girl standing there so prim and pretty. Today her hair looked more coppery than usual, her lips a darker, shinier red, and the shadows beneath her eyes more appealing than ever. A truly lovely girl.

"Remember now," he said, "you're to go direct to Smith's City Tavern. It's on Second Street, Désirée."

"Oh, Nathaniel, please call me just plain Desire from now on."

"And why should I, you funny little sweetheart?"

"Please —"

"Very well, Desire it shall be — like it better myself." He looked deep into her eyes, searching, asked a little sadly, "You will be good?"

[242]

She didn't take offense, just gave him a quick, strangely moving look. "You have been so very generous, dearest, there is no need to be anything else."

"Hup!" barked the coachman.

Bells jingled as the four horses threw themselves into their collars. Nathaniel swept off his hat and its bright cockade flashed in a wide arc.

"*Vale, vale, et si semper indesemper!* In other words, farewell!"

Suddenly, she took fright, wanted to cry out, "Oh, Nat! Nat, don't go!" but she only stood there in front of the posting station waving her handkerchief until tears blurred the vanishing coach.

A resounding kick on the door connecting with the house made Desire pop straight up in bed. Heavens! More brawling? What was going on tonight? Groggily she became aware of early morning.

"Open up, ye damned doxy! Open in the name o' the law!"

The law! Oh dear! What could they want with her?

Bedclothes clutched to her chin, Desire in frozen terror watched the door panels give and shake under a rain of kicks. Suddenly the latch split; there bounded into her room a breathless, brutal-looking individual wearing a dull brown watch cloak. In one hand he was carrying a candle lantern, in the other a length of cord and a cudgel.

The intruder's small, mean eyes fixed her. He tramped towards her favoring what must be a sore foot. "Rouse out of that, and be quick about it."

All eyes, Desire could only gape. "But, sir, I — I have harmed no one."

"Don't yer dast talk back. All you whores are cheats to boot. Never met one who wasn't. Come on, rouse out o' there!"

Too terrified to move a muscle, she merely flinched against the wall. Cursing, the watchman reached under the covers, grabbed her ankle, hauled her kicking out onto the floor with nightshift gathered about her neck.

When, scarlet, she pulled down her nightdress and struggled to her feet, the watchman stood panting, watching, hat cocked over one eye, the loop of greasy cord hanging limp from his red fist. Within Mrs. Norton's house sounded heavy feet, shrieks and rough orders.

The watchman was licking his lips. "Cripes! No wonder old Frenchy does a rushing trade. Pity yer got to cool such a pretty pink bottom in jail."

"Jail? Oh — oh — no!" She had to sail aboard the *Peace & Plenty*. She had to find Nat in Philadelphia. "I can't. I'm going away," Desire choked.

"Yer going away, all right, dearie," the watchman grinned, jerking open a bureau drawer. "Providence is a respectable, law-abiding port; time you fancy-Nancies learned that. No nonsense, now; get into some clothes."

"But, kind sir." Desire raised enormous brown eyes. "I have done nothing dishonest. I swear I haven't."

"So say you," the watchman grunted. "A man was robbed and beaten half to death here this night." Even as he fumbled in the bureau, he kept watching the way her billowy nightshift fell open, exposing breasts.

In the next room Chloë began screaming like a stuck pig. Another girl was shrieking incredibly foul insults. Subconsciously she heard Mrs. Norton, with desperate politeness, trying to buy off a lantern-jawed official whom the other watchman called "Sheriff."

The watchman nodded at the pocket dangling from her wrist. "What's that thing?"

"My — my purse." Her lips felt so rigid she could barely move them.

"Give us a look, dearie." He snatched it, tore it free. When he lifted the pocket, he shot a glance over his shoulder.

"Damn my eyes," he snarled. "Didn't I tell you to get some clothes on?"

In frozen desperation, Desire sullenly commenced to tie petticoats over her nightshift. Hopelessly, she caught up the first gown that came to hand, tucked her feet into her best slippers, then began buttoning her bodice any which way.

A blonde girl was being dragged, weeping, into the hallway. Beyond the open door there a grubby little man with a two days' growth of beard began tying the girl's hands behind her. "Stand still, you cursed hussy."

To think that in another few instants Asa Bennett's daughter too would be trussed, haled through the streets like a common prostitute! Desire almost fainted but remained gasping, staring at that greasy cord in the watchman's grimy paw.

"Hold out yer dukes," he ordered, but when he moved closer he suddenly slipped her purse into his pocket and pointed to the door leading into the lane.

"Say nothin' — an' git!" he muttered.

With the speed of a pursued rabbit racing for the shelter of its burrow, Desire wrenched open the lane door, and with the watchman's sudden shout of "Prisoner escaped!" loud in her ears, ran in headlong terror.

The Bull House

New-Port, Rhode Island
December 27, 1775

Private armed Sloop *Revenge*, burthen about One Hundred and fifteen Tons, or there-abouts, mounting about Twenty-four Guns large and Small, Captain Benjamin Norton, Commander, being bound on a cruising Voyage against the

[244]

Royal Pirate; If any Gentlemen Sailors or others have a mind to take a Cruise in said Sloop let them repair on board of said Sloop Now lying at Mr. Albert Taylor's Wharff, where they may see said Articles of Agreement and be kindly received. Said Sloop wants a Doctor at present.

Thaxter & Son

Certainly many privateers must be ready for sea. But the commissions without which no master dared sail for fear of being hanged as a pirate had not yet been issued. Tim figured the owners had been a little precipitate. The Congress was becoming famous for its vacillations, dilly-dallyings. Why weeks, even months might elapse before any one of these ships dared put out to sea.

The thought of Ira Thaxter's having guaranteed seamen's wages from date of enrolment made him laugh. When the commissions were granted he reasoned the richest prizes should be found cruising around Jamaica. Prizes! His arteries quickened.

The beating of a drum attracted his attention. An officer in blue clumped into sight in front of a couple of drummer boys in smart green and white uniforms. He carried a leather speaking trumpet.

Behind the drummers shuffled a slack-shouldered youth in an old blue militia tunic. He was carrying a white flag which for design, had a green pine tree, or something like that, stitched to its center. Above this arboreal effort the word LIBERTY stood out. Below, AN APPEAL TO HEAVEN. One corner of the banner was trailing in the mud.

When he reached the corner of Thames and Anne streets the officer halted, signaled the drummers to be quiet, and mopped his forehead.

Speaking through the trumpet, he intoned: "Hear ye! All brave, intrepid and able-bodied patriotic seamen, hear ye! The cruiser *Katy* will sail at the first opportunity. Today is the final chance to enlist. Such spirited fellows who are willing to engage will receive a bounty at the end of the war, besides their laurels — "

"Aw pipe down," yelled a voice from the depths of an alley.

The officer went red but repeated, " — Besides their laurels, and fifty acres of land to which every gallant hero may retire to enjoy the gratitude of his country."

"No shares!" a carpenter shouted from the crosstrees of *The Two Friends*. "Pinch-penny! We want prize money!"

The officer shook his fist, bellowed back, "Shut your ugly trap! You bloody privateers will soon enough come whimpering for our help!"

"How are you fixed for men?" Tim asked.

The recruiting officer spat resoundingly into a mud puddle. "I'm still short sixteen hands and may God damn and blast Newport for a hive of self-seeking pirates." He looked worried. "I'm doing all I can, but old Esek is going to raise holy blue hell if I don't find the men."

Uphill in the direction of Bull Street other drums began rolling. "Listen to that, will you? As if we haven't trouble enough, your local patriots figure it's time to begin beating for a home guard regiment."

"I've heard of it," Tim said. How many ages ago had he listened to Joe Child curse over this very unit? "It's handy for local yellowbellies who want to sport a uniform and tend their business at the same time."

Tim was developing an idea. What about the Gardner boys, the Remingtons, Jed Franklin, and Joe Elley? Unless they had been lucky enough to sign on a privateer paying wages from the start, they must by now be desperate for work. Certainly there wasn't room for such a horde of unemployed. He said, "I'm not promising anything, but I will try to scare up some recruits for you."

The officer beamed, wiped a hot red face, cast curious eyes on the Foulke. "I'll never forget it if you will. Old Hop's a devil when he gets r'iled."

"Is Admiral Hopkins really sailing south in a day or so?"

"Yep. You can send your men to the Sabin Inn. I'll be on the lookout for them. Good luck."

Tim was debating his next move when Captain Lawton, proprietor of the Bull House, came splashing across the street, scattering a flock of geese. He called out.

Tim halted, swung about so sharply his rifle barrel rapped a cooper's swing sign.

"Where you been? Looked all over for you." Lawton came puffing up to him and thrust a pudgy hand. "Come along to the Bull House and have a drink."

Tim took the innkeeper's hand. In the past John Lawton had done him no end of small kindnesses.

Once they were seated over leathern jacks of ale, the tavernkeeper said seriously, "Reason I been keen to find you, Tim, was because it so happens I witnessed the sailing instructions your pa gave to George Griffin. You'll recall Griffin commands the *Narragansett?*"

"Yes. That's capital, John. All Pa's records were lost in the raid."

Lawton took a deep draught of ale and smacked fleshy lips ere he said, "Being the smart old feller he was, your pa figured a long time back that the king's ministers would do just what they have done — declare all American vessels taken on the high seas as fair prizes. So he instructed Griffin to undertake enough short cruises 'twixt Saint-Domingue and the Dutch Islands to pay the crew and upkeep. If Griffin heard of British cruisers in the neighborhood, he was to stay in Cap François or Curaçao and wasn't to sail for home until so ordered."

Lawton drank more of the foaming bitter fluid, belched comfortably, then pushed forward a plate heaped with crackers and cheese. They were fine thin crackers and stamped with a bull's head, his private mark.

"Here's 'nother item might pay you to remember and *to keep under your hat.*" The innkeeper bent forward. "I've received word, no matter from whom, that the lords of the admiralty are rigging a great expedition 'gainst the Carolinas in the springtime." He winked. "If the convoys touch at Jamaica to refit after crossing, a smart privateer might pick off quite a few transports and supply ships."

Never in his life had Tim felt so all-fired impatient to be on his way. It would be rare fun cutting out a parcel of fat troopships! The *Narragansett* was plenty fast enough for such work, too!

"Thank you, John. So it's to be a naval raid?"

"More than that," Lawton said gravely. "There'll be troops along, plenty of them. The ministry plans a reg'lar campaign. So God help them Carolinians!"

By end of an hour Tim's hopes were bright as Lawton's pewter. He had arranged for the innkeeper to realize what he could from Asa Bennett's credits. Though Lawton wanted to do the job for nothing, Tim insisted he accept ten percent of anything he collected. By now, he had noticed that a man only did his best when he got paid for it.

Lawton would secure letter of marque papers for the *Narragansett* in triplicate. By separate routes they would be forwarded to Saint-Domingue and by the fastest possible means.

"The privateer brig *Narragansett*, Tim? That sounds fine."

"No. Remember, it's a letter of marque's papers I want."

Lawton paused in the act of refilling a long clay pipe. "That's right; but why ain't you wanting to privateer, plain and simple?"

Slowly, Tim grinned. "We Bennetts have been traders time out of mind, and the *Narragansett* is primarily a merchant ship."

"Then why plan to mount eight guns?" Lawton inquired with amazement.

"Even if I trade, what's to prevent my snapping up prizes now and then? As a letter of marque, I will have two ways of making money. Trading and prizetaking. Your privateersman stands only to gain from his prizes, if any. Figure it out for yourself, John."

With a grubby forefinger Lawton explored a mole on his chin.

"Take after your pa in some ways, don't you?" he grinned. He was silent for a moment. "How d'you figure getting down to Saint-Domingue?"

"I'll sail with Hopkins, as far as Philadelphia anyhow." Solemnly Tim drained the last of his beer. "I need to learn how a man-o'-war is handled."

"But your term of enlistment?" Lawton protested. "You surely don't figure on making the same mistake twice?"

Heat climbed into Tim's face. "No. When I met that recruiting party, I thought of a better way."

The New Flag

The day was cold and raw. A stiff breeze from the northwest was straightening flags set to staffs over in Philadelphia. Bunting snapped also above six vessels of varying tonnage which, set apart from a disorderly huddle of merchantmen, rode to their moorings. Cakes of ice and dingy fields of drowned snow, moving sluggishly out on the tide, bumped and rasped along their sides.

At the foot of Walnut Street sounded cheering and strains of martial music. Unexpectedly, the famous Christ Church chimes commenced to strike a spirited tune. Perceptible to a knot of officers gathered on the quarterdeck of the Continental cruiser *Alfred* was a flashing of bayonets beyond the merchantmen tied up along Front Street.

"Um, the committee seems to have turned out some militia," observed Captain Biddle. "Those horsemen in brown and white will be from the City Troop. "Best thing they do is to parade," he sniffed. Followed by the uneasy glances of his fellow captains, he took a quick turn down the quarterdeck.

They were suspicious of him, Biddle guessed, because he, alone of the new corps captains, had ever held a commission aboard a regular man-o'-war. Other counts against him were that these New Englanders suspected him as a Philadelphian; that his new uniform really fitted. He thought it well conceived; blue with a stand-up collar, cuffs slashed in red, waistcoat of the same color. His blue breeches were close-cut about the knee. He yearned for more of a calf with which to fill his white silk stockings.

As a battery downstream commenced to fire minute guns in honor of the occasion, Biddle's bright blue eyes carefully appraised his fellow captains. They stood bunched, watching a barge festooned with yellow and blue bunting come rowing out through the floating ice.

Twenty, twenty-one. By God, the committee must have granted this old privateersman the salute due a full admiral. How *that* would make the Royal Navy laugh!

Captain Biddle wished he were surer in his mind concerning Esek Hopkins. For all that was said, the Rhode Islander possessed many admirable qualities and he knew all there was to know about seamanship. That heavy undershot jaw of his bespoke determination, unfortunately tempered with a rare obstinacy. Once Esek Hopkins got his back up over a point it required the efforts of the twelve apostles plus the seven devils to get it down again.

No one could truthfully say that the new admiral wasn't a capable judge of men — and a worker. Day and night he entreated, bullied and bluffed to secure for his heterogeneous little squadron the best available supplies. To date he appeared to be one of the few men outside of John Adams, Stephen Hopkins, and Christopher Gadsden who intended the United Colonies to have a real navy.

Best of all was the fact that Esek Hopkins exhibited fear of neither man, God, nor the devil. These were the qualities, Biddle silently decided, which had caused his appointment. His brother, Stephen Hopkins of the committee, would certainly see to it that the new admiral continued to enjoy the Marine Committee's unqualified support.

A particularly icy gust beat over the group of captains. Whipple and Saltonstall swung their arms briskly in the pale sunshine. Captain Hazard, of the *Providence*, in seeking shelter, tripped over his sword so awkwardly that Nicholas Biddle, ex-midshipman of His Britannic Majesty's Navy, winced. Near the color halyard, he came upon the *Alfred*'s first lieutenant. This curious individual was waiting, holding a square bunting tucked under one of his preternaturally long arms. As his senior drew near, short, dark-haired Lieutenant Jones stiffened to attention.

"Well, Mr. Jones," Biddle smiled, "before long our commodore will have taken official command."

"Yes, sir."

"Pray stand at ease, Mr. Jones. We shall have to set the others an example soon enough."

From their first meeting, young Captain Nicholas Biddle and Flag Lieutenant John Paul Jones had got on. Perhaps it was because they both were so terribly eager to put to sea, to begin swapping broadsides with the Royal Navy.

Lieutenant Jones's gaunt, lonesome-looking features relaxed. Though he stood barely five and a half feet tall, he gave the impression of being much bigger. Perhaps his broad shoulders and powerful build created the illusion. The *Alfred*'s lieutenant's gray eyes were sharp and his dark hair was drawn back tight from a high, intelligent forehead. His face was dominated by a pointed nose. When Jones spoke it was with a faint Scottish accent.

"And when, sir, may we hope to put to sea?"

"At the end of this week," Biddle told him and kept one eye on the fast-approaching barge. "Unless Hazard and his sort can manufacture fresh arguments for a delay."

Lieutenant John Paul Jones tightened perpetually compressed lips. "I would to God, sir, the committee would let the admiral take the sea with just you, sir, young Hopkins, and me."

Was it pure chance that he, aged twenty-five, John Hopkins but little older, and young Mr. Jones here should all be of nearly the same opinion on so many points? Biddle thought not. The oldsters seemed hopelessly cautious and "sot" in their ways.

Was there anything to a prevalent rumor that down in Tobago, Jones had killed a seaman in a burst of passion and had had to run to keep from hanging?

"I take it you are going to hoist that flag the committee sent us?" the Philadelphian inquired.

[249]

"Aye, sir, but I don't relish the prospect." Jones cast a contemptuous glance at the bunting he had placed beside the binnacle.

Captain Saltonstall turned a long horse-face over his shoulder and bawled, "Hey, Nick! Better come along. Them barges is getting tolerable close now. Mr. Jones, just you send the fellers to their posts."

Biddle choked. Picture the captain of a British frigate hailing a fellow captain by his nickname, referring to his crew as "the fellers"!

Once the barge of honor came grinding alongside, Captain Biddle could recognize several members of the Marine Committee: Silas Deane with his long Yankee face and wintry eyes; old Stephen Hopkins, in his seventies but still full of energy; the Southerners, Christopher Gadsden, Joe Hewes and Lighthorse Harry Lee; John Adams looked sick — anyhow he was blue-lipped with the cold.

Captain Saltonstall reset an old French sword dangling from his well-filled belt, glanced uneasily about. "Well now, I guess we better stand by the gangway, boys."

Once the barge sweeps had been raised to the perpendicular, Captain Saltonstall flapped his hand at a marine trumpeter, who began a series of flourishes.

Today Esek Hopkins, Commander-in-Chief of the Continental Navy, cut a fine figure. His powerful jaws were pink from a recent shave, his large dark eyes were clear and full of life, his uniform brave with flat yellow buttons, and his scarlet waistcoat was neat and well cut.

"Hoist away!" Hopkins called. A gun roared — another — another.

Bitter-smelling gray smoke whipped across the quarterdeck. The other ships, too, began saluting that ensign climbing to the *Alfred*'s signal yard. Biddle saw that it was of a glaring yellow, that on it coiled the lively representation of a rattlesnake bearing thirteen rattles. Unevenly stitched across the ensign was the motto DON'T TREAD ON ME!

"Gentlemen," John Adams cried in clear carrying tones, "the Marine Committee does now declare these vessels commissioned in the Naval Service of the United Colonies!"

Liberty Island

Amid cheers and to the great relief of God-fearing folk in Philadelphia, the fleet of the United Colonies on January 17, 1776, dropped down the Delaware and re-anchored off Liberty Island only a few miles downstream. The disappointment of those who had expected that the fleet finally was putting to sea was bitter.

"I warned you so," Higsby snarled at Tim. "These vessels ain't never goin' out an' fight the Britainers. Hell's roaring bells! I'm goin' to desert. Other day a feller told me they's some fine partisan skirmishin' fit to break out in the Carolina back country."

"You're crazy," Tim told him amiably.

"No, I ain't neither. He says the Scotchmen that settled along the frontiers are declarin' for the king." Higsby spat into a box of sand.

"Maybe," Tim sighed. "You can't blame the commodore for not putting to sea with half his crew rotten with the pox. Surgeon reports that half the *Cabot's* crew are dying."

A red-headed sergeant of marines occupying a desk opposite Tim's emitted a brassy snort.

"They are all addled — *ad unguem* — to a nicety, one might say." To Tim's astonishment, the marine spoke in a precise, educated voice. "I'll venture that as soon as we're fit for sea, the Congress will, *dextro tempore*, order us to attack the squadron under the noble-spirited Lord of Dunmore.

"It appears that damned old pirate is not satisfied with burning Norfolk flat. Like the heathen, he rages up and down Chesapeake Bay, and every week no end of fine plantations go up in smoke."

"Say, mister, anything in this yarn 'bout two more war boats joinin' us?"

"They won't amount to much. *Experto credite*, perhaps."

The ranger's straight black brows met. "Say, might that lingo be Iroquois?"

The sergeant chuckled. "Scarcely. Tell me, how does one say 'one learns by experience' in Shawnee?"

"O *gone-owe-shesk*," came Higsby's prompt translation. He still regarded the NCO with mistrust. "I put you a question which you ain't seen fit to answer yet. Is that Huron you been talkin'?"

Tim laughed. "No, Sam, it's just Latin. Where do you hail from, Sergeant?"

The marine sergeant's smile faded as he said, "Nantucket. You behold Nathaniel Coffin, scapegrace son of a Loyalist family. Late lieutenant in Colonel William Prescott's regiment of the Massachusetts Line."

Unguardedly Tim said, "I was at the siege, too. Hitchcock's Rhode Island Regiment. I'm from Conanicut. Britishers burned us out middle of last month."

"A sorry business this town-burning. Up in Providence I met the poor devil of a girl whose people got burnt out in Falmouth. Those arrant asses in the ministry must soon give up the practice," Coffin said seriously. "Only serves to outrage the Colonies into further obstinacy." He sighed, "The British got off scot-free at Conanicut, I presume?"

"Not quite, mister, not quite. Here, look at these." Higsby fumbled in his warbag and presently flung three pewter cap plates onto the sergeant's desk. "These here don't touch skelps fer sho proof." His eyes rested steadily on the sergeant's. "I warn't allowed to lift no hair, so I reckon you'll just have to credit me on these. I ain't lyin', honest."

Sergeant Coffin selected a plate, saw that it was silvered and stamped with a foul anchor and the motto: *Per Terram, Per Mare*.

"Very conclusive evidence, I call it. One suspects that the British give few of these away."

Higsby looked relieved; he sure would have made a swipe at that soljer fellow if he had disbelieved. "This here's my tally fer an officer."

From where he stood, Tim could see the grip and guard of a dress sword. The plate was of heavy gold and delicately engraved in elegant script with the name JNO. ST. CLAIR.

"A tidy bit of engraving," observed Coffin, running fingers over the cool ivory of a guard which carved in the shape of a young mermaid.

"How do you take to the sea, Mr. Higsby?"

Tim laughed, "Ask rather what the sea takes from Sam and you've hit the nail on the head!"

Higsby spat. "Anybody who'd go to sea fer pleasure, sez I, would go to hell fer a pastime."

A dispatch boat dropped down from Philadelphia and a messenger delivered to Esek Hopkins a heavily sealed envelope. Once he had read its contents, the commodore ordered his captains to report immediately.

They came, ready with complaints, suspicious and apprehensive. Even when the commodore told them he had good news, their scowls did not disappear.

"We're going to sea, I allow?" Whipple demanded at length.

The commodore flourished a fat envelope dotted with scarlet seals. "Aye, that we are. But there's still better intelligence: off Cape Henlopen we will rendezvous with two more Continental men-o'-war."

Captain Biddle drew himself up, trying to overlook the fact that Hopkins had draped an old plaid shawl over his tunic. "Sir, are you at least permitted to inform us whether we sail to engage the enemy?"

Esek Hopkins scratched his head, looked troubled. "Well now, Nick — er, Captain Biddle, I'd tell you if I knew. You see, my final orders must remain sealed till we get to sea. We all know how hard put the Congress is to collect the powder, naval supplies and cannons for this new fleet that's a-building."

"That is true enough," Saltonstall admitted. "What of that?"

Hopkins said impressively, "It is my considered opinion that we will best serve the committee if we cruise to capture such supplies."

Whipple said slowly, "I guess it's our duty to go after Dunmore."

Tim heard Hopkins chuckle deep in his throat. "Hold on, I ain't done yet about that cruise south for supplies. We could lay siege to New Providence in the Bahamas with even chances of success."

"But there's a big fort there," Hacker protested in deep agitation, "and another, smaller one. I have seen them. So has Lieutenant Weaver."

"I allow it may mean a stiff fight," Hopkins said steadily, "but we should capture the place. The Congress will be vastly pleased with a rich haul of canvas, cannon, and powder. How many of you favor staying in this bay and hunting for the British?"

Three voices called, "Aye."

Grinnell winked, "Will you take a wager on where we go?"

Before Tim could reply, the commodore boomed, "Without counting my vote, we are five to three for attack on New Providence. Therefore, gentlemen, so soon as this gale diminishes, we will set a course for the Bahamas. My orders will reach you before sundown, and mind you obey them to the letter! That means you too, Abe Whipple, you're all of an itch to get off by yourself."

Aboard the *Andrew Dorea*, Captain Biddle began to feel he was making progress. His gun crews could raise gunports, remove tompions, and run out cannon before any of the other men-of-war could so much as cast off their gun covers.

Everybody had heaved a big sigh of relief when first the *Cabot* and then the *Fly* appeared at the rendezvous. This left missing only the *Hornet* and the *Wasp*. Nobody held out much hope that either would come in, though the *Wasp* was bigger than the *Fly*.

Consequently, the excitement became intense when, towards sundown, a schooner was sighted on the horizon. It proved to be the *Wasp*, badly battered and lacking her main topmast. The commodore was so delighted that he ordered a salute fired when the *Wasp* dropped anchor.

Lieutenant Jones grumbled, " 'Tis a zany business to waste good powder. Unless we're uncommon lucky, the Old Man has warned all the Western Bahamas of our presence."

The *Hornet* never did make an appearance.

The First Prizes

Once his course was determined and he found himself cruising on familiar ground, Commodore Esek Hopkins became metamorphosed. His good nature returned, and with it his initiative. On March first, he wore out three gig crews in pulling from one of his ships to the next.

That evening the squadron lined the bulwarks, speculating as to why the sea-stained *Cabot* and *Providence* should mysteriously up anchor and vanish swiftly on a southwesterly course.

Next day they reappeared, escorting a brace of captured Bahamian vessels. They were dingy little fishing sloops quite innocent of paint and sailing under canvas that was brown as any dried oak leaf.

[253]

More consultations resulted and during most of March second, a regular flotilla of captain's gigs floated astern of the *Alfred* with crews cursing at being kept waiting in the heat. Meanwhile, sick and disabled seamen were brought off from the tents in which they had been luxuriating ashore. Everyone prayed that a fumigation of burned sulphur and gunpowder would rid the ships of the pox for good and all.

When, with issuance of the evening grog ration, the news went about that all marines had been ordered to prepare for shore duty, a subdued excitement pervaded the sunburned crew.

A majority of the "leathernecks," as the men persisted in calling them, were ordered into the *Cabot* and the *Providence*; the balance aboard the Bahamian fishing boats.

Tim, smoking a quiet pipe at the break of the *Alfred*'s quarterdeck, sensed a gradual sobering on the part of the crew. Apparently they were beginning to give thought as to what might happen when roundshot commenced flying in two directions. Some at the foot of the mizzen were talking loud enough to be overheard.

"Goin' into an attack, shouldn't wonder," opined a boatswain's mate.

"Attack, where?" demanded a hairy fellow with a battered pug nose.

"New Providence, o' course. Ain't no other real port in these latitudes."

"What's the place like?"

"Dunno. Like most West India ports, I guess — niggers, stinks, and drinks."

"Anybody been there?" asked the pug-nosed man.

The coxswain of the commodore's barge nodded. "I touched there back in fifty-six. 'Twas along of Old Hop, too. We put in to careen and ship water. New Providence was a thriving little port then. I hear it's growed considerable."

"How big?"

"About five thousand people I'd venture and they've a pair of forts defending the place. One's right in town. Don't rightly know where the other lies."

"Guns?"

"Dunno."

By the light of battle lanterns swung in the rigging, activity continued aboard the *Providence* and the *Wasp* until late at night. Men wakeful aboard the other men-of-war could hear the clink of steel, the whine of heavily laden pulleys and much cursing and tramping about.

A rumor circulated that the prizes had reported a big British man-o'-war at anchor in New Providence Harbor. Some were certain that the marines, supported by a picked detachment of sailors, would attempt a night attack on the forts. Others were equally positive that the entire squadron would sail into New Providence Harbor and batter down the enemy by superior weight of metal.

[254]

The chief topic of speculation, however, concerned the number of guns mounted on the enemy fortifications. Were there fifty? Eighty? A hundred? Did British regulars form a part of the garrison? Or was there nothing but militia to worry over? Some wiseacres declared a whole regiment of the line was regularly stationed in Fort Nassau.

Surprise Attack

Just as the bells of the squadron were sounding four notes of the middle watch, Captain Nicholas of the First Continental Marine Battalion appeared on deck. In hushed tones he addressed the sergeant on duty.

"Your men ready, Sergeant?"

"Yes, sir." Nat Coffin left off wondering whatever could have kept that unfortunate Desire St. Clair from joining him in Philadelphia and jumped to attention.

The captain of marines ran an eye over his men. Like corpses on a battlefield they lay huddled about the deck, asleep in grotesque attitudes. Some lay propped against the cannon, some had pillowed their heads on coils of cable or on squares of canvas.

When, silent and ghostly as a shadow, one of the captured sloops came scraping alongside, Captain Nicholas turned to Coffin. "Rouse them. We leave in twenty minutes."

Nat soon deduced that Captain Nicholas was in command of this furtive expedition. Weaver, leather-faced lieutenant of the *Cabot*, was his advisor and responsible for the fifty sailors of the expedition. Weaver was reputed to know the Bahamas as the back of his hand.

Once dawn broke Commodore Hopkins ordered his admiral's flag — thirteen alternate red and white stripes with a rattlesnake crawling diagonally across them — run up to the *Alfred*'s jack staff.

Boatswain's pipes peeped, drums rattled and voices bawled commands throughout the squadron. Aboard the flagship, Flag Lieutenant Jones and Lieutenants Seabury, Pitcher, and Maltbie ran to their stations. John Earle, the sailing master, ordered the head sails raised.

Wearing his second-best uniform and a weather-beaten cocked hat, Esek Hopkins walked the windward rail of his quarterdeck. Tim, detailed to messenger duty, was close enough to get a good look at the old-fashioned, heavy-guarded cutlass which, in a brass-tipped leather scabbard, swung to the commodore's side. The weapon was nothing at all fancy and must have seen a lot of service.

By the growing light, Tim thought he read apprehension written large across Esek Hopkins' big, mottled features.

[255]

Gloomily the commander-in-chief watched the *Cabot*, the *Fly*, the *Andrew Dorea* and the *Columbus* make sail. Turning to Captain Salton-stall, he said, "I'd give a lot, Dud, to know how well those stubborn jack-asses over yonder will follow my orders."

Saltonstall's threadbare shoulders answered with a shrug.

Breaking out sail after sail, the American squadron began coasting the southern shore of Grand Abacco, and as the first rays of sunlight came beating over the horizon, all five vessels broke out their rattlesnake ensigns. Garishly bright, they fluttered against the deep azure of the heavens.

Lieutenant Jones, his slash of a mouth more like an old wound scar than ever, stalked up to Tim.

"Ye ha'e my sympathy, Mr. Bennett," said he. "Had I had my way, we would both ha'e gone wi' the landing party."

Tim smiled on the acid little man. "If half the rumors one hears are to be credited, there should be action enough to satisfy even you, Mr. Jones. At least enough to baptize our flag with a whiff of gunpowder."

Lieutenant Jones's sharp features contracted as he glowered aloft. "That flag, sir, is an abomination. For my part, I shall never see why a venomous serpent should be the combatant emblem of a brave and honest folk fighting to be free. I abhor the device!"

Turning on his heel, he strode off on past the dully glinting breeches of the port battery, a peppery gamecock of a figure.

Fort Montague

Aboard the captured fishing sloops the odors of sweaty clothing, insects and stale fish vied for precedence. Sergeant Coffin lay under the half deck of the leading vessel feeling perspiration pour down his back in sticky, tickling rivulets.

There were much pleasanter situations than to find oneself sprawled on a pile of ballast among ninety other marines and their equipment. Captain Nicholas was lucky to be up there on deck.

Wearing a ragged smock over his uniform and a frayed palm-fiber hat in place of his tricorne, Nicholas looked almost cool as he stood swaying beside the black fisherman-pilot. The only other persons lucky enough to be out in the air were the sloop's black crew and three white sailors in stained white ducks and grimy jerseys.

From the shore an observant individual might at most have deduced that the *Carolina* and her companion, the *Pelican*, rode so low in the water because they had made a fortunate haul at the sponge beds.

Nat, in trying to forget his misery, studied the Conch at the tiller. He wasn't big, but he must be strong as an ox. Whenever he made a movement, the muscles of his gleaming body undulated like poured tar. Must have a lick of Arab blood in him, his nose was so narrow and hawk-shaped.

Captain Nicholas's calm voice impinged upon his contemplation, "We will land directly. Get your gear handy, lads."

"Thank God for that!" gasped a purple-faced marine. "I sure been stewing in my own juice the last two hours."

Sam Higsby, at the far end of the hold, was feeling finer than silk. Now it seemed that nothing could prevent at least a skirmish from taking place. To keep from grinning, he bit off a chaw of tobacco, started to work on it real fast.

Yesterday afternoon, he had cast enough rifle balls to last him for at least three man-sized skirmishes. Maybe today would bring the real scrap he was yearning for. Too bad he was down to the last of those lawn patches.

Lying there with a marine's cutlass sheath digging into his slats, he couldn't help grinning to think of Aggie shivering back in Massachusetts. He bet Aggie never guessed that her petticoat would travel clean down to the Indies.

Captain Nicholas had stood up and was studying the beach with great care. At last he bent and from the stern locker fished out his sword and a brace of big boarding pistols. Lastly he pulled off the smock and put on his cocked hat. He came forward and spoke under the half deck, his silver epaulets bright as a full moon.

"You will line up the instant you reach the beach. Marines in the first platoon, cutlass and pistol men in the second."

On deck the sail whirred down and its gaff made a loud *thump!* as the sponge sloop's keel took the beach. It made soft, rushing noises on digging into the sand.

"Everybody on deck!" the commander snapped. "Lively now!"

Higsby sang out, "Hey, Mister Cap'n, where do I fit?"

"Second line, you're not a marine."

Higsby started to get mad but remembered that his rifle would outrange any musket in the first platoon. The sponge sloop overflowed men. By fives and tens, the landing party splashed ashore, holding muskets and cartridge boxes free of the feeble wash. In the bright, double glare of tropical sun and white sand, everybody acted half blind. The other sponger also was beached and emptying armed men.

"Gonna have some fun now," John Gardner declared with feeling. "Damn redcoats owe me an' Pa a fine tanyard."

Lieutenant Weaver ran up, eyes snapping, his face redder than a beet with the heat. "You'll take a fist in the jaw if you don't keep quiet. Line up, line up! Every minute counts!"

Hampered by very soft and yielding sand, the shore party scrambled about, formed behind Sergeant Coffin and the uniformed marines.

[257]

Long before anybody else, Higsby recognized the two vessels which were running inshore to cover the maneuver. They were the *Providence* and the *Wasp*. Both men-of-war had cannon run out and ready.

Little delay attended the column's getting underway. As soon as it began marching westward beneath a pitiless tropical sun, Higsby's jet eyes commenced to explore a lush, emerald-green fringe of vegetation rising some sixty feet from the water's edge.

All the men hollered to see half-dressed bucks and *mammees* trying to round up pigs, chickens and children that were as crazy scared as they. When the head of the column was still a hundred yards away the inhabitants made for the jungle, leaving in their wake bits of furniture and clothing.

"It's de Spanishers!" somebody was yelling from behind one of the huts. "Best run fast, chillen."

A seaman called through tattooed hands. "We ain't Spanishers. We don't aim to harm you."

"Silence!" barked the Marine captain. "Next man raises a holler will get married to the gunner's daughter!"

Captain Nicholas sounded in earnest and as no one relished a flogging, silence descended. Of Weaver, Nicholas demanded, "What is that village?"

"New Guinea, sir."

"How far from it to Fort Montague?"

"Three-quarters of a mile, sir."

" — And New Providence?"

"Near two miles further on, sir."

As the expedition passed the village, the men couldn't help laughing when a little black boy dashed out of a palm-thatched hut naked as the day he was born and yelling bloody murder. Nevertheless, he clung to a gorgeous blue and gold chamber pot.

The column was slogging over the dazzling sand past a litter of piraguas, skiffs, and fishing gear, when from far up the coast came the reverberating boom of a cannon. It sounded just as if someone had dropped a heavy load of planks.

"Somebody has bungled," Captain Nicholas remarked to his subordinate. "Well, Mr. Weaver, this means if there are British regulars in Fort Montague, we'll be catching particular hell before long."

Sergeant Coffin felt a muscle in his cheek twitch two or three times. The way it had at Breed's Hill. For unsupported troops to charge a fort, the garrison of which lay dozing and unprepared, was one thing. But it was quite another matter to expect half-trained men such as these to advance over a strip of coverless beach in the face of grape shot and musket balls.

Over his shoulder, Nat glimpsed a succession of grim, sunburned faces, all bright with sweat.

Though nothing was said, the whole column guessed what had happened.

Pretty soon Captain Nicholas halted the column, mopped his craggy face, then beckoned Higsby. Together they disappeared into a line of woods which must mask Fort Montague.

Higsby found it all-fired fine to be moving among trees once more; even unfamiliar, strange-looking trees. Picking a route, he preceded Captain Nicholas and moved so quietly that he utterly surprised a group of refugees squatting in a little glade.

When at last they did see him gliding up, they scattered like a covey of quail — all except a weak old man who hid his face behind wrinkled, slate-colored hands and moaned,

"*Piedad! Piedad!* Please doan' kill a po' ol' man, señor!"

Higsby slapped him on the shoulder as he passed, said gently, "Keep yer pants dry, gran'pa, and tell yer folks we Amurricans ain't fixin' to hurt none of you."

On the other side of this point of woods lay a beach identical with that on which the party had landed. But dominating this one was a solid-appearing stone fort.

It wasn't large, nor small either, and a big British jack was set above it. The wind had died out though, and the flag hung limp as a whipped puppy's tail.

Peering around a palm, the Pennsylvanian counted eight embrasures, which probably meant this fort must mount nearly thirty cannons.

Higsby swallowed nothing once or twice. Quite a mouthful! Too bad the *Wasp* and the *Providence* lay such a long way out on the oily-looking sea, becalmed and hopelessly out of range.

Standing very straight and stiff, Captain Nicholas said in rapid, close-clipped accents:

"Men, we move immediately to the assault, for if the enemy secures reinforcements from the town, we will stand small chance of success." He pulled out an ivory whistle carved in the shape of a dolphin. "Mr. Weaver, when you hear this, you and your detachment will assault the east wall. It is not too high to be scaled if your men stand on each other's shoulders. And see that you carry it! I will lead the main attack against the south curtain."

Seamen, furiously swinging their cutlasses, hacked a trail through the flowering but very tough creepers and lianas which, in prodigal profusion, hung from the trees, and presently came in view of the boxlike fort they were to assault.

There was time, Captain Nicholas decided, for the column to catch its breath before undertaking charge. The men, Sergeant Coffin saw, must run nearly two hundred yards, without cover of any sort, and over the soft white coral sand.

"Hi, Cap'n, look!" Higsby pointed and everyone watched a postern gate gradually swing open.

After a brief delay a figure in a scarlet coat came stalking out of Fort

Montague. If one went by the gold braid on his tunic, he must be an officer. An escort of two privates with fixed bayonets followed at a little distance. These also were clad in scarlet but wore white cross-belts and floppy-brimmed straw hats.

The officer advanced, from time to time lifting an espantoon to which a handkerchief had been knotted.

Halfway to the woods, the vivid figure halted and, looking very small and lonely, stood staring at the men gathered among the pale green shadows.

" 'Pears like he wants to parley," observed Captain Nicholas hooking up his vivid green tunic. Dark sweat rings marked both his underarms and sweat had also soaked through at the small of his back.

He crooked a finger at Sergeant Coffin. "Follow me."

To Weaver, he said, "If this fellow attempts treachery, you are to storm the fort at once and secure it. Then, as soon as practicable, you will cooperate with the squadron by attacking New Providence from inland. Capture the governor's palace. It tops a hill, commands Fort Nassau."

Side by side, the two figures in green and white moved out of the woods and set off towards the trio in scarlet. The sun glanced off the sand with a glare that nearly blinded Nat Coffin.

The Englishman proved to be a greyhound-faced individual wearing a lieutenant's single epaulet. He gave Nicholas a grudging salute. Then demanded sharply, "*Qué quiere usted?*"

"Do you mind speaking English?" Captain Nicholas summoned a faint smile. "My Spanish, I fear, is inadequate."

The other's bloodshot eyes narrowed. "Stab me! Why, you talk like an Englishman. Who are you? What are you doing in this infernal, misplaced corner of Hades?"

While the marine captain explained his identity and mission, the Englishman first looked incredulous, then angry.

"Ah. You are merely a pack of rebels, or should I say 'pirates'?"

"I am not here, sir, to call names," Nicholas tartly informed him. "I am here to take yonder fort."

"Take Fort Montague?" the Englishman's heated features contracted. "Plague take such infernal insolence!"

Then he seemed to recall something. "May I send an express to His Excellency the Governor? I daresay he would be interested in learning of your — er — intentions."

The *Providence* and the *Wasp* still lay helpless on the glowing green-blue sea, but their masters had boats out, as if trying to tow. It would be hot work.

Captain Nicholas was saying in his abrupt down-east accent, "Sir, I am directed by my superior, Commodore Esek Hopkins, Commander-in-Chief of the Continental Naval Service, to demand the immediate and unconditional surrender of all forts, military and naval property on this island."

"Oh, do you really?" The lieutenant, a weary-looking career officer of forty or more, lifted a long upper lip in a sardonic grin. "And there is nothing else you would fancy, my good rebel?"

A hard smile flitted over Captain Nicholas's mouth. "If there is, sir, I fancy we will take it. One thing further: provided he is offered no armed resistance, Commodore Hopkins undertakes to guarantee the lives and the personal property of all inhabitants."

At twenty minutes past four o'clock a galloper appeared from the direction of New Providence and rode into Fort Montague. In this afternoon sun, the fort was glowing a deeper yellow. Though it could not have measured over a hundred feet to a side, the fortification looked larger, higher-walled than before.

When the oldish lieutenant reappeared under his improvised white flag, he was sullen and did not salute as he growled:

"His Excellency agrees to — damn, to surrender — " he choked on the word — "this fort, provided the garrison is permitted to retire unharmed."

"Granted," Captain Nicholas replied, "provided you undertake, on your honor, neither to remove or damage any Crown property whatsoever."

The lieutenant made angry little motions, bit his lips. "I fear I have no option in the matter."

"Very well," Nicholas said crisply. He felt sorry for the lieutenant. Poor old fellow! To its loss, the British service was becoming crowded with such friendless and penniless veterans. Good officers, but too poor to afford the purchase of majorities and colonelships.

"We will take possession immediately."

In a column of squads, Lieutenant Weaver's command moved out of the woods, trying to keep step and look soldierly.

It had covered perhaps half the distance to a palisade of mastich wood surrounding the fort as an outwork, when a great blossom of gray-white smoke spurted from embrasures. A split second later, a twelve-pound round crashed into the woods and showered the utterly amazed Americans with a rain of falling twigs and branches. Veterans in the detachment flung themselves flat.

A second cannon thundered, and again a shot screamed by. In the depths of the jungle, it sounded as if some Titan's boy was splitting kindling.

"Down! Lie down!" Sergeant Coffin shouted.

"So I ain't to be cheated after all," Higsby muttered, and with a grunt of satisfaction, cocked his long Leman. But before he could shoulder it, Captain Nicholas rasped:

"Put that damn thing down! You've no order to fire!"

A third twelve-pounder sent its ball tearing harmlessly over the heads of the Americans as Lieutenant Weaver's detachment came floundering back to shelter in a disorderly purple-faced column.

There were no more shots. As the last of the cannon smoke drifted lazily out to sea the fort's flag faltered on its staff, dipped jerkily out of sight.

With the eagerness of small boys exploring a recently abandoned house, the Americans swarmed through Fort Montague. Some ransacked the barracks, others examined the officers' quarters. Everybody admired a cistern which was fed with rainwater by a cleverly designed catchment. The tank must have held at least thirty tons of drinking water. Captain Nicholas at the head of a squad of marines promptly took possession of the magazine.

Of the haste in which the fort had been abandoned there was abundant evidence. Half-eaten food was collecting flies in the enlisted men's barracks, and in the officers' quarters smouldered a mound of half-burned official documents.

As had been anticipated, all the cannon, eight 18's, three 12's, and six 6-pounders had been spiked. The work, however, had been carelessly done. The spikes were too slender and thus failed effectively to seal the vents. By sunset every one of the seventeen cannon was in serviceable condition.

To Sam Higsby's way of thinking, New Providence wasn't much. Why, the whole sleepy-looking little port boasted only half a dozen wharfs and perhaps twice as many red-roofed warehouses that were tinted yellow, white and brown.

Still, he wished Mistress Desire Harmony could see him reconnoiter the advance. He was drifting silently from shed to barn, to the house corner, then across the road to the next dwelling, testing every palmetto clump of every grove of lemon trees. She would have enjoyed coming along, he reckoned. There was plenty of heart in that girl.

Sergeant Coffin found that entering a town captured from the British was an oddly exhilarating experience. Had Alexander, Caesar and Hannibal experienced similar sensations? In command of the uniformed contingent he was marching two paces behind Nicholas.

Save for the persistent yapping of many gaunt dogs, it was deathly still in this dusty, sunlit street. Suddenly a donkey began braying lustily. It sounded so much like Captain Saltonstall hailing a lookout that Nat almost laughed out loud.

It was when the invaders had entered Bay Street and were climbing a hill on which stood the governor's palace, that someone shouted:

"Glad you've come! Hurrah for the American colonies!"

Shutters commenced to swing open. Then everywhere voices began to call, "Down with the ministry!" "To hell with their taxes!" "Welcome, Americans!"

The marines crossed the drawbridge without diminishing their stride in the least, passed under an elaborate keystone engraved with the royal coat of arms. Ahead of them opened a dark and forbidding passageway.

After the glare of the street, Sergeant Coffin found it hard to see. He and the rest stumbled blindly over a wild litter of canteens, bayonets, pikes and pistols abandoned by the garrison. Dozens of Tower muskets stood propped every which way against the walls. A blaze of sunshine gleamed ahead. It was a square courtyard set in the exact center of the fort.

Maintaining a steady cadence, the marines re-emerged into hot sunlight. Immediately Captain Nicholas halted his men. He had just become aware of a solitary figure waiting on the further edge of the court.

This officer's scarlet coat was glittering with so much gold lace Coffin judged he must be at least a colonel. So rigid and unnatural was the lone officer's posture that he suggested a schoolboy's drawing. He carried a ring of brass keys in one hand, the other rested on the hilt of a sword.

Hollowly, Captain Nicholas's footsteps echoed through the courtyard as he advanced.

At a distance of ten feet from that figure so bright against the bluish shadows of a gallery behind, Captain Nicholas halted. He saluted, thinking that never again would he see a human face wear so tragic an expression. Contempt, shame and rage all were expressed.

"I, sir, am Captain Nicholas, First Battalion of Continental Marines, and at your service."

Still the gorgeous figure in scarlet and white made no move. Had not a key turned on his ring and flashed in the sun, he might have been a graven image.

'In compliance with orders from my commanding officer, Commodore Hopkins, I am here to take possession of this fort. Whom do I have the honor of addressing?"

The Englishman narrowed hard blue eyes, obviously steeled himself to speak. "I am His Majesty's duly commissioned governor over these islands." Montford Browne's voice was harsh as the rasp of steel drawn over steel. "I greatly regret that I have lived to — to — surrender my authority to a rabble of disloyal rogues."

The marine captain's rangy figure stiffened, but he controlled himself. "Your views, sir, are your property, but I must request the surrender of your keys."

Landing parties from the squadron, mustering on a dusty parade ground paralleling Fort Nassau, watched with deep interest a small bundle climb a flag on the watchtower. When it could rise no higher into the aching blue of the March sky, the halyards were given a jerk and into the air sprang a flag such as few present had ever beheld.

Straightening under a strong southerly breeze was a design composed of thirteen alternate red and white stripes with a British Jack in its canton corner.

"Now what in the hell is that thing?" one of the seamen growled.

'It's called the Grand Union," an officer told him.

"But, sir, why ain't our yellow rattlesnake flag up there?"

"By Jesus, I got it!" cried a mahogany-faced gunner. "It's them damned leathernecks. They've beat us to it and raised *the army flag!*"

Timothy Bennett spent long hours assembling and making an inventory. Once the work was done, Tim searched for paymaster Lieutenant Grinnell, found him more than a little jingled at the Bull & Otter Tavern. He was consuming a sangaree. Tactfully he sounded Grinnell as to the squadron's next move.

" 'Less I'm way off the course, Hopkins will head for Rhode Island and a hero's triumph, the minute our sick get better." He gave Tim a searching look. "I take it you intend to leave us here and get on to Hispaniola?"

"If the squadron is to proceed no further south."

"It won't." Owlishly Grinnell shook his head. "All we heroes want is to be kissed and praised. Ought to be, too, after this. What's your hurry? Be delighted to stand you to a flip — rum if you prefer."

"Thank you — but my pa used to have an agent here. I was thinking he may know how to get me to the French islands."

Grinnell waved a loose hand. "Have it your own way, m'lad. You're a fool not to come home, though, and be made a little brass god of. Might even forget you're a deserter."

"Now, goddamn you!" Tim's hand flew to the other's neck cloth. "Apologize, or I'll slap your jaws until you do."

Lieutenant Grinnell went red, but didn't like the look of the fist under his nose.

"All right. I 'pologize — my error." Sullenly he added, "You and that damned savage of a rifleman come to the *Alfred* tomorrow and I will pay you off. Expect you'd sooner live ashore anyhow."

John Petty, Esq.

The inhabitants of New Providence, reassured that they would suffer none of the rapine and looting such as had accompanied the Spanish raids of 1684 and 1704, returned, and by consequence, the port's dusty, unpaved streets teemed with traffic.

By the hundreds sailors and marines swarmed and swaggered about the town. Like mischievous boys, they delighted in pinching the buttocks of the slave women just to see them jump and spill the baskets they carried balanced on their heads. Fights over the matter of the flag raised above Fort Nassau raged at almost every tavern.

It lacked half an hour of sundown when Tim paused before a swing board slung above a wide stone arch leading into an inner court. An enormous tiger cat came out from under it, and began to strop itself against his leg.

Badly sun-cracked and faded, the sign was barely legible:

JNO. PETTY, ESQ.
Dealer in Merch'dise of every Nature
Birmingham & Sheffield Goods
China ware, Musical Instruments & Negros

Through the archway floated the melodious tootling of a flute. For some reason the player would, every once in a while, blow an hysterical-sounding sour note but would immediately resume playing.

Deeply mystified, Tim knocked several times then, when no one appeared, he entered the covered passage. Presently he found himself in a sun-dappled courtyard the center of which was occupied by a flaming flamboyant tree. Along one side were parked a pair of two-wheeled carts.

The music, he found, was being played by a plump, jovial-appearing individual who, seated in the shade of a short cloister connecting residence and storehouse, for the sake of coolness had slung his wig to the back of his chair.

To the player's left was a rack full of music. He lolled, half reclining in his chair, and was blowing an ebony and ivory flute as solemn as any judge. Sitting with one of the musician's bare feet in his lap was a small and extremely ragged Negro boy.

After a bewildered instant, Tim perceived that the boy had hold of the flautist's big toe and was, with the point of a long steel needle, attempting to dislodge something from beneath its nail. The black boy braced himself and dug so hard that the musician blew a terrifyingly false note, and sitting up, snatched his foot away.

"A pox on your clumsiness, Jupiter!" he roared. "D'you have to take my bloody foot off to get at a parcel o' chiggers?"

"Oh, nossuh," the little Negro's eyes became perfect circles of white. "Nossuh. Ah goes just so gentle as ah kin!"

"Very well. See that you do. You may resume your efforts. Mind you don't overlook any egg bags."

He had settled himself and was preparing to resume his music when he saw Tim standing in the archway. He waved a plump hand, and bowed sitting down.

"Evening, sir! A very good evening. John Petty at your service. You must forgive my not rising, but I must remain thus at Jupiter's mercy until he has removed the last of these confounded pestiferous insects."

But the moment he learned Tim's identity, Mr. Petty jumped up so suddenly he sent the little boy tumbling backwards across the cloister's bright red tiles.

"Mr. Asa Bennett's son? God bless my body and bones! I am delighted

[265]

to have lived till this happy moment. I am sir, positively overcome with pleasure."

He gripped Tim's hand with fervor. "Wonderful merchant, your respected father. Vastly intelligent. Never shipped me a wrong piece of merchandise — not so much as a button as wasn't salable. Never a word of wrong intelligence. Never once! Adelina!"

The Bahamian's deep voice boomed, making the courtyard resound, and a flock of hens scattered in confusion. Almost instantly in a doorway set at the end of Mr. Petty's vine-draped gallery, appeared a woman who moved with the fluid grace of a doe stepping out of a thicket.

She was slight, perhaps thirty years of age, and had wound about gleaming blue-black hair a bright yellow handkerchief. Her winecolored skirt was in subtle harmony with the yellow and black apron on which she was wiping floury hands. As she hurried forward, Tim noted small circlets of gold let into her ears.

The barefooted merchant stood there beaming. "Adelina, my dove, this is Mr. Bennett of Newport in America. Mr. Bennett, this is my very excellent housekeeper."

To Tim, it was a surprise that any housekeeper could exhibit such an excellent taste in her clothing. Mamba had worn any old thing that happened to be clean.

As Adelina dropped him a flowing curtsey, he realized that she was not merely tanned, as he had at first assumed, but that her skin was of soft brown mellowed with a golden hue. Her nose was pretty, being both short and straight, and when she gave him a shy smile, strong and even teeth flashed behind lips as dark a red as Desire Harmony's.

"Arouse yourself, my dear!" Mr. Petty boomed. "We must make Mr. Bennett welcome, mustn't we? Send Quacko and Jupiter down to the market directly. We will need pigeon plums, plantains, conch meat — we'll give our guest a real Bahamian *fou-fou* — star apples, a duck or two and crayfish — young ones, tell them. You will dispatch Eros to Mr. Forbes's. Present him my compliments, and will he join us at table tonight? Then on to Mr. Parton's, Mr. Drumgold's, Mr. John Card's, and — oh damn, Adelina, we'll bid the whole lot! After all, this is a rare occasion."

Tim noted that so far the woman called Adelina had not uttered a word. Her vivid lips merely curved as she made a small curtsey and retired, earrings flashing. He was debating whether Mr. Petty's housekeeper was a mute when he heard a voice which must have been hers repeating Mr. Petty's orders.

"Yes, sir, we shall have a high old time tonight. My fault if we don't." The Bahamian chuckled until his stomach jiggled beneath a wine-spotted linen waistcoat. "By the bye, how long may I hope to have you as my guest?"

His face fell when Tim explained the necessity of his immediate departure for Cap François.

"D'you prefer rum for the moment, or Madeira?" Mr. Petty queried eagerly. "Maybe a dash of Hollands and bitters? No use our parching while Adelina mixes us a bombo. The dear girl is a trifle deliberate, I fear, but her bombos are fit for the gods in Olympus."

He ended by decanting Madeira into tumblers which, having been fashioned with round ends, must be either drained or held in the hand.

Petty raised his drink towards the fly-clustered ceiling. "Here's luck to our trade together and a blight on His Majesty's advisers! If you prove half the trader your father was, we shall flourish."

"Amen," Tim nodded. Trader? How fine the word sounded!

"I saw Mr. Higsby about an hour ago," one of the Americans told Tim. "He was having the time of his life showing some blacks how to throw a hatchet. I expect they rate him a bigger officer than the commodore. He went out towards the edge of town with some of them."

When Tim came up on Sam Higsby he was dancing to the cadences that a dozen bucks were extracting from an amazing assortment of drums.

The rifleman had on his greasy old hunting shirt, the one that had LIBERTY painted across its chest. Followed by the intent gaze of dozens of the squatting Negroes, the Pennsylvanian spun, whirled and leaped in an Indian dance of some sort.

Now he was pounding the earth with his moccasins in a very difficult and complicated rhythm that delighted his audience. He would bend very low, then spring erect and throw his head back so fast that, like a stallion's tail in the wind, his jet hair lashed his face.

"Ani-kwo-dadu-sto-di, da-tli-de gava," he chanted. "Yum-wi ya tsol-tsi-ski awali ula gisker!"

"Ah-h-h!" cried the audience when he began to swing his war hatchet in glittering arcs. The dance he had done in Tiverton had been as nothing to this fierce upsurgence of energy.

The fire, blazing up, sketched yellow sweaty highlights on Higsby's cheeks.

Tim was about to call out when Higsby, emitting an eerie screech, tossed his war ax high into the smoke. When he caught it, he stood still, panting, grinning.

"Hey-o, Tim!" Higsby greeted. "How you favor my Cherokee eagle dance?"

Relieved to find Higsby sober and ready to accept Mr. Petty's hospitality, Tim expanded, spoke of continuing the voyage to Cap François.

Higsby remained silent until he had done, then drawled, "You won't take it too hard if I say I ain't goin'?"

"Not going? Good Lord, Sam, you can't back out now! Why, what'll I do? From the start I have been planning a berth for you aboard the Narragansett."

The aquiline profile faintly seen in the starlight remained unrelaxed.

[267]

"Why, Sam, I'll give you a chief gunner's share — a mate's — I'll make you so rich you'll never have to starve or fight or — "

"Uh-huh. That's just what I'm afearing. Tim, I set a store by you and I hope we'll stay good friends, but the sea and me is like Hurons and Iroquois," he said simply. "Holy Jesus! I'd liefer have a passel of Wyandot squaws go to work on me than feel like I did sailin' down from Phila-delphy."

Eros trotted, fascinated, between them.

"No, Tim, ain't any skirmishing in this kind o' war and that's all the fighting I know." The rifleman began talking faster. "Heard tell there will be real warrin' in the Cherokee country this summer. Sure to be if old Draggin' Canoe paints himself black an' red."

He gave Eros a lift over a mud hole. "Again, I don't greatly fancy these foreign countries. Folks here sp'ils their vittles with too much pepper."

He gave an impatient snort. "Goddamn it, man, 'twould be different if there was such a thing as a deer anywheres. Bein' as you don't take inter-est in pressin' petticuts, you won't have noticed that in these parts, yer fun's with black wenches or sailor fashion."

"I suppose that's so," Tim admitted slowly. This was a serious jolt to his scheme. All along he had counted on having Sam with him.

Higsby was saying, "Me, I can't stomach these black gals. Smell kinder queer, sourlike. Now a squaw ain't no bunch o' heliotrope, but she's got a woodsy smell to her — kind o' like a well-tanned pelt."

Departure

In the street outside of Mr. Petty's, lines of oxcarts bringing still further supplies for the American squadron began creaking by.

Tim didn't like to think of the ships as about to sail. He had made a good many friends in the squadron: dour, impatient Lieutenant Jones, capable and aggressive Captain Biddle and the commodore himself.

Most of all he would miss Nat Coffin's Latin tags and kindly cynicisms. It was queer about the marine sergeant. When the other NCO's were get-ting drunk or ruffling the yellow girls, Sergeant Coffin remained at the Bull & Otter writing in a book what he wryly described as "Observations."

He would never let anyone see what he wrote. "I'll publish it some day and astound everyone with my wisdom," he'd laughed. "*Amicus humani generis.*"

One night after the Nantucketer had indulged in an extra glass of Bar-bados rum, he had spoken tenderly of a girl back in Providence. Shyly, he admitted he hoped to meet her in Philadelphia on the squadron's return. There had been some misunderstanding between them. Oddly enough, when he inquired as to how soon they would marry, Nat had flushed and murmured: "*Docendo discimus.* There is a matter of deliberation, my friend. There are reasons, plagued sound reasons, I fear, why such a step should not even be considered. Yet — it ain't reasonable — I can't keep from thoughts of my sweet lass. Yon minx is a veritable paragon — sees me as I am, strong here, weak there, yet loves me, I think. Well, Timothy, I fear this is *Vale, frater, et si semper, indesemper vale.* The fleet sails tomorrow at dawn. The seventeenth an I reckoned correctly?" He looked earnestly at Tim. "You will not change your mind?"

"No, Nat, for many reasons, I must reach Cap François as soon as possible."

Coffin eased the pewter buttons of his tunic and settled onto a chair. "*Quo animo?* Why such haste? Surely a dash more of naval experience would not be wasted on a budding privateer?"

Slowly Tim's fingers closed, and he said in a slow voice, "Once the commissions are issued I intend to be among the first on the cruising ground. And where shall you go when the cruise is done?"

"Eventually, to Philadelphia." Nat lowered his voice. "I hope to find the girl I once mentioned. Somehow I feel she would have joined me but for some mischance. *Quo fata ferunt,* as it were."

"Why can't you marry her?" Tim asked with real interest.

A slow flush stained the Nantucketer's tanned visage. "Well, if you must have it, because though but a tyro, she was following a very ancient profession when I met her."

"Ah — I see. A trollop?"

"For God's sake, don't!" The figure in green and white winced. Nat's black-gaitered legs took him quickly the length of the room. "She was not a true trollop. Circumstances had driven her, yet she remained tender and entertained lofty ideals. She is, I fear, a rebel against the present order of society."

Tim frowned, went over to look out of the window into the sunny, lazy street with its dogs, pigs, and naked black children.

"I follow your meaning. I once had a sister who was just that sort of a rebel." He would have gone on, but Nat Coffin's mind was following another track.

"Save for my family, I would marry her straight off." He spread helpless hands. "Dear God, is it right for me to introduce into their placid, well-ordered circle what they could, and with reason, call a 'scarlet hussy'?"

"Take cheer, Nat, your pretty little rebel may never appear to plague you." Tim felt comforted, somehow, to find this companion in adversity. "Probably she will not. It doesn't lie in many women to be constant. Believe me, I know."

[269]

"To be so bitter about it you must have cause," Nat observed, doing up his tunic buttons. "Well, if you decide to write letters home, I'll get them from you at the vendue."

Long after Nathaniel Coffin's almost sedate figure had swung out of sight, Tim lingered, hot and wretchedly undecided, in what Mr. Petty euphemistically referred to as his office.

"Why the devil should I write to her?" he inquired of a tiny, very furry little kitten which came wobbling through the door. It gazed up at him with smoky blue eyes. "Why should I? I did my very best, didn't I? But did she? No!"

The kitten seated itself, opened a tiny pink mouth, yawned profoundly. Tim decided that he would be damned, nay double-damned before he would come crawling back — even by letter. A man's self-respect imposed certain limits.

He seized a quill from the shot jar, and wrote:

March 16, 1776

Mistress Lucy:

I remain at loss to understand your cruel Defection of December last. Nevertheless, I cannot credit that you would entirely of your own Will have Deserted me in my Hour of Need. Yet how am I to think otherwise?

Ah, Lucy, what infatuated you to Abandon your poor lover? If my whole faith in Mankind is not to be Broke — if I am not to deem you the most Faithless of Females, you will repair to the City Tavern on Second Street in Philadelphia town a year come this Date.

Whether we shall ever meet once more, God and you must determine.

Farewell,
Timothy

Next day Tim packed his scanty possessions into a handsome new sea chest Mr. Petty insisted on presenting. His monogram had already been done on it in bright, brass-headed nails so Mr. Petty must have foreseen his decision.

The *Live Oak* set sail on the evening of March the twenty-second and tacked down the eastern channel by the light of a full moon. She met a string of little spongers heading for town. Soft, sweet voices among their crews floated through the balmy air as they prepared their evening meal.

Cooking fires aboard the sloops and schooners painted the sails above them with a palpitating glare. As bright, vibrant panels seen against darkness the canvas glowed, sometimes ochre, sometimes vermilion, sometimes a glaring blood crimson.

When, off Rose Island, the *Live Oak* pointed her stubby bowsprit southwards and began to rise to a series of long and oily-swells, Tim drew a slow breath. Somewhere below yonder horizon the *Narragansett* lay waiting.

In less than a week he should be at Cap François.

[270]

If one counted Indians and blacks, Desire Harmony estimated that over two hundred people had congregated at Congaree Cross Roads. Even after dusk, wagons and pack trains had continued to pull in until whole acres of campfires glowed among the slash pines back of Mr. Joseph Horry's store.

Raucous voices, the sound of axes cutting firewood filled the night. From a freight train drawn up by the woodside came drunken shouts and a girl's squeal of pain.

For some reason Desire felt a sharp, constantly rising uneasiness. It had to do with the advanced condition of her pregnancy, of course. As "Mistress Daisy Montaigne" and an experienced actress, she shouldn't have got so upset over Brian's insistence on starting off with Mark Antony's funeral oration.

Languidly dressing her hair, she could hear babies crying, dogs fighting and snarling, and the trampling of horses. Down in the freighter trains voices were growing louder. Mr. Horry's red rum must be flowing more freely than ever.

Thank fortune the teamsters couldn't get any more liquor — at least not while she was using the space back of the counter for a dressing room.

Last night she and Brian had had a hard time getting through their performance. Somehow, they hadn't easily won approval of an audience as sallow and gaunt-faced as the people around Congaree.

She wouldn't ever forget that audience with its expressionless, flat black eyes, brutish manner and stupid reaction. For a whole hour of singing and acting, Brian had collected only six shillings, four pence. He had been sulky about it all day.

For the first time in her life she was really fearful. Her proverbial luck must work hard tonight if she were to pass unscathed. If Brian hadn't been drinking, ran her thoughts, he would pull them through. He had a genuine actor's gift for winning a hostile or disinterested audience.

People in tidewater South Carolina might appreciate the classics but she judged that to people up here Julius Caesar and Macbeth were just a couple of kings, like King George III maybe.

If last night had been any indication, these primitives both misunderstood and resented Brian Montaigne's Green Room airs and London macaroni manner. His Drury Lane "egads," "zounds," and "prithees" stuck in their craw, made them feel more ignorant than they were — if such were possible!

To her annoyance, she began perspiring profusely under her makeup. Her shepherdess costume felt insufferably hot, a veritable shirt of Nessus. If only the baby would lie still.

She tested her abdomen. Um. Though she had laced as tight as she dared, her pregnancy now was hardly to be concealed. Nervously, she inspected the dingy lace hemming her apron. Oh, bother! It needed sewing again.

" 'Mark where the envious Casca stabbed — ' "

" — Devil take all dirty furriners!" a raucous voice interrupted. "Gi's a song or a jig, dearie. Allus thought a popinjay could dance."

Inside the store, Desire clutched the door latch and began to tremble as she pushed the front door of the store open a little. Of all nights for Brian to get stubborn drunk! Why wouldn't he give this audience what it wanted?

She saw the four torches flaring at Brian's feet, then row on row of unshaven or bearded faces; men, boys, half-breeds, Indians, and mulattoes. Far in the rear a few Negroes looked on eagerly.

A rangy individual in a greasy leather shirt stood up and began shaking a clenched fist. "Jig, damn ye! We want a jig!"

In the front row men in buckskins were passing about a stone jug and talking loudly among themselves. They wore hunting shirts like Sam Higsby's, but the resemblance ended there. There had been nothing bestial or dirty about the Pennsylvanian.

With a sinking heart, she heard Brian's voice grow coldly contemptuous. Sober, he would have humored the crowd, cracked a joke.

"Aw, stow that gab! Sing or dance!" more voices bellowed. "To hell with that fancy lingo. Hey! Er you a man or woman?"

"Stab me, he's a gelding." Someone mimicked Brian's finicky pronuniciation.

Brian, in his flowing toga, made a lordly gesture as if brushing away a troublesome insect. " 'That was the unkindest cut of all — ' "

"*Me — e-o — ow!*" The cry came from among a semicircle of dusty freight wagons, canvas tops of which were reflecting the footlights. Others took up the catcall.

Desire's heart began to pump painfully. Why *wouldn't* Brian come to his senses?

More whistling and catcalls. Suddenly Brian Montaigne broke off, coolly surveyed his malodorous and heavily-sweating audience an instant. Then in his loudest, clearest voice, he exclaimed, "Oh, ye gods! What boots it for an artist to cast his finest pearls before swine?" Turning aside and leaving the stage, he buried his face in his hands and wept drunkenly. In through a side door burst Mr. Horry, his face gray with alarm. "Do something!" he begged. "Some of the orneriest brass-ankles in Carolina is out there. Onct they get roused they'll stop at nothing. Skun a nigger alive last week just fer the hell of it! Most of 'em's ugly drunk. Quick, er they'll be in here and wrecking my stock!"

The audience, Desire perceived, was yelling all manner of threats. Worse still, not so much as a penny had been put into a wooden trencher hope-fully left at the edge of the impromptu stage.

A big, red-haired drover in a green worsted shirt had one foot on the platform as Desire ran to the edge of the stage. Making a dancing half-turn she neatly spun her petticoats garter-high, then reversing the motion gave her audience another glimpse of her thigh.

Back in Trenton the trick had stood her in good stead.

"Patience, kind friends," she called. Then she pirouetted across the whole front of the platform, slender legs alternately revealed and concealed amid a flurry of deftly managed petticoats. The catcalling ceased and so did the whistling.

Heart hammering, she tried to forget the angry, hostile faces at her feet and began a simple country dance which called for a lot of coy winks and head tossing. She found it steadying to fix her gaze on a row of Indians crouched on a log in the background. From their steady unblinking gaze, she gained confidence.

Encouraged, she recited "The Chambermaid's Love Letter" with a pert winsomeness which would not have discredited Mistress Cheer, queen of all soubrettes.

The audience was quiet now except for a couple of drunken teamsters fighting and gouging at each other somewhere among the wagons. As the betrayed chambermaid, Desire found an excuse to show her legs once more, whereat the crowd voiced frank approval of scarlet garters tied in jaunty bowknots.

She was lamenting her indecision as to which lover to marry when a gap-toothed lout in a hunting shirt sang out:

"Don't you worry, Daisy! I'll lick 'em both an' you kin come home with me!"

Behind her, Brian Montaigne was calling in angry whispers, ordering her to retire, complaining that she was stealing his time. The audience, how-ever, would not let her go and insisted she sing again. But Brian snatched at her wrist.

"Come in, you little fool let the canaille yearn!"

Apparently somewhat sobered, Montaigne then scampered out onto the stage to assume the half-witted postures of the unfortunate Launcelot Gobbo.

By now the audience was in such good humor that they applauded, laughed, continued to laugh. When he had done, however, the crowd de-manded Mistress Daisy so she and Brian ran through an end piece entitled "The Beaux's Strategem."

It was received with moderate enthusiasm.

Brian, after bowing acknowledgment, struck an attitude and announced: "Ladies and gentlemen, this concludes our humble offerings for the eve-ning. Most earnestly do we thank you for your patronage — and — ahem

— trust you will generously not overlook the trencher set at the edge of this platform." He bowed deeply. "Hail, fellow lovers of Mimos, and farewell, a long farewell."

"More! More!"

" —If you would again applaud our modest efforts, pray attend the New Theatre in Queen Street, Charleston. Seats are but four pence in the pit."

"To hell with Charleston. We want Miss Daisy!"

"Alas," Mr. Montaigne shrugged, said loftily, "Mistress Daisy is er — indisposed."

"Indisposed? Haw! Haw! *There's* a fancy word for the family way!"

The crowd had largely dispersed, though groups of the more drunken lingered to bicker, boast and belch. Desire had never felt more thoroughly exhausted than when she crawled up a little ladder into the back of the freight wagon, a huge affair dragged by eight gigantic horses.

For a not inconsiderable price, she and Brian had been permitted to contrive beds of a sort among the freight which consisted of harness, spades, and hoes. The train was out of Baltimore and destined for Charleston.

Mercy! It was stifling underneath the canvas cover, but she dared not sit outside because the mosquitoes came out of the swamps in clouds so dense the tormented draft horses, tethered as they were to the wagon tongue, kept up a continual kicking and squealing.

Moving with leaden deliberation, Desire struggled out of her costume and sat panting, half naked in the dark. When she tore her apron hem even wider, her eyes filled and ran over. Come to think of it, though, the rip didn't matter. From now on she just wasn't appearing in public, not after what that brass-ankle had shouted.

Too exhausted to sleep, Desire lay staring up into the hot dark. Poor Brian, he was such a baffling blend of genius and — what else? God only knew!

Down by Mr. Horry's store people must be getting roaring drunk. She could hear yells, and Indians were letting out a screech every now and then. Somebody fired a shot. It outraged the gloomy silence of the swamp with its ringing echoes.

Though she stayed awake a long time, Brian still did not return. She heard him once or twice singing down by the store. He must be drunk as a lord — his voice was so thick and off key. Now, for sure, they wouldn't have a sixpence with which to enter Charleston.

Because of the mosquitoes, Desire pulled Brian's greatcoat up over her head and fell, at last, into a hot, unrestful slumber.

At first Desire thought a drunken Indian was screeching but then, amid a series of agonized screams, she heard her name called,

"Désirée! Help! Don't! Help! Oh-h-h! *Don't!* In God's name don't! Help, Désirée, they kill me!"

Unhandily, because of her swollen figure, Desire scrambled into a shawl and dragged a petticoat up over her nightshift. She didn't even stop to put on her shoes but got down to the ground in a trembling hurry. Even so, those nerve-shaking screams had already diminished to bubbling, whimpering noises like those made by a severely whipped child.

A dying bonfire gilded stalactites of Spanish moss dangling funereally above the crossroads.

"Ya-a-ah! I'm a ol' he-wildcat what likes pretty gals. Come here!" bellowed a drunken trapper and he made a futile grab for her as she sped over the soft, sandy road.

"Désirée," came a weak and breathless cry. "Oh-h — they — they've — hurt me so!"

To her surprise not one of the Cherokees or Choctaws remained in sight. Just four gangling backwoodsmen who, swaying, scowled at her as she ran panting towards the fire. One of them, a gray-haired old villain, was wiping his hands on his breeches.

Said he to a young brass-ankle who was so drunk he could hardly stand, "Shay, le's take 'at goddam shpy's fancy girl inter the swamp."

Never, thought Desire, had she seen so bestial a human face. It was bloated, had furry brows and snaggle yellow teeth.

"Naw," the other mumbled, trying to slip a skinning knife back into its sheath. "Ah don't want no truck with none o' these stage whores. Sting yer fierce. C'mon, Paw, guess we clipped that goddamn macaroni's comb short enough so's he won't want to crow fer a long time."

Beside a dying fire, Brian Montaigne lay on the bare ground with a couple of half-dressed wagoners working over him. From quite a distance she could recognize his painful gasps.

The bigger driver saw her and warned, "You stay away, ma'am. Your husband's hurt. Hurt bad."

"Désirée! Oh-h-h, dear God, why won't somebody kill me?" His voice, from the center of the group, was very weak. Suddenly regaining control of her legs, Desire dashed through a crowd of people in nightshirts.

A tall German with shirt tails jammed into cowhide boots caught her arm. "Nein!" he shook a cropped, pointed head. "Not go, Fräulein. Vot dose *Teuflen* haff done — *aber schrecklich ist!*"

"Let me go! I — I — " She peered wildly about.

From the edge of the woods, a drunken voice invited, "Hey, Mistress Daisy, you come to my wagon and you'll find a *man* in it!"

"*Nein, kommen Sie mit.*" The German tried clumsily to pat her shoulder. He had a round sunburned face and behind his spectacles, he looked immeasurably horrified.

"Come to me, Désirée." Bewilderment and fright was in Brian's voice.

"I can't," she wailed. "They won't let me."

A measure of strength must have returned to him for his voice sounded stronger but still broken, unpitched:

"Use me gently, kind friends — I fear there is naught you can do — "

A motion from the depths of the group suggested that Brian had managed to sit up.

Over his shoulder she glimpsed two men, one a teamster in a broad hat bending over Brian's slowly writhing body. Several blood-darkened rags sketched pale patches on the trampled earth. "Oh, what have you done to him?"

"*Ich und Heinrich? Du lieber Gott!* Ve haff done noddings," the German protested. "It vass dem brass-ankles."

"Brass-ankles? They are — Indians?"

"*Nein.* Vurser. Much vurser!"

When she realized what they had done, the world tilted on edge, her knees went lax and from a great distance she heard the big German's voice saying,

"You to *mein weibe* must come. Ve take care — "

She rallied, "You must let me go. You really must!"

The man supporting Desire patted her cheek in rough kindness. "So — so — he *todt* iss. Dead. Better so. A man should not live as he vass.

"*Kommen Sie mit, Liebchen* — please no more crying. Already Louisa iss so frightened of dis fierce and bloody country. So many savages, so many brass-ankles, so many ruined men."

The Proveauxs

From Maman's glance of warning, Antoinette Proveaux deduced that Papa had something on his mind. When the head of the house had something on his mind, especially at breakfast, everyone from Mrs. Proveaux down to Pansy, queen of the kitchen, moved with caution.

At best, the temper of Louis Proveaux was of the weathercock variety. Antoinette, slipping as quietly as she might into her seat at the breakfast table, read the danger signals. Maman was fluttery; Papa was wearing his oldest coat — a sure sign he was out of sorts.

Roger, however, looked very gay and martial as an ensign in the Second Rifle Regiment of South Carolina. Roger, of course, was what had upset Papa. The Proveauxs had always been merchants, solid Huguenot bourgeois not reconciled to raising their sons as fertilizers for a battlefield. Papa had said so a thousand times.

On Roger, Mr. Proveaux fixed a glance eloquent of disapproval. "At what time may I hope to see *monsieur le maréchal* appear to do some honest work?"

Roger nervously stroked the starched purity of his shirt ruffle. His uniform lapels of burnt orange glowed in the fresh morning sunlight, as he said, "With all due respect, monsieur, I may say that my orders call for a practice march out to Wando's."

"A practice parade, that's what it is! Rubbish! For a merchant's son, a criminal waste of time!"

Roger turned sullen, set a strong blue-black jaw. "Mr. Izard and Dr. Pringle don't speak that way of their sons' service."

The old man jerked the napkin from under his pink double chin. "But certainly they do not! What is time to a planter? Nothing. Pringle, Izard, Lowdnes, Middleton and the rest all are planters. If they need their sons at all, it is only during cropmaking. Bah. Overseers do all the real work."

Antoinette and her mother held their breath. Sycamore's eyes were all whites. Mr. Proveaux seldom worked himself up like this.

"Mark my words. The family which pays strangers to do its hard, unpleasant work cannot long survive!" Louis Proveaux glared into the reddened face of his son. "Now, my fine cockerel, you can tell Major Marion that I will not let you go off again this month. I forbid it! Twice last week, twice the week before. Enough is enough. Do you understand?"

Roger got to his feet and Antoinette braced herself. Her brother was furious with shame.

"Sir," he began stiffly. "Military orders cannot be disobeyed. Especially now that — "

" — Now that what?" Louis Proveaux instantly broke in. "What do you mean? Answer me!"

Roger's eyes wavered and he went scarlet above his lace stock. "I — we — that is, it concerns something we ain't supposed to talk about."

"Tell me."

The wills clashed, then habit won and Roger looked anxiously at his father. "Please, monsieur, you will not repeat? I — I would be punished."

"By now you should have observed that I am no chatterbox," the old man said grimly.

"Well, sir, an express reports that a fleet — a British squadron — is collecting off Cape Fear."

Antoinette glanced at her brother in some surprise. Roger was not given to keeping news to himself.

"Nonsense!" grunted Louis Proveaux. "If there is any fleet at all, it will be our own. One hears that Admiral Hopkins is expected."

Hands clasped behind back, the elder Proveaux circled the breakfast table. He seemed unaccountably disturbed.

"Hm! Hm! Why did you not tell me of this before?" he barked at Roger. "Fine merchant you will make. I warrant Laurens, Richardson and the rest have been up all night trimming their sails to this news!"

"I only heard it last night." The young man shrugged. "Please, monsieur, remember that if you speak of this, I — well, I shall be disciplined."

Buttons gleaming in the fresh morning sunlight, he went over and kissed his mother, patted Antoinette's shoulder and smiling said, "When you go

[277]

to market, don't pay a *sou* over sixpence a bushel for potatoes. There will be a glut in the market."

"Eh?" Louis Proveaux roused from his abstraction. As Roger well knew, such talk was what he liked to hear. "How are hemp prices?"

"Firm, sir, and expected to rise. Colonel Beale's batteaux have just brought in a cargo of fine, water-rotted fibers. Possibly a cargo could be bought cheap."

The old man shot him a quick look. "No doubt. But you forget there is a blockade. Having bought, how is one to ship it?"

Ensign Roger Proveaux paused in the doorway. "By pettyauger to Savannah, monsieur, then by a Dutch vessel to Rhode Island. The ropewalks there starve for hemp."

"And where, my son, did you learn this?" Louis Proveaux was almost beaming.

"From an officer of Continental Marines. He comes from up that way."

"What does a penny-pinching Yankee down here?"

"He is to train marines for that frigate the Marine Committee is to build here." Roger lingered slim and straight in the doorway, one hand negligently posed on the hilt of his sword. Dark, heavily lashed eyes swung to his sister.

"I will bring him home for you to fasten to your chariot wheels, 'Toinette. You have a strange *penchant* for New Englanders, *n'est-ce pas?* I seem to remember that you, Sally Huger and the Laurens girls had an elegant time up in Newport."

Mrs. Proveaux seized the opportunity to get off the dangerous subject. "But yes, ever since those summers in the North, I cannot understand what she sees in such grasping, cold-blooded creatures."

"Strange as it seems, this one is educated and a gentleman."

Antoinette made a pretense of tossing her head. "As if there were no well-bred people in Charleston!"

"But yes, *ma chère* — yet you do enjoy variety in your beaux."

Mrs. Proveaux heaved a delicate little sigh.

"Ah me — this cruel war. I shudder to face another hot summer, Louis. 'Toinette will miss her Quaker Friends."

Market Day

Ominous banks of black and silver clouds were continuing to pile up beyond the Cooper River. Antoinette Proveaux decided it must begin to rain any minute now and was relieved to see the red-tiled roof of the public market looming just ahead. A glance over her shoulder made sure that Lily, Ivy, Marigold and a quartet of small Negresses were following. Her followers made quite a procession with their empty market baskets balanced on their heads.

As her marketing progressed in leisurely fashion, Antoinette inevitably encountered friends, many in-laws and relations. Always they stopped for a few minutes of gossip.

Presently Lily was sent waddling off, her basket heaped high and trailing a comet's tail of pickaninny satellites. Ivy and Marigold stayed, winking and giggling at some young bucks languidly unloading a line of carts.

Ivy reminded timidly, "Fish ain't boughten yet, missy, an' it sho' fixin' t' rain."

The slave was right, Antoinette realized, so, picking up her skirts, she crossed behind the last wagons. They reached the shelter of the fish market just a stride or two ahead of a lashing downpour which drove hucksters helter-skelter to cover. The rain, Antoinette noticed, sketched curious eccentric patterns on the wagon tops and on the broad loins of the teams.

Entering the gloomy interior, she saw the usual dripping baskets of clams, crabs and crayfish. They would always hold a strange attraction for her. Some fish had been laid out on beds of bright green moss or wet straw and were still alive; their gills kept opening tediously, futilely.

"Heah yo' is, mis'tess! Heah is prime pond-chickens, all fat 'n' sassy!"

A shriveled old Negro hurried up offering a basket of colossal, goggle-eyed bullfrogs. Because Papa was partial to *grenouille à la Marseillaise* she bought them.

"Buy mah fine pikes?"

"Mawnin', maum, heah's good rockfish, cheap."

"Dis way, please, maum. Dis way."

The shower was still drumming on the tiles above so Antoinette, drawing her petticoat skirts close, wandered at will over the market's damp and rather slippery cobbles. A family of blacks crouched in a corner were munching shrimps and pitching the shells out into the rain. They looked like wild Negroes and were talking in some unfamiliar dialect. It was Coromantee, most likely. Most of the recent shipments had been secured from that tribe.

In a far corner Antoinette was surprised to discover a lone and very poorly dressed white man crouched behind a counter he had improvised of a plank and two empty kegs.

When she saw his offerings, her eye lit. "My, what elegant snappers! You may wrap me up a dozen."

The fisherman's expression brightened. When he jumped up, she realized he was so thin that his joints looked knobby.

"How much are they?"

"Penny, ha' penny the pound, mum."

Ivy sniffed. Antoinette's smile thinned. "That's a ha' penny more than anyone else is asking."

The vendor's red-rimmed eyes dropped and the eagerness went out of him. "Reckon that's so, ma'am, but me, I can't sell for a farthin' less, mum. They're nice fish," he pointed out desperately. "Fresh caught, still alive, see? I brought 'em in myself."

Antoinette wavered, but Mrs. Proveaux's schooling decided her. "No doubt. But it would be foolish for me to pay above the market price."

The fellow gulped, "Beg pardon, mum, but what does a ha' penny the pound mean to your sort? To me, it's the difference between starvation or a living."

"Starve?" Antoinette's brown eyes grew round. "But why?"

"I'm white, worse luck. I have nobody to feed me when I can't fish; I have nobody to doctor me or my family. There's no one to buy my clothes. If I was black, it would be different."

Dull color crept up into his gaunt cheeks. "I came out from England, mum, for the chance of trading free and equal. They promised us immigrants fair treatment." He spread big-knuckled hands. "But I don't get it. These slave fishermen undersell me at every turn. And why not? Their owner buys them nets, bait, boats — everything. Their owner don't care how many fish his slaves waste just so's he makes a profit."

He indicated a great glistening buck in a ragged gray jersey. "Mr. Hawkin owns him, and him and him. He keeps twenty blacks fishing the bay and the river. Men like Hawkin floods the market apurpose so's to keep the price so low a free man can't manage. What chance is there for a pore feller like me?"

"It don't seem fair," Antoinette admitted uncertainly. "But slaves are an investment, you know. They have to show a profit."

As she started to turn away, the fisherman cried piteously, "Please don't go, mum — please don't tell nobody what I said. I — I'll stand to lose me license. Here, take my snappers at a penny the pound. They'll spoil, else. My children got to eat tonight."

Antoinette remained disturbed long after she had left. Something did seem wrong with the poorer whites. White artisans and mechanics such as the saddlers, shipwrights, smiths, chimney-sweeps, glaziers and painters were emigrating by the hundred, moving into North Carolina or over the mountains into the West.

When she reached the river end of the market, the rain was still falling. She saw that she had guessed correctly; the freighter's train had pulled up in front of Colonel Beale's warehouse.

Idly, she watched a woman scramble awkwardly out of the last wagon and stand there in the downpour, gazing dully about. Finally she tucked a big bundle under one arm and started trudging up away from the waterfront.

The woman, who proved to be only a girl, apparently wasn't noticing the rain, only stumped leadenly along with head bent. She was getting her petticoats all muddy about the hem. When she drew closer, Antoinette tried to see what she was like.

At last she looked up from under a dripping straw hat and stood peering into the fish market. What? Who? It couldn't be! Antoinette looked again, placed the delicate oval of that face, those wide-winged brows and the shadows that lurked beneath them.

She dashed out into the rain, clasped the bedraggled traveler. "Desire! Desire Bennett!"

Ivy, Marigold, everybody, gaped.

" 'Toinette Proveaux — isn't it?"

"What in the world are you doing in Charleston?"

Desire's lips moved stiffly, formed the ghost of a smile. "I don't know. I — I had hoped to find you — someone I knew from — old days. I've had ill fortune and I am so very tired."

Second Company Dismissed!

Their fortnight of field training at an end, the men of the Second Rifle Company answered final roll call, then joyously broke ranks. In groups and singly, the men scattered to their tents, carrying rifles canted every which way. Soon they commenced to depart for home in canoes, pirogues and ahorseback. Because the Second Company was largely composed of tradesmen, a majority of the privates left on foot.

Lieutenant Nathaniel Coffin of the First Battalion, Continental Marines, heaved a satisfied sigh. In two weeks he had been able to accomplish a lot with these plain fellows — far more than he might have with those quick-tempered scions of the aristocracy who wanted commissions in Colonel Christopher Gadsden's First Regiment of Foot, or in Colonel William Moultrie's Second Regiment.

As soon as he learned that construction of South Carolina's contribution to the new navy would be temporarily postponed, Nat had taken an interest in some rifle companies just being formed. There was no trouble about his being granted leave to help train them. Colonel Thomson, a brisk and efficient transplanted Pennsylvanian, was delighted.

Nat found that instruction came easily to him; on the drill field one really got to know men. He wanted to learn about those details in which Carolinians differed from the Pennsylvanians and Rhode Islanders. America was so big. If independence were ever to be achieved, a fellow with a broad understanding might be of some use. Not limited like the local patriots who couldn't see beyond their own county.

Take Higsby for example — there was a fine, representative type. Pity he'd lost track of Sam. It was odd how well he and the rifleman had hit it off on the long cruise back to New England. When he pleased, Sam could lie like a thief on the gallows, but never on essentials; and he always stood ready to do his share of any work he felt he was supposed to.

[281]

Again, the Pennsylvanian possessed a natural philosophy the depth of which was a continual astonishment. Seldom, Nat mused, had he encountered a person less given to self-deception, less easily deceived as to a stranger's true character. He knew his own limitations, did Sam, and was modest, really. He must have caught that habit of bragging from the Indians.

Stripped to his undershirt, Nat Coffin lazed shamelessly on a pallet drenched by late May sunlight. In the distance a woodpecker was hammering lustily on a hollow tree. What he had seen of Carolina during a month was, on the whole, pleasing. Was this because he was held in respect for having twice been under British fire?

Some of the lady visitors had even called him a hero. Exaggeration, he was coming to think, was a Southern failing. Nathaniel Coffin a hero? He couldn't help grinning up at the panel of mildewed canvas above him.

Eyes half shut, he tried to understand the background of Charleston. This flourishing town suggested *multum in parvo* all right. Why should the descendants of French Huguenots and German Palatines be so much more amenable to discipline than those of straight English stock?

Take young Roger Proveaux, for example. The minute Ensign Proveaux understood what was wanted, he executed an order in the smartest, most practical way even if he asked "why" later on. Unlike the other youngbloods, he was neither slack nor careless about details.

Once he was told, Proveaux always made his men test their powder with a prouvette. By consequence, his detachment could outshoot any other unit in either of the city regiments.

A shadow fell across the tent's floor. It was yellow-haired Charles MacIntosh, a sublieutenant in the first Regiment.

"Heyo, Mr. Coffin, we're having a main tonight. Prioleau and Pringle are bringing over their birds. Cocking is dead against the committee's rulings, but you'll come?"

"Why, I — "

"Oh, come along," the other urged. "You'll have to keep your lips buttoned, though."

Nat wavered, "I had thought of visiting in Charleston."

The young fellow, lithe and supple in his blue and white regimentals, stepped inside. "Plague take Charleston! You will have time and to spare for visiting there. Please come. You will be my guest. Pa's plantation lies just beyond Prioleau's."

It would be interesting to observe how these aristocrats acted in liquor. Would they grow boastful, like politicians? Quarrelsome like Morgan's riflemen? Or would they freeze up and get sour like the Massachusetts men?

He hoped that drinking would render them happy and gay like the French and Spanish munitions salesmen he had seen haunting General Washington's headquarters.

By moonlight, Mr. MacIntosh's party tacked up the Wando into a strange and lovely country where great live oaks shed cascades of silvery Spanish moss onto the river's surface. Towering cypresses reared stately sable columns as if supporting the vast inverted bowl of the sky.

From the heart of reed-choked shallows, bull alligators boomed as the sailing skiff slipped smoothly by. Now and then an Indian in a dugout canoe, or a Negro hunter paddling his clumsy pettyauger, ghosted into sight. Everywhere was the squattering sound made by feeding waterfowl.

From its inception, the party was jolly, probably because young Charlie MacIntosh had sent aboard his father's skiff the most sumptuous supper Nat had beheld in many a blue moon. Grinning broadly, his valet and a pair of assistants unpacked hampers of cold duck, turkey, and chicken. Soup and vegetables had been kept hot in a packing of sawdust. Jams, jellies, cakes and fruits of all kind materialized by the dozen. Of wines and cordials, there was a prodigal variety.

For the first time since Nathaniel Coffin had lain on the breastwork of the redoubt on Breed's Hill, he was able to forget the murderous precision with which he had killed a trio of British grenadiers. Yes, he was really beginning to shake off that chill which ever since had dulled a natural heartiness.

Suddenly a messenger broke into the party. "Mr. MacIntosh! Where's Mr. MacIntosh?"

Everyone's head whipped about. On the drive sounded a staccato rattle of hoofs.

"Here. What's wrong?"

"Raise the country! Ride fo' Charleston. Committee's orders."

All the white men ran to the carriage house entrance.

"What's wrong?" rasped Prioleau.

"Plenty," came the breathless reply. "A British fleet is anchorin' off Rebellion Row. A great fleet of frigates, ships o' the line and — and transports. Dozens of 'em. Forty or fifty sail at the very least!"

Charleston, June 1, 1776

For two days Desire Bennett luxuriated in a great four-poster bed that was comfortable to a nearly forgotten degree. She was utterly content just to lie still recruiting her strength, studying with absurd interest a plaster ornament set into the ceiling.

How grand it was to lie once more between linen sheets smelling of lavender! Imagine not having to arise and wonder whether they would have enough money for breakfast. Imagine not having to consider and coddle Brian's mood for the day. Poor, poor Brian!

[283]

Lying there in a soft bed jacket of 'Toinette's she tried to reassure herself that she had done nothing but what she had been forced to. Her affair with John had been honest and they certainly would have married immediately.

Tears welled into her eyes when she recalled him in his scarlet, silver and black sprawled across the frozen ruts. Who had killed him? One of the Gardners? No, they had come up from behind. Another outraged farmer, then? What irony that John had played no part in that tragic, outrageous raid!

Oh, if only John St. Clair had lived at least long enough to hold this child of his that stirred within her. John St. Clair. She was sure now she could never love like that again. Not the way that she had loved John.

Who in the world would have foreseen that her passage money would be snatched from her? She'd had every intention of meeting young Lieutenant Coffin in Philadelphia. He was great-souled, intelligent and so gentlemanly. She guessed he was really in love with her. He would have made a fine husband. Where was he now?

Nat with his deep private thoughts, his ungainly New England frame, red hair and handsome sensitive face. It was pleasant to recall those tender hours together in Providence; peddler's bells ringing in the street below, wagons and coaches rumbling, gulls crying over the river.

It was a crazy world when a girl hadn't the remotest idea of where one's family and nearest friends might be. She didn't really think she had been a bad girl. She hadn't wanted to do — well, do what she had. Only there hadn't been any work.

Once 'Toinette got her to bed, she had slept through the first twenty-four hours without a break and most of the next day, until the stirring of her baby roused her. The child was so very active, she felt it must be a boy.

Suppose she had reached Philadelphia in time to find Nat? How differently things might have gone.

It was fine to abandon the role of Mistress Daisy Montaigne, to be Desire Harmony once more; to be unaffected and genuine in thought and speech.

With the approach of midday, it grew very hot and so humid that Desire pushed off the bedclothes and pulled off her nightshift. She sighed when the air flowed more freely over her swollen figure, her increasingly plump and ever tenderer breasts. Small John gave an energetic wriggle. She smiled, was prompted to try to probe gently in an effort to decide the infant's probable position.

My, having a baby certainly did make a mess of one's figure! Worth it though. When it was all over she would have this part of John St. Clair to cherish for ever and ever.

Her thoughts reverted to Sam Higsby, the gaunt rifleman from Pennsylvania who had come down from the siege with Tim. How nice he'd been that time he had caught her snooping about his leanto. Most men would have taken advantage. She knew now what he'd had every right to think.

There were no grace-notes, no pretty speeches to Sam and he wasn't given to talkativeness. When he did speak in his soft drawl, there was usually sense in what he said. A girl might tie to a man like Higsby. Where would he be now?

Of course, the Proveauxs must be led to believe that John had bequeathed next to nothing, barely enough money to pay her way to Charleston. She would make no mention of Nat, of course, nor of Brian. Chances were slim that anyone who knew her as Désirée or Mistress Daisy would get so far south. Not with the river swollen and the post roads still boggy from spring rains.

Best of all, the British had cut off all coastwise traffic except for the smallest coasters. She'd no wedding ring. What about that? It could have been stolen. Where? Well, say in Wilmington, North Carolina. Wilmington, she must remember that.

Once her confinement was over, perhaps Mrs. Proveaux could secure for her a position as tutor? 'Toinette and the Laurens girls had mentioned the existence of several "dame schools" in and near Charleston. In the old days advertisements had appeared in the Newport papers for "A Genteel Lady to tutor the daughters of a Planter in the Carolinas."

What would Roger Proveaux be like? 'Toinette's brother had never summered in Newport, but she gathered he was fiery, proud and very handsome.

A church bell began to clang, then another, not decorously as for prayer, nor mournfully as for a funeral. Their wild, brazen pealing set up a tingle at the roots of Desire's hair.

Sails Off Rebellion Row

Louis Proveaux gulped a tot of cognac and rubbed his chin, deliberating.

"As yet no one seems certain about the number of ships which have anchored off the bar. But by all accounts, they cannot number less than thirty transports and men-o'-war."

"Thirty?" Grandmère sniffed. "Probably aren't over ten. In a war believe nothing of what you hear and only half of what you see. *Mon dieu! I* know something of war."

For the first time she seemed aware of Desire. "Eh, who is this young lady? Why has she not been presented to me?"

"Mrs. St. Clair is an old friend of 'Toinette's — from Rhode Island," Mrs. Proveaux explained hurriedly. "Mrs. St. Clair is a widow. Her husband was killed in a battle near Newport."

[285]

"Not a battle," Aunt Lobelia testily corrected. " 'Twasn't a real battle, Charlotte. 'Twas a raid. Mrs. St. Clair said so herself."

Louis Proveaux ignored his sister-in-law, spoke to his mother who was sitting as straight as she might and taking in everything with amused calmness.

"As soon as day breaks, the committee will dispatch some expresses to arouse the upcountry. Militia and country regiments will be ordered to muster in marching order."

On short fingers, the merchant commenced to enumerate preparations for a defense. "New earthworks will be raised, a number of merchant ships will be armed. An emergency meeting of the Assembly will, no doubt, decide our future course."

"Then — Charleston will be defended?" Desire asked breathlessly.

Mr. Proveaux cast her an inquiring look. "I fear so. There will be much damage to property, much suffering among the mechanics and poor."

Gradually, the window frames assumed outlines as the early June dawn began to break.

A loud knocking had commenced. Antoinette, glancing out of the window, saw standing on the stoop her father's brother, Marcel. He was spare, as always, dapper and dandy. At this historic hour he wore a coat of moire, a bottle-green — which was the fashionable color — and a waistcoat of canary yellow brocade. His rather thin and colorful nose seemed designed by nature to support those gold-rimmed spectacles without which he was blind as any bat.

At his elbow fidgeted the third partner in Proveaux Brothers & Company. Joseph Proveaux was fat as a pig ready for market. It amused Antoinette to watch his vast stomach undulate under a green-and-yellow-striped waistcoat when he climbed the winding stone stairs.

Puffing, Joseph Proveaux waddled into the hall.

"*Voilà!* Observe what this silly, lunatic defiance of Gadsden, Rutledge and the rest has brought on us!" He gurgled like an angry pigeon, mopped his heavy jaws. "Our trade will be ruined. Aye, ruined beyond repair.

"Some imbeciles would try to defend this port? No. It must not be! *Mon dieu*, our warehouse! our ships! What would become of them? Marcel, Louis!" He turned an anguished countenance on his brothers. "How can you be so infernally calm? Will you take no thought for your wives, your children?"

Marcel laughed and crossed to kiss his mother's blue-veined fingers. "There is no call to worry on that score, old fellow. We have all proved good sires — haven't we? No matter what chances, there will always be enough of our get to carry on the strain."

Even Aunt Lobelia managed a short laugh because Joseph could boast of eleven legitimate children.

[286]

Oak was about to secure the front door when a tall, solidly built officer came tramping in unannounced.

"My service, madame." He made a leg to Grandmère, then clanked over to kiss Mrs. Proveaux's cheek. It was mottled with a tiny threadwork of scarlet veins.

This, Desire deduced, was a Major Barnard Elliott, Mrs. Proveaux's first cousin. He looked reassuringly martial in his artillery uniform of blue turned up in red.

"Quite a family affair I've stumbled on, eh, Charlotte?"

"This is no time for pleasantries," Joseph grumbled.

"Maybe it ain't," the big man admitted as he pulled off gauntlets very redolent of the stable. "It would appear that our loving monarch has sent troops to call. Well, Louis, what do you aim to do?"

Mrs. Proveaux caught at the big man's arm, asked in a subdued voice, "Barnard, can you tell us where Roger is likely to be sent?"

"He will be kept safe, my dear. Main reason I stopped by was to tell you that he's turned up at headquarters with young MacIntosh, Tom Beale and a Yankee friend of theirs. They were still half-seas-over. Young rascals must have been fighting a main."

"Then Charleston really is to be defended?" Joseph demanded fearfully.

Barnard Elliott considered the fat man with no great approval. "To the bitter end, my friend. *Ad extremis*, or something like that."

Louis Proveaux shrugged, fetched a sibilant sigh, "While it is possible to admire the courage of the Assembly, one cannot say the same of its intelligence. Come, Barnard, why will they not face the facts? What serious opposition can this province offer?"

He turned to look out of the window at the distant spars in the Cooper River. "You yourself know we have only five or six undisciplined and badly armed regiments of Provincial troops and militia.

"Have we cavalry worthy of mention? No. We have hardly a piece of field artillery and only an odd assortment of ship cannon to mount on the fortifications. Is that not so, cousin?"

"I fear so," admitted the artilleryman. He shrugged. "Still, if the Yankees were able to beat off regulars from behind breastworks — "

"This is not stupid old Gage we must fight; besides the enemy will have learned."

"Let us hope not," Marcel exclaimed. "I might feel less discouraged if the levies from the back country were to be depended on. As it is, Louis and I know only too well how they envy and hate Charleston and its merchants and planters. I venture those savages might welcome an opportunity of stabbing the tidewater counties in the back."

Joseph Proveaux fiddled still more nervously with his watch fob. "And will the Creeks, Choctaws and Cherokees not rise the moment we strip the frontiers of men? My factors and patroons tell me the tribes have been very restless ever since the Tories and Scotch rose under MacDonald."

"They are always restless," Barnard Elliott pointed out. "But Moore's Creek taught 'em who held the upper hand. Right now I fancy the chiefs do feel aggrieved because we have not been able to deliver the gunpowder due them by treaty."

"Why not send it at once?" Marcel suggested.

"How the hell can we? Don't you know there ain't enough gunpowder in the whole province to fight one major battle?"

"Resistance is madness, if for only one reason," Marcel Proveaux observed in his deliberate, precise way. "There always remains our usual and most deadly peril. Picture the great estates, the villages quite stripped of militia?"

The Siege Begins

President Rutledge lost no time in publishing the new government's intention of defending Charleston. He did this in the last copy of the *South Carolina Gazette* Peter Timothy printed before packing his presses for removal to the back country.

There was much amusement over this, some wags maintaining that the legislators could never function without a record being made of their oratory.

All morning the inhabitants of Charleston remained at upper windows and through gazing glasses fearfully watched new sails appear and maneuver into that formidable array assembling off the long streak of white water which marked Charleston Bar.

With the aid of an old-fashioned spyglass Desire could even distinguish varying classes of men-of-war among the clumsier transports and supply vessels. She and Antoinette had a fine view of the harbor from the second-story balcony on which women of the family maintained look-out for Proveaux vessels overdue from Europe or the West Indies.

"Mercy! There's an awful heap of 'em," Antoinette exclaimed in scared accents. "How many do you make it?"

"Thirty-four," Desire replied abstractedly. Sight of those white ensigns flying out there was conjuring bittersweet memories: His Majesty's ships *Rose*, *Swan*, *Glasgow* and the little *Bolton* lying off Newport; John being rowed ashore, straight and gallant in a flowing boat cloak.

"I make it thirty-six," Antoinette announced. "I think I see two more transports lying behind Dewees Island. Am I right?"

When at length they sought the cool of Antoinette's room, Desire inquired into the Proveaux family's immediate plans.

"Grandmère, Maman and the rest will leave for Magnolia Hill tomorrow."

"Do you wish to go with Maman, Dee?"

"Oh no, no!" came the instant reply. "With everything so upset, maybe I can find employment — "

Truth was, Desire wouldn't for the world have missed witnessing at least the beginning of a siege. She would be in no danger from bursting shells. Her infallible luck would shield her.

"Mama says you must be our guest, at least until after — well, you know." 'Toinette blushed furiously and hurriedly packed a pair of elegant French stays.

Again a generous nod from fortune. Desire wasn't sure what having a baby was like, but she suspected from odds and ends picked up at Mrs. Norton's, that it was nothing extra pleasurable — especially the first time.

"You are all very, very kind and generous, 'Toinette. I vow I will never forget it." She smiled. "I want to stay here and help you take care of Mr. Proveaux and Roger, too, I hope. It will be exciting being in Charleston and really great fun, won't it?"

Antoinette's lively eyes sparkled. "Of course. We shall make Roger invite his handsomest officer friends to dinner. Of course," she flushed, and her gaze, dropping, brushed Desire's swollen figure, "you mustn't expect them to beau — a — a — new widow."

"That is entirely as it should be," Desire said sweetly.

Impatient, bathed in sweat, Lieutenant Nat Coffin continued to supervise the business of measuring the town's supply of gunpowder. Hell, he felt certain, could be no hotter than this small, ill-ventilated magazine.

The inhabitants were moving out with an altogether unnecessary haste. Unless British generals and admirals had changed their ways, everybody had plenty of time to do what was to be done. His Majesty's forces, so far in this war, had moved with stately deliberation. Of course, no immediate attack would be made. My Lords of the Admiralty didn't proceed like hostile Indians or marauding French and Spanish expeditions.

It was so stifling in this tiny octagonal structure that Nat went over to catch a breath of air at the door. Um. Still another line of refugee oxcarts was creaking by, each vehicle loaded to the limit with bedsteads, wardrobes, desks and great, shapeless bundles of cloth. Here and there somebody's portrait stared from amid a tangle of furniture. Trampling hoofs and steel-bound wheels ground the yellow street dust ever thicker and deeper.

Like the blackened and sweat-streaked men under his command, Nat Coffin went barefoot and he had secured his breeches by a length of cord. In a powder magazine, one wasn't inclined to risk a spark struck from an iron belt buckle or a shoe nail. In the magazine itself the hinges, window catches, measuring cups, powder sifters and airing ladles were either of bronze, copper or lead.

A soldier pointed to a huge coach with a shiny blue body and bright yellow wheels. It had been so heavily laden that its body was pressed snug against springs of steel and leather. The vehicle rolled up Church Street at a snail's pace, looming above an assortment of wheelbarrows, wagons and two-wheeled carts.

In the wake of this splendid affair straggled a long line of house slaves. Even the smallest pickaninny carried a burden of some sort; for once, there was not a bit of laughter or foolishness in the blacks. They looked scared half to death.

Several wild Negroes with chains connecting their ankles brought up the tail of the column and marched under the supervision of a hard-faced man who balanced a blunderbuss across his pommel.

"That there is Cicero Ball," remarked the sentry. "Ain't nothin' meaner 'n a mestee who's been granted the whip-hand."

"A mestee? Just what is a mestee?" Nat asked, watching the man in question ride by. Handsome in a coarse, brutal sort of way, the rider's blond hair seemed only just a little crinkly. "You have so many terms for mixed bloods. I can't keep them straight."

Glad of an excuse to relax, the soldier ran a yellow bound cuff across his brows, blotting away a row of pellucid sweat drops. " 'Round Charleston, we-uns rate niggers like this: straight black; then mulatto, which means one-half white; next comes the sambo, he's two-thirds white; then, you've your quarteroon who is only a quarter colored, and you don't often find pretty colored gals with less white blood. A lot of mestees look white 'cause they got only an eighth part colored blood. Last of all come browns, which are even whiter than the mestees."

Nat listened intently. Must remember that. Black, mulatto, sambo, quarteroon, mestee, and brown — but all of them black as black in the eyes of the law.

Lieutenant Coffin worked a little longer then sought the tent in which he had left his clothes. All along he had suspected that there could be nowhere near so much powder in the magazine as a royal ordnance officer's return had indicated. So serious a shortage, he judged, should be reported to Colonel Gadsden with all speed.

Rumors grew wilder, more numerous, with each passing hour but everyone reckoned that at least three, maybe four days must pass before the upcountry companies could appear in any appreciable strength. Soldier and civilian alike speculated on when the first elements of Colonel Thomson's Third Regiment of Infantry, of Lieutenant Colonel Clark's Rangers and of the Raccoon Company of Riflemen would come in. Would the British armada attack before they mustered in strength?

With these and other disturbing questions gnawing at their peace of mind, the remnants of Charleston's population slept ill.

Thanks to Major Barnard Elliott's presence at headquarters, the Proveauxs had not been stampeded into quitting Charleston at once. Weather conditions, Elliott assured them, would prevent for at least forty-eight hours any attempt of the British to cross Charleston Bar. Even under ideal conditions, passage of the bar was a dangerous undertaking.

It was a shining wonder, the big major claimed, that the enemy admiral had not long since sent over some small transports and light men-o'-war to capture the fort standing, less than half completed, on Sullivan's Island. To seize it would be like taking jam off a pantry shelf.

A Yankee serving on Colonel Moultrie's staff, however, had not been so astonished at General Clinton's leisureliness. He maintained that so far British generals had executed their strategy with a truly majestic deliberation.

Comfortably, Major Elliott deduced that no onslaught would be made until the enemy could remove the guns from their ships of the line and run the three-deckers over the bar.

"How big are they?" Desire queried.

"Fourth raters, ma'am."

"Then they will mount around fifty cannons, will they not?"

Major Elliott's bright blue eyes widened and he made a leg in her direction. "Well, I'll be da — blessed! I say, Louis, have you ever heard of a miss who knew a brig from a scow? My compliments, ma'am." A shadow sobered his expression. "We hear that six more transports have arrived and are at anchor."

Desire knew this. She and Antoinette had spent most of the afternoon on the lookout.

By sunset they had counted nearly forty vessels of various sizes riding the Atlantic long rollers off Dewees Island.

Down the street sounded a lot of drumming and fifes began squealing like so many pigs caught under a gate.

By standing on a mounting block, Desire was able to witness the approach of a group of horsemen. There was so much gold and lace work glittered among them, they must be very important.

"There's Colonel Christopher Gadsden," Antoinette cried. "My, ain't he distinguished! And look, honey, that big man with the red face is Colonel Moultrie. Roger says he commands the fort on Sullivan's Island. There's Cousin Colonel Isaac Huger. I think the gentleman beyond is Captain Grimball of the Charleston Company of Artillery. I just dote on the artillery regimentals, don't you?"

"There's the new general." "Horray for Gen'ral Charles Lee!" "Here he comes!" excited voices shouted.

Into Queen Street rode a gangling, hatchet-faced officer astride one of the biggest horses Desire had ever beheld. From Tim's description, Desire recognized Lee instantly.

Blue tunic aglitter with gold, white breeches gleaming, Major General Charles Lee rode at least three horses' lengths in advance of his staff. To Antoinette his bearing was surprising; it suggested that of a conqueror entering a captured city.

A sardonic smile fixed on his lips, the new Continental Commander lifted his cocked hat and saluted with it a few times. Haughtily, he beckoned an aide wearing Virginian regimentals and whispered something in his ear. He must have said something very amusing for the aide laughed so hard he shook a couple of bone hairpins out of his wig.

"Three cheers fer Lee! He'll whip the Britishers!"

The new commander rode by, his leopardskin saddle housing flashing golden in the sunset. The queer, long-haired dogs Tim had mentioned trotted warily at the tall charger's heels.

As they were descending from the mounting block, Antoinette remarked, "I'm right glad I ain't a man — a soldier, I mean. What a sour, sneering look he had! I vow I'm sorry he's to command our troops."

"He ain't going to, ma'am," corrected a uniformed figure. "Not unless President Rutledge grants him leave."

"But why?"

"This gen'ral was commissioned an' appointed by the Continental Congress — not by this province. Till our troops is sworn into the Continental Service, Gen'ral Lee can't give them any orders at all. I'm glad o' that. I don't cotton to no stiff scarecrow like him."

The Wateree Company

Alistair Bryson gave the last cow a gentle slap on her rump and lugged the pail of milk down to a spring house. Like everything Gordon Bryson had built, it was neatly fashioned of enduring stone.

To Alistair, it was a relief to have reached a decision. He would have to enroll if the family wasn't to suffer from the same kind of stupid suspicion which had ruined so many Highlanders in North Carolina. The conviction had come soon after that sore-bottomed express rider had ridden on towards the Wylie and Campbell holdings.

Ever since Flora MacDonald — who apparently would never learn to back a winner — and her handsome young son had raised the North Carolina Scots for Governor Martin and King George III, a spirit of unrest had been prevalent in the Wateree country. Every day the line between Tory and Patriot was becoming more sharply drawn. He must go. There was no doubt of it.

Feyther would make out all right what with young Jock and Angus getting to be such big braw lads. Besides there was Jeanie; she was as strong and useful as a boy.

Alistair felt a peculiar and unfamiliar thrill at seeing hanging above the chimney place the targe and claymore Feyther had carried for the Young Pretender.

It was so bright today he could see the deep notch a dragoon's saber had hacked through the former's tough, brass-mounted leather.

"Why, Alistair!" Mrs. Bryson, surprised, turned a heated face over her shoulder. "What can ye be wanting i' the hoose at this hour? Ye'd best no' let yer feyther catch ye idle."

Seriously, Alistair shook a dark, narrow head. "I have done wi' farming for the now. I've taken a notion to see what a war may be like."

"Oh, lad." Mither's features crumpled. "You canna, mustna — "

"Nay, I must," said he soberly. "Is it no' the part o' gude sense tae have a member of the family on either side o' the fence? Should the Hanoverian usurper's men prevail, I can always go west and it's no great loss. Should the low country people win, then Feyther will have only to say, 'And did we no' send our eldest son to fight against the Crown?' "

"Oh, lad! Lad!" Agitatedly Mrs. Bryson began wiping floury hands on her apron. "Dinna try to be so logical. Feyther knows best. He fought the king and lost every groat to his name!"

"But 'tis not the same this time. I am going anyway."

Heavily, she turned to him. "You'd best break this news to your feyther, lad."

Alistair found the sturdy old man splitting rails which would eventually enclose a fine, new pasture. When he saw his son coming up Gordon Bryson drove his ax-blade deep into a log, then ran the back of a knotty hand across his cheek. His bushy brows merged.

"An' why are ye no' plowing the north field like ye were bid?"

Alistair's heart began to thump. Never before, in all his twenty-six years, had he dared take direct issue with his father.

"Tomorrow, the Wateree Company is mustering at Pine Tree Hill — or Camden as they begin to call it. I am for the war."

Though Feyther was wearing a kilt, he stood naked to the waist and Alistair could see the stringy muscles mapping his chest and arms. Tugging at his ragged gray beard, he demanded ominously, "Ye ken what I think o' this war-r?"

"Aye, Feyther, I ken it verra well." Alistair's gray eyes clung desperately to his father's blue ones.

"You ken naught of war as it really is," the elder Bryson reminded. "The horror, sickness, pain it brings. Maire often than no', ye'll meet with hunger and despair. I ha'e tasted all these things and I would spare my son them."

"I thank you, Feyther, but aiblins the rebels will win."

An uncomfortable silence ruled. They heard the ax blows of Jock girdling trees in the next valley. By autumn still another field would be ready for clearing.

"I — I would leave wi' yer blessing, Feyther."

"Ye go against my will so I'll no' grant ye that," the old man rumbled. "But ye shall carry the auld claymore." His voice thickened a little. "'Tis a good blade and it saw me through my years o' trouble."

"Farewell, Feyther."

Now Alistair was glad he had heeded Mither's plea to don an old kilt of Bryson plaid — dark red with darker edging, light blue and yellow crossings. The village girls kept looking at the group of kilted Scots and whispering amongst themselves. Now and then they would giggle like anything.

Unlike his neighbors, he had been able to bring no rifle to the muster, not even an old musket. Feyther's old long-bladed claymore with its basket guard of bright brass made a brave showing at his hip, though. His baldric, too, was of good leather, broad and liberally decorated with big brass studs.

There were other claymores among the recruits, other tartans. Some were familiar: the Campbells' light green, crossed with darker green, narrow yellow edging; the MacKenzies' blue-green with darker edges and cross lines of red and white. There even was a Munro in red with a broad green stripe, black and yellow checks, and a Cameron and Graeme or two.

Forming another group were the generally fair-haired and brawny sons of settlers from the Palatinate. These spoke German among themselves, and were deliberate in their movements. Probably because the fur trade with Charleston was at a standstill, a surprising number of silent and lantern-jawed trappers enrolled.

The militia captain bore down on Alistair, who was busily munching bread and cheese.

"Bryson, you seem to have a modicum of intelligence. Suppose you act as sergeant over the rest of you Scotch."

"'Scots,' sir," Alistair corrected gravely. "Nae such a thing as a Scotchman exists."

"Call yourselves anything you like." Chesnut grinned. "But for God's sake get lined up."

Aside from his Highlanders, there were around a dozen Germans in broad hats. They were shouldering a weird assortment of muskets, fowling pieces, and blunderbusses.

There must be easily twice as many trappers. In their fringed, neutral-tinted hunting shirts and deerskin hats, they achieved a uniformity of appearance. Invariably they carried a long-barreled rifle and most of them had a war hatchet or a skinning knife swinging at their belts. These "Butternuts," as they generally called themselves, were by far the most profane.

A private was to draw two shillings, sixpence a month and was bound to serve for thirty days, or until all danger of a British invasion was at an end. Men lacking firearms could expect to be issued muskets when the Wateree Company reached Fort Watson.

Making no attempt to keep step, the Wateree Company filed down towards the river. In the largest trunk boat, half a dozen red-and-white cows were fearfully contemplating the slow, snag-dotted current.

Alistair selected a seat near the support of a collapsible mast which was hinged and otherwise designed to be easily lowered when a bridge or low branches barred the channel.

A boy waded out knee-deep in the river and cupping his hands shrilled, "Hey, Paw, mind ye bring me a Britisher's skelp and not his wig!"

Charleston Bar

Begun in January, Fort Sullivan should have been completed long, long since. Now everyone in town demanded to know why only the southern curtain — it commanded that channel along which a hostile fleet must pass — had been completed. Frantic efforts were now being made to nullify this negligence.

Like most of the coast in that region, both Sullivan's Island and Long Island, just to the seaward of it, were merely long, overgrown sand dunes densely covered with myrtle, palmetto and other underbrush.

Lieutenant Nat Coffin, recalling the speedy appearance of mile on mile of entrenchments in and around Boston, felt astounded that so small and simple an earthwork should not have been long since completed. After all, Fort Sullivan was only a simple rectangle strengthened by bold salients at each of its corners.

Resting on the seaward bastion, Nat felt he had found an explanation. At Breed's Hill there had been mighty few officers who couldn't drive a straight furrow or shingle a roof. It now seemed impressive to recall that *in one night* a single small company of Connecticut infantry had raised a breastwork longer than one whole side of this fort.

Black labor, he observed, was miserably inefficient. Why, to accomplish the simplest of tasks an officer had to be in constant supervision. This, he reasoned, was the essential difference between free and slave labor.

A number of eighteen-pounders had that morning been brought over from Charleston in barges. At present they lay on the beach just above the high-water mark. Curiously enough, the carriages on which they were to be mounted had not yet appeared.

There was not a single piece of field artillery in the fort. And, so far as Nat could tell, very little roundshot to fit the nines, eighteens and twenty-six pounders. A fine state of affairs.

He would never understand why Sir Henry Clinton didn't simply land a regiment or two and pull down this shapeless tangle of timbers before it got into shape — certainly the weather was fair enough to permit a boat attack.

Suddenly a lookout began to yell, "They're coming! Fire the alarm! By God, the Britishers are headed for the bar!"

Nat, shading his eyes, was aware of a sharp tingling at the base of his spine. The British commanders then weren't so inept as he'd thought. They would be into Fort Sullivan long before dark, and no doubt about it. All this work was wasted. But that was war.

Stony-eyed, the Nantucketer watched ten, eleven, thirteen crowded transports take advantage of the flood tide, of the ever-freshening south-east breeze. In a straggling line, they set off one by one and steered steadily for the wild white smother marking Charleston Bar.

By the dozen, soldiers, workmen and civilian engineers came running and scrambled up to posts of vantage on the dunes. The slave gangs, welcoming a respite, stared sullenly, incuriously, at those clumps of white canvas moving slowly shorewards.

The leading frigate bore steadily for the bar, which lay less than a mile away. Everyone could see that she was towing her boats. All of these were heavily loaded in order to decrease the man-of-war's draught. The boats reminded Nat of ducklings following their mother.

The ex-pilot's gaze became critical as he followed her advance. "British-ers ought to have lightened her still more. If they try to get them big barns of three-deckers across, you'll see somethin' to remember."

"Why?"

"On the bar they ain't over sixteen foot at high water; most of them ships o' the line draws from eighteen to twenty in commission trim."

Steadily the wind rose, whipped stinging grains of sand up from the beach and into the faces of the watchers on Sullivan's Island. Officers began ordering reluctant men away to secure tents and shelters.

"That vessel in the lead is the *Syren*," announced an officer at the tele-scope. "Next in line looks like the *Sphinx*, frigate. Carries around twenty guns, anyhow."

The bar was now boiling right under the leading frigate's bow. White water surged up, up until it hid the man-of-war's dolphin striker. Smoth-ered cries, yells of satisfaction broke from the men when they saw the *Syren* reel amid that conflict of eddies which perpetually raced over the sandbar. Red copper sheathing gleamed briefly, then all at once the wild swinging of the *Syren's* topmasts diminished.

"Over!" the pilot said, thrusting his head far out. "Now we'll know where we fit — if that bulldog bears port, she only intends to anchor off Five Fathom Hole. If she keeps straight on we'd better get our tails off this sand bank in a hell of a big hurry."

He cast a grim look up to Nat. "Say your prayers, mister."

A second frigate, skillfully duplicating the maneuvers of the first, also passed safe over the bar.

Both of them *steered to port*, headed for an anchorage off Five Fathom Hole.

Bunched by differing speed and handling, seven merchantmen and a lone sloop-of-war were all rushing down on the bar together.

"Bet there's some inspired cussing going on out there," the gunner said. "I thank God *I* ain't aboard that vessel furthest to starboard."

"Look at 'em," a civilian engineer cried. "Look at 'em! They're all crowded together like sheep in a lane."

Nat watched a tall ship, an East Indiaman by her round bows and high sides, shoulder aside a pair of little brigs; she sent them staggering off to port so quickly that they collided. Instantly, their yards locked and, helpless, they reeled 'way over.

A big transport running in their wake had not time to veer aside and smashed into the gilded and elaborately carved stern of the East Indiaman. Under the impact, the Indiaman's mizzen snapped and tumbled — a furious tangle of spars, cordage and canvas — into the water. Hampered, the big, old-fashioned ship swung violently to starboard, began drifting for the breakers spouting along the bar.

The pilot caught his breath with a sharp click. "Watch! Goddamn it, watch!"

The words had scarcely escaped his lips than the big transport which had lost her headsails, reared out of the water like a swimmer reaching a landing and hit the bar with such terrific force that her main and foremasts went crashing by the board.

The two little brigs were the next to strike. As their decks flooded, the crews and troops swarmed into the rigging but were lost as both vessels gradually rolled over on their beams' end.

Other transports found time to come about and begin clawing their way back to join the balance of the fleet in the lee of Dewees Island. As for the vessels which had crossed the bar, they anchored in a hurry and sent out rescue boats.

Standing there on the raw earthworks of Fort Sullivan, Nat Coffin found it strange that these men should have come half across the world just to perish in the boiling water and sand of Charleston Bar.

When, escorted by the stalwart Ash, Antoinette Proveaux ventured out on the morning of June seventh, she sensed tension in the threatened town was augmenting rather than diminishing. For five days enemy ships continued to cross the bar until a really awe-inspiring fleet lay, plainly visible, off Five Fathom Hole.

"As soon as their line of battleships, *Experiment* and *Bristol*, get across," Cousin Barnard Elliott had predicted, "we must expect trouble."

Down by a battery on South Bay, Antoinette got the biggest surprise of her life. All those big solid warehouses which had once stood at the far end of the merchants' wharves had vanished!

Good Heavens. Sunburnt men in parts of uniforms were pulling down the last of Colonel Gadsden's fine counting house! Yonder Mr. Laurens's offices had dissolved into a tumbled heap of bricks.

Where was Papa's counting house? She wanted to break out in tears when she realized that only its foundations remained. Her legs trembled so she had to rest on the nearest doorstep.

As nothing else, this served to bring home the gravity of Charleston's peril.

She went closer. That just couldn't be! — But it was dapper-dandy Uncle Marcel. Minus wig and coat he was working with a shovel right alongside a big, shiny buck Negro. So was old Mr. Pinckney.

As in the popular ditty, the world certainly had been "turned upside down." She could scarcely believe her eyes as she recognized other leading merchants doing slave's work. Why there was Mr. Manigult, Mr. Motte, and yonder was Mr. Middleton! Fearful lest she cause them embarrassment, Antoinette raised her fan and hurried away so fast that Ash had hard work keeping up with her.

From the depths of a trench a muddied figure addressed her.

"Fine mornin', ain't it, Miss 'Toinette?"

She had trouble recognizing Charles MacIntosh until he scrambled up, made her an elaborate bow. "I protest your presence here is more welcome than a mint julep."

"Really, Charles, how you do exaggerate!"

He grinned. "Well, a cooling breeze, anyhow."

"Then I would remain here to refresh Charleston's heroes," she smiled. Dark and petite, she gathered her petticoats and seated herself on a mound of fresh earth. "We are worried, Charles. We have not seen Roger in two days."

"No need. He and Tommy Beale have been ordered with Gadsden's First Regiment out to Fort Johnson." He jerked a blistered, earth-stained thumb toward the northern tip of James Island. "By the by, first chance I get, I want to present an odd and very amusing Yankee; he's a friend of Roger's. May I?"

"Of course. To you, Charles, I will confess I die of curiosity about him. So does my house guest. She is a Yankee, too."

When Antoinette reached home she found it in a turmoil. Pansy and Linden were blocking the doorway, trying to keep out a big Scot in a red-and-green kilt. Obviously, he must be from one of the upcountry regiments.

He was saying gruffly, "Dinna greet, ye blackamoors. If we can leave our farms i' the planting season, yer master can weel spare a leaden gutter and a pewter bowl or two."

When the dark-faced Scot saw her standing so small and trim behind him he turned poppy-red and hurriedly removed the queer little bonnet he wore at a jaunty angle. It sported what looked like a hawk's feather.

"Yer par-rdon, mistress," he gulped. "I hope ye'll no' mistake my pur-rpose." Losh, till now he had never beheld a female so elegant or genteel.

In a small leghorn hat and with a cashmere shawl caught about her slim shoulders, Antoinette Proveaux presented an amazing contrast to the hearty, broad-hipped maids of the Wateree Country.

For her part, Antoinette was little less intrigued with this broad-shouldered fellow who wore a huge brass-hilted sword slung to a leather baldric. From the top of his stocking she noticed projecting what looked like the handle of a dirk.

Ever so often she had heard Papa speak of the fierce Highlanders who during the past fifteen years had been settling in the upcountry. Papa paid unwilling tribute to Scottish perseverance and frugality, while deprecating their intolerance and senseless, sanguinary feuds.

Merciful heavens, this gaunt, bronzed young man dominating her front steps would easily make two of Roger or any of her friends.

Said she, "Pray permit me, sir, to make you welcome. Will you not come in?"

Three other militiamen in kilts grinned and winked when she sailed serenely indoors calling, "Pansy! Fetch these gentlemen a jug of milk and some of your best raisin cookies."

Alistair Bryson, red to the roots of his black hair, entered gingerly. "Aye, 'tis a fine grand hoose ye ha'e here, mistress. Maire is the pity Captain Chesnut has bade us tae take up any and a' lead the citizens can spare."

At the end of an hour the detail had collected a large wheelbarrow full of pure lead weights.

"You ha'e been verra kind," the sergeant declared, his lean features coloring slowly. "I fear ye take us for savages and I wouldna have it so."

She gave him a dazzling smile of reassurance. "I do not think you rude or savage, Sergeant — "

" — Sergeant Bryson, mistress." He fumbled with his bonnet and looked very young all at once for all his heavy sword and brass studded baldric. "I trust ye'll forgi'e me if I observe I hadna thought any Lowland lass could be so bonny. If — if ye find aught in which we can be o' service to ye, Mistress Proveaux, ye've only to send word tae the Third Regiment. We camp for the nonce at Lynch's Pasture."

Antoinette's faintly olive-tinted features dimpled. She smiled, increasingly fascinated by the extraordinary clearness and penetration of the Scot's eyes.

"Perhaps, Mr. Bryson, when Pansy next bakes raisin cookies, I might chance by Lynch's Pasture."

Yes, he resembled some warrior prophet; was more like a dark, avenging deity than an upcountry farmer.

When he swung down the front steps after his men, she noticed that he left behind a faint but remarkably stimulating aura of burned pine, leather and cows.

Enemy Landing

Intelligence that enemy regiments were effecting landing on Long Island produced a tremendous excitement in Charleston. Apparently the almost incredible leisureliness of the British commanders was near an end, for at six o'clock of the morning of June eighth, transports began to discharge supplies of baggage, munitions and hundreds upon hundreds of scarlet- and white-clad regulars.

In endless relays small boats from the fleet rowed across the glassy harbor, then returned.

Once he ascertained that Brigadier General Vaughan and Major General Lord Cornwallis had, unopposed, landed some twenty-eight hundred crack troops, General Charles Lee flew into a towering fury. Sulphurously, he cursed the inexplicable nonarrival of some fine Virginia and North Carolina Continental regiments. Where were they? No one seemed to know.

Caustic, openly contemptuous, he ordered a review of the upcountry regiments. When these raw levies returned to their cantonments, the adventurer's despair became dramatic. He wrung his hands and groaned, asked to know how he had offended heaven that he should be condemned to command "the very canaille of soldiery."

Nonetheless, this ex-English general prepared for a stubborn defense of the city and made an admittedly sound disposition of his troops. He even injected a semblance of order and discipline into his camp at Haddrell's Point and worked himself and his staff until they were red-eyed with fatigue.

One sultry afternoon, he had himself rowed over to Fort Sullivan and inspected the defense with expert attention. His reaction was not one of satisfaction.

"This silly affair more resembles a slaughter pen than a fortification," he succinctly informed Major de Brahm. "Why in God's patience have you designed so flat a slope to the talus? Any cadet in Germany, sir, could see that enemy cannonballs will merely ricochet over the top and plunge into the rear wall."

Easy-going Billy Moultrie got reprimanded because he let his sentries smoke or chew on duty, that his soldiers slouched about and often forgot to salute.

Angrily, the Continental general ordered the construction of a pair of epaulements which would, in a measure, serve to protect the unfinished east and west walls. As a feeble substitute for the still nonexistent north or rear wall a breastwork was to be dug at once.

"If Harry Clinton learned anything at all at Breed's Hill," Lee predicted to the red-faced and furious Carolinians, "he will cross from Long Island and assail this comic fort of yours from the rear. It must fall in short order and you will lose every cannon, every man in this place."

Fortunately for the Carolinians, the task of passing the great three-deckers *Experiment* and *Bristol* over the bar again postponed an attack.

"Give us till the thirtieth and we'll have this job done," Moultrie assured the celebrated privateersman, Captain Lemprière. Along the south curtain now frowned nineteen cannon ranging in size from slim nine-pounders to substantial twenty-eight-pound broadside guns.

Doubtfully, Captain Lemprière fingered a bluish chin. "You've a neat piece of work here, Colonel, but — " Significantly, his gaze wandered out to the heavy concentration of men-of-war.

"We shall beat them handily," came Moultrie's easy assurance. "If only Lee will let us alone."

The Yankee

All the men-of-war now were over the bar; Clinton's troops had regained their land legs, though they could not be having too pleasant a time on the insect-infested flats of treeless, sandy Long Island. Roger, Cousin Barnard Elliott, Mr. Laurens and everybody reckoned that the British would attack on the first of August.

Many respected citizens were looking gloomy. A pity this General Lee had to be so utterly tactless. His arrogant and unbounded egotism was alienating everybody. Again, friction was developing between the city and country regiments. Every morning an increasing number of shooting and knifings were reported. The Virginia and North Carolina Continentals,

[301]

arriving at long last, were given to looking down their noses and asking why South Carolina couldn't boil her own kettle.

All in all, Mr. Proveaux felt that the time had come for Antoinette to join the balance of the family in safety. Desire was to accompany her. The house on King Street would be closed, boarded up like the rest.

Desire, descending from a nap, found Pansy and the other servants bustling about at a great rate. When Antoinette appeared with an extra big basket of flowers Desire raised slim, questioning brows.

"Well, honey, I reckon our last evenin' in Charleston will be one to remember," Antoinette gaily announced. "Roger vows that tonight I shall meet my fate."

"That Yankee friend of his?"

Antoinette bent studiously above the flower basket. "Roger's groom said he would bring him to dinner tonight." She giggled like a small girl. "And what shall I wear to dazzle this cold countryman of yours? The blue chintz or my yellow dimity?"

"The dimity, by all means." Desire felt years older. What would this stray Northerner make of her? Lord's mercy, during the past week she had grown simply enormous and got taken with strange breathless spells when she least expected them.

Antoinette, however, declared that she looked lovelier each day. "I know our Charleston boys. If you ain't married short of six months, honey, I'm a perfect ninny. Besides, Grandmère vows war makes for marriage and babies. Pansy, you take these flowers. Mrs. St. Clair and I must pretty up."

Briskly, Desire brushed and combed her dark red hair. Curious, the only hair which had ever approximated her own in color was Nathaniel Coffin's. Again she wondered where he might be at this moment. Could a girl ever get to know what was going on in the back of his mind?

Sometimes it seemed as if Nat were laughing at her, or was it at himself? Imagine examining life as if it were some strange insect pinned under a reading glass! For all Nat's easy ways, she guessed he must be a rock-ribbed conservative at heart.

She arranged and rearranged one of Antoinette's best cashmere shawls with studied attention. Tonight it wouldn't do for the baby to show any more than was inevitable. She moistened her fingertips and, by the fading light, smoothed her long, gently-arching brows. Her dark-blue gown went well with her hair, her shoes were dainty and her ankles cased in silk.

"It's been a pretty task to get you here," declared Roger's voice, high-pitched and nervous as ever. "Hope Linden ain't forgotten how to mix a bombo Martinico."

Already 'Toinette was hurrying downstairs gurgling hospitality and cordial greetings.

Desire arrived on the top landing in time to witness 'Toinette's curtsey, a thing of fluid perfection. Roger's buttons flashed in the candlelight as he brought forward the guest.

The stranger, Desire perceived, wore an unfamiliar uniform of grass green turned up in white and his epaulet was silver instead of gold. La! This fellow countryman cut a fine, sturdy figure. He looked red-haired, too.

Suddenly, a deep, well-remembered voice declared, "Your humble servant, Mistress Proveaux. This moment has long been anticipated."

Luckily, not one of the three persons below cast a glance upstairs; to save her life, Desire could not have stirred.

Roger said, "Well, honeybunch, have you food enough for a pair of hungry wolves like Mr. Coffin and me?"

"The bombo is quite ready, Roger. I trust Mr. Coffin favors bombo?"

"He does," chuckled Roger. "His bibulous education has made great strides since he came among us. Rascal's got the head of a marble statue, too. Haven't sent him under the table yet."

He turned to Antoinette. "And where are you hiding the ever charming Mrs. St. Clair? Nat, here, is all of a tizzy to make her acquaintance."

Jerkily Desire's hand went up to stifle a gasp that almost escaped when Nat said, "Mrs. St. Clair? *Mirabile dictu*, the name is very very familiar. I wonder — "

On legs which seemed to have no knees at all Desire groped back to her room and stood there staring blankly into space. How foolish it had been to hope. Sooner or later someone would — must — appear, but why — If he sees me like this — he'll think — Oh, what was it I told him in Providence? John was from Maine. Told Proveauxs he was British. Stupid little liar. He mightn't tell them about Mrs. Norton's — but, but Nat would know — Dear God, if Charleston ever learns that the Proveauxs, Roger — 'Toinette — Mr. Proveaux, had been entertaining a common whore.

What a hideous, tangled web her life had become all in a few instants. Ten minutes ago — dreams. Now there never could be a plantation great house for Desire Harmony.

Every time Nat's deep laugh rang out downstairs, it did dreadful things to her heart. Why had chance betrayed her so? Wait! Suppose — suppose she let Nat think the baby — why not? Nat had been ready for marriage and she respected him more than anyone alive. He was very fond of her, too fond, maybe. Don't be a fool. Nat will stand by you if he thinks the child is his. But it is really John's.

She could hear 'Toinette calling from the foot of the stairs, "Dee, honey, Roger and his guest are here!"

Just as she used to before going on the stage, she drew a deep breath and commanded her voice to steadiness. "Yes, dear, I'll come down in a moment."

Catching up a hooded cloak, she descended the back stairs so fast she scared Pansy into spasms. As she darted for the servants' entrance, Marigold called something, but she kept on through the vegetable garden until she reached a deserted back street.

[303]

If she hurried and didn't fall, she might be able to catch the last ferry across the Cooper River.

Dawn, June 28, 1776

Lieutenant Nathaniel Coffin, temporary aide to gouty, doughty Colonel Moultrie, could not sleep. Hot and uncomfortable, he lay listening to clouds of mosquitoes exploring the netting about his head.

How perfectly mistress of the situation Antoinette Proveaux had remained when her house guest had fallen ill with such disastrous inopportunity. If, as Roger had implied, Mrs. St. Clair was pregnant, such a seizure could not be wholly unexpected. Mrs. St. Clair? How curious that within six months he should have heard of two Mrs. St. Clairs and both of them widowed.

It was lucky that Roger had immediately excused himself to go fetch a doctor. That had afforded Miss Proveaux and him a chance to talk, even if she was bravely fighting her alarm — or some similar emotion. It must have been exasperating to have seen her carefully planned dinner go awry.

Lying in the hot gloom of the tent he could visualize ever so clearly her warm, petite loveliness. It was sheer bad luck that, for these several weeks, he had allowed matters of no great consequence to delay his going to the Proveauxs'.

Nat groped for a canteen and took a big swig from it. He wasn't especially tired yet he felt a curious dis-ease. Why? As near as he could judge, he hadn't a fever. Maybe it was sunburn? Yesterday, the heat had become so intolerable that Colonel Moultrie, ever considerate, had ordered all sentries into the shade nearest their posts.

Sweating profusely, the Nantucketer settled back on his blanket, irritably pushed a palm stem from under his ribs.

Presently he dozed. When he roused once more a gray dawning was breaking. Thank God, an easterly wind was blowing away the mosquitoes.

"Five o'clock, an' a-a-all's well!" A sentry's sleepy call floated down from the parapet. They cry reminded Nat of the siege. Imagine the siege being over and Washington's army in possession of starved, smallpox-ridden Boston.

What was happening to Tim Bennett these days? Had he found his ship in Hispaniola, which the French called Saint-Domingue?

R-r-r-tap — tap — r — r — r! He and his tentmate, a humorous Irish surgeon from Beaufort, sat up together. The doctor's dull eyes batted sleepily.

"Faith, Nat," he yawned, "and what has got into that idjit of a drummer bhoy?"

"Something serious must be wrong. That's long roll," Nat was already

[304]

pulling on his breeches. Faintly, the cries of startled ducks and sandpipers penetrated the alarm. Like a gigantic rattlesnake, the drum kept up its dry, terrifying uproar. Pretty soon a second drummer set his sticks to work.

Half or wholly naked men came stumbling out of the tents yelling to know what was wrong. Nat saw Colonel Moultrie waddle by, his shirt tail fluttering as he climbed a bank of gray-white sand marking the unfinished west wall.

The colonel hadn't waited to find his wig so the gray bristles of his natural hair stood up on his scalp like quills on a hedgehog.

Nat Coffin, assigned as aide, plowed along after Moultrie and tried to buckel his sword belt as he ran. When he came up, the commandant of Fort Sullivan had halted. Choking for breath, he peered past the dew-dotted breach of a big twenty-eight-pounder, and at once his heavy jaw shut with a click.

"My God," he groaned softly. "So many. So many!"

Among other members of the staff, Nat ran to a neighboring embrasure. He was struck silent by what he saw.

'Way over on the other side of the dim gray harbor the British men-o'-war were making sail. Some of them were hauling up courses, others were shaking out topsails, gallants and royals.

_Rr-rr-rr-r-r!_ The myrtle woods and the dunes behind the fort resounded to the spiteful rattling of the drums. In the murky half-light, all faces appeared gray and sickly.

Because the tide was still ebbing from Charleston Harbor and the east wind was by no means strong, the enemy men-o'-war — nine in number — made but slow progress. There was plenty of time for gun captains to draw a supply of powder. The magazine lay in an isolated position in the otherwise incomplete north salient but at quite some distance from those batteries covering the channel.

The British had only to navigate a man-of-war or two behind the tip of Sullivan's Island. From that point, they could pour broadsides into the un-protected backs of gun crews manning the south wall. Even a desultory fire would render the fort untenable.

"God help us if the British get any vessels past Sumter Shoals." Roger Proveaux, arriving with a handful of reinforcements, epitomized the gen-eral concern. He looked very spic and span by contrast with the earth-stained garrison.

The lines of his sensitive, almost femininely fine features were drawn taut.

The men quieted as Colonel Moultrie and his staff halted below a short flagstaff which had been hurriedly stepped at the apex of the southeastern bastion.

"Been pondering what sort of an ensign we would show," Captain Ever-leigh told Nat. "Reckon this will be it."

The flag that climbed into the morning sky had a light blue field and bore the word LIBERTY emblazoned in white parallel to its lower edge. In the canton corner some fair hand had embroidered a slim silver crescent.

Colonel Moultrie was smiling, delighted with the device, since his family's coat of arms showed three crescents argent on a field of azure.

His heavy face already bright with sweat, Colonel William Moultrie moved along the gun platform inspecting cartridges, roundshot and, most carefully of all, the quills of fine French powder with which the cannon would be primed.

Here and there, he spoke to a brawny, half-naked gunner — even slapped one on the shoulder. He ended by summoning all officers.

In a curiously detached way, Nat noticed that Colonel Moultrie had a splash of boiled egg on his chin — that Lieutenant Colonel Motte kept working with the tip of his tongue to dislodge a shred of bacon from between his teeth.

"Well, gentlemen," began the commandant, "I reckon I don't have to tell you what we'll be in for inside a few minutes. Being as we have only twenty guns which will bear on the enemy, General Lee figures we can't hold out. It is my firm intention to prove General Lee in error. We'll *have* to prove him so. We local men know that if Admiral Parker gets by us he will be anchoring off Charleston before dark."

Out on the harbor a cannon roared and something passed with an eerie whistling screech. There followed a deafening explosion among the myrtles behind the fort. Great clouds of sand shot high into the air, then leaves, twigs and bits of branches and sand began to fall inside Fort Sullivan.

The First Line

H. M. S. *Thunder* lay about a mile and a quarter offshore and, lest she swing with the flooding tide, her crew anchored her bow and stern.

"Great day in the morning! Will you look at 'em come?" an awed voice asked amid the strained stillness ruling Fort Sullivan.

Slowly advancing under head sails came the *Active*, frigate, twenty-eight guns. H. M. S. *Experiment* loomed near with her triple tier of cannon run out and ready. The great line of the battleship would have made two of the *Active* cruising a few cable lengths ahead of her. In her wake loomed the *Bristol*, Admiral Parker's ship of the line. From her foremast was the admiral's broad pennant. Next in the column sailed another twenty-eight-gun frigate, the *Solebay*.

"Let's see what broadside we kin expect." An ex-privateersman with dark-blue powder burns peppering his cheek began counting. "*Active* and *Solebay* are twenty-eights so they be fifty-six guns in them alone. The liners will mount fifty apiece — "

He whistled, then spat. "Say, boys, this business ain't going to be all beer and skittles. We mount twenty guns 'gainst the Britainers' hundred and fifty-six. And that's *only their first line of ships!*"

Nat began to yawn as he always did when deeply excited. Captain Huger, stripped to his shirt sleeves and wearing a brace of pistols stuck into a fine English sword belt, began to laugh.

"I say, Misto' Coffin, you sho'ly do select the damnedest time to act bored!"

"Our English friends are being overdeliberate." Nat smiled. "They came on faster than this at Breed's Hill."

Deep within him, the Nantucketer was becoming aware of an inexplicable sense of apprehension such as he had not felt at Breed's Hill or at Fort Montague.

Until half past ten, the bombship continued an unsupported bombardment. Her mortars sent shell after shell looping up, up into the air. Everyone could trace the course of these projectiles by the comet's tails of white smoke that trailed after them.

Gradually the *Thunder*'s marksmanship improved until a shell fell among the deserted tents inside the square. The nearest milita scattered but returned sheepishly because the projectile, having plunged deep into the soft sand, exploded without causing the least damage.

The battery captain called, "Round shot! Range about two thousand yards. Battery, fire!" The gun crews promptly leaped clear.

Fascinated, for the first time Roger Proveaux watched a shot fired in anger. Once the gun captain pressed his smoldering linstock to the touchhole a small jet of smoke spurted straight up from the breech of a long twenty-six. A great crashing report followed and madly the steel tube recoiled against a stout cable threaded through its thimble — a ring forged into the breech of the gun itself.

The whole platform trembled as an immense mushroom of choking, silver-gray smoke smothered the number one's embrasure. From his post on top of a merlon, Captain John Blake shouted through cupped hands:

"Number one gun — over by fifty yards! Decrease elevation."

"Shucks!" the hot and excited infantry bellowed. "You powder monkeys couldn't hit a flight of barns!"

Bo-oo-omm!

"Number two gun — short one hundred!"

Even as the third cannon went off, the number two gun was being trundled back by its crew, heaving in unison on the trail tackles. Promptly, a sponger drove a dripping mass of sodden wool and spun yarn far down the still-smoking throat of the piece.

This crew must have been extra-well schooled, Nat Coffin decided. They were taking no chances of leaving a spark in the bore which would blow off the hands of the gunner who would presently ram home a fresh charge.

Roger was by now cursing the day he had joined the infantry — even the select First South Carolina. The artillery, it seemed, would earn a majority of the laurels today.

Monotonously, Captain Blake's voice rose above the rasped commands of the gun captains. "Number three — a bully hit forrard! Try a round of chain shot at her headsails."

Moultrie came hurrying up, the members of his staff trailing after him. "Not so fast! Damn it, Blake. Not so fast!"

"We have hit the *Experiment* twice, sir!" Captain Blake's eyes shone white amid the gloomy billows of burnt powder smoke that were rolling back over the fort.

"Twice! You must hull her *every* time!" Moultrie roared. "We've got no powder to throw away. When the admiral's ship comes up, I want everybody to concentrate on her."

"Say, Colonel, what'll happen when they gits the range?" quavered a little drummer on runner duty.

"We won't have time to get scared, I reckon," came the imperturbable response.

Keeping pace with Colonel Moultrie's halting progress along the parapet, Nat Coffin realized that the easterly wind was picking up, bringing the big ships of the first line into closer range.

The *Active* had a boat out and was about to drop a sheet anchor from it. This, he immediately perceived, was intended to keep the man-o'-war broadside on to the fort.

H. M. S. *Bristol*, looking mountain-tall, took up a position a cable's length astern the *Active*.

Pipes shrilled, yards creaked about as the great ship's anchors went plunging down to the mud on the harbor's bottom amid a wild flurry of spray. Then the flagship's topmen moved out her yards and, in no great hurry, began furling her canvas.

"Look at the admiral's ship," the cry arose. A string of signal flags, pretty and varied as butterflies, was climbing into the *Bristol*'s rigging. Almost at once *Friendship* and *Thunder* ceased firing.

In the uneasy lull which ensued, everybody studied the enemy. How bright those red-painted gunports and muzzles looked. They were as nearly eye catching as the continued flash of steel on the decks and the red coats of marines manning the fighting tops.

Now that the sun was climbing higher, the wind died away until reflections of the men-of-war grew momentarily more perfect. On its staff the fort's blue flag dangled almost motionless.

[308]

Nat bit his lip. His premonition had crystallized into a conviction that when the enemy fired their first united broadside he would be killed. But Captain Oliphant and Lieutenant Lessessue never guessed it when he said: "Looks like it might be wise to get behind a merlon."

Mopping heavy red jowls, Colonel Moultrie turned to Nat. "Mr. Coffin, pray go below and cause the infantry officers to appoint relief gun crews. In this heat our gunners cannot work incessantly. Practiced men are to be preferred, of course."

The Nantucketer had barely reached a set of steps descending to the courtyard than such a hurricane of sound stunned his ears that he could only stand still, clutching the pitchy handrail.

Successive concussions slapped his face so hard he could neither focus his eyes nor collect his thoughts. He was aware, however, that the whole seaward curtain of Fort Sullivan was rocking as if an earthquake had commenced. Over the hissing scream of cannonballs he could hear the fort's palmetto timbers creak and groan.

Grinning because he had survived the first broadside, Nat hauled himself erect, brushed sand from his tunic. He'd better try to set an example. He was supposed to be a veteran — and a Massachusetter!

Though he felt all shuddery inside, Nat winked at Roger Proveaux as he moved on to the next unit. As he ran by on the same errand as himself, young Proveaux was ghastly pale and his eyes looked great with excitement — very like Antoinette's.

The young Carolinian began moving among the men of a badly disorganized company, patting one man on the shoulder, pulling another by the wrist. He would make a good officer some day.

Nat was reporting back to the colonel when a blast of British grapeshot penetrated an embrasure. It reduced an entire crew to mangled pulp, and filled the hot air with the cloying, musty odor of blood. In rivulets, gore leaked through the gun platform onto infantry crouched under the walls.

Once the American gunners got over that initial shock, they settled down and at almost every shot splinters could be seen flying aboard the smoke-veiled men-of-war. One by one yards were being taken down by charges of bar or chain-shot. In festoons severed lines dangled from the flagship's maintop.

Even at the end of an hour, the British cannonade had diminished not a whit.

By shielding his eyes from flying sand, Nat was able to get a good look at the enemy. It was discouraging to discern the enemy ships lying as before, bow to stern. Periodically, gigantic smoke rings spurted from their gunports.

Gradually the deliberate, individually-aimed fire from the fort commenced to take effect. Aboard H. M. S. *Experiment* a topmast gave way suddenly and spilled a tangle of rigging, yards and men into the water.

[309]

As if exasperated by the refusal of this ramshackle fort on Sullivan's Island to crumble, Admiral Parker ordered up his second line of battle.

Very slowly the *Acteon*, *Sphynx* and *Syren* — all frigates — crawled into range. They anchored further out and fired between intervals left by the vessels forming the first line. Soon they added their not inconsiderable weight of metal to the iron hailstorm hammering at Fort Sullivan.

To defend that narrow ford which divided Sullivan's from Long Island, Colonel William Thomson had laid out the simplest imaginable system of breastworks — merely a pair of giant *flèches* with their points aimed at the soon-to-be-disputed crossing.

The ex-Pennsylvanian's greatest concern was over his lack of artillery. Charles Lee had sent him only an eighteen-pounder and a miserable little six-pounder with a range so limited it might as well not have been there for all its usefulness.

Why in blazes, Thomson wanted to know, wouldn't the Continental general stop trying to fight this war as if it were taking place on the plains of Belgium? Why keep whole batteries to defend headquarters?

Sergeant Alistair Bryson and his men had got so used to the sounds of battle from the opposite end of the island that they were able to recognize undertones in the cannonading. There was the bass grumble of a big gun; the staccato crash of an exploding bomb; the nerve-rasping scratch of a ricochet; the juvenile bark of the lighter field pieces. Anxious lest their own retreat be blocked, the Third Regiment and its supporting troops watched lazy pillars of distant gray smoke climb into the brazen heavens.

Occupying a greater part of the line of defense was the Third South Carolina Regiment of Infantry, mostly from the upcountry. No fancy regimentals here. The greater part of the men wore their own clothes and had peeled off most of those.

To the left of the Wateree Company, the Raccoon Company of riflemen had been posted. They wore buckskins and must be very sorry for it, now that the sun was climbing so high. Most of them had already drained their water bottles and were panting like hounds just in from a hard chase.

There was no cover to speak of — not even for the officers. Just a few parched and scarred oleanders and an occasional palmetto with its cabbage-like top.

An oily-looking tide was going out, exposing wide expanses of sedgy flats and attracting hundreds of shore birds.

The flotilla drew nearer, rowing slowly down a channel that wavered through a succession of mud flats.

In all his life Alistair Bryson had never experienced such blinding, intolerable heat. It distorted everything in sight, drew shimmering streamers from the dunes. Fervently, he blessed his ancestors: a kilt admitted air where breeches and trousers would not.

Conversation revived now that the flotilla was really drawing near. In those white-painted boats moved brilliant patterns of color: blue and white of seamen's jerseys, black sailor hats, huddles of scarlet-clad marines and vari-colored revers and cuffs of infantry.

Apparently it was the flotilla's mission to pass by the ford and then to effect a landing in the rear of the American position.

"Look at 'em come!" A sudden startled shout arose from a new direction. "Faces as red as their bloody coats."

Alistair rolled over on the blistering sand and felt his heart flare like a frightened hawk. On Long Island a rank of black shakos seemed to be sprouting from the crest of a gray-white dune. Next, a row of faces came into view, then a blinding flash of scarlet and white cross-belts. Well out in front of the ranks marched a scattering of officers. They were easily recognized by the gold lace on their tunics and the bright smears of light marking the crescent-shaped gorgets which protected their throats.

"Hum. Those yellow facings mean they'll be either the 57th or the 15th," someone in the Raccoon Company announced.

The regulars were trying to keep their ranks dressed, but the yielding sand made that next to impossible. Fifers and little drummer boys trudged along on the flanks of the column playing "Strike, Britons, Home!" for all they were worth.

In successive waves more, and still more, scarlet coats appeared on the skyline and started down the long slope toward the ford.

"Christ A'mighty!" cried Alistair's right-hand companion. "Is there no end to them?"

A Spanish-looking officer came running up, his shirt open clean down to his belt.

"Here they come. Look to your priming."

To the right of Alistair's company fifty riflemen from the Raccoon Company began to fiddle with their sights, and to place bets.

Colonel Dan Horry, reading their impatience, bawled, "Hey, you riflers! Don't you go loosing off without orders. Let the redcoats come on till the smoothbores can range 'em!"

Abruptly a rifleman got to his knees. "Ah, the hell with waiting!" He took quick aim at the leading small boat and fired. The flat, dry report of his rifle rang loud over the mirrorlike channel. A scant hundred yards away an oarsman in a red and white jersey dropped his oar and sagged sidewise. One limp arm dangled over the thwart and an oar went drifting astern. The other rowers flinched, their oars began wavering like the legs of a crippled daddy-long-legs. Startled shouts began to sound in the flotilla.

Furiously Alistair called at the rifleman, "Dinna' shoot so soon! Gi' us a chance to show what we can do."

The insubordinate only squirted tobacco juice at him as he whipped up his powder horn and prepared to reload.

More rifles began to crack as the Raccoon Company's scant discipline went by the board.

For a brief interval the riflemen had a dandy time of it. Fringes flying, they twirled hickory ramrods over their heads and spat half-ounce balls into the bore.

Almost weeping with disappointment, Jamie Campbell shouldered his musket and fired. His Brown Bess boomed mightily, but its ball only raised a miniature geyser yards short of the mark.

Too late, Colonel Horry ran up and began berating the riflemen, knocking up their rifle barrels. "Stop it, you insubordinate slab-sided sons of squaws! I'll see your shoulders smoke for this sure's my name is Horry!"

But there was no restraining these leathery frontiersmen. Confusion spread in the British flotilla. A squad of grenadiers in the nearer boats opened fire, but their smoothbore muskets were no more effective than Jamie Campbell's.

"E-e-eyah! E-e-e-yah!" the riflemen began screeching like so many panthers. A great breathless clamor began to rise from the Carolina regulars posted in the *flèches*.

An officer came panting up to Captain Chesnut and yelled something. Immediately the Wateree Company and a detachment of North Carolinians were ordered out of the little pits they had dug and sent at the double to reinforce Thomson's main body.

Sand filled Alistair's shoes and the claymore dragged hard at his baldric, but he got his men over in a hurry and posted in a shallow hollow above the main position.

The Wateree Company was only faintly aware of an intensification in the bombardment of Fort Sullivan, for now the first ranks of the enemy had reached the water's edge. The officers waded right out, yelling encouragement and waving their swords.

Ankle-deep, the big grenadiers began to advance more and more gingerly. Then the water grew deeper, the officers felt out footing with their swords. The men caught up their cartouche boxes to keep them clear of the surface.

Captain Chesnut said in conversational tones, "Get set, boys; another twenty yards and they'll be in easy range."

All along the hollow the upcountry men were getting ready. Old hands stuck their ramrods into the ground, put bullets into their cheeks and tucked paper wads into their belts. There were so many red, white and yellow facings in the water now that soon even a poor shot could not miss.

Up to their armpits in the coffee-colored tide, the foremost officers halted and began to curse. Alistair could hear them calling to know whether this was the correct spot. Gradually the whole British advance halted, patently unable to advance.

A large man in a major's uniform turned and splashed back yelling, "Tide's dead low, sir — and it's too deep."

A group of particularly resplendent officers appeared and hurried down to the water's edge.

"That must be their general," Alistair deduced.

"Yep, that's Clinton, sure enough," Captain Chesnut nodded.

Arriving at the ford, Sir Henry removed a watch and a packet of papers from his pocket and passed them to an aide. Sword in hand, he then started wading past his half-submerged troops. Those regiments still on dry land shifted in their ranks to see what would happen.

Steadily, and quite ignoring the popping of the six-pounder, Sir Henry Clinton advanced into the slack, tan-colored tide. Water, rising to his chest, stirred the elegant white lace of his jabot. The British Commander kept on until only his gold-trimmed tricorne and white wig remained above water.

"Yon's a rare brave mon," muttered Jamie Campbell. "A rifler could hit him, there's nae doot."

From the American side of the ford rose a mighty yell of derision. Wasn't every day you watched a general get his arse wet!

Grimly, Sir Henry Clinton turned and made his way back to shore. When his troops followed suit, the American force fired a triumphant volley which accomplished nothing because the range was too great; it made them feel better, though, and shots kept crackling all up and down the dunes.

"Ye'd have believed," Lewis Campbell remarked, "that wi' a whole week on his hands, Sir Henry would have made sure how deep yon ford might be."

"Well, there's an end to the Lobsterbacks," someone was calling.

"Like hell," corrected Colonel Thomson. "Most likely Clinton will embark and try to land between us and Moultrie. He hasn't come all this way to stop now."

Gunpowder

Lieutenant Nathaniel Coffin, Continental Marines, found it was somewhat cooler out on the water. He was very glad of that. So were the four Negro rowers and a courier of Colonel Thomson's.

So far Thomson was making out real well, explained the North Carolinian. Only question now was whether Sir Henry Clinton would attempt to land his unhurt army at some point between Thomson and the fort.

The possibility was a real cause for concern. If the British could march across narrow Sullivan's Island, both American positions must inevitably be lost.

Because an occasional stray cannonball came skipping over the harbor's mirrored surface, the black oarsmen required little urging. They made the gig fairly fly across the cove separating Sullivan's Island from Lee's headquarters on Haddrell's Point. Their course lay parallel to a useless footbridge of rum casks and planks.

"The firin' sounds mighty weak from the fo't," Thomson's courier presently observed. "Sounds like they was done fo'."

"They will be if we don't get some powder in a hurry. The enemy could walk right in now, if they only knew it."

They found the commander-in-chief crouched on an observation platform built into a tree. Hatchet features working, Charles Lee was studying the fort through a pocket telescope. When the messengers were announced, he delayed a good quarter of an hour ere he descended a ladder held by two staff officers.

If Nat Coffin had ever beheld an ill-tempered and hostile countenance, it was the major general's.

"Well?" rasped the gangling figure. "Does our high and mighty backwoods strategist at last admit that a veteran of a dozen European wars might know something of siege warfare?"

"I have no information on that point, sir," stated Lieutenant Nathaniel Coffin.

"Come, come! Moultrie is about to get smoked out. May as well admit it."

"Not yet, sir."

Lee's pale brown eyes narrowed and he snapped fingers that might have been cleaner. "Oh, plague take that stubborn Provincial fool." He turned to the courier, "Well, what do you want?"

The North Carolinian saluted, began earnestly, "Colonel Thomson, suh, sho'ly needs reinforcements. He asks please will you land a strong body of troops halfway down Sullivan 'twixt the fo't and the fo'd?"

"Really?" Lee affected great astonishment. "And where does your estimable colonel think I am going to find such troops? Out of a cocked hat?"

A South Carolina major opened his mouth, but before he could utter a syllable Lee roared, "I'll thank you to hold your peace! Things are going badly enough already. Moultrie's pig-headedness will soon lose me all his garrison and Thomson's force also. No. I will not doom another man to destruction on the island. My reputation will suffer enough through this day's work."

Nat seized his opportunity. "But, sir, Colonel Moultrie is not requesting a single man. He only asks that this requisition be honored, and at once." He offered the paper Motte had made out.

Using a bluish forefinger nail, Charles Lee ripped open the requisition. "Only a thousand pounds of powder?" he sneered. "Here's a modest request, stab me if it's not! Gentlemen, dear generous Colonel Moultrie wishes to present the enemy with an additional thousand pounds of our gunpowder!" He glared at Nat. "Present my compliments to your rustic strategist and inform him I will not risk another private or a single gill of powder in the defense of Sullivan's Island! That's flat."

The grumbling boom of successive broadsides from the fleet made the hot air shake.

Tarnished braid flashed on Lee's cuff as he snatched at his pocket telescope.

A growing murmur of dismayed astonishment arose from the staff.

Propelled by just a breath of breeze, all three frigates composing the second line had upped anchor and were setting sail with the obvious intention of rounding the western tip of Sullivan's.

What impended was unmistakable. The *Syren*, *Acteon* and *Sphynx* were circling around towards the little, low-lying fort's quite undefended rear. From that point the frigates could, and undoubtedly would, shatter Moultrie's batteries. At the same time, the garrison's retreat to Haddrell's Point would be cut off.

Pompous and arrogant though he was, the adventurer Lee had been entirely justified in his fears. There could be no doubt now that the fort must fall, and in very short order.

Nothing was to be gained from waiting, so Nat unobtrusively returned to his boat. Bitterly he dreaded the necessity of breaking the news of Lee's refusal to send powder.

As he ran down to the shore, the Nantucketer kept one eye on the three frigates. So light was the wind it seemed as if these men-of-war were being drawn along by invisible cables rather than by the pressure of air on their canvas.

"Wait! Wait!" A captain wearing the regimentals of the First Carolina Line came pelting up. "Plague take that damned turncoat Englishman." He jerked his head towards Lee's headquarters. "How is Colonel Moultrie holding out?"

"Well enough, except for powder. He had only one gun out of action when I left."

"*Only one* — why that's impossible!"

"The palmetto timbers give rather than break under a round shot." Nat turned to the boat crew. "Shove off — "

The dark-faced Carolinian came to the water's edge. "On your word of honor — Moultrie's damage is no greater?"

Nat's color rose above his sweaty white collar. "On my sacred word."

A few yards up the shore were a pair of long, slim pilot boats. Their Negro crews lazed on the beach.

Nat heard the officer bark, "You'll row me to Charleston inside thirty minutes or I'll see every inch of skin is flogged off your backs!"

Jumping abroad, he took the tiller himself and the last Nat saw of that Carolina captin he was alternately calling the stroke and demanding more speed.

The Georgian

A twelve-pound shot from H. M. S. *Experiment* came screaming through an embrasure, shattered the muzzle of a cannon and showered its crew with deadly, jagged iron fragments. Two of Sergeant McDaniel's crew simply disintegrated into mangled lumps of meat. The balance of the stricken crew either fell heavily or rolled crazily about. Bubbling groans, whimpering noises filled intervals in the cannonading. Infantrymen ran to lift the wounded onto stretchers improvised of coats which had been buttoned and turned inside out. Poles had been thrust through the coat sleeves.

A hand that was blue with tattooing landed with a dull thump by the feet of a tall sergeant handling an adjoining piece. His grimy features froze in horror at the slowly relaxing fingers; at the blood slowly crawling over the gritty boards of the gun platform.

"What ails you?" grunted a half-naked gun captain. "A hero from Georgia shouldn't fear a little hot iron."

William Jasper made no reply.

"I never yet seen a Georgian with enough sand to stand up to a field-mouse."

Slowly the big sergeant looked about. "Whoever said that is a damn' liar!"

"Words is cheap," growled the number four of his own gun crew.

Just then the *Bristol* fired such a vicious salvo that the whole curtain trembled under its impact. Squinting over the breech of his piece Sergeant Jasper thought, "Ah'll show these South Carolina bastards! By Christ, ah'll show 'em! How do they get to fancy South Carolina is God's gift to America?"

Colonel Moultrie, looking years older now, came along to inspect the damage. Somebody called, "Hey, Colonel, what the hell has happened to our banner?"

"That last volley carried it off, I reckon," Colonel Moultrie snapped. Seemed to him like an evil omen to see the Moultrie's silver and blue brought down.

"It ain't carried away," a gunner corrected. "It's just the staff is broke. I kin see our flag layin' on the beach."

Jasper sensed a God-given opportunity to shut these fellers up once and for all. He saluted mighty brisk.

[316]

"Colonel, suh, we ought to have a flag to fight under."

"True, but we haven't another."

"Then, suh, ah reckon ah had better fetch that one up."

As the colonel shook his head, another salvo from the enemy rattled against the palmetto logs, sent sand skimming high into the air.

"Don't be a fool. Cannonballs are thicker down there than flies 'round a backhouse."

Jasper, however, was already vaulting over the mess about the ruined gun. He crawled out of the embrasure muttering, "Called me yaller, just 'cause ah comes from Geo'gia! Ah'm gonna show 'em."

A queer buzzing began in his ears when he realized that one of the liners was sure 'nough fixing to fire. Scrambling down a series of splintered logs he was aware, in a frozen sort of way, that those gun muzzles were beginning to protrude through the ports.

Whew! They'd let fly in a minute. He was a great fool to have let them Charleston fellers sass hm into tryin' such a fool trick as this. To keep from worrying too much he tried to count the number of cannonballs stuck between the logs. Six, eight, fourteen, not counting chunks of broken bombshell.

Ha! He saw the blue flag lying down there amid a tangle of broken timbers. The staff had sho' 'nuff been clipped a mean lick — was splintered half its length. Just as he reached the beach, the liner let go her broadside. He could see the water grow all rough under the concussion. Just above his head a roundshot plucked a log out of the southeast bastion, sent it spinning off into the air as if it had been a toothpick.

He felt his bowels pucker. Once he'd come across a nest of young jaybirds too young to fly. All naked and helpless they'd lain there waiting for him to do something to them. He guessed he knew how they had felt.

Zoo-e-e! Tchunk! A cannonball sailed right past his waist, another, falling short, drove a shower of salty sand into his mouth, nose and eyes.

Glory be! A charge of grapeshot, whirring like a covey of gigantic quail, roared overhead. That he had hold of the flag was a surprise. He rumpled it up under one arm, any way it would go.

Shucks! That stitching around the word LIBERTY was no great shakes. If this was a sample of Carolina sewing, he was right glad he came from Geo'gia.

Spurred by the knowledge that another broadside would soon be ready, he scrambled up the log wall as fast as he could and got inside just as the *Bristol* let go.

Safe! It was a crazy thing they'd stung him into attempting. But he'd done it. The Georgian took the flag from under his arm, shook it at them.

"Here's your banner, you goddamn Carolina swamp rabbits!"

When he climbed up and jammed the sponge staff into a crack at the top of a merlon near the southeast salient, Colonel Moultrie snatched out his pipe and joined in the cheering.

Disembarking on Sullivan's Island, Nat noticed parties of infantry deserting that epaulment which fronted Haddrell's Point channel. They knew that by another ten minutes the three flanking frigates would be in position to rake the entrenchment from end to end. Even the officers saw that a defense was hopeless. Their little nine- and twelve-pounders would be quite ineffective.

Lord! How slow the fort was firing. *Age quod agis*, my boy. 'Tend to your business.

Dreading his mission, Nat made straight for the south gun platform. He found Moultrie, Motte and the rest there. They were staring tensely to the westward.

Suddenly, like clockwork set in motion, members of the staff began to cheer, to gesticulate and to pound each other on the back. When he reached the top of the ladder-stair, Nat saw the reason for their jubilation. Either an unsuspected current or the freshening east breeze had caused the *Syren* and the *Sphynx* to foul each other. Yards interlaced, both vessels lost headway and began to drift broadside in the direction of Charleston.

Despite all efforts, the two ships were driven closer and closer together. Soon they lost the last trace of steerageway.

"Watch the third ship," Captain Huger commenced to shout. "Watch the *Acteon!*"

To avoid her entangled consorts, the *Acteon* was bearing away to port, apparently cutting just inside of a very small black buoy. This was one of several which during the past week had mysteriously appeared. Her topsails filling under a strong puff, the frigate drove along so smartly that foam curled away from her cutwater.

Suddenly her progress ceased and her fabric gave an enormous creaking groan. Her bow shot high into the air. Simultaneously all her yards swung wildly over to starboard, catapulting a number of topmen far out over the water.

Wild shouts arose from the fort as the man-of-war settled heavily onto a shoal called the Middle Ground. Gradually the *Acteon*'s canvas canted her so far over to starboard that loose objects tumbled across her decks into the starboard scuppers.

Captain Huger, still unstrung over his sergeant's death, began to hug himself, to laugh until his eyes watered. "Oh, those chuckleheaded fools! Came right on, never taking a bearing! Oh — oh, stab me if this isn't rare. They never suspected that we — oh! oh! — would move their damned buoy hundred feet to port. Oh, burn my breeches. Isn't it wonderful? Look at 'em, Coffin, there's the *Acteon* stuck tight as a duck's foot in the mud!"

Meantime the *Sphynx* and the *Syren* had somehow disentangled themselves, but at the cost of a snapped bowsprit for the former. Her headsails were flapping in a grotesque tangle.

Moultrie roused himself, became lavish with his dwindling supply of powder and roared, "Pour it into 'em, lads."

Joyfully, the handful of guns mounted along the west curtain went into action and at once splinters began to fly and yards to fall aboard the frigates. Punished, they veered off too far and so went sliding up on that same bank of blue mud and sand which was already imprisoning the *Acteon*.

Nat felt his breath come again. Lee, he judged, would be furious because this accident had made a joke of his dire predictions. As for Colonel Moultrie, that stolid gentleman looked mightily relieved, but even yet he did not seem to appreciate how deadly had been his danger.

So many bodies were lugged to the *Bristol*'s rail and dropped into the water that no one could keep accurate count.

"Dum them Britishers," grunted a saturnine fellow with gurry sores all over his hands. "Now I wunt dare taste a crab in a month." His mates roared as if he'd said the cleverest thing.

Helped by a rising tide, the *Syren* and the *Sphynx* floated free of the bar and, unaccountably, abandoned all efforts to deliver their attack from the rear. Sullenly they tacked back to join the fleet and, resuming their original positions, joined in the ceaseless cannonade of Fort Sullivan.

The *Acteon* remained where she was despite the frantic efforts of her crew to get her off.

Around half after four, a sloop was discerned leaving Charleston with a smaller sailboat in her wake. The lowering sun was raising an easterly breeze, so both vessels skirted the helpless *Acteon* and ran into the cove behind the fort.

His features luminous with sweat, a dark-complexioned officer hurried ashore from the sloop and came running up to the fort.

To Colonel Moultrie he panted, "With the compliments of President Rutledge, sir."

Saluting, he presented a fold of paper secured with a flying seal.

As Moultrie read, a smile formed, spread over his unshaven face. "Listen to this!" he yelled at his staff. "Ed Rutledge says, 'I send you five hundred pound of powder. You know our collection is not great. Honor and victory to you and our worthy countrymen with you. Be cool and do mischief!' "

Flight

TO WADBOO, 4 MI, read the bird-stained fingerboard. Mechanically, Desire fanned herself with a soggy handkerchief and hoped her fraying satin slippers would last such a distance. What Wadboo might be like or who lived there, she had no idea.

Dully she realized that that grumbling rumble which had commenced in the early morning was persisting. Of course a terrible battle must be taking place at Fort Sullivan. Terrified fugitives, overtaking her, had brought the wildest reports.

In trying to keep her mind off her heavy, aching body and the fact that her ankles were swelling to almost twice their usual slim proportions, Desire thought backwards.

Why, oh why, did Nat have to reappear just when and as he had? Everything might have worked out if she'd found him without the Proveauxs around. Still, maybe she had been wise, and decent, to leave as she had.

Ahead lay what seemed like a promising stretch of pine woods. It looked really shady there and if she came across a stream, she wanted to sit down and bathe feet which stung as if scalded.

Sure enough, a small runlet was tracing a bright green ribbon across the brown floor of pine wood. It took her some minutes to catch her breath but once she had untied her garters and stripped off the stained remnants of her stockings, the water felt unbelievably fine on her feet. In fact, that cool trickle about her ankles seemed to soothe her whole body.

Way off to the southeast those cannon were still thud-thudding away. Oh dear. It must be a fearful battle. She supposed Nat was in it, and Roger and Cousin Barnard Elliott. When she got a little more strength back she would pray that all of them got —

Quite a heavy noise from behind made her turn her head. At what she saw her fingers flew wide apart and remained fixed in the rigidity of terror. Not six feet away and steadily regarding her from the heart of the myrtle was a fierce black face. One of this Negro's cheeks was puckered by a deep brand.

"Please, maum, please doan't raise no rookus."

"You come out of there!" It wasn't hard for Desire to inject indignation into her tone. "The idea your going about scaring people like that!"

"Yas'm." A strapping young Negro in tattered denims came out to stand uncertainly on the other side of the rivulet.

"Who is that with you?" Desire demanded, feeling the goosepimples subside on her arms.

"It's Eve, maum," he explained. A broad-faced wench appeared, hovered just back of his shoulder. The pair must have been into a lot of briars if one went by the plentiful scratches showing on their sable skins.

She learned that the pair were Barbados-trained and had suffered bestial cruelties at the hands of a Charleston dealer named Ratsch. Cocoa, the man, exhibited heavy welts on arms and shoulders. It was while the slave trader's gangs were being driven to safety in the interior that an opportunity for escape had presented itself.

Desire, her jangled nerves calming, sat with her feet still in the water.

"What do you want of me?" she asked with an amused smile. "Surely you must have seen that I can give you neither food, clothes, nor money."

The branded Negro dropped on his knees as he held out hands joined in supplication. "In de Lawd's name please tek mercy on us, maum. Tek us for yo' people."

"But how — "

Cocoa's eyes rolled. "If you decla'hs, maum, Eve and me is yo' prop-etty, den can't no sodjuhs er patrollers shoot us — tek us up — " He gazed fearfully at the road. "Sway to Gawd, Cocoa an' Eve he'p you plenty. Eve, her puntop cook, fitten belong to quality."

Although she hadn't even the semblance of a plan of action, Desire had learned enough of Southern ways to appreciate that a woman possessing a pair of slaves thereby commanded courtesy and attention — no matter what her state.

So she must once more play a part. The fates, it seemed, had decreed for her the life of an actress.

"Cocoa, I have decided to take you both on." Skillfully, she mimicked 'Toinette's intonations. "While I rest, you go down the road and find what Wadboo is. Eve, fetch my stockings off that bush."

Even at sundown stragglers from militia companies kept limping by. Quite a few of these, so Cocoa said, were riflemen. Because buckskin men must be sho 'nuff strangers in these parts, he wasn't so afraid to address them.

"Evenin', folks, reckon you could stretch yore provender a speck?" Desire gasped, Eve squealed and Cocoa jumped. None of them had had the least warning of this buckskin's approach.

"Sorry, ma'am," said he simply, "I didn't mean for to startle you."

He pulled off a cap of bobcat fur. "I will fix you a real leanto, ma'am, to pay for any vittles I eat."

There was something forcefully reminiscent about that outline, half seen among the trees.

Desire's heart gave a queer little flip as she called aloud, "Well, Mr. Higsby, do you still seek a good fight?"

Sam Higsby jumped as if an arrow had stuck in the tree beside him. Cap still in hand, he bounded forward.

"Why, Miss Desire! What in Gawd's name — ? Tim an' me hunted everywhere."

When, out of sheer relief, she kissed him, Higsby reckoned he was in luck at last.

Long after Eve and Cocoa had gone off to sleep under the pines, Desire and the Pennsylvanian talked, watched the stars wheel slowly by above the treetops.

[321]

At sundown there was no doubt that even so stubborn a fighter as Admiral Peter Parker had had enough. Officers, training spyglasses on the *Bristol* and the *Experiment*, declared both liners to be barely afloat. Why, the flagship alone had suffered along her waterline nearly seventy hits. Had any kind of a sea been running, both liners would undoubtedly have filled and sunk.

Observers described dozens of little scarlet rivulets dripping from the shattered bulwarks and streaking the yellow stripes along the liner's side. Most of the *Experiment*'s yards had fallen and her topmasts canted drunkenly, supporting a hurrah's nest of tangled rigging and sails. On the sea floated splintered sections of bulwark, spars, corpses and stove-in boats.

Thanks to an enforced deliberation, the gunners in Fort Sullivan had, all afternoon, fired each piece as if it were a rifle. It afforded the garrison a poignant object lesson; they, and the rest of America, learned that a single shot, well aimed did more damage than twenty hit-or-miss.

Nat determined to enter this discovery in his "Observations." Um. Had he not arrived previously at such a conclusion? When? At Breed's Hill, of course. There, also, the Provincials had sighted carefully and fired slowly. Maybe it was lucky that the colonies were so dangerously destitute of powder?

At precisely nine o'clock Admiral Parker's ships sullenly fired their last shot, and by the dim and uncertain light of battle lanterns prepared to return to their anchorage.

Standing on a merlon, Nat Coffin enjoyed the evening's cool, and with his foot prodded a roundshot embedded in the woodwork. Below the gun platforms the infantry were commencing to light cookfires. Thoughts of Antoinette Proveaux returned.

Roger Proveaux passed just below him. From where he sat, Nat could see that the Carolinian's shirt was a grimy mess of tatters and that his white nankeen breeches bore grim splashes. He'd see Roger at mess. Right now it was wonderfully quiet on the merlon.

Antoinette! Never had he felt so burning an impatience, so consuming a hunger for any girl. Could this craving for tenderness be born of the death all about? An urge to replace wasted lives?

Colonel Moultrie appeared limping along, dragging his gouty leg. Said he, "Well, now, Mr. Coffin, what do you think of the way us fellers can fight?"

"There can never be a more spirited defense fought by braver men, sir."

"Thank you. I was wondering what a Yankee might say." He winked. "You know you are right fortunate, Mr. Coffin?"

"And why, sir?"

" 'Tain't many of us are privileged to see *both* the British army and navy take a lacing. By God, didn't we surprise our seagoin' friends today? This should sting the king's ministers worse than Breed's Hill."

The receding tide was leaving a lot of half-naked bodies on the beach. They were corpses from the ships. Many of them lacked limbs, heads. Already dozens of great blue crabs were busy with them.

Everybody now was making much of Sergeant William Jasper — putting all kinds of heroic words into his mouth. Perhaps it was just as well that what he had really said, when he got back, wasn't repeated. He certainly had told the South Carolina men what he thought of them in a series of well-chosen four-letter words.

They were doing the same thing about Sergeant McDaniel. He hadn't gasped, "Fight on, my brave boys; don't let liberty expire with me today" — or anything else.

Suddenly he became aware of the smells of boiling ham and frying onions. A gnawing began in his stomach.

He guessed he'd go below and stop in at Roger Proveaux's tent for a swig of straight Barbados. He needed a drink — had earned it, maybe.

On nearing the steps down to the courtyard, he heard the sergeant of the guard barking: "Fall in smartly. You fellers been sittin' 'round on your fat butts all day. Make sure your priming's right."

Halfway down the ladder steps, Nat Coffin paused, aware of a magnificent greenish star glowing above the roofs of Charleston. It must be a planet. If he weren't so tired, he could recall its name. Jupiter? Saturn? Or was it Venus? No, Venus was blue —

From among the guard detail sounded a frightened curse. "Take your finger off that trigger, you fool! Don't you know — "

The musket exploded in Nat Coffin's face, and as he fell the greenish star paled, went out forever.

Cap François

Something wholly unforeseen must have occurred, Timothy Bennett concluded, else why should Messrs. Prenet and Dulac have sent for him posthaste and in the middle of a June day. What the devil could be wrong now?

Irritably, he ran over a string of possibilities. So many obstacles had arisen it was a shining wonder that any more remained.

On deck he flinched at a withering heat which was melting the tar between the deck planks. Like red-hot arrows, heat waves penetrated his white duck coat and trousers.

[323]

He wished to God he had had sense enough to follow the sloppy Creole custom of discarding a cravat and leaving his shirt open clear down to his belt. But somehow he couldn't. It would set a bad example for the men.

This thriving port of nearly thirty thousand souls — black, brown and white — lay jammed tight against the base of a semicircle of high, rugged hills which effectively cut off all the prevailing southerly breezes. Red roofs, gold-tipped cathedral towers, white walls, brown walls, blue walls and gray-white fortifications, all shimmered dizzily under the noonday sun.

Thanks to an unprecedented drought, luxuriant foliage which normally would have showed emerald and sapphire tints had been dried to a pale brown. A shimmering blue haze obscured landmarks further inland than the barracks on the extreme side of town. Crimanently! The towers of the Church of Notre Dame wavered as if an earthquake were in progress.

Captain Freebody emerged from under a spare sail slung over the main boom. "Mr. Bennett," said he, "it's mighty important you get honored our permit to arm. Two more men are down with sunstroke, and three died last week, ye'll recall." His thin ribs were working like bellows. "Half the time I feel giddy as a goat myself."

"I'll do all I can, Freebody," Tim assured him. "You can count on it. Keep the decks wet and the crew under the awnings till four o'clock. We mustn't lose any more men from home."

How to round out the crew was growing to be a serious problem now that more and more would-be privateers were dropping anchors in Saint-Domingue. Most of these latecomers could, and would, pay fancier wages than Bennett & Son. With a stubborn affection, Tim had clung to the name.

Freebody said, "Soon's the sun lowers I'll go ashore. See if I can't pick up a few hands." He jerked his head at a massive ship of the line which had made port the night before. "She may have brought some new blood."

La Dédaigneuse was of the first rating and therefore huge. Mounting a hundred guns, her crew would number around nine hundred and fifty men. She lay off a battery at the near end of the harbor, her enormous gold and white ensign barely astir. When it came to gilding and scroll-work, the great vessel certainly was a creation of rare beauty.

"Boat ready, sir." Below, the coxswain touched his straw hat.

Tim seated himself in the gig's stern sheets but bounced right up. The wooden seat was so unbearably hot that he remained standing while four seamen pulled slowly through a colorful tangle of shipping.

Certainly the harbor Cap François could never have seen busier times. Besides the great *Dédaigneuse*, a pair of frigates, the *Cerf* and the *Surveillant*, a Spanish man-of-war and a Dutch sloop swung to their anchors. Of course, there was a great swarm of French merchantmen, slavers and vessels plying the inter-island trade.

[324]

No fewer than six would-be American privateers lay in the roadstead waiting to take on their armaments. He recognized two of these. Nicholas Brown's fast-looking *Industry* and Abed Thaxter's big, ship-rigged *Retaliation*. The other vessels hailed from Connecticut, Massachusetts and New Hampshire.

The *Narragansett*'s decks had been so stoutly reinforced that no one need worry whether her larger cannon — weighing twenty-three hundred pounds each — would go crashing through into the hold some stormy day.

Sails and rigging had been scrupulously overhauled and all the yards severely tested. If ever his brig need run for her life, Tim intended to feel no fear over the soundness of the *Narragansett*'s top-hamper.

What could have happened to Desire Harmony? In his most recent letter, Captain John Lawton declared that no trace of his sister had been uncovered despite diligent searching. Of Lucy Percival, Lawton merely stated that she was well and occupying herself with the relief of poor and distressed persons in the town.

The instant the letter of marque's gig drew in beside the foot of a flight of slippery, greasy-looking steps at the end of the rue Saint Jean, a noisy swarm of hawkers, pimps, beggars and urchins came charging down.

After his first day ashore in Saint-Domingue, Tim had adopted the use of a native implement, a coco-macaque, which was a species of heavy cane. Flourishing the stick about his head, the Rhode Islander drove before him a dreadfully eager and persistent throng of ragged blacks and mulattoes. He didn't like the looks of these Negroes. They didn't in the least resemble the comparatively easygoing and good-natured blacks he had met in the Bahamas.

Already drenched by torrents of acid perspiration, Tim turned right, heading towards the arsenal and the Parc d'Artillerie.

For several reasons Anatole Dulac had built his mansion on the rue Picolet at the extreme right of the town. It was well away from the noise, smells and bad water at the center of Cap François. For all his casual, slack appearance M. Dulac was long on foresight, very like M. Prenet in this respect.

Um. Why had the Dulac residence been built with such an obvious eye to defense? Most of the many luxurious homes in the capital had not been.

There was, he decided, but one redeeming feature to this wretched excursion. He might get another glimpse of Mistress Jeannette Dulac. He couldn't explain to himself why he had been so thoroughly fascinated by her. Maybe it was because this dainty Creole held for him the very essence of mystery. She was so completely dissimilar to any girl he had ever met. Every word, thought and deed presented a continual, and usually pleasing, surprise.

The time he had first met Dulac's daughter had been there on the street, and he had felt nearly forgotten flames begin to rise. Never had Lucy kindled so consuming an emotion.

[325]

Jeannette Dulac certainly was fashioned along lines calculated to heat a man's vitals. Those wide-set, sloe-lidded eyes, that tapering neck, those fragile shoulders and softly rounded breasts set the blood surging to his temples every time he saw her.

He wouldn't have believed that feet could be so narrow and long, that fingers could be so infinitely graceful. Why, Jeannette Dulac could do things with her fan that held him fascinated for minutes on end; her manipulations were as graceful as the idle wheeling of a seagull.

Then, too, she favored a perfume which made Lucy Percival's scent seem crude.

At night when Anatole Dulac's daughter wore diamonds in her ears and a great glittering necklace of the same stones, she presented a picture to be remembered. She was clever, too, in her small talk; could reel off whole scenes from the plays of Racine, Molière and Corneille.

Nor was Jeannette in the least ignorant concerning politics, or her father's business affairs. It appeared that she kept his letter book in order.

Before he knew it, Tim was ringing the bell-pull before an elaborate iron grille guarding the entrance to M. Dulac's handsome stone residence. He was let in and invited to wait in a stuffy little antechamber. At first he had resented such a delay but soon he had learned that it was only a part of a long-established routine. Nobody who was anybody would dream of receiving a visitor in under twenty minutes.

Crimanently! But he was glad of a chance to cool off. An awning outside cut off the sunlight, and a tiny fountain playing musically in the center of the waiting room at least suggested coolness.

A small object fluttered in through the door and shod feet raced lightly away. By means of a ribbon, a card had been attached to a tiny nosegay of orange blossoms.

Picking it up he read:

Brave Américain:
    For your happiness, it is imperative that you come to the shop of Caumartin, the chocolate maker, at seven tonight.   D.

"D?" Who? Oh! That must be Diane, Jeannette's pretty young sister. What could she be wanting with him? He was still puzzling when a shiny black lackey announced that M. Prenet and M. Dulac requested the pleasure of his attendance in the library.

Undoubtedly the arrival of more, and still more, American vessels was pleasing to Claude Prenet. It showed that his hard work in Philadelphia and Newport, that François Pliarne's efforts in Massachusetts, had not gone for nothing. The Norman's blue eyes were sparkling, and he waved his wineglass with energy when a shoeless black lackey flung back a pair of folding doors and announced, "M. Bennett!"

Both M. Prenet and M. Dulac arose and bowed with decorum. Through a humid semidarkness, Dulac's enormous frame waddled forward.

"Welcome, monsieur," he boomed in good but heavily accented English. "One laments the necessity of bringing you ashore at such a barbaric hour, but," he shrugged, "it becomes necessary for the three of us to take immediate action. It is heard that the king's lieutenant, the Chevalier de Labouisse, is in three days leaving for Cap Jacmel."

"And the cause?" Tim inquired anxiously.

"Your pardon, M. Bennett, I was merely attempting to cover the ground quickly." Dulac indicated a wide settee of superbly woven rattan. "Breakfast will soon be served. Pray render yourself comfortable."

It must have been easily fifteen degrees cooler here than on the street. Tim seated himself and, sighing, unbuttoned his white linen coat. Even this library office was typical of the country. Its latticed but unglazed windows were enormous, and in various pots and jars grew a profusion of tropical flowers. These, arranged against walls of pale blue, created bright splashes of color among the businesslike furniture.

"In brief — " Prenet began, then gave Tim a wry smile, " — in North America, one learns to be brief — we enter a very dangerous, one might say, phase in our negotiations with the M. de Ennery, His Majesty's governor general. If the Chevalier de Labouisse, who is a member of the Superior Council here, cannot be won over, we shall not receive permission to export munitions." He spread his hands, said grimly, "I must confess that M. Achard de Bonvouloir, our agent in Paris, misled my partner and me on this point. We understood that this permission had already been granted."

A cold sensation filled Tim's being. No permission! Great God! He *had* to have his cannons, his munitions.

"M. *le gouverneur* fears we may attempt to corrupt his lieutenant." Dulac smiled. "Which would be indeed gilding the lily!"

"Oh, Lord," Tim groaned, "another bribe! I thought we'd bought everybody from the intendant's groom to the attorney general. You fellows will have to find the money. When I sail, I'll have just one week's pay aboard."

Prenet said smoothly, "There is no call to disquiet yourself, my friend. The bribe money has already been found. There are diplomatic reasons why you must present it. One does not anticipate the least difficulty," he added hurriedly. "Now there remains one other matter which only you can arrange. You must promise M. de Labouisse that you will direct not less than two prizes, taken by you, into Savannah in the colony of Georgia."

"Savannah?" Tim started to object at this dictation but recalled Pa's advice about holding his tongue.

"You have good reason to wonder. Briefly, the worthy chevalier has friends in Savannah who would like to buy fast English vessels." M. Prenet irritably blotted still another row of drops from his brows. "They fear to make purchases further north because there the British blockade is very strong."

"All right," Tim said. "When shall I go see the king's lieutenant?"

"You must make the journey to Les Délices tomorrow," Prenet announced. "Limonade is not far and we shall arrange that you depart in a style suitable to the gravity of your errand. A word of caution, *mon ami*. New England prejudices are best left behind. It is wise to remind yourself that we in Saint-Domingue exist as a tiny white island in a black and savage ocean." Dulac fetched a deep sigh. "Once you see plantation life on the Plain du Nord, you will not conceive a pretty opinion of us Creoles."

Prenet came over too. "Never forget that without this *permis* you are even more hopelessly ruined than we. It is necessary, therefore, for you to favor his every whim."

"You'll have no call to fret on that score," the Rhode Islander assured them grimly.

What lay back of these elaborate warnings? Some of the new hands mentioned bestial, incredible happenings on estates lying back from the sea, but nobody had credited them.

"What about clothes?" Tim demanded. "I only have the rough things I brought down from the north."

"Leave that to me and to Jeannette," Dulac reassured. "She will see that you will command the admiration of Hector de Labouisse."

By half past six of the afternoon Tim had settled with M. Dulac and Claude Prenet what he hoped would prove the final details.

Once a *permis* was secured, the *Narragansett* would be laid alongside M. Dulac's wharf. His was one of the few private yards equipped with a crane powerful enough to handle heavy cannon. It was no coincidence that Dulac's wharf adjoined the busy warehouses of Messrs. Pliarne, Prenet et Cie.

Meanwhile he had just time for an interview with the man he intended to ship as surgeon. In fact, it was the man he had to ship, or put to sea without a medico. These other privateers had snapped up every available surgeon.

Yes, even a drunken Irish surgeon would be better than no doctor at all.

Why should a man of Alexander Boyd's obvious intelligence elect to drink himself into the grave? Yet that seemed to be his end and aim in life. He found the surgeon just about where he had expected — in the courtyard of a third-rate tavern kept by a free mulatto.

Fortunately, Dr. Boyd had not yet become too drunk to talk intelligently.

"I've been mullin' over what yez said the other night, Mr. Bennett. Maybe you're right. Maybe I am a loony to ruin me health over a sad matter that is finished and done with." He cocked a bloodshot eye at Tim. "Ye'll never guess my main reason for signing on?"

"I only know, Doctor, that I'm glad you intend to."

The drunkard waved a loose hand, indicated a seat. "It's because ye've niver inquired why I'm here rotting me gut with cheap rum."

"To tell you the truth, I'd never believe you capable of committing a particularly dreadful offense."

Dr. Boyd stared, his bruised-looking jaw sagging. "And wouldn't ye now? I wish there had been more o' the jury who'd agreed with you," the Irishman said. "Tell you all about it someday. When do you plan on sailing?"

"Next week," Tim said firmly, though he hadn't the vaguest notion as to when the *Narragansett*'s commission would turn up. "You'll come out to the *Narragansett* then, early day after tomorrow?"

"Aye, Mr. Bennett, ye may depend upon it. And now get along, Mr. Bennett, so's I can settle down to steady drinking. If I'm to bid dear old Bacchus a long farewell, I prefer to do it in style."

Tim found the shop of Caumartin the chocolate maker all but deserted. The proprietor proved to be a free Negro with an engaging smile and alert eyes.

"Mlle. Dulac? But yes, certainly, monsieur," the Negro gurgled. "Mademoiselle has instructed your miserable servant to conduct monsieur to her immediately." Tim followed the proprietor through the shop and to a small interior garden. "Monsieur will find mademoiselle in there."

Tim was abruptly reminded of some of Desire Harmony's giddy notions. His sister was always pretending to be this famous historical personage or that. Well, out of consideration for Jeannette, he would humor Diane, find out what was on her mind. Followed by fragrant odors of chocolate and vanilla, he set straight his cravat and strode up to the pergola.

It was much darker inside, but he could see a grass rug, a settee and a couple of wicker chairs.

"Ah, *mon héro!*" Two arms went about Tim's neck and warm, fragrant lips became glued to his. He was much too taken aback to move. The girl clung to him, her hands busy in his hair.

"I knew you would not disappoint poor Diane. Of course, Jeannette lied. It has been *me* you have sighed for all this time!"

God above! The child wore next to nothing above her waist. Quivering like a strained hawser, she pressed herself against his chest. An infinitely provocative perfume eddied about his head.

"Ah, Teem, I love you so dearly," she whispered. "I *must* have you. I will have you! My whole body craves your caress."

"But — but, Mistress Diane," he blurted, "I — my stars and crown, I don't want to marry!"

"Marry? Bah! Who said anything about it?" Her tiny hands fondled his ears, stroked his hair. *Dieu*, but he was firm and smelled of the sea, not of some coiffeur's lotion.

What a conquest! A tame American all her own. Oh, la! la! She would set a new fashion. He was even more desirable than that young English milor' who had come to the British consulate.

"Sit on the settee," she pleaded in low, tremulous tones. "Swear to me that Jeannette has lied, that you never asked her to marry you!"

Tim floundered. Crimanently! Could Jeannette have said such a thing? Futilely, he attempted to disengage this figure clinging so passionately to him. Good Lord! Diane's clothes were so scanty it was just as if she wore nothing at all.

That her perfume was beginning to take effect he realized. Why wasn't he trying to push her away anymore? Her lips were avid — kissing his eyes, his chin, his throat — her fingers kept kneading at the small of his back.

"But Diane," he gasped. "This can't — you're too young. You're only a child!"

"A child?" she murmured, her small nose nuzzling under his chin. "*Bon dieu!* I knew my first lover at twelve and since then — I have had others — many of them."

To the ultimate depths of his being, Tim was horrified. How could any girl talk like this? Worst of all was the realization that she probably wasn't lying.

Diane's blouse had slipped down from narrow shoulders; in this half-light she seemed all at once not so childlike.

"Why do you lie to me, Diane?" He felt his voice thicken. "You *must* be more than fourteen. Tell me so — I — I — need to think — "

For the first time in many months the barriers of his self-restraint began to crack.

Diane's softness surged against his chest, her lips became voraciously tender.

"Entertain no fears, *mon amant*," she breathed, "I will give you no heirs. My *cocote* knows ways."

Tim was unspeakably repelled. "Don't say such awful things."

"One must remain practical," her voice came to him through the twilight, "even during *une affaire*."

She stood an arm's length away, great eyes burning, blouse slipped nearly to her hips.

"Teem! *Mon adoré*."

He couldn't hold back any longer; nature was too strong. He had started to catch her to him when Diane was knocked reeling to one side. A squalling fury pounced on her.

"Miserable imp from hell! Child of the devil! How dare you! How dare you interfere in my affairs?" Jeannette Dulac was not acting; she was fairly sobbing with outrage. "Why must you try to spoil my friendships? Is it not enough that you sleep with every pair of breeches that arouses your fancy?"

Jeannette had pinioned her sister by the hair and, holding her down on the settee, dealt her a series of stinging slaps.

Kicking, panting and weeping, Diane fought back. "Let me go, you fiend! Let me go, you miserable icicle!"

As they struggled about on the settee, legs waving on high, Tim started to intervene but another of Pa's adages restrained him. He could almost hear the old man saying, "A man gets slim thanks for interfering in another's family affairs."

Because she was heavier, Jeannette succeeded in throwing her slighter sister down. Instantly she pulled up Diane's skirts and began to spank her with a slipper wrenched from her own foot.

Every time the leather struck her bare flesh, Diane wriggled, emitted a furious wail.

Diane soon got free and darted across the pergola, hissing like a scalded cat as she rubbed her martyred buttocks.

"I'll kill you for this! I'll poison you!"

Tim thought she sounded as if she meant it.

"You will not! You are too stupid," Jeannette panted, pushing hair from her eyes. "Else how would I know you were here? Oh, you silly, shameless little baggage. The next time you attempt to interfere with my affairs, I'll scratch your cheeks to ribbons. Now get out!"

"We shall see." Diane gave her sister a look dripping with venom, then managed a tearful smile at Tim as she hurried by.

Once the gate at the far end of the garden had slammed shut, Jeannette ran to Tim, bursting into a wild flood of tears.

"Oh, Teem, Teem, what can you think of us here in Saint-Domingue?"

He led the weeping girl to a chair and, kneeling beside her, tried to restrain the spasmodic heaving of her shoulders.

"Please — please don't, Jeannette," he pleaded. "It makes me feel so wretched. I think I understand — "

Her sobs diminished, but she clung to him tighter than ever. "Oh, Teem, please take me from this dreadful island. Save me! Take me away before I become like Diane — and all the rest."

Les Délices

Through whirling clouds of dust raised by six *maréchaussées* forming his escort, Tim made out an imposing stone structure situated halfway up a steep hillside. Clustered below the mansion house were a sugar factory, distillery, overseers' quarters, slave barracks, stables and barns enough to make a miniature village.

[331]

He glimpsed a long driveway lined with royal palms. What had once been elaborate formal gardens swept off to either side. Now these gardens were brown as a winter pasture in Rhode Island.

Here as elsewhere, evidences of a terrific drought were inescapable. Emaciated blacks, retaining barely enough strength to raise skinny hands, had occupied the ditches all the way out from Cap François. Among other grim recollections Tim recalled the sight of a human leg dangling from a post set up at a crossroad.

"It is part of a slave who has for the third time run away," explained a sergeant in command of the *maréchaussée*. Occasionally he would rein in to ride beside the curricle. "The first time a slave runs away, he earns a whipping and loses one of his ears. On the next occasion, the fugitive is generally hamstrung. For a third offense, he is cut into four pieces. His head is mounted before the nearest police station and his limbs are dispatched to the four corners of his parish."

Thank God, this dreadful journey was at an end. Using a lace-trimmed handkerchief, Tim flicked layers of white dust from the splendid coat of burnt-orange colored satin with which Jeannette had equipped him. Tim guessed the garment must belong to one or the other of the Dulac sons who were finishing their education in France.

Tim felt at once ridiculous yet pleased with his silk stockings, white breeches and gaudy green silk waistcoat. Hardest of all to stomach were pumps boasting high red heels and large paste buckles. The Dulacs had been hard put to find pumps large enough. Genuine diamonds flashed on the bosom of his shirt and it was only because he had flatly refused that he was not wearing a dozen finger rings instead of only two.

As the cavalcade turned in off the main road, a bell commenced to clang and clatter. Up at the great mansion house, servants could be seen running in all directions.

The sergeant ordered his men to dismount. The *maréchaussées* dusted themselves and wiped off the blue and silver housings of their saddles, then straightened bows tying their powdered hair. They were mulattoes, nearly all of them — required to serve for two years without pay.

Stiffly Tim descended from the two-wheeled curricle and followed a white major-domo in an elaborate blue and gold livery into a spacious antechamber.

Crimanently! If the folks back in Newport could see him in these macaroni fol-de-rols, in silk stockings with red clocks on them, in high-heeled pumps and sporting diamond and ruby finger rings! He'd like to see the faces of the Second Company if they ever caught him like this.

Suddenly, he couldn't keep from grinning. It seemed a fellow had to do some mighty queer things in making a living, nowadays.

The Rhode Islander was not kept waiting long, and to his surprise, the Chevalier de Labouisse gave him a warm welcome.

"My dear M. Bennett," he cried in tolerably good English, "one is delighted to receive you, positively overwhelmed with pleasure. You could not have called at a moment more thoroughly opportune. It rounds out my party most happily. You must spend the night. You will enjoy making the acquaintance of my good neighbor, M. de Cockburn, and of the Chevalier de Cohars who commands our ship of the line now lying at Cap François."

If Les Délices was unusual, its owner was no less so. The Chevalier de Labouisse must be nearing sixty. Those deep lines about his restless eyes and sloping forehead left no doubt of that. And most of his teeth were false. In his coat of glaring yellow, the Creole's complexion looked as sallow as that of a mulatto. Paint had been applied to the chevalier's cheeks and to his brows as well as to his lips.

By now Tim had learned that in Saint-Domingue a fellow couldn't get down to brass tacks right away. All this waiting and formality was a silly waste of time, but you had to put up with it. He judged it might be smart to butter up the king's lieutenant a bit before he got 'round to talking about the *permis*.

In a sitting room two other gentlemen were throwing dice over a little green table. Watching them stood three white women clad in scandalously scanty fashion.

The host's high heels clicked briskly over the parquet floor. "De Cockburn," he called, "I present to you Monsieur Bennett. He represents a new species. He is an American, one of those rebellious, indigestible rascals who are giving our dear English cousins such bellyaches."

De Cockburn, a huge, bloated individual with pimples standing out all over his face and neck, languidly lifted a lorgnette, surveyed Tim from head to foot:

"How do you do?" he lisped. "Can you play ninepins? Good. You will be privileged to witness a new form of the game I have invented for the benefit of my friend de Labouisse."

The host bowed to his other guest. "The Chevalier de Cohars."

"An American, eh?" In a blue-and-white naval uniform, the captain of *la Dedaigneuse* seemed like a lean and vicious greyhound among overfed lap dogs. "Then you must be one of those beastly anti-Royalists?"

Feeling like a fish out of water, Tim reddened. "We don't have any party except the liberty party. In America we're not anti-Royalist, unless the king ignores our rights."

"Since when do subjects question the divine right?"

"Since the Stamp Act," Tim replied sturdily.

De Cohars turned a hawklike face. "There are no nobles among your sort, I take it?"

"No. Although Lord Stirling and a few others stayed with us, most noblemen in America went over to the king's party."

The girls had been appraising Tim with obvious approbation. They hung in the background, but when the host nodded, a pretty blonde with faintly protuberant eyes came gliding across the floor. She had a pair of dimples that were fascinating to watch.

"This is Adrienne," de Labouisse said carelessly. "She's a good wench, in a bed or out of it. Come along. Our friends wish to finish their game."

"Bah!" snarled the captain of *la Dédaigneuse*. "You Creole savages call a mere thousand livres a throw gambling? At Versailles my lackeys risk as much.

"Come here, Héloïse," he barked at one of the girls. "Kiss every card in the deck. My luck continues incredibly bad."

It astonished Tim that the whole group should so complacently tolerate this nobleman's patent contempt. Why, de Cockburn and de Labouisse were actually smirking!

As the host led Tim and the blonde girl onto a terrace, Tim's blood was congealed by a series of piercing screams. They appeared to emanate from a group of whitewashed buildings at some little distance from the house.

"Good God, sir," Tim burst out, "somebody is being killed!"

"Not killed," twittered Labouisse. "Hurt, perhaps, but not killed."

The girl Adrienne slipped a heavily powdered arm through Timothy's. "There was an unfortunate occurrence yesterday. A mass poisoning. Today come the punishments."

"Poison?"

"Yes," sighed the king's lieutenant, tendering a tortoise-shell snuff box. "These blacks of mine are so lazy. They are fearful that I will grow coffee in addition to sugar."

"But what has that to do with the poisoning?"

"They murder one another so that I will be forced to purchase more slaves. By using my profit in that fashion, I will be rendered unable to expand and so, possibly, require more work of them."

De Labouisse frowned. "On this occasion, one has had to be a trifle severe. This plot has so far cost me a dozen valuable slaves. I will show you."

There was nothing for Tim to do but follow his host's gorgeous figure down a path lined with lemon trees. Brilliants, garnishing his heels, flashed as he led the way, sniffing now and then a yellow rose. The girl Adrienne sidled along beside Tim. She rolled her eyes at him.

"You like me, monsieur?"

"Why, yes, ma'am; you certainly are pretty."

The girl's painted features relaxed and she patted his hand. "Bon! Then Adrienne will be your *amie* while you visit. Money? I don't care about money. How Héloïse can put up with an old boar like that de Cockburn, I will never understand. *Pfui!* His breath is enough to sicken a mule. And as for the chevalier, one cannot know for sure, but I think he is *un vrai vicieux.*"

"But, but — " Tim stammered. "What will — ?"

"Hector de Labouisse? Oh la! la! That is why we are at Les Délices. Madeleine, Héloïse and I entertain his friends. Hector will have nothing but of the purest black."

"Here we are," the host announced. "This is the hospital. You must see what damage the miscreants have caused."

In a dark, stifling-hot room some fifteen or eighteen Negroes of varying age and sex lay quite naked on pallets of dried sugar-cane tops. At first glance Tim knew that eight or nine of the victims were quite dead. Others, lying in dreadfully contorted positions, were barely able to keep their skinny chests in motion. Another group writhed endlessly, whimpered in some Congo dialect.

"This, Monsieur Bennett, is the result of a little ground bamboo added to a bowl of *tassau* and rice."

Here was a sight he could never forget, Tim thought.

"See how the poor creatures suffer," de Labouisse invited. But to the Rhode Islander there was little of genuine pity in his tone.

His painted features animated, de Labouisse took Tim's arm, talked with a confidential air. "At the investigation I learned that one 'village' had managed to poison the other."

"Village?"

"We subdivide the quarters into what are called 'villages.' "

Steadily, the king's lieutenant advanced towards that small square structure from which continued screams arose.

"I forced the guilty villagers to cast lots," de Labouisse continued. "Every fifth person is made to pay for this dreadful crime."

"But," Tim protested, "how can you do that? Innocent folks would have to suffer for something they hadn't done!"

"Undoubtedly!" sighed the Creole. "But what can one do? These rogues are such master liars it would be impossible to arrive at the true criminal, even had one the energy to devote to such a task. As for me, I divided such malefactors into three groups. One is condemned to suffer branding and the loss of both ears. This has already been attended to. The second, to severe flogging. That is what is going on now."

Following a refreshment of champagne and iced cakes, the Chevalier de Labouisse appeared smiling, rubbing his hands. He went immediately to de Cockburn.

Forming a separate group, the house slaves, infinitely better dressed and fed, were assembled along a stone wall. They eyed the congregated field hands with open contempt.

What looked like an old sail was spread over a plot at the end of a long alley of lawn which, miraculously, had been kept smooth and green. At no point did this canvas rise higher than a foot and a half above the earth.

At the opposite end of the alley some chairs had been placed beneath a scarlet canopy. A table laden with pipes, cigars, fruits and various liquors lent a tournament atmosphere.

Tim noted that parallel white lines indicated what looked like a ninepin ground. Save that the alley had a gentle downward slope towards the canvas, the arrangements differed not at all from the regular game.

"Do you play?" demanded de Labouisse.

Tim nodded. "After a fashion. We used to have a pitch at college."

"Capital! Then you and I will form one side, de Cockburn and the Chevalier, the other." So saying he opened a chest, brought out of it what was undoubtedly a ten-pound roundshot.

"Eh?" De Cohars stared. "What's this?"

"An improvement, *mon cher ami*. You will agree presently," smiled the king's lieutenant stripping off his coat. When the others did the same, Tim followed suit.

"Your side must win," Adrienne whispered. "It would make the other girls furious to lose. We have already put up ten livres apiece."

From the sable throng rose a low, inexpressibly dolorous undertone. The guards straightened, peered this way and that. Tim rubbed his eyes; he was almost sure that something beneath had moved the old sail.

"Eight- or ten-pound ball?"

"I imagine I might do better with an eight," Tim answered. "You had best lead off, too."

"Good," smiled de Labouisse. "Very well, Jules!"

The overseer beckoned forward a mulatto guard and, bending, they each grabbed a corner of the tarpaulin and pulled it back. From the slaves rose a deep groan.

Arranged at the end of the long slope and in the conventional V pattern of ninepins, the heads of nine living Negroes were exposed. Buried up to their chins and with turf tamped tight about their necks, they could only roll their eyes. Gags stopped their mouths.

"The prisoners I condemned to death," explained M. de Labouisse. "You bowl first, de Cockburn, this is your invention. By the bye, you are sure their heads will — ?"

" — Like so many eggshells," grunted de Cockburn handling his round-shot.

A next to impossible situation for Tim was relieved when the Chevalier de Cohars gave one amazed glance at the spectacle, turned on his heel and stalked back to the tent saying in frigid accents:

"His Majesty's naval officers do not make a sport of executing felons. Really, after a few years, you Creoles become too much like your property."

Tim cast the captain of *la Dédaigneuse* a bleak smile.

De Cohars said, "You look as disgusted as I feel, monsieur. Let us leave these gentlemen to their — er — sport. I feel a sudden need of champagne."

"Let them go, Hector," snapped de Cockburn quite unruffled. "Takes a real Saint-Dominguais to play this game."

Long before they regained the house, a low and ominous wailing arose among the assemblage.

When Tim got back to Les Délices, he had to run for the lavatory.

When Anatole Dulac learned of Tim's complete success with the king's lieutenant, he sent a slave running to fetch Claude Prenet and dinner that evening approached banquet proportions: seafood, ortolans, guinea fowl and a host of native vegetables, salads and desserts.

Even Diane forgot to sulk.

M. Prenet raised his glass. "*Mes amis,* a toast for the beautiful little *Narragansett!* May her first cruise prove all that we hope!"

"Don't leave out the subsequent ones," called Dulac, his huge stomach indented by the table's edge.

Jeannette added quite gravely, " — And may *le bon dieu* guard and watch over her master."

The Private-Armed Brig Narragansett

To see the brig's batteries finally mounted was a great satisfaction to everyone. The *Narragansett*'s hands could not leave off admiring her eight guns: four each of long eighteens and sturdy nine-pounders.

The cannon looked quite gay, painted as they were, gray with a jaunty scarlet band about their muzzles and boasting a gold stripe around their pomelions.

"French nonsense," snapped Captain Loammi Freebody. "And will you look? Them idjits have painted a big red N on all the gun tackle blocks!" But he was pleased all the same.

Certainly Messrs. Pliarne, Prenet and Dulac had made a thorough job of marking. All the ammunition chests had had the letter of marque's name painted on them, and an N was burned into each of the powder ladles, muskets, blunderbusses and musketoons.

In an unprecedented burst of generosity, the outfitters presented Tim with four fine swivels, peculiarly deadly weapons which could be mounted on the bulwarks and trained fore and aft. Enemy boarders attempting to cross the rail would wither under a shower of lead.

Preoccupied and busy with a familiar round of inventories and inspections, Tim had worked from the first ray of light. Stripped to a cotton jersey and linen breeches, he went up to the quarterdeck.

"Well, Captain, how did the recruiting party make out last night?"

Freebody shrugged. "Well, sir, Mr. Crabtree secured our complement. Mostly in free blacks, though."

Tim nodded. "That's all right. I notice the pure blacks take to discipline better than mulattoes or low-class French. But I don't like it much."

The brig's company now numbered ninety hands. Little more than half of them hailed from the American colonies. Around ten gunners' mates and gun captains were ex-British men-of-war's men.

Now more than ever, he and Freebody lamented the untimely death of Captain Griffin and nearly half the crew of the *Narragansett*. They had perished in agony after eating some tainted dried beef imported from Hispaniola, the Spanish end of the island, when the drought had got very bad.

Because of the necessity of securing properly stamped clearance papers and of taking aboard such last-minute supplies as sea turtles, fruits, fowl and a long boat's load of pigs, Tim did not set out for shore until almost nine of the evening.

As Tim's gig threshed by under the stern of the great, glowing *la Dédaigneuse*, voices and music floated down. Dozens of lanterns glowed high overhead, and through the open gun ports Tim, Loammi Freebody and the men from the *Narragansett* could see hairy members of the battle-ship's crew sprawling in their hammocks, gaming or repairing some item of equipment.

For all the ornate gilding and carved stern galleries, from the liner came fetid odors of stale sweat, rank tobacco and bilge water. Crimanently! She surely made the *Narragansett* seem like mighty small potatoes by comparison.

"Long success to the *Narragansett!*" shouted the harbor master.

"Down with the lobsterbacks!" countered Freebody, and the whole house rang to the cheer that followed. It was certain that these French and Creoles nursed a deep fear and hatred of the Royal Navy. Character-istically, it never occurred to Tim that these foreigners were honestly fond of his cheerful, plain and aboveboard ways, that they might be genuinely hopeful for his success.

A grizzled old Breton who had supplied most of the carpenters came over presently and under his breath said:

"A word of warning, Mr. Bennett. Only today I have received private intelligence from Jamaica. My agent there warns that the English admiral has learned of our activities. This admiral is dispatching from Port Royal a small squadron of cruisers and a heavy frigate."

Tim listened hard over the babble of voices, wished Loammi Freebody could hear this. He found that more and more he was forced to rely on the old privateersman's experience. Well, he intended to learn, to become more than a sort of glorified supercargo on his own ship.

"That's worth knowing. Where are they?"

"Between Cap de la Pristelle, Cuba and Great Inagua." The Breton winked. "In putting to sea one would be astute to avoid the Windward Channel."

Tim nodded his thanks, then asked, "There are English agents here in town?"

"This port teems with them," the Breton assured him. "Your compatriots will be wise to keep a close mouth. A careless word and they will find themselves prisoners."

Off Turks' Island

Bracing himself against the slow, steady roll of the *Narragansett*, Timothy Bennett watched Loammi Freebody make an entry in the brig's log book:

June 27, 1776. This day fine. Moderate breeze from N-NW. POSITION: Longitude 70° 4 min west. Latitude 22° 7 min north. Course: W by S. REMARKS: 9:15 a.m.: Overtook & made Prize of the *Swallow*, schooner, 90 tons, Arthur Watson, Master. Out of Lisbon for Montego Bay, Jamaica. Raised his topsails at dawn. Gave immediate chace. Prize proved very slow. When I fired a gun he came into wind. Haul'd down his Colours at 7:30 a.m. Ten men to secure the Prize. Schooner's lading was found to consist in the Main of Sheffield goods, calicoes, canvas, chinaware, music Boxes, Harnesses, & sev'ral tuns of Oporto Wine. Ship & cargo are Assur'd in the am't of £6500 sterling. Vessel seems well Found. Should fetch a handsome price. Discovering share to Philip Hull, ordinary seaman, who first spied prize. Owner hath ordered prize master to make for Savannah in the Colony of Georgia.

"Not a bad start, Mr. Bennett, not at all bad," Captain Freebody grunted, carefully sanding his entry. "Could wish that some o' the hands showed more keenness, though."

Three days later, Captain Freebody made another entry in the *Narragansett's* log book:

June 30, 1776

2:45 p.m.
Have just rais'd topsails of a large Brig.
Have hoisted Spanish colours and am giving chace. Stranger brig refuses to show colours but hath shap'd a course for Gt. Inagua.

4:05 p.m.
Hull of the Chace now above the horizon. Am closing in fast. Crew restive over large size of Stranger.

5:50 p.m.
Chace is abandoning Boats & cutting away Anchors in effort to better Speed. Continue to overhaul. Hope to Close with Brig before Darkness prevents.

Having completed this entry, Captain Freebody stumped back on deck. With all sails set, the *Narragansett* was fairly hissing over a bright blue sea with her topsails turning gold in the late afternoon sunlight. By God, this was just like the good old days of '61 and '62!

Freebody found his owner pacing steadily back and forth at the break of the quarterdeck and studying the set of the straining canvas. Below, powder monkeys were sanding the deck, stowing loose gear and otherwise preparing for action.

Long since, tompions had been withdrawn from the *Narragansett*'s cannon; roundshot clinked and flashed in all the racks; slow matches, lying on tubs of sand, gave off small blue tendrils of smoke.

Right now the crew, in order to reduce the havoc of flying splinters, was busily lashing hammocks filled with bedding along the tops of the bulwarks. Others were rigging fine chains to supplement vital halyards, braces and stays.

It was a glorious afternoon with a bright blue sky sketching glowing colors in the sea. Quantities of silvery flying fishes kept springing from the wave crests and skittering along parallel to the free-running letter of marque.

If nothing happened, Mr. Bennett would make a good privateersman before long, Loammi Freebody reflected. Under stress, he was calm and foresighted; just like his pa. He was a born fighter, but he might meet up with trouble if he didn't slow down a mite in his judgments.

From its rack beside the binnacle, Loammi Freebody took a heavy, oldfashioned brass spyglass and trained it on the chase. Hum! A fine, strong vessel. Why should she run? A ruse? Or was she really unarmed?

"Well, Captain, and what is she?"

"Might be one of His Majesty's transports," Freebody suggested. "Or maybe another private-armed vessel."

"What makes you think so?" Tim was trying to subdue a fierce excitement.

"The chase is better painted than the average merchantmen."

"Any guns?"

"She shows ports for a broadside of six cannon," the sea captain announced, eye glued to spyglass. "But, being as the lids ain't raised, there's no tellin' whether she's armed or not."

"Mr. Bennett, sir," a voice hailed from the deck. The boatswain shuffled forward, cap in hand. Respectfully enough, he knuckled his forelock. "Mr. Bennett, a lot of us don't like the look of the chase. She's mighty tall and might prove too tough to handle. Hadn't you better sheer off a bit? Feel her out at long range?"

"No! Get back to your post," Tim ordered in the voice he'd used at the siege. "Leave it again and I'll — "

" — Talk easy, sir," Freebody begged. "Remember these ain't no men-o'-war's men."

" — Dock you your share," Tim concluded lamely. He was angry, though, at the impudence of the fellow.

Freebody was quick to capitalize on the boatswain's sullen retreat. "Number one gun, port battery prepare to fire."

The crew shuffled to their posts, the gunport of the port bow chaser was raised and the piece, a long eighteen, was run out.

"Fire!"

The letter of marque shuddered as a great cloud of gray-white smoke went whipping off to leeward. A cable's length ahead of the fleeing brig rose a silvery jet of water. Simultaneously, a British jack climbed to the stranger's signal halyard.

A low cry arose from the *Narragansett*'s gun crews when the chase yawed a little and let fly with a pair of cannons. Her shot screamed by, punching harmless holes in the foretopsail.

"Very light," Freebody snapped. "Reg'lar bean shooters. Let's hope he ain't bein' 'cute and is drawin' us in close for a real broadside."

Encouraged, the *Narragansett*'s crew reloaded, and this time an eighteen-pound shot hit the stranger amidships. Everybody yelled like mad to see a cloud of yellow splinters go aflying. Stung, the chase let fly again. A six-pound ball struck the taffrail, made a loud crackling noise.

To Tim it seemed as if someone had dealt him a hard whack across the forehead. Half stunned, he reeled, clapping a hand to his forehead. Blood began pouring in torrents down his face. The hot sticky stuff filled, blinded his right eye and clouded his left.

A steadying arm went about his waist and he heard Freebody's staccato voice saying, "Hold hard. 'Tain't nought but a splinter graze."

Tim, steadying himself on a back stay, could hear the port broadside let go with a thunderous report. Using the heel of one hand, he cleared an eye and, with a great lifting sensation, watched the brown-and-blue-painted chase come into the wind.

Jerkily, her ensign sank out of sight behind the bulwarks.

The brig proved to be H. M. S. *Growler*, supply vessel, out of Cork for His Majesty's Dock Yard at Port Royal. The minute he set foot to her deck, Tim understood the brig's feeble defense. She was practically unarmed since her armament consisted of four puny six-pounders, little larger than signal guns.

Long and loud, the supply vessel's beefy, red-faced captain cursed and raged at an admiralty which had sworn that no armed American vessel cruised the sea. Sputtering, he stamped about, called the New Englanders pirates and swore he'd live to see his captors swing from execution dock.

He even shook a fist at the rattlesnake flag displayed above his Union Jack.

Not since that November night on which he had met Lucy in the Congress Tavern had Timothy Bennett's heart been lifted so high. It didn't seem real, somehow, to find himself on the quarterdeck of a fat prize taken by his own letter of marque! Yet there rocked the *Narragansett*, less than two hundred yards away, with her topsails backed and her cannon run out. Captain Freebody was taking no chances.

The *Growler*, one hundred twenty tons, proved to be a brand-new vessel. When an army quartermaster sullenly surrendered bills of lading and the cargo manifest, Dr. Boyd scanned them, uttered a piercing whistle.

"Faith, Mr. Bennett, ye must indeed be fortune's favorite! If their lordships of the admiralty had studied to please ye, the rascals couldn't have selected better. Holy Mary! Will yez listen to this?"

Running a stubby finger down the manifest, he read aloud:

> "2,500 pair leggings
> 2,500 pair shoes
> 900 stands of Muskets, King's Arm
> 110 tents, canvas
> 4,800 cartouche Boxes, leather
> 1,500 Bayonets
> 15 barrels of 3F gunpowder
> 4 pieces field ordnance."

When Tim thought of the Continental Army's crying need for such supplies, the golden splinters sparkled in his eyes.

"At a rough guess, Doctor, how much do you think such a cargo will fetch?" He was forgetting the ache of his bandaged head, the burning of the three-inch gash across his forehead.

Dr. Boyd couldn't guess, but Silas Turner, the prize master appointed by Freebody, turned leathery features lit by the deepening sunset. "Mr. Bennett, if this here cargo dunt fetch nigh fifty thousand pounds sterling, I'll eat my wig!"

With Great Inagua a low-lying black smear on the western horizon, the two vessels cruised on parallel courses all night in order that certain choice items of plunder and the iron-bound chest might be transferred to the *Narragansett*.

Just as dawn was sketching lovely turquoise and crimson patterns across the sky, the *Growler* dipped her colors in salute, swung her yards about and departed on her way to Philadelphia.

Locked securely in the transom of Timothy Bennett's cabin was the contents of the quartermaster's chest — nearly twenty-two thousand pounds sterling that would never serve as pay for His Majesty's armed forces in Jamaica.

Nothing was pleasanter for Tim than to heed Loammi Freebody's earnest advice that the *Narragansett* return with all speed to Cap François. Recalling what Mr. Turner had said about privateersmen and their ways, Tim judged it would be wise to remove temptation at the first possible instant.

Privateersmen

Timothy Bennett found there was plenty to occupy him once the *Narragansett* was at sea. The gun crews needed an amazing amount of drill, and under Loammi Freebody's irascible tutelage he was mastering the fundamentals of navigation.

One thing gave him concern. Ever since that brush with H. M. S. *Growler*, the crew kept looking at him as if he were something unusual. Whenever he addressed the petty officers, they seemed markedly reserved, suspicious of him.

On mulling over this impression, he set it down to a lack of confidence in his judgment, or did they lack confidence in their own abilities? Naturally, a crew composed of two races and three nationalities would find it hard to develop into a smoothly operating unit, yet they were no different from most privateer crews.

He frequently encouraged Carradine, the gunner, and Hawley, the boatswain, by reminding them that in the old French war Loammi Freebody had been a successful captain and had always brought his command home safe and comparatively undamaged.

Captain Freebody had wanted to touch at Môle Saint-Nicholas for the needed seamen but he had forgot all about that when the lookouts sighted the topsails of a British frigate crawling along the horizon to leeward.

Tim figured it would be smart to shape a course for Savannah through Crooked Island Passage. First he would sell his cargo of island goods; second, the failure or success of the *Swallow* in reaching safety would become known; and, most important, the needed hands would be American.

The *Narragansett* was clipping along under a fine brisk southeaster, her canvas full and the water flying from her bows in a sparkling white smother when Tim was roused by a long-drawn hail of "Sail ho!"

"Where away?" Freebody demanded through his speaking trumpet.

"Six points off port bow, sir," replied the lookout.

"Masthead, there! How does she sail?"

"Can't tell, sir," came the reply over the whining of tackles and the rhythmic creaking of the freshly painted yellow yards. "She's hull down. Deck! Deck! I spy another sail!" the lookout shouted.

"Where away?"

[343]

"Four points off our port bow, sir."

Men came tumbling up from below, crowded the rigging and lined the bulwarks. A prize? Probably a couple of sluggish merchantmen. More fat pickings. Everybody envied the lookout. He would get two deserving shares for this day's work if the yonder vessels proved fair prizes.

At the end of twenty minutes even those on deck could make out a pair of tiny white specks 'way off to port.

When for a third time the lookout called, "Sail ho!" over the *hush-hushing* of the seas alongside, all hands began to look serious.

Captain Freebody merely ordered the quartermaster to hold the brig on her course.

"Where you going?" Tim queried.

"To the main-top, Mr. Bennett. Figger it's time I take a look my own self."

Soon it became unmistakable that two small vessels were being chased by a large, black-painted schooner.

Freebody turned, wiped wind-started water from his eyes. "Mr. Bennett, it's my judgment we had best put about and steer clear."

"And why, pray? It appears to me that, one way or another, we may take a prize."

His gaunt figure raking across the sky, Freebody set his jaw to an obstinate angle. "Can't say for sure, Mr. Bennett, but I don't like the look of it. That schooner looks turrible spick and span."

"And what of that? She looks no heavier than us."

"Mr. Bennett, that's as may be." He looked desperately uneasy as again he leveled the spyglass.

Tim said, studying the fleeing vessels, "Those look like the kind of snows we build 'round home." Hair, whipping about his forehead, stung the red scar. "They're being chased, Captain. The schooner acts like a picaroon. If she is, I don't intend to stand by and watch them taken."

Freebody said after a long pause, "Mr. Bennett, yonder schooner don't look like a picaroon to me. Too clean. Buccaneers and such are dirty as pigpens." He closed the spyglass with a decisive click. "It is my bounden opinion, sir, that yonder cruises a British bulldog — a reg'lar cruiser o' the Royal Navy." He braced himself against the guard rail of the top. "Mr. Bennett, there ain't but one thing to do and that's to come about, and do it all-fired quick. That schooner's coming up hand over fist!"

Timothy Bennett shook his head. "We will not run away, Captain Freebody. Why do we mount eight carriage guns? What have we been drilling gun crews for? Eternal blazes, man, we are at war with England! It's my conception of duty that we should help those snows escape. You may clear for action, Captain."

"I ain't never questioned an order of yours before, so credit me this time," Freebody pleaded in an undertone. "The hands won't stand for this. For God's sake order the ship about!"

[344]

All along the bulwarks, the crew, in evident uneasiness, were watching the fleeing merchantmen come rushing straight towards the *Narragansett* in a panic-stricken search for protection. One of them was flying a blue-and-white flag; the other, a yellow flag. As yet, the brown-and-yellow-painted schooner was showing no colors whatsoever.

"That's a bulldog!" yelled one of the men. "The *Niobe*, I seen her in St. Kitts last winter."

"Will you clear for action, Captain?" Tim rasped. "Or must I dismiss you?"

This was his owner talking. Habit won. "Aye, aye, sir," Freebody grunted, face like a rock. "But on your head be it!"

Though the bosun's pipe kept shrilling, calling the men to quarters, they only milled excitedly about the deck. By the foot of the quarterdeck ladders a small crowd was gathering, shaking their fists, yelling:

"We'll not fight a bulldog." "She'll blow us to blazes!"

" 'Tain't right. 'Tain't in the articles."

"Get to quarters, damn you!" Tim snatched out his cutlass. "Get the ship back on her course. Sparks! Carradine! Johnson! Get your matches going."

What in God's name ailed these fellows? He couldn't understand it. Why should the very mention of a regular war vessel scare them into spasms? Why, the *Niobe* was obviously smaller.

"Raise our flag!" Tim ordered in the frantic hope that the gesture might inspire discipline. Hardly had the rattlesnake flag straightened out to the freshening southerly breeze than the schooner fired a gun. White ensigns were broken out from her mastheads.

Sullenly, purposefully, the *Narragansett*'s crew came running aft with Carradine, the gunner, out in front.

"Now, Mr. Bennett," Freebody invited acidly, "suppose you handle this?"

Leveling a boarding pistol, Tim shouted, "First man puts foot to this quarterdeck, I'll see hanged for a mutineer." Savagely, he pleaded with them. "See that nearest vessel? She's showing Rhode Island colors. The other's from Massachusetts. We ain't going to stand by and let an enemy smaller than us make prizes of them under our noses!"

"To blazes with 'em," roared Carradine. "We can't fight a king's cruiser. She'll shoot us to bits." He climbed halfway up the quarterdeck ladder, spoke threateningly. "You order this vessel about right away, Mr. Bennett, or there'll be trouble."

Tim realized it was no use. There was nothing to do but run.

"You ain't got the sense of a bedbug," snarled Carradine, helping to grind down the wheel.

Having turned in her tracks, the *Narragansett* commenced to gather headway and started after the snows. Numbly, Tim watched the topmen lie out on the yards, setting every inch of canvas that might draw. The masts groaned, stays creaked and the main boom bent under pressure of the wind.

At half a mile's range the cruiser opened fire and her first shot raised a terrific geyser of water not twenty yards short of the *Narragansett's* stern. Spray fell over the quarterdeck. Solemnly, Dr. Boyd spat in return.

Tim snatched up a leather speaking trumpet. "We can't get away without a fight. Get to your stations, you seamen. Look! The schooner carried only four guns to her broadside. We can lick her if you'll half try."

"No! No! Haul down the flag! Come into the wind," yelled terrified voices.

The deck was crowded with figures running aimlessly about, like hens threatened by a hawk. The few men who did try to man the *Narragansett's* guns were chased away, showered with curses and belaying pins.

The schooner's second shot plowed into the back of an ultramarine roller. Weeping with fury, Tim ran to the one cannon which had been loaded and run out. Rammer, sponger and ladle lay abandoned across its trail but the gunport lid was up and the recoil breeching was adjusted.

"Find me a lighted match," Tim yelled. "We'll show these yel — "

He got no further, for high overhead sounded a thunderous crack. Boyd screamed and like a felled pine the main gaff came whirring down as a shot from the cruiser smashed its jaws to smithereens. Instantly a vast smother of flapping sailcloth blinded the quartermaster, choked the quarterdeck as the main topsail yard broke. Gradually the letter of marque lost way, began to roll.

"We'll fire one gun anyhow," Tim panted, and from his belt pulled the remaining pistol. He fired it full at the touch-hole of the long eighteen.

To see a British jack flying above his brig's rattlesnake flag sent a bitter taste into Tim's mouth. It seemed somehow unbelievable that the thought, worry and planning of these last weeks should so abruptly have come to nothing. And for no sound reason either; that was what hurt.

There had been no earthly reason why the *Narragansett*, shorthanded or not, shouldn't have been able to whip this paltry little cruiser.

To the depths of his soul, Tim Bennett felt sickened, utterly discouraged, and wholly disillusioned. Was there nothing true or dependable in all this world? Twice he'd put forth all his faith — in Lucy and in the *Narragansett*. Which had failed him, hurt him the more deeply, was a question.

He judged he would never be able to understand why the very sight of a royal cruiser was enough to shake the courage of his men. Freebody had been right, all right about this crew. Where lay an explanation for privateersmen's refusal to fight except for cash on the line?

A British prize crew, contemptuous of so spineless an exhibition, shackled the letter of marque's men hand and foot and, jeering, herded them down a ladder into the forehold. A pink-cheeked and arrogant young sub-lieutenant loftily condescended to accept the paroles of Tim, Dr. Boyd and Captain Freebody.

Dr. Boyd alone seemed to comprehend the measure of Tim's grief and bewilderment. Twice, thrice the little man patted his shoulder. "Ye've heard where they're sending us?"

"It can be to hell, for all I care," Tim growled. Every time he saw that neat brown-and-yellow schooner riding the waves but a few hundred yards to windward, he wanted to burst into a string of curses. She must be lighter than the *Narragansett* by twenty tons.

"'Tis into New Providence for condemnation proceedings," Dr. Boyd informed him. "Most likely they'll turn the crew onto the beach as usual and hold us for exchange. Though what they'd swap for me would be the divil of a poor soul!"

To New Providence once more?

There might have been far worse destinations. Fever-ridden Port Royal, for instance. Fervently Tim hoped the new governor of the Bahamas would recognize the validity of his letter of marque's commission. It would be no fun at all to be hanged for a pirate.

Rockcastle Creek, Kentucky

Mike Stoner's moccasins had sketched a series of black prints on the newly fallen snow. Desire Harmony could see them winding down among the beech trees on the far side of the ravine. There were other tracks among the bare sumac and blackberry bushes. Those of several rabbits, of a squirrel, and of course plenty of pug marks left by Snapper.

"That's a mighty fine term fer a bear dog," Sam Higsby had chuckled, fondling the great hound's pointed skull between his knees. "You should have seen him nippin' at that big she down to Crab Orchard bottom last November. Handiest dog I ever see."

Because she couldn't see through the cabin's window of oiled deer's bladder, Desire Harmony Higsby sought the door. Two brown figures could be clearly seen against the snow. Sam and Stoner, the big Pennsylvania Dutchman, were talking beside the carcass of a fresh-killed buck Sam had been flaying.

Sam, she saw, was bloodied, stripped to his doeskin undershirt, while Stoner was weighted down with traveling gear. A long rifle rested in the crook of his arm and he'd a dead rabbit slung to his belt.

She couldn't hear what they were saying because they conversed in the characteristically soft undertones of the frontier. Unless a timber beast got drunk, he would never raise his voice in the woods, or shout, or really laugh out loud.

[347]

Desire knew enough not to call from the doorway. A slender but sturdy figure in gray-brown linsey-woolsey, she crossed a cleared space in front of the fine long cabin Sam and Mike Stoner had put up last autumn. She wished she could wear moccasins, but she couldn't — she had worn heels too long. Her leg muscles ached every time she tried it.

"You will stay to supper, Mr. Stoner?" she invited. She hoped he would accept. It was something to get news, no matter how stale, and it was six weeks since she'd seen a new white face. Skanawati, the Catawba trapper who worked the valleys to the south, would stop by every week or so and sit picking his vermin before the fire a while, but he could talk only a little English and seemed shy of her.

Stoner clawed off a squirrel fur cap. The hair was worn off it on the sides and it was yellowed with grease above the ears.

"Ach, Mrs. Higsby, dot vould I admire," he rumbled from the depths of a shaggy yellow beard, "but I vant I should reach Flat Lick by der moonrise."

What had caused the Dutchman to come so far out of his way — all of fifteen miles off the Warrior's Path? A small stab of anxiety stung Desire's heart.

"Is — there isn't any Indian trouble?"

"*Nein!*" The giant grinned, unslinging his war bag. "All has been still since dot Chief Pluggy got beat so bad at McClelland's Station der end of December." He smiled, teeth gleaming in the depths of his beard. "Und der leetle girl, she iss vell?"

"Oh, yes, thriving. She grows so fast I venture she will match you for size in a short time," Desire laughed, settling a plaid shawl tighter about her shoulders.

"I pring her somedings ven from der settlements I come back," the giant promised. *Gott!* What a beautiful woman! Her eyes and those shadows under them. She was too pretty for the frontier, even if she was strong and willing.

"Really you must stay, Mr. Stoner. We are just about to have a bowl of sagamite. Eve has made a fresh batch of pone today, too."

Stoner shook his head so strongly that long yellow strands of hair mingling with the fringes at his shoulder swayed.

Prettily, Desire passed an arm through Stoner's, led him indoors. "Well, you must at least take along some of Eve's buckwheat souens. She made some this morning."

Sam whistled Snapper in, lest he take to feasting on the deer's head. He slapped the giant between his shoulders. "I'll give you that buck's tongue if you want it."

Stoner was both flattered and pleased. Along the frontier few greater delicacies than a deer's tongue were available. Even smoked, a tongue had lots more flavor than other unsalted meats.

As the three of them stamped into the gloom of the cabin, Stoner looked about and, seeing Sam's spare moccasins drying before the chimney piece, stroked his head in satisfaction.

"*Mein Gott*, Mrs. Higsby, already a home you haff made of it."

"It's prettier than an Indian lodge, anyhow," Desire smiled. She was very pleased that yesterday Sam had finished building a rough wooden barrier which, head-high, divided the cabin two-thirds and one-third. It wasn't nice to have Eve always underfoot and looking on. Now she did her cooking and sleeping at the far end.

"Please, Mr. Stoner, you are very sure there are no Indian signs?"

"Not vun," Stoner reassured her so earnestly that she believed him. "It vass aboudt somedings else I vass talking to Sam."

"Really?"

"Very soon ve in dis country a government must haff." His large head inclined gravely. "Me, Wide Mouth — Colonel Boone, I mean — und some odders t'ink Sam maybe should represent der district in der Virginia Congress."

In the act of smoothing the beaver blanket over Joanna's crib, Desire hesitated. "We — a part of Virginia?" she said. "Why, I thought Kentucky was going to be a separate state."

Sam, reaching up to the shelf over a rough sideboard, said, "All in good time we will be. You cain't raise a oak overnight. Virginny is in a fix to help us better than Caroliny or Pennsylvany." He lowered a big gray-stone jug that gurgled. "I always claimed 'tain't no harm to use a little help when it's needed."

No Indian trouble! Desire was so immeasurably relieved she felt like singing. Ever since Stoner's arrival she'd been wondering whether they'd have to pack their things and "fort-up" at Flat Lick.

She ran over and slipped an arm about her husband's narrow waist. "Sam, I do protest Mr. Stoner is quite right. You *should* run for office."

It was so obvious that Sam was the man for the position. He got along well with everybody along the frontier — with the settlers, the land company agents, the surveyors, the bullies, the faint-hearts, the young and the old; any stray Catawba, Cherokee or Creek who came hunting through the country generally made a beeline for the cabin of Tskili the Black Racer Snake, otherwise Sam Higsby.

Sam, Desire sensed, was settling down into a natural-born leader for those men and women who during the past year had come toiling up through the Cumberland Gap, following the tortuous Wilderness Road to the brand-new outposts of Harrodsburg and Boonesborough.

She was discovering in Sam an unsuspected caution and common sense. For all his ferocious talk, he hadn't taken her and the baby to live and to tremble 'way out on the exposed fringes of the new settlements.

Of course, if the Indians really rose, they were only a little better off here on Rockcastle Creek. The only thing that really bothered her was that Sam had made it plain he didn't intend to homestead. There was nothing of the farmer in him.

So long as game remained plentiful here in the foothills of the Cumberlands they would remain. He figured that if prices stayed anywhere near right — and they should, now that the United Colonies had become the free and independent United States — he'd make all the money they'd any use for. When the game got scarce, they could always pack up and move on.

When the giant Pennsylvania German lumbered over to bend curiously above Joanna's basket of hickory splints, she awoke, balled tiny fists and began screaming.

Sam roared, then gravely informed the squalling infant, "Mike sure ain't no ravin' beauty, but jest you wait, honeybird, till you spy a Shawnee in his feathers and war paint. Mike will look real handsome, then."

Desire emerged from behind the screen carrying some johnnycakes and buckwheat souens wrapped in a cone of birch bark. Her face glowed from the heat of the cooking fire and under her loose-fitting dress, her breasts, heavy with milk, rode easily.

"How are the settlers coming in?"

"Fast enough, ma'am," Stoner replied, running fingers through his greasy yellow hair. "Dot Dick Henderson, Colonel John Williams und fellows in der Transylvanian Company vould haff efferybody believe iss paradise in Kentucky."

"They ain't far wrong," Higsby said offering a bladder of smoking tobacco. "There's fine rich country 'round Boonesborough."

"*Ja?* But suppose Mkahday-wah-may-quah und his Shawnees say, 'Go away, dis iss our hunting land'?"

Desire, who had picked up the baby and was quieting her terrified howls, called over the clamor, "What's that about the Transylvania Company?"

Sam picked up the stone jug, eyed it an instant, but reluctantly put it back on the shelf. Wouldn't do for a feller to get to hankerin' for that red liquor too much.

"Next month maybe I come oudt, Sam, und ve go after bison. Last fall I found a lick down on der Rolling Fork. Bisons, dey vass thick like turds 'round a barn."

"A new lick?"

"*Ja.* I saw plenty of dem t'ings." Stoner's shaggy head inclined towards a huge fossil vertebra doing duty as a stool. "Ach, I nearly forgot! Colonel Boone say vhen he comes by he vants a talk mit you. He likes you, Sam, und he knows you to var haff been. Ho! Ho! Maybe he vants to make you captain, or maybe a general! Ho! Ho! Ho!" The giant's booming laughter again sent the baby off into fists of squalling.

Desire said in perfect gravity, "Really, Mr. Stoner, I don't see why Sam shouldn't be made at least a major. He can read and write, and that's more than most men along this frontier can say."

She kept her gaze fixed hard on Stoner; let him dare to laugh!

"*Ja,* a major anyhow. Vun t'ing, Sam. Chust vatch dese land yobblers don't skin you out of your land title."

The War Bag

Desire Harmony Higsby relaxed comfortably into the deerskin armchair Sam had rigged for her. She guessed she would never cease to marvel at her husband's skill with knife and hatchet. Why, with just those two implements he could approximate the products of a joiner or a carpenter.

He'd even made her a rough sideboard to hold her pitiful store of pewter plates — there would be plenty of them sometime — and their bed was the envy of everyone who saw it. Instead of slats or fir boughs, she and Sam rested on buffalo hides laced to a frame. Four buffalo calfskins served as a mattress and in winter they certainly kept the bed wonderfully warm — even if they did smell a little gamy.

Smiling, she undid the laces at the front of her dress and gave breast to the infant. Joanna gurgled, and clamping her lips down on the nipple, puffed like a little seal.

Out back of the cow shed, Sam and Mike Stoner were laughing like anything — the liquor must be going to work. That was good. Sam loved a good laugh.

Joanna was growing quite a bit of hair now, yellow-gold like John's. Soon there would be enough to support a ribbon. It had been a terrific surprise when Joanna had turned out to be Joanna and not John. She would have sworn the infant would be a boy.

Settling deeper in her chair, Desire Harmony Higsby let her thoughts ramble backwards to that August day on the Watauga when Joanna had been born. Mercy, how hot it had been! If it hadn't been for Sam she guessed she would have gone out of her mind, what with fear, pain and shame.

Right now, staring down at that small pink head in the bend of her arm, she knew she'd try all her life to prove how eternally grateful she was. Never once had Sam inquired into her life subsequent to the raid on Conanicut. Of course he must have wondered, but he expressed no curiosity as to who, or what, Joanna's father might have been. Soberly he had accepted her pregnancy as an accomplished fact.

Because of this she was glad that late next summer she would bear a child of Sam's own. This baby would serve to weld them inseparably.

Every day now she was surer that coming out here had been the right thing to do. The frontiers were Sam's homeland and now that her own world had become a forbidden paradise, the West must be her home also.

They would get ahead. Sam's energy, courage and deep-seated sense of loyalty, reinforced by her New England practicality, her ambitions for the children, and her urge to restore the Bennett strain to respected security, should take them far. This question of running for office might prove the entering wedge.

Even now, after nearly eight months of marriage, she was surprised how little she knew about some things concerning Sam Higsby. All she knew was that he'd been born in York County, Pennsylvania; and that he had roamed the woods since his early teens.

The baby was feeding less greedily now, kneading at the breast with tiny rosy fists.

She had been mightily relieved to hear that Tim was recovered of his wound, that he aimed to fit out the *Narragansett* as a privateer. He would succeed, one way or another. He was stubborn stuff, was Tim.

How strange that Nat Coffin should also have sailed on the expedition against the Bahamas. Yet was it? Even back in Providence, Nat had spoken of joining the Marine Corps. She wished it were possible to learn what had become of him. Probably she would never learn, except by accident. Certainly she wouldn't dare make inquiry.

It was something, though, to know that all of Admiral Parker's great ships and Sir Henry Clinton's fine regiments had not been able to capture Fort Sullivan, let alone Charleston.

She forced away the baby's lips, dried the breast and shifted Joanna to the other. If Joanna grew to look like John, she would make a remarkably handsome girl. John's features had been so regular, his brows so straight, his skin so thin and smooth.

It would be interesting to learn what the Honourable Sir Joseph St. Clair, this child's paternal grandfather, would say were he able to behold his grandchild peacefully nursing in the midst of a howling wilderness. A far cry this from the roar and bustle of London!

Well, Joanna would never learn that she was not Sam Higsby's own daughter. No one in these parts could know that she wasn't.

She heard Eve crawl back through the hutch; so, restoring the baby to her cradle, Desire set about preparing the evening meal. She would have given a year off her life to have sat down tonight to beef instead of venison, to taste some vegetable other than frozen turnip, to swallow real instead of raspberry-leaf tea.

Snapper lay in front of the fire toasting his toes. When she spoke to him, the hound commenced to flog the floor with his heavy tail. At last he got up and stretched his legs, and bowing in his back emitted a small luxurious yelp. At the end of the operation, he came clicking over to her, one ear hopefully cocked.

"Go find Master," Desire told him. "Tell him supper will be ready mighty soon."

When she opened the door, Snapper rushed about in furious circles. Desire knew that he wanted to bark, but he only whined softly; Sam had trained him too well. Sam, she saw, was back skinning the buck. He had slung it from a fork in a big beech tree.

She turned and bent above the pots and pans. She was lucky, Desire realized. Blessed few females along the frontier could boast of a Negro slave woman, of a cow and of a husband so handy in the woods.

By the light of a wick floating in an earthenware bowl of bear's oil, Higsby's face screwed itself into a frown of concentration and he continued working over his second gun. This was a big bear gun, far too heavy to carry about much; but where it hit the fur didn't grow any longer. He had been having trouble with its lock.

"Desire," said he over his shoulder, "trot out the lead kettle, will you? Cast me a few balls for Bella."

"Why, Sam, you're not going off again?" Desire exclaimed. "You've just run your trap lines!"

"Yup. Reckon I'll make a cast down South Fork way. What with all this snow, ought to find a passel of deer yarded up." He winked. "And from the lay o' the land I figger there just might be some beaver dams — but don't tell nobody I said so."

"But Sam, South Fork is quite a way off." She cast him a quick, uncertain look.

"Ain't nothin' to be fearful of, honey; honest there ain't." He smiled, pushing the jet hair back from his eyes. "Too cold. All the Injuns, exceptin' trappers, is holed-up in their lodges.

"Mike told me Blackfish, the Shawnee war chief, has been listening a heap to Hanging Maw — he was the Cherokee got slapped down so hard last fall when he kidnaped them kids near Boonesborough."

He bent further over the gun lock, working with the point of his knife. "Nope, there ain't no Indians south o' the Ohio. You and Eve kin keep house two or three days 'thout no cause to fret. You'll tend the inner trap line?"

"Oh, yes, Sam, I can do that easily," Desire promised. Fetching out a small cast-iron kettle, Desire stirred a bed of hickory coals until they began to crackle and snap, then she set the little pot among them and dropped in the end of a lead bar. Using a turkey wing, she fanned the coals until they glowed white near the pot.

She would have got a bullet mold out of Sam's war bag without being told, but this bag was about the only belonging he kept strictly to himself. Desire could understand why he did this. No woodsman wanted anybody else messing with his kit. In the wilderness it was impossible to replace a lost screw, or a spoiled implement. Besides, a trapper had continually to know the exact state of his replacements. The scarcity of plenty of such essential supplies governed his most important decisions.

She really wasn't curious to go poking about in the war bag — most of such things were indescribably messy — but when she'd nothing on her mind, she sometimes tried to guess what he kept in it. Essentially fair-minded, she never yet had gone nosing about when he was away.

Eve was a good wench, Higsby was thinking, but he sure would like to lay hands on that goddamn worthless Cocoa. The idea of the black bastard's running off to the Indians for no call at all. From the first he had counted on Cocoa to mind the cabin while he was away. Already he had taught the black to dress and flesh a pelt, tedious labor which he would have gladly spared himself.

By God, if he ever found him, the Leman's barleycorn would teach that nigger to run off.

Maybe if the trapping continued good and he found someone to freight the pelts to market, he could clear enough to afford another nigger — *not* one of the fighting kind. 'Course he'd no real call to complain. Eve and Cocoa hadn't cost either him or Desire a copper penny.

Higsby was mightily thankful Eve hadn't run off too. He didn't aim to let so pretty a wife as his grow leathery-faced and crooked-backed from bending over too many fires or from washing too many clothes. He didn't want to see Desire Harmony's fine skin grow tanned looking like a squaw's.

Desire Harmony was a real pretty name. Fit for the prettiest gal he would ever rest eyes on. Sure had to admire her independent ways. She wasn't like other girls, no sir. Different from the rest of them as a cross fox was from a common red. He reckoned he would always recall the cool way she'd stood up to menfolks, to her own pa, even.

Desire? She was right well named at that. Them shadows beneath her eyes weren't there for nothing. He looked pridefully across the cabin. Her hair was red-brown, the color of a prime beaver pelt; and it was every bit as soft.

Everything would be finer than fine if the next baby turned out to be a buck. Along the border a family of boys came in mighty handy. He'd name him for Desire's pa — Asa. It would tickle Desire, and, well — he himself certainly held the old man's memory in high respect. That old Quaker was truly the godliest and humanest man he'd ever come across.

Maybe little Asa would grow up to be a smart scout? Maybe get high up in the army? The Thirteen Fires, as the Indians called the new nation on the seaboard, would surely stand in need of an army for a right long while.

Higsby could look ahead and see the shape of what was to come. Sure as shootin', there would be more and more settlers and movers going west, crowding the Injuns until the Injuns fought back. Not that you could blame the tribes so much.

[354]

Higsby said to his wife, busily stirring the melting lead, "Reach into my war bag for a spare lockpin — there's three of 'em — in that leather pocket furthest to the right. I want the longest screw."

"But, Sam, I couldn't find it. That war bag is a mess. Besides I don't like to go poking — "

"Needn't worry." He grinned at her, dark eyes atwinkle. "Them skelps are done up separate."

"Oh, all right." The bullet lead was beginning to break into silvery little bubbles, so she added, "Lead's ready. Shall I get out a mold at the same time?"

"Yep, but fetch me the screw first."

Desire, crossing to where the war bag hung from a peg driven into the log wall, eyed it curiously. It was a fine new one, of well-oiled elk hide and with long fringes that were hardly torn at all. Some squaw must have spent a lot of time to decorate it so handsomely with red and green quill work.

Standing on tiptoes she began to fumble about.

"Better unhook it. You'll rip the edges, else," her husband told her.

When Desire set it on the elephant-bone stool, the bag made a small clinking noise. Heavens! There must be even more in it than she had imagined. She recognized a whole spare gun lock, a prouvette, two bags of flints, some small pigs of lead, a bladder of pemmican and two or three bullet molds, then some odds and ends of rifle parts.

Her hand encountered a cold, flat metal plate. Pulling it out she held a polished pewter ornament to the firelight. "*Per Terram, Per Mare,*" she read on a scroll winding about an anchor. The king's cipher was on it, too.

"What in the world is this pewter plate for?"

Higsby looked up sharply. "Nothin' much. Came off the cap of one of them Britainers, night o' the raid on Peaceful Haven."

Per Terram, Per Mare. That was the motto of the Royal Regiment of Marine Light Infantry, she recalled.

"Oh!" Desire said in a small voice. It was their first mention of that dreadful night.

Hurriedly, she fumbled deeper, hunting the inner pocket containing the screws. Her fingers encountered something smooth, something heavily carved. In spite of her first instinct, she drew out the hilt and guard of an officer's sword. The grip was gold mounted and protected by an ivory guard carved in the shape of a mermaid.

"Where did you find this?" she asked, stepping over to the fire.

"Shucks!" he drawled amiably. "Ain't nothin' in nature like a woman for curiosity, is there?"

"But, Sam, it's lovely, where did you find it?" She turned it over and over, wondering why it should look faintly familiar.

Higsby grinned, set down the bear gun and began to stuff a red clay pipe he'd traded from Skanawati.

"Ma'am, that there hilt is a token o' the prettiest shot *I* ever made in my life. Near bragged on it a hundred times, but I didn't, 'cause it happened the same night I collected that there hat badge."

Slowly, Desire's eyes sought the guard, remained fixed on it. "You mean the night of the raid?"

"Yep! 'Twas after I'd killed three Britainers up near the barn and I was adriftin' along after the enemy aimin' to pick off stragglers when, all of a sudden, out of the snow and dark comes one of their officers. He was runnin' hell-fer-leather; easy though, just like a deer. You ought to have seen him travel! Show you what a hard mark he made — 'twas snowin', a brisk breeze was blowin'. I got fixed to drop him comin' on but, sez I, 'Sam, you've already bagged three. Let's be sportin' about this.'"

As Desire Harmony stood staring at the hilt, Sam's voice moved further and further into the distance. When she saw the name *Jno. St. Clair*, engraved in a fine script, a cold, killing wind began to roar through her.

As faint and distinct as the tapping of a distant woodpecker, Sam's voice continued. "Yep, I always been mighty proud o' that shot. Sighted center, betwixt his shoulders. Figger it out fer yerself. He was a good sixty yards off and runnin'. I'd have told you 'bout it before, only I didn't want to remind — my god, honey — you ailin'?"

Outlined before the orange glow of the fireplace, his wife's figure stood, a rigid silhouette. When he drew near, he could see that she had turned a ghastly white. Not even when Joanna was being born had her face become so completely drained of color.

"You, you — !" The words struggled through lips twisting like those of a soldier suffering amputation. She held up a rigid, fending hand. "Get back!"

"But, honey, what's the matter. Do you feel sick?"

Through Desire's mind was cascading a white-hot stream of thought. In this same cabin stood the man who had blasted her life's happiness, who had cruelly, in a spirit of sport, robbed her of the only wholly fine force she had ever known.

Because of Sam Higsby she had had to cower, trembling, shivering, in Martin's woodshed. Because he had robbed John of life, she had had to go tramping, hungrily, hopelessly, the streets of Providence. She had had to suffer Mrs. Norton's beating, had had to offer herself to strangers.

Because of this ignorant barbarian in buckskins she had been condemned to the tawdry disappointments of life with Brian Montaigne. Because of that shot she had lost Nat; she had had to flee, like a leper, from the decent home of the Proveauxs.

Crescendo, a sense of outrage clamored at her. She began to tremble.

"Desire —" Sam tried to take her by the elbow. "You look like you're seein' —"

Her fist took him viciously on the side of the jaw. He was so surprised he could only stand staring, puzzled, with one hand clapped to his bruised cheek. With the speed of a snake she lashed out at him with the sword hilt.

"Murderer!" Her voice was shrill, unearthly. "Don't touch me! Keep thy bloody paws off me!"

Higsby fell back a couple of steps, drew himself up, his cheek bones jutting like cliffs. "You gone crazy? Listen, woman, this ain't funny. I ain't done nothin' to — "

" — Haven't done anything?" she panted. "Oh, thee's a filthy savage! Thee's a stinking butcher! And it was *thee all the time!*" Teeth bared, eyes aglow with hatred, she shook the mermaid-guarded hilt before his eyes. "*Thee* killed *him!* I loathe thee. Go away — "

"Shut your trap!" Sam snapped. He was beginning to get mad. No female woman dare address him like this. "I don't know what ails you, but you're layin' terms on me — "

"Oh, I wish I could kill thee as thee killed John St. Clair!"

"Jesus Christ!" The oath escaped Sam amid a whistling gasp of surprise. In a flash he saw it. That officer on the road must have been the whipper-snapper the neighbors had spied leaving the barn with Desire.

He felt the hot blood seethe up to the roots of his hair. So it was that damned Britainer's whelp he was expected to bring up. Like hell he would! Knowing who the brat's father was made all the difference.

He gathered himself, the muscles on his neck growing thick. So she still loved that macaroni feller, not plain Sam Higsby? "You needn't rail at me fer a savage," he snarled. "Fine sort o' gentleman who'd ravish a sixteen-year-old gal!"

"Silence! Thee is not fit to mention John's name." She was looking about as if seeking some weapon.

"Ain't I?" Higsby roared so loud that Eve began to whimper beyond the barrier. "By the livin' God, I wish'd I'd put my foot on that Britainer's dirty neck and skelped him!"

"It's a wonder thee didn't. Thee is lower than the Indians. Kill! Kill! That's all thee thinks of. Stay away from me," she panted. "Don't thee dare ever to touch me again!"

To think she had lain in this man's arms, that she had made love with John's murderer was maddening.

Joanna woke with a startled yelp and began to whimper. Neither of them paid any attention.

"Sit down, else I'll cuff you down!" he snapped.

Desire was the last person to heed such a command. With a furious sob, she hurled the hilt full in his face. The stump of the blade dug into his chin. As a trickle of blood spurted from it, his hand shot out, gripped her arm. Twice, three times, his open hand dealt her slaps that exploded a series of brilliant purple-green lights in her eyeballs. Next he shook her until she was quite breathless, then sent her spinning across the cabin.

Undaunted, she glared up at him. "Hate — thee to — end of my days!" she choked. Her eyes were swimming, her head roaring inside. "Would to God I could tear thy child out of me!"

"By Jesus, I wish you could!" He towered, menacingly black, above her, his breath showing in silvery puffs. "Then my seed wouldn't be asked to grow up along of any Britainer's bastard!"

"Bastard! Oh, you — "

By the distorting play of the flames, they glowered at each other in a white fury.

"Open that trollop's mouth of yours again and I'll ram my fist through it."

Devils looked out of Higsby's jet eyes. So she still loved the Britainer? He couldn't get over it. "You got no right to call me out o' turn, you poor, dirty female critter. I've used you too kind fer yer own understandin'."

He flung about, walking on the balls of his feet like an angry dog. "Eve!"

"Y-yassuh?"

"Get me some food! Pemmican, smoked fish, meal and souens."

Sprawled on the bed and rubbing aching jaws, Desire Harmony could hear his moccasins stalking about. He kept muttering. Once she opened her eyes and met a deadly look.

At the end of ten minutes, he had collected his familiar kit, war bag and all. He poked her with the handle of his war hatchet, spoke in a deep, quivering and unfamiliar tone.

"Attend what I say." He spoke as to an Indian who couldn't speak much English. "We both been pretty hot. Mayhap I'll fergive you — mayhap I won't. I'm goin' down to Rollin' Fork. If I figger I kin fergit about this, I'll be back in two days by sundown. If I cain't, you won't see me ever again."

With that he walked out and slammed the door.

Snapper whined and tried to follow, but Eve grabbed him by the neck. Long before anybody, Snapper could tell if a bear or any other hostile creature was about.

Skanawati

All Eve recalled was waking up to hear the white folks calling each other the most terrible names. Lawd's mercy! Misto' Higsby had been razor-mad, almost.

She wouldn't forget in a hurry the look on his face when he'd stormed out of the cabin with blood dripping from his chin, with his war bag filled and his littler rifle a-swinging to his shoulder. My, my, he sho' had handed mist'ess a couple of mean clips.

What worried the slave most of all was that early next morning Snapper got out and, right away, ran off following his master's trail. She sho' hated to see that hound go hightailing down the ravine. Yessuh, Snapper could scent a Injun or a catamount half the length of Kentucky.

When noon rolled around, she gently approached the brooding girl. "Please, mist'ess, better eat a l'il somethin'. You cain't feed dat baby on sighs. Ah done fixed you a elegant dinner."

"I'm not hungry, Eve," Desire replied with a wan smile.

"Doan' grieve so, l'il buhd," Eve pleaded; she was really devoted to her mistress. "He gwine come back. De men folks gits fractious sometimes, but dey ginerally gits over it when dey dander dies down an' dey craves a mess o' home cookin'."

"I — I hope you're right, Eve."

Desire accepted the wooden bowl of mush and milk with bits of fried pork stirred into it.

"You are right. I suppose I should eat." She brightened. "Let's hope Mr. Higsby will bring home a turkey."

When she had finished eating, Desire rebraided her hair, wound it into a gleaming casque about her head. Humming, she stitched her cashmere shawl in place. Joanna she dressed in the little Indian dress of doeskin Sam had fetched back from Harrodsburg. Though the garment was still a trifle large, Sam might be pleased to see the child wearing it.

For all he had said about Joanna, he was really fond of her.

Abruptly, her fingers faltered, began to fumble. Suppose — suppose Sam *didn't come back?*

The baby emitted a moist gurgle and jerkily flourished a tiny gourd rattle which Skanawati had brought her one day last fall. Desire liked Skanawati better than most of the Indian trappers who chanced by. It was probably because the Catawba didn't go in so heavily for bear grease and had the delicacy not to pick his lice in her presence.

Outside, all at once the cow began to snuffle, to toss her head. Desire heard her horn scraping the wall. Heavens! That meant only one thing. Her heart began to pound. The cow had heard Sam's footsteps.

Hurriedly she put away the account book, smoothed the fur rug over Joanna and, straightening her blouse, ran to the door and eased back the heavy panels.

Not Sam but two Indians were descending the ravine! A single glance disclosed two all-important facts: the foremost savage was carrying his gun with its stock held 'way forward; neither Indian was wearing black or red paint so they were not members of a war party.

Dark and silent against the snow, the two braves came drifting down between the gray trunks of the beeches, theiir heads turning restlessly this way and that.

When she saw a blue turtle painted on the front of the leader's filthy hunting shirt, Desire recognized Skanawati. In her relief she almost sobbed. The other was a strange Indian whose head was clean-shaven except for a coarse crest. He didn't look like a Catawba to Desire but he, too, was of the turtle clan.

Had the caller been any other than Skanawati, Desire would have been terribly frightened; but here he was making the peace sign and holding up a pair of rabbits. In silence he dropped them onto the bare ground before the front door.

Desire smiled a "thank you." She knew what procedure to follow because Sam had told her again and again. One must invite a friendly Indian into the cabin; give him food and a present if possible; ask no questions; a woman should never address a warrior first.

Today Skanawati seemed more dressed up than she had ever seen him. His headdress was composed of scarlet-dyed hickory splints joined to form a sort of crown which rested on his denuded scalp. A clump of brilliant scarlet feathers spurting from this headpiece concealed in their midst a silver tube so arranged that a single eagle's feather, let into it, was left free to revolve.

For weapons, the Catawba carried the usual old French musket, a knife and a war hatchet. But his companion had no more than a bow and a quiver of arrows.

The second Indian, a Shawnee, whose name proved to be Uguku, or Hooting Owl, was shorter than his Catawba friend, and lacked a right eye. Certainly he was no dandy. The blue and orange paint applied in chevrons across his forehead and down his cheeks was smeared and dull, and a weather-beaten heron's feather laced into his scalplock drooped like the tail of a whipped puppy.

Unslinging a mantle of lynx fur, Skanawati followed Desire indoors while his companion stripped off a covering of mangy-looking wolf skins.

The instant the baby saw those painted and bedizened figures she raised terrified wails. Hooting Owl regarded the infant with obvious disapproval. Skanawati kept his attention on the stone jug Desire had laid out in expectation of Sam.

Desire forced a smile and waved to the fireplace. Oh damn! Why did that jug have to be standing in plain sight? Now, if she didn't offer them liquor, the visitors would feel affronted. If she did — well, even Sam admitted an Indian with a few too many drinks in him was a devil and mighty hard to control.

Joanna was still screaming so she guessed she'd better put the baby beyond the barrier. She found Eve trembling like a horse which has scented a bear.

"Don't be silly," Desire warned sharply. "It's only Mr. Higsby's friend Skanawati." She placed the infant on a little rack beside the cook-place. "Eve, you bring some food, quick as you can!"

"Ain' dey hurt us?"

"No, you idiot."

"Lawd! Lawd! If only Misto' Higsby was heah!"

"Well, he will be soon. Now hush your fuss and get busy."

When she went out front again, there was a smell of whiskey in the air; Hooting Owl was covertly licking his lips. The Indians had spread their mantles on the floor and were squatting on them, crosslegged. They sat impassive, expressionless. Only their flat black eyes looked alive. Hooting Owl had set his moccasins to dry at the fire and they were filling the cabin with the rancid smell of stale grease.

"Where my brother, Tskili?" demanded Skanawati at length. He gave Higsby's Cherokee name.

"He went down the ravine a little while ago. He will be here soon to welcome his brothers."

Skanawati blinked. He admired Tskili's squaw for being able to lie so well. All of Tskili's footprints had been made nearly forty-eight hours back. Why should the squaw have lied? No matter. Maybe she would give him bread made of sunflower seeds.

He rubbed his belly. The liquor burned fine. He felt a little guilty about having stolen that drink, but surely an old friend like Tskili would not deny his brothers refreshment. What about another little drink?

Copper bracelets gleamed as he pointed to the stone jug.

Desire hesitated, but gave in. It didn't seem advisable to irritate the Indians when they were so obviously friendly. Besides, Skanawati was dependable. The Indians set the jug to their lips and swallowed several deep gulps.

Desire Harmony Higsby cast anxious eyes at the barrier. What in the world could be delaying Eve? If food could be gotten into these smelly creatures promptly enough, they might not want more to drink.

Whew! The fire, blazing up, had warmed the visitors enough to start them perspiring, and now the whole cabin reeked with their sour, feral odor. Their body smell was rather musky, like that of freshly dressed fox or mink pelt.

Next time the Indians asked for a drink, Desire figured she had better drop the jug and break it. Sam would be hopping mad, but there was no help for it. She didn't like the look of this Hooting Owl at all. He acted a sight too bold.

"Rum," grunted the one-eyed warrior pointing to the stone jug.

"Surely," Desire smiled, and in lifting the jug let it slip through her palms. Unluckily, it only glanced off the wooden bench and rolled, splashing its contents across the floor.

Hooting Owl snarled like a scalded cat and grabbed it up before more than a cupful of whiskey had escaped.

"Kehella!" The chevrons on his forehead flashed as he tilted his head and let the whiskey gurgle freely down his throat until Skanawati snatched it away for his share.

The Catawba, amused to feel the ground sway so pleasantly, was thinking: Tskili is a fool to hunt so far from his lodge. Here are furs worth five big barrels of rum. All good furs because Tskili is a skilled trapper. If something happens to this lodge, can Tskili tell who to blame?

[361]

Skanawati pulled himself up sharp.

"*Ke-we!*" It was bad even to think along these lines. The white man had a very bad way of not forgetting such things.

Hitching up his belt, the Catawba shuffled over to one end of the barrier and considered Eve with inward approval. By experience, he knew the black woman could cook very well, and she looked as if she could stand travel under pressure. Three Tall Feathers, his brother, had a black slave and was always boasting over it.

"Go 'way, Misto' Injun," Eve quavered. "Ah's gittin' yo' vittles fastes' ah kin." She was simply terrified at the blank stare Skanawati gave her.

Soon Eve, trembling and round-eyed, brought in wooden platters heaped high, but Hooting Owl brushed his portion contemptuously aside and went on fingering a prime beaver pelt. The Shawnee was hot now, and bright beads of sweat kept breaking through the paint on his forehead.

To Desire, that red empty eye socket was utterly repellent.

"*Koco ktel-lunsi?*" he mumbled as she went by.

Of course she couldn't understand and unwisely shook her head. The sunset caught her braids.

Wagh! What a rare red color! Hooting Owl felt moved to touch it, but Desire was too quick.

"Tell him to keep his hands to himself," she told Skanawati, but the Catawba was too busy finishing the stone jug to bother.

Desire put her head behind the barrier, whispered urgently, "Take Joanna. Make for the Wilderness Road. Run as fast as you can. Quick!"

The Negress went gray with fright but jerked a nod and began pulling on a shawl. With this responsibility off her mind, Desire turned, surprised to feel less frightened. From somewhere she had gained an ample supply of self-confidence. She could handle these befuddled brutes. Hadn't she been in tight corners before? Her luck was good, too.

Of course Sam would appear now any instant. My! Wouldn't he be mad over the way these smelly savages had made bold with his liquor! Almost impersonally, Desire watched the shaggy, painted figures sway about, inspecting the cabin's least important furnishings.

With alcohol fumes rising in his brain, Skanawati began to speculate again. He was feeling mighty strong, brave and wise — important, too. Why not take prisoner Tskili's woman and the black slave? Why not load them with the choicest furs, set fire to the cabin and leave Cherokee sign about? Hooting Owl had some Cherokee arrows in his quiver.

Belching, he draped an arm over Hooting Owl's shoulder and made the suggestion. Tskili, he pointed out, must be far away, the cow was so still. To ambush him in his camp should be easy: the country was still at peace. Ten dollars from Colonel Hamilton. Maybe twenty.

Desire pretended not to notice anything, merely picked up the food Hooting Owl had spilled. When she heard the slow scrape of the hutch door closing, a deep sigh escaped her. A good thing Eve wasn't fat and had plenty of incentive to put distance between her and the cabin.

The sunset beat hard at bladder windowpanes, dyed them a blinding crimson. Indeed, the whole interior of the cabin glowed with an angry light which brightened the paint on the savages and the copper tones in their skins; it reddened three copper rings set one above the other in Skanawati's ear.

They were up to mischief of some kind, that was plain as day. But what? Should she go on humoring them? Maybe she could load the bear gun? But there it lay with its lock taken apart.

What about Skanawati's antique musket? If worse came to worst, she could grab it up and have nothing to fear because Hooting Owl carried no musket, only a short bow and some arrows stuffed into a quiver of spotted wildcat skin.

Skanawati jerked out his skinning knife and slashed through the cords securing a bundle of fisher skins; at the same time, he shot her a truculent glance, as if daring her to protest. She didn't. Sam could have told her this was an error of the worse sort. To give in to an Indian never placated him, only made him mad, the more eager to assert his dominance.

Both the redskins were drunk as billy goats, kept belching and agiggling foolishly. She watched them explore one bale after another, selecting the most valuable furs. They were pretty clumsy about it, and flung the discarded skins in all directions.

How long had they been here? Nearly an hour, Desire estimated. Sam couldn't be much later since he'd said he'd be back by sunset.

What would the gentle Quaker girls of Newport make of a scene like this? What would Antoinette Proveaux do?

The fossil footstool got in Skanawati's way. The Catawba fetched it an angry kick and howled when he stumped his toes. Desire couldn't restrain a burst of hysterical laughter. This big Indian was so utterly childlike.

"*Gissa!*" Skanawati gave her a vicious slap across the mouth. She had never seen eyes like this Catawba's. They held a clear, merciless, reptilian glitter.

Pressed flat against the cabin's wall, Desire knew now she must make a stand of some sort. Oh, why *didn't* Sam come? She hadn't the least doubt that he would appear, because her luck had never yet failed her. Never! She must cling to that reassuring fact. Hooting Owl scowled at her, then reeled over and looked behind the barrier. When he realized the kitchen end of the cabin was empty a furious bellow burst from him.

Desire thought, I've got to stop him. That red devil can catch up with Eve in no time. If I can only delay him a little while, it will be dark.

"Look!" she cried. "You have not seen the best skins even yet. In that bundle are some beautiful otter skins. I am sure Tskili would like to present them to his brothers."

Eagerly she tugged the bale into the center of the floor — and got pushed sprawling. When her head banged against the wall her eyes filled with tears of outrage. She thought furiously all the same, tried to foresee what might happen.

From the floor, those Indians looked gigantic, monstrous. She must get to Skanawati's musket. Under its threat, she would drive out both intruders and bar the door. Once she had slammed the window's heavy shutter, the savages couldn't get in for quite some time. Sam would be back long before then.

While pretending to collect the far-scattered skins, she worked closer to the Catawba's musket. Suddenly the woodpecker's skin flashed. Hooting Owl was studying her over the stained and broken fringe along his shoulder. Sensing that the Shawnee had guessed her intention, she flashed across the remaining interval, got the weapon cocked and leveled before either intruder could turn around.

"Raise your hands!" she cried. "Quick, both of you! I'll shoot!"

Hooting Owl's dirty hands started upwards, but Skanawati's did not. With a diabolical chuckle he jerked forward his powder horn, tilted it upside-down. Shook it derisively. It was empty. That was really why Skanawati had come to Rockcastle Creek.

Deliberately, the Catawba let go the powder horn and his hand wavered towards his war hatchet, then sought the knife in its fringed sheath. His painted face like that of a clown from hell, he took an uncertain step forward.

"You not tell Tskili!" he said thickly.

"Get back! I — I'll shoot. It's loaded! I know it is!"

Hooting Owl, too, began sidling forward. Wave on wave of horror-stricken terror beat on Desire's intelligence.

"Sam! Sam!" She screamed the name again and again, then in desperation, squeezed the trigger. Only a squalling cry from one of the Indians resulted.

"Oh-h, don't!" she wailed. "Don't hurt me. You — I — Tskili is your brother — "

Nothing would happen, she kept telling herself, nothing serious anyway. She was lucky — always lucky.

A hand tipped with writhing fingers came shooting towards her. Sick with fear, she tried to strike it aside with the musket barrel. The odor of whiskey was stupefying. The world became a pattern of garish colors, yellow-green, blue orange. The woodpecker skin.

She felt herself jerked forward and the gun went clattering to the floor. A foot tripped her and she fell flat.

Her face pressed against a loose fox fur, she screamed in a piercing voice, "Help! Help! Sam!"

What were they going to do to her? *What?* A thousand horrible tales of the frontier flashed across her mind.

Hooting Owl, laughing horribly, went staggering over to the fire on uncertain legs while Skanawati held her pinioned by a knee on the small of her back.

"Sam! Help — they — "

A bare ankle appeared before her glaring eyes, and, instinctively, she bit it as hard as she could. A hoarse scream of pain filled the cabin just before something dealt her a stunning blow. By a narrow margin she failed completely to lose consciousness.

Her senses began swimming. She must not be afraid. Sam was here! At last! At last! She listened for a rifle shot.

Another blow on the head failed to land squarely.

"John," she gurgled. "Help me, John, darling!"

A foot descended, crushed her neck against the gritty clay of the floor. Fingers knitted themselves into her hair, then a pang of unbelievable anguish shot through her head. Spasmodically, her body jerked, twisted.

From far away, she sensed that something was giving, tearing. Cascades of blinding, outrageous pains descended, assaulted her failing consciousness. All the fires in the world began beating upon her head. As suddenly, they went out, leaving it deadly cold.

A sensation of drifting became more pronounced. Desire Harmony felt herself whirled away, thousands on thousands of miles. She smiled because she could see John St. Clair awaiting her.

Wild Horizon

Preface

When one lists what generally are considered to be the decisive battles of the American War for Independence, only Saratoga and the siege of Yorktown as a rule are selected. However, recently it has become realized that there was a third battle, which although involving comparatively few troops, nonetheless served as a very definite turning point in the outcome of that protracted and world-changing conflict. This battle also is important as the decisive engagement of the first civil war — which was fought as a war within a war — by Americans against Americans. In this case embittered Loyalist Americans who supported the British Crown were pitted against American patriots who as fiercely and often just as savagely supported the cause of independence. The Battle of King's Mountain, fought on October 7, 1780, in which only one British regular was present, was unique because of the ferocity displayed by both sides. But for the raw courage of the "Overmountain Boys," patriot refugees and frontiersmen already settled in western North Carolina and Virgina, the War for Independence might have ended as many of the best American generals and statesmen for a time expected — causing a general retreat of their defeated armies and devoted civilians across the Alleghenies where they intended that still another young republic should rise, phoenixlike, from the ashes of defeat.

The first part of this story covers efforts made to prepare a reception for this mass of refugees. Much has been written about the dangers and privations suffered considerably later on by emigrants to the West and to the Far West, but who ever has heard of the sufferings and inarticulate heroism of the members of two expeditions which struggled out to Kentucky and middle Tennessee during the terrible winter of 1779–1780? These ill-equipped and largely inexperienced bands of civilians were led respectively by Lieutenant Colonel James Robertson and Lieutenant Colonel John Donelson, both renowned frontier fighters. Since space did not permit a description of the tribulations and fate of both expeditions, I decided to describe, as well as I could, the adventures and almost incredible hardships suffered by the party which was headed by James Robertson — not that John Donelson's party's long midwinter voyage down the Holston and Tennessee rivers was any less colorful or arduous.

Of all the many characters appearing in this volume only a very few are completely imaginary. These include the Valentine and Colcord families, Dr. Samuel Mason, Saul Black Buck and Parthenia Bryant. All the rest bear at least the names of persons who lived and were present at the time and places indicated. Among such characters are Timothy Murphy, the famous sharpshooter of Saratoga; the Tory George Walker; Major du Buysson and Colonel Armand. Joe Drake, Cash Brooks, Thomas Sharp Spencer, Isaac Bledsoe and other frontiersmen basically are all authentic characters.

A great number of instances and details which might appear to the reader to be products of the author's imagination actually happened, such as the adventures of Jonathan Robertson; the raid on Fairlawn; the punishment of George Walker; and Thomas Sharp Spencer's feats of strength. Needless to say, military engagements and maneuvers are reproduced as accurately as a painstaking and selective research can render them.

September 1779

Seldom, decided Lieutenant Colonel John Sevier, had he more thoroughly appreciated the beauties of such a fine, warm and crystal-clear September day. Riding a few yards in advance of his escort, a file of eight grimy, sunburned troopers who, because they'd been drawn from various units, were haphazardly equipped and uniformed, the colonel made the most of this unfamiliar sense of well-being. Opportunity to indulge in such relaxation had been rare during the past four years. Yes. To be able to slack his reins, to ease his long and wiry body in the saddle and allow his dusty black charger to select its own pace in crossing this wide and nearly treeless plain approached sheer bliss. Frankly, the colonel had had more than his bellyful of battles, cold, heat, interminable marches and death in all its hideous guises.

The hatchet-faced officer allowed cavernous eyes, dull and red-rimmed by fatigue, to wander over a succession of low, gently rounded foothills rising through a faint blue haze towards the red-bronze and yellow slopes of the Bald Mountains and the Alleghenies which towered beyond them.

"*Wagh, ai-yeh!*" as a Cherokee would have cried; it sure was finer than silk to have left the ravaged and hate-filled East Coast so far behind and no longer expect to come upon another burned-out cabin about which buzzards wheeled and squabbled over decomposing bodies or perched hopefully upon trees from which flyblown corpses dangled, limp and pathetic.

Worst of it was, one never could be really sure which side should be held responsible. Such an outrage might just as well have been perpetrated by one of many British-led Tory detachments which vied with bands of equally savage American irregulars in ravaging the back country and murdering without compunction anyone even suspected of favoring the enemy.

John Sevier rubbed weary eyes before again surveying the Alleghenies' eon-softened summits, which suggested a series of gigantic blue-green billows, lying at least another full day's ride farther on.

Even while relapsing to his comfortable half doze, Sevier made note that perhaps a quarter of a mile ahead the narrow track — called the "Charlotte Pike" — disappeared among a clump of scarlet maples flaming about the base of the rock chimney. Idly he noted that on the summit of that tall rock an eagle's nest showed as a crazy tangle of sticks. Long since, the eaglets reared way up there must have spread uncertain wings and flapped away.

The sharp-faced officer briefly debated halting in order to relight his pipe with the tinder pistol he invariably carried, but ended by dropping his pipe into a side pocket. He then roused sufficiently to glance back at his escort.

Judging from the way a pair of troopers were sagging forward in their saddles with forearms crossed over cantles, they must have fallen sound asleep. Others of the bearded or long-unshaven cavalrymen had rendered themselves comfortable by riding sidewise or with one leg hooked over the equipment strapped in front of them. They looked as if all they wanted in life was to dismount, water their horses, fill their canteens and then sleep the clock around.

Sevier calculated that one of the many brooks which came purling and splashing prettily down from the mountains probably would be discovered among those gay, autumn-tinted trees crowding about the rock chimney's base.

After smothering a yawn he called back, "Rouse up, boys! Soon's we reach yonder woods we'll dismount and — "

His sentence remained unfinished, for from the woods ahead burst at least a dozen puffs of smoke instantly followed by as many hard, slamming reports. Musket balls buzzed by like gigantic hornets. Behind Sevier one of his men uttered a piercing yell and fell heavily off his horse. More shots rapped out; then out over the meadow charged a swarm of horsemen, some wearing scarlet tunics, some in Tory green regimentals; others were clad in rough civilian garb. Their screeching yells and whoops beat clearly, menacingly through the warm, still air.

That more of his escort had been hit Sevier knew by screams and agonized cries rising behind him.

Savagely reproaching himself, Sevier bent low in his saddle and spurred hard. How *could* he have allowed himself to get so goddamn careless — especially when bearing intelligence of such vital importance as that with which he'd been entrusted? In a cold rage he snatched out both ponderous horse pistols he carried strapped in heavy holsters at either side of his pommel. Over the quickened drumming of his charger's hoofs he only half heard sibilant *zweeps* caused by sabers being jerked free of their scabbards.

A few pistols banged as in an irregular double rank the enemy at an extended gallop pounded forward to ride down the hopelessly disconcerted Americans.

Sevier, guiding his horse with his knees, cocked both pistols and made straight for a purple-faced British officer galloping well out in advance of his men. A good thing this thick-bodied Britisher — a lieutenant by his single epaulet of tarnished silver lace — hadn't possessed sufficient patience to wait in ambush for only a few moments longer. Had he done so, the American detail must have been destroyed in its entirety.

John Sevier's entire consciousness focused itself on the English officer, who also had snatched out horse pistols. The other's bay horse surged straight at him, a large white blaze on its forehead flashing in the warm sunlight. The colonel extended his right arm to full length, then fired, but was unaware of his pistol's recoil, for the Englishman's flushed, contorted face vanished beyond a sudden blossom of gray smoke; it then reappeared, magically dissolved into a crimson pulp. With a burst of speed, Sevier's charger carried him past the Englishman reeling helplessly in his saddle, on through rotten-smelling clouds of burned powder.

He sensed, rather than saw, a green-uniformed Tory, who seemed to be all wide-open mouth and bared teeth, closing in with saber upswing. Desperately, Sevier slewed sidewise and just managed to dodge the Tory's whistling slash, then used his second pistol to dispose of the fellow. Again and again his spurs raked his charger's barrel. Must get away! *Must.* MUST! No matter how, he must get to Watauga.

Colonel Sevier's Ill News

Flat on his belly just beneath the crest of a steep, wooded ridge which afforded a clear, comprehensive view of Fort Patrick Henry lay Moluntha, eagle-featured war chief of the presently dispersed but still powerful and warlike Shawnee tribe. At the moment Moluntha again was brooding over the treacherous murder of his predecessor, Chief Cornstalk, slain while visiting an American fort under a flag of truce.

Deliberately the Shawnee's wide-set and vivid jet eyes traveled back and forth over the scene below several times, counted the roofs of shacks, huts and cabins crowded together in disorderly fashion behind an absurdly low palisade of rough-pointed pine logs which, as nearly as the Indian could make out, mounted but a single swivel gun. These dwellings also enjoyed the dubious protection of a small, two-story blockhouse.

Moluntha felt pleased on discovering that only fourteen crudely shingled roofs showed *within* that palisade, which could only recently have been erected upon a long, flat and once heavily wooded peninsula. This jutting piece of territory was created by the confluence of the Holston River, deep and fast-flowing, and a busy smaller stream known as the South Branch of the Watauga, which came tumbling down from the mountains of western North Carolina. While a big black ant boldly explored his wrist, Moluntha made note that the fort had been situated with a view to protecting a number of primitive boatyards in which flatboats, gundelows and even a large keelboat lay in various degrees of completion.

Yellow birch bushes and sumac which already had begun to take on the scarlet hues of autumn stirred only slightly when the war chief beckoned Ocondago and Standing Bear to come snaking silently up beside him. The former's face was painted in wide, horizontal red and black bands; the latter had affected a blue and green checkerboard design through which little bright beads of sweat were breaking.

Like their leader, these wiry young braves had taken the precaution of pushing backwards headdresses of frayed and travel-faded eagle feathers tipped in red; customarily, such were worn secured to the scalp lock in an erect position — which instantly would have been spotted by any keen-eyed person down on the peninsula.

Originally Moluntha's scouting party had numbered five, but one brave carelessly had allowed himself to get tripped amid a vine tangle with the result that he'd been fatally gored by a rutting bull elk. Another warrior had been killed quite as dead by a rattlesnake which had slid under his blanket in search of warmth and had bitten him in the neck when the luckless fellow stirred in his sleep.

Now came this alarming discovery of a new fort erected farther west in Virginia — or was it North Carolina? — than any other. Scowling, Moluntha crushed the ant, which, uncautiously, had decided to nip him, but what drew deeper furrows across his yellow-and-blue-painted forehead was the number of those canvas, bark or brush shelters which stood scattered without any semblance of order upon the peninsula behind the fort. *Gissa!* For some time sizable parties of immigrants must have been arriving in this Watauga country.

Several groups of obviously new arrivals were unloading pack animals — there was yet no wagon road across the mountains from any direction — or busy pitching stained and weather-beaten tents among stumps left to mark the never-ending retreat of the forest.

Under the eyes of girls and half-grown boys several herds of pigs, furry brown cattle and flocks of gray-white sheep were browsing on or rooting among those giant canes which grew so tall and succulent along the banks of both rivers.

For over an hour the three Shawnees lay statue-still on the ridge making detailed mental drawings of the blockhouse, its armament and the ridiculous palisade surrounding it. Also they noted how best the defenses might be approached and penetrated when the time came — as surely it must.

At length Moluntha tilted his narrow, strongly modeled head towards his subchief, Ocondago, and whispered, "How many *Americani* does my brother tally?"

"*Kish-kaw-wa!*" Using hand signs, the Shawnee indicated the presence of at least three hundred people, but Standing Bear, hissing like an angry bobcat, indicated his belief that no fewer than five hundred whites were encamped in and around the blockhouse, above which floated the red, white and blue flag of the Thirteen Fires. Although homemade, it was readily identifiable.

Moluntha started to squirm backwards off the ridge crest, but checked his move because a horseman had appeared riding at a slow canter. His mount's hoofs were raising small, regularly spaced puffs of dust along that trail which for countless generations war parties had used in crossing the Bald and Stone mountain ranges when raiding into southwestern Virginia and the Carolinas.

Soon the Shawnees could see that the rider, though small of frame, sat tall and easy in his saddle. He was wearing a black tricorn hat and a dusty blue uniform coat sporting collar, cuffs, and lapels of dull red. Presently it became apparent that this horseman must have covered a lot of ground since sunup; his bay's flanks were streaked with sweat and its strides were short, holding no hint of springiness.

Beneath the cracked and badly smeared paint applied to his forehead, Moluntha's eyes glittered and his hand closed hard over the ponderous British Tower musket lying beside him. "*Gissa!* He who yonder rides is Nolichucky Jack, himself!"

Standing Bear's vitreous black eyes asked a question.

"He is that same Colonel Sevier who helped to beat us so badly at Point Pleasant on the Great Kanawha."

The Shawnee of course had no way of guessing that the travel-stained rider loping along toward the fort was bringing an item of news which ultimately would shape the destinies of several nations —red and white alike.

Once Nolichucky Jack had disappeared, Moluntha and his braves resumed their cautious retreat from the crest. After they had regained the hollow in which their gaunt and rough-coated mounts stood tethered, the Shawnees reerected headdresses and otherwise made ready to move out. Their war chief, however, checked them. "Brothers, from this place we ride together no longer. From what we have seen it is plain that the Long Knives are planning to take away more of our land, but what is of the greatest importance is that *this* time the white men are casting hungry eyes upon the Great Hunting Ground, where by ancient custom even warring tribes may hunt in peace.

A small group of men, bearded or merely long unshaven, sat or stood in uncomfortable silence around a grease-stained trestle table made of rough-finished planks. This hurriedly had been set up near the center of that hot, dirt-floored chamber which included Fort Patrick Henry's entire ground floor and was as gloomy as it was sour-smelling because air and sunlight could only enter through a single narrow door and a row of loopholes let into raw, pitch-dripping log walls.

Lieutenant Colonel James Robertson, occupying a stool near the head of the table, had clear, wide-set and strangely penetrating bright blue eyes which roamed ceaselessly from one weathered, hairy face to the next. His dark-brown hair hung shoulder-long but he had clubbed it, neatly using a length of red-dyed rawhide. Robertson's handsome bronzed features were sprinkled by dark-red fly and mosquito bites.

In a soft, Virginia-accented voice, James Robertson began to speak. "Sorry to have you sent for, boys, but Colonel Sevier here's just ridden in bearin' some pretty serious tidin's. Since he damned near got killed on the way, I reckon you-all had better listen hard to what he's come to say."

[375]

"What kind of tidings?" Amos Eaton demanded, using a dirty sleeve to blot a sheen of sweat from his forehead.

Sevier, looking much taller than he really was, swung a balding head towards the speaker and summoned a bleak smile. "I only hope that you fellows ain't going to do like the kings of old and slay me for being the bearer of ill tidings."

"Ill, you say?" rumbled Donelson.

"Yep, and that's putting it mildly."

James Robertson cleared his throat, steadily regarded the spare figure standing erect in dusty, often-patched and badly faded blue-and-red regimentals. "Your meanin', John, is that lately our side ain't been farin' extra well against the king's armies?"

Sevier's steel-gray eyes made a swift circuit of the dim and crowded room. "Reckon that's about the size of it. By all accounts our people are losing ground, skirmishes and battles up North, down South — everywhere, for that matter."

"Don't tell us dot *verdammt* Prevost has beat us again!" growled middle-aged but still stalwart Fred Stump, who only recently had escaped from a British prison in St. Augustine.

"Yes. Prevost has reinforced the garrison holding Savannah so strongly that our siege of that town most likely will end in a bloody disaster. Charles Town, too, soon will be invested by a powerful force shipped down from New York and New England, and they've brought a whopping big fleet of men-o'-war along to help pound the port into submission."

Sevier sighed, slapping a white crusting of horse sweat from the skirts of his tunic. "And that's not all the bad news, either."

"What else is there?" demanded Edmund Jennings, raising shaggy black brows.

"Up North, British and Tory landing parties have been raiding and burning towns and shipyards along the Connecticut shore of Long Island Sound almost at will; so far, we haven't been able to give them any opposition worthy of mention."

A low growl arose from the listeners.

"What'd ye expect of them damn' cowardly Yankees?" demanded Billy Cocke.

"Stow that kind of talk," rasped Amos Eaton. "They've fought hard and suffered plenty. Go on, Colonel."

"Worse still, our patriotical, high-minded and windy Congress is proving itself ever more incompetent to pay, arm, feed or otherwise supply the miserable Continental regiments we still have left in the field. Every day our Continental scrip-money grows more worthless."

" — Und iss dot possible?" rasped the yellow-bearded German.

The shrill whooping of sunburned and tousle-headed children playing tag on the cramped and uneven "parade ground" just outside beat in through loopholes which also were admitting swarms of fat and loudly buzzing bluebottle flies.

In a gesture expressive of supreme disgust, Sevier flung heavily freckled brown hands wide apart. "Now comes the worst part. 'Tis reliably reported that our French friends are growing mighty sick of their alliance with us and are ready to pull out. All through the Southern Colonies Tory regiments are being recruited and outfitted to help in capturing Charles Town. Once that town's taken the Loyalists swear they'll burn out or hang every last patriot they can catch in the Carolinas. After that, the British are expected to drive north into Virginia ravaging, killing and plundering. Guess you already know that they've captured and burned Norfolk and Portsmouth on Chesapeake Bay?"

Sevier's spurs of tarnished brass jingled softly when he took a few turns before the table. He came to a halt confronting James Robertson and John Donelson. "To sum up, at this moment there appears little reason to doubt that the cause of the United States is doomed." Sevier lowered his voice. "To many, the most disturbing of all these woes is talk that our commander-in-chief for the first time no longer appears confident of eventual victory."

Eaton spoke up, "What you're saying is that even Gin'ral Washin'ton figgers we've lost the war?"

The droning of flies sounded absurdly loud before Sevier nodded and said in a somber tone, "I fear so, for barring divine intervention or a military miracle of some sort, our armies must soon be outmaneuvered and defeated piecemeal, or at best, the remnants will be driven west, away from the seacoast."

"But suppose they surrender?" demanded Billy Cocke in a hollow voice. "What happens then?"

Colonel Sevier's fine features flushed as he almost shouted, "Dammit, man! They don't intend to quit! They've fought too long, and that's the reason why I came here. The commander-in-chief and many of our best generals, such as Knox, Greene, Marion, Harry Lee, along with statesmen like Tom Jefferson, John Adams, George Mason and Patrick Henry, are determined to continue the fight for liberty — "

"Along with a lot of smart land speculators, I expect," interpolated a harsh voice from near the doorway.

Using a scarred and tar-stained forefinger, Donelson scratched at a tangle of sand-colored hair and said slowly, "Well, John, granted that our folks won't be able to whip the Britishers and still don't intend to surrender, what course is left open?"

He in the bedraggled blue-and-red uniform stiffened. "What course is left for our defeated patriots, you ask? Why, sir, they and their leaders mean to fight on, retiring westwards in such a fashion as will cost the enemy very dear should they attempt a pursuit." Sevier's voice swelled until it filled the crowded, gloomy little room. "I tell you fellows we've

[377]

plenty of men left who mean to keep on shooting so long as they've left among 'em a handful of cornmeal, a full powder horn and a bag of bullets. The plan is for our people to withdraw behind what His Excellency terms 'the lofty ramparts of the Alleghenies,' there to settle and build a new free nation which can and will defy tyranny till hell itself freezes over!"

Robertson looked up, inquired, "Is it your meaning, John, that only armed forces will conduct this retreat?"

The shake of Sevier's sun-darkened head was emphatic. "Hell, no! Troops and patriotic-minded civilians alike will emigrate westward — like you already have — taking along their families and as many possessions as they can bring."

"And at the same time," Jennings snapped, scarred features taut, "the handful of us is expected to fight off swarms of the meanest, cruelest savages God ever turned loose in North America! Do you *really* mean that?"

"Und make no mistake, Colonel," Fred Stump grunted, "der tribe vill pounce like hungry pant'ers vunce dey t'inks us vhites mean to settle on der Great Hunting Grount!"

At length Robertson shrugged, then turned to Donelson. "John, everyone hereabouts knows we're figurin' on leadin' expeditions out to the Cumberland country come next spring. So, I hear, are Kasper Mansker, Long John Rains and some others."

"That's so. What's your meanin'?"

"Well, if we wait here till spring before settin' out, why by the time we reach where we aim to go it would be away too late in the season to start clearing land and making crops which could help feed refugees from the East."

"Dot iss so," grunted Fred Stump, who despite several celebrated military exploits remained a farmer down to the soles of his clumsy cowhide boots. Thoughtfully he picked at a hairy nostril. "Neffer could ve plant crops which would come ripe in time."

Robertson heaved himself erect and looked about the dim and increasingly stuffy little room. "That being the truth, I propose that we don't wait for spring but set out for middle Tennessee soon's we can."

At once Cocke stepped forward, thin, parchment-hued features suddenly suffused. "My God, Jimmy!" he shouted. "You gone stark, staring mad? Or are you funnin' us?"

"You know I'm not!" There was more than a trace of anger in Robertson's reply.

"Then you must be crazy to think, for even a minute, about movin' a parcel of men, women, children, freight and livestock above eight hundred miles through an unmapped wilderness *in the dead of winter!*"

Murmurs of agreement circulated the hot and fly-filled meeting place. Unkempt heads were being shaken with varying degrees of violence.

Colonel John Donelson started up, shiny-smooth, full features gone brick-red. "Might have reckoned, Billy Cocke, you'd talk along those lines." He snorted contempt. "Small wonder folks still talk about 'runnin' like Billy Cocke' did before the Battle of Long Island began." The big, heavily built figure glared about him. "Make no mistake, fellers; to even think on attemptin' such a journey calls for plenty more than an average supply of guts."

Said a gray-haired fellow wearing an old linen hunting shirt, "As I see it, having guts and taking a reckless gamble on our lives, our folks and our property — which is all most of us have left in this world — is two mighty different things."

"I can give you my decision right now!" burst out a big, raw-boned man who carried a broad ax he'd been using. "Me and my family ain't joining in no winter march."

"Nor me, either," cried another. "I ain't drove my livestock this far to watch 'em starve and freeze in the forest."

Edmund Jennings, tall and lithe-looking in new, fringed white buckskins, spoke up. "They won't, mister, if yer leader knows his job as well as Jim Robertson does."

Amos Eaton nodded slowly. "Sure, there still are good reasons for delaying till spring — among them the fact that by then we'll have plenty of boats built. And there'll be more of us. Ain't immigrants coming here all the time? By spring we'll have a lot more men ready and able to fight off the savages."

"That's undoubtedly true, Amos," slowly admitted James Robertson, "but what Colonel Sevier's told us still holds true. An we don't have food and shelter ready by the time those people from the East start crossin' the mountains, why, they'll just naturally perish and — " he treated the men lining the walls to a level, penetrating look—"and us, too!"

Fred Stump bit off a chew of tobacco. "So den it seems like ve get kilt no matter vot ve do, hey?"

Sevier quietly pointed out, "You all knew what you were risking when you moved out here." He unslung a pair of pistols which he wore supported by crossbelts of undressed leather. "So, suppose you sleep on the matter, as I suggested, and give me your answer come morning. Right now, I could do with a bait of food — and so could my mount. We've come a far piece in a big hurry."

The Point

At daybreak of a bright, crystal-clear morning in mid-October 1779, Sergeant Daniel Maddox, recently discharged from General Dan Morgan's

Regiment of Virginia Rifles, came to quickly, completely awake. If after three campaigns a soldier hadn't learned to rouse all in an instant he'd likely have become a casualty of some sort.

In a single, lithe motion Maddox rolled out of the ragged woolen blanket he'd brought along after he'd been mustered out, and leaped to his feet. The tall, copper-haired young fellow spat, then yawned and stretched until his joints and back tendons protested.

Somebody's black and tan 'coon dog sniffed curiously while the veteran tugged on light but tough and pliant leggings of snakeskin won at dice from an Iroquois during the Saratoga campaign.

After scratching vigorously under a fringed linen hunting shirt dyed butternut brown he slung on his food pouch, bullet bag and a large brass powder horn bearing the elaborately curling cipher of King George II.

Next he pulled on a wide-brimmed farmer's hat that had been pinned up on one side to support a sprig of hemlock, then stood rubbing a squarish jaw and watching Corporal Tim Murphy, also late of Morgan's Rifles, rake together the few live coals that remained among the ashes of their watchfire.

When a tiny flame wavered into being, Murphy, a dark-complexioned and slightly built but wiry individual, went over to his saddlebags and jerked from them a blackened can in which he would brew the point's morning coffee — which was no coffee at all, only finely cut chunks of potato scorched to a dark brown before being coarse-ground.

Farther on, Colonel James Robertson, tall and powerfully built, was blowing his long, straight nose between his fingers and at the same time relieving himself upon a fallen log. Short-lived twists of steam spiraled up from the puddle thus created.

No doubts lingered in the minds of the two-hundred-odd Long Hunters, frontiersmen, ex-soldiers and former farmers composing this expedition that ruddy and soft-spoken Jim Robertson, who'd first seen the light of day some thirty-seven years earlier in Brunswick County, Virginia, was a born leader and in the very prime of life.

A bandy-legged, leather-complexioned Long Hunter named Joe Drake called for Bruce MacLean, a half-breed Scottish Chickasaw, to help lower an elk's haunch from a sharpened branch.

By the time riding horses and pack animals had been saddled Corporal Murphy called softly — one didn't sing out in the wilderness the way one did in an army camp — "Come along, boys, and get it before I throws it out."

The seven scouts riding as advance guard for the main expedition gathered around to hold out cups whittled out of black cherry or yellow pine.

After gulping his breakfast Dan Maddox went over to the picket line to untie his animals, which consisted of a pair of big, wiry horses of no special breeding he'd bought in Watauga and the bony black jackass he'd ridden all the way out from Lancaster.

Momentarily, the sergeant deliberated whether or not to ease "Ilsa" — that slender, long-barreled rifle he'd fashioned for his personal use just before going off to join the war — into a crude boot of wrinkled and well-greased buckskin. He decided not to stow his weapon on noting that Tim Murphy wasn't putting away his double-barreled Golcher rifle — the same with which he'd mortally wounded General Fraser, "Gentleman Johnny" Burgoyne's most capable general officer. Almost everyone agreed that the loss of General Fraser during the battle of Freeman's Farm had done a good deal to cause Burgoyne's subsequent surrender at Saratoga. Obviously, Tim was going to carry his piece ready for instant use.

In soft, unmistakably Virginian accents Robertson drawled, "Now while we ain't overlikely to bump into a bunch of hostiles in this neck of the woods at this time of year, we just *might* meet up with a big party of Indian hunters on their way home from the Licks —"

" — Or a mess of Iroquois out on a raid," drawled Jennings.

"That's true, so best keep ready for action at short notice." Dwarfed among the giant trees all about him, Robertson squinted at his small brass pocket compass. "All right, boys, mount up. Let's move lively and make the most of this fine weather."

The point, or advance guard, set out along the Kentucky Trace following buck-toothed Joe Drake and the thin-faced half-breed Chickasaw called Bruce MacLean.

Thoughtfully, Maddox watched the leather-clad veterans kick their tackeys — ugly little horses brought up from North Carolina — along the trace at a slow but distance-consuming jog-trot.

A mile and a half to the rear of the point the main body of travelers rode or tramped along in a straggling single file except when the Kentucky Trace, sometimes known as "Boone's Trail," widened briefly and permitted men to travel side by side and speculate about what might happen today.

On reaching the summit of a steep, cedar-covered ridge, Jim Robertson turned in his saddle to cast a long look over his shoulder. Seen at this distance his column suggested a thin, dark cable winding unevenly down the hither slope of a high, heavily forested foothill.

He reckoned he had around two hundred men still with him — only a very few of his followers had lost heart enough to head back to the Watauga country. A good thing that — with one exception — there wasn't a woman or child back there to slow down the expedition's rate of travel. The exception was his eleven-year-old son Jonathan, now riding herd on a small flock of sheep.

While trotting down the ridge's far slope the rangy North Carolinian experienced a pang of conscience — he really had undertaken the easiest part in this dual immigration into Middle Tennessee. He didn't envy John Donelson one little bit his task of floating, in midwinter, more than three hundred men, women and children over a thousand miles from Fort Patrick Henry down the Holston and the Tennessee, transporting also a wide variety of livestock, farm implements, seeds and household furniture.

Maddox learned from gnarled old Joe Drake that the expedition at present was heading for a little settlement on the Duck River known as Whiteley's Station. How far off it was Joe couldn't say.

Again the Pennsylvanian was impressed by the unrelieved loneliness of this vast region in which signs of human activity were so rare. Why, after passing through the Cumberland Gap, two days back, only a solitary spiral of smoke had been sighted and that in the far distance.

All the same, decided the former soldier, this seeming emptiness must be deceptive, or why should big game continue to prove so 'cute and scarce?

In support of this reasoning the advance party yesterday had come upon a pair of bearded, hard-bitten characters who, clad in dirty buckskins, were waiting quietly beside the trace. How they'd learned of Jim Robertson's intent to ride this way was a mystery; but there they were, lugging full packs and bulging war bags.

When James Robertson, tall and supple in his buckskin-covered saddle, had ridden up, one had called out, "Heyo, Cunnel Jim! We'd admire to go along with you an ye're really intendin' for the Great Huntin' Ground."

Robertson tugged at his long, straight nose a moment. "You afoot?"

"Yep. Injuns stole our hosses last summer along with three packloads of pelts."

"Can you walk fast?"

A foxtail attached to the taller man's cap swayed to his nod. "Sure thing. Me and Tom c'n walk and run the legs off'n a bull elk."

While his mount impatiently switched at swarming deerflies and horseflies, the leader's sharp blue eyes considered these shaggy would-be recruits. Finally he drawled, "How're you named?"

The short applicant, who'd a drooping eyelid, exposed gapped teeth in a brief grin. "Me, I'm Cash Brooks and this here porcupine humper's Tom Gordon. We both been rangin' with Boone, Bo'quet and others for many a blue moon."

"Reckon you'll do. For the present you boys will join the main body when it comes along. Tell Major Phillips I said so."

With Caesar, his shaggy, battle-scarred, black and tan bear dog trotting sedately behind his bay gelding, Colonel Robertson advanced until he found Sergeant Maddox and his crony, Tim Murphy, riding a couple of hundred yards in advance of the rest of the point.

"Howdy, Cunnel Jim." Out of habit Murphy touched his hat's brim in easy salute.

Using his chin the leader pointed to a pleasant little valley down which the trace was winding. "I'd like you boys to hurry on ahead and see if you can't come up with some game before it gets frightened off. Try to knock over at least half a dozen head; two hundred men and as many dogs c'n tuck away a powerful lot of meat." His gaze shifted to the rifles they held balanced across their pommels. "I know that's a tall order. Any fool c'n tell game's growing scarcer all the time, but I hear the two of you c'n kill at mighty long range. See you later."

The Mauling

The better part of three hours was required by the meat hunters and their dogs to start and shoot four fat cow elk and a big, white-tailed buck deer — all of which had had to be killed at not less than a hundred yards' range.

Dan Maddox felt particularly pleased over his last shot — a difficult one of nearly two hundred yards' distance — Ilsa *had* remained accurate despite having been rebored, which had had to be done because he'd used his weapon so often during service with the Old Wagoner, as Dan Morgan's men long ago had nicknamed him.

At the first possible moment the meat hunters cut the throats of their quarry, for even in cool weather like this unblooded meat could spoil in surprisingly short order.

Watched by a big brown mongrel, Maddox sank onto his heels and drew his long knife — which was really a carving knife of beautifully tempered Sheffield steel — across the buck's still quivering windpipe. He stood up and watched streams of steamy scarlet arterial blood form a glistening puddle which presently overflowed and went meandering off among fallen leaves, weeds and grass roots. The dogs then advanced and lapped eagerly.

"Reckon that'll about do for now," Tim remarked while tamping down a fresh powder charge and ball — buckshot in this meadow country wouldn't carry far enough.

From his war bag Maddox pulled a strip of white cloth which he tied to a branch high enough above the fallen buck to attract the attention of skinners who, leading pack horses, should soon appear to butcher the carcasses and fetch in the meat.

While slipping his bloodstained knife back into its sheath Tim Murphy shook his head. "B' God, Dan, don't know why cuttin' throats makes me feel so randy, but I've sure got to find me a playsome wench else I'll spoil my britches some night. Ain't bedded a girl in a month, which is uncommon hard on a full-blooded young buck like me."

"My Gawd, Tim, must you always be dreaming of a 'fidgety fork'?"

"Reckon so," grinned the rifleman while swinging up into his saddle. "I'm told my balls are small so I work 'em extra hard to prove they're just as good as big ones."

After checking primings and drawing back their hammers to half-cock, the meat hunters commenced, much more slowly, to follow a newly discovered game trail marked by the fresh spoor of elk and now of *unshod horses!* Which, certainly, couldn't have been made by animals belonging to the expedition.

Hum. These tracks must have been made not very long ago. Pretty soon the trail led to a fair-sized spring where crystal-clear water bubbled from beneath a pile of moss-grown boulders to flow, shimmering, over a streak of yellow sand.

Then, on mucky black earth surrounding the spring, the meat hunters recognized several more or less clearly defined footprints made by moccasins — not shoes or boots. Fervently the meat hunters began to wish they had with them a Long Hunter like Joe Drake, Cash Brooks or Edmund Jennings. Most likely any of them could have told, after having examined that broken arrow and having studied these prints, to which tribe the Indians were likely to belong and what they were up to.

After riding around the circumference of the spring the meat hunters agreed that a party of Indians numbering perhaps a dozen must have drunk and watered their horses here. They watered their horses and washed blood from their gear before drinking from small cherrywood dippers attached to the ties on their war bags.

Scarcely had they remounted than a sudden excited clamor arose from beyond an alder thicket about which one of the bear hounds had been nosing after lapping to wash down the blood he'd consumed. Instantly the other two dogs raised a terrific tumult and raced off among the trees while the meat hunters reined in sharply and stared at one another in lively uncertainty. What had alarmed the dogs? A fox, a panther, or were there Indians hiding among the sun-speckled underbrush? Dogs, they knew, hated the very smell of Indians — probably because the redmen greased themselves with bear fat and never washed.

At length Tim Murphy grunted, "Don't think it's Injuns — dogs are actin' too bold and noisy." He loosened his rawhide reins and rode slowly forward, the stock of the double-barreled rifle halfway to his shoulder.

Tim looked relieved. "By damn! Trust them fool bone-destroyers to chance on fresh bear tracks."

"With Injuns about and all that racket, I reckon our hunt's about over," Maddox grunted. "So let's go kill the critter. Most of the fellows favor bear over venison."

Once the hunters had urged their unwilling mounts into a little clearing carpeted with bright-leaved huckleberry bushes they saw the dogs circling about and then rushing in to snarl about the base of a dead and peeling linden tree. On its lower branches a pair of fuzzy, comical-looking black bear cubs had taken refuge and were whining shrilly while keeping furry round ears pressed flat against their heads.

When he saw what was up, Murphy swung off, tied his horse to a tree, then strode forward a few yards before again raising the Golcher. Two flat, cracking reports sounded in quick succession and the dogs' yelping rose to a crescendo when the cubs came tumbling earthwards and made two dull thuds among bushes beneath the weathered old tree.

Beset by snarling hounds, one cub struggled to rise but collapsed with a dog's teeth in its throat. The other black-brown body stirred not at all despite savage worrying.

Without comment, Maddox dismounted, and with bridle looped over one arm snatched up a stick and began to beat off the dogs. "Good eye. Got 'em both center line."

"Aw, hell! They was easy. Now if only I'd have such luck with women I'd — "

A deep-throated roar caused both hunters to whirl about barely in time to see a huge sow bear come humping, red-eyed, out of a sumac thicket, saberlike claws flashing and long teeth agleam.

Murphy for once had neglected to reload, so dropped the Golcher and went for his sheath knife — too late. The raging animal already was upon him, rearing and lashing out. Tim leaped nimbly back and succeeded in avoiding the bear's first swipes. There wasn't much Maddox could do at that point, for his horse had shied so violently that it tore loose its reins and plunged away, throwing him off balance and spinning him half about.

The sow now shuffled forward with deceptive speed and launched another savage blow at Murphy's reeling figure.

The gunsmith instantly recovered, spraddled legs and whipped Ilsa to his shoulder fast — too fast, because the weapon went off a split second before he was ready.

Beyond a rolling blossom of gray-white smoke Murphy screamed shrilly, again and yet again; there followed snarling growls and wild threshing noises amid the underbrush. Snatching his tomahawk out of its grog, Maddox charged through whirling, bitter-smelling fumes, then pulled up, all standing. From the way the bear was charging blindly about in semicircles and knocking down sturdy young trees Dan sensed he'd been lucky enough to have driven his bullet into the brute's head.

Presently one of the bear's blind rushes carried her off to one side and into a stand of golden-leafed poplars. There, after hugging and snapping at a clump of saplings, the sow all at once sagged to the ground as if suddenly overcome by sleep and lay, muzzle down. Dan sunk his tomahawk's blade deep into the brute's brain before running over to kneel beside his friend.

"You hurt bad?"

Tim Murphy blinked, then stared dazedly upwards, black eyes wide and unfocused. His small, wedge-shaped features looked pasty like a piece of badly cured doeskin rather than their usual bronze-red. "Wha-a'?" His voice barely was audible.

"How bad you hurt?"

Murphy's eyes rolled and he drew a slow, shuddering breath. "Dunno. Ain't checked — guess — ain't no worse off than — after Brandywine, but — reckon I'm in for — session — who's that sawbones in — main column?"

"Mason, Sam Mason. They say he's knowledgeable. Take it easy, Tim — where d'you hurt most?"

"Can't feel much — left side." Tim managed the ghost of a grin. "Lucky — critter missed my balls —"

After slitting the linen hunting shirt's crimson-soaked left sleeve he uncovered a deep, ragged double gash running from Tim's shoulder clear down to his elbow. While the wound was torn and wide, at first glance it didn't appear to be too deep, although dark venous blood and plasma were coursing freely from it.

Maddox contrived a tourniquet out of a stick and a length cut from the long rawhide thong he carried looped over his left shoulder when in the field. He tried to look unconcerned although he knew that such a clawing would prove hard to heal, because bears were partial to eating carrion of any description.

Next, the rifleman took a precaution which — as every veteran knew — was the best possible treatment under the circumstances; he opened his breeches and urinated thoroughly upon the wound and soaked the wad of moss he secured in place using Tim's and his own sweaty neckerchiefs. Nobody ever had explained why this procedure more often than not would keep a wound fairly sweet and open till a physician could dress it.

Samuel Mason, M.D.

The sun had begun to set behind strata of sickly, yellow-gray clouds when the main column straggled onto and spread out over an old beaver fly Colonel Robertson had selected for the night's bivouac.

Dr. Samuel Grineau Mason, Harvard College, class of 1771, felt pleased that this open place had been chosen. Followed by an awkward young man, he rode to the meadow's far side and there prepared to camp in comparative seclusion. Because of what had happened not long before, the doctor hated the sensation of being hemmed in.

Carefully he unloaded first a battered black medicine chest, a flat wooden map case, then heavy saddlebags containing a slender supply of surgical instruments, clysters and a couple of sturdy bone saws all wrapped in oilskins.

[386]

All over the meadow sounded a jingle of harness and trampling caused by nearly a thousand hoofs of all sorts. Soon these sounds became lost in the *ta-chunk!* of hatchets and axes cutting firewood and boughs for bedding.

The spare, square-shouldered physician seated himself on a tussock, and using his thumb, tested the edges of scalpels removed from a scuffed leather wallet. Pretty soon, he knew, the first of this day's crop of injuries would start showing up. Impatiently he looked about for his apprentice, Josh Freedly, a tall, weedy youth of nineteen with the alert, beady eyes of a chipmunk, carrot-hued hair and absolutely colorless eyelashes. Right now he was busy offloading a small, lop-eared jackass which carried the bulk of his master's camping equipment.

Josh drew near and spoke. "Heard the word, Doc?"

"No. What's the rumor this time?"

"Some of our advance party have come acrost fresh Injun sign." Josh was proud to use real frontier terms, but all the same he glanced anxiously about the darkening meadow. "Colonel's ordered outposts set tonight. Hope to God them savages ain't fixin' to assault us."

Stiff and sore as he was from this long day in a most uncomfortable saddle, the doctor chuckled, "An they do, Josh, that carrot thatch of yours will be the first scalp they'll go for."

Josh's pale gray eyes rounded themselves. "Really, Doc? Why for?"

"Old woodsmen among us say that the savages fancy an off-colored scalp above all others. Better stay close to camp tonight. Now pass me a blanket. No, you numbskull, not the one with burrs stuck all over it."

Tonight Sam Mason was lucky; outside of a jackass-bitten patient he'd only had to smear sulphur-and-goose-grease over the foot of a man who'd got it scalded when a stewpot had overturned unexpectedly, and then he'd had to employ forceps to yank a mess of porcupine quills out of a big ex-farmer's leg. During the process the yokel had howled like a moonstruck hound.

Darkness had descended before Dan Maddox walked up to the physician's fire, leading a short-legged and disreputable-looking tackey. On it Corporal Tim Murphy sat, all bunched over and groaning softly.

"Howdy, Doc," Maddox greeted. "Got time for one more?"

"Surely, but I wish you'd come in when the light was better."

Maddox and Josh eased the hurt man out of the saddle. "Sorry we couldn't get here sooner, Doc, but we were a long ways off when Tim, who's always been a lady's man, lost an argument with a she-bear."

"True love always demands a price — so they say." Mason's features, broad-jawed beneath a thin, hawklike nose, gradually tightened while he examined the lacerated arm. Supported by a crude sling, it slowly wept dark-red tears, caused a faint *spat-spat* upon fallen leaves.

During the last hour Tim's arm had swelled considerably and he'd bled freely whenever the tourniquet had been loosed for a little while, but the mauled limb hadn't yet turned that ominous plum-red which Samuel Mason, M.D., always hated to see.

As he stripped off a long-skirted coat of rusty black, the doctor called over his shoulder, "Josh! Fetch plenty of pitch-pine splinters, and you, Maddox, stir the fire under that pot. I'll need a lot of hot water pretty soon."

Dr. Mason's stained red waistcoat glowed in the firelight while from his saddlebags he jerked a thick plug of leather, scarred and indented by the spasmodic clenching of many teeth.

Tim recognized a surgeon's gag the moment he saw it and shook his handsomely homely head. "Keep that for the next feller, Doc. I won't be needin' it — honest. Didn't yell when the sawbones sewed up my leg after Brandywine."

"As you please," Mason said while selecting needles and damp sutures of split deer sinew. "Josh, give this man a swallow of Medford rum. I'll save the laudanum for later."

By now a considerable group of rough-clad, tobacco-chewing immigrants, veteran frontiersmen and greenhorns alike, had been attracted by those flaring pine splinters which Josh had distributed among the onlookers with instructions to "hold these high and steady." Now they crowded around the impromptu operating couch, creating the pool of smoky yellow. Nor was it idle curiosity which drew all of them; here a fellow might acquire a bit of knowledge which sometime might come in handy if he got hurt when off in the woods by himself.

A silence fell in which the faint crackle of the flares sounded sharp and crisp. Using a swab of tow, the doctor began to wipe the long wounds free of flesh particles, clotting blood and urine. "Good thing you are old soldiers and had the sense to piss on such a wound. Now, Maddox, do you grab his good arm and hold hard. Josh, pin down his feet. Lock your teeth, Murphy, I'm about to hurt you."

After deftly snipping away loose little tatters of flesh and skin, Samuel Mason removed a threaded needle from his waistcoat's lapel and went to work.

Revelations by Firelight

Dr. Mason's straight, faintly quizzical brows merged as he strapped shut and then locked his medicine chest. "Maddox, you'll find an extra blanket in that roll. Spread it over the patient so he doesn't wake up. He'll start suffering from chills before long. Another thing, you'd better make sure he gets an easy-gaited nag tomorrow — provided he's fit to ride."

Sergeant Maddox paused to look curiously at the physician. "Say, sir,

[388]

do you know that you talk like some Britishers I've heard? Even if you don't act like them."

"How so, Sergeant? Er — you still are one?" he asked quickly.

"No, but a lot of people keep on calling me 'Sergeant,' so I let 'em 'cause I served out my enlistment and got an honorable discharge along with a soldier's land grant warrant in place of pay-money. It calls for five hundred acres somewhere on public land west of the mountains." Maddox nodded to himself. "That surprised me, sir, 'cause folks in the army claim the Congress has got so stingy they'll try down a mouse for its fat. You're not English born then?"

Methodically, the surgeon wiped blood from his curved needle on a patch of linen, then restored it to his wallet of surgical instruments. "Small wonder you might think so," said he easily. "You see, I was born in Boston and have studied in England."

After a pause Mason said, "Sergeant, I trust you are not expected to report for duty with the advance guard in the morning."

"When the colonel heard Tim was hurt he told Joe and Cash to ride in our space."

"Good. Then you'd better spend the night here and help care for your friend."

"I'd admire to do that, sir." The tall, red-haired Pennsylvanian then leaned his long rifle handylike against a tree. Automatically, he peered up to see what the weather portended — was relieved to glimpse a multitude of stars through the treetops. Wolves hunting along a nearby ridge raised a chorus of eerie, mournful cries.

"Well, Doc, to go back to this Great Huntin' Ground you asked about — if the Long Hunters ain't been lyin' 'tis a great, forested basin — mostly flat but laced by hills and low mountains. Former farmers amongst 'em claim most of the land there's about the richest they've ever seen anywhere, and best of all, it's studded with sulphur springs and salt licks."

"Exactly what is a salt lick?"

Maddox began to rock gently on his heels, like an Indian, to keep blood circulating in his legs and so avoid cramps. "Joe Drake says it's any place where rock salt, which was formed by an old, old sea one hell of a long time ago, shoves up through the earth.

"Almost every kind of animal" — he grinned briefly — "includin' men, crave it; they swear that deer, elk, buffalo, bears, lions, wolves, foxes and even porcupines will travel hundreds of miles just to lick that salt. Maybe that's so, maybe not." When Maddox shrugged, a dark spot on the right shoulder of his hunting shirt indicated where his sergeant's green-worsted shoulder-knot once had rested.

"Why not?"

"Sometimes a body can't readily credit some of Joe's yarns; for example, he vows that sometimes them buffaloes travel so thick that a nimble feller can walk clear across a ravine on their backs." Maddox paused to scratch under his armpit where a louse had gone seriously to work. "All the Long Hunters claim that for time out o' mind the place has been a sort of 'neutral ground' on which the members of any tribe can hunt in peace — guess there must be enough game there for everyone. Yep. They allow as how Cherokees, Creeks, Shawnees, Chickamaugas, Iroquois and even Catawbas who come all the way up from Georgia hunt side by side sometimes. Joe says he's never heard of a regular treaty between the tribes, but 'tis a fact that nations which may be scrappin' elsewhere will leave each other alone while on the Huntin' Ground."

Mason's small eyes narrowed and his lips formed a soundless whistle which expelled his pipe's smoke. "So this is to be our Promised Land?"

A row of coarse thrums or long fringes decorating Maddox's chest stirred as he shifted his position.

"You c'n bet your hat that we're going to get attacked, so the main question is — where, when and how?" With calloused fingers the Pennsylvanian picked a coal from the fire, relit his pipe. "Howsumever, I reckon life in the wilderness never was meant to be easy or long, if a fellow don't act mighty careful *all the time*."

A brief and mirthless laugh escaped Dr. Mason. "One could observe, Sergeant, that you're considerable of a philosopher. I hope you'll forgive my inquiring what prompted you to accompany an expedition which by your own admission seems headed for disaster? Please don't reply unless you feel so inclined. I won't be offended."

After casting still another glance at Murphy's small, blanket-shrouded outline, Maddox picked up Ilsa before settling back against a pack saddle. The fire picked out various bits of brass on the rifle's mountings. "I don't mind — provided *you* tell *me* why a smart, eddicated sawbones like you is willing to risk his scalp in a wilderness he knows nothin' about."

"I presume, friend Maddox, you've already noted that to certain of our company I present something of an enigma?"

"Well, sir, I don't know just what you mean by that five-shillin' word, but if you mean you've got some of our people guessin', you're dead right."

"Well, I know some people rate me a queer duck, which is partially my own fault and that of my parents."

"You ain't to be blamed for what your folks did." Then he added hastily, "Whatever it was."

The bowl of Mason's charred pipe glowed rose-red as he drew a deep puff and chuckled softly. "I'm not a bastard, if that's your implication. My family has lived in and around Boston since 1660, when old Sampson, our first ancestor, who'd been a colonel in Cromwell's Ironsides, was forced to flee for his life following the Restoration.

"I'll spare you further genealogy save to state that my father served in the Ancient and Honorable Company of Artillery when it went to the siege of Louisburg back in forty-five. Incidentally, the Provincials captured that great fortress by themselves without help from the British regular army, which sent not a single soldier to the siege. That's a fact worthy of remembrance in these grim times."

Dan Maddox scratched absently under his shoulder-length, dark-red hair, then cocked an eyebrow. "Am I wrong or wasn't there another siege — later on?"

"That's quite so, Sergeant. General Wolfe took the same fortress back in Fifty-nine after His Majesty's government restored Louisburg to the king of France." Doctor Mason took a small sip, then rolled the cognac over his tongue before continuing. "Know something else? Plenty of people believe that the seeds of this present war were sown when the British government gave Louisburg back to the French without the least 'by your leave' to the Provincials who'd taken the place and, in so doing, discovered that by acting in unison they could accomplish a great deal without British assistance."

"Why'd the Yankees want to take that fort so bad?"

"Needed to rid their shipping of attacks by French privateers and pirates who nested in Louisburg, for one thing. Then there was a much greater danger: for over a century the French, working out of Louisburg, had roused, equipped and led countless Indian raids deep into New England."

On glancing across the fire Mason realized that Sergeant Maddox's round, dark-blue eyes were almost disturbingly intent and fixed unwaveringly upon himself. What was the fellow making of all this?

"Sergeant, am I boring you?"

"Hell, no." The Pennsylvanian grinned and locked hands behind his head. "Tell me, sir, when the trouble began in Boston where did your pa stand?"

"Why do you ask?"

Dan blinked slowly — like a cat dozing in front of a hearth. "It's because I — well, somewheres back in the Watauga settlements I heard tell you've Tory connections. Not that I or any sensible man believe such rumors," he added quickly.

Harsh lines formed around the doctor's mouth, adding years to his appearance. "That is shrewd of you. Too many fool stories circulate and cause all manner of needless grief and trouble." His voice deepened. "Allow me to assure you, here and now, neither I nor any member of my family have ever held the least sympathy for the Royalist cause."

Deliberately, the sergeant's narrow, reddish head inclined. "I'll take yer word on that — sir."

The physician drew a slow, shuddering breath which he expelled in an explosive whirling cloud of vapor. "You'll not be overly surprised to learn that during the late winter of 1776 my lion-hearted little mother perished of hunger and a congestion of the lungs induced by the complete lack of heating in our home."

"Damn' hard lines," Maddox muttered. "And after that?"

"As you know, *our* troops" — the doctor injected a note of defiance into the possessive and stared hard into the gunsmith's slightly oblique eyes — "invested Boston so successfully that scarcely a month after my mother died General Gage was ordered to evacuate his troops to Halifax. Just before the British departed, a party of high-ranking officers who were drinking in a public house were heard to lay bets that, after having been so scurvily treated by his countrymen, Dr. Sam Mason would accept a commission and accompany them to Canada.

"Although I at once and categorically refused this offer I was arrested on the very day that General Washington's troops entered the town and was thrown in jail for a Tory. If I'd imagined that previously I'd suffered injustice I was soon disillusioned," continued Mason bitterly. "I was haled before a drumhead court-martial presided over by a drunken assistant provost marshal who, when I offered depositions attesting my loyalty to the American cause, ripped them to shreds unread. Then he roared, 'Send this damned king-lover to where he can do us no more mischief!'"

It came to Maddox that if his companion weren't telling the truth then he must be a very skilled liar. In the army he'd encountered not a few of them. Hum. Rumor had it that the British were clever about planting spies. Where could one be more useful than on an expedition such as this? The king's generals certainly needed to know how best to pursue beaten patriot forces.

The doctor, in dull monotones, then described his confinement in Newgate, a prison improvised from a worn-out lead mine at Simsbury, Connecticut, in the lightless depths of which convicted or merely suspected Tories were imprisoned without trial. In that ghastly living tomb, some sixty feet below the earth's surface, faint daylight sometimes was visible for maybe an hour, but water seeping from the cavern's roof never ceased its *drip-dripping*. In the course of time, stated the physician, this dripping drove many prisoners insane. In Simsbury Prison the motionless, chill air would penetrate to the marrow of a prisoner's bones and bleach his skin a lifeless, fish-belly white.

"I spent over a year in that hell-hole before I escaped."

Despite himself, the Pennsylvanian was impressed, queried, "How come you got away?"

"By shamming to be a corpse, which wasn't difficult because I'd almost become one," the doctor explained. "Fortunately, when my 'remains' were brought to the surface it was late in the day and the grave diggers were too drunk or lazy to attend to their business straight away so I was left in a shed among the real cadavers to wait for morning. During the night I managed to creep off into the woods. Maybe the burial detail failed to count the dead so failed to notice my absence; anyhow there was no pursuit.

"For months, under false names I wandered among the backwoods of New Hampshire and Connecticut treating the sick and regaining my strength. Finally I felt sufficiently recovered to venture into Hartford, where I communicated with a classmate, one of the very few who'd refused to believe me a Tory. It was thanks to his generosity I was able to assume the identity of a physician who'd been lost at sea and so purchase a stock of drugs and set of instruments.

"I then felt emboldened to offer my services to the Continental Army and was accepted. I was attending wounds after the battle of Monmouth when I was recognized and forced to run for my life." Harsh tones returned to Mason's voice. "After that I dared not remain in the East, so worked my way westward to Fort Patrick Henry, where of course I heard about Colonels Robertson and Donelson's expeditions."

Mason pulled out his silver flask and offered it to Maddox, who, finding it nearly empty, resisted temptation and merely wetted his lips.

"I've told Colonel Robertson my story — most of it, that is — which he professes to credit. Maybe he really does, but I've the notion I'm only here because he sorely needs the presence of a trained physician."

"Why'd you think that, sir?"

"Because he asked so few questions." Mason laughed. "In a way, I flatter myself to believing that I'm more valuable to him than almost anyone else we have with us. Except for — "

Maddox pushed his rifleman's broad-brimmed hat onto the back of his head and yawned. "Except for what?"

"A first-class gunsmith like you. In this most imperfect world it would appear that capable killers are far more in demand than capable healers."

Highlights glinted across former Sergeant Maddox's high cheekbones when he inclined his dark-red head and smothered a yawn; at the same time he began roughly to pat the black-and-brown stray hound which finally had come over to lie beside him.

"Ain't no doubt but that you're damn' handy with your dosin' and your knives, sir," Maddox began in his strong, low-pitched voice. "Well, 'thout braggin', I could say that, in my own way, I'm just about as handy. Me, I c'n work and put together as fine a rifle-gun as any slabsided Dutchman you'll find makin' arms around Lancaster, Reading or Allentown — I ain't lyin'. Anybody in those parts can tell you the same.

"Me, I been makin' and repairin' firearms of all sorts ever since I stood knee-high to a grasshopper and was apprenticed by my uncle to Jake Deckerd, the master armorer. Now, sir, sometimes you'll hear old Jake called 'Deckard,' 'Deckart,' 'Deckheart' or 'Dickert,' and some other ways, too, but 'Deckerd' is the way he really spelt his name. I know. I've stamped it on too damn' many red-hot gun barrels and locks ever to forget the true spellin'." He cocked a heavy brow. "You've heard tell of Deckerd?"

The doctor sighed and pushed his feet in often patched and otherwise worn riding boots across fallen leaves towards the coals. "Of course. The name is known everywhere in America. You were born in Lancaster?"

"No. My Uncle Hank once told me my pa and ma hailed from somewhere near to Philadelphia; said they traveled with a party of Moravians and Mennonites to homestead on the frontier which then was near Lancaster."

The sergeant broke off, then jumped to his feet and looked sharply about, for across the meadow a number of dogs had commenced a furious barking.

Shaggy, shadowy figures by the dozen, roused up, and grabbing arms, immediately sought cover behind the nearest tree. Indians?

" 'Tain't nothin' — this time," Dan said after a pause. "Only a few elk or maybe buffalo over there. Listen and you c'n hear 'em snapping twigs and branches. Critters can't see well in darkness and blunder about considerable."

"Whenever I couldn't answer up pert and correct on a lesson he'd set me to learn, Uncle Hank would frale me plenty fervent. Fact. Then, when I was 'round fifteen years old, he decided to go back East, but before leavin' he apprenticed me to Jacob Deckerd.

"Well, sir, I was just about clear of my apprenticeship when tidings reached Lancaster that a rebellion had been started up in Boston 'gainst the British tyrants.

"Next, we got word of the skirmishes fought around Lexington and Concord and then about a great bloody battle which was fought on a place called Bunker's (or Breed's) Hill. Our people didn't worry much over the war — it bein' Yankee troubles — till New York, New Hampshire and then some other colonies — I still don't mind which ones — raised militia and voted to fight against the king's men.

"Soon as independence was proclaimed the heft of our men and older boys marched off to 'fight for freedom,' so they said, but I reckon they just wanted excitement and to find how a big war was fought."

The doctor chuckled. "So you went early?"

"No, sir. Old man Deckerd wouldn't allow it on account of most of his best artificers had gone off; besides, he claimed he needed more time to make me into a full-fledged gunsmith. So I sweated over the forges and rifling tables till word came that Gen'ral Washington had got licked real bad at a place in New York called Long Island and that another of our armies had been smashed to pieces 'way up in Canada.

"Around then a feller rode into Lancaster sayin' that the king's generals were plottin' to divide our colonies into two parts."

" — Which was true enough," grunted Samuel Mason. "Burgoyne was to march south from Canada while Sir Henry Clinton was to drive north up the Hudson and meet him; thus they would split the colonies apart and fatally weaken them."

"Well, that same feller who brought this news told about a brand-new regiment bein' raised by an old Injun fighter name of Morgan. His first name was Dan'l, same's mine.

"This regiment, says he, was bein' recruited from expert hunters and frontiersmen. Only real crack shots bringin' their own weepons need apply. Well, sir, I liked the sound so I packed a blanket roll, stored my tools with old Deckerd, shouldered Ilsa here" — he dropped his gaze to the wickedly graceful six-foot rifle resting across his lap — "and set out for Winchester there to enroll with Morgan's Virginia Rifle Regiment for two years' service." Dan peered across the fire, "Say, Doc, sure I ain't agein' you with all this chin-music?"

"Not in the least," Mason assured quickly.

"The Long Knives 'mongst us especially were tickled with Dan'l Morgan's notions about how to fight the enemy."

Mason's small, intense eyes bored through the dim firelight. "Just what is a 'Long Knife'?"

"He's a frontiersman who's collected two or more scalps — or says he has. Course to start with, I was green as spring grass and had a pretty rough time till I twice dropped a runnin' deer at near on two hundred yards.

"After that the boys acted more friendly — 'specially Tim Murphy, who was champion marksman of the regiment. That I could mend almost any piece that wasn't really wore out helped a lot, too.

"Yep. Believe it or not, Doc, Ilsa's accounted for near as many redcoats as Tim Murphy's Kitty — which is that double gun over there; 'tis the same he used at Freeman's Farm to mortally wound a famous Scotch Gen'ral named Fraser. Hit him at over three hundred paces.

"Bein' a friend, he says he could have turned the same trick with Ilsa."

"Why Ilsa? Isn't that an unusual name for a rifle?"

Harsh lines deepened upon the gunsmith's leathery features. "Ilsa was the very first rifle I built that I could really brag on — so I named her after Ilsa Bauer, the Lancaster girl I married first time I came back on furlough.

"Her pa, George Bauer, was and is a champion gunsmith — near as good as old Jake Deckerd himself."

Mason's level dark brows lifted a trifle. "So you're a married man? Odd, I'd never have thought of you as such."

Maddox's hands suddenly closed over the long rifle, whereupon the hound beside him lifted his head and briefly thumped his tail on the ground. "I ain't; happened Ilsa perished tryin' to have our first child. Folks said the baby was big, a real buster. Reckon Ilsa must have been built too slim in the chamber to handle such a big bullet. Little feller died, too."

Jonathan Robertson, Aetat Eleven

Only eleven sheep now ran in the flock Colonel Robertson had entrusted to his eleven-year-old son Jonathan. Descended from a strain brought from the Highlands of Scotland to the mountains of North Carolina, these long-legged, sturdy and dirty-white beasts with black faces had proved able to thrive under the most rugged conditions.

Patriarch of this precious flock was Old Scratch, aptly named for the devil by Jonathan after a particularly trying day during which that evil-tempered and wily old ram again and again had proved just as stubborn, strong-minded and persistent as his herder.

As a rule, livestock traveled near the long column's rear, led by Colonel Jim's herd of horses. Some of these, bought earlier in the year near Kaskaskia, revealed Arab-Spanish blood through proudly arched necks, short-coupled conformation and flowing manes and tails. But not too many of Robertson's horses suggested such distinguished lineage; the majority were undersized, tough, cold-bred Carolina tackeys, brutes designed through survival to live on next to nothing and to die hard.

Care and protection of this invaluable herd — which represented most of the colonel's current capital — had been entrusted to Mark and John Robertson, two of Jonathan's several uncles; both were in their mid-twenties and were powerful and energetic.

Jonathan much preferred Uncle John, who, broad-shouldered, fair-haired and with clear blue eyes, suggested his much older brother both in build and temperament. Uncle Mark, on the other hand, was wiry, slightly built and dark of hair and complexion. Mark seldom spoke unless he had to, but everyone respected his undoubted ability; there was mighty little woodcraft he'd missed acquiring from "Uncle" Daniel Boone, that great authority on various kinds of Indians and the savage tricks peculiar to each tribe.

Just behind the horse herd plodded about two dozen cattle, all sharp-horned, furry and nearly as scary and nimble as deer. After these trotted a sounder of smart but ill-tempered swine; mostly they were ridge-backed and brown-black in color.

Once he'd gulped breakfast, Jonathan secured his scant gear for the day's travel before saddling a runty little horse Pa had presented on his last birthday.

While riding into the woods he congratulated himself: Well, so far I ain't lost but one measly old ewe, so mebbe Pa figures I'm earning my salt and ain't too sorry he's brung me along. Who could have guessed a wolf would dare sneak so near to camp without some dog taking notice? Yep. If it weren't for that dratted Old Scratch this here job would be a tight cinch.

Just before daybreak Cash Brooks had roused and sought Colonel Robertson, whom he found rolling out of a blanket. Hunkering down he muttered, "Mebbe I'm loony, Jim, but jist after sundown yester eve I fancied hearin' a bit of shootin' and whoopin' somewheres 'way off 'mongst them hills yonder. You notice it?"

Robertson yawned cavernously, shook his big, handsome head. "No, Cash. Likely what you heard was the crackle of an old tree fallin' and the cry of wolves running' game. Like you know, at a distance such can sound mighty like people hollerin'."

Cash rubbed white bristles standing out all over his chin. "Yep. I know, but one reason my ma's favorite son is still wearin' his hair is on account of when he ain't sure about something he allus goes and takes a look."

Robertson knuckled his eyes. "Generally I do, too, so suppose you and Joe Drake take a quick look-see, but mind you don't ride too far. We need to cover a lot of ground. This fine weather ain't going to last much longer."

Moving at a cautious trot, Drake and his companion soon came onto a well-used game trail, which they followed till they came upon the clearing about which the bodies of several whites lay scattered among underbrush and old animal bones.

Once the column had been alerted, James Robertson and the point made a quick but perceptive survey and through long experience deduced, accurately enough, what had taken place, how and why.

"Well, Cunnel," demanded Drake, "what d'you make of this?"

"The hostiles numbered about ten, but all the same they got hurt pretty bad by only five white people — always provided none have been carried off prisoner."

"What's your notion, Cash?" Drake wanted to know.

"Why, 'tis 'bout the same as yours, Joe," grunted the Long Hunter while studying forms only partially concealed beneath the torn and bloodied remains of garments. "These poor devils, three or four families of 'em, must ha' been makin' for the trace on their way to Whiteley's or mebbe Harrod's Station. From the style their scalps bin lifted looks like some Piankasaws or Miamis bin at work."

Hard-eyed, Sergeant Maddox was all for an immediate pursuit. "Please, Colonel, let's ride; those brutes can't have gone very far — not leading pack horses."

Firmly, Robertson shook his head. "I'd sure like to, but now we've plenty to worry about on our own account; these people were none of ours."

Over the loud buzzing of clouds of flies the colonel said quietly, "While we may be travelin' in a hurry we can't leave Christian bodies to feed the ravens and wild beasts. Couple of you ride and fetch men with spades."

A short while later Jonathan rode his horse into the hollow where a party of hot and red-faced men in galluses and shirt sleeves were hurriedly patting down grave mounds, and he was never to forget his sensations at the sight he beheld. They must have been working hard, for the only bodies visible were those of a shriveled, yellow-faced old woman and a boy only a little younger than himself.

A savage twist flattening his small, lean-lipped mouth, Uncle Mark directed, "Look yonder, Bub."

The dead boy's meager body lay stiff and naked save for a pair of ragged homespun breeches. His fingers and toes were oddly rigid, spread like talons. He'd had plenty of freckles and his light gray eyes peered at the morning sky sadly, wonderingly — as if he hadn't realized what was happening to him. Ugh! The place where his hair had grown showed as a sickening circle of reddish-white bone upon which a peppering of blue-bottle flies had settled and were crawling busily about.

For all Jonathan already had killed, gutted and skinned many a wild creature and once had beheld the corpse of a man who'd accidentally shot himself, he became aware of bitter bile surging from his stomach, up into his throat and mouth. Lordy! He felt the ground shift under him. Sure, he'd heard plenty of talk about scalping, but this! *This!*

He became aware of Uncle Mark's toneless voice grating, "Aye. Take a good, hard look, boy, and *always* remember that this lad perished because his folks didn't have guards posted nor could they have scouted around this place worth a thin damn before they made camp."

Jonathan, angry all at once, felt prompted to retort that he hadn't noticed any such precautions being taken by the expedition. But, wise for his years, Jim Robertson's son kept quiet.

The Giant

The expedition pressed on towards Harrod's Station with Dr. Mason so overworked that Josh Freedly began to wonder how long his master could keep going.

With regard to Corporal Murphy's recovery the physician's manner remained outwardly confident, although he felt deeply concerned. For a couple of days after the rifleman's mauling it seemed that his gashes were going to heal without complications, but then his arm suddenly grew discolored and began to swell with alarming speed; soon threads of incredibly foul-smelling greenish pus commenced to ooze from between stitches and fouled dressings faster than they could be replaced.

When this happened Mason ordered a litter to be contrived from a canvas dodger supported by side bars of lodge-pole pine and strips of ragged tarpaulin. Suspended between two old mules, led by Josh, the patient traveled in reasonable comfort.

This morning Colonel Robertson had ordered Maddox and Brooks to ride well ahead of the point in order to locate and examine a pair of fords reported to exist in the vicinity and to decide which would offer the most practicable crossing.

One glance at the upper ford's wild water flinging clouds of mist and spray high over a formidable barrier of boulders convinced the scouts that they'd better ride on downstream until they came upon the alternative — Uguhu, or Hunting Owl ford.

Without conversation, Maddox and Cash started southwards, dogged by a trio of muddy, burr-stuck and hungry-looking bear hounds.

All at once Cash reined in and bent low in his saddle before pointing at the snow-covered ground. "See that?"

Clearly and recently imprinted in the snow was a line made by several moccasined feet which had emerged from the deep forest to follow the Kentucky Trace.

Breath vapors shifting about their heads, both scouts bent low, studied the tracks at which the dogs had begun to sniff with mounting interest.

Maddox raised a quizzical brow. "Well, Cash, what're you thinking?"

"Ain't nothin' to get yer sweat started. Only four Injuns went this way — mebbe a hour back. Likely they've been out huntin' or followin' trap lines."

"How can you tell?"

"Prints ain't deep or close together, which means they ain't tired or carryin' heavy packs like they were travelin' far."

Preceded by the dogs, the riders had followed the tracks only a short distance when Cash again jerked on his reins and turned, a puzzled look on his weather-beaten features. "Look! What in hell can have scared them redskins so bad they quit the trace in so big a hurry?"

"How can you tell they got frightened?"

Cash looked pained. "Dan'l! Dan'l! Be you blind as a bat? Take note o' the great, long strides each man's suddenly taking!"

Maddox straightened. "God above! What — what made *those*?" Entering the trace from the direction of the river and sharply imprinted upon the snow was a line of impossibly huge human footprints!

Cash knuckled granulated, red-rimmed eyes, then shook his head as if to clear it. "Je-sus! They *cain't* be real. No human man can own such goddamn tremenjus feet."

Incredulous, Maddox studied a particularly clear impression and estimated it to measure around *twenty* inches in length by *nine* in width! Further, he noted that these tracks had been left by someone wearing shoe-pacs, or hard-soled moccasins.

Remounting, they cocked rifles and, after waving the bear dogs forward, started at a slow walk to follow these incredible footprints. In fact they took so much time about it that before long Colonel Robertson, Joe Drake and others of the point trotted into sight.

[399]

Bright blue eyes gone hard and narrow, Robertson growled, "What in hell ails you boys? Trees grow faster than you been movin'. You should have found Uguhu Crossin' an hour since."

Maddox indicated one of the huge footprints. "My God, sir, ain't you noticed *those* tracks?"

The colonel burst into laughter louder than the river's roaring. "My God! So *that's* what's been holdin' up you stupid bug-tits?"

Dan Maddox flushed under his fringe of short, dull red whiskers. "But, but sir! Look at the *size* of them tracks!"

Joe Drake rode up, exposed gapped, amber-hued teeth in a cavernous grin. "My Gawd, Maddox, you ain't seein' no miracle. Them's only Tom Spencer's footprints."

Cash, coldly furious, snarled, "Who's Tom Spencer?"

"Onliest feller I ever see, or hear tell of, who c'n leave tracks the size of bear-paw snowshoes!"

Drake turned to the colonel. "Say, Jim, 'pears to me like Tom's camp oughter to be somewheres close by."

"That could be. I'll take a look and talk with him. Rest of you — except you, Joe, move on and damn' well find that ford. We'll catch up."

Robertson followed Spencer's trail until it turned off the trace, and penetrated an alder thicket and then headed towards a grove of towering sycamores, the scabrous trunks of which showed an unhealthy greenish white in the weak sunshine. Over the tops of these huge trees lingered a thin, blue-gray stratum of wood smoke.

Joe said to his chief, "What say I ride in first? Tom knows me, so he won't likely shoot first and talk later like he gen'rally does. And can that man shoot! I've seen him shoot the balls off'n a squirrel atop of the tallest hickory you ever *did* see."

He cupped hands and called softly, "Heyo! Tom, you thar?"

Presently Thomas Spencer materialized from a clump of junipers. He lowered a long rifle and halted, his vast brown-clad body effectively framed against the snowy background. Maddox found it very easy to credit that the man yonder stood six-feet-nine in his shoe-pacs and that he must weigh well over four hundred pounds. Surely his shoulders measured a full yard across.

Large steel-gray eyes busy with his visitors, Spencer raised a massive arm above a broad-brimmed hat and made the universal peace sign — palm out, fingers straight.

"Heyo, Joe! What're you doin' in these parts?" he boomed in a low-pitched, deliberate voice.

The old Long Hunter's gaunt, Indian-like features relaxed before he pursed leathery lips and squirted an arc of tobacco juice through a broken front tooth. "Why, Tom, we seen yer hoofprints on the trace so I reckoned I'd come over for a little visit."

Colonel Robertson led forward his mount to grip Spencer's enormous hand. Smiling he said, "Well, I'm sure tickled to meet the famous Tom Spencer. I've heard so many tales about you I figured you must be at least half a legend."

The giant's clear gray eyes twinkled. "Well, I ain't no legend, and won't be till I forget someday to look in the right direction."

The two, each impressive in his own fashion, remained a long moment frankly taking each other's measure.

"Well, Cunnel, reckon you're not here just to pass the time o' day?"

"Of course I'm not. I want you to join my party and come with me to the Frenchman's Lick. I've heard you're extra well acquainted with that part of the country. True?"

Solemnly, the gigantic yellow-brown head inclined under his disreputable brown felt hat. "Sure am. It's a choice country, best I ever seen — exceptin' for — "

"Exceptin' for what?"

"That Injuns hunt all over that country. There's hundreds, maybe thousands of redskins from all the tribes rangin' that ground all year." Spencer frowned at his huge feet. "I was damn' lucky, Cunnel, to quit the Cumberland Valley that spring with a few packloads of pelts and my hair in place. I'm not the one to tempt my luck too far."

"Nobody but a fool would doubt that," Robertson admitted, deep-set blue eyes narrowed. "All the same, what d'you say about comin' along with me?"

Deliberately, the giant scratched at a tangle of tawny-brown hair. "Well now, I don't know really how to answer. I might agree to go along with you, and then again I mightn't."

Robertson went over to ease his mount's girth, a precaution he took whenever opportunity offered.

"Suppose I ask first why you mightn't?"

Spencer looked him square in the face, spoke slowly. "There's too damn' many mean Injuns out there for a man's health. They're not gentle playmates at best, but they'll surely go into a rip-snortin' rage an you try homesteadin' their Big Huntin' Ground. Fer another thing, you're headin' for Cumberland Valley at the wrong time o' year and, if I guess right, your party is strung out along the trace — has to move pretty much in single file." The trapper's enormous shoulders rose in a slow shrug that wrinkled his grimy shirt. "You know as well as I, Cunnel, that even a small war party hitting hard from either flank could cost you dear. Such an attack could cut you up so's you couldn't keep on."

"Don't think I'm not aware of that," Robertson said. "But, Tom, how about it? I sure could profit from your advice and experience."

Gradually Spencer's high, reddish-brown forehead furrowed itself. "Cunnel, I'll made a deal with you. I'll come along *provided* you listen to me if I speak up when I think it's necessary."

"Sure will."

[401]

Shortly after Tom Spencer had joined the column it slowed, then ceased to advance; the trace became clogged by tangles of tired men and animals. Some of the immigrants brushed snow from logs and flat rocks, then, easing off their burdens, plunked themselves down to enjoy a breather.

After a while the word was passed back that a wind-felled oak was blocking the trace at a point where the track passed between two almost vertical walls of rock. Apparently there was no way of passing except laboriously to chop through the two-foot-thick trunk.

"Damn!" grunted a gaunt, sad-faced fellow as he sank onto his heels and fell to sucking morosely on an empty clay pipe. " 'Twill take easy a hour to cut the damn' thing through."

"Maybe there's another way," mildly remarked Spencer. "Let me through, boys, and you, Bub," he paused, towering above Jonathan Robertson, " 'bide here and keep an eye on my property till I get back."

Huge pack bobbing, the giant shouldered forward along the line of men and muddied, slowly steaming pack animals.

Spitting and hawking because of his cold, Spencer soon arrived at the van where Colonel Robertson and the advance guard stood looking almighty disgusted and watching a pair of long-haired axmen strip off their gear. He came shoving through the crowd as effortlessly as a bull moose through an alder thicket. "Reckon maybe I can lend a hand." He slipped off his huge pack and stood studying the barrier. Um. This big oak in falling had managed to jam its trunk between sharp rocks rising sheer on either side of the trace. Resting on pointed stone crotches, it suggested a Cyclopean customs barrier.

Thus far the axmen had accomplished little beyond trimming away minor branches and hacking off some bark.

"What's the trouble, boys?" Spencer observed.

Said one angrily, "This here oak's been dead a long time; 'tis seasoned harder'n a mother-in-law's heart!"

"Reckon that's *one* reason I ain't never married," Spencer said mildly, and after wiping his runny nose on his sleeve, strode over the chip-littered snow. "Suppose some of you fellers lop off the rest of the branches you can reach; others had better crawl over the trunk and hew off those on the far side."

Axmen, already red-faced and sweating, fell to work so furiously that, as Cash Brooks put it, they made a racket like a flock of giant woodpeckers gone crazy. Surprisingly soon a yellow-bearded fellow panted from atop the log, "All right, mister, she's all yourn."

"Keep an eye on these." Spencer passed his rifle to Cash Brooks, also his belt with its dangling tomahawk and a big knife in a fringed sheath. Next, the tawny-haired giant spat on his hands and told the axmen to get out of his way.

Cash Brooks muttered, "By damn! If he figgers he c'n heave that log aside he's coon-cub crazy!"

Spencer heard, and a grin spread over his heavy, powder-marked features. "Maybe I can't; had this goddamn cold on me for over a week."

After shaking long brown hair onto his back, he squirmed his prodigious feet through mud and snow down to hard footing, then locked arms as thick as a small man's legs about the trunk. He gave a tentative heave, but the obstacle only quivered and bits of black bark broke off among the imprisoning rocks. Spencer grunted, then straightened in order to work his moccasins still deeper into the ground.

He'll never do it, James Robertson told himself. That tree must weigh a hundred stone— easy.

A penetrating silence descended when Spencer's massive arms once more encircled the oak. Then, hunching knees under the trunk, he drew a deep breath and commenced, very slowly, to heave upwards. His mighty legs quivered and muscles began to stand out in ridges along his reddening neck and to bunch themselves under his tight-fitting hunting shirt.

Gasps and small, incredulous cries arose from the witnesses when, a fraction of an inch at a time, the mangled trunk commenced to rise. The onlookers' cries swelled while Spencer, face purpling, lifted the tree level with his chest, then with his shoulders. Everyone could hear the giant's back tendons crackle when he raised the tree until its trunk was high enough to clear the cleft of rock in which it had lain. With breath bursting through his lips in steaming, explosive puffs, Spencer shoved his burden in a semi-circle until it cleared the trace.

Eyes popping, Spencer gradually removed his support, then stepped clear, gasping, "Reckon you c'n go ahead."

While yells, shouts and whistles made the dark forest resound, the giant unconcernedly started to resling his gear.

Samuel Grineau Mason, M.D., was occupied in sewing up a long gash gouged across a good horse's withers by a flying ax head when, just after the dangerously swift-running Green River had been crossed, Joe Drake trotted up to the physician, his wrinkled, butternut-hued features anxious and spangled with sweat. "Hi, Doc," he panted. "Come quick! Tim Murphy's runnin' a fever that'd melt a stone and has gone clear out o' his haid."

Mason frowned and nodded, then knotted some final stitches before tucking his bloodied needle, suture and all, into his lapel. Grabbing up his instrument case, he started running across the bivouac after Drake. Josh pelted along behind his master, hugging the medicine chest.

Instants before Dr. Mason pushed through a circle of hard-eyed immigrants, standing in silence about the crude litter, he'd recognized the distinctive sickish-sweet reek of gangrene.

Dan Maddox, crouched by the litter's head, was finding trouble in restraining Murphy's spasmodic struggles. Said he, "I'm feared you've come too late, Doc. Tim's fair burnin' and he can't swallow water without choking."

"His condition is grave — to say the least." Mason straightened, small, dark-brown eyes gleaming, and spoke crisply, "I'm going to need a lot of light, so you fellows stand well back. Also, I'm going to need some fine white wheat flour, so find enough — I don't care where — to make a couple loaves of bread."

The shaggy onlookers stared, then glanced curiously at one another. That the doc had been sorely overworked they knew, but for him suddenly to run off his rocker like this!

"White flour?" repeated a gangling, freckle-faced youth.

"That's what I said!" Mason snapped. "And I'll also need a cup of vinegar and a clean bowl." Meanwhile, he slipped off his rusty-black jacket and, apparently lost in thought, began to roll up sweat-stained sleeves.

A dozen men hurried away, broad hats flapping, coontails asway and lugging their weapons any which way.

"Josh! Fetch that bottle of French wine I've been saving." High, smooth forehead furrowed in concentration, the physician then added a cup of cider vinegar to two cups of Burgundy mixed in a tin pannikin. After adding a cup of hot water, he set the mixture to heat over a low fire. Once the utensil began to give off little tendrils of steam he sank onto his knees beside the litter.

Using crisp, English-inflected accents, he directed Maddox to hold steady the patient's head.

"Aye, sir. But what are you fixin' to do?"

"I'm about to attempt a treatment I once heard of in London." He shrugged faintly. "Of course, there's no guarantee it will work in Murphy's case, but, since your friend certainly will die if he continues like this, I feel justified in going ahead."

From the instrument bag Josh had fetched, the physician removed scalpels, two pairs of broad-jawed retractors, a good-sized sponge and a number of swabs of raw cotton.

"You," he flung at a wide-eyed spectator, "no matter how the patient squirms or jerks, steady the wounded arm. Cash, you hold down his feet. Drake, pinion his good arm."

Watched by a circle of onlookers, Mason sliced through a shapeless mass of horrible-smelling bandages until the shiny, purplish-crimson flesh of Tim's upper arm became exposed. Previously applied split-deer-sinew sutures had all but become lost to sight beneath the swollen and fearfully taut skin.

Over his shoulder the doctor snarled at onlookers who had edged closer. "Stand back, you bloody fools, and turn aside unless you want to risk your eyesight. When one lances a wound like this, pus sometimes spurts a long way."

Mason selected a heavy scalpel and turned his head an instant after making a quick incision. As he'd predicted, a jet of incredibly foul-smelling matter squirted high and far while Tim shrieked like some luckless wretch at an Indian torture stake.

"Easy, Tim, easy on!" Mason soothed, while his assistants struggled to restrain the rifleman's spasmodic writhing. He couldn't tell whether the patient either heard or understood him, but he continued all the same. "Now, Tim, most surgeons would amputate your arm right now, but I'm going to try to save it."

This time the leather gag was forced between the gasping, gurgling patient's big, yellowish teeth and tied into place.

"Now," the physician began to speak as if he were lecturing a class at Surgeon's Hall rather than a gathering of rough and generally illiterate woodsmen, "while my assistant uses these retractors to keep the aperture as far open as possible I will employ this number two surgical knife to excise — cut away, that is — such fungus flesh as can be reached without risking the rupture of important blood vessels." The tall young physician then bent and quickly began to cut away shreds of putrescent flesh.

Murphy's small and wiry body commenced a series of convulsive heaves; his congested and bloodshot eyes rolled wildly about their sockets. The men restraining Murphy did an excellent job.

"Next," Mason's clipped, precise voice penetrated the awed and silent crowd, "we press out whatever gleety matter — pus to you — remains in the wound. Then, because the two main gashes lie so close together, I will remove the partition, thus laying the gashes into a single wound."

A hungry jackass, somewhere off in the forest, commenced to bray just as Sam Mason dipped his sponge into steaming hot water and commenced to swab out the single wound. Tim then fainted dead away, ceased to struggle and lay limp.

Mason passed a wrist over his sweat-brightened forehead, selected a fresh sponge, then said in even tones, "Had I some *balsam traumatic* I would use it, but since I haven't, I will make do with this mixture."

He called for the pannikin of heated wine and vinegar, and when Josh, pallid, piggy gray eyes round, brought it, the physician soaked his sponge in the mixture.

"Now you, Maddox, watch carefully how I do this because this procedure must be repeated every hour for perhaps the next twenty-four hours, possibly longer. I cannot perform this service myself since other patients need my services, too. Now give me your undivided attention."

Holding his steaming sponge just a few inches above the wound, Samuel Mason, M.D., squeezed it gently to allow dark, red-brown drops to fall a few at a time into the wound until the cavity was filled. "You must allow these drippings to remain for near ten minutes, then wipe out the wound and cover it with a dressing."

Maddox drawled, "Damn' good thing Tim ain't awake. That slop must burn like hell's own fire!"

"It will burn worse that that," Mason smiled thinly, "but it's worthwhile if this poor devil keeps his arm."

"He'd better," muttered Joe Drake through his ragged, drooping mustaches. "One-armed men don't last extry long in country like we're headin' for."

By the time the surgeon for the second time had started to drop hot wine and vinegar into the unconscious rifleman's wound, Drake returned accompanied by a wizened little man half his size. "Ben here 'lows he's got a bit of white flour — but only a bit — and he wun't give it away lest he gits a few bites for hisself on 'count of his teeth is gone so bad he can't chaw no pone nor biscuit."

The small, shriveled man held out a canvas bag protected from dampness inside an oiled deer's bladder. "Oughter be sufficient for three middlin' loaves; ye c'n have it all, provided I c'n have one for myself."

He beckoned forward a bittern-thin companion wearing a filthy Dutch blanket coat. "Charley here's got a bottle of yeast which he's kept workin'."

"Thank you."

"Doc, ye're sure welcome," Charley said, "but I'd be grateful if ye'd tell us why're so all-fired set on bakin' a mess of white bread."

"In due course I intend to make a poultice," Mason explained.

"What d'ye mean by 'in due course'?"

"I shan't use this bread till it grows moldy."

The wizened man's red-rimmed gray eyes rounded themselves. "You surely ain't going to feed this pore feller on moldy bread?"

Slowly, Sam Mason shook his head. He was very, very weary — worried, too. "No. As I said, as soon as the bread turns moldy I mean to make a poultice of it. I've heard there's nothing like such to draw poisons out of a suppurating wound."

Before his expedition next day resumed its progress towards Carpenter's Station, Colonel Robertson issued orders that a handful of men should remain behind to care for Tim Murphy.

This decision was the result of a brief talk with Sam Mason who'd stated flatly, "To move Murphy at this time would ensure his death, for all his fever has abated for the time being."

"Good. Murphy's too valuable to lose. How's his arm?"

The physician's shoulders lifted under his rusty black coat. "It would win no prizes, but, as I've said, Tim's temperature *is* lower. What he needs is to be kept quiet for another day or two and grant me time to try a dressing I'm preparing."

Robertson gathered his reins, then started his mount towards the trace. "Very well, I'll leave four men behind to help you. You've permission to keep Murphy where he is for two days. After that, you'll have to promise to move him and catch up with the rest of us as quick as you can." The bold blue eyes narrowed briefly. "Can't spare your services any longer for the sake of a sick man — or risk the lives of four healthy men. You can keep Ed Jennings, Maddox and Josh with you."

The white bread baked by the wizened little man turned out to be surprisingly palatable. He accepted his loaf and departed masticating it joyfully between his blackened stumps of teeth. Dr. Mason, however, sliced the remaining loaves into thick slabs which he stuffed into a rotten hollow log.

Joe Drake, Josh and Maddox watched the New Englander. Finally Drake grunted, "You really mean for this fine bread to spoil?"

Mason summoned a wry grin. "That is true; as I told you earlier, I intend to attempt a rare treatment which may save your friend's arm."

Not until late in the afternoon of the day Robertson's column had moved on did the first fibers of sage-green mold begin to appear like a gossamer beard on some of the bread.

Mason muttered more to himself than to his assistants, "Wish to God I could recall exactly how such a poultice is prepared and applied. Question: should the bread be crumbled and rendered into a thick paste, or should slices showing the most mold be bound, whole, over the wound?' After a moment's deliberation he elected the second method.

Tim's fever-parched lips formed a tremulous, pallid smile. "Go ahead, Doc, whatever you decide is all right with me. I don't feel near so feverish as I did."

Breathing a prayer, Sam Mason placed several greenish-white slices of bread over the wound, then, despite Murphy's gasps and half-stifled groans, bound the applications lightly in place with a flannel bandage.

Drawled Joe while biting off a chew, "In my time I've heered of plenty queer notions 'bout physicking, but this one sure beats 'em hollow. Expect that mess to do Tim some real good?"

A hard laugh escaped the physician. "Now isn't that a damn' fool question? Why else would I attempt this technique? Tomorrow should tell whether or not Tim stands a chance of keeping his arm. Right now, I'm so hungry I could eat a horse and chase its driver."

Carpenter's Station

Long before a scout came riding back with news that another expedition was encamped about Carpenter's Station, James Robertson had known about it. Why else should several smoke columns be rising above the forest? Even on a peaceful mission, Indians never would have lit so many fires close together.

Taking along Cash Brooks and his brown-and-black bear dog, Bassoon, Robertson trotted forward to join the point.

"Heyo, Cunnel!" someone sang out. "Any news from Maddox and Murphy?"

Robertson turned in the saddle, shook his head. "Never a peep. Still, I expect they'll be along directly."

The point continued to push on along the west bank of the Green River, anxious to come upon the fortified station not long ago established by a tough old frontiersman named Charley Carpenter. For some obscure reason, here in Kentucky such civilian outposts — no matter how weak or small — had come to be known as "stations."

Robertson readily could visualize what Carpenter's Station would be like; a pair of small, square two-story log houses — each built with a slight overhang to its upper floor and connected with each other by two palisades of roughly pointed logs. One of these curtain-walls likely would be pierced by a small gate flanked by firing platforms.

The courtyard thus created might enclose perhaps a quarter acre of bare ground on which travelers and settlers could take refuge when the Shawnees and Piankashaws or some lesser tribe threw away their peace pipes and replaced them with red-shafted tomahawks.

Joe Drake rode up beside the messenger from Carpenter's, who was a sad-faced, slightly cross-eyed fellow with a gray-streaked beard and wearing a ratty clump of turkey-cock feathers stuck, Indian fashion, into the back of a round cap of fox fur.

"Say, friend, anybody at the station 'side from Carpenter's folks?"

"Yep. Party of settlers from New River in Virginny came in yesterday. 'Tis led by an old-timer called John Rains — and a loudmouth windbag named of Valentine." The cross-eyed man snorted. "How them two ever got together I'll never figger out, 'cept that Rains knows this here country, while the squire, or 'Major' Valentine — as he calls himself — must be carrying plenty of hard money in his saddlebags — " the speaker snickered, "or maybe he's got it hid 'neath his girls' petticuts."

"Then Rains has got females along?" Drake demanded.

"Yep. Four wives, two girls and eight children, two of which is useful, half-grown boys." The scout winked. "Man! Wait till you lay eyes on the Valentine girl-twins; they're pert and handsome as a pair o' speckled pups."

Drake's expression relaxed. "Be they old enough?"

"Sure. Must be all of seventeen. And willing, too — well, one of 'em sure looks like it."

Carpenter's Station turned out to be pretty much as Robertson had anticipated: a pair of plain two-story stronghouses connected by crude palisades of pointed pine logs.

Robertson asked of the cross-eyed man, "Which way is Rains headed?"

"For Harrod's — if it's still there after the Hair Buyer's doin's last year."

"It's still there, friend," Robertson said. "George Rogers Clark and some Virginia troops took Vincennes last winter."

From the small, smoke-veiled encampment outside the station came John Rains limping on a leg which once had been broken and not set correctly. Rains was as dark-skinned as any Catawba, and like them wore his hair in twin braids. A few yards behind Rains strode a thick-bodied individual wearing a bleached, almost white, buckskin hunting shirt and Indian leggings. Ike Bledsoe had a small, round head and enormously long arms.

"How are ye, ye ornery old wampus cat?" called Drake.

"Fit to swaller ye whole 'thout butterin' them hairy ears of yourn," the other yelled back.

To Robertson it was a fine thing to see and hear children again — mostly sunburned and clad in thick linsey-woolsey or homespun garments. As they drew near the little fort a number of significant facts became evident: for instance, a couple of spinning wheels stood in plain sight, and two pairs of heavy cartwheels, tired with iron, rested against convenient trees.

Other members of the point also were pleased by the homely sight of a family's laundry hung out on bushes to dry and by the sound of soft, feminine voices and the excited yells of children.

Even unusually silent Major Phillips, when he appeared at the head of the dangerously strung-out main body, allowed it was mighty fine to watch a flock of red-brown hens and a couple of splendidly lecherous roosters scratching, chasing insects and otherwise making the most of this unseasonably warm November day.

Among Rains's people stood a tall, stoop-shouldered fellow who'd a new scar flaming across his left cheek. Beside him was a handsome, straight-backed young woman whose brown hair was worn tightly skinned back into a neat bun. The couple were ex-militiaman Andrew Dickinson and Peggy, his capable-appearing wife. They were present today in Carpenter's Station chiefly because last July, British, Hessian and Loyalist troops under General Ben Garth and his Tory second-in-command, General William Tryon, had attacked, burned and thoroughly looted the thriving and, to them, pestiferous little port of Norwalk, Connecticut.

When the British forces had pulled out they'd left Dickinson's boatyard a seething mass of flames along with a salt works, two churches, one hundred thirty dwellings — Andrew's among them — eighty-seven barns, twenty-two stores, seventeen shops, four mills and five vessels.

In idle curiosity the Connecticuter viewed the haphazard arrival of Robertson's main body. He paid these shaggy, dusty fellows no real attention until he watched Dr. Samuel Mason's black-clad figure come riding out of the forest and into the clearing. Peggy then heard Andy's jaw shut with a sharp *click!* and watched him shade his eyes against the sun to get a better look at that somber, well-set-up figure.

Peggy Dickinson cast her husband a quick sidewise glance. "What's wrong, Andy?"

[409]

"Don't know yet, but do you mark that tall, red-haired feller with *the* hawk's nose?"

"The one wearing a broad-brimmed black hat?"

"Yes."

"What about him?"

Dickinson's hand crept up to stroke a long, forceful-looking jaw. "I'm pretty near certain I've seen that man before."

"When?"

"Not too long ago. That's what bothers me."

Behind the hurriedly dropped and plentifully mildewed flaps of the only sizable tent in the clearing, the twin daughters of Virginius Virgil Valentine, Esquire, began to comb long, honey-hued tresses — Rosemary for the first, Choice for the third time that day.

Choice sniffed, then her large, dark-brown and velvet-soft eyes sought her twin. "Darling, will you lend me your blue grosgrain hair ribbon?"

Knowing by experience that she'd probably never see it again, Rosemary shook her bright blonde head.

"Oh, please! You know you hardly ever wear it. Besides, I promise to take extra-good care of it."

Rosemary's wide, dark-red mouth firmed itself as she bent over, her small-boned figure gilded by sunlight beating through the travel-stained canvas, to peer through the rear flaps at the dust-clouded clearing. "Sorry, poppet, but you'll have to make do with that black ribbon you borrowed just before we set out on this horrible journey. I'm going to need the blue one myself."

Still fluffing her hair, Choice wrinkled a pert little nose. "All right, *be* a meanie! What do you see?"

"About what I expected. A lot of men, all dirty, ragged and coarse."

Choice came over to join her sister in surveying the new arrivals. "You're right. If there's one man of substance or gentility among 'em, well, I'll be switched — and worse than Papa does it."

Their mother's petulant voice penetrated the canvas partition dividing the tent into two compartments. "Why bother primping for a parcel of timber beasts and assorted scalawags?"

At that moment the tent's front flap was swung apart as an orotund voice boomed, "Not so fast, my love. Not so fast! I have just been in conversation with Colonel Robertson, who leads these new arrivals. Damn, if he ain't a man of parts. And in more ways than one, I'd say. Ha! ha! ha!"

"Mr. Valentine!" Agnes Valentine squeaked in shrill indignation. "Pray do not lower yourself to a level with the coarse manner of our fellow immigrants."

"Tush, woman, and hold your tongue. Mr. Rains informs me this fellow's a Virginian of birth and breeding, much respected in high places. He is also a famed explorer of this infernal wilderness. Moreover, for a long time he served as agent among the Cherokee Indians; handled 'em in masterful fashion. Besides, he holds a bona fide colonel's commission. How does that sound to you young ladies?"

Choice's contralto voice affected a mincing tone. "La, Papa, I shall do my best to earn the colonel's favorable opinion — of our family. Is he married?"

"Don't yet know, but there's no doubt he's influential out here."

Choice finished tying saucy little bows to either side of her softly oval face, then called, "Please, Papa, I must straightaway breathe fresh air or die; I'm fair stifling."

The Valentine family discovered Colonel Robertson sitting with his boots off before a fireplace and chatting easily with Rains and Charles Carpenter while he sipped at a beaker of rum and water. This, the host's only downstairs room, was where he and his numerous family lived, cooked and ate. To go to bed they had to clamber up a crude ladder to a chilly loft where a number of shapeless bough beds were revealed by light filtering through a series of crudely shuttered loopholes.

Imperceptibly, Robertson's attention shifted from the faintly absurd figure gripping his hand to the petite young blondes hesitating behind their father. By God, they certainly were as delicate-looking and as prettily alike as two fresh blossoms on a flowering wild cherry.

Mrs. Valentine acknowledged the tall Virginian's bow with a brief curtsy, then rather diffidently declared herself vastly pleased to meet this raw-boned and weather-beaten but still somehow impressive individual.

"My daughters, sir." Valentine waved them forward to curtsy in their turn and then retire behind their mother.

Once Rains and Carpenter, bearded, sweating and malodorous, had been presented, along with Major Todd Phillips, who came tramping in, there ensued considerable talk and speculation about the progress of the war back East.

With pompous gravity, Squire Valentine presently informed the company that he was emigrating westwards because he foresaw with certainty that the patriot cause was doomed, French help or no French help, and that within a few months there wouldn't be a single American army left in the field.

"No, gentlemen," rumbled the big-bellied man in the militia coat, "we can't possibly win. Everything militates against us — ruined economy and finances, shortages of men and warlike materials indicate a complete British victory within six months — or eight at the outside."

Valentine made a wide gesture and summoned a lugubrious expression. "And that, my friends, is why I decided to abandon a flourishing estate in Bethlehem to hazard life and — ahem, fortune — in order to assist in founding a free new nation in this magnificent Territory of Kentucky."

Three-legged stools were dragged forward to accommodate the ladies

[411]

before lantern-jawed Charles Carpenter produced a stone jug of throat-searing Monongahela whisky and some wooden noggins. Everybody was eager to exchange scraps of news about how George Rogers Clark and his little force nowadays were faring up in Vincennes and whether the British were going to succeed in bribing the Chickasaws.

Rains predicted that next spring the Miamis and Cherokees surely would send out their red sticks. Voices rose once Carpenter's whisky had begun to "spread out." Squire Valentine's big voice dominated the general babble.

From the doorway someone called in clear, ringing tones, "Greetings, gentlemen!"

With cup immobilized halfway to his lips Colonel Robertson wheeled to face the entrance and almost voiced his vast relief on recognizing Sam Mason, M.D., who strode in looking haggard but neatly shaven and wearing a taut smile. Rosemary Valentine cast him a quick glance, thinking she'd never beheld finer or sadder dark eyes than those of this tall young man in rusty black.

Robertson took the physician's hand between both of his. "Glad you're safe. How's Murphy?"

Mason replied in the abruptly quiet room, "We're all here, sir. Murphy still has both arms."

"Good. I began to worry a little when you didn't catch up a couple of days back."

Major Phillips queried, "How's Tim Murphy?"

"As I've said, he's mending well." The physician's thorn-torn finger drummed against the noggin he'd been given. "What that moldy bread did for his festering arm was nothing short of miraculous. But seeing is believing, so — " Mason called over his shoulder, "Maddox! Bring in Murphy, will you?"

Everyone crowding in the smelly little room turned to face the doorway and watched Maddox enter with one arm supporting the Rifleman of Saratoga. The famous sharpshooter looked gaunt, but his dark eyes were bright and his color looked good. He grinned broadly and pointed proudly to his hurt arm now riding in a moss-padded sling.

Robertson said quietly, "Glad to have you back in one piece!"

Murphy reddened. "Thank ye, Colonel. Reckon I'll not tangle with no more bears for a while — she-bears least of all."

"Bet that'll be the only she-critters he'll avoid," grunted Joe Drake, then turned to greet Dan Maddox, but checked himself because the gunsmith, having just caught sight of Mistress Rosemary Valentine, was staring across the room with a foolish grin spreading all over his face.

The Gentle Art of Persuasion

For Colonel Robertson to escape from Squire Valentine's verbosity without injuring that gentleman's sensibilities called for resourcefulness, but he managed to do so by summoning a rueful smile and pointedly shaking the last drops from a whisky flask they'd been sharing.

"'Tis been a rare pleasure, sir, for me to converse once more with a real gentleman," boomed the big-paunched figure; he then departed breathing noisily and moving a trifle unsteadily toward his tent.

Jim Robertson found it wonderfully restful just to sit under the stars beside the Green River with only his dog, Bassoon, for company. For a while he allowed his mind to remain blank and listened to chuckling gurgles caused by the Green's current hurrying over or around exposed stones. Whew! It sure was fine to be shut for a while of Squire Valentine's loud and overbearing voice.

Presently, two quietly treading figures appeared: one was John Rains, who by starlight might well have been mistaken for a Mohawk sachem what with his straight black hair and thin hawk's nose. The other proved to be soft-spoken and usually laconic Ike Bledsoe, who so much resembled Rains that frequently they were mistaken for brothers for all that they were in no degree related.

Rains slipped his dully gleaming long knife from its sheath, then caught up a dead twig and, settling onto his heels, commenced to whittle an Indian "prayer stick" — later on it would prove handy in raising a flame among dying coals.

Foxes had commenced to bark across the river when at last the old Long Hunter spoke. "Well, Jim, what'd you make of my genteel partner?"

Robertson paused in stroking Bassoon's scarred head and grunted, "My God, John, whatever drove you to join shares with such a windy jaybird? Damned if he don't talk longer and louder'n any drunken Choctaw. And what's he doing in those silly regimentals? Bet he'd soil his pants if anybody was to shoot even close to him."

By the light of the waning moon John Rains shook his dark and narrow head. "I'll grant you Valentine's noisy and bone-lazy to boot, but all the same I've the notion that the fellow's no coward, and gen'rally, Jim, I ain't mistook 'bout that quality in a man."

"Even so, why'd you team up with him?"

Thoughtfully, John Rains started cutting another ruff of splinters around his prayer stick. "Ever heard about a useful thing called 'money'? Well, he has some — plenty, I'd say, whilst I ain't seen a pound — hard money — in above a year."

At length Colonel Robertson queried almost casually, "Tell me, John, are you dead-set on takin' your folks to Harrod's place?"

"Yep. Why not?"

[413]

"Look, John, you've ranged all 'round the Frenchman's Lick and must know that the bluff is a far better location for a settlement than Harrod's."

"Why?" Ike grunted.

"Why, the land's wonderfully rich around there."

Rains nodded, said carefully, "That's sure 'nough so, but I ain't forgotten that Harrod's lies in Kentucky and don't occupy none of the Great Huntin' Country. I figure the savages won't bother us much if we settle close by Harrod's."

"No tellin' about that," Robertson remarked quietly. "But that far into Kentucky you're going to be awfully lonesome and spread out mighty thin for a long time to come." He straightened, looked Rains in the face. "Now, John, suppose you were to come along with me to Middle Tennessee and settle along in the Cumberland River Valley — then you'd find plenty of neighbors within easy reach within a few months' time."

"Maybe so, maybe not. What makes you so sure we'd have plenty of neighbors in that there bloody wilderness?"

Robertson began to speak quickly, earnestly. "Here's the reason. What with the war going so poorly back East people already have started flockin' westwards. Most of 'em want to start over, damn' well out of reach of the Crown. Amos Eaton, Kasper Mansker, Jim Freeland and the Buchanans all are headed west that way right now and leading sizable parties — or ought to be."

Robertson waited a while, then inquired briskly, "Well, John, what d'you say? Will you keep on for Harrod's or come along with me?"

A soft sigh escaped Rains. "Dunno. Right now I feel kind of like the feller who knew two pretty gals and could ha' wed either of 'em, but he couldn't decide which he wanted the most. Well, I'm in the same kind of a bind; both Harrod's and the Frenchman's Lick have a lot to recommend 'em."

"It's a hard choice, friend Rains, that much I'll admit." Robertson leaned forward, elbows on leather-covered knees. "And I, too, have had to make a tough decision today."

"How's that?"

"I've been wonderin' how much your families and livestock might slow me up." He arose, slapped twigs and leaves from his seat. Bassoon got up, too, yawned and stretched. "We're behind time already, so we'll have to set a brisk pace if we're to reach the Cumberland before winter really closes in."

Bledsoe asked in a husky whisper, "What'll you do if you find we slow you too much?"

Robertson stared out over the hurrying, white-flecked river. "Well, Ike, I reckon I'd just have to push on and leave you people to follow the best way you can."

[414]

Rains adjusted a coonskin cap. "Which, in this great empty country, ain't a over-comfortin' prospect."

"No, it's not. But that may not happen, and at any rate, you'd be no worse off than if you were to keep on for Harrod's by yourself."

Because he was suffering from a touch of the "rheumatiz," Bledsoe arose stiffly, like an old horse on a frosty morning, then said, "Robertson makes sense."

Rains heaved a deep sigh, then held out a hand. "That's so. Reckon we'll trail along."

As if Providence had set its seal of approval upon this union of the parties the weather for the next two days remained ideal, clear with a bright sun and gentle wind that stung a man's ears only a little.

Next day it was decided that from now on the expedition would have a strong advance guard composed of Ike Bledsoe, Tom Spencer, Cash Brooks, Joe Drake and others familiar with this vast, hilly and forest-shrouded country. John Rains would be in command.

Reluctantly but wisely, Robertson assumed the less exciting but very responsible duty of seeing that the main body kept advancing at its best possible speed.

Now that November had entered its first week no one was much surprised when, as they left Carpenter's Station, the sky assumed ominous silver-gray and black hues and the wind began to nip ever more keenly.

On the third day after quitting the feeble little settlement the weather grew considerably colder and, to make matters worse, a light but all-penetrating rain set in and slanted down hour after hour. Because there wasn't any wind, trees, bushes, men and animals became silver-sheathed by particles which stung eyelids and exposed skin like millions of invisible midges.

Shortly after noon the main body was forced to halt when they found the advance guard had stopped, all bunched up, before a sizable, slate-gray river roaring in white fury over a stone-studded ford which, according to Ike Bledsoe, was known as Mad Bear Crossing.

"Why 'Mad Bear?' " Jonathan wanted to know.

"A few years back, a feller got slain here by a bear that'd just raided a bee tree and had been driven crazy by stings," Bledsoe told him.

"That's sure one hell of a current out there," opined John Rains, fingering his bristle-covered jaw. "Must ha' rained hard as hell somewheres up country."

No one disagreed, since the little river already had begun to overflow its low banks.

Looking about, Jonathan could spy rabbits, skunks, foxes and other non-climbing small animals crouched disconsolately on logs, hummocks and big, moss-covered rocks.

[415]

For a half mile back from Mad Bear Creek men and their livestock collected in knots and cursed this relentless downpour which was turning into rattling, biting sleet. Drovers permitted their charges to wander off the trace to feed halfheartedly on frosty clumps of dead weeds and ferns.

At the river's edge Rains, Robertson and Phillips reluctantly decided that because of the river's dangerously swollen condition and the ever increasing iciness of the weather, serious results would ensue if everybody got completely soaked; some of the women and young folk might readily die of such exposure.

Commented Major Phillips, wiping a pellucid drop from the tip of a knife-sharp nose, "Reckon the only thing is to build a raft."

"Aye, but that's easier said than done." Wrinkles already furrowing John Rains's brow deepened while he scanned the current rushing wildly southwards to lose itself in the Green. "But even so — "

"But even so, what — ?" demanded Robertson in a rare burst of impatience.

"But how're we goin' to keep a raft from bein' carried off downstream? Poling alone won't prevent that."

Tom Spencer pushed to the shoreline with drops of frozen water glittering like silver beads strung along the rim of his broad hat. "Ye're right, John, ain't no earthly use tryin' to pole a raft across that stream and back 'thout its driftin' so far downstream with every crossin' that the people couldn't keep abreast."

His large steel-gray eyes narrowed themselves, then he eased off his enormous pack. "Party I was along of a few years back got in the same fix we're in — only we was worse off 'cause there was a big war party somewhere behind us just hankerin' to lift our hair."

Still in the saddle, Robertson flailed arms to warm himself. "Well?"

The giant Virginian grinned. "Show you, Jim, if you'll just pass the word for the boys to start buildin' a raft of straight logs not less'n a foot and a half acrost their center. Cut 'em twenty, no, thirty foot long. Meantime, anybody who owns a length of stout rope is to fetch it here straightaway."

Rains's weathered features relaxed with comprehension. "I get it. You'll have 'em knotted into two long lines."

"Yep, and use the weaker lengths to lash the raft together."

The necessary orders having been given, Robertson studied the furiously leaping water, then drawled, "Reckon I understand your intention, Tom."

"And that is?"

"You'll hitch long, stout ropes to each end of the raft and, by snubbing them around trees on either shore, control the raft between banks."

Spencer grinned in the depths of his beard. "That's correct, Cunnel. Always did claim us Virginians are smart above the rest."

It having proved impossible to complete a satisfactory raft before darkness fell, the miserable settlers belatedly made camp any which way amid semidarkness.

Never before, decided Choice Valentine, had she felt anywhere near so miserable, untidy and disgusted as on the next morning. How many days had she been wearing these same damp, shapeless and now smelly garments? Of course, there'd been no opportunity for her or any other woman to change clothing. Anyhow, to have done so wouldn't have been practical; on the march everyone's garments got soaked, ripped and dirty in no time at all.

The Valentine family had spent the night huddled close together under a tarpaulin which, carelessly rigged, had permitted cold rain to *drip-drip* onto them as they shivered under half-soaked blankets.

By the time dawn broke, gray and cheerless, Agnes Valentine and the twins had taken colds varying in degree. The old Negress Sally, however, appeared to be immune; Squire Valentine hazarded that perhaps this was because of the snuff the slave woman kept taking.

While scanty breakfasts were being prepared word was passed along the column that on this frigid morning Tom Spencer had added another feat to the legend of his prowess. After stripping to his pants he'd tied a bundle of clothes onto his head, had knotted a slender rope's end about his middle, and had waded boldly into the raging current until forced to swim across white water marking the creek's main channel. Naked as a fledgling bird, Spencer then had endured the freezing wind to kindle a fire with a tinder pistol brought over in a waterproof bag.

Once he'd dressed and got his fire really going Tom pulled across a heavier line which he'd then anchored to a sturdy tree. Once this had been done half a dozen hardy Long Knives had pulled themselves along the submerged rope to arrive on the far shore blue-lipped and with their sodden buckskins clinging as if modeled to their bodies. Once they'd partially thawed themselves at the giant's fire, they'd set about kindling more blazes, since it stood to reason that even folks crossing on the raft ferry couldn't avoid getting pretty wet in places.

Each time the raft made a crossing its progress was further impeded by wild-eyed horses, sheep, and mules and cattle being towed along, willynilly, at the bight of long reins or halter shanks. It proved difficult enough to haul or drive these unwilling animals into the frigid water, but to usefully employ a pole between rearing, threshing bodies proved almost impossible.

Midday found nearly two-thirds of the expedition dripping and shivering on Mad Bear Creek's far shore. The Valentine party and another family of Rains's following were fortunate in having to await their turn for a long while; by then the ferry gangs had grown experienced.

Just before her family started to cross a stretch of trampled mud speckled with broken shale ice towards the ferry raft, Choice suffered a cramp in her bowels so agonizing that she knew, come what might, she simply couldn't any longer postpone a "visit to the bushes." She knew she should have yielded to this embarrassing need much earlier, but she hadn't done so because with such an icy wind snapping at her exposed private parts it was certain to prove a dreadful ordeal. In fact, not a few of the women and older girls all along had suffered from self-induced costiveness because of their reluctance to "seek the bushes."

In the depths of a willow thicket Choice could hear voices — including Papa's — angrily calling for her to hurry and take her place on the waiting raft, but for the life of her she couldn't bring herself to call out. As a result, cold and weary Major Phillips, in charge of loading the raft, yelled to the pole men, "Don't tarry longer. Shove off! She can cross later on."

"Count on Choice to complicate things unnecessarily," growled the squire, then added softly and with relish, "Silly little fool's earned herself another smart switching the first chance I get."

The balance of the Valentine family crouched, huddled together on baggage piled near the clumsy raft's center. Water licking up between hastily aligned logs nipped at their ankles and they felt inclined to agree that this time the head of the family had a real cause for chastisement.

They forgot about the missing girl once the raft commenced to leap and plunge under them.

Choice, on returning pink-faced and self-conscious to the river's edge, found a group of men squatting about a fire and cooking a brace of half-plucked partridges on broiling sticks.

In no great hurry either to face her furious parents or to board the ferry-raft on the next trip, she walked boldly up to the fire.

"My! Don't they look good!" she commented, then treated each of the whiskery, muffled men to a slow look that made them jump to their feet.

Color rushed into Tim Murphy's thin and long-unshaven cheeks. "These birds ain't done yet but ye'll be welcome to a few chaws once they are."

"Thank you. I'll stand here till I get warmed up a bit." Risking a knowing grin, she turned her wind-nipped backside to the heat. Thankfully, Choice accepted the piggin of bitter but steaming hot acorn coffee which Dan Maddox held up to her.

Major Phillips appeared, cold and angry. "What the hell's been keeping you men?"

"We're detailed to the rear guard, sir," Dan explained.

"That may be so, but the colonel's been calling for you, Maddox, and Cash and Murphy."

Maddox immediately got up, slapped wet leaves from his seat, then picked up his pack and rifle. "In that case, boys, reckon we'd better get moving, and ye'd better come with us, Sissy."

Before long the raft was loaded again with some hog-tied pigs that kept shrieking outrage over being piled among baggage near the ferry's center.

To leave their arms free, Tim, Dan and Cash strapped their rifles, muzzles down, between their shoulders, then heaped war bags and belts on the baggage, where Choice sat with skirts hitched high to keep them free of water that kept spurting up between the logs.

Tim's bad arm still wasn't well enough to permit his handling a pole, so he did what he could by encouraging Choice and using a cudgel to keep the terrified pigs under control.

Cash and Dan, legs braced wide apart, drove poles into the rocky bottom and pushed with all their strength when the ferry began to heave and plunge so violently that it appeared ready to disintegrate.

The raft was halfway across Mad Bear Creek when a large, uprooted tree suddenly appeared in the boiling current and neatly severed the ferry's lead rope. At once the raft slewed so violently as to hurl a pair of the regular pole men into the water along with some of the pigs.

Choice tried to shriek but couldn't — she was too terrified.

"Christ A'mighty!" Cash Brooks gasped when, his pole having been wrenched away, he fell flat on his back. The raft yawed and then started to swing on its stern line back towards the east bank.

The sudden increase of pressure on the tail-rope was enough to rip that line from the grip of the men on the east bank. Freed, the raft went plunging and spinning crazily downstream.

At this moment Dan's pole snapped, sent him lurching up to his knees in frothing water.

Uncontrollable now, the raft began to revolve and speed towards a rapids roaring downstream. Maddox groped for one of those ropes which bound the raft together, then with a free hand gripped one of Choice's ankles. Tim, all white eyes, streaming hair and gaping mouth, got the idea and seized the other while the last pigs followed the baggage overboard.

The raft began to rear and plunge like a cruelly spurred horse and the air became filled with sheets of icy blinding spray until the ungainly craft struck a reef with so violent an impact that the ferry captain and his remaining pole man fell into the foaming water.

Mad Bear Creek suddenly narrowed between walls of rock, causing its current to accelerate and carry the raft inexorably towards the rapids — a smother of leaping, twisting white water.

Numbed by fear, Choice tried to pray, but couldn't find the right words — unlike Rosemary, she'd never been very attentive to such matters.

Bitterly, she told herself that what was about to happen wasn't fair; so far, she'd not had very much fun out of life. Without actually formulating the thought, she resolved that should she survive this ordeal she'd never again deny herself a joyous moment, no matter what people said or did.

Time and again the raft collided with snags or struck rocks with such violence that its last bindings snapped and the people aboard suddenly were hurled into the icy, churning current.

Choice managed to hook an arm over a big log and was whirled away, babbling incoherently. "Know — I — wanton — vain. I — too young to die — not for a while. Don't wrinkle — pink gown — no, Ben — Papa might — "

To Choice, only semiconscious, it seemed that she had become immersed in flame clear over her head; she'd no realization that intense cold, not heat, was causing such agony. Her last sensation before losing consciousness was of something tugging savagely at her hair.

When, dazedly, she began to recover her senses, she heard a barely audible voice mumble, "Reckon she — dead?"

"Hell, no! Look, Dan, her tits are beginnin' to stir a little. Here, lend a hand, let's drain some o' the creek outen her."

Then Choice felt herself held upside down by the ankles so that her streaming skirt and triple petticoats fell and muffled her head while she retched quantities of water out of her lungs.

Finally someone remarked, "Well, Cash, can't be much more water left in her. Help ease her down."

"All right, but I hate to do it," said someone else. "Ain't likely I'll soon view another such a pretty white arse."

"To hell with this biddy's arse! Where's Tim?"

"Saw him come ashore below us."

She recognized Dan Maddox's voice when he said, "You sure?"

"Yep. Spied him crawlin' up the bank on hands and knees."

"Say, where's your war bag?"

"Same as yours — in the river — bullet mold, bar lead, picker — everythin'. Now ain't that *hell*?"

Choice felt content to lie where she was, even if sleet continued pitilessly to sting her; it was just as if a million needle-footed spiders were running over every inch of her exposed skin.

Tim bent and in an undertone suggested, "Maybe I'd better rub circulation into yer legs — wouldn't want you to get frostbite."

Not altogether sure that she wanted to protest, Choice nodded, and felt his palms begin to chafe under her sodden underpinnings all the way up her thighs. Presently, when friction began to restore warmth to her lower body, she sighed.

"Oh-h. That's wonderful — don't stop."

Maddox, however, called out sharply, "Leave off, Tim, you've had fun enough. Go collect dead grass."

Once they'd got an efficient fire glowing the men started to dry their footgear. Bronzed by soaring flames, Choice unconcernedly removed and then wrung out stockings of coarse gray wool before toasting sizable but well-formed feet. She would have felt a sight better had she not lost both shoes.

"I'm hungry," Choice announced in a dull voice. "Isn't there anything to eat?"

"No, Sissy," Tim said, "and there ain't nothin' to be done about it now."

The old Long Hunter quit leaping about and scanned the darkening woods. "Don't spy no slippery elm or white oak bark we could gnaw on but there's a tangle of raspberry bushes yonder. Can we find some dead leaves in it reckon I could brew us some 'Liberty' tea. In a fix like this, anything hot in yer gut kind of helps."

Tim nodded. "Now that's a shining idee, old feller, but how're we goin' to heat water?"

Cash held out a slowly dripping copper powder flask. "Maybe this will do, though I hate like hell to spoil it. If we can cut off its top it will serve."

Since no tomahawks remained, Dan was forced to risk ruining the party's only knife for all it had an unusually heavy blade. Employing a rock, the gunsmith soon amputated a brass teat-valve through which powder normally was fed into a rifle.

"Don't look like it'll hold much," Maddox admitted, "but it'll serve to heat around a pint."

Cash nodded, then retied his hunting shirt's throat laces. "Murph, you been banged about pretty bad; you bide here and get this thing aboilin', and you, missy, go pick all the raspberry leaves ye can find. Me and Dan will scout around and rig some twitch-ups, do we come across a rabbit trot."

They found one just before it got really dark and fine, dry little snowflakes started to sift down through naked treetops. They also came across something else of deep significance.

Maddox was whittling a trigger for a snare when Cash hissed, "Listen a spell, then come here quick and quiet as you can."

Bullet in the Back

When Dan Maddox cautiously pushed through a tangle of briars he found Cash bent over a sprawled human body. Both Maddox and Cash saw at once, though the light was fading fast, that this pale-haired corpse had been shot through the back at the level of his kidneys; several trails of dark-brown blood had meandered over a short-skirted deerskin hunting shirt while gouts also had splashed the backs of his leggings. These last immediately attracted Brooks's attention; they had been cut, he observed softly, in the Huron style; therefore the dead man's leggings must have originated somewhere north of the Ohio.

Barely visible amid deepening darkness, the sunken eyes of both men met when the fact sank in that this unknown had on him no powder horn, ax or knife.

Maddox whispered, "Was he one of Rains's?"

"Naw. Ain't laid eyes on a yellow head like that in a 'coon's age."

"How long's he been dead?"

"I figger by the state of the gore 'round that bullet hole he likely got shot early this mornin'."

Balanced on his heels, Cash again studied the sleet-silvered corpse, then reached out to finger a stiff strand of pallid hair. "What beats me, Dan'l, is why whoever jumped this feller didn't foller and lift his skelp. Let's turn him over."

When they'd done so Dan brushed snow from the corpse's tallow-hued face and revealed a short and curly blond beard of rather fine hair; the glazed and staring eyes were of a very light shade of blue. Otherwise, the victim appeared to be about thirty years of age; he was short, lightly built and lay on the snow with dirty, stubby fingers crooked as if he'd been seeking to cling to life.

Fumbling about the corpse's breast pockets Dan Maddox was delighted to discover a flint and steel, a frayed plug of tobacco, a small brass crucifix and a few copper coins.

"What's them?"

"French pennies — *sous*, they call 'em. Burgoyne's Britishers brought quite a few down from Canada with 'em." Dan blinked through the gloom. "What d'ye make over findin' him like this?"

"I'd say he got jumped just when he was wakin' up."

"Sounds reasonable. What happened then?"

"Well, I'd say this Frenchy must ha' been out trappin' by himself and got shot by some lone Injun who'd spotted his camp."

Maddox touched the corpse with the soggy toe of a moccasin.

"Seems likely this feller only found time to hurl his war hatchet and maybe cripple his enemy."

" — And then?"

"Not bein' sure whether his attacker really *was* alone he didn't wait to find out, only took to his heels and ran like hell till he couldn't travel no farther."

A sudden faint crackle in the underbrush caused both men to whirl about, miserably conscious of their helplessness.

"By damn!" snarled Cash. "And us 'thout ary a charge of powder!"

Maddox's heartbeat faltered. The beautiful, deadly-appearing rifles they carried were less useful than a pair of stout quarter staffs. All the same, both men leaped behind trees and cocked their weapons.

Boldly, the gunsmith called, "Come out of there and keep yer hands up high!" Then in rudimentary Iroquois he added, "*Ai-yeh! Kocu Ketellunsi* — Hi, there! What is your name?"

There came no reply in that tangle of honeysuckle and grapevines from which the noise had come.

Cash yelled, "*Gissa, m'majewelan!* You must be an ugly woman who fears to show herself."

More faint crackling noises made Dan mad; for a seasoned campaigner

[422]

to get snared like a recruit on his first scout was absurd! Especially so because he hadn't been careless or used poor judgment.

Slowly, the former sergeant eased Ilsa from his shoulder and leaned the rifle against the tree behind which he was hiding. Next he slipped his skinning knife out of its rawhide sheath. From the corner of his eye he could see Cash getting set, shifting his weight onto the balls of his feet for a quick spring when out into the open moved a sizable, rough-coated dog!

The black-and-white beast advanced uncertainly, sniffed at the dead trapper's body and then peered warily about.

Maddox whistled, then said, "Steady, mister dog. We didn't do in yer master."

The animal wheeled and bared its teeth.

"We ain't Injuns neither," Cash informed. Likely this was the dead man's hunting dog, one who enjoyed tangling with a redskin in preference to anything else.

Wiry and high-shouldered, the dog kept growling until Cash rasped, "Tais-toi, imbécile!"

Surprisingly, the dog stopped snarling, lowered his hackles and then cocked furry ears; but he wouldn't let either man come near.

"What ails the critter?" muttered Dan.

"Dunno. Acts like he smells Injuns nearby. Hope to Jesus he's mistook."

For all that Tim Murphy's injured arm again had begun to ache like a bad tooth he accomplished several chores while the other two men were absent. For one thing he collected a pile of sere brown rushes. Had he been a mite stronger he'd have broken off evergreen boughs to build a single big bed — but he wasn't, so armfuls of reeds would have to do. All the same, it would be pretty bad passing this frigid night with no blankets, no leanto, no food and no weapons to speak of: pity this Valentine girl was so useless and lacking in spirit. Any wench raised along the frontier would have busied herself collecting firewood or building a proper fireplace; all this young female did was to hug the fire, sniveling and complaining about how hungry and cold she was.

Finally, Tim mumbled with a taut smile, "I sure can't feed you, but maybe I can warm you up again."

When he came slipping silently out of the darkness Dan Maddox wasn't much surprised to find the girl huddled before the now roaring fire beside Tim Murphy, who held an arm draped about her shoulders. All the same, Choice was shivering, and her full, clearly limned lips remained lavender-tinted. That she'd lost her shoes, thought Dan, was most unfortunate; to get so delicate a female shod again wasn't going to prove easy. But she'd have to be; in this sort of weather she couldn't travel any distance on stockinged feet.

The gunsmith beckoned Tim out of earshot, told him about finding the

[423]

corpse and repeated Cash's theory about how the stranger had met his death.

"—That's his dog in the underbrush. He'll come in closer once the wolves start cryin'."

Tim looked grave. "So he didn't have a bit of powder on him?"

"Never a bit."

"Too bad, because like always," he tapped his broad belt, "I've got some emergency balls stowed in here. Does anything make you think we may get jumped before daylight?"

"No, but all the same, tonight we'll stand guard by turns."

In the deepening gloom a wolf's howl, infinitely eerie and ominous and not very far off, arose in the forest crowding in on Mad Bear Creek.

As expected, the dead Frenchman's dog moved in and finally made bold to sit on the edge of the firelight with unblinking eyes glowing green-gold.

"Well," Cash drawled, "the brute ain't been extry friendly, yet he ought to warn us if hostiles try to close in. Hi! What's that?"

The dog had leaped to its feet bristling, and all three men froze momentarily before catching up sticks of driftwood; Maddox got his knife out in a hurry. Choice emitted a quavering moan of fear when shrill, agonized shrieks commenced to sound in the woods.

Immediately, Cash hurried over to pat Choice's shoulder. "Don't carry on so, Sissy. That there's only a rabbit which has got itself foul-snared."

Accompanied by the always wary dog which inevitably had been named "Frenchy," the men cautiously entered the woods and were overjoyed to discover that two of the springs, rigged from bent saplings and nooses fashioned from lengths of that rawhide line which Cash habitually carried looped over his left shoulder, held rabbits. One, suspended by a hind leg, struggled and squealed, but the other had strangled quickly and quietly.

The castaways' luck continued fair — for another trap held a half-grown turkey which had been following a rabbit path through dense underbrush.

Warm Interlude

Choice and her companions, although bruised and apprehensive, sank into the deathlike sleep of near exhaustion. By turns the men kept watch and at intervals replenished a fire smoking at the head of that communal bed which proved uncomfortable no matter how they twisted and turned beneath an easily dispersed covering of dead rushes and reeds which offered only a miserably inadequate substitute for blankets.

When Cash roused him, Maddox awoke, feeling considerably refreshed, to view a bright and cloudless dawn etching in detailed silhouette treetops across Mad Bear Creek. He stretched, hawked and spat, then heaved himself stiffly erect, leaving Choice and the ex-rifleman clasped in each other's arms — and very sound asleep.

At first Dan was prompted to awaken them, but Tim looked too peaked, and by now he knew that Choice Valentine wouldn't be of any use, so he decided to let them stay asleep.

Neither man spoke till they'd attended to their natural needs, an example gravely copied by Frenchy upon a piece of driftwood.

Finally Cash cleared his throat. "Dunno what you think, Dan'l, but to me it 'pears like it mightn't be a bad idee to backtrack awhile along that Frog Eater's trail; mebbe we could find his campin' place and mebbe come across some powder and shot and other possibles."

Maddox's coppery head inclined. "Let's do that. If that Frenchman really was jumped by a lone savage who he hurt so bad that the Injun couldn't follow, then his gear still ought to be there."

Before setting out the two brewed raspberry tea in the mutilated powder flask, then gnawed a few shreds of flesh from rabbit carcasses warmed over the coals.

Maddox, looking mightily unkempt, picked up his rifle and paused, small dark-blue eyes narrowed, above the sleeping pair. Even though the girl's honey-blonde hair suggested what sailors would call a "mare's nest" and her clothes remained smeared with mud, Choice Valentine offered a surprisingly stimulating vision as she slept pressed close to the Sharp-shooter of Saratoga. Hum. This female, with lips parted just enough to reveal the ends of small white teeth, *might* have seen less than seventeen summers, but already she surely had everything a grown woman could hope for — and in the right places. To his mild resentment he was fleetingly reminded of his dead wife; she, too, though bigger boned, had been short in stature, blonde and finely proportioned.

Just before he and Maddox set out Cash gave Tim a light kick on the rump, whereat the rifleman came awake all in an instant and snatched up his useless gun. "Hey — wha'?"

Dan shook his head. "Go on sleepin' like that, Tim, and you'll never reach the Frenchman's Lick."

Tim yawned cavernously, then sat up knuckling black and almost round eyes. "What's afoot?"

"Don't know yet," grinned Maddox, "but it seems like a fine day for it."

This was no exaggeration; the sun had commenced to peer over a distant hilltop and sketch delicate crystalline patterns among clumps of sleet-silvered underbrush.

"Now listen; Cash and I are going to try backtrackin' and see if we can find the dead man's camp; considerin' that hole in his back it shouldn't lie too far away. Meantime, I want you to keep a sharp lookout; perhaps some of our people will come lookin' for us though I don't think it's likely. They'll think we've been catfish food long since."

[425]

Cash rubbed his balding scalp. "Now, Murph, better get cracking and 'tend the snares; then fix up some kind of leanto." He shot a glance at Choice, whose gray-stockinged feet protruded from muddied, ill-adjusted petticoats with toes curled against the cold. "After that see if you can figure out some way to get Sissy shod."

He pointed to woodsmoke which, clinging close to the creek's surface, lazily drifted downstream. "That's risky, but I guess there's no help for it — she'd freeze. But if any red bastards smell it and start nosing about, get into the woods and hide."

Once he'd washed his face and hands, Murphy returned to consider the sleeping girl. Little scratches and streaks of charcoal and grease from last night's supper marred the girl's pink and delicate heart-shaped features, but even all tousled and grubby like this Choice looked prettier than a speckled pup. Blood started pumping into his loins.

In what sort of mood would she awaken? Would she try to act hoity-toity, or would she simply rejoice that she still was alive? He decided to find out, so stooped and gently ran his fingers down her back, then over her upturned buttocks. Whew! A goose-down bolster couldn't have felt any softer!

A pleased grin widened over the rifleman's grimy features when, little by little, he eased a hand under her skirts, but she didn't even stir until his rough fingertips were experiencing the warmth and incredible smoothness of her thigh. Finally, Choice sighed, then slowly rolled over onto her back and sleepily batted dark-fringed eyelids.

"Hi, Sissy! You want somethin' to eat?"

Her clear, dark eyes stared blankly upwards. "Wha — ?"

Reluctantly getting to his feet, Tim said, a bit sheepishly, "Best to rouse up. I've got some vittles heatin'."

All at once her intense brown-black eyes rounded themselves. "Mercy! Where are our companions?"

Tim said gravely, "Gone off."

"Gone off? Why — why, have they deserted us?"

"'Tain't nothin' like that. They've only gone to seek the Frenchman's camp and maybe bring in some powder and shot."

"Oh, dear! I only hope they'll return soon. They understand the wilderness — and what to do about this pickle we're in."

Choice took a sip of the raspberry tea before she commenced briskly to rub her feet.

"How do they feel?"

"Bruised and numb."

"Put 'em nearer the fire, Sissy, and they'll soon warm up. Mine did."

"But you're wearing moccasins." Slowly, Choice's dark-red lips assumed a pathetic curve. "I don't know how I'll manage without shoes of some sort."

Despite her obvious hint Tim turned away. "I'd lend you mine 'cept

[426]

they'd be away too great. Besides there's a lot of work to be done afore the boys return."

"But — but, Tim, what *am* I to do? I can't go about like this. Really I can't."

The wide bed crackled softly when Tim sat down beside her. "That's correct and I just been doin' some hard thinking on that subject and maybe I've hit on a good idee."

"What is it?"

More than ever Tim wished he weren't smelling so all-fired high and looking less unshaven and otherwise disreputable.

" 'Tis a pity I've just forgot. But maybe, Sissy, if you was to buss me real nice — heartier than you did yestereve — I might remember."

To his considerable surprise Choice Valentine didn't appear in the least offended. "You mean you know how to make me some footgear?"

"I will, if I have to, but it mayn't be necessary." Tim's dark, deep-set eyes were glinting below heavy but ruler-straight brows. "Well, how about a memory lesson?"

Choice's long black lashes fluttered down, became outlined against her grimy cheeks. Then she pursed lips and tilted her face upwards.

For all his heart had begun to hammer, the rifleman was much too experienced to rush matters, so he kept his lips together when they kissed. He didn't even attempt to pass an arm around her. Apparently his restraint was appreciated, for this slim little creature appeared in no hurry to break away.

Said she demurely while using the back of a hand to rub lips scored by bristles, "Now what about those shoes?"

Fighting an almost overpowering impulse to stay where he was, Tim got up. "That was a beauty of a kiss, so I'll go look into the matter whilst you tidy up a bit."

Softly, she demanded, "Why, where are you going?"

"Into the woods. I'll soon return, so don't you fret."

"Oh, no, no! Please! Don't leave me alone."

He patted her cheek, added seriously, "Don't fear, Sissy, I ain't goin' far, so just neat up and keep the fire goin'."

The Hostiles

Warily, Maddox and Brooks followed the dead man's faint tracks and at times were guided by congealed spots of blood shed by the Frenchman during his flight.

Before long it became all but impossible to make out the trail, for the rising sun had commenced to thaw the ground's covering.

[427]

Several times Cash, employing a mixture of frontier French and various Indian languages, attempted to encourage the dog to trail, but accomplished nothing. Whenever the bareheaded men halted, the furry black and white dog sank onto his haunches, cocked pointed ears and lolled his tongue while casting suspicious and uncomprehending glances at his new masters.

At length Maddox halted. "Cash, it's plain we're wastin' our time just roamin' about like this; had we found the right course we'd have discovered his camp by this time. With such a great hole in him he couldn't have traveled any farther."

Cash broke off a twig of sassafras bush and fell to chewing it. "That's so, but I don't cotton to the idea of not makin' *sure* there weren't other redskins along when that Frog Eater got jumped." He cocked a grizzled brow the color of a wolverine's pelt.

Dan hesitated while a huge and glossy black squirrel sauced him from the top of a towering hickory. "You got any idea which way the Kentucky Trace heads after it crosses Mad Bear Creek?"

"No. All depends which way the country runs — it might even lead north for a while, away from us. Reckon you're thinking we oughter strike cross-country till we cut the trace somewhere?"

"Why not?"

"Because around here lies some of the meanest country *I've* ever seen — it's full of creeks and swamps, tempest-felled trees and deep ravines."

"If that's so, I expect we'd better try to rejoin the column by workin' our way upstream to the crossin'. You got any idea how far we got carried down the creek?"

"Naw. I was that rattled I ain't the least notion; maybe 'twas seven miles — maybe more."

Evergreen growing on the apex of the peninsula permitted Maddox and his companion to scout a narrow stony beach littered with tangled mounds of dryki, heaps of dead canes and jagged shards of drift ice and so obtain a clear view of the confluence of the Mad Bear with the Green. A flock of sheldrake appeared, flashed by, headed downstream, but neither man noticed them. What held their attention was the presence of bluish-gray smoke that was drifting over the Green's tan-colored current!

"My God!" burst out the gunsmith. "Tim's gone crazy to use green wood like this!"

The old Long Hunter caught his breath sharply, "*Look yonder!*"

A canoe had appeared on the Green, apparently headed for the creek's mouth. From the cautious way its four occupants hugged the river's shore they must long since have sighted that fateful stratum of smoke.

The scouts faded skillfully backwards and disappeared in the underbrush.

Off the mouth of Mad Bear Creek the Indians quit paddling for a short while and just drifted on the current. Maddox had begun to hope for the

[428]

best when their paddles again began to dip and flash in the sunshine, driving the canoe towards that peninsula on which he and Cash were concealed.

Cash whispered, "Let's make tracks for the trace; they'll soon jump Murphy and the girl; ain't no use our gettin' scragged into the bargain."

Maddox's lank, coppery hair swayed in negation. "Do as you please, but I'm goin' to try to warn Tim."

"All right. We'll have it yer way, ye bloody ijit."

The two ran ducking under branches, slipping on mossy rocks and circling windfalls, unaware that at the bivouac a far from unpleasant interlude was being concluded.

As soon as Corporal Tim Murphy's leather-covered back became lost to sight amid frosty underbrush, Choice Valentine indulged in some distinctly unladylike scratching at various intimate parts of her anatomy, for like everyone else, she'd acquired vermin. Until now her lice had been chilled into inaction, but, warmed, they were making up for lost time. As best she could, Choice picked the seams of her garments, a proceeding which required so much time that the fire burned dangerously low. Hurriedly, the girl tossed the handiest sticks onto the coals — ignorant that they were of green wood.

Glory! This was such a rare fine day it became almost possible to forget yesterday's miseries. Suddenly she flung wide her slender arms, lifted her face to the sun, laughed out loud and executed a few dance steps.

Choice then stripped off her blouse the better to wash at a little pool where, as she'd recently been taught, she scrubbed herself with fine sand, but winced when the gritty substance encountered various scratches and bruises. Characteristically, Choice was giving never a thought to the anxiety her family must be suffering. She only knew that she was feeling uncommonly joyous, perhaps because Tim Murphy, despite bristle-covered cheeks and leather-hard lips, surely knew plenty about kissing a girl. Of course, the rifleman was no part of a gentleman, but right now that didn't matter a bit.

Once she'd plaited her hair and had scraped as much mud from her clothing as she could, Choice tossed more sticks on the fire before settling onto the bed of rushes in order to resume her hunt for vermin.

In the process she was forced to raise her underpinnings so high that she exposed shapely, pinkish-white legs almost to her hips. Faugh! Her limbs scarcely looked their best in shapeless gray woolen stockings gartered by strips of rawhide.

So silently did Tim Murphy return to the bivouac that, at a flicker of his shadow, she looked up and gasped. When she saw the rifleman he was standing not a yard away, grinning broadly at her déshabille.

Tim's small, black eyes were shining and his uneven, old ivory-tinted teeth peered through a slack smile. His good arm supported his rifle while

[429]

over the other he was carrying a dingy buckskin shirt and a pair of ankle-high moccasins decorated with a few strands of blue-and-yellow beadwork.

God A'mighty! Choice certainly was *something* to look at as blushing bright as a poppy she tugged at her skirts. She looked so fresh and young that he, too, went brick-red.

"Sorry to scare you like that, Sissy, but I ain't seen a girl so — nigh so pretty and soft-lookin' in time out of mind."

She smiled brightly. "Mercy, what a start you gave me!"

Tim advanced holding out the moccasins. "How d'you like the look of these?"

"They look wonderful! Wherever did you find them?" she asked, and after arising in a single graceful movement, hurriedly smoothed out her skirts.

The rifleman chuckled. "Off of that Frenchman the boys found dead in the woods yestereve. But if these moccasins won't fit, reckon Cash knows how to fashion a pair out o' this here leather shirt which looks like it's smoke-tanned. Hi! What ails you?"

The girl's huge, dark-fringed eyes had rounded themselves. "You — you mean you took these things off a *dead* man?"

"Sure." Tim stepped closer, filling his eyes with her disordered loveliness. "He weren't able to make me a present of 'em, so what's the odds?"

He motioned to the couch. "Iffen you'll sit we can try these for size."

Lips compressed, Choice hesitated, then nervously complied, all the while hoping that the moccasins *would* fit, for already she'd noted that small, round hole situated midway down the shirt's back.

Tim squatted onto his heels and tried to keep his hands steady whenever he looked up into the delicate oval of her face. Small, good-natured crinkles spread from the corners of his little round eyes when he began to brush the sole of a stocking free of grit and leaves and discovered that Choice's feet, although long and narrow, were by no means diminutive, so the moccasins proved to be only a trifle large. Yep. Given a little judicious restitching, the Frenchman's footgear would do fine.

Once he'd eased on the other moccasin Tim shifted to sit at the girl's side. She had begun to work her toes, all the while emitting small exclamations of satisfaction.

"Since these things seem to do," he announced softly, " 'twill be easy to fashion a vest for you o' his shirt."

Somehow no longer appalled at the prospect of wearing a dead man's garmets, Choice laughed. "Oh, Tim, how *can* I thank you?"

"Why, that's easy," he informed in a husky undertone. "Suppose you give me a hearty buss?"

Choice not only nodded but turned sidewise to face him. Once he had her inside his arms she fetched a shuddering sigh and at the same time placed a palm between his shoulder blades and pressed her lithe, young body against him as hard as she could. Following a series of lingering kisses which rasped harshly, excitingly on her lips and cheeks, he eased her backwards upon the couch, quivering and with eyes half closed.

To the rifleman's astonished delight she failed to hamper his practiced exploration of her garments — only responded with timid readiness to his boldness.

Spent and short of breath, Tim only emerged from ecstasy when a faint crashing noise sounded in the woods. He sprang to his feet and at the same time sought to secure his belt.

"Criminently!" he gulped. "What the hell was that? The boys can't have come back *this* soon!"

Still dewy-cheeked and with lambent eyes Choice Valentine managed to straighten her skirt an instant before Dan Maddox came loping into sight with Cash Brooks a yard or two behind.

"You 'tarnal fool!" Cash wheezed. "Why the hell did you have to chuck green wood on the fire? Injuns close by!"

Amazed at the man's fury, Tim recoiled. "I didn't, so help me God! Sissy must ha' done so whilst I was away. Injuns you said?"

"Damn' right. Four damn' big bucks."

Cash cut in. "Now everybody listen. If them redskins got useful firearms we're most likely done for, but, if they ain't, let's try to make 'em believe our guns is workin' and grab our chance to jump 'em if they start to act mean."

"You just give the sign," Maddox said.

Cash glowered, "Now remember this, you goddamn greenhorns! There ain't nothin' gets a redskin madder or meaner'n that if he gets the idee a man's weak or afraid of him. So don't anybody act the least bit scared, no matter what happens!"

Showdown

Four Indians in shaggy winter robes appeared climbing lightly over tangles of driftwood cast up on the creek's bank. After them slunk a large and shifty-eyed yellow dog at which Frenchy immediately commenced to hurl rasping threats and growls.

The white party watched with their guns held just as if they weren't completely useless. When the dark-faced apparitions were about fifty yards off Cash called, "*Woopan-a-cheen!* — We are well met!"

None of the savages replied; only kept on advancing, walking stiff-legged and on the balls of their feet like dogs getting ready to fight. The three white men, therefore, moved closer together while Choice got to her feet still clutching a piece of driftwood she'd been about to place on the fire.

"What tribe are they?" Maddox demanded in a casual undertone.

"Piankashaws by their looks," Cash said.

"Must ha' been in a scrap lately," Tim commented. Fresh blood was saturating a rag loosely bound about one Indian's shoulder and another was limping from a gash on his upper thigh.

All three white men were infinitely relieved to note that these intruders carried only one firearm among them — a rusty, old musket — although two others wore powder horns slung over mangy fur mantles.

"Copy me," Cash hissed, while slowly advancing his rifle butt foremost — the armed frontiersman's peace sign.

Attached to the back of his head the Piankashaw leader was wearing a *gus-to-weh*, a sort of headdress composed of four heavy, red-tipped feathers which, having been set in a metal stem, revolved erratically like the arms of a miniature windmill. The leader's broad and brutal-appearing features retained only a few streaks of red and black paint; he carried a few arrows stuck into a quiver made out of a spotted dog's skin and in his left hand he carried a short but powerful hunting bow. His principal weapon, however, was a ponderous *casse-tête* or war club, the rounded head of which was studded with sharp iron points that gleamed evilly in the sunlight.

A pace behind the leader stalked a young warrior who wore a dirty bandage twisted around his left forearm. What immediately attracted Maddox's attention was that a big powder horn was slatting heavily against the Indian's right hip; so the only weapons he carried were a long-shafted tomahawk and a skinning knife.

Although the third Indian, who was bowlegged and afflicted by a ferocious squint, carried the party's only firearm — an ancient Charleville smoothbore — he had no powder horn. Tim quickly noticed that the Charleville was lacking the cover to its priming pan, so this particularly unattractive savage in reality was armed only with a thick-bladed tomahawk.

The fourth savage was lithe and lighter-complexioned than his companions. His head was shaven except for a stiff blue-black crest roached in the Creek fashion. Because of a cut across his thigh which had splashed his deerskin leggings, he limped a little. He, too, wore a powder horn, but carried only a slender spear tipped with a fine, probably French-made, steel point.

The tall Indian flung back his head, then in an arrogant gesture slapped his chest. "Me Orenda, Piankashaw half chief." He pointed with the bandaged shoulder. "Him Big Jack."

Next, Orenda indicated the young, pale-skinned warrior. "Him Tskili." The bowlegged warrior apparently was called Blue Jay.

"Who wounded your friends?" Cash demanded, so abruptly that Orenda was startled into saying, "One sun gone we hunt, got surprised by Shawnee war party. They many, we few. We lose," he held up a hand, fingers spread, "men, much furs, guns."

Cash listened and at the same time tried to foresee what the Piankashaws might do; certainly they must be wondering right now why three frontiersmen carrying fine-looking rifles should have allowed a superior number of strange Indians to march into their camp unchallenged. How long before they caught on to the truth of the situation?

Following a brief conversation carried on in Creek supplemented by considerable use of sign language, Cash informed, "Like this feller Orenda said, he and his people was huntin' close by the Kentucky Trace when they bumped into a swarm of Shawnees busy trackin' a big party of whites — our people, of course."

"How many Shawnee were there?" Tim asked without removing his gaze from Big Jack, who he was pretty sure understood a deal more English than he was letting on.

"He didn't let on beyond sayin' 'twas a big bunch, which might mean anything from ten to fifty — Injuns always talk big about their enemy's numbers — 'specially when they get licked."

Orenda pointed to Maddox's rifle, then held out a hand as if he wished to examine Ilsa. Something in the Piankashaw's expression lent the former sergeant a split second's warning before Orenda whirled up his *casse tête* and sprang. Maddox leaped sidewise and won time to bring Ilsa's heavy octagonal barrel crashing down on the Piankashaw's *gus-to-weh*. Although partially stunned, the half chief lurched aside and raised his club again so swiftly that Maddox only had opportunity to jab at Orenda's solar plexus with his weapon's muzzle. Missing his mark, the gunsmith nevertheless maintained momentum so successfully that he was able to drive his shoulders into the Indian's middle, knock out his wind and sent the half chief sprawling onto the leaf-covered ground. Maddox pounced. While grappling he succeeded in jerking Orenda's skinning knife out of its sheath and driving it between the Piankashaw's ribs.

They rolled over and over with the Piankashaw attempting to shorten his grip on his *casse-tête* sufficiently to jab it against the white man's head. Maddox, meanwhile, kept turning the knife in the wound until Orenda went limp and began to cough up torrents of blood.

Tim also was mighty occupied, for at the same instant Orenda made his move, Big Jack freed his war hatchet, screched *"Kish-kal-wa!"* and charged. In order to win room to use his rifle's butt, Tim sprang backwards but tripped on a stone and went staggering hopelessly off-balance.

As in the grip of a vivid nightmare Murphy glimpsed the Piankashaw's tomahawk flashing downwards bright as an embodied sunbeam. He was bracing to meet the bite of its blade when suddenly it veered aside; Choice had flung her billet of firewood with such astonishing accuracy that it struck Big Jack on the side of his head and sent him reeling aside. Tim instantly whirled up his rifle and brained Big Jack with its brass-heeled butt.

Far more experienced and alert than his companions, Cash disposed of the bowlegged Indian through a lightning throw which sank his knife deep into the base of Blue Jay's throat. Dropping his ancient musket, the Piankashaw spun sidewise with bright arterial blood spurting from between his fingers as, futilely, he struggled to check the flow from his severed windpipe.

Tskili, the pale-skinned young Indian, apparently had no stomach for this fight; when his companions attacked he wheeled and raced for the woods with Frenchy snarling and snapping at his heels.

The encounter came to an end so suddenly that for a long instant the whites remained immobile, panting and incredulous of the situation.

Maddox recovered first and bent to snatch Orenda's war hatchet from its sling. He beckoned Cash. "Come along. That runner may be tryin' to reach their canoe! Tim, take care of Sissy and plunder these fellows."

Without even pausing to charge their rifles from the captured powder horn, the two bounded off like hard-chased bucks, hurdling trash littering the creek's shore. Cash panted, "Hi, Dan, you got blood runnin' down yer back."

"That devil's club must ha' grazed the back o' my neck when I dove at him. Nothin' to fret about."

All the time maintaining a sharp outlook for the cowardly Indian, they ran out on the cedar-shrouded point where the Piankashaws had put in. A moment later they spied the canoe, sheathed with elm bark and clumsily contrived but apparently unharmed, drawn up on a narrow, stony beach. They halted, gasping and fingering their war hatchets, surveyed their surroundings but had no sight or sound of the fugitive. They began to wish now that they'd lingered at the scene of the fight long enough to load their rifles from the bowlegged warrior's powder horn.

Smothering an exasperated curse, Tim strode off stiffly to detach Blue Jay's powder horn. His scowl relaxed when he shook it. "By grabs, Sissy, this damn' thing's near full." He tilted a trickle of coarse black powder down his famous rifle's barrels. "All right, Kitty, drink yer fill, sweetheart. Won't ever let you go hungry again for so long."

After he had spilled and smoothed a priming charge into the Golcher's twin pans and had snapped shut their covers, he extracted a pair of the four musket balls from an emergency pocket stitched to his belt. To have his beloved weapon undamaged and useful once more sent a heartening wave of confidence surging through him.

Gruffly he snapped, "Sissy, go pull the cape off'n that feller Dan killed and wear it, lice or no lice." He was fast losing his anger, so added in a kindlier tone, "Guess you'd better lash that knife of his 'round yer middle."

They then systematically stripped naked all three twisted, bloodied and evil-smelling corpses lying so flat among the trampled and frost-killed weeds.

As soon as there was light enough to see what they were doing, the cast-aways broke camp and found that Maddox had been right about a change of weather. During the night the temperature had dropped considerably and successive squadrons of ragged, lead-hued clouds charged by so low that they appeared ready to trip over the clawlike tops of the taller trees.

Everyone hated leaving the campfire's heat — Frenchy especially; the big, rough-coated dog had to be caught and lifted, growling, into the canoe, but once there he quieted at once and sat peering interestedly over the thwarts.

Because of the freezing weather countless little rivulets and brooks had become iced up and congealed, so today the Mad Bear was running by no means as angrily as it had two days earlier. Nevertheless, the current remained extremely swift, and soon the men's shoulders ached from unaccustomed plying of heavy, shapeless paddles. Sure enough, Mad Bear Crossing did lie ahead; a number of pale, horizontal stripes gouged out of tree trunks by the ferry's snubbing ropes showed faintly through rolling veils of powder-fine snow. But nobody could be seen moving about, and worse still nowhere was smoke visible.

By the time the canoe's prow grated over the landing's gravelly beach an icy wind was whooping and roaring through the treetops and lashing Mad Bear Creek's surface into a white fury.

Tim's heavy black brows were turning white as those of an old man when he yelled over the rushing wind, "Well, boys, and what do we do now?"

Turning his back to the blast, the gunsmith shouted between mittened hands, "We've no choice but to try to overtake them."

Vaguely, Choice dabbed flakes from long, dark eyelashes. "When did our people move on?"

"Sometime yesterday," Cash speculated. "Must ha' figgered we was drownded — so didn't tarry."

They had followed the trace only a short while before they glimpsed their first wolves. Almost invisible, the beasts were ghosting along between tree trunks, and although Frenchy several times raised a racket and offered battle, a good many of the great, gray-black beasts continued to slink along to either side of the trace.

Although it seemed impossible, the snowing increased in intensity into a blizzard, transformed the forest into a dim and confusing icy limbo in which leafless branches flailed like scourges and evergreens swayed and bent as if executing a demoniac minuet while the threshing of their lower boughs often swept the ground bare.

All at once the convoying wolves ran ahead as if to block the party's progress but soon the real reason became apparent; a swarm of snow-plastered wolves were tearing, ripping and slashing over a fallen horse.

When the predators proved dangerously reluctant to leave their feast, Cash slipped off his lock's cover and yelled, "All right, boys. Reckon we'd best touch 'em up 'fore they get real excited and turn on us."

The men had shouldered their pieces and were trying to see through the hard-driven snow when a curious thing happened; several wolves could be seen pointing muzzles towards the invisible sky as if to test the wind, then, like as many embodied phantoms, they vanished into the silvery tumult.

Maddox chafed ice-fringed eyelids. "Wha' the hell!"

Cash shook snow from his cape. "Must ha' scented some deers or bufflers somewheres."

Choice surprised them all because she didn't lag — only plodded on, a small, shapeless figure grown white as Lot's wife.

They had covered possibly half a mile more when Cash again halted and stiffly raised a mittened hand. Once the four grotesquely shrouded figures came together the old Long Hunter yelled over the wind, "Something's wrong!"

"What — you mean?"

"If them wolves was running game — have heard 'em wailing. You heard 'em?"

Nobody had heard any howling.

"Mebbe wind's too great — but something's queer."

Before starting on, Maddox and his companions pulled their caps so low they could hardly see and at the same time hitched snow-thickened mantles up over their noses; nevertheless, ice particles formed at once on their nostril hairs.

Cash began to flounder along so far in advance that on occasion his bent figure became lost to sight. It was after one of these eclipses they found him studying a partially sheltered stretch of ground. There, still clearly distinguishable, moccasined footprints only recently had entered upon the trace from a northerly direction; some of these already were filling up, but a caprice of the drifting snow had left a frightening number recognizable.

"How many are there?" Tim wanted to know while flailing his arms.

"Hard to tell with the ground like 'tis, but I'll hazard they'll number 'round forty. Yep. Those wolves must ha' scented them redskins — that's why they ran off."

The men at once agreed that the only thing to do was cautiously to scout the Shawnee party in hopes of getting near enough to see how many they numbered and, more important, what condition they were in.

From the presence of many discernible footprints it became inescapable that these Shawnees could not be very far off; although ravenously hungry and aware of mounting fatigue, Maddox forced himself to ponder a vital question. Were these Indians slowing down because of the hard going or because they now found themselves close enough to attack the column at will? The latter explanation seemed the more acceptable, for in such frightful weather Robertson's attenuated column could only have been crawling along.

The Surprise

Had it not been for the accumulated experience of Colonel Robertson, Tom Spencer, Edmund Jennings and Joe Drake and several others who had traveled the Kentucky Trace before — a few of them more than once — the expedition must have lost its way with probably disastrous results. As it was, the numbed and discouraged immigrants struggled on through waist- or even shoulder-high drifts forever forming and shifting at the storm's whim. The pitiless sting of sharp particles forced men on occasion to peep through their fingers as they floundered along.

Although growing more and more hopeless, Rosemary nonetheless guessed herself luckier than her twin, who now must be lying stiff and lifeless somewhere at the bottom of Mad Bear Creek. She guessed she'd never get over that awful sensation of helplessness she'd suffered while watching the wildly plunging and spray-smothered raft disappear.

What a pity that plainly handsome, capable and soft-spoken Dan Maddox also had had to lose his life, along with raffish Tim Murphy and that Long Hunter whose name she'd never learned.

Drearily the girl thought, maybe Choice is the lucky one after all. At least she won't die by inches from hunger, cold and exhaustion. Mechanically, Rosemary bent to avoid a half-seen branch, then made efforts to rearrange her traveling cape's hood into warmer folds.

Jonathan felt happy when the order was passed back to make camp. He set about building still another low little shelter out of evergreen boughs. Once it had been thrown together he considered Old Scratch, who was collecting his ewes into a tight circle suggesting a small, slow-moving snowdrift. Nowadays, the boy had begun to admire, even to feel kindly towards that perverse patriarch. Hadn't he on several occasions charged timber wolves sufficiently hungry to reconnoiter the camp's outer rim? Once he'd actually succeeded in butting one of the gray terrors so hard that the brute was sent flying and howling back into the brush.

Since the blizzard set in, Jonathan's task had grown easier, for like all the stock his sheep remained so terrified by what appeared to be a swarm of marauders that they didn't stray and kept near the trace. Most of them now were so thin and poor from hunger that they were glad to lie down whenever they could.

Jonathan dozed off but soon was awakened by a sustained barking of the rear guard's dogs. Their clamor was so fierce he guessed something must be wrong. When a shift in the wind brought the distorted sound of shouts and yells he roused up, pulled his ancient pistol out of a protective bag of greased leather.

Figuring he could safely leave Old Scratch on guard, Jonathan pulled down an oversized fox-fur cap, then wound the precious muffler high and tight about his face before setting out for a wind-flattened fire about which were gathering a ring of snow-covered figures.

"What's up?" he yelled at his Uncle John.

"Look who's just come in."

To the lad's delight he recognized through smokelike clouds of snow the familiar figures of Dan Maddox and Tim Murphy. Then, looming just beyond them, he made out Cash Brooks and what appeared to be a slight young fellow. So they hadn't "drownded"? Criminently! Ed Jennings had been right when he'd said that if anybody could pull the raft's people through Cash could do it. "He's just too ornery to die."

The moment he learned that a sizable band of Shawnees probably was closing in, Robertson summoned his principal subordinates. While wood smoke and stinging snow beat at their whiskery, weather-gnawed faces the leaders swiftly reached a decision.

"What beats me," complained Ike Bledsoe, "is why all these redskins is trailin' us. This time of year they shouldn't be about in any number."

Joe Drake's shaggy head ducked in agreement. "Beats me, too, No savages ought to be found any distance from their villages."

Sour-faced Mark Robertson blew his nose between grimy fingers and growled, "Reckon we're just unlucky. These Shawnees probably were on their way home from huntin' when they cut our trail and then bumped into those Piankashaws Cash spoke of. Because the Piankashaws were so few the Shawnees likely believed they must be followin' only a small party of immigrants."

When dawn finally became more than a presentiment it appeared that the blizzard hadn't abated, not in the least; its biting blasts smote faces like clenched fists and hurled such endless clouds of snow that they all but blinded a man.

Colonel Robertson therefore delayed setting out until his attacking force had consumed whatever food they could come across and had made a final check of their firearms.

Only Jonathan was glad of such weather; amid this whirling tumult his slight, snow-shrouded figure should prove almost impossible to identify.

As the augmented rear guard was moving out, floundering and cursing their lack of snowshoes, the wind abated briefly, just enough to permit a man to make out a companion struggling along at a distance of ten or even fifteen feet.

Glad that he'd kept his old pistol's lock wound in a length of greasy rag and that he'd begged, borrowed or stolen half a dozen paper cartridges and a supply of assorted musket balls, Jonathan decided it might be wise if he worked his way out on the attacking force's right flank as far as possible. He'd seen both of his uncles moving off to the left. Pa, of course, was commanding the center.

Because Tom Spencer's huge outline was easy to identify, the boy kept close behind him, especially while traversing a piece of extra-difficult terrain like a deep ravine in which the snow was piled deep enough to close over the boy's fox-fur cap.

At length the boy's strength started to give out and at the same time he began to conjecture what might happen to him if those painted devils were alert and prepared to charge the immigrants' thin and irregular skirmish line.

He quit wondering when somewhere away off to his left a muffled *boom!* successfully penetrated the noise of the wind. A few faint yells followed, then the boy heard a ragged fusillade that sounded dull — like sticks beating on a wet drumhead.

Copying Tom Spencer and everybody else in sight, Jonathan immediately sought shelter behind a big tree; he lingered there, waist-deep, strained desperately to see through the baffling, ghostly-white atmosphere.

Men began humping forward through the drifts; experienced Indian fighters like Tom Spencer, who hadn't fired yet, were carrying their weapons as high above their heads as they could in case they tripped.

Jonathan's stiff and uncertain fingers were stripping the rag from his pistol when through the shifting whirling storm he suddenly made out the dark outlines of several figures plunging towards him.

Spencer halted, shouldered his piece and, at thirty yards' range, dropped a fur-swathed Shawnee just as he straightened from bending under a low-sweeping hemlock bough; the stricken Indian fell forward and vanished completely beneath the snow. Since he didn't struggle at all, he must have been instantly killed.

Reasoning that if he stuck close to Spencer he probably wouldn't get hurt, the boy continued to follow him.

Somebody shouted, "Look out!"

An Indian who seen through flying flakes loomed even bigger than Tom Spencer, was charging towards him and raising a screeching scalp yell.

To his surprise, Jonathan was able to keep his head; gripping the pistol in both hands he pointed at the center of the Shawnee's snow-spattered hunting shirt, but when he pulled the trigger only a dry *click!* resulted. Panic-stricken, he yanked back the trigger and squeezed a second time, but the weapon remained obstinately silent as the Indian continued to close in with red-and-black-streaked features contorted into a deadly grimace.

Jonathan knew he was going to be killed. What a great fool he'd been in

[439]

trying to play the man! Throat convulsively constricting, he tried to spring aside, but his foot caught on some invisible object and he fell sprawling into deep snow.

He braced 'for the tomahawk's impact, saw it rise, miles above him it seemed, but then unaccountably it wavered aside. That same dog which had just tripped him had left off worrying the Indian killed by Spencer to spring and drive his fangs deep into the Indian's thigh. The force of his charge knocked the Shawnee off his feet so that man and dog rolled over and over in the snow, but the latter hung on to his enemy.

Jonathan swayed to his feet, then clubbed his cumbersome pistol and hovered above the struggling figures waiting for a chance to bring the weapon down on the Indian's head, but somehow the Shawnee got a fresh grip on his tomahawk, beat off his attacker and succeeded in rising to his knees.

Snarling like all of Cerberus's heads at once, Bassoon then grabbed the savage's shoulder, offering Jonathan an opportunity to strike that swiveling black head.

For all the blow was a shrewd one, it still wasn't sufficiently powerful to knock out the Shawnee. Jonathan therefore was forced to hit several times more before his enemy finally went limp and sank forward, half buried in a drift.

Too bewildered to know what he should do next, the boy swayed above his enemy, only partially aware that Pa's bear dog now had the Indian by the throat and had driven his fangs into it so deep that bright blood was beginning to spray the tumbled snow.

For a brief interval none of the men standing with backs turned to the blizzard could believe that the attack had been so completely and overwhelmingly successful. Once the attackers had rendezvoused in the Shawnee bivouac laughing and talking sixty to the minute in their relief, a tally was taken which revealed that not one white man had been killed and that only two had suffered wounds so minor that they weren't even partially incapacitated.

Everybody felt especially fine when a dozen-odd snow-flecked, red-and-black scalps were held up for inspection; moreover, if various claims were to be credited, nearly as many more *coups* lay concealed by the tumbling, ever-shifting snow.

Most of the Shawnees, it appeared, had died when Robertson's central party abruptly had charged, *whoop-whooping*, out of the blizzard to catch their enemies completely unaware; the savages either were lying rolled in their blankets still asleep or numbly were preparing food.

For a while the victors lingered to warm themselves around Indian fires or to seek scraps of cooked foods, after which they set about collecting weapons, warm garments and other useful gear.

Break-Up

As if eager to atone for its previous viciousness, the blizzard abruptly came to an end around noon of the same day that the Shawnees had been beaten and, so everybody hoped, dispersed beyond hope of reunion. It was amazing how quickly the expedition's spirits revived once snow ceased to fall and the razor-edged wind died out. They felt better still when the sun appeared, clear and bright; but it cast little warmth.

Colonel Robertson ordered a real camp made when he realized that even the hardiest veterans seemed ready to drop from exhaustion. Besides, most of the animals had grown so thin and weak that many must have perished had an attempt been made to keep them moving.

Although very few people seemed aware of the fact, this was the first occasion since quitting Carpenter's Station that all members of the combined expeditions had camped together, there being no point or rear guard bivouacked apart.

Thus it came about that the ex-militiaman Andrew Dickinson, who until now had been riding point, caught sight of Dr. Mason for the first time since Carpenter's. Immediately he beat his brain trying to recollect when and where he'd previously seen the physician — if indeed he ever had. To tell the truth, the Connecticuter had been far too occupied with fighting the elements and in obtaining food for his wife and child to rack his memory before this.

Shortly after sunset James Robertson sent out messengers to summon all leaders and heads of families to attend a general conference, with the result that before long nearly fifty gaunt, filthy and bone-weary men collected to stand knee-deep in snow about a huge, soaring bonfire.

Once most of the leaders had appeared, Robertson, standing unbelievably straight in a shaggy bearskin coat, began to speak in a low but surprisingly effective voice. He began by praising them one and all not only for having successfully surprised the Shawnees but even more for their dogged endurance, their ingenuity in solving unforeseen difficulties and especially for their readiness to help one another. With firelight gilding his scraggly, dark-brown beard, the colonel concluded: " — And don't you think I ain't proud, almighty proud to be leading men the like of you!"

Once applause had died away Robertson continued, "Since you all are feelin' so fine you'd best get braced for some bad news. This afternoon Rains, Phillips and I made a survey and found that we now have left only two days' full rations for ourselves while many of our animals are about ready to die of starvation."

His sunken but still piercing light blue eyes slowly surveyed the assembly. "Therefore, I'll put it bluntly. Right away, we *must* supplement our food stores and find forage. Big game hereabouts is scarce at this season and is like to grow scarcer once we start to cross the Barrens.

[441]

"Unfortunately, a big expedition like this can't move fast, 'specially since Doc Mason here reports many crippling cases of frostbite."

Samuel Mason, M.D., sensed, rather than saw, many fatigue-ringed eyes swinging in his direction. One pair especially attracted his attention; they belonged to a tall, cadaverous-looking individual wearing a battered, brown tricorn tied down by a ragged red scarf. Something about the intensity of this fellow's regard proved oddly disquieting.

Had this angular, bony fellow, along with certain others, been taking an undue interest in the sketches he'd made of difficult mountain passes and important fords? As a rule he'd been successful in diverting unwelcome curiosity by remarking that he was only an amateur cartographer making the most of an opportunity to map this hitherto uncharted wilderness. Back East, he assured them, people were ready to pay plenty for even the most rough-and-ready of maps.

One after another, the leaders had their say, but, while their opinions varied considerably, never a one suggested turning back.

Eventually, the principal men agreed on the impossibility of finding sufficient food and fodder for a single, numerous column, so the morrow would be devoted to splitting the expedition into two divisions.

A small, fast-moving force led by Colonel Robertson was to include only physically fit and experienced men who were to ride the strongest horses; they were intended to scout the country around the present campsite for a full day in order to make certain that the Shawnees hadn't somehow got together preparing to dog the expedition in hopes of cutting off hunting parties or herdsmen driving stock in search of feeding grounds.

Further, it was decided that if no evidences of pursuit was discovered Robertson's party would, at its best speed, strike straight across the Barrens for the Ohio River, then hasten to reach the mouth of the Cumberland.

With any luck, this hand-picked party should arrive at the Frenchman's Bluff far enough ahead of the other division, in plenty of time to start the construction of a blockhouse, a few cabins and, it was hoped, to gather corn which James Robertson and some others had planted there the preceding spring.

The "slow" division, which was to be led by Major Phillips, John Rains and Squire Valentine, would be guided around the rim of the bleak and inhospitable Barrens by Tom Spencer, Ed Jennings, Joe Drake and other Long Hunters of equal experience. These veterans had decided to follow a system of southwesterly trending creeks and rivers along which they should find patches of woodlands where it was hoped big game would be wintering.

The "slow" division, it was decided, would include John Rains's original group plus Robertson's sick, disabled and hopelessly inefficient members. It would take along all livestock — including the colonel's priceless Spanish-Arab horses.

By employing a shameless blend of guile and common sense, Tim

Murphy succeeded in making sure that he and Maddox would be assigned to Phillips's division, ostensibly to shoot meat but really because he was determined to remain near Choice, and Maddox seemed more than a little taken with Rosemary.

Dr. Mason's Portfolio

Hawk-faced Major Phillips and skinny, stoop-shouldered John Rains were more than pleased when, on the third day after parting with James Robertson, they encountered a noisy little river which ran so fast that it wasn't altogether frozen over; better still, through some whim of the great three days' blizzard, much less than an average depth of snow had been deposited in a shallow valley through which this stream spiraled towards the featureless, dreary and icy expanse of the Barrens.

Their division also had been fortunate in that hunters snowshoeing well in advance of the column had chanced upon a small band of elk comfortably and conveniently yarded up on a flat, willow-covered island on which reeds, canes and other grasses grew in abundance.

By dint of expert stalking and marksmanship, Tom Spencer, Maddox and Murphy and two other good shots killed four of the beasts outright and so seriously wounded a fifth that it proved no trick at all to drive the cripple into a deep drift and there finish it off as it lay in panting helplessness.

After shapeless, crimson hunks of meat had been equally distributed and then cooked as quickly as possible, the immigrants spontaneously commenced their first jubilation since quitting Carpenter's Station.

After a fife, a fiddle and a guitar began to play, gaunt and sunken-eyed people wearing blankets or shaggy fur robes began to caper about, inventing grotesque dance steps which at the same time served to warm them up. Later, songs and ballads nostalgic of home rose to challenge the eerie wails of the ever present wolves.

Major Todd Phillips kept an eye on a fine marrowbone beginning to brown and char among the coals while his long, blue-black jaws worked steadily on a half-cooked rib. He was losing some of his taut anxiety when somebody touched his shoulder. Looking up he recognized looming above him that refugee from Connecticut called Andrew Dickinson. His flat and narrow mouth was liberally smeared with grease and streaked with elk's blood.

"Please, sir, will you listen to me for a minute? There's need to inform you and some others about something important."

The major in obvious reluctance licked fingers then heaved himself erect. "How important? What's this about?"

[443]

"Well, sir, I can't tell you here, but I think it's something you leaders certainly ought to know about."

Phillips directed irritably, "Speak up, Dickinson! I've still a lot to see about before I turn in, and though I'm dog-tired, I'll listen."

Rains's bulky, mittened hand hooked thumbs over his belt. "Bet you are. Still, I reckon maybe you'd better hear Dickinson repeat what he's already told us."

"Well, sir, as I've just confessed to these gentlemen, from the moment I first clapped eyes on Dr. Mason I've been racking my memory to recall where and when I'd seen him before; finally, just a little while ago, I suddenly remembered."

Phillips coughed and set a cloud of breath vapor spiraling violently away. "How come?"

"We were eating out of the same pot when I heard him mention Norwalk."

"Where's Norwalk?"

"It's a little port on the Connecticut side of Long Island Sound. That's where I used to own a boatyard."

"What has Norwalk to do with the doctor?"

"Well, sir, you probably haven't heard that last summer a British squadron transported a strong body of English, Hessian and Tory troops which, led by that damn' Loyalist ex-Governor William Tryon and a general called Garth, raided and ravaged at will along the Connecticut shore. New Haven, New London, Fairfield and Norwalk all were attacked and, sir, what the enemy did — the Loyalists especially — won't bear repeating."

Over the hiss and snap of a nearby fire, Valentine urged, "Go on. Let Andy tell what took place in Norwalk."

Dickinson's shaggy brows lowered themselves while his voice assumed a harsh, grating quality, "Well, sir, being a corporal in the militia I was called out as soon as the alarm bells rang. 'Fore God, we did the best we could but didn't accomplish much because there were only about fifty of us against near half a thousand trained troops. All the same, we fought from house to house till we ran out of powder and had to surrender.

"After we'd been disarmed some lobsterbacks marched us to our common and kept us under close guard there while the town was being set afire. Buildings had begun to burn all around us when a band of Tories fetched in some more prisoners and among them — " Dickinson paused and looked hard at Phillips — "I could almost swear I saw Sam Mason! He was wearing a Massachusetts Continental officer's coat."

Abruptly, Todd Phillips fought down grinding fatigue, rasped, "So he was a fellow prisoner? What's so terrible about that?"

Andrew Dickinson spat onto the snow, said bitterly, "Well, sir, the doctor *may* have been taken prisoner, too, but he sure wasn't treated like the rest of us. Not one little bit!"

" — And what d'you mean by that?"

[444]

"If you'll just listen, sir, I'll try to explain." The Connecticuter began to speak more rapidly. "When the lobsterbacks set fire to the fine houses 'round our common a few were spared — for the accommodation of their officers, I presume. Be that as it may, come sundown I and the rest of the prisoners were fallen in and started down to the waterfront. It so happened that they halted us for a moment outside Abel Thorne's dwelling and so close that I could look inside and clearly see what was going on."

"Well, what did you see?"

Dickinson's voice rang out, flat and angry. "There was Mason drinking and chaffing with some British officers and some others wearing Tory green. Well, sir, the doctor was being treated like no prisoner I have ever seen or heard of when our guards marched us on."

The major straightened, then strained to peer through the starlight. "This is a mighty serious accusation you're making; are you *absolutely positive* that Doc Mason is the man you saw hobnobbing with enemy officers?"

Dickinson heaved a deep sigh, then dropped his gaze. "I wish I could say so, certain-sure, sir, but please to remember I'd been fighting for a long time and was worried sick over my family and the burning of my boatyard. Besides, I was awful tired and hungry so, well, I'll admit I just *might* have been mistaken; that's what bothers me."

"A pity it didn't bother you before!" rasped Phillips, his sensitive, dark features suddenly grim. "Just what the hell d'you mean by making such grave charges when you're not dead sure?"

He had started to turn away when John Rains made a detaining gesture. "Hold on a minute, Todd."

"Why should I?"

"Because several people say Mason keeps adding to a sort of folder full of notes and drawings he's made."

"That's interesting." Valentine's round, red face momentarily became misted by his own breath. "Hasn't anybody found out what he's doing?"

"No, not that I know of."

Phillips, feeling ineffably weary and yearning to roll up for the night, spoke sharply, "I think you're barking up the wrong tree. Probably, like some others, the doctor's only gathering material for a sketch map. There's nothing suspicious about that."

"Not unless Dickinson's story is true," Valentine said. "But I admit we'd have to examine that portfolio pretty carefully before deciding whether or not the sort of information Mason has collected is either significant or dangerous to our cause."

Rains growled, "Then we damn' well better take a good look at those papers. If the feller's a spy, the sooner we hang him the better. As for me — "

" — Now hold on, John, hold on!" Valentine broke in. "Let's not go off at half-cock. You'd better realize that Sam Mason's a very valuable and respected member of this expedition; plenty of our people owe him their lives."

"On the other hand," Dickinson pointed out, "if he *is* a traitor, uncounted thousands of Americans very likely will lose theirs. Just suppose I'm right and the doctor *is* collecting information about our route to guide an enemy army next year?"

Phillips spoke crisply. "That's worth thinking on. Right now, only one thing seems at all clear; this matter must be dealt with promptly."

Rains's coonskin cap inclined several times. "That's a fact. Me, I don't aim to ride with no traitor alongside, so I say let's take a look at his folder and make sure about him right away."

Whatever his failings, Virginius Valentine never had been one to become easily diverted from his course once he had decided upon it. A little later he beckoned Choice out into the brilliant starlight and demanded, quite casually, after commenting on the beauty of the night, "How much do you like Dr. Mason?"

Choice became almost painfully demure. "Why Papa, you don't think he — "

"I think nothing. Just answer my question, girl!"

"Oh, I like him very well, Papa. Outside of you and Colonel Robertson, he's the only *real* gentleman among us."

" — And how well does he fancy you?"

"While he's kind and polite to me and amusing in that dry way of his, I'm still well aware that he vastly prefers Rosie to me."

After lighting his pipe the squire puffed hard while staring unseeingly over the chill and smoke-wreathed encampment. "Once I've explained, my dear, what I have on my mind, I'll tell you what I expect of you. An you oblige me I — well, I'm sure I can find a certain handsome gold bracelet which might become you."

Choice's black-lashed eyes rounded themselves, then she tilted her head to one side in a curious little mannerism which invariably had proved pleasing to the opposite sex. She stepped closer to her father's ample outline. "What is it you want me to do?"

Once he had explained in detail, her father added, "I don't care how you go about it, but that portfolio must be examined no later than tomorrow if even for a few moments, so you must devise a way to — er — borrow it."

She raised eyes to glance at his face, parted her lips in a slow, inscrutable smile. "Dearest Papa, you may rest assured that I'll do my very best — provided you're not funning me about that bracelet!"

Thankful for even a two-day halt, Virginius Valentine's daughters unlashed bundles in which they hoped to find some reasonably fresh clothing. While sorting out their possessions they could hear their mother on the other side of the tent's partition petulantly ordering Sally to prepare some supper for her owners.

"I expect this will have to serve," Rosemary announced, holding up a clean but wrinkled and utterly shapeless woolen shirt. "I declare, Choice, I'm so sick of being cold and having to go about in dirty, smelly garments I could wail. Do you think we'll *ever* again enjoy privacy, pretty clothes and a hot bath?"

Choice, a taut smile on her dirty, grease-streaked features, continued to peel off thick, often-mended worsted stockings in which several new holes had appeared. "Dream on, dear sister, there's no harm in that. But seriously, I reckon we'll somehow survive this freezing nightmare an we don't encounter another winter storm like that last one."

Rosemary's stiff and dirty fingers awkwardly untied a set of tie-strings securing her blouse, then after momentarily stripping to the waist and pulling on a fresh undervest, she heaved a sigh and donned the wrinkled shirt.

"Of course, we must expect more blizzards but maybe this mild weather will last a few days longer."

She broke off because someone began to scratch at the tent's flap and a small boy's voice shrilled, "Please, Miss Rosemary, you inside?"

"Yes. Who are you and what do you want?"

"I'm Tommy Dickinson."

"What do you want, Tommy?"

"Ma's been took awful sick of a fever."

"Then why don't you find Dr. Mason?"

"I did, but he's too busy fixin' up Mr. Brodhead's busted arm to listen."

"Come in, Tommy," she invited now that her shirt was secured. A tousled yellow head almost engulfed by a huge worsted stocking cap appeared between the flaps. "Which is your tent?"

"It's next to the last one at the back end of the camp, ma'am." Tommy's button-eyes roved briefly over the tent's disorder.

"What seems to be ailing her?"

"Like I said, ma'am, she's got a fever so hard she claims she's fair burnin' up."

"Then run and tell your mother I will come along directly."

An anxious look on her heart-shaped face, Choice watched her twin secure a thick shawl about her and then hook on a traveling cloak. When she reached for the wildcat-skin cap she usually wore, Choice said sweetly, "Suppose you take my marten-fur hat? 'Tis warmer and a lot prettier."

No sooner had Rosemary dropped the weather-beaten flaps into place than Choice ripped off her shirt and as quickly donned the spotted blue blouse just discarded by her sister.

As quickly as she could, the girl then replaited her pale hair into a single braid, all the while emitting disgusted noises over its lank and greasy quality.

[447]

Finally, she tied over her head a red-and-blue-striped scarf belonging to her twin before she hurried to the Brodheads' tent where the Dickinson lad had reported Dr. Mason to be at work. When she entered it was to find him stitching up an ugly wound caused by a compound fracture of the upper arm.

The physician cast the girl a quick glance over his shoulder. "You're just in time, Rosemary; help bandage the patient."

"I fear I can't linger, Sam." Choice attempted to reproduce those small differences in inflection which distinguished her voice from Rosemary's. "The Dickinson woman is so bad with a fever that I must go to her at once."

"She's very sick?"

"Her boy said so. What should I do?"

"Prepare a mild decoction of chinchona, you know, the Jesuits' bark, and administer it."

"But you keep the medicine chest locked."

The physician plunged bloodied hands into a bucket of pinkish hot water, then dried them hurriedly on the seat of his trousers before delving into a pocket and fishing out a key. "You know where the chinchona is kept. Use it sparingly; I'm in short supply and God alone knows when or where I can find more."

Smiling pleasantly to those who greeted her, Choice, for all her heart had begun to pound like an Indian's dance drum, forced herself to proceed at a quick but natural pace to the physician's tent; once there she hastily went to work.

Scarcely ten minutes passed before the girl entered Major Phillips's tent and found it crowded by the presence of her father, Dickinson and John Rains — all anxiously waiting.

Briefly savoring this moment of importance, Choice pulled a worn, black-bound portfolio from beneath her shawl and gave it to Major Phillips. "Here, sir, but I must return it very soon — there's no telling how much longer the doctor will tarry where he is."

Once Phillips had jerked undone the folder's tie strings the other men crowded about to peer over his shoulder like so many naughty schoolboys reading a forbidden book.

Hurriedly Todd Phillips riffled through dozens of sheets bearing remarkably well-done sketches and pages inscribed with long listings of compass bearings and elevations, angles of incline; also included were descriptions of springs, the depth and location of fords and even the kinds of militarily useful timber to be found at various points along the route.

Only a small part of the portfolio's contents had been examined when Tommy Dickinson ran up panting, "Sir! Sir! Doc's packin' his tools and gettin' ready to leave Mr. Brodhead!"

Choice gasped, "Oh dear! Please, sir, I must run!"

"Of course. We've seen enough. It's all-important that this folder should be returned to its place at once," snapped Phillips, wide-set eyes hard and brilliant.

This time the girl had no choice but to risk attracting attention, so ran like a frightened doe, slipping and stumbling across the camp. Gasping for breath, she got the chest unlocked and barely had thrust the portfolio inside when Mason stumped in and, after putting down his bag of instruments, began to kick his boots against each other to rid them of clinging snow.

Leaving the key in the lock, Choice got lightly to her feet, then began to retie her headscarf so nervously that he queried sharply, "What's the matter with you?"

"Nothing, Sam. Really, I'm quite all right."

"No, you're not! I know you too well. Something *has* upset you. What is it, girl?"

She summoned an uncertain smile, then, skillfully mimicking Rosemary's slightly throatier enunciation, said, "Well then, I *am* worried — you're exhausting yourself — working too hard. Won't you try to get more rest — if only for my sake? You look ever so much handsomer when you're not all tuckered out!"

Surprised and pleased, the physician laughed, at the same time wondering why he hadn't noticed previously this warm allure in Rosemary Valentine.

"For your sake, I will try to reform," he smiled. "Oh, by the bye," he remarked, chafing chilled fingers, "I presume you've discovered that I had the Jesuits' bark in my bag all the time; only discovered it after you'd gone out. How absentminded can I grow?"

Choice struggled to keep her voice steady. "So *that's* why I couldn't find it."

Quinine bottle in his hand, Mason bent, lifted the chest's lid, then straightened as if he'd been jabbed by a bayonet. In icy tones he rasped, "My folio is untied! What have you been doing with my private papers?"

She ran over to press herself against him, babbling, "Why, why — Sam, dear — I didn't mean to disturb them. Really I didn't! They — they must somehow have got disarranged while I was s-seeking the b-bark."

"Don't lie to me! You know very well I always keep these papers at the very bottom of this chest!" A pulse began visibly to throb on Mason's temples while he riffled through his folio. "Suppose you explain why these sheets aren't in the order I keep them?"

The girl's smooth and pulpy lips began to quiver. "Oh, Sam, please don't look at me like this. Please! I swear I didn't mean any harm; it's only that so often I've watched you working on those papers and I, well, I've been wondering what they were about."

Small, well-separated brown eyes narrowing, the physician stood over her with hands slowly working by his sides. "Why would you do something so very unlike you?"

[449]

Choice ducked her face behind her hands and stammered, "I — I don't know. Forgive me, Sam, won't you please forgive me? I shall d-die if you d-don't."

"Very well. This time I will overlook the matter." He relaxed and removed his cloak, but then Choice made a serious mistake. "I'm sorry I've upset you so. Do those papers contain — something which should be kept secret?"

He glared at her, then said stiffly, "That's absolutely no concern of yours!" Kneeling, he turned the key in the lock. "Now please go, Rosemary; I've no further need of your services, however able."

Counterfeiting a convincing series of sobs, Choice squelched out into the melting snow only to sight Rosemary plodding towards her on her way back from Mrs. Dickinson, so she merged among shadows cast by a pair of sagging tents.

Once her twin had passed by, Choice scurried to Major Phillips's quarters and blurted out a breathless account of what had happened.

"By damn! Now we've got to act fast!" growled Rains. "Else that bloody spy may try to give us the slip!"

Dickinson, too, was for immediate action, but Valentine only fingered long bristles standing out all over his plump and dimpled chin. "For my part, gentlemen, I believe that we've seen sufficient evidence to act upon, but, just to make sure, let us observe the good doctor's reactions when friend Dickinson tells about what he saw in Norwalk."

" — Or *thinks* he saw," corrected the major. Obviously, he didn't know what to believe.

Nearing Dr. Mason's tent, Rosemary Valentine realized that she was at once relieved and puzzled. Why had Mrs. Dickinson pretended to be so sick when in fact she was suffering from only a slight sniffle and had had no temperature whatsoever? If there hadn't been any real need to send for help, why had she been sent for?

Long accustomed to free access to the physician's tent, Rosemary parted its flaps and stepped inside, a bright smile curving her dark-red lips. "I'm really annoyed, Sam! Mrs. Dickinson wasn't seriously ill at all, so I — "

At this furious expression her smile faded. "Why, Sam, what's gone wrong? You didn't lose Mr. Brodhead?"

The doctor's reddish brows joined in a single, ruler-straight line. "How dare you return here unbidden!"

Rosemary could only gape. "Why, Sam! Why are you so angry? What have I done wrong?"

"You know cursed well, you prying little sneak! How dared you to riffle my private papers?"

The girl's eyes became concentric rings of utter bewilderment. "What are you talking about? I — I've only just now come from the Dickinsons' tent!"

Fixedly, he stared at her, then barked, "Dare you deny that you sought me where I was operating and asked for the key to yonder chest?"

The girl began to grow frightened: this wasn't Sam Mason, but a dangerous stranger who was towering above her. "You must have gone mad — "

"How have you the temerity to — " Mason took a step towards her, but was halted by the abrupt realization that this girl cowering before him was wearing a dark-red scarf whereas she whom he'd just dismissed had been wearing one of dingy blue-and-red stripes.

Perplexedly, his hand crept up to rub his forehead. "Stab me if I know what to think! I was sure 'twas you I just now caught exploring my chest, but I now realize it must have been that precious twin of yours I surprised. She's fixed her hair like yours and was wearing a cap of yours."

"Whatever was Choice doing?"

"She was replacing my — my travel notes in the chest."

"What a stupid, ill-bred thing to do! I'm so — so ashamed of her. But, Sam, why would she want — "

As if to answer the query trampling feet and harsh voices approached the tent. An instant later a group of grim-faced men burst in led by Squire Valentine. Todd Phillips, Andrew Dickinson and knotty John Rains, limping as usual, appeared in rapid succession.

Major Phillips wasted no time, spoke in curt sentences, meanwhile resting a hand on the brass-mounted butt of a pistol stuck into his belt.

Leanly handsome features set in an expression of contempt, Samuel Mason, M.D., drew himself to full height — he'd seen men look at him like this before. "Well, what can I do for you?"

"That, sir, remains to be seen," snapped Phillips.

"I fail to grasp your meaning."

"Thanks to Squire Valentine's daughter," Phillips continued after casting Rosemary a penetrating look as she hovered among shadows behind Sam Mason, "we've had a look at maps, sketches, engineering field notes made by you and kept locked in your chest."

More and more voices, sharp in inquiry and disputation, could be heard increasing outside.

Mason's squarish chin rose as he demanded in a cold and, unfortunately, supercilious tone, "Just what did you expect to find?"

The major's thin, leather-hued lips tightened. "Not what we did. We think you had better explain your purpose in making such careful and expert recordings — "

" 'Expert'?"

"Yes. Since I once served as a sapper I'm able to appreciate your undeniable skill." His voice rose. "We demand to know why you feel moved to collect such information."

Mason cleared his throat. "I resent this illegal and unjustified interrogation, but, since you seem so insistent, I'll have you know that I was directed by General Knox, at whose headquarters I was serving as a military surgeon, to pretend to return to civil life. Then I was instructed to make my way to Watauga with the express purpose of joining Colonel Robertson's expedition. After I had received considerable instruction from various sapper officers I was ordered to prepare a description of the route followed."

Gradually, the physician became aware of hostile eyes boring through gloom in this crowded little tent reeking of wet wool, sour leather and bodies long unwashed.

Phillips made an impatient gesture. "Were you told to select the possible siting of batteries and list tactically important knolls, hills and ridges?"

"I was."

Dickinson broke in excitedly, "That's likely so, but for *whose benefit* are you preparing this information?"

The physician's tone now became that of tolerant contempt. "For the Continental Army's chief of artillery. Who else?"

A sneer distorted the Connecticuter's bony, brutally scarred features. "It's about that we intend to find out. Your information can't possibly be intended for the eyes of Sir Henry Clinton, General Prevost, or possibly that bloody Tory, Patrick Ferguson."

The physician stepped forward with fist balled but halted and recovered himself when Phillips jerked out his pistol. "You're not only an incredibly stupid fool, Dickinson, but a complete swine! Had you not so many friends on hand I'd be pleased to ram those outrageous implications down your miserable throat!"

"Do you deny that you were in Norwalk when the British raided the port last July?"

Following an almost imperceptible hesitation, Mason replied steadily, "I will not deny that I was present and in American uniform."

"What were you doing in Norwalk?" Major Phillips wanted to know.

"I chanced to be passing through that place while journeying to join the sapper regiment with which I was to receive mapmaking instruction."

"You really were taken prisoner?" Valentine prompted.

"Exactly so. Suspecting nothing, I rode into an ambush."

Dickinson stated rather than asked, "At that time you were wearing a Continental officer's uniform — blue with red facings?"

"Quite so."

Dickinson's voice rang out harsh as an eagle's scream. "In that case, why did I personally observe you inside Abel Thorne's house drinking and laughing with British and Tory officers as if you were among good friends?"

Minute beads of sweat suddenly broke out on the physician's badly chapped forehead. "I can explain that. It chanced that some of the British officers you say you saw had known me during the siege of Boston. Being trapped in the town and unable to escape, I was required to doctor not a few of them and their families as well. However, I treated them no better than I attended any patriot who required my services." He made a short, impatient gesture indicative of hopelessness. "I presume it's too much to ask you to believe that my meeting such officers in Norwalk was purely a grievous mischance."

Throat muscles tightening, Samuel Mason scanned the hairy, weather-gnawed faces ringing him in and attempted to detect even a vestige of sympathy and belief. Finding nothing of the sort he drew himself up, said in a steady voice, "Very well, I had hoped it would not be necessary to strain your credulity by mentioning a fact which doubtless will further prejudice you against me."

"Speak up!" prompted a hoarse voice from the tent's entrance. "We'll hear ye out, Doc. Ye've always been good to us!"

"Very well. Here is precisely what happened, so listen with attention. The British somehow had learned about my mission over the mountains — our headquarters, alas, swarms with spies and traitors — "

"You sure should know!" Rains snapped; after all, it wasn't he who had recruited this damned, overeducated fellow.

"General Tryon offered me immediate release on one condition: that I furnish British headquarters with the identical information I was about to collect for General Knox. Since I couldn't carry out my mission were I thrown into a British jail," he looked slowly about him, "and since the enemy had no way of *forcing* me to furnish them with correct findings, I pretended to accede to Tryon's offer."

Aware that a group standing outside the tent had greatly increased and had been listening to everything being said, the major almost shouted, "That, Doctor, settles any doubt in my mind about where your true allegiance lies!"

" — As if there's ever been any doubt about that!" snarled Dickinson.

Phillips's manner changed and he used brisk, military tones, "Some of you tie up the prisoner and keep him under close guard while we decide what's to be done with him."

Before Samuel Mason's tent, the major raised both arms above his head and yelled for silence. "Keep quiet! Now listen, all of you. After discussing the evidence presented against Samuel Mason, a committee of heads of families has deliberated and has found him guilty beyond reasonable doubt of treasonable deeds and intent." Phillips paused, mechanically wetted his lips, and went over to confront the prisoner. "Ordinarily we would string you up without delay — but because you have so long been devoted to your duty and have treated all comers with equal skill, well, we have — we have voted to let you off easy."

Samuel Mason reexperienced the old sickening sensation of helplessness in the face of outrageous injustice. By now he'd learned the futility of impassioned appeals and protests at such a moment, so, quietly, he demanded, "And what do my grateful former patients mean by the term 'easy'?"

Squire Valentine told him in an almost sorrowful tone, "You'll be allowed to keep your horse and some blankets. You will be given a sound gun and a reasonable amount of ammunition and food; then you will be escorted to the edge of camp and shot if you try to turn back. Where you go when you leave us is strictly up to you."

Luke Brodhead shoved to the front of the crowd, his hurt arm cradled in a ragged sling. Angrily, he yelled, "You call *that* lettin' the Doc off easy? You know damn' well he's no part of a woodsman; he can't last two days in the wilderness, so whyn't you heroes be truly merciful and string the poor devil up and put him out of his misery in a hurry?"

Tim Murphy, who with Dan Maddox had just returned from a hunting expedition, pushed forward, shaking his fist and fairly chattering with rage. "By God, any you bastards thinks I'm goin' to stand aside and watch the man who saved my arm and life get driven out to freeze and starve — no matter what he's been accused of — is moonstruck crazy! You can bet the Doc's goin' to outlive the most of you damned yellowbellies, 'cause where he goes, I'm goin' too."

Dan Maddox, deadly lights playing in his sunken eyes, stepped up to the prisoner and jerked undone his bindings. Then he unslung his rifle and stood, alert and ready, beside the accused. Murphy did the same.

Maddox then snapped, "You're acting like addled fools! You've got no *real* proof Sam Mason's a Tory or that he may be lyin' about his mission. Long while ago he told me the truth about what happened to him up in Boston; I credited his story then, and by the eternal, I always will!"

Chance Encounter

Since neither Dr. Mason nor either of the ex-soldiers had even so much as glimpsed a map of this bleak and winter-bound country — if, indeed, any existed — frequent consultations were held regarding the route and direction to be taken.

Right at the start, all three had agreed that nothing would be gained by attempting to find Colonel Robertson's division: first, Dr. Mason certainly would find it difficult, if not impossible, to offer a plausible explanation as to how and why he and his companions had become separated from Phillips's party; second, there was no certainty that Robertson could be found on this vast, rolling and nearly treeless prairie; third, the weather, although it continued clear and bright, daily was growing colder. Probably the mercury in that little Fahrenheit thermometer still reposing in Mason's medicine chest would have shown the temperature as only a few degrees above the zero mark.

For five days the three successfully forced their way through or rode around drifts lying along the course of a frozen creek which seemed to run in the right direction — towards the southeast. The voyagers spoke seldom and then only when necessary.

Sam Mason remained the most taciturn of all and would only brighten up a little after supper had been cooked and eaten. It was as if he were lost again in bitter hopelessness; no doubt he was wondering what would happen to his portfolio. The best he could hope for was that eventually his information would be forwarded to some American authority — always provided that the "slow" division ever reached its destination.

The three "Ishmaelites" — as Mason with wry humor had nicknamed the little party — thus far had made out reasonably well, chiefly because Maddox and Murphy had taken along all their scanty possessions and had demanded their share of food from the meager common stores.

Although they'd not yet located any yarded deer or buffalo, they had discovered a number of dense thickets along the riverside in which rabbits, grouse, partridges and even a few turkeys had elected to winter.

One afternoon during a halt to rally their energy all three men heard the distinctive *crack! crack!* of rifles being fired somewhere beyond a low, snow-covered ridge that presented a glittering barrier in the near distance. Cautious reconnaissance disclosed a pair of tiny black figures snowshoeing towards a fallen animal; the distance was too great to make sure what it was they'd just shot.

"They whites?" Mason mumbled through a breath-frosted muffler.

"Must be," Maddox told him. "No redskin would be crazy enough to go huntin' in weather like this. Besides, those shots sounded good and loud."

"What do you mean by that?"

"Injuns can't afford to use a deal of powder, so as a rule they don't charge their weapons so heavy."

Maddox, as most experienced on the frontier, told Mason to stay and guard the horses against some hungry predator which might attempt an easy meal. "Besides," muttered the gunsmith, "those fellows out there ain't goin' to be so wary of two men as they would be of three."

Maddox was careful to raise a long "hallo-o" before he and Murphy snowshoed over the skyline. Both of the distant hunters ceased to bend over their quarry and, snatching up guns, flung themselves flat behind the fallen animal.

Repeatedly making the peace sign, Tim and Maddox advanced until they were able to make out fur caps barely showing above the dead buffalo's snow-smeared bulk and two pair of eyes squinting behind gleaming iron rings made by rifle muzzles.

"Hey there!" sang out one of the hunters. "Keep them rifles pointed up and halt where you stand!"

When they had complied the other stranger called, "Who are ye?"

[455]

"Me, I'm Dan'l Maddox, and this here half-pint is Tim Murphy."

"You fellers from Robertson's?"

Dan thought quickly while shouldering Ilsa in a gesture intended to be reassuring. "That's correct."

"How come you're wanderin' 'round?"

"We were out huntin' meat for him when a blizzard cut us off. We've looked around a lot, but we ain't seen any sign of him."

"Then ye're lost?"

"That's the way 'tis and there's no 'tiser," grinned Tim. "We're damn well lost and powerful hungry, too. All three of us."

The taller stranger promptly slung his gun in line with Murphy's stomach. "*Three!* Where's the other man — or are there more of you somewheres around? Now speak true, else we'll surely blow you fellows apart!"

Maddox spoke up in a hurry. "Take it easy, mister! 'Fore God, there's only Sam Mason behind yonder ridge; he's guardin' our nags."

"All right, you kin come on in. But don't make no sudden motions."

Maddox and the rifleman then shuffled forward, light snow spraying rhythmically from under their bear-paw shoes. Solemnly, they stripped off their mittens to offer filthy, clawlike hands.

Eyes bright and restless, the strangers rose from behind the buffalo and advanced slowly, watchfully. Both were stockily built, brown-bearded and appeared to be in early middle age. One, wearing a shaggy wolfskin coat secured by a wide, brass-buckled belt, had a frayed and broken turkey feather stuck into the back of his cap; the other was protected from the weather by a long-skirted and dingy white Dutch blanket circled by a blue band. For a moment the four men lingered on this vast white plain with sharp snow particles eddying about their legs.

Finally, Tim inquired, "You fellers trappin'?"

Said he in the Dutch coat, "Naw. We're huntin' meat out of Kasper Mansker's place."

"Mansker?"

"Yep. The Dutchman's building a station hard by Sulphur Springs."

"That far off?"

"'Tain't close. Barrin' another storm it lays at the end of two, mebbe-three days' hard travel."

"You mounted?" Dan demanded in carefully subdued anxiety. Men afoot might go to any lengths to get horses.

"Yep. Got a pair of tackeys tethered hard by. Oh, I forgot to say," the bushy-bearded fellow wearing the wolfskin tapped himself, "me, I'm Haydon Wells and this here no-good son of a woods colt goes by the name of Humphrey Hogan."

"Pleased to meet you."

Hogan grinned. "Me and Haydon would admire to have you along. The both of you look like you know how to handle a rifle."

Dan slung Ilsa across his back, then jerked out his skinning knife and

[456]

pointed to the buffalo which lay with tongue lolled out and steaming and glazed black eyes staring fixedly on squadrons of ragged, silver-gray storm clouds which had begun to charge out of the northwest. "Let's get this critter's skin off whilst he's still warm."

When the gory job was completed Hogan slowly wiped his blade on fringed elkskin leggings. "Wal now, reckon we've plenty to stay our bellies with till this new tempest blows over."

"Let's hope so," Wells said, then turned to Tim, who was cutting out the tongue. "Your hatchet sharp? We'd best start cuttin' up."

Dan said, "Mine is, so I'll help butcher. Meantime, Tim, you trot back and fetch in *Mister* Mason — " he stressed the "mister" — "and the mounts. Hurry; looks like we'll get hit by another mean storm before long."

He was right. The new blizzard proved even more vicious and prolonged than that which lashed the expedition after crossing Mad Bear Creek. During four whole days, the men were forced to huddle, half-frozen, in a shelter contrived of the buffalo's hide and blankets stretched over a rough frame made from willows growing around a frozen pond.

The sky had finally cleared and they were loading their scant possessions and what remained of the meat when Mason said thoughtfully, as if thinking aloud, "I'd be surprised if either party has survived this long."

Curtly, Wells shook his head. "If they were caught 'way out on the Barrens I reckon there won't be anything seen of 'em except bones when the spring thaws uncover 'em. They were plain crazy to try traveling in midwinter."

Dan Maddox finished cinching his ribby horse before drawling, "Think you're at least half wrong; bet you even money most of Jim Robertson's party will win through."

"What about Rains and Phillips and their people?" Hogan queried as he caught up his reins and prepared to lead out.

The gunsmith shrugged. "Sorry as I am to say it, I won't grant 'em the chance of a snowball in hell!"

Mason nodded. "I fear you're right and that's bad; I must recover my records. I can't afford to wait for 'em to be forwarded hit or miss and at no particular time. They've got to reach General Knox in the spring if they're to serve any useful purpose."

"Just how you fixing to recover 'em?" Tim demanded while slinging his famous rifle.

"Don't know, but I've *got* to. Right now I'm chiefly interested in remaining alive."

When the daylight came and the wolves had retreated to a reassuring distance, Maddox yawned cavernously, then trained a speculative eye on the doctor. "Didn't sleep so good last night, did you?"

The physician passed a bony and dirt-glazed hand over his thick, inch-long, dark-red beard which served, aside from shielding his face from bitter winds, to conceal many of the harsh lines that had become engraved upon it. His dark-brown eyes had retreated even deeper into their sockets while his cheekbones now stuck out like hatchet blades, but his voice remained clear and strong. "No. I was wrestling with that uncomfortable thing called a conscience," he explained simply.

In a gesture unusual for so undemonstrative a man, Dan Maddox placed a hand on his friend's shoulder. "Come on. What in hell's troubling it, Sam?"

" — Whether or not I should make an attempt to find Rains and Phillips. You see, if they keep on in the southeasterly direction they were keeping when we — er — when we parted, they'll be attempting to cross the Barrens at their widest point, or so Hogan tells me."

"Wells says the same," Maddox said, then turned aside and unconcernedly relieved himself onto the snow. "He allows they'll never live to reach the far side. When them old-time Indians burned off this country for a buffalo pasture they sure did one fine job. Been at it for ages, so they tell me."

"Do you think anything ought to be done about locating our former companions?"

"I ain't sure," drawled the rifleman. "Hate to think of all those poor fools dyin' so slow and painful after all they've been through."

Once the men had eaten and began to flap snow from ragged blankets preparatory to rolling them, Sam Mason raised his voice, "Hold it a moment, fellows, I've got something important to say and I hope you'll hear me out."

"Spit it out," Hogan rasped. "Time we was movin'. What's on yer mind?"

" — That I've decided an effort must be made to locate Phillips's party."

Tim's bearded jaw sagged. "My God, Sam! You gone clear out o' yer wits? Why, those people will surely shoot you like a dog the minute they recognize you!"

Haydon Wells's shaggy head snapped about so fast that the horses raised their heads. "What's that?" he demanded sharply. "Why fer would anyone want to kill Sam Mason?"

There was nothing for it now but to tell, as simply as possible, the whole sorry and complex story. Maddox did a good job, omitted no pertinent fact, then steadily regarded Haydon Wells, whose permanent half smile had vanished. "Well, there you have the whole story, boys, as short and plain as I can make it. You'd best make up your minds who's right in a hurry."

Wells fingered his salt-and-pepper-colored mustache. "Don't know what Hump thinks, but, as for myself, I think the doc's been done dirty by."

Hogan's gap-toothed grin lifted grease-shiny round spots on his cheeks. "Reckon ye're right, Haydon. Me, I figger that two good men who've knowed the doc for so long wouldn't have elected to take their chances along with him if he'd been a wrong one."

After deliberation, it was decided that in case Spencer, for some reason, had elected to depart from his original route, Haydon Wells would guide Mason and Murphy to the southwest while Hogan and Maddox would search due south. It was reaffirmed that, if three days' scouting produced no sign of the column, all hands would turn back and rendezvous at the nearest meat cache the scouts had established on the way to Kasper Mansker's station. Nobody even mentioned the grave possibility that none of these men so stiffly loading their horses might ever be seen again.

Camp Misery

Many times during the past fortnight, Choice Valentine had imagined that she'd touched the ultimate depths of despair, but right now she realized that she'd been quite mistaken. Nothing which had occurred in the past could even compare with the appalling conditions at present prevailing in Camp Misery, as this desolate, disorderly encampment aptly enough had been nicknamed.

Three days back so many immigrants had taken scurvy or had otherwise fallen sick — with several lingering close to death — and losses among the remaining skeleton-thin livestock had become so serious that, when the head of the column entered a wide natural bowl created among a group of low ridges on which a good supply of brown buffalo grass was visible, the harried and increasingly desperate leaders decreed a long halt.

Perhaps it was the death of Agnes Valentine that prompted this decision, but more likely it was the fact that Tom Spencer, their principal guide, at last had succumbed to snow blindness, which was afflicting everybody more or less. In addition, he'd fallen victim to a mysterious complaint in his bowels that for hours on end kept the giant groaning and doubled up in agony.

In a way, Choice was relieved that poor, dear Mamma had died so suddenly — of what nobody seemed to know; now at least she wouldn't have to go on starving and freezing.

She wondered how much longer Papa would remain absent. Over an hour ago he'd been called to another of those interminable councils which never seemed to arrive at a decision — right or wrong — and usually ended in wrangling as futile as it was bitter. Despite her wretchedness, Choice was becoming aware that Papa — who now was weighing forty pounds less than he had three months ago — had become influential among the leaders.

[459]

If only he'd been able to prevent that stupid driving away of Sam Mason and Tim and Dan Maddox! Until recently she'd not appreciated how much the last two had done for her family. Choice snuffled, then wiped a red, badly chapped nose on her sleeve. Admittedly she missed Tim, with his easy laughter, eager lips and ready virility whenever a moment's privacy became available, but to her growing surprise it was of the gunsmith she had thought the most often of late. Maybe it was because Rosemary definitely was "sweet" on him? All her life she'd set out to win whatever her twin wanted. Dan Maddox, she decided, she'd have for her own.

Employing the jerky motions of a woman thrice her age, the girl wearily pulled Mamma's best cashmere shawl over her own dirty gray one, then braced herself and stepped out into blazing sunlight to be momentarily blinded. Lord! How her eyes ached and burned from continual exposure to acrid wood smoke and the fearful glare of sunlight glancing off these interminable snow-blanketed Barrens.

The first person she encountered was young Jonathan Robertson, who, supporting himself on a staff — he'd suffered a touch of frostbite in both feet — was stolidly limping along driving the ram and three surviving ewes out to graze. Poor little fellow! He tried to smile even though he knew he'd be out in the wind all day ready to use that funny old pistol of his on any predator that dared to come too close. Wolves — and there were several sizable packs of them prowling about — daily were growing bolder, perhaps because they no longer could feed on that long line of carcasses dotting the division's tortured route.

When Old Scratch started to stray among the sagging, smoke-stained tents, Jonathan used his staff to fetch the ram a resounding *whack!* which a few weeks earlier certainly would have earned him at least an attempted butt, but today the ram merely coughed before lunging heavily across a snowbank in the right direction; dispiritedly, the ewes followed.

Briefly Jonathan wondered what the outcome to today's council would be. Would the head men decide to stay where they were awhile longer or try to move on? If only Joe Drake, Cash Brooks or some of the other old-timers hadn't gone with Pa! For some time Jonathan had suspected, privately of course, that neither Tom Spencer nor Ed Jennings had been too sure about where they were going. If only there had been a few unmistakable landmarks around to set them right; but there hadn't been a one. Jennings, at least, had admitted that he was lost.

Jonathan painfully started to traverse his gaze but suddenly checked the slow turning of his head. Were his eyes tricking him or had three dark specks appeared to move slowly along the summit of a ridge running roughly parallel to the one on which he stood? Shading his eyes with both hands the boy stared until burning tears started to draw cold lines down his cheeks.

Shucks, what if those were only a few stray buffaloes! He caught his breath and stared harder at those distant silhouettes. No, by grabs, those *were* horsemen yonder and, better still, they couldn't possibly have come from Camp Misery! Criminently! Maybe big Tom Spencer had been right all along and a settlement lay somewhere nearby?

Air bit at his lungs with icy teeth when he filled them to yell, but he sensed that his high-pitched shouting wouldn't travel anywhere near far enough. Besides, dang the luck, those strangers were riding upwind and away from him!

Jonathan started to snowshoe wildly down the slope, but halted halfway down, aware that this effort would prove futile. Those horsemen must be riding at least half a mile off. Worse still, it now looked as if they were headed away from Camp Misery and about to disappear below the crest. Oh, God! How could he attract their attention?

Then he remembered his pistol, and praying that its priming was good, leveled in the strangers' direction and squeezed the trigger.

Eternal seconds seemed to elapse before the smoke cleared away. Had they heard? Yes. They'd reined in and were swinging their mounts to face him.

He waved and jumped up and down like an oversized jumping jack, all the time yipping shrilly, Indian-fashion.

Indians? A sobering thought: what if those tiny dark figures turned out to be redskins scouting for a large party? If such proved to be the case, would he be allowed time to snowshoe back and raise an alarm?

But almost immediately he became sure those were white men whose horses now were rearing and plunging often breast-deep through deep drifts covering the floor of that little valley which separated the two ridges.

Pretty soon Jonathan began to knuckle his eyes and to believe that his empty belly must be tricking him. Danged if that tall fellow riding in the lead didn't look a lot like Doc Mason — and — by grabs! That *was* Tim Murphy all bundled up in a tight-belted bearskin coat. The other man he couldn't recognize.

Snowshoes kicking up successive sprays of dazzling white, Jonathan plunged down the slope. "Doc! Doc! Is that really you?"

"In body if not in spirit," called the foremost rider. "By God, Jon, I'm delighted not to find you frozen stiff!"

The boy grabbed Mason's leg out of the stirrup and hugged it.

Tim's grin widened as he inquired, "How's everybody in camp?"

"Gee, Mr. Murphy, we're powerful bad off. Hungry and lost, I reckon. Doc's going to be awful busy." Then he remembered something. "One of Squire Valentine's girls been took terrible sick."

"Which one?" Tim and the doctor demanded simultaneously.

"Why, 'tis Miss Rosemary; she's been poorly ever since her ma died. She's been bedridden three-four days now." The boy's windbitten features peered up through a cloud of breath vapors. "You'll come quick and fix her up?"

"I expect so — if I'm allowed."

Once the four of them had come up with the grazing sheep the rifleman queried, "Now look, Jon, what, well, what kind of a greetin' kin we expect?"

Wells asked sharply, "Are they hungry enough down there to listen to reason?"

"Yep. Reckon they'd do most anythin' fer a good feed."

Murphy gathered braided rawhide reins while his gaze flickered across the glaring plain and came to rest on the encampment's irregular dark outlines. "If that's so, I reckon, Doc, you'd best play it safe and keep these here sheep company whilst me, Wells and the boy go find out whether it's safe for you to come in. Maybe we can talk sense into Rains, Phillips and the rest of them numbskulls."

While Old Scratch and his diminished harem continued to paw snow from the browse, Doc Mason with Jonathan Wells, and Maddox — back from the encampment — watched a party of horsemen quit Camp Misery and head for the grazing ground.

Suddenly, Jonathan fixed bleared eyes on his companions. "Any you fellers spare me a charge of powder and shot? Used my last to signal you."

His crooked smile widening, Haydon Wells bent in his saddle and offered a powder horn along with a pair of dull-gray musket balls which seemed small enough to fit into the bore of the boy's antique weapon.

"Thanks, Mister. Thanks a lot!"

The scout chuckled. "Ye're welcome, but tell me, Bub, what're ye reloadin' fer?"

Jonathan squared thin shoulders under a sheepskin cloak fashioned from the fleece of that ewe which had died of eating ivy. "I figure to kill the first man who tries to hurt or drive the Doc away again!"

As matters turned out there was no call for Jonathan to use his pistol. Squire Valentine, suggesting a gaunt, bearded and not unattractive caricature of his former self, appeared astride an equine scarecrow a few yards ahead of hollow-eyed and fuzzy-bearded Major Phillips and a pair of bundled-up heads of family Mason recognized only by sight.

While pulling in his frost-rimed mount, Valentine managed a vague salute and then dismounted to offer his hand. "Ah — Doctor. I, well, I trust that you will be sufficiently generous to — er — overlook suspicions which now appear to have been quite baseless."

"That's very handsome of you, sir." Mason's tone was sardonic. "Do I take it correctly that you speak for your colleagues as well?"

Major Phillips forced a bleak smile onto long and somber features. "We do, sir. Pray forgive our hasty decision and action. It's, well, it's just that during this war we've suffered so damned much from treason that — "

"I quite appreciate that, sir," came the physician's cold assurance.

Valentine then broke in, "May I say, sir, we are more than eager to have you resume your very skillful ministrations! Incidentally, Tom Spencer and my daughter should receive your first attention."

"Is — is Rosemary badly off?"

"She is gravely ill, I fear."

"I regret to hear this." Then the physician recalled the other obligation, demanded crisply, "You will return my portfolio with its contents intact?"

"It will be returned the moment we reach the encampment. You have my word on that, sir."

No Band of Brothers

The day was so exceptionally warm and pleasant for early February that Captain Barry Colcord told his wife to fetch little Patrick out onto the half-finished porch where the baby could enjoy the sunshine. Having just pulled off boots muddied during a ride around his property, the dark, well-built young Carolinian relished the comfort of going about like this in stocking feet; it was even better to drop into a wicker armchair, relax and just sit for a while; he'd been out since sunup inspecting dikes being raised to enclose a series of new rice fields situated along the northern border of his plantation.

Again Barry experienced exasperated frustration that this seemingly endless war should so seriously have slowed and otherwise have hampered the development of Ricelands, the well-situated and otherwise promising plantation he'd bought on the Sampee River just before his marriage to Laura MacDonald. The property lay due north of the little town of Georgetown, South Carolina.

They'd only been married a few months when news of the battle of Breed's Hill had arrived from the North along with a ringing call to arms. In quick response, he and his brothers, Augustus and Robert, had mounted their hunters and had ridden away, lightheartedly enough, during the summer of '76 to enroll in Francis Marion's newly formed Partisan Legion. At that time the "Swamp Fox," as he now was becoming known, had been a mere lieutenant colonel with most of his brilliant career still before him.

His wife raised that ruddy and angular but far from unattractive face which so clearly revealed her Highland ancestry and reached up to pat his cheek, murmuring, "Ah, Barry, Barry, my dearest, 'tis fair to have you by me. How much longer can this idyll continue?"

Pouring milk, Colcord replied gravely, "Another full week — if my luck holds. Rob and I were granted the same leave; 'Gustus, too." When he grinned some of the weary lines disappeared from his powerfully modeled features. "When the colonel wants to get shut of the Colcord clan he don't believe in doing it piecemeal!"

A small smile curved Laura Colcord's wide and pleasantly shaped mouth. "Of course it hasn't occurred to you that Colonel Marion might feel that three men going on leave together might travel safer?"

"Good of him — but unnecessary. Since we chased Prevost from before Charles Town last fall that esteemed general and Colonel Campbell appear quite content to remain in Georgia waiting to find out what Lincoln and Moultrie may have in mind. Actually, I expect that both sides must be waiting for reinforcements before undertaking serious operations."

Frowning, Laura tilted milk into the baby's shiny rosebud of a mouth; next, she smoothed gleaming, raven hair, tightly braided about her head. "That's good, so long as British or Tory patrols don't start raiding this far north. What really worries me is that — "

" — Is that some of our dear Loyalist neighbors will begin to make trouble before long? Well, I'll admit they're a force to be reckoned with since we failed to recapture Savannah and took that licking at Briar Creek — which I'll not forget in a hurry. Yes, the king's friends *are* growing steadily bolder and more outspoken. It's unfortunate, also, that the governor's finding it hard to raise new militia companies."

"Why?"

"Because they're afraid to enter Charles Town since that outbreak of smallpox killed so many people last fall. On the bright side, a good many volunteers are coming into Charles Town and Lincoln's camp at Purysburg. Beyond this," he continued seriously, "we've heard news that General Washington already has ordered south the Virginia and North Carolina Continentals who have been serving with him."

Barry sighed; what luxury it was simply to sit like this on his own front porch, watching great, dark, ever-shifting strings of ducks, reed birds and other waterfowl continually climb, dip and swirl like smoke above the broad and tawny Sampee flowing so leisurely to join the Pee Dee above Georgetown and then to drown itself in the Atlantic.

After a while Laura murmured over the baby's avid suckling noises, "Tell me, dearest, since we have suffered so many defeats of late how do most of our people — of the ordinary sort, I mean — feel about who is going to win this eternal war?"

Colcord's look of contentment faded, and for a brief instant he eyed his wife almost cautiously. "Why ask about that? Have you heard news I haven't?"

Her nod was curt. "Yesterday afternoon, while you were riding the fields, a stranger stopped by here."

Colcord's voice grew edged as he watched a flush suddenly creep out over his wife's prominent cheekbones. "What did he want? Why haven't you mentioned this before?"

"Because I didn't want you needlessly upset; not while you're on leave."

"Well, then, why did this fellow come here?"

"He was bearing a message from my brother."

[464]

Straightening abruptly in his chair, Barry demanded, "The Whig one, I hope?"

"Aye. 'Twas from Jamie. He sent word that with the British now holding Savannah in greater strength than ever and having won control over all Georgia, enemy commanders are very busy recruiting among the Loyalists. Also, their agents are traveling in our hill country and rousing the mountain Scots of North Carolina — my people."

Colcord's lean, red-brown and weather-roughened features contracted; he looked her in the eye. "That's no recent news. Wasn't there anything else this messenger had to say?"

"Yes, that's not all." Nervously, Laura began to stroke her son's head. "Jamie has heard reliable reports that last fall Sir Henry Clinton gathered a strong fleet and a great army up in New York, and he thinks that at this very moment it is sailing south to Savannah."

"What!" Barry jerked a nod. "It stands to reason, doesn't it, that Sir Henry would want to join forces with the British in Georgia?"

"Jamie feels sure that the enemy will attack Charles Town as soon as they can." Laura summoned an uncertain smile. "Of course, as we both know, Jamie *may* have been listening to wild rumors, but he says that my — my other brothers are all excited. Charles is reported to be raising a Loyalist company while Colin has mysteriously disappeared. He is supposed to be riding southward."

Barry started to speak out, but contented himself by reminding her that Benjamin Lincoln, the portly, lethargic but often brilliant New England general whom Congress had sent down to command its Southern army, had captured Beaufort and had won a smart minor victory at Kettle Creek — that same battle in which the Colcord brothers had led their light cavalrymen in a successful charge.

Straightening, Barry made an effort to break the tension. " 'Twould appear that our young soldier has drawn sufficient rations for the moment." He reached out and, with awkward gentleness, wiped milk from Patrick's chin before briefly stroking the baby's curly blond hair.

Replete, Patrick refused to rouse even when his mother draped him over a shoulder and began to pat his back. All at once Barry, deeply moved, bent to kiss his wife, but was checked by a suddenly intent look in her large, black eyes.

Following her gaze, he spied a faint, cone-shaped cloud of yellow dust arising above a narrow road which followed the tops of dikes separating his ricefields from his father's.

He felt a small chill creep down and spread over his back. That rider was coming in a hurry. Um. People didn't ordinarily spur like that over trifles.

As the rider came nearer he recognized him by his immensely wide and powerful shoulders and the characteristic way he sat, rather than posted in the saddle, as his younger brother, Robert.

Since childhood, Robert Colcord never had been given to minimizing his account of any event — no matter how trivial; in fact, his friends long since had claimed that Rob could stumble over a stick and make his report of that incident sound more important than the Second Coming of Christ. His broad, good-natured features agleam with sweat, Rob flung himself off a lathered gray hunter and, after looping his reins over an arm, hurried to his brother.

"From that unusually serious set on your silly phiz," Barry observed acidly, "I judge you're bringing some news of real importance."

Panting slightly, Lieutenant Colcord burst out, "'Fore God, Barry, it couldn't be more serious!"

"Well, are your tidings good or bad?"

Rob kicked aside an overcurious hound, then dashed sweat from his eyes. "They're both!"

"For God's sake, don't riddle me at a moment like this! What's this all about?"

"Seem's a courier passed through Georgetown this morning carrying news that a great fleet of enemy transports and men-of-war — over a hundred of 'em — has been sighted off Tybee Island heading for Edisto Inlet!"

"Oh, my God! All that many! Are you sure about this?"

"Oh, yes! Yes. General Lincoln is sending word for all militia and state troops to report to Charles Town as soon as may be, so we're off again."

"What's the good part of the news?"

Grinning hugely, Rob clapped his brother on the shoulder. "Cheer up! This means that we're going to get another crack at the lobsterbacks and square accounts for Briar Creek and Savannah! Ain't that wonderful?"

Grimly, Barry shook his head. "What's so wonderful about that? I'm heartily sick of campaigning."

The younger brother's elation vanished. "Sorry — since I ain't married I'll admit I don't see things the way you do, but I do understand you hate to leave Laura in her — er — present condition."

" — And that's not the half of it!" Barry drew a slow, deep breath. "Well, Rob, I suppose this means we're bound for Charles Town in a big hurry. Who are we supposed to report to?"

"Colonel Moylan's Horse — if we can find them. If not, to a Major Vernier who commands what's left of Pulaski's dragoons."

"Why dragoons? We're light-horse."

"I've no idea, but those were the orders I got. The message wasn't written out, so maybe the fellow was mistook. As for myself, I'd say we'd better attach ourselves to the first organized cavalry force we come across."

"That makes sense till we learn more."

They tramped into the house to find Laura changing the baby's diapers. a soft sigh escaped her when she straightened up and slowly shook her head. "Glad to see you, brother Rob, but I'm terribly discouraged over your news." She looked away quickly with wide but narrow lips compressed. "Oh! Rob! Rob! This isn't right! This isn't fair! Our time together has been too short, too happy. Why must you go again? Haven't you two done more than your fair share of fighting?" she almost wailed. "Why, oh why, couldn't you have enjoyed your entire leave?"

Rob went over diffidently to pat his sister-in-law's back. "Don't take on so, honey. Near as I know, a war ain't never been designed to fit any particular man's convenience. Take heart, dear girl. This time we're surely going to smash the redcoats and Tories so hard they'll just have to holler quits! Then we'll be home for keeps."

"Why so serious, Rob? Whenever we've gone campaigning before you've acted gay as a catbird on a pump handle."

The muscular and taller younger brother frowned before lowering his voice, "Reckon this time it ain't quite like before."

"Why not?"

"Heard anything lately about those poor whites who live down in Shell Town?"

Over his glass Barry nodded. "Now and then. What about them?"

"Well, those rascals have managed to arm themselves — God knows how."

Barry's dark-blue eyes met his brother's of clear gray. For all Rob inevitably had aged during the past three years, his curly, roughly clubbed, collar-length brown hair and his smooth, almost unlined features continued to lend him an almost boyish aspect.

"Towards which side do those swamp rabbits incline?"

Frowning, Rob gnawed his lip. "Can't answer that; no one can. But Pa and I expect they're waitin' to see which way the cat's going to jump before they choose sides."

"Who leads 'em?"

Rob slowly revolved his wine glass between short but powerful fingers. "A mean-looking, yellow-beard fellow name of Jasper Skelton; it was he who, at the head of a gang of scalawags, rode up to Tranquillity, bold as brass, yesterday morning and, grinning like a horse collar, told Pa he wasn't to fret if us boys got called back into the field; he and his neighbors stood ready to protect all Colcord property."

Robert's eyes began to shine. "As for himself, the Old Man snapped, "I'm ready, willing and damn' well able to protect any and all Colcord property.' Skelton — he's scrawny, sallow-faced and a little cockeyed — sneered, 'Well, it's just as you say, Squire — but these days ain't nobody can be *sure* about nothin'! We just might have to call on ye to supply us someday, willy-nilly.'

"Damn the sassy fellow!" Rob rasped. "I only hope he grants us an excuse to burn that human hogsty flat! Should have been done a long while ago. What about a body servant?"

"Think I'll take along Saul Black Buck."

Robert's brows went up. "Saul? You mean that mustee hunter you bought last year?"

"He's the one. While Saul's a little long in the tooth, he's still damned knowledgeable in swamps and wooded country."

"He's part Indian, ain't he?"

"Yes, Half Creek, half Nigra — or maybe less. He don't know himself."

"He own a firearm?"

Barry put away the decanter. "No, but I'm lending him that German rifle-gun I picked up at Kettle Creek. He's learned to shoot it pretty well, but he's still handier with a bow."

"Well, Barry boy, I'm off now to see who can be coaxed or threatened into enlisting."

Long after the hollow sound of hoofbeats had faded along the dike road Barry remained silent, slumped in his chair and feeling all of ten years older. Why in God's name had Rob had to add to his anxieties by mentioning Jasper Skelton's visit and his implied threats? Everybody in this part of Georgetown County for a long time had considered Shell Town, that unimportant hamlet downriver, as no more than a squalid disgrace to the community. Most Shell Towners certainly were smugglers and probably pirates as well. Granted the opportunity, they were reported ready to row out under cover of darkness to plunder defenseless little coasters.

Barry took apart and expertly cleaned the locks to his heavy, brass-mounted saddle pistols. After that he stitched tight a fraying seam in his saddle of fine English pigskin. He ended by poking up the fire and running bullets to fit his carbine and side arms. By midnight the young captain's saddlebags bulged with fresh underwear, stockings and even a ruffled dress shirt against the possibility that it might be required for a formal occasion.

Barry felt increasingly sure that his decision to take along Saul Black Buck was sound. Aside from acting as a body servant, the half-breed was certain to prove invaluable in scouting or on patrol duty. He cast a look across the room at Black Buck, as he preferred to be called, busily braiding a fresh pair of bridle reins. How strange that, in a cross between an Indian and a Negro, characteristics of the former race should almost invariably predominate. Saul's slightly hooked nose was thin and high-bridged, and his grizzled hair wasn't really kinky — only wavy — while his skin was the hue of copper-black velvet.

Nothing was said when the old mustee silently appeared around the house leading Barry's favorite hunter, Eclipse — so named, rather unoriginally, because the long-legged mare hadn't a single white hair on her. For himself, Saul Black Buck had found a bigger-than-average brown tackey which, judging by its long legs, might have counted a blooded animal somewhere among its ancestors.

Only when Barry began to pull on his gauntlets did Laura, for the first time in her life, begin to quiver and then burst into uncontrollable tears "Forgive me," she choked, "I — I fear I'm acting like a silly child and no part of a good soldier's wife, but I — I can't help it." Almost angrily she slapped her bulging abdomen. "Perhaps this is to blame for my weakness."

He put gentle arms about Laura, hugged her to him and kissed her wet features again and again while gamecocks in their walks behind the house announced the breaking of the new day. "Ah — darling, dearest, please don't take on so. Look. Right now I swear to return in plenty of time to greet our new heir."

He kissed her again, then, setting his riding cloak aflutter, he swung up onto Eclipse, wheeled, and with the day's first light drawing dull gleams from his helmet, reined the mare about and clattered off towards Tranquillity. At a more sedate pace Black Buck and the pack horse moved out after him.

Behind Ricelands the foxhound Juno began to emit doleful sounds.

Rebel! Rebel!

When the Colcord brothers, with crested brass helmets glinting, left behind the small but fast-growing port of Georgetown, they were leading what was termed a "half troop," consisting of twenty-four passably well-mounted recruits. They set off along a sandy, little-used back road which led less comfortably but more directly to Monck's Corner than did the comparatively wide and roughly graded King's Highway.

Only a few of the troopers were clad in parts of uniforms from several units. Although this was winter, most of the men, who for the most part were hard-eyed farmers or small tradesmen, wore fraying broad-brimmed straw hats, sleeveless jackets of strouding, frieze or osnaburg. The rest of their costume consisted of knee breeches or pantaloons of coarse linen and stockings of heavy thread. Without exception, these new cavalrymen's foot gear was well worn and home-cobbled.

To war a sergeant's green worsted shoulder knot, Barry Colcord designated taciturn Gavin Wilcox, a silent, grimly efficient, sheep-faced veteran of the siege of Charles Town in '76. For corporals he selected Paul Skene and Oliver Peete, both time-expired militiamen who swore that they'd served last year under Colonel Laurens during General Lincoln's costly and unsuccessful attempt to recapture Savannah. For his lance corporals he selected a quartet of hard-looking characters said to have fought in Georgia with patriot partisans under Captain John Dooley against Tory forces led by the redoubtable and able Colonel Boyd.

[469]

Lending the half troop a slightly professional air were several swords and sabers of varying design and a few battered helmets of brown or black leather.

This inland section of the South Carolina coast was flat as any platter, sandy and overgrown with useless slash pines, pin oaks and palmettoes. An occasional grove of huge, moss-draped and silver-gray live oaks helped to relieve the landscape's depressing monotony. The half troop continually was forced to ford or even swim across a seemingly interminable succession of brooks and creeks flowing eastward to feed those vast marshes which lined the coast all the way up to North Carolina.

Hereabouts, what farms there were looked poverty-poor. Few and far between, they usually consisted of no more than a ramshackle slab shanty or an old-time log cabin standing lonely amid sandy-gray fields on low, brick supports, with only a privy, a cowshed or a rickety corncrib to keep them company.

Rob, jogging along beside his brother, all at once raised a hand to shade his eyes against the pale winter sun. "Notice all those buzzards wheeling up ahead? Wonder what interests 'em?"

"Probably someone's butchered a hog — or maybe they're just waiting for some sick horse or cow to die."

All at once Black Buck rode up alongside with so intent an expression that Barry straightened in his saddle, asked quickly, "What's wrong?"

"Me know this place, sar. Is little public house around next bend. Vultures swinging low close by."

A moment later the sandy track straightened sufficiently to reveal a great swarm of black-and-brown turkey buzzards flapping, wheeling and planing above the charred skeleton of a small structure standing under the scorched limbs of a gigantic water oak.

From the lower limbs of a nearby tree three attenuated, half-naked bodies dangled six feet clear of the ground. They remained quite motionless except when brushed into gentle motion by the wings of buzzards swooping and striking at the dead bodies with gruesome patience. Because the buzzards had no way of obtaining purchase, thus far they hadn't had much success.

While kicking forward Eclipse, Barry, as well as his followers, realized that a ragged piece of paper had been affixed to the shirt of each corpse. Most of the veterans present guessed what had been scrawled on those placards. It would be something like A REBEL DOG, or SO, TO ALL THE KING'S ENEMIES.

"What do you make of this?" demanded Captain Colcord while uncocking his pistol.

"Reckon the destructives couldn't ha' been here later than yesterday," volunteered Corporal Skene. "Nothin' burning. Ashes are cold."

Disregarding his orders to report to Monck's Corner with all speed, Captain Colcord ordered his men to dismount, then in a gruff voice instructed Sergeant Wilcox to cut down the murdered men and start digging bury holes.

The half troop's veterans, having already viewed similar atrocities, worked in grim silence while a row of shallow graves was being scooped out of the sandy soil, but the recruits raged, cursed and vowed terrible revenge.

After a delay which had lasted about an hour Colcord pulled on his helmet and told Sergeant Wilcox to remount the command.

"Stand to horse! Prepare to mount! Mount!" bawled the sergeant, then in the customary column of twos the Ricelands Rangers trotted off along a road which, if a weathered finger board was to be trusted, eventually should bring them to Cobb's Mill; the road sign, however, gave no indication of how far off the place lay. Possibly they might, at Cobb's Mill, encounter other troops on their way to join General Lincoln — or a band of Tory destructives? Devoutly, they hoped to come upon the latter.

Tory! Tory!

Cobb's Mill, South Carolina, consisted, in the winter of 1780, of about sixty largely wooden dwellings, three churches, a dozen-odd shops and stores; well and handsomely constructed of red brick were the Eagle Tavern, the county courthouse and the adjacent jail. The prosperous little town's population nowadays numbered three hundred souls of all ages and various colors; but for this war, its inhabitants undoubtedly would have numbered many more.

Sheltered by a magnificent grove of water oaks, Cobb's Mill had been built on the convex bank of a wide and leisurely bend in the Upper Cooper River. Nowadays the services of a clumsy, flat-bottomed ferry-scow were much in demand. One Hubert Rugely owned a rough wharf with a shed standing at its land end which accommodated pirogues, canoes and small flatboats bringing deerskins, furs and other products in from settlements springing up in the back country farther west. Dingy little sloops, snows and pinkies which managed to sail up from Charles Town also tied up at Rugely's Wharf.

By the time Barry and Wilcox *clip-clopped* into the town's dusty and unpaved main square almost all soldiers had moved out, so it appeared that, for a while at least, the inhabitants of Cobb's Mill would have their pretty little tree-shaded town to themselves.

Hopeful of purchasing sufficient cloth of any shade of brown to make uniform jackets for his followers, Barry pulled up before a shop marked A. BENBOW, DRAPER, swung lightly off Eclipse and, passing his reins to Wilcox, said, "Sergeant, reckon I'll go see if he's got anything useful in there."

The captain started up the draper's steps only to collide with the proprietor, a fat, round-faced little man wearing square-lensed, steel spectacles.

"— One moment, sir," Barry began, "d'you have brown-dyed yard goods of any description?"

"Lord love you, no, suh. Not anythin', any color. Been cleaned out of all yard goods since near a year ago." The draper, who was selecting a brass key when he noticed the frayed silver epaulet on Colcord's right shoulder, said, "Sorry, Cap'n, but bein' as how I don't aim to miss what's about to happen, reckon I'll lock up for a space."

Under the visor of his helmet Barry's dark, wide-set eyes narrowed. "What's all this fuss about?"

"Why, sir, there's about to be a trial."

"What are you talking about?"

"Well, sir, last night our Committee of Safety finally got around to arrestin' George Walker."

"Who's Walker?"

"Why, sir, 'tis him who owns and runs the Golden Lion."

"What's that?"

"Why, sir, 'tis a fine big tavern on the ferry road."

"For what did they arrest this man?"

"Why, sir, plenty of people livin' around here take George Walker for a Loyalist sympathizer," the shopkeeper blinked shortsightedly while putting away his key, "but near as many others stand ready to swear he ain't a Tory." The draper chuckled and began to button up a well-cut gray overcoat. "Be that as it may, sir, in a little while we aim to make sure about his politics."

A Tory! Yesterday's scene returned in full and horrifying detail. Under his chin strap Barry's jaw set itself. He went over to where Wilcox was and remounted Eclipse.

What had prompted this decision was an abrupt realization that by no means all of Cobb's Mill's inhabitants were hurrying towards a pair of lofty, moss-draped oaks towering above the Court House and the jail alongside. A good number of angry-looking persons had gathered into little groups and were talking in savage undertones.

"Sir," grunted Wilcox, "looks like some of these folks already have made up their minds what the verdict's going to be."

"What's your meaning?"

"Just look over yonder, sir." The sergeant pointed down a rutted side street in which an iron cauldron of tar was being lowered over a fire so big that men working there had to keep shielding their faces against the soaring, crackling flames.

Another great, discordant shout went up when the jail's ponderous, nail-studded door cracked open again and a quartet of semiuniformed militiamen in broad hats and cross belts tramped out and at once lowered their muskets to the horizontal in order to force the screaming, fist-shaking mob to back away from the table and chairs.

"Hurray fer Judge Thompson!" someone shouted. "Hurray! Hurray fer justice!" "Come on, yer worship," howled another decent-looking citizen. "Make George Walker swear or just hand that dirty king-lover over to us!" "That tar hot yet? Somebody fetch a feather pillow! Get a rope ready in case he won't swear!"

The next figure to appear provoked such an explosive outcry that horses shied and women stopped their ears. From where he sat vainly attempting to calm his mare, Barry could tell that the prisoner was a tall, well-built fellow who still appeared distinguished though his chin showed a purple bruise and his light-brown hair hung like a gapped fringe before blazing black eyes. The prisoner wasn't able to brush aside the dangling locks for the simple reason that his hands were tied behind him.

Pandemonium swelled. "Tory! Tory! Test the goddamn bloody Tory!"

All at once the church bell stopped clanging, which, oddly enough, had the immediate effect of subduing the outcry.

The next to appear was the sheriff, a bittern-thin fellow whose long beak of a nose emphasized the similarity. He was followed by a short, plump individual who, judging by the quill pen he carried thrust over one ear and the folio of papers tucked under his arm, must be clerk of the court. Judge Thompson parted the skirts of his long black coat and gravely seated himself behind the table under the tree.

Only the excited yipping and snarling of dogs and an undertone of angry voices on the square's far side broke a comparative stillness when the judge donned gold-rimmed spectacles and queried briskly, "Your name?"

"Why ask that, Edward Thompson? Ain't we served on the same vestry for going on ten years? If your memory's that poor, you ought to give up law."

The judge's already taut mouth contracted into a thin and colorless line. "Never mind the advice, George. Answer me!"

"Very well, your worship. My name is Walker; George Huger Walker — and be damned to you! How can you, presumably a man of law and integrity, dare to countenance the arrest of a peaceful, law-abiding citizen without a warrant?"

Judge Thompson spoke in grave, almost sad tones, "George Walker, you stand before this tribunal accused of entertaining Loyalist sympathies inimical to the cause of American independence. How plead you?"

"This ain't a proper court of law!" wheezed the prisoner still deathly pale and fighting for breath. "So, Ed Thompson, I'm damned if I'll plead one way or another!"

Out of a side street rumbled a two-wheeled farm cart drawn by an aged and heavy-footed white horse. Its ungreased axles screeched like fiends undergoing torment.

[473]

"Quiet, everybody!" roared the sheriff. "His worship will now administer the test oath!"

While waiting for the shouting to die down, the clerk picked up the pitcher and filled a glass with an amber-hued fluid which apparently was a rum toddy.

Solemnly, Judge Thompson got to his feet and, merging heavy brows, picked up the glass. In a clear, rich voice he said, "George Walker, will you swear before the ever-living God and the world that our war against Great Britain is just and necessary? That you have not and will not aid or abet the forces of Great Britain? Will you pledge faith and true allegiance to the Sovereign State of South Carolina?" He held out the toddy glass. "Will you seal this solemn oath by drinking to the health of George Washington, of the Continental Congress and to the damnation of King George III and all the rascals about him?"

A taut stillness descended in which people elbowed, shuffled and craned necks to obtain a clearer view of that small, cleared space before the jail.

The tavernkeeper, breathing noisily, continued to stare straight ahead, made no sound.

Angrily, the sheriff prompted, "Get on with it, Walker! Before we're done we intend to find out where your true sympathy lies!"

Two guards had started to hustle the prisoner forward when, all at once, the publican shook off their hands and, of his own accord, advanced to the table and cried in a strangled voice, "All right, I *will* drink!" His hand shot out and seized the glass which he held poised before his lips. He then glared wildly about and screamed, "I drink — eternal damnation to your congress of traitors, to George Washington and all the rascals around him! Long live the king!"

Such an uproar swelled that Barry's hunter reared and he was barely able to restrain her outraged plunges. But so eager was everyone present to hear what was about to be said that the mob quieted at once.

"You shall immediately be stripped of your clothes, tarred and feathered and then placed in a cart in which you will be carried about town for two hours to suffer pelting with filth."

The judge paused to catch his breath, "Next, you will be placed in the stocks and have water flung into your face for another hour. Finally, you shall be taken down to the dock and thrown into the river."

The prisoner, his eyes rolling like a madman's, broke into shrieks of hysterical laughter. "Oh, thank you! Thank you, my kind friends and neighbors! Is — is this all the punishment you rebel dogs can devise?"

"There's gratitude for sparing his life," snarled one of the militiamen and grabbed Walker by the hair. "Come along, you bastardly king-lover."

That same afternoon a fish peddler trundled his barrow into the half troop's bivouac and proved ready and eager to describe with ghoulish satisfaction how thoroughly George Walker's sentence had been carried out.

[474]

Hard-eyed and still outraged by the Piggott atrocities, the Ricelands Rangers gathered about to listen.

"Yes, boys, 'twould have done yer hearts good to hear that bastard squall when the tar, which must ha' been damn' near on the boil, hit his dirty hide." The peddler chuckled. "You should ha' seen how crazy he looked there in the cart with all them white feathers stickin' out of him like a porkypine's quills.

"Well, as they were takin' him down to the river some ugly young gal began jabbin' at his face with a sharp stick. If he ever again uses his left eye I'll be surprised, 'cause its eyeball was hangin' down over his cheek."

Rob Colcord, from deep in his throat, rasped, "Hope the dirty dog drowned when he hit the water."

"Maybe he did. When they flang him into the river he was in pretty pore shape and was complainin' they'd busted his ribs, but, all the same, the bastard was still strong enough to grab aholt of a snag that came drfitin' by. Last we saw of him he was clingin' to it and moanin' like a cheated whore."

Even Black Buck looked impressed.

Colonel Washington's Headquarters

All morning long a slow, silver-gray drizzle had come slanting down soaking the Ricelands Rangers to the bone and dimpling an endless succession of lead-hued puddles dotting the road. But now the sky seemed to be brightening and dark clouds were commencing to lift, which encouraged Captain Barry Colcord to hope that this all-penetrating downpour soon would cease. He squirmed shoulders under his riding cloak and started yet another trickle creeping down his back like an icy little snake.

For a change he elected to ride at the little column's rear in company with wrinkled old Black Buck. The mustee appeared almost cheerful perhaps because that morning he'd come across a fine, red-tailed hawk's wing feather which he'd stuck into his disreputable felt hat at a jaunty angle.

From his position Barry was able to consider each individual composing his command, which no longer could rightly be termed a half troop, for on the march down from Cobb's Mill the Colcord brothers had attracted and enlisted a number of unattached horsemen more or less aimlessly riding in from the back country. Fighting down an impulse to enroll numbers at the expense of quality, they'd accepted only reasonably young and able-looking fellows astride large, strong horses. Regretfully, they'd turned aside would-be recruits who were too old or too young or were mounted on those short-legged but durably tackeys found in profusion all over Georgia and the Carolinas. While such beasts were wonderfully tough and could live on almost nothing, they couldn't run very fast or far carrying any considerable weight — as many a dragoon commander had discovered to his sorrow.

Towards midday the troop, riding in the usual column of twos, neared a crossroads beside which a pair of discouraged-looking vedettes in rain-soaked capes were slouching in their saddles. Off to the left, as Barry knew through long experience, lay Governor Edward Rutledge's mansion, a handsome, white-porticoed structure of red brick effectively revealed against a background of moss-hung live oaks.

Gentle pressure by Colcord's knees sufficed to set Eclipse trotting to the head of the troop in time to halt his command on the main road, at present flanked on both sides by deep ditches overflowing into adjacent tobacco fields.

One of the vedettes was wearing a hussar's busby covered in ratty-looking fur and a frogged, once-brilliant blue uniform. When he splashed by the other vedette, a wiry, short-legged fellow whose pointed, yellow-brown features suggested a fox's mask, he was offered a vague salute.

Barry glared. "You can do better than that!"

The fellow stared, then stiffened and offered a regular's crisp salute, which Colcord returned with equal precision.

"I'm in search of Colonel Moylan's cavalry regiment. Where is it?"

The hussar's sloping shoulders rose under his long and mud-splashed cape as he replied in an unintelligible language which Barry, through his service before Savannah, reckoned must be Polish — there had been a lot of Poles among the French and other foreigners in Count Pulaski's legion. The hussar crooked a finger to his companion, who under his cape was wearing the dark-brown-and-red shell jacket of Colonel Daniel Horry's South Carolina Light Dragoons.

"Sorry, suh, he's jest another dumb ferriner. Kin I he'p you?"

"I'm looking for Moylan's regiment. He commands the Virginia Continental Light Horse, I believe."

"Yessuh, but he's went into Charles Town; rode off early this mornin'." The dragoon brushed a beading of crystalling raindrops from the visor of a weather-beaten leather helmet before tilting his head towards the driveway leading to the governor's mansion. "Howsumever, the most of his men is camped over yander."

"Who's in command around here?"

"Why, right now, suh, 'tis Cunnel Washin'ton, but they do say Gen'ral Huger — " he pronounced the name "Hew-gee" — "will soon come to take over."

"You are referring to Colonel William Washington?"

"Yessuh."

"Where is he?"

"On a mean day like this reckon you'll find him holed up in the big house."

Barry clicked muddied brass spurs, then pulled off his helmet, tucked it in the crook of his left arm, bowed and addressed a big-bodied, broad-shouldered individual who had a long straight nose and the same bold, aggressive jaw as his cousin George. "Colonel Washington, sir?"

Deliberately, Washington finished his play, then faced his cards before looking up. "Well, sir, and what might your business be?"

Once Colcord stiffly had reported his troop's arrival, the colonel smiled while reaching for a delicately etched brandy glass that appeared to be engulfed by his powerful, brown hand. "Delighted to welcome you among us, Captain. 'Tain't every day we receive a well-mounted troop led by experienced officers — and more's the pity. Sorry Moylan ain't around right now, but in any case I wouldn't assign you to him. Too many other regiments are seriously under strength."

Washington's big, dark-brown head swung to his left. "Captain Colcord, meet Colonel Horry — Daniel Horry." He elevated a quizzical brow. "You won't object to serving under a fellow South Carolinian, eh?"

Colonel Horry, who'd undone his neckcloth and looked to be feeling better for a few brandies, arose to offer a hairy fist. Some time ago he must have taken a saber slash across the face; there was a deep nick in the bridge of his nose and his left cheek was almost caved in. He grinned like a friendly dog. "How do, Captain Colcord. You're more than welcome to my command; what with one thing or another, my regiment right now has less than a hundred men ready and able to ride against the enemy."

Colonel William Washington gestured towards the fireplace. "Shed that damn' wet cloak and go stand over there. We've enough puddles in here already." Next, he shouted for an orderly to bring in another glass, after which he held out a squat brandy bottle which, if the thickness of the dust coating it meant anything, must be of respectable age.

Once a secretary had prepared orders enrolling the Ricelands Troop — Colcord quietly requested that it be so designated — into the service of the state of South Carolina, Washington over one shoulder bellowed for his aide. "Walker! Write requisitions for such rations, blankets and fodder as Captain Colcord may need for the moment. We'll see about arms and other equipment when and if that damn' supply train ever arrives from Charles Town."

He glanced at Barry, warming his hands before the flames. "Anything else you stand in immediate need of, Captain?"

Hesitantly, lest he appeared to be crowding his luck, Barry mentioned the need of sufficient cloth to uniform his men — at least from the waist up.

Queried Major Vernier, twirling his brandy glass, "Why this urgency to uniform your men?"

"Well, sir, I feel it's important if I'm to maintain the kind of discipline I want." He smiled faintly. "As you know, Major, uniforms help build and maintain discipline."

"*Mais oui.* Of a certainty, uniforms help."

Colonel Baylor grinned at the hussar officer. "What with your presently reduced numbers, Paul, I presume you might spare our friend sufficient tunics?"

The Frenchman parted long, expressive hands. "*Oui.* That is possible, *mon ami*, but *hélas*, they are certain to prove much too small for your tall American bumpkins. They always have."

"In that case," Colonel Washington said, "Captain Colcord, you'd better go in town tomorrow and see what cloth — if any — you can come across." His wide, thin-lipped mouth spread in a brief smile. "Oh, by the way, tell Mr. Walker that I expect you and your brother to mess with me until further notice."

In an obvious gesture of dismissal the commandant of General Lincoln's cavalry picked up his cards; his companions also returned their attention to the game.

Threatened City

For all that the morning dawned silver-dimmed by fog and posing the threat of continued rain, Lieutenant Robert Colcord was feeling, as his brother was fond of putting it, "as happy as a flea in a fox's ear." Noticing everything of significance, Rob rode past those inadequate raw earthworks which had been thrown up so hastily last summer when General Augustine Prevost's small army of British regulars reinforced by hundreds of Tories had threatened to capture Charles Town.

Once he reined Hector into Broad Street Rob commenced a systematic canvass of drapers' and clothiers' shops, but invariably proprietors shook their heads, mumbling, "Sorry, sir. Got sold of all yard goods long ago." This remained the usual reply until one said, "Might have some, sir, once they've auctioned the cargoes of those transports our cruisers prized last week, but there ain't no telling what kind of cloth it might be or of what color."

How considerate of dear old Barry to send him in town in his stead, saying that there were many requisitions to be filled and important information to be gleaned at cavalry headquarters. Brother Barry, of course, had sensed that he just might be eager to catch another glimpse of Amelia Trefont, that lovely young girl who'd been completely orphaned because her mother had perished of smallpox only a few weeks before her father had been killed during Sir Henry Clinton's first siege of the city during '76.

Uncle William, a distant relative of Amelia's father, generously had taken the girl under his roof, ostensibly as a companion for sixteen-year-old Betsey, that child of his later years whose bearing had cost him his wife's life.

While on duty in Charles Town the previous summer, Rob at first had taken only a passing interest in the gay young orphan with the gently oval features, curly red-gold tresses and wide, pale-blue eyes, but, gradually he'd come to pay her more heed; not that he'd advanced beyond the formal kissing of her hand. But just once, on the eve of his departure to join the Allied armies besieging Savannah, he'd lightly kissed her cheek. Even so, the aspect of pert little Amelia Trefont had the trick of appearing, unbidden, in his mind's eye, especially when he was about to waken or to go to sleep.

Dark-haired and self-centered Cousin Betsey, however, remained in his estimation just another saucy, empty-headed chit who, as he laughingly maintained, should have been drowned at birth.

Twice he had to steady his tall, dappled-gray hunter when groups of drunken sailors off the feeble little squadron of privateers and Continental men-of-war presently anchored off Battery Point came reeling and yelling out of grog shops and taverns. Fog-veiled Broad Street continued to be obstructed by creaking wains, carts and covered wagons laden with every imaginable sort of freight.

After turning into Church Street, the broad-shouldered young officer continued riding towards Battery Point, on which stood Uncle William's familiar and quietly elegant white-trimmed brick dwelling. Arriving before the Colcord residence he reined left down a short, cobbled drive towards a pretty little garden which in a few weeks' time again would burst into a symphony of carefully planned color. How smart of the Charlestonians to ensure privacy by building their homes with the public rooms facing towards the side or the rear, safely removed from the dirt and noise of the street.

Seizing an elaborate silver knocker which in happier times had had the name Colcord engraved upon it in flowing script by a famous London silversmith, he knocked loudly, because Uncle William's venerable butler, Euripides, recently had grown very hard of hearing. The gleaming white door, therefore, was drawn back with commendable promptness. "Why, Mistuh Rob! Do please come in, suh. Sho' is one measly day, ain't it? Dey's a blaze in de library, suh. Better you go in dere."

Bowing continually, Euripides backed indoors, reporting that his owner had gone out to attend a meeting of the Fellowship Society.

"Yassuh. Jes' wait a little; Massa gen'rally come home to eat, lessen — " the butler grinned, blinked rheumy, yellowish eyes — "lessen Massa doan stop at Misto' Strickland's tavern."

A tinkle of feminine voices upstairs caused the caller to raise his brows in unspoken query.

"De young Mist'is an' Miz Amelia is busy fixin' up fo' a socialable."

Rob handed the Negro his mud-spattered cloak and then a long-peaked forester's hat of green felt. "Pray inform the ladies that I am below and would be pleased for an opportunity to offer my respects."

[479]

The screech and whine of ungreased axles and the *clip-clop* of hoofs on Church Street became less noticeable once Euripides fetched into the library a pineapple-shaped carafe of pale yellow arrack together with a plate of spices, lemon peel and a copper pot of steaming hot water.

"De young ladies send wu'd, suh, dey soon be down." The slave's liver-colored lips twitched. "Reckon you knows, Massa Robert, dat 'soon' don't mean 'di-rekly.'"

"Ah yes. Tardiness is a feminine failing — and privilege, I presume. At least they think so."

Before leaving, the old Negro went over to place more logs on the fire, but, being damp, they hissed and steamed a good while before reluctantly taking fire.

To savor its fragrance Rob held the steaming toddy under his nose before taking a swallow and allowing its heat to warm his belly. He was conjecturing whether Amelia Trefont might have matured a bit since he'd last seen her, when the front door knocker banged insistently. At a quick shuffle the butler hurried to draw a pair of brass bolts; in these uncertain times no Charles Town citizen in his right mind ever left any ground-level door unlocked — even during the daylight — as he would have during those blissful, almost forgotten years of peace.

Rob guessed who was causing all that racket even before a deep voice boomed, "Beelzebub's balls! A fine to-do when a man has to wait in the wet outside his own home! Damn you, Rip, why're you so slow answering? Rheumatics worse?"

"Nossuh, Massa Tom, ah come de quickest ah could."

"Bah! Trees grow faster than you move these days."

"Tom!" Rob surged to his feet and ran out into the hall to fling arms about his favorite first cousin, who was nearly of the same age and was about as big-framed as himself; he also had the same weathered look and his red-faced, blue uniform reeked just as pungently of horses and wet leather.

Delightedly, Tom beat upon Rob's shoulder blades. "By God, this *is* a wonderful surprise!"

"When did you get back from the frozen North?"

Tom finally ceased pounding his cousin's back. "Less than a week ago. When spies told Light-Horse Harry that Clinton was collectin' troops and ships fo' a Southern campaign he let me go on detached duty — indefinitely."

"Good thing. How is Colonel Lee these days?"

"Busy as a fox in a forest fire and still the best cavalry leader we've got on our side — barrin' Francis Marion, of course."

Once Rob had mixed Tom an arrack toddy and a second for himself, the long-legged cousins fetched chairs up to the fire. After a considerable exchange of news concerning births and deaths among relatives and friends and an account of the formation of the Ricelands Troop, Tom abruptly abandoned his light manner and looked his brown-clad cousin steadily in the eye. "You've heard how many men the redcoat generals already have brought against us?"

"Only hearsay. As I said, we only reported in to Billy Washington's headquarters yesterday. What can you tell me?"

"Plenty. I've just left a staff meeting at General Lincoln's headquarters. Oh, by the way, I've only today been assigned to duty with Colonel Theodorick Bland's regiment. They say he's a real piss-cutter.

"Well, to return to the subject, it's been reliably reported that Clinton and Cornwallis right now have with 'em at least six thousand of the king's regular establishment and near twenty-five hundred Northern Tories they've brought down from New York, New Jersey and Pennsylvania — real mean fellows by all accounts — and lots more are reported to be on their way south."

The dark-faced young man hunched forward, elbows on knees and locked fingers around his glass. "When you add these numbers to General Patterson's regulars, who are due from Savannah any day now, you'll appreciate our side's up against one hell of a lot of excellently trained and equipped troops. Worse still, strong reinforcements under Lord Rawdon are on their way from New York. And so far I've not even mentioned their naval forces."

"When's Rawdon supposed to arrive?"

"It's anybody's guess."

Rob, by rubbing his chin, caused a soft rasping sound. "How many men-of-war do the lobsterbacks have on hand?"

Beneath chestnut-colored bristles Tom Colcord's chapped and concave cheeks flattened. "At headquarters just now they circulated a tally." He fumbled in a side pocket and pulled out a crumpled sheet of paper. "Here's my copy. Read it, my lad, and weep."

Frowning, Rob scanned the names of an awesome number of ships of the line headed by Vice-Admiral Mariot Arbuthnot's gigantic flagship *Romulus;* ten frigates also were identified, along with a depressingly long list of brigs, sloops, bomb ketches and transports. The fleet presently anchored off Johns Island numbered well over a hundred vessels mounting at least a thousand cannon of varying weights and ranges.

Rob frowned over his half-consumed toddy. "And what do we have to oppose this armada?"

His cousin pulled out a second piece of paper. "Very few real men-of-war of any consequence. Our best are vessels bought from the French when they pulled out from Savannah last year." He wrinkled his brow, read on. "Well, there's the *Bricole,* a forty-four-carriage-gun frigate, the *Queen of France,* a twenty-eight-gun sloop, *La Truite* carries twenty-six pieces, the brig *Notre Dame* with sixteen, and then there are one or two small craft which mount about a dozen cannon between 'em."

"And what do we have for American-built ships?"

"Says here, the *Providence* and the *Boston*, both sloops carryin' thirty-two guns; the *Adventure*, a brig mounts twenty-six; the *General Lincoln* and the *Ranger* are schooners which together mount around twenty old cannon."

A spark snapped out of the fireplace; Tom yelped when he tried to extinguish it with a stockinged foot.

"Who commands our squadron?"

"Commodore Whipple, a lanky, blue-nosed Yankee."

On a brass fender enclosing the fireplace Rob absently scraped a curd of black muck from his boot. "What about Whipple?"

"They say he's both able and brave and so far has had a fine record. Be that as it may, all you've got to do is contrast the weight of broadsides on each side and you'll appreciate how hopeless Whipple's position is. What makes it especially bad for him is that his rag-tag crews are made up of ex-smugglers and privateersmen — rascals who won't put their hearts into a fight 'less there's enough prize money in the offin'."

Once the cousins had refilled glasses and packed yellow Maryland tobacco in yard-of-clay pipes lifted from a mahogany rack above the hearth, they reseated themselves.

After a while Rob asked through a cloud of smoke, "What sort of horses do they breed up north — in Pennsylvania, I mean?"

"Hardly any thoroughbreds exceptin' around Philadelphia; aside from that, they only rear heavy-boned farm stock or saddle horses we wouldn't even look at twice." Tom pursed weather-cracked lips to expel a perfect circle of gray-blue smoke. "Yes. Harry Lee's been very hard put to mount his men even reasonably well." He sighed. "What few good animals there were got swept up by British and Tory raiders early in Seventy-seven."

Tom further eased his short-skirted, blue-and-buff cavalry jacket revealing a light blue waistcoat lacking several buttons. "By the bye, speakin' of raiders, have you heard that that devil Banastre Tarleton is reported to be among the officers Clinton's brought from New York?"

The harsh quality which entered his cousin's voice caused Rob to elevate an eyebrow. "And who, pray, is Banastre Tarleton?"

A grating laugh escaped Tom. "Seems he's a young, hell-for-leather, damn-all London rake who at present is supposed to be servin' with Lord Cathcart's Light Dragoons. He's brimful of ambition, a first-rate tactician and a magnificent swordsman — but he's got no more sense of honor in a bedroom than on a battlefield."

"Meaning — ?"

"Captured officers report that whenever opportunity offers this Tarleton fellow will bed a brother officer's wife or mistress quick as a buck rabbit and never mind the consequences.

"Nevertheless, the Green Dragoon, as they call him up North, is a darin' and a successful leader. Seems he's got boundless energy and is so ruthless he's been known to saber a surrendered man rather than bother to take

[482]

him prisoner. He took a major part in that horrible massacre of Mad Anthony Wayne's men at Paoli."

"Paoli?"

"It's a hamlet near Brandywine in Pennsylvania.

"Nevertheless, Light-Horse Harry swears Tarleton's the best cavalry leader on either side."

"Can you imagine it? He's barely twenty-six, yet, without benefit of influence at court, he's been promoted from cornet to lieutenant colonel in less than two years! There's no doubtin' that his havin' played a big part in the capture of our eccentric General Charles Lee in New Jersey had much to do with so amazin' an advancement."

Rob was about to inquire the whereabouts of Bland's Horse when light footsteps and a sibilant swishing of skirts and petticoats sounded on the hall staircase a moment before plump little Betsey Colcord ran in with a jauntily flowered bonnet bobbing from its ribbon ties over her shoulders. Dark eyes lighting, she flung arms wide and, skirts flying, rushed towards her cousin. "Oh, Cudd'n Rob! What a *wonderful*, wonderful surprise!"

Because Betsey was only a young sixteen Rob felt it still proper to catch her in a bear hug, sweep her clear of the floor, then kiss her resoundingly on both cheeks.

Set down, she burst into a torrent of questions. "How is Cudd'n Barry? And Uncle Frederick and Juno? Has she had more puppies? If she has, may I have one?"

Tom groaned in derisive disapproval. "Try to forgive her, Rob! I fear the brat won't ever learn manners. Too bad she's too big to spank — used to be lots of fun."

All at once Tom checked his ribaldry and offered a slight "leg" when into the library floated a slight, straight-backed figure clad in faint green taffeta which contrasted effectively with short, reddish-gold curls bunched to either side of pale, gently oval features.

"And how are we today, Amelia — Mistress Trefont, I mean."

Rob released his cousin and hurriedly attempted to recover a measure of dignity before offering the Trefont girl a bow infinitely more courteous than Tom's. She made a graceful little curtsy and lowered her gaze as became a well-bred young lady, then she looked him full in the face and summoned a bright smile. "'Tis fine indeed to see you looking so well, Mister Colcord," she murmured, happily unconscious of the banality of her words.

He was right. By God! Amelia Trefont's eyes *were* a baffling shade of greenish-blue and the passage of half a year had done quite a bit towards filling out her bodice. But what a tiny thing Amelia remained. Even on tiptoe she couldn't stand above five feet. Suddenly he knew now how to describe her complexion — it was the delicate pinkish-white of newly burst apple blossoms.

"Good day to you, sir." She merely tilted her nose in Tom's direction.

She didn't much like Betsey's brother; he was such a clumsy tease and never would take anything she said or did in the least seriously. Besides, the big oaf invariably reeked of sweat, horses and liquor of some kind.

"Mercy!" giggled Betsey, setting straight her bonnet. "I declare, Cudd'n Rob, you look even handsomer and more distinguished than ever."

"'Out of the mouths of babes and sucklin's,'" Rob laughed without removing his eyes from Amelia. "Tell me, where are you young ladies going in such a flutter?"

Betsey whirled a light camlet cloak about her shoulders. "Oh, dear! We must leave for Mistress Mazyck's this very minute! She and her friends there are going to teach us how to tear bandages, pick lint and fashion pledgets."

"Lawd! Lawd! Such serious work for dainty hands," grunted Tom, then stalked over to the fireplace and used tongs designed for the purpose to relight his yard-of-clay with a coal from the grate.

Amelia's long lashes fluttered several times before she peered almost boldly up at Rob's broad, red-brown features, then said a little breathlessly, "Will you excuse me a moment? I'll be right back."

She departed running upstairs with unladylike speed and returned almost immediately carrying his brass helmet in one hand and a short, emerald-green ostrich plume in the other.

"Amelia!" burst out Tom's sister. "How dare you to be so — so bold!"

"You see, I noticed that that pretty, bright helmet of yours is lacking a plume." Smooth cheeks flushed, she said hurriedly, "So I wonder whether you would care to wear this until you find a more suitable one?"

Good Lord, thought Rob, in Horry's Horse an officer's plume is supposed to be either yellow or dark blue. Nevertheless, he bowed, smiled and spoke softly, "I shall be most honored to wear your gift, Miss Trefont. Since I deem this a lovely lady's favor, I trust you will put your plume in place?"

Cousin Tom snickered in the background. Rob cast him a warning look. Good God, couldn't he appreciate that this girl was entirely in earnest and quite unaware of the implications of her act?

Once the bright green feather's quill had been well seated in a short, brazen tube, Amelia, holding out the garnished helment, offered it with a bright but tremulous smile that Rob wouldn't forget in a hurry.

"Miss Trefont, please accept my earnest thanks. I — I hope that I shall always wear this with honor."

"Oh, for heaven's sake, 'Melia, do come along! We're already terribly late and I really *must* find time for a chat with Sally Colleton and her mother." She flashed a gleaming smile at Rob. "They're *ever* so genteel."

"Maybe so," grunted Tom, leaning resignedly with one elbow on the mantlepiece, "but everyone around here knows Sir John Colleton's just another damn' king-lover."

Betsey flared right up. "That may be true, my dear brother, but nevertheless, Sir John remains a true son of South Carolina. Nobody can truthfully say he's taken part in any Tory activity."

Tom inquired acidly — he didn't like to hear of any relation of his defending a Loyalist — "Why are you so all-fired eager to gab with Lady Colleton?"

Hurriedly, Amelia broke in, "Why, Tom, 'tis this way. Lady C. has kindly invited us to visit at Fair Lawn and keep Sally company if — well, just in case Charles Town grows too — too crowded to be safe, or if — "

" — Or if the redcoats start to bombard us," snapped the lieutenant of Horry's Horse, "which they're surely goin' to do just as soon as they complete their batteries across the Ashley. 'Twon't be over-healthy here once they start."

When at the end of an hour Uncle William still had failed to return home, Rob regretfully drained the last of his arrack, called for his horse and made ready to depart. "You'll ride out to see us, eh, Tom? Barry would be that pleased!"

"Sure 'nough. Where are you?"

"Bivouacked on the governor's property — but how long we'll stay there I've no idea. Come over real soon and fetch along some of those measly gamecocks you're always bragging on. Might fix up a main and do a little serious drinkin'."

First of the Green Dragoon

During the month which followed the arrival of the Ricelands Troop — as the unit now had become designated officially — the Colcord brothers did not endlessly drill their men or scheme for supplies in vain. Few cavalry units under General Benjamin Lincoln's command could boast a comparable improvement. Further, the troop had been recruited selectively to a strength of seventy enlisted men, which made it one of the largest on duty in the vicinity of Charles Town.

To top things off, Barry finally had come across an ample supply of fine duck sailcloth brought in by the last privateer able to pierce Admiral Arbuthnot's now impenetrable blockade. Next, the troop commander searched until he found a dyer who could and would stain the tough white material a weatherfast butternut brown.

Once the troop's new jackets had been faced with white duck out of the same lot and ornamented with some of the late Count Pulaski's buttons, the Ricelanders strutted about, mighty proud of uniforms which wouldn't have won any praise from a competent military tailor.

By now the troop had become comparatively well armed: cumbersome long-barreled muskets and fowling pieces had gradually been replaced by short-barreled carbines or naval blunderbusses. At short range the latter weapons had a murderous effect — and were infinitely easier to handle on horseback. In addition, all troopers by now had been issued either a sword or a saber of some description, but few of these were supported by proper frogs or slings; they dangled loosely secured by rawhide whangs and straps to any convenient part of a rider's saddle.

An aide hurried up. "Gentlemen, General Huger and Colonel Washington present their compliments, and will you please come with me?"

They hurried into Thomas Bee's pine-paneled study to find the general and several of his staff questioning a mud-splashed cornet of Bland's regiment who looked as if he'd just been hauled backwards through a bramble-filled swamp.

Absently, General Huger was stroking a strong, deeply cleft jaw while Colonel Washington, with brow furrowed, riffled through a sheaf of morning reports.

The general wasted no time. "G' day, gentlemen. Mr. Boyle, here, has just fetched in intelligence of considerable significance which is to the effect that Sir Henry Clinton's main force is advancing in this direction behind a screen of British and Tory cavalry commanded by that same Colonel Tarleton who surprised and cut up Boyle's outpost on the Edisto two days ago. Boyle was taken prisoner but managed to escape last night. Mr. Boyle, pray convey your information to these gentlemen."

Wearily, the ex-prisoner passed the back of a dirty, thorn-raked hand over a forehead smeared with black swamp muck and addressed Horry. "Sir, I was held under guard close by Colonel Tarleton's tent, so close in fact that just before I got away I overheard plans being made for a raid on Sir Toby Gascoyne's stud farm with the object of seizing as many tall horses as possible."

Daniel Horry cast a quick glance at the pale and hollow-eyed cornet. "Did you form any impression of when the enemy expects to call on Sir Toby?"

The slim youth, who looked as if he had neither slept nor eaten in many hours, swayed a little but continued to stand at attention. "Sir, I can't be sure, but my guess is that the raid will take place sometime this afternoon. Colonel Tarleton was most insistent that no time be lost in securing remounts."

General Huger arched heavy, iron-gray brows and demanded crisply, "Mr. Boyle, approximately how far from here does this stud farm lie?"

"Sorry, sir. Not being from these parts, I wouldn't know."

Colonel Horry spoke up. "Sir Toby's property lies on the Edisto Ferry Road about ten miles away."

"That's good," snapped the general. "Horry, see that every effort is made to cut off Tarleton's retreat. Every tall horse that falls into enemy hands will cost us dear. I'm told Tarleton is determined to capture animals strong enough to carry those big dragoons he's brought down from New York."

It seemed difficult to realize that death was lurking somewhere among these sunlit, early spring woods in which wild cherry, dogwood and Judas tree buds were beginning to burst. Migrating songbirds — towhees, tanagers, bluebirds, cardinals and an infinite variety of warblers whistled and sang while flitting from tree to tree but Sergeant Gavin Wilcox noticed them not at all. He was again experiencing a gradual tightening of muscles crisscrossing his lean belly. The veteran was devoting disapproving attention to the noisy and haphazard fashion in which Lieutenant Ballard and the men from Moylan's regiment were advancing in a wavering line of skirmishers through myrtle and honeysuckle tangles and around stands of holly and red-trunked slash pine. Here and there a cottontail rabbit or an occasional deer would bound away with white stern flashing.

Presently, Barry arm-signaled a halt, then, with newly burnished helmet agleam in dappled sunlight, rode over to confer with chunky little Lieutenant Ballard, who appeared anxious and not at all sure either of himself or of his troopers.

After issuing detailed instructions, Barry showed his silver whistle. "Now remember, Mr. Ballard, at all costs keep your men quiet till I sound this. After they've fired a volley, they're to mount and charge with the saber down onto the road. Make 'em whoop and yell like the devil was after 'em."

When finally the mustee rode back to report that the road lay not far ahead, the cavalry deployed along the crest of a low, thickly wooded ridge, then dismounted, unevenly spaced for the sake of cover. Just behind and below the ridge crest stood knots of horse holders, each man holding four animals in addition to his own.

Barry was encouraged to see how effectively Rob, his green plume jauntily asway, along with Wilcox, Skene, Peete and other veterans, steadied troopers, reminded them that after they'd fired the first and only volley they'd have time for they must mount quickly, draw sabers and charge, making all the noise they could.

While Private Black Buck, his wrinkled features devoid of expression, expertly soothed Eclipse a few yards behind him, Barry eased himself into the depths of a clump of holly already bright with shiny new leaves and was cautiously thrusting the branches aside to see better when the mustee hissed and pointed to the right. An instant later the captain thought he heard faint sounds coming from that direction. Softly he cursed, because a squirrel had started to chatter furiously somewhere down the road.

Soon the faint jangle of curb chains, the clink of iron stirrups colliding and a low and continuous thudding made by many hoofs became clearly audible. Veterans among the ambushers wriggled as flat as they could amid the underbrush, then checked flints before snugging carbine stocks

[487]

tight against their shoulders. Sweating in streams, green men followed their example.

In Rob's imagination eons seemed to elapse before a knot of men wearing forest-green jackets and black-crested helmets banded with brown fur trotted briskly into sight around a bend in the road. That the enemy's point was alert Rob appreciated at once and felt his mouth beginning to go dry, as it usually did in anticipation of a fight. The point kept peering carefully at both sides of this narrow sunlit track.

The raiders' advance guard now appeared riding four abreast carrying their carbines with brass-shod butts supported upon their hips.

Moments later the main body rode into sight; they were big men who mostly were wearing green, but there were a few scarlet jackets among them, also a number of men in drab-hued civilian clothes. These last, Rob decided, must be local Loyalists who'd just joined up and hadn't yet found time to get into uniform. Behind them appeared a single figure. Short but powerfully built, he was wearing a Lincoln-green dragoon tunic, buckskin breeches, glossy knee boots and a brass helmet resplendently crested in white-and-crimson horsehair.

The stallion this solitary rider bestrode was the most magnificent piece of horseflesh Rob had sighted in a very long time. By God, that thoroughbred down there must stand well over seventeen hands!

There was something about yonder officer's erect, almost arrogant posture in the saddle as he trotted nearer which instantly attracted and held Barry Colcord's attention. Now the smoothly posting figure drew near enough for the ambusher to make out light-brown side whiskers sweeping down almost to the point of a short and almost femininely rounded jaw. Barry couldn't tell anything about the other's eyes, they being hidden below the helmet's visor. Just the same, he felt certain that Lieutenant Colonel Banastre Tarleton, the Green Dragoon, was riding into pistol range.

Barry waited for the enemy's point to pass Ballard's end of the ambush and at the same time marveled why some woodswise Tory among the raiders hadn't taken alarm at the racket raised by that fool squirrel; a homegrown Britisher, of course, couldn't be expected to notice such a sign. Once the raiders' rear guard began to round the bend Colcord clapped the whistle between his teeth, drew a deep breath and aimed a long-barreled saddle pistol at the nearest officer before sounding three shrill, ear-piercing blasts. He fired, but even before the ponderous weapon roared and its recoil jolted his arm clear up to the shoulder, he sensed that he'd missed. Meanwhile the ridge, for a distance of two hundred yards, bloomed with puffs of woolly gray-white smoke. The reports of small arms firing a ragged volley sounded like a gigantic pile of dry brushwood set afire. Beyond a curtain of burned powder smoke sounded the wild trampling of hoofs followed by yells, shouts and the screams of wounded men and horses.

Without delaying to learn what might be happening on the woods road Barry dashed back, grabbed his reins from the mustee and swung into the saddle bellowing, "Draw sa-a-bers! Charge! At 'em, Ricelands — keep on yelling!"

As he kicked forward his horse, Black Buck threw back his head and raised a heart-stopping scalp yell: "Whoop! Whoop! Hi ya-a-h. Yah!"

Indescribable confusion prevailed upon the road. Everywhere horses were neighing, rearing, plunging and bumping into each other. To the ringing clash of meeting blades and a barking of horse pistols, more saddles became emptied.

Ignoring pistolballs that hissed past, Barry lay out on the mare's neck, bunched his weight behind his sword point and aimed at that muscular little officer with the brown side whiskers.

Barry wasn't two horses' lengths short of his target when out of dust clouds raised by the melee dashed a wounded trooper who charged into him and sent Eclipse staggering off balance for a few strides. Despite everything Barry kept his attention on Tarleton's long-nosed face, now become visible beneath his visor.

Correcting his aim, Barry yelled, "At you, sir!"

Tarleton heard. Baring his teeth, the Green Dragoon swung his charger about, whirled his blade high above his head, then spurred to meet his attacker. All the while Tarleton kept screaming for his men to rally.

Only a split second before Barry counted on driving home his point, a wild-eyed riderless horse blundered into his opponent and knocked him aside at the critical moment. Before the Carolinian could manage to wheel, a tangle of cursing, slashing, stabbing men became interposed.

When next he sighted the Green Dragoon it was to see him galloping towards the head of his column all the while striking at his men with the flat of his sword and shrieking for them to stand fast.

But the retreat wasn't to be checked. British and Tories alike bent over their horses' necks and, raking their flanks with bloody spurs, thundered away in the direction of Goose Creek, leaving the road littered with equipment, dead men and groaning wounded.

Letter to Laura

After hunting up a piece of planking for a desk Captain Barry Colcord seated himself, rested his back against a tree and braced for the ordeal of penning a letter; his writing always had been deplorable, while his spelling had been the despair of every schoolmaster under whom he'd smarted. Brow furrowed, he unscrewed the small leaden ink bottle he used in preparing reports and other official documents. Laboriously, he then used his penknife to shape a new point on his quill but paused to cast a look at the fast-darkening afternoon sky; briefly, he debated whether he might not justifiably postpone the letter, but the call of duty prevailed, so after smoothing a sheet of foolscap on his improvised desk, he scribbled painfully:

Munk's Corner,
S. Carolina
13th Aprill, 1780

Respect'd Madam:

I trust by this time you rec'd my last Letter in witch I enformed you of the Tragicall death of yr. bro. Colin in a Tavern fight in Charles Town. I hope, my Deerist, you have not been undully Greeved but How sad it is to think of such a Fine yung Man cut down in the very Flour of yuth.

Nearly 3 Weeks have passed since I last wrotte you and what a Tragickall 3 Weeks theese have been.

Our ennemies are said to Nummer above 10,000 Men now and only 2 days ago succeeded in crossing the Ashley and are now on Charles Town Neck ware they are throwing up Earthwurks at a furius rayte.

Worse News piles up on the Bad. 2 days ago a scoutt-Sloop out of George-towne sightted a strong Fleet of Ennemy Men of Warr with many Trans-portts saling towards Charles Towne. This is thought to be Lord Rawdon bringing neer 3,000 more Reglars to join Gen'al Clinton in the Seege. Theese, added to the 10,000 men already under Sir Henry's Command, plus 5,000 Seemen makes a very formidibel Force for our little Garrison to stand off— Gen'l Lincoln has only 2700 Contital Soldiers and about the same number of Millitia who may, or may Not be Dipendable! We, the Cavalry that is, have been drove back until now Wee are camped near Munk's Corner wich lyes about 30 myles above the Towne.

We have nearbye 2 small Reg'ts of Infantrie garding Biggen Bridge. Every-one is in low Spirrits because iff Gen'l Lincoln is to save our last reel Army in the South he must *Retreat at Once!* whilst wee still can keep open a lyne of Retreat for him to the Cooper River Crossings. This is a verry difficult feet, thanks to the Acktivittys of that devill-on-Horseback, Colonel Tarelton who seams to have now found sootable Mounts for all his Men.

I am pleezed to say our Troop maintains its Discipline and Courage. My Bro, as usuall, is a Very Tower of Strengthth.

We howrly expect to engage Tarleton who is reliable Reportted to be sumwhere in the Vicinity and in grate strengtht. Would to God wee knew just where he is!

Momentarily, Barry raised eyes to watch a tall and neatly dressed mu-latto go galloping by on the road to Charles Town. He had no difficulty in recognizing the rider as Cudjo Jim, General Huger's trusted mulatto body slave. He thought, yonder perhaps goes the last man who stands a chance of winning through to the city.

Barry returned to writing. When a shadow crossed his letter he glanced up to find Sergeant Wilcox standing at a respectful distance with his long sheep's face set in a mighty anxious expression. After saluting, he broke out, "Sir, I just returned with the watering detail and I feel you better hear about something that happened down by the stream."

Glad to be relieved of penning, Barry nodded. "What was it? You've never been one to bark at a knothole."

Gilded by the sunset the ungainly, semi-bald figure looked uneasy. "Sir, you remember that time up to Cobb's Mill when that Tory got tarred and feathered?"

Barry stuck the quill over one ear. "Yes. 'Twas a fellow called George Walker if I remember right. What about it?"

Wilcox forgot himself long enough to scratch vigorously under his new dark-brown tunic. "Well, sir, just as we was finishing watering I chanced to look across the stream and saw, not thirty yards off, a trooper in a green jacket sitting his horse on a little knoll, bold as brass. How long he might have been there I got no idea; might ha' been quite a while 'cause he was pretty well disguised among the trees and bushes."

Barry said, getting to his feet and stoppering his ink bottle, "Did you give chase?"

An unhappy expression appeared on Wilcox's weather-beaten features. "We tried to, sir, but by the time me and a couple of the boys got across the stream the feller had faded back into a thick woods. We looked everywheres but couldn't find no sign of him. Think likely, sir, he was a enemy scout?"

"Seems entirely likely," Barry admitted and gratefully dropped his piece of plank. "Come along. Headquarters ought to hear about this."

While hurrying to his tent he folded his letter, then buckled on his sword and snatched up his helmet. At the same time he yelled for the mustee to saddle Eclipse.

Twenty minutes later, hot and breathless, the master of Ricelands was demanding an interview with the cavalry commander. He found General Huger in heated conference with his staff. Perpetually haggard and sallow from recurrent malaria, he cut them short, then curtly demanded Colcord's errand. Although still red-faced and short-tempered, the commanding officer kept quiet long enough to hear an account of Wilcox's experience.

A tall, one-eyed major glared at Colcord. "Impossible! The enemy *can't* possibly be scouting this far north! More likely 'twas just some deserter or straggler of ours your man saw. Remember, sir," he turned to Isaac Huger, "plenty of our units are wearing green these days — Baylor's Fourth Troop, for instance."

The general turned on George Baylor, snapping, "That correct?"

"Aye, sir. My Fourth Troop have green jackets turned up in red."

"Was this fellow wearing red facings?" sharply demanded Colonel Washington.

"I don't know, sir. Wilcox didn't say. But — "

" — So your man may have been mistaken," growled Colonel Horry. "Still I think — "

"Oh hell!" persisted the one-eyed major. "Not even Tarleton can possibly have advanced so close! Why, only this noon he was reported bivouacked near the siege lines, which, as we all know, lie thirty-odd miles away!"

"Nevertheless," Colonel Horry pointed out acidly, "the fellow disappeared when the sergeant and his men crossed the stream."

"If he was a straggler or a deserter he wouldn't be apt to linger, would he?"

"Be that as it may," Horry insisted, "seems to me the better part of wisdom is to order our pickets and patrols to be advanced a good distance in the direction of Charles Town."

Colonel Washington rapped an angry curse and changed the subject. "Oh, to hell with such trifles! What I want to know is why Ben Lincoln doesn't get off his fat arse and get to hell out of Charles Town sometime tonight. Tomorrow will be his last opportunity to save his neck. After that 'twill be too late. If only he weren't keeping back the North Carolina and Virginia Continental Line — the only real soldiers we've got left. God! To think of those veterans penned up like sheep behind those feeble earthworks."

With hands slapping each other behind his back, General Huger took a short turn over the Red Hart taproom's bricked floor — that rough and ready little tavern recently pre-empted by his adjutant. Grimly, Huger halted and faced his staff.

"Gentlemen, please believe that I've done everything possible to persuade our commander-in-chief that he *must* abandon the town at once! This same afternoon I have written to emphasize his dire peril, and to encourage him, I described the location of our supporting patrols as well as the disposition and strength of my forces." Angrily, Huger flung up his hands. "Yes. Not an hour ago I sent my servant, Cudjo Jim, to him."

"My God, sir," cut in Baylor, "you didn't entrust such a message to a nigger?"

"Yes, I did, because I figured that being black he'd stand a better chance of getting by any British patrols he might encounter.

"To add weight to my plea I requested Major Vernier, here, to add the warning of a veteran campaigner."

Paul Vernier vigorously inclined his narrow, dark head. "*Mais oui.* I wrote to *le général*, begging him in the name of common sense to retreat at once, while he can. Also I advised him that only for a short time longer will we be able to keep open his route to the river crossings. *Nom de dieu!*"

Everyone in the crowded, smoke-filled taproom, thought Barry, looked as gloomy and depressed as if he'd lost his last friend. They would, however, have appeared infinitely more anxious had they known that, at this very moment, Cudjo Jim, General Huger's dispatches and all, was being hustled into the presence of Lieutenant Colonel Banastre Tarleton.

Monck's Corner

Barry Colcord's dream was a jumbled but frighteningly realistic reconstruction of the battle of Moore's Creek Bridge. In awful clarity he heard once more the sharp, vicious crackle of musketry, the thunderous roar of cannon and, more particularly, the eldritch wails of bagpipes and nerve-crisping shrieks from the wounded.

He heard again Campbell's kilted Highlanders screaming "King George and the Broadswords!" as they launched their valiant, foredoomed charge across the bridge's naked stringers. Again, all the world seemed to be staring eyes and red, wide-open mouths lurching through the battle smoke.

God above! *This was no dream!* Convulsively, the Ricelands Troop's commander flung aside his blankets and sat up. By the brilliant blue-white starlight he glimpsed a black, shifting pattern of half-seen figures eddying confusedly among the tents. Then arose a gale of frightened howls, curses and shouted commands, followed immediately by the *boom! bang!* of heavy horse pistols going off interspersed by the sharper sounding *crack! crack!* of carbines.

Out of the shadowy woods appeared a wave of screeching, saber-swinging cavalry who charged headlong into the encampment and began slashing and pistoling down their half-awakened and hopelessly confused enemies.

Coatless and stocking-footed, Barry had barely time to snatch up his sheathed sword in one hand and his French pocket pistol in the other. He had started out of his tent when a yelling, brass-helmeted horseman blundered into it and buried him under wildly flapping canvas.

His wind effectively knocked out, Barry Colcord lay writhing, vainly struggling to fill his lungs and only half aware of hoofs trampling all about him. Now shrill, frightened yells arose: "Quarter!" "I surrender." "Quarter! Grant me quarter!" "*No! Don't!*" "Can't you see I've surrendered? "Quarter! Spare me! Quarter!" Followed by screams of "For God's sake have mercy!" "No! No! *Don't!*"

Vaguely, he heard his brother shouting, "Ricelands! This way, Ricelands! Rally to me! Quick! Quick!"

Unshaven and otherwise slovenly guards lounging about the captured American headquarters stood to attention when out of the Red Hart's

[493]

front door strutted Lieutenant Colonel Banastre Tarleton, whose short and stout but wiry figure Barry recognized immediately.

Flushed and swaggering, the Green Dragoon was bareheaded, so his curly red-brown hair fell in untidy coils to brush his shoulders. The victor stepped out into the sunshine and at the same time peered for a long minute at the scarecrows standing, still bound, among the peach trees. After taking a deep pull from a pewter pot of liquor, he bellowed, "Guards! Any of their so-called officers out there?"

A big, raw-boned Tory sergeant saluted. "Yes, suh! An they h'ain't been lyin' in their teeth, there oughter be a major and a couple of capt'ns 'mongst them."

"Very well. Fetch the mangy rascals inside. I want to talk to 'em."

When he was shoved inside, Barry saw that several severely wounded American officers had been placed on the taproom's long oaken serving tables. They were moaning or just breathing stertorously while their blood, flowing unchecked, caused a soft pattering noise upon the bricked floor.

Aching in every muscle along his hurt side, Barry Colcord remained much too exhausted and miserable to get any sleep in a corner of that dusty, half-filled corncrib into which he and three other officers had been shoved to join a multitude of rats.

In the near distance wounded men under the trees still were making noises like thirsty cattle; from around the Red Hart sounded bursts of drunken laughter and singing.

What could have befallen brother Rob, Wilcox and the other dependables who'd created reasonably disciplined and steady soldiers out of a mob of unruly recruits? How well he now understood the Roman emperor Augustus Caesar's anguished cry of "*Varus! Varus!* Give me back my legions."

He was too deeply plunged in an orgy of self-reproach to notice a faint *thud*! as if someone had dumped a sack of grain behind the corncrib. But he did notice what seemed to be a large rat's persistent squeaking.

Barry raised his head, listened with care. What the hell? Weren't these squeaks too rhythmic and too often repeated to be natural?

Squirming towards the corncrib's rear over the sprawled bodies of his companions, he pursed lips and squeaked back — one long, two short, one long note; next he cupped a hand to his ear and caught sounds as faint as the whispering of a wild duck's wings high in a night sky. Black Buck was murmuring, "Cappen? Mistuh Barry. You there?"

Pressing his mouth against a ventilation slat let into the building's whitewashed side, Barry muttered, "Yes. What's up?"

"Guard dead. Me unlock door now. You come out quick."

"Right. But first I must rouse the rest."

"Sure. But don't let fellas make noise nor follow too quick."

When the plank door's crude lock clicked and its hinges creaked, Barry slipped out into the starlight, and on hands and knees crawled as fast as he could around to the rear, where he glimpsed the dead guard lying on his side as if suddenly overcome by sleepiness rather than eight inches of razor-sharp steel between his ribs.

Gapped teeth faintly agleam, the mustee passed over the dead guard's carbine, but kept his saber for himself. Black Buck beckoned towards a dense holly thicket. Silent because he was in his stocking feet, Barry plunged into the woods, where it proved hard work to keep his slave in sight. The mustee must be able to see uncommonly well in a dim light, so unerringly did he follow a faint footpath which evidently led to a big swamp lying behind the village called Monck's Corner.

Following careful reconnaissance, Black Buck, wading most of the way, presently led to a small wooded and bush-covered island which at the moment was occupied by an indeterminate number of bedraggled officers and men. Present were tragic-faced and tight-jawed General Huger, Colonel Washington and a handful of regimental commanders. Few carried arms of any description and all were dressed just as they'd been when Tarleton had swooped. Many were bootless and some were wearing only underdrawers.

A few horses, mostly minus saddles, were standing listlessly among the shadows off to one side; Barry's heart gave a joyful surge when he recognized Eclipse's familiar outline.

Brigadier General Isaac Huger began to speak slowly, tonelessly, like a man who is just coming to realize his responsibility for an overwhelming and, worse still, inexcusable defeat. "Gentlemen, I feel that our most sensible course is to scatter before daybreak and individually make our way across the Cooper as best we can."

Fair Lawn

The clanging of the big iron bell set on a post in front of the slave quarters awakened Amelia Trefont from a comfortable sleep. She was lying, warm and cozy, beside Betsey Colcord in a big, brocade-canopied four-poster. Blinking like a sleepy kitten, Amelia turned onto her side and peered groggily about. "What's that?"

Betsey moved, reluctant to rouse, but when she did, the chubby little creature sat bolt upright, clutching the bedclothes before her. "What — wha' amiss? Why, 'tis still dark. Oh, that awful bell! Make them stop!"

"Must be a fire," Amelia hazarded, then raised her fallen night rail to cover pink-pointed breasts and slender, sloping white shoulders.

On both floors of Sir John Colleton's house could be heard the padding of feet and excited Negro voices. Quickly the girls realized that one by one, candles had begun to glow outside the guestroom door. The girls, eyes huge and white-ringed with fright, hurried to pull on a few garments.

Someone knocked hastily, then Lady Colleton appeared shading a candle with one hand. The old lady was wearing a rose-tinted nightgown over which she had .pulled a loose, lace-trimmed housecoat. Although she must have known that her gray hair was sprouting in ludicrous elf locks from under an enormous nightcap, she remained calm and patrician.

"Good girls! It's fine that you've kept your wits enough to get dressed. I've no idea what is taking place at the village, but rest assured, my dears, everyone will be safe inside this house!"

Pale-haired Sally Colleton now appeared, suggesting an animated ghost in a dressing gown of flowered yellow lawn. "Oh, Mamma, Mamma! What are we to do?"

"Stop whining and keep your wits about you!" cried her mother. "Above all, keep quiet. Oh, dear! If only your papa hadn't insisted on riding over to Cobb's Mill yesterday. Drat the man! Why does he have to be away at a moment like this?" Lady Jane Colleton appeared to be talking more to herself than to the three wide-eyed young girls she was leading down a broad, gracefully winding staircase towards the ground floor.

Curtly, the old lady ordered her trembling and white-eyed butler to locate the footmen, a pair of young, strong Negroes, and to close and bar all doors and windows opening to the outside on the ground level. Unfortunately, not every window shutter in the place could be secured; a lot of them simply wouldn't close due to the careless application of paint.

Once these precautions had been taken, the straight-backed old lady marched the girls, pale and subdued, into Sir John's handsome, walnut-paneled study.

A moment later young and darkly handsome Mrs. Greenslit, who lived on an adjoining property, hurried in, followed by a bony and much older sister — a confirmed spinster named Dayton. Their eyes were red and streaming and their hair flying witch-wild.

"Oh dear, oh dear!" wailed the tall young woman. "It's so dreadful!"

"What?"

"Soon after the fighting began," Mrs. Greenslit began to sob, "our carriage house was set on fire. Paul went to put it out and, and he — he hasn't come back — nor have any of our servants." She ran to fling arms about Lady Jane. "Oh dear! Oh dear! I hope you don't mind, but we were all alone and so — so frightened by all that smoke and flames. When the fire began spreading to the barn and dairy house we ran out of the back door and came here. I — I hope you don't mind. You're so strong, and always know what to do."

"There, there, my dear! Of course you're welcome, both of you. Here, take some hot coffee."

Within the next half-hour two other groups of women and a pair of young children reached Fair Lawn, so by sunup over a dozen bedraggled people sat about the study talking ninety to the minute and attempting, without much success, to reassure one another that soon everything would turn out all right.

Once her guests had munched buttered beaten biscuits washed down with steaming hot acorn coffee, Lady Jane Colleton quietly excused herself and disappeared upstairs; presently she returned carrying a silver-mounted dueling pistol.

"I am about to make a tour of the property," announced Lady Jane, "and I invite anybody who understands the use of this — this thing to accompany me."

Delicately pointed features flushing, Amelia spoke up. "I do, ma'am."

"You?" Betsey, Sally and the rest began to laugh. "You, of all people!"

"Yes! My papa taught me. He was a soldier," she added with pride, "and a fine one."

"Capital!" smiled Lady Jane. "Then take this, my dear, and come with me. We shan't venture far, but I feel I must make an 'estimate of our situation,' as Sir John would say."

A brief inspection of the property revealed that apparently all the slaves, including house servants, had vanished into the swamp. They weren't likely to emerge from it, remarked Lady Jane, until all was peaceful.

Amelia's misgivings returned when she and her bony-faced hostess sighted single riders or small groups of armed and uniformed horsemen in the distance. As a rule these men were trotting across fields which stretched away from Fair Lawn on three sides but were staying comfortably well away from the mansion.

Apparently, observed Lady Jane, the king's troops at present must be occupied in running down survivors of the defeated forces. Since it seemed unlikely that more fighting would take place in the vicinity of Fair Lawn, Lady Jane led her guests out to the semidetached, deserted cooking house and there supervised the preparation of a breakfast which quickly was carried into the big house.

Betsey ate like a hungry fledgling and Amelia also made a good meal now that the danger appeared to be by, but Sally Colleton, always a pallid and colorless little creature, refused to touch her food. Instead of eating, she kept crossing to an unshuttered window to peer out.

All of a sudden she emitted a gasping cry. "Oh, Mamma! Mamma! Some riders are coming this way!"

Amelia ran to another window, and by peering through a crack in its shutter, glimpsed some twenty green-coated horsemen in crossbelts and dirty white breeches. Several were wearing red fox-tails in their broad hats. They were closing in on the mansion in an irregular line abreast. Short cloaks aflutter, they circled the mansion to its rear and made straight for the stables. Almost at once their disappointed curses could be heard on finding nothing more useful than a pair of worn-out, gray-muzzled mules.

Led by a gray-haired officer with alert bronzed features, the detachment clattered back to the front of the house. The officer then dismounted and went up to hammer on the wide white door with the pommel of a brass-guarded sword.

"Open up!" he roared. "Open up and be damn' quick, else we'll burn down this rebel rat's nest with everybody inside of it."

"Hold hard, sir!" called Lady Jane, then unbolted the door, swung it open and stood glaring defiance.

The green-coated officer, who was no longer young, stared in amazement at this apparition standing framed in the entrance. "And who might you be, you scrawny old hen?"

"I, you unmannerly lout, am Lady Jane Colleton. I blush that any servant of our king — by your jacket you must be a Tory — should prove so uncivil." She glowered down her long, broad nose. "This is my home and since you are uninvited guests, you and your verminous rascals had better get off this property at once or you'll wish you had when Sir Henry Clinton hears about this inexcusable discourtesy." She then added, "Sir John Colleton always has been loyal to His Majesty."

While running a finger inside his helmet's sweat band, the officer jerked a nod. "Very well, ma'am, I'll accept your word on that. Servant, ma'am. I'm sure you'll be safe here till the Crown's authority is reimposed."

"Better not believe her, sir," called Corporal George Walker. "The people around here need only the least excuse to turn their coats when the wind blows to suit 'em."

The brown-faced officer turned and spoke in acid tones. "That will do! If this lady passes her word that there ain't no rebel soldiers in her house, that's all there is to it — no matter what people of your kidney may imagine."

The Tory offered a sloppy salute and just had remounted when, in the distance, an outpost raised a fox-hunter's view-halloo and, standing in his stirrups, pointed to a brief and badly scattered stream of horsemen galloping heavily across a field green with new vegetation.

"There go some Yankee bastards! Come on!" The Tory officer pulled out his sword and spurred down the driveway followed by his detachment.

After pushing his men and desperately wearied horses to the limit of their endurance the Tory leader decided to abandon the chase and ordered his patrol to fan out and reconnoiter a dense patch of woods in which enemy stragglers might conceivably have taken refuge.

When the patrol was well into the grove and deployed into a thin line abreast, Corporal George Walker deemed it a good time to veer out of contact and set about his own business, along with three other Carolinians who had suffered much and lost everything.

On a signal from the one-eyed man, they pulled up, listened to diminishing noises made by their companions in crashing through the underbrush.

Once certain that no one would notice them, the deserters wheeled their mounts and at a brisk trot set off in the direction of Fair Lawn.

Since the occupants of Sir John Colleton's home had failed to resecure the mansion's front door following the Tory patrol's departure, it was simple for the corporal and his hard-faced companions, Troopers Barker, Middleton and Rolfe, to march indoors. They stood in the hall, muddied boots marking the gleaming parquet floor while they stared at gilt-framed portraits, crystal candle sconces, a handsome bull's-eye mirror and well-polished mahogany furniture such as George Walker once had owned.

Stung by memories, he shouted down the deserted hall, "Everybody listen to what I want done! I want every nigger out of here inside of two minutes; everybody else will come to the drawing room *at once!* God help anybody who tries to delay or escape."

A string of resounding curses beat up the stairwell to the second floor, where the women and girls all were. "Get down to the drawing room, you addle-brained bitches, and bring your whelps along, else we'll take the lash to you!"

Amelia remembered her soldier-father. "You do as you please," she announced in a small, taut voice, "but I'm going to stay up here. See? I've got Lady Jane's pistol."

In the frozen silence of utter terror the girls heard women begin to wail shrilly below.

His remaining eye red and narrowed, George Walker rubbed his stubble-covered chin, while with the careful deliberation of a housewife about to select from a coop a fowl suitable for her table, he surveyed the weeping and terrified captives.

Finally, he rasped, "Is everybody here?"

"Everybody!" snapped Lady Colleton in icy tones. "Now, what do you want of us?"

Rolfe, a brutally handsome blond young fellow who had new and old pimples standing out all over his face, drawled, "Say, George, reckon there still must be somebody upstairs; heard a noise from there just now."

Sally Colleton lost her head, whimpered fearfully, "Oh-h, please don't be angry. Everybody's here except Betsey and Amelia."

Walker emitted a snarling laugh. "So that's how it is? Well, since we're in a hurry, Barker, just you get right up there, find those shy little ladies and bring 'em down instanter — drag the bitches if they won't come peaceably!"

Because Amelia had been careless and had only half-cocked her pistol she couldn't fire it when, after several attempts, the bedroom door burst open and in lurched a dark-complexioned, shock-haired fellow who had tufts of chest hair spurting through an unbuttoned green-and-white tunic. Like a hawk stooping on a wood pigeon he pounced on Amelia Trefont and wrenched away her pistol before slapping her so hard across the face that she reeled across the room.

[499]

"Try to shoot me, eh?" Wearing a slack grin, he closed in on her. "Now ain't you the bobcat's kitten? C'mere!"

For both Betsey and Amelia it proved most unfortunate that they should just have removed those few garments they'd donned so hurriedly when early that morning the slave bell had begun to clang and not yet had found time to dress properly, so now they were fluttering about wearing only short and semitransparent lawn undershifts.

Gesturing like a farm boy shooing chickens to the door, the deserter demanded, "C'mon along, my pretty little pullets. Really, ye should have obeyed orders."

"Oh! No, no!" screamed Betsey, and tried to dodge aside, but Barker's hand promptly closed over her wrist. Ineffectually, Tom's sister tried to brace bare feet on the rug, but got hauled along all the same.

The invader turned to Amelia, "You comin' quiet-like or — ?"

"Don't touch me!" Amelia cried in a small, flat voice. "I — I'll come without your help."

When the girls arrived in the drawing room the one-eyed corporal tramped over and dropped onto a fragile gilded parlor chair that creaked under his weight while he balanced a naked saber across patched knees. "All right. The old hens among you take your brats, get off this place *and keep running!* The boys and me have business to transact with a mind towards squaring accounts for what your gentle, high-minded patriots have done to us and our folks."

Like sleepwalkers, Lady Jane, the old-maid sister, the other women and their children prepared to depart.

Once they'd downed the contents of a brandy decanter, the invaders, laughing uproariously all the while, employed the flat of their blades to drive the unwanted captives out-of-doors. Left behind were Betsey, Amelia, Sally and that handsome young matron named Greenslit. All four remained in the drawing room's center pressed together, their eyes huge and unseeing.

For all of a minute Walker and his fellows studied their captives, then the one-eyed corporal kicked over his chair, strode forward and grabbed Amelia's wrist, announcing in a thick voice, "I want this one! You boys take your pick of the rest!"

He hauled the Trefont girl, wildly struggling, out of the parlor and up the staircase. "Come along, sissy. Since we're going to have fun together we may as well enjoy ourselves in comfort."

Amelia tried to scream, but she seemed to have lost control of her throat muscles and could only gasp and gurgle. Not so the other females; once the hot-eyed invaders seized them they shrieked like pigs being hoisted for butchering. Only Mrs. Greenslit made an attempt to struggle, but it was no use; squalling and kicking futilely in her captor's arms, she was carried out towards a couch in Sir John's study.

The raiders had started to scatter to various rooms when Barker sang out from the landing, "Hey, fellers! C'mon upstairs. There's a plenty of fancy beds up here."

At that Betsey fainted, but Barker carried her plump, pink figure, already half-revealed by the disorder of her lawn undershift, up Sir John Colleton's gracefully designed hanging staircase.

Amelia tried to go limp and heavy but at once felt herself clutched so tight to Walker's chest that his uniform's buttons dug painfully into her newly budded breasts. Moreover, his body was giving off a reek of stale sweat and horses so nauseating that, amid a semidaze, she gagged and struggled only ineffectually.

On gaining Sir John's bedroom the Tory set her down; deliberately seating himself on an armchair still covered with feminine garments, he ripped off a filthy neckcloth. Next, without once removing his gaze from the girl, Walker slowly undid his sword belt and stripped off his torn and faded green tunic and a flannel shirt dark with sweat stains.

After that he said softly, "Now, honey, you can start walking back and forth before me." He sat studying Amelia while she hesitated, barefooted, in the middle of the room all unaware of how effectively sunlight beating through French windows was revealing her body under a nimbus of white lawn.

"D'you know," announced George Walker, "I've always admired watching a likely filly parade before the judge's stand?"

Lost in a frantic turmoil of emotions, Amelia could only shake her head and mumble, "Oh-h, I — I don't understand wh-what you want."

When she hesitated, the one-eyed man leaped towards her and, causing a brief, snarling sound, ripped off her shift, left her swaying in the center of the room stark naked save for long strands of gold-red hair with which she vainly attempted to conceal her private parts.

"Start moving! I told you to dance," he rasped. "Dance, damn you!"

When she only turned horrified greenish eyes in his direction and made a pathetic little gesture did George Walker use his sword belt to smack her twice, thrice across the thighs. "Dance, you rebel slut!" he choked, ravaged features working and going scarlet. "You'd better dance real good — till maybe I feel better about Cobb's Mill!"

Amelia gasped and attempted to comply with a few steps from a Christmas masque she'd once performed but her slender white legs could execute only stiff and halting movements.

"Jesus Christ!" snarled Walker, "I've seen gracefuller trulls prance about my tavern many's the time! Well, sissy, since you can't dance, let's see if you make love any better!"

He caught the slim young girl about her waist and flung her, hair flying, to lie whimpering and spraddle-legged across that same canopied bed from which Lady Jane had roused so hastily long hours ago.

Simply because he'd been up inspecting the troop's picket line Rob

Colcord had not been quite as surprised as the rest of the Ricelanders when outposts — who had not, despite Major Vernier's earnest advice, been sent out nearly far enough — came tearing wildly through the light-less woods yelling that a great force of enemy cavalry was hard on their heels.

Rob barely had time to grab up his sword and shout at the top of his lungs, "Turn out! Turn out!" then, "Wake up, Barry! Enemy's here!" just before Tarleton's men appeared in a howling, saber-swinging mass of indistinct figures.

Out of nowhere Black Buck appeared through the darkness. He was riding bareback and reported that he'd seen the captain taken prisoner and carried off God knew where. Then the mustee disappeared into the gloom.

With Wilcox and a few others strung out behind him Rob headed towards that great swamp which lay behind Monck's Corner.

Dawn revealed his hatless and sadly bedraggled little party which, ominously enough, now numbered thirteen, occupying a small, thickly grown islet situated near the swamp's rim. There, Saul Black Buck rejoined them, reported the captain's escape and his order to rendezvous at Lenud's Ferry.

By late afternoon Rob Colcord decided it might be safe to move out in search of food, weapons and clothing. Nothing living remained in sight except for a few stray pigs, skulking dogs and some wounded horses limp-ing and grazing about the fields.

The survivors had come within half a mile of the conflagration when they sighted a gray-haired woman stumping along, stiff-legged with fatigue. She was using a broken sapling for a walking stick and was follow-ing a cart path that skirted the great swamp.

Rob trotted forward, then slipped off his nag and bowed to this pathetic old lady with the wildly disordered hair. Incredibly, she was wearing a tattered housecoat over what appeared to be a nightgown.

He was shocked and surprised to learn that this harridan was Sir John Colleton's lady.

"Lady Colleton!" A fearful possibility struck home. "Please, ma'am, is Amelia Trefont visiting you?"

Tiredly, Lady Jane's reddened eyes raised themselves. "Yes, unfortu-nately she is."

"Please, ma'am, where is Mistress Trefont now?"

"Still at Fair Lawn — I fear."

" 'Fear'? What do you mean by that, ma'am? What has happened?" he demanded while his scarecrow companions rode up.

The barefoot, bedraggled old lady leaned more heavily on her staff as if to prevent herself from falling. "Sir, I wish to God I knew! And then again, I'm glad I *don't!*"

"For God's sake, ma'am, can't you tell me *something?* I'm Betsey Colcord's cousin, Robert."

"*You* are Robert Colcord?"

"I am."

"Oh, my God! Not long ago four ruffians in Tory uniform invaded my home; my daughter, Amelia and two other young ladies were detained when those villains drove us older women and the children out of my house."

At first glance Fair Lawn was seen to be intact, but several outbuildings on an adjoining property, Will Greenslit's place, had been reduced to smoldering ruins.

Four horses were drowsing and switching flies before a hitching rail before the mansion. Listlessly, these raised heads when the newcomers clattered up.

Rob had begun to feel a trifle reassured when inside the handsome ivy-grown brick mansion sounded a thin, choking wail redolent of fear and pain; this was followed by a burst of raucous laughter.

Rob didn't delay to secure his mount, but slipped to the ground and, carrying only a naked sword, rushed up the front steps. Just then a burly, yellow-haired young man appeared in the front doorway. Although bootless and stripped to the waist, he was holding ready a brass-barreled carbine.

From behind, Wilcox shouted a warning, but Rob raised his blade and kept on. Just as he mounted the last step the half-dressed fellow fired and Rob's life ended amid a blinding sheet of flame; his body went bumping and rolling back down the front steps.

Snarling incoherent curses, Gavin Wilcox started to rush the murderer but someone screeched, "Turn back, Sergeant!"

Wilcox checked his stride and cast a backward look when Black Buck yelled, "More hostiles!" The mustee already had started to gallop towards the haven of the swamp.

Less than a quarter of a mile away, a line of horsemen, this time wearing red coats, were deploying across the fields at a fast trot.

Flotsam of Defeat

Cautiously Captain Colcord reined his mare at the edge of a steep, heavily wooded ridge in order to view a wide stretch of the coastal plain of South Carolina. In vain he attempted to ignore the insistent throbbing of a long though shallow gash in his scalp — the result of a saber cut only partially parried. At length he dismounted, and when Black Buck came forward to take Eclipse's reins she at once extended her long neck, no longer sleek or well filled, to nibble at nearby tufts of grass.

One by one the wounded officer's haggard, ill-clad companions followed his example, stretched legs and then checked the condition of their mounts' shoes and hoofs.

Three of Barry's ragged and wild-appearing followers were of the original Ricelands Troops who'd enlisted at the start; all of them lived in the immediate vicinity of Georgetown. The sixth and last member of this weary little party was a smallpox-scarred major of infantry named Spurling. His property, he claimed, lay on the seacoast some twenty miles northeast of Tranquillity and Ricelands.

Like Barry and his handful of veterans, Spurling barely had escaped with his life following Colonel Buford's sanguinary defeat at the Waxhaws. With Buford's undoing, the last force of organized American troops remaining in South Carolina had been shattered and scattered.

So horrible had been the cold-blooded massacre of surrendered men after the Waxhaws defeat that for the balance of the war Banastre Tarleton invariably became referred to as "Bloody Tarleton." "Remember the Waxhaws!" became a rallying cry and "Tarleton's Quarter!" a warning to the enemy that no prisoners would be taken under any conditions.

Bone-weary and never so discouraged, Barry fell to worrying over what he would find when and if he ever reached Ricelands again. What a nightmare this summer campaign had been! In the past he'd experienced and survived some pretty hard going — but nothing comparable to what he'd just been through. Nowadays the country was crawling with little groups of dispirited soldiers struggling furtively homewards as best they could. Such stragglers had to remain eternally alert to avoid British and Tory patrols combing the backcountry.

Soon after Lincoln's surrender, Lord Cornwallis had made for him unusually swift and skillful use of the forces left under his command by Sir Henry Clinton after that general had sailed for New York, confident that the rebellion, in the South at least, had been crushed for good.

Once they'd devoured the last of their rations, the stubble-bearded fellows stretched out under trees and promptly fell asleep.

Barry remained awake long enough to dip a rag in the brook and attempt to remove flecks of dried blood marking his jacket's lapels; no point in frightening Laura any more than he had to. Too bad he couldn't conquer this mounting anxiety over what he might find at Ricelands; his only encouragement was to remember that, in so vast an area, the enemy might have occupied themselves with more tempting targets than a half-finished plantation house. Thank God he'd not much longer to wait to find reassurance.

Laura must have borne their second child by now. How had she weathered the ordeal? Who had attended her? Papa, of course, would have made sure that she'd receive the very best of care. How shameful to realize that he'd not the least notion whether his wife had presented him with a son or a daughter.

Everyone on the patriot side grimly agreed that something *must* be done — and in a big hurry — to check Lord Cornwallis's projected conquest of Virginia and North Carolina. To conduct this campaign, the new British commander-in-chief could rely upon plenty of capable subordinates, among them Lord Rawdon, Banastre Tarleton and that great if vindictive Tory leader, Patrick Ferguson.

While fanning insatiable flies from his head, Barry closed his jaws convulsively. Oh Lord, if only those more than two thousand fine Continental troops hadn't been surrendered so stupidly, so needlessly at Charles Town!

Because Eclipse had been, and probably still was, the fastest horse foaled in Georgetown County in many a year, Barry Colcord raced along the Sampee's shore leading Sergeant Wilcox by a good hundred yards. The rest of his following became strung out over a quarter of a mile.

A strangled, breathless sensation seized the Carolinian when, on rounding a bend in the road, he sighted Ricelands for the first time — in an eternity, it seemed.

The house itself, standing among great oaks, appeared to be intact although flames were beginning to curl up from the horsebarn and the slave quarters behind it. However, as he was turning into his driveway a tentative wisp of smoke rose from Ricelands' western exposure and he sighted a swarm of dark figures hurrying in and out of his home like ants about a disturbed hill.

In a frozen, deadly rage, the Carolinian roweled his mare until she began to run as she had not since the start of the war. His remaining saddle pistol he knew to be useless, it recently having suffered a broken lock — so he wrenched out a heavy dragoon saber he'd picked up after the Battle of Waxhaws and, in deadly silence, charged straight at a milling crowd of looters clad in parts of uniforms or rough civilian clothes. They were too busy piling furniture into a pair of farm wagons pulled up before the front entrance to notice him until he got quite close.

A mad gleam in his eyes, Colcord slashed at raiders lugging Laura's chest of drawers down the front steps. Screaming, they dropped their loot and tried to protect themselves, but two of them immediately went down under the thick, curved blade. Next, the berserk master of Ricelands made for a bearded, narrow-shouldered fellow who hurriedly dropped a chair he was preparing to heave onto the nearest wagon and tried to get away.

Barry felt his arm jarred all the way to his shoulders as he brought his saber crashing down squarely onto the looter's head and split his skull to a level with his brows. Wrenching free his weapon, Barry raced about the wagons. Then, for the first time, he wished he'd delayed long enough to allow his companions to come up, for now a group of mounted men appeared around a corner of the house and rode straight at him. Their furious yelling penetrated the crackling roar caused by flames consuming wood dried by the long and rainless summer.

"Laura! *Where are you, Laura?*" screamed Colcord, then wheeled to meet a wide-shouldered and pale-bearded fellow in a tattered red tunic. He came rushing up a few yards in advance of his companions, jeering, "She ain't goin' to see you, Cap'n — nor anyone else anymore!" Barry got a brief but indelible impression of burning blue eyes, a long jaw and a ruddy, stub nose rushing toward him behind a leveled pistol.

He swung his saber in a short arc — no time for a full swing — and struck with all his strength, but Eclipse was moving too fast to permit his hitting the target fairly. He was carried past the red-coated rider before he knew it. All the same, he knew he hadn't missed altogether; his point had encountered brief resistance and he glimpsed his enemy reeling in his saddle while clutching at a crooked cut that had started blood spurting through his sparse yellow beard.

Barry tried to turn back, but couldn't; Eclipse was too outraged by his merciless spurring to heed him. In desperation the frantic Carolinian again and again threw his weight against the bit in a series of violent jerks which opened his wounded scalp and sent a warm rivulet coursing down his neck.

By the time Colcord succeeded in wheeling, his companions, although heavily outnumbered, had commenced a melee in front of the house. Above the ever-increasing roar of flames, he heard scattered shots, then blades began to flicker in the sunrise. Horses backed and lunged in all directions. By the time Barry could close in again, several figures lay still on the dusty ground and wounded men were trying to pull out of the fight.

Barry thought he recognized the sandy-haired man he'd slashed; he was dismounted and running towards a row of horses snorting and rearing at a hitching rail.

When, through shifting clouds of dust, Barry realized that Wilcox, Black Buck and two others were falling back, he charged for a third time, but this time a swarthy fellow in a black-and-white calfskin jerkin saw him coming and sang out, " 'Ware! Heah comes the young mastuh ag'in!" and whipped a carbine to his shoulder.

Barry dropped flat along the mare's neck and drove his point into the fellow's hairy chest barely in time to spoil his aim, but then another musket roared and it seemed that his whole left side was caving in. By instinct alone, he clung to his saddle until a red-streaked wave of blackness engulfed him.

The Fugitives

Sergeant Wilcox and Saul Black Buck unloaded the unconscious and deathly pale captain from a spring wagon and placed him on a mattress which four husky Negroes maneuvered up a winding staircase to the room Barry had occupied during his youth.

Old Dr. Jessup, fetched from Georgetown in a racing chaise, made a careful examination, then stated that a heavy bullet had passed cleanly through the patient's side, but in doing so had cracked two, possibly three ribs. He was forced also to stitch the reopened gash in Barry's head.

Thoughtfully fingering a long, silver-gray beard, the physician drawled, "Well, Frederick, I wouldn't worry overmuch if the boy weren't in such a damnably poor condition. Even so, he may be riding in two months' time. D'you know what really concerns me?"

"No, Edward, I don't. What is it?"

"How will your son react when he learns about the doings at Rice-lands?"

As for Barry, he lingered in a curious half-world. Much of the time he felt light-headed and feverish because the weather continued windless, hot and dreadfully sultry. Endlessly, he muttered, turned and twisted on sweat-sodden sheets.

After Dr. Jessup's second visit Frederick Colcord followed him out to the mounting block and asked quietly, "Now, Edward, not as a doctor but as an old and dear friend, is Barry making any progress — will he recover?"

Dr. Jessup merged slender, silvery brows and heaved a deep sigh. "I could answer that better were I certain that Barry *already* knows the worst — that his wife and the baby girl are dead, that his home and outbuildings have burned to the ground."

The colonel fingered his strong, box-like jaw. "While I can't be positive, Edward, I *feel* that he knows."

"Why?"

"Understanding my son as well as I do," the old officer said heavily, "I think that since he hasn't tried to rally enough even to ask questions, it seems obvious that he's aware of what's happened and that he's unwilling to make the effort to recover." The colonel straightened, said with a touch of asperity, "Well, since I don't intend to lose Barry, suppose you tell me what I must do?"

"Somehow you're to rekindle Barry's interest in life. Possibly constant reminders that his son is alive and well and needs him may do the trick. Failing that, Frederick, you must find some other incentive."

The sun was up and already making its heat felt when Barry opened gummy eyes and realized that today was so windless that even minor noises could be heard beyond the mosquito bar of white muslin protecting his bed. Reaching out, he rang a silver hand bell and almost at once recognized Aunt Minnie's elephantine tread on the back staircase.

"Lawd be praised!" She beamed like a dusky moon when she saw him for the first time sitting somewhat propped up among his pillows.

He managed a wan smile framed in a dense growth of dark stubble.

"Want to eat something, Auntie; real food, mind you — no invalid's hog-wash."

"Nossuh! Oh, praise de Lawd! Ah fix you de bestest omellette eveah ah make! Anythin' else, suh?"

"Present my respects to my father and ask him to come and see me at his convenience."

Frederick Colcord's rugged, deeply lined and ivory-tinted features lit when he beheld his second son regarding him with a clear light showing in his sunken, brown-ringed eyes. "Oh, Barry, Barry! Thank God you're getting better! Should have known you would, but I — I've been so — so goddamn bloody fearful you mightn't — well — want to live." Colonel Colcord offered an apologetic shrug as he crossed to take the invalid's hands very gently between his. "You never were any part of a coward, my son." The veteran thumbed a trace of moisture from his cheek and his manner underwent an abrupt change, became brisk. "I must leave you now to speak to some uninvited guests. You may have heard them arrive last night?" Frederick Colcord drew a deep breath. "How much do you recall about what happened at Ricelands — the fate of Laura and her new baby?"

The bandage-swathed head inclined almost imperceptibly. "Yes, Pa, I've overheard enough to guess most of what's happened."

"Good. That spares me a dreadful task." He smiled. "By the bye, you'll not have to listen hard to hear Patrick playing a game of tag with pick-aninnies back of the house."

Barry blinked. "Thank God at least he was spared. How did that happen?"

Barry listened to a militarily succinct account, nodded, then said, "What about those people you spoke of, sir? I mean the ones who came here last night?"

"They're fugitives from another terrible defeat we've suffered. At the moment the poor devils are still sleeping like dead men. The senior officer is a Colonel Armand. With him are a lieutenant from Maryland named Tarrant and a Frenchman who calls himself the Chevalier de Buysson; seems he was an aide to a foreigner called Baron de Kalb. He says the baron was killed at Camden."

Late in the afternoon Colonel Colcord ushered in two of his visitors. One was Colonel Charles Armand, who not only was an aristocrat from Virginia but like his host had served for many years as a regular in the British army, during which he'd done extensive campaigning in the Low Countries, aside from having taken part in General Wolfe's famous siege and capture of Quebec.

Otherwise, Charles Armand was a hatchet-faced, wiry individual who stood almost as tall as General George Washington, on whose staff he had served for over two years as a personal aide. The Virginian, because his tunic was being mended, at present was outfitted in one of his host's velvet housecoats. His were level but penetrating gray-blue eyes, deep set in a narrow head which appeared to be close-shaven under a short and yellowed campaign wig. Because remarkably few wrinkles creased the visitor's fine, patrician features, his age might lie anywhere between fifty and seventy.

Colonel Armand's companion, Major le Chevalier du Buysson, was Norman and as French as French could be — although not typically so, he being big of body, blue-eyed and quite deliberate of speech and manner. Moreover, his plentiful hair was coarse and straw-colored, as was his large and ragged mustache.

Later it came out that the Chevalier du Buysson had reached America quite early in the war in the retinue of the Marquis de Lafayette and, because he spoke fluent English — for all he hated the "Goddamns" with a passion — he had been attached almost immediately to the commander-in-chief's headquarters, where he'd served until that unlucky day when he and Colonel Armand had been detached and ordered south in a desperate attempt to reach General Horatio Gates in time to help him devise a plan of campaign which would be to drive the enemy out of Georgia and the Carolinas and, in so doing, destroy Lord Cornwallis's army.

"I feel," the veteran commenced, "that perhaps what the chevalier and I have to tell you, Captain, is best related in two parts. The first concerns a major engagement fought near the village of Camden in North Carolina." He inclined his head towards the big Norman who sat on a ladderback chair with arms folded across his chest and thick, hairy legs sticking out from an old, brown-and-blue banyan of Augustus's. "Since Major du Buysson was longer in the thick of battle than I was, I shall ask him to give you an account of what happened."

Once the men sitting about in the darkened bedroom had swallowed a few sips of mint and brandy, the Frenchman continued his story. "We 'ad marched for about four hours along a narrow, sandy and wood-cloaked road that ran between mosquito-filled swamps, when suddenly the night became streaked by musket flashes." Angrily, the Norman broke off, tilted back his big yellow head and took a long gulp. "Our advance guard 'ad blundered into the enemy, who also were undertaking a night march in the 'ope of surprising us at dawn. Voilà! They were as astonished as we, but much better trained."

Du Buysson bowed towards his companion. "Since Colonel Armand was in command of the American legion, 'e can tell you better than I what 'appened to our van when the infantry of Tarleton's legion came up and opened fire."

Weak from diarrhea, the disorganized Americans had taken one look at those lines of scarlet-and-white-clad figures advancing steadily behind a hedge of twinkling steel points and around two thousand of them dropped their muskets and, without so much as pulling a trigger, fled in a headlong panic which at once communicated itself to a Maryland brigade held in reserve.

"*Alors, monsieur le capitain,*" the Norman spread hands in a gesture infinitely expressive of disgust — "being a veteran yourself, you readily can perceive the sudden 'opelessness of our situation with our left and center in complete confusion and terrified men running in every direction save towards the enemy. In vain did my chief, the Baron de Kalb, send for the remnants of our reserves. These Maryland men came up bravely, but, *hélas,* by then it was far too late. Milor' Cornwallis 'ad launched his best regulars in a furious attack upon our left flank which crushed it — " Slowly, the Norman shook his head. "I ask you, what choice 'ad we but to fall back?"

"What followed?" Barry murmured after a brief silence.

"Disaster, complete disaster! *Figurez-vous, mon capitain,* of our poor little army more than a thousand men were killed, wounded or captured, along with all of our baggage train, supplies and artillery."

Finally, Barry asked, "And what, may I ask, was General Gates doing during the battle?"

Father and son were taken aback by the violent curses which erupted from both visitors. Their vehemence so startled Colonel Colcord that he arose and hurriedly ordered a fresh round of drinks.

"Well may you ask, Captain, how our valiant commander-in-chief occupied himself!" Charles Armand, with bony jaw jutted, commenced to stride agitatedly back and forth on slippered feet. "Believe it or not, sir, the moment the battle was joined, that vast, lily-livered poltroon became so numbed by fear that he could not issue a single order! During the entire engagement he sent never a word to his subordinates! Instead," snorted the Virginian, "the general — I, myself, saw him do it — mingled with the first flood of runaways which, as the chevalier has told you, were green, half-sick volunteers from North Carolina.

"That miserable coward completely lost his head, and being mounted on Fearnaught, the fastest horse in the army — " he glanced at Frederick Colcord — "which is a son of Colonel Baylor's famous racer of the same name, you'll no doubt remember, sir — our general soon outdistanced his fellow fugitives and never drew rein till he reached Charlotte, which lies a long sixty miles to the north of Camden."

" — And there, sir, you have the whole ugly and disgraceful story of Camden!" concluded Armand, angrily draining his second julep. "Never was a victory more complete nor a defeat more total! What remains of our troops now have become all but hopelessly dispersed, hiding in swamps and forests. Most of 'em, we fear, have abandoned their weapons and are too disgusted to even dream of taking them up again — and after what's happened this last year who can blame the poor fellows?

"Aside from this, our Continental paper currency is altogether worthless, while in the South there remains no reserve of arms, ammunition or other materials of war.

"What with the French," he bowed to du Buysson who made a rueful grimace, "having retreated to their West Indies and displaying little inclination to continue the war, the future couldn't appear more hopeless especially since one hears persistent rumors of disaffection and even mutiny breaking out among troops serving in the Northern states."

The Virginian fetched a long, long sigh. "To render our situation more desperate, hardly an American man-of-war now remains at sea, so our ports are subject, at will, to enemy raids. Meanwhile, the enemy's vigorous blockade of our coasts is strangling our commerce and cutting off aid from abroad while the Congress continues to prove itself ineffectual — incapable of acting with either wisdom or vigor."

Last Resort

Barry had had a long nap when Aunt Minnie rapped and peered inside, beaming because she was wearing a new orange-and-blue kerchief knotted neatly over kinky gray hair. "De gennamuns say dey be up direckly, suh — if yo' cares to see dem."

"Send them up by all means. I'm feeling much better."

On this occasion Barry's previous visitors were accompanied by a small, jockey-sized young lieutenant named Tarrant who, as the chevalier explained humorously, had been sleeping like six dead men ever since his arrival at the plantation.

After offering courteous greetings Colonel Armand lost no time in coming to the point. Barry prepared to listen with bandaged head resting against a mountain of pillows.

"As you must have gathered from what we told you earlier, Captain Colcord, our cause at this moment totters on the edge of ruin." The Virginian's hard, steel-gray eyes fixed themselves on Barry's dark-blue ones. "Many of our best and most intelligent leaders, both civilian and military, are now convinced that, barring a miracle, the forces of the Crown cannot fail to destroy what is left of the United States, and that within a few months' time. However, as I have already indicated, there are others in high places, George Washington among them, who do not concur with this dismal view and have sworn never to surrender or to accept a royal government.

"Shortly after news was received of that inexcusably stupid capture of General Lincoln's troops," Colonel Armand continued after casting a curious glance at his host, who sat staring moodily out into the night, "a secret council of war was convened in His Excellency's headquarters, one which only the ablest and most trustworthy of his officers were invited to attend. It was then that weighty decisions were arrived at and agreed upon."

The Virginian paused long enough to permit Colonel Colcord a question. "And what were these decisions?"

Barry struggled up on his bed, Lieutenant Tarrant turned to face the speaker and Colonel Colcord stopped looking out of the window as Armand said, speaking slowly and impressively, "Among other things we decided that, if all were lost in the field, we would under no conditions tamely lay down our arms and submit to the king's pleasure!"

Fascinated in spite of himself, Barry drew a deep breath and wished he hadn't. His cracked ribs caused such stiletto-like stabs of pain that he gasped, "Oh, damnation!"

Misunderstanding, the Virginian cast him a sharp look. "Shall I desist, sir? Or does what I'm saying meet with your approval?"

The haggard young officer caught his breath and nodded. "It does, sir. Kindly continue."

"Very well. Certain of us who escaped from the defeat at Camden now feel justified in carrying out the council's first instructions."

" — And they are?" queried the master of Tranquillity from among the shadows.

"We, sir, are to scatter and range through the South to find groups of stragglers and time-expired veterans and fragments of broken regiments to tell them two things: first, those who are willing to fight on must remain in small, mobile groups which will be capable of avoiding British and Tory patrols. These are gradually to work their way into North Carolina where they are to assemble in the vicinity of Hillsboro, or at some other rally point to be determined later on."

"What about those who've had a bellyful of the war?" queried Barry. "I fear they will form the great majority of the fugitives you seek."

"Such men who refuse to fight but don't intend to live under British rule will be instructed to prepare themselves and their families to cross the mountains when spring comes, settle beyond them and thus enable us to continue our form of government in this new land."

Colonel Colcord stroked his chin a moment, then asked, "So is it the intention of the council you've mentioned that patriotically minded people should emigrate to settle in Kentucky and Tennessee?"

"That is our intention."

" — And what preparations, if any, have been made to accomplish this migration successfully?" This was a veteran field officer speaking.

"Surveys of possible routes across the mountains have been and still are being made. For example, Mr. Tarrant, here, was sent west earlier in the summer on just such a mission."

"Then why is he here?" Barry asked unexpectedly.

Tarrant flushed and looked acutely unhappy. "Why, sir, I was making my way towards the Watauga settlements when my party — which numbered only six in all — was surprised by a band of outlaws who murdered all of us saving myself. I was lucky enough to have been off exploring a nearby ford at the time they struck."

Barry reached for water to quench a suddenly burning thirst. Meanwhile, his father said, "So you failed in your mission?"

"Only partially, sir; I was able to bring back valuable information about the state of the Charlotte Pike as far as the Smoky Mountains which lie about two-thirds of the way to Watauga."

"Wherein, then, did you fail?" Barry asked.

Tarrant sighed and slapped a mosquito. "In that I had orders to locate certain agents who had been sent last winter to find out about what preparations had been made to receive immigrants and troops retreating from the South and East."

The diminutive officer hesitated and glanced about the darkening room. "It isn't generally known, sir, that, last autumn, the council dispatched certain agents to the westernmost Watauga stations and urged settlers already established there to take along any newcomers and push farther west — all the way out to the mouth of the Cumberland River. On arrival, they were to build forts or stations — as I believe they call 'em — clear land and start plantations sufficient to feed immigrants arriving from the East."

Young Tarrant looked increasingly embarrassed. "My failure lay in that I did not reach Sycamore Shoals, which is the chief settlement of the Watauga country."

" — And because of this," broke in the chevalier, "we of the council remain in ignorance of what 'as 'appened beyond the mountains. For all we know, expeditions led by Colonels Robertson and Donelson may 'ave been wiped out, or may 'ave been so decimated before reaching their destinations that the survivors 'ave been reduced to 'elplessness."

"On the other hand they might conceivably have got through," commented the Virginian. "If they have, we must swiftly find out how they are faring. We have heard absolutely nothing definite nor have received any maps of their routes or a description of the country they traveled through, although such were promised us."

A servant knocked, then brought in a pot of fragrant real coffee, glasses and a gleaming decanter of cognac. Conversation briefly was suspended in favor of banal comments on the weather and an exchange of topical jokes everyone seemed to have heard.

Finally, Colonel Armand set down his cup and addressed Barry. "Suppose, sir, that I come directly to the point? In the light of what you have heard from us you can understand why the council must dispatch a few dependable and experienced officers across the Alleghenies. Our agents must evaluate the situation in the West and then, as quickly as possible, send us the maps and information we need — and *make sure* that they get to us."

[513]

Leaning forward, he lowered his voice, "Captain Colcord, we very much hope that you will consent to be one of these men."

Barry uttered a short, mirthless laugh. "Why me, sir? I know nothing about the frontier."

"Nevertheless, you have campaigned for years in wildernesses no less difficult than those to which I hope you will go."

"But," insisted the wounded man, "I speak no Indian language at all and know nothing of the savages' ways."

"— But your mustee manservant does," promptly stated the chevalier. "I 'ave 'ad some interesting conversations with 'im. This Saul Black Buck, 'e speaks Creek, Cherokee and Shawnee and several dialects. And, of course, 'e is part Indian. Is that not so, *monsieur le colonel*?"

Barry's father inclined his handsome head. "That is so, and besides, Black Buck hunted with the Creeks and Cherokees until he was captured and enslaved."

Curious, young Tarrant inquired, "How in the world did he ever come here, sir?"

"I bought him years ago from an Indian trader who happened to be passing through Charles Town. At the time I stood in need of a good hunter for this place. I gave him to my son when Barry got married."

"— And so," Armand resumed, "if Black Buck accompanies you, you will, in effect, have at your disposal the special knowledge required for a successful mission.

"Aside from that, Major du Buysson and I are agreed that you are excellently well qualified in matters of integrity, courage and intelligence — let alone military experience." He stood up. "Will you undertake this mission?"

Barry sat completely upright for the first time and studied the solemn faces surrounding his four-poster. "Gentlemen, I am no more ready to call quits than you are. So, to the best of my ability I will endeavor to oblige you."

"Oh, God," sighed the master of Tranquillity. "Must you go? You've already done so much!"

"No more than many others, sir. Pa, I — I'm pretty tired, so please advise me. What would *you* do in my place?"

The old man sighed. "Just what you're going to do, I expect."

"Thank you, Pa. And now, gentlemen, do you care to inform me further about this assignment?"

The Virginian said, "As soon as you are able, you will follow the Charlotte Pike to Sycamore Shoals in the Watauga country. You will take Saul Black Buck with you and not more than two other companions — a larger party might attract unwelcome attention. Feel free to adopt any expedient which will get you surely to the Watauga country as fast as possible.

"Upon arrival you will endeavor to find either Colonel Sevier or Colonel Shelby — both of whom enjoy the council's complete confidence. Once you have obtained the required intelligence, maps and reports, you will forward them at once to General Washington's headquarters."

The Chevalier du Buysson added gravely, "*Mon capitaine*, there is still another matter which requires your investigation. Last fall we ordered to Fort Patrick Henry a Dr. Samuel Mason with secret orders to attach himself to Colonel Robertson's expedition before it set out for the Frenchman's Bluff."

"Where is that?"

"It lies somewhere near the middle of the Tennessee country. A similar agent accompanied Colonel Donelson's waterborne expedition, which was intended to descend the Tennessee and other rivers to the Ohio and then proceed up the Cumberland to join Robertson's people at the bluff. Although both parties are rumored to 'ave reached their destination, we 'ave 'eard nothing at all — no maps, no news, either from Dr. Mason or our other agent. You can comprehend our desperate need for definite information, *hein?*"

Colonel Armand jerked a nod. "Yes. One of your principal duties will be to discover what has become of these men and their information.

"There is no need to point out that yours will be a most perilous journey, for, as Mr. Tarrant here has discovered, the hill country, and the whole frontier for that matter, are swarming with banditti, masterless men and gangs of outlaws wanted by the British Crown and our own government."

After a long pause the big Frenchman queried, "Now, 'aving 'eard all this, *mon capitaine*, are you still prepared to cross the mountains?"

"I am. As quickly as I'm able to travel I'll set out with Saul Black Buck." His gaze then sought his father's erect figure. "Speaking of outlaws, sir, has there been any news of Skelton?"

Colonel Colcord snapped his fingers. "Damn my forgetfulness! Only this morning my overseer told me that a straggler had ridden in to beg a meal and said that just a few days ago he'd passed a party fitting the Shell Towners' description. He said they were hurrying towards the mountains as if eager to get beyond them."

Phoenix Republic

For all this was only mid-September it was inescapable that fall was setting in. On and near the summits of Stone Mountain Range, hardwoods, showing as bright patches on a dark blanket of evergreens, were turning yellow, orange or red — especially the maples, beeches and birches.

On the Charlotte Pike, a rough trace which wound in a generally northwesterly direction over the Stone Mountains from Morgantown in North Carolina, Captain Barry Colcord of the dispersed and defeated Ricelands

Troops reined in Eclipse, his long-limbed mare, on the range's highest crest.

Turning in his saddle, Barry Colcord peered back along the Charlotte Pike — so-called even though it remained impassable for wheeled vehicles over most of its length — and perceived that Tom Calloway, a hungry-looking young Georgian who usually wore a cheerful expression on his flat and sallow face, had dismounted to tighten his saddle's girth.

It had struck Barry as significant that Calloway when he'd asked if he might go along out West hadn't volunteered any details concerning his immediate past.

Saul Black Buck also had halted. Odd, mused Barry, how many subtle changes had taken place in the mustee since they'd set out from Tranquillity. Of late Black Buck had taken to wearing his slightly kinky, gray-white hair in twin braids and had mounted a pair of eagle feathers in his battered straw hat. His hooked beak of a nose and thin lips more than ever resembled those of a full-blooded Indian. Ever since they'd entered the foothills of the Stone Mountains the mustee's jet eyes had begun to flicker, ceaselessly probing his surroundings.

With his ragged cloth hunting shirt billowing in an updraught from the valley below, Calloway led his horse to stand staring out over these many ridges, which, all blue with haze, lay ahead.

"Say, Cap'n," drawled the Georgian, "how soon you figger we'll come to the first o' the Watauga settlements?"

"No telling. Maybe tomorrow, or the day after, or the day after that. Why?"

"Just been wonderin' why right-minded people ever would want to settle in such a God-awful, lonely wilderness!"

Colcord beckoned Black Buck. "Ever hunt this country?"

"No, mastuh. Me lived more west 'mong Creeks and Cherokees on edge of Great Hunting Ground."

Colcord turned to Calloway. "What about you?"

"Naw, suh, ain't never been this way afore, but I done heard plenty 'bout the Watauga ground from my Uncle Sam. Him and old Jacob Brown wintered and trapped out this way back in Seventy-cne. When he come back to Georgia to fetch his family out there he told us young 'uns all about the Watauga country; said they's plenty of game and rich land out that way."

Captain Colcord's newly lined features relaxed a trifle. "It's magnificent, all right. How far ahead of us would you say the next party is traveling?"

The mustee grunted, " 'Bout two, mebbe three mile."

A few thin columns of gray-blue smoke rising in the middle distance suggested that other groups of emigrants already had pulled off the pike to make camp for the night.

The mustee remarked softly, "Fum now on, mastuh, us bettah look out sharper'n we bin. Plenty Cherokee live beyond this gap."

"What of that? They made peace five seasons ago with Colonel Robertson."

"True, but dey plenty Creek 'round here, too, an' 'breeds an' white outlaws. None of 'em goin' pass up takin' a easy scalp." The mustee's narrow and nearly lashless jet eyes slitted themselves. "Mastuh, now us must journey like we scoutin' Tory country."

"All right." Colcord mounted Eclipse, swearing softly at barbed pains shooting through his tender side.

On sighting a fairly level little clearing hemmed in by lofty evergreens and carpeted with frost-killed ferns, which should offer easily-come-by bedding, Barry pulled up and announced that this night would be spent here.

Once the horses had been unsaddled and their single pack animal off-loaded, Black Buck was preparing to use a flint and steel on a small pile of shredded cedar bark when two shots sounded not very far away. Almost before the reports ceased to echo and reecho through the fragrant-smelling fir forest, Colcord and his companions were behind trees with weapons cocked and ready.

"How far off?" breathed Tom Calloway, small, pale-brown eyes intent.

" 'Bout a whoop off," muttered the mustee.

Colcord listened a long moment, then spoke softly. "Tom, you mind the animals whilst Saul and I take a look. Most likely 'twas nothing more than some fellow shooting his supper."

Noiselessly as panthers stalking a grazing deer, they started along the pike a few yards out on either side. They had progressed only a short distance when a series of shrill and unearthly screams that lifted the hairs on a man's neck beat through the purplish twilight. At the same time Barry heard a loud crashing as if several horses were traveling downhill at a gallop.

Drifting, shadow-quiet, from tree to tree, Barry closed in on that point whence had come the shrieks.

He glimpsed Black Buck's dark outline keeping abreast, then saw a fire burning in a small open space barely visible through the trees. When, cautiously, Barry parted a clump of laurels just enough daylight remained to reveal a man's long-legged body lying loosely sprawled on the ground; a slender youth was kneeling and keening shrilly beside it.

Once Barry had made sure that no one else remained in the vicinity, he ventured into the clearing, at the same time calling in a soft undertone, "Don't be afraid, lad. We're friendly."

Briefly the mustee exposed black-and-yellow tooth stumps in a flat, tight grin. "Saul's eyes may be growin' dim, mastuh, but he kin tell dat ain't no boy, for all dem britches an' short hair."

Only vaguely did Parthenia Bryant recognize the sound of advancing footsteps, then raised her eyes from the body lying so incredibly flat, and through blinding tears watched the approach of a tall, wide-shouldered figure.

When the stranger drew near, Parthenia leaped to her feet with catlike speed, at the same time unsheathing a long, slim-bladed knife. Emitting a squalling snarl, she sprang at the apparition with such violence that, had she been any heavier, the impact must have sent Barry Colcord staggering off balance.

As the blade flickered towards his throat Barry brought the barrel of his carbine down on the girl's forearm, forcing her to drop her knife. By the shrill way his sharp-featured and freckled assailant screamed Barry knew Black Buck was right; this meagerly built individual with slanting, hate-filled pale eyes and short, dark hair was no youth but a girl of about eighteen.

When his assailant staggered aside, Colcord flung an arm about her waist, but she must have known something about wrestling, for she escaped his grasp and started to run. She might have escaped had not the mustee tripped her so effectively that she fell hard enough to knock out her wind and lay on the fallen leaves writhing spasmodically, like some small animal run over by a wagon.

Barry picked up the girl's knife, then stood peering down at her through the fast-deepening dusk. "My God, Saul, I've met up with gentler bobcats."

The mustee grunted, "Mastuh, better me tie her up?"

"No! No! Please — don't tie!" The girl stopped struggling and began to sob wildly. "You — you've broke m-my wrist, y-you bloody murderer!" She sat up glaring about. "You aimin' to slay me, too?"

Colcord snapped harshly, "Suppose you stop talking nonsense and tell me what's happened here."

"I — I won't! Y-you're one of the k-killers!"

"What's your name?"

"Parthy Bryant, and be damned to you!"

He pointed to the roughly dressed corpse. "Who was he?"

"Billy — my brother."

Barry began to wonder why a couple so seemingly destitute should have had at least five horses in their possession. He had counted as many severed halter shanks dangling from nearby trees.

"Saul, go fetch in our animals."

As soon as Saul returned with Tom Calloway to the little clearing, Colcord undid blanket rolls and got out a folding tin candle lantern and Tom concocted a stew from lumps of greasy and slightly tainted venison boiled with Indian cornmeal and a rasher of salt pork.

Once the stew had begun to simmer, Colcord carried a gourd dipper of it over to the sullen-faced girl. He sank onto his heels. "We had nothing to do with your brother's death, so eat this, you pathetic little fool, and maybe you'll feel better."

From under dark lashes the girl's faintly slanted and pale gray eyes peered upwards; a fleeting half smile appeared on her clearly delineated lips. "Thanks, mister. Guess I — I must ha' been too shook up to think straight. I won't cause no more fuss, really I won't."

As Parthenia Bryant's slim and grimy hands closed over the gourd she seemed to shrink in size and to appear even slighter and thinner than ever. Although the stew remained smoking hot this wild, barelegged creature in the tattered and shapeless homespun shirt and breeches used black-nailed fingers eagerly to cram lumps of meat into her mouth.

In his deep and slightly hoarse voice, Calloway said, "Say, sissy, you say yer last name's Bryant?"

"Aye. My pa was Long George Bryant — one of the finest Long Hunters." Then she added with a hint of pride, "Him an' Dan'l Boone was cousins — sort of."

Feeling uncommonly good-natured, Calloway invited, "Go on, sissy. You talk a heap like my Uncle Sam."

"Don't go on callin' me sissy," snapped Parthenia. "I ain't got a brother now."

Barry relit his pipe and expelled billows to join the campfire's smoke. "All right. From now on we'll call you Parthy."

"When the trouble with the redcoats begun, Pa took down his long rifle, filled up his war bag with possibles and told Ma, 'Ye c'n expect me back, Millie, when you sight me.'"

Wearily, Parthenia pushed strands of greasy brown hair from before eyes circled by lavender shadows. "Well, in near two years' time Pa come home but he weren't nice to look at or hear, 'cause he was half crazy and had a great shot hole in his neck that never did heal up; said he'd took that hurt in a great battle fought 'way up in Pennsylvany — wherever that is."

Colcord extended hands towards the flames and nodded. "I take it he never recovered?"

"Naw. 'Though Billy, the neighbors and me nursed him bestest we knew how, Pa kept on failin' till he perished."

" — Where was yer ma?" Calloway drawled while picking broad, yellowish teeth with his knife's point.

"She'd died a piece before Pa got back."

"How long ago did yer pa perish?"

The girl shrugged thin, gracefully sloping shoulders. "Don't rightly recall when, but 'twas towards this summer's end. He gave Billy —" Her oblique, light-gray eyes filled as they sought that patch of leaves yet darkened by her brother's blood. "Anyhow, all Pa left of worth was his gun and his soldier's land warrant. Me and Billy decided to move on, so we sold Pa's cabin and got hardly enough to buy a little travelin' gear and a couple of no-count tackeys.

"Well," her voice grew strained again and she glowered at the flames, "we was ready to set out for Watauga when Billy chanced to fall in with some trifling fellers who claimed they was quittin' the war 'cause they reckoned us folks sure 'nuff was going to get licked. Anyhow, they got Billy to join 'em in a raid on some Tory's farm in the valley next to ours. Well, they pulled it off all right an' come back with some valuables and a herd of real good horses."

"After resting and drinkin' for a couple of hours the other fellers took their share of the horses and rode off without no by-yer-leave."

Barry roused a little. "Did they say where they were going?"

"Naw. They just lit out, like I said. I was glad. They were a mean lot and even tried to pester me some, but Billy wouldn't let 'em — nor would I.

"We lit out the very next day for the mountains fixin' to settle somewheres out there."

"Are you sure those men weren't just common horse thieves?" Colcord suggested casually.

Abruptly, Parthenia broke into another freshet of tears. "Oh-h, I — I don't rightly know! Even if them horses mightn't truly have belonged to a Tory, my brother weren't no thief!"

Calloway yawned cavernously. "Say, Parthy, ain't it possible that them horses' rightful owner might ha'e caught up with ye?"

"Who knows? All I know is they slew poor Billy 'thout no warnin'!"

Colcord stretched and sighed. It had been a hard day but he'd no intention of going to sleep just yet. "Did you see anything of the attackers — enough to recognize them, I mean?"

"No. I — I was mindin' my business 'in the bushes' when those cowards killed Billy; reckon that's the only reason I ain't dead, too. I was just tying up my britches when, next thing I know, I heard shots, then a big feller came ridin' fast right past me towin' some of our horses towards the pike. The others was further off."

"Others? How many were there?"

"Mebbe three of them."

"Tell me, how well did you see this man?"

The girl, whose loose shirt seemed to be only moderately filled, jerked a nod. "For all the poor light I think he was tall, like you, only he'd a yellow beard which weren't so thick I couldn't spy a big red scar."

"Shaped how?"

"Like a pot hook, kind of."

Barry Colcord's voice sounded harsh as a blade being dragged across a steel sharpener. "Like a pot hook?"

Parthenia blinked. "Sure. Like I said, I spied a scar shaped like that through the feller's beard."

"I'm looking for a fellow who looks something like that," Colcord admitted, then added with a harsh little laugh, "Back where I come from he was called Skelton, Jasper Skelton. I'm mighty keen to come up with him."

Calloway asked drowsily, "Was he a — a Tory?"

"I'm not sure about that. All I know about Skelton is that he's a cold-blooded murderer."

Parthenia, astride the pack horse, rode behind its canvas-covered load with small feet dangling slack from her knees. Barry noted, however, that the girl's reflexes remained unimpaired; whenever her mount slipped or stumbled her long, sinewy legs instantly clamped themselves around the beast's barrel.

All in all, Parthenia Bryant presented an unlovely if pathetic figure, for if the girl possessed a comb she hadn't used it to untangle her boyish dark-brown locks, which appeared to have been hacked off rather than trimmed above small, flat ears.

The gray and cheerless afternoon was well advanced when Black Buck, who had been riding a few rods ahead of the rest, halted and pointed to a ravine over which a lacy stratum of gray-blue smoke was drifting just above the treetops.

The mustee blinked. "Careful, mastuh. That plenty people."

Could Skelton be in the camp below? Barry turned to young Calloway. "You and Parthy stay here. Saul, come with me."

Maintaining a brisk lookout, Colcord kicked forward Eclipse. It seemed advisable to warn these strangers of his approach, so he started to sing in a strong but sadly off-key baritone.

He barely had commenced a second stanza when a gruff voice warned from the depths of a thicket, "'Bide right there! Don't you move!'"

When the former cavalry officer halted, Saul Black Buck slipped off his horse, quick as a pouncing lynx, to take shelter behind a thick oak; already he had an old carbine ready for use.

Colcord made no effort to shift his own weapon from its crosswise position on his pommel. "Take it easy, friend. We mean no one harm." Desperately, he tried to visualize the challenger; too bad he'd never heard Skelton speak.

"How many do ye number?" the unknown demanded from among a stand of blue spruces.

"There are two of us here and a couple more — one's a girl — waiting on the pike. We're peaceable folk on our way to Watauga."

"You better be tellin' strict truth."

Colcord could see the speaker now; he was black-haired and didn't in any way resemble Skelton as he crouched among the spruces leveling a long-barreled Tower musket. His garb was a hunting shirt of coarse brown linen and a jockey cap of black leather that had its peak pinned up in front with a sprig of evergreen tucked into it — ranger fashion.

Barry raised a hand in casual greeting. "Come on out, stranger, and let's get acquainted."

"Well, seein' as you put it that way, I just might. But don't make a quick motion; the same goes fer yer tame savage behind the tree."

Out of the thicket stepped one of the biggest men the Carolinian had ever beheld. He must have stood at least six foot three and was broadly built. This clean-shaven stranger's complexion was a healthy red-bronze hue and he wore his black hair braided into a single, orderly queue bound by a greasy, black ribbon.

To complete the unusual this big fellow's knife, war hatchet and cartridge box, along with a bayonet — of all things — were supported by once-white canvas crossbelts of the type worn by British grenadiers. With a start of surprise, Barry recognized an oval pewter ornament stitched to the fellow's cap.

Bending in his saddle, Barry shook hands, saying, "Seem to recognize that badge of yours — North Carolina Rangers, ain't it?"

"Well, I'll be dogged! That's right. How *d'you* know that?"

"Seen some fighting down South."

"Who air you?" After a perceptible pause, he added, "sir."

"Barry Colcord, late captain of the Ricelands Troop — Colonel Horry's Light Horse." He called over his shoulder, "Saul! You can come out."

Walking lightly on the balls of his feet the mustee sidled into the open, elevating his carbine's barrel as he advanced. His battered brown hat and the two feathers on it were still drooping and soft from rain.

The big man's full lips curved. "Me, I'm Arthur Jennings, recently sergeant in Major Dixon's company of North Carolina Rangers."

Somehow a warm, indefinable current passed between the veterans when they struck hands.

"Suppose, sir, you and your tame Injun and the rest of you —" he paused, raised a bushy brow — "sure there's only two more?"

"Sure, and one of them, as I've said, is a wild sort of girl we found beside the pike. If you're interested, friend Jennings, I'll tell you more about it later on."

"All right. Since night's nigh, suppose you camp with us? My wife and the rest of us are halted in yonder hollow."

Barry couldn't suppress a grin. "Somehow I'd guessed that you've women with you. How many?"

"'Bout a dozen — all ages. Got some sprats along, too."

Wasn't this sheer, bull luck? Now, perhaps he could get rid of Parthenia and go on with his mission.

"Cap'n, I want you should meet Mr. Tom Drayton," said Jennings as they reached the settlement.

The other, a square-built and slightly pop-eyed individual, offered a curt head bow. "Your servant, sir."

"Mr. Drayton," Arthur Jennings explained, "is a surveyor. He's going to Sycamore Shoals, where he's supposed to meet some fellow surveyors from Virginny. Together, they're supposed to run a boundary line 'way out west. Way things stand nowadays, ain't nobody in Watauga knows whether his land lies in Virginny or in God's country—" he laughed—"which is North Carolina. Mr. Drayton's been sent by our legislature to make sure us Carolinians don't get to hold the dirty end of the stick. It's important 'cause there'll be a pile of people headin' this way from now on."

A faint smile flitted over Mr. Drayton's squarish, insect-mottled features. "If running a true line is *all* I'll have to worry about I'll be well satisfied."

Something in the surveyor's voice prompted Barry to inquire politely, "What are you driving at, sir?"

"— Why, just before leaving Edenton I read a report that Georgia and South Carolina have been conquered and that a pair of British Indian agents by the name of Stuart and Cameron are busy trying to raise the Cherokees, Chickamaugas and Chickasaws against us. Seems these gentlemen are spreading reports that fugitives from the East intend to establish a number of settlements in the Indians' Great Hunting Country. Naturally, the savages don't fancy the idea."

Three women herding children of varying sizes, all round-eyed with curiosity, drew near.

When suddenly all the dogs in camp started to bark, the men jumped for their weapons while, with practiced swiftness, the women dragged their offspring into the underbrush.

"Rest easy," Barry called out. "Those are only my other companions coming in."

When Calloway and Parthenia rode into sight, Lucy Jennings at first was fooled into believing that the latter was a lanky boy, but then recognized her mistake and caught a quick breath. "Good land of Goshen! Why, that lad's *female!*" Then she turned to Colcord, demanded sharply, "What's wrong with her? Why don't she pay attention? Is she sick?"

As briefly as he could, Barry described the murder of Parthenia's brother and the theft of the Bryants' horses. In conclusion he shot a sharp glance at the former sergeant. "Now perhaps you'll understand why I must know if anyone has overtaken your party in the last day or so."

"Well," Jennings said, "ever since we crossed the mountains we've been passed by a lot of soldiers — mostly stragglers and maybe some deserters, I'd say. Howsumever, they all minded their own business and went on by, peaceable and friendly — like they weren't looking for loot or trouble and only wanted to get shut of the war."

George Harrison glanced at Jennings, said, "That's so, but only this mornin', just before sunup, we heard a passel o' horsemen — sounded like there might ha' been five or six of 'em — ride by our camp along the pike.

[523]

We wondered why they didn't halt for news and a bait of food. Folks goin' over the mountains gen'rally do."

A big woman whose vast bosoms rode easily under a calico shirtwaist approached Parthenia, said, smiling, "I'm Betty Harrison. Come on, sissy, we're friendly folks — as you can see — so there's no call to look so down at the mouth."

Snarled Parthenia, slanted eyes glittering, "Don't you dast touch me!"

"Why, you pert little baggage! I only — "

Jennings's wife intervened, soothingly, "Don't take on so, my dear. Nobody's going to force you to do anything. Land of Goshen! You *must* have had a hard time lately, you look *that* starved and weary. Come along to my tent."

A sigh of relief escaped Barry when Parthenia nodded and obediently trudged off after the former sergeant's wife.

The Road to Watauga

By now September was so far advanced that brooks had started to form skim ice along their edges at night and long V's of migrating geese could be seen flapping southward; their musically eerie honking was to be heard at almost any hour.

Now that Barry Colcord and his companions were acting as scouts in front of the column, Jennings and Harrison devoted most of their time caring for a small but precious herd of brown-and-white milch cows and a rambunctious little red Durham bull which, on account of his truly magnificent genitals, was known as "Gentleman Johnny Burgoyne."

Parthenia, still uncommunicative and moody, tried to help Jennings's wife Lucy about the cook fire but wasn't of much use. Her gaze was so blank that three Negro slaves belonging to the party wondered whether this mysterious young female weren't "tetched in de haid."

Shortly after the parties merged, Jennings and his men became insistent that Captain Colcord assume overall command. Former rangers Jennings and Harrison and their sober, grimly determined fellows guarded the main body while Black Buck and Tom Calloway scouted well out on the column's flanks.

Parthenia begged for scout duty, but Colcord curtly ordered her to the rear to herd the livestock. The rangy young thing looked daggers at him but ended by obeying sullenly.

On the third day after the union Colcord had turned the point over to Black Buck in order to ride back to see how the main body was faring when he glimpsed Parthenia Bryant riding well out to one side and cantered over to her.

"Why aren't you where you're supposed to be?"

Her pale eyes shone coldly from under a ratty fur cap someone had given her. "I ain't no soljer. I — I guess I c'n ride where I please."

Colcord grabbed her bridle, snapped, "Whilst I'm responsible everyone does what they're told, you included! Now, get back where you belong and keep on herding the stock or I'll paddle your backside."

Parthenia scowled before turning her mount and heading for the rear. She'd lived in a black mood ever since Mrs. Harrison had warned that once they reached the Shoals she'd have to wear a shirt and otherwise act like a decent female. While she'd said nothing, rebellion had begun to seethe in her soul.

Around noon Black Buck came back to report that he'd sighted a dead horse lying beside the pike; apparently it had died so recently that wild beasts had had no time to tear it.

Nobody in the column heeded the carcass lying stiff and forlorn in a little gully beside the track until Parthenia drew abreast. When she saw it, she uttered a thin scream, leaped off her mount and ran over to clutch the fallen animal's head to her chest. She began to curse and weep.

Exasperated at such nonsense, Colcord rode over. "What the hell ails you, girl?"

"He was my horse. They've killed him, damn them!"

"How d'you know he was your horse?"

Parthenia raised streaming eyes. "S-see that c-cross-shaped b-blaze on his forehead? I — I'd know it anywhere 'cause I p-picked him for my own from among the herd Billy and those fellers b-brought back."

Parthenia checked her sobbing. "If I'd been ridin' him he'd not have broke that there leg." Convulsively, she fingered her long-bladed sheath knife. "For that I'm goin' to slay some of them villains."

Tom Calloway drawled from behind her, "That'll take time, sissy, so 'bide yer chance and get back to drivin' stock."

Parthenia cast the Georgian a look of pure hatred before swinging back onto her tackey. "I'll kill 'em! By God, I will — and sooner'n anybody thinks!"

When she sneaked out of camp Parthenia Bryant had stolen, along with a carbine and powder and bullets, a square of old tarpaulin cloth which had been slit near its middle to make what later would be termed a poncho. Only this kept her slender, shivering body from being completely soaked, as using a broken branch for a whip, she drove her tackey splashing along the pike at its best pace. The animal was a clever little brute, which was fortunate, because it seemed able to follow the track when she herself couldn't see through the blinding storm more than a yard or two ahead.

Long before the beast slowed to a walk, then halted, Parthenia had been listening, and with ears sharpened by the frontier, thought to detect faint sounds other than those made by the wind and rain.

Barely in time she was able to rein off the pike and into a clump of balsams; heart hammering, she watched a big man ride by. He had his head bent into the storm and wasn't looking where he was going; like her, he was leaving things up to a big, bony gray which plodded ahead of two heavily laden pack horses following in single file with heads held low.

Once the little column had vanished amid a wild welter of lashing rain and flying leaves, Parthenia delayed a good while before returning to the pike — no point in getting jumped by anyone who might be following that lone rider.

Shielding her eyes and peering between fingers stiff with cold, the girl kept on. She guessed she might have felt as miserable before but she couldn't remember when. By now she was soaked to the skin, shivering violently and, worst of all, because she was riding bareback — she hadn't dared delay long enough to swipe a saddle — her wet buttocks were beginning to chafe and ache like fury. Her main concern, however, was to keep an oily rag she'd wound around the stolen carbine's lock in place and at the same time to not lose the bullet bag clutched under her poncho.

She must, Parthenia reckoned, have covered about another two miles before the sky cleared completely and the lowering sun's rays drove a measure of chill from her bones, but she kept on shivering; huge trees kept on dripping and trickling onto her as heavily as a spring shower.

The tackey splashed doggedly along rivulets which all too often followed the track's trampled, manure-browned course. Still there was no sight or sound of the men she was seeking and she was feeling almighty low when, on rounding a bend, she noticed, about a hundred yards ahead, a curl of bluish smoke hanging above a shallow ravine that cut across the pike.

To wait proved difficult, but she thought about Billy and her horse and forced herself to stay quiet until dusk began to gather; while it still was light enough to see clearly she set out through the underbrush making no more noise than a hunting vixen. True darkness was about to set in as Parthenia gained the lip of a little ravine from which smoke still was rising. Ah! She caught a faint glimmer of flames beyond the black pattern of sodden leaves.

Tethered between her and the campfire were three of the horses Billy and his companions had brought back. She recognized them beyond any shadow of uncertainty, so lay flat and kept as still as a hiding rabbit while making a careful survey of the group huddled about the fire. A fresh sense of outrage surged through her and momentarily dropped a transparent scarlet veil before her eyes. In this hollow were lounging those same villains who'd murdered Billy without granting him the least chance of defending himself.

Easily she recognized the tall, thin, yellow-bearded fellow, but not before she had mistaken Skelton for another bearded individual who also was wearing a ragged green uniform jacket and closely resembled him in build.

While she lay with teeth clenched to keep them from chattering, the girl thought about a story told long ago by a very old man. She recalled that many years back a woman named Hannah Dustin had been captured by Indians somewhere up in New England and had been forced along with her children, to undertake a long, hard march towards Canada. Parthenia recalled the old gaffer's saying that Mrs. Dustin had waited one night till her captors all had fallen asleep. Then that old-time frontierswoman had seized the nearest tomahawk and successively had slain each and every one of her captors! How strange that she should remember the ancient's adding, "What's more, Hannah scalped them redskins and brung home their hair!"

Parthenia hoped that since these men had been drinking hard, they should fall asleep early. Soon they obliged her, and, after throwing wood on the fire, rolled up into shapeless outlines around the firelight's perimeter.

At length everyone seemed to have fallen asleep, and fortunately, the fire still burned brightly enough to show where the sleepers lay. Cautiously, Parthenia got to her feet but was so wet and stiff she could barely move during the several minutes required to unwind the wrappings on the carbine.

Fierce joy surged through her while with infinite care and delicacy she drew back the icy-feeling hammer through half, all the way back to full-cock. For the first and only time that day she blessed the rain which had so drenched this hollow that no twig snapped nor did any leaf rustle. Lugging the carbine in her left hand Parthenia soundlessly parted branches, dodged bushes and otherwise made her way towards that hand ax stuck in the tree.

Bent well forward, Parthenia neared the fire until she found herself standing directly above a fellow who lay face down, with his hat fallen off. The same half-strangled sensation she'd suffered when her brother had been murdered returned, only stronger this time. Expertly, her cold hand hefted the hatchet as she straightened and while raising her arm remembered what a Long Hunter once had said — that the only sure way of killing a man outright, without raising an outcry, was to strike him squarely on the center of his poll.

Parthenia put all her weight and muscle behind the blow and did just that. The hatchet caused a soft *ta-chunk!* as if it had only split a ripe melon. The sleeper never even stirred.

To free the blade proved more of a task than the girl had bargained for, but by planting a foot on the fellow's shoulders, she succeeded, and was preparing to strike again when a panther high on the hill screeched. Immediately the three remaining outlaws roused from their blankets, cursing and fumbling for their guns as they peered stupidly about the hollow.

"Ye bastards!" Parthenia threw at a figure who was halfway erect. Her hatchet caught him flush on the side of his head and sank in deep; emitting a hoarse, choking cry the fellow swayed an instant and fell heavily.

At the same moment Parthenia whipped the carbine loosely to her shoulder and, recognizing Jasper Skelton, fired a snap shot. The weapon kicked like an angry mule and flew out of her grasp amid billowing smoke. She saw Skelton convulsively fling wide his arms and go staggering backwards until he collapsed across the dull red campfire.

Parthenia didn't delay but wheeled and tore off through the sodden woods back to the pike and began running and tripping towards her tackey.

Sycamore Shoals

In very few ways did Choice Valentine now resemble that delicate young lady whose family had set out from Bethlehem, Pennsylvania, well over a year ago. Her body, rid of adolescent fat, had lengthened and narrowed while her pretty pink-and-white complexion had turned a not unpleasing shade of light brown. Her now stringy honey-colored hair had turned a shade darker. The only things that remained unchanged about Choice were the fullness of her generously rounded breasts, the hue of her black-fringed somber eyes and the dark-red contours of her small, full mouth.

In skirt and breeches of bleached buckskin bright with beads and quill work she suggested a proud young Amazon who thought nothing of carrying a knife and a brace of little pistols clipped to her belt.

Slouched comfortably in her saddle she heard Dan Maddox ask a fellow who was returning to Sycamore Shoals from Fort Patrick Henry how much farther on lay their destination.

"Ten, mebbe fifteen miles, I reckon," drawled the wizened old man. "Ought to git thar in time to watch the sun set." His effort to bite off a chew exposed ruinous black-and-yellow teeth. "Ye'll find it quite a place. Yep, this last year the Shoals hev growed into a considerable burg. Above five hundert folks live there, or real close by, and there'll be more refugees showin' up all the time till winter sets in fer keeps."

Dr. Samuel Mason, astride a ribby bay gelding, only half heard the ancient's observation; he was much too preoccupied in wondering how his wife might be coming along. Wouldn't it be just his infernal, continual bad luck to be away when Rosemary would be delivered of their child? Of course, he had given Josh detailed instructions about what to do if anything really went wrong; but nothing should. There were plenty of "wise women" among those feeble stations which, during the spring of '80, had sprung up around the fairly sound fort James Robertson had built on the Frenchman's Bluff. Now the place was known as Bluff Station and provided a refuge for nearby weaker stations.

Mason reined to allow ex-Sergeant Dan Maddox, big, calm and steady as ever, to ride up beside him.

Tim, of course, was keeping Choice company, but everyone around Nashborough — as some people were beginning to call Bluff Station in honor of General Francis Nash, a patriot who'd got himself killed in action early in the war — was aware that whatever might have passed between them during the winter march was now over and done with.

The gunsmith was feeling more contented than he had been for some time, in fact, ever since a trapper had appeared at the Bluff bringing the exciting rumor that Dan'l Morgan was about to reassemble his riflemen in a desperate, final effort to save the republic. Unexpectedly, several immigrants had volunteered to return to the wars but hadn't been able to get themselves equipped in time to accompany Dr. Mason and Major Valentine to Fort Pat Henry.

Yes, sir, if what that trapper had said about Dan'l Morgan's returning to the war was true — well, he and Tim Murphy were figuring to be among the first to rejoin the Old Wagoner. But, of course, no one could credit even a little of the rumors which sometimes seeped across the mountains.

Absently he stroked Ilsa's glowing tiger-striped maple stock, but frowned over the presence of too many bruises and scores marring that beautiful satiny surface. Yep. First thing he'd do when he reached the Shoals would be to find a gunsmith and borrow the use of his tools for a while. For some time Ilsa had needed a new pan cover and a set-screw to hold a flint firmly in the cock's jaws. Nor had he been able, with all his skill and the tools at his disposal, to fashion a first-class frizzen out of nothing. Tim's double-barreled Goucher also stood in need of considerable attention; the right barrel's lock by now simply couldn't be trusted any longer to handle more than a moderate powder charge.

Tim came up growling, "That gal's so all-fired set-up with the idee of meetin' some fancy new men she won't even pass the time of day with an old friend."

Why in God's name, he wondered, hadn't Choice said the word? If she had, by God, he'd never have even glanced at another woman — for a while, anyway. Why, when they'd known each other so damn' sweetly on so many occasions, hadn't the memory of them made a difference? Maybe it was because she'd never got pregnant, for all he'd tried his best to bring that about. A terrible possibility struck him for the first time. Was she afraid he was sterile and couldn't father a brat?

Choice, riding up to join the leaders of the little party, pulled in beside the doctor. It had proved quite a blow to the girl's vanity that, despite

[529]

proven wiles, she hadn't been able to lure Sam Mason from Rosemary. Of course, some small-minded folk could claim that Sam and Rosemary weren't *legally* married yet. Colonel Robertson had felt himself qualified as a civil official to preside in the absence of an ordained minister, so, solemnly enough, he had read the marriage service one blustery March morning when the log palisade protecting Bluff Station was only half raised.

Major Valentine rumbled to the old guide, "Do we sight the Shoals from the top of the next rise or don't we?"

"Likely you will, Squire, or I don't know my way around these parts."

Sam Mason shifted in his saddle, glanced at a waterproof bag protecting the original black portfolio he'd compiled despite so many difficulties and dangers. What could have happened to the copy he'd forwarded to Fort Patrick Henry in Captain Blackmore's care? Even now, he'd learned nothing except that Blackmore had disappeared and that the papers never had reached their destination. God send they'd fallen into the hands of truly wild Indians unable to comprehend their importance. Yes. Probably Blackmore's scalp and that of a Long Hunter sent along to protect him right now were decorating some Shawnee's smoke-filled wigwam.

Bitterly, Samuel Mason, M.D., lamented those weeks which had elapsed before the arrival of a messenger sent by Colonel Sevier to inquire why his information had never reached the fort. Well, this time Sam Mason intended to place his data in John Sevier's own hands or in those of his immediate deputy.

From the brow of a steep little hill the saddle-weary travelers from Middle Tennessee obtained a fine view of the town called Sycamore Shoals. Established on land purchased from certain Cherokee chiefs of questionable authority, the place soon had become populated largely by sturdy Scotch-Irish immigrants from the hills of North Carolina, but there were also a good many rough-and-ready backcountry Virginians and more than a scattering of sober, industrious and curiously superstitious Pennsylvania Dutch.

Nowadays this burgeoning little town included over a hundred log cabins and pine-slab habitations of varying sizes built on rich bottomlands created within a wide sweeping bend in the Indian River. The sprawling town lay under the guns of a well-built fort which had risen right after the still-disputed Treaty of Sycamore Shoals had been signed back in 1772.

"What an admirable situation for a town," Virginius Valentine commented. "I'd venture yonder's a natural focus for trade routes crossing the mountains."

"Aye," nodded the old guide. "We got mebbe five or six pikes, traces and roads all leadin' straight to the Shoals."

Dr. Mason made no immediate comment because he was experiencing a lifting sensation on sighting a crude version of the Stars and Stripes fluttering above the fort's lookout tower. All at once he realized he hadn't beheld an American flag in nearly two years. In fact, he'd continually been astonished that so few of the people going out to Tennessee had ever even seen the flag of their country.

The physician gathered his reins and called over his shoulder, "Since it's downhill and not much farther to go, suppose we take up a trot?"

News of Parthenia Bryant's amazing exploit had preceded the Jennings party into Sycamore Shoals, with the result that when a lone, hard-looking individual herding several good-looking horses appeared, the surviving Shell Towner promptly was arrested for confinement in the guardhouse of the fort. Meanwhile, the animals were impounded pending his trial.

In a way, Barry Colcord was feeling well pleased because Parthenia's arrival was diverting curiosity from himself and his mission, and also because he'd no longer feel responsible for this pathetic, half-wild young female.

Strangely enough, once Parthenia had achieved her revenge she'd quit being quite so bristly and unfeminine; she'd even taken to hiding her worn and patched breeches beneath a short, fringed skirt of buckskin pressed upon her by Mrs. Jennings.

Once the Jenningses and their companions had pitched camp on the edge of that rich plain on which Sycamore Shoals had risen, Barry signaled Saul Black Buck and Calloway and, followed by them, made for the fort, which when one got close to it didn't look like much — at least not from a regular soldier's point of view; nevertheless, the palisade was high and stout, while its curtain walls and corner blockhouses mounted a respectable number of cannon and swivels.

If any sort of interior guard was being maintained it wasn't noticeable, Barry decided; only a pair of long-haired fellows wearing dirty crossbelts and faded blue jackets seemed to be on duty before the main gate. Both had stood their muskets against the palisade and, watched by a circle of boys and stray dogs, were flipping knives in a game of mumblety-peg.

"Is Colonel Sevier in the fort?" Barry asked stiffly. God above! Discipline around here seemed to be even worse than in Carolina.

"Yep. Ye'll find Johnny up in the commandant's office."

Barry crossed the grassless, sunburned parade ground, which no doubt was designed to double as a refuge for settlers and their stock during an Indian raid.

He found Lieutenant Colonel Sevier bent over a table desk and immediately was impressed that the commandant's blue-and-white uniform really fitted him and that his gold epaulets and buttons were clean and shining. Perhaps because of his crisp white wig, John Sevier's long, clearly chiseled features appeared coppery hued as any Indian's.

Smiling, the tall North Carolinian heaved himself to his feet and offered a hand. "And whom have I the pleasure of addressing, sir?"

Standing to rigid attention, Barry stated his name, rank and former command, though it hurt to mention the Ricelands Troop.

Sevier waved to a seat of rawhide laced over a hickory frame. "Please to sit, sir, and tell me more of the situation in Carolina."

After dispatching an orderly to fetch leathern jacks of scuppernong wine, Colonel Sevier permitted penetrating gray eyes to consider his caller.

"— And now, Captain, suppose you tell me what's brought you here?"

Once Colcord had given a cautious description of the mission on which Colonel Armand had sent him, the commandant nodded thoughtfully. "So that's it. Well, Colcord, I presume you know that both Shelby and I share the council's confidence, so I'll say it's timely you've shown up this soon after Dr. Mason's arrival."

"Dr. Mason's here?"

"Yes. He only reached this place yesterday evening, along with some people from those new settlements along the Lower Cumberland River. After identifying himself, the doctor made only a preliminary statement, but he left some — er — documents in my custody." He studied the younger man with care. "After I have studied them and when Colonel Shelby returns, we'd better talk again."

"Sir, to which state does your county belong?"

"Some tell me it's Virginia, some say North Carolina. At the moment," Sevier said carefully, " 'tis believed we belong to the latter state, but no one can be sure till surveyors, already at work, have run a line out west."

"And what, sir, is Colonel Shelby's responsibility? I gather you are in joint command here?"

"He's colonel of Sullivan County, just as I suffer the same responsibility here in Washington County."

" — And just what is the kind of colonel you speak of?"

Sevier laughed briefly. "Why, in effect, we're sort of half-arsed, civilian-military subgovernors with only temporary authority from the state of North Carolina. Damned if either of us has any clear idea about our powers."

Outside a dull hubbub began. The lounging guards caught up their arms and ran to block the gate but were too slow. A short, thick-bodied man on a fast-looking badly lathered horse already had pounded through it. He dismounted immediately and, after yelling something at the sergeant of the guard, ran up to the commanding officer's door.

His face and beard were speckled with dust. Wide dark sweat marks showed on his back and under the arms of a faded brown canvas uniform coat.

"Sir, Cunnel Cleveland's done sent you a proclamation just wrote by Major Patrick Ferguson — damn his Tory soul to hell!" growled the messenger. He spat savagely, then fumbled in a shot bag and pulled out a crumpled sheet.

"Where did you come by this?"

[532]

"Near the Cowpens. An officer of the cunnel's done give it me two days back and he says, says he, 'Ride like hell to Watauga and give this to the commander there.'"

Sevier's heavy black brows merged. "Where is Colonel Cleveland now?"

"Cain't say. Only he was headed for Morgantown Gap and herdin' a gre't passel o' homeless folk from Carolina; they're bein' chased by the Tories so hard there ain't no tellin' just where they're to be found right now."

"About how many folks is Cleveland guarding?"

"Mebbe a thousand souls, mebbe half ag'in that many more." Without invitation the messenger plunked himself down on a three-legged stool. "Ain't ye goin' to read what I've rid so hard to bring ye?"

"Haven't you read it?" demanded Sevier.

"Naw, I ain't lettered, nohow."

John Sevier's blunt, brown fingers began to unfold the crumpled rain-and-perspiration-stained broadside. "How many fighting men would you say Colonel Cleveland's got with him?"

"Search me," the messenger grunted, then got up on badly patched cowhide boots to tramp over and help himself from a bucket of drinking water. "Four to five hundret 'twould be my guess — but I ain't nowise knowledgeable."

The colonel of Washington County slowly smoothed the sheet of paper; then, as he read, a rich red flush appeared above his neck band and shot to the roots of his hair. "Now, by God! This really tears it!"

"How?" Colcord queried.

"Read this!" He passed over the proclamation.

To see more easily, the Carolinian moved to the nearest of three small windows imperfectly illuminating the commandant's office and read in poorly set type:

To all Rebels Lurking beyond ye Mountains:

Herewith you are summoned to lay down your Arms and Disperse at once. You will then return peaceably to your Allegiance to His Britannic Majesty, King George the Third.

Should you fail in this I will march my Forces over ye Mountains, Hang your Leaders and so Waste your Country with Fire and Sword that a Buzzard flying over it will find Naught on which to Feed excepting the Bodies of Dead Rebels.

> Patrick Ferguson
> Major, Commanding His Majesty's
> American Volunteers in North Carolina

Watched by the grimy messenger, the commandant for several moments strode back and forth before his desk. Finally he halted before Colcord, growled, "Well, at least one thing's plain. We'd better fight his army to the east of the Smokies — so, if we get licked, as well we may — we still can retire through the gaps and defy those bastards to follow."

Once the courier had clumped out, grinning like a horse collar, John Sevier returned his attention to the cavalryman. "And now, sir, will you tell me how the war goes beyond the Alleghenies?"

Seating himself, the commandant listened intently to Barry's description of disasters occurring the past few weeks.

Only when the handsome young Carolinian mentioned Colonel Armand's visit to Tranquillity did the neatly uniformed figure straighten and speak. "Thank you, Captain. I feel well informed." He paused, then lowered his voice. "Before we go any further, did Colonel Armand and his friend give you words by which you and I can positively identify ourselves?"

Colcord went over to close the door, which had been left slightly ajar, then bent over the commandant's desk and in a low voice said, "Xenophon."

Sevier nodded and in equal gravity gave the countersign, "Cincinnatus."

At once, Sevier sent a runner to fetch Dr. Mason, who with Major Valentine and his daughter was lodging in a rough little inn called the Sachem's Head.

With truly surprising speed the physician appeared and repeated the council's words of identification. At once Barry Colcord became deeply impressed by this brown-eyed stranger's bearing and mode of speech. He took Samuel Mason, M.D., to be some seven years his senior — around thirty-four years of age. They were about of a height — five foot nine — but the newcomer was heavier built and his small, round eyes were dark brown while his own were dark blue.

"Before we go any further with this business," Sevier announced, "I believe we'd best repair to my hut. The walls around us are leaky and the floors so thin that if a mouse scratches its whiskers in here it can be heard in the guardroom below."

The doctor picked up the large and awkward leather-covered case he'd brought in and kept between his feet. Silently he prepared to follow his host.

By the means of judicious bribery Major Virginius Valentine had secured a temporarily vacated bedroom for a private dining room but retained small hopes that the meal would in any way prove cheerful. Major Ferguson's proclamation had fanned sentiments already bitter into blazing resentment.

All along the haphazard streets of the settlement, refugees who'd been hurt or who'd been forced to witness the burning of their property or the hanging of friends and relatives listened to semidrunken orators proclaim that a day of reckoning was drawing near.

Mason considered his sister-in-law when she came in. *Certes!* Choice was a vision of loveliness; somehow she'd managed to bring along an Eastern-made dress. Further, during the afternoon she'd found opportunity to wash and comb her honey-colored hair and even had tucked little bows of faded blue ribbon above her ears.

The two men smiled when Choice lamented because she'd no real slippers left and had been forced to wear Indian moccasins; this she hated because a lack of heels made her appear even shorter than she was.

Choice's large dark eyes glistened and her red lips formed a teasing smile. "This offers to be the event I've dreamt of so long! A real gentleman actually is coming to dine!"

While drying his hands, Samuel Mason wondered just how his wife might appear at present. Certainly Rosemary's waist would be nowhere near so slender nor her hair half so lustrous as her twin's.

Choice pleaded, "Sam, please be sweet and tell me more about this dashing Southerner. Has he a pleasing manner?"

"Yes, and without being affected about it," the doctor assured her. "To my mind he's the first thoroughly well-bred individual I've encountered in many a blue moon." He winked at Valentine. "Aside from my father-in-law, of course."

" — And his voice? Does he have a nice voice?"

"Sounded pleasant enough to me."

Choice drew a quick breath. "Is — is Captain Colcord married?"

"No. I believe recently he has lost his wife and a child under tragic circumstances."

"Oh, what a dreadful pity," Choice murmured, then fluffed her hair and went to peer out of the window. "I do hope he won't be late. I vow I'm fairly perishing to — "

She broke off, hearing footsteps mounting the inn's stairway of half logs. Came a knock and then Barry Colcord appeared in the improvised dining room's entrance; he blinked through rank-smelling fumes given off by the beef-tallow dips.

Choice's bright, brown-black eyes rounded to their limits; never before had she experienced a sensation like this — so powerful and so deliciously unique.

The electric moment ended when Dr. Mason performed introductions, but its impact lingered.

A coarse but nourishing meal of pork chitlings, applesauce, boiled turnips and sweet potatoes was consumed with ever-decreasing diffidence. Before long, Choice found herself describing with considerable vivacity and humor young Jonathan Robertson's running feud with Old Scratch, who'd survived the midwinter journey to beget a goodly number of lambs whose dispositions, happily, seemed at variance with that of their cantankerous sire.

" — And what's become of the lad?" Barry inquired, gaze riveted on the raconteuse.

"He's growing like the proverbial weed," Major Valentine interrupted. "During the troubles last summer he took after his father and assumed a man's stature — especially after his brother James got murdered by the savages."

"Come, come!" Sam Mason broke in. "Let us not burden Captain Colcord with our woes. I'm sure he's had plenty of his own."

Colcord held up a hand. "That's most considerate, sir, but, if you don't mind, I'd like to hear more about what happened after your expedition reached the Frenchman's Bluff."

Major Valentine stroked his large nose a moment, then described how, shortly after the overland column's fast-moving division had crossed the frozen Cumberland and had reached their goal on a particularly frigid New Year's Day, the construction of Bluff Station had been commenced right away.

Rains's and Todd Phillips's slow division, which had tarried at Mansker's, had arrived some weeks later. After that, several weak or badly sited stations had been thrown up along the river close by Bluff Station, which had been planned and constructed by Colonel Robertson himself.

About a mile and a half downstream from the Frenchman's Bluff, Amos Eaton, who had come west with a small party of his own, had raised a cluster of unfortified but fairly comfortable cabins. Dr. Mason had elected to settle there with his bride, chiefly because Eaton's Station was so centrally located.

Thanks to some tolerable Monongahela whisky absorbed by the men and Choice's determined efforts to be gay, the occasion ended in an atmosphere of something approaching cheerfulness.

Finally, Barry got to his feet and bent over Choice's hard little hand. "Ma'am, I hesitate to desert such pleasant companionship but I fear I must return to the fort. Colonel Sevier has offered me accommodations there. Thank you, Major, and you, Doctor, for your courteous hospitality."

He bowed to the men, then brushed the girl's hand with his lips. When he straightened, their glances met and clung so long that Valentine and the doctor exchanged amused glances.

Choice murmured in soft and urgent undertones which Tim Murphy might have recognized. "For me, sir, this has been a — a — the most delightful evening. I — I trust — we, that is, will see you again?"

To his considerable surprise Barry Colcord, while riding Eclipse out to witness the hanging of the surviving Shell Towner, sensed no consuming hatred for the man — rather, he felt more like a legal representative obligated to witness an execution.

Not so Parthenia Bryant. She rode up with pale eyes dilated and bright as those of a night-hunting house cat. "Hope to God they don't break his neck when they swing him. Hope the villain strangles real slow an' kicks an' struggles the longest while! Hangin's a heap too good for the likes of him!"

At least half a thousand people must have assembled to watch an oxcart convey the condemned man, sobbing and shivering with fear, to the base of a stunted oak. Around the prisoner's neck already dangled the rope which pretty soon would choke the life from his body. As the cart creaked forward, curses and primordial sounds arose — very similar to noises which once had arisen at Cobb's Mill.

Parthenia grated, "Look at him, Mister Cap'n. Only hope the devil's pitchfork is good and hot and ready to catch his soul!"

In something like astonishment at her vindictiveness, Barry considered this lithe young creature beside him, then realized that she'd attempted to improve her appearance. Parthenia actually had washed her face and neck; her short hair looked considerably less untidy. Excitement, moreover, had heightened her color. In fact, at the moment Parthenia Bryant, because of her buckskin skirt and a clean cloth shirtwaist, appeared more attractive, more feminine than he'd ever seen her.

When the oxcart halted under a thick limb a minister, the Reverend Samuel Doak, tried to climb up to speak with the condemned man, but the crowd pulled him back yelling, "Let the murderin' whoreson die uncomforted!"

As a barefooted youth shinnied out on the limb and quickly secured the rope, the doomed man screamed in a shrill, inhuman voice, "Spare me! For God's love, spare me! Oh, no! Don't! Please, friends, please don't kill me. I ain't fit to die!"

Parthenia jumped off her tackey and raced over to the cart, shaking her fist and squalling, "Damn yer black soul! Ye're as fit to die now as ye'll ever be! Swing him! Swing him!"

Barry dismounted, caught Parthenia by her wrist and dragged her back. "That'll do! Does you no good to sink to that poor devil's level."

To his amazement the girl all at once broke into tears, flung arms about him and clung, sobbing. "Hang onto me! I don't know how to think no more! What if 'twasn't him shot Billy?"

A curious semigroan rose from the crowd when the ox driver used his goad, yelled, "Hup! Git! Git!"

Even Parthenia was satisfied with the length of time the attenuated figure kicked and writhed before its motions gradually slowed and a fine trickle of urine began to drip proving that the man was dead.

Only because Lieutenant Colonel Isaac Shelby, originally from Maryland, already had started back from the race meeting at Jonesborough did he appear in Sycamore Shoals so early the next morning. With him came his brothers, Evan and Moses; a third brother, James, would arrive later and bring along as many recruits as could be mustered in that part of the country.

Since Shelby already had heard about Ferguson's threat his naturally hot blood had cooled somewhat, but he still was mad clear through and in his deep-set blue eyes lurked dangerous lights.

It didn't take long for Shelby and Sevier to assemble a council of war which included citizens representing various settlements scattered about the Watauga country. Right away a rider was sent to hurry up those riflemen who'd left Bluff Station after Dr. Mason had set out.

Once the council convened there wasn't much oratory or discussion; everybody agreed with the co-commanders it was wiser to fight the Tories east of the Great Smokies than wait for them to invade and ravage the settlements.

This course also would preclude the possibility of an outbreak by pro-British tribes already stirred up by Crown agents; these would be only too eager to pounce and exterminate defeated Americans and nullify, in torrents of blood, the one-sided Treaty of Sycamore Shoals by which many hundreds of square miles had been ceded to the whites by Creek and Cherokee chiefs through dubious negotiations.

A decision also was taken to dispatch messengers to leaders of patriot irregulars thought to be operating east of the mountains urging them to come as fast as they could to Sycamore Shoals or, if unable, to join the Western Volunteer Army just east of Jonesborough; failing that, they must appear somewhere on the Wilderness Road between the mountains and Morgantown.

"Now that that's settled," drawled the colonel of Sullivan County, "all we need do is to find out how many troops Major Ferguson has along and how good they are."

It was decided that an immediate appeal should be hurried to Colonel William Campbell of Virginia, whose militia from time to time had been opposing Ferguson's advance. Campbell, someone volunteered, was supposed to be leading four hundred weary and hungry men.

Also to be located were other patriot commanders: that elusive North Carolinian Colonel Cleveland, as well as Colonel James Williams and Colonel William Graham from the same state.

Aside from these was mentioned Colonel Ben Williams and an aged General McDowell, also from North Carolina, but no one knew how many followers these officers were leading or where they could be found.

Nevertheless, riders were sent in search, hurrying along the Wilderness Road towards Morgantown Gap.

Captain Barry Colcord, sitting quietly to one side, was both amazed and stimulated by the grimly determined manner of the meeting.

An important question then arose: who would assume overall command once the scattered forces became united? For this responsibility Sevier and Shelby, both lieutenant colonels, favored hard-faced William Campbell of Virginia — a redoubtable frontier fighter who held the commission of full colonel.

Jollification

For the next few days Colonels Sevier and Shelby's Overmountain Boys began to arrive at the Shoals; usually they came in alone or by twos and threes but sometimes even a dozen would report to the fort at the same time. Most were reasonably well mounted and all carried long rifles, shiny tomahawks and scalping knives slung to their belts.

Hunting shirts of various sorts and colors from white to dark brown or black were so usual that these came to constitute a sort of rough and practical uniform. For baggage each new arrival carried only a blanket, a kettle and a fodder sack in addition to an ammunition bag and a greasy haversack containing a scant supply of food.

Loud and generally obscene greetings were exchanged whenever new arrivals rode into town. Often these hard-bitten characters were accompanied by favorite bear dogs, so some mighty noisy and often bloody fights took place when they tried conclusions with local canines.

Everyone felt vastly encouraged when the first elements of Colonel William Campbell's thin and footsore Virginia Volunteers appeared and went into camp near the fort. With them they brought fresh tidings of disaster; Major Ferguson, it seemed, had chased these Virginians for several days with a well-trained and equipped army supposed to number nearly two thousand.

Later, reports came in that the Tories had halted on the other side of the mountains close to Gilbert Town and were in a position to block the retreat of Colonel Elijah Clark, who was attempting to guard a motley column of defeated patriots and their families trying to escape westward from Georgia and South Carolina. Also it was rumored that Ferguson had appealed to Lord Cornwallis for quick reinforcements — by Tarleton's British Legion if possible.

When, on the twentieth of September, Colonel James Williams of North Carolina came in leading another hundred rangy and hard-eyed riflemen, a decision was taken to wait no longer. On the morrow the little army would set out along the well-traveled Wilderness Road towards Morgantown Gap.

To his mild astonishment Dan Maddox actually found himself anticipating another sight of that girl who'd so tickled his interest when first she'd appeared at the smithy. When finally she did appear, Parthenia examined his work with an experienced and critical eye. At last she smiled and her smooth brown face lit and softened.

"Say, Mr. Maddox, there's a real first-rate mendin' job. Thanks a heap!" She fumbled in a small leather pouch slung to her belt and offered a handful of coins. "Just take out what you figger's comin' to you."

The ex-ranger laughed and was glad that for the moment no one was within hearing distance. "All right, sis, I'll just do that!" Before she suspected what Dan intended he'd grabbed her close and planted a resounding smack full on her mouth.

Parthenia's reaction wasn't what he expected; the girl just stood there looking as if someone had clubbed her on the head; her eyes gradually rounded and her thin brown lips parted until she raised a hand to rub its back across her lips.

"What's wrong, Parthy? Was that so bad?"

She felt blood rush up to heat her features. " — N-no, Mr. Maddox, but this is the very firstest time I ever got bussed by anybody 'ceptin' Ma."

Hands on hips, the leather-aproned gunsmith surveyed his client, a foolish half grin decking his features. "Well, and how do you feel?"

"Don't know," came her surprising reply. "Like Ma said once upon a time, 'One robin don't make a spring.' "

That night began a spontaneous jollification. An enormous bonfire was kindled in a harvested cornfield near the river. Liquor flowed freely from various sources. Drums, fiddles, flutes and even a trumpet or two assembled into what might be misnamed a band of music.

By the hundreds, residents and transients flocked to the scene while taverns reluctantly disgorged happily inebriated customers attracted by all that singing, shouting and stamping down by the water.

Along with a few other officers Barry Colcord handed Choice to a small rise from which the party viewed the frolics without risk of getting jostled or assaulted in drunken camaraderie. He'd seen Major Valentine's daughter several times, having become attracted not only by her piquant good looks but also by her seemingly genuine desire to be near him whenever possible. Only the night before, he'd been surprised to find himself describing, for the first time since it had taken place, the destruction of Ricelands and the murder of his wife and child.

"I don't see how you can ever get over it."

"Maybe I never will; not altogether, that is, but, as wiseacres say, time is the great healer. All the same, right now I doubt whether I wish ever to return to Georgetown County."

"Are you certain?" Choice asked almost too readily.

"Of course I don't know, but somehow I feel that when this confounded war ends — if it ever does — I'll send for my son and take up land somewhere around here."

Choice had caught her breath, said hurriedly, "Whatever you decide, Captain, for heaven's sake don't even dream of going so far west as the Tennessee stations."

"Don't think I will," said he seriously. "I'm far too green on the frontier to last long, but perhaps I may settle somewhere around Watauga. Think that's a sound idea?"

She did.

Faces tinted red-gold by the bonfire's glow, they listened to gaunt, hairy men sing tunes which had crossed the Atlantic long, long ago, many of them during the reign of Elizabeth, the Virgin Queen.

"I was only wondering," said Barry, "how many of those men singing and dancing down there will be alive after we've met the Tories. A stupid, morbid thought, is it not?" Before he knew what he was doing he'd slipped a hand around her waist.

She made no effort to move aside. "I presume a good many women and children are wondering the same thing."

"No doubt. At least their men are lucky enough to have someone worry over what may happen."

Choice turned, reached up and kissed him on the cheek. "Oh, Barry, you'll have someone, too; with all my heart I'll pray for you. Should you — if you ever could want me I'll wait for you here."

"You'd really wait?"

"Oh, my dear, forever, if you tell me to."

Dan never joined the jollification. Recalling the Bryant girl, he shook off his companions and sought the Jennings camping place. Only two or three women were sitting in semidarkness, gossiping and vainly attempting to disguise their dread of the morrow.

Dan wasn't overly surprised to find Parthenia sitting in front of her tent chipping sharper edges onto some fine-looking gun flints.

"Heyo, sis."

She looked up half smiling. "Heyo yerself, Mr. Maddox. Why ain't ye whoopin' and prancin' with the rest of them drunken ijits?"

He squatted on his heels beside her. "Why ain't you?"

"Because I ain't a ijit and I don't fancy crowds nohow."

"No more do I," he said, then helped her to her feet. "Suppose you and me walk along the shore a piece and watch the goin's on from a distance?"

Before she put away her instruments she held out a handful of dully glistening red-brown flints. "Here, these are fine French stones. I want you should have 'em."

"Why for?"

"Likely you'll have need of such 'fore you kin tack that devil Ferguson's hide to a barn door."

When she started to leave her ragged little tent she realized Mr. Maddox was blocking its exit, also that he seemed to be having trouble with his breathing. She guessed it must be the liquor he'd guzzled; his breath fairly reeked of rum.

"Parthy," he began thickly. "Parthy, I — I — " He stepped inside the tent, which stood at considerable distance from the rest. "Parthy, I don't know what's come over me, but — but Ilsa's been a long time dead now. Since she died I ain't touched never a female woman. I — I, well, I want — "

Parthy retreated a couple of steps, said softly, "I know. I know and I'd sure be pleased to oblige you and I will, but — " through the dim light her

[541]

eyes bored intently into his — "I don't aim to become no man's leman. Ma, she taught me better, God rest her soul."

"Amen. But, Parthy, I ain't drunk and I — I've just *got* to have you. You're the only one I've ever wanted since Ilsa died." He put his arms around her slowly, gently. "*You* know what the frontier's like, *you* understand the meaning of fear, hunger and hardship."

She didn't resist when he drew her close enough to feel again the wondrous, delicate softness of a woman's breasts.

"Oh, Parthy, I've seen how good you work and heard how you, you 'venged yerself on those murderers all by yerself and, by God, that shines!" He tightened his arms about her, felt his blood heating past endurance and hungrily crushed her mouth.

At first Parthenia didn't resist; in fact, she pressed lips and body so hard against him he figured that, sure enough, he was home and dry with her.

But when Dan tried to slip a hand inside her shirt she suddenly twisted out of his grip and ran out of the tent. "I'm meanin' it when I say, Dan'l, I'd sure admire to live with you and bear you a lot of children — but I don't aim to, lest we visit a preacher first."

As, trembling a little, Dan hesitated before the slim, resolute figure, an overwhelming need seized him. He muttered, "Perhaps we'll do that — but why're you so confounded dead set?"

"The reason I'm so dead set," she explained seriously, "is 'count of I'm what some folks would call a 'woods colt' — same's a bastard in the frontier country. You see, Pa already had a wife when he married my ma. Me, I don't want none of my get to suffer like I have."

Dan Maddox gave in with a readiness which surprised him. "All right, Parthy, we'll have it yer way. But who is there to tie the knot?"

The girl's teeth glimmered in the dark oval of her face as she laughed softly, "Why, dearie, I *just* happened to hear they's a minister up to the fort — the Rev'rend Doak, I think."

When he held out his hand towards her Parthenia grabbed it and hugged it to her breast. "Well, come along, girl," he said. "Let's go and try to find this Bible-pounder. Ain't likely a man of God would be triflin' around a jollification."

When, not much later, they found their way back to Parthenia's tent they made awkward, violent love — as man and wife.

"The Sword of the Lord and of Gideon"

Not long before sunup a milling swarm of horsemen began to try to form in eight columns of twos on a big, vacant tobacco field lying on the southeast side of Sycamore Shoals, for when dawn had begun to glimmer, soldiers in the fort had fired a cannon as a warning for volunteers to assemble.

In the lead, as commanding officer for that day, rode Lieutenant Colonel John Sevier. He no longer was clad in neat, immaculate regimentals but wore a knee-length hunting shirt of butternut-dyed canvas such as he always used when in the field. The only indication of his rank was a pair of silver lace epaulets that flopped, awkwardly pinned to his shoulders.

In the interests of security, Dr. Samuel Mason rode with a rear guard composed of Overmountain men he knew and trusted, because he was carrying his original drawings, maps and notes describing Robertson's route to the Frenchman's Bluff. Captain Colcord, entrusted with a set of copies made during the past week, traveled in the van with the headquarters staff.

More through force of habit than anything else, Dr. Mason was prompted every evening to scribble in his journal a brief summation of the day's happenings.

26, Sept. 1780. This Day passed through Morgan-Town Gap and soon were joined by a very old North Carolina Gen'l who had with him about a Hundred-and-Sixty mounted Riflemen. Cols. Shelby, Sevier and Campbell wished Gen'l McDowell, because of his Superior Rank to assume Chief Command, but, he being Aged and Feeble, he declined the Honour in favour of Col. Wm. Campbell.

His next entry read:

Colonel Shelby today is Furious and Distracted because two previously Trusted Men belonging to his Headquarters Co. have Deserted and are Presumed to be riding straight to Major Ferguson to apprise him of our Strength and Intention.

Yesterday, we passed a Place called The Cowpens where it was learned that the Enemy, hearing of our Presence, has commenced a Retreat from Gilbert Town. It is Generally felt that the Tories will fall back upon the British Outpost called Ninety-six where Considerable Reinforcements and Supplies are said to be awaiting him.

A night or so later Mason wrote:

There is much Jubilation amongst us for at last we have met the elusive Col. Cleveland. He and his Troops entered on the Wilderness Road and met us purely by Chance. For us this is a most Fortunate Occurrence since he Commands near Four hundred Men as Tough and Bitter as any I have Beheld all during this War. They are Burning with Outrage over the Barbarous conduct of the King's Followers since our Defeat at Camden. Frankly, I would not Wish to be taken Prisoner by any of them were I a Loyalist.

When the little army halted for the night of October fifth, an escaped prisoner was brought to the headquarters tent before which Colonels Campbell, Sevier, Shelby and Cleveland were wolfing half-cooked suppers.

[543]

It appeared that this ragged fellow had got away only two days earlier, and when he began to recite his observations more and more high-ranking officers came to listen. The ex-prisoner satisfactorily answered all manner of questions designed to determine his honesty. His most valuable single piece of intelligence was that the American commanders were mistaken in believing the Tory forces to be falling back on Fort 96. Major Ferguson, instead, had turned away in a southeasterly direction, apparently with intention of joining Lord Cornwallis, the security of whose left flank had been entrusted to him and his corps of Tories.

"You're positive about this?" demanded florid-faced Colonel Campbell.

"Yep. I'm sure as a feller can be about anything in this crazy war. For a fact, I overheard some Tories from Noo Jersey laugh because they figgered to have sure 'nough fooled you fellers into believin' they was headed for Ninety-six."

Colonel Shelby, sucking on his pipe, made little watery noises. "All right, we'll credit that. Now, tell us, friend, does Ferguson have any regular British troops along?"

"Naw! Not a single goddamn one! All he's got with him is a lot of damn' tough Tories."

"What regiments are with him?" Colonel Williams wanted to know.

"Ain't exactly sure, but he's got some from a Noo Jersey volunteer regiment, some from the King's American Rangers and the Queen's Loyal Rangers. Both of 'em are from Noo York, but the heft of his people come from Georgia and the Carolinas — and a meaner lot I never want to see!"

Colonel Cleveland inquired, "About how many men would you say Major Ferguson has brought together?"

"Somewheres 'twixt a thousand or fifteen hundred of the murderin' bastards; most of 'em carry rifles and look like they know how to use 'em. Make no mistake about it, gents, if, and when, you come up with Ferguson, ye'll be tanglin' with first-class fighters."

King's Mountain

A small flock of passenger pigeons flying over King's Mountain in pursuit of the main migration which had followed this route the day before flared on sighting a low, club-shaped ridge which was about half a mile long and rose only about sixty feet high on the average. At its widest point this eminence was only a hundred yards wide and ran in a generally northeast-southwest direction. Near the club's head a few canvas-covered wagons were visible, surrounded by a sprinkling of tents.

Had they been interested, the birds also would have noticed a long and very thin column of mounted men traveling towards the base of that ridge known to mere humans as King's Mountain. It being still early in the day, the horses below, refreshed after a night's rest, were moving at a brisk trot.

Only a strong sense of duty prevented Dr. Samuel Mason from entrusting his portfolio to some reliable officer and then pushing ahead to join the hand-picked vanguard along with Tim Murphy, Dan Maddox and other volunteers from Middle Tennessee.

Now Mason was riding with those unlucky volunteers who'd come in on foot or whose mounts had broken down; altogether these numbered about four hundred — all of them spitting mad for fear the battle might be fought before they could join in and exact payment for their losses and sufferings.

Since he was a medical man, it appeared only his duty to remain with the wagons and be prepared to receive wounded men as soon as they appeared.

This, the morning of October 7, 1780, dawned without anybody's foreseeing that on this day the greatest battle of the first American civil war soon would be joined. Only much later would it be appreciated that the *only* professional British soldier to serve in the impending conflict was Major Patrick Ferguson himself, that on both sides, all combatants were Americans.

About two hours after daybreak a galloper came racing through the unlit woods to bring the electrifying news that the advanced contingent had succeeded in their mission! The Tory army had been found. It had camped and had taken up a defensive position on the summit of the long, low hill locally known as King's Mountain. The galloper couldn't say just how many men the Tory leader now was commanding, but it was thought that there were plenty of them.

Early in the morning, scouts reported to the advanced division's commanders that the enemy apparently had elected to decide the issue on or around King's Mountain. Later, it was reported that when Patrick Ferguson had learned of the enemy's approach he'd shouted, "I defy God Almighty and all the rebels out of hell to overcome me here!"

His point was well taken, since that redoubtable and very able officer had under his command some eleven hundred troops. Of these around a hundred were expert riflemen selected from New York and New Jersey Loyalist regiments; the bulk of his forces, however, were battle-hardened Southern Tory militia. Most of these, in place of nonexistent bayonets, had been equipped with long steel blades which, driven down the bore of a piece, converted a gun into a spear which could prove useful at infighting when no time was left for reloading. Such weapons, of course, couldn't be fired once these improvised bayonets had been inserted.

Observed Colonel William Campbell, "Reckon we've got just about sufficient men with us to surround yonder pesky ridge."

A local volunteer stepped forward and, employing a twig, traced the outline of a blunt, long-handled club on ground whitened by splotches of passenger pigeon droppings.

Intently, Colonel Campbell's staff followed the movements of the twig now being manipulated by the commanding officer himself.

"Now, I want you all to look close. This is about where we're standing. See? Right below the head of this here club head. Now, I want you, Lacey, Winston, Cleveland and Hambright, to stay put right here under General McDowell's direction.

"Meanwhile, Ike Shelby and you, Jim Williams, will lead your fellows along the ridge's north side till you reach the handle's end. Me and Johnny Sevier will do the same thing; only we'll advance around the south slope."

His gaze circled the intent brown faces about him. "Now, you fellows wait till you hear my men raise the war whoop Johnny Sevier's taught us. When you hear it, yell like hell, then we'll all swarm up that ridge the fastest we're able."

He spat and fingered a long knife at his belt. "Best of it is, I don't believe Ferguson's got any real notion of how many men we've brought along so he's apt to start shootin' at whichever crowd gets to the top first; probably he'll hurry his reserves to drive 'em back, which should grant us a fine chance of reachin' the summit without gettin' hurt too bad."

Colonel Campbell squinted up the hardwood-covered slope. "I want you all to remember this: if the enemy charges like he means it, just you fall back down the slope, drifting from tree to tree and killing every enemy you can. Now I figure, and I think you'll agree, that when Ferguson hears the whooping from another direction on the hill he'll most likely order his men back to the top to meet the new threat; that's when you start back up the slope — screeching all the while."

It was only natural that Maddox and Tim Murphy should elect to serve under John Sevier, most of whose three hundred riflemen had lived beyond the Alleghenies. So they joined up with a party of hard-eyed men from Western Virginia because they looked as if they really could handle themselves in a hot fight. Many of them had pinned up floppy-brimmed hats on one side, then had tucked a piece of paper into the fold to avoid being mistaken for Loyalists in civilian garb. A lot of patriots were taking that precaution.

Steadily, the mounted riflemen picked a route westwards through hardwoods growing along the sides and base of King's Mountain. Already men began to fidget and check their gear against the moment they'd be told to dismount.

Briefly, Dan thought back to other battles he'd been in and came to the conclusion that this fight would be different and possibly more deadly than any he'd known. For one thing, this time the enemy wasn't a lot of ramrod-stiff, drill-yard-trained redcoats who'd been taught the only way to fight a battle was to point, not aim, their muskets and deliver as many devastating volleys as they could at an enemy who should, according to the rules, be advancing in obligingly solid ranks. After that, it would be a "fix bayonets," charge and drive survivors into panic-stricken retreat. No. This time the men on top of the little ridge were no wooden-headed Europeans but a lot of fellow Americans, all too often the fathers, brothers or cousins of men beginning to take position along the base of the heights.

Gradually the forward movement of the troops ahead slowed, then an order was passed back for everyone to dismount and tie their horses to trees rather than turn the animals over to horse holders — apparently every last man was going to be used once the climbing and shooting began.

Grimly silent all at once, the riflemen got off, then tied coats and un-necessary gear to their saddles; with them, aside from their firearms, they would carry only ammunition bags, knives and war hatchets. Dan noticed that not a single bayonet was anywhere in sight.

Obedient to arm signals from their officers, the volunteers began to drift forward in a long, loose line abreast, but when they reached the foot of the wooded slope they were ordered to halt and wait for that whooping from Colonel Campbell's direction which would start them climbing and screeching like scalp-hungry redskins.

As Dan had anticipated, here was a novel experience. To tell the truth, until now he'd never been altogether sure about just *what* he was fighting for. He held nothing personal against those red-faced, often strange-talk-ing Englishmen — they hadn't cost him property nor had they murdered people he knew, but these fellows up on the ridge were different, except that they were fighting for King George III, same as the lobsterbacks he and Tim had been battling over all these years.

A rail-thin fellow to his right reckoned this must be about noontime, account of the sun shone almost directly overhead and all shadows were short.

Crouched behind a big, gray-barked beech, Tim, his small body taut and compact, fiddled with the Golcher's rear sight, adjusted it for close range. As near as he could foresee this tussle was going to develop into a nearly hand-to-hand affair offering a sharpshooter little chance to prove his skill.

Finally, from the left where Colonel Campbell had led his men some-one raised a clear, blood-chilling yell: "Whoo! Whoo-whoop!"

Even from a distance of eighty yards Colonel Sevier's men heard Billy Campbell shouting, "There they are, boys! Now shout like hell and fight like devils!"

Tom Calloway soon realized it was fine that the summit of this ridge was treeless; when he reached the top he'd know it. While he was jumping from behind one tree to the next he recalled how he'd begun this war as a red-hot patriot; then, because the Sons of Liberty kept getting whipped and most of his neighbors called themselves Loyalists, he'd signed up in Capt'n Catlin's troop of Georgia Tories and even had fought in a few skirmishes. But after a party of drunken king-lovers had murdered Pa and raped his young sister, he'd switched sides again — this time for keeps even though it had seemed like a mistake after what happened at Charles Town. Even now, Tom still felt right hot over Pa and Sis.

Over an increasing rattle of shots he heard whooping and shouting from above and the shrill screaming of a badly hit man. A moment later Tom sighted a broad-chested fellow slipping and sliding downhill; a bayonet gleamed at the end of his gun. Checking his descent the Tory squatted behind a mossy log and was looking about for a target when Tom threw up his rifle and fired a quick shot. Whether he hit or not, the Georgian had no time to find out. Suddenly where one bayonet had caught the sunlight now there were a dozen. There was something heart-stopping about the deadly shine of them.

Tom was still priming his pan when somebody shouted, "Fall back, boys! Them Loyalist bastards have got bayonets and it's too soon for knives and hatchets!"

Although a fearful racket was exploding on the top of King's Mountain, the Tories attempted a second bayonet charge, but it seemed considerably less forceful than their first. Shelby's men fell back again, but in doing so exacted a stiff price. Quite a few bodies came tumbling downhill. As before, the enemy's advance was checked less than halfway down the slope, and again the men in green or brown went laboring back to the summit.

On the far side of the handle of the club Dan Maddox, Tim Murphy and the rest of John Sevier's men were adopting much the same tactics. As they did so Dan became aware of murderous impulses sweeping through him as they had not since that frozen fight with the Indians after the crossing of Mad Bear Creek. Bayonets he'd seen in plenty before, but most of his companions had not, so felt less confident.

Twenty minutes after the first shots had crackled, the battle roared towards a crescendo because volunteers climbing up the club's head were nearing its summit. A fierce, ear-piercing clamor arose as, successively, Cleveland's, Hambright's and Winston's men emerged panting and sweat-soaked on the plateau.

Black Buck found a peculiar satisfaction in dropping a white who was wearing a single epaulet. Too bad he'd been forbidden to take that particular scalp; it plus the epaulet would have counted for plenty money after the battle. Unfortunately, Colonel Campbell had been most emphatic that no scalps were to be taken under any circumstances.

Everywhere sounded yelling and whooping and men crashing about, so the old mustee cunningly stayed where he was and took time to tighten the set-screw holding his flint in place. No use, at this late date, in getting knocked over by a stray bullet. Once he'd reloaded, he started up again, wishing his bony, bowed legs were stronger, like when he'd been a young buck full of piss and vinegar.

Dan Maddox, on emerging onto open and fairly level ground, quickly

[548]

perceived what was taking place; the main fight now had become centered near the head of the ridge where the wagons and tents were.

In quick succession, Campbell's and Shelby's breathless followers appeared and formed a line across the center of the handle of the club. Effectively their leader cursed, forcing them to wait for reinforcements from below. Nevertheless the raging riflemen didn't waste time; they kept on shooting point-blank into the disorganized mass of Tories, who were paying no attention to a handful of brave mounted officers who were riding back and forth and using the flat of their swords trying to form the now completely surrounded men into some sort of order.

Conspicuous on horseback, these officers were shot from their saddles in quick succession; soon only two remained visible.

A South Carolinian Maddox had eaten with the night before sang out, "See that busy bastard on the tall black horse? That there's *Ferguson himself!*"

Hearing him, Tim made a quick estimate of the range. Jesus! Ferguson wasn't riding above a hundred yards away!

Continually bumped and jostled, Tim tried to take a decent sight but simply couldn't, so, angrily, he used his left barrel to kill a big officer who amid clouds of rolling dust seemed to be rallying some men. Next, he debated whether or not to stop and reload Kitty's empty barrel. Hell no! He'd still a charge left so why not work his way ahead, get closer and wait for an opportunity to get a clear shot?

To any experienced officer the Tory situation had become desperate, if not hopeless; Major Ferguson, who certainly was one, nevertheless continued to rage back and forth, shouting and waving his sword. Because he'd long since lost his hat, his white wig shone bright in the hot sunlight and a silver gorget slung about his neck kept winking like a bright star.

The men who'd scaled the handle of the club then began to advance along the plateau, but paused when a glimmer of white cloth fluttered above the struggling throng. Tim watched Ferguson's sword flash as he cut down the surrender flag, then he did the same to a second. Ferocious, animal-like noises rose from the volunteers along with growls and infuriated shouts of, "Remember the Waxhaws!" "Remember Monck's Corner!" "Give 'em Tarleton's quarter!" "Shoot 'em, hew the bastards down!" "Kill, kill 'em!"

By some freak of battle the clumps of men in front of Tim suddenly separated long enough to afford him a brief, unimpeded view of that raging figure on the black horse. This time, by God, Tim told himself, it wouldn't be skill but the purest kind of luck if I succeed in killing Patrick Ferguson. Shouldering his beloved Kitty, he sighted as quickly as if shooting at a leaping buck, then pulled evenly on the Golcher's front trigger. Ha! Fierce delight flooded him when he saw Ferguson suddenly stiffen and then crumple over his pommel. The Tory commander clutched at his side, then sagged off his horse and disappeared among men milling desperately about him.

"By God!" Tim whooped. "Now don't that shine? Got him! Fraser with the left barrel, Ferguson with the right! Now I reckon I can die happy!"

Just an instant later he did just that, for an uncommonly brave Tory who had remained in the lee of a wagon well outside the swarming mass shot Tim Murphy through the heart.

Aftermath

As usual with undisciplined troops the effects of a victory proved almost as disorganizing and confusing as a defeat. For a while the victorious Volunteers remained where they were as if they couldn't comprehend that they'd won and, better yet, that most of them still were alive and unhurt. Once the initial shock wore off the victors began to look about and then move dazedly over the battlefield. Soon basic instincts asserted themselves. B'God, wasn't this just the right time to come by a good pair of boots, a fine or at least a sound rifle, a warm coat, or a bit of jewelry?

Most Volunteers began to rove about in search of dead bodies and among the bushes and weed-grown little gullies they found and stripped around one hundred and fifty-seven. Most of the enemy wounded also were plundered; if these protested, they died and not pleasantly, either. Wildly excited and vengeful riflemen continued to prowl everywhere along the crest and sides of King's Mountain, often quarreling as they found the fallen. They stuffed their pouches and carefully examined ownerless weapons.

Nobody paid the least attention to enemy wounded, no matter how a man moaned and pleaded — what had happened at Monck's Corner and the Waxhaws was still too fresh in their memories.

Once the sullen and generally terrified prisoners had been placed under a guard from Colonel Cleveland's hard-bitten North Carolina Militia Regiment — which was about the only unit to preserve even a semblance of discipline — the bodies of twenty-eight Patriots were collected for burial.

Some time before this happened Dan Maddox had come to realize he hadn't sighted Tim Murphy since Sevier's men had started sweeping along the plateau towards the club's head.

Anxious, he yelled at an Overmountain Boy he recognized, "Say, you seen anything of Murphy?"

The fellow's coonskin cap inclined as he swung by carrying a fine English saddle. "Sorry, friend, I guess he's got himself kilt."

"What!" Dan swayed as if struck by a strong wind. "You *sure?*"

"Yep, the little feller got knocked off towards the very last. It he ain't been carried off already you oughter find his corpse in a little hollow beyond the farthest wagon."

Successive ripples of icy water seemed to flow down Maddox's back to penetrate his heart. Oh hell! What was he getting so upset about? This fellow could hardly have known Tim at all; he must be mistaken! Nothing could ever happen to Tim Murphy — wasn't he as tough and durable as shoe leather?

Dan was wrong. He found Tim's small body lying all huddled up in a little gully as if he had been sleeping and had got cold. But this wasn't so; on the bottom of this depression his blood had created a glistening little pool.

For a long minute Dan Maddox stood frozen, trying to face this incredible fact. At the same time he recalled a flood of scenes: those campaigns they'd fought together up in New York State; that time an Irish bawd near had bitten his tongue through; the time Tim got carried about on his fellows' shoulders because he'd killed Burgoyne's general the way he had.

After supper Sam Mason, having helped to treat the last of the wounded, departed in search of Colonel Campbell's headquarters and to his delight came across Captain Colcord sorting captured documents by the light of a pine-knot flare. The Carolinian jumped up beaming to pump hands. "By God, Doctor, I'm mighty happy you got through all right." He hesitated, then his glad expression faded. "It's too bad about Tim Murphy."

"What about him?"

"He was killed."

"Oh God! How dreadful. He was a great friend and a wonderful man — there'll never be another like him." The physician bit his lip. "You're sure he's dead?"

"Yes, and I wish I weren't," Barry sighed, and thought of his brothers and so many other good men gone. "His friend Maddox came and reported his death. The poor fellow seemed to be taking it very hard, to say the least."

Colcord folded away a sheaf of papers, then looked up. "By the way, Maddox says he is setting out for home in the morning. I presume you'd like to go with him?"

"Yes, I, too, need to get back to my wife even more than Maddox, but — "

"But what — ?"

"Well, I feel I ought to carry my report to Hillsboro personally." He smiled thinly. "Or do I appear quixotic?"

Without hesitating a second the Carolinian replied, "You do not. I see no need for you to go there — unless you want to."

"You're sure about that?"

"Absolutely! Your portfolio will be safe with me and well guarded all the way."

Samuel Mason, M.D., drew a long, slow breath. "Perhaps you're right."

"Of course I am. There's no reason why we both should go and meet that dreadful fellow Gates." Barry closed a field desk with unnecessary vigor. "Hope I arrive in time to see his replacement, General Greene, become commander-in-chief. All of us down South will feel a lot better the minute he does!"

"This is very handsome of you," the physician observed softly. "I — I hope I'm not being derelict in my duty, Barry."

Barry Colcord smiled. "You've also a duty to your wife — and my future sister-in-law — haven't you, Sam?"

"True enough, I suppose. Well, good night." He started to turn away but checked himself.

"Have you any special message for Choice?"

"Yes," smiled Barry. "Pray say that I'll come for her the very first moment I can."

"Then you'll not be going back to Carolina?"

Slowly Frederick Colcord's remaining son shook his head. "No, Sam, I don't think I'll do that. Of late I've come to believe that a better future for us all lies across the mountains."

Next morning, a band of lean, leather-clad riflemen broke camp early with the new sun warming their backs and again turned their faces toward the wild horizon.

Eagle in the Sky

Preface

In preparing this volume the author's intent was not only to re-create in lively, largely contemporary phraseology an account of how people typical of the period 1780–1781 believed, lived and acted, but also to describe, as accurately as thorough research permitted, certain events of deep historical significance while the long and bitter war for American independence was approaching its end. The story moves against backgrounds as diversified as Boston; West Point, New York; the Danish West Indies; the Maine District of Massachusetts; and York Town, Virginia.

It has been the author's further ambition to emphasize and to place in proper perspective the decisive importance of the part played by the infant republic's alliance with France, or to be more accurate, with the government of Louis XVI. Certain it is that lacking French support, American independence could not have been obtained, at least in that day and age. The new nation, having no fleet of her own, was dependent upon France's powerful navy to make possible the delivery of money, troops and essential military supplies of all kinds. Without the power of Admiral de Grasse's great ships of the line the allied troops never could have bottled up Lord Cornwallis in York Town and eventually forced his surrender.

Instructions and examples afforded by the French king's professional officers and well-disciplined regulars proved invaluable in converting into real soldiers those raw levies who only at this late date became ready to admit that patriotism and undisciplined valor simply were not sufficient in the long run to win against Britain's stubborn, well-drilled but often poorly led troops. History has established beyond reasonable doubt that the French king's ministers were not moved to encourage the rebellious colonies out of altruism; even less did these gentlemen admire those rights and principles for which the ex-colonists were fighting so desperately to attain. In simple truth, the French government granted assistance only in hopes of regaining from the ancient enemy certain strategically important segments of that vast empire they had ceded to Great Britain under the Treaty of Paris in 1763.

Only gradually did the average American come to appreciate that there must be something of value in European methods of training, commanding and supplying troops. Thus, by degrees, there came into being the regiments of the Continental Line. Although woefully few in number, they proved to be very dependable fighters no matter from which state or district they had been enlisted. Time and again a handful of Continental units steadied mobs of wavering militia sufficiently to snatch victory out of impending defeat.

In describing the practice of medicine of that time I have drawn exclusively from contemporary diaries and letters — a rich but confusing source of information, since many diseases were known under a variety of names and the treatments or remedies for these varied so much it seemed wise to mention only easily recognizable ailments and injuries. Dr. James Thatcher's invaluable and wonderfully detailed diary of his service with the Continental Army forms the basis for information concerning medical episodes included in this tale.

Certain readers may be inclined to dispute the small size of the *Grand Turk III* in view of the huge crew she carried on departing from Boston. To these I can only point out that her dimensions, rigging and armament were practically identical with those of the *Rattlesnake,* a privateer which in that same year shipped an even more numerous crew.

Intensive research through the Naval Record Society and in the British Museum revealed certainly that Captain David Graves, commanding the flagship *H.B.M.S. London* during the decisive engagement off the capes of Virginia, indeed must be held responsible for hoisting contradictory signals — an error which produced momentous effects upon American history and that of all the world, for that matter. Probably the fact that Captain Graves was a son of the admiral in command of the British squadron allowed him to escape almost unscathed Vice Admiral Hood's and Rear Admiral Drake's bitter censure. He also managed to avoid disgrace at the hands of King George III's ministers.

Just how Major General Lord Charles Cornwallis felt about Captain Graves's egregious blunder while his sword was being surrendered to the Franco-American allies outside York Town can only be surmised.

GLOSSARY OF MEDICAL TERMS

Late Eighteenth Century | *Twentieth Century*

Late Eighteenth Century	Twentieth Century
Animal Economy	Bowel Movements
Corruption	Infection
Commotion	Concussion
Costiveness	Constipation
Canine Madness	Hydrophobia
Cramp Colic	Appendicitis, also Typhlitis
Clyster (Glyster)	Enema
Extravasated Blood	Rupture of Blood Vessel
Falling Sickness	Epilepsy
Flux of Humour	Circulation
French Pox	Venereal Disease, Syphilis and/or Gonorrhea
Green Sickness	Anemia
Hip Gout	Osteomyelitis
Hallucination	Delirium
King's Evil	Scrofula
Long Sickness	Tuberculosis
Lues Venera	Venereal Disease, Syphilis and/or Gonorrhea
Lung Fever	Pneumonia
Mania	Insanity
Mortification	Infection
Nostalgia	Homesickness
Putrid Fever	Diphtheria
Remitting Fever	Malaria
Sanguinous Crust	Scab
Screws	Rheumatism
Ship's Fever (Jail Fever or Camp Fever)	Typhus
Sore Throat Distemper	Quinsy
Strangery	Rupture or Stricture
Venesection	Bleeding

Eve of the New Year, 1780

Sabra Stanton extended slim hands to the fire and over her shoulder watched her uncle's goosequill pen drive deliberately, precisely, over a new sheet of foolscap on his desk. Dr. William Townsend's students could tell anyone who might be interested that he never permitted himself to become hurried; even during the more critical moments of an amputation he took enough time to work surely and steadily.

The clear, yellow-red flame of a single whale-oil lamp projected her uncle's aquiline profile and neat club wig in faithful silhouette against the study's furthest wall.

That wind, roaring in from the sea and over Boston Harbor, was so cruelly edged that Sabra wished she had selected a thicker cloak for bringing Uncle Will Mamma's invitation to New Year's dinner. She wouldn't be a mite surprised if at any minute snow began to fall.

Sabra's wide gray eyes wandered upwards and came to rest upon a small plaster bust of Galen glaring down from its pedestal above the entrance to the study. Poor Galen! He sadly needed dusting again. Mamma was right; black Sophie would never make better than a tolerable housekeeper. Still, old Sophie's lack of gumption was fortunate — else she might not have chanced in to witness what was promising to become a significant little ceremony.

Lord. Uncle Will and his three apprentices were looking solemn as so many stuffed owls — and about as talkative. Quietly, Sabra eased her slippered feet out of those damp, white pine pattens on which she had crossed the treacherous ice and mud of Bennett Street and made a little scuffling noise, but nobody cast her a look. Why, a body could easily delude herself into believing a coroner's inquest to be in progress. Not once during the past two years could she recall having seen Lucius Devoe sit so very still.

Again her gaze came to rest upon her uncle's thin and slightly stooped shoulders. She realized, all at once, that he was wearing his Sunday coat of mulberry velvet adorned by dark blue cuffs and a double row of gilt lead buttons. Glory! This must be more of an occasion than she'd realized. Like most Boston physicians, William Townsend customarily attended to his practice in a suit of unrelieved black. On reflection, Sabra decided that Uncle Will had not spruced up in honor of his apprentices, but in order to celebrate this eve of the New Year in the company of his fellow surgeons on duty at that army hospital away out in Jamaica Plain.

La! How uncommon dashing Lucius Devoe was looking this evening. Hastily Sabra dropped her eyes, aware that a warm current had commenced to mount, tingling towards the rim of her bodice. It was irritating, thought Sabra, to realize that not once in many minutes had the lean young Jamaican's intense, brightly somber eyes become fixed upon her. Instead, they were following every movement of Dr. Townsend's softly scratching goosequill.

A bold impulse offered itself. Dared she, on such short notice, invite a comparative stranger into Papa's house? Why not? Hadn't Papa bade her bring in whomever she chose, to sample a goblet or two of prime Madeira? As a rule Papa was most strict, but judging from the jovial manner in which he had been holding forth when she had left for Uncle Will's, he wouldn't object. Maybe he'd retire early? Mamma invariably accompanied her spouse up to bed, so she and Lucius — or Asa Peabody, perhaps, since Lucius was proving so provokingly inattentive — might find an opportunity to sit by themselves for a while.

Deliberately William Townsend, M.D., thrust his quill deep into a glass filled with birdshot and with his one good eye considered the writing he had just completed. At length he nodded absently, redipped his pen and then with a bold flourish signed his name.

In his usual leisurely fashion Dr. Townsend wrote the word "Certificate" in large letters across its top; then, for an instant, the old physician's gaze flickered over to consider Peter Burnham, a broad-shouldered and solid young fellow of near twenty-five years. Townsend saw dark red hair clubbed by a smart tie of dark green grosgrain ribbon framing a squarish face dominated by wide-set, dark-blue eyes, a short nose and a jaw so strong as to verge on the pugnacious.

Dr. Townsend felt confident of one thing — Peter Burnham would fight for whatever he held to be right; God grant that also he might acquire a greater measure of patience. Unless all signs failed he should rise high in his chosen field — that unfashionable and sadly neglected branch of medicine described as male midwifery.

The old physician's massively modeled countenance, now blotched with the brown flecks of advancing years, relaxed. What a deep satisfaction it was to prepare this third and last certificate. Of these three students only Asa Peabody possessed the emotionally level but endlessly inquiring mind of a possibly great physician; trust young Peabody to pounce upon illogical elements in even the most approved treatments. The Lord, and Dr. Townsend, knew how willing Asa Peabody was to work. The young fellow had nigh ruined his eyes from studying too late by the feeble light cast by cheap and malodorous beef-tallow candles.

On this third certificate, William Townsend altered his text a trifle to read:

CERTIFICATE

TO ALL WHO SHALL SEE THESE PRESENTS GREETING:

Asa Peabody hath sev'd Apprenticeship under me for two Years, two Months, in Ye Studie and Practice of Physicks and Surgery, during which

Time he hath prov'd himself Uncommon Studious, Able and Gift'd. Therefore, I can, with full Confidence, Recommend him to Ye Publick as a Bachelor
of Medicine excellently Qualified in Ye above Branches.

Wm. Townsend, m.d.

Boston, Massachusetts
1st January 1780.

Dr. Townsend reached into the tail of his best coat, and producing a
yellow silk handkerchief, wiped from the chill-reddened end of his sharp
nose a pellucid drop. Weather-beaten countenance creased in a smile, he
got to his feet, remained absently rubbing together large and deceptively
clumsy-appearing hands.

"Sabra, my dear, pray summon Sophie and instruct her to fetch four of
the small glasses and a decanter she will find in the corner cupboard."

Sabra returned shortly with Sophie, who set down a salver before Dr.
Townsend.

"Ahem." Doctor Townsend cleared his throat, peered about in rare
amiability. "Young gentlemen, pray I trust you will join me in a tot of
Spanish brandy? His blind left eye gleamed white as that of Galen's
plaster bust as he raised his glass in Sabra's direction. "My winsome niece,
I am pleased you chanced by." Townsend put down his glass and adopted
a grave mien. "Gentlemen and fellow physicians; now that you have
joined the ancient, honorable and merciful company of physicians and
chirurgeons I bid you welcome."

The old man's single pale-blue eye studied his ex-apprentices for the last
time. Tallest by half a head, Asa Peabody revealed his country origins in
clumsy, homemade brogues, white cotton-thread hose, and the old-
fashioned cut of a homespun coat. His waistcoat was secured by cherrywood buttons — probably whittled by his own hand. To some people Peabody's features might have seemed a little long and his mouth too wide,
but the eyes peering steadily from beneath straight and rather heavy
brows were large and set well apart.

Probably because Peter Burnham's body was thick and his legs and arms
powerfully constructed he appeared bigger than Peabody; yet he wasn't.
Such copper-red hair and bold blue eyes were distinctive enough, but
Burnham's features were so handsomely proportioned that in later years
they would inspire Mr. Rembrandt Peale to reproduce them on canvas.
Burnham's costume suggested him to be exactly what he was — the son of
a prosperous hardware merchant. He wore a dove-gray coat of fine French
gabardine, equipped with flat pewter buttons bearing his monogram; black
thread hose, black knee breeches. His vest was a gay, sky-blue satin affair
lavishly embroidered with yellow flowers of some unidentifiable variety.

Nearest to the fireplace stood Lucius Devoe, looking miserably poor in
his only suit, of threadbare black serge. Today, in honor of the occasion,
he wore at his throat a pathetic scrap of torn and mended lace. The young

Jamaican's extreme poverty further could be read in frayed shirt cuffs, patched shoes and the shiny state of his coat collar. Lucius Devoe's features, a shade less dark than olive, were almost never in repose. His forehead, nose and cheekbones were cleanly modeled and well proportioned. But what one noticed first about him was the alertness of his very dark blue eyes.

Mechlin lace at Dr. Townsend's wrists gleamed briefly when he picked up a certificate. "In the past you have heard me speak many times — doubtless at too great a length on occasion; therefore my final remarks will be brief."

He went stalking across the study and the gilt buttons of his waistcoat flashed as his big, heavily freckled hand closed on Asa's. "Dr. Peabody," said he gravely, "in your regard I entertain the fondest expectations. May your admirable concentration on anatomy reward both you and mankind."

"You — you are very kind, sir," was all Asa could find to say; Lord, how he yearned for the gift of eloquence.

Godfreys! I've made out! he thought. Why, why I am a full-fledged physician. Oh, if only Pa could know about it.

The texture of this certificate between his fingers was sure enough evidence that this long-hoped-for hour indeed had arrived. Yes, behind him stretched the years of toil at net, handline, and trawl; why, even yet he retained remnants of calluses at those points where his thumbs would close over a dory's oars. Well, he was now a bachelor of medicine. So far so good. He intended some day to add the venerated initials M.D. to his name. Right now, not twenty medical men in all Massachusetts held that coveted degree.

As from afar, Asa heard Dr. Townsend's dry precise voice saying, "Dr. Burnham, my best wishes will accompany you wherever you fare." The old physician's one eye twinkled. "I'm thinking that red hair and those blue eyes will carry you a long way — in more than one fashion."

Peter Burnham's hand closed over his certificate. "Thank you, sir. Always I shall endeavor to remain a credit to you, your skill, and your principles." Then he grinned a grin which, like oil on water, spread all over his ruddy features and became reflected in merry blue eyes.

"Dr. Devoe." Sabra looked up expectantly in time to see her uncle draw himself to full height. He spoke less lightly. "You have labored industriously and under great handicaps; though a stranger to our land and to this city you have made friends and won respect. For you I have one final word of counsel. Weigh your every decision with care — and probity."

Alone of the three Devoe bowed, and without affectation. "Dr. Townsend, as long as I live I shall cherish your precepts."

"Gentlemen" — Dr. Townsend's gaze included all three of the oddly contrasting figures before him — "to our beloved and sorely beset country! I adjure you to remain constant to her cause. Too many brave men already have given it their lives." A wry smile wrinkled the old surgeon's parchment-hued features. "I feel confident that you will serve our country second only to humanity."

The Red Lion

Peter Burnham and Asa Peabody descended the long slope of Hanover Street with care. Footwalks did parallel that thoroughfare but their surfaces were so irregular, so dotted by frozen puddles veiled beneath new snow, that footing was treacherous. Ear tips atingle, the two men bent their bodies against a wind driving flurries of fine dry snow in from Massachusetts Bay. These flakes had such sharp edges that they cruelly stung a wayfarer's face and created a distinct singing noise high in the sky.

Tonight lights glowed in unusually many houses. A stray, rough-coated cur crept out from under a doorstoop, sniffed discouragedly at Peter's heels, then scurried off into the driving snow.

In this part of Boston stood a few new houses constructed to replace habitations torn down to warm General Gage's British troops during that dreadful, never-to-be-forgotten winter of 1775–1776. Even now, five years later, only the trunks of very young saplings could be seen about town, for in their desperate efforts to find fuel, the redcoats had hacked down every sizable tree in Boston and the vicinity.

"Godfreys! How'd you like to be at sea tonight?" Asa panted over the roaring wind.

"Fine, if I look as addled as you talk," Peter yelled back. " 'Tis certain-sure three-B weather."

"Three-B?" Asa had to cup his hands.

"Aye!" Peter roared in deep-throated merriment. "Bed, blonde and bottle weather, as we call it down in Connecticut."

"Where is this Red Lion?" Asa demanded. "I'm colder'n a codline in February and so peckish I could gnaw the bones out of my landlady's Sunday stays."

"It ain't far now," Peter encouraged. "Besides, we both felt colder waiting for old Doc Townsend to sign those certificates."

All the grog shops and quasi-brothels situated nearest the waterfront were roaring, crowded to capacity. From them pipe music or the twanging of Spanish guitars beat out into the street. The out-and-out bordellos, Peter explained, were less brilliantly lighted, but from them the scraping of fiddles sounded louder and one could catch the thump of feet mingled with a deal of high-pitched laughter and an occasional scream.

Presently a swing-board adorned with a prancing red lion loomed ahead.

"Hold your hat and look alive," Peter cautioned. "We'll find no prayer meeting going on in there."

In the wake of six or eight soldiers clad in a weird miscellany of blue, brown and even gray uniforms they bore down on a wide doorway through which were rushing blasts of hot air reeking of tobacco smoke and pungent with odors of sweat, lemon peel, cloves and rum.

Asa blinked and Burnham gasped. "Whew! That's a genuine six-cornered stink!"

To describe the Red Lion as packed to overflowing would have constituted a stark understatement; seated at long hurdle tables ranged at right angles to the entrance were mahogany-faced Spaniards, nervous, feverishly gay Frenchmen, stolid half-breed Indians and Dutchmen. There were even a few Negroes. Riggers, shipwrights, armorers, rope spinners, chandlers, and a swarm of heavily sweating laborers crowded each other and drank deep draughts of ale from wooden noggins or jacks of copper-bound waxed leather.

"What's this? What's this?" Mr. Perkins, the proprietor, fat features fiery, was flinging a sheaf of clean white Continental bank notes onto the beer-marked table before a thin, red-nosed soldier — a sergeant by the green worsted knot on his right shoulder.

"That's money, mister," he growled. "Take it and like it."

"I'll do neither and damn yer eyes fer a bold rogue. Expecting to pass such trash."

"'Tain't trash. Law says it's legal currency," rasped a big private in a faded brown uniform. He coughed heavily and Asa noted that his eyes were hollow, that the gray-pink tinge of recent sickness stained his cheeks.

"Legal fiddlesticks," snorted the publican breathing hard through a bulbous and red-veined nose. He dropped his voice. "Ain't you fellers got just a leetle hard money?"

"No. We ain't out o' no hole-in-the-wall privateer." The sergeant got up, his hands nervously opening and shutting. His companions followed suit, scowling and closing in, shoulder to shoulder.

The innkeeper hesitated, decided to temporize, spoke less belligerently. "Now, boys, ain't no one can rightly say Joel Perkins is hard on the defenders o' this fair land of ours." His little blue eyes narrowed. "Being as this is the eve o' the New Year, I'll accept Noo York or Connetycut notes at fifty per cent discount."

"Look, mister, we ain't no cheats," the thin soldier said bitterly. "Honest, we got nawthin' but what we're paid in — Continental notes."

Mr. Perkins aimed a slap at a passing and quite inoffensive pot boy, then leveled a hairy sausage of a finger at the doorway. "Get out! The pack of ye! Them notes ain't worth a thin damn. Next time you want charity go seek an almshouse."

The soldiers glowered, hesitated, then a corporal in a dirty gray uniform pulled a sheaf of notes from each of his side pockets. "Here, you goddamn fat-bellied patriots. Help yerselves to this bum wad!" The corporal flung the double handful of Continental notes up against the smoke-browned and fly-specked plaster above his head. The white bits of paper fluttered, scaled briefly about like a flock of miniature gulls. The only man who bothered to pick up a note used it as a spill to light his pipe.

The sergeant paused on his way to the door, shook his fist at the smoke-veiled room. "That was my first pay in six months. I pray God some day soon the lobsterbacks will come back and burn down this goddamn rat trap called Boston over yer ears, you goddamn ungrateful crotch-festered civilians!"

A sudden commotion in the kitchen caused nearby patrons to witness the abrupt entrance of a scrawny, gray-faced man. Nearing middle age, he wore a soiled, bottle-green waistcoat, greasy durant breeches and ragged worsted stockings. Scant, ginger-colored hair straggled untidily downwards as if attempting to conceal the grime on his neck and a very dirty stock of brown leather.

"Wot have we here?" demanded a pimply merchant's clerk. "A musicker, I'll be bound! Well, old gaffer, do you aim to play us the minooet?"

The dirty old man made but slow progress between the tables because in one hand he was carrying a flageolet while with the other he tried to manage a crude crutch. The musician's left leg, Asa noted, was shrunken and several inches shorter than its companion.

"If ye'll only make way, kind friends," he was pleading in a whining, high-pitched voice, "ye'll greet the New Year on the wings o' the sweetest music. I vow ye've a rare treat in store, gentlemen."

"Go ahead, Gimpey — let's hear what ye can do."

In rough good humor the revelers drew aside, permitting the cripple to thump along towards a small clear space formed by the junction of tap-room and bar. The musician held the crowd's attention just long enough to permit the comparatively unobserved appearance of a black-haired girl wearing a dingy, red-and-white-striped skirt and a Robinson vest of faded blue. Over this last she had crossed a ragged yellow shawl. At a quick estimate Asa guessed this small, ghastly pale creature could not yet have attained eighteen years. A double row of small metal discs jingled softly along the rim of the curious little hand-drum she carried at her side.

"So this is old Gimpey's treat?" Peter commented over his toddy. "What a dirty little vixen it is! Stab me," he added suddenly. "What remarkable eyes!"

He was right, Asa decided; the girl's large and very black eyes were heavily lashed, and lifted, ever so faintly, at their outer corners. Lips compressed, the girl struck as hard as she could at hands reaching out in attempts to pinch her buttocks or to snatch off her garters.

"Quite the little hellcat, eh?"

"Can you blame her?" Asa felt mad clear through to see the way these revelers, now far gone in liquor, made a game of this luckless waif and, quite without shame, offered incredibly obscene invitations.

When she brushed by Peter's table he could tell that her petticoat must have been cut for some woman considerably taller than this girl; its spotted fabric trailed a path through the spit and sawdust on the floor. This pallid little creature had made an effort to secure abundant black hair with a band of faded yellow silk ribbon; but the knot must have been badly tied for in a minute it would fall away.

She had almost succeeded in joining the musician when an unshaven young teamster in a brown and white calfskin waistcoat dexterously flipped up the girl's ragged petticoat and venting a raucous guffaw, jerked undone a pathetic rag garter. The would-be entertainer's lumpy black stocking slipped and fell, gathering in ungainly wrinkles about her slim ankle.

Small pointed teeth bared, she whirled and used her hand-drum to slash at the teamster's head. "Satan trample your beastly guts!"

"Ho! Kitty's got claws!" roared Peter, in huge delight because those metal discs on the drum had sketched three bloody lines across the fellow's cheek.

"You — you goddamn viper!" Still clutching the garter, the teamster surged up, but was pulled back to a sitting position by his companions.

"Let be, Abner! Ye won yer prize, ain't yer? Even if ye've had to pay for the doxy's garter, ye can brag all over Essex County on it."

"A spirited piece," Peter chuckled, raising a second toddy. "Notice her leg? 'Twas shapely, my lad, shapely. Were a man to scrub hard enough, I'll wager he might find real looks under all that dirt."

In the clear space the cripple had rested his crutch against a table and was wetting blue, pinched-looking lips before sounding a few experimental notes on his flageolet.

Though mightily embarrassed, Asa kept his attention on the girl, watched her swiftly rip a strip from the hem of her petticoat and with it resecure her fallen stocking.

The buzz of conversation slackened. "For yer pleasure, kind friends," the musician whined, "Mistress Hilde will now sing —"

"Mistress Hilde's a bloody whore!" came a raucous call from the depths of the bar. "Three pennies weekdays, six pence Saturdays —"

" — Nonetheless," the cripple insisted hurriedly, "Mistress Hilde now will entertain you. For God's sake sing out lass."

Once her companion had struck up a lively air, Mistress Hilde forced onto her pallid lips such a pitiful caricature of a smile that her expression reminded Asa of an occasion back home in Machias, when some children had cornered a half-grown cat. They were pelting the unhappy creature with clods until he'd put an end to their sport.

Thin hands violently atremble, the girl called Hilde nodded to her companion and commenced an accompaniment on her little hand-drum. Presently she tilted back her head and began a lively Irish ballad in a stronger voice than her fragility suggested to be possible. The quality of her notes was fairly true, Peter decided, settling back. Hands plunged in pockets, he listened carefully though his blue eyes were becoming heavily lidded with the heat and liquor. "Well, Asa, what do you think?"

"She has pretty hands," Asa commented. "But if ever I've beheld a person fairly primed to take the long sickness — "

"Pox for a blue-nosed sobersides!" Peter grinned and, once the girl had ceased singing, called, "Catch!" and spun her a silver sixpenny bit. Dexterously she caught the coin in her little hand-drum, then curtsied, at the same time flashing an uncertain smile.

Suddenly Asa's hand closed on his companion's wrist. "Of all things — see that symbol painted on the drumhead?"

"That blue thing?" the red-haired doctor demanded. "What of it?"

"Yonder's a Micmac totem! — that of the Turtle clan. Strange. How d'you suppose it got so far south as Boston?"

"Sing again, lass!"

"Good enough. Let's have some more."

Patrons tossed out into the sawdust of the clear space coppers or creased and dirty paper notes of varied origin. The cripple hopped about paying small attention to the paper, but carefully retrieving any hard money from the thick sawdust. The girl, however, remained where she was, uninterested, erect, and somehow infinitely aloof from the smoke and stenches of the taproom.

Eventually the musician picked up his pipe and prepared to play. "Mistress Hilde will now regale ye one and all wi' a sad love song — by Mr. Henry Carey. She does real good by it."

His reed sounded an introductory flourish, then the black-haired girl commenced to sing.

> "Of all the girls that are so smart
> There's none like pretty Sally;
> She is the darling of my heart
> And she lives in our alley.
> There is no lady in the land
> Is half so sweet as — "

She faltered, then continued, despite the fact that out in Cross Street was sounding a distinctive, shivering clash recognized by more than a few of the seamen present as that of Moorish cymbals. The clangor sounded louder. More heads swung expectantly towards the door; the crowd lost interest in raven-haired Hilde and her sad love song.

Donnybrook Fair

A few minutes short of midnight a second group of privateersmen came stamping into the Red Lion. A single glance betrayed the fact that they had been patronizing an imposing number of waterfront grog shops. Their leader was a black-browed, bandy-legged fellow wearing an elaborate green uniform adorned with sergeant's stripes done in white. Followed by a roistering gang of deckhands in knitted stocking caps, wide leather belts, brass-buckled brogues, and stained petticoat breeches, he swaggered in and, swaying slightly, surveyed the taproom in insolent self-assurance.

Like hounds on finding their yard is invaded by a strange pack the *Grand Turk*'s men stiffened, gathered their feet under them and closed in together. As Luke Tarbell had done, the marine sergeant tossed a handful of small gold and silver coins ringing onto the bar and bellowed.

"Name yer tipple! The drinks are on me. Everybody's agot to drink to the *Dauntless* — best damn' privateer afloat!" Belligerently, he added, "An' I won't take no for an answer!"

" 'Twas the *Dauntless* prized one o' Gen'ral Henry Clinton's store ships last month and her with nigh ten thousand golden guineas aboard!" someone muttered at a table nearby Asa's.

"To hell with you and yer drinks," Tarbell rasped. "We don't drink with no puddlerakers. Go fry yer fat butt somewheres else!"

Asa, reading the omens, roused himself, muttered, "Rig for a squall, Peter," and, after pushing his table further away from the wall, seized a Madeira bottle by its neck.

"What hulk-scrapin' say dat? Mebbe it was you, little boy?" A big, yellow-skinned mulatto wearing a tarred round straw hat drove an elbow viciously hard into the ribs of one of the *Grand Turk*'s crew. "Make room for a real fightin' man!" he roared waving an enormous fist. "Ah's got me one powahful thirst!"

"Stow it, you sassy half-baked 'coon!" snarled the *Grand Turk*'s man and swung his tankard at the mulatto so quickly the other couldn't duck and so caught the heavy stone mug full on the chin. Half dazed, the mulatto reeled into the arms of a shipmate.

"Faith and 'twill be ould Donnybrook Fair all over again!" exulted an Irish teamster joyfully balling his fists.

Before Asa could even bat his eyes the taproom had become a battle-ground. The rival privateersmen caught up chairs, platters, bottles, anything handy and, howling obscenities, strove earnestly to bash in each other's heads.

Babbling futile curses, Mr. Perkins struggled towards the door. "Watch! Watch ho!" he yelled. "Come quick, for God's sake! Ahh-h. Let the lads have their frolic." A wooden piggin sailed through the air, narrowly missed the publican's brown scratch wig, but splashed him with ale.

Asa and Peter tipped their table on edge, legs outwards, and, in a fine impartial spirit, hurled whatever missiles came to hand at the heaving, flailing combatants.

Once the tide of battle surged up to him, the cripple, swearing frightful oaths, took his crutch by its toe and laid about him with surprising effectiveness. Flattened against the wall behind her companion the black-haired girl stood flinching, one grimy arm raised to shield her pointed little face.

One of the *Dauntless*'s crew unwisely fetched Peter a shrewd clip on the jaw, whereupon that red-haired individual ripped off coat and waistcoat and plunged very effectively into the battle. His attack took the trouble-making privateersmen on their flank, which unexpected assault turned the course of the brawl in the favor of the *Grand Turk*'s sadly battered and outnumbered crew.

"Watch! 'Ware the watch!" Somebody began shouting and, sure enough, the distinctive staccato rattle of several heavy wooden kloppers could be heard in Cross Street.

"The watch! Out o' my way! One side!" Such of the combatants as were able snatched what possessions they could and went leaping, crashing through the kitchens and so out the back door leaving in their wake a hurrah's nest of overturned tables, chairs, and benches. Noncombatants, proceeding with caution, emerged from their refuges to stand anxiously watching the captain of the watch glare about.

"Take 'em!" he snapped to his hot and breathless roundsmen. At once they commenced to uncoil short lengths of cord.

Three privateersmen, apparently badly hurt, lay groaning; and sitting on the floor among the wreckage was a young apprentice dazedly attempting to staunch a deep knife slash in his forearm. Blood kept spurting from between his hairy fingers.

"Help! It — it won't stop!" the apprentice began to cry. Asa started foward, but one of the watchmen thrust a heavy oaken staff to bar his path.

"Stand where ye are."

"That man's radial artery has been severed — I — I'm a physician."

"That true, Mr. Perkins?"

The landlord overheard and, setting his wig straight, hurried over. "Leave him be, Tom. He's a physicker, sure enough. He took no part in it. I saw him stand aside," the innkeeper lied, then he caught Asa by an arm. "For God's sake sew the clumsy bastard up; he's bleeding all over my place. Lord's mercy! And I try to run a respectable ordinary."

"I will — if you'll let be my friend Dr. Burnham. He was provoked into this brawl."

Peter was not a lovely sight as he stood there panting, red hair loose, shirt minus a sleeve and splashed with blood drops from a split lip. At Mr. Perkins's nod the watchmen turned away in search of likelier quarry.

"Gorry! The cranium of *homo sapiens* is a plagued hard affair," Peter observed, rubbing swollen knuckles. Asa had been fashioning a tourniquet from a billet of wood and length of codline. Once he applied pressure,

[569]

the hemorrhage ceased. "What have we here?" Peter shook the hair out of his eyes to bend over the wounded apprentice. He used a pen knife to cut away the sodden woollen sleeve.

"Thank'e, sir," babbled the youth. "I couldn't stop it no how. Is — is any muscles cut?"

A maidservant ran up to Mr. Perkins, muttered something in his ear which prompted him to rip a curse and come back over to where the two physicians were working.

"One o' my doxies got hurt," he growled. "Will one o' you gents attend her? But mind, I ain't payin' no fees — "

"You go, Asa, I'll sew this lad up in jig time. Hey! You with the pot belly, fetch me a needle and some linen thread."

Asa entered the kitchen to discover a group of scullery maids, cooks and spit boys collected in one corner. They were chattering like so many jays, but doing nothing whatever about a figure lying limp at their feet.

Against the dirty sawdust the girl Hilde's quaint, finely featured face was now completely colorless, her scrawny arms and legs were wide flung and her jet hair powdered with bits and chips of wood. In her garish blue and red costume she suggested nothing so much as a rather soiled puppet tossed carelessly away.

"Jest my brimstone luck!" the crippled musician was complaining. He had just doused the unconscious girl with a gourd of water. "Here 'tis New Year's Eve and this little no-good bitch won't be fitten' to sing another note." The fellow's tired, rather frightened brown eyes roved in search of sympathy. "Dunno why I took her on. Wherever that damned Hilde goes, bad luck follers ahorseback."

Not much time was required to decide that her wound was of minor importance. Asa deduced that some missile had struck the singer just above her left ear hard enough to cut the scalp and to render her unconscious.

"She needs fresh air and quiet," he told the circle of the hot and excited faces above him. "Where can she come by it?"

"There's a cubby off the wine cellar," someone volunteered. "Mebbe that would serve?"

When Asa collected the inert figure in his arms he was not much surprised to discover that she proved a very slight burden, so treading easily, he followed a paunchy little man down some creaky stairs into the chill dark of a cellar. A wavering Betty lamp presently lit a small nook in which the discarded straw packing of wine bottles offered soft if moldy-smelling bedding.

"Mr. Perkins will be hollerin' fer me," the guide explained, placing the lamp on the floor. "I got to hurry above else he'll dock me. He's a main hard master is Joel Perkins — God rot his greedy bones!"

By the Betty lamp's wavering and uncertain light Asa made a more careful examination of the cut and was relieved to discover that the bleeding had ceased. Invisible damage, however, might have been caused to the os temporal by the impact. Once a basin of warm water was fetched by a sympathetic kitchen girl, he commenced an exploration by first washing away dirt accumulated in the vicinity of the wound; then he succumbed to a sudden temptation to cleanse the balance of the singer's features.

The kitchen girl shook her head in envy, spoke more to herself than to the big young physician, "My, ain't she the pretty one?"

To Asa's mounting surprise the singer's skin proved to be a clear, almost translucent white and of a very fine texture. Even by this uncertain light he could tell that her brows were slender, gently arched and so fine they might have been cut from moleskin. Her eyes were distinguished by a faint bluish pattern of veining in their upper lids. He searched for her pulse. He'd never been able to afford a watch; consequently he'd learned to toll off the seconds pretty accurately. Um. Normal but soft.

Once the contusion had been thoroughly cleaned, Asa contrived a pledget of his last good handkerchief and secured it into place with a strip torn from the bedraggled red petticoat. Characteristically, he was unaware that this last operation had exposed the singer's straight, very thin legs until flesh showed above the tops of her often-darned black cotton stockings.

His next step must be to restore the girl's consciousness. "Find Dr. Burnham and request him to fetch down a dram of spirit," he instructed the wide-eyed scullery maid.

Then, awkwardly, he set about easing those tie strings securing Hilde's skirt and petticoats but confining her diaphragm. Soon he perceived his patient's respiration was even more seriously hampered by her tight-laced stays. To find the knot securing the coarse spun yarn doing duty as laces was difficult, but Asa persisted and was rewarded by an immediate improvement in his patient's breathing. All at once he heard the tap-tapping of a crutch advancing across the floor and straightened hurriedly.

"By God, Doc," sniggered the cripple, "yer a sight slicker'n I figgered; never did see a female's underpinnin' cast adrift quicker." Leering, he hobbled forward extending a tremblingly eager hand. "I'll thank ye fer two shillin's, Doc, then old Jabez will give yer leave to indulge yer every fancy."

"For your information, this girl is exhausted and half starved to boot. First sickness she takes will be the end of her."

"'Twill be a mercy." Jabez seated himself on an empty rum barrel. "It's a pity she's so danged stubborn — so set above herself. Old Lizzie's taken a strap to her more'n once, but it ain't done no good."

Concerned, but not overly moved, Asa considered the short oval of the singer's features at the moment silhouetted against the sable tangle of her hair. To her quickening breathing, breasts almost childishly small and immature barely stirred beneath her sweat-stained shift. What the devil had become of the spirit he'd sent for? Peter must still be engaged in tying off the apprentice's severed artery.

[571]

"Where does this Hilde hail from?" More to make conversation than out of any curiosity, Asa put the question.

"Hilde says she's from New Scotland but she claims she don't know just where. Only one thing is sure; old Lizzie Wright bought her bond off'n a Scotch Papist from up Canady way. Swore she'd make a prime doxy, he did; then took his money and walked off." Jabez spat untidily. "He lied like Lucifer — Lizzie claims she's never been given more trouble by any wench in her whole life and, mark you, old Lizzie ain't noways unreasonable, neither."

"How'd you come to have this Hilde along with you tonight?"

"Sometimes I rents her off Lizzie to sing for me in the taverns." Jabez sniffed. "Stand to lose three shillings on this night's work; main hard luck on a poor old soldier, it is."

After a brief silence Asa said, "I sent up for some grog quite awhile back. Be a good fellow and go see what's happened to it, will you? And there's no need to look at me like that."

"Fancy yer to be trusted, Doctor," Jabez admitted grudgingly.

The veteran still was clumping up to the kitchen when a sharp sigh drew Asa's attention. The girl's long, blue-black lashes were stirring a trifle, her spidery thin fingers began uncertainly to flex themselves.

"Can you hear me?" he inquired gently.

The violet-blue lips moved several instants before any sound was emitted.

"Eh?"

"*We-la-boog-we.*" The girl called Hilde sighed, then added something like, "*We-loo-lin.*"

Asa started, bent closer, thought, Godfreys, it's Micmac she's talking! In Passamaquoddy — a related dialect of Algonquin — the speech of nearly all the Indians in the vicinity of Machias, he inquired her name.

"*Kwee-a-lin,*" she whispered.

"Little Dove? Is that it?"

The girl's eyes still unseeing opened just a little. "*Kway!*" She gave the word of greeting.

"*Kway!*"

"Why — why — " She struggled to rise but he placed a restraining hand on her forehead.

"You'd best lie quiet. You've been hurt." She lay back breathing faster and faster, staring up in wonderment at the broad and friendly face above.

"You — you are a physician?"

"Aye. You are not badly harmed. There is nothing to fear."

"You'd better go away — " she faltered. "I — I can't pay you."

"A matter of no importance," he reassured. "You'll need care though, lest a commotion arise."

She turned her head aside, then in an odd gesture briefly pressed both hands hard over her lips. "Where do you live? I will go there. Indeed I will."

He soothed her and became so much absorbed in a consideration of her frail state that he quite missed the implication of her promise. "I lodge at the Widow Southeby's in Sudbury Street. It's number fifty-one; I'm generally in after supper. That cut should be examined, certainly within two days' time. But if you experience any dizzy spells you must send for me."

Judas Maccabeus! A realization came over Asa; he was actually prescribing! It'd be something to receive his first patient — even a nonpaying one — in what he chose to call his consulting room, though for a fact it was no more than an unused storeroom of Mrs. Southeby's.

He stared happily into space. Tomorrow he'd hang that little sign he'd whittled during early winter evenings and the world would know that "Dr. Peabody" had set up practice for himself. It was a fine sign. Even back in Machias, where clever carvers were the rule, everyone admitted that Morgan Peabody's third son was extra clever with his jackknife. In fact, while studying with Dr. Townsend, Asa owed a good part of his living to the skill and industry with which he fashioned butter stamps, lard paddles and all manner of piggins, noggins and other wooden tableware.

On glancing at his patient he was disconcerted to watch two small tears well from under the singer's tight-shut eyelids and go slipping down over her cheeks. "Does your head hurt?"

"Where is Jabez?" she inquired. "I — I'll get a beating for this."

Suddenly outraged, he burst out, "If either he or anybody else lays a finger on you just you tell me and I — well, I'll have the law on 'em."

"You have been — good, Doctor, too good. Please, what are you called?" Asa told her.

"You spoke Algonquin?" the girl inquired timidly. "Or was I dreaming?"

"Always each spring a few Micmacs visit a 'Quoddy camp across the river from my home."

"Home?" Hilde lingered on the word.

"Machias, in the Eastern District of Massachusetts." He smiled. "It's away beyond Frenchman's Bay near to Nova Scotia. Where do you come from?"

The girl called Hilde closed her eyes as if infinitely weary. "I wish I knew."

A Small, Convivial Gathering

That the Samuel Stantons had been, and were, entertaining on a scale far more elaborate than Sabra's casual invitation had suggested, Lucius Devoe surmised the instant he set foot beyond the great, white-painted front door and its brass dolphin knocker. A black manservant in a powdered wig and chocolate livery was gravely trimming candles in graceful candelabra and girandoles while a younger slave rearranged silver cups and some glasses about a punch stand decorated with holly and evergreens of varying kinds.

Mrs. Stanton, long crippled by rheumatism, was seated in a big wing chair but received her daughter's guest pleasantly enough. Her spacious white-painted drawing room was empty, temporarily deserted by her guests.

To the Jamaican, Sabra's tiny mother represented something new in his experience — an American lady of quality. On the lady's carefully coiffed and powdered hair had been placed a precisely pleated palisade cape of muslin adorned with a rose-colored ribbon. Mrs. Stanton's party gown of brocade and rose-colored silk lace was a handsome affair festooned in flounces and bound with silver gimp. All in all Mrs. Stanton appeared so delicately diminutive that, perched in her big chair, she suggested a huge French doll. Her voice, when she acknowledged Lucius's presentation and careful bow, was deeper and more compelling than he would have expected.

"Pray make yourself at home, Doctor, and assist us in giving the New Year a hearty welcome."

During his first few minutes inside the old merchant's imposing mansion Lucius Devoe suffered acutely; he felt hopelessly out of place. His plain, poorly cut and threadbare suit, his darned gray wool hose and well-patched shoes he knew had been covertly, but thoroughly, noted by little Mrs. Stanton's sharp black eyes.

Flushing red as a turkey gobbler's neck, he adopted a fresh attitude. Since there was nothing immediately to be done about his sorry appearance, Lucius at once employed a familiar private tactic; he pretended that he stood clad in the most elegant of London-cut Lincoln green velvet; that his stockings were of Italian silk, brave with scarlet clocks; that Valenciennes lace glistened at his wrists and throat. Why not? They'd be there some day, sure enough.

To Sabra's surprise and partial pique, he seated himself beside Mrs. Stanton and set about to entertain her with cleverly told tales about Jamaica and his life there. When he had obtained her complete attention, he described, in detail, a fine, if purely imaginary, cattle penn near Constant Spring, once owned by the Devoe family. Lucius took care, though, not to paint the former Devoe property as too imposing.

" 'Twas an ill day, ma'am," he declared soberly, "when Papa fell in an affair of honor; 'twas with an officer of the Port Royal garrison. Poor Mamma had no head for business and, alack, her intendant was a glib rascal. The villain not only embezzled her profits, but cozened my mother about the true situation of our estate until, all at once, he declared us to be quite ruined."

The delicate lines of Mrs. Stanton's pink and white features softened.

She fetched a little sigh. "Poor, deceived creature. I declare, women should be allowed more education in matters of business, so often do widows lie at the mercy of the first unprincipled rogue. Tell me, Dr. Devoe, did you have brothers and sisters?"

"Three, ma'am," Lucius told her, truthfully enough. "They and my dear mamma all perished of the *coup-de-bar* fever which desolated Port Royal in Seventy-three. I," sadly, he dropped his gaze, "was left friendless, penniless and alone."

Lucius observed that not rag rugs but a deep and soft Turkey carpet graced Stanton's polished hardwood floor. Brass fire tools, andirons and an ornate fender protecting the wide fireplace showed hours of polishing; they glowed as if fashioned of yellow gold.

Lucius hated to estimate the cost of the spermaceti candles lighting this gracious room. They gave off no pungent, smoky reek of beef tallow, only a deliciously clear yellow light.

This house, he was silently resolving, set a pattern for the quietly opulent manner in which Lucius Devoe, M.D., intended to live — before not very long, too. It was to make possible such luxuries that he'd quit Port Royal and the dubious security of his father's squalid little house, which might be well enough for a carpenter's mate employed at His Majesty's dockyard — but not for that man's son.

A number of men's voices maintained an uneven obbligato in the dining room where, as Mrs. Stanton stated, Mr. Stanton and his guests were lingering over port and churchwarden pipes. Every now and then a deep, and hastily muffled, burst of laughter would break in on the Jamaican's discourse.

After a while from that room sounded a scraping of chairs, then doors banged back and the voices swelled louder. Evidently a majority of the gentlemen had decided to patronize a pair of comfortably warmed brick privies standing amid a little orchard in Samuel Stanton's backyard.

Sabra's father appeared, his pumpkin-round red face agleam with perspiration. He'd a splash of cranberry sauce on his waistcoat of pale blue satin and specks of snuff speckled his lace.

"Well, well," he cried on spying Lucius Devoe. "Who have we here? Eh? Who is he, my dear?" On heavy but still muscular legs, the merchant traversed his salon, keen gray eyes busy with his daughter's guest. He reminded Lucius of a rich East Indiaman entering port.

"Mr. Stanton," Mrs. Stanton informed him evenly and at the same time signaling her spouse to remove the snuff specks, "this is Lucius Devoe, an acquaintance of Sabra's, or should I say Dr. Devoe?"

"You're one of Billy Townsend's students, eh? How is the old rascal — still pickling cats and rats?"

"Papa, please! Dr. Devoe is a student no longer," Sabra broke in. "Uncle Will certificated Dr. Devoe, Asa Peabody, and Peter Burnham tonight. I — I chanced to be there."

"Young man, pray accept my hearty best wishes," Mr. Stanton offered a pudgy pink fist. "My brother-in-law ain't easy to satisfy — none of that family is."

Lucius bowed deeply, gracefully. "Your humble obedient servant, sir."

Over his shoulder Mr. Stanton called to a gentleman just entering the salon, "You'd best look lively, Aspinwall; you've fresh .competition in town."

The Jamaican's second bow was the essence of deference; his heart was hammering wildly. To think that he was being presented to the great Dr. Aspinwall!

One by one, other gentlemen appeared, surreptitiously picking their teeth with small gold picks kept in their vest pockets. Lucius took care to catch each and every name, to memorize them. Long since, he had perceived how ridiculously flattered most men are to be recognized by name.

The man with a fat, larval face was Briggs Hallowell — Lucius recognized the name immediately. It appeared regularly in the *Boston Gazette* as auctioneer over many a prize vessel. Hallowell appeared in company with a sunburned, broad-shouldered individual who walked with the peculiar swinging gait of a seafaring man. The stranger presented a striking figure in a truly magnificent coat of sky-blue velvet adorned by silvered vellum lapels and ornamented with a profusion of silver lace. Lucius's fingertips began to tingle. Jupiter! Those looked like solid gold buckles secured to the stranger's yellow morocco pumps. Yellow bristles faintly blurring the point of his jaw indicated that Mr. Hallowell's friend might be blond, though there was no being sure; his carefully curled chop wig was white as any snow field.

"Mrs. Stanton," Hallowell bowed awkwardly. "This is Mounseer Fougère, master of His Most Christian Majesty's sloop-of-war, *Ecureuil*."

The Frenchman made a very elegant bow, then bent to brush Mrs. Stanton's fingers with his lips. His vivid blue hair ribbon — its ends were nocked into neat swallow's tails — fluttered so bravely that Sabra's sister Theodosia gave a little ecstatic sigh and bit her lips cruelly hard behind her fan to give them color.

"*Cette honneur m'accomble,*" declared the French naval officer in deep and very resonant tones. "Consider me your most devoted slave, madame."

Lucius couldn't have been more surprised. Such Frenchmen as he had met while serving aboard the *Active* had been almost without exception dark, hairy and small-sized fellows, quick and nervous as racehorses at the barrier. This solid young wind-beaten giant was something new. From hard blue eyes to powerful legs, he could not have differed more from the common concept of a Frenchman.

Mrs. Stanton considered M. Fougère with sharp attention. So this chap commanded one of the French king's vessels-of-war, did he? If he was typical of the officers commanding the vessels of Admiral de Ternay's squadron, Messrs. Arbuthnot, Graves and Hood were due for some surprises.

Lucius realized suddenly that not only Sabra but both of her sisters were lost in a shameless admiration of M. Fougère's apparel. In open envy they studied his exquisitely fine Alençon laces, the sheerness of his white silk stockings and the elegant shape of yellow morocco pumps supported by high heels of a brilliant scarlet.

The slender young Jamaican was taking care not to address too much attention to Sabra, although, whenever she dared, she cast him a slow and lovely smile. Jupiter! How very sweet and warm-looking she appeared in her blue and rose dress. Only once did he seize an opportunity of addressing her privately. When Mrs. Stanton demanded birch logs to brighten the fire he'd sped to fetch them, found Sabra a step behind. Intoxicated with the trend of the evening, he had made bold to give her slim fingers a quick squeeze.

"When shall I see you again?"

"Possibly day after tomorrow. I intend to fetch some comforts to Dr. Blanchard's marine hospital for Mamma."

"When?"

"Oh, about three of the afternoon."

"Capital." Her acumen delighted him. As a rendezvous the hospital presented the most natural place imaginable.

When, unobtrusively, he reappeared, liquor-warmed conversation was causing the Stantons' salon to reverberate.

"We can't let the Southern states go British, Greenslett." Dr. Aspinwall shook his white-wigged head so vigorously that its black tie ribbon fluttered like a blackbird caught in a squall of wind.

"But Savannah is already lost and the betting's five to one Charleston will fall to Clinton and Graves within a matter of weeks. The Carolinas are British already to all intents and purposes."

"I don't agree. Ben Lincoln's down there with near five thousand men — and they claim he's a damned able general."

"Fiddlesticks!" snapped Greenslett. "Old Granny Lincoln's not another Greene or even a Wayne. Even that Frenchy boy, Lafayette, is more able. No, Will, I fear we must abandon the Southern colonies. Come now, is it not wiser by far to reach a compromise with Parliament? Once we have assured our own independence here in the North we must build up our strength, create a strong army and navy. Then, and only then, can we sensibly attempt to include the Southern states." The speaker took an agitated pinch of snuff. "Gad, Doctor, if you haven't seen Georgia and the Carolinas you've no concept of how poor and underpopulated they are — "

"Never, sir, never!" Dr. Aspinwall's tone was incisive as one of his own scalpels. "Our Southern neighbors should, and must, be considered an

[577]

integral part of our union — quite as much as Massachusetts or New York!"

Sabra's mother spoke to M. Fougère. "Gossip is running that the French king is to abandon his alliance with America because King George's Parliament has agreed to return all Canada to French sovereignty. The French forces are then to assist the British in subduing us. I trust there is no truth to it?"

Everyone looked at the big blue-clad Frenchman. *"Impossible! C'est impossible! Jamais, mes amis! L'idée est ridicule!"*

"Perhaps. I hope so. Have you heard this tale before, William?" Stanton demanded of Dr. Aspinwall.

The doctor nodded. "Aye! In my opinion 'tis but some Tory's trouble-mongering. Eh, M'sieu Fougère?"

The naval officer's assent was vehement. Never would Louis XVI break his pledged word or abandon his obligations to the Congress. The present alliance with America was presenting what His Most Christian Majesty and his ministers most earnestly desired — an opportunity to humble England's arrogance and boastful pride.

Color tinging his bronzed cheeks the big Frenchman looked about, blue eyes gleaming. Were mesdames and these gentlemen aware that the Dutch were on the verge of joining Spain, France and America in their coalition against George III?

Only Mr. Langdon had heard the good news. A small cheer arose and the girls clapped softly.

"Let's drink to that," Mr. Stanton suggested. "I say, what the deuce *is* the Dutch king's name?"

Nobody seemed to know so Lucius Devoe spoke for the first time. "I believe, sir, the Dutch had no king but a *Stadtholder*. He is William the Fifth and rules through a body called the States-General."

"Stateholder or king makes no mind," called Hallowell. "Let's toast something in a hurry; my whistle's drier than a charity sermon!"

Down the street a church bell commenced to clang and bong; another bell increased the clangor. Then, like a soprano joining in a deep male chorus, the hall clock added its silvery tones to announce the moment of midnight and the start of the new year.

The company faced about as the front door opened suddenly to admit a tall officer who whipped off a cockaded tricorn but never paused. His long stride into the salon caused his riding coat to fly apart, disclosing travel-stained doeskin breeches, blue tunic, deep red lapels and several gilded but tarnished buttons.

"Oh, Joshua!" Theodosia screamed and ran forward, but Sabra checked her impetuous rush.

Mrs. Stanton half rose, perforce fell back and in a choked voice faltered as young Captain Stanton knelt to kiss her hand. "My son, oh, Joshua, Joshua, my son!"

[578]

There was a distinctive Stanton set to this young officer's wind-reddened features; his eyes were bright and piercing as his mother's.

"Praise God, it's my boy!" old Mr. Stanton cried. "Home and safe. Welcome, lad. Welcome home from the wars. Don't cry, you silly girls, just because your brother's home."

Gallows Tree

Snow, fallen during the night, had not only spread a dazzling new blue-white covering over the farmers' fields, but veiled also those old entrenchments and redoubts scarring Boston Neck. Sometimes formidable drifts over the road to Dorchester Heights had barred Asa Peabody's way and delayed his progress. In addition the hired horse had proved to be ill-shod and so aged that its lower lip hung loose.

After sunup the temperature unexpectedly had dropped and now a brisk breeze out of the west was nipping savagely at Asa's nose and so much of his ears as showed above the rough gray muffler. This being of a Sunday's morning, the rented two-wheeled cart encountered little traffic beyond a scattering of citizens tramping into Boston to attend services.

Godfreys! But this wind was keen. Even at this late hour the cattle still stood close to their barns or nosed dispiritedly at snow-capped straw stacks in the stableyards. Once the physician's cart turned to traverse a wide cornfield and a flock of crows reluctantly rose from among the shocks of sere, wind-whipped stalks. More already were winging in from the slate-gray mud flats along Back Bay where a rising tide had halted their restless quest for offal, clams and stranded fishes. In ragged formation the sable column joined, headed for a woods beyond the outskirts of Dorchester; their cawing sounded sharp and clear in the blue winter sky.

Presently the horse panted around a turn in the deeply rutted road. Asa raised his gaze from the beast's steaming and furry rump to behold his goal. Stark, lonely and black against the sky, the gallows tree stood on the summit of a little knoll rising from the midst of a broad field. The tree, a gale-twisted red oak, had been struck by lightning a few years back and half killed. Asa shielded his gaze against the glare, was not particularly surprised to discern quite a small crowd gathered about that lonely oak.

Over his shoulder he cast a glance at Peter Burnham's figure lying huddled under a horse blanket on a pile of straw at the bottom of the cart. He was, at the moment, snoring manfully and clutching his cloak about him. Phew! What a head he'd have when he came to. Asa himself wasn't feeling any too spry this morning, thanks to three of Mr. Perkins's hot rum toddies. He drew several deep breaths of the crisp and invigorating morning air.

Because of increased desertions and other crimes committed by troops garrisoned in Boston, executions had become frequent. This would explain the small size of the crowd waiting in a loose circle about the gallows tree.

Asa's cart jolted near to the tree and he spoke to the lieutenant of the execution company.

"Beg pardon, sir; I seek Captain Morgan," he began politely.

"Oh, you do, do you now?" The officer cast Asa's black-clad figure a glance devoid of interest.

"Yes."

"Well, he ain't here," the lieutenant grunted. "Lucky bugger's sleeping off last night's jollification. I'm Lieutenant Anson. What the devil d'you want?"

Asa bent suddenly, somber brown eyes on the speaker. "Civility, sir, is common property. Why not avail yourself of your share?"

The lieutenant stared, then snorted, "You can stow the preaching. I've asked you already, what d'you want?"

"Here." Asa bit back his resentment, thrust out the order prepared by Captain Morgan.

Frowning in a glare off the snow the lieutenant scanned Asa's paper; his unshaven mouth tightened in a contemptuous grin. "So you've come abody-snatching, eh?"

Asa's wide brown features went a darker hue, but he hung onto his temper. After all, if he was to study the effect of a sudden interruption of the flow of blood to the liver, spleen and lungs, he badly needed this cadaver.

The unshaven lieutenant's nod was brusque as he returned the permit. "Seems in order. But mind, you'll have to cut the rogue down yourself. Damned if I'll have my men do it." He paused. "Well, Doctor, here comes your gallows' fruit," the lieutenant grunted in a half-hearted effort to atone for his previous churlishness. "Red Tom Duneen ought to keep you busy whittling for a good spell; he's a powerful big bruiser." He turned to the drummer boy. "Well, let's get on with it. Get ready to beat the 'Rogue's March.'"

"Yes, sir." The drummer boy nodded, tried by blowing on his chilled fingers to warm them.

No scaffold had been built beneath the oak, so the only indication of what impended was the presence of a noose dangling from a powerful lower limb. Starkly yellow, it swayed against the brilliant winter sky.

Asa debated waking Peter Burnham; still, despite a swollen jaw and slightly blackened eye the Connecticuter looked so comfortable he allowed him to sleep on.

Now the oxen were wading much closer, heads bent against the slope, their breathing creating silvery billows about their horns. To either side of the hay sledge three purple-faced infantrymen marched knee deep in the snow; every now and then the early morning sunlight would draw a blinding reflection from their needle-sharp bayonets. The ox drover, a bearded old farmer, walked close enough to his sledge to grip the hickory rail and yet manage his span.

The prisoner's seat — an empty powder keg — was not so low but that one could fail to witness his blank despairing expression; that his hands, pinioned tightly behind his back, were clenched. The condemned man, the onlookers perceived, was wearing a ragged brown uniform jacket — from which all buttons had been cut away — ragged black breeches and white woollen hose. One of his stockings had slipped, exposing the sinewy, hair-covered calf of his leg.

The other passenger was a spectacled little priest in clerical black. Adjusting his balance, he swayed awkwardly to the motion of the sledge, all the time reciting prayers.

The infantry forming the square momentarily moved apart to permit the sledge passage. It was at that precise instant that the prisoner, a hulking red-haired fellow, sprang suddenly to his feet and, with a thrust of his shoulders, knocked the priest out of the sledge so violently that the ministrant's shovel hat and prayerbook flew far out over the snow.

Though hampered by bound arms, Duneen, screaming in hoarse insensate defiance, cleared the hay sledge's low rail, but on landing lost his footing and went floundering, rolling, over and over in the snow.

Snow-covered from head to foot, Tom Duneen regained his feet, thought to detect a gap and charged towards it, still screeching his terror, his revolt at what was about to be done to him. Someone tripped him, whereat a trio of guards dropped their muskets, and like hounds on a deer, flung themselves upon him.

Duneen's foot lashed out desperately, caught one soldier such a kick in the crotch that he doubled up screaming out his agony. With a desperate thrust of massive shoulders the prisoner bowled another clean off his feet, but still remained hemmed in.

"Ah, no, lads! Mercy!" the prisoner was gibbering. "Don't hang poor Tom Duneen. I can't, I — I won't die. Mercy, for the love of Mary. Help! Please, please, Lieut'nt Anson, don't let 'em kill me. Crogan! Ye'll help me? Don't we come from the same village?"

"Be still, ye treacherous murdering dog," snarled the sergeant. "'Tis spoiling a very pretty hangin' yez are."

"Hang him! Hang him!" shrilled one of the women gazing in wide-eyed fascination upon Duneen's struggles.

Several minutes elapsed before the guards succeeded in applying additional bonds and were able to lug the condemned man, still struggling and screaming back onto the hay sledge.

The execution detail shifted nervously in their ranks and breathed mighty hard because the doomed man kept up his inhuman screaming. It was so poignant of a searing, tearing fear that Asa felt hairs on the back of his neck stir and rise.

"Gag him, you Goddamned fools!" the lieutenant yelled. "Crogan, if you don't shut that bastard up in two minutes, I'll break you back to ranks."

Once the prisoner's dreadful sobbing cries had been stifled by a scarf twisted about his mouth, the lieutenant hawked, spat and then drew from his belt a scroll of blue paper. He glanced at the civilian group. Evidently in the grip of a macabre awe, a few women had turned aside, but most of them looked on, open-mouthed, in delicious horror.

"Hear ye, hear ye, one and all!" Lieutenant Anson intoned. "Having been duly tried by a competent court-martial, former Corporal Thomas Duneen, B Company, Second Massachusetts Infantry, has been found guilty on two counts of murder, three of desertion, and one of counterfeiting the currency of the Sovereign State of Massachusetts. The court-martial therefore has ordered this prisoner, the said Thomas Duneen, to be conducted to this place of execution" — Lieutenant Anson paused to catch his breath — "and on the morning of January the first, in the year of our Lord 1780, the said Thomas Duneen shall be hanged by the neck until dead, dead, dead. May God take mercy on his soul." Using absurd care, Lieutenant Anson folded the scroll and tucked it back into his sword belt. He then drew a sword, a slight dress weapon equipped with a slender, useless curved blade. In a low voice he called, "Drummer, sound off!"

Once the complicated cadence of the "Rogue's March" began to beat through the clear winter air, the hay sledge slid forward. Squarely under that noose swaying against the sky the driver halted his oxen.

The prisoner's struggles slowed, then ceased altogether. Two infantrymen raised Duneen to his feet; they had to support him by his elbows because the murderer's knees wavered like those of a man far gone in liquor.

"Will yez behave?" the sergeant demanded while adjusting the noose. "Ye can make a speech, then."

Duneen nodded and had his gagging scarf removed. Asa could tell that the prisoner had calmed and, though his bloodshot eyes still rolled, he stood straight and still; handsome in a bold, brutal fashion.

" 'Tis steady I am again, bhoys," he called in a loud, clear voice. "Forgive me for the trouble I've given yez for 'tis a Judas-guilty sinner that I am." Blinking from the glare off the dazzling snow fields he looked about. "Father, will yez pray the Blessed Virgin, in her great mercy, to overlook my crimes?" The priest nodded. "Then, Sergeant, dear, let's get on wi' this business; ye'll be terrible dry 'fore 'tis done."

The lieutenant's sword glistened in an upward movement, remained up, shone blue-white like an icicle in the wintry light. The drum commenced to roll, slowly at first, then fast, faster, and yet faster. Asa felt his throat close, sweat break out on his mittened hands.

The ox drover shifted his chew of tobacco and kept one eye on the sword as, expectantly, he lifted his ox goad. The sergeant and his fellows retreated to the front of the sledge, leaving Duneen precariously balanced on the keg.

In a glittering arc the lieutenant's sword swept downwards and, almost simultaneously the drover jabbed his near ox. "Hup, you Judy!" he sang out. "Hup, you Jack!" Obedient, the great creatures bent their heads and settled into the oaken oxbows, steam clouding their heads. The sledge's runners creaked in the snow.

A pang akin to nausea made Asa's stomach tighten, his bowels contract, when he watched Duneen's brown-clad figure topple awkwardly off the keg. Under the sudden drag the big oak branch bent but snapped back, and bits of dark brown bark rained down to speckle the snow.

Tom Duneen's fall was a scant three feet; he suffered no broken neck.

Impressions of what followed remained engraved in Asa's memory as long as he lived; a burly figure revolving slowly at the end of the rope, twisting, bucking in powerful but futile contortions which endured for nearly five minutes. All this while the green-faced drummer boy kept beating the long roll; horrified and keeping eyes fixed on his officer.

When, at long last, Tom Duneen's body hung motionless, a dark outline against the raw blue of the sky, Lieutenant Anson lowered his sword and rasped, "Sergeant, take over." The lieutenant fished in the pocket of his coattail, brought out a small stone bottle from which he took a long, long drink. "Have a drink, Doctor?"

Still numbed and shaken to the depth of his being, Asa shook his head. How easy it was to take life, he was thinking, and how very difficult it was to save.

"Drink?" Peter Burnham's disheveled red head appeared over the edge of the cart. Straw stalks clung to his tangled ruddy hair and lent him a comical appearance. "For God's sake, give me a swallow. My mouth's drier'n a damn' chalk pit."

The lieutenant gaped at this sudden apparition; then laughed and passed over his bottle. "Yer main lucky to have missed this bad business. Help yourself." Sword tucked under arm and threadbare gray cape aswing, Lieutenant Anson ran after the ox sledge and jumped aboard.

Soon only the two young physicians remained below the gallows tree.

In a Dark Cellar

Frayed and greasy, the rope tautened until the tackle block creaked and its roller commenced slowly to revolve. Presently, rapid dripping sounds filled a damp stillness pervading the cellar and drowned out the soft panting of three men heaving on the line.

"Sway away! Smartly now," Asa gasped, keeping an eye on the brim of

[583]

a brine tun. Slowly, smoothly were appearing the sodden head and pallid shoulders of ex-Corporal Tom Duneen's cadaver. Lank red hair dangled stringily, hid the dead man's features and all but concealed a sharp steel hook lifting the corpse by its chin. Briny odors, reminiscent of a fish-pickling works, grew stronger.

"Lower away — handsomely now!" Asa directed. "Grab the bastard's ankles, Lucius, and steady him down."

A soft *bump!* marked the impact of the cadaver's heels; by easing on the hoist line the ghastly figure was permitted to collapse gradually. Because the skin of the dead man's legs already had been removed clear up to his thighs, their musculature now was revealed, blue-black, in a sharp and fascinating relief.

Lucius crossed the cellar to trim one of their two whale-oil lamps into greater efficiency. "If you two butchers are about ready to begin your hacking, I'll get after my own work."

From a shallow pickling tub the Jamaican removed an old market basket containing the executed criminal's vital organs. This he deposited, leaking copiously, upon a small table after hurriedly pushing to safety sheets of sketching paper, pencils and a number of water colors. Sighing softly, Lucius selected the bloody, purplish spleen, and after testing the edge of his knife, commenced to section it — hard work because the yellow-red lamplight was abominably inadequate. Due to a violent popular prejudice against dissections, they hadn't dared take advantage of two carefully boarded-up windows which might have admitted considerable daylight into Widow Southeby's cellar.

"Have you any special desire to work on poor Tom's murderous heart?" asked Asa.

"No, I'm for a knee joint today," Peter replied slowly. "Quite an improvement, this, on attempting conclusions from old Fothergill's anatomical charts, eh what?"

"Good old Tom Duneen," Asa mumbled and bent over the great jelly-like clot of the heart.

"Fothergill, I'm sure, is wrong about the extent and use of the quadriceps tendon of the knee." Peter's lips compressed themselves. "God's truth, Asa, why should people object to the dissection of a human body? How're we to learn what's wrong with 'em if we don't know what's right? Steady all!"

Presently Peter observed, "Old Townsend was thorough, granted; but d'you know, Asa, he's omitted a cardinal item in our training?"

"Eh?" Asa glanced up.

"Hardly a word has he imparted concerning female anatomy, let alone afford us opportunity for dissection."

"Of course not," Lucius snapped over his shoulder. "Willie Townsend's an eminently respectable old fogey. Chance a scandal? Not he."

"Yes," Peter continued as if he had heard nothing, "females are structurally very different from men — as we have had the pleasure of discovering on occasion. For instance, a woman's femur sets into her pelvis at an angle very different from that of a male. It follows, therefore, that there must be no end of important variations in the structure of other joints — particularly in the pelvic region." He continued cutting, bending low in the uncertain red-yellow glare of the lantern. Abruptly he straightened, faced his companions, "I mean to dissect a female before the winter's out, come what may."

"Avast there," warned Asa, a grim set to his features. "The time for that lies somewhere in the future. Don't risk ruining your career at its start by treading such all-fired dangerous ground."

"Your hardihood and curiosity exceed your discretion, my lad," Devoe told him earnestly. "Jupiter! The Boston public is dead set enough even against the dissection of criminals. Were you ever detected exploring the tender mysteries of the female form divine you could count yourself lucky to escape with a suit of tar and feathers and a term in prison."

The big, redheaded young doctor lowered his voice and looked up, one hand still grasping the great aductor tendon. "In fact, my friends — I — " He hesitated, blinked, then continued in tones of scarcely suppressed excitement, "I have — we — you may, if you wish, have an opportunity of — "

Asa's broad figure straightened; the expression of his dark brown eyes was intense. "Peter — you *haven't?* You haven't gone hunting female cadavers."

"Yes." His tone was a trifle defiant. "I entered conversation with a certain carter last night; for the modest sum of five pounds, hard money, this fellow vows he can procure the corpse of a young woman."

"Impossible!" Lucius stared over his half-completed watercolor sketch. "He'd not dare rob a graveyard for such a sum!"

Peter grinned. "For him there is no need. The rascal's brother is an undertaker. I tell you it's safe."

Dr. Peabody's Patient

Lizzie Wright splashed another — and final — bucket of hot water into her establishment's one hip bath; then, panting, pushed a strand of sand-colored hair from before small and piggy blue eyes. Though battered and much dented, the bath was her pride and joy. Of real copper, it certainly was the only such convenience in all the neighborhood — a fact which put firm ground under Lizzie's oft-repeated contention that her wenches were the cleanest to be found anywhere in Battery Street. Actually, the bath gathered dust thirteen days a fortnight.

"The good Lord alone knows why I toil like a black slave to accommodate such a worthless, finicky, la-de-dah baggage like you, Hilde. Yer a lucky girl, but too addled in the head to know it."

The madam used her chapped and black-nailed forefinger to scrape from her brow a thin film of sweat. Resentfully, she regarded her doxy's slight figure seated, shivering violently, on the bed's edge. "Just you understand me well, Hilde. Now that ye'll be fresh-washed as any nabob's fancy-girl, yer to demand *and get* ten shilling, else ye'll taste the strap again, and twice as hard."

"Yes'm." Hilde Mention kept miserable black eyes fixed on her own dirty bare toes curling against the chill of the floor. "I'll do the best I can, indeed I will. I — I'll give this one a real, first-class tumble. I really will."

For all she'd been asleep near fourteen hours Hilde still felt uncommon sleepy and weary, incapable of further revolt. She sighed and shivered when warm air from the bath fanned the black hair hanging so limp and greasy over her forehead.

"You'll not regret this kindness, Mrs. Wright. The — this doctor's queer about soap and water. Why, he — he washed me himself."

"I'll wager he did and had ye, too, ye cheating little vixen."

Dr. Peabody had been so kind, honest-spoken and steady. The only other such person she'd known had been Mooinaskw; she'd dearly loved her Micmac foster mother, for all that the old woman smelled much like the she-bear for which she was named.

"He'd better pay well — hard money too. Mind ye git back here by five. There's a nice sea capt'n been taken by yer looks, though God knows why he'd want a bag o'bones like you." Lizzie Wright wiped her hands on a dull blue apron. "Ye've been livin' here on the fat o' the land these past three months and 'ave yet to earn me a pound. Declare, I can't figger what ails ye."

The madam paused, hands on hips, blotchy features set in an expression of frank bewilderment. "You get my fanciest gent customers fair slobberin' fer you and yet ye freezes 'em. Why, they'd buy ye laces an' farthingales an' rings an' mebbe furs if ye'd only study to please 'em. What for do ye want 'em to swear they loves ye? Pah!" Mrs. Wright spat resoundingly. "That's fer love! Fer all their silly tales men an' boys don't come to Battery Street lookin' fer love — only to glut their lust and try the fancy games they dassent to at home. And you, you silly ninny, keep on moonin' of a knight in shinin' silver armor who'll come aridin' to carry you off ter everlastin' bliss."

Overcome by the girl's unreasonableness Ma Wright caught up a stick of kindling and fetched Hilde such a resounding whack on her thigh that she gasped and cringed. "Mebbe that'll warn ye to get such notions out o' yer head. Just you come back empty-handed and I'll have Jack give you such a hidin' yer won't walk fer a week!"

The perfect answer occured to Hilde as, slowly, she rubbed the smarting spot. A slow, wise smile curved her lips, thin and blue, but still subtly lovely.

"I — I guess you're right, ma'am. There are no longer any knights. From now on I — I shall cease to look for one."

A sharp west wind beating through the garret's floor lifted little puffs of dust and sent chills climbing up Hilde's thin legs as Lizzie Wright waddled out, enormous buttocks rolling under her faded callimanco skirt like ground swells across a sandbar. Said she over a huge and flabby shoulder, "Mind ye, miss, yer bound in my employ fer two more years. God help ye if yer minded to run off and try to bilk me."

Hilde dried herself and lingered a moment to let the unaccustomed warmth play over her back, thin little buttocks and legs; thank goodness the welt was fading. What, she wondered, could be causing this faintest imaginable greenish tinge in her skin?

First, she was going to discharge her debt to Dr. Peabody — or attempt to. How amazing; she was almost glad at the prospect of going to a man. Surely he would be gentle and tender? If only she had met Dr. Peabody when first she'd reached Boston: of course now it was too late — much too late.

Hurrying into her only other shift, she was surprised to feel hungry, ravenously so. Of late she had become quite accustomed to enduring the pangs caused by an empty belly. There being nothing to eat, Hilde swallowed several deep gulps from a lead-mended jug standing beside her bed. Sure enough, the water took an edge off her appetite.

In a hurry now, Hilde laced up a brown velvet bodice, adjusted the set of her green-and-brown-striped kersey skirt, then flung a frayed gray shawl about her shoulders. What a pity there was no mirror; she would like to have learned whether this heat she felt burning in her cheeks had relieved the customary dead-white of her complexion.

For a last time Hilde's hands crept out to the dying coals. She felt fine as satin at the prospect of quitting this wretched, icy box of a room, those sordid rags of underclothes dangling so uglily from wooden pegs driven into beams gray with cobwebs and dust. God pity the next poor female who must inhabit these dreary surroundings. One would probably be moved in tomorrow; what with the hard times, the war, and the ever-lengthening casualty lists, girls and young women aplenty came drifting from up and down the coast into Boston, a thriving metropolis where twelve thousand souls made their homes.

The January air was cold enough in itself, but driven by the westerly breeze that was blowing, it stung Hilde's body through the scant protection of her petticoats, shawl and skirt like the bite of a wasp, and nipped cruelly at her uncovered and still-damp head and ears. Luckily, a brief winter sun was shining, drawing pale yellow reflections from windows of the fine new houses dotting Beacon Hill.

Hilde knew that the distance to Sudbury Street was not very great, but her legs were feeling so queerly uncertain she wondered how much time would be consumed in reaching Dr. Peabody's address.

Although breathing painfully hard, Hilde started upwards, the dirty snow crunching under her square-toed shoes; many of the oaken pegs securing their soles had dropped out and now admitted cold and slush.

It is an odd thing to have gone through life lacking any idea of who one really is, she mused as she struggled along. Her last name seemed right for some reason — Mention. Plenty of people had commented on her oval features, slender hands and narrow feet — and on the very faint slant of her eyes. Where her name of Hildegard came from, Hilde knew well enough; Frau Schroeder had called her that, piously declaring it shameful that a white and presumably Christian girl should be known by the outlandish Indian name of *Kwee-a-lin.*

Outlandish or not, Hilde reflected, those savages, the Micmacs, were the kindest people she'd ever met. How she had loved their lazy good nature and their simple sense of honor and justice.

If only the Reverend Neidiger had left her alone. She was completely happy that day playing, dirty and half naked, among those dark-complexioned children in the bark wigwam of Wejek, subchief of the Micmacs. A stiff smile curved Hilde's lips. Wejek and dear old Mooinaskw could be stern, but generally were most indulgent with her. It being the Algonquin custom for children to adopt their mother's clan, Mooinaskw had her inducted into her Turtle clan. How proud and happy she had been.

Oh why, of all the Indian villages in Nova Scotia, had the Reverend Hugo Neidiger to wander, lost and on the point of starvation, into their village? But for that her life might have continued a happy one. Unluckily the pastor noticed her, a pale-skinned little savage girl, packing dried blueberries in birch-bark cones.

Br-r-r-r. The wind roaring down Sudbury Street tore anew at Hilde's shawl and gnawed her cheeks. She sighed and started on.

She wondered what arguments the Reverend Dr. Neidiger used on Wejek and what price he paid for her ransom. Wejek wasn't one to give things away — except to friends. How she had kicked, clawed and squalled at being parted from Mooinaskw. She remembered scratching four scarlet furrows across the Reverend Dr. Neidiger's cheek before he gave her a box on the ear and tossed her frightened half to death onto the bottom of the old canoe Wejek gave him.

Hilde supposed Minna Schroeder and Helmuth, her huge stupid-looking husband, meant to do their Hanoverian best by her, but from the start they were over-ready to whip her for even the least disobedience of rules she couldn't understand. And that wasn't all that made her miserable; the little Schroeders, all ten of them, hated her for being so different. How they had tormented her every waking moment in a hundred ways, how they had mocked and ridiculed her poor efforts to learn their ugly language.

At last number fifty-one Sudbury Street loomed before Hilde's eyes. There could be no doubt that this was the correct address; a new, hand-carved sign read: A. PEABODY, B.M.

Praying that the doctor might not be out, Hilde drew a deep breath, climbed three steps and reached for a tarnished brass knocker and rapped timidly. She listened, but heard only her heart. It was pounding like the hoofs of a runaway horse.

She was rearranging her shawl when the door to number fifty-one creaked open and a wrinkle-faced little woman stuck her head out. When she noticed the caller's lip rouge she drew back a little before demanding sharply, "Well? What do you want here?"

"I — I seek Dr. Peabody," Hilde faltered. "He told me I was to come here for — for treatment."

Asa came to the door and called briskly, "Please to enter."

At first he failed to recognize this small, black-haired young woman hesitating on his threshold; details of that brawl at the Red Lion already had faded from his memory. All the same he saw at a glance that this girl was deathly pale and thin as any bittern.

"Good afternoon, Dr. Peabody, I — I see that you do not remember?" His caller sounded surprised and regretful.

A wide and friendly smile dispersed the uncertainty on his broad features. "Why, as God's my life, 'tis Mistress Hilde. So you obeyed my instructions? Do come in. I am very glad to see you."

"Are you?" she demanded, her great dark eyes flying wide open. "Are you really, Doctor?"

"Of course. Please be seated. You've been resting? Eating as I advised?" he demanded, noting her labored breathing and the complete lack of color in her meager cheeks — they should have been glowing on a day cold as this. Those pale brown demi-lunes beneath her eyes, though oddly attractive, should not have existed at all. Um — and what of that very faint but still noticeable greenish tinge to the skin about her neck and near her temples?

At the same time he was aware that her intense black eyes were taking him in from scuffed shoes to carelessly combed brown hair. A wavering smile crossed lips which, beneath their trace of paint, were lavender-hued.

His hand went out towards her head. "So long as you are here, Hilde, let me examine that cut."

A single glance reassured him that the contusion was just as insignificant as he had remembered; moreover it was healing well. Why then had this young female come to him? Surely she had not walked so far — weak as she most evidently was — just to invite examination of this trivial hurt?

"Is — is it mending, sir?"

[589]

"Aye, a firm sanguineous crust has formed," he reassured. "But you must be careful with your comb not to dislodge it."

By this clear light he could distinguish very distinctly the blue veins in Hilde's eyelids. What the devil? Her eyes kept narrowing as if she were very weary. Prompted by a sudden curiosity he took her hand and tested her pulse; his misgivings multiplied at finding it so very slow and weak.

"Tell me," he inquired once more, "have you been reposing as I instructed you?"

"Oh, yes, Doctor. I — well — Mrs. Wright let me lie abed yesterday all day long."

"You have had plenty to eat?"

Not being a practiced liar she only dropped her eyes to regard her wrist still imprisoned between his strong stubby fingers.

"Look at me, Hilde," he directed very gently, "and tell me the exact truth. Have you had enough to eat these last few days?"

A long sigh escaped her. "Well, not exactly. You see, Doctor, I — I haven't been earning much, and — "

"When did you last eat?"

"Yesterday at noon."

"Of what did the meal consist?"

"Bread."

"Is that all?"

"Yes, sir. Mrs. Wright said 'twas all I deserved."

"Lucifer take such a woman!" Indignation boiled within him. How far more cruel people could be to one another than the beasts of the forest.

Asa left the room and called for Mrs. Southeby, but she had stepped out, most likely to borrow some item from a neighbor.

The kitchen cupboard yielded half a smoked herring, a lump of cheese, some skimmed milk and the very stale heel of a loaf. If only he could come across a bit of real tea; right now something hot and mildly stimulating would restore his patient better than anything else. All he found in the canister was a miserable substitute called "liberty tea" — in reality dried raspberry leaves.

As usual, a tea kettle sat on the back of the stove sending up wandering feathers of steam, so he flung some leaves into the cup and stirred it until the brew took on an amber color. Then, loading the food onto a wooden trencher, he returned to the consultation room.

To Asa's surprised annoyance the room was empty, but a soft noise from upstairs prompted him to call out, "I say, Mistress Hilde, where are you?"

"Up here," her voice sounded low and quivering. "Please come — "

What the devil? She'd no business up there. Leaving plate and cup on his desk, he took the stairs two at a time and found the door to his room just a trifle ajar. On pushing it wider he emitted an incredulous gasp. There standing beside his bed was his patient, her garments forming a white and green puddle at her feet. Save for white stockings and yellow ribbon garters supporting them Hilde was quite nude, though she yet held her petticoat dangling from one hand. Further, she had loosened her abundant black hair, permitting it to tumble in a sable cascade over one shoulder. It was so long it reached almost as low as the red marks her petticoat ties had sketched about her waist.

Straight, thin and white as some medieval craftsman's carved ivory representation of Eve, Hilde stood waiting, her immature, pale-pink-tipped breasts lifting very rapidly to her respiration.

Every detail of her rib structure was recognizable, also the planes of her pelvis and shoulder bones. Scarlet to the brows, Asa remained rooted, will-power momentarily atrophied. For all his medical training, never, until this moment, had he beheld a mature female completely nude.

"Wh — what — " he choked. "Have you gone mad?"

"Oh, no." Her eyes wavered, fell. "You see, I — I haven't any money and since you were so — so very good and kind to me the other night — I — "

Suddenly he collected himself, turned aside his head. He was sweating like a stevedore and about as clever. "For heaven's sake put your things on again."

She covered her face with both hands, commenced to sob. "I had not deemed myself to be so very undesirable. Please forgive me." Then in a muffled voice, *"Mon Dieu, c'est bien le fin — je ne peux plus —"*

At the sound of a faint thud Asa spun about to find that Hilde Mention had lost consciousness. Thin limbs awkwardly outflung, she lay inert on the bare pine floorboards with her jet hair streaming in all directions like spilled ink.

Conscience-stricken, he hurried to pick up the frail figure and was about to place the senseless girl on his bed when a voice, shrill with outrage, demanded.

"Well, sir! What sort of scandalous conduct is this?" A cone of sugar still in one hand, Mrs. Southeby was glaring from the doorway. "Never in my born days have I seen the like of it!"

"Mrs. Southeby! Please pull back the coverlet when I lift her." Right now, Asa Peabody was far from suggesting a grave young physician capable of dealing with any and all crises. "My arms are full."

"So I see," she snapped in icy tones. "Here's a pretty howd'y'do. The idee your carrying on like this in my decent house when my back's turned."

Correctly, he realized that his landlady was beyond reasoning, so he almost flung Hilde onto his bed, took the widow by both shoulders and shook her gently. "Just you listen to me, Mrs. Southeby; listen, and stop this witless ranting."

"Ranting! How dare you!"

"You deem yourself a real Christian, don't you?" he demanded, dark eyes glowing. "Answer me, Mrs. Southeby. Answer me!"

"A fine one, you, to put such a question even while your — your leman defiles this house."

"You do neither yourself nor me much credit by such talk," Asa grimly informed her. "Now listen. This is God's truth. This young woman came here very ill — "

"Why'd she strip herself nekkid as an egg?"

"She was out of her senses with fever and fainted as you came in."

"A likely tale!" sniffed the landlady, but ceased trying to break away. "Just you take your hands off me, Asa Peabody. You know right well if I hadn't come home the minute I did you'd be with her in that bed. I — I hate you!"

"Have I ever before given you cause for complaint, ma'am?"

Fluttering, smoothing her sleeves back into place, she evaded his look. "Not exactly, but this — "

"Then, please — I need your help."

He turned, drew a patched and faded crazy quilt over the motionless, marble-pale figure.

"Please see if you can't rouse her. You, as a doctor's widow, ought to know how. I'll go fetch some stimulants."

"I'll wager she's shamming." Breathing heavily, Mrs. Southeby bent, took the girl by one emaciated bare shoulder and shrilled right in Hilde's ear, "Wake up! Get your clothes on and get out of here!"

"Oh, for heaven's sake, ma'am, stop such nonsense. The girl's ill, I tell you. Look at that green tint to her skin."

He was right, she saw. This strange girl with the devil's brand on her lips lay motionless, an almost shadowy figure so colorless against pillow-case and counterpane. Her narrow chest remained quite motionless.

At that Mrs. Southeby straightened her mobcap and stood erect.

"Forgive me, Doctor." She held out a pleading, work-wrinkled hand. "I — I don't rightly know why I've been acting like I did. I ought to have known you would never cause me shame."

The First Patient of Dr. Burnham

"God love me, 'tis wonderful to be ashore and home again." Captain Robert Ashton, master-owner of the twelve-gun privateer brig *Grand Turk III*, sighed comfortably while brushing a scattering of yellow johnnycake crumbs from his Sunday best waistcoat of Turkey red silk. Once he had pushed his chair back from the dining table, Harriett, darker-haired of Rob and Andrea Ashton's twin girls, instantly scuttled from her seat with the speed of a small white rabbit to return from the living room clutching a pipe, tobacco canister and tinder pistol. After smiling sweetly on her father, Harriett turned, and in triumph, stuck out the tip of a pink tongue at Susan, her twin.

Presently Andrea Ashton appeared, smiling from her clear, gold-splintered hazel eyes as well as with her lips. "Captain Ashton, your elder son enjoys an Ashton appetite. I thought he'd never have done."

Rob Ashton chuckled, placed an arm about his wife's waist — still a slender one for all that she had borne him four children in as many years — and brushed her cheek with his lips.

Playfully she tapped the captain's hand. "La, sir, 'tis ever the gallant gentleman you remain. Those French and Spanish hussies keep you in practice, I'll warrant."

His squarish, weather-beaten features relaxed. "Of course, my pet, of course; every evening and twice of a Saturday. You'll join me in a glass of Madeira?"

Rob, a sturdy, brown-haired man looking a little older than his actual thirty-two years, poured two glasses of Madeira and raised his glass. "Your health, my love; you shine as a mother, and as a wife."

Andrea turned quickly, tenderness bright in her expression. "Thank you, sweeting," she whispered. "And to you, sir; 'tis wond'rous fun being married to you, Captain Ashton. Let us proceed to the living room. I'd sit on your lap if the girls weren't about."

"They've gone aloft — "

" 'Upstairs,' you incorrigible sea dog."

A little while later Rob crossed the room to select a coal from the hearth and, in a pair of brass tongs, held it to his pipe bowl. Only then did he notice his wife's abstraction. Patricianly handsome in her flowered gown of yellow damask, Andrea was sitting as erect as usual, but considering with unseeing eyes the wonderfully delicate ivory and bone model of a French bugalet — an odd, outlandish rig calling for two masts — which he'd discovered years ago, aboard a prize.

"Wherefore the brown study, my love?"

Andrea looked up quickly, hazel eyes earnestly questioning. "Rob, dearest one — do you plan to go to sea again soon?"

All through Sunday dinner Rob had dreaded her asking just that question. The devil fly away with his brig's first officer! Why had Gideon Pickering, that lanky and taciturn Connecticuter out of Groton, felt it incumbent upon him to stop by and raise the question of a sailing date?

Rob's sturdy legs, well outlined in white Italian silk stockings, took him to the far end of the living room and halfway back. By the mantelpiece he paused, a solid, dependable sort of man. Above his best jabot of sparkling Valenciennes lace a frown creased his features.

"You may as well learn now," he told Andrea evenly, "that we shall sail soon because I have serving aboard the *Turk* at present the best-trained crew I have ever signed. Should I delay too long in port, I'll likely lose most of my best hands — and I can't afford to part with a single gunner."

Andrea bit her lip. "Oh, Rob — must you go again so soon? Why, we've hardly had you with us a fortnight."

"I fear so. I have received intelligence that Sir Henry Clinton, down in New York, is expecting the arrival of a convoy from Cork."

Joyous cries raised by the twins, now romping upstairs, filled an uncomfortable silence. Rob put down his cold pipe, commenced to drum absently upon the mantel of gleaming yellow pine.

"Pray believe that I lament this necessity of putting to sea so soon, sweeting; 'fore God I do."

"Why continue privateering at all?" Andrea demanded tensely. "You hate fighting, you know, quite as much as you enjoy trading. You have amassed for us a very sizable fortune — you own three vessels outright and a warehouse filled with Sheffield and West Indies goods. Here in Boston you are extremely well regarded and have connections with all the best merchants." She reached out, took his hands. "And, Rob, need I remind you that now you have quite a family to look after?"

A faint smile lit his weathered features. "No. We seem to have done extra well in that respect, too."

"Rob, for our sakes, won't you give over privateering? For near five years you have been monstrous fortunate; stop now, whilst you may. Oh, darling, some day one of those fast new British frigates they speak of will come up with the *Grand Turk* and then — and then you'll be killed or captured — and the admiralty won't exchange seamen any longer. Won't you take up trading abroad again? Mr. Phillips, Mr. Leverett — oh, everybody — vows that now that the French and Spanish are at war against England, trade over here will become ever so brisk."

The captain's stubby fingers continued their drumming. "Everything you say is true," Rob admitted, "except that last. To be sure trade may flourish, but it will be a chancy traffic. Neither the Dons nor the Frenchies will send their prizes here for sale because there's no hard money to be had. Deprived of the goods we fetch to prize auctions in our privateers, Boston trade would stagnate." He spoke carefully, selecting his words, "You speak of trading abroad. Tell me, my dear, what chance has an unarmed merchant vessel of reaching her destination these days?"

Andrea sighed, made a small helpless motion with one hand.

"Again, what would I use for money? Real goods are the only worthwhile currency at present. No standard currency exists in all North America, unless you count an occasional piece-of-eight, or Spanish dollar." He stared out into the street. "To top everything, I heard Lem Abbott swear at the coffeehouse yesterday that the Congress is about to declare all Continental notes invalid. Tell me, sweeting, how I can do business deprived of currency and credit?"

"If you feel the *Grand Turk* must go to sea again why not put Mr.

Pickering in command for this cruise? You've always thought so highly of him."

"Gideon's a good and able officer," Ashton admitted, frowning at the brass fender by his feet. "But there's a vast difference between a good first officer and a satisfactory skipper. Gideon's a born pessimist and over-severe in the matter of discipline."

From above sounded faint and sleepy whimperings. Master Robbie at last. Instinctively Andrea's fingers commenced to untie her bodice laces. She'd better hurry upstairs before the baby really got to howling and up-setting the other children. Oh bother! The twins now were racing around like a pair of squirrels.

She paused in the living room doorway, the strings of her bodice hang-ing loose and her breasts swelling ripe and round against the sheer lawn of her undershift. "I'm sure you know best, Rob," she told him, smiling. "Still, I wish you'd mull over my suggestion about sending Pickering in your stead."

Captain Ashton got up, moved towards his wife. "My darling, because you never have spoken in this strain before," he began in his soft Virginian voice, "I will give the matter my deepest — "

The words died on his lips, banished by a thin scream and a gasp, followed by something bumping and thumping down the stairs. Andrea stifled a cry and whirled about. "Rob! Come quick! Oh, God have mercy!" she gasped, swooping down on Susan. The child lay motionless at the foot of the staircase, her left arm thrust from under her at a shocking and un-natural angle.

A single terrified glance apprised Rob that from his daughter's elbow was protruding a slim splinter of bone. White and sharp-looking as a small bayonet, it had pierced the child's pale-blue muslin sleeve; already a bright red stain was soaking the fabric.

Rob picked up Susan's limp, diminutive form and placed the white-faced little thing on the living room divan. It was entirely characteristic of Andrea Ashton that she indulged in no hysterics, broke into no useless lamentations — only her eyes betrayed her anguish.

Rob started for the door. "Whom do you employ as physician?"

"Dr. Chase," Andrea called, at the same time slipping a cushion under her daughter's dark head. "Oh dear! It's a long way to his house."

"Is no doctor any nearer?" The captain's voice had assumed a metallic quality any of his officers would have recognized.

"No. Wait! Hester said a new doctor has set up practice just around the corner in Charter Street."

"His name?"

"I don't know, but — oh Rob, fetch him. Quickly! *Quickly!*"

Without delaying for hat, coat or cape, Rob Ashton went pelting out down Snow Street. A moment later he was rounding the corner into Charter Street searching for a physician's name on one of the housefronts.

He saw it almost at once, a modest shingle bearing the name P. BURNHAM, B.M. nailed below a ground-floor window. Captain Ashton was pounding up a short ash-strewn walk when a young fellow appeared at the door.

"Your pardon," Rob panted. "There has been an accident. I seek a Dr. Burnham."

"I am he, sir, and at your service."

"Please to follow me and at once, please. My daughter has fallen the length of the stairs and has broken her arm and God alone knows what else."

"In an instant, sir, I will accompany you."

Once in the privateersman's living room, Peter ran to the divan, slit the child's sleeve and, watched in miserable silence by the Ashtons, made a rapid examination. As he feared, his first patient had suffered a compound fracture; unluckily both the radius and the ulna bones had been broken. What made the fracture dangerous was that the ulna protruded jaggedly a full two inches through the flesh and that the puncture was bleeding freely.

Captain Ashton cleared his throat gruffly, then announced, "I am conducting Mrs. Ashton outside. I will return immediately."

"No, no! I don't wish to go," Andrea protested. "Susan is my child, too. You know I am no coward."

"That I know — and well. But believe me, this is a different matter."

To break the news to his wife that an amputation of Susan's arm necessarily must take place would require tact and preparation. Rob stared on his daughter from miserable eyes. It revolted his soul to realize that this bright, merry little creature was doomed to go through life maimed, a spinster, and an object of pity, but if Susan were to survive, no other course was open. On shipboard, as everywhere else, a compound fracture resulted in gangrene and dreadful death — failing immediate amputation. Such a wound became turgid and filled with malignant pus.

Rob swallowed hard. He felt all green and gray inside as he led Andrea stony-faced and walking stiffly back to his office. There he placed both hands on shoulders quivering beneath his touch.

"We have weathered many trials together, dear," he reminded her, the pain he was suffering written across his bronzed face in harsh and ageing lines. "This is the greatest; let us meet it courageously."

"Yes, but Rob, Rob — she's so little, so soft, so — so innocent."

"Her life, at least, will be assured," Rob reminded. He was trying to be soothing, but his fingertips left reddish marks on his wife's arms.

"Oh, Rob, Rob!" Her hazel eyes were terrible in their fear. "She's such a b-baby. He c-can't — he must not c-cut her."

He gave his wife a heartbroken look. "Then you — you understand?"

Andrea's eyes closed and she swallowed spasmodically. "Quite. Only last month the Hartwell boy broke his leg the same way. Dr. Appleby was forced to — to cut it off. It being a pierced break he had no choice — so Dr. Appleby declared."

When Rob came back into the living room Susan was still unconscious. Young Dr. Burnham, a bit pale and very serious of mien, had removed his coat and was rolling up the sleeves of a worn linen shirt. On a chair beside the sofa reposed the open instrument case. The glitter of steel shining within it made Rob flinch.

He swallowed hard. "Well, Doctor?"

"Your daughter, sir," Peter explained, blue eyes intent on the sea captain's deep-set brown ones, "has either swooned from alarm and anguish or has suffered a commotion. However, I can assure you that no other bones have been fractured."

"Please proceed. What — what of my child's arm?"

Peter drew a long slow breath. "As a privateer captain you must have beheld many fractured limbs; you are aware, therefore, of the usual treatment for such injuries?"

"Aye."

"Few such fractures, even if expertly set, escape with a mere discharge of laudable pus. Therefore amputation is resorted to."

Burnham passed a hand over his curling red hair. He was debating fiercely within himself. Here lay his first patient — he must not lose her! And yet, and yet, was it not worse certainly to maim this poor child for life?" "In a child so young," he observed, "once corruption takes hold there remains but small hope of recovery."

Ashton fixed unseeing eyes upon a shaft of sunlight sketching a brilliant rectangle on the white marble of his hearthstone.

"Are you inclined, Captain, to accept a risk?"

"What risk?"

"That I attempt to preserve your daughter's arm — "

"Of course!"

"Wait. I'll not disguise that such an effort will be made at the risk of her life."

Rob's hand closed hard on the doctor's shoulder. "What are you sayin'? Speak plainly, suh." His Virginian accent was, all at once, very noticeable.

"That I may be able to save your daughter's arm — provided you and Mrs. Ashton understand that she may perish in the attempt. I — well, I feel confident of success, else I would not mention it."

Ashton hesitated, slowly beat one fist against the other. At length he looked up. "Suh, I believe I would rather see Susan dead than — than an unhappy cripple."

Why in Tophet had his first case to be like this? What a damned fine start for his practice.

Adieux

In solid satisfaction Asa Peabody, B.M., surveyed the new traveling chest, admired his initials sketched in bright, brass-headed nails ornamenting its wooden lid. Part of his satisfaction stemmed from the fact that he had come by this fine chest so cheaply. Till recently it had been the property of a carpenter who, unluckily for him, had signed articles aboard the privateer schooner *Freedom*, eight guns, out of Chatham. Barely at sea, she'd been taken by H.B.M.S. *Iris*, formerly the U.S. frigate *John Hancock*. During a brief running engagement the carpenter had lost his head in more senses than one, or so the auctioneer had pointed out in macabre waggishness.

The most treasured of its contents was Dr. Townsend's unexpected gift of a not new but very handsome set of French surgical and trepanning instruments.

"You'll need these, lad," the old doctor had said in his gruff way. "Full well I know good knives and such are scarcer than scarce with the army." He'd brushed aside all thanks, though such elegant instruments must have cost him a very pretty penny.

Asa smiled happily to himself, and his whole being thrilled. Tomorrow, Asa Peabody of Machias would commence his long journey southwards, into a strange country and towards a most unpredictable future. Judas Maccabeus! Ever since he'd been a little tacker in homespun dresses he'd yearned to journey far and wide. He allowed he'd have to do some tall riding before he fetched up to Fort Arnold at West Point. All he knew about the fort was that 'twas situated on a great and historic river, the Hudson. Folks claimed the Hudson was near thrice as wide as the frozen Charles out yonder — even at its broadest point.

At the door to his consulting room sounded a light knock, then Mrs. Southeby appeared to stand with hands held behind her.

She fetched a deep sigh. "I'm real grieved to see you leave, Dr. Peabody. You've been a fine good lodger, you have — and — and nobody ever whittled a prettier cracker stamp than you. I — I — " From behind her she produced a pair of bright red mittens. "I hope you'll not think me bold, but I — I've made these for you. I hope they will prove useful."

"Why, Mrs. Southeby!" Asa felt his throat thicken. "They're fine — really beautiful mittens, full-pegged and everything."

"Finest wool I could come across in Boston," Mrs. Southeby avowed simply. "Mind you don't dry 'em by a hot fire, else they'll shrink down to fit a cat. Take care of 'em, Doctor, and they'll keep your fingers warm for your work, even if you get soaked through. When do you leave on your travels?"

"Tomorrow, ma'am. I lodge tonight at Captain Stanton's. Barring accidents, we leave for Providence by post sleigh first thing in the morning." He took her small and wrinkled hands. "You have been mighty kind to me, Mistress Southeby, and patient with my poverty and queer hours and — and, what's been going on in your cellar. I'll endeavor to justify your good opinion of me."

"You will, Doctor, I'm certain-sure of it."

"Did Dr. Burnham — ?"

"Yes, this morning he fetched the last of that miscreant away."

"And my humble thanks again in the matter of — of my first patient."

"Rubbish. It was only Christian to take in the poor creature."

Fluttering much like a small brown hen surprised by a wind squall, Mrs. Southeby retreated toward the kitchen.

Asa was on the point of locking his clothes chest when, on the staircase, light steps sounded. It was Hilde, her hair brushed and glossy and her green shawl stitched neatly in place — pins were far too expensive for such a purpose. Spots of color glowed in the pale smooth sheen of her cheeks.

"What in Tophet are you doing out of bed?" Asa demanded in rough kindness.

"I — well, I heard of your impending departure." The girl paused on the second step from the bottom; even so she remained just a bit below the level of his eyes. "Anyway, I feel ever so much stronger now."

He shook his head. "Shouldn't have got up, you know. Three days ago you would have lost a wrassle with a mouse and you still ain't overspry. So, Mistress Mention, you'd best return to your room. I'll look in for a final examination. Really, I will."

Hilde's huge black eyes probed his features. "I am most profoundly grateful," she stated, clinging to the banister with a slender blue-veined hand, "but I am leaving now."

"Leaving? Why?"

Her gaze fell away. "I — I must, really I must. Please don't press me, Doctor. I — I wish there was some way I could prove my gratitude for — for all you've done."

"No call to fret yourself on that score," he assured her awkwardly. "Most of what ailed you, Hilde, was hunger. I will be frank — you have a touch of green sickness, especially dangerous to a girl of your tender years. Whatever chances, you must eat heartily."

"Oh, yes, Doctor." During these past three days and blissfully warm and comfortable nights Hilde had pondered her future, and, with a return of strength, she had arrived at a firm decision. Rough though her life among the Micmacs had been, it yet remained her only experience with happiness and security. Something deep within her nature craved the empty serenity of the woods, reassociation with those smells and sounds loved of her early childhood. By now, Hilde felt sure she could never feel truly at home among white people because her sense of values, her judgment seemed always at fault regarding her own race.

Therefore, she was determined, by hook or crook, to win her way back to Nova Scotia, back to the lodge of Mooinaskw and Wejek.

[599]

"Yes, Doctor, please be assured I have decided on a wise course," she informed him — just as if she knew when and how she was going to regain Wejek's village.

"May *le bon Dieu* bless your generous clean soul!" Hilde Mention suddenly descended the last step and, in an unconsciously graceful movement, knelt on one knee in front of the ungainly but commanding figure in black. Before Asa divined her purpose her soft lips were pressed to the back of his hand.

Red to his hairline, Asa lifted Hilde to her feet, attempted rough good humor. "Come now, Hilde, up to Machias we'd say that's no way for a pretty girl to kiss a man."

Her soul soaring into wide black eyes, Hilde looked up at him. "You don't really want me to kiss you — on the mouth?"

Spurred by some unfathomable impulse, Asa caught her in his arms, planted a hard kiss on her parted lips. He grinned sheepishly after that and, as he put her down, said, "Whatever's happened to you, Hilde Mention, and I allow it's been aplenty, it ain't mucked you. Why, I hold you no more of a real harlot than," the name came tumbling out, "than Sabra Stanton."

Hilde's pointed, somberly lovely features became transfigured. "You really believe that? *Really?*"

"As I live and breathe, Hilde. We can't all rule our destinies." Confused and embarrassed he turned into his consulting room. "Look, I'm going to write you a letter to a friend of Dr. Townsend, my instructor. 'Tis a female who maintains a most respectable lodging house."

Asa opened his traveling desk, and scrawled a recommendation.

If he understood William Townsend as he thought he did, the old surgeon would do whatever possible for this delicate, shy little creature. In folding the sheet Asa enclosed a Rhode Island ten-shilling note which ought to fetch six almost anywhere in Massachusetts.

Hilde's shadowed eyes came to rest upon the new chest. "Why are you leaving Boston?"

He methodically packed his quill. "I have accepted a surgeon-mate's commission with the army."

New Prospects

In an obscure corner of the Golden Ox Yoke, an ordinary particularly favored of teamsters, horse dealers and the like, Dr. Peter Burnham leaned well over his beer-stained table and considered, with shrewd attention, the blunt and battered features of Murdo Moore, his companion. That worthy represented himself as driver to a busy but none-too-sober undertaker of the town.

Beneath black and bushy brows which merged into a single line, Murdo Moore narrowed red-veined blue eyes and spoke in a hoarse whisper reeking of rum and chewing tobacco. "Aye, yer honor, I offer ye as choice a young female corpse as ye'll behold in yer lifetime! 'Tis a chancy business, but I'll manage it an' ye meet my price."

Peter glanced over his shoulder to reassure himself that all present were quite uninterested in his affairs. Wouldn't do to tolerate eavesdropping — not in so desperately risky a matter as this. "Of what did she die?"

The other blew his nose between his fingers, then wiped them on leather breeches shiny with use and dirt. "Why, yer honor, 'twas of love, ye might say — er — she was what ye'd call a doxy." Moore's red-lidded eyes shifted. "That's the only reason I'd risk snatching a female body."

"I don't follow you."

"There'll be none to worry, or ask questions, over what becomes o' such a pore and friendless baggage's mortal remains."

Peter put down his beer pot and studied his ill-favored companion with sudden suspicion. "When you say she died of 'love,' you don't mean the *lues venera?*"

"Lor' love ye no, sir," the ill-smelling rogue's gaze examined their surroundings before he muttered. "The bawdykeeper claimed 'twas from some seizure o' her vital organs. The poor wench suddenly and without no warning at all fell dead. 'Tis a fine-lookin' healthy corpse, purty, too — only a day old."

"Now look you, Moore, you'll swear you've come by this body honestly?"

Without checking his gulping, the teamster nodded several times. "Aye, the bawdykeeper wants three pound, ten sterling. Fer that he'll even write a bill of sale."

"Surprising, considering dangers involved; still, I'll accept your word on it." But for all that, doubts lingered in Peter's mind concerning the legality of such a transaction. God in heaven, what an opportunity to push aside, even just a little, the thick veil of ignorance concerning the physiology of the human female.

"The corpse — where is it?"

Murdo Moore frowned, considered a spot of mutton grease gleaming on the shiny planks on the table. "That's as may be, yer honor. First, suppose ye tells what will ye pay — hard money?"

"Five pounds, or nothing — I'm no haggler." That was a great deal of money, more than he could afford. Still it wouldn't do to have this ill-favored rogue wagging a dissatisfied tongue.

"Why then — 'tis a bargain."

Slowly Peter passed a hand over his dull red hair, sighed and took his decision. "Where shall I find you, and when?"

"Ten of this night, yer honor. At the river end o' Green Lane ye'll find an old disused stable — 'tis called Bramwell's barn. I'll fetch the body there, and no further."

"So far so good, but how am I to get the cadaver to my — my study?"

"That's fer yer honor to figger out," growled Moore, and no amount of persuasion or bribery would shake the teamster from his determination.

Peter's sense of elation vanished. Damn! The task of transferring the illegal remains from a cart into the Widow Southeby's cellar would require the efforts of at least two men. On whom dared he call? The obvious solution was Lucius Devoe. That ambitious student would be eager to participate in subsequent dissection.

The other spat into the foul sawdust at his feet, then bent forward and spoke in a hurried undertone. "When ye reach Bramwell's barn ye'll hum a stave o' 'The World Turned Upside Down.' Understand? Then I'll show you to the cart; ye can return it to Tim O'Brien's stable."

Great was Peter's astonishment to find a letter awaiting him at his lodgings. Increasingly dismayed, he read:

Respected Friend Peter:

Word hath just reached me that my Family in Machias is in dire Straits. Filial Duty leaves me no choice but to Repair thither at once and I shall have sailed ere you Receive this. Since now there can be no Army Career for me I have writ Doctor Townsend suggesting you in my Place with Gen'l Washington's Staff so pray seek him at once. Am confident you will receive ye appointment. May good luck attend you always. Vale!

Y'r humble and obed't Servant,
A. PEABODY, B.M.

Impulsively, Peter clapped on a buckled gray hat and fairly sprinted down to a livery on the corner to rent a saddle horse. By continually kicking his mount, a short-legged cob, he kept up a jolting trot which fetched him into Bennett Street and before Dr. Townsend's doorway within twenty minutes.

An hour later Peter Burnham emerged from his former instructor's familiar brick house. Remounting, he grinned on passersby, whistled cheerily and fair rode on feather beds. Tomorrow, come hell or high water, he'd become Surgeon's Mate Burnham.

Damn! If he knew where to find Murdo Moore he'd cancel the whole affair, but he didn't. No more could he fail to appear at the rendezvous. To leave the poor rogue waiting indefinitely at the barn, risking discovery and probably lynching, wouldn't be fair. The Burnhams were famous for keeping their commitments. The devil take that poor girl's cadaver! Was it time yet to look in on Captain Ashton's daughter? No. He'd better locate Lucius first.

For a second time that day, Peter encountered the unexpected. When he did come up with Lucius, it was to discover the Jamaican emerging from a Mr. Levin's haberdasher's shop on Hanover Street.

What a transformation. In place of the familiar rusty black coat and patched shoes, Lucius created the impression of a modish young gentleman of the town. He was garbed in a fine coat under which showed a snuff-colored suit; a jabot of good but inexpensive Flemish lace glistened at his throat, and black thread stockings outlined his lean legs. There was an unfamiliar assurance to the way Lucius's well-built shoes — they boasted new bathmetal buckles — pressed the grimy snow of Hanover Street.

"Lucius! Is it indeed you?"

The Jamaican treated his friend to a quick, singularly engaging smile. "Aye, Peter, the goddess of chance at last has smiled on me. Right royally, I might add. Last night I could not seem to lose."

There was, Lucius felt, no call to amplify his explanation — which, in a way, was entirely truthful. Had it not been due entirely to chance that, through Sabra Stanton, he had come to know Mrs. Fletcher and so to learn of her imaginary ailments?

Peter led the way into a tobacconist's and there disclosed the news of Asa's abrupt change of fortune.

Lucius frowned, bit his lip. "Poor devil. Really, Asa deserved better than banishment to a backwoods hamlet." Then he gave Peter a sharp glance. "Who's to fill his appointment?"

"Dr. Townsend wishes me to take Asa's place. Blanchard and Captain Stanton also approve. Naturally, I accepted."

Lucius offered his hand. "Congratulations, old friend. For a second time they have chosen well." It stung, though, that Dr. Townsend twice should have passed him over. Some day, and before very long, Dr. Townsend and the rest would be constrained to admit their blindness.

"Come along to my lodgings," Peter was inviting. "I've more news of interest to you."

"Indeed? And what, pray?"

The taller of the two grinned. "I am about to make you a most expensive gift — also a rare opportunity. I'll tell you when we get to my quarters."

Before a fire in Peter's lodging the matter of Murdo Moore's cadaver came out. Lucius looked at once fascinated and a little frightened. "Jupiter! You're running a fearful risk. Why go through with it?"

"I don't want to, but I can't find Moore."

"Um. I see." Lucius gnawed his lip in thought and swift calculation. "Let me understand correctly. My part is merely to wait at Mrs. Southeby's, to help you unload, and then drive the empty cart back to O'Brien's stable?"

"Yes. Wish I could stay to work on that dissection! It'll be years, most likely, before I'll come across another such chance. What's wrong? Ain't you pleased?"

"Oh, yes. But for all you're so easy about it, more than one physician has been stoned to death for a similar attempt."

[603]

"Each profession has its hazards; any physician worth half his salt must expect to run risks, time and again."

"True enough," Lucius admitted, fingers rubbing up and down his port glass. "I presume you have decided on your route to Mrs. Southeby's? Wouldn't do to make any mistakes."

"From Bramwell's barn I figure I'll follow Green Street to Unity then descend Sudbury Lane; by that time of night that whole neighborhood will be sound asleep."

"Sounds reasonable," the Jamaican agreed. "Very well. You can count on me to be waiting at half after ten in Mrs. Southeby's woodshed."

"Take heed how you unbar the backyard gate," Peter warned. "Damned hinges on it screech like a pair of banshees."

Lucius nodded soberly, then offered his hand. "Best wishes on your appointment."

Beaming, Peter clapped him on the shoulder. "I'll find a post for you, too, soon's I get settled down there. You can count on it."

Count on it? Not much. What ambitious young officer in his right mind would introduce his staff to a man who could, and would, constitute a dangerous rival? Again, the underfed, unpaid and semimutinous Continental Army had become so diminished in numbers it wasn't reasonable to suppose there would be many new posts open; not for a good long while.

The Body of Jennie McLaren

Dr. Peter Burnham sat hunched on the seat of the rented two-wheeled cart and bent his head towards a fitful southeast wind. So far all had progressed to plan — with never a hitch to rouse his alarm. To all intents and purposes, his cart conveyed nothing more worthy of note than a load of wheat straw.

Timothy O'Brien's unexpectedly spirited livery stable horse moved smartly along, iron-shod hoofs ringing disconcertingly loud on the cobbles of Green Street. In Unity Street, that older part of town, the houses had been built very close together along a narrow thoroughfare. Here the street presented a confusing pattern of silver-blacks, dark grays and jet shadows, lanced here and there by an occasional gleam of candlelight. Near the intersection of Sudbury Street it was black as the Old Nick's heart, but at half after ten there was little or no pedestrian traffic.

All the same Peter wondered at a persistent sense of uneasiness. To be sure, Murdo Moore's manner had been furtive; that would be only natural under the circumstances. But need the teamster have grabbed his fee and bolted out of the barn immediately to become lost in the darkness?

What a crying shame he might not profit by this purchase. Vividly he could recall unhooding a dark lantern to make sure he had not been bilked. He hadn't been. The light had disclosed the colorless, placid features of a rather plain young woman whose dead eyes peered up at him almost reproachfully through their half-closed lids.

One recollection, and a disturbing one, came as, nervously, he slapped the reins across the cart horse's broad rump. For those of a trollop, the dead girl's garments had appeared sedate and of exceptionally fine quality. How come? Whores generally were poor and improvident.

Cape tossing in the raw wind, Peter shivered, made an effort to rally his wits. The heavy darkness, tension and imagination were combining to create chimerical dangers. Of course everything would continue to proceed smoothly; no reason to doubt it. Within another ten minutes he'd be driving into Mrs. Southeby's backyard. Pray God, Lucius would be punctual, ready and waiting.

Peter guided the horse around a frozen pool, expertly steadied the animal when, a few rods further along, it slipped on ice hidden in a deep rut. Gorry! He'd never imagined Unity Street to be so long. Peter took a firmer grip on the reins and braced his knees against the heavy jolting of the cart. Lord! How loud those iron tires rasped in this empty blackness. Steady now. Within five minutes he'd have accomplished the trickiest part of this expedition. Beyond Charter Street he would regain a quiet residential district.

A roundsman clumping along with staff and lantern cast the two-wheeled cart an incurious glance, then a pair of patrons staggering out of an inn yelled something to which Peter called a gruff "Good night, to you!" When they shouted some further question he urged the livery horse into a jolting trot.

After another hundred yards Peter realized he could turn into the comparatively idle length of Snow Street — in fact he could have turned off this tavern- and inn-lined thoroughfare sooner — though it would have prolonged his journey. Come to think of it, he didn't much resemble a teamster in his triple cape. Sweat broke out on his palms and along the lining of his stylish buckled beaver hat.

His breath entered with a soft gasp when, at the entrance to Middle Street, he noted a small knot of roisterers collected under the signboard of the Eagle Tavern, or were they just rum-warmed citizens leaving for home? Something about their stance and the quick way they swung to face his cart set Peter's nerves to crisping. Though desperately he yearned to turn aside, he had no choice but to keep on. Any other course would certainly invite suspicion. A tall watchman strode out into the middle of the street, raised his staff in one hand and lantern in the other.

"Halt!" he commanded. "Pull up there. State yer name and business abroad at this hour."

As the peace officer swung his thick hickory staff crosswise, barring further progress, certain of the bystanders drifted off the sidewalk to assist in blocking the street. Keen barbs of apprehension stabbed at Peter's brain as he reined in, but he assumed a bold attitude.

"I'm minding my business, sir, and am molesting no one. Pray allow me to pass."

"I demand yer name and business," growled the watchman and strode forward in the obvious intention of seizing the cart horse's bridle. The yellow-red rays of his whale-oil lantern disclosed narrow, unshaven cheeks and hard eyes peering belligerently from beneath his tricorne hat.

"I am Paul Bradstreet," Peter replied in as easy a tone as he could manage. "I have here a load of straw from Roxbury. My horse fell and I've been delayed."

"Stuff! Yer nag's as fresh as a daisy. Dismount, Mr. Bradstreet, whilst I take a look." To the gathering crowd he snapped, "I'll lay long odds he's got more than straw in that cart. Smuggling's profitable, I hear."

"Git down thar!" "Pull up!" "What's he got in that there waggin?"

Attracted by the watchman's loud summons, door after door opened, disgorged groups of curious onlookers. The watchman's lantern now was lighting many faces, gilding them, making his eyes appear extra large. Frightened by the hands reaching for its bridle the horse commenced to snort and back up despite Peter's efforts to control it.

Peter insisted, "You've no right to halt me. This is my horse and load of straw. I'm breaking no law, so you've no call to stop me like this."

The minute the words left his lips Peter knew he'd made a terrible mistake.

"He's lying," a voice called. "Yonder *ain't his horse!* That there rig's hired from Tim O'Brien's stable. Used it myself two days back."

The watchman made a snatch at the nag's bit and so startled the creature that it shied violently but the peace officer made good his hold all the same.

"Git down, I tell ye. Git down in the name o' the law!"

"Yep — he's a smuggler all right. Dismount, you!"

The crowd yelled and closed in, an ominous and rapidly shifting black pattern.

"What've ye caught, Caleb?"

"Wager 'tis a horse thief?"

A drunken black-bearded fellow began to bellow, "Come join the fun. We've took a horse thief!"

"Mister Bradstreet," roared the watchman, "will ye git down or must I drag you out o' that waggin?"

A swift estimate of the situation advised against violence. The watchman was big and beefy and stood poised ready for overt motion. Although arguing furiously all the time, Peter obeyed. Of all the outrageous mischances! His only hope now lay in the exercise of brazen effrontery.

"Keep your filthy hands off me," he warned a pair of pot-valiant fellows who came closing in. "Else you'll answer to a magistrate."

"Very likely, very likely," growled the watchman. "That's what all rogues say." He bent over the tail of the cart and plunging an arm into the straw clear up to his elbow he began feeling about. Almost instantly he emitted a triumphant "Ha!"

"What's he got there? What's he got?"

The crowd thickened until Unity Street was filled from one gutter to the other, more shutters commenced to bang back allowing sudden beams of light to fall into the street.

" 'Tis something heavy wrapped in sailcloth," the watchman announced. "Knew he was a bloody smuggler."

"What is it? Sugar? Coffee? Metal goods?"

"Somebody hold up my lantern." Once the flame could illumine the floor of Tim O'Brien's cart the peace officer flinched back uttering a stifled cry of horror.

"Why! Why — he's got a dead body! A woman's body — a young woman's body, by God!"

A terrible clamor broke from the nearest of the spectators. "Bodysnatcher!" Infinitely menacing, the cry swelled louder and louder. "The villain's stole some poor female's corpse."

Aware of his deadly peril, Peter unhooked the clasp of his cloak, swung it from his shoulders and in the same motion moved to back up against the high wheel of the cart.

"It was not stolen," he shouted at the scowling roundsman. "I've a bill of sale for proof. Look here — "

Peter might as well have attempted to argue back the onrush of a storm wave charging up a beach. When three or four burly citizens flung themselves forward, Peter, by no means ignorant of the art of rough and tumble, ducked under their wildly flashing arms. Fists flying, he charged, suddenly and effectively employing his weight.

His nearest assailants he sent reeling, tripping over each other. At the same time a savage and unfamiliar exhilaration kindled fires in his brain. The mob ringed him around. Those behind sounded very brave indeed and already were clamoring for his life; those in front recoiled mindful of the two fallen figures, but only for an instant.

"String him up, the dirty defiler of womankind!" "Hanging's too good for a body-snatcher." There was a dreadful, menacing quality to the crowd's outcry. By the dim light of a few lanterns and a pineknot torch or two, Peter glimpsed clawing hands, clenched fists, open yowling mouths and furious eyes.

He rained blows at this wall of flesh converging upon him, and with such effect that again it retreated. He might then have won free had not a clod of frozen mud come whizzing out of the dark to strike him on the forehead and send him reeling aside, conscious only of innumerable vivid meteors whirling about in his eyeballs.

They'd have killed him had not O'Brien's horse become so maddened that it reared, plunged and struck at the crowd with its front feet. The cartwheels crushed more than one foot and evoked sudden howls of agony. The roundsman who still stood in the cart was forced to hang on for dear life as loose straw commenced to fall out into the street. Then, in seeming reluctance, the girl's corpse slipped over the tailboard and fell out onto the street, garments indecently awry. It lay rigid with hands clenched and teeth faintly agleam in the wavering torchlight.

The glassy eyes and tumbled hair were so sharply etched against the trampled snow that the mob froze into a stunned immobility.

"Cover her for God's sake! It's shameful to leave her like that."

Then a well-dressed citizen cried out, "Why! Why,. that's Jennie McLaren's body!"

"Are you sure?"

"Aye, she been a neighbor of mine for years. Died day before yesterday."

Their sense of outrage redoubled, the onlookers turned to wreak their will on the offender.

Because quantities of stones, faggots and more clods were whizzing quite indiscriminately through the air, several of the rioters were dropped senseless, and the men pinioning Peter ducked and loosened their grip. Instinct warned him that he'd not be offered a second chance to break free. Though his head still spun, Peter drew a great breath, set his shoulders and surged towards that point where the throng seemed thinnest. Strengthened by terror of impending death, the young doctor drove a path through the mob and though hands grabbed, wrenched and tore at his clothing, he was able to maintain momentum.

The very numbers of his enemies began to react in his favor; most of them couldn't recognize him. By stooping suddenly amid a flurry of flying fists, he tricked his persecutors into striking at each other; at once, a series of helpful free-for-alls commenced. But, inevitably, somebody recognized and tripped him and, before Peter could rise, a very heavy fellow dove upon him, driving every bit of wind from his lungs.

"Here he is!"

In terror-stricken helplessness the doctor squirmed under a torrent of kicks and blows; boots crushed his fingers and smashed against his ribs. Yielding blindly to the instinct of self-preservation he continued to struggle until a kick caught him in the jaw and dazed him. Into his mouth surged a gust of salty hot blood; it burst in a fine spray from his writhing lips and spattered the filthy snow.

"We'll preserve decency in this town." "Hang the bastard!" "String him up!" "A rope!" "Somebody fetch a rope."

"There's a dandy one in my stable yonder," an aged voice cackled. "Wait till I fetch it."

A pair of scowling teamsters heaved Peter to his feet; they had to hold him erect since his legs were wavering like saplings in a breeze.

"Look at him, the foul, body-snatching dog!" yelled one of them. "Look at him, the indecent wretch."

Spittle splashed into the young physician's eyes and fingers tore out strands of his long red hair. A primordial fear of death sickened him as they hauled him, sagging and stumbling, down the street to a place where some blacksmith's sign was dangling from its heavy, wrought-iron bracket.

Feigning even greater weakness than he felt, Peter struggled, despite the continual impact of blows and offal, to clear his senses. They made little progress, probably because his guards were bellowing protests at being pelted so indiscriminately with their prisoner.

A youth, horsed high on the crowd's shoulders, quickly unhooked and brought down the blacksmith's sign. Menacingly, the stark iron bar stuck out over the street.

"Ah-h, that's it — that's the right idea!"

Exerting a final supreme effort of the will, Peter slowed before his eyes this mad whirling scene, relaxed every muscle to simulate a swoon. His knees buckled and his battered head sagged forward, dripping streams of blood onto the frozen snow. The infernal uproar swelled, continued.

"Rouse the villain! Let's see him hang higher'n Haman!"

"Here's yer rope! 'Tis a fine new one and I want it back after," piped the old man from the stoop of his house. Everybody glanced in his direction; and the crowd fell back to give the aged man passage.

Endowed with that desperate strength which comes to those in mortal peril Peter gave a sudden violent twist that broke the relaxed grip of his unwary captors and charged along the path being opened for his would-be hangman. Peter's recovery and subsequent tactics consumed so little time that for a few priceless instants the mob remained unaware, barely long enough to permit him to butt, whirl and plunge his way a short distance to the entrance of an alley.

Always a fine runner, Peter hurtled blindly along a winding passage at once both lightless and treacherous. His feet slipped on garbage; he stumbled over firewood and once a bucket sent him reeling breathless and terrified into a wall.

"Stop him!" "Stop thief!" The blood-hungry yelping of his pursuers was fearfully close behind.

Head swimming, Peter sensed rather than perceived an opening to his right; for better or for worse, he plunged through it because the foremost of his enemies was running not twenty yards in his rear.

"Oh God, help me!" he wheezed. A tall wooden fence barred his course. Rallying rapidly failing strength, Peter flung himself over the palings, only half heard a sharp snarl of tearing cloth. The skill with which he negotiated this hazard lent him confidence — and perhaps an additional fifty feet of lead. Now his breath was only drawn in agonizing, sucking little gasps. Where he ran, he had not the least notion, but whenever he glimpsed empty blackness ahead he ran for it. Such blackness meant space, precious life-giving space.

With strength rapidly abandoning him, Peter blundered around the corner of a shabby brick dwelling, fearfully conscious that he was not shaking off the hue and cry. This time he found himself in a dead-end alley — a short cul-de-sac ending in a high brick wall. Aware that his vaulting ability was a precious asset, Peter charged straight for the six-foot barrier. God help him! Too late he realized that this wall was crowned by a thick cap of broken glass set in cement!

No turning back was possible, so he grabbed for the top, felt immediately the searing bite of glass slashing deep, deep into his hands. Then, when he heaved over the top, the shards gouged savagely at his knees. Blood was spurting from his hands, and pouring down his legs — Christ! He had been cut to ribbons.

"There he goes!" "I saw him." "Yes, over the wall!" "Run around and cut him off."

Cruelly hurt and spattering gore as he ran, Peter lurched across some citizen's backyard in which bare fruit trees loomed dimly stark. A watchdog, rousing from its kennel, emitted a rasping snarl and flew at him. Only by the sheerest luck did the fugitive land a kick which altered the brute's threats to a pained and high-pitched yelping.

Sobbing for breath and sweating at every pore, Peter tried a door giving onto the orchard. Though latched, it gave under his weight and flew inwards, permitting the fugitive to struggle along a corridor and into a room. Here he tripped over some half-seen furniture.

Upstairs, frightened outcries arose, but now Peter managed to locate the front door; so slippery with blood were his fingers that they failed in their first attempt to release the bolt. Ha. Now he could peer out into the street. Praise God, it looked empty and, better still, a lane opened directly opposite. The householders upstairs now were summoning the watch at the top of their lungs.

Although Peter thought he had traversed the street quite unseen, he was wrong. Inexorably, the hue and cry arose again, swelling even louder. How hard it was to breathe; blood kept welling into his wounded mouth and, falling down his throat, half choked him.

Thanks to easier going in the lane, he lengthened his lead. Ah, a large square appeared before him, offering the choice of a lumber yard opening to his left and a tannery to his right. Both should afford likely hiding places — provided he didn't leave too broad a blood trail.

The tanner's yard presented the less inviting shelter, yet he decided upon it for just that reason. He could hope that his pursuers might tire themselves out in rummaging about the many stacks of lumber yonder. Too utterly spent to continue, Peter ran to take refuge in one of perhaps a dozen great casks and vats occupying the tannery yard.

Thank God, the snow about them had been so heavily trampled it might not betray his course. Exerting his last ounce of strength, he pushed aside the wooden cover of a vat and tumbled inside to find himself standing knee deep in icy cold tanning fluid and wheezing like an overworked draft horse. All the same he took care gently to ease the heavy lid back into place.

For a long time Peter was unable to do anything more than stand in the blessed darkness of the vat and attempt to recapture wits and breath. For the moment an overwhelming numbness mercifully blunted his pain. Gradually his breathing leveled until at length he felt able to attempt an estimate of his situation and condition.

Several facts appeared self-evident; he was yet far from safe. As a physician, he could tell that in his flight he had suffered very serious hurts and wounds. His left hand, for instance, was frightening in its continued disobedience; his mouth was swollen all out of shape; several of his teeth had been loosened and two were missing. In addition, a couple of his ribs certainly had been fractured — nothing else could explain such blinding flashes of pain whenever he drew breath.

Thrice his pursuers had explored the tannery yard, cursing and poking about the uncovered barrels. Luckily, they were by now too much fatigued and discouraged to lift the vat lids, and eventually had tramped off.

By degrees cold generated by the tanning fluid crept upwards until a paralyzing chill was groping beyond his knees. Once the immediate peril had faded, a reaction set in, so robbing him of his strength that he floundered onto all fours in the bitter-smelling fluid. The acid's stinging at his lacerated hands and knees drove him back to a crouching position.

Had he in reality shaken off his enemies? One thing was certain — he couldn't remain where he was. But what to do? Granting that the hue and cry had subsided, what would be his wisest course? Tomorrow, of course, his true identity would become known — after all, Boston had been his home for nigh on three years and plenty of people knew him and could identify a man with auburn hair. Demands for his arrest and conviction would be screamed from the housetops of the unco'-gude.

No. Most certainly he must not return to his lodgings, especially since his landlord viewed all physicians with an abiding suspicion and had only tolerated such a person because Daniel Burnham's son paid regularly and well. A mean-souled and unimaginative little tailor, he was forever quoting, "He that sinneth before his Maker, let Him fall into the hands of the physician."

Peter emerged from his sanctuary just as the clock in the Old North Church boomed three sonorous and reverberating notes. Now, if ever, Boston Town would be still. Three o'clock. Great God! What eons had not passed since he had guided Tim O'Brien's cart into Unity Street?

By slinking, limping from shadow to shadow and doorway to doorway, towards dawn he found himself, weak and still bleeding, crouched behind a pile of firewood stacked in a shed at the rear of Captain Robert Ashton's residence.

Apparently this shed had been designed not only to preserve firewood from rain but also to ward wintry blasts from the kitchen door. No little willpower was required on Peter's part to pause and, nursing his agonizing left hand in the bosom of his shirt, to look backwards. Wouldn't do to expose the Ashtons to questioning. As near as he could tell, he'd left no bloodstains on the snow of Captain Ashton's backyard.

He locked his teeth to silence moans that almost broke from his lacerated lips. At first he rapped softly, then, receiving no reply, louder and louder. Pains now were shooting like red hot arrows up his left forearm. Maybe it had been fractured; its hand refused to answer his least command.

At length a small dog roused itself indoors, set up a shrill alarm which continued until a ray of light appeared, shifted, crept out from under the door.

"Quiet, Growler." A bolt slid back, Peter recognized Captain Ashton's deep voice demanding, "What the devil d'ye want at this ungodly hour?"

"Dr. Burnham," Peter was able to gasp. "Help me."

"Burnham? What's amiss?"

"Help, for God's sake. I — I'm in bad case."

Immediately the kitchen door swung open, releasing a rush of wonderfully warm air.

"Here, let me assist you." The privateer captain lowered a huge, brass-bound boarding pistol and gripped Peter's elbow.

The Virginian helped him to a rush-bottomed kitchen chair; then, by the light of his candle, cast a single intent look at this apparition. Lank red hair was dangling in sodden strands over the young physician's purplish and grotesquely swollen features. Already a small, bright scarlet pool was forming below his lax left arm.

"Good God, man, you're cut to ribbons." Captain Ashton ran out, reappeared with a bottle of Jamaica rum. "Take a big swig, and ye needn't talk less you've a mind."

Somehow Peter raised his head, summoned a twisted smile. "I'd better tell you — you may not want to harbor me."

"Stuff."

"No. I beg you to listen."

Captain Ashton, gathering a yellow and red banyan about him, hooked bare toes over the rungs of his chair to keep them above the draught.

Captain Ashton held a flaming spill to his study lamp, which, being filled with pure winter-pressed whale oil, cast a fine clear light. When Peter regained semiconsciousness, he discovered that his right eye wouldn't open. For all that, he could see well enough to tell that he'd never lack cause to remember what had happened tonight.

"Ha. Thought you'd be coming to pretty soon. Sit steady now."

He was laying lax on an easy chair and Robert Ashton was washing the mud, blood, and slime from his injured left hand — and was hurting him abominably.

The rum strengthened Peter, cleared his head enough for him to realize that while his right hand had suffered two long, deep, and very painful gashes across its palm, no tendons or nerves had been severed. But God in heaven! How terribly his left hand and wrist had been mangled and slashed by that broken glass. His third, fourth and little finger utterly refused to respond to his most earnest efforts to move them. No use. He could even see the ends of severed muscles in the depths of a hideous gash across the heel of that hand. Successive waves of despair set Peter to trembling. Could he ever operate again?

His broad bronzed face intent, Rob Ashton was, at Peter's insistence, pouring brandy over the gasping physician's mutilated flesh when, her gray eyes wide and questioning, Mrs. Ashton appeared carrying a Betty lamp.

"Mercy save us, it's Dr. Burnham!"

Andrea did not tarry to ask questions; she flew back upstairs and presently returned, a number of linen strips aflutter in her hand. Following the patient's directions, she contrived pledgets to staunch a slow, persistent hemorrhage from the wounded hands, then bound them deftly into place. Next she treated vicious cuts on the fugitive's knees, and ended by bathing with hazel water the many little cuts and contusions disfiguring his features.

"I've a vial of laudanum," she announced. "Will you take some?"

Peter's distorted mouth made a grotesque effort to form a smile. "It's as you prescribe, Dr. Ashton," he mumbled. No use to mention his hurt side. Maybe the ribs were only cracked. No telling just yet. Every deep breath lanced his side with devilish sharp bodkins.

The Ashtons helped him, one on each side and murmuring encouragements, to a small warm bedroom on the second floor. Then, casting him a compassionate look, Andrea Ashton withdrew leaving her husband to help Peter out of the foul wreckage of his clothing.

The clocks of Boston were disputing the exact moment of five when Andrea Ashton reappeared carrying a tumbler of laudanum and water. Obedient as any six-year-old, Peter swallowed it, every drop.

"How is Susan faring?" Become a little lightheaded, Peter wanted to rise, to examine the child's broken arm. "Need to see for m'self — mustn' lose — arm. Mus' really go — see."

"Certainly — in a moment or two. Just settle back for a little, first," Andrea soothed.

The soporific took almost instant effect whereupon Peter lapsed into a deep slumber.

[613]

"Poor man," sighed Andrea, picking up the rags staining her floor. "Why can people, supposedly civilized, Christian people, be so vastly cruel to one another? I wonder what's happened."

Rob Ashton told her what Peter had insisted on reporting, then, casting a thoughtful look at the unconscious physician, remarked, "Let us not deceive ourselves; he is in trouble, my dear, serious trouble. How grave is his danger we will not learn at once."

It was only late of the next afternoon that the privateer captain came to appreciate that he was harboring what appeared to be a felon. Everywhere, broadsides, notices and public criers were offering a handsome reward — fifty pounds no less — for the apprehension of one Peter Burnham, a physician of the town. He stood near five feet, eight inches in height, had blue eyes and red hair.

The crimes of which he stood accused were the theft and illegal possession of the corpse of one Jennie McLaren, stolen from the residence of Zebediah McLaren, the deceased's father and a thoroughly respectable chandler. There was no doubt over one thing; Boston was fairly boiling with a righteous indignation over this scandalous affair. Not for many a long year would Dr. Peter Burnham dare to walk Boston's streets without fear of arrest.

A Broom at the Masthead

Seated in the stern sheets of Captain Ashton's own gig, Peter Burnham surveyed the outline of that brig which in all probability he would call home for the next six months — perhaps longer. Like a dainty woman drawing aloof from a jostling crowd, the *Grand Turk III* lay at anchor on the fringes of the rest of the shipping. Seven or eight other privateers swung to moorings along the gig's course; a small ship, three brigs, three schooners and a snow or two completed the tally of private men-of-war. Carpenters were hard at work on a big, black-painted schooner, mending ominous-looking shot holes in her bulwarks, or, nearer her water line, replacing with seasoned planking temporary coverings of sheet-lead or green hide.

The *Grand Turk*'s gig sped smoothly over the slate-hued waves of Boston Harbor, her oarsmen bending to their oars in rhythm to a chant raised by the coxswain.

The more Peter considered Captain Ashton's brig, the more he understood why the Virginian's admiration for his vessel verged on love. An amateur sailor whose nautical knowledge was confined to a few pleasure cruises in Long Island Sound, Peter could not have begun to explain why the brig's lines appeared so unusually harmonious; come to think of it, Captain Ashton once had said that originally she had been French.

[614]

The *Grand Turk* was somewhat smaller than he had expected, not ninety feet in length — she was actually eighty-three at the water line — and quite narrow — about twenty feet in the beam. Though of but two hundred tons burthen, she looked larger, perhaps because her two topmasts rose some ten feet taller than would be the rule in a vessel of her dimensions.

Even Peter could tell, when the gig rowed closer, that her figurehead was not the original one. While the turbaned and bearded Turk who, clutching a scimitar, stared fiercely out over the water was not badly done, the workmanship was infinitely inferior to the execution of the delicate scrollwork streaming so gracefully aft from the bows.

His convictions on that point presently became stronger because decorations about the brig's stern revealed so much imagination and well-considered design. For instance her three stern ports, though harmoniously proportioned, were yet large enough to permit a medium-sized carriage gun to be fired through them.

A chill wind came beating up the harbor, caused Peter to gather his boat cloak closer. The debilitating effects of his fever were still upon him. How fortunate he'd been not to lose his left hand under the laborious ministration of that same earnest but ignorant physician who, during the blank period of his own delirium, without necessity — Peter was convinced of that point — had amputated Susan's arm just as it was promising to heal. In a way, learning about that amputation was the hardest blow with which he'd had to cope. "Catastrophe" might be the only word adequate to describe the shock he'd suffered when, weak and struggling to regain strength, he'd learned how Dr. Chase had preyed upon the fears of Susan's distracted parents until they'd consented, most reluctantly, to an amputation of the little girl's arm.

Peter stared at the lid of the medical chest reposing between his knees. Criminanently! Susan's arm *would* have healed in time. Under close questioning, Mrs. Ashton — no hysterical flibbertigibbet at any time — admitted that the swelling of the fractured arm had commenced to subside.

Ironically, it was only because of his own high fever and suppurating wounds that Mrs. Ashton had insisted on summoning to her house myopic and jovial Dr. Chase. Peter had heard Dr. Townsend mention Chase as a practitioner belonging to the old school, completely unimaginative and wedded to methods approved some fifty years earlier. 'Twas said the Dr. Chase would bleed a canary to death in trying to cure the bird of an earache.

Peter roused from this miserable reverie to hear the coxswain yell a string of warning curses at bumboats clustered about the foot of the *Grand Turk*'s ladder. Reluctantly they rowed out of the way.

"Deck there! Officer coming aboard!" bawled the coxswain steering the gig bobbing into the *Grand Turk*'s lee. A member of the watch caught the painter expertly flung by the number one oarsman.

Because of his injured hand — it seemed to have no strength at all nowadays — Peter only clumsily swarmed up a rope ladder dangling over the brig's dark blue side just forward of the quarterdeck's break. A flush of shame clouded his expression because two deckhands were forced to catch him by the armpits and assist him across the rail. A lean officer with the face of a heartbroken horse came running up and looking quite unhappy.

"I'm the surgeon; my name — "

"Devil take your name. Goddamn it, sir, the quarterdeck; salute the quarterdeck!"

"Beg pardon?"

The deck officer's long face went scarlet. "Salute the quarterdeck, you dungerhead. 'Tis the custom aboard men-o'-war."

Though he couldn't perceive the least sense in it, Peter raised his black tricorn in the general direction of the stern.

"Who in tunket are you?" snapped the officer, a human beanpole of a fellow garbed in a greasy blue and brown uniform which bore but a single epaulette of tarnished gold lace.

"Mr. Burnham, surgeon for this cruise, so ye'd best mend your manners," Peter advised.

"Why?"

"Suppose I were called to take off your arm?"

The horse-faced officer stared, then smiled sourly and offered his hand. "Damn, mebbe you'll do. Anyways, I'm Pickering — first officer aboard, and don't you ever forget it."

So this was Gideon Pickering, hailing from Groton in the state of Connecticut? As Rob Ashton had said, he looked it.

"So you're signing on as sawbones?" The first officer's yellowish and bony features betrayed no emotion.

"Yes."

"You'll address your superiors as 'sir' aboard this vessel," Pickering snapped. He beckoned a tall young lad of perhaps fourteen years. "Boy! Show Mr. Burnham to the cockpit."

While the air in the cockpit was not quite noxious, the atmosphere there certainly was lifeless and reeked of bilges but a few feet below Peter's bunk.

Was he actually expected to exist in such a fetid hole?

Quite discouraged, the new ship's surgeon seated himself upon the clothes chest. Damnation! Since childhood he'd abominated confined spaces. Oh God, why had he ever listened to Murdo Moore's lying tongue? A plague on Jenny McLaren's remains! Miserably, Peter peered about, aware that his head was beginning to throb because of the bad air. Still, as the boy had pointed out, he had at least space to himself, whereas in a larger man-of-war he'd most likely have to put up with some midshipman. Probably a surgeon's mate would be there also to plague and crowd the cockpit. Yes. Despite everything he was well off. Ashton had taken pains to explain that in a regular vessel of war a ship's doctor ranked just above the schoolmaster and therefore rated near the lowest of the afterguard. They must expect to take leavings by way of accommodation.

"Har-rump!"

Peter turned to observe another of the *Grand Turk*'s officers; he differed from Mr. Pickering as sharply as a man could.

"This our new pullguts?"

"Dr. Burnham, Mr. Doane — second officer."

Abel Doane's body seemed constructed in a series of superimposed ellipses; he walked on thick, bowed legs and carried a sizable paunch; his perfectly round head seemed to be supported by no neck at all. Mr. Doane's eyes shone a lively brown and his cheeks were the color of Winesap apples. All in all, he put Peter in mind of a robin after a rain, when the worms were plentiful and easy to get.

"How are you?" Uneven teeth gleamed in the afternoon sunlight when Mr. Doane offered a thick red hand. "Welcome aboard the *Grand Turk*, Dr. Burnham. Let's hope you'll enjoy this cruise, and return from it gunnel deep with your share."

Pickering jerked a nod, stalked over to the rail to superintend the hoisting aboard of bags of round shot.

"You're about to inspect the crew, hey?" Doane remarked. "Well, best get cracking — skipper'll be aboard by six bells o' the afternoon watch. Parkins!" he roared, "Parkins! Fetch Mr. Burnham a table and stool, and step lively about it."

"Avast, you men!" The boatswain, a big burly fellow wearing a brown furze coat, began herding the men into loose ranks which must have included roughly a hundred men — a very considerable number for so small a man-of-war, thought Peter.

The *Grand Turk*'s crew displayed a heterogeneous variety of sea clothes; some wore brogans; some stood in heavy, wooden-soled boots; a few even went about in rope-soled shoes; most wore leathern breeches or petticoat-breeches of stained white canvas. Some few had adopted bits and pieces of blue or brown uniform apparently at random and indulging the individual's fancy. Here and there shone a gold hoop, though the style for earrings was waning. In only one respect was there any uniformity. All the men wore their hair clubbed and secured in an eelskin or by a bit of ribbon.

On the whole they impressed Peter as able and healthy-appearing. Obviously the pick of the port had elected to cruise aboard this privateer. Wasn't Rob Ashton known to be an all-fired able captain? And lucky too? Whoever sailed along of him stood good chances of returning to port with a tidy sum knotted in his handkerchief.

Among the men staring curiously at the two officers approaching them were half a dozen Negroes and at least twice as many full-blooded Indians; more numerous still were half-breeds. Impassively, their opaque, obsidian-bright black eyes followed the efforts of Parkins to arrange Dr. Burnham's table.

Soon Peter ascertained that although the heft of the crew was American, almost every seafaring nation in Europe was represented. There were French, Swedes, Dutch, Danes; even a slant-eyed Finn with the palest imaginable blue eyes, and a trio of dark-skinned fellows out of some petty Italian kingdom. His greatest surprise came when a baker's dozen of the able seamen answered his questions in accents characteristic of Devon, Cornwall, Lincoln and Dundee.

In an aside, Doane informed him that for the most part these were deserters from the Royal Navy, good hands all, because they sailed with a halter about their necks and hated the king's service with a passion. Doane said the British were particularly adept at sailmaking and carpentry while Americans made superior topmen and gunners; the Indians and Negroes rated highest in their ability to board and, in hand-to-hand fighting, to sweep clean an enemy deck.

Looking sheepish, the men commenced to shuffle by. Peter told them to open their mouths — he wanted no toothless men aboard — peered down their throats, felt their abdomens for rupture and peered inside their shirts for evidences of the dread *lues venera*, or French pox.

Whoever had signed on this crew must have known what he was about; Peter felt justified in refusing not one of the *Grand Turk*'s company — nor in ordering all heads to be shaved and clothes to be boiled. Of course two or three seamen had bad colds and a few, he suspected, would become afflicted with *lues venera*, but there was no being sure of it. It went without saying that, once the brig was out to sea, all manner of minor ailments would, all at once, be brought to his attention.

Moving with short jerky strides, Captain Ashton came swinging aft, acknowledged Mr. Pickering's salute before running an expressionless eye over the little group of officers lined up before the helm.

"Mr. Pickering."

"Aye, aye, sir?"

"We will weigh anchor at seven bells sharp."

The First Prize

Three days of westerly gales harried the *Grand Turk* far out to sea, flung stinging clouds of snow across her deck, making life a frozen misery for lookouts and helmsmen. However, once the brig traversed the thirty-sixth degree of latitude, the weather grew fairer; seasick men, Peter among them, emerged to revel in the sunlight.

Thus far the brig's surgeon had found little call for his art and therefore he devoted himself to learning, as quickly as possible, pertinent facts concerning the *Grand Turk*'s rigging, design and armament. Soon he commenced really to understand the reasons necessitating the intricate routine of life aboard a well-handled man-of-war.

Once his brig was indisputably clear of the blockade, Captain Ashton relaxed his stiff and curt manner — though he never did unbend as he had when ashore — and took to chatting. One fine morning he ordered the *Grand Turk* to cruise under easy canvas and beckoned his surgeon to share his privileged position by the lee rail.

"I'm coming to appreciate what a really lovely vessel you have, sir."

"Aye. That she is, Doctor. She's a love. To sail a moderately well-found ship in peacetime is fine, suh, but come war, the best ain't any too good." He nodded to the guns constituting his starboard battery. "Now you take those cannons, for instance; they look pretty much like any others, don't they? They ain't, though. Those lilies on their breeches proves they're, every damned one of 'em, French-made of fine bell metal."

"Why bell metal?"

"In a hot engagement guns get heated so a crew either has to cease fire or cool 'em down with seawater. Plain iron guns will crack and burst if you douse 'em when hot. These guns *won't*; therefore we can maintain our rate of fire whilst the enemy's slackens. Aye, the French cast the best ordnance in all creation. 'Tis sheer murder to send men to sea with half the guns we are casting in America right now."

"In peacetimes you wouldn't find half so many men aboard," Ashton remarked after a pause, dark brown eyes continuing to sweep the horizon.

"I was wondering on that. Why so big a crew?"

"Should we take prizes I'll have to supply crews to sail 'em home."

Gradually Peter adapted his life to the routine, proved himself ready to learn; and, recognizing his capabilities, the afterguard lent him every assistance.

Nor did Peter neglect his medicine; hour after hour he studied, queried and made notes. Especially useful in the light of his present assignment was Dr. John Jones's *Practical Remarks on Wounds & Fractures*, a standard book on military medicine. The more he digested the opinions of that eminent Welsh surgeon the more he concurred. Particularly apt was his opening paragraph.

As every Operation is, of necessity, attended with a certain Degree of Bodily Pain, as well as terrible Apprehension to the patient's mind, a good Chirurgeon will be, in the first place, well Assured of the necessity of an Operation before he proceeds to perform it.

Such a sharp pain suddenly went shooting through Peter's crippled hand that he studied that member, all crisscrossed as it was by dull red scars. The pang of course meant some severed nerve was trying to heal. Every night since sailing he had devoted an hour in his malodorous hutch to flexing, patiently bending those stiff fingers, though they hurt like fury. By now he no longer deluded himself that the third and fourth fingers of that hand would ever again become articulate. Question: could he train the other three still obedient digits to perform the work of their senseless fellows?

Peter quitted the rail to take a short turn amidships, then debated whether he should climb, to join for a while the lookout braced inside a hoop secured to the foretop. He could see the seaman, a full-bred Penobscot, standing with stubby brown legs braced inside that hoop which kept him from plunging below. The Indian's head was turning in slow circles so that the wind whipped his long black hair over first one shoulder and then the other.

Sharp against the lighter blue of the sky shone the Indian's blue-and-white-striped jersey, and sunlight, reflected from the sea, drew coppery flashes from his face and arms.

The lookout's attention was casual only because the *Grand Turk* was standing southwards and out of the customary trade routes. In these latitudes nobody really expected anything to happen.

Peter had barely put foot to the fore' ratlines when the lookout suddenly sang out, "Sail ho!"

If the ship had struck a reef, more activity could not have ensued.

"Where away?" Pickering's acid voice demanded.

"T'ree point off de starboard bow, sar. Two spars, sar."

"What course does she sail?"

"No can tell yet."

To watch Captain Ashton, his officers and crew under these circumstances was a revelation; there was no excitement which was not sternly subdued, no rushing around. Events followed in an orderly sequence. The solidly built Virginian remained infinitely calm, but alertly so, because he detected any fault or omission. He never raised his voice, nor did he curse.

After a bit, Captain Ashton himself ascended the main shrouds, carrying his spyglass with him; Doane swarmed up to join the lookout in the fore' crosstrees. Though the call to quarters had not been beaten, the brig's gun crews formed about their pieces, expectant and watching their captain focus his heavy glass.

Presently Captain Ashton closed the cover of his telescope lens, tucked it under one arm and returned on deck. Mr. Doane followed suit.

To Gideon Pickering's unspoken query, the *Grand Turk*'s master stated, "She's a brigantine, old-fashioned English or Dutch designed. Been through a storm, too, because she's juried to her fore and mizzen. From the slack way her sails are trimmed, I'll wager she's shorthanded to boot. Mr. Pickering, beat the men to quarters," Ashton directed. "If she proves a privateer, she'll carry heavier metal than us, for all her sorry state."

Not yet hoisting her huge battle ensigns, the *Grand Turk* stood boldly towards this slovenly, brown-painted brigantine wallowing along to leeward. So far she was showing no colors whatsoever. From her master's failure to make sail it was judged that he was resigned to the hopelessness of his position.

Shading his eyes against the glare of the morning sun, Captain Ashton remained clinging to the lee shrouds and evidently estimating his chances. Presently, the Virginian came to a decision.

"Bend on, and hoist, Dutch colors," he instructed Greenleaf.

The deckhands alternately were studying this old-style vessel and casting curious eyes at their own quarterdeck, while the gun crews stood at stations, ready but not tense. Apparently no one expected a fight and, indeed, none developed. When the *Grand Turk* bore steadily down until her maximum range of two hundred yards was reached the stranger ran up British colors.

A Britisher! That meant a prize certain-sure. A yell of delight burst from the privateer's men.

Easily as a hare circles a cow, the *Grand Turk* steered boldly across the stranger's bows and could have raked her cruelly. Peter cast Ashton a quick look just as the privateer captain nodded. Mr. Pickering caught up his speaking trumpet.

"Hoist our colors! Up gun ports!" he roared.

Even as the Dutch flag sank, fluttering, to the deck, three huge Stars and Stripes shot skywards, flinging defiance.

Not even a warning gun was required to send the stranger up into the wind, to lie wallowing helplessly and losing steerageway. Peter guessed he'd always remember this bright sunlight, the two vessels lying not over two hundred yards apart in this great and empty dark-blue ocean.

Making not a single hostile gesture, the stranger brought his ensign jerkily downwards. Then, and only then, did the *Grand Turk* also come into the wind, taking position slightly ahead of the brown brigantine.

To an accompanying trill of the boatswain's pipe the privateer's longboat went smacking down alongside.

Brown features imperturbable, Ashton beckoned Peter. "Mr. Burnham, prepare to accompany the boarding company. I'm minded that something is confounded wrong aboard yonder vessel; might have plague aboard." This seemed more than likely, as ominously few heads were visible along the stranger's rail.

"Aye, aye, sir." After dashing below for his medicine case, Peter none too adroitly followed Mr. Doane into the brig's longboat now bobbing in her lee. Despite everything, no precautions were being spared; a swivel gun was mounted on the longboat's bow and her crew were armed with cutlasses and boarding pistols.

"What ship is that?" Doane yelled through cupped hands, once the longboat had pulled over under the stranger's stern.

"Ship *Hammond*," came an answering hail, "forty-three days out of London for Tortola."

That the *Hammond* had suffered severely from the elements there could be no mistaking. Jagged gaps in her bulwarks had not yet been mended and short jury masts rising to the stumps of her fore and mizzen had been but clumsily rigged.

"Ahoy! Look alive and heave us a line," Doane directed, once the long-boat was rowed expertly into the lee of the wallowing brigantine.

"You — you'll not torture us?" cried the spokesman, a fat, stupid-looking fellow wearing three days' beard. "You'll spare our lives?"

"We ain't pirates, damn your ugly eyes," Doane snapped. "Don't ye know an American flag when you see one?"

"Begging your pardon, sir." The officer on the quarterdeck still looked scared half to death. "I ain't never seen such afore, sir."

"Who in hell are you?" Doane, now on the deck of the *Hammond*, was still angry over the fellow's cowardice.

"I'm Brandon, sir, second mate."

"Huh! Mr. Brandon, you can trot out your manifest, and no nonsense. Dr. Burnham, have the kindness to learn whether there is sickness aboard. Damned few cargoes are worth chancing sickness aboard the brig."

Accompanied by a brace of the *Grand Turk*'s men, Peter followed an aged Irishman down into the main hold. There, he was informed, were quartered a party of women and children on their way out to Antigua, Tortola and adjacent islands.

"Spare us!" "For the love of God, spare our lives!" "Have mercy, kind sirs!" "Don't kill us!" Frightened cries reverberated from an area subdividing the passengers from the cargo. Some ten women, and nearly twice as many children of all ages, clinging together and holding out hands clasped in piteous supplication, were collected in a group. Most of the children wept in an access of terror, but a few were attempting to conceal themselves among the cargo and baggage. A few of the younger women were kneeling, clutching Bibles to their breasts and moaning pleas for mercy.

One figure dominated the entire scene; that of a tall young woman who alone stood bolt upright.

"Be quiet! No harm will be done you," Peter called as he strode forward, the two seamen at his heels. "Now, madame — "

"Stop where you are!" The central figure cried sharply and the muzzle of a small pocket pistol was swung steadily in line with Peter's chest. "Halt, or I fire!"

"Really, ma'am, you have nothing to fear. We are in truth no pirates, but privateersmen obedient to the laws of war."

"Bah!" her bosom lifted convulsively. "Between a pirate and a Yankee privateer there is not even a small difference."

"Your pardon, ma'am. I fear you have read too many lying English gazettes. Look." He pulled out his medicine case. "I am in truth a physician."

"These are lies!" The young woman's eyes of blue hardened. "You — you can kill me, but shall not force me."

"Oh, stop playing the fool, I tell you I'm Peter Burnham, surgeon aboard the private armed brig out yonder. And who, ma'am are you, may I inquire?"

The lovely, silver-blue head rose proudly. "I am the Baroness Katrina Varsaa, lady-in-waiting at the court of Köbenhavn."

"Your servant, ma'am."

Gradually the Baroness Varsaa's taut attitude relaxed; lips, etched like symmetric crimson scars across the pallor of her features, formed an uncertain smile. "You are indeed a doctor? Good. Here there is much need of your art."

Once Peter Burnham could vouch that no pox, cholera, or any other plague was aboard the *Hammond*, a signal was made to that effect; good news promptly acknowledged by the brig. Now captor and prize were cruising under light canvas separated by less than a quarter of a mile of water. Presently, the captain's gig was lowered, came pulling over to the old brigantine.

There could be no doubt that she constituted a true prize; both owners and registry were British. Had not the *Hammond*'s company included so many women and children, Captain Ashton probably would have removed her cargo and scuttled this weary old hooker. Leaking badly, a fact attested by the continual suck and creak of her pumps and otherwise ill-found, she'd not fetch much of a price at a prize sale.

"'Tis a pity to waste a prizemaster on a tub like this," the Virginian observed, "but her cargo's confounded bulky — and it'd never do to cruise with all those females aboard the *Grand Turk*. There'd be knifings in no time." Again, though he didn't mention it, women weren't considered lucky aboard ship — almost as unchancy as ministers and rabbits.

"Right you are, sir," Mr. Doane nodded owlishly. "When women come aboard, harmony takes to the maintop, and that's a fact."

"Well, I reckon she's just about worth taking over and sending her in."

"Where, sir?"

"Have to think on that," Ashton said.

One of the privateersmen having bent an American ensign to the signal yard and hoisted it above the *Hammond*'s faded British ensign, a cheer came ringing over from the *Grand Turk*. In this bright sunlight the privateer looked trim and graceful as a print fresh from an engraver's shop.

Eventually Ashton decided to send aboard his quartermaster's mate for prizemaster, along with five able seamen; they should be sufficient to fetch the vessel into a friendly port.

[623]

She'll never reach Boston nor Charles Town this time of year — and in this state, Ashton was thinking. She's so damned slow she'd never slip through old Arbuthnot's blockade. The French islands? Maybe.

Ashton had remained undecided when, up from below, appeared the straight-backed figure of Baroness Varsaa, and unbidden, stalked in regal composure up to the table over which the *Grand Turk*'s officers sat scanning the *Hammond*'s invoices and bills of lading. She wore a pert straw bonnet secured by long blue ribbons below her chin and carried a bulging pocket.

"I will go at once aboard your ship," she informed Captain Ashton, quite serenely. "This dreadful vessel is all smells and sails so very slow. Send one of your men to bring my trunk from below."

The Virginian arose, bowed, then reseated himself, his gold epaulettes atwinkle. "I vow 'twould be a rare pleasure to indulge you, ma'am — "

" — Get to your feet." The young woman's bright blue eyes flashed in the shade of her wide-brimmed bonnet. "I am not accustomed to being addressed by a seated man." Her trace of foreign accent became more marked in her excitement.

In perfect good nature Rob Ashton smiled, but remained seated. Said he mildly, "This ain't a royal levee, ma'am, nor do you, or anyone else, give orders aboard a prize of mine." He was at pains to be patient in amplifying his position. "Account of this is wartime and we're likely to be in action time and again, I can't have you aboard my brig. You are going to stay aboard this vessel."

The baroness stamped a slim, well-slippered foot. "I will not stay! I detest this stinking old tub of a ship and those dreadful common women below." The tall young woman's manner then underwent a change; she spoke very sweetly now, hands in their black lace mitts gently kneading at her pocket. "Besides, I am a neutral and no ordinary person. My father is chamberlain to His Majesty Christian VII, King of Denmark and Norway."

"Is this true?" Ashton demanded of the *Hammond*'s anxious and thoroughly discouraged second officer.

Before that beefy individual could make reply, the girl in blue and yellow swung her pocket across Ashton's face. "Boor! Savage! How dare you question the word of a Varsaa? Why I'll — I'll — "

The Virginian arose and, rubbing his cheek, promised in a flat even voice, "Any similar nonsense, mistress, and I'll surely turn you over my knee and spank you right in front of everybody. Now you can clear out. You've wasted too much of my time as it is. Benson!" He beckoned his quartermaster's-mate. "Escort this lady to her cabin and return immediately."

"Oh-h. I am most regretful." The Baroness Varsaa concealed her face behind slim, very white fingers and commenced to weep. "How am I ever going to arrive at Annaberg? I must get to Annaberg — *soon*. Can you not understand?" She seemed on the verge of desperation.

Peter's gaze wandered from her ringless hands to her breast, to her waist, and then up to the exquisite pink and white oval of her face. She deduced his train of thought and flushed.

"Please come aside just for a little. I — I have to talk with you, *Herr Doktor*."

"You still have time and to spare," were his first words.

"Oh, but it is not that. I am — I am to be wedded — my marriage must not be delayed."

Peter wanted to comment, "Obviously," but didn't.

"Where is Annaberg?"

"As I have said, on our island of Saint Jan in the Danish West Indies."

"Is it far?"

"Not very, Mr. Brandon says."

Peter looked at her narrowly. "That'll be a neutral port, isn't it?"

"We are not at war, sir," she replied, obviously puzzled by his ignorance.

Peter went up to Captain Ashton on the quarterdeck.

"You said, sir, this vessel ain't fit to make the run for America?"

"I did. What of that?"

"So she'll have to try for a French or a neutral port? Then, sir," Peter suggested evenly, "is there any good reason why this vessel can't be sent into the Danish islands? They're fairly near to hand and, being neutral, won't be patrolled by the lobsterbacks."

The privateer captain frowned, sucked his lower lip between his teeth a moment, then shrugged. "That's not a bad idea, Doctor. Fact, 'tis a very sound suggestion, suh. Aye. We can touch there and pick up our prize crew on the way home."

Peter hesitated, then demanded boldly, "Can the lady be dropped at Saint Jan? She was distraught just now, and is most contrite."

"She's a pretty piece," the Virginian remarked. "Well, if Benson runs no risk at it, I suppose he may."

Fortunes of War

The *Grand Turk*'s surgeon had not long enjoyed sleep before her boatswain's whistle shrilled insistently. The first light of dawn was revealing topsails on the horizon. Barefooted, both watches were sent tumbling aloft and out along the yards. Then the privateer cracked on sail on sail with such speed that, as the sun came slipping redly above the sea, she had brought under her guns a trig schooner of perhaps a hundred tons burthen.

Although new, the *Soldier's Endeavour* was not fast; the shipwrights of Bangor had constructed her along traditional British lines, sacrificing speed for more ample hold room. Mightily, the privateer's crew rejoiced. The prize proved to be a military supply ship, deep in the water with stores which now would never reach His Britannic Majesty's garrisons in Jamaica.

Gallantly, if unwisely, the schooner had fired a couple of guns and so earned a broadside from the *Grand Turk* which sent her foretop crashing overboard.

A rich prize this, Ashton smiled, one which should prove very welcome among supply officers of those threadbare regiments defending Charles Town against Lord Cornwallis's well-drilled regiments. All stores Ashton left as they were, but ordered two chests of military specie sent aboard his brig. Huzzas arose when the privateer captain, always understanding of human nature, had opened the treasure chests that one and all might feast their eyes and hopes on rich, red-gold coins, all new-minted and stamped with the well-hated effigy of "German George," by the Grace of God King of England, Ireland, Scotland, and France.

With a crew of four, Captain Ashton sent Quistion Savage aboard as prize master over the *Soldier's Endeavour* and gave orders to sail this prize into Boston or New London, whichever seemed to offer the greater chance of success.

Three days later they fell in with the brigantine *Hope*, a Maryland vessel prized by the *Hussar*, privateer out of Liverpool. Again this crew proved a lucky capture, in that she retained aboard her original crew, and so no member of the *Grand Turk*'s company was required to man her. All the same her sale would bring full shares to the *Grand Turk*'s crew. Five members of the British prize crew were added to prisoners populating the brig's forehold.

With each passing day — it was now late February — the weather grew increasingly warm and the seawrack thicker. Just across the twenty-first degree of latitude, the privateer's lookouts sighted and, at the conclusion of a mighty brisk two days' chase, overhauled the *Jolly Tar*, a big privateer captained by one James Hannah.

She mounted twelve guns and wanted to fight, but her ordnance must have been extra cheap and imperfect, for during her second broadside, the number five gun blew up and made mincemeat not only of its own crew but of those of the adjoining cannons. The resultant carnage cost Peter Burnham two sleepless days and nights, and opportunity further to test the usefulness of Dr. Jones's *Treatise on Wounds & Fractures*.

So big a ship — she was all of two hundred fifty tons — justified an experienced prizemaster and a crew to match. Unfortunately, the *Jolly Tar*'s company consisted solely of stubborn, and dangerously resentful, Englishmen; never a foreigner or an Irishman was found aboard. Accordingly, Rob Ashton detailed no less than eighteen of the *Grand Turk*'s

[626]

crew to bring this, the richest prize to date, into a friendly port. The *Jolly Tar*'s fifty-man crew were secured below the forehold hatch gratings only at pike points.

Although Rob Ashton hated to part with his jovial second officer, he put Abel Doane in command of the captured privateer. For all his easygoing ways, Doane was a clever seaman; if anybody could fetch this prize into port it would be he. The detaching of an officer and four men each to the *Hammond* and the *Soldier's Endeavour* had somewhat diminished the *Grand Turk*'s company, but the departure of eighteen more meant a reduction evident in more ways than one; the watches commenced to grumble at extra work.

Reverie

The wind having quite died out at sundown, the *Hammond* brigantine lay aimlessly rattling her standing rigging under the impulse of an endless series of glass-smooth swells. Once her steerageway was lost, the ancient vessel fell into the trough of the seas and commenced a monotonous rolling which in short order rendered seasick nearly all the women and children on board. To make matters worse, a humid, near-to-suffocating heat closed in.

Baroness Varsaa decided no longer to respect the prizemaster's order that after dark all save his prize crew and two of the Irishmen must remain belowdecks. Not very many arch glances were required to persuade Quartermaster's-mate Benson to relax his injunction.

"Well, then, ye may come on deck after dark, ma'am, and ye'll find a bench waiting nigh the main shrouds."

Trina thanked the prizemaster and heaved a vast sigh of relief. Of course, Magda *would* fall seasick again, leaving her no choice but to comb out her own hair. Stroke. Stroke. Why did the servant class invariably surrender so readily to assaults by the elements — and get drunk so easily?

Trina was deciding that she never fell seasick because for generations unnumbered the Varsaas had followed the sea. Papa, in his early days, had risen to vice admiral of the Royal Navy, and at this very moment brother Antoine commanded a stumpy little corvette. She needed no spyglass to help her distinguish a bugalet from one of those clumsy howkers which came plowing northwards from the Netherlands. Ketches in their various forms were commonplace, as were Norwegian cats, recognizable by stumpy masts and huge, high bows. Once or twice she recalled sighting a patache, far from its native Mediterranean waters.

Of His Danish Majesty's Indies horrific tales were current. Every child at home knew of a slave insurrection on this same Saint Jan's Island. Back

[627]

in '33 the blacks had revolted and, during a three-day reign of terror, had massacred seventy-six of the hundred and ten white residents inhabiting that island.

An officer of the Royal West India Company had described it all to Papa one night over pipes and many glasses of fiery schnapps. The colonial was drunk enough to omit none of the ghastly details of tortures inflicted first on the whites then on the reenslaved blacks.

The Lesser Antilles, Kapitan Tornquist declared with conviction, were a sink of bestial cruelty, a hell of blasting heat, and a gehenna of soul-crushing boredom. A few planters made a prodigious profit out of the sugar cane their windmills ground and the rum distilled by their cauldrons, but the rest of the colonials worked — and drank — themselves into early graves.

Trina Varsaa became aware that, for all her déshabille and the night air, she was perspiring heavily. Her fine pale hair began sticking about her forehead and to her neck. If it was like this at night on Saint Jan, she knew she couldn't stand it long.

After loosely securing her bodice strings Trina crossed the deck and seated herself on one of the futile little cannon with which the *Hammond* pretended to defend herself. An American privateersman on duty at the break of the quarterdeck saw her and signaled an obscene invitation. She turned her back and felt so low in her spirits that when he moved away she produced from her petticoat pocket a small flask of very fine cognac and, half defiantly, took a swallow. The liquor was so warm it set her to coughing.

Wearily, Trina's mind tramped back over that oft-traveled path to the moment of her downfall. Ever so clearly she could revisualize the candlelit card room of the palace; the brilliant velvets, satins, silks and brocades; the odors of beeswax, pomatum and French scent strong because of huge fires kindled against the bite of a November gale screaming about the battlements of Kronberg Castle.

There she was, herself, gay as never before and so lovely in a new ball gown of celestial blue that all the gentlemen had stared, forgetting, for the moment, to make their court bows. For such a state occasion as the king's birthday ball she had worn her necklace of tiny pearls and Aunt Klara had lent some magnificent sapphire ear bobs.

What had rendered her especially radiant was the receipt of glorious news. Mathias was returning home from duty in Iceland! To think that in a few days big bold Major Baron Mathias Lynge would take her in his arms and crush her into blissful breathlessness.

The more she thought on the subject the more likely it appeared that Prince Karl must have added a liberal measure of brandy to that champagne bubbling in the heavy silver goblet he'd fetched while she stood watching some scarlet-coated Royal Guard officers playing the English game of Hazard.

Yes, she must have been a bit tiddily; otherwise His Majesty's brother would not, for once, have appeared uncommonly attractive when, a moment later, he muttered, "This afternoon a ship made port from our West Indies. Her captain brought one lovely bird, all bright blue, green and gold. *Gott!* It is nearly as beautiful as you."

"You flatter me, Your Highness."

"Come and view the bird; no one else has seen it, or will. It shall be yours."

Like a silly idiot, she had followed her prince down the long, draughty corridor leading to a small and seldom-used music room. Sure enough, there was such a bird, an adorable, dainty little thing. When she whistled to it the finch cocked a glistening black eye.

She was turning to admire it when, in an avalanche of lust, Prince Karl flung himself upon her, thrusting her, terrified and furious, backwards onto a French settee. When she attempted to scream, his hand, moist and reeking of tobacco, clamped down over her mouth, half smothering her.

On one thing she could look back with satisfaction; she had struggled a long time, and had drawn great bloody scratches across the roughness of his cheeks. At length she lay, pinned beneath Karl's tremendous weight, her garments in wild disorder. Just then the door banged open and there, her heavily powdered face a quivering mask of outrage, stood Her Majesty Julianne-Marie, the dowager queen.

Even now, aboard this miserable vessel, Trina couldn't bear to remember the vile terms laid upon her by this royal termagant; she had used language such as charwomen shrill at each other in rage.

In the pink-gray of the following dawn a coach, its windows heavily curtained, conveyed her back to Count Varsaa's crumbling castle at Hornbaeck and to the frightened stares of her mother. Count Olav Varsaa, impoverished and sensing the utter ruin of high hopes built upon her future, had turned a lean back, pushed her aside, and had refused to listen to a word. Poor Mamma, browbeaten, and timid as a mouse, had listened and understood. What mostly concerned her was that no tangible consequences of the rape should ensue.

Mamma's prayers had been to no avail; by January it had become certain that Karl's seed had taken root.

So she would marry Stephan Frydendahl. As nearly as she could tell, he would be a man of about forty, so her father had said. Word already had gone forward announcing her arrival and her predicament; the dowager queen, thorough and essentially practical, had indicated that in due course Stephan Frydendahl might hope for a court appointment as reward for relieving a more than embarrassing situation. The Varsaas, moreover, were well connected and of ancient lineage.

Trina continued to stare into the dark, trying to visualize Stephan Frydendahl. But what she saw was Peter Burnham, stalwart and bronzed-looking in a yellow shirt, blue coat and gray breeches.

How strange that this savage of an American should so cling to her thoughts. Yes, it was surprising and disturbing the way his plain, good-natured features kept invading her mind like some gallant entering her boudoir unbidden.

Were Frydendahl anything like *Doktor* Burnham, some little happiness might emerge from the wreck of her dreams.

If only Mathias Lynge had returned a few days earlier. Poor dear. Scarcely had he set foot on his native soil than an admiralty order sent him sailing off again — away to the Faroes. Her Majesty the dowager queen was leaving nothing to chance. She wanted a whole ocean between Trina and her wretched son. And no chance of revenge from the gallant Lynge.

The Cockpit

During the next twenty-four hours the weather worsened until the *Grand Turk* was plunging southwards along the sixty-fifth degree of longitude, under double-reefed topsails and a single storm jib. Following seas caused the privateer to pitch heavily, a treatment to which her fabric protested; a couple of minor leaks were sprung.

On the second day the wind increased to a full gale which sent spindrift flying up the crosstrees and caused the Muslim figurehead to douse his forked beard deep into the backs of an endless succession of gray-green rollers. It was then that a stay parted during the night and catapulted a seaman into a roaring and lightless turmoil. A cry like that of a tern lost in a fog rang out; then all was wind and flying spray again; to put out a boat was impossible. Gloom settled over the brig's company.

On the fourth day the gale diminished somewhat, but the seas remained mountainous.

A lookout, clambering into the crow's nest, had barely settled into place than he shouted through cupped hands, "Sail ho!"

Just arrived on deck to draw a breath of fresh air, Peter glanced at his heavy silver watch — landsmanlike he still reckoned time by hours and not by bells. It was, he noticed, exactly nine-thirty on the morning of February the twenty-first, 1780. So long as he lived, Peter Burnham would never forget that date.

"Summon the skipper," bawled the officer of the deck, Eldad Greenleaf. Regularly he served as the *Grand Turk*'s quartermaster, but in Pickering's absence he had been promoted to acting first officer. Everybody knew that had Eldad been less prone to viewing a bottle through its small end, he long since would have been commanding a ship of his own.

Captain Ashton, red-eyed and fresh from his bunk, clumped upon deck carrying a brown, leather-bound brass telescope tucked under one arm.

He took up a post near the binnacle. The only other occupant of the brig's tiny quarterdeck was Jan Vanderhyde, the Dutch gunner and marine officer, his flat red face intent. Above the roar and crash of the seas, Ashton hailed the masthead through his speaking trumpet.

"How does she sail?"

"Standing north'ards, sir, wi' a half-starboard tack," came the wind-distorted reply.

Considerable effort was required of Ashton to steady his glass sufficiently to survey the strange vessel which, under topsails and a reefed forecourse, appeared to be coming directly on.

Some kind of flag was flying from the ship's signal peak, but at this distance there was no recognizing it. All that could be learned at present was that the other vessel's hull was painted dull brown and that her sails were far from well trimmed.

Another quarter hour found the two vessels perhaps a mile apart but steadily closing in on one another; the *Grand Turk* was standing due south; the stranger, a big sloop, sailing to the north-northeast.

"Yonder's a merchantman," Greenleaf grunted to Peter. "You'd never find a ship o' the Royal Navy so badly braced and atowing a longboat."

"Hoist Swedish colors," directed the *Grand Turk*'s master.

For the first time this cruise, his seventh and therefore lucky one, Robert Ashton wavered on the brink of indecision. A fine, new-built ship such as this one bearing down on him should fetch a *very* pretty penny at prize court, yet an indefinable uneasiness was pervading him. Why? Maybe yonder sloop was too big?

Ashton did, for him, an unusual thing. He asked of his acting first officer, "What do you make of her?"

"She's a mite large, sir," Greenleaf replied. "But I allow we can take her measure in jig time."

Peter thought, if we take this vessel my share will amount to more than enough to send me abroad. Flexing his stiff fingers, the physician drew a deep breath. Just one more action and then, well, maybe he could piece together a future.

Captain Ashton faced sharply about, his brown features set in taut and unfamiliar lines. "Mr. Greenleaf, we will clear for action."

Already the gun crews, reeling like drunken men, were removing their sponges and rammers from the racks. The four younkers appeared laboring from below, thin shoulders stooped under the weight of leathern powder buckets.

"We'll turn a pretty sixpence out o' this one," predicted Larry Lord, swinging past Tom Laughry on his way to the magazine.

The older powder boy grinned. "Bet yer sweet life — if Cap'n feels generous we ought to make near a hundred Spanish dollars, or I'm a monkey's uncle. Shake a leg there, Spurgeon! We're overhaulin' the chase, hand over fist."

Once the "clear for action" order was shouted, Peter went below, followed by his two assistants; a wizened fellow named Larkin who had once attempted to study pharmacy, and a gangling but very strong Negro youth named Frye. Peter suddenly found himself thinking it unfortunate, perhaps, that the *Grand Turk* had thus far cruised unscathed. Despite patient and very tedious drilling on Peter's part, his assistants remained miserably inexpert and uncertain of their duties.

Once they got the great lantern alight — after many failures due to the brig's frenzied pitching — they folded a pair of old staysails and a tarpaulin across two empty arms chests, then lashed their crude operating platform fast to eyebolts let into the deck.

"I want sand, plenty of sand," Peter told Larkin. "With this motion, spilt blood will prove slippery as grease. Yes, and you'd best rig some lifelines or we'll crack our skulls if ever the brig falls into the trough."

"Down that Swedish flag!" Captain Robert Ashton commanded. "Break out our battle ensigns and let's see what their colors are."

A deep, defiant cheer arose from the *Grand Turk*'s streaming decks as to the fore signal yard and the main gaff climbed the Stars and Stripes, instantly to flatten in the wind as if they had been cut out of sheet metal.

Still the chase refused to show her colors, only kept up the losing bid for escape.

The carpenter waited in lee of the foc's'le head, together with his hammer, nails and sheets of lead ready to nail over shot holes. Long since, all hammocks had been stowed and the brig's two longboats cast adrift. Should a shot have struck them the resultant hail of splinters could have wiped out a dozen men.

A slight commotion drew Rob Ashton's attention. The captain of the number four gun had jumped suddenly down from the bulwarks on which he had been studying the chase and had slipped on the wet deck to stun himself against the carriage of number six gun. Two of his gun crew dragged him, semiconscious, to a hatch grating and left him there, dazed and gasping.

From the start of this chase Captain Ashton had been aware that hardly enough hands remained aboard his brig to handle her sails in such a blow and also to man her batteries. When it became apparent that the starboard broadside would become engaged, he directed that only those guns be readied.

Having set topgallants and all jibs, the *Grand Turk* now was closing in more rapidly. Acting-Lieutenant Eldad Greenleaf kept his full attention on the set of the sails.

In frozen dismay the privateersmen watched the progress skywards of a white ensign — it meant that the chase was a regular man-of-war of the Royal Navy! Magically, those badly adjusted sails were trimmed and the warship wore smartly to port, disclosing gun ports already triced up. Rob Ashton felt as if a fist had landed at the base of his skull: his adversary was displaying a broadside of eight heavy-looking cannon!

As if to clinch this terrible disillusionment, the stunned gun captain roused up on the hatch long enough to bellow, "For God's sake, sir, turn aside. I was acomin' to warn ye. Yonder's H.B.M.S. *Albany*, sloop-o'-war, sixteen guns. Saw her up at Penobscot."

To avoid being raked, Captain Ashton instantly ordered his helm put down hard. The brig responded handsomely and, as she veered off to port, her guns were run out to an accompanying rattle and a whine of tackles. Now the privateer's gun captains blew hard on their matches, watched all the while their crews who had hard work to avoid sliding all over the deck.

"Fire!" shouted Ashton, hopeful of getting in a perhaps demoralizing first blow. At that precise instant, however, the *Albany* let fly a broadside. Fearful screeching sounds preluded a noise such as a whole crew of lumbermen might make in splitting kindling. Magically, a great gap appeared in the privateer's starboard and bulwarks, and splinters flew hissing upwards to slash the lower canvas. Causing sharp reports, half a dozen taut stays parted, one of them unfortunately was that of the forecourse sheet.

"Fire!" repeated the Virginian, broad features drained of color. "Aim at her spars, men. Load chain or bar shot! Fast, fast for your lives!"

It was well enough to call for rapid fire, but so violent was the rolling of the brig that her gun crews, already hampered by severed ropes, kept dropping their instruments and went reeling wildly off balance. A roundshot, escaping from the grip of a number two man, went thundering along the deck and smashed into a bloody pulp the ankle of a gun pointer on number four gun.

Splinters occasioned by that first enemy broadside had not only damaged the rigging but also had stretched several figures on the *Grand Turk*'s deck. Bright crimson streams spurted from them tracing zigzagging patterns over the well-holystoned decking.

One after another the brig's starboard battery went into action and two of her guns scored hits; it was easy to see the effect of her gunnery because the wind instantly snatched from the muzzles of the cannon clouds of rotten-smelling, gray-brown smoke. Although the privateers were habituated to easy victories, discipline, long implanted, asserted itself a moment later. The brig's cannon recommenced their desperate efforts at defense.

Keeping his eyes on the big sloop-of-war, Rob Ashton strove desperately to keep his head. In all his five years of privateering no comparable calamity had ever struck his vessel. No doubt that he was as badly outgunned as he had been outwitted. Who could have imagined a British man-of-war's skipper capable of daubing his vessel's sides so sorry a shade of barnyard brown?

Provided the *Grand Turk*'s rigging remained standing, he figured he might outsail the *Albany* in a fight to windward — on the other hand, His British Majesty's sloop seemed a fast sailer and she might blow him out of the water long before he could beat out of range.

Another course suggested itself; he might be able to lose speed suddenly enough to pass under the Britisher's stern and so run before the wind. By jettisoning cannon, anchors and by starting his water casks he might win free.

Accordingly, Ashton ordered his brig headed across the wind and, despite her damage, the *Grand Turk* commenced promptly to swing onto the port tack. The *Albany* fired again, hulling the luckless privateer and decimating the crews of number two and number four guns. The privateersmen commenced to falter in the service of their pieces; they weren't accustomed to seeing their fellows lying about the deck as shattered, shapeless masses of gory flesh and broken bones.

Ashton bellowed as he had not during all his seafaring career. "Fire on upward roll! *Only on upward roll!*"

Praise God! The *Albany*'s gunners fired high, doubtless deceived by a sudden rolling of the gun deck.

Ashton ordered canvas made — sent the topmen scampering aloft. One was shaken from his hold and disappeared in the stormy sea.

Survivors of the two forward gun crews were lugging horribly shrieking messmates below; time and again the *Grand Turk*'s violent motion threw these bearers off balance, and the injured, perforce, were dropped to create great scarlet splotches on the deck.

Somehow Vanderhyde got his gun crews back under control and three of his guns managed to anticipate the next British broadside. Once those great gray mushrooms of smoke belched from the *Grand Turk*'s cannon, a curious, whirring sound — such as might be made by a covey of gigantic partridges — filled the air. Double charges of chain shot were shrieking across some seventy-five yards of wind-whipped water.

"Ha-a-a!" yelled the privateer's gunners when, in magical suddenness, the British cruiser's foresail split into furiously flapping shreds. Simultaneously, two of the *Albany*'s jibs vanished as if snatched away by an invisible hand.

Vanderhyde himself trained the remaining number six gun and touched it off — a fraction of an instant before the sloop fired her fourth broadside of the engagement.

The concerted impact of her enemy's heavy roundshot caused the *Grand Turk* to heel 'way over and, at the same moment, a great flash of blinding light shone in Rob Ashton's eyes. An instant later he crumpled, inert, onto his quarterdeck.

Again came an enemy broadside, but, praise God, it seemed to have flown high. All the same, six wounded already lay in a bloody wallow and more were struggling below. Two men lying face down on the trampled sand partially blocked that narrow passage to the operating platform. Over these struggled the newer cases.

Peter found another figure stretched before him on the scarlet-stained tarpaulin and, by applying forceps, drew an iron bolt from its position deep in the back of a German lad of eighteen; hurriedly Peter stuffed the hole with lint and despite the anguished screams of the patient knotted a pledget into place.

The dimly lit cockpit degenerated into a bedlam of outrageous sounds; groans, whimperings, screams and odd, lowing sounds like those made by thirsty cattle. One topman, whose whole right side had been crushed, kept on screching until one of the walking wounded snatched up a caulking mallet and cracked him on the top of the head.

When the *Grand Turk* changed course, the rolling became so violent that not even four men could keep a patient on that ghastly scarlet tarpaulin.

Surely hell could be no worse than this, Peter thought. He realized he was helpless for the present. He grabbed at the wrist of a powder monkey who had just lugged below a shattered marine. "Pass immediate word to the captain; I can't operate till this rolling abates."

"Aye, aye, sir." It was young Prescott, his smooth young face gone whiter than that of any living being Peter had ever beheld. The boy's eyes were twin pools of horror.

If Captain Ashton entertained any notion of surrendering it wasn't visible. The rumble of gun carriages being run in for reloading continued to sound on deck. Peter, locking his teeth, crawled on hands and knees along the row of wounded, worked as best he might.

Eldad Greenleaf straightened from a hurried inspection of Captain Ashton's unconscious figure and cast a critical eye aft to where a brace of barefooted helmsmen heaved at the *Grand Turk*'s tiller.

The *Albany* now was forging ahead with the obvious intention of raking her cruelly mauled adversary. With the master dead or nearly so, with the brig's gun deck a shambles — only three guns remained in firing condition — there remained only one sensible course.

"God curse the luck!" Greenleaf snarled. "We'll have to strike." He felt a chill strike the pit of his stomach. All too well he knew what would follow surrender: imprisonment in a stifling and noisome forehold, kicks, blows, and swill for food, eventual internment in some heatless British prison.

There was no longer any hope of exchange, either. Since last year, His Majesty's ministers had come to appreciate that in the revolted colonies there were none-too-many seamen, but press gangs could always round out the crew of a Royal man-of-war.

"Strike the colors!"

But when the seaman ran towards the signal halyard, he slipped on blood issuing from Captain Ashton's sagging jaw, and fell heavily.

Greenleaf, sensing the imminence of a fourth broadside, started for the halyard himself. In doing so he cast a last despairing glance at H.B.M.S. *Albany*. To his amazement the sloop appeared to be losing way. Why? Then he noticed how many severed stays and halyards streamed from her tops.

"By God! Look! Look, sir!" One of the helmsmen was leveling a blunt forefinger at a crack opening above a shot hole showing halfway up the *Albany*'s mainmast. Even as Greenleaf watched, the crack expanded and, clearly visible against the sloop's brown paintwork, ran like lightning towards the deck.

Then it happened. The royal cruiser's mainmast snapped just below its crosstrees and, to a violent threshing of yards and wild flapping of canvas, the spar went crashing over her starboard rail. Water was flung high into the air and the sloop heeled over until her port strakes showed.

Bowlines and stays leading to the foremast held a brief instant bending that spar like a bow; then the lines parted under the terrific strain. The foremast recovered but, creating a grinding, crackling roar, the mizzenmast tottered and, dragged by the dead weight of the sodden maintop, followed the mainmast over the lee rail. The *Albany* was halted just as effectively as if she had struck a reef.

Um. Total casualties numbered thirty-nine! A pretty grim tally. Greenleaf licked his pencil point. Let's see. Thirty-nine out of fifty-three leaves seventeen able-bodied men to sail a badly mauled brig of two hundred tons burthen. His heart sank.

Eldad Greenleaf knew that he alone of the ship's company was qualified to navigate unless Captain Ashton recovered — which seemed mighty unlikely right now. Um-m. To try for home in this condition wasn't practicable, not by any remote stretch of the imagination. So few hands couldn't be expected to handle sail in those late winter winds prevailing along the American coast at this season.

Sundown. The crew was tired out, exhausted physically and emotionally. It had seemed callous to dump the dead overboard with never a prayer said over them nor a hammock to swing them down to Davy Jones. He'd no choice, though. The *Grand Turk* had suffered four shot holes between wind and water which were admitting such quantities of seawater that, despite the carpenter's best efforts, the pumps had to be kept going and that required the continual efforts of four men.

The brig must seek shelter promptly; Greenleaf blinked nervously when he thought of how much temporary planking and sheet lead were in use to keep the *Grand Turk* above water. Such stopgap measures would suffice only so long as the weather remained fine and the ocean smooth. Where to head? Where? Lord, Lord. The only other officer surviving was Dr.

Burnham, and he knew mighty little concerning navigation or the management of a vessel.

Eldad tried to figure things out just as if he were younger and hadn't consumed so plagued-many gallons and gallons of rum. Well he knew that those gallons had done little to whet his once lively intelligence. A long time went by before he came to the conclusion that the best thing was to head for Saint Jan. If all went well he'd pick up there Benson and the four men who'd sailed away in charge of the *Hammond*.

Yessiree. The more Greenleaf turned the matter over in his mind, the more he figgered that this was the proper ticket. He'd lay a course for Saint Jan. The Danes, smarting under an arrogant application of the British embargo, very likely would give even a stricken American privateer a handsome reception.

Once safe in the shallow and neutral waters of Coral Bay in Saint Jan's, the brig could be careened and her not inconsiderable water-line damage repaired. Greenleaf figgered on sending down the main topmast; a chance shot from the enemy's second broadside had cut it nigh on a third through. Tomorrow he'd have it fished; that spar would never survive a stiff breeze.

A curse out of Tophet on being so short-handed! Of the seventeen sound men, four must always be at the pumps and three in the cockpit tending the wounded. Two more were required to manage the helm, which left but eight dog-tired hands free to make sail, assist the carpenter at his desperate efforts to stop the leaks, to bend on new canvas and to repair the rigging.

For a long time to come there'd be precious little sound sleep for anybody aboard. Greenleaf ran his eye about the horizon while speculating on how soon some of the more lightly wounded hands might be returned to duty. Only one man could settle that question. Accordingly, the acting master made his way down to the cockpit.

By the afternoon following the engagement, Peter had got a canvas ventilator rigged which, while not really efficient, nonetheless directed a little fresh air into the cockpit. So far he'd not been able to prepare a report list for the captain — twenty-four wounded men required a deal of attention. He told Greenleaf so.

Said he, "Don't bother about that list — Cap'n won't be wanting it."

Burnham's red head jerked up and his hollowed eyes narrowed. "He's hurt?"

"Aye, sir, and badly."

"Why wasn't I told?"

"He wouldn't let me. Insisted you had enough to do for the others."

"I'll examine him the minute I finish this job."

So exhausted that his every motion required a distinct effort, Peter Burnham made his way over debris still littering the companionway and climbed on deck. Like Greenleaf, the first thing he did was to draw a dozen deep breaths then pause blinking at the pure blue of the sky. Just how many ages ago had he made his way below, blissfully unwitting of the horrors in store?.

"God Almighty!" One of the crew flinched at the sight of him. Then Peter realized that from his shoes to the crown of his head he was spattered and spotted with fresh and dried blood. His new apron resembled that of a butcher at the end of a long day's work. Wouldn't do to appear before the skipper like this — especially if Ashton was hurt as badly as Greenleaf had implied.

Moving on lead-heavy feet, Peter Burnham descended into that small but elegantly appointed cabin in which he had enjoyed so many cheerful repasts. Except for a litter of charts scattered during Greenleaf's efforts to locate those he needed, Captain Ashton's cabin seemed about as always.

Peter was brought up sharp, though, by his first sight of Robert Ashton. He lay asleep at the moment — or was he unconscious? In any case the *Grand Turk*'s master lay very flat, breathing hoarsely on the neatly folded blankets of his bunk.

On hurrying over, Peter realized that Ashton had gone a gray-white and his usually carefully clubbed dark brown hair was streaming loose over his pillow. What caused Peter's liveliest concern was that from either nostril thin threads of blood had sketched irregular streaks over the stubble on the captain's cheeks to drip onto the pillowcase.

God above! Robert Ashton was in bad case, indeed — one had only to listen to his breathing.

Using every care, Peter removed the Virginian's garments, then wrapped his cruelly bruised body in a soft wool blanket. Luckily, the weather was growing hotter so there'd be no necessity of piling bedclothes across that injured chest. Eyes burning with sleeplessness, Peter Burnham fetched a basin and pulled out the mechanical lancet he bought when he'd thought he was going to adopt the army. It was a very neat French invention. One had only to press a little trigger to release a sharp blade which, with a deft flick, would open a vein as neat as you pleased. Um. He figured to draw off about ten ounces.

Until this moment, Peter had not realized how very great was the depth of affection he felt for this quiet Virginia gentleman. Memories of that serene, quietly elegant home back in Boston arose to plague him. For the sake of lovely and spirited Andrea Ashton and her children, he would do all in his power to save the *Grand Turk*'s master. Perhaps he could? The Virginian's fiber was tough and he was young — a little over thirty at the most.

Only reluctantly did Peter Burnham respond to a continued shaking of his naked shoulder.

"Wha — wha's matter?" he mumbled and roused up on that bunk which had been occupied by Abel Doane ere he'd gone aboard the *Jolly Tar* as prizemaster.

It was Tom Laughry, the only remaining boy of the ship's company. "Dr. Burnham, sir, wake up! Wake up, sir!"

Peter swung his feet to the deck, but ashamed to be found stark naked beneath a single sheet, hugged the covering to him. It had been so infernally hot in Doane's cabin that he couldn't bear the thought of a long nightgown.

"What's amiss?" he asked. "Speak up, boy."

"Sir, Cap'n's come to; he's askin' fer you. Wants you should come to him right away."

Captain Robert Ashton, of Norfolk in Virginia, lay on his berth breathing shallowly. When he forgot and attempted to draw a deep breath, a dozen red-hot pike points seemed to pierce the right side of his chest. By now he was becoming resigned to this hateful and overwhelming weakness.

Ashton didn't know quite what to think. Since boyhood he had been ever hale; never a sick bed had been his lot. Yet somehow he knew his vitality was near spent. The angel of death, whose wings he had heard many and many a time during a hard-fought action, was about to lay chill fingers on his brow and say, "Come with me."

Robert Ashton knew for sure he was about to die, though he couldn't tell why. Lying there hot and so very weary, he regretted that never again would his hands caress the wonderful cool warmth of his wife's white shoulders. Never again in all this world would he be privileged to watch the delicate deviltry of her eyes, the tenderly mocking twist of lips that still spelled heaven.

It was something, Rob Ashton felt, to know that he'd done what he could in a quiet and unspectacular way towards serving his country. Aye. He'd risked death time and again to keep alive that trade which was the very lifeblood of the new nation. Come to think on it, during the seven cruises on which he had embarked, the *Grand Turk II* and *Grand Turk III* had prized some twenty British vessels.

It came as a relief to realize that never once during his maritime career had he ever been needlessly harsh to prisoners fallen into his power, nor had he handled his crews with anything but fairness and generosity. How many other privateer owners could say the same?

Then the captain's mind ran for a while on the *Desdemona*'s long, tortured voyage which, on some reefs off Somerset Island in the Bermudas, had ended in disaster.

A thin smile curved Ashton's fever-dried lips. Well, if anything the rector said was true, before long he'd see Peggy.

In a way Rob wasn't sorry that the end was at hand; at bottom, he'd never been a man of violence. Always he had yearned for peace, but had found none during this endless, senseless war.

The children, Rob reckoned, would make out all right; but what of the

[639]

United States? Bankrupt and near exhaustion after five long years of strife, could the new nation survive? What a vast pity he wouldn't be privileged to learn what would chance.

The familiar noises of his ship under way proved soothing. From where he lay he could see most of this comfortable, familiar little cabin, a fact which reassured him.

Rob closed his eyes and only roused when he heard a footstep, felt someone's hand testing his pulse. He couldn't see very well, so he asked, "That you, Burnham?"

"Yes, Captain." Peter Burnham's voice now sounded nearly as soft and gentle as Andrea's.

Peter replaced Ashton's icy hand on the counterpane miserably aware that not even the greatest physician in Europe could long avert death.

Rob Ashton's voice was little more than a whisper. "I am going, ain't I?"

"Yes, there's no use lying, sir. And very soon, I fear." He had hard work to blink back hot, most unprofessional tears.

"My thanks for your honesty, Peter. Always cling to that integrity. And now — you'll undertake to see the shares fairly divided?"

"Aye, sir."

"You're to divide half of my prize money among the wounded for 'twas my stupidity — " The dying man's eyes closed momentarily and he sighed. "Take my hand, Peter, I — I feel so lonely in this half light. There, that's better."

"Yes, sir?"

"Pray present my tenderest compliments," he employed the old, genteel phrase, "and ever enduring affections to — to — " he faltered, licked lips turning blue-lavender, "to my darling Andrea."

"As quickly as I return to Boston, sir. Never doubt it."

"And pray inform Peggy — " his breathing grew shorter and more labored.

"Peggy? Who, may I ask, is she?"

"My first wife, dead the last six years. I fear through ignorance I used her ill."

Peter's fingers tightened on the cold hand under them.

"I am certain you didn't willingly do so. Is there any special commission you wish to charge me with?"

But Robert Ashton was wavering on the threshold of eternity. He lay silent and so motionless that Peter pressed his ear over Ashton's heart.

"He's gone — " Peter muttered, but he was wrong.

Ashton's voice sounded quite clearly amid the darkness. "Andrea, beloved." Then, indeed, the *Grand Turk*'s master fell forever silent.

"Doctor, what'll you aim to do?" asked Eldad Greenleaf.

"I expect I'll continue my studies," Peter replied.

"But yer almighty artful right now — never have seen such a handy sawbones. The men swear by you."

"My thanks, Captain. This cruise has taught me, among other things, how little — how very small is the sum of my skill. I intend to journey abroad — to Holland, France and Italy." He turned, abruptly facing his companion. "How much do you suppose my share will amount to — at the very least?"

"Only lady luck and the prize courts can answer you that, Doctor. God granting that a couple o' the prizes make port I'd say ye can figger on fifteen hundred pounds sterling." He arose. "Well, sir, I'm to bed; we'll begin raising anchor afore dawn. Goodnight, Doctor."

Peter made no move to go below; it was balmy and cool on deck; besides, his mind had begun to run again on Trina Varsaa.

Peter thought, "Right now Trina must be settling her new home down yonder on Saint Jan. How will she make out? Maybe that fellow Frydendahl — that was his name, wasn't it? Yes, Stephan Frydendahl — might take agreeably to the notion of receiving a ready-made heir for a wedding present; foreigners are funny about such matters." All he knew was that Danes were something like Swedes, speaking different dialects of the same tongue.

Greenleaf, too, knew little about Denmark save that it turned out some pretty able mariners and was a small but rich kindgom on the very northern rim of Europe. Also he claimed the Danes could drink like porpoises and maintained large interests in the slave trade.

It was the last day of May. Bits of greenery and an occasional coconut went floating by; numbers of gloriously colored dolphins appeared to play about under the brig's cutwater and flying fish became so common that no one paid them the least heed.

Now tiny thrushes, warblers and finches, blown out on the sea, settled exhausted and forlorn in the rigging; once an exquisite little hummingbird fell onto the deck. None of these castaways lived long; quite early the crew wrung the necks of the larger birds and tossed them into a stew pot.

Eldad Greenleaf ordered the brig's canvas reduced.

"I aim to raise Saint Jan just about daylight," he explained to Peter while bent over a fine new admiralty chart.

"By which channel do you aim to approach, sir?" inquired the acting mate, a half-breed Wiscassett from Cape Cod. "Drake's Channel, mayhap?"

Greenleaf sucked his lower lip in between his teeth and slowly shook his head. "Nay. I'm minded to sail down King's Channel, but presently I'll veer into Saint James Passage and then bear sharp to starboard and stand in to Saint Jan from the south'ard. That should allow us wide berth of any cruisers on patrol off Tortola; figger those British bastards might keep a bulldog or two stationed in Sir Francis Drake's Bay. Again, by putting into Coral Bay from the south'ard we'd find plenty o' room should need arise to run for it past Saint Croix and so out into the Carib Sea."

The land smell momentarily was growing more pronounced — so said the older hands. Though no moon shone, the stars were so brilliant that a sharp-eyed man might discern a cay half a mile distant.

Silently the *Grand Turk* maintained her course, until both lookouts at the same moment called, "Land ho!"

"What do you see?"

"Two cays off the starboard bow." Then almost immediately, "There's three islands off the larboard bow, sir, big ones and dead ahead."

Greenleaf clambered stiffly up into the shrouds, and stood leveling his night glass in obvious uncertainty. Presently, he uttered a short cry of satisfaction.

"Ha! Yonder looks like Thatch Cay. Come half an hour, we should raise Saint Thomas to starboard."

Before long the brig emerged from Sundet Sound and sailed boldly out into the Caribbean, now showing faintly gray by a false dawn. At once the *Grand Turk* commenced to parallel the southern coast of Saint Jan.

Here and there gleamed an occasional shore light and, up in the foot-hills, reddish campfires flickered.

After a bit, Greenleaf anxiously commenced to study his topsails — ordered mainsail and forecourse set. "Dag nab it! Pesky wind's afadin' out," he grunted. "Was afraid it might. Often does in these latitudes, just about daybreak."

Dawn found the *Grand Turk* still cruising parallel to the southern shore of Saint Jan. Because the Caribbean was so calm, Peter found little difficulty in surveying a big, well-protected bay, lying beyond the Ram's Head.

"Right smart lot o' craft in port," Greenleaf remarked. "Looks like two of 'em are making sail."

What immediately captured Peter's attention was the presence of a tall ship of the line — she looked like a third-rater of maybe sixty guns but towered over the rest of the shipping as a giant oak rises above underbrush. His brown nut of a face screwed into a knot behind the eyepiece of his telescope, Greenleaf was watching her crew shake loose sail after sail.

"My eyes ain't so good as they once was," Greenleaf muttered. "Can you make out her flags?"

"Aye, she flies a red flag bearing a white cross from each of the tops."

"Are they cut swallow-tailed?"

"Yes."

"Then she'll be Danish, praise God. 'Twouldn't do fer us to git caught by an enemy liner in a flat ca'm like this."

The privateersmen lined their rail to watch the third-rater's slow, almost sluggish approach. There could be no mistaking now the identity of those flags flying from her tops — they were Danish, all right. If she held her present course she must pass within seventy-five yards of the becalmed privateer.

The privateersmen fell to waving their caps and cheering the foreigner, now sailing almost abeam of the *Grand Turk*. Everyone aboard the brig started when aboard the liner a bugle started to sound a discordant series of calls. At the same time a loud rumbling reverberated across the placid sea as through the liner's ports were run the muzzles of perhaps twenty-five cannons, their red-painted ends glaring at the lesser vessel like so many angry eyes.

To a sharp whirring noise the Danish flags shot down and up rose the flag of a rear-admiral of the Blue Squadron in His Britannic Majesty's Navy.

Silence, characteristic of complete and shattering surprise, pervaded the *Grand Turk*'s men — in horrified astonishment they watched appear on the quarterdeck a number of figures in blue and white. Only fifty yards distant, a great red-faced fellow wearing an enormous cocked hat bellowed, "Surrender, ye rebel dogs!"

Eldad Greenleaf recovered, shouted right back, "These are neutral waters. Ye've no right to attack us."

"Tosh. Make but a single move and I'll blow your tub out o' the sea. Haul down that rag ye fly."

The Master

Lying abed and waiting for daylight, Stephan Borgardus Frydendahl, Friherre of Annaberg Station, felt in more than usual ill humor. All night long a pain, stabbing in his back, had kept him sweating and squirming on sodden sheets. Hour after hour, he'd been listening to a voracious humming of insects flitting outside that gauze mosquito bar which protected his great four-poster bed. Though the netting kept such pests at a distance, its fabric also effectively cut off any breath of air straying in from the sea. What a dog's life this was, even though one grew rich at it.

By now Frydendahl felt convinced that he was afflicted by the stone. A weakness in that direction seemed to be the lot of all the Frydendahls. His father had died of a kidney stone. The big toe of his left foot also pained him, gave promise of gout. To imagine that great ass of a physician, Cornelis Bodger, telling him to modify his eating and drinking. *Gott!*

What a fool! Suppose one cut out eating and drinking, what would be left? Only the black girls and, in this climate, only so many of them might be enjoyed each week.

Stephan parted his mosquito bar and paused, half out of the bed. If Katrina had been a trifle less haughty on arrival — no, surely this was just another attempt to make game of the Frydendahls. The Varsaas would never forget that the Frydendahls for generations had paid them homage.

So? What effrontery to wish an embarrassing bastard brat on him. Well, Count Varsaa was to learn that things had changed; the Frydendahls would tolerate no further humiliations.

Stephan Frydendahl's watery blue eyes considered the landscape, wandered over his cane flats near the coast, then shifted to a quartet of windmills which, situated on a series of hilltops, ground his sugar cane.

He leveled a telescope, through which he studied various gangs of slaves already hard at work in his cane fields. Klaas, the young Dutchman in charge of number three gang, must be reprimanded; he wasn't driving those surly black brutes of Mandingoes half hard enough.

Ach! A pang from the vicinity of his kidneys dealt Stephan a twinge sharp enough to evoke a groan and to half close his eyes. He couldn't stand such torture much longer. Sweat broke out along the Dane's broad forehead. Craving a drink of cold water, Stephan Frydendahl used a heavy walking stick to pound angrily on the flagstones beside him.

"Trina!" he bellowed, picking up a cane of supple bamboo. "Blast your lazy soul, Trina, you blonde bitch, rouse out and fetch your lord a jar of cold water!"

Between powerful brown hands he flexed the terrible cane.

Out from the shadows of a short colonnade appeared Trina Frydendahl, his wife. Her eyes, because of the crescents beneath them, appeared more huge than they really were. In dank, colorless strands her fair hair dangled low, as if to hide, in an ashamed way, the single garment of coarse gray cloth covering a body swelling into an ungainly convexity.

Wearily, Trina inquired, "You called?"

"My lord husband!" Stephan prompted, staring at her over the bamboo stick ominously bowed between his hands. "God blast your treacherous eyes, must I teach you respect all over again?"

Trina's dirty bare feet — she was allowed no bathing privileges — whispered away into the house. Once inside, she moved more slowly; it was becoming increasingly hard to ignore the unsupported drag of breasts grown heavy and tender. A black woman, risking a shy smile of sympathy, passed Trina a long stone bottle.

Mechanically, Trina tested a damp film on its outside attesting the fact that evaporation had cooled the water within. Feeling desperately short of breath, she paused; it was time to remind herself that, after all, she was a Varsaa.

Even yet she found herself still unable fully to appreciate the enormity of this situation into which she had become trapped. No doubt now that the promised explanatory letter had never been forwarded by the court of Köbenhavn. Who could have failed her? Probably one of the dowager queen's sycophants.

In the distance the sound of a bell, jangling loudly, startled her. That would be that *Herr Doktor* Bodger, whose principal claim to distinction lay in his boast of having sired well over a hundred mulatto brats.

"Trina! Bring my water."

The flagstones burned the soles of her feet; not yet were they toughened sufficiently to endure such a heat. Toes flinching, Trina carried her water jar across to Frydendahl's gross, half-naked figure lolling on a wicker chair facing on Leinster Bay. She had bent to serve him when his stick dealt her a stinging cut across the thigh.

"Kneel!" he roared. "Kneel when you serve me, you disgraceful trollop."

Eyes filling, Trina sucked the linings of her mouth between her teeth to keep from weeping. There was nothing to do but obey; there was nothing to be gained by offering resistance.

"I'll have fresh sheets on my bed," Stephan told her, thick lips suddenly buckling with pain. "For the sake of your hide see that tonight the wind sail is properly adjusted outside my window. Last night I nearly smothered. After that, get to your room and await my orders."

Trina forced herself to bend her head and mutter, "Yes, lord husband," before waddling back to the welcome blue-white shadows of the colonnade. She was finding it most difficult to walk barefoot. Stephan had forbidden her high-heeled slippers — shoes of any sort, for that matter. As a result the great tendons along the backs of her legs ached from an unaccustomed tension.

Once Trina gained the miserable yet welcome shelter of that narrow cubicle into which Stephan Frydendahl locked her most of the time, she collapsed onto a rough blanket on her cot. Softly, the unhappy young woman commenced to weep. Why did Stephan have to be so hateful?

At a slight sound from the direction of her door Trina started up violently. Was Stephan coming to taunt and curse and maybe beat her again? No. It was Mamma Bellona who slipped past the heavy, iron-bound portal. The old Negro woman advanced with a finger held tight against great, purplish, clam-like lips. She carried a small stone jar — Trina knew what it contained — a salve rich in coconut oil.

Obediently, Trina pulled up her single unlovely garment and lay down so that Mamma Bellona might anoint the distended skin of her abdomen and so, perhaps, she might avoid those *striae* often enduring long after childbirth.

Long held a slave in Jamaica, Mamma Bellona spoke English far better than Danish. Besides, it seemed safer to converse in the first language. None of the other Negroes understood anything but Danish or Dutch.

"Missy, two days gone by in Coralhaven young buckra gemmun speak yo' name."

"A buckra?" Out of a semistupor induced by her misery Trina struggled to understand. Buckra? Oh yes, that usually was applied to Englishmen and, more recently, to Americans. "He spoke my name?" Trina's heart gave a sudden leap and her eyes flew wide open.

"Yessum. Fo' true." Mamma Bellona was far from stupid.

To win Mis' Trina's gratitude — and the possibility of eventual freedom — she risked at most twenty lashes. Friherre would never set her free. Half a century ago, among certain sour-smelling jungles fringing the Niger, one of the tribal storytellers had recounted a fable — that of the bandicoot. It appeared that the little bandicoot had gnawed through a tether imprisoning his friend the king of the jungle. Because of that small and kindly act, the bandicoot lived long and only died of overeating at my lord the elephant's table.

"A — stranger?" Trina sat up on her cot. "His hair — ?"

"Lak de sunset, missy."

"Oh-h, go on. For the love of God, go on!"

"De buckra gemmun come ober fum Tortola, two, t'ree days gone. At Frederick Five Tavern gemmun he ask if young princess come from the white country. He ask an' ask agin. When no one tell he ask, 'Whar gone de Baroness Varsaa?' "

Despite the humid heat gathering in her cell-like room, Trina grabbed Mamma Bellona's skinny shoulders.

"What did he look like, Mamma?" Suddenly, it seemed not at all strange to call this withered, gray-blue hag "mother."

"He tall, fo' true, tall lak r'yal palm, lak Coromantee warrior."

Trina's naked breasts lifted to a very deep breath; for the first time in many weeks she smiled. "You are sure this gentleman had hair like the sunset?"

"Fo' true, missy — not many such."

Trina's spirits revived. No longer did she feel so completely alone; but of Dr. Burnham — how well she recalled his name — how much help had she any right to expect?

Trina lay back again breathing quickly, her skin softly gleaming amid the humid gloom. The old Negress nodded to herself as she recommenced her massage. So this was how the breeze blew? Chaw! Things might happen at Annaberg ere long.

Down a miserable, rain-gullied road leading to Coralhaven from Annaberg rode Frydendahl's steward bearing gold and an urgent invitation to the American doctor to visit Stephan Frydendahl on professional matters.

Late the next day therefore a two-wheeled *volante* deposited at the massive door to Annaberg a red-haired individual garbed in a faded blue coat, wrinkled white duck trousers, and a cocked hat, the gold braid of which seawater had clouded with verdigris. The visitor's luggage was unimpressive. It consisted merely of a small sea chest, a medicine case, and a carefully fashioned wooden case measuring perhaps two feet by a foot.

The blazing sun beat hard at Peter's face while the rasp of the iron tires of the *volante* diminished beyond a hedge of oleanders fringing the driveway. As he stood on the drive listening to the *volante* follow the circling road downwards to distant Coralhaven, Peter recognized that the windows of Frydendahl's residence were so aligned as to permit defenders to enfilade the entrance; also, though cunningly disguised, embrasures had been designed at each corner of the house to permit musketeers to fire downwards with a minimum of exposure. Peter was soon to learn that since the fearful slave revolt of 1733, nearly all plantation houses were constructed along these lines.

So this was the home Trina had come to? How would she greet him? How would he be able to bear himself — right now his heart was thudding like an Iroquois tomtom.

In any case I'll see her very soon, Peter thought, then tugged at a brass bell handle. Somewhere in the depths of Annaberg a bell jangled and a big dog brayed furiously until a deep voice could be heard roaring something in Danish — a language of which Peter understood less than nothing.

Presently a series of bolts *click-clucked*, then an elderly, light-colored Negro, barefoot and shirtless but wearing a green livery coat and pantaloons, pulled back a massive front door liberally strengthened with iron bands and fairly studded with great nailheads.

"You de doctuh gemmun, *Baas?*" He inquired after bowing nearly to the ground.

"Yes, I am Dr. Burnham."

Presently a couple of little black and white monkeys came gambolling out of a passageway to grab at Peter's coat skirts. Chittering, they then leaped up onto the shoulders of Peter's guide.

The little procession after a considerable progress along a series of empty corridors finally halted in a huge sleeping chamber, the ceilings of which stood a good ten feet in height. The bed, Peter perceived to be a massive affair of carved mahogany set on a sort of dais and hung with a net of fine gauze; each of its legs stood immersed in a copper water pot. This precaution, he had learned, was designed to discourage the approach of creeping insects.

Two very tall windows, heavily barred, afforded a magnificent view of the ocean and of a small harbor lying perhaps two hundred feet below. From them one could see for miles and miles away out to where a number of palm-crowned cays gleamed green and white in the sometimes sapphire blue, sometimes emerald sea.

"De Marster, *Baas*, say please when freshed to come out on de piazza," the butler said, bowing for a third time. Hesitantly, he raised liquid brown eyes. "My name Wulf, *Baas*, yo' humble obedient slave; bell you ring, Wulf come."

It was a relief to strip off coat and shirt and, at an elaborate brass and mahogany washstand, to sponge himself from poll to waist with fresh cool water.

I'm acting the fool, he reflected. I never should have come over to Saint Jan. Trina would be a colossal idiot even to consider leaving all this for a penniless, disgraced physician.

Aye, he was penniless, all right; the *Hammond* had fallen into British hands once more off Tortola and her prize crew was on their way to England. So, unless by great good fortune some of the *Grand Turk*'s more important prizes had won passage through that screen of enemy cruisers prowling from Georgia to Nova Scotia, he was no better off than he'd been back in January.

Standing there, blotting himself dry with a great fluffy towel, Peter took a firm resolution; no matter what chanced here at Annaberg, he wasn't going to betray by so much as a quiver of an eyelid his hapless devotion for Trina Frydendahl.

Luck had favored him in one direction at least; when herded up onto the deck of H.B.M.S. *Raisonable* Peter had not for a minute supposed that his captors would permit him to retain his medicine and instrument chests, nor that Rear Admiral Sir George Collier would respect his claim of being a noncombatant and therefore exempt from imprisonment. All the same Sir George *had* listened and finally had agreed to set him at large — a surprising decision, considering his recent and brazen violation of Danish neutrality.

After laying away his gear, Peter clubbed his hair with a length of dark blue ribbon presented by Dr. Robert Tunney, Surgeon General to the Royal Colony of Tortola. Tunney had proved a decent sort, going out of his way to befriend and advise a luckless colleague. During many a long hour he and the surgeon general had bickered over various points of physick and surgery and so had come to conceive a mutual respect and admiration. If ever this blighting war came to an end Peter Burnham was immediately to seek out Robert Tunney, M.D., at Surgeon's Hall in Windmill Street in London. But all that lay in the far future.

Some mighty depressing news had been brought into Coralhaven by a British army victualler blown off her course to Barbadoes. In no time at all news circulated that, on the twelfth of May last, some three thousand Continental and South Carolina troops and seamen under the command of General Benjamin Lincoln had allowed themselves to become penned up in Charles Town and, being cut off from relief, had been forced to surrender at discretion.

The war, British sea captains boasted along the waterfront, couldn't last much longer now. Why, the only major port left in rebel hands was Boston, where all the trouble had begun.

[648]

Very likely Louis XVI of France and his ministers would think twice before further reenforcing their forces in America. What use to stiffen an already broken reed?

Diagnosis

Seated in a most comfortable wicker chair Peter studied Friherre Stephan Borgardus Frydendahl — and could think only of a fox. Crimanently! This gentleman's florid coloring, his small, tawny eyes set so close to a long and roseate nose, suggested Renard grown tremendously. Frydendahl's every gesture, the way he handled his eyes, were essentially vulpine, and the Dane's whole bearing suggested wariness, unrelenting and perpetual.

The Dane put down a lithe bamboo stock equipped at one end with a horsehair fly whisk and got ponderously to his feet.

"Velcome, Dr. Burnham, velcome to Annaberg," he boomed in tolerable English. "You haff your bedroom found?"

"I regret the necessity of keeping you waiting," Peter smiled as they shook hands. "I was so very travel-stained I needed a wash."

While the sun sank, quantities of insects commenced to sing and chirp as the two men sat on the piazza, sipped their drinks and, smoking long very thin cigars, conversed quite amicably. All the time Peter kept an ear cocked for the whisper of a woman's petticoats — for the rich sound o˙ Trina Varsaa's voice. At dusk great, wide-winged bats commenced to swoop about a double rank of papaya trees lining a walk leading down into an elaborate garden. Still no mention was made of a mistress of Annaberg. It was very strange, thought Peter.

"And now, sir," he ground out his cigar stump, "regarding this ill health of yours — ?"

"Can you tell anything by simple observation?" Frydendahl wanted to know.

The American shrugged. "I'd hazard that you suffer from the stone. During the last hour I have seen you wince a dozen times."

"*Ja!* Dot iss it," the Dane grunted. "God, how I haff suffered."

Further description of symptoms left no doubt in Peter's mind that his big red-faced host suffered from a chronic mortification of the uretha and a stone in his bladder.

"What treatment have you taken?"

"Oh, dot old fool Bodger has made me drink *aqua animalis*."

Peter glanced up in surprise. Not in many years had that concoction been prescribed back home. "It relieved your pains?"

"No, though it tasted bad enough to."

"I'm not surprised," Peter told him. "Do you know of what this *aqua animalis* is made?"

"No — be good enough to tell me."

Peter delved into his pocket, brought out a copy of William Salmon's *Pharmacopoeia Bateana* he'd come across in Coralhaven. He read: " '*Aqua Animalis*, The Animal Water of Horsedung. *Bate. Take of Horse-turds newly dropped, add of Whitewine a Gallon; Sweet Fennelseeds, Parslyseeds, avis Grocers Treacle, or: Polypode of the Oak, Butchers Broom, Liver-wort, ana MIj.: Ginger.: mix and distill according to Art, with a gentle Fire.*"

"While I have no doubt but that you are afflicted with the stone, sir," Peter went on, "I must understand your diet, observe the balance of your humors and your way of life before deciding what should be done."

Frydendahl suddenly flew into a temper. "I vill not vait. I suffer too much. Damn your soul! Are you a physician or a fortuneteller?"

"Pray calm yourself, Mr. Frydendahl. During a few days I must make observations on your condition."

The Dane glowered a moment but ended by subsiding. "And so?"

"You will save your night water in a clean jar. You will eat no spiced food nor drink anything stronger than tea."

Frydendahl's big hands jerked apart. "Impossible! Vithout good food, vines and liquors I cannot live or vant to."

"You delude yourself, sir." A smile curved Peter's lips and his brows climbed a little. "However, if you prefer to continue suffering, that is entirely your affair and I shall leave at once." He intended to stay, however, at least until he had seen Trina.

"Forgiff me, *Doktor*, I spoke in haste yust now; in my back is lodged like a white-hot pitchfork."

"Then, I take it, you agree to follow my directions?"

"*Ja*."

"If I remove your stone, my services will cost you five hundred rix dalers."

Frydendahl's lips pursed themselves and he sat heavily back in his great rattan chair; fright was written all over his round and florid features. Suddenly he held out his hand. "Good, it iss a bargain — five hundred golden rix dalers." He shrugged, lit a fresh cheroot from a small brass lamp burning on a coffee table. "After all, such a sum is nothings to escape from this hell of pain." His yellowish eyes came to rest on Peter's face. "I know not why, *Doktor* Burnham, but I feel you can be trusted. Yes, I know not so many peoples I vould trust so far."

After an enormous supper of rabbits stewed in onions, roast pork, goose stuffed with truffles, two kinds of fish, papayas, custard, bananas, coffee and four varieties of wines, Peter puffed uncomfortably on his yard-of-clay pipe. "I will require, during the cutting for your stone, the assistance of two intelligent white men," he informed his host. "Can you find such?"

Frydendahl frowned, passed a hand over his turbaned pate. "So? That iss not easy; you vould not vish for Dr. Bodger?"

"No. I prefer two gentlemen with little or no medical training."

"Ha, you are afraid they might observe your method?"

Peter treated his host to an irritated glance. "Since you appear to lack confidence in my ability, sir, I venture you had best call on someone else." He spoke sharply. He was beginning to find out that, like most bullies, Frydendahl failed to respond to politeness.

Frydendahl heaved himself to his feet, laughing uproariously. "I should not haff said dot, perhaps. No, no, I trust you very vell, *Doktor* Burnham. Vell, let me see. Maybe dot Carleby, Carolus Carleby of Carolina plantation; he is anxious of buying some timberland of me. Yes, he vill come. And Ditlev Reverdil, my cousin. Vhen you vish them here?"

"Only the day before I operate." Peter drew a deep breath and essayed to speak noncommitally. "In Coralhaven the pastor of the Lutheran church told me you are married. Is that so?"

"Vhat concern is it of yours?"

"Only that we physicians have learned that, during convalescence, it is best for the patient to be nursed by his wife."

Frydendahl's heavy head swung sharply under its enormous palm fiber hat and his eyes stabbed at Peter's bland expression. "*Ja.* I vass married two, three months ago. My vife is avay, visiting Fra Holmstrup over on St. Thomas Island."

"Now, sir, please listen to my instructions."

When Peter had concluded, the master of Annaberg made a flatulent noise with his lips, then spat noisily. "So you vill allow me no drink but beer?"

"Exactly," Peter replied, trying to recall Dr. Townsend's discourse on the subject. "You will consume nothing but fruit, milk, and soft foods — no meats at all."

Frydendahl glared. "I think you must be trying to kill me before that — that business. I vill not — " Frydendahl just then must have suffered a pang, for his face writhed. He groaned. "It shall be as you say. It has never been vorse than today. Now I shall go and sleep." He beat the flagstones with his stick, roaring for his servants.

"In the cool of the morning I will come bleed you," Peter warned, and said nothing of the clyster he proposed to throw up.

"This house is yours, *Doktor*, except for the vest ving," the planter announced. "If you vish to amuse yourself with fishing or shooting, tell Klaus; he iss my gamekeeper. If you are fool enough to vish to risk riding in this *verdammt* climate, Leon vill find you a saddle horse. Good night." And the big fellow went shuffling off.

Why should there be no sign of Trina, Peter wondered. Had he not heard in Coralhaven those accounts of a wedding taking place at Annaberg he might well consider himself in error. Surely any normal man would have been uncommon proud of having wedded so very beautiful a girl.

Certainly Frydendahl had no possible means of learning that he, Peter

Burnham, was aware of Baroness Varsaa's existence and, even less, that the child she must be carrying was not his. Why? Why, then, this complete denial of her very existence?

Peter settled back in his armchair, considering the wondrous brilliance of the stars.

Um. Even before this operation took place, he would have touched a tidy sum. If his work proved a success he guessed he'd be in the way of earning a small fortune in these Virgin Islands. If only he had available a text of William Chelsenden's treatise on *High Operation for the Stone.* Along with William Smellie, Percivall Pott and that great Quaker, John Coakley Lettsom, Chelsenden had been one of Dr. Townsend's principal heroes. Peter couldn't help chuckling when he recalled a little jingle current in medical circles:

> *The patients sick to me apply*
> *I physicks, bleeds, and sweats 'em*
> *If, after that, they choose to die,*
> *What's that to me?*
> I. Lettsom.

Peter ran a finger around the inside of his shirt collar. Lord, even after dark the heat was something one must experience to understand. A little guiltily, he slipped his feet out of their ponderous pumps and happily wriggled his toes while running over in his mind the most approved procedures for the removal of a stone — or stones — from a patient's bladder.

Speed in operation he knew to be essential. Chelsenden was reliably reported to have removed a stone in something under one minute and a half; Dr. Townsend attributed that surgeon's high percentage of success to his swiftness with his knife and an attendant lack of shock suffered by the patient.

The next morning humid heat beat against Peter in waves, warning that a hot day was commencing; presently a slave appeared carrying a goatskin of water with which he commenced to spray the flagstones of the portico. Peter guessed his most sensible course of action would be to retire to his room and doze until the late afternoon.

At present he could not detect a sign of activity anywhere. Even the watchdogs which roamed the ground floor of Annaberg slept, panting.

Right now, he told himself, might be a propitious time to undertake certain reconnoiterings? He casually circled the one area denied him and found that the west wing was in reality but a spur off the main body of Frydendahl's great, yellow-tinted plantation house.

Simulating an absorbed interest in those varied and brilliant flowers which, in regular beds, paralleled the foundations, Peter explored the west wing. At the same time he whistled, very softly, a series of old English tunes.

He had nearly reached the end of a row of windows ranged along the south face of the west wing when a flash of something white falling among the flowers shone in the corner of his eye. The physician took care to betray no surprise, only treated his immediate surroundings to a more thorough inspection. Only after a long interval did he work over towards a bed of nasturtiums glowing like a floral brazier in the cruel sunlight. Under pretense of examining some particularly gorgeous blossoms, he was able to find and to palm a short strip of cotton before continuing his leisurely inspection of the flower bed.

Not to hurry at once to his quarters proved difficult, but Peter forced himself to survey, in the main hall, the mold-speckled portraits of several long-dead Frydendahls.

A brindle mastiff blinked baleful yellow eyes, rose from a cool corner and, in friendly fashion, came over to sniff at Peter's ankles. Such canine guardians roamed every plantation house on Saint Jan and, saving those who fed and cared for them, would attack any black on sight.

Reassured, the dog snuffled, then returned to his corner and flopped down, muzzle on paws, but kept amber-hued eyes open and alert.

Peter told himself, Um. This evening I think I shall do a bit of wild pigeon shooting? 'Twould be handy to know where Frydendahl's guns are kept.

Once in his quarters, he locked the door before inspecting a strip of cloth which appeared to have been ripped from the hem of a petticoat. Written upon it in rust-colored letters were the words: *Doktor, Help me for the love of God. K. Varsaa.*

For a long time Peter remained seated on the edge of his great bed staring at this irrefutable evidence of disaster.

Why was Trina Varsaa being held prisoner? The explanation presented itself at once. Men far less ill-tempered and selfish than Stephan Frydendahl would become anything but agreeable over the prospect of supporting another man's bastard.

Um. Just what was Frydendahl doing to his bride? One fact stood out in sharp relief — Trina must be reached in all speed. Knowledge warned that, being so far advanced in pregnancy and quite unacclimated to this blasting heat, she stood in desperate need of medical attention. Whatever course he followed, he must proceed with the greatest of caution. At Annaberg Stephan Frydendahl was a law unto himself, and on Saint Jan's Island, also, for that matter.

Lithotomy

With the hour for the operation on Stephan Frydendahl drawing close Peter was annoyed to detect traces of anxiety in himself. This was odd, because he had made up his mind about each step to be followed and knew exactly what he was to do. Perhaps his uneasiness stemmed from a realization that the merest flick of certain muscles of his right hand, guiding a razor-sharp edge, could set Stephan Frydendahl's blood to spurting in such uncontrollable jets that no power on earth could check them.

Back and forth the physician paced his bedroom; he guessed he had planned pretty well, too, concerning the problem presented by Stephan's wife. For at least a week after the removal of his stone Frydendahl would be kept in bed; a week during which Peter's plans for Trina would be put into effect.

Lost in thought, the physician stood staring out between the sturdy bars of his bedroom window and absently massaging the stiff fingers of his left hand. By now he had become convinced that never would he fully regain their use; those tendons severed by the glass on that wall top in faraway Boston would not mend. Though a surgeon's left hand he knew played an important role in cutting for the stone, he figured his handicap wouldn't hamper him to any serious degree.

As to his assistants, they were barely adequate; one was a big, slow-witted fellow who had to be rehearsed in his part again and again. Carolus Carleby, Peter decided, would only be useful because of his ox-like strength. Ditlev Reverdil, on the other hand, was quick to learn and clever. Above fifty years of age, he was nervous as a cat, surly and quite as suspicious in his manner as Frydendahl.

The shadows of palms sheltering the garden were growing long and sharp; it was nearly time. Peter turned back into the room to inspect his preparations. Because Frydendahl had seemed to expect it, he would wear for the occasion a ruffled shirt and his blue coat, into the lapels of which he thrust a trio of curved needles already threaded with silk.

A taut smile on his mouth, Peter picked up his case of instruments and strode along the great hall towards his operating room — a small bedroom located, for the sake of a possible breeze, on the northeast corner of the house.

After considerable debate with himself, Peter had decided upon a single bed with four posts that would do for tying down the patient should he grow fractious.

Finding his operating room empty, Peter tested yet again those linen bands with which Frydendahl's hands would be secured to the bedposts. Across the center of the bed was waiting a firm bolster in a yellow silk cover. Peter felt it, made sure it would be firm enough for his purpose. Praise God! His self-assurance was returning during the familiar preparations.

Waiting on a marble-topped side table was a copper bleeding basin and a second wash basin for cleansing his hands of blood. Next the New Englander laid on his instrument table — a pretty gilded wood and majolica affair — a sounding staff. Slim and bearing a groove in its blunt end, it was nearly a foot long. From a jar of goose grease he dipped some fat and with it rubbed the whole length of the staff. Then he arranged the scalpels he intended to use — they were sharp as an unkind look — beside a gorget and a pair of blunt forceps.

Peter next occupied himself by selecting bandages and bundles of lint from his medicine chest, then dropped some ligatures into the wash basin to soften.

Why the devil didn't Frydendahl and his friends appear? With every passing minute his nervousness grew. It was difficult not to think of Trina and a temptation soon to be faced.

At length, with Carleby towering beside him, Frydendahl came in clad in a billowing, lace-trimmed nightgown; about his head was fastened a bandage designed to keep the sweat from pouring down into his face. He was pale and sweating in apprehension.

"You have nothing to fear," Peter reassured him. "If you give me no trouble, five minutes will see the matter concluded."

Reverdil closed the door and locked it as Carleby, from a waistcoat of orange-tinted linen, transferred into his breeches pocket a short-barreled pistol. At the same time he treated Peter to a black look which made it quite clear that if the patient failed to survive this operation said pistol would be used.

"Get onto the bed," Peter instructed Trina's husband; then, more because it was expected than for therapeutic reasons, he produced his lancet and bled the Dane a scant six ounces. Next he pulled out a pulse watch and gravely counted the patient's heartbeats.

Peter readjusted his turned-back sleeves, then snapped, "Sit on the bolster, then lie back."

Once Frydendahl had obeyed, Peter employed a pair of broad linen bands to tie the patient so that his knees were raised but secured well apart. Though Frydendahl grumbled and the two other Danes scowled, Peter bound the planter's hands to the bedposts.

Trembling the least bit, Peter gave Reverdil the sound staff. "Introduce this — slowly and gently, as I have told you."

"Damn it, keep his legs steady," Peter flung at Carleby. "Under no conditions let go until I say so."

Peter felt sweat breaking out on his forehead when he felt the scalpel's cool ivory handle beneath his fingers. He drew a deep breath, bent and seizing his lower lip between his teeth, drove the knife deep through the first skin, then a layer of fat and deep into the taut flesh; ridiculous how easily this incision could be made. Swiftly and surely, Peter drew his instrument downwards then outwards; and immediately he introduced the first two fingers of his left hand into the wound he had created well to the left of the midline of the patient's perineum.

Frydendahl emitted a bubbling screech, then commenced cursing in Danish.

"Hold that staff steady!" Peter growled at Reverdil. Employing the fore-finger of his right hand, he groped until he located, through the hot tissues, that lump which identified the tip of the staff. His scalpel cut towards it in such a fashion that a second incision had been made upwards from below.

It was the work of an instant for Peter to pass his gorget down the groove in the rod. At the same time he passed the blunt forceps through the wound and into the bladder where it came into contact with the staff and gorget. Quickly he moved the forceps deeper into the incision. Ah! Now they came in contact with a hard object. Unluckily Frydendahl chose that moment to give a spasmodic heave so the forceps closed on nothing, and blood coursed ever more freely from the incision.

"God blast your soul, Carleby!" Peter panted. "Hold him tight! Tight! You let him wriggle like a speared eel!"

Again he manipulated the forceps' jaws until he felt them meet and grip the stone, then carefully he worked his forceps slowly outwards until he could withdraw them. Sweat was stinging Peter's eyes, yet he saw, clearly enough, that his blood-stained forceps were gripping a large chalk-white stone.

"It's out — steady now. Steady everybody. You may withdraw the staff, Reverdil!"

"Wonderful," panted Carleby; the giant was white-faced while emitting a small gasp of satisfaction.

Peter dropped stone and forceps into the water basin then, in almost the same motion, he jerked a needle from his lapel and passed it beneath the spurting veins until its point pricked the fingers of his left hand held in such a position as to protect the intestines.

Peter guessed even Asa Peabody, a perfectionist in such matters, would have admired the dexterity with which he tied the ligatures and then stitched up the wound. As a last step, he bound over the wound a pair of lint pledgets well soaked with blood. He straightened and went to wash his hands.

"Get on vith it," gurgled Frydendahl, eyes rolling wildly. "Vhat kind of a butcher are you?"

Peter held the stone where his patient could see it. "There, sir, is your stone. The operation has been completed."

Peter made his way to his patient's room to make a post-operative check. An hour before the operation Frydendahl's clerk had brought into Peter's quarters a canvas sack containing the agreed five hundred golden rix dalers.

The patient winked. "You treat me well because I am rich, heh?"

"No. It is because you are my patient. I do my best to give all patients the same consideration."

"Vhat! You vould use the same art on a — a *kerl* as on me?"

"I don't expect you would understand; however, that happens to be the case."

The planter settled back against the bolster, his florid hands and countenance creating vivid splashes against the pillow slips.

The laudanum Peter had given him began to take effect, and shortly Frydendahl slept, making little bubbling noises through his lips.

Long since, the physician had taken two precautions: to make fast friends of the mastiffs, Krakadil and Löke, and to gain access to the armory of Annaberg. In this connection, he had gone so far as to try wing-shooting some of those huge green doves which inhabited a patch of woods down near the ocean — and the plantation's tidy little fishing harbor off Leinster Bay.

Peter sent Frydendahl's valet to fetch a pitcher of flip, an errand he estimated would require five minutes to discharge. Keeping one eye on the bed, the physician undertook a systematic search; suddenly he realized that the brass key he sought was not likely to be found in Frydendahl's temporary bedroom.

Quickly changing the scene of his activities, he discovered shortly afterwards that which he sought in a not-so-secret drawer of the Dane's writing cabinet.

From the armory Peter appropriated a light flask of powder, a handful of balls suitable to be fired from the small but effective French pocket pistol he had taken to carrying — a fine example of compactness and exquisite workmanship.

At ten of the second night following Frydendahl's operation, Peter strolled out of his room and down that great hall in which night lights drew dim flashes from the armor and antique weapons arranged in panoplies along its walls.

Immediately the dog Löke arose, came gravely forward, his toenails clicking loudly on the mahogany flooring. Peter patted him two or three times, then Löke sighed and clicked back to his mat.

For a long five minutes Peter waited outside of Trina's prison, every faculty keyed to observation. Finally he felt positive he was not being observed.

The instant his key slipped into the lock he heard, on the far side of the door, a scurrying sound; therefore he took the precaution of pushing open the door before entering. It was well he did so, for crouched in the half light like a wild animal ready to spring and leveling a wicked length of steel was the wrinkled old black woman known as Mamma Bellona.

"Ah. Doctuh!" While he was closing and locking the door behind, she concealed her knife, then shuffled forward to drop on her knees and kiss his hand.

The old creature's eyes reminded Peter of a cat's, yellow with intense black centers. He followed her bent figure into a small room.

[657]

The old woman clung to his hand. "Is good you come to mist'ess. Evil spirits work 'gainst her. Me do all me know; she fin' no rest."

Stephan Frydendahl's wife lay on her back, her swollen abdomen mountainous beneath a stained and heat-rumpled sheet. Her eyes opened to the sound of his tread and, when she beheld that big figure almost filling the door frame, a glorious look of hope brightened her delicate features.

"Trina!" he cried hoarsely, "Trina! Oh, to find you again."

"Oh, *Doktor* Peter — at last! Peter."

When she struggled to raise herself on one elbow he gently forced her back; so she contented herself by pressing his hands to her cheek; by the Phoebe lamp's dim rays he saw two large tears well from beneath her lowered eyelids and go slipping over the wasted contour of her cheek.

Trina emitted a smothered little sound. "Peter, Peter! Never will you leave me again?"

"No," he promised in a thick voice, "not ever again, as long as I shall live." When, very gently, he kissed her brow Trina put an arm about his neck and drew his lips down on hers.

"*Mon chevalier,*" she sighed, and smiled in a pathetic attempt at gaiety.

After administering an opiate Peter sat for a while beside his love, stroking her fingers and seeking to reinstill hope and courage. He intended, he told her, to take her away from Annaberg in two days' time. Did Mamma Bellona know of some nearby cay where they might find refuge? The old woman thought a moment then, her eyes round as ever, nodded slowly.

"Of Saint Jan and the nearby islands Mamma Bellona knows everything," Trina replied drowsily. "Dear Peter, you will surely take me away?"

"As I hope for God's mercy. The important thing, my dear, is that you rest until then and recruit your strength. He — " he nodded towards the other end of the house, "will be unable to quit his bed for another three days at least. I believe I have frightened him beyond danger of disobedience."

By the afternoon of the third day after the operation of Frydendahl, Peter's plans were formed, but were characterized by an essential flexibility. He now knew where a fishing boat well suited to his purpose customarily was moored. It looked to be fast and sturdy and was equipped with an easily managed lanteen sail. Many and many a summer off New London he had handled a very similar rig.

Peter had halted in the shade of some trees, for though the sun was sinking beyond the summit of Camel's Back Mountain the day remained so confoundedly hot he was debating a plunge in a nearby stream when a sound of running feet drew his attention. Presently there appeared on the path a Negro boy of perhaps twelve years, who was running as if all the seven devils were hot on his trail.

Recognizing him, the runner halted, gasped out, "*Baas! Baas!* Mamma Bellona say — "

[658]

Peter waited to hear no more of the message but started pelting, full-tilt, up the path leading to Annaberg.

Once indoors, Peter immediately noted that the plague room door was open and that a scared-looking girl was lugging in a copper pot of steaming water. One glance into Trina's room told him everything — and that he was too late. From the cot over which Mamma Bellona bent sounded a feeble moaning. Splashes of blood had marked walls, sheets and floor, and on a grimy pillow lay something swathed in a roll of rags.

"Gustavus," breathed Trina. "Gustavus Varsaa. I am content." Then she sank into an exhausted slumber from which Peter made no effort to arouse her.

Shaking his red head Peter handed the child to Mamma Bellona. In this climate few white infants of full development stood much chance of survival, perhaps one in five. For a premature baby less than no hope existed. Why, the infant's mouth was far too tiny even to accept a nipple. This child would die — a martyr to Stephan Frydendahl's hatred.

Nonetheless, he bound and trimmed the umbilical cord, directed that stone hot-water bottles be placed to either side of the mewling mite, then redirected his attention to Trina.

To be sure, she had lost quite a lot of blood, but hardly more than was normal. All the same, he refused to allow her to remain in this breathless, ill-ventilated hole.

Two days more elapsed, two days during which Stephan Frydendahl's strength became so greatly restored that all of Peter's persuasion was required to keep the master of Annaberg in bed. But that must be done. Certainly in not less than four days could Trina recover sufficiently from the double shock of the miscarriage and the loss of her infant to undertake a trip down to the fishing harbor.

When Peter came next to check on his patient, Frydendahl spoke only briefly. "My friend, you are vun great surgeon. You vill make a huge fortune." Bald head agleam he sank back on the pillows. "Send Wulf to me. Now I vill rest."

Peter went to his room.

Although Peter could not analyze his apprehension, something in Frydendahl's manner had been vaguely disquieting. Maybe he was imagining it. Trina was mending rapidly. She had abundant natural strength and her humoral balance appeared to have been restored, despite the weeks of bad food and mistreatment; yet it would be so easy to induce another hemorrhage.

Stripped to the waist, he sat sweltering in his room, the inevitable halo of flies buzzing about his head. He drew out his French pocket pistol and fell to admiring its wickedly slim outlines.

Time now to visit his second patient, to take her pulse, to change dressings, and to administer tonics both medicinal and mental.

He found her sitting propped up and looking lovely again beyond all description. A pair of pale blue bows had drawn the lustrous silver-blonde tresses to either side of her face. For the first time a trace of rosiness had reappeared along her cheekbones. To watch instinctive fear vanish from her eyes as he quickly closed the door behind him was thrilling beyond description.

"How do you feel?" he demanded taking her pulse.

"So much stronger, Peter. It is wonderful. And now most of the bruises have disappeared."

Um. Her pulse beat normally, but was not overly strong. Accordingly, Peter knelt beside her bed, turned down the covers and placed an ear over her heart. A thrill of relief invaded him. The soft *thud-thudding* was markedly stronger than it had been even twenty-four hours ago.

Meanwhile her fingers played with his coppery hair. "Peter, do you understand what my heart is saying?"

Peter was drawing breath to reply when suddenly he felt Trina's fingers go rigid; he whirled aside, facing the entrance. Yonder the door had swung silently open and there, his face an empurpled mask, towered Stephan Frydendahl. Snarling noises escaped him.

In surprising agility the Dane sprang aside, aimed at the kneeling Peter a murderous blow with a ponderous walking stick nearly six feet long and topped with a heavy knob of ivory.

Simply because Peter was quick did the weapon fail to cave in his skull and only caused a glancing but agonizing blow to land on his shoulder. Frantically, the physician rolled onto his back, at the same time wrenching for the French pistol. Damn! It was hung up in his pantaloon pocket.

"So? So?" roared Frydendahl. Having lost the element of surprise he dropped the stick and from under his banyan produced a heavy short-barrelled pistol. Trina screamed, flung her pillow at Frydendahl and so caused him to dodge. With death but a split second postponed and the Dane's gleaming barrel leveled on him, Peter fired from the floor.

Trina screamed again. Peter scrambled crab-wise to gain his feet, but anticipated that second explosion which would snuff out his life.

No pistol bellowed, but some heavy object clattered onto the floor. Through the eddying fumes of acrid smoke he glimpsed Frydendahl standing as before, except that a bluish-red dot had appeared in the exact center of his forehead. Almost immediately Frydendahl crashed forward, his body pinning down Peter's legs.

Exodus

Peter did not delay but ran down the hall towards his room, bellowing, "Wulf! Klaus!" Everything depended on whether Sverdrup, the overseer, in his house a quarter of a mile distant, had heard the shot.

Wulf appeared in trembling anxiety. *"Baas?"*

"Fetch Klaus and carry Friherre Frydendahl to his room," Peter told him. "There has been an accident; he is not badly hurt."

The only two men servants tolerated inside of Annaberg by Krakadil and Löke quickly obeyed Peter's succinct commands and soon had the planter back in his room.

"Stay with your master, you two, and bathe him with cold water while I summon help." He scowled. "If either of you sets foot outside this room before I return I'll see your backs sliced to ribbons."

Klaus and Wulf nodded. Though laboring under a terrible uncertainty, they respected the authority in his voice; besides, the *Baas's* wound was very small and little blood was in evidence. It never occurred to them that their master would die in a few days' time, running down gradually, like a clock someone has forgotten to wind.

When Peter returned, Mamma Bellona was in attendance on Trina. Already tied into a bundle were her clothes and other odds and ends. Peter wound a soft blanket about Trina Varsaa, handed her his instrument case and then slung the medicine chest by a strap to his back. Then he picked her up and carried her out into the growing darkness. A penetrating silence prevailed over Annaberg; if any of the house servants had taken alarm, there was no way of telling so.

Through eyes narrowed against a sparkling sea, Trina and Peter watched an outrigger canoe come tacking in from that faint blue smudge on the horizon made by Saint Jan's Island. Side by side they lay on the warm white sand, happily considering those changes which the past two months had wrought in their lives.

When Trina arose and walked out to the end of a small sandspit extending into the infinitely clear, blue-green water he noted how the sunshine had darkened her fair skin to a delicate and fascinatingly light bronze. While she stood outlined against the sunset her hair, as so often happened, escaped once more from the crude pins she used to secure it and floated free from under a crown of scarlet blossoms encircling the small, proud head. The single blue cotton garment she wore concealed little of Trina's magnificent figure as its fabric eddied lazily under the offshore breeze. He clenched eager hands, trembling to caress again the incredible, maddening softness of her smooth body. Lord, but it was wonderful to lie here, like some pagan demigod caressed by a fragrant and balmy wind, plunged deep in the magnificent adventure of a great love bestowed and perfectly returned. How little was understood, back in staid old Connecticut, about the magnificent splendor of love in its various facets.

At the base of a wind-twisted palm, he rolled onto his back and lay staring at the gentle motion of the bright green fronds and whispered, "Yonder stands my wife, Mrs. Peter Burnham."

Peter guessed most folks back home wouldn't set much story by their marriage rites, performed by Hippolyte Cohû, patriarch of the village. His service would remain unrecognized by the Church of England or the Lutheran Church, though for nearly a hundred years his simple Creole-French phrases had served to bind in well-respected wedlock the black, brown, and yellow young people of Congo Cay.

How beautiful Trina had looked that day in her white gown and neck-lace of blue and yellow seashells; bracelets and a tiara to match had completed her wedding regalia. "They are just as lovely," she'd told Ti Annette, "as the jewels of our royal family."

An excited Negro appeared on Congo Cay one crystal-clear morning. He had come sailing out of Coralhaven, making good time before a strong southeast breeze. If the truth was in him, a government sloop would depart the following day with intent of surveying the hardwood stand on Congo Cay. The colonial surveyors, so the messenger declared, would examine every foot of this long, low-lying cay.

Mamma Bellona sniffed, told Trina that the fellow was lying; once two silver Spanish dollars had clinked into the messenger's pink palm, a great deal of his agitation had evaporated. And yet — there was no being sure, Peter reflected. Neither he nor his wife understood Negro nature.

To risk capture and imprisonment in a filthy dungeon would be asinine — as unforgivably stupid as it would be disastrous. Justice in Charlotte-Amalie on Saint Thomas, capital of the Danish West Indies, would be neither swift nor impartial.

Repeatedly Trina reminded herself that Baroness Katrina Astrid Maria Varsaa, Danish noblewoman, had perished in order that Mrs. Peter Burn-ham, American citizen, might exist. When alone she drilled herself to correct her accent. Again and again she tried to reproduce, for the benefit of the stone crabs and pretty little parakeets, Peter's pronunciation of certain words difficult for her. Yes, she must forget those too-correct sen-tence structures, such as always identify a person who has learned English by rule.

"It is no use taking a risk that this baboon is lying. We must leave, my Peterkin."

Thus it came about that at sunset of the next day a small lugger bought with three of Stephan Frydendahl's golden rix dalers put out to sea and left astern the friendly fires of Congo Cay.

The French islands of Marigot and Saint Martin's, Peter knew, lay to the south-southeast and in their direction he determined to shape his course. Principally, he wished to avoid Tortola, the vicinity of Jamaica, and the British Antilles to the northwest of the Virgin group. By setting sail near midnight, he calculated to have left traffic plying the Tortola Strait safely astern before sunup.

Letter to West Point

Mistress Sabra Stanton closed the door to her room behind her. A small sigh of relief escaped her. Mercy! If it could grow so dratted hot in Boston, how terrible must be those temperatures prevailing further south. Thrusting forward her under lip Sabra blew damp hair free of her forehead.

Sabra thought, while advancing towards the center of her room, "La! I'm getting near to becoming an old maid — why, I'm nineteen and going on twenty."

The sun must be beating harder than ever at the brick walls; the lifeless hot air of her room seemed so smothering that she undid the limp cambric kerchief clinging to her neck, flung it carelessly onto a chair. Then, mechanically her fingers untied a series of apple-green bows securing the front of her pale yellow lawn bodice.

Heavens to Betsy; it was a mercy to be out of that dress. A wicked, unladylike impulse occurred — sent delicious, if shameful, currents to mounting from her loins to her shoulders. To release her stay cover required less than a moment. Then, flushed and breathing quickly, she undid the ties securing her five muslin petticoats, let them ripple to the floor in rapid succession.

What gave her the greatest joy was to cast loose her stays, cruel hickory-splinted affairs which restricted her waist like the inexorable and unyielding claws of a demon. Ah-h-h. To feel the air commencing to cool her skin was a subtle sort of ecstasy. Only her perspiration-dampened shift remained as clothing. Sabra hesitated. What she was about to do undoubtedly was wanton, but she didn't care — the impulse was too great to be resisted.

Her cheeks went hot and her rounded breasts began to tingle at the idea of completely disrobing while not preparing for bed. In a defiant twist of her lithe young body Sabra rid herself of the shift; stood nude save for shoes and neatly gartered stockings. Her fingers rubbed hard at the vertical dark pink indentations caused by her stays. Air evaporated perspiration, dewed her skin and caused gooseflesh to rise on it. La! It was wonderfully stimulating to stand like this, permitting a faint breeze to cool her body. For all that sister Phoebe had once or twice passed her a grudging compliment, never had it occurred to Samuel Stanton's second daughter that she might be uncommonly well built.

Sabra's fingers trembled a little as they selected a goosequill with a nice sharp point. Brows joined in concentration Sabra wrote in a pretty, quite formless, hand:

Boston, ye 30th of August 1780.

Dear my Heart's Beloved:

Yr two *precious* Letters arrived by ye stage yesterday. I am Transported with Joy to learn how well You fair. Bro. Joshua hath wrote several Times to Papa. He spoke of yr quick Success which he says surprizes everyone — saving me! O, my darling, yr Sabra is so *vastly* Proud of yr Advancement and ye Promise of that Fine new Post at Hartford.

By this time you must have received Papa's letter granting his Consent — I yet can scarce credit that he did. Oh, my Darling, I near swoon with Delight when I consider that our nuptials are but one short month removed. Another thirty Days then I shall, O so Truly, pledge you my Troth, and become MISTRESS LUCIUS DEVOE! What a career we shall build for you. All my Heart and Head will Labour towards yr advancement. You may rely upon it. You will soar to Fame's pedestle. I know it as surely as I sit here —

Sabra blushed a trifle, though it was just as well that Lucius could not see her sitting as she was.

Papa hath no doubt made clear to You that Sister Phoebe and I will commence our Travels — O happy hour — to West Point on ye 19th of next month — unless the accidents of war forbid. Would cruel Father Time could dissolve his hours and already I could sense yr very dear arms about your loving Sabra. We shall journey under ye protection of a Friend of Papa — one Major Amos Clark. Cured of Grievus Wounds he is about to Rejoin his Regiment serving under dear General Washington.

Oh, Dear Heart, could you but behold ye many beautiful things Mamma and her Friends have bestowed for my bridle Chest. Ere many days You shall admire them, each and every One.

Among other Things my Aunt Matilda hath presented me with a cannistre of cane sugar and most wonderful of all a pound of Mocha coffee which Mamma intimates she did Acquire three Years agone, when near a hundred Indignant Boston Dames invaded ye warehouse of an unpatriotick Merchant, and so took Possession of his stock of Sugar and Coffee, the which he refused to sell for less than Six shillings ye pound.

You failed of a missive from me last Month, because Mamma, Phoebe and I Voyaged to New Port in Rhode Island, there to Visit Aunt Abigail who hath suffered severely from an attack of Megrims. By a most fortunate Accident we witnessed ye arrival of a great French Fleet and an Army.

Oh, Lucius, be of good Chear! With such powerful Allies we cannot fail to win this War! I hear You asking, how many Men are in this Foreign Army? It is an *Immense Array* — near six Thousand of the French King's best troops.

You say we are for a space to have Quarters at ye Fort? How many Chambers are there? Shall we have a Man Servant? Major Clark says probably. I am learning simple Modes of coiffing my hair, though it will be Difficult to do without a Hairdresser. What will the other Wives be like? Are they young like Me, or old and Shrewish?

Until we reach King's Ferry, my Love, where I shall once more delight my lips with yours —

[664]

A sound of steps on the stairs sent Sabra flying to snatch a pale green negligee from her wardrobe. She thought to recognize sister Phoebe's quick step.

Flushing at having so nearly been trapped in such immodest, if lovely, nudity, Sabra hurriedly snatched the pile of her clothes from the floor and flung them onto a chair before unlatching her door.

That moment at which Samuel Stanton could remove his wig was the pleasantest of any hot summer's day. Eben, the butler, placed the dreadfully expensive, carefully curled affair of horsehair on its block within a powdering closet to the right of the entrance. After a narrow inspection for chance vermin, Eben combed the chop wig and expertly reset one of the ivory pins securing its side curls in position.

Another wonderful comfort Sabra's father found was in shedding his snuff-brown gabardine coat and waistcoat of yellow silk. Absently, he noted that perspiration had stained the coat's armholes.

"Big day, suh?"

"Not so big as it couldn't be a deal better, Eben. Trade is slow, confounded slow these days." Stanton jerked a kerchief from his breeches pocket and mopped the close-cropped contour of his skull, then vented a gentle sigh. Thankfully, he sank onto the woven rush seat of his ladder-back.

"Well, well," he remarked, as always, when Eben poured out a glass of lemon water. Stanton slipped onto his nose a pair of heavy, steel-rimmed spectacles then hesitated between perusal of the *Boston Gazette & Country Journal* and the *Massachusetts Weekly News Letter.*

Deciding on the latter, he shook out its folds and starting on the back page of that single, once-folded sheet; immediately he became absorbed. Merchantlike, he left the news to the last, and studied the shipping news with great alertness.

"Entered inwards, schooner *Neptune* from Falmouth; ship *Peggy* from Philadelphia." Lips pursed, he ran on down the list. "Prizes of War." His interest sharpened. "Arrived this day, the ship, *Lovely Agnes*, prize to the Massachusetts privateer brig *Grand Turk III*; Gideon Pickering, prize-master."

God above! This *Grand Turk*'s luck was as infallible as ever. Why, only a fortnight ago her prize the *Jolly Tar*, a fine new brig, had made port under command of one Abel Doane.

Stanton reversed his newspaper. Um. It would appear that the Hessian General Knyphausen had been attempting to invade New Jersey. The correspondent claimed that this mercenary's purpose was to test the effect of the surrender of Charles Town upon the American public. Good old Nathanael Greene, however, had checked Knyphausen in a smart little battle fought at Springfield in New Jersey and the Hessians had been sent plodding back into their defenses near New York.

Another item informed the reader that a strong British fleet yet cruised off Point Judith, effectively blockading in Newport Admiral De Guichen's French squadron.

Disturbing news had been received from upper New York. Incredible though it might seem, the Tory General Sir John Johnson and Chief Joseph Brant of the Six Nations once again had closed upon some settlements in the Mohawk Valley the horrors of Indian warfare. Sam Stanton's jaw tightened. What could the Royal Tyrant hope to gain loosing such red hellions on his former subjects. Nothing but an undying hatred.

Stanton tossed aside the *Weekly News Letter* and shifted in his chair before commencing to read the *Gazette* in hopes of more encouraging news. He found none at all; quite the contrary.

That ineffable Horatio Gates, leading an army to the relief of the Carolinas, had permitted himself to be surprised by inferior forces and roundly trounced on the nineteenth of August before a place called Camden in South Carolina. General Gates, it was reported, had retreated with precipitation some eighty miles to escape pursuit by Lord Cornwallis.

The account continued:

This mortifying disaster following that at Charles Town gives a severe shock to our Army. It must be Productive of the most important & Serious Consequences as respects the welfare of the Southern States. The Continental troops display'd their usual Courage and Bravery, but at the first onset of the Enemy the whole Body of the Militia became panic struck, were completely routed & ran like a Torrent, leaving the Continentals to oppose the whole force of the Enemy.

This Defeat was not without Loss on the part of the Foe, they having upwards of Five Hundred Men with Officers in proportion kill'd & wounded. The whole number of Continental officers killed & wounded & missing is forty eight. Among our slain is Baron de Kalb, Major General. While leading on the Maryland & Delaware Troops he was pierc'd with Eleven Wounds and soon after Expired. He was a German by birth, a brave and meritorious Officer and a Brigadier-General in the Armies of France; serv'd three years of High Reputation in the American Army.

True, a French army under Count de Rochambeau *had* arrived, but it was small and blockaded in Newport; the French king's Second Division was reported to be rotting in Brest while waiting for a break in the British blockade.

Yes. The new nation's military and financial situation was desperate, all right. Joshua's letters, very explicit concerning the general aspects of strategy, had made it so clear that even a child could foretell what would follow should Sir John Johnson and his painted Indian devils succeed in descending the Mohawk Valley towards New York and should General Clinton march north to effect a junction. Only the fort at West Point could prevent such a fatal meeting.

Stanton finally went to sleep and roused only when Eben knocked and entered, his shiny black face grinning above his white stock. The butler's fat, gray-black hands trembled a little as, on a silver salver, he offered an envelope secured by a red paper wafer.

After eagerly breaking the seal, Samuel Stanton re-adjusted his glasses, then read:

> At Headquarters
> Tappans, New York
> Ye 1st Aug. 1780.

Um, the letter must have traveled express to have arrived so very promptly.

Respected Sir:
  Pray make my duty to my Mother and Sisters.
  Of late we have seen much activity; seeming endless marching and counter-marching because the Enemy have brought Vessels, so our spies inform, to launch a great Attack against the French new-arrived in New Port. At this Intelligence Gen'l Washington set our Army in Motion at once across the Hudson River and moved in threatening array upon the Island of Manhattan, the which caused our Enemies to think Better of sailing northwards.
  News of the arrival of the French Troops hath done much to mitigate our Army's Discomfiture over poor Gen'l Gates' Shameful and total rout at Camden. Indeed our Troops had begun to melt away near as fast as last Spring. Only on the Continentals can we count. The Militia—a plague on 'em all—are as chancy as a young girl's whims.
  I am glad, most Respected Sir, you share my opinion that Young Mr. Devoe would make an excellent Husband for our Sabra. Since we rode out together January last, I have had considerable Opportunity to study him under the various Rigors and Conditions peculiar to Field Service, and can truthfully vouchsafe that the Promise he offered at the Beginning hath been Sustained. This young Physician is a tireless worker but enjoying an inventive turn of mind which hath earned the earnest Commendation not only of Doctor James Craik, his immediate Superior, but even that of the Director-Gen'l of the Medical Department, Doctor William Shippen.
  For the moment quiet prevails in New Jersey and New York & it is well that this is so. The Discipline in our Forces is very low indeed; mere Children of fifteen and sixteen are being paid Fifteen Hundred Dollars for Nine Months service in order to fill the ranks.
  As for myself, I confess considerable concern in securing *Absolutely Necessary* supplies for my Battalion. I have drawn no Pay since February the last, and the Merchants hereabouts dun me without let. Respected Sir, I hesitate once more to Trespass on your Generosity, but if you can alleviate me to some Extent I shall be Ever Appreciative. All too many of us Field Officers find ourselves, through no fault of our doing, in my Predicament. We cannot fathom why the Congress does not take Steps to Pay us in currency of some value.

[667]

I trust Mamma endures the Summer's heat agreeably and that her Rheumaticks are no Worse.

Permit me, Sir, to offer my filial homage. I hope to obtain Leave again this Autumn that I may once more clasp you by the Hand and embrace Mamma and my Sisters.

Y'r Most respectful, obedient son,
JOSHUA

The Invitation

Doctor John Fletcher of Nottingham, Maryland, yawned a prodigious yawn and gazed through the window of that small cottage he shared with Lucius Devoe. For some moments he watched the Hudson, flowing so smoothly and clearly under a heavy log boom and great chain barring progress upstream from West Point. They formed mighty effective obstructions, Fletcher reckoned, blocking the channel as they did all the way across to Constitution Island. An enemy vessel attempting to pass the boom inevitably would be delayed long enough to permit her being sunk or disabled by heavy guns firing from the Chain Battery or from Fort Arnold, above.

From where he stood, the Marylander couldn't see Fort Arnold — the principal fortification among a dozen lesser forts and batteries — since it stood some distance back on heights dominating this narrow bend in the lordly Hudson. But he could make out a cluster of houses dotting a small plain between it and the river landing.

Fletcher turned, yelled, "Jennings! Goddamit, Jennings! Where in hell are you?"

"Coming sir." The orderly appeared, rubbing heavy eyes.

"Good God, Jennings! Can you do nothing but sleep?"

"Yessir." He stifled not very effectively a yawn. "But there's nawthin' else to do."

"Is Dr. Devoe back from across the river?"

"Nawsir. But I allow he will be soon. Thorne rode for 'e landing with a saddle hoss near a hour ago."

Hesitantly, John Fletcher passed a hand over a humorous-appearing brown face. Short, he lent the impression of being taller, perhaps because his head was so narrow and his shoulders not even ordinarily wide.

"Apprise me as soon as Dr. Devoe returns," he instructed, then swung over to his desk and commenced drafting a requisition for a pair of cupping cups — the type he needed were brass-mounted glass, equipped with a membrane valve which could be used to control the flow of blood.

The beating of a drum indicated that the garrison was being summoned to stand Retreat. Fletcher smiled his satisfaction. An almighty change for the better had characterized discipline at West Point since Major General Benedict Arnold had assumed command. Genial, easy-going General MacDougall had been content to let disciplinary matters follow the line of least resistance.

It was encouraging for one and all to hear that the works would soon be repaired and strengthened. General Arnold himself had conducted a penetrating, and sometimes embarrassing, inspection of stores accumulated in various souterraines and magazines.

Rumor had it that Arnold was extra anxious to improve his command because, last spring, he had so narrowly escaped being cashiered for peculation. But for the intercession of his commander-in-chief, Arnold would have been dismissed — everybody was aware of that.

Something of an amateur artist, Fletcher fetched from his field trunk a piece of drawing paper and pencil and, moving out onto the porch, fell to sketching those craggy heights across the river. Yonder, eagles nested in the spring, and all manner of birds and beasts took their rest.

Raising eyes from his drawing he noticed that the military ferry was on its way back. Right now the little craft's stained sail was hanging limp, but the oars of the bateau men kept it moving. Their long ash sweeps were raising little showers as they pulled for the landing.

As a ferry yonder craft wasn't much; nowhere near as elegant as the commanding officer's barge which nowadays was continually plying the river. Some days General Arnold's barge descended the Hudson as far as Verplancks' Ferry and Stony Point. The King's Ferry–Stony Point crossings were by far the most useful remaining in American hands and by them passed all land communication between New England, New York and Southern states.

Fletcher's pencil quickly filled in those bold headlands looming beyond the Lantern Battery which guarded the main boat landing for Fort Arnold.

Returning to his drawing, Fletcher sketched on the margin a trio of bateau men engaged in throwing a hunting knife at a peg driven into the ground and became so intent on his art that he became aware of his roommate's presence only when a shadow fell across his sketch book. Devoe was grinning as he tossed his riding gloves onto a settle on the porch, patted a sagging pocket.

"Compliments of his sublime and unpredictable majesty, our commanding officer. Tonight, we will drink Arnold's health in Canary."

For all he must have had a tiresome journey across the Hudson, down to the Robinson house and back, Lucius was in high good spirits.

"Well, John, what do you think has chanced?"

"At headquarters you plucked a few more soft plumes to feather your nest."

"No, no; seriously."

"You're to act as physician to General Arnold and family?" the Marylander ventured.

"Yes, that's it. My fee will be a mere twenty pounds monthly." Lucius stripped off his coat and yelled for Jennings to bring a wet towel. "Lord, John, you should see in what elegance he lives! What silver, what fine linen — and the general's lady." In ecstasy the Jamaican rolled dark eyes towards the flyblown ceiling of their porch while casting loose the new glass buttons of a long waistcoat. "Lord, John, Mrs. Arnold's a raving beauty; her hands are tiny and each little nail glistens like mica."

Fletcher failed to respond to his companion's enthusiasm. "You didn't notice any Union Jacks embroidered on her petticoats, did you? The whole Shippen family she springs from are known to be red-hot Tories."

"No, I wouldn't care a fig if I did. John, John, here's the really good news. You and I are bidden to take supper at headquarters next Friday!"

Their orderly uncorked the dark green bottle Devoe had brought and looked about for glasses until he came across two of varying design. Into them he poured the clear yellow wine.

Fletcher, smilingly, offered a fold of paper. "And now it's my turn with good news. Thanks to Dr. Thatcher, you have been bid to mess tomorrow at the quarters of His Excellency, Major General Frederick von Steuben."

Devoe recalled their orderly. "Look to my uniform, Jennings, and mind you burnish its buttons better than you did the last time. I shall want it tomorrow night."

Though Lucius spoke carelessly, Fletcher laughed. Very few medical officers had elected to bear the expense of purchasing a uniform; yet it was entirely in keeping with Devoe's character.

"I learned something at headquarters today," Devoe remarked suddenly. "Did you know that Dr. Shippen has been cleared of the charges brought against him by Rush and Morgan — his predecessors?"

" — And well he should have been," Fletcher declared stoutly.

Never had Lucius watched guards present arms with such an automatic and uniform precision, seen sentries stand so very erect in uniforms evincing such painstaking care, he thought as he sat at von Steuben's long, linen-draped table. No wonder that the commander-in-chief's personal bodyguard were almost without exception of German origin. Only these docile foreigners would surrender enough individuality to follow instructions to the letter, to drill like so many obedient children. No American could or would tolerate such discipline, such a loss of personal self-expression. All the same, General Washington's own bodyguard was the object of wonder and admiration of all who saw it on duty.

For Lucius the occasion afforded one thrill after another. Why, tonight the guest of honor was Major General Greene, spoken of throughout the army as the commander-in-chief's alter ego.

What a strange character was Quartermaster General Nathanael

Greene. At the outbreak of the war a simple blacksmith, one of whose legs was a full inch and a half shorter than its fellow, he had through sheer ability and a very intimate understanding of the military principles embodied in Caesar's *Commentaries* risen from a humble subaltern in the Rhode Island militia to a reputation second only to that of George Washington — in the eyes of the fighting men.

True, there were also Anthony Wayne, capable but impetuous; and Henry Knox, dependable, but quiet and impassive as any of those oxen which drew his trains of artillery through one long campaign to the next. But they had their limitations, and Greene hadn't.

Looking down the table, Lucius immediately noticed the blue and white uniform and glittering gold lace worn by Major L'Enfant, who had laid out the original defenses of West Point. The majority of the male guests wore blue turned up in scarlet for the artillery, light blue for the infantry, yellow for the cavalry, and so on.

Toasts galore were offered to His Excellency the Commander-in-Chief, to the Congress, to His Most Christian Majesty of France, to Count Rochambeau, to general this and general that, until Lucius's eyes were swimming. Director-General Shippen wore black and sat three places nearer the head of the table than Lucius, his angular and slightly mottled face red by the candlelight.

Struggling to rally his wits, the Jamaican settled back and listened attentively to the table talk. Come to think on it, already he had progressed quite a way from that poverty-stricken hovel near Kingston.

If only his several brothers and sisters could behold him now, sitting in the company of great noblemen, famous generals, and even a statesman or two of the first importance! The best of it was that he had come this far thanks to no one but himself. Silently he reminded himself, this is only the beginning. Yes. A far-sighted fellow might achieve almost any goal during the social upheaval now taking place in America.

Take General Washington's favorite aide, Major Alexander Hamilton; everyone knew him to be the illegitimate sprig of a Nevis Islander — one of the least important West Indies. It made no odds that Hamilton was a bastard; his opinion was held in high importance by the commander-in-chief, who listened to Hamilton as to few others.

After the war what great estates might not be carved out of that rich wilderness reported to lie to the northwest? If a few generations earlier the Schuylers, Phillipses, the van Rensselaers and the van Wycks had been able to fashion baronies for themselves, why should a Devoe not be able to do the same?

The two goblets of Malaga he had consumed continued to warm Lucius's innards, to titillate his imagination. Jupiter! Why in time should there not be a Devoe Township, nay, a Devoe County? It seemed possible, entirely possible.

Gradually, almost imperceptibly, the Jamaican became aware of someone's regard. Drawing a deep breath, he looked up and saw, seated almost directly opposite, a handsome young woman of about his own age. She was richly clad in a gown of dark blue velvet trimmed in crimson and wore, at the division of her breast, an enormous broach of gold set with pearls. Inexplicably, his breath quickened as he summoned a shy smile and his fingertips buzzed.

"Of course, Major," he overheard her say to her companion, "the defeat in South Carolina was most discouraging; yet our army has suffered far worse reverses at Quebec and Long Island."

Lucius became lost to all other considerations; equally he neglected the plump young woman to his left, and the bird-faced wife of Colonel Birchard to his right, except to inquire of her, "I confess to being very awkward about names. Can you give me that of the young lady in blue who sits directly across the table?"

Mrs. Birchard smiled faintly before directing a quick glance across the table. Said she evenly, "You must mean Mrs. Wynkoop?"

"Ah, yes. Mrs. Wynkoop." Lucius lingered on the name, converted it into a question.

"Emma Wynkoop, for your further information, is a widow, I believe, of a year's standing." Mrs. Birchard's manner suggested disapproval that the young widow no longer wore weeds — even had tucked a few wild gentians in luxuriant black hair. "She owns an estate up the river and is very rich, I am told."

Wise enough to let the matter drop, Lucius put forward a question concerning a picnic projected for the following week, yet, try as he would to keep his gaze from Emma Wynkoop's roundish white face and its large, navy-blue eyes, he couldn't.

After dinner the necessity of manufacturing diplomatic and possibly fruitful conversation with Dr. Shippen presently removed Mrs. Wynkoop from Lucius's thoughts. When an hour later the ladies emerged to rejoin the gentlemen gravely sipping port under the fly, he wasn't in the least surprised that Emma Wynkoop, in masterly casualness, came sauntering almost directly up to him, dark eyes alight and friendly.

"You," she began, "must be the clever and very promising Dr. Devoe we have heard so much about?"

Unaccountably, Lucius stammered, "Why, Mrs. Wynkoop, ma'am, I — I do protest, I deserve — no — such fine description."

"But was it not you who caused the construction of a flying hospital built along the design of an Iroquois longhouse?"

"Why yes," he admitted blushing to his ear tips. "I presume I was responsible." He needed to display a becoming modesty and so indulged in a rare bit of frankness. "The idea, however, was not mine to begin with, only its application here at West Point. 'Twas devised by Dr. Tilton. Last winter he employed it in New Jersey with much success." Somber eyes riveted to the face so eagerly lifted, Lucius burst into explanation. "In my

[672]

type of hospital, you see, our heating fire is built in the exact center of a ward on an open hearth and is served by no chimney at all."

"But, Dr. Devoe, what of the smoke?"

"If the ward room doors are the right size" — he made brief gestures with his hands — "the smoke circulates high up and passes off through an opening about four inches wide let into the ridge of the roof and takes the poisonous exhalations of wounds with it. The draught thus insured maintains a continual supply of fresh air so often lacking in sickrooms.

"I place my patients with their heads next to the wall and their feet turned towards the fire all round the room. Further," he lowered his voice, aware that several of the guests were regarding them, "I may point out that smoke combats contagion, but without giving the least offense to the patients." His voice rang once more with enthusiasm. "In this way, dear lady, I am able to accommodate, with impunity, double the number of patients possible in any other ward of comparable size."

"Why, this is amazing!" Mrs. Wynkoop clapped hands in gentle enthusiasm. "Were I to send some victuals for your sick, will you sometime show me your flying hospital?"

"I would be charmed," he burst out. "But these days victuals are plagued hard to come by, as we here at the fort know only too well."

As a group of other guests bore down towards them, Emma Wynkoop murmured, "Though I hesitate to suggest so long a ride in hot weather, perhaps, Doctor, you would care to come to my estate and make a selection of supplies?"

Instantly, he replied. "I would be charmed to do so. When?"

Without any greater hesitation, she said, "Come next week, the tenth — if Mrs. Arnold can spare you. Anybody in Kaaterskill village can tell you how to reach my estate." She manufactured a bright laugh and turned. "Good evening, Captain!" She acknowledged the deep bow of William North, one of Arnold's favorite aides. "You have been neglecting me most shamefully. What a very modish wig!"

The aide started to talk but fell silent because the Baron von Steuben's guttural bass was booming out. "Duels! *Pfui!* To them must come an end. Vot nonsense, this murdering of goot officers. Haff you heard, *Herr* General Greene?" The Inspector General breathed heavily through a long and pointed nose, while offering a well-polished silver snuffbox.

Greene said he hadn't heard. "Another duel?"

"*Ja wohl*, on the twenty-ninth vas another such affair between a *Leutnant* Offut and Mr. *Herr* Parr of Colonel Maryland's dragoons regiment. Vot follows? *Leutnant* Offut kills *Herr* Parr and iss himself gravely wounded in the thigh. Vot stupidity! Vot criminal nonsense! *Ach!*"

In spite of special care and every treatment Drs. Thatcher and Craik could devise, Brigadier General Poor of the New Hampshire Troops succumbed to putrid fever. Lucius thanked his stars for having been summoned to consultation at Paramus only at the very last moment. No one could rightly state that he had lost so distinguished a patient.

The weather having turned unseasonably warm, there could be no delay concerning a funeral. Lucius never forgot that sad ceremony because it served as his first occasion to observe at close range the American Army's well-beloved command-in-chief.

Long campaigns probably had done less than ceaseless bickering with the Congress to etch careworn lines in General Washington's powerful features. Everybody moved warily since His Excellency's temper was mighty short these days. Jimmy Thatcher claimed it was because his false teeth fitted so badly — for all that no less an expert than Paul Revere had fashioned them out of the finest quality of Indian elephant ivory.

Lucius welcomed the excuse to share a tent with Thatcher, that indefatigable note-taker and diarist, and to remain at Paramus for General Poor's obsequies.

Lucius watched his colleague writing about General Poor's funeral, at the same time wondering why Providence should have elected to strike down so well-beloved and so capable an officer. Why should Poor have been spared during so many battles and skirmishes, only to fall victim to a loathsome disease?

Thatcher locked his writing case and, looking up, sighed, "Well, that is that. God rest the poor gentleman's bones." He helped himself to a pinch of snuff. "Have you determined on going up to Kaaterskill?"

"I scarce know," Lucius smiled. "Why?"

"Were I you, I'd accept. Breedon visited at Ramsdorp last spring and claims it to be one of the very finest estates along the entire Hudson Valley." Thatcher winked. "She's a handsome young lady is Mrs. Wynkoop; and owning a fortune of near ninety thousand pounds shouldn't make her look any plainer, either." James Thatcher, Jr. showed irregular teeth in a grin. "You were always a shy speaker, Lucius, yet you sat aside with her at von Steuben's instead of getting decently drunk with the rest of us. Phew! That old Prussian's brandy must be distilled in hell. How I wished for a lid to the top of my head next morning. You've heard, I presume, that His Excellency will be riding north in a week's time?"

Lucius was annoyed that so significant an item of information had not sooner reached him. "He's to meet the French commander?"

"Aye, that's it. We're all praying that General Washington succeeds in coaxing a bit of hard cash out of our gallant allies." Thatcher looked mighty serious all at once. "God knows what will chance should he fail.

Last week there were two near-mutinies, but the paymaster grandly handed a few line regiments pay due since last January."

"During His Excellency's absence who's to succeed in command of the army?"

"Nat Greene, of course. Who else?"

The Jamaican bent, commenced packing saddle bags for his return to West Point. "Why not Arnold; he's senior?"

Thatcher cast his friend a sharp look. "But for the commander-in-chief's good offices, your friend Benedict would have been dismissed from the service last summer."

Thank fortune, thought Lucius, Sabra was due to arrive at the Fort within another fortnight. He'd make a valuable friend of Emma Wynkoop for the two of them.

Jupiter! What a pother was in prospect. News of the Devoe-Stanton engagement had circulated far and wide — chiefly because Major Joshua Stanton was so universally known and well liked. Lieutenant General Knox, Chief of Artillery, was swearing that during the next campaign he'd make young Stanton a colonel, come what might.

Suppose he accepted Mrs. Wynkoop's invitation to visit Ramsdorp? Gossip would travel many a dusty lane, faster than a swallow's flight — conjecture would enter the officers' mess at the fort. Let the idle tongues wag! He wasn't going, really, to see Emma Wynkoop, but to procure support and supplies badly needed for his patients — and always there seemed to be more. Nowadays, hardly ever did a seasoned veteran turn up among replacements for the garrison.

What a pity he and Emma Wynkoop could not have met but a few months earlier! As no other female, she commanded his attention and respect. He remembered her low crisp voice and direct reasoning complicated by no feminine circumlocutions.

Irritably, Lucius beat his heels against the nag's furry sides. Damnation! With Sabra to become his wife in so short a time he'd no right to be even thinking of Emma Wynkoop, whose only relatives now dwelt in New York and were fire-eating Tories. Who could blame them? Patriot forces, in the fighting around New York back in '76, had burnt and plundered their property without mercy.

Reluctantly, he decided against a visit to Kaaterskill.

To Dr. Devoe's vast astonishment, a note regretting, in the most polite of terms, his inability of making a visit to Ramsdorp, resulted in the arrival at West Point of three oxcarts heavy with choice supplies for his hospital. Carts, oxen and all had been sailed down the river aboard Mrs. Wynkoop's own flatboat.

Soldiers off duty at the fort gathered by the dozen beside the landing enviously to watch the great, two-wheeled carts come creaking ashore freighted high with vegetables, salted meat, bacon and hams. Later inspection revealed also numerous heavy Dutch blankets and a box of linen shirts; these last could not have been more highly esteemed had they been of pure cloth of gold.

The arrival of this magnificent gift elevated Lucius in the esteem — and envy — of his fellow officers because Hans Hodenpuyl, the broad-faced Dutchman in charge, loudly announced that the shipment must be receipted for by Senior Surgeon Lucius Devoe and no one else.

Hodenpuyl brought from Emma Wynkoop, a curious letter; one which implied that she understood his reasons for failing to visit Ramsdorp and respected him accordingly. She had, Emma wrote, thought over his remarks concerning those stringent problems confronting the medical service. Possibly they would find opportunity to discuss them further since it chanced that she had been bidden to make a visit to her old friend Mrs. General Arnold whom she had met in Philadelphia.

"I shall be their guest," Emma wrote, "during four days, beginning the twenty-third of September. Perchance your official duties will bring you to Robinson house at least once during that period?"

The twenty-third? Lucius passed a hand over his jaw. Um. If all went as planned, Sabra should reach King's Ferry not later than the twenty-fifth. Again, he congratulated himself on his decision to avoid visiting Kaaterskill. The impact of Emma Wynkoop's charm and personality on his imagination somehow was terrifying.

Major Joshua Stanton stopped in on the way to Paramus from his post at Fort Ticonderoga. He was sunburned, hearty and full of enthusiasm over the task of remounting on limbers a number of fine old French cannon he'd discovered there. Characteristically, he had scoured the countryside until he'd located some wheelwrights and now they and a crew of carpenters were turning out an impressive number of caissons and limbers.

"I've near enough to equip a whole regiment," he exulted to the senior officers' mess at Fort Arnold. "By God, you can't beat the Dancing Masters when it comes to casting fine guns. For all they're sixty years old, they're the best I have ever seen."

On arrival at Lucius's quarters, Sabra's brother flung his hat onto the settle and stood using a hazel switch he had cut somewhere on the way down, to slap the dust from his sweat-whitened riding boots.

"Well, well. The great day draws nigh, eh, Lucius?" He grinned. "Who'll you have to tie the knot?"

"The Reverend Dr. Enos Hitchcock, Josh. He's chaplain to General Patterson's brigade."

"A good man," Joshua agreed. "Hails from Beverly, I think, back home." Joshua tramped indoors in search of drinking water. There he cocked a curious eye at Lucius's uniform, hanging, brand-new and brave with gold lace, in a wardrobe. "So they've slapped you pullguts in uniform at last? It's a good thing, makes you seem really a part of the service."

Somewhere far to the south sounded the unmistakable *boom!* of a field-piece. Faintly the report reverberated along that deep trough through which the Hudson flows at West Point. Glancing off first one rock wall, then another, it sounded like a giant's game of ninepins in progress.

Joshua flung his companion a quick look. "What the deuce does that firing mean?"

"I've no idea, unless some battery is at practice."

Their conversation resumed and had continued but a few minutes before it was interrupted by a second report, then a third.

The *clip-clopping* of a horse trotting slowly up that road which led down to the river sounded progressively louder.

The rider proved to be a bandy-legged sergeant of dragoons. Perspiring heavily, this cavalryman dismounted, read the names painted on a shingle nailed to the doorframe; then, with his saber's ferrule sketching a furrow in the dust, he rapped.

"Dr. Devoe, sir?" He gave Lucius a smart salute.

"Yes. What can I do for you?"

"I've a message for you from headquarters, sir."

The note proved to be brief. Mrs. Arnold, it appeared, had become so indisposed as to require immediate medical attention. Dr. Devoe would please attend her with all speed?

"So you're personal physician to the commanding general's wife." Joshua whistled briefly. "Is there no height to which you can't fly? Well, keep it up. I'm off to the ordnance officer." Again he clapped his future brother-in-law's slight shoulder, then his big, well-knit figure went swinging off across the scant, dusty brown grass covering Fort Arnold's parade ground.

Lucius had barely drawn rein before the Beverly Robinson house than an orderly ran forward from a guard tent and led away his horse just as an infantry officer hurried up, looking very anxious.

"Dr. Devoe? I am Major Franks, special aide to Mrs. Arnold. Kindly follow me."

At the foot of a staircase leading above, Major Franks advised in a low voice. "Best be extra civil. The general's in a curs'd foul mood. He's just returned from downriver and is weary out of all conscience. This way, Doctor, I'll show you your quarters. There you may prepare presently to attend Mrs. Arnold."

While bathing his face and hands Lucius wondered what could be ailing Mrs. Arnold. A touch of dysentery most likely; it was very prevalent hereabouts. God forbid that she should be afflicted with the cholera morbus!

"Whew, it's damnation hot in here!" In an attempt to secure some cross-ventilation, he opened his door. Someone else must have been activated by a similar impulse for, across the hall and slightly to his left, another door opened.

"Good evening, Doctor," smiled Emma Wynkoop and curtseyed. This evening she was most effectively gowned in dark green, and cherry-red ribbons secured her dark-brown hair.

For a long moment neither moved; the widow's gaze remained fixed on his; gradually the lids parted until her great dark eyes were narrowly, but completely, ringed by white. It was a curious effect, one which held Lucius in delighted fascination.

Yes, seen thus by the vivid sunset glare Emma Wynkoop presented a memorable image, lower arms and bosom agleam above her Lincoln-green bodice, teeth glinting behind slightly parted dark red lips.

"Why — why — " Lucius stammered, then recalled his manners enough to make as elegant a leg as was possible in the cramped space of the hallway. "I am overwhelmed, ma'am. The gods of chance have been uncommon kind. There is so much to thank you for, dear lady."

A serving girl wearing a striped blue and white petticoat and a neat white shawl was advancing timidly along the hallway.

"Mrs. Wynkoop, ma'am. Please fetch in the doctor. Mistress Arnold is ready."

The Jamaican drew a deep breath and made a successful effort to assume his professional manner; grave, dignified and yet displaying a profound concern over his patient's symptoms.

Lucius followed the maidservant along a winding corridor towards the opposite end of the house.

Emma Wynkoop had preceded him and was saying, "There, there, Peg, my poppet — Dr. Devoe is here; I am positive your malady will prove nothing grave."

"I pray you are correct," a man's deep voice interrupted. "Where's that dratted sawbones?"

On the opposite side of the room lingered Major General Benedict Arnold wearing definitely informal attire. He yet retained the white riding breeches he must have worn on his trip downstream, and wore in addition blue morocco slippers and a ruffled shirt. Obviously, he had been keeping on with his drinking. A toddy glass was in his left hand.

There could be no denying that Benedict Arnold presented one of the handsomest figures Lucius had ever beheld. The general's florid profile was strong and dominated by a very long, straight nose jutting out over a bold, well-rounded jaw which was growing fleshy. The slender black brows were straight but rose sharply at their inner ends. The commanding officer's neck emerged as a heavy red pillar from the ruffles of his stock.

Quite easily Lucius could understand why Benedict Arnold, when seen in profile, was said to resemble his great good friend George Washington.

Lucius bowed stiffly. "Sir, Senior Surgeon Devoe has the honor to report himself."

The commandant drank thirstily of his toddy. "Mrs. Arnold complains of pains in — ahem — the digestive region. Damn, Emma, don't you ever again permit her to drink iced water! I vow that has been the cause of her undoing." He shuffled over towards the door. "I'll see you at mess, Devoe. You're to sit at my table."

"Oh, no, Benedict," Peggy Arnold raised a protesting white hand. "I have ordered a tray for Dr. Devoe sent upstairs. There are many things I need to discuss with him. You will not desert me, will you, Doctor?"

"It's as you command, ma'am," was all that seemed tactful to say.

"Very well. I fancy Emma and Dr. Devoe can give you proper care. My service, darling!" From the doorway General Arnold cast a glance eloquent of real devotion to this small China doll of a woman. He paused. "And how is our lad?"

"Doing splendidly, sir," Emma Wynkoop told him. "He teased the cat this afternoon and got well scratched for his pains."

A Door in the Night

When Lucius closed the door to his bedroom it was tilting pleasantly, not sickeningly, about his head. Lord above! General Arnold's sack had seemed mild and fragrant as a spring breeze in the lee of an apple orchard. No, it couldn't have been that which had set his tongue to clacking, to fancying himself the very soul of wit? Probably it was the sherry? Or was it the applejack he'd sampled last of all? Had he appeared as monstrous clever as he'd imagined?

Lucius seated himself on the edge of his bed and, grasping its coverlet, essayed to recover complete control of his equilibrium. Jupiter! How Mrs. Wynkoop's dark beauty had shone forth! Why, right now he could ever so clearly visualize her smile flashing in the candlelight. Praise God, the general's lady was suffering from nothing more serious than a touch of summer complaint which the bismuth and paregoric he'd administered should relieve in short order.

Seated in the dark, Lucius wondered whether he was correct about a curious impression that, for all his outward gaiety, General Arnold's manner had remained restless and constrained. All evening long, he had kept glancing out of the windows. Perhaps his uneasiness stemmed from the approach of a rainstorm which now was rolling down from the north?

Like salvoes fired by a whole brigade of heavy artillery, thunder began to reverberate along those natural battlements ranging the Hudson all the way from Kingston down to Verplanck's Ferry.

Ha! Lucius felt steadier once the air commenced to freshen. Through his window he could see branches beginning to be thrown into sharp relief by lightning and their tired autumn leaves beginning to stir and toss.

"Damned roads will be sopping tomorrow," Arnold had grunted.

Still dressed, Lucius sank back onto his bed; though he hated to admit the fact, he remained a bit too dizzy to contemplate disrobing.

"Mus' think of Sabra — sweet li'l Sabra," he reminded himself. "Goin' to be my wife. I love her. Not Emma. Gen'leman can't go back on his word, and I'm a gen'leman. Mus'n' think about Emma."

But Emma was only a dozen yards away. Emma was rich; Emma was ambitious; Emma was experienced, too, no doubt of that.

Was he drunk? No, not really. Couldn't he think? Couldn't he move in perfect balance? Of course; then he wasn't jingled — intelligent men never let themselves become befuddled. Once Peter Burnham' had got that way — what had chanced with Peter Burnham? Strange, not a word had been heard of him in Boston, or anywhere else, after that frosty night back last January.

Lucius squirmed on the hard and narrow bed. He'd not intended for anything untoward to happen to Peter; really, he hadn't planned for such a tragedy. Only it had seemed so *very* necessary for Lucius Devoe to receive that junior surgeon's commission.

A door kept banging softly; so far not loud enough to warrant an investigation. But now the storm closed in, and, raising an eldritch shriek, swooped down upon the Hudson River Valley. Under its assault little branches were torn loose and hurled against the roof of Colonel Beverly Robinson's house. At the same time the lightning fired a *feu de joie* and the rain lashed so wildly at his open window that Lucius roused himself and dropped the sash. More violently still raged the storm, pounding in baffled fury on the windowpanes.

The banging of that door down the hall grew more insistent. Lucius thought, it'll disturb my patient. Yet he lay still a full five minutes before, finally, he swung stocking feet to the floor and got up.

Breathing with unaccustomed rapidity, Lucius left his room, closing his door after him. Again a furious draught of air flung open Emma Wynkoop's door. Looking inside the physician saw a modest chamber done in nail-rust red and a single figure bent over the washstand and apparently oblivious to his presence. Emma Wynkoop, hair unbound and in her night shift, was measuring something into a tumbler.

Only when a particularly violent crash of thunder shook the house did Emma Wynkoop see him standing on the threshold. Three things leaped to her attention, the vivid black of his eyes, his unbound hair streaming free and the tense curve of his mouth.

"Your door — I heard it slamming. What are you about?" he inquired in a strained voice.

"Why, why, the storm upset my stomach —" Emma straightened, turned and held up a small bottle. "I thought perhaps an elixir —" Even by this uncertain light he could tell that her nightrail was of light, very fine lawn. No other fabric save silk could fall so lightly loose from her shoulders. How white the cloth shone under the dark torrents of her hair.

"What is that stuff?"

"Why — 'tis an elixir," she explained, added quickly, "don't be a ninny, for heaven's sake. Either leave or come in and shut that wretched door; its latch seems to be broken."

Lucius looked about and presently located a cloth-covered door stop, which silenced the banging all in a moment.

"Aren't you clever? I never thought of that," Emma said with a half smile. "Isn't this storm terrifying?"

Lucius agreed, but directed his attention to the elixir bottle. "That stuff serves no useful purpose. Allow me to fetch you a draught of elecampane. 'Tis capital for an upset digestion."

"Oh, no! Pray don't disturb yourself."

But he darted out; reappeared a moment later, a vial in his hand.

"Thank you. I was beginning to fear that I had contracted Mrs. Arnold's complaint," Emma said. "I feel much better, now."

"I must leave. Suppose someone came here?"

"Let them. Please stay with me a little longer. The other evening at General von Steuben's you spoke concerning a balance of humors. What is your theory on the subject?"

"All physicians, ma'am, nowadays are instructed that four elements or humors are present in every human." He hesitated, swallowed hard on nothing. "I do not wish to be indelicate — "

"Pray continue," Emma urged, all the while smoothing the bedclothes until they outlined, all too effectively, the graceful outlines of her legs and thighs.

"For near a hundred years the best scholars of Europe have believed that four humors exist in every human."

" — And they are?"

" — Blood, phlegm, black and yellow bile," Lucius explained hurriedly. "Other schools describe these humors as 'sanguine, phlegmatic, bilious or choleric, and melancholy.' We are told that when one humor overbalances its fellows, illness ensues. To restore health the volume of that excessive humour must be reduced."

From his seated position at the foot of the bed the Jamaican shifted to occupy a chair nearer its head. Though he seated himself on some of her intimate garments, Emma offered no protest.

Although it seemed impossible for the rain to sluice down any harder — it did so; the kettle drums of thunder, however, now were thudding further down the Hudson and nearer to New York.

All at once Lucius was astonished to find himself speaking of Jamaica, confessing his humble origin and the desperate poverty of his family. In vivid detail he described his adventures at sea; his fixed ambition to study medicine and to win greater than local acclaim. He spoke even of Sabra, of being affianced to her — but nothing of his impending nuptials. Most

[681]

likely, she knew of them through her intimacy with Peggy Arnold. No point in dwelling on the matter.

Emma's nearness and a scent of lavender had a magical and an unprecedented effect upon him as wine fumes, suddenly rising again, clouded Lucius's mind. Her candle commenced flickering towards the end of its life, reminding him of an old lady he had once attended on her deathbed. She had still been lovely for all her failing vitality.

He was describing the scene to Emma Wynkoop when the wick fell over, and in her bedroom existed only the faintest kind of light cast by a fire cheering some guard detail. Ineffective and faintly red firelight came slanting in the shutters' slats to create weirdly dancing streaks of light.

It seemed as if a gale far more overwhelming than that still roaring outside were pressing him forward, until at length he lay beside her with heated features pressed to the intoxicating softness of her breast.

An Express from Colonel Jameson

During the early hours of the dawn, in vain Lucius attempted to reason with himself — to thresh the matter out in all its implications. He, hard-headed Lucius Devoe, could not possibly have become so senselessly infatuated. Senselessly? Um — maybe not. He began to suspect that cold, if subconscious, logic rather than physical passion had, from the start, attracted him to Emma Wynkoop.

From every practical point of view, the widow promised to make a more useful and socially adroit wife for an ambitious young surgeon than refined but inexperienced and insular Sabra Stanton. Above all, he judged he could understand a woman of Emma's type far more thoroughly than a girl like Sabra.

And yet, and yet, Lucius, somehow, could not bring himself so cruelly to hurt Sabra — his affianced wife, even now travelling happily southwards. To wound her forthright, true and tender love would be sheerest wickedness. No doubt existed in his mind that, loving him profoundly, she would remain true through thick and thin.

Another point. How would his brother officers, his superiors, judge a fellow who broke his solemn pledge to a sweet and trusting young girl? For one thing, Joshua Stanton could be dangerous, once his New England calm was shaken. No, sir. Josh would not suffer passively such a mortal affront to his sister — particularly since he had encouraged their match.

The morning of Monday, September 25, 1780, proved so sparklingly beautiful that Lucius felt moved to whistle while lathering in preparation to shaving. During the night he had reached a final and irrevocable decision; come what might, he would keep his word and marry Sabra Stanton. Now he felt at peace with the world.

Probably over at West Point he'd discover a message announcing the arrival at King's Ferry of Sabra and Phoebe. Aye. Almost certainly within twenty-four hours he would clasp her in his arms.

It facilitated matters that Mrs. Wynkoop was not present at the breakfast table; nor were any of the other officers' ladies. When Lucius entered, General Arnold glanced up quickly, then nodded and went on eating, hugely, as usual. Captain North, his personal aide, had reappeared from delivering troop movement orders to Colonel Lamb commanding at Fort Arnold, and was leafing through documents destined for the general's attention.

Other officers on duty at headquarters lounged about, drawing on after-breakfast pipes and scanning newspapers, for all that the bulk of them were quite young.

Conversation then ran on local problems and events.

Someone asked, "Suppose you all heard that cannonading Saturday afternoon?"

"Yes. What the devil was it?" demanded Major Franks.

"Odd thing; a British man-o'-war, a sloop called the *Vulture*, came sailing upstream, bold as brass, and dropped anchor off King's Ferry. Stayed there, too, until some of our artillery got into battery and peppered at her till she dropped down to Teller's Point where the river is wide enough for her to escape our shot."

On seating himself, Lucius immediately became aware not only of an unaccustomed activity but the presence of two strange officers: a big burly major and a gentleman dressed in the usual black garb of a physician. They were, he learned, Dr. McHenry and Major Shaw, both aides to General George Washington, who had ridden in expressing regrets that the commander-in-chief unexpectedly had decided to inspect the north and middle redoubts on the Hudson's east bank, and therefore would not arrive in time for breakfast.

This, of course, accounted for that extra neatness of uniform about the mess. Everyone was speculating on what might have happened as a result of the recent interview at Wethersfield between General Washington and Count Rochambeau, the French commander.

"Judson, fetch me some more eggs. I seem to have a prodigious — " Arnold broke off and his big head swung sharply towards the window, watching the headlong approach of a horse and rider. Without awaiting instructions, Lieutenant Allen bolted out onto the porch.

By craning his neck Lucius glimpsed a red-faced officer wearing a lieutenant's single epaulette, hurling himself from the saddle of a foam-lathered horse.

"For General Arnold's personal attention!" Everybody could hear the messenger's breathless cry.

Allen reappeared with the heavily breathing officer at his heels. "It is for your hand alone, sir," he explained.

[683]

"Where are you from?" Arnold demanded.

" — From Colonel Jameson's command, sir, at Westchester." The courier stood very straight and held out a sweat-marked letter.

Major General Arnold's black brows joined. In a harsh monotone he demanded, "Do you know the nature of this dispatch?"

"Only that it deals with a matter of the first importance, sir."

The clinking of a dish, set on the table by an orderly, sounded very loud in the penetrating silence. Every eye in the room watched Arnold score the seal with his thumbnail. As the general's bold black eyes flickered over the dispatch Lucius noted a muscle begin to twitch in the fullness of Arnold's cheek while gentle perspiration commenced to spangle his forehead just below the wig line.

"Gentlemen, pray excuse me. This matter requires my immediate personal attention over at the fort," he announced, shoving back his chair. "You will continue your breakfasts, gentlemen, and carry out such orders as you have already received to prepare West Point for General Washington's inspection."

Heavy epaulettes of gold bullion surmounted by their twin stars of silver flashed in the bright sunlight when Arnold got to his feet. All over the mess room gilt buttons began winking as the various officers turned to see what was going on. Lucius noted that General Arnold's lower lip had become gripped between his teeth. Almost hurriedly, the general's big figure limped out through the door. Lucius heard him snap, "Captain North, see that I have a horse immediately."

"Any particular charger, sir?"

"Blazes no! Get me a horse, I said. I'm in a tearing hurry; even a farm horse will do. And you — " he flung at Allen, "gallop down to the landing and have James Lowery get my bateau men turned out on the double and ready to row."

Various officers stared at each other in bewildered conjecture. "What the devil can be up?"

"What's amiss?"

" 'Fore God, I've never seen the old boy in such a swivet!"

Those on the ground floor heard Arnold's limping tread on the staircase, heard the door to his wife's room bang shut.

Pulling on his boat cloak the general came *clump-clumping* back down the stairs, his black eyes strangely bright against the leaden background of his features. Pausing only long enough to snap at Lucius, "Attend my wife, she has been taken ill again," he hurried out of the Robinson house and, spouting curses, he struggled into the saddle of a common trooper's mount led up by Captain North himself.

"Shall I come with you, sir?" the aide demanded anxiously. "Is there aught gone wrong?"

Arnold gathered the reins, shook his head. "No. Wait here to greet His Excellency. I — I'll see him on the other shore."

[684]

Without further ceremony Arnold jabbed spurs into the bony gelding he bestrode and wrenched its head about. Together with half the staff, Lucius watched their commander go galloping off, cloak aflying, then soberly the physician made his way upstairs to find Mrs. Arnold sprawled in a dead faint on the floor. A terrified chambermaid was bent over her, rubbing her wrists.

"Oh, dear God — 'tis a lie! No! 'Tis not possible," were the first words Peggy Shippen Arnold choked out once Lucius's sal ammoniac had returned her to consciousness. The distracted creature's great blue eyes rolled wildly, her fingers clenched and unclenched themselves and her diaphragm heaved convulsively.

"He's made to say such things! Benedict would never do such a thing!"

Major Franks, the aide detailed to Mrs. Arnold's service, came running in. "Pay no heed to her words, Doctor! She is undergoing a frenzy and knows nothing of what she speaks."

Lucius nodded. It was well known about the post that Mrs. Arnold was subject to fits of what was properly called "frenzy."

"He is *not* a traitor!" Mrs. Arnold screamed at the top of her lungs. "He is not! Not for all the gold in England!"

Lucius pressed a cold cloth over the congested features, managed in a measure to muffle her outcries.

"I'll kill myself — where's my child? I'll kill him, too, rather than he should live in shame. Kill me, Doctor — I — I can't support this disgrace."

"Pray calm yourself, ma'am," Major Franks implored, hastily shutting the door behind him. He shot Lucius a desperate look. "Quiet her, for God's sake, or we are all undone."

"Whom Can We Trust Now?"

Lucius Devoe's patient had scarcely lapsed into a drugged slumber than voices outside began bawling, "Turn out the guard! Turn out the guard for the commander-in-chief."

Bugles sounded flourishes, guard details came pelting up on the double. Then one could hear the trampling of many horses advancing along the driveway.

"Atten — shun! Present — harms!" rasped the officer of the day. Out of the window Lucius could see two platoons of smart-looking infantry drawn up and presenting their pieces as General Washington, accompanied by General Lafayette and General Knox, chief of artillery, and a small staff came riding up to the porch and there acknowledged the adjutant's salute.

Dr. Craik, in a tone that brooked no argument, said, "Dr. Devoe, you will accompany me across the Hudson. His Excellency has expressed a lively interest in your Indian longhouse hospital."

[685]

"Yes, sir. I'll go for my saddlebags immediately."

Upstairs he beat at Emma Wynkoop's door and found to his amazement that she was just then rousing from sleep.

"Why, Lucius — what's afoot?" she yawned.

"More than I can explain in a moment. Pray attend Mrs. Arnold when she wakes," he begged. "I'm ordered immediately across the river."

Down at the river Arnold's barge, of course, was nowhere to be seen, so while the commander-in-chief was waiting for another barge to be readied, he observed to Knox:

" 'Twill be a pleasure to inspect West Point once again. I expect our indefatigable Arnold has put things to rights, and will be burning to display his accomplishments." The general, Lucius thought, showed the effect of his long ride up into Connecticut; but not so much as his staff. "It is one of the sorrows of war," Washington continued, "that old companions-in-arms so often become separated. During the early days of this war, what a pack of troubles did we not meet and overcome as best we could. Arnold was, indeed, as the shade of a rock in a weary land back in 'Seventy-six and 'Seventy-seven."

General Knox blinked his little blue eyes; otherwise his heavy inverted egg-shaped face remained impassive. Lafayette's delicate, cameolike profile contracted. It was well known he had small use for Arnold — two such spirited leaders were bound to clash.

To the growing surprise and vexation of the commander-in-chief — ever expectant and appreciative of the courtesies of war — no guard detail was waiting, drawn up on the landing platform of Fort Arnold. No cannon thundered salutes.

In fact, surprisingly few soldiers of any description were to be seen anywhere and these were occupied with usual and commonplace duties. Nor was there any sign of Major General Arnold's barge — a fact commented upon by Dr. McHenry.

Eventually Colonel Lamb, in immediate command of Fort Arnold, came galloping down from the fort, very red-faced. He declared himself mortified and, noting the angry lines about Washington's mouth, stammered apologies for not having been warned of his distinguished visitor's approach.

The staff commenced exchanging glances as General Washington demanded sharply, "How is that possible, sir? Did not General Arnold cross over to this fort not two hours ago?"

Colonel Lamb looked dumbfounded. "General Arnold, sir? There — there must be some error, sir." The unhappy colonel spread his hands. "We have not seen General Arnold in a week's time."

Washington drew himself up, mouth clamped into a tight line. "This is a most extraordinary and irregular situation. I shall expect a written explanation. Colonel Lamb, dispatch messengers in search of General Arnold;

pray present him my compliments and instruct him to report to me at once. In the meanwhile I will inspect your works."

Lucius was laying out a series of saw blades preparatory to sharpening them — there would be some amputations that afternoon — when, from their emplacements in the fort above, a cannon boomed, then in rapid succession a whole series of reports.

"The general alarm signal, by God!" Like hornets from a disturbed nest, the handful of troops remaining in garrison in and about West Point ran to man their posts. Only then did it become apparent how very destitute of troops was Fort Arnold. What with the absence of wood-cutting and foraging parties and troops away on maneuver, not one gun in five could be manned.

Speculating wildly on what could have chanced, Lucius ran for his post at the hospital and thus came across John Fletcher. He was talking to a wildly excited courier.

"Yessir. Y' should ha' seen Gen'r'l Washington's expression when Major Hamilton handed him them papers. They wuz forwarded by Major Tallmadge down to White Plains. There's no doubt — "

" — They concerned General Arnold?" Lucius broke in.

The courier spat and caught up his cap now that Fletcher had applied sticking plaster to a branch slash across his nose. "By God, that they did, sir," growled the rider. "Proved fer a fact old Arnold was plotting to sell this here post to the British, lock, stock and barr'l."

"Well, I'm damned," gasped the Jamaican, as all manner of minor incidents fell into a pattern terrible in its implications.

"You were there?"

"Yessir. You should ha' seen His Excellency's expression when he finished reading. 'Arnold has betrayed us,' he sez, and tears were runnin' down his cheeks. Then he says to Gen'r'l Knox in a choked-up kind o' voice, he says, 'Whom can we trust now?'"

Tension, engendered of Arnold's plot with Lieutenant General Sir Henry Clinton, commander of all His Majesty's Forces in North America, reigned over West Point. On the twenty-seventh of September two regiments of the Pennsylvania Line arrived after forced marches up from the Continental Army's encampment at Tappan's.

Fort Arnold, hastily rechristened Fort Clinton, in honor of General George Clinton — there were four general officers of that name in this war — was readied against attack. All leaves granted the officers were canceled, no passes were issued, and as quickly as possible those garrison troops so treacherously dispersed by Arnold were recalled.

Vigilance became the order of the day; every person entering or leaving West Point was subjected to the severest scrutiny. Of course, wild rumors burgeoned. The British were reported marching up the Hudson to attack the all but betrayed fortress. Arnold had been apprehended and shot on the spot. This and that officer had been implicated in the plot and were being held under close arrest. Executions by the dozen were bound to follow. All these tales were, of course, nonsense, and pretty soon the facts came out. Arnold had been quite alone in his treason.

Alas that his opposite number now held for espionage proceedings at Tappan's, should have been the gay, clever and amazingly handsome Major André, adjutant general to Sir Henry Clinton and the scion of a distinguished English family.

Poor fellow, he was doomed even before trial. Beyond any question of doubt he had been captured down in Westchester, wearing not his regimentals but civilian clothes lent him by one Joshua Hett Smith, now sharing Major André's captivity. He was bound to meet the same tragic fate as Captain Nathan Hale of Connecticut, who also had been detected in disguise.

There were stormy scenes at the commander-in-chief's headquarters; persistent questioning of everyone belonging to the traitor's staff. A pair of tough Pennsylvania Continentals came tramping into his hospital bearing an order for him to accompany them to the Robinson house. In the end, Lucius Devoe was acquitted of active complicity, at least; but was directed to remain in the immediate vicinity of Fort Clinton.

Just when he became aware of Emma Wynkoop's continued presence at the Robinson house, Lucius could never be sure. Probably it had been the evening of that memorable day when Major André had been conducted up from Fishkill, calm and dignified but, in his borrowed clothes, much resembling a broken-down country squire. He saw her then, peering out from the window of that room in which Mrs. Arnold lay prostrated.

After a dinner rendered constrained by the presence of so many hard-bitten and weather-browned officers, it was only natural that Emma and he should take a stroll. Presently they were occupying a bench so arranged as to overlook the Hudson.

Spasmodically, Lucius's fingers closed over Emma's. His gaze sought the distant lights of Fort Clinton. The wisest course? How easy to say but how hard to recognize! Here was another major turning point in his life. He tried to think clearly, dispassionately. If only Joshua hadn't mentioned old Sam Stanton's many mercantile reverses. Marriage was a mighty serious affair and, well, divorce was practically unknown.

I have only one lifetime, he thought. Instinct I've never acknowledged as a true force, but perhaps now I had better respect it. Sabra's pretty and sweet, but Emma's handsome, too. Best of all, I know what I'll get by way of a bedfellow if I marry Emma. Sabra might prove difficult, cold as a fish. Think on it! Emma owns outright a vast fortune and is far more intelligent than Sabra. Of course if I marry Emma there'll ensue a scandal, but now Arnold's disgrace and treasons are filling all minds, folks won't heed such a small matter. Stands to reason Joshua and his folks will be pretty mad, but such things blow over. After all, I have done Sabra not the least harm, while I owe Emma loyalty for — for the other night. Some would declare that I'm constrained to marry her.

Emma started to draw away her hand; in the semidarkness he could read in her eyes a pained expression.

On the seat he turned abruptly and took her into his arms. "Oh, Emma, Emma dearest," he cried, "I want you to be my wife and as quickly as possible."

"Oh, yes, yes, yes, yes!" After a little, she straightened, smoothed her hair. "The Reverend Dr. Carver is still at the Robinson house, I believe. Since the betrayal, I have been dwelling in the overseer's house."

"What of the banns? They're required to be posted a fortnight."

"A pox on the silly custom," Emma laughed softly. "Have you never learned that a pair of golden sovereigns can erase time as easily as a chalk mark?"

A little before midnight that night, Emma Wynkoop and Lucius Devoe in the overseer's house joined hands before the Reverend Dr. Carver. Piously, the minister raised his eyes and commenced to recite: "Dearly beloved, we are gathered here —— "

Reflections by Firelight

Three or four years earlier, Major Joshua Stanton in all probability, would not have bothered to slap Dr. Lucius Devoe's face before the whole mess; nor would he have dispatched young Captain Calvert of Colonel Smallwood's Maryland Dragoons to convey a challenge. He would merely have seized an opportune moment to beat the lights and liver out of the scoundrel.

As it was, the practice of dueling — imported by Southern officers — had become so thoroughly accepted in the army that no other course occurred to Joshua Stanton. And he made the challenge to Lucius.

Seated alone and miserable in his quarters, Lucius realized that he stood every chance of losing his life. Of swordplay he knew nothing at all and it came as thin consolation that Sabra's brother was reputed to possess only a field soldier's skill with pistols. A shiver mounted his back. He knew that Joshua Stanton was going to kill him; the conviction became rooted in his soul.

Even now Major David Page's icy tones beat at his memory. "Second you? Never. I'd sooner second the devil himself than a rascal so lost to all sense of honor."

Captain Carl Schmidt had grunted in his best Pennsylvania Dutch accent. "*Nein*. Only for gentlemans do I act. Excoose me."

As a last resort Lucius had had to fall back on the services of one Captain Gustave Delacroix, a none too savory appendage of the Marquis de Lafayette's headquarters. This saturnine individual had agreed to act, frankly admitting that his participation was prompted by a certain penchant for duels — and for no other reason.

A long pull of hard cider did little to ease the physician's self-accusations. What a great, lop-eared jackass he'd been to blunder out of his depth like this! Emma had appeared utterly amazed at his failure to foresee this duel as the inevitable result of a flagrant affront to the sister of a respected and popular veteran of the commander-in-chief's own family. When he'd told Emma about the challenge, the soft lines of her face had faded.

"What else did you expect, you ninny? A fine pickle you've let us in for," she'd snapped. "Why didn't you tell me your Boston wench was on her way down to marry you?"

"But I thought you knew — " and he was sure this was so — "why, talk about our wedding was all over the post."

"Nonsense! Can you be so purblind as not to perceive that there's a world of difference twixt breaking off an engagement at long distance, and marrying another woman under your affianced's very nose?"

Consumed by that acid rage which afflicts a shrewd man who has outmaneuvered himself, Lucius stared at scarlet-gray embers dying in the fireplace.

One other man, he guessed, must also feel pretty badly tonight. On the morrow, October the second, Major John André, courageous and almost too truthful adjutant general of His Majesty's Army, would be conducted to a place of execution and at high noon hanged by his neck until dead. Poor André. He at least would die with honor and in the service of his king.

Sunrise Above the Hudson

A blanket of silvery mist was yet concealing the river when Joshua Stanton and Captain Paul Calvert reined in at the edge of a small and level clearing situated a good half mile upstream from the Shelburne Battery, most northerly of the defenses at West Point. To their surprise, three saddle horses already were tethered in a clump of birches near the middle of the clearing.

Although Joshua didn't know Dr. Fletcher well, he nonetheless recognized Lucius's former roommate; he wore a black coat and very politely lifted his silver-bound tricorn hat. Waiting beside the physician stood he who had agreed to act as president of the meeting, a Lieutenant Colonel Dickson from the Cape Fear region in North Carolina.

Captain Calvert looked mighty easy in his saddle as he circled the clearing to appraise its peculiarities, if any. He saw that fairly long hay stubble covered that stretch of even ground on which the duelists would meet; also that the rising sun would within a quarter of an hour strike directly sidewise across the proposed positions and favor neither antagonist. Calvert nodded. Colonel Dickson, an old hand in affairs of honor, had chosen well.

As he rode up to dismount he heard the Carolinian say, " 'Tain't spo'tin' for' Devoe to insist on such close range — fifteen paces don't call fo' pretty shootin'."

Joshua shook his head. "Probably doesn't know any better."

Dickson frowned, took a pinch of snuff. "Sho'ly, his second should have insisted on a decent interval."

Fletcher said, "Captain Delacroix, they say, doesn't care a damn so long as somebody gets killed."

"For sure, this is a senseless way to settle a quarrel. Here am I, Pa's only son, risking death and without the opportunity of taking some damned lobsterback along to balance the account. If it's in any way possible, I am going to kill that little rat simply because I don't want him to drill me. Mamma surely will die of a broken heart if I get slain in a duel."

Major Stanton had stood in mortal danger far too many times to feel rattled or jumpy — as he had that long-gone day up on Boston Neck. Lord, he'd shivered then like a sick dog and his hand had been so unsteady he'd scarce been able to reprime his musket.

What chiefly surprised him was that he experienced about this business none of the exhilaration he had come to associate with going into battle. In this quiet clearing sounded no banging of muskets or thundering of cannon; lacking was the inspiring rattle of drums or screaming of fifes. There was no thrill to be found in the fact that, on this morning of October 2, 1780, polite murder was about to be committed.

Hoofbeats sounded on that trail which led up from Fort Clinton. The foremost figure proved not to be Dr. Devoe but a thin, waspish individual wearing a very sharp-pointed mustache. Despite the fact that Delacroix wore an American light cavalry uniform, he suggested nothing other than the French cavalryman he was. A few paces behind Captain Delacroix rode the man Joshua Stanton had come here to kill. Right now, the physician looked scared half to death and ridiculously small astride his bony white nag.

Somberly, Joshua watched the Frenchman dismount, gather the reins over his left arm and smartly salute first the president and then witnesses. Apparently Lucius had received some coaching in the niceties, for he raised his hat to the officials.

In some amusement Joshua noticed that Lucius wasn't wearing his uniform today — just his old black costume.

Now the seconds were standing to rigid attention before Colonel Dickson, listening to the president's final instructions. Beneath a scarlet-leaved sumac, John Fletcher was laying out instruments and dressings and in his nervousness kept swallowing on nothing at all. Meanwhile the seconds drew from a covered wicker basket carefully primed and loaded pistols for instant use on either principal who committed a breach of the rules.

A coin was spun and Delacroix called the turn. As a result the president walked over to Lucius Devoe, offering a second basket. His was first choice of two pistols, the butts of which protruded uglily from beneath a clean white napkin.

Joshua watched Devoe, gone very pallid beneath his dark skin, draw forth a weapon and stand curiously considering it. Now the remaining pistol was being brought over to him.

A faint singing noise commenced to sound in Joshua's ears when the president, his long gray cloak stirring gently in a sudden breeze off the Hudson, moved to a point midway between the two parties. Colonel Dickson placed a handkerchief between boots glowing with polish, then, watched by everyone, stepped off fifteen even strides. Again he bent and placed a handkerchief between his boot toes before walking back to his post a few feet opposite the midpoint.

"You have all in readiness, Dr. Fletcher?"

"Yes, sir."

"Dr. Devoe, are you ready to fire?"

Lucius must have answered, but his voice was so faint Joshua could not hear it. He warranted the Jamaican must be terrified. That was well; wouldn't do for the last male Stanton to die here.

"Major Stanton, are you ready to fire?"

"Yes, Colonel, whenever you wish."

Colonel Dickson's big voice rang out so loud that the tethered horses pricked their ears. "You will advance to your marks, gentlemen, and turn your backs to one another. I shall count three; once you hear the word 'three' — and not an instant before — you will turn and exchange shots at will. Seconds will shoot either gentleman who anticipates my count of three."

"Ready yourselves, gentlemen!"

Colonel Dickson's voice rang out, sharp and clear. Maybe the voice of God announcing the arrival of judgment day would sound like that?

In the depths of the birch woods a jay now was fairly shrieking at his squirrel enemy.

"One!"

Joshua recalled the first deer he ever shot —

"Two!"

— A grenadier of the British Forty-second rushing at him once more, with bayonet leveled.

"Three!"

Joshua bent his right knee and, as Calvert had taught him, pivoted his whole body until there rushed into his scope of vision a black and white figure. Leveling his pistol with care, Major Stanton fired, but at that same, precise instant something struck him so violently that it spun him about. Off balance, Joshua fell onto his back and saw the treetops go wheeling crazily about; nothing more.

Reprise

For all that Asa Peabody could tell, Boston had changed very little during the past year and a half. Surely it must have been longer ago than that he had followed young Morgan to board the *Sally*? Late summer, he noted, had robbed the lawns and gardens of greenness, and yellow patches marred the leaves of elms fringing the Common. Children and ordinary folk still went barefoot, and under this late August sun goats, chickens and pigs scavenged, happily and numerously, along Boston's streets.

Ah! Up the street had materialized the pale pink brick of Dr. Townsend's house and, almost opposite, the façade of Mr. Samuel Stanton's fine residence. When he walked a bit closer he noticed that both residences could do with some paint.

Was Sabra within — was she now less than a hundred feet distant?

While diminishing the interval to William Townsend's front door Asa found time to wonder how Joshua's military career was shaping up. The exciting possibility presented itself that Lucius or Peter might be in Boston! How good it would be to see either of them. Strangely enough, he recalled his first patient — that dark, sickly and big-eyed wench. What had been her name? Helen? No. Then he remembered; Hilde, Hilde Mention, that was it!

The silver plate affixed to Dr. Townsend's door remained bright as ever and the same old Negro woman responded to his knock. She threw upwards her hands.

"Fo' de good Lawd's sake! Ef it hain't Misto' Peabodeh!"

"Afternoon, Sophie. Is Dr. Townsend in?"

"Yassuh, an' he'll sho' be pleased to see yo'. Come right in, suh, jes' come right in." Sophie stepped back into the house, began calling, "Doctuh Townsend, suh! Oh, Doctuh Townsend! please come down directly, suh. Yo' is in fo' one mighty nice surprise."

Asa made bold to tramp down the short hallway while snuffing the familiar odors of camphor, nitre and the other drugs.

"Good afternoon, sir!" he called. "May I have a little of your time?"

"Eh? Who's that?" Dr. Townsend appeared at the head of the staircase.

"Mr. Peabody, sir."

The old physician halted momentarily, blinking in his incredulity, then,

[693]

to Sophie's giggles of delight, he pattered down to the ground floor. "Asa! My boy!"

To the younger man's surprise Dr. Townsend not only wrung his hand but put both·hands on his shoulders, held him at arms' length and studied his face.

"As God's my life! 'Tis really you. I've hoped, nay prayed, that you might return to use, and to improve, your skill. Come in, come into the consultation room."

Dr. Townsend waved his guest to an armchair and asked Sophie to fetch some rum. "Now tell me, lad, what's chanced with you?"

"Tell me, sir, what do you hear of my friends Burnham and Devoe?" asked Asa, after he had recounted his own adventures briefly.

Most of all he wanted to inquire concerning Sabra, but somehow he couldn't bring himself to, right away — needed to brace himself against the almost certain disclosure of her marriage.

"Now about Burnham, let me see, let me see — " Dr. Townsend removed his spectacles, rubbed his one good eye and looked mighty thoughtful. "You knew that he was selected to fill that post which you — er — could not accept?"

"I hoped for as much. Pray continue. I have had no word from Boston since I departed. I'm sure he has done excellently."

"Alas, you are wrong."

"Wrong?"

As briefly as he could, the old physician described the scandal concerning Jenny McLaren's body, told of the hue and cry and of Peter's subsequent complete disappearance.

To Asa the account came as a profound shock. What a tragic ending to so promising a career.

" — And nothing since has ever been heard from him?"

"Nothing. I fear he must have died that very same night. 'Twas a great pity; young Burnham possessed courage, imagination, and a rare capacity for learning although he never could match your surgical skill, nor that Jamaican lad's gift for diagnosis."

" — And what of Lucius?"

Dr. Townsend put down his glass and took a turn down the room. "I fear, Asa, you were unlucky in your fellow apprentices. Devoe, after brilliant beginnings, proved a great scoundrel."

"Scoundrel? What do you mean, sir? Has he — "

"You recall my niece, Sabra Stanton?"

A chill tide of apprehension rose within him. "Indeed I do, sir."

"Well, this rascal — this, this villain, played upon Sabra's sensibilities until she fell very much in love with him. Also he cozened her father and her brother — "

" — Captain Stanton?"

"He became a major upon his return to the army. As I was saying, Sabra became affianced to this fellow."

An icy trickle started from the base of Asa's brain and crept down his spine.

"They — they were married?"

"No." Red invaded the pink and white pattern of Dr. Townsend's wrinkled features. "Almost on the day they were to become espoused, Devoe deserted Sabra for a rich woman from the Hudson River Valley. Oh, Asa, it was very shameful business and particularly painful for Sabra because near the whole army knew of her impending wedding." Dr. Townsend broke off, motioned to the rum bottle. "The instant my nephew learned what had chanced, he yielded to a natural, if reprehensible, impulse, and challenged Devoe to a duel."

"Reprehensible, sir?"

"A duel, Asa, is the most mistaken mode of avenging a wrong." Slowly, the old physician shook his head. " 'Twasn't like Josh to do such a thing; I am sure he must have acquired the idea from some of those corrupt Southerners. Folks say the Virginians and Carolinians will attempt to blow each other's head off over the vainest of excuses."

"But what of Joshua?" Asa begged. "He killed Lucius, of course."

"No. Through sheer bad luck — Devoe, they say, was no part of a marksman — Joshua took the rascal's pistol ball through his shoulder, where it so grazed the bone that a mortification set in."

"Joshua survived?"

"Aye. Though he lay at death's door for weeks, and would have perished but for the care his sisters bestowed upon him. My nephew is yet serving with our army, but it is known that he will never regain the full use of his right arm."

" — And Lucius?"

"The rogue escaped unhurt." Dr. Townsend sniffed his disgust. "The devil cared for his own that morning."

"What of Sabra? How is she? Where is she?"

The old man's single eye surveyed his caller with renewed interest. "You *were* fond of her, Asa, weren't you?"

"Yes, sir, far more than she ever realized; far more than I did, for that matter. Where is Sabra now?"

"She lingered long at Fort Clinton to nurse her brother. She has not yet returned to Boston, but she may be on her way home. I imagine Sam Stanton could answer that."

Asa started to get up, but the old physician raised a detaining hand. "No, stay just a little longer, Asa. I have something to say."

Once Asa had reseated himself, Dr. Townsend said, "It is perhaps providential that you should have returned just now. You see, I would like to confine my activities to instruction. I fear I grow too old to go running

[695]

about at all hours." He looked Asa squarely in the eyes. "Would you care to take over my practice?"

"Take over your practice!" Asa's jaw dropped. Judas Maccabeus! William Townsend's practice was one of the richest in all Massachusetts. "Of course, sir, but having no money, I could not even begin to buy — "

"I believe I said nothing about *selling* my practice?" Townsend smiled quietly. "I possess quite enough of this world's goods to provide for the remainder of my span."

"But — but, sir. Why offer *me* this — this honor?"

"I believe that during the course of my life I have instructed near three hundred apprentices. Of them all I consider you to be the most promising. Tut! Tut! No protests, please. That's the plain, unvarnished truth as I see it. Well, Asa, what do you say?"

The offer was so completely unexpected Asa for a time could only smile helplessly. "I'd admire to accept, sir, and will; if you're of the same mind after this war ends. However, I conceive it to be my duty first to offer my services to the medical department."

Quite deliberately, Dr. Townsend refilled their glasses, made a little tinkling noise when the trembling of his hand allowed the bottle to touch against the rim of his goblet.

"I respect that sentiment in you, sir. May I add that I am not surprised, only pleased. My practice will keep — and this war soon must end, one way or another. America is near exhaustion and the French are disgusted; but, also, the British people have become deeply discouraged and the Parliament grows more conciliatory every day.

"A decisive victory for one side or the other will settle the issue." Dr. Townsend arose, offered his hand. "Er — if you should need some — er — pecuniary assistance, you won't hesitate to call on me?"

"No, sir."

"Then get along over to Sam Stanton's. I expect you'll find him in at this hour."

Mr. Stanton had aged perceptibly; those chocolate-hued liver patches freckling his neck and hands were darker. His back, however, was still straight and his voice steady.

"Sabra — is she returning home?" Asa asked after the two men had greeted each other.

"No. She remains with Joshua, for all that I've pressed her to return. Mayhap she's fallen in love again — "

" — And Joshua?"

"His last letter declared that our army is preparing to march on Philadelphia."

"But doesn't Sir Henry Clinton still hold New York?"

"Aye, and in force. The ways of our military minds are strange indeed."

Asa spent that night at Dr. Townsend's, and early the next morning, purchased a seat on the Wethersfield coach. Bad weather aside, he should reach White Plains, New York, within four days.

The Road to Annapolis

Early autumn in Maryland was a wonderfully gay and brilliant affair, thought the French troops; the scarlet dogwood and sumac leaves, the yellow hickory trees and the fields of tired green suddenly became refreshed with bursts of goldenrod and purplish blue asters.

The country here was reminiscent of home — with its gently rolling terrain and so many broad, lazily flowing rivers such as the Patapsco, Patuxent and the Gunpowder. Somehow, to one's eye it seemed not quite so new as the lands they'd traveled further north.

How incredible, they assured one another, that this interminable march, which had commenced, aeons ago it seemed, up in Newport on June the ninth, now in September was nearing its conclusion. How many stifling, dust-choked and thirsty miles did not lie behind? *Nom de Dieu!* Could one ever forget those weary leagues and the curious friendly towns marking that route, Philadelphia, Whippany, Paramus, King's Ferry, and Wethersfield?

By now, the faces and hands of the Comte de Rochambeau's men were burned quite as brown as those of any American. Being intelligent, the men of the Saint Onge, the Soissonsais, Deux-Ponts and Bourbonnais regiments had learned very quickly to avoid the middle of the day as a marching time.

Although a few misanthropes grumbled, a vast majority of the rank and file had come to love this great, sprawling, and nearly empty country. The friendly open-handedness of the natives never ceased to astonish these sons of peasants accustomed from birth to suspect and to distrust all strangers. These Americans betrayed a flattering and sometimes embarrassing curiosity concerning the customs and habits of their allies.

What particularly surprised and impressed the inhabitants was that, like the British, the Frenchmen always marched arranged in precise companies, battalions and regiments; for them there was no tramping comfortably along in a straggling column with muskets held any which way and with the forage and baggage wagons God knew where.

Their discipline, too, was a shining example. 'Twas said that French troops would camp in an orchard full of ripe fruit and leave without having touched a single apple, plum or peach. A far cry, this, from the ruinous depredations committed by state troops or militia.

The men of the Bourbonnais and Soissonsais regiments had proved famous for an unconquerable gaiety; always they were ready to plant a kiss

[697]

or snatch a swift embrace from the brown-cheeked country girls standing barefoot and giggling by the roadside.

The Saint Onge regiment, in green cuffs and green piping, for some reason appeared to be a slightly soberer lot; but for all that, they boasted the best band of music in the whole French Expeditionary Force.

It was for the Royal Deux-Ponts regiment, however, that local inhabitants reserved their greatest enthusiasm. Perhaps this was because they, alone of the French infantry, wore light blue tunics most effectively turned up in yellow at their lapels and cuffs.

Somehow the Maryland people, like the Pennsylvanians and the rest, interpreted this wearing of blue as a gesture of courtesy towards their American allies who several days earlier had traveled this same road.

There had been among these many state troops, including General Mordecai Gist's three fine, new regiments of the Maryland Line. But they had all, with the exception of the Continental Line regiments, confiscated or stolen everything that hadn't been nailed down — and a lot that was.

From a light, two-horse carriage purchased for her in Philadelphia by Hector, Chevalier de Lameth, Hilde Mention smiled and waved happily at the population of a tiny crossroads village which was raising a cheer for the Royal Deux-Ponts regiments. She heard it because today her mettlesome dappled grays were carrying her along almost among the regiment's rear guard.

Hilde, politely — if a trifle inaccurately — addressed throughout the Expeditionary Army as "Madame de Lameth," had no intention of being left behind, once light transports, dispatched by the fleet of Admiral de Grasse, took aboard these dusty troops belonging to His Most Christian Majesty.

A long-drawn command, transmitted from the van where rode Colonel Count William Deux-Ponts and his principal officers, caused the rear guard to halt. Another order sent them scattering under the trees to avoid the hot September sun — all save the musicians who, unlucky dogs, must now strike up a tune. This they presently did, and their playing of "Les Grands Chevaux de Lorraine" caused these simple country folk to grin in shy wonderment and approval.

Sunburned children, clad only in homespun smocks or jumps, were the first to approach, quite round-eyed and ready to scurry back to the underbrush as quickly as quail chicks.

Because their thousand-mile-long march was very near its end, the Deux-Ponts felt in high good spirits. A few light infantrymen commenced to sing — more joined in. They even drank cheerfully of such vinegar and water as remained in their canteens and then lit their pipes. *Pardieu!* Was it not something to continue in such good condition after marching near a thousand miles over the most execrable roads in all the world?

Long ago Hilde had learned to avoid country taverns; without exception, their furniture was filthy, their parasites beyond calculation and their food miserable. She decided to remain by her carriage while some of the company went inside the local inn. Even while dismounting onto the sundried ground, Hilde kept an eye on the road. Unless Colonel Deux-Ponts had detained him during this customary mid-afternoon halt, Hector would soon appear, pointed dark features alight with tender anticipation.

Even while Jacques was unhitching the grays, the nearest Deux-Ponts troops bowed to this so beautiful little lady and raised their hats. A lieutenant ran up, silver gorget awinking in the sunlight, to inquire if he might be privileged to assist.

By now, even the dullest drummer boy serving in the Royal Deux-Ponts recognized this cheerful, dark-eyed girl who had kept house for Captain, the Chevalier de Lameth, back in friendly little Newport, Rhode Island.

No less did the men of the Troisième *Compagnie* admire their captain. *Nom d'un nom!* He was the gallant one, the Chevalier de Lameth. Though barely twenty-one years of age, the chevalier had afforded his men more than necessary proof of his courage, and amid an army in which officers maintained a studious disregard of their men, *le capitaine* was forever bribing, threatening, conniving with the commissary to procure the best possible for the Third Company. Yes. That was why every man and boy was quite willing to follow Hector de Lameth wherever he led.

"*Garde à vous!*" The blue-and-white-uniformed men beneath the trees began springing to their feet; noncommissioned officers hurriedly adjusted their buttons. From the road sounded a delicate patter of hoofs, and a second later, Hector on his golden chestnut mare, Victorine, cleared the pasture fence of split rails as easily as a gentleman could lift his hat. Delicate ears cocked and moving with the effortless grace of a wave up a beach, Victorine cantered to the carriage.

"*Ma petite fleur* — my heart!" Hector called and, swinging his leg back over the cantle, dropped from his saddle as lightly as a bluebird descending from a limb to the ground.

Reins trailing from the crook of his elbow and with the sun glaring off his golden epaulettes, Hector de Lameth kissed Hilde again and again, in full sight of the resting infantry. Silently, they approved. *Ma foi!* What a Sèvres figurine of a woman was this. At length the chevalier produced a lace-trimmed handkerchief and with it wiped from his peeling and cruelly sunburned forehead a generous beading of sweat.

"Tomorrow, little dove," he assured her, "you will have suffered your last ride over these cursed, incredible roads."

"We near Annapolis, then, my soul?"

"But yes, I have sent Pierre riding ahead to engage us decent quarters in this village of Annapolis."

They went and sat under a tree, watching Victorine.

"*Dis-donc, chéri,*" she demanded, "there has been fought a great naval battle, no?"

"Yes."

"With what result?"

"So far we do not know." The Frenchman's almost too finely modeled features fell into worried lines. "Monsieur de Viomesnil merely stated that a dispatch boat has reported a naval action of the first importance taking place at the entrance to this Chesapeake Bay."

"And where is that?" Hilde slipped an arm through his.

"What does it matter, *ma mie?*" He shrugged. "Such a huge country — it is almost terrifying. *Mon Dieu*, so very big and so empty."

"Yes; you like it?"

His lips brushed the back of her hand. "Always I shall love America because here I found you, flower of my heart. You are not too tired?"

"Oh, but no," she laughed. "Today the road has not been difficult at all and as always Jacques is most solicitous of my comfort."

Hector shifted on the grass to view the road. Along it from the direction of Baltimore was traveling a two-wheeled chaise. In the warm air the hoofbeats of a pair of dusty bay horses sounded very loud. A postilion was astride the lead nag — although the word really was too elegant a description for the sullen-faced boy who wore a crumpled straw hat, patched boots, a linsey-woolsey shirt and leather breeches.

In the chaise sat a single figure so effectively masked, bonneted and gloved that not even Hector de Lameth's discerning eye could estimate her age or condition.

When the Royal Deux-Ponts called out greetings the passenger waved absentmindedly, but took no other heed. As the chaise passed her Hilde noticed an unusually small calfskin-covered portmanteau strapped underneath its seat just before the vehicle became lost to sight beyond a dim and shifting pall of yellow golden dust.

Once the chaise had disappeared and the curiosity of the Deux-Ponts had subsided, Hector eased a traveling stock of white wash-leather, idly snapped his finger at Victorine, then tossed his hat on the grass at his knee.

"Do you know something, my darling? I am consumed with impatience to commence the fighting."

Hilde's fingers tightened on the pale green stem of her wine glass.

"Yes, dearest, I know — since you are by tradition a soldier, it is only natural." She tried to hold steady her voice. "There is news?"

"Yes. De Custine swore this morning that we will find Milor' Cornwallis pinned against the River of York. Yes. It is planned that we shall converge on him from all directions. The American generals de Lafayette and Greene from the southwest, *le grand* General Washington from the west, ourselves from the north, and the West Indian troops of the Marquis de Saint-Simon will advance eastward, from the direction of the River of James. *Enfin*, at last we shall roundly trounce *messieurs les anglais.*"

Hilde's eyes sought the field flowers in her lap. "But will they fight hard?"

"In that direction lies the greater honor. *Mon Dieu,* the sacred English always fight their best against us. Do not doubt that many of yonder brave fellows," he indicated his troops adjusting gear by the roadside, "will remain forever in America. Am I not in a macabre mood? I wonder why?" Hector laughed shortly, then raised his glass in a characteristically gay flourish. "A toast, queen of my heart, to a hard siege and confusion to our enemies!"

Hilde's fingers came to rest on her lover's light-blue sleeve, played with its texture an instant. "Hector?"

"Yes, darling?"

"Never imagine that I would wish you — an officer of the famous Deux-Ponts — to avoid any part of your duty; yet I beg you to promise that you will not seek out danger for its own sake."

Epaulettes atwinkle, Hector twisted his shoulders until he could press her lips with his. He laughed lightly. "Ha, jealousy at last! Now there is a fine promise to exact from me! Danger! Here's to that fickle wanton. Next to you, my love, I find her the most irresistible witch in all the world."

Impulsively Hilde dropped her glass, flung a slim arm about his neck. "You will take care? Promise," she insisted. "Promise. Should anything happen to you I — I would not care to live."

In some surprise de Lameth peered into her passionate features, said a shade more soberly, "What a strange, intense little creature it is here. If once he were to see you I am convinced Papa would consent to our marriage — *dot* or no *dot.*"

Hilde's dark red lips curved themselves into a small, mechanical smile. "You must not delude yourself, Hector. Are you not the last bearer of a name that was already great when the English were driven out of Calais? No, my lover, for you there must be a great marriage and many children to restore the family. The wife of the last Chevalier de Lameth must bring him position, domains, and many, many *louis d'or.* Your little Hildegarde can bring you only — "

" — The most perfect, the most priceless of all dowries — true love." He shrugged. "As for the rest — the domains, the monies, the titles — I shall win them with my sword — as did my ancestors." His voice filled, resounded with earnestness and a complete conviction. "But come, *mignonne,* we become too serious for so beautiful a September afternoon in Maryland; this will never do."

Somewhere, up near the head of the column and far up the road, a drum commenced its dry, imperative rattle.

"*Voilà.* The march resumes itself." He jumped up, slapping dried grass from the travel-stained white breeches. "Now attend what I say. You will seek, in this Annapolis town, a tavern called the Reynold's, and there I will seek you out tonight as quickly as our camp can be pitched."

Onto his carefully curled and powdered hair Hector swept his tricorn, bravely supporting a new blue, white and yellow cockade — a panache symbolizing the alliance of America, France and Spain. "Until that felicitous hour, my queen, I have the honor to bid you *au revoir*."

Mistress Susan Stevens

The Annapolis road ascended another long low hill and up it were panting the grenadiers of the Bourbonnais regiment — and well they might gasp for breath, swathed as they were in tight and heavy woollen uniforms, and carrying sixty-five-pound knapsacks. All light troops of the Expeditionary Force, those lucky devils, had been embarked at Head of Elk and already were concentrated in the vicinity of Williamsburg.

The distinctive light blue of the Royal Deux-Ponts became visible. Possibly half a mile distant, they were bracing themselves for the climb and Hilde, leaning far out of her carriage window, thought to recognize Hector and Victorine upon that distant slope.

Faintly, drum and fife music cheering on the sweating infantry drifted back along the road.

In Hilde's brief life but three men had ever treated her with a selfless kindness. What could have become of that demigod Dr. Peabody, back in Boston? Never as long as she breathed would she forget his gentleness and humanity towards a bedraggled, soiled little creature who had fainted so inconsiderately in his bedroom. Come to think of it, it was really Asa Peabody she must thank in the first instance for knowing the Chevalier de Lameth — and all that his love had brought.

Almost with first sight of the Chevalier de Lameth she had fallen so hopelessly in love with him that somehow to share his bed and the fortunes of war had seemed never less than perfectly natural. Oh, Hector, she thought. Ever since then you have proved so steadfast, so gentle and very understanding.

Twice he had asked her hand in marriage, but she loved him too much — for, more or less tactfully, officers of the Royal Deux-Ponts at various times had made it entirely plain that such a step surely would not only ruin Hector's military career but precipitate a disastrous break with the old Marquis de Lameth.

By dint of patience and tact, finally she had brought him to agree that the wisest course would be to await the end of this war, then return to France and to allow the acid old marquis to see for himself how truly, how profoundly they adored one another.

Hilde began thinking how wonderful it would be to reach Annapolis. A finger board, passed a little while ago, declared that town to lie but a dozen miles distant. Were this distance correct her carriage should arrive before the Reynold's Tavern long before darkness set in.

All at once Jacques reined in and applied his brakes as a voice called, "Oh, please stop. I — I am in such trouble."

Before Jacques could reply, Hilde donned her mask and peered out to recognize, some yards ahead, that same chaise which had rolled by during the afternoon halt. The vehicle lay crazily tilted in the weed-choked ditch with one axle resting on the thoroughly mashed remains of one of those overslender wheels.

The two nags, traces loosed, were nibbling eagerly at dusty herbage beside the road. Under the direction of his passenger, the surly postilion was engaged in unstrapping the portmanteau from its position at the rear of the chaise.

Hilde called, "How can I be of assistance, ma'am?"

"Oh! A lady!" The distracted young woman in a dark-blue cloak vented a small cry of astonishment. "Oh yes! You see what has chanced and I — I must continue my journey; really I *must*."

"You are for Annapolis?" Hilde demanded through the window. The stranded traveler, she judged, could be little older than herself but a bit heavier in build.

"Yes, madame. I know 'tis a great imposition, but I wonder whether you would consider — " reaching into a petticoat pocket, she produced a not very heavy purse. "Possibly I could purchase conveyance of you?"

As the woman by the roadside removed her traveling mask Hilde received an impression of chestnut hair, of cool gray eyes and wide sweeping brows. She added anxiously, "I am on my way to Virginia, to a town called Williamsburg."

Hilde said pleasantly, "You are welcome to share my carriage — but please first put away your purse."

Hilde turned the handle of the carriage door and gave Jacques rapid instruction in French which sent him leaping down to unfold the steps and then secure the stranger's portmanteau. The girl in blue hurried forward, smiling widely.

"Really, you are uncommon kindly, madame — "

"Who are you?" Hilde demanded.

The strange girl hesitated just a moment before replying, "I am Mistress Susan Stevens of — of Hartford, Connecticut. I told that donkey of a post boy not to turn so sharp, but he would in spite of everything."

Producing some silver, Mistress Stevens pursed full red lips, then turned to confer with her postilion, who immediately aided Jacques to strap her portmanteau onto the luggage rack of Hilde's carriage.

"Just now you spoke French, madame?" Mistress Stevens inquired.

"I am Madame de Lameth, and originally I came from Nova Scotia where many people speak French," Hilde informed. "And you come from Connecticut — a fine city?"

Her guest nodded gravely, then steadied herself to a swaying of the body caused by Jacques's return to his seat. "*Allez-y!*" The carriage lurched into motion once more.

"I can't begin properly to thank you," Susan Stevens presently declared. "I really don't know what I would have done if you had not chanced along. I suppose I'd have mounted one of the chaise horses," she said more to herself than to her companion. "Or maybe one of your baggage wagons would have assisted me. Your troops are so very courteous."

"I am glad there was no need to put their gallantry to such a test."

"When I crossed over to New Jersey from New York, I did not know of this great march to the South," Mistress Stevens declared, eyes busy first with the handsome luggage, the brocade curtains, then with her companion's modish attire and tiny blue morocco shoes. "So for days on end I have become entangled with the troops of either our army or of yours. Travel, you can imagine, has become most difficult, since every horse of any quality has either been bought or stolen."

The iron tires rasped out onto a ford where presently the horses halted to drink thirstily of tawny water slipping silently over the gravel.

"Madame de Lameth, do you fancy I will meet with many difficulties in attaining Williamsburg?" Susan Stevens inquired, as, emitting a sigh, she undid the bonnet strings. For all her mask and bonnet, her pleasantly open features proved to be both sunburned and dusty.

"Such a journey at this time will not prove easy," Hilde predicted. "There are many troops in that vicinity."

"Oh, dear! I don't know what to do and my money — well, I believe I will have just enough. Let me see — " Lost in calculations, she stared fixedly at her dusty shoe tips.

Hilde became interested. "You are perhaps to visit friends or relatives?"

The girl in the blue traveling cloak stirred and blinked several times. "No, not exactly. You see, ma'am, I am most anxious to — to find someone who was very dear to my heart."

"I trust he is not ill — or wounded?"

"So do I, but I don't know. He serves under contract to — " Susan sat straighter — "well, to one of the enemy regiments."

In her turn, Hilde drew herself up. "Did you say he serves with an *enemy* regiment?"

"Yes, ma'am. But don't mistake me. My — my friend is not a soldier, nor does he hold a king's commission. He is, in fact, a physician dedicated to the saving of human life. Does it matter in what army he labors?"

"No. You need not explain further, Mistress Stevens." Hilde's voice softened. "I quite understand, because it chances that I owe a vast debt to a physician."

"Where does he practice?"

"In Boston," Hilde replied, "but that was long ago."

On the outskirts of Annapolis, Hilde's carriage was overtaken by a strong detachment of cavalry which in the vivid glare of sunset presented such a brave sight that both she and Susan Stevens — who had proved to be no part of a Loyalist — waved and smiled at these big, blue-jacketed fellows in black jack boots, white waistcoats and breeches.

Their helmets, Hilde noted, were of brass, sported white horsehair crests and had a band of brown bearskin bound across their fronts. For arms they carried carbines slung across their backs and beneath their left knees curved, useless-looking sabres swung downwards towards dust raised by the hoofs. These, she learned later on, were a troop of Continental dragoons.

Although the bulk of the French troops were encamped beyond Spa Creek, little cooking fires flickered under trees fringing the side streets of Annapolis. From them odors of saffron and garlic, unfamiliar but inviting to native nostrils, drew crowds of onlookers to view those large cauldrons in which was being prepared that magnificent *soupe* which ever has proved a boon to French armies.

Only by dint of the most skillful driving was Jacques able at length to guide his carriage around Church Circle and so bring it to a triumphant halt before the Reynold's Tavern.

"*Mon Dieu!* Miss Stevens, what *can* have happened to my husband?" Hilde, who had been looking eagerly for Hector, asked.

"In all this crowd 'tis no wonder he is hard to discover," Susan remarked.

"But certainly he will be here. Ah-h! There! There he goes. Hector, *chéri! Me voici!*" Hilde leaned 'way out of the window and commenced blowing kisses and waving her scarf. Susan watched in some astonishment. What odd ways the French had of greeting one another.

"*Holà!*" Hector waved and began pushing through a mob of French and American officers thronging the tavern's entrance. Even before he was halfway to the carriage, Hilde had alighted and was running up to be clasped in his arms.

Oh, dear. Will anyone ever rush to hold me like that? Susan Stevens gazed enviously on their obvious and mutual adoration before remembering to avert her attention. Presently the de Lameths commenced a rapid conversation punctuated by many expressive gestures.

To find shelter for tonight will be difficult, my girl, Susan told herself. Aren't I the silly fool to get myself in such a pickle?

Madame de Lameth came back almost dancing, the small oval of her face radiant. "Mam'selle Stevens, the Chevalier de Lameth has returned to seek the patron of this inn. He will do what he can, but in any case you must share my quarters. The chevalier insists upon it."

Susan shook her dark brown head and answered softly, "I'd much sooner sleep in your carriage than to separate you from your husband."

Hilde's pale-green-gloved hands rested briefly on those of her traveling companion. "Do not worry. My Hector, like most Frenchmen, is a fine provider. He has a way with him. You will see."

Susan nodded. During those agonizing and mortifying weeks in New York she had come to learn how quickly the gleam of gold can transmute the sourest expression into a beatific smile.

Things turned out very much as Hilde had predicted. Tall and spare as a lance, the Chevalier de Lameth soon reappeared in company with a short, plump and very jolly officer of Smallwood's Maryland Cavalry.

Gravely, Hilde performed the presentation to Susan Stevens of her cavalier. It was quite something to behold that easy grace with which the Chevalier de Lameth bent to kiss Mistress Stevens's dusty blue glove. In turn he waved forward this rotund, middle-aged Marylander.

"Mademoiselle Stevens, permit me the honor to present Major Joseph Ridgely of Colonel Smallwood's Horse."

Susan found herself looking into genial, ruddy features, and two of the merriest gray eyes she had ever beheld.

"Your obedient servant, M-Mistress Stevens," he boomed in a big and hearty voice. "You are most welcome t-to Maryland. Captain de Lameth" — to Hilde's surprise he pronounced the name correctly — "explained y-your situation — and m-makes it possible for me t-to indulge myself by inviting you to make use of m-my quarters."

Occupy a strange officer's room? Mercy to goodness, no! Susan flushed. "You are most kind, sir, but I could not think of putting you out."

Major Ridgely uttered such a hearty laugh that the coach horses started, then turned questioning heads. 'God bless you, ma'am, there are other beds at my disposal in Annapolis. Oh, my soul, yes!"

Before Susan could voice further protest, Hector de Lameth clapped Ridgely on the shoulder. "Ma'm'selle Stevens, one suspects, observes only the niceties in her refusal. Eh, *mon ami*? Come, shall we move in the ladies' things?"

"I would be flattered, Miss Stevens, if you would accept a small measure of that Parisian scent you so admired." While she spoke, Hilde's eyes strayed to Susan Stevens's portmanteau, then widened momentarily. Painted in clear letters across the inside of its lid was: SABRA STANTON, BOSTON, MASSACHUSETTS. *Nom de Dieu!* Faint as a cry of a bird lost in a storm, came a voice saying, Somewhere, sometime you have heard that name before now.

Delightedly, Susan accepted the perfume, but sensing an obligation to reciprocate, sought her portmanteau. After a brief search she produced a tiny silver and enamel bosom bottle — one of those fragile receptacles designed to keep fresh flowers alive when tucked into the front of a bodice.

Too late, she saw her name betrayed, but only casually closed the chest. A moment later she turned, smiled sweetly innocent. "I fancy I am now as ready as possible, madame. This scent is indeed divine!"

To her who had called herself Susan Stevens the evening proved unforgettable. Under the benign influences of the Chevalier de Lameth's Moselle and Major Beau Ridgely's Madeira, most of Sabra Stanton's doubts and sorrows seemed to melt away.

After they had eaten and were in Sabra's quarters, Hilde's expression sobered and her straight black brows crept closer together. "My dear Susan," she began, "I am not of the curious sort, perhaps because I have met with much sorrow in my life — and many difficulties. I have come to like you more than a little. Can I be of — well, of any assistance?"

Sabra's smile faded as she looked her companion full in the face. "What leads you to imagine that I stand in need of assistance?"

"As a rule young ladies do not travel towards a battle for mere pleasure alone — least of all, unescorted," Hilde pointed out.

"You see many women and girls riding both animals and the baggage wagons."

"Yes, but very few nice girls," Hilde returned quietly.

The wine perhaps had released a measure of Sabra's natural reserve. "Why do you deem me — unhappy?"

"You *are* Sabra Stanton, are you not?"

Sabra's eyes flickered over to the portmanteau. "Yes. That is my true name. I have good reason to travel under another."

"No doubt. Please say no more. I am perhaps indiscreet in having said so much."

"Oh, no," Sabra burst out. "I want to talk to you. For weeks I have been stifled for lack of conversation."

They seated themselves on the bed, Sabra leaning against its footboard, Hilde's doll-like figure propped against the bolster and pillows.

Sabra indulged in no self-palliative preambles, but spoke in disarming frankness. "You see, Hilde, last year I became affianced to a certain officer on service with our army. I was madly in love with him."

" 'Was'?" Hilde murmured.

Sabre flushed, shrugged. "It is possible that I still am. I don't know. It is that very uncertainty which plagues me, night and day. Although I have endeavored to do so, I seem unable to put him out of my mind." Her voice softened. "Lucius possesses — well, qualities which prompt me to believe that I don't fully understand the reasons back of his abominable conduct."

Hilde merely regarded her hands. "Abominable conduct?"

"Yes," Sabra began talking faster. "I journeyed down from Boston to King's Ferry — a place on the Hudson River. We were to be married two days later, I forgot to tell you that." Sabra sighed. "Well, you can imagine how thunderstruck I was to learn, in Kingston, that Lucius — my intended husband — had that very day espoused another woman; a very rich lady, I believe."

"I think," Hilde announced evenly, "you are most fortunate to be shut of so great a fool."

The shake of Sabra's head was instant and vigorous. "No. That is just what is wrong. Lucius is no part of a fool!" Her hands commenced closing restlessly in her lap. "Mayhap I'm a loony, yet I cannot rid myself of a notion that, somehow or other, Lucius was forced into this maneuver. You see, Hilde, I *know* he loved me until that time. You should have read the tenderness of his letters. Oh, they had a way of creeping into the very core of my heart. Really, I cannot have been so badly mistaken." Sabra's voice gradually had lowered itself until, in order to hear, Hilde had to lean forward.

"You have my sympathy." She was thinking of her long fruitless passion for Dr. Peabody. "And after you learned that he had betrayed you?"

"There was a duel. Lucius remained unhurt, but shot my brother through the shoulder, and very nearly killed him. Surely, if Lucius had been as guilty as it appeared, God would have punished him, and not Joshua?"

"One has yet to hear of *le bon Dieu* serving as president in an affair of honor," Hilde commented drily.

"Be that as it may, it was well that Phoebe and I were there to care for Josh. Sometimes we feared he would never shake off that terrible fever. Eventually he did, and recovered rapidly because he is strong. It was only then that I — "

" — That you felt impelled to find this Lucius and question him face to face?"

"You are very clever, Hilde."

"Oh, no, Sabra, I am a very simple person, indeed I am. But of life I have observed a little."

"You are quite right. I can find no peace. I cannot continue my life until I see Lucius, hear his story, and judge whether any excuse exists for what he did. Then, and only then, can I banish his memory from my mind and heart. Am I so foolish?"

"Not in the least." Hilde's fingers closed gently on her companion's hand. "But it is really unfortunate that you have undertaken to seek this Lucius during such terrible days and in so dangerous a region. Tell me; how did you learn of his presence in Williamsburg?"

"Would that Lucius were there! No. I fear him to be in York Town. You see, Lord Cornwallis gave up Williamsburg some weeks ago — was driven out, rather."

"But how can you be sure this Lucius is indeed in this York Town?"

"Because I traveled to New York in search of him. There I sold my wedding clothes, the linens I had been given to set up housekeeping. As it turned out, I arrived in New York only to learn that a few days before Lucius had sailed as contract surgeon to certain reinforcements being dispatched to the assistance of Lord Cornwallis."

"Do you know with what regiment he serves?"

"Not for sure," Sabra replied gloomily. "Last I heard, he was on duty with a German regiment — the Anspach. All the same, I shall find him, and then I will know whether I still love him."

"His wife accompanied him?"

"Not she. After the scandal and the duel she retired to her estate and left Lucius to scurry away to New York."

Scout Ship

Captain Andrew Warren came to the conclusion that this evening of September 4, 1781, was pretty near the loveliest he could recall. Out of the north-northeast a breeze was blowing just strong enough to send his new command, the *Grand Turk III*, surging southwards at a speed thrilling to one appreciative of a vessel's sailing qualities.

God above, what sheer luxury it was to feel a deck tilt and lift once more beneath his feet. Though Warren hated to admit it, this privateer was a damned sight handier in the wind than any of the regular naval vessels he'd ever sailed in. Watch cloak blowing free, Andrew Warren strolled across the otherwise deserted quarterdeck to its weather rail. From where he stood he could discern the black outlines of the starboard watch huddled among those long eight-pounders with which this brig's original battery had been replaced.

A soft sighing of wind through the shrouds, the gentle tap-tapping of reef points against taut canvas and the steady *hiss whiss,* of the waves alongside played a familiar symphony in his ears. If only this handsome brig had been a regularly commissioned naval vessel instead of a privateer under charter to His Excellency, Admiral de Barras, Andrew Warren's cup of happiness would have overflowed.

At the sound of footsteps he swung sharply about. "Good evening, Dr. Burnham. You are up late."

"Good evening, Captain. When do you imagine we will raise land?"

"Around sunup, I expect."

"Any sign of a British squadron?"

Andrew Warren's teeth glistened amid the bold planes of his features. "I followed our Dancing Master's instructions so we sail well to the east'ard of any bulldogs. 'Tis a handy vessel you and Mrs. Ashton own, Doctor. For all her two hundred tons she handles dainty as a yacht. She's handy into the wind, yet I'll warrant she can run downwind like a scalded cat."

"Thank you, Captain. You see, this vessel means considerably more to me than just an — an investment." Peter Burnham experienced a deep sense of satisfaction at hearing the *Grand Turk III* thus praised, especially as his present captain had proved to be a grim, hard to please fellow.

From the start, though, it had been clear that Captain Warren knew his duties from A to Zed. Why, in three days' time he got the brig's crew jumping about as smartly as if he yet commanded a regular man-of-war.

An odd character, this Andrew Warren. Peter Burnham thought back to that day near a month ago when he'd come across this lean, black-haired giant studying shipping notices affixed to an inn's notice board. Noting the anxious and bitter lines about this stranger's intelligent-looking eyes, he'd entered into conversation with him, had brought him home for dinner and for further observation because the *Grand Turk* needed a capable master.

Lord, how the poor fellow had eaten! Presently it turned out that he was a returned prisoner, with a wife and child to support and down to his last stiver.

When first Peter had beheld a vessel which resembled the *Grand Turk* to a marked degree, she had been standing in past Beaver Tail Point towards Newport Harbor and he had refused to credit his eyesight. He could, though, when halfway out to this brig riding under the guns of the *Concord*, frigate, with the French flag flying above a British Jack.

H.M.C.S. *Concorde*, later investigation revealed, had run down and recaptured the *Grand Turk* off Saint Kitts.

Captain Warren went forward to bellow a command to the watch, and Peter, seeking the taffrail, peered over the stern.

What fine luck that all Ashton's prizes save the *Hammond* had reached friendly ports. I made no mistake in buying a half share of the brig, he told himself. Already she's earned Mrs. Ashton and me a tidy sum. Poor woman, she'd a thousandfold rather have her husband alive and well.

When he'd announced his purchase, Trina had thrilled at the thought of his owning that vessel which had played so critical a part in her life.

The only discordant note about the present moment was the fact that Trina again was big as a house with child, so big that her infant would be born within the next two or three weeks — certainly while he was absent. A comforting aspect of this situation was the fact that she'd have level-headed and supremely capable Minga Warren on hand to serve in the dual role of friend and nurse.

Well, mused Peter Burnham, here he was, under contract as surgeon to the squadron of Admiral Vicomte Paul François Jean Nicolas de Barras, who, commanding eight lumbering ships of the line, by now must be sailing at least a day and a half astern of the fleet little *Grand Turk*.

This voyage to the Chesapeake might have required much less time had not Admiral de Barras so fully appreciated the extent of his responsibilities. Did not the transports he was convoying carry in their holds the only siege train in North America? Therefore he had elected to cruise far away from the American coast, in an effort to reach the James River without risking capture at the horny hands of admirals Graves, Hood and Drake.

It was entirely logical that a chartered privateer, swift and handy into the wind, should have been dispatched as scout ship. No less reasonable was the idea that he, Peter Burnham, should sail aboard her that he might set up in Virginia a flying hospital ready and capable of receiving the sick and injured of de Barras's squadron. Peter figured he'd made no mistake in picking Andrew Warren for the *Grand Turk*'s new master.

Now she was stepping towards the Chesapeake with the speed of a lance hurled by a powerful arm. Peter felt pretty certain that this ex-naval officer was eating his heart out for fear he wouldn't be allowed to engage the enemy. Lord, how he doted on those new French eight-pounders!

A falling star streaked brilliantly across the western sky and, for a wonder, Warren made comment. "Let us hope, Dr. Burnham that yonder presents an omen."

"Omen?"

"Yes. The decline of the British navy. Would to God that the United States could play some part in its fall!"

Curiously, Peter Burnham surveyed his employee. "Is America indeed so destitute of sea power?"

Andrew Warren gripped the taffrail with both hands. "At this moment, sir, only two wounded and homeless frigates, the *Alliance* and the *Deane*, comprise our navy. May I assure you, Doctor, but for the French fleet we would long since have been smashed."

"Tell me, Captain Warren, why is it so extremely distasteful for you to sign aboard a privateer?"

"I'll not answer that." Warren's laugh was bitter. "Ashore they warned me, 'Be civil to your owners and you'll get ahead.'"

Peter Burnham's jaw closed with a click. "I had deemed you more intelligent, sir, than to address such a remark to me."

"Your pardon, Doctor. Very well, I will speak the truth. Had I been content to ship aboard a privateer three years ago I reckon I could have made my fortune twice over. Many less capable than I have done so." He stepped closer, hungry-looking features taut. "But damn my soul, sir, our union can't survive without a navy and a strong one. Can't you understand? Without naval strength we are nothing and can become nothing great. Mark my words, if our Dancing Master admiral doesn't rendezvous with the French West India fleet and whip old Granny Graves and his bright lads, Cornwallis will be reenforced, and this war lost for good and all!"

"I ask your pardon." In friendly fashion Peter Burnham placed a hand on the other's arm. "Knowing perhaps something of the meaning of disappointment and frustration, I can admire your constancy in persisting so long in a luckless service — and without recognition or hope of reward."

Once Dr. Burnham had cast a final look at sea and sky before going below, a strange restlessness pervaded Andrew Warren's being. Hourly a conviction was growing in his imagination that tomorrow would prove a vastly significant day. Come dawn, his brig would commence to shape a course directly for capes Henry and Charles which marked the entrance to the vast and rich waters of Chesapeake Bay. The big question was — would he sight Admiral Graves's fleet bearing down to blockade the bay? Nobody knew where the British ships really were.

He passed the word below to summon Mounseer Aristide Loubet, who under the terms of the charter was his first officer. Not that Warren had found grounds for complaint. M. Loubet had proved both clever and imaginative; besides, he could speak to that half of the crew which spoke no English at all. M. Loubet displayed many evidences of gentle birth, for all his slipshod dress and foul language. Warren suspected that this first officer must have come to grief in the French king's navy; cards perhaps, or an unfortunate duel.

For third in command, Warren had signed on that same Abel Doane who had sailed under Captain Ashton. Warren estimated Doane as the kind of man who would never command a ship of his own except by accident; a natural-born second mate, that's what Doane was.

Andrew Warren went below and for a space remained bent above his charts, calculating and recalculating his brig's position. That the *Grand Turk* should win through to Lynnhaven Bay was imperative; no less a personage than Admiral de Barras had emphasized the fact only the day before.

How nervous the admiral had been. No wonder. His shrift would prove short indeed should his eight line-of-battle ships become intercepted on their way to the Chesapeake by Graves's infinitely superior squadron.

Locked in Andrew Warren's personal clothes chest reposed a box carefully weighted by strips of lead. It contained most urgent dispatches destined for the immediate attention of Lieutenant General the Count of Rochambeau and Major-General the Marquis of Saint-Simon.

When the privateer's captain reappeared on deck it was to find dawn painting glory in the east and flinging bright golden lances against the broken purple-blue surcoat of defeated night.

To his surprise Abel Doane, usually a slugabed, already had appeared and was bending his globular figure over the flag locker. M. Loubet, he noted, had ordered a shortening of the forecourse probably because the wind now was blowing very fresh out of the northeast.

Once again, an inexplicable premonition of impending drama gripped Andrew Warren. In a tense and mounting suspense, he and his first officer stood watching the first bright fingernail-paring rim of the sun slide over the horizon and commence to gild brisk and feathery whitecaps. But for all that, neither of them could have predicted that a most decisive day in America's war for independence was dawning.

The sun barely had cleared the horizon than a lookout posted in the maintop yelled down, "Sail, ho-o-o-!"

Immediately Andrew Warren shouted through cupped hands, "Where away?"

"Broad off t' starboard bow, sir."

"What rig?"

"Can't make out yet, sir, she bein' hull down. I only caught the flash o' her sails."

Foremast hands, crowding excitedly up on deck, noticed that the sea was changing from dark to light blue, and was losing some of its previous sparkling transparency.

"River silt," Doane grunted, pointing to an occasional streak of sand-colored water.

Warren nodded agreement and felt relieved. His vessel was off the mouth of Chesapeake Bay, all right, but far enough south and east of the capes to avoid the attention of a chance British watch frigate, he hoped.

He picked up a leather speaking trumpet. "Masthead, there! What course does the stranger sail?"

" 'Pears like she's sailin' 'bout west-southwest, sir."

Excitement mounted because just then the foremast lookout shouted suddenly, "Sail, ho! Two points off our sta'board bow and hull down, sir!"

The crew began to look anxiously at each other. This second ship must be cruising many miles distant from the first.

"How does she sail?"

"South-southeast, sir; looks like mebbe she's a frigate."

"If that first vessel is a Britisher," Doane remarked, "then I allow yonder's a French ship, cruising on lookout."

Warren's manner grew crisp and his dark eyes sparkled. Enjoying the weather gauge of both strangers, he didn't feel in the least concerned.

Both lookouts sang out in unison. "Sails! Many sails, sir! Broad off our starboard beam, sir."

"Mr. Doane, take the deck. Monsieur Loubet, come with me."

With that Andrew Warren went swarming nimbly up to the main cross-trees. Loubet followed only a few ratlines below; the Breton's scarred, blunt face had assumed a wooden aspect.

Warren felt his heart quicken as one after another many tall ships, six, seven, eight of them, poked their tops over the horizon.

Ever the efficient officer, Warren glanced at his watch and read the time as seven o'clock. Below, the brig's whole crew had swarmed to her starboard rail, watching sail after sail flash in the morning sun. Even the least intelligent among them guessed that, beyond a shadow of doubt, yonder, sailing southwards, was an impressive number of men-of-war. Of what nationality were they?

"*Violà la flotte Britannique*," Loubet announced. "*Vous êtes d'accord, mon Capitaine?*"

Andrew Warren, spyglass glued to eye, nodded. "You are quite correct. By their course and position that must be Admiral Graves's squadron coming down from New York. How many tall ships do you count?"

"Fourteen for sure, *mon Capitaine*," Loubet called over the creaking of the yards and braces. "And you, monsieur?"

"I tally sixteen heavy frigates or line-of-battle ships."

The passage of half an hour proved them both wrong. Steering a roughly parallel course, but sailing nowhere near as fast as the *Grand Turk*, cruised no less than nineteen majestic ships of the line! Perhaps as many more transports, tenders and victuallers were struggling along in the wake of the men-of-war.

Once he became convinced that Cape Henry, southernmost of the Virginia Capes, indeed loomed ahead, the *Grand Turk*'s master ordered his vessel on a course calculated to send her running straight into the six-mile-wide entrance of Chesapeake Bay. Ah! There they were. Cape Henry off the port beam and Cape Charles blue off the starboard bow.

The day continued fine and produced a breeze still and steady enough to delight any honest sailor.

All was going almost too well, Warren mused. As if to justify his apprehension there materialized from under the land a cruiser — she looked like a big sloop-of-war or a light frigate. She was crowding on sail as if running to beat the privateer into the entrance and proved so fast that presently Warren determined to bear up and force the unknown vessel to make clear her intentions.

Within half an hour the stranger — she was a frigate, all right — cruised near enough to permit observation of a predominantly white flag snapping from her signal yard.

"Might be a French flag — or a British white ensign," Doane told Peter Burnham. "Skipper's right to haul his wind and look lively. Stranger's got the metal of us and plenty to spare."

"Looks like a Frenchie to me, sir," remarked the quartermaster presently.

"Aye," Doane agreed. "Yonder'll be one of old de Grasse's watch ships streaking in to raise the alarm. He'll be barely in time. Look up yonder." Away off to the northeast had reappeared a string of white dots heralding the approach of the British squadron.

The words were hardly spoken when the watch frigate commenced firing alarm guns, then ran up to her signal yards a string of varicolored flags. From his chosen position in the *Grand Turk*'s main crosstrees, Warren in growing anxiety watched the British ships commence to maneuver as if seeking battle position.

"God help de Barras if he comes up now," Andrew Warren muttered.

"He'll blunder straight into that array." Then he leveled his speaking trumpet at the quarterdeck. "Send Manning to me!"

The ex-naval officer's deep-set eyes were aglow now, his lips drawn hard and flat against his teeth. Because it had escaped its tie ribbon, his dark brown hair was flying.

"Will you be able to recognize any of those enemy liners to windward?" he inquired when the boatswain came up, hand over hand, to join him.

"Yes, sir, very likely, sir," panted Manning. He shaded his eyes. "I can be surer in a little while."

It had become apparent meanwhile that the British armada was even more numerous than previously estimated. All lookouts agreed that standing majestically in towards Cape Charles cruised nineteen liners, a fifty-gun ship, no less than six frigates, and what much resembled a fire ship.

The British, without exception, were sailing the port tack and in no particular order. Apparently, Vice Admiral Sir Samuel Graves had not as yet decided upon his order of battle.

"Must be waiting to learn what his spy ships will report," Warren reasoned. "Well, he's still got plenty of time."

Half an hour dragged by, during which those aboard the *Grand Turk* watched in mounting awe a series of maneuvers that concluded by dividing this vast fleet into three lesser squadrons. By now George Manning commenced to recognize certain of the enemy.

"That for'ard ship, sir," he called over the rushing of the wind, "is the *Alfred*, she's a seventy-four; behind her sails the *Belliquex*. She's only a third-rater, sixty-four guns. The third ship in line I don't recognize, but the fourth is the *Barfleur*, a first-rater, ninety guns. The red pendant to her maintop shows she's got an admiral aboard, Sir Sam Hood, most likely, and may God rot his guts!"

"What's that blue pendant showing 'way off in the third division?"

"That will belong to the admiral commanding the division, probably Rear Admiral Sir Francis Samuel Drake."

"And where'd you calculate Admiral Graves will be showing his flag?"

Manning hesitated, shielding his eyes from the glare of the sun. "See that only other first-rater, sir, right in the center of the fleet? She's the *London*. See how she towers above the rest?"

From a close study of some excellent French charts, Andrew was aware that although the gap separating the two capes was a good six miles in width, a shoal called the Middle Ground in reality divided the entrance into two comparatively narrow channels, of which the southernmost was the wider.

Under every stitch of canvas that would draw, the brig now was fairly flying along with her American ensign standing out, crisp and clear, against the flawless September sky.

For a while Warren felt confident he could successfully enter the bay, but then something happened which caused him to order the helm hard down astarboard and send his crew scrambling aloft to shorten sail.

Crowding around the dull green and sandy yellow bluffs of Cape Henry shone the canvas of another fleet, quite as great as that standing in from the Atlantic — and New York. On the privateer's deck, First Officer Loubet slapped his thigh and fairly danced in his excitement as Warren slid down a back stay to resume his normal post before the binnacle.

"*Alors, voilà Monsieur de Grasse! Maintenant commence la lutte des titans!*"

Peter Burnham was frankly awed by the grandeur of those two great fleets with their tall canvas, bristling guns and varicolored sides.

"The Frenchies," Coane explained, "are fixin' to get out to sea in time to take formation before meeting the British. See, there come the lead ships of the French van." He pointed to two or three frigates, one blue, one bright green and the third dull yellow, rounding Cape Henry with battle flags flying and guns run out.

"The tide, Mr. Doane?" Andrew snapped. "How runs the tide?"

"Near the flood, sir," Doane replied. " 'Twill ebb sharply soon."

The *Grand Turk* now was practically retracing her former course, but stood more to the southwards and as near to the yellow dunes of Cape Henry as Warren dared take her. It was really too risky to try for the passage when a single excited liner might make a mistake and blow his little brig to kingdom come. Ship after ship, singly and by twos and threes, the French came crowding out of both channels, all huddled together like sheep chased out of a fold.

Now signal guns commenced to bang and boom among the ships to the northwards. Like bright-colored and demented butterflies signal flags shot up, then disappeared.

Warren determined that the British admiral was ranging his squadron into a "line-ahead" formation which would place Rear Admiral Sir Samuel Hood's division in the van, Graves himself would take the center, leaving Rear Admiral Sir Francis Drake to bring up the rear.

In bitter envy, the ex-commander of the U.S.S. *Diligent*, through his glass, watched those huge two- and three-deckers go surging into position. The screen of lighter ships, sloops and frigates promptly formed out on either flank. Far, far behind, the transports and victuallers idled, awaiting the outcome of this impending battle.

At last the French *avant-garde*, clear of the entrance at last, commenced also to assume a "line-ahead" formation. Aristide Loubet identified the leading man-of-war as the *Pluton*, seventy-four guns commanded by d'Albert de Rions; then came the *Marseillaise*, another seventy-four. That Loubet at some time must have held a staff position Warren now was certain; how else would he be able to reel off the names of the vessels as they fell into line? *Duc de Bourgogne*, seventy-four; *Diadème*, seventy-four; *Saint Esprit*, eighty, and so on.

"That fourth vessel in line," he was explaining in explosive French, "is the flagship of the van, commanded by Admiral de Bougainville — she is called the *Auguste* and mounts eighty guns."

Considering his orders, Warren had no choice but further to shorten his canvas, back his topsails and stand back and forth — a mere spectator of this rapidly developing clash of titans — until an opportunity presented itself to dash through the South Channel and, with all speed, head for the mouth of the James River.

Closer and closer sailed the great French line-of-battle ships, their lofty top-gallant masts climbing dizzily high into the heavens. To Warren's experienced eye, the French van was being quite as smartly handled as Sir Sam Hood's huge vessels.

All at once — Andrew Warren and Loubet both wondered why — instead of bearing down with all his strength upon the French as they came struggling out of the entrance to Chesapeake Bay, Admiral Graves now ordered his whole fleet to wear and shape courses out to sea; why, now they were bearing approximately east-southeast!

Incredible though it seemed, the British admiral was actually allowing the French opportunity to reorganize and to properly space their *avant-garde*. Not only that, but, with each passing moment, more of King Louis's great blue, white and gold ships of the line were running out of the South Channel and gaining the open sea.

The Signals of Admiral Graves, September 5, 1781

That stiff breeze which since sunup had been blowing steadily out of the north-northeast gave no indication of diminishing, and under its compulsion both fleets went steering out to sea — the British clinging doggedly to their priceless advantage of the weather gauge.

By a quarter to two of the afternoon the last French ships had cleared Cape Henry, and with the last of the *arrière-garde* in tolerably good formation were starting after the center and the dangerously detached *avant-garde*. All the same, this forward division remained perilously far ahead of the main fleet.

Soon the French center division began passing not a quarter mile to windward of the impotent little *Grand Turk*. First the *Pluton*, seventy-four, then the *Caton*, sixty-four, next the *Souverain*, seventy-four, and after her the enormous *Ville de Paris*. She was the flagship of the irascible Provençal, Admiral Comte de Grasse, Loubet exulted. When her captain so decreed, her crew could run out one hundred and four guns to hurl death and destruction upon the enemies of His Most Christian Majesty.

Like a mosquito circling a battle between two huge swarms of beetles, the brig maneuvered downwind and waited her chance to run for the entrance.

Both fleets were now arranged in an orderly "line-ahead" formation — with the British sailing almost due east and de Grasse heading for the broad Atlantic on a course slightly south of east.

At two-fifteen in the afternoon, a number of signal flags appeared at the *London*'s signal yard.

Doane, eyeing a broad expanse of tan water opined, "They'll be about three miles apart. Give 'em a half-hour and we will see what happens."

For once Andrew Warren neglected to check the disposition of his crew. Jerusha! Before his eyes was developing a major naval engagement between two closely matched fleets — that experience dreamed about and passionately yearned for by every good naval officer. Right from the start, he had perceived Graves's missed opportunity of destroying the French piecemeal at the entrance. Now it would appear that Graves was committing a second blunder by advancing his line at a long, obtuse angle towards the French, instead of closing in by divisions and fighting on a parallel line. If a sudden flurry of flags on the *Barfleur* meant anything, Rear Admiral Hood wasn't being backwards about protesting these tactics.

The *Grand Turk*'s master barked at Manning. "What means that signal from the *London?*"

" 'Keep more to starboard,' sir."

Now both fleets were sailing sluggishly — liners were never fast — but majestically away from the entrance. Even the dullest eye could tell that the British vessels were by no means as handy sailers as their enemies.

Time seemed to halt for those aboard the privateer — they were watching the lead ships of the British van, that which had been the rear until the line reversed itself — come bearing down on the now rigidly correct formation of Rear Admiral de Bougainville.

Loubet groaned, "*Nom de Dieu!* Had we the weather gauge, our whole fleet might now attack." He clasped his hands. "*Sainte Vierge!* Change the wind. Now! Now! We can enfilade the whole *maudite* fleet of Albion."

The wind, however, remained in the north-northeast and the British van under Drake and those of de Bougainville drew closer. More French ships sailed by, passing the little brig not two cables' lengths distant — roughly fourteen hundred feet.

Andrew Warren's mouth went dry and his soul burned. Oh, curse the luck! Damn it! God damn it! Why must he and his command be forced to stay on the outskirts of this fight like some shy bitch watching the two great hounds join battle? Yet to a naval officer, orders were orders. That his brig, with her pitiful battery of twelve eight-pounders, could no more affect the outcome of this engagement than a man clapping his hands on the forecastle, never occurred to Andrew Warren.

Nearer and nearer sailed these marine mammoths, heeling well to starboard under the northeast breeze. The *Grand Turk* sailed as close to them as Warren dared; he wanted those Frenchmen to see, if only as a token, the huge American ensign streaming at his gaff. Nobody paid the least attention.

The weather remained so fair that everyone about the *Grand Turk* received a clear impression of the beginning of the engagement, when all of a sudden the British, at a cable's length, let fly a tremendous broadside at the *Réfléchi*, fifth vessel in the French column. Everyone saw gray-white smoke burst from the sides of the *Shrewsbury* and *Intrepid* then, seconds later, heard the roar of the discharge.

"*Mon Dieu!*"

"My God, look at the *Réfléchi!*"

Under an iron hail dispatched by the British guns great jagged sections of the French liner's fabric — she was the smallest in line — sailed high into the air, her masts swayed and her previously orderly canvas sagged, flopped crazily on broken yards. All the same, Captain Bondel's men fired back a reverberating, deafening defiance, then a great billow of gray-white smoke formed and briefly concealed the *Réfléchi*.

"Look! Look at that!" Manning was biting his knuckles. "See that vessel bearing down? That's the *Princessa*, Drake's own ship."

Thirty-five cannon composing the *Princessa*'s starboard battery began spouting flame and roundshot as that tall seventy sailed straight at the seventy-four-gun *Diadème*. Soon not two hundred feet of sand-colored water separated the two contestants. Every time a broadside thundered, those aboard the *Grand Turk* could see the lower sails writhe under the concussion. Deafeningly, the reports of salvoes beat out over the waters, momentarily flattening the waves.

Open-mouthed, Peter Burnham stood watching ship after ship of the two vans begin to fire, then become locked in a death struggle. Scarlet, blue, green and gold glimmered through dense, greasy-looking clouds of powder smoke.

Now the huge *Saint Esprit* came up, half of her eighty guns spouting fire.

Lying as she was to leeward of the fight, great clouds of rank, rotten-smelling smoke presently drifted down and enveloped the American brig, set her company to coughing, cursing and rubbing their eyes. For a time Peter could see nothing at all. Lord! His eardrums ached. It was as if a continuous and savage thunderstorm were raging a quarter of a mile to windward.

Once the battle smoke had drifted by, Warren shouted, "I say, Manning, what ails old Tom Graves? Why don't he bring up his rear?"

Manning laughed a little wildly. "God knows; must be something wrong, sir. Ha! There's the cause. D' you spy that pendant, sir, the striped one at the *London*'s yard?"

"Aye, and what of that?"

" 'Tis our — their signal for 'line-ahead.' Now can you read also a red flag with the white Saint Andrew's Cross flying just below, sir?"

"Aye. I see that, too. What does it signify?"

"Yon's the signal for 'close action,' " Manning yelled. "By God, old Graves has Hood nicely fixed. The admiral's flying *contradictory orders!*"

Immediately Andrew Warren's experienced eye sought the British rear division and perceived a distinct uncertainty present there.

Sir Sam Hood's division, apparently, had commenced to change course in compliance with the "close-action" signal, quite ready and eager to grapple with the nearest French ships. But now that the "line-ahead" signal had reappeared they were floundering, hesitating before returning, ever so reluctantly, to obey the flagship's orders.

Meanwhile, the French *avant-garde* and de Grasse's center were concentrating their enormous fire power on the luckless and outnumbered British van — Admiral Graves's center had not yet closed range. H.B.M.S. *Terrible* and *Ajax* must be suffering heavy damage.

Warren watched a topmast and several yards go spinning up above the smoke clouds; terrific explosions ensued. Nor were the French ships going scatheless. Gulls wheeled frantically away from sails and pieces of fabric flying high into the air as the rumbling thunder of guns set the air aquiver and presently surpassed all description. All the sea seemed peopled by ships wearing, tacking and changing sail. Away off to the rear, some British ship was badly afire and another nearly dismasted.

During the late afternoon the wind changed, forced Admiral de Grasse to wear and sail more to the southwards, with the British still trying to close in. The parallel fleets had become stretched across the ocean for a distance of over three miles and everywhere the sails of lesser men-of-war dotted the sea.

By the set of their sails Warren knew that these British ships were not going to come any closer, so when a huge seventy-four — she was the *Invincible* — came surging by at near three cables' length, he snatched up his speaking trumpet.

"Guns number two, four and six, one round! Sight on that vessel." Immediately followed the familiar screeching of blocks and tackles and the dull *thump, thump* of mallets knocking loose quoins.

Warren caught a deep breath, then shouted, "Fire!"

The three guns belched smoke and flame then recoiled savagely against their breechings. When the wind carried off blinding clouds of smoke Warren bit his lips and watched his brig's three cannonballs raise quite harmless waterspouts a good hundred yards short of the *Invincible*'s dull yellow beam.

Particularly galling was the fact that this liner did not deign to fire even a musket by way of reply.

"Cease fire!" A sharp stinging manifested itself in Andrew Warren's eyes as, sadly, his gaze sought the *Grand Turk*'s ensign. Surely, so beautiful a flag deserved a finer showing? Well, by God and by gravy, some day he'd see that flag better served by a damned sight.

Like men emerging from a trance the *Grand Turk*'s company shook off the spell induced by this overwhelming spectacle. Before a strong but diminishing stern wind the *Grand Turk* pointed her dainty bowsprit towards the Middle Ground and commenced to sail straight into a sun sinking ever lower over Chesapeake Bay.

The Circle Forms

Already anchored in Lynnhaven Bay were those numerous transports and supply ships which de Grasse had conveyed up from Saint Domingue. From them had been debarked all of the thirty-one hundred men destined to fight under the command of the Marquis of Saint-Simon.

From the *Grand Turk*'s quarterdeck next morning, Dr. Peter Burnham viewed this crowded bay with a lively interest. He noted that all the transports had buoyed their anchor ropes and were ready to cast loose and run at a moment's notice. Clearly, their masters must remain on tenterhooks until a final outcome of the fleet action was announced.

Once Andrew Warren had delivered his dispatches he ordered the *Grand Turk* thoroughly cleaned and her stores and water restocked. Would de Barras, with his eight liners and the convoy transporting that all-important siege train, manage to slip through in safety? Along with Generals Washington, Rochambeau, Lincoln, Saint-Simon and a few hundred others, Warren lived in a ferment of anxiety.

He learned, for instance, that when that doughty Provençal, de Grasse, had sailed out to meet the British he had left behind sufficient ships to maintain his blockade of the York and James rivers. Besides, it was known that H.B.M.S. *Charon*, a fifty-gun ship, and the frigate *Guadaloupe*, thirty-two cannon, and a number of smaller men-of-war were riding under the protection of Lord Cornwallis's batteries at York Town.

Engaged in preventing a British retreat across the James were the *Experiment*, fifty — taken from the enemy by d'Estaing off Rhode Island — and the *Andromaque*, also of fifty guns. Escape across the lower reaches of the York were secured by the *Vailliant*, sixty-four; *Glorieux*, seventy-four, and *Triton*, sixty-four — all third-class ships of the line.

By degrees Peter deduced that French and American forces, while awaiting de Barras's arrival, were concentrating on the south bank of the York, slowly but surely driving the besieged British in on a hamlet grandiloquently called York or York Town.

His Lordship Major General Lord Charles Cornwallis, so spies reported, was beside himself for fear that Graves had been driven away and that no reinforcements would come sailing up this broad, tea-colored river.

On the afternoon of the ninth, a despatch boat came racing in from the capes firing signal guns and flying flags informing all and sundry that de Barras's fleet had been sighted standing into the entrance. Andrew Warren, perceiving the implications of this successful passage, so far forgot himself as to dance a little jig in his cabin. Next morning the crews of all the ships at anchor lined the rails to watch the great *Duc de Bourgogne*, eighty guns, the *Neptune*, of equal power, and six lesser ships of the line come sailing in to salvoes of welcoming salutes. They were escorted by three frigates, one of them that same *Concorde* which had recaptured the *Grand Turk III* off St. Kitts.

Even greater delight was displayed ashore when transports from Rhode Island commenced to discharge the all-important — and only — train of siege artillery. These magnificent and ponderous pieces of ordnance, everyone calculated, would treat Lord Cornwallis and his troops to one of the sharpest and most unpleasant surprises recorded during this war. Not one of them dreamed that a heavy train of artillery existed in all of North America.

It came as no surprise that on being apprised of de Barras's arrival Admiral Graves had thought hard — and then had decided to return north to refit. Much could be advanced in favor of this decision since the French fleet now numbered thirty-four ships of the line against his battered eighteen — the *Terrible* having had to be burned as unseaworthy. Moreover, wild gales inevitably attendant on the equinox were due any day now.

So, very reluctantly, the British squadron headed back to New York, thereby abandoning Lord Cornwallis, General O'Hara and deservedly well-hated Colonel Banastre Tarleton to fate and their own slender resources.

Two days before de Barras added his ships to this great and still-growing fleet in Virginian waters, the *Grand Turk*'s longboat sailed up to the very entrance of the York River and there set ashore Dr. Burnham together with his precious chests of medical supplies.

Once on land, that capable physician lost no time in commandeering a house and two large hay barns which would serve well enough as a flying hospital — he preferred the more accurate description of "field hospital."

Whilst he stood superintending the removal of trash from his hospital-to-be, a baffling experience befell Peter. Some of the Agenais regiment — troops of the French West Indies contingent — were marching up the York Town road, when the aspect of a young officer on a tall black charger drew Peter's attention. When Peter lifted his hat the other smiled, turned in his saddle and returned the courtesy before riding on.

Peter stared after the white-coated figure. Gorry! Where had he seen that finely chiseled and sensitive face before? In Newport? Couldn't be; these troops hailed from Saint Domingue. Then the impossible impression offered itself that the face he recalled *was that of a girl!* Impossible. And yet, yet he knew that somewhere in the past he had viewed an almost exact duplicate of that handsome young officer's oval visage. Where? Where?

Of an infantryman delayed by a broken shoelace, he asked, "Can you give me the name of your commander — that officer on the black horse?"

The soldier made immediate reply. "Monsieur, he is Major the Marquis de Menthon. Monsieur, perhaps, has met him at Cape François?"

Peter rubbed his chin, smiled perplexedly. "That is just what puzzles me, my friend. I am sure I have never met the marquis, yet somewhere I have encountered a person who resembles him to a marked degree. Does he perhaps own a twin brother?"

The soldier stared, then shook his head. "But no, monsieur. We of the Agenais know the family well. Monsieur le marquis has two brothers, both much older than he."

"A sister?"

The Frenchman shook his head. "One has not heard that Monsieur le marquis has a sister."

Long after the infantryman had shouldered his musket to set off after his company, Peter stood where he was, mulling the puzzle over and over. By grabs, he *had* seen this marquis before — or his very spit and image. Sure enough, halfway back to the barns he remembered. So startling was the recollection that he halted and laughed right out loud. It wouldn't have seemed half so funny if he hadn't been perfectly certain of his memory. A vivid impression of the Red Lion Tavern in Boston, of that dark-haired young trollop who, on the eve of the New Year, had sung a ballad just before that famous free-for-all had commenced.

Governor's Palace

Moodily, Dr. Asa Peabody, senior surgeon and commandant of the Medical Department's general hospital in Williamsburg, Virginia, studied a sheaf of returns made by his subordinates. Plague take it, this siege was yet of a week's duration and already his slender stock of drugs, pledgets and bedclothes had run low — most discouraging of all was the lack of nurses. Frowning, Asa considered a double row of sycamore trees reluctantly shedding yellow-gold leaves beyond the broken windows of what had once been the royal governor's palace.

Sitting at his desk in a small rust-red chamber immediately to the head of the staircase, Asa Peabody thoughtfully leafed through his requisition lists. Where, where to replenish his supply of essential drugs and physicks? To canvas the various flying hospitals he knew would prove quite useless. Such crude installations near to the entrenchments were even more hard pressed for necessities because more often than not the rascally regimental surgeons in charge of them were selling precious supplies to private buyers. The best of these flying hospitals occupied barns or churches which quickly became horribly malodorous and, in his private opinion, encouraged the spread of disease.

To staff his hospital, Asa felt he had been lucky in the matter of surgeons and physicians — but where, oh where, could he find additional nurses? His face, when he bowed his weary head, felt uncommon hot and dry between his hands.

His thoughts ran on. I'd better mount up tomorrow and visit headquarters — maybe the surgeon general will listen. Yes, I can safely leave Jimmie Thatcher and John Fletcher in charge — they can handle the younger physicians perfectly well.

Through John Fletcher he'd learned nearly two months back all about the scandal attached to Lucius Devoe's marriage. Fletcher proved well informed on the matter and small wonder — he having shared quarters with Lucius at West Point.

From Fletcher he ascertained also that once Sabra had nursed her brother back to health and seen him ride off to rejoin his unit — then in Philadelphia — she'd let on that she was starting back to Boston — but had gone to New York instead. Just why Sabra Stanton should have risked crossing the Neutral Ground, of infamous repute, to reach the occupied seaport of New York, Fletcher couldn't attempt to explain.

Irritably, the senior surgeon slapped a fly from his cheek, then tilted 'way back in his chair and stared at the smoke- and water-stained ceiling. Alas, that John Fletcher knew no more of Peter Burnham's fate than did anyone else.

How long ago seemed that night when the three of them had sat on the edge of their chairs watching old Dr. Townsend write out their certificates. Eons seemed to have elapsed since he and Peter celebrated their certification at the Red Lion.

A knock at the door roused him from his abstraction. "Come in." That would be Dr. Thatcher in from his rounds.

To his surprise an orderly appeared. "Leddy to see ye, sir." He jerked his thumb down the corridor.

"A lady? What in God's name is a woman doing in here?"

The fellow shrugged apologetically. "Couldn't nowise stop her, sir. Says she's heard yer short o' help." He lowered his voice. "She's a mighty fancy piece, sir, dressed kind o' foreignlike."

"Is she French?" Asa demanded sharply.

"Mebbe so, sir. Leastways she's got some kind of furriner orderly to her kerriage."

"Very well, you may show her to my office."

A Frenchwoman, eh? Amazing though it seemed, not a few ladies of quality accompanied their men to war — an old custom in Europe, so it seemed. At the sound of light feet climbing the staircase he got to his feet and stood waiting behind his desk.

Sounded a whisper of petticoats, then, in the doorway, appeared the diminutive, black-masked figure of a lady clad in the peak of quiet elegance. The caller's Capuchin cloak and gown were of dark green silk, her bodice of yellow, richly embroidered brocade.

In a quick movement she allowed her calash bonnet to fold back, revealing sable hair puffed and pinned into symmetric ringlets. All the while she held a black velvet mask in place by the silver mouthpiece gripped between her teeth. This left her white-gloved hands free to undo the scarlet ribbon ties securing her cloak.

"Well, Dr. Peabody, and what do you think of your patient now?" his caller demanded, a trifle uncertainly as she removed the mask.

Asa gaped like any bumpkin at a strolling juggler. "Why, why you're Hilde."

"Yes, Doctor, I am Hilde Mention — or was."

"Judas Maccabeus! Why, only this minute I was thinking of you!"

Suddenly Hilde extended both hands over the desk; they stood silent and transfixed a long moment as their eyes met. "Dr. Peabody! How can I tell you how very glad I am to find you again?"

"And I you, little Hilde," he smiled gravely, offered silent reassurances as to his discretion. "How are you addressed nowadays?"

"I am Madame Hector de Lameth. My husband," Hilde flushed at the technical untruth, "serves as a captain in the Royal Deux-Ponts regiment."

"Then you are married and happily, too, I'd hazard; my sincere good wishes."

Her first hero had aged, Hilde perceived, and was thinner, but his features had gained in character. Yes, Asa Peabody looked as innately distinguished as any man in all North America.

He was pushing forward a rush-bottomed chair. "Pray seat yourself."

When she had done so she said, "Only today I heard your name spoken and learned that you were — here. I came at once, as fast as my carriage could travel over from the tavern."

"Then you are — er quartered here in Williamsburg."

"Yes. I have accommodations at the Raleigh."

While the sun drew longer and longer shadows from the sycamores shading the former royal governor's palace, Hilde described quite frankly, all that had happened since she had run pell-mell out of Mrs. Southeby's house.

" — And so," she concluded smiling softly, "I am come to discharge my debt to you in offering my services and those of my companion — a young lady who shares my rooms at the Raleigh." Hilde smoothed her skirt. "For reasons best known to herself, my friend calls herself Susan Stevens, but I am not sure that really is her name because another is painted in the lid of her portmanteau. Although I have not known Susan long, she is most anxious to be of service to our army; morever, she has what I lack — experience in attending the sick and wounded. You will allow us to assist as best we may?"

"On one condition." Asa's manner became serious. "You shall attend only the wounded — not the sick."

"It shall be as you say," came her quiet assent. "When shall we appear?"

"At seven of tomorrow morning. It is then we commence washing the patients and changing their dressings," he told her then smiled at her modish costume. "Best wear your plainest gowns, both in your interest and that of my patients. Wouldn't do to rouse their — er — enthusiasm too quickly."

Hilde arose and picked up her mask. "I shall bring what I can by way of dressings and delicacies."

"By the bye," Asa inquired curiously, "what was the name in the lid of Susan Stevens's trunk?"

"Sabra Stanton from Boston. I wonder if you have ever heard the name up there?"

York Town Besieged: The Second Parallel

Since the first of October when the siege had commenced, the French batteries hardly ever had been completely silent. And now, emitting deep-throated bellows, the siege guns from Newport were hurling heavy cannonballs at the enemy lines or into the crumbling village beyond. Time and again, clouds of lazily climbing bluish wood smoke betrayed the fact that another of the sixty or seventy houses comprising York Town had taken fire.

Happily, each passing day brought an increased mutual respect among the allies. The Americans could not wonder enough at the magnificent skill and profound knowledge evinced by the French sappers and artillerists. On the other hand, the French greatly admired the remarkable ability of their allies with small arms. The Americans could, and did, display amazing marksmanship. They were also complimentary concerning works planned by old von Steuben and constructed by eager American troops who certainly knew a lot more about the handling of a spade than about laying a siege piece.

To Major Joshua Stanton's envious eyes those great cannon of the siege train represented the ultimate, nay, the *ne plus ultra* in ordnance. Lovingly the New Englander's eyes dwelt on these magnificent, perfectly proportioned pieces, each one of which was engraved near its breech with the lily coat-of-arms of France and the personal cipher of Louis XVI. What fine, sturdy carriages, what solid wheels skillfully tired in massive iron bands; they even had cleats welded across their treads to prevent undue recoil.

Jehosophat! What a mort of powder was required to charge one of these black-throated monsters which, slowly but surely, were knocking the British parapets, bastions and salients to bits. Fortunately, the French never seemed to be afflicted with that shortage of powder which throughout this war had proved the bane of General Knox's corps of artillery.

By a considerable margin these siege guns outranged the heaviest cannon mounted on the British works, mostly fetched ashore from H.B.M.S. *Charon*. Long since she had been nearly stripped of her ordnance to reinforce Lord Cornwallis's light fieldpieces.

His envy vying with his genuine admiration, Major Stanton walked towards his own batteries. Most of the guns they fired also were of French manufacture; a few of these pieces had been dragged all the way down from that fort which M. de Vauban had designed at Ticonderoga — hundreds of miles nearer Canada.

His American gun crews, Joshua noted, invariably seemed more intent on the business in hand. To these bronzed, inelegant men, each shot appeared as a personal affair. Whether they hit or missed was, in their way of thinking, a matter of life and death.

All the same they were ready to raise a cheer for General Washington whenever they scored a prettily placed salvo. Unlike the French, the American artillerymen stood around their piece any which way; each one trying to learn as much as he could about the fine points of sighting, loading and firing. These hickory-brown men drank no wine, only squirted tobacco juice upon the dusty ground. When they got hot they plunged their heads into the same wooden water buckets used for sponging the bore after every shot.

Captain Rich, a cheery fellow from the eastern shore of Maryland, raised his hat when he noticed Major Stanton advancing, then, glancing abruptly to his left, pointed to a glittering group entering the battery from its rear. "Three cheers fer General Knox!"

At General Knox's approach Joshua Stanton drew himself up straight and saluted as smartly as his injured arm would permit. Red-faced, potbellied old von Steuben quite unexpectedly nodded — he wasn't much for recognizing mere field officers.

"*Ach!* So you are back, Major Stanton," he grunted, digging at the ground with a gold-headed walking stick. "Goot. You are just in time for Lord Cornwallis's country dance."

This battery being from his own battalion, Stanton hoped that these rough-and-ready artillerymen would behave. They were deplorably prone to make flatulent noises, take mincing steps and kiss hands to one another whenever even the highest-ranking officers of the Auxilliary Forces appeared. Perhaps these grimy and unshaven gunners were too tired to misbehave, but for a miracle they stood to attention, well-muscled brown torsos agleam with sweat and their greasy hair dangling any which way about their ears.

Colonel de Villefranche drew General Knox aside and commented interestedly upon the fact that these Americans, in order to diminish the recoil of their pieces, had built a counterslope back of their gun carriages. Further, they had lashed bags of sand to the trail of each piece.

"You taught them this, Your Excellency?" Villefranche demanded of von Steuben.

The German puffed out his cheeks, laughed a little. "*Nein, mon Général*, always these monkeys think up new tricks. *Ja*. After four years, I haff come to egpect it. Now let us see vot your poys can do, Captain Pitman."

Stanton ran forward when, without looking, von Steuben called his name. The old Prussian had climbed up onto the embrasure and, through his telescope supported on the end of a fascine, was studying the *Charon* as she lay, perfectly mirrored by the placid waters of the York.

"Dot iss extreme range," he grunted. "Tell your poys I send them vun case of Rhine *wein* if they hit dot sheep in less than six shots."

Everyone present turned to watch two men on gun number one lower a pair of tongs slung from a bar into that blinding glow generated by the well-bellowsed charcoal fire. So intense was the heat that these gunners had to make three tries before the claws of their bar-tongs succeeded in closing upon a glowing cannonball. The sphere gave off bright little sparks — it was a truly impressive projectile weighing all of twenty pounds.

The other gun crews stood watching attentively. In a moment would come their turn and they intended to profit by any advantages or mistakes committed by their predecessors.

Von Steuben leaned hard on his tall walking stick, glared angrily around. "Captain Pitman! Vhere iss your cup?"

Joshua Stanton cursed silently. Of course, something would have to go wrong! There wasn't any cup ready to hand. Everything therefore was held up — the cup being that concave metal rammer especially designed to ease a glowing projectile out of the tongs and into the bore.

At this point, veterans among the witnesses unobtrusively sought what shelter offered itself. That wet wad, they knew, would cool the cannon and sudden heat as from a red-hot iron ball had, in the past, been known to split a defective barrel upon discharge and send murderous iron shards hissing in all directions.

"Fetch a cup, you dunderheads!" roared Captain Pitman. "There's one in the magazine."

To which the gunners added, turning aside streaming scarlet faces. "Stir your arses, for Christ's sake! We're fryin' with this damn' thing."

Once the cup was brought up, they heaved the glowing ball to the lip of the bore and one of the crew brought his brass cup beneath the projectile. At the command of "Ease," the tong men lowered their burden into the waiting receptacle.

When the red-hot sphere went rolling down the bore a great plume of steam gushed out and a sharp hissing noise resulted as the glowing iron came in contact with that sodden wad. At almost the same instant, a crewman held out his linstock and touched his match to the priming. Instantly, a thin jet of smoke spurted vertically from the touchhole, the cannon emitted a deafening report and vomited a huge cloud of gray-white smoke while, under the recoil, its ponderous carriage backed half-way up the earthen ramp.

From their embrasure, General Knox and his guests followed the projectile's flight high, higher into the sky, saw it attain the zenith of its parabola and then rush earthwards. Raising a brief cloud of steam, it plunged into the York River some fifty yards short of the anchored man-of-war. They watched the *Charon*'s deck teem into sudden activity; like ants in a disturbed hill, the tiny black figures of her crew rushed hither and yon.

When the number two gun took its turn, Captain Pitman, Indianlike features tense, ordered the angle of elevation increased. This time the glowing ball carried over the *Charon*'s tops, but plunged into one of the transports. Very quickly flames broke out on the unlucky vessel's forecastle and sent tendrils of blue-gray smoke spiraling into a nearly windless sky.

The battery just missed sampling General von Steuben's Rhine wine, for not until their ninth shot did the gunners plump a red-hot ball smack through the *Charon*'s gun deck. They cheered all the same and now that the range had been determined all four pieces commenced, at will, an increasingly accurate cannonade.

By twilight, H.B.M.S. *Charon* presented a sight to remember as, ablaze from stem to stern, she swung to her moorings with flames soaring high above her tops and creeping out along her yards in brilliant parallels.

When above nine thousand human beings find themselves contained within an area some twelve hundred yards long by five hundred yards across, together with their animals, supplies, weapons and vehicles, not much vacant space is left. Crowded within a perimeter described by ten redoubts and sixteen batteries, lay seven thousand two hundred fifty-seven officers and men of the regular British establishment, eight hundred forty seamen, several hundred refugee slaves — their lot especially was pitiable — and half a thousand horses.

Necessarily, what one person or group of persons did immediately affected their neighbors and in general irritated them, no matter how worthy or innocent the act might be.

On the afternoon of the eleventh of October, Dr. Lucius Devoe found himself in an especially foul humor. Every one of the few houses remaining more or less intact in York Town was already jampacked with sick and wounded and the sick lists were growing steadily longer.

It was terrible how this smallpox was spreading. Soldiers of half a dozen famous regiments lay dying in backyards on piles of the autumn leaves. These poor devils had only their greatcoats with which to shelter themselves from the still broiling sun of midday and the sharp chills of night. Down on the riverbank, where the soil was sandy and digging easy, long trenches had been opened. Into these the dead were tumbled twice a day in the most perfunctory manner.

Once shells from the besieging French and American batteries had begun to range York Town itself, conditions had worsened rapidly, and continually one encountered nightmarish scenes. Men killed by bursting shells lay unburied for days at a time, until, bloated and hideous, they created such an intolerable stench that sullen Negroes, driven at the bayonet point by brutal German mercenaries out of the Seyboldt and Anspach regiments, gingerly passed loops of ropes about the dead men's ankles and with the aid of starving horses dragged them down to the burial pits.

Largely unlisted, the dead sank into a common grave. Side by side, stalwart veterans from the élite First and Second Life Guards lay among raw replacements for the Eighteenth of the Line; men of Fraser's Eighty-second and McDonald's Seventy-sixth Highlanders lay with their campaign-stained tartans sprawled across the blue-clad corpses of German mercenaries or the green tunics of some Loyalist who had paid his last bitter tribute to his king. Occasionally the bodies of seamen, landed from the sunken *Charon*, were added to this mephitic pile of human debris.

"They're killing o' our pore starving 'orses," grunted a patient in the uniform of Tarleton's dragoons. "They're luckier than us. At least they shoots those pore creatures and puts them out o' their misery."

"Cheer up, chum," said another. "This business carn't last much longer. We're done for."

"Aye! 'E bloody rebels and the Dancing Masters 'ave done us in this time."

But another said, "Nah, we'll 'ang on. Mark my words, any day now old 'Arry Clinton, 'Ood and Graves will come asailing up this bleeding river and we'll hand the Froggies another drubbing."

At length Lucius finished operating and swayed out into the fresh morning sunlight and away from the reek of that dead horse. At a pump in the backyard he washed a measure of the dried blood and serum from his face and arms. Jupiter! Sleep he must have, and soon. His hands were shaking as if palsied.

He wandered over to a small orchard and leaned against a tree in the shade. Never had exhaustion so nearly conquered him. His eyes ached and burned like fury, and as he stretched out on the ground the sound of ax blows delivered by sappers working to repair a stricken battery sounded maddeningly loud.

He closed his eyes. What would Emma be doing now? She must be getting very large with his baby — or was it his? Stronger than ever, doubt rankled in his mind. A smart girl, Emma, and an exquisitely passionate bed companion to boot. How long before his arms once more could clasp her vibrant warm smoothness?

Certainly Emma must have been pleased to learn about his appointment as surgeon-in-chief to Lord Cornwallis's forces in Virginia. Yes, sir. If British arms prevailed, despite this impending disaster, he could count on a fat appointment from the royal governor. Emma had reasoned it all out extremely well. Was she not even now supplying food for the patriot armies at very low cost?

An ant crawled onto his chin, and absently he brushed it away. Then an unhappy thought came to plague him. How had Sabra weathered the dual blow he'd dealt her? Never had he been quite able to forgive himself for his defection, and the last he'd heard Joshua was lying at death's door. Very probably he had died, long since. Who'd have thought he'd come out so well in that awful duel?

Well, despite the misadventure at West Point, he was again forging steadily to the top. Certainly, he had outdistanced both Peter Burnham and that big, trusting clod of an Asa Peabody.

General Hospital

The old cart's long ungreased axles screeched loud as battling tomcats, but their plaint sounded in Asa Peabody's ears as sweet music. He still couldn't get over having secured so many supplies from the troops just in from Newport. Allowing his body to sway to the cart's lurching progress, Asa grinned from ear to ear.

At first he simply couldn't credit his eyesight, but there indeed was Peter Burnham, all-fired dignified and polite, conducting a party of French officers about the flying hospital he'd set up amid a grove of towering sweetgum trees.

At first they'd stood there like a couple of dolts, simply gaping on each other, then had followed a joyous beating of each other's shoulder blades and wringing of hands. When they'd loosed a torrent of questions, the amused gentlemen of General Viomesnil's staff had turned tactfully aside to inspect a ward they had already seen.

How utterly amazing, how wonderful to find big, red-headed Peter again! Imagine his being married to a lovely Danish noblewoman. The only sobering element about their reunion was the sight of Peter's cruelly scarred left hand, but there'd been no time then to inquire about how he'd come by such an injury.

Dear old Peter! They had agreed to dine together as soon as one or the other was freed of the press of duty.

The prospect of greeting Hilde de Lameth was definitely cheering. That diminutive young woman sparkled through the dark wards like a bright ray of sunlight and displayed a strength surprising in so fragile a figure.

"I hope, sir, you'll not object to my quitting my duties a little early tonight?" she asked Asa when he came upon her sponging the feverish forehead of an old soldier. Her fringed eyelids dropped. "You see, my husband is riding over to call on me."

"Naturally not," was Asa's instant reply. "I trust to be honored in meeting so fortunate a gentleman."

In company with Dr. Fletcher, he made a round of the sick wards, then finally climbed from an octagonal hallway up to his own little office situated by the head of a sadly scarred and gritty staircase. To his vast astonishment Sabra Stanton was waiting just outside the door.

"May I — see you, Doctor?" she demanded in a low voice. "I have waited some time to find sufficient courage to address you."

Puzzled and intensely excited, Asa closed the door behind them, shut out the hospital noises. He bowed. "I had hoped you would call sooner Mistress Stevens, or should I say Mistress Stanton?"

His heart began drumming like a partridge's wings when at last he faced her squarely, regarded the well-remembered, modest loveliness of Sabra's features. Yes, she *was* beautiful in a newly grave and mature way, despite heated features, disordered hair and work-stained apron.

Sabra's chestnut head averted itself to gaze out of the window. "I came to warn you that Madame de Lameth's devotion to her duties quite exceeds her strength. On our way back to the inn last evening she practically swooned. Please, Doctor, forbid her to return here for a few days. I — I have met a farmer's wife — she has agreed to assist me in the wards. We can manage very well until Hilde recruits her strength."

Chevalier Pierre Louis Marie Phillipe de Menthon, major of the Agenais regiment, drew rein before the long, white clapboard façade of the Raleigh Tavern.

"To you, *mon ami*, I will confess," said he to his companion, Captain de Berthelun of the Gatinais regiment, "that I have welcomed this opportunity to visit the village of Williamsburg."

"Indeed?" De Berthelun shifted in his saddle and allowed himself to appear politely intrigued.

"Since we have landed here in Virginie a number of persons have mentioned the presence here of a young woman who is reported married —" just a trifle he emphasized the word — "to young de Lameth — you know of the family, of course." De Menthon kicked his right foot free of the stirrup preparatory to dismounting. *"Pardieu!* No less than five officers of the Deux-Ponts, that amiable red-haired American surgeon, and two American officers have observed of an incredible resemblance between this lady and myself."

"To be so closely resembled must give one an uncanny feeling, monsieur," de Berthelun smiled, guiding his charger over to the inn's mounting block, "especially when your counterpart wears petticoats."

Once his orderly had come trotting up to take charge of the horses, de Menthon, very slim and graceful, brushed dust from a perfectly fitting white uniform faced in rose. The orderly bent, wiped more dust from the Marquis de Menthon's tall black leather boots. "The spurs, too, you idiot. Go around to the innyard and wait."

"Oui, mon Commandant."

"Let us hope that we are fortunate enough to find the lady at home," de Menthon smiled, straightened his stock and, followed by his companion, entered the famous old tavern. They were exploring the Apollo Room in search of the publican when the tinkle of an overturned glass a few tables distant drew de Menthon's attention to a large, black-clad individual — a physician by his dress. As if on a phantom, this broad-featured medical man stared at him. No less startled of aspect was his companion, evidently a fellow physician.

"My God! Look, Thatcher! *Look there!* Am I deluded?" Asa Peabody passed a hand before his eyes. For a moment he thought Hilde was masquerading, perpetrating some mad prank, but as quickly realized that this undoubtedly was a man.

"Your pardon, sir," he apologized as the marquis drew near. "Forgive my staring so, but — "

De Menthon smiled. "Ze resemblance she strikes you, too?" he inquired.

"It's, it's incredible," Thatcher agreed wiping spilt coffee from his waistcoat. " 'Pon my word, sir, save in identical twins, I wouldn't have dreamed so precise a resemblance possible." His eyes narrowed. "You and Hilde ain't twins, are you?"

"Hilde?" De Menthon's manner remained unruffled. "I know no lady of zat name. You permit zat I present myself, ze Marquis de Menthon; and ze Captaine de Berthelun."

With the names "Mention" and "de Menthon" resounding in his brain, Asa pushed forward a pair of chairs and would have given an order, but the marquis clapped his hands for the drawer. "Ez zere per'aps cognac?"

"Afraid not, sir," Thatcher supplied. "British cleaned the cellar out last winter. But our host can serve passable rum."

De Menthon's silver epaulettes rose in a resigned shrug. *"Ron! Ron!* Always ze rum. On Saint Domingue we almost drowned in it, eh Louis? If ever again one be'olds *la belle France* nevaire will one taste a drop of ze stuff."

Captain de Berthelun produced an elaborate tortoise-shell snuffbox, offered it.

De Menthon spoke carefully. *Bigre!* here was a mystery of the first rank. "It would appear, *messieurs les médicins,* zat you both are — how you say it? — friendly with zis Madame de Lameth?"

A host of conflicting impulses made a battlefield of Asa's mind. Of one thing he was sure; under no circumstances was he prepared to reveal the whole sum of his knowledge concerning the past of Hilde Mention.

Thatcher's craggy features contracted. "She is really Dr. Peabody's old friend."

"Ah, eendeed?" Silver buttons winked to the Marquis' half-bow. "My felicitations. Thees *mystère* ees of ze most eenterest to me. You met — ?"

"In Boston. As Mistress Hilde Mention she was a patient of mine. I attended her for several days."

Up flew the Marquis's slender black brows in an expression uncannily reminiscent of Hilde. " 'Men-shun'? *Comment* — 'ow did she spell her name?"

Asa told him while de Menthon wrinkled thin nostrils over a rum and water brought by a perspiring Negro.

"Since then she has become Madame de Lameth." A look flashed between the American and the Frenchmen — a look which confirmed a mutual understanding of Hilde's true status. Asa went on, "Here, she has been assisting at my hospital — too vigorously, I fear."

"*Hélas.* She 'as spoken possibly of 'er origins?"

"Very little. Hilde was orphaned at a very early age — by a shipwreck off Canada, I believe."

" 'Ow, mos' *romantique.*" The Marquis sighed. "One is puzzled, very puzzled. Between ze names 'Menthon' and 'Mention' one perceives ze closest similarity, no? And yet — one 'as no seestairs, but several *cousines* — all of whom one knows. Um, per'aps *grandpère* — " He broke off, smiled quickly. "Per'aps, you weel do me ze *honneur* to present — ?"

"Certainly, major. It'll be a pleasure. I'm just as mystified about your resemblance as anyone." Asa accepted a pinch of de Berthelun's snuff. "We are waiting to see Madame de Lameth ourselves," he vouchsafed. "Unfortunately, she and her husband have gone out to take the air. They should return soon."

"One 'opes so. Soon we mus' return to ze siege and eet ees a long ride back to York Town, no?"

More drinks were brought as conversation shifted to the present campaign. All four of them felt convinced that the enemy soon must surrender. Warmed by the rum, Captain de Berthelun hinted that an attack soon would be made on those two redoubts which secured the British left.

All too soon, church bells of the town sounded nine sonorous notes.

"*Peste!*" de Menthon growled. "What a meesfortune." He checked the time against his own handsome gold chronometer and nodded to his companion. *"Hélas,* we mus' return to our duties." He arose. "Be assured, *monsieur le médicin,* one will return at ze first opportunity. If you please, my compliments to ze lady and to my old friend, Monsieur de Lameth."

Asa, too, was tired of waiting. Once he and Thatcher had watched the Frenchmen ride off, he penned a brief note of instructions. Hilde was to repose herself and to avoid the hospital for forty-eight hours at the very least. Mistress Stevens had undertaken to see that all duties would be performed in her absence.

Evening Star

Warm and clean-smelling air drifted through that little woods where Hilde lay, weary but irrepressibly content, with her cheek pressing against Hector de Lameth's tunic. It being unbuttoned, she could feel the warmth of his skin through the fine lawn of his ruffled shirt.

"My darling, I can hear the beating of your dear heart," she murmured drowsily.

"Do you know what it is saying?" His finger skewered one of the curls lying across her partially bared shoulder. "No? Well then, it repeats over and over again, 'I love you, I adore you; I love you, I adore you!' and so it will until the end of my days."

"That is a great deal for one heart to say."

His fingers brushed her cheek, found it unusually hot. *"Mon ange,* are you quite well?"

"But, of course, Hector, why not? I am well — and, oh, so very content now that you are by me."

"At supper tonight I thought your eyes very bright and your color higher than usual."

" 'Twas caused by the prospect of meeting my lover after four endless days of separation."

"Bon." De Lameth settled back against the bole of a huge sycamore, vastly comfortable because his cloak lay folded beneath his shoulders.

"Ma foi! It grows so late. Look, do you see that evening star? Why it shone above these branches when we came; now it is ready to set."

"Which star?"

"That huge pure white one," he explained gently and indicated it. "See, like none of her fellows, she displays just a touch of blue. Such a gay and pure star reminds me of you, my sweet little nightingale."

Hector is worried, Hilde told herself. He never makes conversation like this unless he has concerns. She wriggled up into a sitting position. "Hector, please to look in my eyes. There will be an attack — very soon?"

Sharp profile picked out by the afterglow, Hector watched the evening

[735]

star sink towards the skyline. Said he ever so tenderly, "Even the longest and dullest of campaigns end in a few battles."

"Then there will be one tomorrow?"

Hector de Lameth suddenly swept her back into his arms and kissed her. "You guess well," he admitted. "But remember, *chérie*, the storming of a redoubt is not like delivering charge *à la baïonnette* across an open field. *Mais, non.* Besides, our little business will be attended to under cover of darkness."

Hilde pleaded. "Hold me tighter, my hero, then tell me more of France."

Obediently, the young officer spoke on and on. He dwelt on their future. Should Papa refuse his consent to a marriage they would return to America. True, he had not yet come to love America as well as *la patrie*, but still it was a wonderful land. So much lay waiting to be accomplished here.

"Oh, look, Hector," Hilde cried suddenly. "My star! It is ready to disappear."

Again he kissed her fondly. "As so am I. Comte Guillaume will be furious over my tardy return. Come, my lovely one — tidy yourself. We must return to the inn."

Hilde's arms swept out to clasp his neck and almost desperately, she pressed herself to him. "In trying to forget this assault of tomorrow, I shall dwell upon this most perfect of afternoons and evenings," she whispered. Her laugh was a little choked when Hector, rising, swept her off her feet and carried her a few steps on the way back to Williamsburg.

Bayonets in the Dark

Biting his knuckles in mingled envy and anxiety, Major Joshua Stanton watched, by the starlight, two dense columns of infantry, the one dark, the other light, form upon a level field just to the rear of the first parallel. Because of shell holes, half-dug trenches and debris, they were experiencing a little difficulty in ordering their files, but presently both columns moved off in nearly perfect silence.

The Americans, thanks to their dark-blue uniforms, quickly became lost amid the gloom. Yonder went picked troops: two full regiments of the Maryland and Pennsylvania lines. For a long time Joshua would remember dark and handsome Lieutenant Colonel Alexander Hamilton listening attentively to the last-minute instructions of Major General de Lafayette.

Sabra's brother was following the progress of that long column of French troops now filing off to the left, towards redoubt number nine. Picked grenadiers of the famous Gatinais followed hard after a detachment of sappers and axmen. Fresh laurels for the colors of this ancient regiment — it had been organized during the reign of Henri IV — lay within reach. Most impatient for action were the stalwart Provençals and Auvergnats of the Royal Deux-Ponts who were no less anxious to come to grips and to acquit themselves well under the eye of their colonel, Comte Guillaume de Deux-Ponts.

Joshua experienced a familiar constriction of his diaphragm; he had experienced such a sensation before, at Saratoga and again at White Plains. The staff stood conversing quietly on a little knoll commanding the dimly seen parapets of the two threatened redoubts. Beyond could be heard the occasional *clank* of musket barrels colliding and the trampling noises caused by nearly six hundred men. General Washington himself peered intently after the two columns with fingers drumming on gloves tucked into his belt. Knox, Joshua knew, was keeping his attention to the left where lay that battery which would fire a signal for the attack to commence.

Occasional clouds briefly obscured the stars, but luckily, what breeze there was blew from over the York and redoubt number ten at the extreme left of the British line.

The commander-in-chief's deep voice inquired, "Major Tilghman, what o'clock have you?"

"It lacks but ten minutes of eight, Your Excellency."

"How the time drags at moments like these," Washington observed.

A puff of the river breeze brought once more a faint sound of clinking accouterments and the trampling of feet. Now both columns had become lost in the darkness.

Under this damp wind Joshua's crippled shoulder began to ache. Minutes dragged by. Would the British be surprised?

At the head of the second battalion of the Maryland troops Major Thomas Offutt, swinging along with bared sword ready in hand, felt his breath come faster. He reckoned this was very like putting a fast, but green young hunter at a high and very solid post and rail fence.

To the men about him, Offutt whispered, "We have no axmen to cut us a path and must get over those palisadoes any way we can. You'd better hoist one another over the first obstacles."

A concerted sigh of relief arose when the first of the signal bombs sailed high up into the sky. Its fuse had been cut so short that the projectile burst — creating a brief but dazzling golden-red blossom in the night sky — when at the zenith of its trajectory. By its brief red glare Offutt could see his men's faces, all shadowy eyes and stiff, motionless mouths. Briefly their shadows became sketched on the trampled earth, then the report came, loud as a giant's handclap. Another bomb hissed upwards followed by yet another.

Raising a mighty yell the whole dark column surged up a slight incline, bayonet points swinging in quick arcs to their stride.

Surprisingly, from above them came no sound until a startled voice shouted, "*Wer da?*"

[737]

"Hurray fer America!" "Hurray fer Washin'ton!" The infantry at Offutt's heels were just yelling, crying nothing intelligible.

"Come on! Come on, you bastards." Shrieks, screams and panted curses beat through the smoke clouds. For the moment Major Offutt could see absolutely nothing and to keep himself from becoming spiked on a friendly bayonet thought it wise to shout, "This way, Maryland, this way."

Allied batteries meanwhile were raining death and destruction on the British supporting areas, as fast as their clumsy guns could be loaded and laid.

Almost before Offutt realized it, he and a knot of his men stood swaying on the parapet. So far as he could tell not a single American had discharged his musket, but, like a sleet of steel, their bayonets now were slanting downwards.

Through choking, confusing smoke, Offutt glimpsed a number of dark figures running pell-mell across the redoubt, obviously in hurried retreat.

"Forward! They're running!"

Followed a sound of steel striking wood, grunts, screams, a few more shots, then an English voice called out, "Quarter! Quarter! For God's sake grant us quarter."

Among the foremost of his men Captain the Chevalier de Lameth crouched in the fosse before redoubt number line cursing that incredible deliberation with which the sappers were hewing down the palisadoes just ahead. With each passing minute, the British and German fire was increasing in effectiveness. Already dreadful screams and groans were rising on all sides; every so often some grenadier would collapse, kicking blindly, uselessly like a beetle impaled upon a pin.

Hector sensed, rather than saw, indecision seize the men of his company. *"En avant! Pour Dieu et Saint Louis!"* he screamed, just as had his forebears at Crécy and Agincourt.

An outstretched leg tripped him and, sobbing for breath, Hector was just recovering his feet when something like a hot branding iron was laid across his left thigh. All the same he limped on, sword held high and yelling encouragements. Ha! Now more and more white figures had gained the parapet and were thrusting downwards at a series of white cross-belts. The Gatinais must be over the opposite parapet. Hector judged so by the changed pitch of their cries.

All at once Hector de Lameth found himself on the parapet and looking down onto a little lake of struggling men and flashing weapons. A tall British grenadier jumped up onto the berm snarling, " 'Ere's for yer, ye bloody Dancing Master."

De Lameth evaded a savage thrust by the fellow's bayonet, leveled his sword and sank it deep into the grenadier's throat. Another enemy, however, had clubbed his musket and with terrible effectiveness swung it against the Chevalier de Lameth's side.

[738]

Amid a great blaze of light, and a torrent of whirling sparks, Hector de Lameth collapsed, fell miles backwards into an unbroken blackness.

The British commander's failure to order a counterattack, coupled with the perfection of the surprise, left many beds vacant in the flying-hospital that were expected to have been filled. Not even the most optimistic of the allied tacticians had anticipated such light casualties — less than a hundred and fifty injured was indeed a cheap price for so valuable a gain. In fact, there was so little to do that Peter Burnham found himself feeling resentful and foolish at having left his own hospital in which lay the sick and disabled of de Barras's fleet.

Peter was attempting to determine the nature of one young captain's injuries when Colonel Dubois came up.

"Ah. He is the tough one, this Chevalier de Lameth. Imagine it! He has suffered a musketball passing through the left thigh and a shallow sword slash of the right shoulder."

Gazing down at this patient resting on the sheets arranged across a deep pile of straw, Peter thought he noted a fleck of blood or two on the young fellow's unshaven chin.

"It is a pretty flower that I grow, no?" wheezed de Lameth and tried to laugh, but ended by coughing instead. A faint, rose-colored spray burst from his lips and despite everything he grimaced in agony.

"It hurts you to breathe, does it not?"

Hector de Lameth's pallid and sweat-spangled features contracted. "Most damnably," he admitted.

The sky streamed smoke and the reverberations of the guns were deafening when Peter led Asa into the officers' ward.

"Ah, Captain de Lameth. Glad to find you looking so well." Asa tried hard to appear casual.

"Ah, Pea-bodee, *mon ami*." A faint smile curved the wounded officer's lavender-tinted lips. Asa felt a great wrench at his heart; this hollow-cheeked, sunken-eyed wretch little resembled that gay young officer who only a few nights before at the Raleigh had led the guests in songs and dancing.

That the patient was delighted to behold Asa's familiar face was inescapable.

After a little, Peter took Asa aside and only then gave a detailed description of de Lameth's condition.

"You expect me to operate, Peter?"

"I think you will. You possess the skill requisite to meet such a problem. I — " he held up his crippled left hand, smiled sadly. "I, well, I haven't."

Asa put down his saddlebags, noticed that a house door lay supporting a thin mat upon a pair of saw horses. Um. So he was expected to operate was he? Well, Peter at least had selected a favorable hour of the day; at

[739]

two of the afternoon the sun was still high and its light, striking through the canvas, was strong yet diffused.

The tricorned and powdered head of a sergeant appeared at the flap.

"*Vous êtes prêt, monsieur?*"

Peter nodded, and a moment later Hector de Lameth's litter was brought in. Surgeon Colonel Dubois followed a few paces in its rear. Hector de Lameth lay very white, his jet eyes sunk deep into their sockets.

"*Alors,*" he whispered, managing the faintest imaginable smile. "You are about to deliver a fresh bayonet charge?" His hand, veined in blue and pallid beneath the sunburn that lent it a yellowish tinge, beckoned Asa. "And how goes it with my lady — my wife?"

"Splendidly. She is more beautiful than ever."

Asa was lying in his teeth and he knew it. Hilde had not returned to the hospital after her two-day vacation and Sabra Stanton reported her to be feverish to the point of lightheadedness. Her symptoms, Asa thought, suggested a touch of la grippe.

"Please to proceed, messieurs — I — fear I — " his eyelids sagged closed. "I am most impolite, but one is a trifle fatigued."

Quickly, Peter exposed de Lameth's chest and Asa's eyes widened when he noted the extent of that mottled, mulberry-hued discoloration.

Asa, stripped to breeches and shirt, mopped the sweat from his brow before bending low over de Lameth's inert figure. "You must understand, monsieur, that — well an operation of this gravity is not always successful. Have I your permission to proceed?"

The young officer spoke without opening his eyes. "There is but one condition."

"And that is?"

"Should you fail — you will convey to madame — my wife," he emphasized the title, "that my last thoughts were of her and of the great love she so generously gave to me."

At length Asa made an incision and guided the forceps into it, gripped the splinter and worked it free, using immense patience and delicacy.

When at length Asa had tied the last of the bandages and straightened, Dubois offered his hand. "My most sincere compliment on your art. One would not have deemed it possible to withdraw such a large splinter without rupturing the lung case."

Peter beamed. "You're a shining wonder, Asa. Are there any further instructions?"

"Only that the patient be kept warm, and if he becomes demented a watch be kept to assure the position of his bandage. Though I'd admire to linger, I fear I must leave at once," he apologized. "It would seem that a storm is brewing."

He was quite right. Towards sundown, a shrieking, howling gale blew out of the southwest; a storm so violent that great trees went crashing

[740]

down, small ships were driven ashore, and crews of the men-of-war down-stream were set to putting out extra anchors.

All night long the wind raged and, in so doing, thwarted Lord Corn-wallis's last and most desperate attempt to break out of the trap into which he had thrust himself. Displaying a surprising if belated energy and hardi-hood, the unhappy earl under cover of darkness attempted to ferry his doomed command across to Gloucester Point. From there he might have attempted a long, long retreat northwards. As it was, the river boiled like a stew pot and the carefully collected small boats were either sunk or driven ashore under the lashing of the wind.

General O'Hara and the Sword

The siege guns and field artillery had not fired in near two full days; even so, after nearly three weeks of almost incessant bombardment neither be-siegers nor besieged could quite accustom themselves to this sudden silence. For a second time during this war — and, curiously enough, on the anniversary of Burgoyne's capitulation at Saratoga — a British field army had asked permission to surrender its colors and to lay down its arms.

Those officers and men who, during six long years, had fought King George III's courageous and well-disciplined soldiers had to pinch them-selves to realize that at last, at long last, the victory was theirs. Those Massachusetts soldiers who had first thrown their sights on a redcoat in the spring of 1775 — there were precious few of them left — remained espe-cially thoughtful. Through their minds surged half-forgotten and confused recollections covering not only half a hundred raids, skirmishes and bat-tles, but even more poignant memories of chill and miserable retreats.

Virginians, Pennsylvanians, Marylanders, and New Yorkers shared their scanty liquor supply and went round with fixed grins decorating their bronzed features. This time the news seemed just too good to be true.

To think that Lord Charles Cornwallis, that merciless scourge of the Southern states, must soon surrender his sword. The news soon got about that in the Articles of Capitulation there was a specification that Corn-wallis must hand his sword to that same General Benjamin Lincoln — re-cently exchanged — who had been forced, under humiliating conditions, to surrender his own sidearms last year in Charles Town.

Around noon of October the nineteenth, 1781, elements of the victor-ious armies commenced to move from their positions in order to line a two-mile route leading out from York Town to the field to surrender. Lazy dust clouds arose and settled on the marching men who soon com-menced to sweat.

Rank on rank, regiment on regiment, wearing new or freshly cleaned uniforms and with accouterments newly burnished, the French maneuvered to line the left-hand side of this road leading from the enemy positions. The Americans, garbed in their usual weird assortment of uniforms, formed up along the right. Some of their units — the Virginia militia in particular — wore no uniform at all, only cross-belts secured over a second-best suit of civilian clothes.

Mighty picturesque, on the other hand, were companies of mountain men, whose faces were burned to a hue almost identical with that of their fringed buckskin hunting shirts. These sinewy fellows carried long rifles and wore scalping knives or war hatchets at their belts. Once the order "stand easy" was given, everybody began to talk sixty to the minute and to crane his neck in the direction of York Town.

Very near to the field of surrender, but not adjacent to it, rode General George Washington and a whole company of general officers. Smiling, chaffing one another, they sat their horses, dusted their coats and reset their stocks.

Between the commander-in-chief and the town were posted that backbone of America's endeavor — the Continental regiments of the Line. In firm, erect ranks these regulars stood just as choleric old von Steuben had taught them, with buttons bright and their blue and buff uniforms clean, though stained through hard campaigning.

At irregular intervals were posted regimental standard bearers, together with their guards. Lazily, these varicolored banners stirred in a cool wind blowing up the river from Chesapeake Bay. The day was a glorious one, clear and crisp, but warm in the sun.

Behind their infantry the Allied Army's handful of cavalry was drawn up. Bravely, the sun glanced from the brass helmets of the dragoons and the cheek pieces of their horses' bridles. These troopers must have been currying since sunup because their mounts shone like newly minted coins.

French array displayed many distinctive colors. Most noticeable in the long line were the light blue of the Royal Deux-Ponts and the dark blue coats of the Sayonne regiment of those French Marines who had fought so well across the river at Gloucester Point. Dozens of regimental ensigns, blazoned with the records of two hundred years of warfare, stirred lazily.

The surrender hour, two o'clock, remained half an hour distant, so, accustomed to the age-old military maxim of "Hurry up, then wait," the French and Americans commenced to call to each other across the twenty-yard interval and exchange cheerful insults.

"'Allo, you Yankee son-a-beech!" greeted a towering sergeant of the Soissonsais.

"Hullo, yerself, ye sister-seducing frog-eater!" boomed an equally huge Virginia militiaman. When he kissed his hand and made the Frenchman an awkward bow, roars of laughter arose from both sides of the route.

Because he belonged to no particular unit, Captain Andrew Warren, together with his officers Loubet and Doane, stood on a small knoll on the American side. He had sat up late at night burnishing the buttons of his old American naval uniform — never having been retired by the Marine Committee, he guessed he retained a right to wear it. No trace of verdigris stained his single epaulette, earned in such bitter disillusionment — and unswerving loyalty. Not a few curious glances were directed towards him.

Nearly a quarter of a mile nearer York Town, Brevet Lieutenant Colonel Joshua Stanton chatted happily with lesser members of General Knox's official family.

Jerusha! What a memorable day this was proving! First a promotion, and now what looked like an end to this war. From his position between colonels Nicholas Fish and Walter Stuart, Joshua found that he could enjoy a fine view of the French senior officers. Quite a few of them he knew by sight — Colonel William Deux-Ponts, for example, and the Comte de Custine, standing next to the always picturesque Duc de Lauzun, who still wore Madame de Coigny's black heron feather nodding in his hussar's busby.

He even received smiling nods from General Choizy and the Baron de Viomesnil, with whom he had had much to do of late. Yonder, mopping his face, was his old friend the Marquis de Chastellux, General Rochambeau's principal aide.

Of Colonel Fish, Joshua learned that a bandy-legged, heavy-set officer looking most uncomfortable ahorseback was Admiral de Barras.

At the extreme end of the French array, Admiral Comte de Grasse sat his horse more comfortably while chatting gravely with Lieutenant General the Comte de Rochambeau — faithful, patient and able Rochambeau.

Opposite the French high command and occupying the extreme right of the American line, the commander-in-chief sat easily astride his fine bay charger.

No trace of haughtiness or pride manifested itself on General Washington's countenance — only serenity. To the left of his commander was General Benjamin Lincoln. Solid and red-faced, he was fully occupied in controlling a tall gray charger.

Never again, during this war, would so many famous ranking officers come together; big-nosed, red-faced von Steuben, General Trumbull, Colonel Cobb and General James Clinton of New York — no doubt happier today than his namesake on the British side, Mad Anthony Wayne, Major General Henry Knox and shrewd, opportunistic Colonel Alexander Hamilton.

The only major architects of this victory not present were the great Nathanael Greene — he was occupied far away, retaining Lord Rawdon in Charles Town, South Carolina, and Major General de Lafayette who, over at Gloucester Point, was preparing to receive the surrender of Colonel Banastre Tarleton's garrison.

While minute after minute dragged by, horses fidgeted, switched at flies and pawed the ground and the officers began to grow both irritable and suspicious. Weren't the British coming out after all?

Ha! A deep, muffled cry came rippling along the double ranks. Everyone tried to see down the road. There it was; a thumping of drums in the distance. *Boom-a-rattle — ta-tat. Boom! Boom!* Although distant, voices of officers could be heard calling their troops to attention.

Joshua recognized the flashes of hundreds of bayonets being brought to "present arms." In gradually increasing volume, came the music of many fifes and drums beating a march, but they were yet very far and many minutes must pass before the surrendering army approached this sector.

Joshua's gaze sought the commander-in-chief's tall figure and saw that, calm and dignified as ever, Washington was looking skywards. Presently he turned on the leopardskin housing of his saddle and said something to Knox. Several of the French, following the direction of the commander-in-chief's interest, also gazed upwards and Lauzun tilted his fine head backwards so far that braids of false white hair to either side of his lean face swung to the rear. "Ah. And what kind of a bird is that?"

"He is an eagle, suh," called one of the Virginia officers. "He is what we call a bald eagle."

Lauzun laughed joyously. "Ah, *mes amis*, have we not here an omen — like the Romans of old?" His voice rose. "Gentlemen of France, look upwards and behold that eagle in the sky — an American eagle and free as the air in which he flies! Today, my friends, a new nation soars to take a sure place in God's world."

"Hurray for you, suh!" yelled a Virginia colonel. "That's right well spoken, suh."

Drums now began sounding louder and, by craning his neck a little, Joshua could distinguish a line of scarlet and gold breasting a rise nearly half a mile away. In a moment more he could make out the lift and swing of gaily painted drums as they responded to the stride of the little drummer boys; soon he recognized the flash of sunlight on their brass-mounted drumsticks.

On foot, and a few yards to the rear of the field music, a contingent of scarlet-coated officers were marching straight and stiff as so many ramrods. High behind them appeared the thick black outlines of dozens of color staffs; all British flags were cased because, at Charles Town, Sir Henry Clinton had, in his arrogance, decreed that no American — "rebel," he'd called them — colors might be displayed.

"Where is Cornwallis?" "I don't see Cornwallis," voices cried in undertones. "Where's their commander?"

One after another, the allied units presented arms to the defeated officers marching by at the head of a seemingly endless scarlet column flowing up between the ranks of blue-and-white-clad infantrymen.

That singing noise commenced to play again in Joshua Stanton's ears. "It's six years since I first saw a redcoat on Boston Neck," he reflected. "I was only a lad then, a scared little lieutenant, who didn't know his arse from his elbow about soldiering, and now I'm seeing them whipped at last."

Nearer and nearer tramped the field music, red in the face from playing so long and marching so far but rendering "The World Turned Upside Down" tolerably well.

"That ain't Cornwallis. Where is the bastard, anyhow?"

The black and gold revers of a British general officer had become visible through the veiling dust. Mounted, the stranger rode between a French and an American officer. The three tried to keep abreast but the American's horse curvetted and caricoled.

"Where's Cornwallis?" called a grizzled militia colonel, eyes glowing in hatred. "He's the one to make surrender!"

"Shamming sick," someone replied disgustedly. "Old Charley ain't got the stomach to admit he's been licked."

Now appeared a row of blue-clad figures. Colonel Fish muttered that this was von Saybothen of the Hessian troops and his aides; next came a group of green-coated Loyalists who, especially, must feel that their world was turned upside down. Following these marched the blue coats of a dozen naval officers, then more scarlet and gold tunics.

Almost before Joshua realized it, General Charles O'Hara, Cornwallis's second-in-command, was passing, his mottled cheeks thin and his hooked nose sharp-looking as a knife.

On a signal the music halted and fell back towards either side of the road. The surrendering troops also halted. Now that the music was silenced, everyone present could hear General O'Hara in a choked voice inquire, "Where is General de Rochambeau?"

The French Adjutant General, Comte de Dumas, misunderstanding the Englishman's intent, indicated his superior, but when O'Hara urged his mount in Rochambeau's direction, Dumas spurred ahead fast enough to overtake O'Hara before he could draw rein before the French commander.

The Comte de Rochambeau took no notice of O'Hara's intention except to indicate General Washington sitting impassively to his right. General O'Hara of His Britannic Majesty's Coldstream Guards advanced toward the American commander, his lips drawn thin and colorless over his teeth. A deep and general sigh could be heard as O'Hara held out Lord Cornwallis's sword — he had carried it across his pommel.

Washington, quite imperturbable, despite the Englishman's attempted affront, halted O'Hara with a brief gesture. "Pray address General Lincoln."

Because Cornwallis's sword glittered so brilliantly several horses curvetted and began to snort. Benjamin Lincoln, at Washington's left, drew in his big stomach and accepted the sword. "Not from so worthy a hand," he rumbled and, reversing the weapon, he returned it hilt first to O'Hara.

"God bless my soul! You are most generous, sir." Everyone heard the guardee's startled words then saw tears suddenly slip down over his ruddy cheeks.

The surrendering general and his staff immediately were conducted to one side where, in tents previously erected, they refreshed their drooping spirits. Meanwhile the field music struck up again and, directed by a pair of American sergeants, the head of that long, red-coated column advanced into a field about the limits of which had gathered swarms of seamen, cooks, sutlers and camp followers.

On the trampled brown grass the British laid down their arms.

Descent into Darkness

On the day after the last of the enemy troops, sullenly and ill-temperedly, had stacked arms before being marched away under guard, American pickets on the Williamsburg road were astonished to see a young woman driving into battered York Town. Beside her, in a decrepit chaise, shone the scarlet coat of a paroled British officer — he had been taken prisoner during an unsuccessful sortie attempted earlier in the week.

"Aye, madame, 'twill require small imagination on your part to comprehend our sufferings." Three golden buttons adorning his cuff glittered when he indicated shattered windows, crumbled brick fences and dozens of houses, the walls of which were pierced through and through. Loose bricks, scattered over the road, caused the chaise to bounce sharply once they turned into the village square.

"I can vouch for the fact that your people did all they could to make miserable our lives. My word, my ears still ring from a shell which burst so near as to knock me off my feet. Why I wasn't slain, madame, I'll never understand." He grinned. "Maybe I was born to hang — Grandma always said so."

Once Sabra's eyes grew wide and she pinched her nose. The chaise was approaching what appeared to be an extra-wide trench. Horrors! A shiver chilled her heart; this was no trench at all, but a common grave nearly overflowing with grotesquely tumbled dead bodies.

All at once aware of her strained expression, Captain Staniforth — of the Second Life Guards and very proud on that score — said, "Even before the siege began, Dr. Devoe was well and favorably known, ma'am. A deuced clever surgeon, if I may say so. Came down under contract to von Seybothen's Anspach troops. Would you credit it? Inside of a month he became senior corps surgeon to the Guards, and later surgeon-in-chief to our luckless little army?"

"Yes," Sabra said. "I can believe it. I am not at all surprised."

Sidewise, the guardee regarded this remarkably handsome young woman, then ventured, " 'Tis most urgent business with this Dr. Devoe brings you so promptly to York Town?"

"As you say — most urgent business."

Sabra refused to be drawn out. On attempting to understand her present sensations, she found that she simply could not. All manner of emotions and ideas were swimming about her mind like peas boiling in a pot. It was somehow frightening to know that, in a very few minutes, she and Lucius Devoe would meet again.

"Please, let us proceed to — to Dr. Devoe's hospital." Sabra tried hard to steady her voice, but it was difficult, because in a very few minutes now she would know for sure what course the rest of her life was to follow.

"Well, I'm damned," Staniforth reined in, looked hurriedly about. "Hullo! That house there — that was his hospital. I'm certain on it! But look — "

The roof was gone, the windows blown out and a great section of wall had collapsed into the yard. Fire had scorched the bricks.

A broad-faced Yorkshireman wearing the uniform of the Twenty-eighth of the Line nodded solemnly. "Ay, zur. Was hospital till struck by a pair o' gradely bombs, zur. Roof fell in. Moved what was left to yonder barn."

" 'Tis most unchancy, ma'am. I trust nothing's gone amiss with Dr. Devoe." Captain Staniforth dropped the reins across the beast's dusty back. "Your pardon, ma'am, but I fancy you'd best wait here whilst I make inquiries."

Fighting down a rising nervousness, Sabra forced herself to remain on the lumpy and moldy-smelling seat of the chaise. Half expecting to recognize Lucius's small and wiry figure emerging from the barn she tensed herself. Ah! But there appeared only the guardee in the company of a tall, gray-eyed individual wearing an apron marked with new blood.

"May I present Dr. Reinhoff?" Staniforth said as the other bowed gravely.

"Good day, sir," Sabra murmured, "but it is Dr. Devoe I came to see."

Dr. Reinhoff gave a tired shake of his head. "I t'ink you are yet in time, *Fräulein*. In dot shed lies *mein* poor colleague."

"Lucius is — he's hurt?"

"*Nein*. He iss dying," Reinhoff shrugged. "A great loss, *Fräulein*. He most inderesting ideas hat. *Ja*. Next to me, Devoe iss der cleverest surgeon in America."

Sabra bit hard on her lip. Lucius dying? Why, it didn't seem comprehensible.

"You are sure, there is no room for hope?"

"*Nein, gnadige Fräulein*." The German looked genuinely unhappy. "An arm he lost, but his real hurt iss in der belly; it vass slight, but mortifications began und so — " Reinhoff made a circular motion about his head.

[747]

Sabra only stared. How curious that the possibility of Lucius being injured had never even occurred to her.

Only two figures occupied the woodshed; an orderly of sorts, and a figure lying on an officer's cot bed. A flash of perception told Sabra that Lucius's right arm had been amputated at the elbow.

The Jamaican's dark eyes, sunk deep in his head, slid slowly open. The always sharp outline of Lucius Devoe's cheeks and chin now were more than ever pronounced beneath a black stubble covering his cheeks and chin. A blue cloak had been folded to support his head and, covering him, was some officer's greatcoat.

Captain Staniforth was tactful and turned to look out of the door as, skirts aflutter, Sabra hurried across trampled straw covering the floor.

" 'E's out o' 'is 'ead, mum," the orderly warned.

"No, not any longer — Lucius's voice sounded faint indeed. "I am quite sensible."

He wasn't so sure, though, when he thought to behold Sabra Stanton bending above him, lips parted in a tortured smile and hands uncertainly extended. To raise his head a little he tried, but couldn't. That settled matters; as a physician he recognized the import of this deadly chill which gradually had been advancing inwards along his limbs — such as remained to him. Before long, that chill must reach, and silence, his heart. The possibility, somehow, didn't trouble him now. He felt tired, so very tired.

The orderly suggested, " 'Ere's a bit o' rum, ma'am. Shall I give it to 'im?"

"I think you had better do so."

The dying man's head, outlined against its halo of dark disordered hair, inclined ever so slightly. "Is — is that really you, Sabra?"

"Yes, Lucius," she whispered, dropping onto her knees. "It is really I. You can feel my hand." An instant she rested her fingers along his forehead.

Several moments passed as they gazed on each other and Sabra succeeded in ignoring a terrible odor pervading the shed; in Williamsburg she had become accustomed to noisome smells, but the terribly swollen condition of the stricken physician's abdomen was not lightly to be dismissed.

"Lucius." She knew, even as she spoke, that no overwhelming surge of tenderness was smoothing her voice. "Lucius, why — why did you desert me?"

" 'Twas ambition," he sighed. "Ambition reinforced by circumstances. I beg you to believe one thing — I have never loved — truly — anyone — but you, Sabra."

Gently, the kneeling girl fanned away a swarm of dreadfully persistent bluebottle flies. His teeth all at once seemed abnormally prominent and when he spoke again his eyes remained shut.

"I confess I loved you — yet, in my ambition I have wounded you — and others who befriended me."

Steady footfalls, raised by a file of troops passing down the street, beat through the shed door. "Water please — bad for abdominal wounds — but can't harm me now." When he had sipped a little of the lukewarm fluid, he spoke a bit more clearly. "Please hear me out, Sabra. Peter was my friend, yet I ruined him by spreading a rumor — which set a mob upon him and may have caused his death."

"No! No. It didn't. He got away and is doing well."

"Praise the — Lord." By a Herculean effort Lucius thrust his remaining hand from beneath the gray overcoat. "Can they ever forgive my trespasses, Sabra?"

His last conscious sensation was of her hair brushing his cheek, the faint scent of that allspice with which he had always associated her. All but imperceptible came the cool pressure of her lips on his forehead as he traversed that horizon which divides life from eternity.

Asa Peabody, B.M.: His Journal

Although a definite chill pervaded Dr. Peabody's office he was patient; as soon as the sun rose high enough to warm the slates not far above his head, it would disappear. Right now his eyes felt uncommon hot and tired.

Several moments passed before he perceived, lying among the papers on his desk, an envelope heavily sealed with brilliant yellow wax. Picking it up he turned it over and noted that a coat-of-arms he did not recognize was clearly impressed upon the seal. Something of this letter's general aspect piqued his curiosity. He ripped it open, glanced at the signature and, in mounting interest, read the signature as that of the Marquis de Menthon. Odd — this name was uppermost in his mind at that moment. He unfolded the letter, smoothed it and read in the handwriting of somebody other than the marquis:

My dear Dr. Peabody:

Fortune plays many tricks. This day a naval officer of the fleet of M. de Barras was struck by that same resemblance which has puzzled us all, and approached me. An explanation of our little mystery becomes quite simple. It appears that my great granduncle, André, having incurred the displeasure of Madame duBarry, was exiled to the interior of Canada. For fear of a worse fate the Comte André de Menthon gave out that he had been slain at an Iroquois ambush. Actually he voyaged with his family to an obscure region far to the north of Quebec where he and his descendants have lived as *petits seigneurs* ever since.

The last male of that line having died, she who had married the grandson of the original refugee determined to return to France to claim the title for her infant daughter. *Hélas*, the vessel was cast away on the coast of Nova Scotia and only those in the boat occupied by Captain de Riom, who tells me this tale, were believed to have survived.

Because of the amazing family resemblance it cannot be doubted that your maid of mystery is other than the Comtesse Adrienne de Bussac-Menthon.

At the first opportunity I shall avail myself of the Pleasure of kissing my fair cousin's hand. Until then, please accept, most distinguished sir,

My respectful service.

Well, there it was. Asa put down the de Menthon letter and stared for a long while at the scarred door panels opposite his desk. So Hilde of the Red Lion Tavern was in fact of noble descent. But what good could this knowledge do now?

Hum. So Hector de Lameth was mending and would live to bring further distinction to his name. That at least was good news.

Slowly, Asa reviewed the past forty-eight hours while rubbing his hands together to rid them of stiffness. As if his quill weighed pounds instead of ounces, the physician dipped its point deep into a portable lead ink bottle. Carefully, he then wrote:

CASE NO. 246.
The matter of H.M. (dL)
Female
Aged Approx. 20 yrs.
Symptomia:

A grippe resolving into a severe Chill followed immediately by a Fever, Pulse high, 120 to the Minute.

Query: Why doth no truly accurate thermometer exist? Record of the exact Degree of fever would appear of First importance. Thus could Danger be recognized & prompt treatment afforded.

Asa stopped writing. There could be no doubt that he and Peter had followed the most recent and highly considered treatment for peripneumony. All the same, Hilde de Lameth had grown increasingly feverish.

It was only then that again and quite reluctantly they had resorted to bleeding — although neither of them held that age-old practice to be definitely beneficial. For a little while Hilde had calmed down, but then her fever soared until she had relapsed into a further hallucination.

Eyes staring and rolling wildly, the stricken girl kept crying piteously for Hector. At length she had commenced talking in a language strange to eter, but which Asa recognized as Micmac. An incoherent jumble of German, French and English phrases escaped her pallid lips.

Asa's head sagged forward onto his chest and he tasted so great a bitterness that a groan escaped him. Savagely, he reproached himself.

"Should I have bled Hilde? I don't hold with the practice and yet — "

[750]

What benefit could be derived from blistering a failing patient, despite opinions held by the most learned authorities? Why should it not be possible earlier to arrest, or eliminate the formation of a purulent tumor?

"Dear God," he prayed, "grant me the courage, the intelligence to seek the truth along paths yet untraveled."

His fingers were rasping over bristles standing out along his jaw when the office door suddenly swung open, admitting a brilliant flood of clean morning sunlight. Sabra stood there, hesitant, her eyes yet inflamed by the tears she had shed. Diffidently, she advanced towards the big figure sitting so crushed and weary behind his desk.

"Asa — oh Asa." She placed a light hand on his shoulder. "I can only guess how very downcast you must feel this morning. I wish to say by way of comfort that no living physician could have struggled harder, could have done more to save poor Hilde. Please Asa — don't reproach yourself so, I — I — can't bear it." Her voice softened. "The Lord's will was being fulfilled. Think on how your art saved Captain de Lameth — your art and no one else's. You and Peter did everything possible for Hilde."

"Aye, Everything — and nothing," Asa muttered and got to his feet.

In silence, he gave to Sabra the Marquis de Menthon's letter, then watched surprise briefly animate her weary features, a surprise which soon gave way to an expression of infinite sadness.

"How tragic this letter came only now," she murmured. "Poor Hilde wanted so desperately to learn who she was, and to whom she belonged." Sabra looked up, gray eyes brimming. "This intelligence at least will afford Hector de Lameth some consolation. He will be greatly pleased to learn she was as gently born as himself. The French are odd about such things, aren't they?"

"Yes, they set quite a store by family," Asa replied heavily. "You are most kind to — to have come to see me, Sabra, especially when you lack even more sleep than either Peter or I."

"Asa?" A sudden intensity in Sabra's expression surprised and puzzled him.

"Yes?"

"I have something to tell you."

"Yes?"

"You know I went to York Town?"

"Yes, Sabra, I heard that you did."

"I went to seek out Lucius Devoe."

"*Lucius!*"

"Yes," Sabra explained, "I had reason to believe him to be serving with the Anspach regiment."

Asa frowned. "You sought Lucius, after — "

"Yes. I found him, Asa, and watched over him as — as he died."

"Poor, unhappy devil — Did you really love Lucius?"

Slowly Sabra's eyes rose. "I believed that I did, Asa, but I know now

[751]

that my love for Lucius was unreal as a false dawn which precedes true daybreak and, I — I — oh, Asa, try to comprehend — to — "

"Sabra! Sabra! How much happiness we have lost — but how much more lies before us."

As easily as a doe slips into a thicket, Sabra Stanton entered the stout protection of his arms.

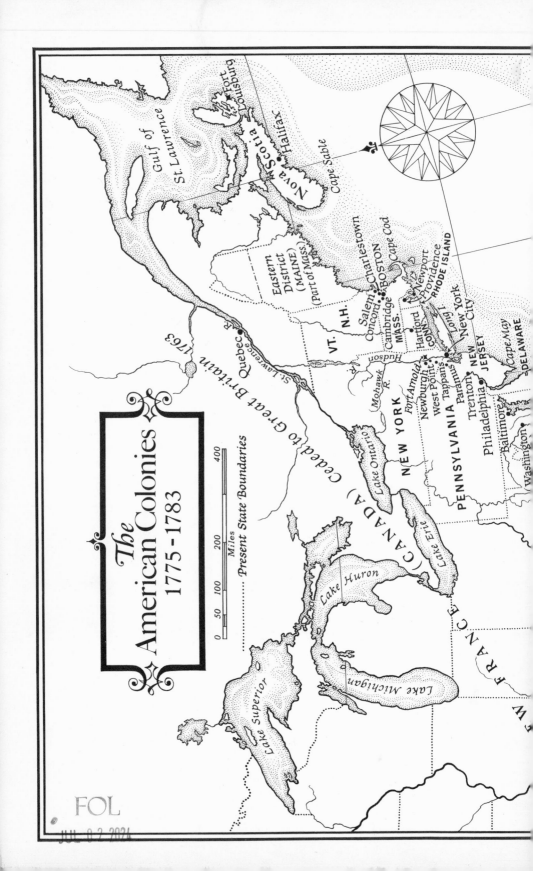

The American Colonies 1775–1783

Miles

0 50 100   200   400

.... Present State Boundaries

Lake Superior

Lake Michigan

Lake Huron

Lake Erie

Lake Ontario

(CANADA) Ceded to Great Britain 1763

St. Lawrence R.

Quebec

Gulf of St. Lawrence

Fort Louisburg

Nova Scotia

Halifax

Cape Sable

Eastern District (MAINE) (Part of Mass.)

VT.

N.H.

Salem
Concord
Cambridge
BOSTON
MASS.
Charlestown
Cape Cod

Hartford
CONN.
Newport
Providence
RHODE ISLAND
Long I.
New York City

NEW YORK

Mohawk R.
Hudson R.

Fort Arnold
Newburgh
West Point
Tappan
Paramus
NEW JERSEY
Trenton
Philadelphia
PENNSYLVANIA
Baltimore
Cape May
DELAWARE
Washington

(NEW) FRANCE